D1716119

LABOR LAW IN THE CONTEMPORARY WORKPLACE

Third Edition

■ ■ ■

Kenneth G. Dau-Schmidt

Willard and Margaret Carr Professor of Labor and Employment Law
Indiana University–Bloomington, School of Law

Martin H. Malin

Professor of Law and Director of the Institute for Law and the Workplace
Chicago-Kent College of Law, Illinois Institute of Technology

Roberto L. Corrada

Professor of Law and Mulligan Burleson Chair in Modern Learning
University of Denver, Sturm College of Law

Christopher David Ruiz Cameron

Professor of Law
Southwestern Law School / Los Angeles

Catherine L. Fisk

Barbara Nachtrieb Armstrong Professor of Law
University of California, Berkeley, School of Law

for

THE LABOR LAW GROUP

AMERICAN CASEBOOK SERIES®

WEST
ACADEMIC
PUBLISHING

American Casebook Series is a trademark registered in the U.S. Patent and Trademark Office.

West, West Academic Publishing, and West Academic are trademarks of West Publishing Corporation, used under license.

Printed in the United States of America

ISBN: 978-1-64242-486-7

Collectively, the authors dedicate this book to the late Clyde W. Summers, a long-time member of The Labor Law Group, whose six decades of path-breaking scholarship in almost all areas of the law governing the workplace and whose deep and loyal friendship have inspired all of us. Individually, we dedicate this book as follows:

To: Betsy, my muse and partner, and the mother of my three children.

> "Let us be lovers, we'll marry our fortunes together."

Paul Simon

K.D.S.

To: Joyce, my wife and best friend, and our daughters Martha and Catherine. There is no force stronger than a father's love for his daughters.

M.H.M.

To: My beloved family: Theresa and Amelia.

R.L.C.

To: Samantha, Alexandra, and Andrew.

> "A truly rich man is one whose children run into his arms when his hands are empty."

Anonymous

C.D.R.C.

To: Jeff, Adam, Alex, Mara, Kim, Andrew, and Sarah.

C.L.F

FOREWORD

THE LABOR LAW GROUP

The Labor Law Group had its origins in the desire of scholars to produce quality casebooks for instruction in labor and employment law. Throughout its existence, the hallmarks of the Group have been collaborative efforts among scholars, informed by skilled practitioners, under a cooperative nonprofit trust in which royalties from past work finance future meetings and projects.

At the 1946 meeting of the Association of American Law Schools, Professor W. Willard Wirtz delivered a compelling paper criticizing the labor law coursebooks then available. His remarks so impressed those present that the Labor Law Roundtable of the Association organized a general conference on the teaching of labor law to be held in Ann Arbor in 1947. Professor Robert E. Mathews served as coordinator for the Ann Arbor meeting, and several conferees agreed to exchange proposals for sections of a new coursebook that would facilitate training exemplary practitioners of labor law. Beginning in 1948, a preliminary mimeographed version was used in seventeen schools; each user supplied comments and suggestions for change. In 1953, a hardcover version was published under the title *Labor Relations and the Law*. The thirty-one "cooperating editors" were so convinced of the value of multicampus collaboration that they gave up any individual claims to royalties. Instead, those royalties were paid to a trust fund to be used to develop and "provide the best possible materials" for training students in labor law and labor relations. The Declaration of Trust memorializing this agreement was executed November 4, 1953, and remains the Group's charter.

The founding committee's hope that the initial collaboration would bear fruit has been fulfilled many times over. Under Professor Mathews's continuing leadership, the Group's members produced *Readings on Labor Law* in 1955 and *The Employment Relation and the Law* in 1957, edited by Robert Mathews and Benjamin Aaron. A second edition of *Labor Relations and the Law* appeared in 1960, with Benjamin Aaron and Donald H. Wollett as coeditors of the book and cochairs of the Group, and a third edition was published in 1965, with Jerre S. Williams at the helm.

In June 1969 the Group, now chaired by William P. Murphy, sponsored a conference to reexamine the labor law curriculum. Practitioners and full-time teachers, including nonmembers as well as members of the Group, attended the meeting, held at the University of Colorado. In meetings that followed the conference, the Group decided to reshape its work substantially. It restructured itself into ten task forces, each assigned a unit of no more than two hundred pages on a discrete topic such as employment discrimination or union-member relations. An individual teacher could then choose two or three of these units as the material around which to build a particular course. This multiunit approach dominated the Group's work throughout much of the 1970s under Professor Murphy and his successor as chair, Herbert L. Sherman, Jr.

As the 1970s progressed and teachers refined their views about what topics to include and how to address them, some units were dropped from the series while others increased in scope and length. Under Professor Sherman's leadership, the Group planned a new series of six enlarged books to cover the full range of topics taught by labor and employment law teachers. Professor James E. Jones, Jr., was elected chair in 1978, and he shepherded to completion the promised set of six full-size, independent casebooks. The Group continued to reevaluate its work and eventually decided that it was time to convene another conference of law teachers.

In 1984 the Group, now chaired by Robert Covington, sponsored another general conference to discuss developments in the substance and teaching of labor and employment law, this time in Park City, Utah. Those discussions and a subsequent working session led to the conclusion that the Group should devote principal attention to three new conventional length coursebooks: one devoted to employment discrimination, one to union-management relations, and one to the individual employment relationship. In addition, work was planned on more abbreviated coursebooks to serve as successors to the Group's earlier works covering public employment bargaining and labor arbitration.

In 1989, with Alvin Goldman as chair, the Group met in Breckenridge, Colorado, to assess its most recent efforts and develop plans for the future. In addition to outlining new coursebook projects, the Group discussed ways to assist teachers of labor and employment law in their efforts to expand conceptual horizons and perspectives. In pursuit of the latter goals it cosponsored, in 1992, a conference held at the University of Toronto Faculty of Law at which legal and nonlegal specialists examined alternative models of corporate governance and their impact on workers.

When Robert J. Rabin became chair in 1996, the Group and a number of invited guests met in Tucson, Arizona, to celebrate the imminent fiftieth anniversary of the Group. The topics of discussion included the impact of the global economy and of changing forms of representation on the teaching of labor and employment law, and the impact of new technologies of electronic publishing on the preparation of teaching materials. The Group honored three of its members who had been present at the creation of the Group, Willard Wirtz, Ben Aaron, and Clyde Summers. The Group next met in Scottsdale, Arizona, in December 1999, to discuss the production of materials that would more effectively bring emerging issues of labor and employment law into the classroom. Among the issues discussed were integration of international and comparative materials into the labor and employment curriculum and the pedagogical uses of the World Wide Web.

Laura J. Cooper became chair of the Group in July 2001. In June 2003, the Group met in Alton, Ontario, Canada. The focus there was on "labor law on the edge"—looking at doctrinal synergies between workplace law and other legal and social-science disciplines—and "workers on the edge"— exploring the legal issues of highly compensated technology workers, vulnerable immigrant employees, and unionized manufacturing employees threatened by foreign competition. The Group also heard a report from its study of the status of the teaching of labor and employment law in the nation's law schools and discussed the implications of the study for the Group's future projects. Members of the Group began work on the casebook on international labor law at this meeting. During Professor Cooper's term, the Group also finished its popular reader *Labor Law Stories*, which examines the stories behind many of the most important American labor law cases.

In July 2005, Kenneth G. Dau-Schmidt became the chair of the Labor Law Group. Shortly after his election, the Group held a meeting in Chicago with nationally recognized practitioners to discuss how best to teach students about the practice of labor law in the new global economy of the information age. The outline that resulted from this meeting served as the basis for *Labor Law in the Contemporary Workplace*. Following the Chicago meeting, the Group met several times to work on new editions of its books and develop new projects: June 2006 in Saratoga Springs, New York; June 2007 in St. Charles, Illinois; and June 2010 in Lake Arrowhead, California. Group projects that grew out of or benefited from these meetings include *International Labor Law: Cases and Materials on Workers' Rights in the Global Economy* and *A Concise Hornbook on Employment Law*. The Group also hosted: a November 2007 symposium on the problems of low-wage workers, the proceedings of which were published in the *Minnesota Law Review*; a February 2009 symposium on the American Law Institute's Proposed Restatement of Employment Law, the proceedings of which were published in the *Employee Rights and Employment Policy Journal*; and a November 2010 symposium on labor and employment law policies under the Obama administration, the proceedings of which were published in the *Indiana Law Journal*.

Marion Crain became chair of the Group at the beginning of 2011. That same year, the Group sponsored a one-day conference on the crisis confronting public-sector employment, the proceedings of which were published in the *ABA Journal of Labor and Employment Law*. In 2011 the Group also hosted a meeting of experts in Chicago to consider the ongoing Restatement of Employment Law project. The proceedings of this meeting were published in the *Employee Rights and Employment Policy Journal*. In June 2012, the Group met in Asheville, North Carolina, and approved the formation of an editorial policy committee charged with establishing policies to ensure that the Group's products continue to reflect its tradition of close collaboration and high standards. The Asheville meeting served as the genesis for a labor arbitrator training workshop for academics in Chicago in December 2012. In February 2013, the Group cosponsored a symposium at the University of California-Irvine School of Law on alternatives to the Wagner Act and employment law models of workplace protection. The proceedings of the conference, called "Re-imagining Labor Law: Building Worker Collectivities After the NLRA," was published in the *UC Irvine Law Review*. In June 2014, the Group met in Ithaca, New York.

Stephen Befort and Melissa Hart became Co-Chairs of the Group at the beginning of 2015. In that year, Group members voted to approve a partnership between the Group and the Chicago-Kent College of Law, Illinois Institute of Technology to oversee the publication of the *Employee Rights and Employment Policy Journal*. In November of 2016, the Group hosted a third conference on the American Law Institute's Restatement of Employment Law. This conference was held at Indiana University–Bloomington and its proceedings were published in the *Employee Rights and Employment Policy Journal*. In December of 2016, the Group met in Los Angeles, California. Melissa Hart stepped down as Co-Chair of the Group in December of 2017 after being appointed a Justice on the Colorado Supreme Court.

At any one time, roughly twenty-five to thirty members are actively engaged in the Group's book publication work; this has proven to be a practical size, given the challenges of communication and logistics. Coordination and editorial review of the projects are the responsibility of the executive committee, whose members are the successor trustees of the Group. Governance is by consensus; votes are taken only to elect trustees and to determine whom to invite to join the Group. Since 1953, more than eighty persons have worked on Group projects; in keeping with the original agreement, none has ever received anything more than reimbursement of expenses.

The Labor Law Group currently has nine books in print. West Academic has published *Public Sector Employment: Cases and Materials* (Third Edition) by Martin H. Malin, Ann C. Hodges, Joseph E. Slater, and Jeffrey M. Hirsch; *Principles of Employment Law* by Peggie R. Smith, Ann C. Hodges, Susan J. Stabile, and Rafael Gely; *Labor Law in the Contemporary Workplace* (Third Edition) by Kenneth G. Dau-Schmidt, Martin H. Malin, Roberto L. Corrada, Christopher David Ruiz Cameron, and Catherine L. Fisk; *Disability Law: Cases and* Materials, by Stephen F. Befort and Nicole Buonocore Porter; International *Labor Law: Cases and Materials on Workers' Rights in the Global Economy* by James Atleson,

Lance Compa, Kerry Rittich, Calvin William Sharpe, and Marley S. Weiss; *Employment Discrimination Law: Cases and Materials on Equality in the Workplace* (Eighth Edition) by Dianne Avery, Maria L. Ontiveros, Roberto L. Corrada Michael L. Selmi, and Melissa Hart; *ADR in the Workplace* (Third Edition) by Laura J. Cooper, Dennis R. Nolan, Richard A. Bales, and Stephen F. Befort; and *Legal Protection for the Individual Employee* (Fifth Edition) by Kenneth G. Dau-Schmidt, Matthew W. Finkin and Robert N. Covington. Foundation Press has published *Labor Law Stories*, edited by Laura J. Cooper and Catherine L. Fisk.

This is the third edition of *Labor Law in the Contemporary Workplace*. The first edition was published in 2009 and the second edition was published in 2014, both by the same authors as the third edition: Kenneth G. Dau-Schmidt, Martin H. Malin, Roberto L. Corrada, Christopher David Ruiz Cameron, and Catherine L. Fisk.

THE EXECUTIVE COMMITTEE

STEPHEN BEFORT (CHAIR)
RICHARD A. BALES (TREASURER)
NICOLE BUONOCORE PORTER (SECRETARY)
RUBEN GARCIA
JEFFREY HIRSCH
CYNTHIA NANCE
KERRY RITTICH
NOAH ZATZ

PREFACE

The purpose of the book is to prepare students for the contemporary practice of labor law. Following the practice of the Labor Law Group, this book had its origin in a meeting of Group members and distinguished practitioners who met in 2004 to discuss a new labor law book. At this meeting there was a remarkable consensus that the newly-imagined book should convey to students the excitement and challenge of the contemporary practice by focusing less on the traditional doctrine and its historical development and more on the economic and social struggles taking place in today's diverse workplace in the context of a more global economy. The authors' work has benefited greatly from these initial discussions, as well as later comments by Group members and practitioners. As a result, this book reflects not only the collective experience of the authors as practitioners and scholars, but also that of the other members of the Group and practitioners representing both labor and management, and past members and/or staff of the National Labor Relations Board and the United States Department of Labor.

The book differs from existing labor law casebooks in four respects. First, the book is organized around contemporary cases and problems as a means of teaching the core principles of labor law. Although the book contains many of the older cases that form the labor law canon, we have reduced some of the old cases to notes and use recent cases to illustrate how the law is developing. Because the book combines the classic cases with recent developments, and contains introductory discussions of every topic, it can be used by the experienced and the novice labor law teacher alike.

Second, although the focus is on collective bargaining law in the private sector workplace under the National Labor Relations Act, the book makes extensive reference to the Railway Labor Act and public sector labor law, the statutes covering sectors where union density remains high. The book also shows how labor law increasingly intersects with other laws of the workplace, including federal, state, and local laws regulating wages, hours, and benefits; immigration; discrimination; occupational health and safety; political organizing; and plant closures.

Third, the book examines the practice of labor law in the global economy. Throughout, the book discusses the impact of international migration of labor and capital on the practice of labor law, and introduces students to the ways in which contemporary employers and unions are affected by and use international law and cross-border negotiation and cooperation.

Finally, the book allows students to learn skills and to understand the dynamics of labor law practice through classroom simulations. To that end, the book includes extensive problems for discussion and, significantly, the teacher's manual shows how the entirety of labor law can be taught through simulation exercises. Two of us teach labor law through simulations, while three of us use a more traditional lecture and discussion format. The variety of teaching methods used by the authors helps ensure that the book works with a variety of pedagogical styles.

The book follows an organization that is straightforward, yet non-traditional compared to that that found in other labor texts. Recognizing that many professors prefer to teach the material in their own order, the book is written without assuming that students will read it from start to finish. Chapter 1 covers the development of the modern employment relationship and the history of the principal labor laws. It then goes on to discuss the unique collective rights regime of labor law and the way that union organizing occurs in the economy of today. Chapter 1 can be assigned as background reading or can be discussed in the first week of the semester.

Chapter 2 covers the feature of federal labor law that makes it unique in American law: statutory rights are accorded to workers primarily as collectives, and only secondarily as individuals. The scope of protection for "concerted activity" for "mutual aid and protection" has been an area of significant ferment in the last two decades as many forms of worker activism are collective but are not always engaged in for the immediate purpose of joining a labor union. The chapter examines the classic issues through the lens of recent controversies, including whether the National Labor Relations Act should protect social media activity and expression by workers, worker collective action through class arbitration and litigation and the impact of the statute on employer rules and policies. The chapter concludes by examining the statutory protections for strikes, picketing and protest, and the variety of statutory limitations on strikes.

Chapter 3 examines two of the most hotly contested and rapidly changing questions governing the law of the workplace: which workers are considered "employees" who are entitled to assert the protections of labor law, and which entities are considered "employers" that are obligated to respect those protections. As to the first question, the chapter treats the status of contingent workers; union organizers; apprentices, including graduate student teachers, trainees, and house staff; and transborder workers, including undocumented, foreign, and multi-country workers. As to the second questions, the chapter treats supervisors; managerial and confidential employees; workers for public sector entities; workers for multiple entities that actually constitute a single employer (the "single employer" doctrine); and transborder employers.

Chapter 4 examines the process by which workers exercise their right to choose (or refuse) union representation. The NLRA protects both rights, and much of the recent law of organizing has arisen in connection with the strategies employers use to persuade employees to exercise their right not to join a union. The chapter begins with the definition of labor organization and how the National Labor Relations Act should treat workplace committees. The chapter then examines the law regulating union access to employees and employer speech and behavior. It then examines the processes by which employees express their preference for or against union representation, including the NLRB-administered election process, voluntary recognition, the use of card-check and neutrality agreements, and the designation of a union as a representative through a bargaining order. The chapter also covers the law regulating the use of picketing and protest to secure union recognition.

Chapter 5 covers the collective bargaining process. It contrasts the processes envisioned under the NLRA, the RLA and in the public sector. It then focuses on the different aspects of the duty of bargain in good faith under the NLRA, followed by consideration of the scope of mandatory bargaining.

Chapter 6 examines the law on economic pressure. It begins with the constitutional protections for picketing, boycotts, and other forms of labor protest. The chapter then examines the legality of management tactics to discourage strikes, including the use of replacement workers, and the legality of union tactics to encourage solidarity during strikes. The chapter then turns to the legality of the dominant employer economic weapon, the lockout. Finally, it examines statutory protections for employers, including the prohibition of secondary boycotts and hot cargo agreements.

Chapter 7 studies the operation of the workplace under a collective bargaining agreement. It begins with the judicial enforcement of the agreement to arbitrate and then takes a glimpse at the way that arbitrators enforce collective bargaining agreements. The chapter then covers the enforcement of the no strike clause and the availability of injunctions against employer conduct pending arbitration. The chapter then examines the union's duty of fair representation in contract negotiation and administration. Finally, the chapter covers the interplay between the contractual grievance procedure and enforcement of "external" law, including the NLRB's deferral to arbitration and the question whether courts will conclude that an arbitration agreement precludes litigation of statutory claims under civil rights and other workplace laws.

Chapter 8 is unique to this book in that it examines the laws relating to unions and new forms of worker collectives as local, national and global political actors. It begins by examining union involvement in contemporary initiatives on workplace regulation. The chapter then examines new forms of labor organization, particularly worker centers and other local, national, and international worker networks. The chapter then examines the international laws and agreements that are relevant to worker collective activity today, including the use of trade sanctions and various forms of contractual arrangements such as codes of conduct. The last part of the chapter covers the laws regulating internal union affairs, including the collection of dues and fees from members and nonmembers, union internal governance and finances, and union treatment of dissenting members.

Chapter 9 examines the circumstances and methods under which employers might attempt to end the bargaining relationship. The covered subjects include the situations in which an employer can legally withdraw recognition or seek decertification of the union. The chapter also examines employer efforts to limit or avoid collective bargaining through corporate reorganization, including double breasting, and successorship doctrine. Finally, the chapter deals with the possible rejection of a collective bargaining agreement by an employer that has sought the protection of bankruptcy law.

Chapter 10 examines federal preemption of state labor law. The chapter treats the three basic forms of preemption under the NLRA: *Garmon* preemption, which precludes state regulation of conduct that is "arguably" protected by Section 7 or prohibited as an unfair labor practice under Section 8; *Machinists* preemption; which precludes state regulation of areas that Congress intended to leave unregulated; and Section 301 preemption, problem, which precludes state law claims that are "inextricably intertwined" with the interpretation of a collective bargaining agreement covering the same employee rights.

One other prefatory note about the editing of the cases and other materials: for the sake of readability, we have not used ellipses to indicate material cut from cases. Ellipses do not tell the reader anything about what was omitted; besides, they are distracting. Additions, however, are noted in brackets. We generally omitted citations within cases and materials except where they were important to communicate something specific about the authority relied upon.

KENNETH G. DAU-SCHMIDT
MARTIN H. MALIN
ROBERTO L. CORRADA
CHRISTOPHER DAVID RUIZ CAMERON
CATHERINE L. FISK

July 2018

ACKNOWLEDGMENTS

This book was a group effort, and many people besides the authors made significant contributions. The authors' work benefited greatly from: the superb administrative support of Sharon Wyatt-Jordan and Melanie Barrios; the diligent editing of Rue Toland; and the skilled research assistance of Arthur Traynor, Kurt Kline, Ben Ellis, Ryland Sherman, Paul Newendyke, Sadie Dillon, Steve Bassett, Carolina Flores, Tracy Scholnick Gruber, Shawna Ruetz, Adam Ray, Alicia Kim, Russell Kalvelage, Michael Oswalt, Dylan Saba, and Daniel Schieffer.

The authors would also like to thank the members of their labor law classes and the members of the Editorial Policy Committee and of the Labor Law Group whose comments on drafts immeasurably improved the First, Second and Third editions.

In addition to the comments and suggestions of various members of the Labor Law Group, this book benefited greatly from the thoughtful comments of: Craig Becker, past Member of the National Labor Relations Board, current General Counsel for the AFL-CIO; Barbara Berish Brown, Partner, Paul Hastings Janofsky & Walker LLP; Wilma B. Liebman, past Chair of the National Labor Relations Board and current Adjunct Professor at New York University; Daniel Nielsen, Mediator and Arbitrator, past staff member of the Wisconsin Employment Relations Commission; David A. Rosenfeld, Partner, Weinberg, Roger & Rosenfeld; Eugene Scalia, Partner, Gibson, Dunn & Crutcher, past Solicitor for the Department of Labor; Patricia C. Slovak, Partner, Schiff Hardin, LLP; and Jacalyn Zimmerman, Arbitrator and past Chair of the Illinois Labor Relations Board. In particular, the Second Edition of the book benefited greatly from detailed comments provided by David A. Rosenfeld.

The authors would like to acknowledge the support and comments of their colleagues, and the financial support of their respective institutions during the hours they spent working on this book. Professor Dau-Schmidt would like to thank Willard and Margaret Carr whose generosity financed his summer support for this project and the taxpayers of Indiana who financed his sabbatical work on the Second Edition. Professor Malin acknowledges financial support for summer stipends and research assistants from Chicago-Kent College of Law. He also thanks his Chicago-Kent colleague Professor César Rosado Marzán who has used the book and provided very helpful feedback. Professor Corrada thanks his Dean, Bruce Smith, and the Workplace Law Program (including Professors Rachel Arnow Richman, Beto Juarez, Marty Katz, Nantiya Ruan, Catherine Smith, and Adjunct Professor Joe Goldhammer) at the University of

Denver, Sturm College of Law, for support of his efforts on this book. Professor Cameron thanks Dean Susan Westerberg Prager and the family of the late Justice Marshall F. McComb Southwestern Law School for their support of his work on the Third Edition. Professor Fisk thanks Dean Kate Bartlett of Duke Law School and Dean Erwin Chemerinsky of the law schools at the University of California at Irvine and Berkeley for their support of this project. Finally, the authors would also like to acknowledge the debt of patience and love they incurred to their family members during the years this book took to produce. No person is an island, or at least no happy and productive person.

THE LABOR LAW GROUP

Executive Committee

Stephen Befort
Chair
University of Minnesota

Richard A. Bales
Treasurer
Ohio Northern University

Nicole Buonocore Porter
Secretary
University of Toledo

Ruben Garcia
University of Nevada–Las Vegas

Jeffrey Hirsch
University of North Carolina

Cynthia Nance
University of Arkansas–Fayetteville

Kerry Rittich
University of Toronto

Noah Zatz
University of California–Los Angeles

Editorial Policy Committee

Catherine L. Fisk
Co-Chair
University of California–Berkeley

Michael Selmi
Co-Chair
George Washington University

Lance Compa
Cornell University

Ann C. Hodges
University of Richmond

Pauline T. Kim
Washington University–St. Louis

Thomas C. Kohler
Boston College

Orly Lobel
University of San Diego

Members

Brian A. Langille
University of Toronto

Orly Lobel
University of San Diego

Deborah Malamud
New York University

Martin H. Malin
Illinois Institute of Technology, Chicago–Kent College of Law

Mordehai Mironi
University of Haifa

Robert B. Moberly
University of Arkansas (Emeritus)

Charles J. Morris
Southern Methodist University (Emeritus)

Cynthia Nance
University of Arkansas–Fayetteville

Dennis R. Nolan
University of South Carolina (Emeritus)

Maria L. Ontiveros
University of San Francisco

Angela Onwuachi-Willig
Boston University

Nicole Buonocore Porter
University of Toledo

Robert J. Rabin
Syracuse University (Emeritus)

Kerry Rittich
University of Toronto

Brishen Rogers
Temple University

SUMMARY OF CONTENTS

TABLE OF CONTENTS

TABLE OF CASES

The principal cases are in bold type.

LABOR LAW IN THE CONTEMPORARY WORKPLACE

Third Edition

CHAPTER 1

THE EVOLUTION OF THE CONTEMPORARY WORKPLACE

■ ■ ■

A. INTRODUCTION

"The unwritten story here is that when you strip people's voice for so long and you take so much from them, there is a point at which people will stand up."

> —Randi Weingarten, American Federation of Teachers National President

Beginning in West Virginia, and then spreading to Oklahoma, Arizona, Kentucky, Colorado and beyond, the spring of 2018 saw thousands of teachers bind together and walk off the job to seek higher wages and better working conditions.

Although each state had its own context, these labor disputes had several common themes. With the state budget shortfalls of the Great Recession and Republican election victories of 2010, many states undertook austerity budgets that cut state funding for education. Teacher wages and benefits suffered while class size increased and support resources declined. At the same time, "education reform" programs undermined teacher professionalism by requiring teachers to "teach to the test" and maximize student standardized test scores. Low wages and poor working conditions have resulted in a teachers shortage across the country as many teachers retire or leave the profession and enrollment in education programs has dropped.

In West Virginia, the average teacher's salary in 2016 was $45,622, ranking 47th among the states. By 2018, the West Virginia teachers had not had an across the board raise since 2014. Among the strikers was Rebecca Diamond, who earned just $39,000 a year after 19 years on the job and who worked as a part-time cashier at Hardee's to help support her family. Rebecca told reporters that when she started teaching, she knew it wouldn't make her rich, "but I thought it would be enough."

West Virginia Governor, Jim Justice, offered the teachers a 1 percent raise for each of the next five years, less than the current 2 percent rate of inflation. Adding to the pain, West Virginia told its school employees that they would have to start paying $300 more a month in health care premiums. At this point the teachers decided to strike, even though strikes *by public employees are illegal in West Virginia and all the teachers could have been fired. The strike ended after nine missed school days when the governor signed a bill giving the teachers a 5 percent raise effective July 1, 2018 and promising to address the issue of rising health insurance costs through a state task force. Teachers in West Virginia and across the nation celebrated this victory. As summed up by Carrena Rouse, a West Virginia high school teacher, "I love my students. I love my fellow teachers. And I'm glad we don't have to be hanging around here (the capitol) anymore."* Steven Greenhouse, *The West Virginia Teacher Strike Was Just the Start,* N.Y. Times, Mar. 7, 2018, https://www.nytimes.com/2018/03/07/opinion/ teachers-west-virginia-strike.html*; John Bacon, West Virginia Teacher Strike Ends, Some Schools to Reopen Wednesday,* USA Today, Mar. 6, 2018, https://www.usatoday.com/story/news/nation/2018/03/06/tentative-deal-re ached-end-west-virginia-teacher-strike-governor-says/398850002/.

NOTES AND QUESTIONS

1.   Why do workers want to organize into unions and collectively bargain with their employers? What purposes do unions and collective bargaining serve in the workplace? Does society as a whole benefit from the existence of unions and their representation of workers' interests in the workplace and in the legislatures? Do we need more or less union representation in the United States?

2.   Why did the teachers strike? Was the strike the fault of the teachers or the state? Like most states, West Virginia does not allow strikes by public sector employees and the teachers strike was illegal. Why didn't the school districts fire the teachers who struck?

3.   West Virginia does not have a comprehensive public sector collective bargaining statute. Teacher raises and benefits are enacted into law by the state legislature and the governor. Are there ways to formulate the conduct of collective bargaining so as to allow the parties to jointly determine the terms and conditions of employment but minimize the need for strikes?

4.   In *Janus v. Am. Fed'n of St. Cnty. & Municipal Employees Council 31*, 138 S. Ct. 2448 (2018), the Supreme Court over-ruled 40 years of Supreme Court precedent to hold that it violated the First Amendment for state governments to make and enforce agreements with unions requiring union-represented employees who choose not to join the union to pay a "fair share" fee to the union equal to the proportionate costs of their representation. Under our system of exclusive representation, if a union is elected as the representative by the majority of employees in an appropriate bargaining unit, the union is legally required to fairly represent all of the employees in that bargaining unit, whether they are members of the union or not. Thus, the *Janus* decision leaves public sector unions in the position where they are legally required to provide services to all bargaining unit employees, but those same employees cannot be obliged to pay for those services. What would you predict would be the result of this decision? Could a TV cable company succeed

if it were required to provide cable service to customers, but customers were not required to pay? If the *Janus* decision weakens public sector unions, will that help those workers resolve workplace disputes with their employers without strikes, or, perhaps, will those disputes fester and grow as they did in the case of the teacher strikes? It should be noted that all of the 2018 teacher strikes occurred in "red states" that already prohibited the enforcement of fair share fee agreements and all of these states had significant legal restrictions on teacher collective bargaining. See Joseph Slater, *Janus: Damaging Labor*, Jurist June 29, 2018, https://www.jurist.org/commentary/2018/06/joseph-slater-impact-janus/.

* * *

As the teachers' strikes illustrate, the practice of labor law in the contemporary workplace is an exciting and challenging vocation that starts with knowledge of a variety of federal and state laws, but also requires knowledge of policy arguments and practical skills such as strategic thinking, problem-solving, and creativity. To represent either the teachers or the state government in the above dispute, one would have to have a working knowledge of the relevant federal and state laws, as well as state and federal politics. The primary purpose of this book is to give you an introduction to federal labor law and its interaction with other federal laws, state law, and international treaties in the contemporary workplace. Although this book focuses primarily on the application of the National Labor Relations Act (NLRA) to labor relations, at appropriate times we also address the application of the Railway Labor Act (RLA), state public sector laws, and other federal and state laws.

The teachers example is also useful to illustrate many of the premises on which this book is based, as well as some of the specific policy questions we will be considering in studying labor law. A brief outline of these premises and questions follows.

1. *Successful employment relationships are of fundamental importance to individuals and the functioning of a healthy society.*

The teachers and state governments both have a fundamental interest in their relationship of employment. For the teachers, the quality of their employment relationship determines the quality of their lives. The standard of living that they and their families enjoy, their social relationships and status, how they live their lives day to day, and even fundamental elements of their identities, are all tied up in their employment. For the state governments, the success of their schools is dependent on a productive relationship with the employees. Without the talents and efforts of the teachers, the state's pupils and populace will suffer. Indeed, at least at some minimal level, workers and employers always share a mutual interest in eachother's success. Employees want to work for a successful and profitable employer, while employers want to maintain productive employees. Despite this basic interest in each other's success, employees and employers inevitably experience conflicts in the determination of the terms and conditions of employment. The teachers would like higher wages, deference to their professional judgment, fair treatment on the job, medical insurance, and a pension while the state and school boards resist such improved wages and benefits because they increase costs, decreasing monies that can be spent elsewhere or requiring an increase in taxes.

On the larger societal level, the success of a society depends on the quality of the employment relationships of the people in that society. Indeed, the employment relationship is the basis for the organization of most institutions in society. The quality of that relationship determines the effectiveness of our institutions and the viability of our economy. Moreover, as we have already established, workers spend the bulk of their waking hours engaged in employment that has a fundamental impact on the quality of their lives. Because the majority of our citizens spend so much time in paid employment, the quality of employment relationships determines the basic health of our society, the level of control people are able to exercise over fundamental issues in their lives, and the degree of respect for human dignity that exists in our civilization.

2.   *Society should regulate our system of work relations to promote efficiency, equity, and employee voice in the resolution of conflicts in the employment relationship.*

Due to its importance to people's lives and the structure of society as a whole, it is essential that a modern society establish useful goals for the regulation of the employment relationship. The importance of economic prosperity dictates that one societal goal for the employment relationship is that it be productive. In a competitive economy this means that the terms of employment must be efficient in that the benefits of each term to the parties exceed their costs, and that both the employees and employer earn at least a competitive return for their contributions to the firm.

However, ours would be a stifling or even oppressive society if efficiency were the only goal. Because employees invest a portion of themselves in their work, employment is not simply an economic transaction. Respect for the dignity of human life requires that the fair treatment of all workers on the job be a fundamental societal objective. Accordingly, the regulation of the employment relationship must strive for the equitable treatment of employees both in the division of the proceeds from the firm and for their treatment on the job. Moreover, the importance of self-determination to human dignity, and the operation of a free and democratic society, requires that employees enjoy effective participation in the work-related decisions that affect their lives. Employees are not mere cogs in some gigantic machine, but instead human beings that must be free to express their concerns and interests in the important endeavor of work. Thus, there are at least three objectives that must be part of any rational regulation of the employment relationship in a democratic society: efficiency, equity, and employee voice. John W. Budd, Employment with a Human Face: Balancing Efficiency, Equity and Voice 1–2 (2004).

    3. *Collective action plays a fundamental role in an optimal system for resolving employment conflicts in a productive and fair society.*

    The teachers found that they could not achieve efficient or fair terms of employment through individual bargaining. Individual teachers didn't have the bargaining power to induce their employer to raise wages or change working conditions at the expense of tax revenue. Although it is true that the teachers were free to work elsewhere, employees do not always have viable alternatives and, even if they do, their leaving communicates little about what is wrong with the job. Moreover, for reasons of efficiency and fairness, many terms and conditions of employment are shared by all employees: the hours of work, the system of evaluation, systems for retention and promotion, the terms of the company health insurance, the speed and safety of the work process, etc. Since all of the employees are exposed to many of the same terms and conditions of employment, those terms and conditions are a "public good." How can the workers effectively negotiate over issues that affect them all without some coordination or collective action? Finally, individual employees have trouble strictly enforcing their contract rights during the life of the agreement. If they sue their employer to enforce their rights before the end of their employment relationship, they risk alienating their supervisors and negatively influencing future employment decisions.

    One alternative to leaving the determination of the terms and conditions of employment to individual bargaining would be to enact legislation that requires certain minimum terms of employment. Indeed, the Fair Labor Standards Act specifies certain minimum wage and overtime payments for covered workers (teachers are exempted), while the Civil Rights Act prohibits discrimination on the basis of race, gender, religion and nationality. Similarly, the Occupational Safety and Health Act prescribes certain minimum conditions for workplace safety while the Employee Retirement Income Security Act also sets certain minimum standards for pensions and benefits if the employer chooses to provide such benefits (public employers are exempted). However, even these minimum standards may be inadequate to meet the needs of the employees. For example, many workers who earn the federal minimum wage still live in poverty. Moreover, state and federal legislation generally provides a "one size fits all" solution to problems that are enforced by some underfunded government agency. The workers themselves may want to devise a solution that meets their needs and the needs of their industry, and which they themselves can enforce. Protective legislation is generally associated with the societal objectives of equity and voice, although legislation can also ameliorate inefficiency caused by failures in individual bargaining.

A final alternative is for workers to bind together and take collective action to address their grievances against their employer. In the example, the teachers organized to petition their state legislatures and bargain collectively to achieve higher wages and better working conditions. By binding together, workers can solve many of the problems associated with individual bargaining. As a group, the teachers will have more bargaining power in negotiations with the state and gain better working conditions, wages and benefits. As a group, the workers can also express their interests with respect to workplace issues that are public goods and affect them all, whether it is in collective bargaining or before the legislature, administrative bodies or the courts. Finally, the terms of a collective bargaining agreement are generally enforceable for the life of the agreement, and the employees can collectively set up and administer grievance mechanisms and job security measures that allow them to enforce their contractual rights effectively without inordinate fear of retribution. Collective bargaining and advocacy can give the employees a say in the governance of their workplace in a way that cannot be achieved through individual bargaining or legislation. Collective action can result in a solution that is particularized to the needs of the affected employees and industry that the employees can themselves effectively enforce. Collective action is generally associated with the societal objectives of equity and voice, although it can also ameliorate inefficiency caused by failures in individual bargaining.

4.   *Government regulation can help improve the performance of employee collective action in resolving employment conflicts.*

West Virginia does not have a comprehensive public sector collective bargaining statute. Teacher wages and benefits are set through legislation passed by the state legislature and signed by the governor. There is no formal system for consultation between the teachers and their school boards to address problems in the workplace. Also, although the teachers have a constitutional right to associate, West Virginia has no statutory obligation to bargain with the teachers and there is no statutory protection against discrimination against teachers who support the union. Although largely absent from the teacher strikes, employer efforts to resist employee collective action can also include discharging union leaders and threatening their supporters with discharge and blacklisting.

Although employee collective action can have desirable effects from the workers' and society's perspective, employers resent the loss of control and increase in costs that generally accompany employee organization. From the employees' perspective, organization is a public good that allows them to solve many of the problems of individual bargaining. If the employees can overcome the temptation to "free ride" and let others carry the burdens of organizing, they can improve their bargaining position relative to the employer and achieve a voice in workplace governance. To resist organization, employers sometimes try to exacerbate this free rider problem by increasing the individual costs of union support through discharges and discrimination. Even if the workers succeed in organizing, there is no guarantee that the unpleasantries will cease. Rather than focusing on solutions that allow the firm to succeed for both parties' benefit, either the workers or the employer may engage in strategic behavior such as discriminatory discharges, lockouts, or strikes to try to gain an advantage at the expense of the other party.

Government regulation can improve the functioning of employee collective action in resolving workplace disputes. Private sector employees under the NLRA, and public-sector employees in states that have comprehensive public employee collective bargaining statutes, have redress to statutory protections that prescribe a system for selecting employee representatives, prohibit discrimination on the basis of union support, and require the parties to collectively bargain "in good faith" with each other. By providing a low cost means for determining employee representation, discouraging discrimination on the basis of union support and requiring good faith bargaining, the government can help foster the cooperative resolution of disputes between the parties through collective bargaining. Kenneth G. Dau-Schmidt, *A Bargaining Analysis of American Labor Law and the Search for Bargaining Equity and Industrial Peace*, 91 Mich. L. Rev. 419 (1992). It is perhaps not a coincidence that the 2018 teacher strikes occurred largely in states without statutory systems to govern collective bargaining.

In this book we will examine the law governing collective bargaining in the United States in the context of the contemporary workplace. We will examine: who are "employees" and "employers covered by bargaining statutes such as the NLRA (Chapter 3), the prohibitions on employer and union behavior or "unfair labor practices" (Chapters 2, 4, 5, and 6), the NLRA's election procedure (Chapter 4), the conduct of collective bargaining (Chapter 5), enforcement of the collective agreement (Chapter 7), and efforts to end the collective bargaining relationship (Chapter 9). In the contemporary workplace, the introduction of information technology has led to a new more decentralized organization of production and new work relationships. With the decline in the traditional employment relationship and the rise of global trade, traditional collective bargaining has declined, and workers have had to find new and creative ways to take collective action and influence their employers. We will examine some of the new means that workers are using to address conflicts with their employers at various places throughout the book, but especially in Chapters 6, 7, and 8. Finally, we will examine the circumstances in which state regulation of workplace issues must give way to federal regulation—the doctrine known as labor preemption (Chapter 10).

In the remainder of this chapter we will examine the history of the employment relationship, the American labor movement, and American labor law. As you will see, the recent adoption of information technology is not the first time that changes in technology and transportation have driven changes in the employment relationship and the optimal system for regulating that relationship. We undertake this historical analysis not only to give you insight into the origins and meaning of the current law, but also the origins and precedents for the current conflicts in the employment relationship.

NOTES

1.   *The Importance of Work:* In considering the importance of work, it is sometimes useful to reflect on your own career choices. Why do you want to be a lawyer? Is it the tasks you see yourself doing? The prestige? The income? Do you want to provide some public service through your work? Not surprisingly, recent empirical work suggests that income, hours, and job satisfaction vary greatly across the legal profession according to the type of job one undertakes. Lawyers in large private practices work the most hours (about 2600 hours per year) and make the highest incomes ($137,400 per year in 2018 dollars five years after law school), but suffer the lowest job satisfaction and the lowest satisfaction with the balance of work and family. At the other extreme, government and public interest lawyers work somewhat shorter hours (about 2400 and 2100 hours per year, respectively) but make significantly less money (about $75,900 per year in 2018 dollars five years out of law school) and enjoy higher job satisfaction and satisfaction with work/family balance. Kenneth G. Dau-Schmidt et al., *"The Pride of Indiana": An Empirical Study of the Law School Experience and Careers of Indiana University Law Alumni*, 81 Ind. L. J. 1427, 1457–1462 (2006). Indeed, there seems to be a negative relationship between income and job satisfaction in the legal profession as a whole. Why would this be? Could hours worked be the key? Other job characteristics? Where do you see yourself fitting into the profession? It should be noted that, as little as 15 years out of law school, almost a third of people with law degrees are not practicing law, but instead are managing businesses, serving as elected or appointed public servants, teaching, or working in some other capacity. *Id.* A legal education can be a good basis for a career outside of the practice of law. What do you want to do with your life?

2.   *Societal Purposes in Regulating the Employment Relationship:* Do efficiency, equity, and voice adequately represent all of the important societal purposes in designing a system to address issues in the employment relationship? How can we apply these lofty concepts in a practical policy governing work relations? How should these purposes be balanced when they are in conflict? In discussing these purposes, consider the opinion of no less an authority than Pope John Paul II in the Centesimus Annus ("The Hundredth Year" 1991):

> The State, however, has the task of determining the juridical framework within which economic affairs are to be conducted, and

thus of safeguarding the prerequisites of a free economy, which presumes a certain equality between the parties, such that one party would not be so powerful as practically to reduce the other to subservience.

The State must contribute to the achievement of [dignity at work, a just and secure wage, and humane working conditions] both directly and indirectly. Indirectly, by creating favorable conditions for the free exercise of economic activity, which will lead to abundant opportunities for employment and sources of wealth. Directly, by defending the weakest, by placing certain limits on the autonomy of the parties who determine working conditions, and by ensuring in every case the necessary minimum support for the unemployed worker.

Other religious authorities have also addressed the importance of the employment relationship and the moral conduct of such relationships. In Judaism, Talmudic decisions concerning workers' rights reflect a consistent imperative for "social justice", which leads to standards regarding the payment of wages, hours of work, and sickness and disability pay. Michael S. Perry, Labor Rights in the Jewish Tradition (1993). Under Islamic beliefs, various hadiths promote justice and fairness, while particular hadiths can be interpreted as prohibiting discrimination and requiring a living wage and an equitable distribution of wealth. Khahil-ur-Rehman, The Concept of Labour in Islam (1995). Buddhist beliefs celebrate work as an essential element of self-realization. The Buddhist point of view sees three functions to work: to allow a person to develop his or her skills, to allow a person to overcome ego-centeredness by joining with other people in a common task, and to produce the goods and services necessary for existence. To organize work in such a way that was meaningless, boring, or nerve-wracking would be little short of criminal, indicating a greater concern for goods and the material aspects of this world than the people. E. F. Schumacher, Small is Beautiful: Economics as if People Mattered 54–58 (1975).

3. *Balancing Societal Goals in Regulating the Employment Relationship*: In some situations, the societal goals of efficiency, equity, and voice will be mutually reinforcing. A productive employment relationship provides the resources necessary to support equitable treatment of employees and to include employee voice in the decision-making of the firm. Similarly, the fair treatment of employees and the consideration of their concerns will reduce employee turnover with its attendant search and training costs, and harness workers' ideas for increasing productivity and quality. Indeed, many modern theories of efficient management rely on employee input through employee committees or "quality circles" to insure production efficiency and quality control.

However, the question naturally arises as to what our society should do when the goals of efficiency, equity, and employee voice are in conflict? Should efficiency dominate, based on the importance of economic sustenance? Should equity and voice take precedence on the theory that we hold the values of human dignity even dearer than economic prosperity? Or should we engage in a balancing of these important competing values when they conflict in our system of employment relations? In the law, conflicts between efficiency on the one hand, and equity and voice on the other, often play out as conflicts between the employer's contract or property rights, which are identified with efficiency, and the workers' free speech and associational rights, which are associated with equity and voice. As we will see in the *Jones and Laughlin Steel Corp.* decision later in this chapter, such fundamental conflicts are the stuff of which landmark labor and constitutional law cases are made. This conflict is also a recurrent theme in the interpretation of the NLRA. *See e.g. Lochner, infra* this chapter, *Jones and Laughlin Steel Corp., infra* this chapter, and *Lechmere, infra* Chapter 4.

4.   *Who Decides?* Does our current system of addressing issues in the employment relationship rely too heavily on individual bargaining? Regulation? Collective bargaining? What is the appropriate balance among these methods of addressing issues? Are there certain issues that are best addressed through one of these means? Why might this be so?

The simple comparative institutional analysis among individual bargaining, regulation, and collective bargaining presented above is just one way to consider and discuss the best means to address the needs of employees and employers in the work place. A more direct method that might be meaningful for many students is to consider the question of who decides an issue in the employment relationship under each of the examined methods and how that decision is made.

Under individual bargaining, the usual state of affairs is that the employer makes a unilateral offer with respect to the terms and conditions of employment. This offer is subject to the employee leaving for a better offer elsewhere, and, although rare, there are some opportunities for bilateral negotiations. What are the pros and cons to having the employer set the terms of employment in this way? Are there particular issues or situations in which individual bargaining will work particularly well or particularly badly?

Under regulation, the terms and conditions of employment are determined by the legislature, subject to lobbying by the parties and the desire to get re-elected. Is the legislature a good forum for the resolution of issues in the employment relationship? Are there particular problems with this method and how should they be addressed? Public choice theory tells us that legislatures are subject to undue influence by small, well-organized, moneyed groups of people with a continuing and particular interest in a given subject. How do we protect our democracy from undue influence by such "special interest groups"? Who are these people anyway? In the absence of a healthy American labor movement, will worker interests receive adequate attention in the legislature? Are there particular issues or situations in which regulation will work particularly well or particularly badly?

Finally, under collective bargaining there is generally much more of a bilateral negotiation, or discussion between the employer and the representatives of the employees. The outcome of these negotiations is subject to the relative bargaining power of the parties and the exercise of their economic force. Is this a fair way to decide issues in employment? Is it efficient? Is there utility in the exchange of information that occurs in collective bargaining? Do you think this exchange of information has an impact on the terms and conditions of employment regardless of the relative bargaining power of the parties? Are there particular issues or situations in which individual bargaining will work particularly well or particularly badly?

B. A BRIEF HISTORY OF AMERICAN LABOR LAW

The history of American labor law is an interesting subject, worthy of study in itself. The development of the interests of the parties and their reflection in the law represents the very nexus of the interests of labor and capital in the organization of society. Conflicts in defining and accommodating employer property rights and the speech and associational rights of workers represent fundamental conflicts in the organization of society with respect to the purposes of efficiency, equity, and voice. As will be seen, throughout the history of American labor law, the impact of changes in trade and technology on the employment relationship have often driven the concerns of the parties that labor and employment law have sought to address.

1. THE ARTISANAL PERIOD: THE TRANSITION FROM EMPLOYMENT RIGHTS BASED ON STATUS TO "FREE LABOR" CONTRACTS

a. The Organization of Production and Labor

ARTISANAL PRODUCTION IN THE NINETEENTH CENTURY[1]
Katherine V.W. Stone
From Widgets to Digits: Employment Regulation for the Changing Workplace
pp. 13–22 (2004)

[Work During the Artisanal Period]

[The] 1733 painting ["Overmantel"] by John Heaten depicts eighteenth-century life on the Marteen Van Bergen farm in New York's Hudson Valley. There is a house and an expansive yard populated by a well-dressed husband and wife, several young children, two black slaves tending livestock, and a white household servant, probably indentured, engaged in a transaction with a Native American. On the roadway in front of the house is a milk-wagon driver, and approaching the house is a well-dressed man followed by two lads, possibly a merchant-craftsman and his

---

apprentices. The painting thus depicts the dominant forms of labor in the early years of the Republic—family members, slaves, indentured servants, craftsmen, and apprentices. There are no wage workers in the picture.

The picture portrays America in its formative years. In the seventeenth and eighteenth centuries, American economic life consisted of the daily travails of people who, like those in the painting, were in relationships defined by fixed legal obligations, such as husband, wife, parent, slave, indentured servant, craftsman, and apprentice. The notion of a labor market in which individuals freely sold their labor did not exist. In fact, until the nineteenth century, there were practically no people in employment relationships. Merchants, artisans, and members of the learned professions all engaged in remunerative activities, but they did not work for wages. Merchants sold their wares, professionals charged fees for their professional services, and artisans were self-employed craftsmen who sold the products they produced.

Wage labor emerged only gradually throughout the course of the nineteenth century, evolving from several sources. One was the perpetual journeymen, the craftsmen-in-training, who never acceded to the ranks of master. In the nineteenth century, master craftsmen, in their quest for cheap labor, abandoned customary norms and began increasing the number of apprentices they kept. Accordingly, by mid-century, there were a large number of journeymen who worked for masters and were paid wages, yet lacked any realistic hope of becoming a master themselves. Conflicts over wages, quality standards, and hours frequently arose, leading journeymen to form societies and trade unions to protect their interests.

Newcomers were another source of wage labor in the second half of the nineteenth century. Some were former slaves who migrated to northern cities after the Civil War to find work. Some were unmarried women who left farms and flocked to factories in industrial centers where they worked as machine tenders until they married and dropped out of the paid labor force. Boatloads of immigrants and their children also arrived and found a place in the urban factories of the New World. These groups, together with the skilled journeymen, comprised the new group known as "free labor."

With the advent of free labor, the factory became the dominant locale of production. Many types of manufacturing activities moved from homes or workshops owned by master craftsmen to factories owned by merchant-manufacturers. Life in the factory was grim for unskilled workers. They worked long hours in dangerous conditions for paltry pay. They were vulnerable to sudden layoffs and unannounced pay cuts, and were subjected to harsh disciplinary rules and confiscatory fines. But skilled workers fared differently. They retained a dignity that came from their exclusive knowledge of the mysteries of the craft and a power that came from their labor organizations. The skilled workers saw production as a partnership in which they determined what needed to be done and how to do it, while the manufacturers provided the workplace, raw materials and marketing. [T]he skilled workers rather than the manufacturer hired the helpers and supervised their work.

Labor Organizations in the Artisanal Era

The craft unions had their origins in the 1830s, when many journeymen felt the need to form separate associations from the master craftsmen. Many trade societies were organized in cities, and there were numerous local strikes of journeymen against masters. Beginning in the 1850s, national craft unions were formed. The National Typographers Union was formed in 1853; the Cigar-Makers International Union in 1864; the International Association of Machinists in 1888, the United Mine Workers of America in 1890. By the end of the century, sixty-two national craft unions had been formed in diverse trades: they included the Bakers and Confectioners Workers International Union, the Boot and Shoe Workers' Union, the United Hatters of America, the Tin Plate Workers, and so forth. [In 1886, the American Federation of Labor (AFL) was founded in order to join together the individual national trade and craft unions to further the interests of workingmen. The national unions favored legislative reforms that would protect labor's right to organize and engage in collective action.]

Radical and Reform Political Programs

While the craft unions strove to protect the skilled workers' skill, status, and privileges, other worker-based reform movements were formed to secure progressive political and legal reform. [For example,] the Knights of Labor (KOL) was formed [in 1872 as an] organization of the American working class, including artisans, unskilled workers, shop-keepers, and small manufacturers as members. The Knights grew quickly, so that by 1884, it had local assemblies all over the country. The Knights believed that the economic problems of the era were the result of the rise of monopolies, particularly in the key areas of transportation, communications, and the financial system. Their political program was focused on advocating antimonopoly measures. By the century's end, membership of the Knights of Labor dwindled severely as a result of the difficulty of keeping so many disparate types of workers united in the face of adamant employer opposition. The other political labor reform movements also declined in importance, so that by 1900 the national craft unions were the dominant form of American labor organization.

NOTES

1.   Under the English common law inherited by our fore-parents during the colonial period, the legal basis of the employment relationship, or "master and servant" law, grew out of the law of domestic relations by virtue of the fact that "servants" were often a member of the "master's" household. As a result,

the legal rights and responsibilities of masters and servants were largely based on their status as such, rather than a contractual theory of bargained for exchange. Under the common law of master and servant, the master was generally obligated to employ and maintain his servants for a period of a year, during which time the servant was to serve him dutifully and the relationship could be ended only upon "reasonable notice." 1 William Blackstone, Commentaries 413 (1765).

2.   Why did the first craft unions form? How did the interests of the masters and the journeymen change as technology changed and the scale of production expanded? Could all journeymen reasonably expect to one day run their own shop, and if not, how could they address issues in their employment relations?

3.   Some economists have likened craft unions to price-fixing cartels such as OPEC. Is this a fair and accurate characterization? OPEC country oil ministers meet periodically to discuss whether the price of oil is too high or low, and then adjust output goals accordingly. How did the craft unions differ from such a price-fixing cartel? Did they unilaterally "fix" prices by adjusting quantity supplied? Did they have other functions?

4.   Why did the first unions form among craft workers? Would unskilled workers have as much interest as skilled workers in organizing a given type of job? Would unskilled workers have as much bargaining power as skilled workers?

5.   In recent years the media has focused much attention on immigrant workers. As the basis for "immigration reform", President Obama argued for enhanced border security, a pathway to citizenship for undocumented immigrants, and "modernizing" the legal immigration system. He and immigrant advocates argued that immigration makes the country stronger and should be encouraged. Elise Foley, *Obama Calls for Immigration Reform Movement*, The Huffington Post (Mar. 25, 2013, 12:25 PM), http://www.huffingtonpost.com/2013/03/25/obama-immigration-reform_n_2949063.html. President Trump was elected on a platform that included further restrictions on both legal and illegal immigration including the construction of a wall across the southern border of the United States with Mexico and increasing deportations. Nicholas Kulish et al., *Trump's Immigration Policies Explained*, N.Y. Times, Feb. 21, 2017, https://www.nytimes.com/2017/02/21/us/trump-immigration-policies-deportation.html. Did immigration play an important role in the shaping of the American labor movement in the artisanal period? What role did immigrant labor play?

b. Collective Action During the Artisanal Period

Early in the artisanal era, collective action was usually undertaken by journeymen of a single craft on a firm or city-wide basis. A society of shoemakers, saddlers, cigar makers, tailors, etc. would strike and picket the workplace of a master, or all of the masters in a city, to secure the masters' agreement that they would pay the society's piece rate for production, and conduct a "closed shop" that employed only members of the journeymen's society. Sometimes the unions of the various crafts would coordinate collective action on a city or even multi-city basis to address some issue of common concern. For example, in 1835, the members of various craft unions in Philadelphia conducted a joint work stoppage for the purpose of establishing a ten-hour workday from 6:00 am to 6:00 pm with an hour off for lunch and dinner. Employers resisted abandoning the existing "sun up to sun down" system arguing that "to be idle several of the most useful hours of the morning and evening would lead [the workers] to intemperance and ruin." Despite employer resistance, the movement spread to other parts of the country and by the end of the 1830s, the ten-hour day had become the norm. Foster Rhea Dulles, Labor History in America 61 (3d ed. 1966).

However, as mechanized methods of production and transportation improved, the economy became organized on a regional or even national basis. Goods were no longer produced merely for local consumption in a single city, but were produced in several cities for sale across a region or the entire country. As a result, if shoemakers in a single city struck for a higher piece rate, shoes produced in other parts of the country could be imported to undermine the strikers' bargaining position. Thus it became clear that in the future workers would have to organize and take collective action on a national basis.

Perhaps the first significant national strike was the railway strike of 1877. The economic depression of the 1870s had left the nation and the railway industry in ruin and turmoil. Some of the railways had declared bankruptcy and were being operated in receivership by the federal courts. All of the railways had decreased wages and payrolls, leading to spontaneous strikes by their employees on all three of the main east-west trunk lines across the country. To ensure that no trains moved without their agreement, workers in Indianapolis occupied the station. Federal Judge Walter Gresham cited the workers with contempt for interfering with his orders to operate the railroad in receivership and, himself, led a posse to help federal troops dislodge the Indianapolis strikers. Judges in other jurisdictions followed Gresham's example (absent the John Wayne impersonation) and used contempt citations and troops to break the strike, sometimes with tragic consequences. In Pittsburgh, the first battalion of militia sent to disperse the railway workers joined them on the picket line, but the second battalion to arrive opened fire with a Gatling gun, killing and wounding many. The railway owners and other employers were impressed by the power of the federal courts to quell the strike through injunctions and the deployment of troops. They would find reasons to call upon this power to limit worker collective action many times in the future. Walter Nelles, *A Strike and Its Legal Consequences—An Examination of the Receivership Precedent for the Labor Injunction*, 40 Yale L. J. 507 (1931).

The mid 1880s found the nation once again in the midst of economic depression and labor strife. In 1885, the Knights of Labor conducted a successful strike against Jay Gould's railroads and achieved the repeal of a wage cut. The success of the Knights of Labor saw their membership swell, and gave impetus to the nationwide movement for an eight hour day. Labor organizations called for a national strike in support of the eight hour day on May 1, 1886, and conducted this protest without a major incident. However, just two days later, police intervention in an altercation between strikers and replacement workers at the McCormick Harvester plant in Chicago resulted in the deaths of four strikers. In response to these deaths, a small anarchist organization called "Black International," made up largely of German and Polish immigrants, organized a demonstration for May 4th in Chicago's Haymarket Square. The May 4th demonstration had virtually concluded, when a detachment of 200 police arrived to disperse the crowd. At this point, someone in the crowd threw a bomb at the police, killing one police officer and wounding several. The police opened fire, which was returned by some of the workers, and in the ensuing melee seven police were killed and fifty-seven injured while four workers were killed and fifty more injured. Paul Avrich, The Haymarket Tragedy (1984).

Chicago, as well as the rest of the nation, was outraged by the bombing and the ensuing "Haymarket Riot." The Chicago police rounded up eight anarchist leaders who had organized or spoken at the meeting, and charged them with murder. Although some of these leaders had previously advocated violence, and there was evidence that at least one had previously constructed bombs, there was no evidence that any of them had anything to do with the bombing of May 4th or the ensuing riot. Three of the defendants were not even at the Haymarket that night and three more had left before the explosion. After a one-sided trial, all of the defendants were convicted, with seven sentenced to death and one sentenced to 15 years in prison. Ultimately four of the defendants were hanged, one committed suicide in jail, and three were pardoned after six years in jail. The harsh treatment of the Haymarket defendants became a cause célèbre in the international labor movement. The annual May 1st demonstrations on behalf of the defendants and the eight hour day were the genesis of the annual "May Day" labor celebrations undertaken in the rest of the industrialized world.

NOTES

1.   Why were so many of the first nationwide strikes focused on the railways? Were these workers skilled? Did they have a strong community of interest? Might their employers enjoy supra-competitive profits because of their market position, or "market rents", which the employees would want to share?

2.   The ethnic identity of Hispanic workers and their organization by ethnicity is an important development in the contemporary workplace. *See,*

Janice Fine, *Worker Centers: Organizing Communities at the Edge of the Dream*, 50 N.Y.L. Sch. L. Rev. 417 (2006); Victor Narro, *Impacting Next Wave Organizing: Creative Campaign Strategies of the Los Angeles Worker Centers*, 50 N.Y.L. Sch. L. Rev. 465 (2006). How does this development compare with the historic participation of immigrants in the American labor movement? Why would immigrants play such an important role in the movement? Is it appropriate that Hispanic immigrants now annually demonstrate on May 1st for immigration reform? What might the German immigrants who helped popularize that day as a day for celebrating the achievements of labor say if they were invited to speak at a modern May 1st rally over immigration issues?

c. The Judicial Response to Collective Action: The Doctrines of Criminal and Civil Conspiracy

The early efforts by journeymen to organize for their mutual aid and protection brought a hostile reaction from the courts. The first American case testing the legality of collective action came in 1806, in what has become known as the *Philadelphia Cordwainers* case (*Commonwealth v. Pullis*, Philadelphia Mayor's Court (1806)). In the fall of 1805, journeymen members of a society of cordwainers (shoemakers) in Philadelphia called a strike to demand higher piecework rates. The strike lasted several weeks and ended in failure. Nevertheless, the leaders of the strike were charged in the Mayor's Court of Philadelphia with the common law crime of conspiracy. Walter Nelles, *The First American Labor Case*, 41 Yale L. J. 165 (1931).

Although there was no doubt that the men could have individually refused to work for the proffered rate, the novel legal question was whether the men could act in concert to refuse to work with the purpose of gaining higher pay. Despite the fact this was a case of first impression in the United States, the magistrate asserted in his charge to the jury that it was settled law that the combination of workmen to raise wages was illegal, citing English authority that acts done in concert to the detriment of the public could be a criminal conspiracy. The reporter's charge stated that demand and quality were the "usual means" of setting the price of work and that collective bargaining was an "unnatural" means that would inevitably result in injury to the public. Based on these instructions, the jury convicted the cordwainers and each was fined eight dollars and costs.

Despite its questionable application to such cases, the criminal conspiracy doctrine became the first law under which courts evaluated the legality of workers' collective action in the United States. Over the course of the next few decades, dozens of strikes were broken by judges who invoked the doctrine to enjoin strike activity and punish union leaders. This application of a doctrine, which made unions themselves illegal, did not achieve broad acceptance among the public. In a few notable cases, juries stubbornly refused to convict workers of this crime, despite instructions from the judge. Some cases even sparked mass protests. By the 1840s, even the courts had lost confidence in its application to labor cases.

The first break in the application of the criminal conspiracy doctrine to labor cases came in the case of *Commonwealth v. Hunt,* 45 Mass. 111 (1842). In that case, seven members of the Boston Journeyman Bootmakers' Society were convicted of criminal conspiracy for forming "an unlawful club, society and combination" and following its "unlawful by-laws, rules and orders." In accordance with the Society's by-laws, the journeymen had refused to work for masters who employed journeymen who were not members of the Society, which, according to the indictment caused "great damage and oppression, not only of their said masters but also of divers other workmen and against the peace and dignity of the Commonwealth." Walter Nelles, *Commonwealth v. Hunt*, 32 Colum. L. Rev. 1128 (1932).

On appeal, however, the Massachusetts Supreme Judical Court in an opinion by Chief Judge Shaw rejected the prevailing views concerning the legality of trade union activities and reversed the convictions. Shaw found that, absent a contractual obligation to work for a given employer, the allegations that the defendants had agreed not to work for any employer who employed a nonunion worker were insufficient to support a conviction. The court also ruled that a conspiracy to impoverish another workman, who was alleged to have lost his employment because he was not a union member, was not in itself unlawful; that illegality would depend upon the means used. "If it is to be carried into effect by fair or honorable and lawful means, it is, to say the least, innocent; if by falsehood or force, it may be stamped with the character of conspiracy." Thus the court rejected the idea that combinations of workers were, in and of themselves criminal conspiracies, and opened the inquiry to an examination of the union's purpose and means. The court defined an unlawful conspiracy as "a combination of two or more persons, by some concerted action, to accomplish some unlawful purpose, or to accomplish some purpose, not itself unlawful, by unlawful means." Shaw's "ends and means" analysis would receive further elaboration under what became known as the "civil conspiracy doctrine".

Although an improvement over the criminal conspiracy doctrine, the inquiry into ends and means required under the civil conspiracy doctrine proved too vague and malleable to constitute a workable national labor policy. It provided well-heeled judges considerable leeway to indulge their own social philosophies in assessing the objectives of organized workers. The Massachusetts case of *Vegelahn v. Guntner*, 167 Mass. 92 (1896) is often presented as an example of the limitations of the civil conspiracy doctrine. In that case, Vegelahn, a manufacturer of furniture, sought to enjoin picketing by his upholsterers, led by Guntner. The upholsterers had walked off the job after being denied their demands for a set schedule of wages and a nine hour work day. Vegelahn attempted to continue production by employing replacement workers and, in response, the upholsterers set up "patrols" in front of his place of work, to convince people not to work for him. The patrols usually consisted of two men, but at times grew to numbers large enough to present a physical obstacle to people desiring to enter the plant door. The patrols used various means of persuasion including reasoned arguments, appeals to sympathy, coarse language, epithets and threats of bodily harm. At the hearing for final decree, Justice Holmes, who reported the case for consideration by the full court, concluded that the use of "persuasion and social pressure" was a lawful means to use in seeking better wages and hours, and could not be enjoined. In particular, he allowed the defendants to establish two man patrols to give notice of the strike and to persuade others to refuse to do business with the plaintiff. Holmes maintained the injunction against physically blocking the plaintiff's door, threats of violence, violence or interference with existing contracts.[2]

Upon consideration by the full court, the majority expanded the injunction to prohibit any "patrols" in front of Vegelahn's business "for the purpose of annoying, hindering, interfering with, or preventing any person in the employment of the plaintiff, or desirous of entering the same, from entering it"; thus enjoining even the peaceful patrols by two men that did not interfere with existing contracts allowed by Holmes. The majority reasoned that:

> Intimidation is not limited to threats of violence or of physical injury to person or property. It has a broader signification, and there also may be a moral intimidation which is illegal. Patrolling or picketing, under the circumstances stated in the report, has elements of [such] intimidation.

Moreover, the majority rejected the strikers' argument that their harm to Vegelahn was justified because they had just refused to work and picketed to secure higher wages.

> This motive . . . does not justify maintaining a patrol in front of the plaintiff's premises, as a means of carrying out their conspiracy. A combination among persons merely to regulate their own conduct is within allowable competition, and is lawful, although others may be indirectly affected thereby. But a combination to do injurious acts expressly directed to another, by

---

[2]   Holmes' final decree was as follows: "[I]t is ordered that the defendants, be enjoined from interfering with the plaintiff's business by obstructing or physically interfering with any persons in entering or leaving the plaintiff's premises, or by intimidating, by threats, express or implied, of violence or physical harm to body or property, any person or persons who now are or hereafter may be in the employment of the plaintiff, or by in any way hindering, interfering with, or preventing any person or persons who now are in the employment of the plaintiff from continuing therein, so long as they may be bound so to do by lawful contract."

way of intimidation or constraint, . . . is outside of allowable competition, and is unlawful.

Accordingly, the majority found that the workers' patrols were an "unlawful means" under the civil conspiracy doctrine, even if they pursued the lawful end of higher wages, and enjoined all such patrols.

Justice Holmes rejoined with one of his most famous dissents. He argued that he had already given Vegelahn the full protection of the law by enjoining violence, intimidation, threats, patrols larger than two men that might physically block the door and interference with existing contracts. Holmes asserted that "It appears to me that the judgment of the majority turns, in part, on the assumption that the patrol necessarily carries with it a threat of bodily harm. That assumption I think unwarranted, . . ." Moreover, Justice Holmes argued that, just as the harm inflicted by business competitors is legally justified, so too the harm inflicted on Vegelahn's business by the workers' combination to refuse work and peacefully picket was justified.

> [I]t has been the law for centuries that a man may set up a business . . . although he expects and intends thereby to ruin someone already [in business], and succeeds in his intent. In such a case, he is not held to act "unlawfully and without justifiable cause," . . . . The reason, of course, is that the doctrine generally has been accepted that free competition is worth more to society than it costs, and that on this ground the infliction of the damage is privileged. . . I have seen the suggestion made that the conflict between employers and employed is not competition. . . .. If the policy on which our law is founded is too narrowly expressed in the term free competition, we may substitute free struggle for life. Certainly the policy is not limited to struggles between persons of the same class competing for the same end. It applies to all conflicts of temporal interests.

Holmes went on to argue:

> One of the eternal conflicts out of which life is made up is that between the effort of every man to get the most he can for his services, and that of society, disguised under the name of capital, to get his services for the least possible return. Combination on the one side is patent and powerful. Combination on the other is the necessary and desirable counterpart, if the battle is to be carried on in a fair and equal way.

NOTES

1.   *Remedies at Law*: Tortious interference with a business is a private nuisance and subject to tort damages. Physical harm and threats of physical

harm would be a crime. Is it clear that plaintiff's remedies at law are inadequate? What is the basis for equitable jurisdiction in this case?

2.   *Unlawful Means*: What are the union's purpose and means in the *Vegelahn* case? Does the majority object to the union's purpose or the means it uses to achieve that purpose? Holmes and the majority agree that the picketer cannot use threats of violence, violence, physically blocking the door, or interference with contract to achieve their objectives. Would any form of union picket be lawful under the majority's decision?

3.   *Unlawful Ends*: In applying the civil conspiracy doctrine, judges were also very skeptical of the "ends" that unions sought to achieve. The courts' application of the "objectives test" generally excluded indirect union action to build bargaining power. For example, in the case of *Plant v. Woods*, 176 Mass. 492, 57 N.E. 1011 (1900), the Supreme Judicial Court of Massachusetts disallowed a strike by workmen to recruit an employer to their side in a jurisdictional dispute with another union. Similarly, in *Duplex Printing Press Co. v. Deering*, 254 U.S. 443 (1921), the Supreme Court condemned the union's strike to recruit secondary employers in a boycott of the employer with the primary dispute. The courts' application of the objectives test was also subject to the criticism that the judges applied different standards in evaluating the organization of capital and the organization of labor. For example, compare the result in *Plant*, in which the union was enjoined from striking an employer until he agreed to employ only members of that union with the result in *Bowen v. Matheson*, 96 Mass. 499 (1867), where a combination of shipping masters were allowed to refuse to supply seamen to shippers who employed seamen furnished by the plaintiff.

4.   *Too Much Discretion? Who Should Regulate?* The "ends and means" test of *Vegelahn* and *Plant* gave the courts a lot of discretion in determining what collective action workers would be allowed to undertake. As *Vegelahn* demonstrates, if the judge has a sufficiently negative view of unions, almost any means can be suspect. Moreover, the determination of which ends can "justify" or "excuse" the damage to plaintiff under the prima facie tort test used in *Wood* is inherently subjective. As previously discussed, the employment relationship is one of the fundamental relationships in peoples' lives. Did the civil conspiracy doctrine give too much discretion to courts to exercise in the governance of labor relations? Would it be better if such discretion were exercised by our elected representatives in the legislature and the executive?

5.   *The Theory of Countervailing Power*: In his dissent Holmes argues that "Combination on the one side [capital] is patent and powerful. Combination on the other side [labor] is the necessary and desirable counterpart, if battle is to be carried on in a fair and equal way." This idea has come to be known as the "theory of countervailing power" in the industrial relations literature and has been used as an argument in favor of collective bargaining and laws encouraging employee organization. John Kenneth Galbraith has argued that a society needs countervailing power in the economy and politics in order to be a healthy functioning democracy. John Kenneth Galbraith, American Capitalism: The Concept of Countervailing Power (1952).

What do you think of the argument? Can you think of historical or current examples in which the relative power of capital and labor in a society have become imbalanced to the detriment of that society? Do we have a good balance now in American society?

d.   The End of the Artisanal Era

Toward the end of the nineteenth century, continuing improvements in technology and transportation further increased the optimal scale of production and set the stage for the new systems of mechanized mass production that were to come. The artisanal system of production stood as a barrier to these changes because under this system the skilled craftsmen, whose economic and social position would be undermined by the new mechanized processes, determined the method of production and the system of wages. In order to adopt new mechanized methods of production, employers had to destroy the old system of production, and, in particular, wrest control from the unionized craftsmen. Thus, by the end of the century, manufacturers in many sectors were determined to break the union work rules and destroy the skilled workers' monopoly of knowledge about production. These employers formed trade associations and national organizations like the National Association of Manufacturers to wage a concerted "open shop campaign" against the unions.

The first significant battle for control of the production process took place in 1892 at the Carnegie Corporation's Homestead Steel Works. Andrew Carnegie and his chief officer Henry Frick resolved to eliminate the union at Homestead and designed a plan to this end. Before contract negotiations in 1892, Frick built a barbed wire fence, complete with towers for sentinels and riflemen, around the Homestead Works. Inside the fence, Frick built barracks to house strikebreakers. Frick manned his fortress with three hundred guards from the notorious Pinkerton Detective Agency. After the union contract expired, Frick locked-out and dismissed the union workers and announced that from now on the Works would operate nonunion. The workers fought the Pinkertons, sheriff, and state militia to prevent replacement workers from entering the plant, incurring dozens of casualties. After four months, federal troops interceded to quell the violence, breaking both the strike and the union. The Works reopened with strikebreakers and operated nonunion for the next fifty years. The Carnegie Corporation then used spies and blacklists to eliminate the union from the rest of its plants and mills. Katherine V. W. Stone, From Widgets to Digits: Employment Regulation for the Changing Workplace 24–26 (2004).

Other firms followed Carnegie's lead and sought to destroy their unions. The demise of the craft unions allowed employers to abandon the artisanal system of production and create one that did not depend upon the cooperation of skilled workers. In the early twentieth century, they set out to accomplish this feat.

2. THE LABOR RELATIONS SYSTEM OF THE INDUSTRIAL ERA

a. The "Labor Problem" and the Development of Industrial Management Practices

THE LABOR SYSTEM OF THE INDUSTRIAL ERA[3]

Katherine V. W. Stone

From Widgets to Digits: Employment Regulation for the Changing Workplace
pp. 27–41 (2004)

The Twentieth-Century "Labor Problem"

After the skilled workers' unions were broken and their skills downgraded, employers found themselves with a crisis of discipline and morale on the shop floor. In the artisanal era, skilled workers saw themselves as partners in production, so that the problem of motivation did not arise. But with the command and control style of supervision of the post-Homestead era, skilled workers no longer were self-motivated. Instead, the issue of how hard workers worked became an issue of conflict.

The homogenization of the workforce produced another problem that employers had not anticipated. With the old skilled/unskilled dichotomy disappearing, there was a greater possibility than ever that those workers would see their interests in class terms. While the American Federation of Labor (AFL) was conservative and apolitical, the American Socialist Party and the Industrial Workers of the World were growing rapidly. Employers feared anarchism, socialism, and, after 1917, Bolshevism inside the plant gates.

Both the problem of worker motivation and the problem of deterring concerted radical opposition were aspects of what was known, at the turn-of-the-century, as the "labor problem." To solve the labor problem, employers embraced theories of scientific management and personnel management—two complementary and overlapping approaches to the problem of work organization. The approaches resulted in new methods of wage payment, new promotion policies, and paternalistic welfare policies. These practices were designed to bind the worker to the firm and create incentives for hard work.

Scientific Management and the Problem of Worker Motivation

The first step in establishing the new job structures was the development of a new payment system. Factory managers learned early on that when workers were paid by the day, they had no incentive to maintain a reasonable work pace. To combat [shirking], employers instituted piecework systems [in] which they paid a fixed sum for each unit produced.

---

[3] Copyright © 2004 Katherine V. W. Stone. Reprinted with the permission of Cambridge
Additional: University Press.

[However piecework systems often failed because, as workers increased their productivity and pay under the piecework system, employers became tempted to cut the piece rates so that the workers earned income closer to their traditional levels.] Once workers experienced a rate cut, they were thereafter careful to restrict their effort so as not to "spoil the job."

In 1895, Frederick Winslow Taylor proposed a different system of wage payment. Taylor's "scientific" system [for determining appropriate levels of production and compensation] was comprised of two techniques to develop productivity benchmarks from which to set the "correct" rates for each job—job analysis and time study. Job analysis entailed extensive observation and experiments to determine how long each task should take. [Taylor] and his disciples broke all work tasks into their component motions and determined the best way to perform each [job]. [They] also redefined the jobs [to] break down job duties into smaller and narrower categories. Taylor also invented systematic time and motion study to give employers a yardstick by which to measure how long each job should take. [Taylor] would select a "first-class man," observe his task performance, eliminate all unnecessary motions, and then, once the job was performed in "the one best way," time [the job] with a stop watch.

[Taylor's methods of scientific management were applied to various methods of mass production. In 1908, Henry Ford built a factory in Highland Park, Michigan, to produce his Model T. After five years, he introduced a moving assembly line so that jobs could be subdivided and materials could move quickly through the production process. Ford's system differed from Taylor's in that differential piece rates played little role in encouraging productivity. On the assembly line [management set] the speed of the line [and thus] the pace of productivity. However, like scientific management, Fordism involved deskilling tasks, defining jobs narrowly, and encouraging long-term attachment between the worker and the firm. As in Taylorism, the assembly line aimed to remove knowledge from the control of workers, but, in contrast with Taylorism, knowledge was reposed in the technology of the assembly line rather than in the planning department.]

Personnel Management and the "Human Factor" in Production

In the early 1900s, a new school of personnel management coalesced around the problem of [worker] turnover. To reduce turnover, the personnel management theorists advocated that firms institute a systematic promotion plan in order to motivate employees to give greater effort, to build loyalty, to diminish turnover, and to provide a systematic mechanism for skill development. [These systematic promotion plans were generally based on seniority with workers moving up "job ladders" from low skill to higher skill jobs within the firm over the course of their career. Secondly, the personnel management theorists encouraged firms to establish "corporate welfare" programs including profit-sharing, insurance and pensions. These welfare policies, like job ladders, were a means to encourage long-term ties between the employee and the firm.]

The ideas of the scientific management and personnel management movements spread rapidly amongst American firms. By 1927, forty percent of firms surveyed by the National Industrial Conference Board reported the use of seniority for layoffs. Many others had welfare programs and personnel departments that instituted promotion ladders and mechanisms to enhance job security. Thus by the end of the 1930s, scientific management and personnel management had become the dominant human resource policies within large U.S. manufacturing firms.

NOTE

What do you think of the labor relations system of the industrial age? Work becomes more routine and less skilled, but also more accessible to more people. Employers become more powerful in employees' lives, but also are a source of security and benefits. The increased output that resulted was, of course, a great boon to the comfort and satisfaction in many people's lives. How does the labor relations system of the industrial age compare with the workplace today?

b. The Early Industrial Period (1890–1932): The Gilded Age, the Progressive Era and the Roaring Twenties

i. Labor Relations During the Early Industrial Period

At the beginning of the industrial age, the American labor movement included both conservative and radical elements. The dominant form of unionism in the United States at this time was a very pragmatic variety sometimes referred to as "bread and butter" unionism. The best examples of this type of unionism were the craft unions of the American Federation of Labor (AFL), and there was no greater advocate of this bread and butter unionism than the federation's able leader, Samuel Gompers. Proponents of bread and butter unionism accepted capitalism as the basic method for organizing production and merely sought to further workers' interests within that system through the process of collective bargaining. Thus, rather than seeking a new organization of society for the benefit of working people, these unionists sought only to collectively negotiate with their employers on "bread and butter" issues such as wages and hours. Although these unionists were politically active, seeking to influence legislation and elections, they generally eschewed the formation of a separate political party to serve workers' political interests. The member organizations of the AFL were autonomous national trade unions, organized according to craft. The AFL was formed to resolve jurisdictional disputes among member organizations, provide support for member organizations engaged in important boycotts or strikes, and to educate the public and the legislature on the problems of workers.

However, there were members of the American labor movement who sought more fundamental changes in the American economic system. The Industrial Workers of the World (IWW), or "Wobblies," was founded in 1905 on syndicalist principles seeking the eventual control of business by workers. As an intermediate step, the Wobblies attempted to organize workers not by craft, but in "one big union." The IWW leadership initially came out of the Western Mine Federation and included such folk heroes as Joe Hill, Big Bill Haywood, and Mother Jones. Although the Wobblies' greatest strength lay in the mines and logging camps of the West, their most notable success occurred in the Lawrence, Massachusetts, textile mills in 1912 (the "Bread and Roses" strike). There the Wobblies successfully organized the largely immigrant workforce of the mills and undertook a strike that achieved not only a wage increase, but a 54 hour work week for women and children.

Another labor leader who sought fundamental change in our economic system was Eugene V. Debs. Debs was the son of French-Alsatian immigrants who settled in Terre Haute, Indiana and kept a grocery store. He began work in the railways at fourteen and eventually was elected President of the American Railway Union. Debs catapulted to national prominence in the American labor movement in 1894 for his role in conducting a national railway strike to support striking Pullman workers. For his part in the strike, Debs was arrested for interference with the U.S. mails and violation of a court injunction, and sent to jail. *In re Debs*, 158 U.S. 564 (1895). The strikers faltered without their leader, and by the strike's end 13 workers had been killed, 57 wounded, and an estimated $80 million worth of property had been damaged. Debs became a leader of the Socialist Party of America and ran as their candidate for President five times, receiving over 6% of the vote in 1912.

Employers used a variety of strategies to resist employee organization during this time. Employers sometimes required employees to agree not to associate with or support a labor organization as a condition of employment. These agreements, referred to as "yellow-dog contracts," were useful to employers both to directly discourage employee organization and to act as the basis for tort damages or an injunction against union organizers for "interference with contract." Employers also sometimes maintained "black-lists" of employees who supported unions, declining to hire them again in the future. Such lists could be devastating to workers' livelihoods when used by major employers or shared among employers. A less hostile, but still effective, employer strategy was to organize an employer sponsored "company union" that would represent the employees in discussions or even contract "negotiations" with the employer. Employees who became invested in the employer sponsored union were less likely to participate in organization of an independent union, and the company union contracts could serve as the basis for an injunction against independent organization on the tort theory of interference with contract.

However, some employers were not restrained in their hostility to employee organization and even employed "guards" or "militia" to beat up and kill union members and their families. One of the most outrageous examples of the use of this strategy occurred in a 1913 strike against John D. Rockefeller's Colorado Fuel and Iron Company when company agents attacked the miners' camp while the men were away, shooting and burning to death several of the miners' wives and children. Because the tent city was located near Ludlow, Colorado, the murders are generally known as the "Ludlow massacre." Howard Gitelman, Legacy of the Ludlow Massacre: A Chapter in American Industrial Relations (1988).

The entry of the United States into World War I brought government suppression of American radicals and protection for bread and butter unionism. Although Gompers and the leaders of the AFL supported the war effort, the leaders of the IWW and Debs actively opposed the war as a sacrifice of working class boys for the interests of the moneyed class. Most of the Wobblies' leaders were prosecuted and imprisoned for their opposition to the war under the Espionage Act of 1917 and Sedition Act of 1918. With their leadership in jail, the Wobblies declined rapidly, ceasing to be an effective labor organization in the early 1920s. Debs was also imprisoned for sedition, although this did not prevent him from running for President from jail in 1920 and receiving almost 1 million votes. Debs' conviction for his opposition to the war was upheld by the Supreme Court in the infamous case of *Debs v. United States*, 249 U.S. 211 (1919). To promote industrial peace during the war, President Wilson created the Taft-Walsh War Labor Conference Board to develop a code for industrial relations during the war. This code recognized the workers' right to a living wage, the norm of the eight hour day and the maintenance of the status quo with respect to union security in organized shops. Although there were no penalties for strikes or lockouts, the code stated that such tactics should be suspended for the duration of the war. Wilson also appointed Samuel Gompers to the National Council on Defense which advised the President on federal labor policies during the war.

The Roaring Twenties brought a lean time for the American labor movement. With the end of the war, employers renewed their efforts to eliminate unions. The success of the communist revolution in Russia brought increased charges of "Bolshevism" with every act of employee collective action. To promote their drive against unions, the National Association of Manufacturers organized "open shop" associations across the country. The National Association of Manufacturers dubbed their open shop movement "the American Plan" and tried to associate operating union free with "American virtues." This public relations campaign, along with the general dominance of business interests in the public policy of the 1920s, created a favorable environment in which employers could use their anti-union tools of yellow-dog contracts, black-lists, company unions, and intimidation. Moreover, the economic prosperity of the time and employer policies of corporate welfare fostered employee contentment even in the absence of independent unions. For many employees it did not make sense to risk the wrath of their employer when employment was steady, wages were relatively good, and their employer's policies sought to bind them to the firm in long-term employment through pensions and promotions up "job ladders." Of course the "bubble" of economic optimism and congeniality that existed during the 1920s was about to burst.

ii. The Courts' Response

"Freedom of Contract"

In the courts, the rise of the industrial age was accompanied by greater employer control of the employment relationship through individual contract. As has previously been discussed, between the artisanal and industrial period, the legal basis for the rights and responsibilities in the employment relationship shifted from the status of a person as a "master" or "servant" to the terms and conditions the parties specified in their contract for employment. Indicative of, and instrumental in, this change was the courts' abandonment of the "English Rule" on the period of employment in favor of the "American Rule" of "employment-at-will." Under the English Rule, employees were presumptively employed for one year during which time they could be discharged only upon "reasonable notice." Under the doctrine of employment-at-will, an employee can be discharged at any time for "any reason, good or bad," unless he expressly contracts for employment security or a contract for a definite period.[4] Moreover, in combination with the doctrine of unilateral contract, the at-will doctrine allows the employer to unilaterally change the employees' terms and conditions of employment at any time that suits her needs. If an employer decides that the hours, wages, or benefits she has previously established are not sufficiently profitable, she can "end" that at-will relationship, and offer different terms that the employees accept for prospective work by performance. Absent sufficiently attractive alternatives, the employees have little or no input to the terms of employment.

In the early industrial period, the courts guarded the employer's ability to control the terms and conditions of employment even against state and federal legislation under the constitutional theory of "freedom of contract." In *Lochner v. New York*, 198 U.S. 45 (1905), the Supreme Court struck down a New York statute limiting to 60 the number of hours bakers could work in a week, under the theory that this limitation

---

[4]   The at-will rule was first identified by Horace Wood in an 1877 treatise on the master-servant relationship. Horace Gay Wood, Master and Servant 272–73 (1877). Mr. Wood's reading of American case law in identifying the rule has been subject to more than a little criticism. *See,* Theodore St. Antoine, *You're Fired!*, 10 Hum. Rts. Q. 32, 33 (1982); Clyde Summers, *Individual Protection Against Unjust Dismissal: Time for a Statute*, 62 Va. L. Rev. 481, 485 (1976) (the rule has "doubtful antecedents"). *But see* Andrew P. Morriss, *Exploding Myths: An Empirical and Economic Reassessment of the Rise of Employment At-Will*, 59 Mo. L. Rev. 679 (1994).

unconstitutionally infringed on the employers' and employees' "liberty" to contract for longer work hours, as protected in the 14th Amendment. The Court, per Justice Peckham, reasoned that the state could only infringe on such liberty pursuant to a valid exercise of its police power to protect vulnerable classes of people, regulate particularly dangerous activities, or safeguard the general health and well-being. The Court held that the New York statute did not represent a valid exercise of the state's police power because there was no showing that bakers were of lesser mental or physical capacity than most men, that baking was a particularly hazardous occupation, or that the bread produced by bakers working more than 60 hours was less safe or healthful than other bread. Justice Holmes dissented citing precedents of Sunday laws, usury laws, and other protective legislation that had been upheld and arguing that the Courts opinion enshrined the theory of "laissez-faire economics" in the Constitution. In Holmes' view, the majority's use of the word "liberty" to frustrate the legislative will of the majority was a perversion of the term, unless the majority had infringed on fundamental legal principles. Justice Harlan, joined by Justice White and Justice Day, also dissented, citing presented evidence that bakers suffered greater health problems and died earlier than other workers and that long hours in hot dusty conditions was an important cause of these problems. Harlan predicted that the Court's decision would "involve consequences of a far-reaching and mischievous character; [and] seriously cripple the inherent power of the states to care for the lives, health, and well-being of their citizens."

Justice Harlan's prediction proved true with a vengeance. During what would later be known as "the Lochner Era" the judiciary used the theory of "substantive due process" under the 5th and 14th Amendments to strike down over 200 federal and state statutes which, in their view, impinged on liberty and freedom of contract without adequate justification. Some of the most notable of these cases include: *Adair v. U.S.*, 208 U.S. 161 (1908) (invalidating section 10 of the Erdman Act prohibiting "yellow dog" contracts); *Coppage v. Kansas*, 236 U.S. 1 (1915) (invalidating a state statute prohibiting "yellow dog" contracts); and *Adkins v. Children's Hosp.*, 261 U.S. 525 (1923) (invalidating a federal statute establishing a minimum wage for women and children in the District of Columbia). Even in cases involving child labor, where the Supreme Court would admit to a legitimate exercise of state police power to protect a particularly vulnerable group of people, the Court's narrow view of federal power under the commerce clause denied power to the Congress to pass federal protective legislation, leaving any state that adopted child labor laws at a competitive disadvantage. See e.g. *Hammer v. Dagenhart*, 247 U.S. 251 (1918) (striking down federal child labor law as exceeding congressional power under the Constitution); *Child Labor Tax Case*, 259 U.S. 20 (1922) (striking down federal tax on child labor). As the economy continued to grow and develop into a national economy, the problems of ham-stringing federal and state legislative power under the *Lochner* doctrine became more and more apparent. See, James Gray Pope, *Labor and the Constitution: From Abolition to Deindustrialization*, 65 Tex. L. Rev. 1071 (1987). Nevertheless, it was not until the exigencies of the Great Depression brought a dramatic transformation of the political landscape that the Court would be forced to rethink its view of the constitutional role of government in the regulation of the economy.

NOTES

1.   *Employment-At-Will:* The primary arguments in favor of the employment-at-will doctrine are that it allows employers to easily get rid of bad employees and that it allows employees freedom to move from a bad employer to a good one. Should an employer really be able to get rid of an employee for any reason, good or bad? What if the employer fires the employee for refusing to violate the law? *See Petermann v. Int'l Bhd. of Teamsters*, 174 Cal.App.2d 184, 344 P.2d 25 (1959) (discharge of employee for refusing to commit perjury held in violation of public policy). What if the employer gets rid of a salesman to avoid paying him a commission on a sale he has already secured? *See Fortune v. National Cash Register Co.*, 373 Mass. 96, 364 N.E.2d 1251 (1977) (discharge after commission earned to prevent its payment violates implied covenant of good faith and fair dealing). Is this really the best balance between efficiency and equity that is possible in our system of regulating labor relations? What sort of voice do at-will employees have in the running of the workplace?

2.   *Lochnerian Laissez-Faire:* The decisions of the *Lochner* era outlined a very limited role for the proper intervention of the state in personal affairs. The state was to: encourage private exchange through enforcement of contract law; ensure the compensation of losses imposed on third parties through tort law; and protect voluntary exchange, property, and bodily integrity through enforcement of the criminal law. Save for very limited intervention under the police power to address general issues of public health or the interests of people who were physically or mentally infirm, or subject to extraordinary risks, the state was prohibited from legislating to address unfairness or distributional inequities in the private dealings of people. With respect to the definition of property rights and the distribution of wealth, the status quo was held constitutionally sacred. Although the state was apparently allowed to pass legislation to facilitate the organization of capital in larger and more powerful entities, it was prohibited from addressing inequities that this organization caused or to protect or facilitate the organization of labor to bargain with these entities. Thus, "bargaining" between employers and employees under "Lochnerian laissez-faire" often occurred between large powerful corporations who set the terms of employment for individual employees whose primary method of influencing the terms of employment was to leave for another job, if one existed. Is this an efficient or fair basis for addressing disputes in the employment relationship? Is it constitutionally mandated as the only means?

3.   *Criticisms of Lochner:* The *Lochner* decision has been subject to a number of criticisms. First, it is argued that the *Lochner* doctrine is just not a very good reading of the Constitution. The due process clause does not mention freedom of contract, let alone suggest substantive protection of such a right. Second, as Holmes suggested in his dissent, the opinion seems to enshrine economic laissez-faire in the Constitution unduly limiting legislative power to regulate a modern economy. Indeed the Court used the doctrine for the next three decades, along with a narrow interpretation of the commerce clause, to upend both state and federal legislation aimed at regulating the economy. The fixture of contractual relations and property rights in a narrow interpretation of the Constitution when such rights are inherently a creation of law has struck some as arbitrary rather than inevitable or profound. Cass R. Sunstein, *Lochner's Legacy*, 87 Colum. L. Rev. 873 (1987). Finally, it has been argued that the *Lochner* decision and its narrow interpretation of allowable legislative action constituted an unnecessary and improper incursion of the courts into the legislative powers of Congress and the state legislatures. Litigation under the doctrine consisted more of a rearguing and reappraisal of the legislative decisions as to whether to pass a regulation than a principled argument as to whether the legislature had properly exercised its powers and responsibilities subject to fundamental personal rights. *See e.g.* Brandeis Brief in *Muller v. Oregon* (1908) in which the then lawyer Louis Brandeis set forth massive documentation, not only of judicial precedent, but also legislative evidence and "precedent" in favor of special legislative protection governing the employment of women.

What do you think? Is *Lochner* a good reading of the Constitution? Did the Court assume the role of the legislature? Is the Court competent to make such decisions? Can a government run a modern economy under a system of *Lochnerian* economic laissez-faire?

* * *

"Governance by Injunction"

The institution of collective bargaining flew in the face of the doctrine of "freedom of contract" championed by the courts during the early industrial period. The combination of workers into associations to compete with the captains of industry for a larger share of the benefits of production violated the model of atomistic worker competition inherent in the judges' conception of the best practices of laissez-faire economics. The fact that many of these unwashed workers were also immigrants only added to the judges' sense that worker power violated the established norms for propriety and order. Employers had taken note of the success of the federal courts in quelling the railway strike of 1877, and sought to expand the courts' power to grant injunctions and contempt citations to imprison strike leaders and ham-string collective bargaining. Although unions were no longer treated as criminal conspiracies, they could be enjoined under the ends and means test of the civil conspiracy doctrine. Commonly drawn from the upper classes, judges were often suspicious of both the ends sought by the associations of workingmen, and the means they used to achieve those ends. In the absence of national legislation to regulate the conflicts in collective bargaining, the courts were left to mediate collective labor relations through what was derisively referred to as "governance by injunction." Felix Frankfurter & Nathan Greene, The Labor Injunction (1930). Under this largely common law system for governing labor relations there were several bases on which an employer might be able to obtain an injunction of employee collective action.

Violence or the threat of violence associated with employee collective action was of course an unlawful means and could serve as a basis of injunction under the civil conspiracy doctrine. Often, this violence was instigated by "security" personal retained by the employer to break the strike, for example—the murders of the miners' wives and children in the Ludlow massacre that occurred in the 1913 miners' strike against John D. Rockefeller's Colorado Fuel and Iron Company. As in the *Vegelahn* case, 167 Mass. 92, 44 N.E. 1077 (1896), discussed *supra*, state and federal judges were sometimes quick to infer that employee collective action would inevitably be violent or coercive, and enjoin it on that basis. Moreover, under the law of conspiracy, unions could be held responsible not only for the acts of their leaders, but for the acts by any member by virtue of the fact that they were members and thus part of the "conspiracy." In the *United States v. Debs*, 64 F. 724 (N.D. Ill. 1894), *affirmed on other grounds*, 158 U.S. 564 (1895), the union was held responsible not only for the acts of its members, but also its sympathizers, even though union officials did everything possible to discourage illegal activity. These broad interpretations of union responsibility under the conspiracy doctrine made it relatively easy to find a factual basis for the injunction of collective activity on the basis of violent or coercive activity.

"Yellow-dog contracts" provided employers with another argument that employee collective action constituted an unlawful means to achieve employee objectives. Because these contracts required employees to abstain from associating with unions as a condition of employment, union solicitation of support, and collective action were found to constitute the tort of "interference with contract." The Supreme Court affirmed this doctrine and the appropriateness of an injunction of union organizing activities in the landmark decision of *Hitchman Coal & Coke Co. v. Mitchell*, 245 U.S. 229 (1917). After the *Hitchman* case, yellow-dog contracts achieved widespread popularity among employers. Professor Bernstein has estimated that no less than 1,250,000 workers were required to sign such agreements during the 1920's. Irving Bernstein, The Lean Years: A History of the American Worker, 1920–1933, at 200 (1960). The widespread use of such agreements allowed injunctions that effectively curtailed organization in some industries. For example, under the notorious "Red Jacket injunction" Judge John J. Parker effectively barred the United Mine Workers from organizing in virtually the entire West

Virginia coal industry. *United Mine Workers v. Red Jacket Consol. Coal & Coke Co.*, 18 F.2d 839 (4th Cir. 1927). As previously discussed, federal and state efforts to limit the use of yellow-dog contracts were consistently struck down as unconstitutional interferences with "freedom of contract" during this time under the *Lochner* doctrine. *See Adair v. United States*, 208 U.S. 161 (1908); *Coppage v. Kan.*, 236 U.S. 1 (1915).

"Company unions" provided yet another basis for an injunction under the doctrine of civil conspiracy. A "company union" is a worker organization that is formed or dominated by the employer. In the wake of Colorado Fuel and Iron Company strike of 1913, John D. Rockefeller tried to remake the industrial relations image of his firm by forming the Employee Representation Plan (ERP), which allowed workers to elect representatives to meet with company officials to discuss working conditions and settle grievances. Many other employers followed suit so that by 1928 approximately 1.5 million workers were covered by company unions and 3.5 million workers were members of AFL unions. United States Department of Labor, Characteristics of Company Unions, 1935: Bulletin of the United States Bureau of Labor Statistics, No. 634, at p. 27 (1937). Company unions served as a bulwark against genuine organizing since the officers of the company union could generally be called upon to campaign against an independent union. Moreover, if the employer signed a contract with the company union, organization by an independent union for the purposes of negotiating wages and working conditions would constitute interference with contract, enjoinable under the civil conspiracy doctrine. *Newton v. Laclede Steel Co.*, 80 F.2d 636 7th Cir. 1935), *aff'g*, *Laclede Steel Co. v. Newton*, 6 F. Supp. 625 (S. D. Ill. 1934).

The antitrust laws provided a final basis for granting injunctions—and treble damages—against union boycotts and strikes. In 1890, Congress passed the Sherman Act and made "every contract, combination . . . or conspiracy in restraint of trade" a crime. 26 Stat. 209 (1890), as amended 15 U.S.C. §§ 1 et seq. (2012). The Attorney General was given the power to prosecute Sherman Act violations, but the aggrieved parties were given the power to sue civilly for treble damages under Section 7. Although the obvious objective of the act was to eliminate price-fixing agreements among producers and suppliers of goods, the statutory language was broad enough to apply to employee collective action. Even if the government did not prosecute collective action under the Sherman Act, the fact that it might be illegal added one more arrow in the quiver of employer lawyers to gain an injunction under the means test of the civil conspiracy doctrine. The possibility of treble damages under the Sherman Act posed an ominous threat to the economic viability of unions and their members. In 1908, in the "Danbury Hatters' case," the Supreme Court confirmed that the Sherman Act applied to combinations of workers, at least where they sought to boycott goods that were transported across state lines. *Loewe v. Lawlor*, 208 U.S. 274 (1908). Seven years later, the Court upheld a treble damage award that allowed the boycotted hat manufacturer, Loewe, to collect his damage award by seizing the bank accounts and houses of union members. *Lawlor v. Loewe*, 235 U.S. 522 (1915). A national collection by the AFL prevented any of the Danbury Hatters from being turned out of their homes, but the decision incensed working people across the country.

In 1914, President Wilson called for revision of the antitrust laws, and labor saw its chance to gain an express exemption of union activity from the Sherman Act. Although there was some resistance to a complete exemption for labor in Congress, Section 6 of the Clayton Act was titled "Antitrust Laws Not Applicable to Labor Organizations" and expressly stated that "the labor of a human being is not a commodity or article of commerce" and that "[n]othing contained in the antitrust laws shall be construed to forbid the existence and operation of labor, . . . organizations . . . or to forbid or restrain individual members of such organizations from lawfully carrying out the legitimate objects thereof. . . ." 38 Stat. 730 (1914) as amended 15 U.S.C. §§ 12 et seq. (2012). Section 20 of the Act went on to specifically prohibit injunctions in disputes between "an employer and employees . . . unless necessary to prevent irreparable injury . . . for which there is no adequate remedy at law" and to declare that "no such restraining order or injunction shall prohibit any person or persons, . . . from ceasing to perform any work . . . or from ceasing to patronize . . . any party, or persuading others by peaceful means to do so. . . ." *Id.* Organized labor was ecstatic with this legislative accomplishment which Samuel Gompers christened "Labor's Magna Carta."

However, in 1921, the Supreme Court dashed labor's hope of escaping the antitrust laws by reading the labor exemption of the Clayton Act as a nullity. In the case of *Duplex Printing Press Co. v. Deering*, 254 U.S. 443 (1921), the Court interpreted section 6 of the Clayton Act as only exempting the activities of labor organizations and their members that were legal before passage of the Act. The Court interpreted Section 20 as establishing the existing common law standards for injunctions and applying merely to the employees of a particular employer, and not employees as a general class—thus providing no protection against injunctions of national boycotts. It would be decades before a later Supreme Court would once again breathe life into the words Congress had written in the labor exemption of the Clayton Act.

This system of "governance by injunction" aligned the judiciary with the interests of management to such an extent that it undermined the reputation and authority of the courts. Felix Frankfurter & Nathan Greene, The Labor Injunction 200–05 (1930). The one-sided issuance and enforcement of temporary restraining orders to quash collective action caused the courts to be identified with the interests of employers in the minds of many working Americans. The taint of such bias led the Senate to reject the nomination of Judge Parker to the Supreme Court in 1930, principally on the basis of his infamous *Red Jacket* injunction prohibiting the United Mine Workers from organizing in West Virginia. The fact that most judges were from wealthy backgrounds reinforced the idea that they were in league with management against the working class. To support the view that labor could not get a fair hearing in court, one had only to cite any number of opinions under the courts' adherence to a fairly extreme view of freedom of contract, the disallowance of protective labor legislation under the *Lochner* doctrine and the effective evisceration of the labor exemption of the Clayton Act. The distrust of the courts by proponents of the working class engendered by the courts' decisions during this time would have an impact not only on the American labor movement, but also the formulation of our labor laws that is still felt today.

Moreover, the regime of "governance by injunction" provided a poor basis for developing a national policy on labor relations. In undertaking to regulate labor relations in this way, the courts exceeded not only their constitutional authority, but also their institutional competence. The courts had expanded "a simple, judicial device to an enveloping code of prohibited conduct, absorbing, *en masse*, executive and police functions and affecting the livelihood, and even lives, of multitudes." Felix Frankfurter & Nathan Greene, The Labor Injunction 205 (1930). The "remedy" of granting broad and devastating injunctions against only one side of the dispute, without addressing the underlying social and economic problems that led to the dispute has been described as "akin to tying the lid on a boiling kettle of water and stuffing a rag down its spout." Walter E. Oberer, Timothy J. Heinz & Dennis R. Nolan, Labor Law: Collective Bargaining in a Free Society 80 (5th ed. 2002). As the economy expanded to become a national economy, it became clearer and clearer that we needed a *national* labor policy enacted by our elected representatives in *Congress*, not dictated by the courts.

NOTES

1.   In addition to substantive objections to "governance by injunction," critics of the time raised several procedural and practical problems with this system of governing collective labor relations. In brief, these objections were:

a)   The courts often issued temporary restraining orders on an *ex parte* basis so that they heard only the employer's side of the dispute. This practice occurred even when the employer knew the identity and address of the leaders of the workers and had time to serve them and give them an opportunity to appear.

b)   Temporary restraining orders were frequently based on the affidavits of guards and private detectives employed by the employer, produced in a stereotyped form and followed by pro-forma complaints. Critics argued this evidence was unreliable and based more on a legal formula than the actual facts of the case.

c)   Although temporary injunctions are, in theory, merely an interlocutory remedy, in reality they often broke the strike. The employees' ability to apply economic pressure on an employer can be undermined by an injunction of even a few days that undermines the employees' faith in the union and collective action, or allows the employer to move perishable or distressed goods.

d)   The courts' orders were often phrased in complex legal terminology which left the average working man to only guess at what they prohibited.

e)   The employer's armed guards, who had given the affidavits to support the injunction, were often sworn in as deputy marshals to enforce the decree. This left the enforcement of the court's order to highly partisan and often violent personnel, intimately associated with the employer.

f)   If violence or breaches of the peace did occur, employees or union officers who were prosecuted did not receive the usual procedural safeguards of a criminal prosecution before a jury. Instead, they were held to account in a contempt proceeding before the same judge who had issued the order.

Felix Frankfurter & Nathan Greene, The Labor Injunction (1930). *See also* Judge Amidon's opinion in *Great N. Ry. v. Brosseau*, 286 F. 414 (D. N.D. 1923).

iii. The Railway Labor Act

Even while the courts pursued a fairly radical regime of individual contract and governance by injunction, pressure began to build for federal legislation to govern collective labor relations. In 1926, Congress passed the first such federal statute governing labor relations in the railway industry. There were several reasons why federal labor legislation was developed first in the railway industry: the industry was highly organized with powerful unions facing powerful employers; the industry was organized and conducted on a national basis and clearly required a federal legislative policy; strikes in the railway industry were very disruptive to the economy as a whole creating pressure for legislation to encourage cooperative labor relations; and the legislative solution adopted in the Railway Labor Act (RLA) was first agreed to by representatives of the affected unions and employers before Congress considered the bill. 44 Stat. 577 (1926) as amended; 45 U.S.C. §§ 151–88 (2012).[5] Although the RLA at first governed only railroads, it has since been expanded to the airlines, and the principles developed in the RLA served as a legislative precedent to the broader National Labor Relations Act (NLRA) passed in 1935. Even today, judicial opinions interpreting the RLA can serve as important precedents in interpreting the NLRA, and vice versa.

---

[5]   The text of the Act, as amended, may be found in the Statutory Supplement.

RAILWAY LABOR ACT OF 1926

Charles M. Rehmus
The Railway Labor Act at Fifty: Collective Bargaining in
The Railroad and Airline Industries, Chapter I (1977)

Legislative History

In December of 1924, President Coolidge urged the carriers and the railroad unions to jointly work out a procedure to ensure labor peace in the industry. During 1925, a committee of railway executives met with union representatives and a draft bill was agreed upon. Supported jointly by the railroad industry and its unions, and opposed only by the National Association of Manufacturers, the new bill was passed 381 to 12 by the House in March and 69 to 13 by the Senate in May 1926. No changes of substance were made in the course of hearings or enactment. [T]he President signed the Railway Labor Act on May 20, 1926. [T]he Act remains operative [to this day and] is the oldest continuous Federal collective bargaining legislation in the Nation's history.

Nature of the 1926 Act

The underlying philosophy of the law was, as it still is, almost total reliance on collective bargaining for the settlement of labor-management disputes. When bargaining broke down, the law provided for mandatory mediation but arbitration only if the parties agreed. A major innovation was the specific provision for creation by the President of emergency boards, a device by which neutrals might make non-binding recommendations for procedures and terms on which a dispute might be settled. Reliance was thus based on the hope that public opinion would force compliance with otherwise non-enforceable decisions and recommendations.

The Act's five basic purposes were set forth in Section II:

1. To prevent the interruption of service.

2. To ensure the right of employees to organize.

3. To provide complete independence of organization by both parties.

4. To assist in prompt settlement of disputes over rates of pay, work rules, or working conditions.

5. To assist in prompt settlement of disputes or grievances over interpretation or application of existing contracts.

A major feature of the 1926 Act was to set forth a specific procedure for settling disputes over the terms of new or renewed agreements. The basic mediation function under the Act was to be undertaken by a five-member [National Mediation] Board. The parties were required to give 30-days' notice of a desire to reopen contracts and, failing agreement, the

Board was to mediate. If agreement did not result from this stage, the Board was to attempt to obtain the parties' agreement to submit the dispute to arbitration.

[Another] major innovation in the 1926 statute was the detailed provision for procedures in the event mediation failed and one or both of the parties proved unwilling to arbitrate. In a dispute that would in the judgment of the Board "threaten substantially to interrupt interstate commerce" the President might, "in his discretion," create an *ad hoc* emergency board "to investigate and report respecting such disputes" within thirty days. During this period, any carrier involved was to refrain from changing conditions of employment and employees were prohibited from striking.

Constitutionality of the 1926 Act

A test of the constitutionality of the new statute was not long in the making. In May, 1927, the Brotherhood of Railway Clerks presented the Texas and New Orleans Railroad with a set of proposed wage improvements. [The carrier] decided to discharge union members and only deal with a newly-created company union. The Clerks sought an injunction to restrain the carrier from interfering with the employees' right to select their own representatives under Section 2 of the act. The Carrier responded that the Railway Labor Act was unconstitutional in that it violated the Company's rights guaranteed under the First and Fifth Amendments to operate its property, including the selection and discharge of employees, as it saw fit.

The case reached the Supreme Court [in 1930], and the Court disagreed. It had no doubt of Congress' right to prohibit interference in the choice of bargaining representatives under its constitutional power to regulate commerce.

The Railway Labor Act of 1926 does not interfere with the normal exercise of the right of the carrier to select its employees or to discharge them. The statute is not aimed at this right of the employers but at the interference with the right of employees to have representatives of their own choosing. As the carriers subject to the act have no constitutional right to interfere with the freedom of the employees in making their selections, they cannot complain of the statute on constitutional grounds. *Tex. & New Orleans R.R. Co. v. Bhd. of Ry. and S.S. Clerks*, 281 U.S. 548, 570 (1930).

NOTES

1. *The Railway Labor Act Today:* Although the Railway Act of 1926 proved reasonably successful in inducing peaceful settlement of contract disputes in the railway industry, it failed to promote freedom of association where it did not exist. As late as 1933, a majority of the largest railroads still maintained company unions. These compromised unions continued to exist

because the statute merely promoted independent unions rather than prohibiting company unions. The statute also lacked adequate enforcement machinery and imposed no effective penalties for non-compliance. With the election of Franklin D. Roosevelt and a Democratic majority in 1932, the presidents of the railway unions saw their chance to amend this situation, and the Act.

2. *The New Deal Amendments:* In 1934, Congress passed a set of substantial amendments to the Railway Labor Act. In general, the amendments were hailed by the national labor organizations as an important legislative victory. The President signed them on June 21, 1934. Among the most important provisions were:

1)   The prohibition of yellow dog contracts and company unions in the railway industry. The carriers were not to influence employees in their choice of representatives and were directed to bargain collectively with certified representatives.

2)   The establishment of a permanent, bipartite National Railway Adjustment Board (NRAB), to hear grievances submitted by either labor or management. Provision was made for neutral referees to decide disputes if the partisan members of the Board could not agree on a decision. Provision was also made for the enforcement of Board orders in court.

3)   The membership of the National Mediation Board was reduced from five to three members, ostensibly because the Board's workload no longer included grievance disputes. The Board was empowered to conduct representation elections.

In 1936, the provisions of the Railway Labor Act were extended to air carriers. Provision was made for the creation of a National Air Transportation Adjustment Board, but the air transportation industry and its unions have always preferred to maintain local system boards for grievance resolution.

3. *Post New Deal Amendments of the RLA:* Although the basic provisions of the RLA were all in place with the 1936 amendments, a few notable changes have occurred since that time. In 1951, the prohibition of the closed shop passed in 1934, was substantially reversed. The union shop was made a permissible form of required union membership. In addition, dues deductions were permitted. In 1966, in an attempt to relieve caseload pressure on the NRAB, Congress approved the creation of Special Adjustment Boards to hear and resolve grievances on a local basis. Finally, in 1970, Congress made further changes designed to relieve caseload congestion at the NRAB, increasing its permanent membership to 34, half appointed by the carriers and half by national labor organizations.

iv. The End of the Early Industrial Period: The Great Depression and the Norris-LaGuardia Act

The Roaring Twenties came to a screeching halt on "Black Thursday" October 24, 1929. On that day, stock speculators, many of whom had bought stock on margin, began to panic and sell off their shares. A group of Wall Street bankers intervened to stabilize the market for a brief time by buying blue chip stocks at inflated prices. However, the following week the market entered a free fall losing over 24% of its value. Compounding the nation's woes, many banks were heavily invested in the market and its decline forced them into default either directly or by undermining people's confidence in the security of their deposits. These defaults forced the banks to recall loans, restricting the availability of credit and causing a contraction in the money supply. As the nation's wealth and money supply contracted, aggregate demand for goods and services declined, depressing prices and wages, and causing employers to lay off employees. With fewer people working, aggregate demand spiraled down further and the nation entered the long dark period known as the Great Depression. For over a decade, the nation's unemployment rate exceeded 10% and reached heights estimated at 25–30%. By 1933, the nation's gross domestic product had dropped by a third. The seriousness of this economic calamity would shake the American people's confidence in capitalism. John Kenneth Galbraith, The Age of Uncertainty 213 (1977); *see also* John Kenneth Galbraith, The Great Crash 1929 (1997).

The decline in the American economy prompted employers to renege on the promises of the corporate welfare programs developed under the new systems of personnel management. Pension plans, medical benefits, and the long-term employment relationships these benefits were designed to promote, became a liability in the new economic environment. These programs, along with many of the employees, were rapidly discarded. The at-will employment doctrine facilitated this change since it allowed employers to unilaterally change the terms and conditions of employment prospectively, or end the employment relationship. Almost all of the pensions of the day had long vesting requirements of 25–30 years of employment, and even then were written under the "gratuity theory" of pensions so that, like the promise of a gift, they were only enforceable once the benefit was actually given. *See e.g. McNevin v. Solvay Process Co.*, 32 A.D. 610, 53 N.Y.S. 98 (1898), *aff'd per curium* 60 N.E. 1115 (1901). At the same time, many employers paid full dividends on common stock as a way of shoring up their stock prices to preserve their ability to raise capital. Needless to say, the facility with which employers were able to jettison long term commitments and benefits to employees under the existing regime of freedom of contract contributed to a growing political consensus on the need for government regulation and guarantees of benefits.

Initial government reactions to the crisis were minimal or even counterproductive. President Hoover argued that the nation's problems could be solved through "belt-tightening." He reasoned that, in such a time of uncertainty, the government should be stable—balancing its budget and shoring up its currency. Unfortunately, these measures further contracted the money supply and decreased aggregate demand. There were also those in Hoover's administration who believed that the pain people were enduring would have a therapeutic effect on the economy. Secretary of the Treasury, Andrew Mellon, argued "Liquidate labor, liquidate stocks, liquidate the farmers, liquidate real estate. . . . [That] will purge the rottenness out of the system. . . . People will work harder, live a more moral life . . ., and enterprising people will pick up the wrecks from less competent people." Herbert Hoover, The Memoirs of Herbert Hoover, vol. 3: The Great Depression, 1929–1941, at 9 (1951). However, in Congress, at least some representatives were ready for a change. Republicans George Norris and Fiorello LaGuardia ushered through the act that would bear their names and would outlaw yellow-dog contracts and attempt to free unions from the burden of "governance by injunction." President Hoover begrudgingly signed the Norris-LaGuardia Act on March 3, 1933—his last day in office. 47 Stat. 70 (1932), 29 U.S.C. §§ 101–15 (2012).[6]

The Norris-LaGuardia Act sought to solve the problems of the existing labor relations system by taking the federal judiciary out of the business of regulating those relations through injunctions. Section I of the Act declares, "No court of the United States, shall have jurisdiction to issue any restraining order or temporary or permanent injunction in a case involving or growing out of a labor dispute, except in conformity with the provisions of this Act." The under-lying philosophy of the Act was to cure the existing defects in the common law and antitrust laws, without directly encouraging employee organization. In so doing, it sought to establish a "laissez-faire" system for labor relations, in which the federal government neither hindered nor fostered employee organization.

Mindful of the Court's nullification of the previous efforts to limit labor injunctions in the Clayton Act, the drafters of the Norris-LaGuardia Act sought to leave no loophole for later judicial mischief. In Section 13, paragraph C of the Act, a "labor dispute" is broadly defined as "any controversy concerning terms or conditions of employment, or concerning the association or representation of persons in negotiating . . . terms or conditions of employment, regardless of whether or not the disputants stand in the proximate relation of employer and employee." Section 4 of the Act states, "No court of the United States shall have jurisdiction to issue any . . . injunction in any case . . . growing out of any labor dispute to prohibit any person . . . interested in such dispute . . . from doing, whether singly or in concert, any of the following acts." Section 4 then goes on to

---

[6]   The provisions of the Norris-LaGuardia Act can be found in the statutory supplement.

meticulously describe as protected activities all of the activities necessary to undertake the traditional union weapons of strike and boycott, exempting for possible injunction only conduct involving violence or fraud.

Even where violence or fraud is alleged, Section 7 of the Act specifies that an order restraining such conduct may be issued only after a hearing that produces certain findings of fact. This hearing must be preceded by "due and personal notice . . . to all known persons against whom relief is sought" unless failure to issue an order without notice would cause "substantial and irreparable injury to complainant's property," and even in this dire circumstance the Act limits the restraining order to "no longer than five days." The court's findings must be based upon "the testimony of witnesses in open court (with opportunity for cross-examination)." Among the specific findings the court must make to issue an injunction are that "as to each item of relief granted greater injury will be inflicted upon complainant by the denial of relief than will be inflicted upon defendants by the granting of relief," and that "the public officers charged with the duty to protect complainant's property are unable or unwilling to furnish adequate protection." Section 9 of the Act states that any restraining order or injunction granted pursuant to Section 7 must be narrowly tailored to prohibit only the violent or fraudulent activity that is the basis of the injunction. Section 10 of the Act provides for expedited appeals in cases involving the issuance or denial of a temporary labor injunction, giving such matters "precedence over all other matters except older matters of the same character" in the courts of appeal. Finally, Section 11 of the Act specifies that any person charged with contempt of an order issued under Section 7 shall have the right to a jury trial.

The Norris-LaGuardia Act went on to attempt to remedy some of the other imperfections of the common law that had "dogged" union organizing to date (pun intended). Section 3 of the Act outlawed the infamous "yellow-dog contracts" declaring that any contract in which either party agrees "not to join, become, or remain a member of any labor organization or of any employer organization" is "contrary to the public policy of the United States, shall not be enforceable in any court of the United States and shall not afford any basis for the granting of legal or equitable relief by any such court." Moreover, Section 6 of the Act sought to limit the threat of vicarious liability to union members by stating that "[n]o officer or member of any association . . . participating . . . in a labor dispute, shall be held . . . liable in any court of the United States for the unlawful acts of individual officers, members, or agents, except upon clear proof of actual participation in, or actual authorization of, such acts, or of ratification of such acts after actual knowledge thereof."

Although the Norris-LaGuardia Act dealt only with federal courts, the social and political forces that produced the Act also produced similar statutes in many states. These statutes, commonly referred to as "little

Norris-LaGuardia Acts," are generally modeled on the federal act and deny jurisdiction to state courts to issue injunctions in cases involving labor disputes, except under carefully prescribed conditions.

NOTES

1.   The Norris-LaGuardia Act was effective in ending the system of governance by injunction. However, under existing doctrine, union officers are nevertheless obligated to follow even clearly illegal injunctions, until they are overturned by a court. 42 Am. Jur. 2d Injunctions § 315. Given this and the effectiveness of even temporary injunctions in quelling a strike, to what can we attribute the fact that the Norris-LaGuardia Act has been effective?

2.   *Modern Applications of the Norris-LaGuardia Act*: As will be discussed in Chapter 6, the Supreme Court has developed several qualifications to the protections of the Norris-LaGuardia Act to "accommodate" it to the provisions of Section 301 of the Labor Management Relations Act, enacted in 1947. Nevertheless the Norris-LaGuardia Act continues to provide significant protections against injunction for employee collective action. Consider the facts in *Jacksonville Bulk Terminals, Incorporated v. International Longshoremen's Ass'n*, 457 U.S. 702 (1982):

On Christmas day, 1979, the Soviet Union invaded Afghanistan. The international diplomatic response was severe. President Jimmy Carter stated that the Soviet incursion was "the most serious threat to the peace since the Second World War." He organized an international embargo on grain and technology exports to the Soviet Union and a boycott of the 1980 Summer Olympics in Moscow. Humanitarian aid and low tech exports such as fertilizer were not included in the embargo.

In January of 1980, the members of the International Longshoremen's Association (ILA) decided to do President Carter and the international community one better. The President of the ILA announced that "in response to overwhelming demands by the rank and file members of the Union, the leadership of the ILA today ordered immediate suspension in handling all Russian ships and all Russian cargoes in ports where ILA workers are employed. . . . People are upset and they refuse to continue the business as usual policy as long as the Russians insist on being international bully boys."

In accordance with this resolution, members of the ILA employed by Jacksonville Bulk Terminals, Inc. (JBT) refused to load fertilizer components on to ships bound for the Soviet Union. JBT had a collective bargaining agreement with the ILA that included a broad no strike clause which stated "during the term of this Agreement, . . . the Union agrees there shall not be any strike of any kind or degree whatsoever, . . . for any cause whatsoever." The contract also had an arbitration clause that required "matters in dispute" to be submitted to arbitration. In response to this work stoppage, JBT brought an action against the ILA, alleging that the work stoppage violated the collective bargaining agreement, seeking to compel arbitration, and requesting a temporary restraining order and a preliminary injunction pending arbitration.

May a federal district court grant an injunction under the Norris-LaGuardia Act based on these facts? Section 13 paragraph c of the Norris-LaGuardia Act defines a "labor dispute" as "any controversy concerning terms or conditions of employment, or concerning the association or representation of persons in negotiating . . . terms or conditions of employment, regardless of whether or not the disputants stand in the proximate relation of employer and employee." Is this political boycott conducted by the Longshoremen a "labor dispute" protected by the Act? What about the fact that the union has promised not to strike, and instead to arbitrate disputes, during the life of the agreement? In fact the Supreme Court has held that injunction of strikes over an issue encompassed by a contractual grievance arbitration clause does not violate the Norris-LaGuardia Act, *Boys Market, Inc. v. Retail Clerks Union, Local 770*, 398 U.S. 235 (1970) and *Buffalo Forge C. v. Steelworkers*, 428 U.S. 397 (1976), *infra* Chapter 6, but is the Soviet's invasion of Afghanistan really an issue that can be resolved through contract arbitration by JBT and the ILA? *See Jacksonville Bulk Terminals, Inc. v. International Longshoremen's Ass'n*, 457 U.S. 702 (1982) (term "labor dispute" defined to include even disputes that have their origin in political protests rather than economic self-interest, underlying issue of union members' outrage over Soviet invasion of Afghanistan not arbitrable).

c. The Middle of the Industrial Period (1932–1950): The New Deal, World War II, and Its Immediate Aftermath

In 1932, Franklin Delano Roosevelt (FDR) and the Democrats were swept to power on a tidal wave of discontent with President Hoover and the policies of the Republican Party. FDR carried 42 of the 48 states while his Democratic Party picked up100 seats in the House and 12 seats in the Senate. Roosevelt's stirring inaugural address made it clear that the government was, at long last, willing to take responsibility for direct aid to workers, farmers, and industry and to enact programs to help right the economy. As the President declared "the only thing we have to fear is fear itself," the country took hope and felt it had found the leadership necessary to get out of the Depression. In his presidential campaign, FDR had promised a "New Deal" for the American people that would provide work, security and a voice in the running of the economy. For the first time in our nation's history, a government had taken power that would make the welfare of industrial workers a matter of primary concern and which would act on the principle that only organized labor could deal on equal terms with organized capital to bring about a proper balance between the two forces in capitalist society.

i.   *The National Labor Relations Act (the Wagner Act)*

a)   *Legislative History of the Act*

THE NATIONAL LABOR RELATIONS BOARD[7]
Frank W. McCulloch[8] and Tim Bornstein
(1974)

I.   BEFORE THE WAGNER ACT

During the famous Hundred Days following Roosevelt's inauguration, Congress followed his leadership in approving a number of innovative approaches to revive the economy. Surely the boldest of these was the National Industrial Recovery Act (NIRA), which swept through Congress on a tidal wave of urgency and was signed by the President on June 16, 1933. The scheme of the NIRA was to relax the antitrust laws to permit employers within a single industry to enter into cooperative codes of fair competition so as to increase employment, establish minimum wages and hours, and accelerate production and purchasing power. In effect, the Act permitted price-fixing in exchange for industry's willingness to maintain employment and agreed-on wage levels.

In order to encourage the labor movement's cooperation in the programs generated by the NIRA, the White House and Congress agreed to an obscure provision in that statue—Section 7(a)—patterned largely after the policy declarations in the Norris-LaGuardia Act. In substance, Section 7 (a) required every code of fair competition under the NIRA to include the following terms:

(1) The employees shall have the right to organize and bargain collectively through representatives of their own choosing, and shall be free from the interference, restraint, or coercion of employers . . . in the designation of such representatives . . . or in other concerted activities for the purpose of collective bargaining or other mutual aid or protection;

(2) That no employee and no one seeking employment shall be required as a condition of employment to join any company union or to refrain from joining, organizing, or assisting a labor organization of his own choosing.

Although Section 7(a) was scarcely more than a declaration of policy, it seemed to have a remarkable energizing effect on the labor movement. [In hundreds of organizing campaigns, unions used Section 7(a) as the basis for telling unorganized workers: "President Roosevelt wants you to join the union!"] In combination with other causes, Section 7(a) was a

---

[7]   Reproduced with permission of Greenwood Publishing Group, Inc. Westport, CT.

[8]   Frank W. McCulloch was Chair of the National Labor Relations Board from March 7, 1961, to June 2, 1970.

catalyst for a frenzy of organizing, employer resistance, and strike activity throughout the county.

In response to widespread labor unrest, President Roosevelt appointed a National Labor Board in August, 1933, to bring about compliance with Section 7(a) and to mediate labor disputes. As chairman of this board, the President named his old friend and ally Senator Robert Wagner of New York as the public member. Other members were named as representatives of labor and industry.

In May, 1935, the shaky edifice of voluntary codes created by the National Industrial Recovery Act collapsed. A fatal blow was stuck by the Supreme Court in that month in the famous "sick chicken" case, *Schechter Poultry Corp. v. U.S.*, which declared the NIRA unconstitutional. While the Supreme Court in its austere chambers was writing the obituary for the NIRA, several thousand feet away in the Capitol, Congress was at work on a comprehensive new labor statute, the Wagner Act.

II. THE WAGNER ACT AND THE BIRTH OF THE NLRB

Legislative History of the Wagner Act

In the congressional elections in November, 1934, an overwhelming Democratic majority was sent to Washington. Both the mood of the country and the spirit of Congress were ripe for formulating long-term and fundamental national labor policies. Senator Robert Wagner introduced his famous bill, S. 1958, on February 15, 1935. Ironically, President Roosevelt was rather cool to Senator Wagner's bill until virtually the eve of its passage. Roosevelt preferred a more consensual statute, one that could be jointly agreed on by labor and management, like the Railway Labor Act of 1926.

Despite intense opposition from management and, perversely, from the Communist Far Left (which regarded the bill as a cruel "deception" of workers), Wagner's bill passed the Senate by a lopsided vote, sixty-three to twelve. At this point, the White House publicly endorsed the bill for the first time, and it easily passed the House of Representatives by a voice vote. Insignificant differences between the Senate and House bills were easily resolved by a conference committee, and the agreed-on bill was overwhelmingly approved by the entire Congress in late June.

On July 5, 1935, without the pomp and ceremony that often accompany the signing of historic legislation, President Roosevelt quietly signed the National Labor Relations Act and issued a low-key message. It said, in part:

> A better relationship between labor and management is the high purpose of this act. By assuring the employees the right of collective bargaining it fosters the development of the employment contract on a sound and equitable basis. By providing

for an orderly procedure for determining who is entitled to represent the employees, it aims to remove one of the chief causes of wasteful economic strife. By preventing practices which tend to destroy the independence of labor it seeks, for every worker within its scope, that freedom which is justly his.

Years later the historian James MacGregor Burns would write that the Wagner Act was "the most radical legislation passed during the New Deal, in the sense that it altered fundamentally the nation's politics by vesting massive economic and political power in organized labor."

* * *

b) The Purposes of the Wagner Act

Congress was forthright in stating the "Findings and Policies" behind the Wagner Act expressly in the statute. Section 1 of the Act states:

> The denial by employers of the right of employees to organize and the refusal by employers to accept the procedure of collective bargaining lead to strikes and other forms of industrial strife or unrest, which have the intent or the necessary effect of burdening or obstructing commerce . . .

> The inequality of bargaining power between employees who do not possess full freedom of association or actual liberty of contract, and employers who are organized in the corporate or other forms of ownership association substantially burdens and affects the flow of commerce, and tends to aggravate recurrent business depressions, by depressing wage rates and the purchasing power of wage earners in industry . . .

> It is hereby declared to be the policy of the United States to eliminate the causes of certain substantial obstructions to the free flow of commerce . . . by encouraging the practice and procedure of collective bargaining and by protecting the exercise by workers of full freedom of association, self-organization, and designation of representatives of their own choosing, for the purpose of negotiating the terms and conditions of their employment or other mutual aid or protection." 49 Stat. 449 (1935).

NOTES

1. *The Purposes of the Wagner Act:* As McCulloch and Bornstein observed, two of the primary purposes of the Wagner Act were expressly stated in Section 1 of the Act.

Industrial Peace: The most common argument made in favor of the Wagner Act was that fostering collective bargaining through a regulated system of selecting bargaining representatives and negotiating agreements would decrease labor relations strife or promote "industrial peace." Although this argument was framed with an eye towards justifying federal intervention into labor relations under the commerce clause power, the supporters of the bill genuinely intended that the Act encourage and regularize collective bargaining as a means of peacefully resolving labor relations disputes.

Equity in Bargaining Power: Another theme in the passage of the Wagner Act was that the economy would be strengthened by independent unions which could insist upon more equitable division of profits, thereby increasing purchasing power. Thus, the bill was seen as a means to fight the depression era contraction in aggregate demand that and pump money into the economy. Unionization was seen as a positive means of rebalancing employee and employer bargaining power for the benefit of the economy and society.

Industrial Democracy: A final theme of importance in the passage of the Wagner Act was that of encouraging democratic processes in the work life of employees. Although not expressly mentioned in Section 1 of the Act, the idea of "industrial democracy" was important in the floor debates and the public presentation of the Act. Just as democracy was good for government, so too the drafters thought that some form of industrial democracy would benefit the machinations of the workplace. Although vaguely defined, the idea of industrial democracy included collective, and thus fairer, representation of individual employees and the joint creation of private law through collective bargaining. Through collective bargaining, employees would have a more effective voice in determining the conditions of employment, thereby achieving a higher level of human integrity and dignity. James B. Atleson, Values and Assumptions in American Labor Law 40–42 (1983).

2.   *Interpretation of the Act in Light of Its Purposes:* The purposes of the Act have not just been flowery pronouncements long since forgotten, but in fact have been touchstones for the Board and Court in interpreting the provisions of the Act.

Various Board and court decisions have interpreted sections of the NLRA in light of its purpose of promoting industrial peace. *See e.g. Fall River Dyeing & Finishing Corp.,* 482 U.S. 27, at 38–39 (1987) ("The upshot of the presumptions [of a continuing majority] is to permit unions to develop stable bargaining relationships with employers, which will enable the unions to pursue the goals of their members, and this pursuit, in turn, will further industrial peace."); *Charles D. Bonanno Linen Serv. v. NLRB,* 454 U.S. 404, 412 (1982) (stating that rules on multiemployer bargaining were designed to promote industrial peace); *Mallinckrodt Chem. Works,* 162 N.L.R.B. 387, 392 (1966) (holding that, in defining an appropriate unit, the Board will take into account the interest of employees and the public in stability of labor relations and accordingly uninterrupted operation of facilities); *Teamsters Local 174 v. Lucas Flour Co.,* 369 U.S. 95, 105 (1962) ("We approve that doctrine [of finding implied no-strike clauses in agreements to arbitrate]. . . . [A] contrary view would be completely at odds with the basic policy of national labor legislation to promote the arbitral process as a substitute for economic warfare.") (footnote omitted); *Textile Workers Union v. Lincoln Mills of Ala.,* 353 U.S. 448, 455 (1957) ("It [the Labor Management Relations Act] expresses a federal policy that federal courts should enforce . . . agreements [to arbitrate] . . . and that industrial peace can be best obtained only in that way."); *Buffalo Broad. Co.*, 242 N.L.R.B. 1105 (1979) and *Marion Power Shovel Co.*, 230 N.L.R.B. 576 (1977) (stating that bargaining history is given weight in determining the appropriate unit largely because continuing an established unit is viewed as promoting stability in labor relations and thus industrial peace); *see also United Steelworkers v. American Mfg. Co.*, 363 U.S. 564, 567–68 (1960); *United Steelworkers v. Warrior & Gulf Navigation Co.*, 363 U.S. 574, 578–85 (1960); *United Steelworkers v. Enter. Wheel & Car Corp.*, 363 U.S. 593 (1960).

Similarly, Board and court decisions discuss the Act's purpose of promoting equality in bargaining power in interpreting provisions of the Act. *See e.g. NLRB v. E.C. Atkins & Co.*, 331 U.S. 398, 404 (1947); *NLRB v. Jones & Laughlin Steel Corp.*, 301 U.S. 1, 23 n.2, 33–34 (1937); *Lewis v. Quality Coal Corp.*, 270 F.2d 140, 143 (7th Cir. 1959), *cert. denied*, 361 U.S. 929 (1960) (holding that a union's threat to strike does not create unfair bargaining power in favor of employees sufficient to render employment contract illegal); *Beckwith v. United Parcel Serv.*, 703 F.Supp. 138, 141 (D. Me. 1988) (noting that the NLRA is concerned with equating bargaining power between employer and employees), *aff'd.*, 889 F.2d 344 (1st Cir. 1989); *United States v. Int'l Union, United Mine Workers*, 77 F.Supp. 563, 567 (D. D.C. 1948) (stating that organization is the *only* means by which employees can achieve a measure of equality of bargaining power with employers); *Nat'l Mar. Union v. Herzog*, 78 F.Supp. 146, 155–56 (D. D.C.) (statutory three-judge court holding that Congress sought to promote equality of bargaining power not only by guaranteeing employees the right to act collectively but also by protecting an elected union's exclusivity as a bargaining agent and imposing on employers the duty to bargain in good faith), *aff'd*, 334 U.S. 854 (1948); *Kinder-Care Learning Ctr., Inc.*, 299 N.L.R.B. 1171, 1172 (1990) (finding that employees are at a disadvantage in bargaining with their employer unless they are able to organize and bargain collectively); *Meyers Indus.*, 281 N.L.R.B. 882 (1986) (holding that NLRA contemplates collective action as a means of achieving equality of bargaining power), *aff'd sub nom. Prill v. NLRB*, 835 F.2d 1481, 1484 (D.C. Cir. 1987).

Although somewhat less common, Supreme Court precedents have also acknowledged the importance of the purpose of promoting industrial democracy in interpreting the statute. *See e.g., Steele v. Louisville & Nashville R. Co.*, 323 U.S. 192, 202 (1944) ("Congress has seen fit to clothe the bargaining representative with powers comparable to those possessed by a legislative body both to create and restrict the rights of those whom it represents. . . .[T]he organization . . . [must] represent all its members, the majority as well as the minority, and it is to act for and not against those whom it represents."); *Nu-Car Carriers, Inc.*, 88 N.L.R.B. 75, 76 (1950), *enf'd*, 189 F.2d 756 (3d Cir.), *cert. denied*, 342 U.S. 919 (1951) (holding that for an employee to try to influence his union's policies, criticize his union's leadership, and generally debate the goals of his bargaining representative with other members is protected concerted activity under the NLRA); *NLRB v. Allis-Chalmers Mfg. Co.*, 388 U.S. 175, 180 (1967) ("National labor policy has been built on the premise that by . . . acting through a labor organization freely chosen by the majority, the employees of the appropriate unit have the most effective means of bargaining for improvements in wages, hours, and working conditions."); *Emporium Capwell Co. v. Community Org.*, 420 U.S. 50, 64–65 (1975) ("vesting the representatives of the majority with this broad power [of exclusive representation,] Congress did not, of course, authorize a tyranny of the majority over minority interests. . . . [I]t undertook in the 1959 Landrum-Griffin amendments to assure that minority voices are heard as they are in the functioning of a democratic institution. . . . [W]e have held, [that] by the very nature of the [power of exclusive representation,] Congress implicitly imposed upon [the union] a duty fairly and in good faith to represent the interests of minorities within that unit. . . . And the Board has taken the position that a union's refusal [to represent minorities] is an unfair labor practice."). *See also*, James Y. Moore & Richard A. Bales, *Elections, Neutrality Agreements, and Card Checks: The Failure of the Political Model of Industrial Democracy*, 87 Ind. L. J. 147 (2012); Charles B. Craver, *Mandatory Worker Participation is Required in a Declining Union Environment to Provide Employees with Meaningful Industrial Democracy*, 66 Geo. Wash. L. Rev. 135 (1997); Karl E. Klare, *Workplace Democracy and Market Reconstruction: An Agenda for Legal Reform*, 38 Cath. U. L. Rev. 1 (1988).

c) The Provisions of the Wagner Act

Section 2: Covered Employers and Employees

Section 2 of the Wagner Act sets forth definitions of many of the most important terms used in the statute. The definitions of "employer" and "employee" in this section set the basic parameters for the coverage of the Act.

Section 2(2): Defines "employer" to include "any person acting as an agent of an employer" but to exclude "the United States or any State or political subdivision thereof, or any person subject to the Railway Labor Act." This definition is intentionally broad, but expressly excludes public employers and employers governed by the RLA. Public employers were excluded because, under our federal system, there were serious questions about the constitutionality of a federal law governing the relationship of the states with their employees. With respect to the federal government, it was thought that it was a more benevolent employer, and its employees were not in as great a need of collective bargaining. As will be discussed later in this chapter, most public employers are now covered by federal or state statutes specifically governing public sector labor relations.

Section 2(3): Defines "employee" to include "any employee, and shall not be limited to the employees of a particular employer," and to exclude agricultural laborers, domestic servants, and any person employed by his parent or spouse. The provision that the definition "shall not be limited to the employees of a particular employer" was an attempt to avoid the fate of the labor exemption of the Clayton Act before the courts. Important qualifications to this definition of "employee" were added in the Taft-Hartley Amendments of 1947. We discuss the definition of employee and employer under the Act in more detail in Chapter 2.

Section 7: The Right to Organize

The heart of the Wagner Act is Section 7, "Rights of Employees." Based on Section 7 of the NIRA, this section sets forth the employees fundamental rights to organize, collectively bargain, and undertake collective action for their mutual aid and protection.

> "Employees shall have the right to self-organization, to form, join, or assist labor organizations, to bargain collectively through representatives of their own choosing, and to engage in concerted activities, for the purpose of collective bargaining or other mutual aid or protection." 49 Stat. 449 § 7 (1935); 29 U.S.C. §§ 157 (2012).

Each of its three primary components—the right of *self-organization,* the right to engage in *collective bargaining through freely chosen representatives*, and the right to engage in *concerted activities*—has been given specific meaning by the Board and courts in a variety of factual situations. The remainder of the statute is designed to implement these fundamental rights and make them real.

Section 8: Unfair Labor Practices

Based on his experience under the NIRA, Senator Wagner believed that in order for the NLRA to succeed, it needed to specify the activities that impinged on employees' collective rights under Section 7. Accordingly, Section 8 of the Wagner Act specified five prohibitions against employer activities, called "unfair labor practices," which encroached on employees' collective rights. It was not until the Taft-Hartley Amendments of 1947 that Congress would define unfair labor practices for unions in the provisions of Section 8(b).

Section 8(a)(1): Forbids employers to "interfere with, restrain, or coerce employees in the exercise of the rights guaranteed in Section 7." Congress left it to the National Labor Relations Board (NLRB) to apply this general prohibition in the light of the infinite combinations of events which might be charged as violative of its terms. In general, it has been interpreted to prohibit management threats, surveillance, espionage, restrictions on employee solicitation and communication, violence, and promises of benefit.

Section 8(a)(2): Attempts to ensure independent unions by providing that employers shall not "dominate or interfere with the formation or administration of any labor organization or contribute financial support to it." The term "labor organization" is broadly defined in Section 2(5) as "any organization of any kind . . . in which employees participate and which exists for the purpose . . . of dealing with employers concerning grievances, labor disputes, wages, rates of pay, hours of employment, or conditions of work." As we will discuss later in Chapter 4, this broad prohibition against company unions has posed an obstacle for employer sponsored employee committees.

Section 8(a)(3): Prohibits "discrimination in regard to hire or tenure of employment or any term or condition of employment to encourage or discourage membership in any labor organization." Workers are protected from various acts of employer retaliation for union affiliation, including: discharge, wage cuts, layoffs, and reassignment A proviso to Section 8(3) authorizes union security agreements—agreements between the union and the employer that employees will provide certain support to the union as a condition of employment.

Section 8(a)(4): Provides that employers shall not "discharge or otherwise discriminate against an employee because he has filed charges or given testimony under this Act" in order to ensure employee cooperation in enforcement of the Act.

Section 8(a)(5): Requires employers "to bargain collectively" with the representatives of employees. Combined with the definition of what it means to "bargain collectively" added later to the statute in section 8(d), this provision requires employers to engage in good faith negotiations with a labor organization properly selected as the majority agent of employees. What it means to bargain "in good faith" will be discussed extensively later in Chapter 5.

Section 9: Representation Elections

In Section 9 of the Wagner Act, Congress set forth three fundamental concepts that govern the selection of the bargaining representative: exclusive representation, an appropriate bargaining unit, and majority rule.

Section 9(a): If a representative has been selected by a majority of employees in an appropriate unit, that representative becomes the "exclusive representative of all the employees in such a unit for the purposes of collective bargaining." The adoption of a system of exclusive representation makes our industrial relations system somewhat unique in the world since most countries allow multiple, or "plural" unions in the same unit, generally under some system of proportional representation. This section also specifies the subjects of collective bargaining as "wages, hours of employment, or other conditions of employment." As we shall see later in Chapter 5, this delineation of the subjects of bargaining in the Act has led to the distinction among "mandatory," "permissive", and even "prohibited" subjects of bargaining.

Section 9(b): Congress defined the concept of an "appropriate bargaining unit," and directed the NLRB "to decide in each case where, in order to insure to employees the full benefit of their right to self-organization and to collective bargaining . . ., the unit appropriate for the purposes of collective bargaining." The determination of an appropriate bargaining unit is important because only employees within the approved unit may vote in the representation election, and the employer's obligation to bargain is limited to employees in that unit. Moreover, as will be discussed later in Chapter 7, the union is under an obligation to "fairly represent" all employees in the unit, whether they are supporters of the union or not.

Section 9(c): Within an appropriate unit, Congress specified that the exclusive representative was that chosen by a majority of the unit as indicated by secret-ballot elections or by "any other suitable" means. The formal election provisions of the NLRA are another facet that makes American labor law largely unique in the world, although in more recent times unions have come to rely more on less formal means of establishing majority representation such as card checks and voluntary recognition.

Other Provisions: Administration of the Act

To administer the National Labor Relations Act, Congress created the National Labor Relations Board (NLRB or "the Board") composed of three members appointed by the President and confirmed by the Senate. Congress later increased the number of Board members to five. Board members serve staggered five year terms. The Board is charged with administering both the unfair labor practice provisions of Section 8 and the election provisions of Section 9. The Board's authority and procedures for determining whether an unfair labor practice has occurred are set forth in Section 10. The Board's authority to conduct elections is set forth in Section 9. The Board is empowered to investigate charges, issue "complaints," conduct hearings, determine whether violations have occurred, and issue orders to stop and remedy violations. Upon finding a violation, the Board can issue a "cease and desist" order against the violator and take such other "affirmative action, including reinstatement of employees with or without back pay," as is necessary to effectuate the purposes of the statute. The primary limitation on the Board's power in fashioning "affirmative actions" is that the NLRA is expressly a remedial statute designed to stop and redress illegal conduct, but not punish it. The Board's orders are not self-enforcing, so the Board is authorized to petition for enforcement in the appropriate federal court of appeals.

NOTES

1.   *Section 7 Rights*: The declaration of Section 7 that "[e]mployees shall have the right to self-organization, to form, join, or assist labor organizations" seems fairly straightforward, but what does it mean "to engage in concerted activities, for the purpose of . . . mutual aid or protection?" Do you have to be represented by a union to act "in concert?" What would "mutual aid" mean besides collective bargaining and contract enforcement? If Section 7 allows

employees "to bargain collectively through representatives of their own choosing," do they have to "choose" their representatives through the Section 9 election procedure, or will other means serve? What other means?

2.   *Section 8 ULP's*: Section 8(a)(1) forbids employers to "interfere with, restrain, or coerce employees in the exercise of the rights guaranteed in Section 7." Can an employer tell her employees what a bad idea it would be for them to organize? Can she tell them it may cost them their jobs because it will drive the firm out of business? What about the Section 8(a)(3) prohibition on employer discrimination? If an employer knows an employee is a good welder, but is applying for a job just to organize his shop, does he have to hire that welder? If the employees do organize and after a few years of operating with the union and making modest profits the employer decides to sub-contract the welding to save money, laying-off the union welders, is this discrimination?

3.   *Section 9 Elections*: How do we decide what is an "appropriate unit" for an election under Section 9(b)? Should it be all employees in a certain craft? All of the employees in a plant? All the employees in all of the employer's plants? On what basis should we decide who needs to be included? Should the Board just let the employees organize in any unit they want, subject to the express provisions of the act?

ii. The Courts' Response: The Constitutionality of the Wagner Act

Even before the ink had dried on President Roosevelt's signature on the Wagner Act, American employers denounced it as unconstitutional. The National Association of Manufacturers issued a memorandum arguing that the Act was unconstitutional the very day it was signed. Several weeks later, the American Liberty League, an organization of many of the country's largest employers, issued a 127-page treatise that argued that the Act was unconstitutional and urging employers to ignore it. Frank W. McCulloch & Tim Bornstein, The National Labor Relations Board 26 (1974).

There was good reason for employers to doubt the constitutionality of the Wagner Act. As previously discussed, the Supreme Court had consistently invalidated other major New Deal statutes as exceeding the federal government's constitutional powers. With these decisions as their guide, the lower federal courts issued nearly one hundred injunctions against the operation of the Wagner Act and the NLRB between 1935 and 1937. In 1935, the Supreme Court had invalidated the National Industrial Recovery Act and in 1936 it struck down the labor provisions of the Bituminous Coal Conservation Act and New York's minimum-wage law.

In November of 1936, Franklin Delano Roosevelt was re-elected by a landslide. He complained bitterly of the tyranny of the Supreme Court's "nine old men," who were undermining the statutory foundation of the New Deal which the vast majority of the American people had elected him to pursue. In February of 1937, Roosevelt surprised the nation with a plan to appoint one new Supreme Court justice for each justice over age seventy, up to a maximum of six. This scheme was dubbed the "court-packing plan" by its critics and, overnight, it provoked a national controversy about the proper bounds of executive, legislative and judicial powers.

The stage was set for one of the most important legal contests in our nation's history. At stake was not only the survival of the popular legislative agenda of the New Deal legislation and Roosevelt's credibility as a leader, but also the integrity of the Supreme Court. During the spring of 1937, as the controversy brewed on Capitol Hill and across the country, the question of the constitutionality of the Wagner Act reached the Supreme Court in five test cases. The most important of these cases was the *Jones & Laughlin Steel Corp.* case, excerpted below.

NLRB V. JONES & LAUGHLIN STEEL CORP.
301 U.S. 1 (1937)

CHIEF JUSTICE HUGHES delivered the opinion of the Court:

In a proceeding under the National Labor Relations Act of 1935 the National Labor Relations Board found that the respondent, Jones & Laughlin Steel Corporation, had violated the act by engaging in unfair labor practices affecting commerce. The unfair labor practices charged were that the corporation was discriminating against members of the union with regard to hire and tenure of employment, and was coercing and intimidating its employees in order to interfere with their self-organization. The discriminatory and coercive action alleged was the discharge of certain employees.

The National Labor Relations Board, sustaining the charge, ordered the corporation to cease and desist from such discrimination and coercion, to offer reinstatement to ten of the employees named, to make good their losses in pay, and to post for thirty days notices that the corporation would not discriminate against [union] members. As the corporation failed to comply, the Board petitioned the Circuit Court of Appeals to enforce the order. The court denied the petition holding that the order lay beyond the range of federal power. We granted certiorari.

Contesting the ruling of the Board, the respondent argues (1) that the act is in reality a regulation of labor relations and not of interstate commerce; (2) that the act can have no application to the respondent's relations with its production employees because they are not subject to regulation by the federal government; and (3) that the provisions of the act violate section 2 of article 3 and the Fifth and Seventh Amendments of the Constitution of the United States.

The facts as to the nature and scope of the business of the Jones & Laughlin Steel Corporation have been found by the Labor Board, and they are not in dispute. The Labor Board has found: The Corporation is organized under the laws of Pennsylvania and has its principal office at Pittsburgh. It is engaged in the business of manufacturing iron and steel in plants situated in Pittsburgh and nearby Aliquippa, Pa. [and is] the fourth largest producer of steel in the United States. With its subsidiaries—nineteen in number—it is a completely integrated enterprise, owning and operating ore, coal and limestone properties, lake and river transportation facilities and terminal railroads located at its manufacturing plants. It has sales offices in twenty cities in the United States and a wholly-owned subsidiary in Canada. Approximately 75 percent of its product is shipped out of Pennsylvania.

We think it clear that the National Labor Relations Act may be construed so as to operate within the sphere of constitutional authority.

[I]n its present application, the statute goes no further than to safeguard the right of employees to self-organization and to select representatives of their own choosing for collective bargaining or other mutual protection without restraint or coercion by their employer.

That is a fundamental right. Employees have as clear a right to organize and select their representatives for lawful purposes as the respondent has to organize its business and select its own officers and agents. Discrimination and coercion to prevent the free exercise of the right of employees to self-organization and representation is a proper subject for condemnation by competent legislative authority. Long ago we stated the reason for labor organizations. We said that they were organized out of the necessities of the situation; that a single employee was helpless in dealing with an employer; that he was dependent ordinarily on his daily wage for the maintenance of himself and family; that, if the employer refused to pay him the wages that he thought fair, he was nevertheless unable to leave the employ and resist arbitrary and unfair treatment; that union was essential to give laborers opportunity to deal on an equality with their employer. *Am. Steel Foundries v. Tri-City Cent. Trades Council*, 257 U.S. 184. We reiterated these views when we had under consideration the Railway Labor Act of 1926, 44 Stat. 577. Fully recognizing the legality of collective action on the part of employees in order to safeguard their proper interests, we said that Congress was not required to ignore this right but could safeguard it. Congress could seek to make appropriate collective action of employees an instrument of peace rather than of strife. Hence the prohibition by Congress of interference with the selection of representatives for the purpose of negotiation and conference between employers and employees, "instead of being an invasion of the constitutional right of either, was based on the recognition of the rights of both." *Tex. & New Orleans R.R. Co. v. Ry. & S.S. Clerks*.

[Questions under the Commerce Clause]

The congressional authority to protect interstate commerce from burdens and obstructions is not limited to transactions which can be deemed to be an essential part of a "flow" of interstate or foreign commerce. Burdens and obstructions may be due to injurious action springing from other sources. The fundamental principle is that the power to regulate commerce is the power to enact "all appropriate legislation" for its "protection or advancement" (*The Daniel Ball*, 10 Wall. 557, 564). That power is plenary and may be exerted to protect interstate commerce "no matter what the source of the dangers which threaten it." *Second Employers' Liab. Cases*, 223 U.S. 1. Although activities may be intrastate in character when separately considered, if they have such a close and substantial relation to interstate commerce that their control is essential or appropriate to protect that commerce from burdens and obstructions, Congress cannot be denied the power to exercise that control. *Schechter Corp. v. U. S.*

Giving full weight to respondent's contention, the fact remains that the stoppage of [its] operations by industrial strife would have a most serious effect upon interstate commerce. In view of respondent's far-flung activities, it is idle to say that the effect would be indirect or remote. It is obvious that it would be immediate and might be catastrophic. We are asked to shut our eyes to the plainest facts of our national life and to deal with the question of direct and indirect effects in an intellectual vacuum. Because there may be but indirect and remote effects upon interstate commerce in connection with a host of local enterprises throughout the country, it does not follow that other industrial activities do not have such a close and intimate relation to interstate commerce as to make the presence of industrial strife a matter of the most urgent national concern. When industries organize themselves on a national scale, making their relation to interstate commerce the dominant factor in their activities, how can it be maintained that their industrial labor relations constitute a forbidden field into which Congress may not enter when it is necessary to protect interstate commerce from the paralyzing consequences of industrial war?

Experience has abundantly demonstrated that the recognition of the right of employees to self-organization and to have representatives of their own choosing for the purpose of collective bargaining is often an essential condition of industrial peace. Refusal to confer and negotiate has been one of the most prolific causes of strife. This is such an outstanding fact in the history of labor disturbances that it is a proper subject of judicial notice and requires no citation of instances. The opinion in the case of *Va. Ry. Co. v. Sys. Fed'n No. 40*, points out that, in the case of carriers, "a prolific source of dispute had been the maintenance by the railroads of company unions and the denial by railway management of the authority of representatives chosen by their employees." The opinion in that case also points to the large measure of success of the labor policy embodied in the Railway Labor Act. And of what avail is it to protect the facility of transportation, if interstate commerce is throttled with respect to the commodities to be transported!

Questions under the Due Process Clause and Other Constitutional Restrictions

Respondent asserts its right to conduct its business in an orderly manner without being subjected to arbitrary restraints. What we have said points to the fallacy in the argument. Employees have their correlative right to organize for the purpose of securing the redress of grievances and to promote agreements with employers relating to rates of pay and conditions of work. *Tex. & New Orleans R.R. Co. v. Ry. S.S. Clerks.* Restraint for the purpose of preventing an unjust interference with that right cannot be considered arbitrary or capricious. The provision of section 9(a) that representatives, for the purpose of collective bargaining, of the majority of the employees in an appropriate unit shall be the exclusive representatives of all the employees in that unit, imposes upon the respondent only the duty of conferring and negotiating with the authorized representatives of its employees for the purpose of settling a labor dispute. This provision has its analogue in section 2, Ninth, of the Railway Labor Act, which was under consideration in *Va. Ry. Co. v. Sys. Fed'n No. 40.*

The act does not compel agreements between employers and employees. It does not compel any agreement whatever. It does not prevent the employer "from refusing to make a collective contract and hiring individuals on whatever terms" the employer "may by unilateral action determine." The act expressly provides in section 9(a) that any individual employee or a group of employees shall have the right at any time to present grievances to their employer. The theory of the act is that free opportunity for negotiation with accredited representatives of employees is likely to promote industrial peace and may bring about the adjustments and agreements which the act in itself does not attempt to compel. The act does not interfere with the normal exercise of the right of the employer to select its employees or to discharge them. The employer may not, under cover of that right, intimidate or coerce its employees with respect to their self-organization and representation.

The act has been criticized as one-sided in its application; that it subjects the employer to supervision and restraint and leaves untouched the abuses for which employees may be responsible. But we are dealing with the power of Congress, not with a particular policy or with the extent to which policy should go. We have frequently said that the legislative authority, exerted within its proper field, need not embrace all the evils within its reach. The Constitution does not forbid "cautious advance, step by step," in dealing with the evils which are exhibited in activities within the range of legislative power. *Carroll v. Greenwich In. Co.,* 199 U.S. 401.

The question in such cases is whether the Legislature, in what it does prescribe, has gone beyond constitutional limits.

Reversed and remanded

[*The dissenting opinion of Justice MCREYNOLDS, joined by Justices VAN DEVANTER, SUITHERLAND and BUTLER has been omitted.*]

NOTES

1. *The "switch in time that saved nine":* At the time the constitutionality of the New Deal legislation was being considered, the Supreme Court was split between the conservative "Four Horsemen" (Justices James Clark McReynolds, George Sutherland, Willis Van Devanter, and Pierce Butler) and the liberal "Three Musketeers" (Louis Brandeis, Benjamin Cardozo, and Harlan Stone) with the balance of power held by Chief Justice Charles Evans Hughes and Justice Owen J. Roberts. The first major realignment on the constitutionality of New Deal legislation occurred in *West Coast Hotel Co. v. Parrish*, 300 U.S. 379 (1937), when Roberts joined Chief Justice Hughes, and Justices Louis Brandeis, Benjamin N. Cardozo, and Harlan Fiske Stone to uphold a Washington State minimum wage law, five to four. The same majority upheld the constitutionality of the Wagner Act on April 12, 1937. These victories for the New Deal, combined with growing public opposition to the court-packing plan, saved both the Wagner Act and the Supreme Court.

2. What is the extent of the federal government's interstate commerce power outlined in the opinion? Is this power adequate to regulate a national economy? What about now that the United States economy is enmeshed in a global economy? How can the government effectively regulate a global economy? Was the Supreme Court's recent opinion in *National Federation of Independent Business v. Sebelius*, 567 U.S. 519 (2012) (upholding the Affordable Care Act's individual mandate as a valid exercise of federal tax power, but in which five justices in separate opinions stated that the individual mandate and the expansion of the Medicaid program exceeded federal power) consistent with the view expressed by the Supreme Court in *Jones & Laughlin*? Are the *Sebelius* opinions consistent with a federal power adequate to regulate a national or international economy?

3. What happens in a national economy if organized labor and management cannot even agree on basic rules for the resolution of representation questions and contract negotiation and enforcement like those represented in the National Labor Relations Act? In England, class divisions have historically been much stronger than they are in the United States and the working class has been even more suspicious of Parliament and the courts as tools of the ruling class. As a result, organized labor resisted national labor legislation in England until relatively recently, opting instead to resolve such questions based on the strength of their membership's solidarity and willingness to strike to get what they need from employers. Even disputes over the interpretation of collective agreements were resolved through strikes if the employees felt strongly enough about the issue. The result was that until

recently England has suffered a rate of work days lost to strikes more than twice as high as that in the United States. Kenneth G. Dau-Schmidt, *Labor Law and Industrial Peace: A Comparative Analysis of the United States, the United Kingdom, Germany and Japan under the Bargaining Model*, 8 Tul. J. Int'l & Comp. L. 117 (2000).

4.   *Good Lawyering:* After the passage of the Wagner Act, the American Liberty League advised its members to ignore the Act as unconstitutional. Clearly in retrospect this was not good substantive legal advice, but prospectively was it good lawyering? Is there a difference between arguing that Congress should not pass an act because it is unconstitutional and advising clients that they need not follow an act because it is unconstitutional? Should lawyers ever advise their clients to violate the law?

5.   *The Changes Over Time That Saved Clayton Act Sections 6 and 20:* The Court's change in attitude, combined with significant changes in personnel[9] and a consistent legislative agenda of establishing minimum labor standards and promoting collective bargaining, led the Court to reexamine its interpretations of the Sherman and Clayton Acts as they apply to labor.

In *Apex Hosiery Co. v. Leader*, 310 U.S. 469 (1940), the Supreme Court examined whether a union was liable for treble damages under the Sherman Act for the conduct of a strike that prevented the company from shipping its product to customers in other states. Based on the legislative history of the Sherman Act, the Court stated that the Act was aimed primarily at combinations of capital or "trusts" that sought to fix prices on goods and services in interstate commerce. Although a combination of workers restrains competition among those workers, such a combination was not prohibited at common law and Section 6 of the Clayton Act made it clear that labor was not a commodity or article of commerce for purposes of the antitrust laws. Thus, the Court held that unions could not be liable under the Sherman Act for collective action such as a strike to raise wages, even though that strike or the wage increase might have an effect on interstate prices. The Court left open potential liability if a union conspired with one or more employers for the purpose of raising prices. The Court disingenuously asserted that its past interpretations of the Sherman Act were consistent with these principles.

In *United States v. Hutcheson*, 312 U.S. 219 (1941), the Court reexamined the labor exemption in Section 20 of the Clayton Act in light of the broad restrictions on labor injunctions contained in the Norris-LaGuardia Act. The Court found that it would be incongruous to continue to read Section 20 as allowing the criminal prosecution of activity that was expressly protected from injunction in the Norris-LaGuardia Act. Moreover, the Court acknowledged that the Norris-LaGuardia Act was a disavowal by Congress of its *Duplex Printing* decision. Accordingly, the Court overruled *Duplex Printing* and held that collective action, even among employees who were not employees of the

---

[9]   Roosevelt appointed Justice Hugo Black in 1937, Justice Stanley Reed in 1938, Justices Felix Frankfurter and William Douglas in 1939, and Justice Frank Murphy in 1940.

same particular employer, was protected from prosecution under the antitrust laws by Section 20 of the Clayton Act.

Despite, or pursuant to, the *Apex Hosiery* and *Hutcheson* decisions, the antitrust laws remain relevant to labor relations in cases where: a union acts as a conduit for a price-fixing conspiracy among employers; employees and non-employees combine together to engage in certain secondary activities; and independent contractors bind together to take collective action for higher wages or better working conditions.

iii. The Rise of Industrial Unionism Under the Wagner Act: From the Great Depression to World War II

The industrialization of the American workplace created the need for a new type of unionism. Since the inception of the American labor movement, union organization had developed largely along craft lines. In a plant, generally only the skilled workers would be organized, and then in unions particular to their specific craft. There were several reasons why craft workers organized first: they strongly identified with their craft, they would likely benefit from negotiated improvements over the rest of their career, and they were hard to replace. Accordingly, tradesmen had the greatest incentives to unionize and the lowest costs from unionization, and thus more readily organized. Moreover, during the artisanal period, skilled workers were essential to production and thus workers could effectively bargain with an employer by organizing on merely a craft basis. However, with the industrialization of work and the rise of Taylorism, production knowledge was incorporated into the assembly line as tasks were broken down for routine performance by less skilled workers. As a result, skilled workers became less important to employers, and workers in many industries needed to organize all production workers in order to effectively bargain with their employer. Appropriately, organizing all of the workers in a plant on a "wall-to-wall" basis came to be referred to as "industrial organization" or "industrial unionism."

Although industrialization created the need for industrial unionism, it was the Great Depression that gave impetus to industrial organization and the passage of the Wagner Act that provided the opportunity for it to succeed. After the passage of the Wagner Act, leaders of the existing industrial unions—John L. Lewis of the United Mine Workers, David Dubinsky of the Ladies Garment Workers, Charles Howard of the International Typographical Union and Sidney Hillman of the Clothing Workers—sought to persuade the other leaders of the AFL to seize the opportunity and organize the mass production industries of steel, autos, glass, and rubber. To accomplish this task, these men and the leaders of six other unions formed the Committee for Industrial Organization (CIO) in 1936. Although they sought to work within the AFL, industrial organization inevitably lead to conflicts with the trade unions as the unions tried to organize employees in the same shops. Relations became so strained that, in August of 1936, the AFL expelled the ten national unions that started the CIO, and those unions then formed the *Congress* of Industrial Organizations (CIO) under the leadership of John L. Lewis.

The CIO embarked upon the most ambitious and successful organizing drive in American history. Led by Philip Murray, the CIO's Steel Workers Organizing Committee attacked the basic steel industry with four hundred organizers. In a stunning victory for the CIO, the largest steelmaker, U.S. Steel Corporation, agreed to recognize the steelworkers' union in March, 1937, without a fight. However, the leaders of the smaller steel companies, known collectively as "Little Steel," fought back, resulting in the long and violent "Little Steel strike" of 1937. The workers ultimately lost the strike against Little Steel after the "Memorial Day Massacre" in Chicago. Walter Reuther and his brothers, Victor and Roy, led the organizing effort in the auto industry in Detroit. While organizing Ford's River Rouge plant, Walter and UAW organizer Richard Frankensteen were assaulted by company security officers in what became known as "the Battle of the Overpass." Despite the company's intimidation tactics, the Reuthers led several successful "sit-down strikes" in which the auto workers occupied their plants to prevent replacement workers from taking their jobs, and successfully organized the Big Four auto companies. CIO organizers had similar success in other industries including textiles, rubber, electrical parts, glass, and clothing. The CIO's success spurred increased organizing efforts from the AFL as the Machinists, Electrical Workers, Carpenters, and Teamsters entered the field to organize industrial workers. By the end of 1937, the CIO had 3.5 million members and the AFL claimed over 4.5 million members. As the 1930s wore on, the economy continued to improve, but now the specter of World War loomed on the horizon.

Just ten days after the attack on Pearl Harbor, President Roosevelt convened a conference of national labor and business leaders to plan for industrial cooperation during the wartime crisis. The conferees agreed on a three point war time program: no strikes or lockouts for the duration of hostilities, peaceful settlement of industrial disputes, and the creation of a tripartite board to resolve disputes made up of representatives of labor, business, and the public. In January of 1942, President Roosevelt reconstituted the War Labor Board by Executive Order and appointed a tripartite membership under the leadership of Attorney William H. Davis and Senator Elbert D. Thomas. As the nation struggled to produce arms both for itself and its allies, shortages of raw materials and labor developed resulting in upward pressure on wages and prices. The War Labor Board dealt with this problem by adopting a formula for resolving price and wage disputes developed by the little steel producers based on the cost of living index. Through their cooperation and effort, and the efforts of the War Labor Board, American labor and management succeeded in making America "the arsenal of Democracy" and achieved what President

Roosevelt described as "the greatest production achievement in the world's history." Foster R. Dulles, Labor in American History 332–34 (1966).

Once the war was over, the gloves came off in American industrial relations. The mass production industries had been organized only shortly before the war and collective bargaining had been frozen almost immediately by wartime controls. Labor sought to make up for years of waiting for wage increases in these industries. Moreover, despite the efforts of the War Labor Board, wages had not kept pace with the demand for labor during the war. Workers felt that they had sacrificed more than their employers to maintain industrial peace during the war, and they felt they had some catching-up to do. As a result, a wave of strikes swept the basic industries in late 1945 and all of 1946. In November, 1945, the United Auto Workers led a strike of 180,000 workers against General Motors that lasted 113 days. In the spring of 1946, the United Mine Workers conducted a strike in the soft-coal industry that caused industrial consumers and homeowners great inconvenience. No sooner was this strike settled than John L. Lewis and his union threatened another nationwide strike. In May, 1946, 300,000 railroad workers struck nation-wide. The strike statistics for 1946 were staggering: 5,000 strikes, involving 4,600,000 workers and a loss of 107,475,000 man-days of work. More man-days were lost through strikes in February of 1946, than in 1943 and 1944 combined. For war-weary Americans who longed for a return to "normalcy," the labor strife in the first year after World War II was a tremendous disappointment.

In the 1946 congressional elections, the voters elected a Republican Congress for the first time since 1930. The Republican slogan for the campaign was simply: "Had enough?" Labor problems were not the only subject in the minds of voters in that election, but the new congressional leadership had been elected over labor's opposition and in response to public sentiment against "labor's excesses"—a phrase commonly used in 1946 and 1947. The Eightieth Congress felt it had a mandate to "put labor in its place." It seemed all but inevitable that changes in the Wagner Act lay ahead. Frank W. McCulloch & Tim Bornstein, The National Labor Relations Board 35–37 (1974).

iv. *The Taft-Hartley Amendments to the NLRA*

a) *Legislative History of the Amendments*

THE NATIONAL LABOR RELATIONS BOARD
Frank W. McCulloch & Tim Bornstein
pp. 39–42 (1974)

From the moment the Wagner Act had become law; large segments of the business community had sought to repeal it or to amend it in ways acceptable to employers. Leading the fight for amendments to the Wagner

Act were the National Association of Manufacturers and the U.S. Chamber of Commerce, both of which made revision of the Wagner Act a top legislative priority. Ostensibly, the goal of the business community was to make the law more equitable and, in particular, to cure its one-sided application to management of unfair labor practice restrictions. In reality, its more significant purpose was to curb the growing economic and political power of organized labor. The legislative debate over the merits of revision in the law masked a classic confrontation—a power struggle—between the business community and the labor movement.

When the Eightieth Congress organized itself in January, 1947, Senator Taft became chairman of the Senate Labor Committee. His counterpart in the House of Representatives was a little-known congressman from New Jersey, Fred A. Hartley, Jr. Both the Senate and House committees held hearings on labor bills that were introduced in the early days of the Eightieth Congress. Although the House and Senate bills had many features in common, the House bill was far more punitive and restrictive from labor's point of view. Because of the differences between the bills, it was necessary to convene a conference committee. Representative Hartley later wrote that his strategy in the House Labor Committee was to write the toughest bill he could, so that in conference the Taft bill would seem moderate and reasonable by comparison. On June 4, the House approved the conference bill by a vote of 320–79 after a debate of one hour. The Senate passed the bill by 57–17 on June 6.

The pressure that had been on Congress during the Taft-Hartley debates now was directed at the White House. Business and most farm groups wrote and telegraphed the President to sign the bill, while labor and liberal groups urged a veto. Rallies of union members were held throughout the country to denounce Taft-Hartley as a "slave labor bill." Proponents and opponents spent huge sums for radio and newspaper advertisements. On June 20, President Truman sent a veto message to Congress. It was a strong message, which, according to the *New York Times*, used twenty-four adjectives, such as "dangerous," "unworkable," "harsh," "arbitrary," and "drastic," to attack the Taft-Hartley bill. That same evening, he addressed the nation on radio and explained his reasons. Senator Taft followed in a separate radio address defending the bill. The same day, the House overrode the veto within an hour after receiving the President's message. Three days later the Senate, too, overrode the veto by a wide margin. The Taft-Hartley Act became effective on August 22, 1947.

b) Provisions of the Taft-Hartley Amendments

Section 7: The Right Not to Organize

To the Wagner Act's pronouncement of the right to organize and engage in concerted activities set forth in Section 7, Congress added language expressly affirming workers' right NOT to engage in such activity, subject to union security agreements authorized under Section 8(3).

Section 8(b): Union Unfair Labor Practices

Responding to the claim that the Wagner Act was one-sided in that it regulated only *employer* unfair labor practices, Congress defined six union unfair labor practices in the Taft-Hartley amendments.

Section 8(b)(1): Prohibits unions from interfering with employees' Section 7 rights, provided this section does not impair unions' ability to set rules on the acquisition and maintenance of membership. It also protects the right of management to select its own representatives for purposes of collective bargaining.

Section 8(b)(2): Makes it unlawful for a union to cause an employer to discriminate against an employee in violation of Section 8(a)(3). Basically it provides that unions cannot pressure employers to engage in discrimination against employees, either to encourage or discourage union membership. This prohibition, read in conjunction with amended Section 8(a)(3), declares the closed shop illegal, although other forms of union security agreements are still allowed.

Section 8(b)(3): Imposes on unions an obligation to "bargain collectively" similar to that imposed on employers by the Wagner Act. The meaning of this obligation was spelled out in Section 8(d) discussed below.

Section 8(b)(4): Is known as the "secondary boycott" prohibition. It makes it unfair for a union that has a "primary" dispute with one employer to put pressure on a second employer to cause her to stop doing business with the first employer. This section also prohibits strikes in jurisdictional disputes between unions where one union has been certified. Section 8(b)(4) has been the source of endless litigation and overwhelming confusion. Congress again tried to make the law of secondary boycott clear and precise through amendments in the 1959 Landrum-Griffin Act discussed below. As we will see, the secondary boycott prohibition has proved particularly debilitating to unions in the new "boundary-less" workplace.

Section 8(b)(5): Prohibits unions from charging excessive dues or initiation fees. This prohibition was enacted on the basis of evidence that a few craft unions charged exorbitant dues and initiation fees in order to exclude workers and create an artificial labor scarcity in order to keep their wages high.

Section 8(b)(6): Prohibits the practice of "featherbedding"—requiring employers to pay for services not performed. There has proved to be a tension between this provision and the laudable union objective of maintaining employment.

Related to the new union unfair labor practices were two other provisions of the Taft-Hartley amendments, Sections 8(c) and (d).

Section 8(c) is commonly known as the "free speech clause." It provides that the expression of views, arguments, or opinion "shall not . . . be evidence of an unfair labor practice . . . if such expression contains no threat of reprisal or force or promise of benefit." This provision was enacted in response to some Board decisions during the Wagner Act years that required employer neutrality in the conduct of representation elections and had punished some employer anti-union statements as unfair labor practices.

In Section 8(d), Congress defined the meaning of the duty to "bargain collectively" as "the mutual obligation of the employer and the representative of the employees to meet at reasonable times and confer in good faith with respect to wages, hours, and other terms and conditions of employment." However, section 8(d) states that "such obligation does not compel either party to agree to a proposal or require the making of a concession." The section also provides that the parties reduce their agreement to writing if requested by either party. Finally, Section 8(d) requires a sixty day "cooling-off" period in any situation in which a party wants to terminate or modify an existing contract.

Section 9: Changes in the Law of Representation Proceedings

Congress directed the Board to afford special treatment to four classes of employees: supervisors, professional employees, craftsmen, and plant guards. Supervisors are excluded from coverage under the act under the theory that, since modern corporations can only act through their agents and supervisors, those employees ought to owe a duty of loyalty solely to the employer. Accordingly, supervisors cannot be included in bargaining units with other employees and cannot even organize units of their own under the act. Professional employees are covered by the act, but are not to be included in a bargaining unit with nonprofessional employees, unless a majority of the professionals vote for inclusion. Craftsmen are covered by the act, and cannot be denied a petition for a separate craft unit solely on the ground that a different unit had been established by a prior unit determination, unless a majority of the craftsmen vote against separate representation. This provision sought to address the conflict between the AFL and the CIO on the proper specification of craft units in the midst of "wall to wall" industrial organization. Finally, plant guards are covered by the Act and can have their own bargaining units, but are excluded from unions including non-guard employees on the theory that, if the employees go on strike, at least someone should be working to guard the plant.

Congress also added two new kinds of elections, supplementing the Wagner Act election to certify a bargaining agent:

1.   *Elections on employer petitions.* Under the Wagner Act only a union or employees could file an election petition. The Taft-Hartley amendments allowed an employer faced with a union's demand for recognition to request that the Board conduct an election.

2.   *Decertification election petitions.* Congress established an election procedure for employees to decertify a union and oust it as their bargaining representative.

Changes in the Structure of the Board

Congress created an independent general counsel for the NLRB, to be appointed by the President. The general counsel would be in charge of the Board's prosecutorial functions and supervise all of the Board's attorneys, except for direct legal advisers to the Board. The theory of establishing an independent prosecutor within the agency was that the Board should function like a court and be totally divorced from the prosecutorial function. Providing the Board members with legal counsel independent of the general counsel was an important step in this regard. Congress also expanded the Board from three to five members and authorized it to sit in panels of three members to exercise its various powers.

Section 14(b): State "Right to Work" Laws

Congress saw fit to allow states to pass statutes prohibiting union security agreements. Consistent with the rhetoric accompanying this provision, these laws are called "right to work laws" because they give employees the right to work without joining or paying money to the union that represents them. The problem of course is that such laws encourage free-riding on union efforts and undermine union power. Currently, 27 states and one territory have such laws in effect.[10]

Sections 206–210: National Emergency Strike Provisions

Congress provided that, if the President believes that an actual or threatened strike or lock-out "imperils the national health and safety," then he can impanel a board of inquiry to investigate the "causes and circumstances" of the controversy. Once he receives the report of the board, if the President determines that the strike or lock-out is a threat to national health or safety he can direct the Attorney General to seek an injunction in federal court. During the injunction, the parties are to continue to negotiate with the aid of the Federal Mediation and Conciliation Service (FMCS). If no agreement is reached after 60 days, the board of inquiry submits another report to the President, including the final offer of the

---

[10]   Alabama, Arizona, Arkansas, Florida, Georgia, Guam, Idaho, Indiana, Iowa, Kansas, Kentucky, Louisiana, Michigan, Mississippi, Nebraska, Nevada, North Carolina, North Dakota, Oklahoma, South Carolina, South Dakota, Tennessee, Texas, Utah, Virginia, West Virginia, Wisconsin, and Wyoming. Missouri enacted such a statute in 2017 but the Missouri voters rejected it in a referendum in August 2018.

employer. The law requires that the affected employees have the opportunity to vote on the employer's final offer. Whether or not the employees accept the employer's final offer, the injunction must be dissolved within 80 days from its initiation.

Section 301: The Enforcement of Collective Bargaining Agreements

Congress provided that suits for violation of collective bargaining agreements in industries affecting interstate commerce can be brought by or against labor organizations in federal court. Before this time, collective bargaining agreements were enforceable, if at all, under state common law in which the union might be a principal to the agreement or an agent of the employees. As will be seen later in Chapter 7, the passage of Section 301 was instrumental in the development of a consistent federal common law on the enforcement of collective bargaining agreements.

NOTES

1. *Section 8(b), Union Unfair Labor Practices*: Section 8(b) places prohibitions on unions that are similar to those on employers in Section 8(a). Unions are prohibited from interfering with employee Section 7 rights, discriminating with respect to union membership and failing to bargain in good faith. Do you think unions are as likely to commit such unfair labor practices as employers? For example, what would be the point of a union refusing to bargain with the employer?

In Graph 1 below, we report the average number of unfair labor practice charges made against employers and unions for each presidential term from Franklin Delano Roosevelt in 1937–40 to George W. Bush in 2005–06. One would expect the number of charges filed to depend on the level of union organizing activity, the level of employer resistance and the parties' estimation of whether the Board will favorably act on their charge. The number of union elections was generally about 8,000 a year, until the 1980s when they crashed to levels of fewer than 4,000 elections a year. The number of unfair labor practice charges per election started out at about two during the forties and grew to about six to nine charges per election from 1975 to the present. Union faith in the Board and its prosecution of unfair labor practices suffered a substantial decline in the 1980s with President Reagan's appointments to the Board. In terms of the relative levels of unfair labor practice charges against unions and employers, after 1952, the number of union unfair labor practice charges varies from a high of 34.6% of all charges in 1969–72 to a low of 24.3% in 1993–96.

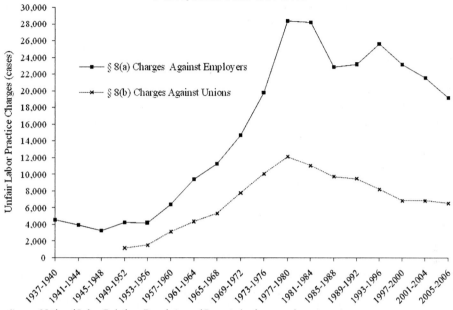

Graph1: Unfair Labor Practice Charges Alleged, Average Number for Each Four Year Period, Fiscal Years 1937-2006

Source: National Labor Relations Board, Annual Reports (various years).
Prepared by Dae Hwan Kim for use in LABOR LAW IN THE CONTEMPORARY WORKPLACE.

2. *Union Security and "Right to Work" Laws*: Provisos to the antidiscrimination provisions of sections 8(a)(3) and 8(b)(2) allow labor and management to negotiate "union security agreements" that can require, as a condition of employment, that employees pay "agency fees" to support the union's work as exclusive representative. The purpose of such agreements is to prevent employees from enjoying the benefits of union representation without paying for them. These benefits might be as general as enjoying higher wages and benefits or as personal as receiving union financed legal representation in a personal grievance. Under our system of exclusive representation, the union is legally obligated to fairly represent all employees in the unit, whether they are dues paying members or not, and the union can be sued in federal court for failing to do so. Union advocates argue that without union security agreements that require all unit employees to pay at least an agency fee to cover the costs of representation, some workers will "free ride" on the union's efforts, undermining its bargaining power and its ability to organize and represent workers. As a result, without union security agreements we can expect less union representation and lower employee wages.

Section 14(b) of the Taft-Hartley amendments allows states to enact "right-to-work" laws[11] that prohibit such union security agreements and make

---

[11]   The common use of the term "right-to-work law" in these debates is quite a coup for the proponents of such laws and is quite controversial among their detractors. Although the term sounds positive and affirming, the detractors would point out that no one actually gets a right to work under these laws but instead gets the right to receive union services without paying for them. As a result detractors sometimes call them "right-to-shirk laws."

them unenforceable. The general argument in favor of such laws is that some employees object to unions and should not be required to provide financial support to one as a condition of employment. Proponents of right-to-work laws also argue that they improve the business climate and increase employment. Since the 2010 elections, the proponents of right-to-work laws have had some success pitting one state against another and arguing that if their state passed a right-to-work law, businesses would relocate there. Amid much controversy and debate, Indiana enacted a right to work law in 2012 (I.C. 22–6–6–1), followed shortly by Michigan also in 2012 (MCL 423.14), Wisconsin in 2015 (WC 111.04, et seq.), West Virginia in 2016 (WVa Code § 21–1A–3), Kentucky in 2017 (KRS 336.130) and Missouri also in 2017 (Mo Code § 290.590(1)) (2016). The Missouri statute, however, was rejected in a voter referendum in August 2018.

It is of course very tough to separate out the effect of one law on union support, wages, and "state business climate;" nevertheless, there is a long-standing body of empirical work on the impact of right-to-work laws on workers and the economy. Empirical studies suggest that employee "free-riding" on unions makes it harder for unions to organize in states with right-to-work laws. A simple analysis of the extent of union organization for 1997 showed that the percent of the workforce that was organized was 7.6% in right-to-work states, compared with 16.8% in union security states. However, it may be that low union density leads to state politics that allows right-to-work laws rather than right-to-work laws that cause low union density. More sophisticated analyses that attempt to account for this endogeneity estimate that the negative impact of right-to-work laws on union membership ranges from about 10% to 30%. Raymond Hogler & Steven Shulman, *The Law, Economics, and Politics of Right to Work: Colorado's Labor Peace Act and Its Implications for Public Policy*, 70 U. Colo. L. Rev. 871, 929–30 (1999).

It does seem that right-to-work laws result in lower wages and benefits for both union and nonunion workers in states that adopt them. In a 2012 study, Martin Wolfson compared the average wages and benefits in right-to-work and non-right-to-work states and found that the average compensation was $7,835 higher in non-right-to-work states. Marty Wolfson, *'Right to Work' Lowers Wages—and That's a Fact!*, Higgins Labor Studies Program, University of Notre Dame, January 3, 2012. Inferring causation merely from arithmetic means is once again problematic since states with better educated populations also have higher wages and tend not to have right-to-work laws. A more sophisticated analysis by Heidi Shierholz and Elise Gould that tried to control for such factors found that in right-to-work states 2.6% fewer workers had healthcare benefits, 4.8% fewer workers had pensions, and overall wages were 3% lower. Heidi Shierholz & Elise Gould, *The Compensation Penalty of "Right-to-Work" Laws*, Economic Policy Institute Briefing Paper #299, February 17, 2011, http://www.epi.org/publication/bp299/. See also Elise Gould & Will Kimball, *"Right-to-Work" States Still Have Lower Wages*, Economic Policy Institute Briefing Paper #395, Apr. 22, 2015, http://www.epi.org/public ation/right-to-work-states-have-lower-wages/.

However it does not seem that passing a right-to-work law has a significant impact on the "business climate" of a state or increases the state's economic prosperity. Several researchers have examined the question and found no positive impact on economic growth for right-to-work states. Dale Belman, Richard Block & Karen Roberts, *Economic Impact of State Differences in Labor Standards in the United States*, 1998–2000, Employment Policy Research Network (Feb. 2009); Lonnie K. Stevans, *The Effect of Endogenous Right-to-Work Laws on Business and Economic Conditions in the United States: A Multivariate Approach*, 5 Rev. of Law & Econ. 595 (2009); Gordon Lafer & Sylvia Allegretto, Does *'Right to Work' Create Jobs?* Answers from Oklahoma, Economic Policy Institute (Mar. 1, 2011). What do you think of the "right-to-work" debate?

3.   *National Emergency Strike Provisions*: The national emergency strike provisions of the NLRA have not been invoked many times. Most recently, they were used by President George W. Bush in 2002 to enjoin job actions by both the International Longshore and Warehouse Union (ILWU) and Pacific Maritime Association (PMA) (an employer association) in west coast ports. To support their demands in contract negotiations, ILWU members engaged in a slowdown in unloading ships. The PMA retaliated with a lock-out giving the Bush administration the opportunity to enjoin any further work stoppage. Ultimately, an agreement was reached. Prior to this incident, you have to go back to President Carter's efforts to enjoin a coal strike in 1977 to find the invocation of these provisions. At least one expert on the subject has concluded that the national emergency strike provisions of the NLRA are largely irrelevant to the functioning of American labor relations. *See* Dennis R. Nolan, *"We Didn't Have Time to Train the Monkeys!": The 2002 Presidential Board of Inquiry on the Work Stoppage in the West Coast Ports*, in 57 Proceedings of the National Academy of Arbitrators 55 (2005).

4.   *The Board's Quorum Requirement*: As previously mentioned, the Taft-Hartley Act increased the size of the National Labor Relations Board from three members to five, but allowed the Board to delegate its authority to groups of three members. The Act specified the Board's quorum requirement under these procedures as follows:

> The Board is authorized to delegate to any group of three or more members any or all of the powers which it may itself exercise. . . . A vacancy in the Board shall not impair the right of the remaining members to exercise all of the powers of the Board, and three members of the Board shall, at all times, constitute a quorum of the Board, except that two members shall constitute a quorum of any group designated pursuant to the first sentence hereof. 29 U.S.C. § 153(b).

In December of 2007, the Board found itself with only four members and, expecting two more vacancies by the end of the month, delegated its powers to a group of three members. On December 31, 2007, the appointment of one of the three-member group expired, but the others continued to decide cases as a two-member quorum of a three-member group. This situation continued for the next 27 months, during which time the two-member quorum decided more than 500 cases. Two of these decisions sustained unfair labor practice complaints against the company New Process Steel, L.P., which sought review, challenging the "two-member Board's" authority to issue orders. The Seventh Circuit ruled for the Board, concluding that the two members constituted a valid quorum of a three-member group to which the Board had legitimately delegated its powers. *New Process Steel, L.P. v. N.L.R.B.*, 564 F.3d 840 (7th Cir. 2009). However, in June of 2010, the Supreme Court reversed 5 to 4, holding that section 3(b) requires that a delegee group maintain a membership of three in order to exercise the delegated authority of the Board. *New Process Steel, L.P. v. N.L.R.B.*, 560 U.S. 674 (2010). The Court, per Justice Stevens, reasoned that this reading of section 3(b) is the only way to give full effect to all of the provisions of section 3(b) and that if Congress had intended to authorize two members to act on an ongoing basis, it could have used straightforward language to this effect. The dissent, per Justice Kennedy, argued that the Board's interpretation was a reasonable interpretation of the Act and that the majority's interpretation, requiring that the delegee group maintain three members, had added a requirement that was not in the language of the statute.

d.   The Late Industrial Period (1947–1970): Post-War America

The United States emerged from WWII as the only intact industrial power in the world. Indeed, due to government investment in production facilities during the war, the United States emerged from the war even stronger economically than when it entered. During the next three decades, while the rest of the world rebuilt, the United States economy operated largely free of international competition. As a result, American industry and labor enjoyed profits and wages unburdened by the pressure of international competition, and the American regulatory scheme, operated effectively without the need to coordinate with an international legal regime.

During this post-war period, America's captains of industry believed that the "best" management practices were to build a large vertically integrated firm, supported by a stable workforce. Firms "vertically integrated," performing all of the stages of producing their product in house, to ensure coordination of production and to achieve economies of scale. A classic example of such integration was Ford's River Rouge plant where it was bragged that the production process went "from iron ore to Mustangs under one roof!" Firms wanted a stable workforce to ensure their supply of this valuable resource in coordinating production. To maintain workforce stability, firms developed administrative rules for the retention, training, and promotion of workers within the organization. Economists refer to these systems of administrative rules as the "internal labor market," because, although these decisions are made in reference to external market forces, they define the terms of compensation, and promotion within the firm in a way that is not directly determined by the "external" market.

The vertical integration of firms facilitated the retention of employees over the course of their careers because integrated firms had layers of positions within the firm for employee advancement. For example, at IBM from the 1950s to the 1980s, Thomas Watson, Jr., was famous for fostering a program of hiring employees largely on the basis of "character" and then training them for different positions within the firm as they progressed through their career. Thus, the employer became a major source of training and security throughout the course of the employee's life.

i. Labor Relations During the Late Industrial Period: The Cold War, the Seizure of the Steel Plants, the AFL-CIO Merger

The American labor movement hit its stride in the decades just after World War II. The percent organized in the private sector grew to a post-war high of 33.2% in 1955. Even the limitations on union power sought in the Taft-Hartley amendments did little to check the effective operation of American unions during this time. This was because the methods of organization and representation that developed during this time fit well with the post-war economic environment, the prevailing management practices, and the system of regulation under the NLRA.

The NLRA system of choosing an exclusive representative through an election in an appropriate unit and resolving disputes through collective bargaining worked relatively well in the post-war period. Because of the large-scale vertical integration of production, the NLRA definition of who was an "employer" generally defined the party that had control over issues of concern to the people defined under the NLRA as the relevant "employees." Moreover, because jobs were well-defined and long-term, bargaining units were relatively well-defined and stable. Employees had a long-term interest in their jobs and a particular employer and thus had incentive to invest in organizing a workplace to reap future benefits. Employers were relatively insulated from international competition and were more concerned with maintaining production than maintaining low wages.

Moreover, the NLRA's traditional single-unit system of bread-and-butter collective bargaining worked well in resolving issues in the workplace during this time. Traditional collective bargaining gave employees a useful voice in the administrative rules of the internal labor market, allowing them to address the issues of greatest concern to them in their work life. Their demands for benefits, seniority, and job security were compatible with management's objective of the long-term retention of skilled workers. Moreover, due to the large-scale vertical integration of most firms, employees could address their concerns to the party with control over those issues—their employer under the NLRA. The firm that signed their paycheck was also the firm that decided how much to produce, what methods to use, and how to market production. Employee co-determination and enforcement of the administrative rules of the internal labor market played an important role in the best management practices. Union representation and its accompanying system of grievance and arbitration provided a fair and efficient means of enforcing the agreed-upon administrative rules of the workplace.

In the aftermath of World War II, the Soviet Union and the United States vied for political and economic influence in the organization of the world. The United States sought to promote democracy and capitalism while the Soviet Union sought to promote single-party communist states and state organized production. To meet the Soviet threat, President Truman devised the strategy of "containment," developed programs of military and economic aid for allies and organized several alliances including the North Atlantic Treaty Organization (NATO). Although the two primary adversaries never directly engaged in hostilities, there were many important surrogate conflicts and the competition was intense in this "cold war." Although there were still some socialists in the American labor movement, the great majority of American workers, and their leaders, were bread and butter unionists who only wanted a better deal within the free enterprise system. Even the socialists within the movement were generally loyal Americans who were appalled at the totalitarianism of the Soviet system. Nevertheless, in 1949 and 1950, as the Korean War began, American labor leaders undertook a major effort to remove communists from positions of power in the American labor movement. In 1949, the delegates to the CIO Convention voted to expel the United Electrical, Radio, and Machine Workers (UE), on charges of pursuing communist policies. Within a year, the CIO had expelled ten more unions for communist influence. New unions, such as the International Union of Electrical Workers (IUE), were chartered by the CIO to raid the members of the expelled unions and take their place in the Congress of Industrial Organizations.

During the Korean War the country suffered an "employer strike" in the steel industry. Wages and prices had once again been brought under government control to further the war effort. When negotiations for a new contract between the United Steel Workers and the steel industry broke down near the end of 1951, the dispute was referred to the Wage Stabilization Board. The Board investigated the dispute for three months, during which time the union agreed not to strike. Once the Board made its report, the union accepted its recommendations, but the companies objected to the inclusion of a union security clause and the proposed wage increase. When the Economic Stabilization Director rejected requested increases in the price of steel, the steel companies rejected the proposed agreement with the Steelworkers and the union made ready to strike.

Rather than invoke the emergency provisions of the Taft-Hartley Act, which had been passed over his veto, President Truman seized the steel plants under his power as Commander-in-Chief in order to continue steel production and maintain the war effort. Although this act was controversial, President Truman reasoned that the workers had abstained from a strike during the work of the Wage Stabilization Board, and accepted their recommendations, so it was the Steel Companies, not the workers, who were instigating the strike. Ultimately the Supreme Court ruled that President Truman's seizure of the steel plants exceeded his constitutional power. *Youngstown Sheet & Tube Co. v. Sawyer*, 343 U.S. 579 (1952).

In November 1952, William Green, President of the AFL for nearly thirty years and Philip Murray, President of the CIO for over a decade, both died. They were succeeded by George Meany and Walter Reuther, respectively, both men of vigor and foresight. Since AFL activists now accepted that industrial unionism had a place in the American labor movement alongside craft unionism, the primary issue that had separated the two organizations had subsided. The two organizations undertook greater efforts at cooperation and began contemplating merger. In June 1953, representatives of the AFL and CIO negotiated a no-raiding agreement, which was eventually ratified by a majority of the constituent unions in the two organizations. In February 1955, a joint committee announced an agreement for the full merger of the two organizations which was ratified in December 1955. The new AFL-CIO, with about 15,000,000 members, was headed by George Meany with Walter Reuther as the head of the Industrial Union Department. The new federation included labor organizations that represented 86% of the unionized employees in the country.

ii. Labor Legislation of Post-War America: The Landrum-Griffin Act and Public Labor Relations Acts

a) The Landrum-Griffin Act

ORIGINS OF THE LMRDA
Martin H. Malin
Individual Rights within the Union pp. 34–48 (1988)

The growth of the labor movement resulted in increased public attention to internal union affairs. As a result, [in 1956] the Senate created the Select Committee on Improper Activities in the Labor and Management Fields, composed of eight senators under the chairmanship of Senator John McClellan (D. Ark.).

The McClellan Committee held 270 days of public hearings, recording 20,432 pages of testimony from 1,526 witnesses. It investigated several unions, focusing primarily on the Teamsters, Bakery and Confectionery Workers, United Textile Workers, International Union of Operating Engineers, and Allied Industrial Workers. It also investigated several management consultants, including Nathan Shefferman, Vincent Squillante, Marshall Miller, and Equitable Research Associates, headed by John Dioguardi. The Committee found that the unions which it investigated lacked democratic procedures, abused their powers to place subordinate bodies under trusteeships, were infiltrated by racketeers, engaged in violence, abused organizational picketing and that their officers colluded with management and embezzled [or] otherwise misused union funds. It [also] found improper and illegal actions by employers and their agents. The AFL-CIO, in an effort to forestall unfavorable legislation, adopted a series of ethical codes in 1956 and 1957 [and] expelled or suspended several unions including the Teamsters and the Bakery and Confectionery Workers.

[There were several factors that gave impetus to the adoption of some type of legislation governing internal union affairs. First, many legislators wanted to fulfill the democratic function of collective bargaining. One of the fundamental purposes of the Wagner Act, was to give workers a voice in determining the terms and conditions of employment. Collective bargaining can serve this purpose of industrial democracy only if the union is democratic. Secondly, anti-union forces and some employer organizations supported the legislation because they hoped that it would reduce the effectiveness of unions economically and politically. In part, they hoped to use the momentum of such legislation to curb the unions' economic weapons—a hope realized in provisions added to Title VII restricting picketing and boycotts. Clyde S. Summers, *American Legislation for Union Democracy*, 25 Mod. L. Rev 273 (1962).]

[The Labor Management Reporting and Disclosure Act, popularly known as the Landrum-Griffin Act, was signed into law by President Eisenhower on September 14, 1959. Public Law 86–257, as amended; 29 U.S.C. §§ 401–531 (2012).[12]] Title I of the LMRDA contains the "Union Members' Bill of Rights." It includes: the right to attend, participate in, and vote at meetings and elections; the freedom to meet and assemble with other members; the right to testify, to communicate with legislators, and to bring suit; the right to obtain or inspect copies of collective bargaining agreements and to be informed by the unions of the rights granted by this law; the right to notice and a fair hearing before any disciplinary actions; and protection from certain increases in union dues and assessments. Title II of the LMRDA requires the annual filing of a financial statement regarding the union and its officials with the Secretary of Labor that are then available to members and the public. Title II also requires that unions file their constitutions and bylaws, containing provisions and procedures

---

[12]   The text of the LMRDA can be found in the Statutory Supplement to this book.

regarding membership requirements, disbursement of union funds, the calling of meetings, and discipline or removal of officers, with the Secretary of Labor. Title III of the LMRDA provides controls on the use of trusteeships by national and international unions to run local unions. Under Title III, trusteeships may be established over subordinate unions only in accordance with the superior union constitution and bylaws, and for one or more of the following reasons: to address corruption or financial malpractice, to assure the enforcement of collective bargaining agreements and other duties of a bargaining representative, to restore democratic procedures, or to otherwise carry out the legitimate objects of the labor organization. [Finally, Titles IV through VI of the LMRDA regulate the election and conduct of union officers subjecting them to regular secret ballot elections at least every five years and subjecting them to a fiduciary duty.]

NOTES

1.   *Labor Racketeering:* Although it is the common stuff of Hollywood movies, the vast majority of unions have no connection with organized crime. Organized crime gained a foothold in some labor unions in the period known as the "Labor Wars" of the 1930s in which both employers and unions sought the aid of gangsters to counteract violence committed by the other side. Once organized crime gained a foothold in a union, they consolidated their power through intimidation and patronage. Such labor racketeering was largely confined to the unions investigated by the McClellan Committee. In the late 1950s and early '60s James R. Hoffa, the President of the International Brotherhood of Teamsters, rewarded friends with low interest loans from the Teamsters' Central States Pension Fund. As Attorney General, Robert F. Kennedy investigated these loans and other irregularities. Hoffa was ultimately investigated for failure to pay taxes and was convicted of trying to bribe a grand juror. However, it is apparent that Hoffa was less beholden to the Mob than his successor Frank Fitzsimmons, since upon his release from jail he was kidnapped and killed to prevent him from again being elected President of the Teamsters. Michael J. Goldberg, *Cleaning Labor's House: Institutional Reform Litigation in the Labor Movement*, 1989 Duke L. J. 903, 913; James B. Jacobs & Ellen Peters, *Labor Racketeering: The Mafia and the Unions*, 30 Crime & Just. 229, 230 (2003).

2.   *Federal RICO Trusteeships:* Starting in the 1980s, federal prosecutors undertook a series of lawsuits under the Racketeer Influenced and Corrupt Organizations Act (RICO) to try to end Mob influence in certain unions. *See e.g. United States v. Local 560, Int'l Bhd. of Teamsters*, 581 F.Supp. 279 (D.N.J. 1984). With rare exception, these suits were brought against just four international unions or their locals: the International Brotherhood of Teamsters (IBT), the Hotel Employees and Restaurant Employees International Union (HEREIU), the Laborers International Union of North America (LIUNA), and the International Longshoreman's Association (ILA). The government's strategy was to use the RICO statute to establish a federal

trusteeship of the mob-influenced union, and to use this control of the union to establish democratic and legitimate practices within the union, and disclose corruption in union locals. James B. Jacobs, Eileen M. Cunningham & Kimberly Friday, *The RICO Trusteeships after Twenty Years: A Progress Report* (2004) http://www.ipsn.org/rico_trusteeships_jacobs.htm. In these cases success in restoring democratic principles and honest practices has been noticeable. For instance, in the case of the Teamsters, "the federal civil RICO suit . . . and the court-imposed trusteeship that it produced . . . has led to a major transformation of the [Teamsters]." James B. Jacobs & Ellen Peters, *Labor Racketeering: The Mafia and the Unions*, 30 Crime & Just. 229, 249 (2003). Over 120 organized crime figures have been purged from the leadership and at least three international elections have been deemed "competitive" in the free and fair sense. *Id.* at 249–50.

3.   *Union Elections:* Although one can certainly find instances of unions violating democratic principles in their elections, the available empirical evidence suggests that such cases are the exception, not the rule. In their analysis of Department of Labor data on LMRDA violations for fiscal years 1965–74, Richard Freeman and James Medoff found only 239 violations, out of a total of approximately 200,000 union elections, for a violation rate of only 0.1%. Freeman and Medoff also found the unions experienced a 40–60% turnover in local union officers and a 9–12% turnover in national officers in each election. Richard B. Freeman & James L. Medoff, What Do Unions Do? 210–11 (1984). The typical turnover in Congressional elections is only 3–4%. More recently, in examining Department of Labor records for the fiscal years 1998–99, the General Accounting Office found only 162 LMRDA election violations of any kind, out of approximately 40,000 union elections. In 62 of these violations the Department of Labor took no action against the defendant and in 47 of them the case was resolved through voluntary compliance. United States General Accounting Office, Administering the Labor-Management Reporting and Disclosure Act, GAO/HEHS–00–116 at 45 (June 2000).

4.   *Union Trusteeships:* Although he was one of the grand old men of the American labor movement and a pivotal founder of the CIO, John L. Lewis had a propensity for silencing dissent within the United Mine Workers by expelling his rivals or putting their locals in trusteeship. Clyde Summers, *Union Trusteeships & Union Democracy*, 24 U. Mich. J.L. Reform 689 (1991). At least since the passage of the LMRDA, trusteeships have not been so prone to abuse. The LMRDA restrictions on voting the delegates of locals in trusteeship and taking local resources have significantly decreased the incentive for abuse. Moreover, the LMRDA time limits and procedures for a trusteeship restrict the possibilities of abuse. In examining Department of Labor Records on LMRDA cases for the fiscal years 1995–99, the General Accounting Office found 353 new trusteeships, 35 LMRDA violations and that, of those 35 violations, only 5 required legal actions to gain compliance. During this same time unions ended 259 trusteeships. United States General Accounting Office, Administering the Labor-Management Reporting and Disclosure Act, GAO/ HEHS–00–116 at 36–37 (June 2000).

b) Public Sector Labor Relations Acts

It was not until the 1960s that public employees began to achieve statutory protection of their right to organize and collectively bargain similar to that enjoyed by most private employees under the RLA and NLRA. Up until that time, labor relations in the public sector were largely governed by court-made law that denied public employees the right to strike, collectively bargain or arbitrate disputes, and allowed public employers to enforce yellow-dog contracts, form company unions, and fire employees for supporting a union. *See, e.g., Frederick v. Owens,* 25 Ohio C.C. (N.S.) 581 (Ct. App. 1915); *City of Jackson v. McLeod,* 199 Miss. 676, 24 So.2d 319 (1946), *cert. denied,* 328 U.S. 863 (1946). In the absence of state and federal statutes governing public sector labor relations, the "rules" and regulations that did exist on employee collective action in the public sector were largely issued by mayors, school boards, and department heads, and these rules often prohibited employee organizing. Court challenges to these rules on the basis that they infringed constitutional rights were invariably rejected. *See e.g., Perez v. Board of Police Comm'r,* 78 Cal.App.2d 638, 178 P.2d 537 (1947); *Seattle High Sch. Teachers Chapter 200 v. Sharples,* Case No. 209483 (Super. Ct. King Cnty. Wa., May 28, 1928). Although some public employees succeeded in organizing even under this regime, their collective action was often limited to informal discussions and agreements enforced through political action. Joseph E. Slater, Public Workers 71–81 (2004).

There are several reasons why the right to organize and take collective action was recognized so late in the public sector. As in the private sector during the first half of the twentieth century, public sector employees had to contend with the extreme conceptions of freedom of contract and negative views of unions held by many members of the judiciary. Courts cited the government's freedom of contract to uphold rules prohibiting public employee organization. *See, e.g., McNatt v. Lawther,* 223 S.W. 503 (Tex. 1920), and characterized union membership as "disloyal," "inimical to proper discipline," "inefficient," and "detrimental to public welfare" to rationalize the enforcement of public sector yellow-dog contacts and discriminatory discharges. *See, e.g., Perez v. Board of Police Comm'r,* 78 Cal.App.2d 638, 178 P.2d 537 (1947); *Hutchinson v. Magee,* 278 Pa. 119, 122 A. 234 (1923). When public employees asserted a constitutional right to free speech and association, the courts generally acknowledged those rights, but held that the First Amendment afforded no protection against discrimination in public employment due to the exercise of such rights because public employment was a "privilege." In the words of Justice Holmes in *McAuliffe v. New Bedford,* 155 Mass. 216, 29 N.E. 517 (1892), "The petitioner may have a constitutional right to talk politics but he has no constitutional right to be a policeman." Additionally, public sector workers faced the obstacle that some people thought public sector collective bargaining was inconsistent with democracy. Judges and legislators asserted that if the government negotiated with unions over wages and terms of employment that had previously been set by administrative rule or executive fiat, this would constitute an unconstitutional delegation of governmental power to private parties. *See, e.g., City of Springfield v. Clouse*, 356 Mo. 1239, 206 S.W.2d 539 (1947). These arguments were never squared with the fact that governments regularly negotiated contracts for goods and services with businesses that could then be enforced in court. Some feared that collective bargaining by state employees would lead to strikes by essential employees such as fire fighters and police. Indeed, one of the earliest experiences with public sector collective bargaining in the United States resulted in the infamous Boston police strike of 1919. It was sometimes thought that the government was a more benevolent employer and that public employees had less need for collective bargaining. In particular, some public employees enjoyed civil service protection which limited arbitrary treatment by their employer. Finally, until the 1960s government employment was not a large enough percentage of the workforce to draw the attention of larger labor organizations. During the 1930s through 1950s the largest national labor organizations focused on organization in the private sector. Joseph E. Slater, Public Workers 81–96 (2004).

Just as in the private sector, this system of judge-made law could not last. Several factors coalesced to foster a change in the 1960s. First, the public sector experienced tremendous growth in employment in the 1950s and '60s.[13] This growth was in part due to a rise in government programs under the New Deal and the Great Society, but more importantly due to an increase in demand for government educational and social services in the late 1950s and 1960s as the "Baby Boomers" entered school and increasing numbers of people survived into retirement. Second, by the 1960s, the United States had experienced almost two decades of stable and productive relations under the NLRA in the private sector. People could begin to imagine productive work relations under a similar system in the public sector, including alternative methods of resolving disputes such as mediation, fact-finding, and arbitration—or even strikes of non-essential public workers. Third, in 1964 the Supreme Court established the principle of legislative apportionment on the basis of "one person one vote," *Reynolds v. Sims*, 377 U.S. 533 (1964). This decision ended the ability of rural, nonunion, voters to disproportionately influence state and federal legislation. Fourth, by the late 1960s, the courts began to take a more positive attitude toward employee collective action and the prospect of constitutional protections for public employees' rights. Courts began to uphold public employees' claims of constitutional rights, rejecting the previous "rights/privilege" distinction of Justice Holmes, *Keyishian v.*

---

[13]   The number of public employees as a percent of the civilian workforce increased from 6.2% in 1929 to 15.6% in 1975. Most of the growth in public employment occurred in state and local government and outside of essential services. See the notes following this section.

Board of Regents, 385 U.S. 589 (1967). They found that, at least under some circumstances, public employee expression and association for the purpose of collective action enjoyed constitutional protection. *See, e.g., Pickering v. Board of Educ.*, 391 U.S. 563 (1968); *AFSCME v. Woodward*, 406 F.2d 137 (8th Cir. 1969). Courts that had previously accepted the idea that collective bargaining would be an unconstitutional delegation of legislative power came to reject this argument. *See, e.g., Independence-Nat'l Educ. Ass'n v. Independence Sch. Dist.*, 223 S.W.3d 131 (Mo. 2007), overruling *City of Springfield v. Clouse*, 206 S.W.2d 539 (1947). Finally, the 1960s and early '70s was a period of experimentation and social change. People were more open to "far out" ideas like public employee organization. Joseph E. Slater, Public Workers 193–95 (2004).

In a "chicken and egg" situation, new legislation regulating collective bargaining in the public sector fostered greater organization among public workers and greater organization among public workers prompted further legislation regulating public sector collective bargaining. In 1959, Wisconsin became the first state to enact a general public sector bargaining statute. The Municipal Employee Relations Act (MERA) gave local government employees the rights to organize and bargain collectively, and prohibited employer and union interference with those rights. Since that time, a total of thirty-one jurisdictions have enacted "comprehensive" public employment labor relations acts[14] and eight have enacted measures governing significant sectors of their public employees such as teachers, utility workers, transit workers, or police and fire fighters.[15] Typically these statutes are modeled after the NLRA, guaranteeing the rights to organize and collectively bargain, providing election procedures to determine majority representation and outlining employer and union unfair labor practices. Although as many as eight states have allowed some public employees a limited right to strike by statute,[16] these states generally require mediation and/or fact-finding before a strike can be undertaken and all prohibit strikes by "essential employees" such as police and firefighters. Four other states have recognized a limited right to strike for some non-essential public employees by court decision.[17] States that regulate public sector collective bargaining but do not allow strikes

---

[14]   Alaska, California, Connecticut, Delaware, District of Columbia, Florida, Hawaii, Illinois, Iowa, Kansas, Maine, Maryland, Massachusetts, Michigan, Minnesota, Missouri, Montana, Nebraska, New Hampshire, New Jersey, New Mexico, New York, Ohio, Oregon, Pennsylvania, Rhode Island, South Dakota, Vermont, Washington, Wisconsin, and Wyoming. https://www.afscme.org/news/publications/for-leaders/public-sector-collective-bargaining-laws.

[15]   Georgia, Idaho, Indiana, Kentucky, Nevada, Oklahoma, Tennessee, and Texas. In addition, in these and other states some state employees are granted collective bargaining rights by executive order or court decision. Milla Sanes and John Schmitt, *Regulation of Public Sector Collective Bargaining in the States*, Center for Economic and Policy Research, Appendix (2014), http://cepr.net/documents/state-public-cb-2014-03.pdf.

[16]   Alaska, Hawaii, Illinois, Minnesota, Ohio, Oregon, Pennsylvania, and Vermont allow at least a limited right to strike to some public employees by statute.

[17]   California, Colorado, Louisiana and Montana.

generally have a system of mediation and fact-finding, leading ultimately to interest arbitration, to determine the terms of collective agreements when the parties cannot agree. *See e.g.* 20 Iowa Code 20.19–20.22. Martin H. Malin, *Public Employees' Right to Strike: Law and Experience*, 26 U. Mich. J.L. Reform 313 (1993).

Federal employees first gained the right to organize and bargain collectively in 1962 when President Kennedy issued Executive Order 10988. Since that time many federal employees have gained the right to collectively bargain by statute. The principal statute is the Federal Service Labor Management Relations Statute (FSLMRS), also known as Title VII of the Civil Service Reform Act of 1978. Federal funding statutes at times have also fostered public employee organization. For example, the Urban Mass Transit Act (UMTA) of 1964 provided funds for local governments to take over previously private mass transit systems, but required that the collective bargaining rights of transit employees be preserved in the process. The need to comply with UMTA led many states to enact legislation granting public employees collective bargaining rights. Joseph Grodin, June Weisberger, and Martin H. Malin et al., Public Sector Employment: Cases and Materials 364–65 (3d ed. 2016).

The Great Recession of 2008 caused a drop in tax revenues and an increase in government budget deficits across the country. At first, much of this shortfall was made up for by federal stimulus money designed to maintain state services and employment in the depths of the recession. However, once the stimulus money ran out, state and local governments began to look for ways to cut their budgets and meet balanced budget requirements—including public servant wage cuts and lay-offs. The passage of the Affordable Care Act, Pub. L. 111–148, 124 Stat. 119 (2010), and rising budget deficits galvanized conservative voters in the 2010 elections, resulting in many Republican successes, including retaking the House of Representatives and many governorships and state legislative houses. With great concern over the economy and budget, and new-found political power, the Republican Party was poised to promote or undertake not only significant cuts in government services and employment, but also a larger agenda limiting public employee rights.

The larger agenda against public employee rights was prepared by conservative activists financed by billionaires. The billionaire Koch brothers and their corporate allies not only financed Republican candidates across the country, but also financed model legislation drafted by the American Legislative Exchange Council (ALEC) and research and opinion columns to support their causes. These efforts included model legislation to eliminate or limit public employee collective bargaining, regulate the terms of public employment, prohibit public employee dues check-off, reverse prevailing wage legislation, and make union security agreements unenforceable. Critics assert that this legislative agenda to constrain public employee unions is driven as much by a desire to silence organized political opposition by working people as it was to eliminate public employee collective bargaining. William Cronin, *Who's Really Behind Recent Republican Legislation in Wisconsin and Elsewhere?* (Hint: It Didn't Start Here), http://scholarcitizen.williamcronon.net/2011/03/15/alec/. Critics argue that ALEC's campaign amounts to the largest power grab by the upper class since the end of the artisanal period when Andrew Carnegie and other industrialists sought to destroy the trade guilds.

The 2010–12 legislative sessions saw efforts in many states to limit or end public sector collective bargaining using ALEC-drafted model bills. New restrictions on public sector employees were passed in twenty-one states and significant restrictions on public sector collective bargaining were enacted in twelve states.[18] In Indiana, Governor Mitch Daniels had previously revoked the executive order authorizing state employers to collectively bargain with representatives of state employees, and used the legislative session to: restrict the subjects of school teacher collective bargaining, make it a crime for state officers and officials to collectively bargain with public employees, and to pass a "right-to-work" law which made it a crime to negotiate a union security agreement in either the public or private sector. In Wisconsin, newly elected Governor Scott Walker proposed a 2010 "budget" in "Act 10" which not only trimmed public employment rolls and cut remaining employees' wages and benefits 9%, but also stripped the public employees of the right to collectively bargain over any issue other than wage increases up to the rate of inflation. The bill also required unions of public employees to annually reaffirm their majority status through elections that they won by 51% of the eligible employees, with all non-voters counted as "no's." In Ohio, newly elected Governor Kasich promoted Senate Bill 5, which limited the subjects of public sector collective bargaining and prohibited strikes by public employees where nonessential public employees had previously been allowed the strike. However, opponents of Ohio's Senate Bill 5 collected the necessary 230,000 signatures to place the bill on the November 2011 ballot as a public referendum where it was rejected by 62% of the voters, thereby negating its enactment under the Ohio Constitution. Kenneth G. Dau-Schmidt and Winston Lynn, *The Great Recession, the Resulting Budget Shortfall, the 2010 Elections and the Attack on Public Sector Collective Bargaining in the United States*, 29 Hofstra Lab. & Emp. L. J. 407 (2012). Since that time, similar bills significantly restricting public employee collective bargaining rights have been enacted in several states including Iowa and Missouri.

Today public sector employees constitute a significant share of the American labor movement. Graph 2 reports the average union density (percent of employees organized) for non-agricultural workers for each four

---

[18] Indiana, Wisconsin, Ohio, Michigan, Arizona, Idaho, New Hampshire, Oklahoma, South Carolina, Tennessee, Utah, and Wyoming. The Ohio and Idaho enactments were overruled by voter referenda.

year presidential term from 1929–32 to 1945–48 and the average union density for both private and public sector employees for the presidential terms from 1949–52 to 2013–16. Graph 2 also shows the average union density for all workers in both the private and public sectors for each four year presidential term from 1949–52 to 2013–16. As can be seen in Graph 2, union density averaged over 35% for private sector workers during the period 1953–56 when only 11% of public sector workers were organized. Yet in the most recent period of 2013–16, union density in the private sector averages only 6.6%, while 35.2% of public sector employees are represented by unions. Indeed, 48.7% of the 14.8 million employees who belonged to unions in 2017 were public employees.[19] Examining average union density for all workers including both private and public employees, we see that average union density has declined from a height of 32% in the period 1953–56 to a low of 11% in the most recent period 2013–16. *See also* Richard B. Freeman, *Through Public Sector Eyes: Employee Attitudes Toward Public Sector Labor Relations in the United States*, in Public Sector Employment in a Time of Transition 59–83 (Dale Belman et al., eds. IRRA 1996). As discussed in the notes, the constitutional prohibition on agency fee arrangements in the public sector announced in *Janus v. AFSCME Council 31,* 138 S. Ct. 2448 (2018) will undoubtedly result in a decline in union membership in the public sector in forthcoming years.

---

[19]   In 2017 there were 14,811,500 union members in the American workforce (10.7% of the total), 7,600,200 of these members were in the private sector (6.5% of private sector workers) and 7,211,300 of these members were in the public sector (34.4% of public sector workers). Barry T. Hirsch & David A. Macpherson, *Union Membership, Coverage, Density, and Employment,* http://www.unionstats.com.

Graph 2: Union Density in the American Private Sector, Public Sector and All Workers, Average Percentage for Each Four-Year Period, 1929-2016

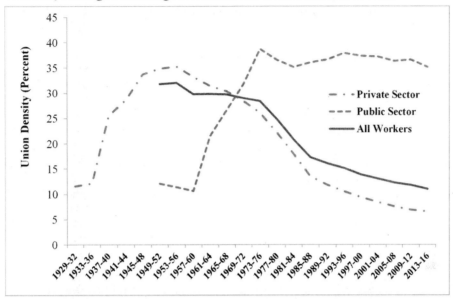

Sources: Richard B. Freeman, *Spurts in Union Growth: Defining Moments and Social Processes* (Nat'l Bureau of Econ. Research, Working Paper No. 6012, 1997); Leo Troy & Neil Sheflin, Union Sourcebook: Membership, Finances, Structure, Directory (1985); Barry T. Hirsch & David A. Macpherson, *Union Membership, Coverage, Density, and Employment*, http://www.unionstats.com. *Note*: The figures for nonagricultural workers are from Freeman, *supra*; the figures for 1949-1983 are from Troy & Sheflin, *supra*; the figures for 1984-2016 are from Hirsch & Macpherson, *supra*. Prepared by Dae Hwan Kim for use in this book.

NOTES

1.   The United States is somewhat unusual among industrial democracies in its late development of the right to collectively bargain in the public sector. The English accepted public employee organization shortly after World War I under the Civil Service National Whitely Council. Public Sector union membership grew dramatically in Britain during the 1920s and by the mid 1920s British law provided for mandatory arbitration in public sector labor disputes. On the whole, British laws never made the sharp distinction between private sector and public sector employees that existed in the United States. Similarly, the French government accepted public employee organization in 1926 and union membership among public employees rose sharply in the period from 1926–1932. The French constitution of 1946 guaranteed public employees the right to join unions. As in Britain, French law generally makes few distinctions between private and public employees. Joseph E. Slater, Public Workers 92–93 (2004).

2.   *The Growth of Public Sector Employment:* As previously mentioned, public sector employment has grown as a percent of the civilian workforce since 1929, primarily at the state level. With the New Deal programs and the advent of World War II, federal employment sky-rocketed from 1.1% of the civilian labor force in 1929 to 5.2% in 1945. However, since the end of World War II the

federal sector has steadily shrunk and has now leveled off at approximately 2% of the civilian workforce. State government employment started at about 5.1% of the civilian labor force in 1929, increased steadily to 7.3% in 1955, and then grew more rapidly as the Baby Boomers went off to school and more people survived into retirement, increasing to 10.3% in 1965 and 12.5% in 1975. State government employment has remained at about this same level from 1975 to the present. The Economic Report of the President 1967, Tables B-20 and B-25; The Economic Report of the President 2000, Tables B-33 and B-44; The Economic Report of the President 2016, Table B-14.

3.   *Mediation, Fact-finding, and Arbitration:* Public sector statutes often prescribe one or more neutral procedures to resolve conflicts in collective negotiations while minimizing or prohibiting strikes. Under "mediation," the parties meet, either together or separately, with a neutral expert chosen through their mutual assent, who mediates the dispute. Although the mediator has no authority to decide the disputed issues, a skilled mediator can facilitate agreement by helping the parties to minimize problems of personality, communicate their core interests, and discover areas of mutual benefit. Under "fact-finding", a fact-finding board, generally consisting of a management representative, a union representative, and a neutral chosen by the parties, conducts a formal hearing on the issues in dispute to "find facts" as to how the issues should be resolved based on the situation of the parties and how similar issues have been resolved by parties in "comparable" jurisdictions. Although the results of fact-finding are not binding on the parties, it is hoped that the fact-finders' opinion will be persuasive, if for no other reason than that the opinion will help sway public opinion in favor of one side's bargaining position or the other's. Under "arbitration," a neutral expert appointed by the parties conducts a formal hearing to determine the issues in dispute according to the situation of the parties and how similar issues have been resolved by parties in "comparable" jurisdictions. When an arbitrator *determines* the terms of the collective agreement, this process is usually referred to as "interest arbitration" to distinguish it from the more common "grievance arbitration" in which the arbitrator finds facts and *interprets* the terms of the contract negotiated by the parties. Sometimes by statute, or agreement of the parties, the interest arbitrator is bound to select the "last best offer" between the proposals actually offered by the parties in negotiations rather than determining some middle result. The purpose of such "last best offer arbitration" is to give the parties incentive to make their best offers in negotiations rather than conducting negotiations with an eye towards arbitration.

4.   *Union Security and "Right to Work" Laws in the Public Sector*: As in the private sector, the federal and state laws and executive orders governing collective bargaining by America's federal and state employees generally require that collective bargaining be done by a union that is the representative of the majority of employees in an appropriate unit, as the exclusive representative of all employees in that unit, and that the union fairly represent all employees in the unit whether they are members of the union or not. To prevent "free-riding" by employees who benefit from union representation, but

do not join the union and pay dues, unions in both the private and public sector have historically sought to negotiate "union security agreements" that, in modern times, have required all employees in the unit, as a condition of employment, to either join the union or pay an agency or "fair share" fee equal to a proportionate share of the cost of collective bargaining in that unit. Charging non-members for political expenditures was expressly prohibited.

At the outset of 2018, union security agreements were prohibited and unenforceable for federal employees and state employees in twenty-eight states. For federal employees, the Civil Service Reform Act requires both: (1) that any labor group representing non-management staff in an agency must represent all the non-management employees, regardless of whether they join the union; and (2) that federal workers are not under any obligation to pay a representation fee to the union. *See* 5 U.S.C. §§ 7102, 7111(a), 7114(a) (2012). For state employees, as previously discussed, 27 states and one territory have passed "right to work" laws that prohibit the enforcement of union security agreements covering private sector employees, and those same states generally prohibit the enforcement of union security or "fair share agreements" covering public employees either in the same statute, a separate statute, or by court opinion.[20]

In June of 2018, the Supreme Court handed down its decision in *Janus v. AFSCME, Council 31, et al.*, ___ U.S. ___, 138 S.Ct. 2448 (June 27, 2018), extending a constitutional prohibition against the enforcement of union security or "fair share" agreements to all state and federal employees. The majority over-ruled the forty-year old precedent of *Abood v. Detroit Bd. of Ed.*, 431 U.S. 209 (1977) to hold that, despite the fact the fair share fees included only the cost of services the union was legally required to provide and NOT political expenditures, the obligation to financially support a labor organization of which the employee was not a member was an infringement of the employee's First Amendment rights. This holding of course puts public sector unions in a very tough place as it allows and gives incentive for employees to "free ride" on union efforts, enjoying the benefits of representation without paying for them, even though the employee actually favors union representation.

At the very least, it would seem that the *Janus* decision will diminish the vitality of public sector unions in the twenty-two states that previously allowed fair share agreements. The decision will undoubtedly result in a drop in union membership in those states as now, in deciding whether to join the union, employees will choose between non-membership (no dues) and membership (100% dues), whereas before they chose between non-membership with a fair share fee (85–90% of dues) and membership (100% dues). Teacher unions in Wisconsin and Michigan saw drops in membership of 57% and 21%, respectively, after their states adopted public sector "right to work" laws in

---

[20] Those states include Alabama, Arizona, Arkansas, Florida, Georgia, Guam, Idaho, Indiana, Iowa, Kansas, Kentucky, Louisiana, Michigan, Mississippi, Nebraska, Nevada, North Carolina, North Dakota, Oklahoma, South Carolina, South Dakota, Tennessee, Texas, Utah, Virginia, West Virginia, Wisconsin and Wyoming. Missouri enacted such a statute in 2017 but the Missouri voters rejected it in a referendum in August 2018.

2011 and 2013.[21] This drop in membership will also undoubtedly result in a decrease in public sector union resources in these states. In Wisconsin, teacher union revenues have dropped 70.6% since the enactment of a public sector right to work law, and in Michigan teacher union revenues have dropped 24.6% since the enactment of its law. *Janus*, and new laws restricting public sector collective bargaining, may also result in unions shifting resources from collective bargaining to political action and lobbying. In Wisconsin, the teacher unions have more than doubled their average contribution to candidate campaigns since the adoption of Wisconsin's public sector right to work law. Bradley D. Marianno & Katharine Strunk, *After* Janus, 18 Education Next (Fall 2018), http://educationnext.org/after-janus-new-era-teachers-union-activism-agency-fees/#. Some have argued that *Janus* will lead to public sector unions paying more attention to their members, both listening and communicating the value of membership. The hotel, restaurant and culinary unions in Nevada have demonstrated that unions can maintain high membership rates even when fair share agreements are prohibited. Dave Jamieson, *The Las Vegas Union That Learned To Beat The House*, Huffpost, June 12, 2018, https://www.huffingtonpost.com/entry/the-las-vegas-union-that-learned-to-beat-the-house_us_5b182984e4b0734a993a56f7.   Although some attribute this unusual success to the uniquely profitable status of casinos. *Nevada's unusual, powerful unions*, The Economist, Aug. 10, 2017, https://www.economist.com/united-states/2017/08/10/nevadas-unusual-powerful-unions. Finally, *Janus* and new laws restricting public sector collective bargaining, may also result in greater uncertainty and conflict in public sector labor relations as the resources spent on constructive collective bargaining decline. The recent spate of teacher strikes has occurred in states with public sector right to work laws and restrictive collective bargaining regimes and teachers have cited the weakness and frustration of their unions as reasons behind the strikes. *Is This Supreme Court Decision the End of Teachers Unions?* NPR, June 27, 2018, https://www.npr.org/sections/ed/2018/06/27/617893848/is-this-supreme-court-decision-the-end-of-teachers-unions?utm_source=facebook.com&utm_medium=social&utm_campaign=npr&utm_term=nprnews&utm_content=20180627.

It is possible that *Janus* may be the beginning of the unraveling of our current system of exclusive representation by majority unions. If we recognize the First Amendment right of union dissenters not to financially support collective bargaining, shouldn't our laws also recognize the right of union supporters not to pay to represent those dissenters? If unions escape the bonds of exclusive representation and start to negotiate "members-only" contracts, why require elections if the union represents only employees who join as

---

[21]   Indeed, in the wake of the *Janus* decision, there has been some evidence that well financed employer organizations will actively solicit public employees to drop their union membership. *In Response to Janus Decision, Governor Cuomo Signs Executive Order to Protect Union Members from Harassment and Intimidation*, New York State, June 27, 2018, https://www.governor.ny.gov/news/response-janus-decision-governor-cuomo-signs-executive-order-protect-union-members-harassment.

members? What do you think will be the implications of *Janus* for public sector labor relations in the United States?

5.   *If Teacher Strikes are Illegal, Why are There so Many of Them?*: As discussed in the opening example of this chapter, this edition is written in the midst of the largest spate of significant teachers' strikes since the 1990s, or 1970s. To date all of these strikes have occurred in states where teachers' strike are prohibited. What's going on?

The current teachers' strikes are a great example of the limits to prohibitory power and the value of regulated collective bargaining. It is now manifestly evident that the budget-cutting and legislative "reform" of state educational systems that occurred in the wake of the Republican victories in the 2010 elections were a counter-productive over-reaction. Although teachers may have had better benefits than their private sector counterparts, they have never been over-compensated relative to competing opportunities for college graduates in the private sector. Kaitlin Mulhere, *These 7 Charts Explain the Fight for Higher Teacher Pay*, Money, Ap. 11, 2018, http://time.com/money/5228237/teacher-pay-charts/; Kenneth G. Dau-Schmidt & Mohammad Khan, *Undermining or Promoting Democratic Government? An Economic and Empirical Analysis of Public Sector Collective Bargaining*, 14 Nev. L. J. 414, at 433–39 (2014). The teacher wage and benefit cuts enacted in the austerity measures passed in the wake of the 2010 election only made the profession economically less competitive, while the education "reforms" undermined the status of the teaching profession. The predictable increase in dissatisfaction within the profession has led to increased exits and retirements and a decrease in people entering the profession, resulting in a nation-wide teacher shortage. Jack Lessenberry, *Senator Knollenberg shocked by Michigan's teacher shortage. Let me explain what happened.*, Nov. 2, 2017, http://michiganradio.org/post/sen-knollenberg-shocked-michigans-teacher-shortage-let-me-explain-what-happened. Given this context, it is not surprising that teachers, en masse, are willing to risk their jobs in an effort to force legislators and governors to act to better their wages and benefits. It is also not surprising that school boards do not avail themselves of their "remedy" of firing the illegally striking teachers and trying to replace them all by offering substandard wages and benefits. The power of the prohibition on strikes is limited by the parties' economic alternatives and the commitment of the teachers to act collectively to address their interests. A superior solution that might have avoided these strikes would be to have a system of regular and meaningful negotiations between the teachers and their school boards to address wages and working conditions—a regulated system of collective bargaining.

6.   *The Practical Perils of Criminalizing Collective Bargaining*: Each year the Indiana State Fair Commission needs to employ trained stage hands to set up and operate its 16 day program on the State Fair Grounds. The best, probably only, source of trained stage hands for short term employment is the hiring hall of Local 30 of the Stage Hand Union in Indianapolis. Each year the Commission contacts Local 30's hiring hall and requests that the union send

out about a dozen trained stage hands for work on the state fair. The Commission can participate in the union's hiring hall because it agrees with the union in a contract, renegotiated about every two years, to pay wages and benefits according to the union's scale with other temporary employers. In the contract, the Commission retains the power to reject recommended stage hands, to direct and control their work, and to discipline them or fire them for poor performance. After the enactment of I.C. 4–15–17–4 in 2011, making it a crime for Indiana public employers to collectively bargain with their employees, can the State Fair Commission continue to secure trained stage hands in this way? Indiana public employees still have a constitutional right to associate in unions, and many still do. Short of participating in a union hiring hall, can an Indiana public employer voluntarily consult its employees' union to determine how best to handle lay-offs or benefit cuts under the governor's budget? What important public policy would be upheld by a law prohibiting even voluntary consultations with worker representatives?

Realizing the State Fair Commission's dilemma, one state attorney suggests amending the agreement with Local 30 to state that the union is the employer of the stage hands and a sub-contractor with the state. Can this problem really be solved so easily? Can the parties just state that the union is the employer or do they need to actually change the relationship between the parties to give the union real control over which employees do the work and how the work is done in order to make the union an employer? What if the State Fair Commission contracted with the union as a "temporary services provider" who provided the names of "independent contractors" who would work for the state on a temporary basis under terms set by the union like a temporary service agency or a "platform" service provider like Uber? If the parties can just designate the union as the employer, service agency or platform provider, what's to stop other public employee unions in Indiana from claiming they are employers, service agencies, or platform providers and their members will not show up to work until the state meets their "sub-contracting" or platform demands? Is this the solution to the current debate over public sector collective bargaining; make the public employee unions sub-contractors, service agencies, or platform provides so that the work is now "out-sourced" to the "private sector" and allow the unions to bargain and lobby like other government sub-contractors?

3. THE RISE OF THE NEW INFORMATION TECHNOLOGY AND THE GLOBAL ECONOMY: THE MARKET DRIVEN WORKFORCE AND THE CHALLENGES OF ORGANIZING IN THE CONTEMPORARY WORKPLACE

a. The Organization of Production in the New Economic Environment

In the 1970s, the post-war system of trade and technology that served as the foundation for the system of industrial unionism under the NLRA began to change. With the rebuilding of Europe and the rise of the economic power-houses in Asia, international trade began to make serious inroads into the American economy. The impact of international trade was first felt in low-capital industries such as textiles and shoes, but the oil crisis of the 1970s facilitated significant inroads into even the capital-intensive auto and steel industries. With the quadrupling of the price of oil after the 1973 OPEC embargo, the auto and steel manufacturers in Europe and Asia enjoyed some real competitive advantages with more fuel-efficient designs, up-to-date production facilities, superior management, and lower wages. Manufacturing jobs began to migrate overseas or disappear entirely as industry strived to become more efficient. At the same time demand for services expanded. As a result, the American economy became more service-oriented. Service employees proved less amenable to organization under the traditional industrial model, in part because some deemed employee organization "unprofessional" and in part because the focus and priorities of the existing industrial unions did not meet their needs.

After 1970, the United States also saw great changes in the demographics of the American workforce. African Americans took advantage of new opportunities afforded by the civil rights movement of the 1960s and began to move into jobs from which they had previously been excluded. In the 1970s, women entered the paid labor force in unprecedented numbers, taking on new roles and coming to dominate important sectors of the economy and professions. Beginning in the 1980s, men began to suffer obstacles to educational opportunities that had previously been open to them, thus limiting the types of jobs they could get. Also during this time, the United States experienced a boom in immigration, first from Latin America and then from Asia. Beginning in the 1950s and '60s with only a few hundred thousand workers under the Bracero program, documented and undocumented immigration from Central and South America grew to over 8 million in the decade of the 1990s before declining to 6.5 million in the decade of the 2000s. Since 2009, the number of immigrants from Asia has exceeded the number of immigrants from Central America adding further diversity to the American labor force. Gustavo López & Jynnah Radford, *Facts on U.S. Immigrants*, 2015, Pew Center on Research (May 3, 2017), http://www.pew hispanic.org/2017/05/03/facts-on-u-s-immigrants/#2013-fb-authorized-pie.

This diversification of the American workforce has created new challenges for the labor movement. Although unions have significantly improved internal race relations, historically some unions actively discriminated against African Americans and some employers exploited race divisions to frustrate employee organization and collective action. Women brought to the workplace a new emphasis on concerns such as gender discrimination, sexual harassment, flexibility in hours, and childcare, which unions have learned to accommodate. Hispanic workers have their own issues concerning language and cultural identity, and undocumented workers have trouble enforcing their legal rights without facing deportation. Because they have often experienced employee organization in their native land, Hispanic workers are generally amenable to employee organization, especially through Hispanic worker centers as part of their larger ethnic identity. Allegations about the exploitation of Asian immigrants to the United States, have haunted the American technology industry.

In the 1980s, new information technology accelerated globalization and allowed for the efficient horizontal organization of firms. Information technology allowed employers to coordinate production among various suppliers and subcontractors around the world. Employers no longer had to be large and vertically integrated to ensure efficient production; they just had to be sufficiently wired to reliable subcontractors. The "best business practices" became those of horizontal organization, outsourcing, and subcontracting as firms concentrated on their "core competencies"—or that portion of production or retailing that they do best. In this economic environment, employers sought flexibility, not stability, in employment; the number of "contingent employees" who work part-time, or are leased or sub-contracted, reached new heights in the American economy. The new horizontal organization of firms broke down the job ladders and administrative rules of the internal labor market, and firms became more market driven. New technology allowed "bench-marking", or the checking of the efficiency of a division of a firm against external suppliers, thus bringing the market inside the firm in a way not previously experienced. Perhaps the most extreme example of these horizontal methods of production is the Volkswagen truck plant in Resende, Brazil, where the employees of various subcontractors, under one roof, assemble trucks made from parts from around the world, with only a handful of actual Volkswagen employees on hand to perform quality control. Peter Cappelli, The New Deal at Work: Managing the Market Driven Workforce (1999); David Weil, The Fissured Workplace: Why Work Became So Bad for So Many and What Can Be Done to Improve It (2017).

The new information technology also facilitated first the rise of the "big box" retailers and then the rise of on-line shopping sites to a position of unprecedented world-wide economic power. The simple bar code allowed Walmart to master inventory control, coordinate sources of product supply world-wide and grow into an international economic powerhouse with unprecedented power to determine wholesale prices and thus determine the wages and employment of its suppliers. *See Is Walmart Good for America?* (PBS Frontline Report 2004), http://www.pbs.org/wgbh/pages/frontline/shows/walmart/view/. No sooner had the big box retailers attained global dominance than their position began to be challenged by on-line retailers. Over the period 2010–16, Amazon's sales in North America quintupled from $16 billion to $80 billion. Derek Thompson, *What in the World Is Causing the Retail Meltdown of 2017?*, The Atlantic Apr.

10, 2017, https://www.theatlantic.com/business/archive/2017/04/retail-meltdown-of-2017/522384/. Brick and mortar retailers responded by increasing their on-line efforts, with the result being a significant decline in retail jobs. Quartz Media LLC, There are 170,000 fewer retail jobs in 2017—and 75,000 more Amazon robots (2018), https://qz.com/1107112/there-are-170000-fewer-retail-jobs-in-2017-and-75000-more-amazon-robots/. Of equal importance, the "big box" retailers and on-line retailers have provided an extensive retailing network for foreign producers, facilitating the inroads of foreign production into the American economy and accelerating globalization.

In the 1990s the global labor market experienced a near doubling of the relevant labor force with a concomitant downward pressure on wages and benefits that is yet to be fully felt in the American economy. Since 1990, the collapse of Communism, India's turn from autarky, and China's adoption of market capitalism have led to an increase in the global economy's available labor force from 3.3 billion to 6 billion. Because all of these countries were relatively capital poor, their entry into the global economy has brought no corresponding increase in global capital, and as a result, the capital-to-labor ratio in the global economy has dropped approximately 40%. This abrupt change in the ratio of available labor and capital in the global economy has put tremendous downward pressure on wages and benefits on workers in developed countries that are subject to global competition, and dramatically increased earnings on capital. Low wage competition from elsewhere in the world has contributed to American employers' desire to subcontract work to low-wage countries and to entice immigration of low-wage employees from Central and South America. The downward pressure on wages and benefits exists not only in manufacturing, but in any service in which work can be digitalized and sent to qualified people elsewhere in the world. Richard B. Freeman, America Works: Critical Thought on the Exceptional U.S. Labor Market 128–40 (2007).

In 2008, the United States—and the rest of the world—suffered the worst financial crisis since the Great Depression. The burst of a speculative bubble in the American real estate market threatened the economic viability of financial institutions that had heavily leveraged their positions to invest in mortgage instruments. Credit markets ground to a halt as financial institutions became afraid to loan money to each other because of uncertainty about the borrower's exposure in mortgage instruments. Panic in the financial markets lead to panic in world stock markets and a substantial decline in stock prices word-wide. To prevent the failure of American banks and mortgage institutions, the Bush administration intervened by buying troubled mortgage instruments and taking equity positions in distressed institutions under the Troubled Asset Relief Program (TARP). After he took office, President Obama completed the TARP program and sought to maintain aggregate demand and rekindle economic growth by covering state government deficit spending and undertaking federal stimulus spending under the American Recovery and Reinvestment Act (ARRA). However, concern over state and federal deficit spending and the divided government that resulted from the 2010 elections left the United States with no coherent recovery strategy. Although unemployment declined to historically low levels, wages stubbornly refused to rise in the face of low wage competition world-wide and labor force participation remained down. The continued stagnation of wages would undoubtedly have an impact on union organization and labor relations world-wide.

The new information technology has also accelerated the automation of the workplace. Beginning at the dawn of the Twenty-first Century and accelerating during the Great recession, the global economy and especially the developed nations, experienced an increase in the rate of the replacement of human labor with computers and automated labor. By one estimate, 45% of America's occupations comprising 47% of the workforce will be automated within the next 20 years, including jobs in transportation, logistics, production labor, administrative support, various sales and service clerks, and construction. Carl Benedikt Frey & Michael A. Osborne, *The Future of Employment: How Susceptible Are Jobs to Computerisation?* Oxford Martin School Working Paper 37–38 (Sept. 17, 2013), https://www.oxfordmartin.ox.ac.uk/downloads/academic/future-of-employment.pdf. The impact of automation using the new information technology has not been uniform across the American economy. The new technology has raised the productivity and wages of some employees, predominantly professional employees who exercise discretionary judgment that cannot be easily automated. On the other hand, the new technology has resulted in the obsolescence of many workers who performed rote physical or mental tasks that are more easily automated, displacing those workers largely down into the low wage labor market. The resulting "job polarization" or disappearance of mid-skill, mid-wage level, jobs, has resulted in greater income inequality in the United States and decreased the traditional opportunities for people to rise in the income distribution. Kenneth G. Dau-Schmidt, *The Impact of Emerging Information Technologies on the Employment Relationship: New Gigs for Labor and Employment Law*, 2017 U. Chi. Legal F. 63, 85–91 (2017). For the most part, economists remain sanguine that, as with previous bursts in automation, these displaced workers will eventually retrain or transition to new jobs, some with even higher wages, but technologists have argued that the adoption of "artificial intelligence" has permanently altered the relationship of labor and capital and that we may have to transition to an economy and society in which a growing share of the population cannot maintain themselves through their own labor and perhaps never work. *Id.* Some have suggested that people in developed countries will have to establish systems of "basic income"—government provided minimum benefits and income support to all legal residents—through legislation rather than systems of individual or collective bargaining. *See generally* Basic Income: An Anthology of Contemporary Research (Karl Widerquist et al., eds., Wiley-Blackwell 2013).

The new age of trade and technology that has developed since the 1970s has not been kind to American workers. Although historically the wages of American workers have kept pace with the growth in their productivity, since at least 1980, the wages of American workers have remained flat despite significant growth in productivity. This recent divergence between wages and productivity, known as the "wage gap", is shown in Graph 3 below. The wealth generated by the increases in productivity since 1980 did not just disappear, but instead became ever more concentrated in the owners and managers of major businesses and other high income earners. As a result, "labor's share" of the Gross Domestic Product (GDP) has been declining in recent years and the distribution of income and wealth in America has become more unequal. Since 1980, the share of non-farm domestic product going to non-supervisory employees in the form of wages and benefits has declined from 35% to 27% of the total. Kenneth G. Dau-Schmidt, *Promoting Employee Voice in the American Economy: A Call for Comprehensive Reform*, 94 Marquette L. Rev. 765, 795 (2011). Economists have provided three interrelated explanations for the decline in "labor's share" of GDP and the rise of inequality in the U.S. The first is that the improvements in technology wrought by the new information technology have improved capital's productivity and thus it's earning power—increasing capital's share of GDP. Second, globalization has undermined the bargaining power of workers in developed countries, particularly low-skill workers, as they have been thrown into competition with low-wage workers across the globe. Finally, changes in national labor market policies, for example decreases in the real minimum wage and declining support of public education and labor unions, have undermined workers' bargaining power. Although it is difficult to determine how much each of these three factors has contributed to the "wage gap", Mishel, Bernstein and Allegretto have argued that a reasonable estimate is that each factor is responsible for about a third of the currently observed gap. Lawrence Mishel, Jared Bernstein & Heidi Shierholz, The State of Working America 2008/2009, at 7 (2009).

Graph 3: The American "Wage Gap" as Represented by the Difference Between the Percentage Growth in First Quarter Nonfarm Worker Productivity and Worker Wages, 1947-2018

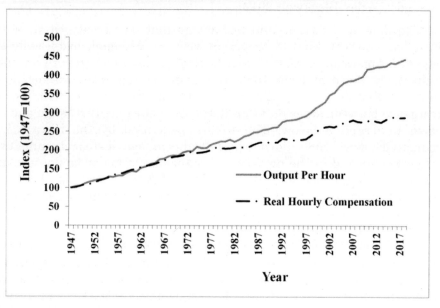

Source: Bureau of Labor Statistics Data Sets,
http://www.bls.gov/lpc/#data, http://www.bls.gov/data/
https://fred.stlouisfed.org/series/COMPRNFB
https://fred.stlouisfed.org/series/OPHNFB?utm_source=series_page&utm_medium=related
_content&utm_term=related_resources&utm_campaign=categories

The declining fortunes of the American worker have led to turmoil in American society. Stagnation in income and declines in labor force participation contributed to an approximately 26% decline in the marriage rate between 1970 and 2011, with the decline felt most harshly by low-income men. Michael Greenstone & Adam Looney, *The Marriage Gap: The Impact of Economic and Technological Change on Marriage Rates*, The Hamilton Project (Feb. 3, 2012), https://www.brookings.edu/blog/jobs/2012/02/03/the-marriage-gap-the-impact-of-economic-and-technological-change-on-marriage-rates/. This decline in the marriage rate is of course associated with an increase in out of wedlock births, especially among lower income women. June Carbone & Naomi Cahn, *The Gender/Class Divide: Reproduction, Privilege and the Workplace*, 8 Fla. Int'l U. L. Rev. 287 (2013). Declining job prospects have contributed to incarceration rates, especially among working class Black men. John Pawasarat & Lois M. Quinn, Wisconsin's Mass Incarceration of African American Males: Workforce Challenges for 2013, Employment and Training Institute, University of Wisconsin-Milwaukee (2013), https://www4.uwm.edu/eti/2013/BlackImprisonment.pdf. The declining fortunes of the working class have even been linked to the booming opioid addiction epidemic and the rise of suicides among middle-aged White people. Anne Case & Angus Deaton, *Mortality and Morbidity in the 21st Century*, Brookings Papers on Economic Activity, 397 (Spring 2017).

The declining fortunes of unions has left working people with a decreasing voice in the American economy and American politics. Many Republican legislators have sought to further decrease the economic and political clout of unions seeing them as reliable allies of to their Democratic opponents. Calls to address the problems of the displacement of workers due to international trade and automation have largely gone unheeded. Republican concerns over immigration and social issues has fanned divisions within the American electorate based on gender, race and ethnicity. Within the Democratic party, the adoption of identity politics along those same lines of gender, race and ethnicity has left American workers fractured in addressing their common interests. In the presidential election of 2016, voters in Black, Hispanic and union households favored Hillary Clinton while White working-class voters from non-union households helped deliver several key midwestern states to Donald Trump. President Trump has promised to address the concerns of American workers in international trade, but it is yet to be seen how successful his efforts will prove. The early results are not encouraging. Edward Helmore, *Harley-Davidson: Trump's Tariffs Pose Grave Threat to Famous American Name*, The Guardian, March 10, 2018, https://www.the guardian.com/us-news/2018/mar/10/harley-davidson-tariffs-trump-motor cycles. It is also unclear how American workers will speak with a clear and consistent voice in addressing their economic and political concerns in the new global economy of the information age.

NOTES

1.   *The Impact of International Trade on the American Economy*: Even simple international trade models predict that when high wage, high capital countries trade with low wage, low capital countries, the result will be increased total wealth but decreased wages and increased payments for capital in the high wage country as the high wage workers struggle to compete with low wage workers. Robert C. Feenstra, Advanced International Trade: Theory and Evidence 31–63 (2004). This simple prediction seems to have born fruit in the developed countries of the world as global trade seems to have increased total wealth but decreased labor's share of total product relative to capital's share. The trade models also predict that over time workers displaced by foreign trade will retrain and transition to new jobs, and the balance of trade between the trading counties will equalize. However, at least with respect to trade with low wage developing countries, in particular Mexico and China, these transitions have proven much slower and more costly for American workers than originally expected. Since the ratification of NAFTA in 1993, the United States has lost an estimated 850,000 jobs to Mexico. Robert E. Scott, The effects of NAFTA on US trade, jobs, and investment, The Economic Policy

Institute, https://econpapers.repec.org/article/elgrokejn/v_3a2_3ay_3a2014_3ai_3a4_3ap429-441.htm. Similarly, since the entry of China into the WTO in 2001, the United States has lost an estimated 2.4 million to China, with no real countervailing job gains. These job losses were concentrated primarily in Midwestern and Southeastern manufacturing, and for the affected workers resulted in: substantial periods of unemployment; a loss of value in firm and industry specific human capital; and substantial wage losses. America's trade deficit with China shows no signs that it will right itself and this deficit retards job growth in the United States. Although it is clear that trade with low-wage countries results in a redistribution of income and wealth from American workers to American management and capital, the adjustment costs this trade has proven far larger than anticipated and it is not yet clear that the benefits of that trade exceed these costs. David H. Autor *et al.*, *The China Shock: Learning From Labor Market Adjustment To Large Changes In Trade*, 8 Ann. Rev. Econ. 205 (2016).

American trade unionists and small businessmen have also sometimes argued for "fair trade" or "principled trade" rather than "free trade." How and why should American workers and businesses be asked to compete with companies in countries that don't even enforce basic labor standards or environmental standards? If there are valid reasons for our basic standards for work, production and trade in our economy, as established by our government, asking our companies and workers to compete with companies in countries that don't enforce those same standards undermines those standards and the primacy of our democratic decisions. It also unfairly undermines the strength of our economy. Keith DauSchmidt, *Free trade. Fair trade. How about principled trade?*, Minnesota Business, Sept. 28, 2016, http://minnesota business.com/free-trade-fair-trade-how-about-principled-trade.

What should be American policy with respect to international trade? Does it matter that there are winners and losers in free trade? Are there ways to have the winners aid the losers so that all can benefit from international trade? What should be done to help American workers transition to better jobs in the new global economy? Should tariffs be used, perhaps to off-set the cost savings of substandard working conditions and environmental standards? Can we make trade among the various countries both fair and profitable?

2. *Recent Trends in Immigration*: As recently as 1970 there were only 9.6 million immigrants living in the U.S., constituting 4.7% of the nation's population, but by 2014 the number had more than quadrupled to a record 42.2 million immigrants, constituting 13.2% of the population. The percent of immigrants living in the U.S. now rivals the record 14.8% set back in 1890. Since the passage of the Immigration and Naturalization Act in 1965, there has been a dramatic shift in the region of origin among the immigrant population residing in the U.S. In 1960, 84% of immigrants living in the U.S. were born in Europe or Canada, while only 9.5% were from Latin America, 3.8% were from Asia, and 2.7% were from other areas. By 2014, European and Canadian immigrants made up only 13.6% of the foreign-born population, while Latin American immigrants made up 51.7%. Asian immigrants made up

26.4% and 8.3% of immigrants were born in other regions. In the early 2000s, the number of newly arrived Hispanic immigrants greatly outnumbered the number of newly-arrived Asian immigrants, but with the Great Recession, Latin American immigration slowed, especially from Mexico, while Asian immigration continued to grow. Since 2009, the number of newly arrived Asian immigrants has exceeded the number of newly arrived Hispanic immigrants each year. Anna Brown & Renee Stepler, *Statistical Portrait of the Foreign-Born Population in the United States, 2014*, Pew Research Center (Apr. 19, 2016), http://www.pewhispanic.org/2016/04/19/statistical-portrait-of-the-foreign-born-population-in-the-united-states-2014-key-charts/#2013-fb-authorized-pie; Migration Policy Institute, *U.S. Immigrant Population and Share over Time, 1850–Present*, http://www.migrationpolicy.org/programs/data-hub/charts/immigrant-population-over-time.

There are important differences among immigrant groups as to how they enter the country, their likely educational achievement and their family income. Like the European immigrants of the turn of the Twentieth Century, Latin American immigrants tend to be impoverished or working-class people in their country of origin, who come to the U.S. to earn higher wages in low-skill jobs. Asian immigrants tend to be from the merchant or upper classes in their country of origin and come to the U.S. for education or a technical or professional job. As a result, in 2013 Latin American immigrants were less likely to have a college degree (12%) than the American population as a whole (32%), while Asian immigrants were more likely to have a college degree (50%). Mexican immigrants particularly were at a disadvantage with respect to education as only 5.8% of them had college degrees and 58% had not graduated from high school. Similarly, in 2013 Latin American immigrants had a lower median household income ($39,000) than the American population as a whole ($52,000), while Asian immigrants had a higher median household income ($69,000). Latin American immigrants are less likely to be proficient in English (39%) than Asian immigrants (54%). Latin American immigrants who are employed are much more likely to work in construction, agriculture and mining (18%) than Asian immigrants (2.6%) and much less likely to be in management or a profession (18%) than their Asian counterparts (52%). Ana Gonzolez-Barrera, *Appendix A: Mexican and Asian Immigrants Compared* (Nov. 19, 2015), http://www.pewhispanic.org/2015/11/19/appendix-a-mexican-and-asian-immigrants-compared/. Finally, in 2013, Latin American immigrants were more likely to be unauthorized immigrants (40.5%) than their Asian counterparts (13.1%). Brown & Stepler, *supra*.

Economic theory provides two arguments concerning the impact of immigrants on the wages of native born workers. To the extent that immigrants compete directly with native workers, the simple economic model would predict that an increase in labor supply from immigration would depress wages. To the extent that immigrants perform work that native workers will not do and which stimulates economic growth or complements domestic labor, immigration can actually raise domestic wages by making it more productive. A recent survey of the economic literature found that the empirical work suggests that immigration has a modest positive overall effect on native wages,

David Card, *Is the New Immigration Really So Bad?* 115 The Econ. J. F300 (2005), but there is evidence that immigration has depressed the wages of college graduates and (especially) those without high school degrees. George Borjas & Lawrence Katz, *The Evolution of the Mexican-Born Workforce in the United States, in* Mexican Immigration to the United States (George Borjas ed., NBER Conference Report 2007); George J. Borjas, *The Wage Impact of the Marielitos: A Reappraisal*, NBER Working Paper No. 21588 (2016).

While most immigrants are legally authorized to be in the country, it is estimated that in 2014 there were 11.1 million unauthorized immigrants, or about 25.5% of all immigrants. Among the authorized immigrants, 19 million or 43.6% are naturalized citizens, 11.7 million or 26.9% are authorized permanent residents and 1.7 million or 4% are authorized temporary immigrants. The nation's unauthorized immigrant population grew rapidly between 1990 and 2007, reaching a peak of 12.2 million. Since then, the population has declined to about 11.1 million, where it has remained. Unauthorized immigrants from Mexico make up half of all unauthorized immigrants, and have been a driver of the group's population decline. Since 2007, the number of unauthorized Mexican immigrants fell from a peak of 6.9 million to 5.8 million in 2014. Brown & Stepler, *supra.* As will be discussed later in the book, unauthorized immigrants have special problems enforcing the law since, even if the law protects such immigrants, they fear reporting violations and possibly being deported. It has been argued that President Trump's harsh policies on the deportation of unauthorized immigrants has also slowed the flow of unauthorized immigrants across the border. Jenny Beth Martin, *Trump Immigration Policies Working*, Wash. Times, July 5, 2017, http://www.washingtontimes.com/news/2017/jul/5/trump-immigration-policies-working/.

How does this wave of immigration compare with the earlier waves of European immigration? How are the problems of these people the same, and how are they different? Immigration policy has been a hotly contested subject in Congress and election campaigns. What policy should the U.S. adopt with respect to immigration?

3.   *Race and the American Labor Movement*: As suggested in the text, some members of the American labor movement have actively discriminated against African Americans. As you will see later in this book, the "duty of fair representation" was first imposed on unions in a case in which the defendant union excluded Blacks from membership and negotiated a contract that expressly discriminated against Blacks with respect to job assignments and pay. *Steele v. Louisville & Nashville R.R. Co.*, 323 U.S. 192 (1944). Unfortunately, this was not an uncommon practice in the railway and other industries. *See also Bhd. of R. R. Trainmen v. Howard*, 343 U.S. 768 (1952). Even in the absence of intentional discrimination, union practices such as hiring halls or seniority provisions sometimes served as a barrier to new groups, such as African Americans, who sought to enter a craft or workplace. Employers also sometimes tried to use racial divisions as a way of frustrating employee collective action, for example using Black workers to replace striking

White workers. *See* Herbert Hill, *The Problem of Race in American Labor History*, 24 Rev. Am. Hist. 189 (1996); *Negro Non-Unionist Kills Meat Striker; Colored Strike Breakers Clash With Rioters in Chicago*, N.Y. Times, July 27, 1904, at 1.

However, as a rule the members of the American labor movement have done much better on the issue of race relations in recent years and African Americans have been active supporters of collective bargaining once they were given the chance to join the union. Unions are subject to the anti-discrimination provisions of the Civil Rights Act. Between 1935 and 1985, the number of African Americans in labor unions increased from an estimated 50,000 to more than three million. P. Frymer, *Race, Labor Unions, and American Political Development in the 20th Century*, Paper presented at the annual meeting of the American Political Science Association, Philadelphia, PA (2003). Indeed, the labor movement has become a positive force on the side of civil rights. In one particularly fine moment in this regard, President Walter Reuther and the UAW were proud supporters of Dr. Martin Luther King, Jr. and the March on Washington. As early as 1961, Walter Reuther invited Dr. King to speak at the UAW's 25th Anniversary Dinner in Detroit. In preparation for the March on Washington, Dr. King organized a march in Detroit working out of Solidarity House, the UAW's international headquarters. The speech that Dr. King gave at the "Great March in Detroit" is considered the first version of his now famous "I Have a Dream Speech" that he delivered to over 200,000 people at the March on Washington, August 28, 1963. Thousands of UAW members joined in the marches in Detroit and Washington, and Walter Reuther shared the podium with Dr. King at both occasions.

4. *Men and Education:* The obstacles that women and minorities have faced in the labor market are well documented in the academic literature. Much less attention has been paid to the obstacles men face in education. Currently, boys are only 46% of high school graduates, and 40% of college graduates. Although this gender gap in education exists across all races and classes, the problem is the worst for poor African American males—particularly those from households where no father is present. Among African Americans, men constitute only 43% of high school graduates and 33% of college graduates. Jay P. Greene & Marcus A. Winters, *Leaving Boys Behind: Public High School Graduation Rates*, Manhattan Institute for Policy Research Civic Report No. 48 (2006), http://www.manhattan-institute.org/html/cr_48.htm; Tom Chiarella, *The Problem with Boys*, Esquire, July 2006, at 94. One reason for this problem is that, since the 1980s, the percentage of female teachers and administrators in primary and secondary education has increased from 80% to 90%. As a result young boys, especially those with no father in the home, have a paucity of educated male role models. Moreover, it seems that the increasingly female dominated educational establishment has increasingly come to rely on teaching methods and definitions of "intelligence" and "good behavior" that are geared to girls. *Id.*; Thomas S. Dee, *A Teacher Like Me: Does Race, Ethnicity or Gender Matter?*, 95 Am. Econ. Rev. 158 (2005); Thomas S. Dee, *The Why Chromosome: How a Teacher's Gender Affects Boys*

and Girls, 6 Education Next, Fall 2006 at 68; Thomas S. Dee, *Teachers and the Gender Gaps in Student Achievement*, 42 J. of Hum. Res. 528 (2007); Richard Whitmire, Why Boys Fail: Saving Our Sons from an Educational System that's Leaving them Behind (2010); Nicole M. Fortin, Philip Oreopoulos & Shelley Phipps, *Leaving Boys Behind: Gender Disparities in High Academic Achievement*, 50 J. Hum. Res. 549–579 (2015). How can we best provide educational opportunities for men and make the most of all of our nation's human resources?

5.   *Growing Income Inequality in the United States:* During the post-war period from 1947 to 1979, the income for all income groups in the United States grew in the same proportions at an approximately 3% annual growth rate, roughly doubling over that time. However, since 1979 the fortunes of the rich and poor have dramatically diverged in the American economy. Since 1980, the average pretax income of adults in the bottom 50% of the income distribution has stagnated at about $16,000 per adult (in 2014 dollars), while average national income per adult has grown by 60% to $64,500 (in 2014 dollars). As a result, the bottom 50% income share has collapsed from about 20% in 1980 to 12% in 2014. In the meantime, the average pretax income of adults in the top 1% of the income distribution rose from $420,000 to about $1.3 million, and their income share increased from about 12% in the early 1980s to 20% in 2014. The top 1% of income earners now enjoy an income share that is almost twice as large as that received by the bottom 50% of income earners, a group that is by definition 50 times more numerous. Government redistribution through taxation and transfers has offset only a small fraction of the increase in pretax inequality. Even after taxes and transfers, there has been close to zero growth in real income for working-age adults in the bottom 50% of the income distribution since 1980. Although government transfers have increased since 1980, these increases have been aimed largely at the elderly and people in the upper half of the income distribution. The increase in income inequality since 1980 was driven primarily by wages increases among the wealthy during the 1980s and '90s, but since 2000 the increase in income inequality has been driven by increases in equity and bond income among the top 1% of income earners. Thomas Piketty, Emmanuel Saez & Gabriel Zucman, *Distributional National Accounts: Methods and Estimates for the United States*, 133 Q. J. of Econ. 553, 557 (2018). What are the implications of growing income inequality for the American workplace? For the American economy as a whole? For our democracy? *See generally*, Jake Rosenfeld, What Unions No Longer Do (2014).

Graph 4: Percent of National Income Received by the Top 1% and Bottom 50% of Income Earners in the United States, 1962-2014

Source: Thomas Piketty, Emmanuel Saez and Gabriel Zucman, *Distributional National Accounts: Methods and Estimates for the United States*, 133 Q. J. of Econ. 553 (2018), online appendix http://gabrielzucman.eu/usdina.

b. Labor Relations in the New Economic Environment

The NLRA system of collective bargaining through an exclusive representative chosen by an election in an appropriate unit has not worked well in this new economic environment. The NLRA definitions of who is an employee, who is an employer, and what constitutes an appropriate bargaining unit have all become increasingly irrelevant—at least as interpreted by the Supreme Court. Workers may labor as subcontractors, temporary workers, subcontracted workers, or employees of a subcontracting employer when the *real* economic power in the relationship resides with a "third party" producer or retailer, or the producer of an "on-demand" or "crowd-sourcing" app. Jobs are not well-defined or long-term, as employees work in situations of decentralized decision-making and progress through their careers among multiple employers. The decentralization of decision-making in the new economic environment poses a particular problem for the definition of employees and employers under the NLRA due to the Court's broad interpretation of the supervisory and managerial employee exceptions. As the NLRA definitions of employee and employer have lost their meaning in the new economy, so too has the definition of an appropriate bargaining unit, which depends on these definitions.

Even putting aside the problems of definitions under the NLRA, employees and employers are less amenable to traditional NLRA organization in the new economic environment. In the new economy, employees have less long-term interest in the job and thus less incentive to organize a particular employer. Why should employees incur the risks and costs of organizing a particular employer when they may well be working for a different employer next year? Employers are more concerned with ensuring low prices and flexibility in production than with maintaining production or a stable workforce. As a result, employers are more inclined to resist employee organization and take advantage of the many strategies for delay and intimidation available under the current law. Although the potential remedial awards that could be levied against an employer for engaging in intimidation or delay are relatively small, such employer tactics can significantly raise the costs of organizing to employees and unions. Statistics suggest that employers engaged in approximately 28,000 instances of reprisals against union proponents in 2006, with an average back pay award of only $2,700. Because the workforce has become more diverse, it has become more costly to organize on an industry-wide basis. Employees need to overcome the divisions of race, gender and ethnicity in order to organize for their mutual aid and protection. Of course, employers sometimes attempt to exacerbate these divisions as a means of preventing worker solidarity. An AFL-CIO estimate suggests that it costs a union as much as $1,000 per worker to undertake an organizing campaign. Finally, the increased flux in work and production in the new economy makes maintaining a given level of organization in a given industry more difficult. Due to increased employee turnover, employer reorganization, and outsourcing, workers who are organized do not necessarily stay organized long. A recent AFL-CIO estimate suggests that it will take 20% of the organization's budget just to organize and replace those members who are lost due to attrition, reorganization, and outsourcing.

Finally, traditional single unit, "bread-and-butter" collective bargaining does not always work well in the new economic environment. Unions have had trouble successfully negotiating higher wages and benefits in recent years. The entry of the former Soviet Republics, India, and China into the world economy has ensured that there are some real wages and benefits bargains available to employers in sectors that are open to international trade. New information technology allows employers to more easily relocate or outsource work to replace employees and cut wage costs. Moreover, in the new economic environment, employers strive to maintain flexibility in production and employment and to resist the promises of job security, seniority, and benefits that employers once used to bind employees to their jobs. With the decline of the internal labor market and the rise of a market-driven workforce, there are fewer managerial rules for unions to help determine and administer, and thus less for unions to achieve through traditional collective bargaining. Moreover, the new decentralized organization of production among contractors and subcontractors, rather than in large, vertically integrated firms, and the rise of the "big box" and on-line retailers mean that workers are less likely to be "employed" by the party with real economic power in their employment relationship. The restrictive definition of employer and the existing restrictions on secondary boycotts under the NLRA significantly hamper workers' ability to address the issues of most concern to them with the party having control over those issues through traditional collective bargaining. Kenneth G. Dau-Schmidt, *The Changing Face of Collective Representation: The Future of Collective Bargaining*, 82 Chi.-Kent L. Rev. 903, 915–18 (2007).

NOTES

1.   *A Change in Government Attitude?*: It has been argued that labor's recent problems in organizing the workforce and conducting collective action arise in part from a shift in the government's attitude towards the problems of workers and employee organization. During the period of 1930–70, the federal government was focused on maintaining low unemployment through Keynesian fiscal policies and fostering employee organization under the NLRA. Then in 1981, President Reagan fired and replaced the striking members of Professional Air Traffic Controllers Organization (PATCO). Although the PATCO members had struck in violation of the law, it has been argued that President Reagan's treatment of these employees evinced a less than beneficent attitude toward organized labor and collective action. Moreover, since at least the 1980s, both Republican and Democratic administrations have been less concerned with employee wages and collective representation and more concerned with productivity and international competitiveness. Since 2010, governors and legislators in states such as Wisconsin, Michigan, Maine, Iowa and Missouri have become aggressively anti-union. Federal senators and state legislators have even sought to interpose their personal antiunion perspectives into firm organizing campaigns, threatening future government subsidies and favorable tax treatment if the plants organized, even when the employer had agreed to remain neutral in the organizing campaign. Alec MacGillis, *Bob Corker Devastated Organized Labor in Chattanooga. Let It Be a Lesson.*, The New Republic, Feb. 18, 2014, https://newrepublic.com/article/116653/bob-corkers-uaw-intervention-chattanooga-vw-vote-speaks-volume. Detractors argue that these changes in the attitude of the federal government have engendered or reinforced changes in attitudes by employers and the public at large. Herbert R. Northrup, *The Rise and Demise of PATCO*, 37 Indus. & Lab. Rel. Rev. 167 (1984); Michael K. Burns, *10 Years After PATCO Strike, A Legacy of Labor Bitterness*, Baltimore Sun, Aug. 4, 1991, at 4E, 1991 WL 5891560.

2.   *A Change in Employer Attitude?*: Some academics have argued that American employers have become more aggressively anti-union in the period since the 1970s. They cite employers' increased use of anti-union consultants in thwarting union organizing drives and permanent replacements in response to strikes during this time. Department of Labor statistics show that the number of instances in which the NLRB ordered reinstatement for discriminatory discharges by employers during union organizing campaigns

almost doubled from an average of 1500 a year in the period 1971–75 to an average of just under 3000 a year for the period 1981–85. Commission on the Future of Worker-Management Relations, U.S. Department of Labor, Fact Finding Report, 84 exhibit III-4 (1994). Some attribute this change in attitude to the government's change in attitude discussed above and a general move to conservative thinking among business managers. However, the increased competitive pressures on employers in the global economy have also undoubtedly played a role. *See* Michael H. Leroy, *Regulating Employer Use Of Permanent Striker Replacements: Empirical Analysis of NLRA and RLA Strikes 1935–1991*, 16 Berkeley J. Emp. & Lab. L. 169 (1995).

3.   *A Change in Employee Attitude?*: There has undoubtedly been some change in the public's view of unions and collective bargaining since the 1930s and '40s. Back in the heyday of industrial unionism many American's considered it a sign of good citizenship that a person was a union member, alongside attending church regularly, serving in the military, and voting. The reputation of the American labor movement suffered some in the public's mind with the post-war strikes in 1946, the hearings of the McClellan Committee in 1956, Hollywood's general obsession with the view of labor leaders as gangsters, and the conservative "Reagan Revolution" of the 1980s. Nevertheless, American workers seem to have maintained a remarkable interest in elected representation in the workplace. In a recent survey, Professors Richard Freeman and Joel Rogers found that 87 percent of workers would like some form of collective representation in discussing firm decisions that affect their employment conditions, and almost half favor traditional union representation. However, workers fear employer reprisals if they openly support unionization. Richard B. Freeman & Joel Rogers, What Workers Want 39–64 (2006).

c.   Opportunities for Unions in the New Economic Environment

The rise of the global economy and the implementation of new information technology pose some serious problems for traditional organizing and collective bargaining under the NLRA. Because of the changes in the employment relationship that these developments have wrought, the costs of traditional organizing have increased while the benefits of traditional collective bargaining have decreased. It is thus not surprising that the percentage of the private sector workforce organized in the United States has declined precipitously over the past thirty years. There currently exists a vigorous debate within the American labor movement as to how to respond to this problem. The crux of the debate seems to be whether to commit resources to innovative methods of organizing and then to rally the new membership to address limitations in the current law, or to commit resources to politics in hopes of amending the law to facilitate future organizing. Although we do not yet know how this debate will be resolved, it is useful to observe some of the ways in which the current economic environment also presents some interesting opportunities for the labor movement.

First, and most obviously, new information technology provides new means for communication and coordination. In undertaking any form of collective action, there are major problems and costs associated with collecting and dispersing information and coordinating efforts. To the extent that new information technology lowers these costs, it can be a boon to employee organizing and collective action. Moreover, each new generation of workers shows more adaptation to, and reliance on, new information technology to conduct their lives. Unions are beginning to use new information technology to transmit information on wages, benefits, work disputes, and boycotts, as well as to coordinate efforts in collective action both locally and around the world. The labor movement should fully exploit this new technology, especially as it attempts to organize the e-generation.

Second, the vertical disintegration of firms and the rise of contingent employment have created a need for an institution to coordinate benefits and training over the course of employees' careers and to represent their interests on a multi-employer and societal basis. Private firms could offer benefit plans for individual purchase; the government could also increase its health insurance and pension programs. However, unions seem well-situated to marshal the necessary resources and to administer these benefits on an industry-wide basis in the absence of long-term employment with a single employer. Indeed, unions have an ample history of administering multi-employer benefit programs in the construction industry, where worker-union affiliation is more stable than the typical employment relationship. Similarly, unions or professional associations could coordinate employee training and advancement among multiple employers to provide some semblance of career ladders in the new information age. As discussed below, some unions and professional organizations have already started to focus on promoting training and career continuity for their members over the course of their work lives. Also, even in the absence of traditional collective bargaining agreements, workers need labor and professional organizations to represent their interests in their respective industries, as well as in society at large. Labor organizations and professional associations can represent their members by providing aid and expertise in the negotiation and enforcement of individual contract rights and in the promulgation and enforcement of statutory and constitutional rights. Indeed, as discussed below, the implementation of new information technology and the rise of the global economy have raised some important issues of risk bearing and equity that will need to be addressed on a societal or international level. Unions can play a pivotal role in representing workers' interests in these debates.

Finally, the adoption of new production methods and the rise of the global economy raise important issues that need to be addressed on a collective basis. The use of new information technology to adopt decentralized production methods, which involve more short-term employment relationships, has led to the devolution of risk from employers to employees. As the provision of benefits as a method to bind employees to employers has declined, employees have come to shoulder a greater share of the risk of illness and disability and have taken on greater responsibility for the marshaling and investment of their retirement resources. As employers have abandoned lifetime employment schemes, employees have also taken on greater responsibility for retraining if their skills become obsolete, and shoulder a greater risk of periods of unemployment during their work lives. This devolution of risk onto individual employees aggravates important problems that can be addressed on a collective basis, either at the firm, professional, or societal level. Indeed, the problem can perhaps *best* be addressed through a collective plan for direct risk reduction and efficient risk spreading. The only question is whether such collective solutions should be undertaken through the market, internal employer rules, or societal programs. It would seem that these risk issues raise an important question for workers to address through collective workplace or political action.

Moreover, although globalization and the new information technology have led to economic growth, they have also led to economic dislocation and inequality. As discussed in the notes of the previous section, economic models of international trade demonstrate that, although trade may increase total wealth, there will be "winners" and "losers" in such trade with workers in high-wage countries losing jobs to workers in low-wage countries and bargaining power to the owners of capital. Automation using the new information technology also produces "winners" and "losers" making capital and some workers more productive and more highly paid while displacing other workers into the low-wage labor market. The displacement and loss of earning power that international trade and automation have caused American workers have resulted in economic, social and political upheaval in American society. These issues of displacement and increased income inequality in the United States, and developed countries in general, pose important questions for workers to address through collective action in the workplace and in the political arena.

The need to address the issues of dislocation, risk, and income inequality provides a basis for a broad-based social and political labor movement. Globalization and automation may be inevitable, but it is still an open question whether we will use these processes to raise everyone up or leave some workers behind. Since we use the market as a means for rationing so many things, including medical care and education, this question goes to the fundamental fairness and structure of American society. Furthermore, the growing inequality appears to be undermining the functioning of our democracy. There is also a need to readdress the government's role in helping people to bear risk, save for retirement, and obtain useful training. Our system has long been a mixed system of basic government programs and private-employment-based benefits and training. As employment becomes more contingent and less long-term, employers will be less willing to invest in benefits and training for a given employee because they will reason that the employee may soon be working for someone else. Moreover, the competition of the global economy will mean that private employers cannot provide benefits unless they directly and immediately increase productivity. As a result, we will have to rely more on government programs to meet these needs. At a minimum, there is a need to retrain employees displaced from their jobs by the machinations of the global economy. Unions and professional organizations can play an important role in promoting, shaping, and monitoring the administration of such programs in workers' interests. This discussion must be conducted on a larger societal basis, or even an international basis, because such problems can no longer be effectively addressed at the employer level in a global economy. Kenneth G. Dau-Schmidt, *The Changing Face of Collective Representation: The Future of Collective Bargaining*, 82 Chi.-Kent L. Rev. 903, 918–21 (2007).

NOTES

1.   *Recent Efforts to Amend the National Labor Relations Act*: Since the 1970s there have been several efforts to amend the National Labor Relations Act in various ways to address deficiencies and bring the Act up to date with current economic realities. Most have languished from filibusters in the Senate, although one was vetoed. None have become law. The Labor Law Reform Act of 1977 was aimed at the NLRA's problems of administrative delays and inadequate remedies. Although the Reform Act had majority support in both the House and the Senate, and would have been signed by then President Carter, it died for want of cloture in the Senate. A less ambitious attempt at reform the next year also failed. William Gould, IV, A Primer On American Labor Law 123–33 (1982). The Workplace Fairness Act of 1992 would have prohibited employers from using permanent replacement workers to break strikes, although it allowed the continued use of temporary replacements. The Act failed by three votes to get the necessary 60 votes for cloture in the Senate. Even a bi-partisan amendment by Senators Packwood (R-Oregon) and Metzenbaum (D-Ohio) to allow permanent replacement where the union had refused an offer of binding arbitration failed to garner the necessary majority to bring the bill to a vote. In 1995, members of the 104th Congress proposed the TEAM Act, that would have allowed an exemption to the company union provisions of Section 8(a)(2) for joint committees of employee and management representatives in nonunion workplaces to address matters of mutual interest including, but not limited to, issues of quality, productivity, efficiency, and safety and health. This bill passed both houses but

was vetoed by President Clinton. More recently supporters of organized labor proposed the Employee Free Choice Act which would amend the NLRA to allow employee organization on the basis of membership cards without an election; provide for mediation and arbitration of first contract disputes; and significantly increase penalties for unfair labor practices. The Employee Free Choice Act passed in the House in 2007, but failed to overcome a filibuster in the Senate. The Employee Free Choice Act languished during the first two years of the Obama administration and then died after Republicans regained control of the House in the 2010 elections. Since the Republican takeover of the ederal government in 2016, there has been talk among Republicans in Congress of a national right to work bill and amendments to the NLRA to further decrease union power. Commentators have recommended a number of possible reforms including: providing penalties for unfair labor practices rather than just remedies, speeding Board administration particularly of elections, allowing abbreviated elections or the selection of bargaining representatives on the basis of signed representation cards, allowing secondary job actions, easing the restrictions of Section 8(a)(2) on management-employee committees, broadening the definitions of employer and employee under the Act, and promoting elected employee committees. Paul Weiler, *Promises to Keep: Securing Workers' Rights to Self-Organization under the NLRA*, 96 Harv. L. Rev. 1769 (1983); William B. Gould IV, *Labor Law and Its Limits: Some Proposals For Reform*, 49 Wayne L. Rev. 667 (2003). What reforms to the National Labor Relations Act do you think Congress should adopt?

2. *Worker Centers, An Idea Whose Time Has Come?*: In the last decades of the Twentieth Century, in response to the restructuring of the labor market and the decline of traditional unions, workers began to associate together in a new type of civic organizations called a "worker center." The workers who organized together into worker centers consisted primarily of low-wage immigrant labor who sought a way to deal with the problems of exploitation and racism that they suffered in the workplace and in the larger society. These workers are found primarily in service industries including building and construction, landscaping, hotels and restaurants, and domestic work. The workers' association through a worker center can help them address individual and collective problems with immigration, on the job, or in the larger society through collective economic or political action. There are approximately 250 worker centers in the United States with five major worker center networks, a network of worker center networks and several solidarity networks with unions and other social and political organizations.

Worker centers sometimes have a close association with organized labor. Worker centers may consult with unions to gain access to union resources or expertise. Some worker centers view themselves as a precursor for workers seeking union representation. Unions often admire worker centers for their creativity in developing organizing campaigns, their commitment to worker justice and their ability to connect worker struggles with community issues to fight for victories beyond the workplace.

In 2006, the AFL-CIO's Executive Council unanimously passed a resolution, "Creating a National Worker Center Partnership," that called on organized labor to build and strengthen ties with worker centers in their communities. Since 2011, the AFL-CIO has partnered with philanthropic institutions to provide grant money for the organization of worker centers through the Labor Innovations for the 21st Century (LIFT) Fund. This fund helped support major organizing campaigns of worker centers like the CLEAN Carwash Campaign, National Day Laborer Organizing Network and the National Domestic Workers Alliance. Union partners such as the Laborers (LIUNA) and Steelworkers (USW), as well as central labor councils and state labor federations from various cities and states, also benefited from these efforts. These partnerships between unions and worker centers have led to significant worker victories in local policy campaigns against wage theft and other forms of worker exploitation and solidarity support for worker organizing campaigns. Victor Narro, Saba Waheed & Jassmin Poyaoan, *Building A Movement Together: Worker Centers and Labor Union Affiliations*, The UCLA Labor Center (June 2015) http://theliftfund.org/wp-content/uploads/2015/09/LIFT-Fund-Worker-Center-Union-Affiliation-Study-June-2015.pdf.

Are worker centers a good substitute or complement to traditional labor unions? Why might they be able to grow even when traditional unions are in decline? To date worker centers have grown primarily among low-wage immigrant workers. Can this model be used for other workers in the American economy? Are worker center "labor organizations" regulated under the NLRA and other federal laws, or are they something else? What else?

CHAPTER 2

COLLECTIVE ACTION IN THE WORKPLACE

■ ■ ■

A. INTRODUCTION

Enderby Electronics, Inc. manufactures LCD and LED ultra high definition television sets, tablet PCs, and other electronic goods with a workforce that includes recent immigrants from Somalia, most of whom are Muslim. To accommodate the Somalis' need to pray during the workday, Enderby converted a conference room, outside the production area, to a prayer room. The location of the conference room was inconvenient because to get to it required leaving the company's "secure area" and then again passing through company security checkpoints to return to production. Most of the Somali immigrants work in entry-level positions at the bottom of the employer's wage scale. Recently, Enderby announced five new "lead worker" positions that earned higher wages. Although several Somali workers applied for these jobs, every person promoted to the positions was a native born Christian American. When the winners of the new lead worker positions were announced, fifty-seven Somali employees walked off their jobs in protest.

After leaving work, the Somali employees gathered at the Somali Community Center in town to assess the situation. They agreed they would not go back to work until their issues were resolved. They decided to establish a picket line at Enderby and distribute leaflets. They returned to Enderby that afternoon and set up a picket line on the sidewalk in front of the main entrance. The leaflets and picket signs asserted that the employer discriminated on the basis of race and religion and that the employer's insistence that employees go through security checkpoints to enter and leave the production area to get to the prayer room precluded them from having enough time to pray. They also complained that the Somali workers suffered ethnic slurs from supervisors and other workers. Some of the picket signs read, "Enderby Electronics is Racist" and others said, "No Religious Freedom for Workers at Enderby."

In addition to the picket signs, several of the Somali workers posted on Facebook describing the incident and decrying Enderby as a racist and anti-religious workplace. Enderby has an Electronic Communications Usage Policy that prohibits employee posted material that is "obscene, defamatory, harassing or abusive to any person or entity associated with Enderby." Enderby also has an Employee Handbook that requires employees "to be courteous, promote harmonious relationships, and otherwise abide by basic standards of civility."

NOTES

1.   What is this association of Somali workers? Is it a union? Is it a community organization? Is it a religious organization? The absence of the Somali workers has significantly slowed production. Assume the employer regularly dismisses individual employees who do not show up to work. Can the employer fire the striking workers? Is there a reason why this case should be treated differently than the case of an individual worker who just cannot get her act together to get to work? Should the employees have fewer or more rights when they act in concert? Or the same rights? Even if the employer cannot fire the Somali workers, should it be able to hire new workers to continue production?

2.   What if Enderby fired the Somali workers who posted on Facebook? Should an employer be able to fire employees who post on Facebook or tweet about happenings at work? What if the employee posts only went to a limited number of close friends? Should an employer be able to regularly track tweets or Facebook posts of employees? What about Enderby's Employee Handbook requiring employees to be "courteous" and "civil"? Do you think the policy would deter Somali workers from protesting unfair working conditions because they might be viewed as discourteous or uncivil?

3.   Should Enderby have the right to fire the workers who walked out for the day? Would it matter whether the workers who were fired were in fact undocumented? Would it matter if the company singled out for firing only those workers who were known supporters of a union? What measures, if any, should the company be allowed to take to keep production going? Should it matter why the workers struck or who organized it?

* * *

The courts have long puzzled over how to treat employee collective action within the context of our legal system based on individual rights and responsibilities. As discussed in Chapter 1, the courts' initial reaction to employee collective action was to treat it less favorably than individual action. As the *Philadelphia Cordwainers* and *Commonwealth v. Hunt* cases described in Chapter 1 reveal, unions were generally viewed as conspiracies in which the combination of the workers made worker actions more dangerous, and thus a prohibited threat to society. Accordingly, courts often enjoined union members from striking, even though individually they all could refuse to work lawfully.

Eventually, the courts developed positions that were less hostile to employee collective action. As discussed in Chapter 1, the majority view in the early industrial period was that unions were not per se illegal, but their activities could be enjoined if they sought an illegal end or employed prohibited means. Of course, under so subjective a standard, individual judges would inevitably apply their own personal views on the desirability and appropriateness of employee collective action in deciding whether the workers had sought appropriate ends or used appropriate means. Some judges saw employee collective action as inherently coercive and violent. Others, like Justice Oliver Wendell Holmes, viewed the combination of labor as the "necessary counterpart" to the combination of capital in a capitalistic system. As he explained in his dissent in *Vegelahn v. Guntner*, 167 Mass. 92, 44 N.E. 1077 (1896), set out fully in Chapter 1:

> "One of the eternal conflicts out of which life is made up is that between the effort of every man to get the most he can for his services, and that of society, disguised under the name of capital, to get his services for the least possible return. Combination on the one side is patent and powerful. Combination on the other is the necessary and desirable counterpart, if the battle is to be carried on in a fair and equal way." *Id.* at 1081 (Holmes, J., dissenting).

Eventually, Congress developed a federal labor policy addressing the question of how employee collective action should be treated that captured Holmes' philosophy in *Vegelahn*. In Section 7 of the National Labor Relations Act (NLRA), Congress declared that concerted activity is not only legal, but protected, and that workers should be free to engage in it, without coercion from their employer. Later, in the Taft-Hartley amendments, Congress also clarified that employees were free to decide not to engage in collective action. Section 7 of the NLRA states:

> "Employees shall have the right to self-organization, to form, join, or assist labor organizations, to bargain collectively through representatives of their own choosing, and to engage in other concerted activities for the purpose of collective bargaining or other mutual aid or protection, and shall also have the right to refrain from any or all of such activities." 29 U.S.C. § 157 (2012).

This focus on preserving the rights of workers as a collective body is what distinguishes labor law from other laws designed to protect workers. Individuals have rights under the NLRA, but all in the context of serving the collective good of employees in any given workplace. One might consider Section 7 to be a broad anti-retaliation law protecting workers who engage in group action around workplace issues from being retaliated against by an employer. The Supreme Court has viewed favorably a host of anti-retaliation laws in various labor and employment statutes. *See, e.g., Burlington Northern & Santa Fe Railway v. White*, 548 U.S. 53 (2006); *Crawford v. Metropolitan Government*, 555 U.S. 271 (2006); *Thompson v. North American Stainless*, 462 U.S. 170 (2011). Of course, most anti-retaliation provisions are available to individual employees (including the

NLRA's Section 8(a)(4)), but these are often more limited protections for using available legal processes to vindicate rights.

The right of workers to organize collectively and independently is at the heart of the statute, but certainly is not absolutely protected. Throughout the statute, the protection of worker voice and collectivization is offset by competing employer interests in property and efficiency. Unfortunately, much of the balancing between labor and employer interests has not been accomplished in the NLRA itself. Rather, the National Labor Relations Board (NLRB) has been tasked with identifying the proper accommodation, which it has chosen to do mostly on a case-by-case basis with oversight by the federal courts. As the Supreme Court stated in *Republic Aviation Corp. v. NLRB*, 324 U.S. 793, 798 (1945), "[t]he Wagner Act did not undertake the impossible task of specifying in precise and unmistakable language each incident which would constitute an unfair labor practice. On the contrary, that Act left to the Board the work of applying the Act's generally prohibitory language in light of the infinite combination of events which might be charged as violative of its terms." Accordingly, the statute leaves open many questions. The materials in this Chapter introduce the NLRB decisions and federal court cases that explore the beginning tensions between management and worker interests and the lines that have been drawn in the attempt to balance both sets of competing interests in the context of what constitutes concerted activity for mutual aid and protection.

B. CONCERTED ACTIVITY FOR MUTUAL AID AND PROTECTION

1. CONCERTED ACTIVITY

Section 7 of the NLRA protects the right of workers to engage in "concerted activities." Concerted is defined as: "1 a: mutually contrived or agreed on <a concerted effort> b: performed in unison <concerted artillery fire>" Merriam Webster Dictionary. The second definition, "performed in unison," connotes simultaneous activity by more than one. The first definition, however, "mutually contrived or agreed on," seems not to be bound temporally. In human terms, the definition suggests that individual actors working alone may, as part of a broader effort, be involved in concerted activity. The difference in the two definitions, however, is enough to create disparities in interpretation.

COMMUNAL RIGHTS

Staughton Lynd
62 Tex. L. Rev. 1417, 1423–1427 (1984)

a. The Right to Engage in Concerted Activity

I suggest that the right of workers "to engage in concerted activities for . . . mutual aid or protection" now guaranteed by federal labor law is an example of a communal right. More than any other institution in capitalist society, the labor movement is based on communal values. Its central historical experience is solidarity, the banding together of individual workers who are alone too weak to protect themselves. Thus, there has arisen the value expressed by the phrase, "an injury to one is an injury to all." To be sure, at times particular labor organizations, and to some extent trade unionism in general, fall short of this communal aspiration. Yet it is significant that trade union members still address one another as "Brother" and "Sister" and sign their correspondence "Fraternally yours." These conventions evidence an underlying attitude and practice fundamentally different from that in business and even in academia, where one person's job security subtracts from, or at most is separate from, another's.

On the one hand, the protection of concerted activity in Section 7 of the NLRA makes it "perhaps the most radical piece of legislation ever enacted by the United States Congress." On the other hand, the American Civil Liberties Union predicted at the time the Act was passed that it would "impair labor's rights in the long run, however much its authors may intend precisely the contrary." I have felt for some years that this assessment by the ACLU was correct:

> [I]t took a lot of backtracking by the Supreme Court to get there, but maybe that was part of the prediction, at least in its more sophisticated form: no matter how the law was written, once you had the government that far into controlling the labor movement, given the nature of power in American society, it was going to wind up controlling the labor movement for the sake of business. But from my point of view, the historical miscarriage of the NLRA makes it more and not less important to "celebrate and seek to restore to its intended vigor the right to engage in concerted activity for mutual aid or protection."

It may not be immediately clear why this right is so different from other rights. The best approach to understanding the special features of this right is to examine the underlying forms of struggle from which the right is derived. Consider the following example.

After Anna Walentynowicz was discharged from her job as a crane operator in the Lenin shipyard in Gdansk in August 1980, her workmates struck demanding her reinstatement. Other shipyards struck in sympathy. In two days the workers at the Lenin yard had won their demands.

[Walentynowicz along with Lech Walesa, the leader of the Polish "Solidarity" Union, were reinstated and the Polish government promised to build a monument honoring workers killed in the strike of 1970.] The strike would have ended in failure, however, had it not been for the intervention of two individuals, Walentynowicz and her friend Alina Pienkowska. As Walentynowicz tells the story:

> Alina Pienkowska and I went running back to the hall to declare a solidarity strike, but the microphones were off. The shipyard loudspeakers were announcing that the strike was over and that everyone had to leave by six P.M. The gates were open, and people were leaving. So Alina and I went running to the main gate. And I began appealing to them to declare a solidarity strike, because the only reason that the manager had met our demands was that the other factories were still on strike. I said that if the workers at these other factories were defeated, we wouldn't be safe either. But somebody challenged me. "On whose authority are you declaring this a strike? I'm tired and I want to go home." I too was tired, and I started to cry. . . . Now, Alina is very small, a tiny person, but full of initiative. She stood up on a barrel and began to appeal to those who were leaving. "We have to help the others with their strikes, because they have helped us. We have to defend them." Somebody from the crowd said, "She's right!" The gate was closed.

The strike that gave birth to Polish Solidarity followed.

I believe that this piece of history embodies a good deal of what legal workers for a new society care about. In Gdansk, one worker was fired and a whole shipyard walked off the job in protest. Although one recounts this as if it were an everyday occurrence, I have never known a university faculty to do this for a colleague who had been fired or denied tenure. It does, however, occur regularly in the labor movement. Ed Mann tells of an incident in Youngstown in the late 1960s:

> We had a man killed in the open hearth. . . . He had seven days to go to retirement. Two or three months before that I'd filed a grievance, requesting that certain safety features be adopted. The grievance was rejected out of hand. He was killed by a truck backing up. One of the items on the grievance was that trucks backing up have a warning system. The guy gets killed. Everybody liked him. He'd worked there . . . how many years? . . . you know. All right, I led a strike. I had to scream and holler, drag people out by the heels, but I got them out, shut the place down.

In Gdansk, after the first yard struck in protest, workers at other shipyards also left their jobs. As is often the case in wildcat strikes, the workers developed their own demands, in addition to demanding

Walentynowicz' reinstatement. When the question was posed whether the Lenin yard strikers should stay out on behalf of the demands of other shipyards, Anna Walentynowicz took the position that only if the Lenin workers continued their strike on behalf of the workers at the other shipyards would they be "safe." Clearly she was saying that workers, to secure their rights, need above all else to preserve their solidarity.

This distinctive experience of solidarity, underlying the right to engage in concerted activity, has . . . unusual attributes. First, the well-being of the individual and the well-being of the group are not experienced as antagonistic. Justice O'Connor has written that "the concepts of individual action for personal gain and 'concerted activity' are intuitively incompatible." This is the view from the outside, the view of someone who has not experienced the wage worker's elemental need for the support of other workers. Learned Hand came much closer to the reality in a passage written soon after the enactment of Section 7:

> When all other workmen in a shop make common cause with a fellow workman over his separate grievance, and go out on strike in his support, they engage in a "concerted activity" for "mutual aid or protection," although the aggrieved workman is the only one of them who has any immediate stake in the outcome. The rest know that by their action each one of them assures himself, in case his turn ever comes, of the support of the one whom they are all then helping; and the solidarity so established is "mutual aid" in the most literal sense, as nobody doubts. So too of those engaging in a "sympathetic strike," or secondary boycott; the immediate quarrel does not itself concern them, but by extending the number of those who will make the enemy of one the enemy of all, the power of each is vastly increased.

I have heard a rank and file steelworker use almost identical language in trying to persuade fellow workers to support each other's grievances. What is counterintuitive to Justice O'Connor is the common sense of those engaged in the struggle.

Second, the group of those who work together—the informal work group, the department, the local union, the class—is often experienced as a reality in itself. Thus, Hand's rationale misses something crucial to the right to engage in concerted activity. I do not scratch your back only because one day I may need you to scratch mine. Labor solidarity is more than an updated version of the social contract through which each individual undertakes to assist others for the advancement of his or her own interest.

In a family, when I as son, husband, or father, express love toward you, I do not do so in order to assure myself of love in return. I do not help my son in order to be able to claim assistance from him when I am old; I do it because he and I are in the world together; we are one flesh. Similarly in a workplace, persons who work together form families-at-work. When you and I are working together, and the foreman suddenly discharges you, and I find myself putting down my tools or stopping my machine before I have had time to think—why do I do this? Is it not because, as I actually experience the event, your discharge does not happen only to you but also happens to us?

NLRB v. WASHINGTON ALUMINUM CO.
370 U.S. 9 (1962)

JUSTICE BLACK delivered the opinion of the Court:

January 5, 1959, was an extraordinarily cold day for Baltimore, with unusually high winds and a low temperature of 11 degrees followed by a high of 22. When the employees on the day shift came to work that morning, they found the shop bitterly cold, due not only to the unusually harsh weather, but also to the fact that the large oil furnace had broken down the night before and had not as yet been put back into operation. As the workers gathered in the shop just before the starting hour of 7:30, one of them, a Mr. Caron, went into the office of Mr. Jarvis, the foreman, hoping to warm himself but, instead, found the foreman's quarters as uncomfortable as the rest of the shop. Jarvis exclaim[ed] that "if those fellows had any guts at all, they would go home." When the starting buzzer sounded a few moments later, Caron walked back to his working place in the shop and found all the other machinists "huddled there, shaking a little, cold." Caron then said to these workers, ". . . Dave [Jarvis] told me if we had any guts, we would go home. . . . I am going home, it is too damned cold to work." Caron asked the other workers what they were going to do and, after some discussion among themselves, they decided to leave with him. One of these workers, testifying before the Board, summarized their entire discussion this way: "And we had all got together and thought it would be a good idea to go home; maybe we could get some heat brought into the plant that way."

When the company's general foreman arrived between 7:45 and 8 that morning, Jarvis promptly informed him that all but one of the employees had left because the shop was too cold. The company's president came in at approximately 8:20 a.m. and, upon learning of the walkout, immediately said to the foreman, ". . . if they have all gone, we are going to terminate them." After discussion "at great length" between the general foreman and the company president as to what might be the effect of the walkout on employee discipline and plant production, the president formalized his discharge of the workers who had walked out by giving orders at 9 a.m. that the affected workers should be notified about their discharge immediately, either by telephone, telegram or personally. This was done.

On these facts the Board found that the conduct of the workers was a concerted activity to protest the company's failure to supply adequate heat in its machine shop, that such conduct is protected under the provision of § 7 of the National Labor Relations Act which guarantees that "Employees shall have the right . . . to engage in . . . concerted activities for the purpose of collective bargaining or other mutual aid or protection," and that the discharge of these workers by the company amounted to an unfair labor practice under § 8(a)(1) of the Act, which forbids employers "to interfere with, restrain, or coerce employees in the exercise of the rights guaranteed in section 7."

The Court of Appeals took the position that because the workers simply "summarily left their place of employment" without affording the company an "opportunity to avoid the work stoppage by granting a concession to a demand," their walkout did not amount to a concerted activity protected by § 7 of the Act.

We cannot agree that employees necessarily lose their right to engage in concerted activities under § 7 merely because they do not present a specific demand upon their employer to remedy a condition they find objectionable. The language of § 7 is broad enough to protect concerted activities whether they take place before, after, or at the same time such a demand is made. To compel the Board to interpret and apply that language in the restricted fashion suggested by the respondent here would only tend to frustrate the policy of the Act to protect the right of workers to act together to better their working conditions. Indeed, as indicated by this very case, such an interpretation of § 7 might place burdens upon employees so great that it would effectively nullify the right to engage in concerted activities that section protects. The seven employees here were part of a small group of employees who were wholly unorganized. They had no bargaining representative and, in fact, no representative of any kind to present their grievances to their employer. Under these circumstances, they had to speak for themselves as best they could. As pointed out above, prior to the day they left the shop, several of them had repeatedly complained to company officials about the cold working conditions in the shop. These had been more or less spontaneous individual pleas, unsupported by any threat of concerted protest, to which the company apparently gave little consideration and which it now says the Board should have treated as nothing more than "the same sort of gripes as the gripes made about the heat in the summertime." The bitter cold of January 5, however, finally brought these workers' individual complaints into concert so that some more effective action could be considered. Having no bargaining representative and no established procedure by which they could take full advantage of their unanimity of opinion in negotiations with the company, the men took the most direct course to let the company know that they wanted a warmer place in which to work. So, after talking among themselves, they walked out together in the hope that this action might spotlight their complaint and bring about some improvement in what they considered to be the "miserable" conditions of their employment. This we think was enough to justify the Board's holding that they were not required to make any more specific demand than they did to be entitled to the protection of § 7.

Although the company contends to the contrary, we think that the walkout involved here did grow out of a "labor dispute" within the plain meaning of the definition of that term in § 2(9) of the Act, which declares that it includes "any controversy concerning terms, tenure or conditions of employment. . . ." The findings of the Board, which are supported by substantial evidence and which were not disturbed below, show a running dispute between the machine shop employees and the company over the heating of the shop on cold days—a dispute which culminated in the decision of the employees to act concertedly in an effort to force the company to improve that condition of their employment. The fact that the company was already making every effort to repair the furnace and bring heat into the shop that morning does not change the nature of the controversy that caused the walkout. At the very most, that fact might tend to indicate that the conduct of the men in leaving was unnecessary and unwise, and it has long been settled that the reasonableness of workers' decisions to engage in concerted activity is irrelevant to the determination of whether a labor dispute exists or not. Moreover, the evidence here shows that the conduct of these workers was far from unjustified under the circumstances. The company's own foreman expressed the opinion that the shop was so cold that the men should go home. This statement by the foreman but emphasizes the obvious—that is, that the conditions of coldness about which complaint had been made before had been so aggravated on the day of the walkout that the concerted action of the men in leaving their jobs seemed like a perfectly natural and reasonable thing to do.

The activities of these seven employees cannot be classified as "indefensible" by any recognized standard of conduct. Indeed, concerted activities by employees for the purpose of trying to protect themselves from working conditions as uncomfortable as the testimony and Board findings showed them to be in this case are unquestionably activities to correct conditions which modern labor-management legislation treats as too bad to have to be tolerated in a humane and civilized society like ours.

Reversed and remanded

NOTES

1. *Section 7 Protection Is Not Limited to Union Members or Union Organizing.* The workers in *Washington Aluminum* were not members of a

union. They simply had a mutual and serious complaint about their conditions of work. Without Section 7 of the NLRA, their actions in leaving work without employer permission could easily result in substantial employer discipline, including discharge. The very end of the Court's decision suggests there are times when worker concerted action may be classified as "indefensible." Where is the line drawn between what action is protected against employer reprisal and what action is unprotected? And, who gets to draw the line? Can you think of actions the *Washington Aluminum* workers might have taken to make their conduct "indefensible?" Many employment lawyers do not appreciate that Section 7 protects the rights of all workers, not just unionized ones, to engage in concerted activity without employer reprisal. You would do well to remember it.

2.   *Are All Walkouts over Working Conditions Protected?* Recall the Somali worker problem at the beginning of this Chapter. Like the workers in *Washington Aluminum*, the Somali workers also walked out of the workplace without notice to their employer. Are the situations the same? Does a walkout to protest a promotion in the workplace amount to a "term or condition" of an individual's employment like the unbearably cold conditions in *Washington Aluminum*? Also, in *Washington Aluminum*, the workers had a history of complaining about the temperature in the workplace, and, although the employer in that case viewed the complaints as mere gripes, would you say the employer in the Somali workers' problem had the same general notice? Should it make a difference according to the Court's opinion in *Washington Aluminum*?

3.   Assume that nonunion production line workers arrive at work one morning only to find that management has painted the production floor over the weekend, leaving the production work area in disarray and creating an unsafe work area in which it is impossible to perform work. If workers decide to leave as a result, can they be disciplined or discharged? In light of *Washington Aluminum*, would it make a difference if the workers could be assigned to other work, and paid for their time, while the area was cleaned? Should it make a difference that the workers were not protesting a company policy or condition? What if the area could be made safe and workable in just an hour? See *Vemco, Inc.*, 314 N.L.R.B. 1235 (1994) (walkout was concerted and protected), *rev'd*, *Vemco, Inc. v. NLRB*, 79 F.3d 526 (6th Cir. 1996) (walkout was concerted but not protected).

4.   *Can Workers Walk Out Over Any Issue?* Does it matter whether or not there is a labor dispute at the heart of the controversy? A labor dispute is defined in the Act as a "controversy concerning terms, tenure or conditions of employment, or concerning the association or representation of persons in negotiating, fixing, maintaining, changing, or seeking to arrange terms or conditions of employment." 29 U.S.C. § 152(9). In *Northeast Bev. Corp. v. NLRB*, 554 F.3d 133, 138 (D.C. Cir. 2009), several employees left their jobs to go to the union hall to find out about the status of their employment as a result of a company merger. The NLRB held there was a labor dispute and the employee walkout was protected, but the D.C. Circuit disagreed, finding that

"a mere quest for information is not a labor dispute." *Id.* at 140. The court distinguished *Washington Aluminum* because there the employees were seeking to change their working conditions. *Id.* However, where employees leave the job and their interest in information stems from concern about employer discrimination against union supporters, the employee action is protected. *See Fortuna Enterprises v. NLRB*, 665 F.3d 1295, 1301 (D.C. Cir. 2011).

NLRB v. CITY DISPOSAL SYSTEMS, INC.
465 U.S. 822 (1984)

JUSTICE BRENNAN delivered the opinion of the Court:

James Brown, a truck driver employed by respondent, was discharged when he refused to drive a truck that he honestly and reasonably believed to be unsafe because of faulty brakes. Article XXI of the collective-bargaining agreement between respondent and Local 247 of the International Brotherhood of Teamsters, Chauffeurs, Warehousemen and Helpers of America, which covered Brown, provides:

> "The Employer shall not require employees to take out on the streets or highways any vehicle that is not in safe operating condition or equipped with the safety appliances prescribed by law. It shall not be a violation of this Agreement where employees refuse to operate such equipment unless such refusal is unjustified."

The question to be decided is whether Brown's honest and reasonable assertion of his right to be free of the obligation to drive unsafe trucks constituted "concerted [activity]" within the meaning of § 7 of the National Labor Relations Act (NLRA or Act). The National Labor Relations Board (NLRB or Board) held that Brown's refusal was concerted activity within § 7, and that his discharge was, therefore, an unfair labor practice under § 8(a)(1) of the Act. . . . The Court of Appeals disagreed and declined enforcement. At least three other Courts of Appeals, however, have accepted the Board's interpretation of "concerted activities" as including the assertion by an individual employee of a right grounded in a collective-bargaining agreement. We granted certiorari to resolve the conflict, and now reverse.

I

The facts are not in dispute in the current posture of this case. Respondent, City Disposal Systems, Inc. (City Disposal), hauls garbage for the city of Detroit. Under the collective-bargaining agreement with Local Union No. 247, respondent's truck drivers haul garbage from Detroit to a landfill about 37 miles away. Each driver is assigned to operate a particular truck, which he or she operates each day of work, unless that truck is in disrepair.

James Brown was assigned to truck No. 245. On Saturday, May 12, 1979, Brown observed that a fellow driver had difficulty with the brakes of another truck, truck No. 244. As a result of the brake problem, truck No. 244 nearly collided with Brown's truck. After unloading their garbage at the landfill, Brown and the driver of truck No. 244 brought No. 244 to respondent's truck-repair facility, where they were told that the brakes would be repaired either over the weekend or in the morning of Monday, May 14. Early in the morning of Monday, May 14, while transporting a load of garbage to the landfill, Brown experienced difficulty with one of the wheels of his own truck—No. 245—and brought that truck in for repair. At the repair facility, Brown was told that, because of a backlog at the facility, No. 245 could not be repaired that day. Brown reported the situation to his supervisor, Otto Jasmund, who ordered Brown to punch out and go home. Before Brown could leave, however, Jasmund changed his mind and asked Brown to drive truck No. 244 instead. Brown refused, explaining that "there's something wrong with that truck. . . . [Something] was wrong with the brakes . . . there was a grease seal or something leaking causing it to be affecting the brakes." Brown did not, however, explicitly refer to Article XXI of the collective-bargaining agreement or to the agreement in general. In response to Brown's refusal to drive truck No. 244, Jasmund angrily told Brown to go home. At that point, an argument ensued and Robert Madary, another supervisor, intervened, repeating Jasmund's request that Brown drive truck No. 244. Again, Brown refused, explaining that No. 244 "has got problems and I don't want to drive it." Madary replied that half the trucks had problems and that if respondent tried to fix all of them it would be unable to do business. He went on to tell Brown that "[we've] got all this garbage out here to haul and you tell me about you don't want to drive." Brown responded, "Bob, what you going to do, put the garbage ahead of the safety of the men?" Finally, Madary went to his office and Brown went home. Later that day, Brown received word that he had been discharged. He immediately returned to work in an attempt to gain reinstatement but was unsuccessful.

On May 15, the day after the discharge, Brown filed a written grievance, pursuant to the collective-bargaining agreement, asserting that truck No. 244 was defective, that it had been improper for him to have been ordered to drive the truck, and that his discharge was therefore also improper. The union, however, found no objective merit in the grievance and declined to process it.

On September 7, 1979, Brown filed an unfair labor practice charge with the NLRB, challenging his discharge. The Administrative Law Judge (ALJ) found that Brown had been discharged for refusing to operate truck No. 244, that Brown's refusal was covered by § 7 of the NLRA, and that respondent had therefore committed an unfair labor practice under § 8(a)(1) of the Act. The ALJ held that an employee who acts alone in asserting a contractual right can nevertheless be engaged in concerted activity within the meaning of § 7:

> " '[When] an employee makes complaints concerning safety matters which are embodied in a contract, he is acting not only in his own interest, but is attempting to enforce such contract provisions in the interest of all the employees covered under that contract. Such activity we have found to be concerted and protected under the Act, and the discharge of an individual for engaging in such activity to be in violation of Section 8(a)(1) [of the Act].' The NLRB adopted the findings and conclusions of the ALJ and ordered that Brown be reinstated with backpay."

On a petition for enforcement of the Board's order, the Court of Appeals disagreed with the ALJ and the Board. Finding that Brown's refusal to drive truck No. 244 was an action taken solely on his own behalf, the Court of Appeals concluded that the refusal was not a concerted activity within the meaning of § 7.

II

Section 7 of the NLRA provides that "[employees] shall have the right to . . . join or assist labor organizations, to bargain collectively through representatives of their own choosing, and to engage in other concerted activities for the purpose of collective bargaining or other mutual aid or protection." 29 U. S. C. § 157. The NLRB's decision in this case applied the Board's longstanding "*Interboro* doctrine," under which an individual's assertion of a right grounded in a collective-bargaining agreement is recognized as "concerted [activity]" and therefore accorded the protection of § 7. *See Interboro Contractors, Inc.*, 157 N.L.R.B. 1295, 1298 (1966), *enf'd*, 388 F.2d 495 (2d Cir. 1967). The Board has relied on two justifications for the doctrine: First, the assertion of a right contained in a collective-bargaining agreement is an extension of the concerted action that produced the agreement; and second, the assertion of such a right affects the rights of all employees covered by the collective-bargaining agreement.

A

Neither the Court of Appeals nor respondent appears to question that an employee's invocation of a right derived from a collective-bargaining agreement meets § 7's requirement that an employee's action be taken "for purposes of collective bargaining or other mutual aid or protection." As the Board first explained in the *Interboro* case, a single employee's invocation of such rights affects all the employees that are covered by the collective-bargaining agreement. This type of generalized effect, as our cases have demonstrated, is sufficient to bring the actions of an individual employee within the "mutual aid or protection" standard, regardless of whether the employee has his own interests most immediately in mind. See, e. g., *NLRB v. J. Weingarten, Inc.*, 420 U.S. 251, 260–261 (1975).

The term "concerted [activity]" is not defined in the Act but it clearly enough embraces the activities of employees who have joined together in order to achieve common goals. What is not self-evident from the language of the Act, however, and what we must elucidate, is the precise manner in which particular actions of an individual employee must be linked to the actions of fellow employees in order to permit it to be said that the individual is engaged in concerted activity. We now turn to consider the Board's analysis of that question as expressed in the *Interboro* doctrine.

Although one could interpret the phrase, "to engage in other concerted activities," to refer to a situation in which two or more employees are working together at the same time and the same place toward a common goal, the language of § 7 does not confine itself to such a narrow meaning. In fact, § 7 itself defines both joining and assisting labor organizations— activities in which a single employee can engage—as concerted activities. Indeed, even the courts that have rejected the *Interboro* doctrine recognize the possibility that an individual employee may be engaged in concerted activity when he acts alone. They have limited their recognition of this type of concerted activity, however, to two situations: (1) that in which the lone employee intends to induce group activity, and (2) that in which the employee acts as a representative of at least one other employee. The disagreement over the *Interboro* doctrine, therefore, merely reflects differing views regarding the nature of the relationship that must exist between the action of the individual employee and the actions of the group in order for § 7 to apply. We cannot say that the Board's view of that relationship, as applied in the *Interboro* doctrine, is unreasonable.

The invocation of a right rooted in a collective-bargaining agreement is unquestionably an integral part of the process that gave rise to the agreement. That process—beginning with the organization of a union, continuing into the negotiation of a collective-bargaining agreement, and extending through the enforcement of the agreement—is a single, collective activity. Obviously, an employee could not invoke a right grounded in a collective-bargaining agreement were it not for the prior negotiating activities of his fellow employees. Nor would it make sense for a union to negotiate a collective-bargaining agreement if individual employees could not invoke the rights thereby created against their employer. Moreover, when an employee invokes a right grounded in the collective-bargaining agreement, he does not stand alone. Instead, he brings to bear on his employer the power and resolve of all his fellow employees. When, for instance, James Brown refused to drive a truck he believed to be unsafe, he was in effect reminding his employer that he and his fellow employees, at the time their collective-bargaining agreement was signed, had extracted a promise from City Disposal that they would not be asked to drive unsafe trucks. He was also reminding his employer that if it persisted in ordering him to drive an unsafe truck, he could re-harness the power of that group to ensure the enforcement of that promise. It was just as though James Brown was reassembling his fellow union members to reenact their decision not to drive unsafe trucks. A lone employee's invocation of a right grounded in his collective-bargaining agreement is, therefore, a concerted activity in a very real sense.

Of course, at some point an individual employee's actions may become so remotely related to the activities of fellow employees that it cannot reasonably be said that the employee is engaged in concerted activity. For instance, the Board has held that if an employer were to discharge an employee for purely personal "griping," the employee could not claim the protection of § 7.

In addition, although the Board relies entirely on its interpretation of § 7 as support for the *Interboro* doctrine, it bears noting that under § 8(a)(1) an employer commits an unfair labor practice if he or she "[interferes] with, [or] [restrains]" concerted activity. It is possible, therefore, for an employer to commit an unfair labor practice by discharging an employee who is not himself involved in concerted activity, but whose actions are related to other employees' concerted activities in such a manner as to render his discharge an interference or restraint on those activities. In the context of the *Interboro* doctrine, for instance, even if an individual's invocation of rights provided for in a collective-bargaining agreement, for some reason, were not concerted activity, the discharge of that individual would still be an unfair labor practice if the result were to restrain or interfere with the concerted activity of negotiating or enforcing a collective-bargaining agreement.

To be sure, the principal tool by which an employee invokes the rights granted him in a collective-bargaining agreement is the processing of a grievance according to whatever procedures his collective-bargaining agreement establishes. No one doubts that the processing of a grievance in such a manner is concerted activity within the meaning of § 7. Indeed, it would make little sense for § 7 to cover an employee's conduct while negotiating a collective-bargaining agreement, including a grievance mechanism by which to protect the rights created by the agreement, but not to cover an employee's attempt to utilize that mechanism to enforce the agreement.

In practice, however, there is unlikely to be a bright-line distinction between an incipient grievance, a complaint to an employer, and perhaps even an employee's initial refusal to perform a certain job that he believes he has no duty to perform. It is reasonable to expect that an employee's first response to a situation that he believes violates his collective-bargaining agreement will be a protest to his employer. Whether he files a grievance will depend in part on his employer's reaction and in part upon the nature of the right at issue. In addition, certain rights might not be susceptible of enforcement by the filing of a grievance. In such a case, the collective-bargaining agreement might provide for an alternative method of enforcement, as did the agreement involved in this case, or the agreement might be silent on the matter. Thus, for a variety of reasons, an employee's initial statement to an employer to the effect that he believes a collectively bargained right is being violated, or the employee's initial refusal to do that which he believes he is not obligated to do, might serve as both a natural prelude to, and an efficient substitute for, the filing of a formal grievance. As long as the employee's statement or action is based on a reasonable and honest belief that he is being, or has been, asked to perform a task that he is not required to perform under his collective-bargaining agreement, and the statement or action is reasonably directed toward the enforcement of a collectively bargained right, there is no justification for overturning the Board's judgment that the employee is engaged in concerted activity, just as he would have been had he filed a formal grievance.

III

In this case, the Board found that James Brown's refusal to drive truck No. 244 was based on an honest and reasonable belief that the brakes on the truck were faulty. Brown explained to each of his supervisors his reason for refusing to drive the truck. Although he did not refer to his collective-bargaining agreement in either of these confrontations, the agreement provided not only that "[the] Employer shall not require employees to take out on the streets or highways any vehicle that is not in safe operating condition," but also that "[it] shall not be a violation of this Agreement where employees refuse to operate such equipment, unless such refusal is unjustified." There is no doubt, therefore, nor could there have been any doubt during Brown's confrontations with his supervisors, that by refusing to drive truck No. 244, Brown was invoking the right granted him in his collective-bargaining agreement to be free of the obligation to drive unsafe trucks. Moreover, there can be no question but that Brown's refusal to drive the truck was reasonably well directed toward the enforcement of that right. Indeed, it would appear that there were no other means available by which Brown could have enforced the right. If he had gone ahead and driven truck No. 244, the issue may have been moot. Respondent argues that Brown's action was not concerted because he did not explicitly refer to the collective-bargaining agreement as a basis for his refusal to drive the truck. The Board, however, has never held that an employee must make such an explicit reference for his actions to be covered by the *Interboro* doctrine, and we find that position reasonable. We have often recognized the importance of "the Board's special function of applying the general provisions of the Act to the complexities of industrial life." As long as the nature of the employee's complaint is reasonably clear to the person to whom it is communicated, and the complaint does, in fact, refer to a reasonably perceived violation of the collective-bargaining agreement, the complaining employee is engaged in the process of enforcing that agreement. In the context of a workplace dispute, where the participants are likely to be unsophisticated in collective-bargaining matters, a requirement that the employee explicitly refer to the collective-bargaining agreement is likely to serve as nothing more than a trap for the unwary.

In this case, because Brown reasonably and honestly invoked his right to avoid driving unsafe trucks, his action was concerted.

JUSTICE O'CONNOR, with whom THE CHIEF JUSTICE, JUSTICE POWELL, and JUSTICE REHNQUIST join, dissenting:

Under the *Interboro* doctrine, an individual employee is deemed to have engaged in "concerted [activity]" within the meaning of § 7 of the National Labor Relations Act (Act) if the right he reasonably and in good faith asserts is grounded in his employer's collective-bargaining agreement. On this view, the reasonable, good-faith assertion of a right contained in the collective-bargaining agreement is said to be an extension of the concerted action that produced the agreement; alternatively, the reasonable, good-faith assertion of the contract right is said to affect the rights of all the other employees in the work force. Thus, if the employer "[interferes] with, [restrains], or [coerces]" the employee in response to the latter's assertion of the alleged contract right, the *Interboro* doctrine enables the employee to file a § 8(a)(1) unfair labor practice charge with the National Labor Relations Board (Board). Although the concepts of individual action for personal gain and "concerted activity" are intuitively incompatible, the Court today defers to the Board's judgment that the *Interboro* doctrine is necessary to safeguard the exercise of rights previously won in the collective-bargaining process. Since I consider the *Interboro* doctrine to be an exercise in undelegated legislative power by the Board, I respectfully dissent.

In my view, the fact that the right the employee asserts ultimately can be grounded in the collective-bargaining agreement is not enough to make the individual's self-interested action concerted. If it could, then every contract claim could be the basis for an unfair labor practice complaint. But the law is clear that an employer's alleged violation of a collective agreement cannot, by itself, provide the basis for an unfair labor practice complaint. Congress once considered a proposal that would have given the Board "general jurisdiction over all alleged violations of collective bargaining agreements." But it realized that "[to] have conferred upon the National Labor Relations Board generalized power to determine the rights of parties under all collective agreements would have been a step toward governmental regulation of the terms of those agreements." Thus, Congress expressly decided that, "[once] [the] parties have made a collective bargaining contract[,] the enforcement of that contract should be left to the usual processes of the law and not to the . . . Board." By basing the determination whether activity is "concerted" on the assertion's ultimate grounding in the collective-bargaining agreement, the *Interboro* doctrine's extension of the concerted activity proviso transfers the final authority for interpreting all contracts and for resolving all contract disputes back to the Board. This arrogation of power violates Congress' decision to the contrary.

This Court has previously recognized that the labor laws were designed to encourage employees to act together. *See, e. g., NLRB v. J. Weingarten, Inc.*, 420 U.S. 251, 260–264 (1975). Even a single employee acting in good faith and asserting a right contained in the collective-bargaining agreement may be too fearful, inarticulate, or lacking in skill to relate accurately either the event being investigated or the relevant extenuating factors. Other disinterested employees, especially knowledgeable union stewards, can assist the employee and the employer in eliciting the relevant facts and in preventing misunderstandings and hard feelings. The participation of other employees may save production time, reduce administrative expenses, and avoid unnecessary discharges and disciplinary action. By providing an increased degree of statutory coverage to employees participating in that process, the labor laws encourage and preserve the "practice and procedure of collective bargaining." The fact that two employees receive coverage where one acting alone does not is therefore entirely consistent with the labor laws' emphasis on collective action.

The Court and the Board insist that, because the group has previously expressed interest in the right now being asserted, the individual's self-interested expression must be treated as "concerted" to ensure that meaning is given to the contract rights. This argument is mistaken. It confuses the employees' substantive contract entitlements with the process by which those entitlements are to be vindicated. When employees act together in expressing a mutual concern, contractual or otherwise, their action is "concerted" and the statute authorizes them to seek vindication through the Board's administrative processes. In contrast, when an employee acts alone in expressing a personal concern, contractual or otherwise, his action is not "concerted"; in such cases, the statute instructs him to seek vindication through his union, and where necessary, through the courts.

Finally, the *Interboro* doctrine makes little sense when applied to the facts of this case. There is no evidence that employee James Brown discussed the truck's alleged safety problem with other employees, sought their support in remedying the problem, or requested their or his union's assistance in protesting to his employer. He did not seek to warn others of the problem or even initially to file a grievance through his union. He simply asserted that the truck was not safe enough for him to drive. James Brown was not engaging in "concerted activity" in any reasonable sense of the term, and therefore his employer could not have violated § 8(a)(1) of the Act when it discharged him. The fact that the right asserted can be found in the collective-bargaining agreement may be relevant to whether activity of that type should be "protected," but not to whether it is "concerted." The *Interboro* doctrine is, in my view, unreasonable in concluding otherwise.

I do not mean to imply by this dissent that conduct should not be considered "concerted" because it is engaged in by only a single employee. The crucial issue is, as the Court notes, the precise nature of the relationship that must exist between the action of an individual employee and the actions of the group. An employee certainly engages in "concerted activity" when he acts with or expressly on behalf of one or more of the other employees. And, as several of the Courts of Appeals have concluded, the statutory language can even be stretched to cover an individual who takes action with the proven object of inducing, initiating, or preparing for group action. But it stretches the language past its snapping point to cover an employee's action that is taken solely for personal benefit.

NOTES

1. *Individual Invocation of Statutory Rights*. In *Alleluia Cushion Co.*, 221 N.L.R.B. 999 (1975), the Board expanded its view of concerted activity beyond the confines of the local workplace and its collective bargaining agreement. In that case, a worker wrote a letter to the California Occupational Safety and Health Administration complaining about safety issues at Alleluia Cushion. The Board held the worker's action concerted even though no other workers expressly supported his campaign. As with the applicability of the Board's *Interboro* doctrine to collective agreements, the Board found that the invocation of statutory rights is inherently concerted. The Board's holding in *Alleluia Cushion* proved controversial, and was rejected by several federal circuit courts. *See, e.g., NLRB v. Bighorn Beverage*, 614 F.2d 1238 (9th Cir. 1980); *NLRB v. Buddies Supermarkets, Inc.*, 481 F.2d 714 (5th Cir. 1973). The Board has consistently failed to view the invocation of worker statutory rights, by itself, as concerted activity since the late 1980s despite its holding in *Alleluia Cushion. See Meyers Indus., Inc.*, 268 N.L.R.B. 493 (1984) (Meyers I), *rev'd sub nom Prill v. NLRB*, 755 F.2d 941 (D.C. Cir. 1985) (Prill I); *see also Myth, Inc.*, 326 N.L.R.B. 136 (1998). The courts, however, have upheld the Board's findings on the issue not as a matter of statutory interpretation, but rather as a matter of deference to the Board's discretion, leaving open the possibility that a later Board may go the other way on the question of what may constitute "constructive" concerted activity. *Prill v. NLRB*, 835 F.2d 1481, 1484 (D.C. Cir. 1987) (Prill II); *Meyers Indus., Inc.*, 281 N.L.R.B. 882 (1986) (Meyers II).

2. *Is the Act of Filing a Charge Itself a Type of Concerted Activity?* Consider what the result should be if an individual worker was fired for filing a workers' compensation claim on his own behalf. Under the reasoning in *Alleluia Cushion* and *City Disposal*, shouldn't the act of filing be concerted, not just because workers' compensation laws are statutory products of group process, but also because workers in the particular workplace have an interest in the enforcement of workers' compensation laws that exist to enhance worker health and safety? See *Krispy Kreme Doughnut Corp.*, 245 N.L.R.B. 1053, 1053 (1979) (yes, "[s]uch benefits also arise out of the employment relationship and are of common interest to other employees"); *Krispy Kreme Doughnut Corp. v. NLRB*, 635 F.2d 304, 308 (4th Cir. 1980) (no, "the action of the solitary employee in this case [did not] intend[ ] or contemplate[ ] any group activity").

3. *When Is Individual Action Concerted?* Although the line between the isolated action of a single worker and the concerted action by one worker involved with others remains murky, a variety of scenarios have been considered by the Board and the courts. For example, individual attempts at preliminary discussions that do not result in concerted action may nonetheless be concerted. *See, e.g., Gran Combo de P.R.*, 853 F.2d 996, 1004 (1st Cir. 1988). A single complaint is sometimes enough to be concerted if others share the complaint, *see Mike Yurosek & Son, Inc.*, 306 N.L.R.B. 1037 (1992), *supplemented by* 310 N.L.R.B. 831 (1993) (four workers refused overtime, and though they acted singly and identically, the concerns of the workers were "logical outgrowths" of concerns held by the group). Sometimes single complaints are not concerted even though they are shared by others. *See, e.g., NLRB v. Portland Airport Limousine Co.*, 163 F.3d 662 (1st Cir. 1998) (refusal to drive a tractor motivated by individual safety concerns not concerted even if the concerns communicated to another worker who also refused). A single employee's action may be concerted if the employee is seeking representation in a one-member bargaining unit. *See, e.g., International Transp. Serv., Inc.*, 344 N.L.R.B. 279 (2005). But, generally, actions are viewed as concerted if they consist of either an inducement to action, *see, e.g., Martin Marietta Corp.*, 293 N.L.R.B. 719 (1989), or if they are encouraged by others, *see, e.g., Phillips Petroleum*, 339 N.L.R.B. 916 (2003).

The Board overturned an ALJ decision finding that an employee had not engaged in concerted activity when confronting a supervisor in front of other workers. *Wyndham Resort Dev. Corp.,* 356 N.L.R.B. 765 (2011). The ALJ had found that an employee's complaint about the employer's change in dress code made to a supervisor in front of other employees but without prior consultation or conferral with those employees did not constitute "concerted activity." *Id.* at 7. The Board reversed stating that "the Board has consistently found activity concerted when, in front of their coworkers, single employees protest changes to employment terms common to all employees. The Board reasons that an employee who protests publicly in a group meeting is engaged in initiating group action. The concerted nature of an employee's protest may (but need not) be revealed by evidence that the employee used terms like "us" or "we" when voicing complaints, even when the employee had not solicited coworkers' views beforehand." *Id.* at 8. The Board concluded that the employee had sought to induce group action by using terms like "us" and "we."

Assume in the Somali workers problem at the beginning of this Chapter that only one, not fifty seven, walked out after promotions to non-Somali workers were announced, but that he did not leave until talking to at least ten other Somali workers who exclaimed their disgust at the Enderby action. Is he engaged in concerted activity or not?

4.   *Discussion of Wages/Rates of Pay as Concerted Activity.* Discussing rates of pay, wages or benefits is considered concerted activity whose prohibition by an employer is unlawful. *See, e.g., Quicken Loans, Inc.,* 359 N.L.R.B. 1201 (2013); *Taylor Made Transportation Svcs,* 358 N.L.R.B. No.427 (2012); *Radisson Plaza Minneapolis,* 307 N.L.R.B. 94 (1992) (mere rule is unlawful whether phrased as mandatory or not and whether enforced or not); *Heck's Inc.,* 293 N.L.R.B. 1111, 1119 (1989) (employer's maintenance of a rule "requesting" employees not to discuss their wages with each other unlawful in the absence of a business justification—such a prohibition "constitutes a clear restraint on the employees' Section 7 right to engage in concerted activities for mutual aid and protection concerning an undeniably significant term of employment"). An employer's preemptive action to discharge an employee before she could discuss wages with other employees was a violation of the Act despite the fact that no actual concerted activity had yet taken place. According to the Board, "in order to prevent [an employee] from having further conversations with employees about wages and discrimination in the setting of wages is the type of unlawful intent alleged in the complaint—'to discourage employees from engaging in these or other concerted activities.'" *Parexel Int'l, LLC,* 356 N.L.R.B. 516, at 7–8 (2011).

5.   *The NLRB Website, General Counsel and Advice Memoranda:* The NLRB has an excellent website, *nlrb.gov,* that contains charge forms and current information about labor board matters. Attorneys and others can also use the website to find important policy memoranda that may otherwise not be officially published. For example, the General Counsel's Office and the NLRB Division of Advice release advice memoranda involving new areas of regulation for which there is no existing case law. *See nlrb.gov/cases-decisions/advice-memos; nlrb.gov/reports-guidance/general-counsel-memos.*

6.   *Concerted Activity and Social Media.* The newest challenges to the law related to Section 7 protection and the scope of concerted activity have come from worker use of social media. The Board has found that employees used social media to engage in concerted activity when a single employee acted "with or on the authority of other employees, and not solely by and on behalf of the employee himself." *Design Technology Group LLC d/b/a Bettie Page Clothing,* 359 N.L.R.B. 777 (2013), *aff'd* 361 N.L.R.B. 876 (2014) (company violated Section 8(a)(1) by terminating workers for Facebook postings discussing supervisor performance and work-related concerns and for discussions related to looking through textbook involving worker rights to determine company violation of labor laws). How would you frame an unfair

labor practice charge on behalf of an individual employee disciplined for Facebook or Twitter posts to make it more likely that the Board would determine that the individual was engaged in concerted activity? Using the word "we" rather than "I" in framing a charge may help on the issue of whether the action was concerted. Do you agree?

2. MUTUAL AID AND PROTECTION

Clearly, actions of a group of employees in a particular workplace concerning labor issues in that workplace will be for mutual aid and protection of the employees. Thus, in most labor disputes, there is no question that worker efforts are for mutual aid and protection. However, circumstances involving two extremes of the question have continued to bedevil the Board and the courts. The first of these involves subject matter—specifically, whether labor issues of a state or national scope that nonetheless have at least an indirect impact on particular workers qualify as being close enough to workers' localized concerns to constitute efforts for mutual aid and protection. The other of these circumstances involves identity—specifically, whether efforts on behalf of only one worker, though engaged in by a group, qualify as being for mutual aid and protection.

Should an individual worker's request to have a union representative at an interview with a supervisor that may result in discipline be considered concerted activity for mutual aid and protection? What if the worker is the only person who will benefit from the representation? In *NLRB v. J. Weingarten, Inc.*, 420 U.S. 251 (1975), a case involving a unionized worker, the Supreme Court upheld the NLRB's position that such a request, and indeed the representation itself, is protected by Section 7. In so holding, the Supreme Court stated,

> The action of an employee in seeking to have the assistance of his union representative at a confrontation with his employer clearly falls within the literal wording of § 7 that "[employees] shall have the right . . . to engage in . . . concerted activities for the purpose of . . . mutual aid or protection." This is true even though the employee alone may have an immediate stake in the outcome; he seeks "aid or protection" against a perceived threat to his employment security. The union representative whose participation he seeks is, however, safeguarding not only the particular employee's interest, but also the interests of the entire bargaining unit by exercising vigilance to make certain that the employer does not initiate or continue a practice of imposing punishment unjustly. The representative's presence is an assurance to other employees in the bargaining unit that they, too, can obtain his aid and protection if called upon to attend a like interview.

Id. at 260–61. The Court found that union worker representation requests were concerted activities for mutual aid and protection. The Court also substantially limited the right, finding it exists only when the employee requests representation, and only in "situations where the employee reasonably believes the investigation will result in disciplinary action." *Id.* at 257–58. In addition, the Court spelled out the parameters of the right vis-à-vis the employer, explaining that exercise of the right may not interfere with legitimate employer prerogatives, that the employer is under no obligation to interview the employee and may choose not to do so rather than ask questions with a representative present, and, finally, that the employer is under no obligation "to negotiate with any union representative who may choose to attend the interview," *id.* at 258–60, even though the representative does have a right to speak during the interview. *See Talsol Corp.*, 317 N.L.R.B. 290 (1995). The *Weingarten* Court also noted that an employee could make a "knowing and voluntary" waiver of the right, 420 U.S. at 257, and after *Weingarten*, the Board held that a union could waive workers' *Weingarten* rights by collective bargaining agreement. *See Prudential Ins. Co. of Am.*, 275 N.L.R.B. 208 (1985).

The Board and the courts have continued to flesh out the contours of the *Weingarten* right, finding no right to representation if the employer merely seeks to inform the employee of a disciplinary decision already reached, *see, e.g., Brunswick Elec. Membership Corp.*, 308 N.L.R.B. 361 (1992); *NLRB v. Certified Grocers of Cal., Ltd.*, 587 F.2d 449 (9th Cir. 1978). The *Weingarten* right exists only if the employee is interviewed about subjects that fall within the definition of statutory terms and conditions of employment, *see, e.g., Harrah's Lake Tahoe Resort Casino*, 307 N.L.R.B. 182 (1992). But the right does apply to polygraph and drug tests, even though, in the case of a drug test, no interview is involved. *See Safeway Stores, Inc.*, 303 N.L.R.B. 989 (1991) (drug test); *Consol. Casinos Corp.*, 266 N.L.R.B. 988 (1983) (polygraph). Also, an employer violated the Act when it discharged an employee for secretly audiotaping a meeting that the employee reasonably believed would result in discipline. The employer had denied a request by the employee to have a union representative present during the meeting. *Stephens Media, LLC*, 356 N.L.R.B. 661 (2011).

What should the remedy be for an employer violation of the *Weingarten* right? Should the employees whose rights are violated have the underlying violation expunged from their records, or, if terminated, be reinstated with backpay? Maybe there should be an exclusionary rule that provides no information gathered during the interview can be used in meting out discipline? Should the violation be viewed as *de minimis*, with the employer only being penalized if the discipline imposed by the employer is a direct or indirect result of the employee's invocation of the *Weingarten* right? Which of these would you choose, and why? See *Taracorp Indus.*, 273 N.L.R.B. 221 (1984) (make whole relief not appropriate under § 10(c) where employee was properly terminated for a reason other than assertion of *Weingarten* rights or ULP), and compare it to the Board decision it overruled, *Kraft Foods, Inc.*, 251 N.L.R.B. 598 (1980) (make whole relief, including reinstatement and back pay, available for remedy of employer denial of *Weingarten* rights).

If the right to a representative is safeguarded in the unionized setting, does it stand to reason that the right should exist in the nonunion arena as well? After all, the language of Section 7 itself grants the right to engage in concerted activity for mutual aid and protection equally to unionized and non-unionized employees. Consider, however, the NLRB's latest stance on the issue, reversing its prior position.

IBM CORP.
341 N.L.R.B. 1288 (2004)

CHAIRMAN BATTISTA and MEMBERS MEISBURG, SCHAUMBER, LIEBMAN, and WALSH:

The sole issue in this case is whether the Respondent, whose employees are not represented by a union, violated Section 8(a)(1) of the Act by denying the Charging Parties' requests to have a coworker present during investigatory interviews that might result in discipline.

On October 15, 2001, the Respondent, prompted by allegations of harassment contained in a letter it received from a former employee, interviewed each of the Charging Parties. None of them requested the presence of a witness during the October 15 interviews. On October 22, the Respondent's manager, Nels Maine, denied Charging Party Bannon's request to have a coworker or an attorney present at an interview scheduled for the next day. On October 23, Maine interviewed each of the Charging Parties individually after denying each employee's request to have a coworker present during the interview. All three employees were discharged approximately a month after the interviews.

[Ed: The Board recounted in this part of its opinion the history of the issue of *Weingarten* rights in the nonunion workplace. In *Materials Research Corp.*, 262 N.L.R.B. 1010 (1982), the Board found that the *Weingarten* right extended to the nonunion workplace. The Board emphasized that the right stemmed from Section 7's protection of concerted activity for mutual aid and protection. Three years later, the Board changed its view in *Sears, Roebuck, & Co.*, 274 N.L.R.B. 230 (1985), emphasizing that without a union, an employer can deal with employees on an individual basis. A remand by the Third Circuit in *E. I. DuPont & Co.*, 289 N.L.R.B. 627 (1988) led to the Board's conclusion that its view in Sears was based on a permissible, not mandatory, interpretation of the statute. Twelve years later in *Epilepsy Found. of Ne. Ohio*, 331 N.L.R.B.

676 (2000), the Board once again concluded, based on its reading of Section 7, that the *Weingarten* right extended to the nonunion setting.]

D.   Policy Considerations Support the Denial of the *Weingarten* Right in the Nonunionized Workplace

In reviewing the policy considerations underlying the application of the *Weingarten* right, we follow the teaching of the *Weingarten* Court that the Board has a duty "to adapt the Act to changing patterns of industrial life. . . . The Board has the 'special function of applying the general provisions of the Act to the complexities of industrial life.' " *Weingarten*, 420 U.S. at 266. The years after the issuance of *Weingarten* have seen a rise in the need for investigatory interviews, both in response to new statutes governing the workplace and as a response to new security concerns raised by terrorist attacks on our country. Employers face ever-increasing requirements to conduct workplace investigations pursuant to federal, state, and local laws, particularly laws addressing workplace discrimination and sexual harassment. We are especially cognizant of the rise in the number of instances of workplace violence, as well as the increase in the number of incidents of corporate abuse and fiduciary lapses. Further, because of the events of September 11, 2001 and their aftermath, we must now take into account the presence of both real and threatened terrorist attacks. Because of these events, the policy considerations expressed in *DuPont* have taken on a new vitality. Thus, we reaffirm, and find even more forceful, the result and the rationale of *DuPont*. We hold that the *Weingarten* right does not extend to the nonunion workplace.

The *Epilepsy* result does not take into account the significant policy considerations relevant to a nonunion work force. The critical difference between a unionized work force and a nonunion work force is that the employer in the latter situation can deal with employees on an individual basis. The Board's decision in *Epilepsy* does not take cognizance of that distinction. It forbids the employer from dealing with the employee on an individual basis. Thus, for this reason as well, grounded in national labor policy, we choose not to follow *Epilepsy*. Further in this regard, our colleagues suggest that the term "dealing" is confined to the Section 2(5) definition of "labor organization." That is not true. The Board uses the phrase "dealing" to condemn direct contacts between a unionized employer and employees. Our point is that, prior to *Epilepsy*, a nonunion employer could have such contacts with individual employees. Today we return to that doctrine.

4.   *The presence of a coworker may compromise the confidentiality of information.* Employers have the legal obligation, pursuant to a variety of federal, state, and local laws, administrative requirements, and court decisions, to provide their workers with safe and secure workplace environments. A relatively new fact of industrial life is the need for

employers to conduct all kinds of investigations of matters occurring in the workplace to ensure compliance with these legal requirements. An employer must take steps to prevent sexual and racial harassment, to avoid the use of toxic chemicals, to provide a drug-free and violence-free workplace, to resolve issues involving employee health matters, and the like. Employers may have to investigate employees because of substance abuse allegations, improper computer and internet usage, and allegations of theft, violence, sabotage, and embezzlement.

Employer investigations into these matters require discretion and confidentiality. The guarantee of confidentiality helps an employer resolve challenging issues of credibility involving these sensitive, often personal, subjects. The effectiveness of a fact-finding interview in sensitive situations often depends on whether an employee is alone. If information obtained during an interview is later divulged, even inadvertently, the employee involved could suffer serious embarrassment and damage to his reputation and/or personal relationships and the employer's investigation could be compromised by inability to get the truth about workplace incidents.

Union representatives, by virtue of their legal duty of fair representation, may not, in bad faith, reveal or misuse the information obtained in an employee interview. A union representative's fiduciary duty to all unit employees helps to assure confidentiality for the employer.

A coworker, however, is under no similar legal constraint. A coworker representative has no fiduciary duty to the employee being questioned or to the workplace as a whole. Further, it is more likely that a coworker representative in casual conversation among other coworkers and friends in the workplace, could inadvertently "let slip" confidential, sensitive, or embarrassing information. Not only is this upsetting to the employee directly affected, it also interferes with an employer's ability to conduct an effective internal investigation. The possibility that information will not be kept confidential greatly reduces the chance that the employer will get the whole truth about a workplace event. It also increases the likelihood that employees with information about sensitive subjects will not come forward.

To be sure, under *Weingarten* and *Epilepsy*, the employer can conduct the investigation without the presence of the employee. However, in many situations, the employer will want to hear the story "from the horse's mouth," i.e., directly from the employee. *Weingarten* and *Epilepsy* foreclose that approach unless the employee is granted the presence of another employee.

The presence of the other employee causes its own problems. As discussed above, the presence of the other employee may well inhibit the targeted employee from candidly answering the questions posed by the employer. And, if he does candidly respond, there is a concern that the assisting employee will reveal to others what was said. Finally, the employer may have an interest in keeping quiet the fact of the inquiry and the substance of the questions asked. There is a danger that an assisting employee will spread the word about the inquiry and reveal the questions, thereby undermining that employer interest.

We recognize that many of these same concerns exist in a unionized setting as well. However, the dangers are far less when the assisting person is an experienced union representative with fiduciary obligations and a continuing interest in having an amicable relationship with the employer. Further, there is no merit to the dissent's reasoning that the existence of these concerns in the unionized setting necessarily means that the *Weingarten* right must either be available in both unionized and non-unionized workplaces, or it must be foreclosed in both workplaces. Such reasoning is contrary to the conclusions of the Third Circuit in *Slaughter*, the D.C. Circuit in *Epilepsy*, and the Board's decision in *DuPont* (to which we return today), which all concluded that both limiting the *Weingarten* right to unionized employees and extending it to all employees are permissible interpretations of the Act.

[Concurrence by Member Schaumber is omitted]

MEMBERS LIEBMAN and WALSH, dissenting.

Today, American workers without unions, the overwhelming majority of employees, are stripped of a right integral to workplace democracy. Abruptly overruling *Epilepsy Foundation of Northeast Ohio*, a recent decision upheld on appeal as "both clear and reasonable," the majority holds that nonunion employees are not entitled to have a coworker present when their employer conducts an investigatory interview that could lead to discipline.

Workers without unions can and do successfully stand up for each other on the job—and they have the legal right to try, whether or not they succeed. The majority's predictions of harm, in turn, are baseless. There is no evidence before the Board that coworker representatives have interfered with a single employer investigation since *Epilepsy Foundation* issued in 2000. We are told instead that everything has changed in "today's troubled world," following "terrorist attacks on our country," the rise of workplace violence, and an increase in "corporate abuse and fiduciary lapses." But allowing workers to represent each other has no conceivable connection with workplace violence and precious little with corporate wrongdoing, which in any case seems concentrated in the executive suite, not the employee cubicle or the factory floor. Finally, we would hope that the American workplace has not yet become a new front in the war on terrorism and that the Board would not be leading the charge, unbidden by other authorities.

As we will explain, the right to coworker representation, in nonunion workplaces as well as in unionized ones, has a strong foundation in the Act. Two of our colleagues, at least, recognize that *Epilepsy Foundation* is "a permissible interpretation of the Act," but they invoke "policy considerations" (which a third colleague joins) for refusing to adhere to it. To the extent that the majority raises any legitimate concerns, they easily can be accommodated without abandoning that right, which—as applied in unionized workplaces and as it presumably would apply in nonunion workplaces—is quite limited. Under the Board's application of *Weingarten*: the employer has the option to forego an interview; the union representative may not obstruct an investigation; the right to have a witness present does not apply to every conversation or workplace matter; and the employer has no duty to "bargain with" the representative.

III.

Our colleagues argue that differences in the union and nonunion settings justify denying nonunion workers the right recognized in *Weingarten*. The real question, however, is whether these differences mean that the right to representation can be grounded in Section 7 only where a union represents workers. Clearly, they do not, for reasons convincingly explained in *Epilepsy Foundation*.

From the perspective of Section 7, at least, it makes no difference whether, like union representatives, coworker representatives (1) represent the interests of the entire workforce, (2) can redress the imbalance of power between employers and employees, or (3) have the skills needed to be effective. The majority makes a powerful case for unionization, but a weak one for refusing to recognize the rights of nonunion workers. As the *Epilepsy Foundation* Board correctly observed, "Section 7 rights do not turn on either the skills or the motives of the employee's representative." The majority here simply confuses the efficacy of a right with its existence.

According to the majority, there is a "critical difference between a unionized work force and a nonunion work force" that is relevant here: "the employer in the latter situation can deal with employees on an individual basis." This contention was refuted by the Board in *Epilepsy Foundation*, drawing on a decision of the Third Circuit. 331 N.L.R.B. at 678, *citing Slaughter v. NLRB*, 794 F.2d 120, 127 (3d Cir. 1986). The District of Columbia Circuit, in turn, has rejected the majority's point. Simply put, requiring a nonunion employer to permit coworker representation (if it chooses to conduct an investigatory interview) is not the equivalent of requiring the employer to bargain with, or to deal with, the representative. Describing the argument as based on the "historic distinction between unionized and nonunion employers," as opposed to the Act itself, does not save it.

Aside from its attempt to distinguish union and nonunion workplaces, the majority claims that employers have an overriding need to prevent interference with workplace investigations mandated by law. But there is no basis to conclude that coworker representation has had, or likely will have, any of the harmful consequences that the majority conjures up. The solution here is to strike a balance, not to pretend that nonunion employees have no Section 7 interest that must be respected. Although the majority does not bother to detail the sources of employers' legal obligations to conduct effective workplace investigations, we will assume that employers do have such a legal obligation, in some circumstances. Further, we will assume that nonunion employees' right to representation makes it harder, in some measure, for employers to discharge that obligation—just as observing other legal requirements or moral norms does (Star Chamber proceedings, in contrast, were wonderfully efficient). Even making these assumptions, however, it is impossible fairly to reach the majority's conclusion: that nonunion workers are never entitled to a coworker representative in investigatory interviews.

First, to the extent that employees' rights under the Act may be in tension with legitimate employer interests or the goals of other federal statutes, the majority never explains why it is that Section 7 must give way, always and completely. Surely the process is one of balancing and accommodation, conducted case-by-case, as federal labor law has long recognized in other contexts. If, as we believe, the right to representation is guaranteed by Section 7, then any infringement of that right is presumptively a violation of Section 8(a)(1), but the presumption may be overcome, in appropriate circumstances (a point we will address).

Second, the majority has simply failed to make the case that a nonunion employer cannot conduct an effective investigation if employees are entitled to coworker representation during interviews that reasonably may lead to discipline. Here, too, the majority contrasts union representatives and coworker representatives, arguing that union representatives may actually facilitate an effective investigation and that in any case, their special legal status makes them less likely to violate confidentiality.

In any case, there is no evidence before the Board either that unions have interfered with employers' investigatory obligations since 1975, when *Weingarten* was decided, or that coworker representatives have caused harm since *Epilepsy Foundation* issued in 2000. Nothing in the record shows that investigations have come to a halt because of the presence of a coworker at an investigatory interview, or that information obtained during such an interview has been compromised. Rotely repeating the unsupported assertions of employer advocates in their briefs to the Board, the majority shows a startling lack of interest in what is actually happening in American workplaces.

NOTES

1. The NLRB is a five member body, with one member designated as Chair. Each member is appointed for a five-year term by the President with Senate approval. Labor policy in the U.S. is extremely political and politicized, and for the Board, this has meant that various labor doctrines are subject to reversal at each party shift in Presidential elections. As you can see from the history of the issue in the *IBM* case, the *Weingarten* rights of unrepresented workers is one of those politically volatile questions. The Bush Board reversed several longstanding precedents of the Clinton Board (and previous Boards), and the Obama Board overturned those, and the Trump Board has begun rejecting the Obama Board rules. The Trump Board General Counsel Peter B. Robb issued a Memorandum, *Mandatory Submissions to Advice,* outlining and naming the Obama Board precedents for which the General Counsel's Office "might want to provide the Board with an alternative analysis." *See* Peter B. Robb, *Mandatory Submissions to Advice,* MEMORANDUM GC 18–02 (Dec. 1, 2017) ("Alternative Analysis Memorandum"). For more on NLRB flip-flopping/ oscillation and potential pitfalls, see Samuel Estreicher, *Policy Oscillation at the Labor Board: A Plea for Rulemaking,* 37 Admin. L. Rev. 163, 163–69 (1985) (lamenting the instability and unpredictability of labor law due to NLRB reversals of previous decisions).

2. The *Weingarten* right has been extended to Federal public sector employees by statutory mandate. *See* Federal Labor Relations Act, 5 U.S.C. § 7114(a)(2)(B) (2006); *FLRA v. NASA,* 120 F.3d 1208 (11th Cir. 1997). State public sector law, however, does not generally extend *Weingarten* protections. *See, e.g., New York City Transit Auth. v. Public Employment Relations Bd.,* 8 N.Y.3d 226, 832 N.Y.S.2d 132, 864 N.E.2d 56 (2007) (New York's Taylor Law has no *Weingarten* protection for lack of statutory language prescribing "mutual aid or protection"); *but cf. Robinson v. State Pers. Bd.,* 97 Cal.App.3d 994, 159 Cal.Rptr. 222 (1979) (plaintiff state employee was entitled to have a union representative present at the meeting with his superiors). The right also has not been extended to unionized employees covered by the Railway Labor Act. *See Johnson v. Express One Int'l, Inc.,* 944 F.2d 247 (5th Cir. 1991) (The RLA does not contain language of Section 7 of the NLRA granting the right to engage in "concerted activity for mutual aid and protection" from which the *Weingarten* right is derived).

EASTEX, INC. V. NATIONAL LABOR RELATIONS BOARD
437 U.S. 556 (1978)

JUSTICE POWELL delivered the opinion of the Court:

Employees of petitioner sought to distribute a union newsletter in nonworking areas of petitioner's property during nonworking time urging employees to support the union and discussing a proposal to incorporate the state "right-to-work" statute into the state constitution and a Presidential veto of an increase in the federal minimum wage. The newsletter also called on employees to take action to protect their interests as employees with respect to these two issues. The question presented is whether petitioner's refusal to allow the distribution violated § 8(a)(1) of the National Labor Relations Act by interfering with, restraining, or coercing employees' exercise of their right under § 7 of the Act to engage in "concerted activities for the purpose of . . . mutual aid or protection."

The newsletter was divided into four sections. The first and fourth sections urged employees to support and participate in the union and, more generally, extolled the benefits of union solidarity. The second section encouraged employees to write their legislators to oppose incorporation of the state "right-to-work" statute into a revised state constitution then under consideration, warning that incorporation would "[weaken] Unions and [improve] the edge business has at the bargaining table." The third section noted that the President recently had vetoed a bill to increase the federal minimum wage from $1.60 to $2.00 per hour, compared this action to the increase of prices and profits in the oil industry under administration policies, and admonished: "As working men and women we must defeat our enemies and elect our friends. If you haven't registered to vote, please do so today."

Petitioner contends that the activity here is not within the "mutual aid or protection" language [of section 7] because it does not relate to a "specific dispute" between employees and their own employer "over an issue which the employer has the right or power to affect." In support of its position, petitioner asserts that the term "employees" in § 7 refers only to employees of a particular employer, so that only activity by employees on behalf of themselves or other employees of the same employer is protected. [I]n petitioner's view, under § 7 "the employee is only protected for activity within the scope of the employment relationship." Petitioner rejects the idea that § 7 might protect any activity that could be characterized as "political," and suggests that the discharge of an employee who engages in any such activity would not violate the Act.

We believe that petitioner misconceives the reach of the "mutual aid or protection" clause. The "employees" who may engage in concerted activities for "mutual aid or protection" are defined by § 2(3) of the Act to "include any employee, and shall not be limited to the employees of a particular employer, unless this subchapter explicitly states otherwise. . . ." This definition was intended to protect employees when they engage in otherwise proper concerted activities in support of employees of employers other than their own.

We also find no warrant for petitioner's view that employees lose their protection under the "mutual aid or protection" clause when they seek to improve terms and conditions of employment or otherwise improve their lot as employees through channels outside the immediate employee-employer relationship. The 74th Congress knew well enough that labor's cause often is advanced on fronts other than collective bargaining and grievance settlement within the immediate employment context. It recognized this fact by choosing, as the language of § 7 makes clear, to protect concerted activities for the somewhat broader purpose of "mutual aid or protection" as well as for the narrower purposes of "self-organization" and "collective bargaining." Thus, it has been held that the "mutual aid or protection" clause protects employees from retaliation by their employers when they seek to improve working conditions through resort to administrative and judicial forums, and that employees' appeals to legislators to protect their interests as employees are within the scope of this clause. To hold that activity of this nature is entirely unprotected—irrespective of location or the means employed—would leave employees open to retaliation for much legitimate activity that could improve their lot as employees.

It is true, of course, that some concerted activity bears a less immediate relationship to employees' interests as employees than other such activity. We may assume that at some point the relationship becomes so attenuated that an activity cannot fairly be deemed to come within the "mutual aid or protection" clause. It is neither necessary nor appropriate, however, for us to attempt to delineate precisely the boundaries of the "mutual aid or protection" clause. That task is for the Board to perform in the first instance as it considers the wide variety of cases that come before it.

The Board determined that distribution of the second section, urging employees to write their legislators to oppose incorporation of the state "right-to-work" statute into a revised state constitution, was protected because union security is "central to the union concept of strength through solidarity" and "a mandatory subject of bargaining in other than right-to-work states." The newsletter warned that incorporation could affect employees adversely "by weakening Unions and improving the edge business has at the bargaining table." The fact that Texas already has a "right-to-work" statute does not render employees' interest in this matter any less strong, for, as the Court of Appeals noted, it is "one thing to face a statutory scheme which is open to legislative modification or repeal" and "quite another thing to face the prospect that such a scheme will be frozen in a concrete constitutional mandate."

The Board held that distribution of the third section, criticizing a Presidential veto of an increase in the federal minimum wage and urging employees to register to vote to "defeat our enemies and elect our friends," was protected despite the fact that petitioner's employees were paid more than the vetoed minimum wage. It reasoned that the "minimum wage inevitably influences wage levels derived from collective bargaining, even those far above the minimum," and that "concern by [petitioner's] employees for the plight of other employees might gain support for them at some future time when they might have a dispute with their employer." We think that the Board acted within the range of its discretion in so holding. Few topics are of such immediate concern to employees as the level of their wages. The Board was entitled to note the widely recognized impact that a rise in the minimum wage may have on the level of negotiated wages generally, a phenomenon that would not have been lost on petitioner's employees. The union's call, in the circumstances of this case, for these employees to back persons who support an increase in the minimum wage, and to oppose those who oppose it, fairly is characterized as concerted activity for the "mutual aid or protection" of petitioner's employees and of employees generally.

[The dissenting opinion of JUSTICE REHNQUIST, joined by CHIEF JUSTICE BURGER, is omitted.]

NOTES

1.   *What Is Too Attenuated? Eastex* suggests that "at some point the relationship [between the activity and the worker's job] becomes so attenuated that an activity cannot fairly be deemed to come within the 'mutual aid or protection' clause." 437 U.S. 556, 568 (1978). When is that point of attenuation reached? Consider again the Somali workers' problem. Assume that one of the Somali workers testified before the City Council that Enderby should not be considered for any government contracts because the company was not sufficiently insured to undertake public projects. Would it matter if the worker testified that Enderby should not be considered until it improved its labor relations and increased the ethnic diversity of its management corps? See *Tradesmen Int'l, Inc. v. NLRB*, 275 F.3d 1137 (D.C. Cir. 2002) (a union organizer's testimony before a city board encouraging the requirement of a surety bond for employer's city work, while concerted, was not sufficiently related to improving terms and conditions of employment to be viewed as being for "mutual aid and protection"). *But see Five Star Transp. Inc. v. NLRB*, 522 F.3d 46 (1st Cir. 2008) (bus drivers engaged in concerted, protected activity when they wrote letters and email to school district critical of bus company and urged that the bus company not be awarded a contract; though not in direct employment relationship with bus company, letters were aimed at safeguarding employment conditions).

2.   *What Are the Interests of Employees as Employees?* Does *Eastex* provide unqualified worker protection for distribution of political literature related to labor issues in the workplace? The Court states that there may be "types of conduct or speech that are so purely political or so remotely connected to the concerns of employees as employees as to be beyond protection." Consider that in *NLRB v. Motorola, Inc.*, 991 F.2d 278 (5th Cir. 1993), the Fifth Circuit reversed an NLRB decision upholding, in line with *Eastex*, employee distribution of materials related to a local ordinance banning workplace drug testing after employer announcement of a mandatory drug testing plan.

According to the Fifth Circuit, the employees involved were not acting as employees, but as "members of outside political organizations." Which do you think is stronger, the nexus between non-minimum wage workers and national minimum wage legislation upheld as not too attenuated in *Eastex* or the nexus between an employer drug testing policy and local drug testing legislation rejected in *Motorola*? Is *Motorola* consistent with *Eastex*? Should the fact of employee affiliation with "outside political organizations" make a difference when considering whether actions are concerted and for mutual aid or protection within Section 7? What about protests surrounding sexual harassment or sex discrimination in the workplace, or more national protests like those encouraged by the #MeToo movement? *See, e.g., Ellison Media Co.,* 344 N.L.R.B. 1133 (2005) (one employee encouraging another employee to report sexually offensive comments is for mutual aid and protection).

3.   *How Long are Workers Protected?* Once worker activity is found to be concerted and for mutual aid and protection, how long does protection last? Is the activity protected indefinitely under Section 7? In *Quietflex Mfg. Co.,* 344 N.L.R.B. 1055 (2005), the Board upheld an employer discharge of eighty three workers engaged in a twelve hour work stoppage. The majority found that the work stoppage lost the Act's protection when it endured beyond a "reasonable time." In upholding the discharges, the Board applied a balancing approach in which it weighed the workers' Section 7 rights against the employer's private property rights. In doing so, the Board weighed ten factors: 1) the reason for the stoppage, 2) whether the stoppage was peaceful, 3) whether the stoppage precluded employer access to property or interfered with production, 4) whether workers were able to present grievances to the employer, 5) whether workers were warned of consequences, 6) the work stoppage's duration, 7) whether workers were represented or had a grievance process, 8) whether workers remained beyond their shift, 9) whether workers attempted to seize property, and 10) the ultimate reason for discharge.

The Board majority found that the length of time of the stoppage and the fact that the workers were discharged for refusing to leave the premises, combined with various opportunities to present grievances to management weighed in favor of the employer. Dissenting Member Wilma Liebman maintained that because the work stoppage did not involve the production areas of the plant and involved no real harm to the employer, the employer's property interest was "nominal" and could not outweigh the Section 7 rights of the workers. *See also Cambro Mfg. Co.,* 312 N.L.R.B. 634 (1993) (discharge of eleven workers upheld after a few hours despite peacefulness of stoppage and worker assembly in dining room and hallway, not production areas); *Waco, Inc.,* 273 N.L.R.B. 746 (1984) (discharge of nine workers upheld after only three and one-half hour peaceful work stoppage); Calvin William Sharpe, *"By Any Means Necessary"—Unprotected Conduct and Decisional Discretion under the NLRA,* 20 Berkeley J. Emp. & Lab. L. 203, 212 (1999) (criticizing *Cambro*); Craig Becker, "Better Than A Strike:" *Protecting New Forms of Collective Work Stoppages under the NLRA,* 61 U. Chi. L. Rev. 351, 367 (1994) (criticizing *Cambro*); Amy J. Zdravecky, *"If I Only 'Had a Brain' . . . I Could Figure Out the Contours of Concerted Activity Versus Other Competing Rights": Quietflex Manufacturing and Its Ten Factor Balancing Act for Determining How Long a Protected Concerted Work Stoppage Can Continue on the Employer's Premises,* 22 Lab. Law. 69 (2006) (collecting authority and analyzing *Quietflex Mfg.*).

In *Atl. Scaffolding Co.,* 356 N.L.R.B. 835 (2011), the employees delivered a letter demanding an increase in pay and per diem rate to their supervisor and refused to work. They were then ordered to take buses to the parking lot, and then, when ordered, some went to a vacant lot across the street. Later the employees were asked to leave the vacant lot and complied. The employees did not return the following day and were discharged for job abandonment. The Board found the work stoppage was peaceful, there was no attempt to deny anyone access to the property, and the employees moved when asked. Further, there was no cognizable interference with production. The employer cited *Cambro* and *Quietflex* saying that the employee's absence from their jobs interfered with the employer's ability to get work done. The Board found the case to be distinguishable from *Cambro* and *Quietflex* because those cases were on employer property and even when the employees were asked to leave, they did not. Also, in those cases the employer was deprived of property for an unreasonable period of time. In *Atl. Scaffolding Co.,* the Board found that there was no need for *Quietflex* balancing because time and interference were minimal. Do you agree with the way the Board distinguishes *Quietflex/Cambro* and *Atl. Scaffolding*? Doesn't it rather seem that the Board in *Atl. Scaffolding* is trying to limit the reach and possible holding of *Quietflex*? Note that Trump Board General Counsel Peter Robb has singled out *Quietflex* as one of the cases and case applications for which his office may want to give the Board "an alternative analysis." In his memorandum, Robb specifically mentions cases which allegedly give "heavier weight to those factors that tend to favor protection [by the NLRA]." *See Alternative Analysis Memorandum,* at 2.

4.   *Scope of Protection.* Consider whether the following are activities taken for mutual aid and protection:

a.   Two workers walk out because of cold and drafty working conditions when a particular door was left open, but the other workers felt the workplace was too hot when the door was shut. *NLRB v. Jasper Seating Co.,* 857 F.2d 419 (7th Cir. 1988) (despite disagreement by employees, walkout protected because aimed at a dispute with the employer).

b.   Union, after trying to pass legislation requiring employers to pay employees a fair, living wage and to live up to community and environmental obligations, objects to construction permits sought by nonunion companies. *Petrochem Insulation, Inc. v. NLRB,* 240 F.3d 26 (D.C. Cir. 2001) (for mutual aid and protection because objections related to "area standards," overall local attempts to influence employee wages and conditions).

c.   Worker fired after attempting to persuade other employees to use an ESOP (Employee Stock Ownership Plan) to buy out the company. *Harrah's Lake Tahoe Resort Casino*, 307 N.L.R.B. 182 (1992) (advances employee interests in being owners, not in being employees and thus unprotected).

d.   Several workers leave work to participate in an all-day immigration rally, taking place nationally in every city, to protest governmental policies, including and especially related to immigrant work. What if the workers participating in the immigration rally are off-duty? For a discussion of the Section 7 issues surrounding this activity, *see* Michael C. Duff, *Days Without Immigrants: Analysis and Implications of the Treatment of Immigration Rallies under the National Labor Relations Act*, 85 Denv. U.L. Rev. 93 (2007) (making a case for some Section 7 protection). *Compare* Kaiser Engineers, 213 N.L.R.B. 752 (1974) *with* Reliable Maintenance, Case No. 18-CA-18119 (Advice Mem. Oct. 31, 2006). Would the workers be protected if they had left both to protest the employer's policy and also to protest on immigration policies? What about *Washington Aluminum* and *Eastex*? Do they provide support?

FRESH & EASY NEIGHBORHOOD MARKET, INC.
361 N.L.R.B. 151 (2014)

CHAIRMAN PEARCE and MEMBERS HIROZAWA, SCHIFFER, MISCIMARRA, and JOHNSON:

This case raises the issue of whether an employee was engaged in "concerted activity" for the purpose of "mutual aid or protection" within the meaning of Section 7 of the National Labor Relations Act when she sought assistance from her coworkers in raising a sexual harassment complaint to her employer. The judge found that she was not, and the Acting General Counsel excepts. We find that the employee was indeed engaged in concerted activity for the purpose of mutual aid or protection. We also agree with the Acting General Counsel that, to the extent the Board's divided decision in *Holling Press, Inc.*, 343 N.L.R.B. 301 (2004) would require a finding that the employee's activity was *not* for mutual aid or protection, that case—which lies far outside the mainstream of Board precedent—should be overruled.

I.   FACTS

On August 24, 2011, employee Margaret Elias, a cashier at the Respondent's grocery store, asked supervisor Bruce Churley if she could participate in training related to the sale of alcohol, known as "TIPS." Churley told her to write a note to him on a whiteboard in the breakroom, which Elias did on August 25. Her message read, in relevant part: "Bruce . . . Could you please sign me up for TIPS training on 9/10/11?"

On August 26, Elias saw that the word "TIPS" had been changed to "TITS" and that a picture of a worm or peanut urinating on her name had been added to her original whiteboard message. Elias asked Michael Anderson, her team leader, about filing a sexual harassment complaint and showed him the whiteboard. When Anderson asked why she would want to do so, Elias left the breakroom, angry at his reaction. Afterward, Anderson telephoned Churley and, when informed of Elias' plan to file a sexual harassment complaint, Churley told Anderson to take a photograph of the altered whiteboard message and erase it.

That same day, Elias hand copied the whiteboard picture and the altered message to a piece of paper. She asked Anderson and two coworkers, Krista Yates and Victoria Giro, to sign the document. All three did so. Regarding the substance of Elias' conversations with those employees, the credited evidence establishes the following: Before Anderson signed, Elias told him that she wanted to depict what was on the whiteboard and to file a sexual harassment complaint in connection with that content. Likewise, before Yates signed, Elias indicated to her that she wanted to file a complaint. When Giro signed the document, she knew Elias was upset by the whiteboard alteration and, at some point during their conversation about the document, Elias mentioned wanting to file a complaint. Giro, who testified that she personally found the whiteboard alteration inappropriate, suggested that Elias report the matter to Churley so he could review the breakroom cameras, find out who altered Elias' message, and take appropriate corrective action. As found by the judge, during these conversations Elias was loud and angry.

At the time that Anderson, Yates, and Giro signed Elias' document, only the hand-drawn picture and the altered whiteboard message appeared on the paper. At some later point, Elias added the following statement: "Someone changed the board to 'TITS' instead of TIPS and [sic] and put a worm pissing on my name. I take this as sexual harassement [sic]. This has been on the [b]oard since I got here at 2PM." Elias testified that although she did not intend that statement to be a joint complaint, "I was offended and I believe that the other girls were offended too. And it just seemed that if we were to file a harassment charge that it wouldn't happen again." Elias also testified that she felt the altered message was "sexual-based harassment" for her and the two other women who were working that night.

Later on August 26, Churley returned to the store and saw the photograph of the altered whiteboard that Anderson had taken. Churley then reviewed the breakroom's video footage and identified Gary Hamner as the employee who altered Elias' whiteboard message. Churley emailed Employee Relations Manager Monyia Jackson to report the incident. He also spoke to Anderson, Giro, and Yates about Elias' request that they sign her handwritten reproduction of the altered whiteboard message. The three stated that they believed they were only witnessing that Elias' reproduction was correct, that they did not want to help her bring a sexual harassment complaint, and that they felt forced to sign the document. Nonetheless, Giro testified that she would not have liked the whiteboard alteration if it had happened to her and thought that management should have been notified in some way so that disciplinary action could be taken. In fact, Giro testified that, the day after she signed Elias' document, she went to Churley and told him that she thought the whiteboard alteration was inappropriate and that she hoped he would "take care of it."

In the following days, Yates made a formal complaint against Elias for "bullying" her into signing the statement showing the reproduced whiteboard message and accused Elias of altering the statement after Yates signed it. In addition, Hamner complained that Elias cursed at him upon his arrival to work on August 26.

Employee Relations Manager Jackson then began an investigation into the whiteboard incident and the complaints against Elias. After interviewing Anderson, Yates, and Hamner, Jackson telephoned Elias on August 31. Jackson spoke to Elias about her sexual harassment complaint, as well as her coworkers' complaints against her. When Jackson questioned Elias about why she felt that she had to obtain her coworkers' signatures on the statement, Elias responded that it was for her own protection. Jackson also instructed Elias not to obtain any further statements so that Jackson could conduct her investigation into the incident. She told Elias, however, that Elias could talk to other employees and ask them to be witnesses for her. Elias was never threatened with and did not receive discipline for her actions. Upon completing the investigation, Jackson concluded that the whiteboard alterations were inappropriate, disciplined Hamner for making the alterations, informed Elias of her decision in writing, and assured Elias that she would be protected against retaliation. Jackson found no merit to Yates' and Hamner's complaints against Elias.

III. DISCUSSION

Elias Engaged in Concerted Activity for the Purpose of Mutual Aid and Protection

To be protected under Section 7 of the Act, employee conduct must be both "concerted" and engaged in for the purpose of "mutual aid or protection." Although these elements are closely related, our precedent makes clear that they are analytically distinct. As described more fully below, whether an employee's activity is "concerted" depends on the manner in which the employee's actions may be linked to those of his coworkers. See *NLRB v. City Disposal Systems*, 465 U.S. 822, 831 (1984). The Supreme Court has observed, however, that "[t]here is no indication that Congress intended to limit [Section 7] protection to situations in which an employee's activity and that of his fellow employees combine with one another in any particular way." *NLRB v. City Disposal Systems,* 465 U.S. at 835. The concept of "mutual aid or protection" focuses on the *goal* of concerted activity; chiefly, whether the employee or employees involved are seeking to "improve terms and conditions of employment or otherwise improve their lot as employees." *Eastex, Inc. v. NLRB,* 437 U.S. 556, 565 (1978).

Under Section 7, both the concertedness element and the "mutual aid or protection" element are analyzed under an objective standard. An employee's subjective motive for taking action is not relevant to whether that action was concerted. "Employees may act in a concerted fashion for a variety of reasons—some altruistic, some selfish—but the standard under the Act is an objective one." *Circle K Corp.,* 305 NLRB 932, 933 (1991), enfd. mem. 989 F.2d 498 (6th Cir. 1993). Nor is motive relevant to whether activity is for "mutual aid or protection." Rather, the analysis focuses on whether there is a link between the activity and matters concerning the workplace or employees' interests as employees. As one court has explained:

> The motive of the actor in a labor dispute must be distinguished from the purpose for his activity. The motives of the participants are irrelevant in terms of determining the scope of Section 7 protections; what is crucial is that the purpose of the conduct relate to collective bargaining, working conditions and hours, or other matters of "mutual aid or protection" of employees.

Dreis & Krump Mfg. Co. v. NLRB, 544 F.2d 320, 328 fn. 10 (7th Cir. 1976).

1.   *Elias was engaged in concerted activity*

In *Meyers I*, the Board defined concerted activity as that which is "engaged in with or on the authority of other employees, and not solely by and on behalf of the employee himself." *Meyers I*, 268 NLRB at 497. In *Meyers II*, the Board clarified that the *Meyers I* definition of concerted activity includes cases "where individual employees seek to initiate or to induce or to prepare for group action, as well as individual employees bringing truly group complaints to the attention of management." *Meyers II*, 281 NLRB at 887. The requirement that, to be concerted, activity must be engaged in with the object of initiating or inducing group action does not disqualify merely preliminary discussion from protection under Section 7. In this regard, "inasmuch as almost any concerted activity for mutual aid or protection has to start with some kind of communication between individuals, it would come very near to nullifying the rights of organization and collective bargaining guaranteed by Section 7 of the Act if such communications are denied protection because of lack of fruition." *Mushroom Transportation Co. v. NLRB,* 330 F.2d 683, 685 (3d Cir. 1964). In addition, it is well established that "the activity of a single employee in enlisting the support of his fellow employees for their mutual aid and protection is as much 'concerted activity' as is ordinary group activity." *Whittaker Corp.*, 289 NLRB 933, 933 (1988).

Here, Elias sought her coworkers' assistance in raising a sexual harassment complaint to management, by soliciting three of them to sign the piece of paper on which she had copied the altered whiteboard message in order to "prove" the harassment to which she had been subjected. Although she did not intend to pursue a joint complaint, her testimony establishes that she wanted her coworkers to be witnesses to the incident, which she would then report to the Respondent. Two of those coworkers testified that they were aware of her intent to memorialize the incident for the purpose of reporting it to management. Even without more, under *Meyers II* and its progeny, Elias' conduct in approaching her coworkers to seek their support of her efforts regarding this workplace concern would constitute concerted activity. Elias did not have to engage in *further* concerted activity to ensure that her initial call for group action retained its concerted character. The Board has previously found similar action to support a finding of concerted activity. See *Holling Press,* 343 NLRB at 302 (employee appealing to her coworkers to support her sexual harassment claim was engaged in concerted activity).

In concluding that Elias was not engaged in concerted activity, Member Miscimarra and the judge maintain that Elias was raising a personal complaint not shared by others and that her coworkers signed the statement only to stop her "annoying" conduct. But under Board precedent, concertedness is not dependent on a shared objective or on the agreement of one's coworkers with what is proposed. See, e.g., *El Gran Combo*, 284 NLRB 1115, 1117 (1987), enfd. 853 F.2d 996 (1st Cir. 1988); and *Meyers II*, 281 NLRB at 887. The concerted nature of Elias' request would not be diminished even if Elias' coworkers did not agree with her sexual harassment complaint, or, as Member Miscimarra argues, did not want to sign the document. The Board has also recognized that activity such as Elias' solicitation in this case may be protected even if the solicited employee is uncomfortable with the request. See *Frazier Industrial Co.*, 328 NLRB 717, 719 (1999), enfd. 213 F.3d 750, 341 U.S. App. D.C. 393 (D.C. Cir. 2000). It is also well established that an employee may act partly from selfish motivations and still be engaged in concerted activity, even if she is the only immediate beneficiary of the solicitation. Thus, Elias' initial request, on its own, establishes concerted activity, regardless of whether her coworkers signed or refused to sign the document and notwithstanding their irritation with the manner of her request for their assistance.

Member Miscimarra further contends that our decision today will result in unprecedented Section 7 protection for an employee soliciting assistance from his or her coworkers in raising a complaint to management even if the solicited employees are unwilling to help or file their own complaint against the employee seeking assistance, they do not have a shared interest in the matter raised by the employee, and the complaint raised by the soliciting employee lacks merit. However, what our colleague deems unprecedented protection is, in fact, consistent with decades of Board precedent. As noted, solicited employees do not have to agree with the soliciting employee or join that employee's cause in order for the activity to be concerted. See *Mushroom Transportation*, 330 F.2d at 685; *Circle K Corp.*, 305 NLRB at 933. Nor do the solicited employees have to share an interest in the matter raised by the soliciting employee for the activity to be concerted. See El Gran Combo, 284 NLRB at 1117. Further, the protected, concerted nature of an employee's complaint to management is not dependent on the merit of such a complaint. See *Spinoza, Inc.*, 199 NLRB 525, 525 (1972), *enfd.* 478 F.2d 1401 (5th Cir. 1973). It is thus clear that, in finding Elias' conduct to be concerted, we are applying established precedent. Our colleague's criticisms, therefore, represent a dispute with existing Board jurisprudence.

2.   *Elias' concerted activity was for the purpose of mutual aid and protection*

We turn now to the question whether Elias' concerted activity was for the purpose of mutual aid or protection. Our finding that it was flows from the Supreme Court's endorsement, in *Eastex*, of the view that Congress designed Section 7 "to protect concerted activities for the somewhat broader purpose of 'mutual aid or protection' as well as for the narrower purposes of 'self-organization' and 'collective bargaining.' " 437 U.S. at 565 (emphasis added). Thus, the "mutual aid or protection" clause encompasses "much legitimate activity [by employees] that could improve their lot as employees." *Id.* at 567. The Court concluded that it was appropriate for the Board to draw the precise boundaries of that clause "as it considers the wide variety of cases that come before it." *Id.* at 568.

In *Meyers II*, the Board "acknowledged that efforts to invoke the protection of statutes benefitting employees are efforts engaged in for the purpose of 'mutual aid or protection' " and reiterated the Supreme Court's view that "proof that an employee action inures to the benefit of all" is "proof that the action comes within the 'mutual aid or protection' clause of Section 7. 281 NLRB at 887. In exercising the authority affirmed by the *Eastex* Court, the Board has found that a broad range of employee activities regarding the terms and conditions of their employment falls within the scope of the "mutual aid or protection" clause. See, e.g., *Dreis & Krump Mfg.*, 221 NLRB at 314 (employees' complaints over supervisory handling of safety issues); and *Tanner Motor Livery,* 148 NLRB 1402, 1404 (1964), *enfd. in relevant part* 349 F.2d 1 (9th Cir. 1965) (employees' protest of racially discriminatory hiring practices). See also *Ellison Media Co.*, 344 NLRB 1112, 1113–1114, 1119 (2005) (conversation between two employees was for mutual aid or protection where one employee, who had previously complained about offensive comments from a supervisor, urged a second employee to report sexually suggestive comments from same supervisor); and *Owens Illinois,* 290 NLRB 1193, 1204–1205 (1988), *enfd.* 872 F.2d 413 (3d Cir. 1989) (employee's action in contacting OSHA was protected). As those cases indicate, Elias' activity unquestionably would be deemed for "mutual aid or protection" had she attempted to join forces with another employee who likewise had been the victim of alleged sexual harassment by Hamner (or anyone else in the Respondent's workplace for that matter). Thus, the question presented here is whether Elias' solicitation of support from her coworkers should be treated any differently simply because, on this occasion, Elias was confronting misconduct that Hamner seemingly directed at her alone. After a review of well-established precedent, we answer that question in the negative.

In other contexts, the Board has found that an employee who asks for help from coworkers in addressing an issue with management does, indeed, act for the purpose of mutual aid or protection, even where the issue appears to concern only the soliciting employee, the soliciting employee would receive the most immediate benefit from a favorable resolution of the issue, and the soliciting employee does not make explicit the employees' mutuality of interests. In *IBM Corp.,* 341 NLRB 1288, 1294, 1307 fn.13 (2004), for example, the Board reaffirmed that the "mutual aid or protection" element is satisfied where a single employee, facing a disciplinary interview, requests assistance from a coworker. The Supreme Court has held the same. See *NLRB v. J. Weingarten, Inc.,* 420 U.S. 251, 260, 95 S. Ct. 959, 43 L. Ed. 2d 171 (1975) (single employee's appeal for help from other employees implicates "mutual aid or protection" even though only that employee may have had an immediate stake in the outcome). Discipline, of course, is often highly individualized—and the *IBM* Board certainly did not suggest that concerted activity exists only where the employee asked for help has engaged in the same or similar alleged conduct for which his coworker is being investigated. Likewise, in *El Gran Combo,* 284 NLRB at 1116–1117, the Board found that an employee who, unlike his band mates, did not receive a share of the band's album sales nonetheless acted for the purpose of mutual aid or protection by soliciting fellow band members to support his individual demand for a share of the group's earnings. Similarly, in *Circle K Corp.,* 305 NLRB at 932–934, the Board found that even where an employee may have been motivated by personal concerns in soliciting a coworker to sign a letter to management regarding terms and conditions of employment of concern to all employees, the employee was nonetheless engaged in concerted activity that satisfied the "mutual aid or protection" requirement. In *Rock Valley Trucking Co.,* 350 NLRB 69, 69, 83–84 (2007), the Board found that a truck driver who was assigned lower mileage than his coworkers was engaged in protected conduct when he raised the disparities with his coworkers and his manager and asked a coworker to bring the issue to management. Although the driver was the one who directly suffered from the unequal assignment, the

Board agreed that his actions were aimed not merely to secure a personal benefit, but also sought a change from a flawed assignment process that could affect all employees.

Although arising in widely varying circumstances, all of those cases are grounded in the "solidarity" principle. In enacting Section 7, Congress created a framework for employees to "band together" in solidarity to address their terms and conditions of employment with their employer. *City Disposal Systems,* 465 U.S. at 835. "[M]ak[ing] common cause with a fellow workman over his separate grievance" is a hallmark of such solidarity, even if "only one of them . . . has any immediate stake in the outcome." *NLRB v. Peter Cailler Kohler Swiss Chocolates Co.,* 130 F.2d 503, 505 (2d Cir. 1942). By soliciting assistance from coworkers to raise his issues to management, an employee is requesting that his coworkers exercise vigilance against the employer's perceived unjust practices. See *El Gran Combo de Puerto Rico v. NLRB,* 853 F.2d 996, 1005 fn. 4 (1st Cir. 1988), quoting *J. Weingarten,* 420 U.S. at 260–261. The solicited employees have an interest in helping the aggrieved individual—even if the individual alone has an immediate stake in the outcome—because "next time it could be one of them that is the victim." *Id.* "An injury to one is an injury to all" is one of the oldest maxims in the American labor lexicon.

Applying that bedrock principle here would lead to the conclusion that Elias, too, was acting for the purpose of mutual aid or protection in soliciting her coworkers' assistance in complaining to management about an incident of alleged sexual harassment. Nevertheless, we recognize, as did the judge, that such a finding appears to be foreclosed by the Board's decision in *Holling Press.* In that case, over a dissent by then-Member Liebman, the Board found that an employee, although acting concertedly, did *not* act for the purpose of mutual aid or protection when she sought a colleague's assistance in connection with her sexual harassment complaint. In doing so, the Board concluded:

> [W]here one employee is the alleged victim, that lone employee's protest is not concerted. And, even if the victim seeks support from another employee, and that seeking of support is concerted activity, the "mutual aid or protection" element may be missing. The bare possibility that the second employee may one day suffer similar treatment, and may herself seek help, is far too speculative a basis on which to rest a finding of mutual aid or protection. [343 NLRB at 303–304.]

Thus, *Holling Press* effectively nullifies the solidarity principle when it comes to claims of sexual harassment involving conduct directed at only one employee. In doing so, Holling Press seemed to create a special exception for sexual harassment claims.

The General Counsel asks us to reverse Holling Press in that respect. Drawing on the Board's decision in Meyers II, above, he argues that when an individual employee effectively invokes statutory protections benefitting employees—here, protections against sexual harassment in the workplace—that employee's efforts are for the purpose of "mutual aid or protection" under established Board and Supreme Court precedent, discussed above. We agree that Holling Press cannot be reconciled with that precedent.

We hold that an employee seeking the assistance or support of his or her coworkers in raising a sexual harassment complaint is acting for the purpose of mutual aid or protection. This decision applies equally to cases where, as here, an employee seeks to raise that complaint directly to the employer, or, as in *Holling Press*, to an outside entity.

NOTES

1.   *Flip-Flop?* The *Fresh and Easy* case was the Obama Board's response to the Bush Board's decision in *Holling Press*. Conservatives and progressives generally split on the issue of whether or under what circumstances a single worker can invoke the protections of the NLRA for the purpose of mutual aid and protection. Indeed, Peter Robb, the General Counsel of the NLRB, appointed by Donald Trump, issued a Memorandum on December 1, 2017, listing several cases in which the General Counsel's office "might want to provide the Board with an alternative analysis. . . ." *See* Peter B. Robb, *Mandatory Submissions to Advice,* Memorandum GC 18–02 (December 1, 2017). One of the cases targeted in the Memorandum is *Fresh & Easy Neighborhood Market.* The General Counsel characterized *Fresh & Easy* as "[f]inding conduct was for mutual aid and protection where only one employee had an immediate stake in the outcome." *Id.* at 2.

2.   *Squaring with Title VII and Other Sexual Harassment Protections.* One might ask how NLRA protections against sexual harassment square with Title VII or state law protections. Generally, the focus of laws like Title VII are on the individual while NLRA rights might be viewed more as group protections. However, on a broader level, worker solidarity can be reinforced through both regimes. Moreover, the NLRA has a different enforcement scheme, making it easier for those without the means to fund litigation to bring sexual harassment claims. *See NLRB Holds that the NLRA Protects Workers Seeking Colleagues' Assistance in Filing Sexual Harassment Complaints: Fresh & Easy Neighborhood Market, Inc.,* 128 Harv. L. Rev. 785, 790–791 (2014) ("Persons asserting their individual Title VII employment rights to improve their workplaces face increasingly difficult legal obstacles. . . . In light of these legal developments and practical realities, protecting group efforts to vindicate individual rights might provide positive value in advancing employment law's goals of creating safe and healthy work environments.").

3. UNPROTECTED CONDUCT

Under certain circumstances, conduct that is literally concerted and for mutual aid and protection may be held to be unprotected for policy reasons. For example, a group of employees who assault a particularly oppressive supervisor may be acting concertedly for mutual aid and protection but their conduct would not be protected under section 7. What are the limits of this category? Consider the following case.

NATIONAL LABOR RELATIONS BOARD V. PIER SIXTY, LLC
855 F.3d 115 (2nd Cir. 2017)

CABRANES, CIRCUIT JUDGE:

[T]he NLRA generally prohibits employers from terminating an employee based on that employee's union-related activity. But even an employee engaged in protected activity "can, by opprobrious conduct, lose the protection of the [NLRA.]" We are thus required to resolve whether an employee's Facebook post insulting his boss's mother and encouraging other employees to vote for the union ought to receive protection under Sections 8(a)(1) and 8(a)(3) of NLRA. . . .

We . . . affirm the NLRB's determination that Pier Sixty violated Sections 8(a)(1) and 8(a)(3) by discharging Hernan Perez since Perez's conduct was not so "opprobrious" as to lose the protection of the NLRA. Our decision rests heavily on the deference afforded to NLRB factual findings, made following a six-day bench trial informed by the specific social and cultural context in this case. We note, however, that Perez's conduct sits at the outer-bounds of protected, union-related comments for the reasons laid out below.

BACKGROUND

Pier Sixty operates a catering company in New York, N.Y. In early 2011, many of its service employees began seeking union representation. Following what the parties substantially agree was a tense organizing campaign that included threats from management that employees could be penalized or discharged for union activities, Pier Sixty employees voted to unionize in an October 27, 2011 election.

Two days before that election, Hernan Perez was working as a server at a Pier Sixty venue. A supervisor, Robert McSweeney, gave Perez and two other servers various directions in what the NLRB's opinion describes as a "harsh tone. These directions included "Turn your head that way [towards the guests] and stop chitchatting," and "Spread out, move, move." McSweeney's attitude in delivering these instructions upset Perez, who viewed them as the latest instance of the management's continuing disrespect for employees. About forty-five minutes later, during an authorized break from work, Perez used his iPhone to post the following message on his Facebook page:

> Bob is such a NASTY MOTHER FUCKER don't know how to talk to people! ! ! ! ! Fuck his mother and his entire fucking family! ! ! ! What a LOSER! ! ! ! Vote YES for the UNION! ! ! ! ! !

"Bob" referred to McSweeney. Perez knew that his Facebook "friends," including ten coworkers, would be able to see the post; the post was also publicly accessible, although Perez may not have known so at the time. Perez took down the post three days later, on October 28, 2011. The post had already come to the attention of the management of Pier Sixty which, following an investigation, fired Perez on November 9, 2011.

— Fired

Later that day, Perez filed a charge with the NLRB alleging that he had been terminated in retaliation for "protected concerted activities." On December 15, 2011, Evelyn Gonzalez, who had led organizing efforts at Pier Sixty, filed a second charge, alleging various unfair labor practices in violation of Section 8(a)(1) of the NLRA. On August 24, 2012, NLRB Region Two issued an amended complaint consolidating those two charges. On April 18, 2013, the presiding Administrative Law Judge ("ALJ") issued a decision finding, as relevant here, that Pier Sixty had violated Sections 8(a)(1) and 8(a)(3) of the NLRA by discharging Perez in retaliation for protected activity. Pier Sixty filed exceptions, and a three-member panel of the NLRB affirmed the ALJ's decision, with one member dissenting. The NLRB filed an application for enforcement, and Pier Sixty filed a cross-petition for review that are now before this Court.

— ALJ

DISCUSSION

B. The NLRB's Decision That Pier Sixty Violated the NLRA by Discharging Perez

We now turn to . . . whether the NLRB's petition for enforcement should be granted. That question itself turns on a more particular one: was Perez's Facebook post so "opprobrious" as to lose the protection that the NLRA affords union-related speech?

— Issue

The NLRA generally prohibits employers from discharging an employee for concerted or union-related activity. Specifically, Section 7 of the NLRA guarantees employees the right "to engage in . . . concerted activities for the purpose of collective bargaining or other mutual aid or protection." Determining whether an activity falls within the meaning of Section 7 is a task that "implicates [the Board's] expertise in labor relations" and is for "the Board to perform in the first instance."

This right to engage in union-related activity is protected by Sections 8(a)(1) and 8(a)(3) of the NLRA, which prohibit an employer from discharging employees for participating in protected, union-related activity under Section 7. But even an employee engaged in ostensibly protected activity may act "in such an abusive manner that he loses the protection" of the NLRA. *City Disposal Sys., Inc.*, 465 U.S. at 837, 104 S.Ct. 1505. The parties disagree about the proper framework for identifying "abusive" behavior. The "abusive" behavior at issue here is Perez's use of obscenities in the workplace. Traditionally, the starting point for evaluating whether an employee's "uttering of . . . obscenities" in the workplace qualifies for protection under the NLRA has been the four-factor test established by the NLRB in *Atlantic Steel*. 245 NLRB at 816. That test considers: "(1) the place of the discussion; (2) the subject matter of the discussion; (3) the nature of the employee's outburst; and (4) whether the outburst was, in any way, provoked by an employer's unfair labor practice."

But the *Atlantic Steel* test has come under pressure in recent years. In *NLRB v. Starbucks*, 679 F.3d 70 (2nd Cir. 2012), this Court concluded that the *Atlantic Steel* test gave insufficient weight to employers' interests in preventing employees' outbursts "in a public place in the presence of customers" and we suggested more balanced standards for evaluating "opprobrious" conduct in that context. *Id.* at 79. We remanded the cause to the NLRB to develop an appropriate test for determining the NLRA's "protection for an employee who, while discussing employment issues, utters obscenities in the presence of customers." *Id.* at 80.[35]

At about the same time, the General Counsel's Office began developing new guidance for evaluating an employee's use of social media that went in a more employee-friendly direction and that limited the ability of employers to issue rules regarding use of social media, even where employees were posting public criticisms of their employers and workplace.[36] This new guidance built upon a regularly-observed distinction between activity outside the workplace and confrontations in the immediate presence of coworkers or customers. In light of the General Counsel's new guidance, the Board has utilized the nine-factor "totality of the circumstances" test in recent social media cases.[38]

---

[35] On remand, however, the Board "assume[d] that [the] conduct lost the protection of the Act" but found a violation of the Act on other grounds. See *Starbucks Corp.*, 360 NLRB 1168, 1169 (2014).

[36] *See* NLRB OFFICE OF GEN. COUNSEL, REPORT OF THE ACTING GENERAL COUNSEL CONCERNING SOCIAL MEDIA CASES, MEMORANDUM OM 12–59 (May 30, 2012); NLRB OFFICE OF GEN. COUNSEL, REPORT OF THE ACTING GENERAL COUNSEL CONCERNING SOCIAL MEDIA CASES, MEMORANDUM OM 12–31 (Jan. 24, 2012); *see also* NLRB OFFICE OF GEN. COUNSEL, REPORT OF THE ACTING GENERAL COUNSEL CONCERNING SOCIAL MEDIA CASES, MEMORANDUM OM 11–74, at 5–6, 12 (Aug. 18, 2011). We note, however, that advice memoranda from the General Counsel do not constitute precedential authority and are not binding on the Board, *see Midwest Television, Inc.*, 343 NLRB 748, 762 n.21 (2004), much less on the courts.

[38] *See, e.g., Richmond Dist. Neighborhood Ctr.*, 361 NLRB No. 74, 2014 WL 5465462, at *2 n.6 (Oct. 28, 2014) (holding, in the absence of exceptions to applying a totality-of-circumstances test, that egregiousness of a private Facebook conversation could be examined using such a test); *accord Fresenius USA Mfg.*, 358 NLRB 1261, 1267–68 (2012), *superseded on other grounds by* 362 NLRB No. 130, 2015 WL 3932160 (June 24, 2015).

In the present case, after adopting the ALJ's factual findings, the Board analyzed Perez's Facebook post using the nine-factor "totality of the circumstances" test. While we are not convinced the amorphous "totality of the circumstances" test adequately balances an employer's interests, Pier Sixty did not object to the ALJ's use of the test in evaluating Perez's statements before the Board. For that reason, we need not, and do not, address the validity of that test in this opinion. Instead, Pier Sixty argues that the Board's decision—that "Perez' comments were not so egregious as to exceed the Act's protection"—is not supported by "substantial evidence" in the record. It is not entirely clear whether Pier Sixty is challenging the factual findings of the Board or its legal conclusions. Regardless of whether we are reviewing the factual findings under a "substantial evidence" standard or the legal conclusions under a "considerable deference" standard, the Board's decision in this case is justified. Several factors inform our conclusion.

First, even though Perez's message was dominated by vulgar attacks on McSweeney and his family, the "subject matter" of the message included workplace concerns—management's allegedly disrespectful treatment of employees, and the upcoming union election. Pier Sixty had demonstrated its hostility toward employees' union activities in the period immediately prior to the representation election and proximate to Perez's post. Pier Sixty had threatened to rescind benefits and/or fire employees who voted for unionization. It also had enforced a "no talk" rule on groups of employees, including Perez and Gonzalez, who were prevented by McSweeney from discussing the Union. Perez's Facebook post explicitly protested mistreatment by management and exhorted employees to "Vote YES for the UNION." Thus, the Board could reasonably determine that Perez's outburst was not an idiosyncratic reaction to a manager's request but part of a tense debate over managerial mistreatment in the period before the representation election.

Second, Pier Sixty consistently tolerated profanity among its workers. The ALJ found that Pier Sixty had not previously disciplined employees for widespread profanity in the workplace, including the words "fuck" and "motherfucker," among other expletives and racial slurs. The Board relied on evidence that, in the context of daily obscenities, Pier Sixty only issued five written warnings to employees for such an offense in the six years prior

---

The "totality of the circumstances" test for evaluating an employee's use of social media may consider the following factors: (1) any evidence of antiunion hostility; (2) whether the conduct was provoked; (3) whether the conduct was impulsive or deliberate; (4) the location of the conduct; (5) the subject matter of the conduct; (6) the nature of the content; (7) whether the employer considered similar content to be offensive; (8) whether the employer maintained a specific rule prohibiting the content at issue; and (9) whether the discipline imposed was typical for similar violations or proportionate to the offense. *Pier Sixty, LLC,* 2015 WL 1457688, at *3.

The aforementioned tests, though most relevant to the conduct at issue here, are not the exclusive frameworks through which the Board has evaluated whether employee conduct is entitled to NLRA protection.

to Perez's discharge. And there was no evidence that Pier Sixty has ever discharged an employee solely for the use of offensive language. The ALJ specifically credited employee testimony that Chef DeMaiolo and McSweeney cursed at employees on a daily basis including screaming phrases such as "What the fuck are you doing?," "Motherfucker," and "Are you guys fucking stupid?" We recognize that one could draw a distinction between generalized scatology (or even cursing *at* someone), and, on the other hand, cursing someone's mother and family. But one could reasonably decide, as the ALJ did in this case, that Perez's comments "were not a slur against McSweeney's family but, rather, an epithet directed to McSweeney himself." Under the circumstances presented here, it is striking that Perez—who had been a server at Pier Sixty for thirteen years—was fired for profanities two days before the Union election when no employee had ever before been sanctioned (much less fired) for profanity.

Third, the "location" of Perez's comments was an online forum that is a key medium of communication among coworkers and a tool for organization in the modern era. While a Facebook post may be visible to the whole world, including actual and potential customers, as Pier Sixty argues, Perez's outburst was not in the immediate presence of customers nor did it disrupt the catering event. Furthermore, Perez asserts that he mistakenly thought that his Facebook page was private and took the post down three days later, upon learning that it was publicly accessible. We thus conclude, according appropriate deference to the Board's factual findings and interpretation of the NLRA, that the Board did not err in ruling that Perez's Facebook post, although vulgar and inappropriate, was not so egregious as to exceed the NLRA's protection. Nor was his Facebook post equivalent to a "public outburst" in the presence of customers and thus can reasonably be distinguished from other cases of "opprobrious conduct."

holding

In sum, Pier Sixty has failed to meet its burden of showing that Perez's behavior was so egregious as to lose the protection of the NLRA under the Board's "totality-of-the-circumstances" test. However, we note that this case seems to us to sit at the outer-bounds of protected, union-related comments, and any test for evaluating "opprobrious conduct" must be sufficiently sensitive to employers' legitimate disciplinary interests, as we have previously cautioned. We have considered all of Pier Sixty's objections to enforcement and have found them to be without merit.

NOTES

1. *Rudeness.* If Perez's tone was not of the "egregious" type that would lose the Act's protection, what is? Consider whether a worker's statements in the context of union organizing that the employer is a "pig" and a "laughing stock" are enough to be unprotected. Would it matter if the worker is an assembly line employee? A professor? See *Carleton College*, 328 N.L.R.B. 217

(1999) (a professor's sarcastic and vulgar language is nonetheless protected), *rev'd, Carleton College v. NLRB*, 230 F.3d 1075 (8th Cir. 2000) (given a college's interest in maintaining collegiality and respect among faculty, a professor's sarcastic and vulgar language is unprotected). Should the statement or conduct's relationship to terms and conditions of employment matter in determining protection? See *New River Indus. v. NLRB*, 945 F.2d 1290 (4th Cir. 1991) (letter ridiculing company's show of gratitude to workers by serving free ice cream unprotected because the court viewed it as simply ridiculing the company instead of legitimately protesting working conditions). "Employees are permitted some leeway for impulsive behavior when engaged in concerted activity, but this leeway is balanced against an employer's right to maintain order and respect." *Piper Realty Co.*, 313 N.L.R.B. 1289, 1290 (1994).

Rule

The *Atlantic Steel* factors discussed and applied in *Pier Sixty*, have been applied to find that an employee has lost the Act's protection because of "egregious behavior, including displaying 'an opprobrious or abusive manner.'" *Verizon Wireless*, 349 N.L.R.B. 640, 646 (2007).

2.   *Disparaging the Employer's Product or Service*: Employee conduct disparaging the employer's business may be protected concerted activity if the disparagement relates to labor relations or working conditions and is not too extreme. In *NLRB v. International Bhd. of Electrical Workers, Local Union No. 1229 (Jefferson Standard Broadcasting Co.)*, 346 U.S. 464 (1953), after reaching an impasse in bargaining that had lasted for over five months, the union began daily peaceful picketing of the employer's station. The placards and handbills named the union representing the picketing workers and emphasized the station's unfairness to its employees and its refusal to move on the specific bargaining demand at issue. The workers did not strike. Instead, they continued to work their regular hours at full pay, and demonstrated with placards and handbills during off duty hours. This type of conduct continued without incident for almost a month and a half. However, without warning, several of the workers began an attack on the quality of the station's programming. They printed 5,000 handbills that were distributed and mailed to various businesses and public places throughout the city. The handbills cited the station's stale programming, lack of local and sports programming, lack of investment in equipment, and seeming indifference to the importance of the city ("Is Charlotte a Second Class City?"). The handbills made no mention of the union, a labor controversy, or collective bargaining. The attack continued for a couple of weeks until the station terminated ten workers involved in the disparagement.

The Supreme Court agreed with the employer that the handbills were "a demonstration of such detrimental disloyalty as to provide 'cause'" for termination. The Court emphasized that the attack was not related to any company labor practice or working conditions and that, instead, the attack focused on finance and public relations, the province of management. Moreover, the attack asked for no public sympathy or support and was conducted while the workers were being paid by the employer. According to the Court, "[n]othing could be further from the purpose of the Act than to require an employer to finance such activities." The Court concluded by stating the conduct involving product disparagement would have been unprotected even if the NLRB found, which it had not in this case, that the attack was "concerted activity wholly or partly within the scope of Section 7."

Since *Jefferson Standard*, the Board and Courts have generally tended to find conduct by strikers disparaging employers' labor relations to be protected by the Act while finding conduct by nonstrikers or, especially, on-duty workers disparaging the employer's product or service to be unprotected. For example, in a case similar to *Jefferson Standard*, but with facts more favorable to the workers, the NLRB had a more difficult time deciding the issue. *See Patterson-Sargent Co.*, 115 N.L.R.B. 1627 (1956). There, as in *Jefferson Standard*, the workers published and distributed handbills to consumers disparaging the product of the employer, a paint company. Unlike the Jefferson Standard workers, however, these workers were on strike, as indicated on the handbill, and the disparagement related to the dispute, alleging that the quality of paint made by replacement workers was not as good. The full NLRB split 3–2 on the question of whether the disparagement was protected, with the majority finding that the untruthful product disparagement crossed the line and would have even if truthful. The dissenters felt the conduct should have been protected since the workers were not being paid for work by the employer and the handbill indicated a connection with a labor dispute.

In *Sierra Publ'g Co. v. NLRB*, 889 F.2d 210 (9th Cir. 1989), the Ninth Circuit upheld a Board decision finding that a letter sent by the union to a publishing company's retail advertising customers advising them of the dispute between the union and the company and stating that the company's circulation had plummeted and the company was speedily going downhill was nonetheless protected because the letter was clearly related to the labor dispute and the product disparagement was not so severe as to cross the line of protection. According to the court, *Jefferson Standard's* intent was not to "equate every critical comment with unprotected disloyalty."

The United States Court of Appeals for the Eighth Circuit upheld a Board decision (2–1) that MikLin Enterprises, Inc. d/b/a Jimmy Johns violated Sections 8(a)(1) and (3) of the Act by terminating employees who put up posters disparaging the Employer's product in the context of a labor dispute. See *MikLin Enterprises dba Jimmy Johns v. NLRB*, 818 F.3d 397 (8th Cir. 2016). According to the case, MikLin Enterprise employees upon being hired are given Jimmy John's Rules for Employment, Rule 11 of which states: "Find your own replacement if you are not going to be at work. We do not allow people to simply call in sick! We require employees and managers to find their own replacement! NO EXCEPTIONS!" *Id.* at 401. After the Industrial Workers of the World lost a union election at MikLin, several employees placed posters featuring two identical side-by-side photographs of a sandwich on community bulletin boards in the public area of several of MikLin's stores. Above the left sandwich was a label stating "Your Sandwich Made By A Healthy Jimmy John's Worker." Above the right sandwich was a label stating: "Your Sandwich Made By A Sick Jimmy John's Worker." Below the photographs, in larger white letters, the poster stated: "Can't Tell the Difference?" In smaller red letters, the poster stated: "That's Too Bad Because Jimmy John's Workers Don't Get Paid Sick Days. Shoot, We Can't Even Call In Sick." Below that, in even smaller white letters, the posters stated: "We Hope Your Immune System Is Ready Because You're About To Take the Sandwich Test . . ." Below that, in white letters approximately the same size as the labels at the top of the posters, the posters asked readers to "Help Jimmy John's Workers Win Sick Days. Support Us Online At www.jimmyjohnsworkers.org." Managers removed the posters. *Id.* at 402.

In upholding a Board finding that MikLin's termination of the employees for being the "leaders and developers" of the sandwich campaign was an unfair labor practice, the Eighth Circuit found that the employee's conduct in developing and putting up the disparaging posters was protected by the Act and did not lose protection for crossing the line into unlawful disparagement. The court found that the statements in the posters, developed in the context of a labor dispute about paid sick leave, were not made with "reckless disregard of truth or falsity," or were even "materially false and misleading." *Id.* at 405, 405 n.3. The court also cited employee testimony that employees were directed to work while sick, actually worked while sick, and observed other employees working while sick." *Id.* at 406.

However, the United States Court of Appeals for the Eighth Circuit in an *en banc* decision reversed the Eighth Circuit panel decision in the Jimmy Johns case. The en banc majority held that the Jimmy Johns employees who posted flyers with pictures of two identical Jimmy Johns sandwiches, one labeled a sandwich made by a healthy Jimmy Johns worker and one labeled a sandwich made by a sick Jimmy Johns worker protesting the absence of paid sick days, and the requirements that employees calling off sick find their replacements or face discipline was disloyal under the *Jefferson Standard* rule and therefore not protected by section 7. *See MikLin Enterprises, Inc. v. NLRB*, 861 F.3d 812 (8th Cir. 2017) (en banc).

Consider again the Somali workers' problem at the Chapter's beginning. What if the employees who had walked off the job had printed handbills distributed to the Muslim community indicating that Enderby refused to promote Muslim employees and therefore was "a company that had a heinous and invidiously discriminatory religious outlook" that loyal Muslims should not acquiesce to by purchasing Enderby television sets or PC tablets? Would your response change if the handbill revealed the dispute between the workers and Enderby but indicated that "Enderby TV sets and PC Tablets are made with cheap parts and a manufacturing process that cuts corners"?

3.   *Confidentiality*: The Board and the courts have consistently found worker release of legitimately confidential company information as well as its unauthorized acquisition to be unprotected. *See, e.g., IBM Corp.*, 265 N.L.R.B. 638 (1982); *Laminated Prods., Inc.*, 294 N.L.R.B. 816 (1989). However, protection has been extended to workers when employers have promulgated overly broad confidentiality rules and when employers have prohibited

employee discussion of wages. *See, e.g., Handicabs, Inc. v. NLRB*, 95 F.3d 681 (8th Cir. 1996); *Longs Drug Stores Cal., Inc.*, 347 N.L.R.B. 500 (2006).

4.   *Email & blogging related to Section 7 rights: Pier Sixty* involves the application of Section 7 in the context of cyberspace. An increasing number of cases involving Section 7 protection result from employee action over the internet. Is labor law in general, and the NLRA in particular, ready for these challenges? Part of the answer materialized in the NLRB's decision in *Purple Communications, Inc.*, 361 N.L.R.B. No. 126 (2014) ("Consistent with the purposes and policies of the Act and our obligation to accommodate the competing rights of employers and employees, we decide today that employee use of email for statutorily protected communications on nonworking time must presumptively be permitted by employers who have chosen to give employees access to their email systems."), discussed more fully in Chapter 4. For some useful general exploration of email and internet-related use issues, *see* Katherine M. Scott, *When is Employee Blogging Protected by Section 7 of the NLRA?*, 2006 Duke L. & Tech. Rev. 17 (2006) (exploring definition of concertedness and mutual aid and protection and arguing that courts and the Board should consider the purpose of an entire blog, not isolated posts, in making determinations about whether blogging is protected under Section 7 of the NLRA); Christine Neylon O'Brien, *The Impact of Employer E-Mail Policies on Employee Rights to Engage in Concerted Activities Protected by the National Labor Relations Act*, 106 Dick. L. Rev. 573 (2002) (discussing "business only" email rules in the context of various NLRB decisions and memoranda).

Even if employers have a property interest in email at work, to what extent does an employer's concern extend to social media? Can an employer discipline workers for their Facebook postings about work? Consider the following case.

HISPANICS UNITED OF BUFFALO
359 N.L.R.B. 368 (2012)

CHAIRMAN PEARCE and MEMBERS GRIFFIN and BLOCK

At issue in this case is whether the Respondent violated Section 8(a)(1) of the Act by discharging five employees for Facebook comments they wrote in response to a coworker's criticisms of their job performance. Although the employees' mode of communicating their workplace concerns might be novel, we agree with the [administrative law] judge that the appropriate analytical framework for resolving their discharge allegations has long been settled under *Meyers Industries* and its progeny. Applying *Meyers*, we agree with the judge that the Respondent violated 8(a)(1) by discharging the five employees.

The relevant facts are as follows. Marianna Cole-Rivera and Lydia Cruz-Moore were coworkers employed by the Respondent to assist victims of domestic violence. The two employees frequently communicated with each other by phone and text message during the workday and after hours.

According to Cole-Rivera's credited testimony, Cruz-Moore often criticized other employees during these communications, particularly housing department employees who, Cruz-Moore asserted, did not provide timely and adequate assistance to clients. Other employees similarly testified that Cruz-Moore spoke critically to them about their work habits and those of other employees.

This "criticism" issue escalated on Saturday, October 9, 2010, a nonworkday, when Cole-Rivera received a text message from Cruz-Moore stating that the latter intended to discuss her concerns regarding employee performance with Executive Director Lourdes Iglesias. Cole-Rivera sent Cruz-Moore a responsive text questioning whether she really "wanted Lourdes to know . . . how u feel we don't do our job. . . ." From her home, and using her own personal computer, Cole-Rivera then posted the following message on her Facebook page:

> Lydia Cruz, a coworker feels that we don't help our clients enough at [Respondent]. I about had it! My fellow coworkers how do u feel?

Four off-duty employees—Damicela Rodriguez, Ludimar Rodriguez, Yaritza Campos, and Carlos Ortiz—responded by posting messages, via their personal computers, on Cole-Rivera's Facebook page; the employees' responses generally objected to the assertion that their work performance was substandard. Cruz-Moore also responded, demanding that Cole-Rivera "stop with ur lies about me." She then complained to Iglesias about the Facebook comments, stating that she had been slandered and defamed. At Iglesias' request, Cruz-Moore printed all the Facebook comments and had the printout delivered to Iglesias. On October 12, the first workday after the Facebook postings, Iglesias discharged Cole-Rivera and her four coworkers, stating that their remarks constituted "bullying and harassment" of a coworker and violated the Respondent's "zero tolerance" policy prohibiting such conduct.

In *Meyers I*, the Board held that the discipline or discharge of an employee violates Section 8(a)(1) if the following four elements are established: (1) the activity engaged in by the employee was "concerted" within the meaning of Section 7 of the Act; (2) the employer knew of the concerted nature of the employee's activity; (3) the concerted activity was protected by the Act; and (4) the discipline or discharge was motivated by the employee's protected, concerted activity. See also *Correctional Medical Services*, 356 NLRB No. 48, slip op. at 2 (2010). Only the first and third elements are in dispute here: whether the employees' Facebook comments constituted concerted activity and, if so, whether that activity was protected by the Act.

The Board first defined concerted activity in *Meyers I* as that which is "engaged in with or on the authority of other employees, and not solely by and on behalf of the employee himself." In *Meyers II*, the Board expanded this definition to include those "circumstances where individual employees seek to initiate or to induce or to prepare for group action, as well as individual employees bringing truly group complaints to the attention of management."

Applying these principles, . . . there should be no question that the activity engaged in by the five employees was concerted for the "purpose of mutual aid or protection" as required by Section 7. As set forth in her initial Facebook post, Cole-Rivera alerted fellow employees of another employee's complaint that they "don't help our clients enough," stated that she "about had it" with the complaints, and solicited her coworkers' views about this criticism. By responding to this solicitation with comments of protest, Cole-Rivera's four coworkers made common cause with her, and, together, their actions were concerted within the definition of *Meyers I,* because they were undertaken "with . . . other employees." The actions of the five employees were also concerted under the expanded definition of *Meyers II,* because, as the judge found, they "were taking a first step towards taking group action to defend themselves against the accusations they could reasonably believe Cruz-Moore was going to make to management."

Our dissenting colleague contends that the employees' Facebook discussions about Cruz-Moore's criticisms were not undertaken for the purpose of their "mutual aid and protection." Specifically, he states that a group action defense to Cruz-Moore's criticisms could not have been intended because Cole-Rivera failed to tell her co-workers that Cruz-Moore was going to voice her criticisms to Iglesias. We disagree.

In *Relco Locomotives, Inc.,* 358 NLRB No. 37, slip op. at 17 (2012), the Board reiterated established precedent that the "object or goal of initiating, inducing or preparing for group action does not have to be stated explicitly when employees communicate," citing *Whittaker Corp.,* 289 NLRB 933, 933 (1988). Even absent an express announcement about the object of an employee's activity, "a concerted objective may be inferred from a variety of circumstances in which employees might discuss or seek to address concerns about working conditions. . . ." *Id.* Relying on this authority, the Board in *Relco* found unlawful the discharge of two employees for discussing among themselves and other employees their "concern" about the rumored discharge of a fellow employee. Notwithstanding that the two never "talk[ed] specifically about working together to address their concerns about [the employee's] termination," the Board adopted the judge's finding that they "engaged in concerted activities when they communicated with other employees about their concern . . . [and i]t matter[ed] not that [they] had not yet taken their concerns to management—their discussions with coworkers were indispensable initial steps along the way to possible group action" *Id.,* slip op. at 17.

Here, too, Cole-Rivera's Facebook communication with her fellow employees, immediately after learning that Cruz-Moore planned to complain about her coworkers to Iglesias, had the clear "mutual aid" objective of preparing her coworkers for a group defense to those complaints. Contrary to our colleague, Cole-Rivera was not required under *Relco* to discuss this object with coworkers or tell them it was made necessary by Cruz-Moore's impending visit with Iglesias. Her "mutual aid" object of preparing her coworkers for group action was implicitly manifest from the surrounding circumstances. *Timekeeping Systems, Inc.*, 323 NLRB 244, 248 (1997).

As to the third element of the violation, whether the employees' concerted activity was protected, we find that the Facebook comments here fall well within the Act's protection. The Board has long held that Section 7 protects employee discussions about their job performance, and the Facebook comments plainly centered on that subject. As discussed, the employees were directly responding to allegations they were providing substandard service to the Respondent's clients. Given the negative impact such criticisms could have on their employment, the five employees were clearly engaged in protected activity in mutual aid of each other's defense to those criticisms.

The Respondent does not argue that the employees' comments were unprotected because they were made via Facebook. To the contrary, the Respondent asserts that, "regardless of where the comments and actions of the five terminated at-will employees took place, the result herein would have been the same." According to the Respondent, it was privileged to discharge the five employees because their comments constituted unprotected harassment and bullying of Cruz-Moore, in violation of its "zero tolerance" policy. The judge rejected this argument, and so do we.

First, as the judge found, the Facebook comments cannot reasonably be construed as a form of harassment or bullying within the meaning of the Respondent's policy. Second, even assuming that the policy covered the comments, the Respondent could not lawfully apply its policy "without reference to Board law." *Consolidated Diesel Co.*, 332 NLRB 1019, 1020 (2000), *enfd.* 263 F.3d 345 (4th Cir. 2001) As the Board explained in *Consolidated Diesel*, "legitimate managerial concerns to prevent harassment do not justify policies that discourage the free exercise of Section 7 rights by subjecting employees to . . . discipline on the basis of the subjective reactions of others to their protected activity." *Id.* Here, as in *Consolidated Diesel*, the Respondent applied its harassment policy to the discharged employees based solely on Cruz-Moore's subjective claim (in a text message) that she felt offended by the Facebook comments. As the United States Court of Appeals for the Fourth Circuit noted in enforcing the Board's decision, "[s]uch a wholly subjective notion of harassment is unknown to the Act," 263 F.3d 354, and discipline imposed on this basis violates Section 8(a)(1).

In sum, because we have found that the Facebook postings were concerted and protected, and because it is undisputed that the Respondent discharged the five employees based solely on their postings, we conclude that the discharges violated Section 8(a)(1).

NOTES

1.   *"Mere Griping" versus Inciting Concerted Action.* The Board has held many times that mere griping is not protected by the Act because it does not constitute "mutual aid and protection?" The Third Circuit held in *Mushroom Transportation Co. v. NLRB,* 330 F.2d 683 (3rd Cir. 1964) that for an individual complaint to be deemed protected concerted activity, "it must appear at the very least that it was engaged in with the object of initiating or inducing or preparing for group action or that it had some relation to group action in the interest of the employees." Do the Facebook postings by the HUB workers meet this test? Do you think the employees would, if polled, say they were protesting because they feared for their jobs and wanted to increase their leverage by soliciting opinions of other workers? Can the *Mushroom Transportation* test be met in any case by allegations or proof that the employee's complaints were intended to elicit co-worker support? What about the Facebook posts by the Somali workers in the problem beginning this Chapter? Are they merely gripes or an attempt to initiate, induce, or prepare for group action?

2.   The Facebook postings in *HUB,* and in the Somali worker problem, were made by workers posting on Facebook from home while the Facebook posting in *Pier Sixty* was made during a work break. Do the employer's work rules extend to postings about work or other workers that are made from a home, and not a work, computer or phone? Should it? What if the postings are limited to Facebook friends or Twitter followers? Can the employer impose its work rules on postings made from home to a private network of friends? *See Public Service Credit Union,* No. 27-CA-21923, 2011 WL 5822506 at *1 (Nov. 1, 2011) (*NLRB Div. of Advice*).

C. INTERFERENCE, RESTRAINT AND COERCION OF CONCERTED ACTIVITY

1. WAIVER OF RIGHTS TO COLLECTIVE LITIGATION

EPIC SYSTEMS CORP. V. LEWIS
128 S. Ct. 1612 (2018)

JUSTICE GORSUCH delivered the opinion of the Court:

Should employees and employers be allowed to agree that any disputes between them will be resolved through one-on-one arbitration? Or should employees always be permitted to bring their claims in class or collective actions, no matter what they agreed with their employers?

I.

The three cases before us [including *Epic Systems Corp., Ernst & Young, LLP,* and *Murphy Oil USA, Inc.*] differ in detail but not in substance. Take *Ernst & Young LLP v. Morris.* There Ernst & Young and one of its junior accountants, Stephen Morris, entered into an agreement providing that they would arbitrate any disputes that might arise between them. The agreement stated that the employee could choose the arbitration provider and that the arbitrator could "grant any relief that could be granted by . . . a court" in the relevant jurisdiction. The agreement also specified individualized arbitration, with claims "pertaining to different [e]mployees [to] be heard in separate proceedings."

After his employment ended, and despite having agreed to arbitrate claims against the firm, Mr. Morris sued Ernst & Young in federal court. He alleged that the firm had misclassified its junior accountants as professional employees and violated the federal Fair Labor Standards Act (FLSA) and California law by paying them salaries without overtime pay. Although the arbitration agreement provided for individualized proceedings, Mr. Morris sought to litigate the federal claim on behalf of a nationwide class under the FLSA's collective action provision, 29 U.S.C. § 216(b). He sought to pursue the state law claim as a class action under Federal Rule of Civil Procedure 23.

Ernst & Young replied with a motion to compel arbitration. The district court granted the request, but the Ninth Circuit reversed this judgment. 834 F.3d 975 (2016). The Ninth Circuit recognized that the Arbitration Act generally requires courts to enforce arbitration agreements as written. But the court reasoned that the statute's "saving clause," see 9 U.S.C. § 2, removes this obligation if an arbitration agreement violates some other federal law. And the court concluded that an agreement requiring individualized arbitration proceedings violates the NLRA by barring employees from engaging in the "concerted activit[y]," 29 U.S.C. § 157, of pursuing claims as a class or collective action.

Although the Arbitration Act and the NLRA have long coexisted—they date from 1925 and 1935, respectively—the suggestion they might conflict is something quite new. Until a couple of years ago, courts more or less agreed that arbitration agreements like those before us must be enforced according to their terms.

But recently things have shifted. In 2012, the Board—for the first time in the 77 years since the NLRA's adoption—asserted that the NLRA effectively nullifies the Arbitration Act in cases like ours. *D.R. Horton, Inc.,* 357 N.L.R.B. 2277. Initially, this agency decision received a cool reception in court. See *D.R. Horton,* 737 F.3d, at 355–362. In the last two years, though, some circuits have either agreed with the Board's conclusion or thought themselves obliged to defer to it. . . . More recently still, the disagreement has grown as the Executive has disavowed the Board's (most recent) position, and the Solicitor General and the Board have offered us battling briefs about the law's meaning. We granted certiorari to clear the confusion.

III.

Even if the Arbitration Act normally requires us to enforce arbitration agreements like theirs, the employees reply that the NLRA overrides that guidance in these cases and commands us to hold their agreements unlawful yet.

Seeking to demonstrate an irreconcilable statutory conflict even in light of these demanding standards, the employees point to Section 7 of the NLRA. That provision guarantees workers "the right to self-organization, to form, join, or assist labor organizations, to bargain collectively through representatives of their own choosing, and to engage in other concerted activities for the purpose of collective bargaining or other mutual aid or protection." 29 U.S.C. § 157. From this language, the employees ask us to infer a clear and manifest congressional command to displace the Arbitration Act and outlaw agreements like theirs.

But that much inference is more than this Court may make. Section 7 focuses on the right to organize unions and bargain collectively. It may permit unions to bargain to prohibit arbitration. Cf. *14 Penn Plaza LLC v. Pyett,* 556 U.S. 247, 256–260 (2009). But it does not express approval or disapproval of arbitration. It does not mention class or collective action procedures. It does not even hint at a wish to displace the Arbitration Act— let alone accomplish that much clearly and manifestly, as our precedents demand.

Neither should any of this come as a surprise. The notion that Section 7 confers a right to class or collective actions seems pretty unlikely when you recall that procedures like that were hardly known when the NLRA was adopted in 1935. Federal Rule of Civil Procedure 23 didn't create the modern class action until 1966; class arbitration didn't emerge until later still; and even the Fair Labor Standards Act's collective action provision postdated Section 7 by years. And while some forms of group litigation existed even in 1935, Section 7's failure to mention them only reinforces that the statute doesn't speak to such procedures.

A close look at the employees' best evidence of a potential conflict turns out to reveal no conflict at all. The employees direct our attention to the term "other concerted activities for the purpose of . . . other mutual aid or protection." This catchall term, they say, can be read to include class and collective legal actions. But the term appears at the end of a detailed list of activities speaking of "self-organization," "form[ing], join[ing], or assist

[ing] labor organizations," and "bargain[ing] collectively." 29 U.S.C. § 157. And where, as here, a more general term follows more specific terms in a list, the general term is usually understood to " 'embrace only objects similar in nature to those objects enumerated by the preceding specific words.' " *Circuit City Stores, Inc. v. Adams,* 532 U.S. 105, 115 (2001) (discussing *ejusdem generis* canon). All of which suggests that the term "other concerted activities" should, like the terms that precede it, serve to protect things employees "just do" for themselves in the course of exercising their right to free association in the workplace, rather than "the highly regulated, courtroom-bound 'activities' of class and joint litigation." *Alternative Entertainment,* 858 F.3d, at 414–415 (Sutton, J., concurring in part and dissenting in part) (emphasis deleted). None of the preceding and more specific terms speaks to the procedures judges or arbitrators must apply in disputes that leave the workplace and enter the courtroom or arbitral forum, and there is no textually sound reason to suppose the final catchall term should bear such a radically different object than all its predecessors.

The NLRA's broader structure underscores the point. After speaking of various "concerted activities" in Section 7, Congress proceeded to establish a regulatory regime applicable to each of them. The NLRA provides rules for the recognition of exclusive bargaining representatives, 29 U.S.C. § 159, explains employees' and employers' obligation to bargain collectively, § 158(d), and conscribes certain labor organization practices, §§ 158(a)(3), (b). The NLRA also touches on other concerted activities closely related to organization and collective bargaining, such as picketing, § 158(b)(7), and strikes, § 163. It even sets rules for adjudicatory proceedings under the NLRA itself. §§ 160, 161. Many of these provisions were part of the original NLRA in 1935, see 49 Stat. 449, while others were added later. But missing entirely from this careful regime is any hint about what rules should govern the adjudication of class or collective actions in court or arbitration. Without some comparably specific guidance, it's not at all obvious what procedures Section 7 might protect. Would opt-out class action procedures suffice? Or would opt-in procedures be necessary? What notice might be owed to absent class members? What standards would govern class certification? Should the same rules always apply or should they vary based on the nature of the suit? Nothing in the NLRA even whispers to us on any of these essential questions. And it is hard to fathom why Congress would take such care to regulate all the other matters mentioned in Section 7 yet remain mute about this matter alone—unless, of course, Section 7 doesn't speak to class and collective action procedures in the first place.

Telling, too, is the fact that when Congress wants to mandate particular dispute resolution procedures it knows exactly how to do so. Congress has spoken often and clearly to the procedures for resolving "actions," "claims," "charges," and "cases" in statute after statute. *E.g.,* 29 U.S.C. §§ 216(b), 626; 42 U.S.C. §§ 2000e–5(b), (f)(3)–(5). Congress has likewise shown that it knows how to override the Arbitration Act when it wishes—by explaining, for example, that, "[n]otwithstanding any other provision of law, . . . arbitration may be used . . . only if" certain conditions are met, 15 U.S.C. § 1226(a)(2); or that "[n]o predispute arbitration agreement shall be valid or enforceable" in other circumstances, 7 U.S.C. § 26(n)(2); 12 U.S.C. § 5567(d)(2); or that requiring a party to arbitrate is "unlawful" in other circumstances yet, 10 U.S.C. § 987(e)(3). The fact that we have nothing like that here is further evidence that Section 7 does nothing to address the question of class and collective actions.

In response, the employees offer this slight reply. They suggest that the NLRA doesn't discuss any particular class and collective action procedures because it merely confers a right to use *existing* procedures provided by statute or rule, "on the same terms as [they are] made available to everyone else." But of course the NLRA doesn't say even that much. And, besides, if the parties really take existing class and collective action rules as they find them, they surely take them subject to the limitations inherent in those rules—including the principle that parties may (as here) contract to depart from them in favor of individualized arbitration procedures of their own design.

Still another contextual clue yields the same message. The employees' underlying causes of action involve their wages and arise not under the NLRA but under an entirely different statute, the Fair Labor Standards Act. The FLSA allows employees to sue on behalf of "themselves and other employees similarly situated," 29 U.S.C. § 216(b), and it's precisely this sort of collective action the employees before us wish to pursue. Yet they do not offer the seemingly more natural suggestion that the FLSA overcomes the Arbitration Act to permit their class and collective actions. Why not? Presumably because this Court held decades ago that an identical collective action scheme (in fact, one borrowed from the FLSA) does *not* displace the Arbitration Act or prohibit individualized arbitration proceedings. *Gilmer v. Interstate/Johnson Lane Corp.,* 500 U.S. 20, 32, 111 S.Ct. 1647, 114 L.Ed.2d 26 (1991) (discussing Age Discrimination in Employment Act). In fact, it turns out that "[e]very circuit to consider the question" has held that the FLSA allows agreements for individualized arbitration. *Alternative Entertainment,* 858 F.3d, at 413 (opinion of Sutton, J.) (collecting cases). Faced with that obstacle, the employees are left to cast about elsewhere for help. And so they have cast in this direction, suggesting that one statute (the NLRA) steps in to dictate the procedures for claims under a different statute (the FLSA), and thereby overrides the commands of yet a third statute (the Arbitration Act). It's a sort of interpretive triple bank shot, and just stating the theory is enough to raise a judicial eyebrow.

Perhaps worse still, the employees' theory runs afoul of the usual rule that Congress "does not alter the fundamental details of a regulatory scheme in vague terms or ancillary provisions—it does not, one might say, hide elephants in mouseholes." *Whitman v. American Trucking Assns., Inc.,* 531 U.S. 457, 468, 121 S.Ct. 903, 149 L.Ed.2d 1 (2001). Union organization and collective bargaining in the workplace are the bread and butter of the NLRA, while the particulars of dispute resolution procedures in Article III courts or arbitration proceedings are usually left to other statutes and rules—not least the Federal Rules of Civil Procedure, the Arbitration Act, and the FLSA. It's more than a little doubtful that Congress would have tucked into the mousehole of Section 7's catchall term an elephant that tramples the work done by these other laws; flattens the parties' contracted-for dispute resolution procedures; and seats the Board as supreme superintendent of claims arising under a statute it doesn't even administer. . . .

What all these textual and contextual clues indicate, our precedents confirm. In many cases over many years, this Court has heard and rejected efforts to conjure conflicts between the Arbitration Act and other federal statutes. In fact, this Court has rejected *every* such effort to date (save one temporary exception since overruled), with statutes ranging from the Sherman and Clayton Acts to the Age Discrimination in Employment Act, the Credit Repair Organizations Act, the Securities Act of 1933, the Securities Exchange Act of 1934, and the Racketeer Influenced and Corrupt Organizations Act. Throughout, we have made clear that even a statute's express provision for collective legal actions does not necessarily mean that it precludes " 'individual attempts at conciliation' " through arbitration. *Gilmer, supra,* at 32, 111 S.Ct. 1647. And we've stressed that the absence of any specific statutory discussion of arbitration or class actions is an important and telling clue that Congress has not displaced the Arbitration Act. Given so much precedent pointing so strongly in one direction, we do not see how we might faithfully turn the other way here.

The employees rejoin that our precedential story is complicated by some of this Court's cases interpreting Section 7 itself. But, as it turns out, this Court's Section 7 cases have usually involved just what you would expect from the statute's plain language: efforts by employees related to organizing and collective bargaining in the workplace, not the treatment of class or collective actions in court or arbitration proceedings. Neither do the two cases the employees cite prove otherwise. In *Eastex, Inc. v. NLRB,* 437 U.S. 556, 558 (1978), we simply addressed the question whether a union's distribution of a newsletter in the workplace qualified as a protected concerted activity. We held it did, noting that it was "undisputed that the union undertook the distribution in order to boost its support and improve its bargaining position in upcoming contract negotiations," all part of the union's " 'continuing organizational efforts.' " *Id.,* at 575, and n. 24.

In *NLRB v. City Disposal Systems, Inc.,* 465 U.S. 822, 831–832, 104 S.Ct. 1505, 79 L.Ed.2d 839 (1984), we held only that an employee's assertion of a right under a collective bargaining agreement was protected, reasoning that the collective bargaining "process—beginning with the organization of the union, continuing into the negotiation of a collective-bargaining agreement, and extending through the enforcement of the agreement—is a single, collective activity." Nothing in our cases indicates that the NLRA guarantees class and collective action procedures, let alone for claims arising under different statutes and despite the express (and entirely unmentioned) teachings of the Arbitration Act.

* * *

The policy may be debatable but the law is clear: Congress has instructed that arbitration agreements like those before us must be enforced as written. While Congress is of course always free to amend this judgment, we see nothing suggesting it did so in the NLRA—much less that it manifested a clear intention to displace the Arbitration Act. Because we can easily read Congress's statutes to work in harmony, that is where our duty lies. The judgments in *Epic,* No. 16-285, and *Ernst & Young,* No. 16-300, are reversed, and the cases are remanded for further proceedings consistent with this opinion. The judgment in *Murphy Oil,* No. 16-307, is affirmed.

[A concurrence by JUSTICE THOMAS is omitted.]

JUSTICE GINSBURG with whom JUSTICE BREYER, JUSTICE SOTOMAYOR, and JUSTICE KAGAN join, dissenting.

The employees in these cases complain that their employers have underpaid them in violation of the wage and hours prescriptions of the Fair Labor Standards Act of 1938 (FLSA), 29 U.S.C. § 201 *et seq.,* and analogous state laws. Individually, their claims are small, scarcely of a size warranting the expense of seeking redress alone. *See* Nantiya Ruan, *What's Left To Remedy Wage Theft? How Arbitration Mandates That Bar Class Actions Impact Low-Wage Workers,* 2012 Mich. St. L. Rev. 1103, 1118–1119 (Ruan). But by joining together with others similarly circumstanced, employees can gain effective redress for wage underpayment commonly experienced.

To explain why the Court's decision is egregiously wrong, I first refer to the extreme imbalance once prevalent in our Nation's workplaces, and Congress' aim in the Norris LaGuardia Act (NLGA) and the NLRA to place employers and employees on a more equal footing. I then explain why the Arbitration Act, sensibly read, does not shrink the NLRA's protective sphere.

I.

It was once the dominant view of this Court that "[t]he right of a person to sell his labor upon such terms as he deems proper is . . . the same as the right of the purchaser of labor to prescribe [working] conditions." *Adair v. United States,* 208 U.S. 161, 174, 28 S.Ct. 277, 52 L.Ed. 436 (1908) (invalidating federal law prohibiting interstate railroad employers from discharging or discriminating against employees based on their membership in labor organizations); accord *Coppage v. Kansas,* 236 U.S. 1, 26, 35 S.Ct. 240, 59 L.Ed. 441 (1915) (invalidating state law prohibiting employers from requiring employees, as a condition of employment, to refrain or withdraw from union membership).

The NLGA and the NLRA operate on a different premise, that employees must have the capacity to act collectively in order to match their employers' clout in setting terms and conditions of employment. For decades, the Court's decisions have reflected that understanding. See *Jones & Laughlin Steel,* 301 U.S. 1, 57 S.Ct. 615, 81 L.Ed. 893 (upholding the NLRA against employer assault); cf. *United States v. Darby,* 312 U.S. 100, 61 S.Ct. 451, 85 L.Ed. 609 (1941) (upholding the FLSA).

Relevant here, § 7 of the NLRA guarantees employees "the right to self-organization, to form, join, or assist labor organizations, to bargain collectively through representatives of their own choosing, *and to engage in other concerted activities for the purpose of collective bargaining or other mutual aid or protection.*" 29 U.S.C. § 157 (emphasis added). Section 8(a)(1) safeguards those rights by making it an "unfair labor practice" for an employer to "interfere with, restrain, or coerce employees in the exercise of the rights guaranteed in [§ 7]." § 158(a)(1). To oversee the Act's guarantees, the Act established the National Labor Relations Board (Board or NLRB), an independent regulatory agency empowered to administer "labor policy for the Nation." *San Diego Building Trades Council v. Garmon,* 359 U.S. 236, 242, 79 S.Ct. 773, 3 L.Ed.2d 775 (1959); see 29 U.S.C. § 160.

Unlike earlier legislative efforts, the NLGA and the NLRA had staying power. When a case challenging the NLRA's constitutionality made its way here, the Court, in retreat from its *Lochner*-era contractual-"liberty" decisions, upheld the Act as a permissible exercise of legislative authority. See *Jones & Laughlin Steel,* 301 U.S., at 33–34, 57 S.Ct. 615. The Court recognized that employees have a "fundamental right" to join together to advance their common interests and that Congress, in lieu of "ignor[ing]" that right, had elected to "safeguard" it. *Ibid.*

B

Despite the NLRA's prohibitions, the employers in the cases now before the Court required their employees to sign contracts stipulating to submission of wage and hours claims to binding arbitration, and to do so only one-by-one. When employees subsequently filed wage and hours claims in federal court and sought to invoke the collective-litigation procedures provided for in the FLSA and Federal Rules of Civil Procedure, the employers moved to compel individual arbitration. The Arbitration Act, in their view, requires courts to enforce their take-it-or-leave-it arbitration agreements as written, including the collective-litigation abstinence demanded therein.

In resisting enforcement of the group-action foreclosures, the employees involved in this litigation do not urge that they must have access to a judicial forum. They argue only that the NLRA prohibits their employers from denying them the right to pursue work-related claims in concert in any forum. If they may be stopped by employer-dictated terms from pursuing collective procedures in court, they maintain, they must at least have access to similar procedures in an arbitral forum.

C

Although the NLRA safeguards, first and foremost, workers' rights to join unions and to engage in collective bargaining, the statute speaks more embracively. In addition to protecting employees' rights "to form, join, or assist labor organizations" and "to bargain collectively through representatives of their own choosing," the Act protects employees' rights "to engage in *other* concerted activities for the purpose of . . . mutual aid or protection." 29 U.S.C. § 157 (emphasis added); see, *e.g., NLRB v. Washington Aluminum Co.,* 370 U.S. 9, 14–15, 82 S.Ct. 1099, 8 L.Ed.2d 298 (1962) (§ 7 protected unorganized employees when they walked off the job to protest cold working conditions).

Suits to enforce workplace rights collectively fit comfortably under the umbrella "concerted activities for the purpose of . . . mutual aid or protection." 29 U.S.C. § 157. "Concerted" means "[p]lanned or accomplished together; combined." American Heritage Dictionary 381 (5th ed. 2011). "Mutual" means "reciprocal." *Id.,* at 1163. When employees meet the requirements for litigation of shared legal claims in joint, collective, and class proceedings, the litigation of their claims is undoubtedly "accomplished together." By joining hands in litigation, workers can spread the costs of litigation and reduce the risk of employer retaliation.

Recognizing employees' right to engage in collective employment litigation and shielding that right from employer blockage are firmly rooted in the NLRA's design. Congress expressed its intent, when it enacted the NLRA, to "protec[t] the exercise by workers of full freedom of association," thereby remedying "[t]he inequality of bargaining power" workers faced. 29 U.S.C. § 151; see, *e.g., Eastex, Inc. v. NLRB,* 437 U.S. 556, 567, 98 S.Ct. 2505, 57 L.Ed.2d 428 (1978) (the Act's policy is "to protect the right of workers to act together to better their working conditions" (internal quotation marks omitted)); *City Disposal,* 465 U.S., at 835, 104 S.Ct. 1505 ("[I]n enacting § 7 of the NLRA, Congress sought generally to equalize the bargaining power of the employee with that of his employer by allowing employees to band together in confronting an employer regarding the terms and conditions of their employment."). See also *supra*, at 1634–1636. There can be no serious doubt that collective litigation is one way workers may associate with one another to improve their lot.

Since the Act's earliest days, the Board and federal courts have understood § 7's "concerted activities" clause to protect myriad ways in which employees may join together to advance their shared interests. For example, the Board and federal courts have affirmed that the Act shields employees from employer interference when they participate in concerted appeals to the media, *e.g., NLRB v. Peter Cailler Kohler Swiss Chocolates Co.,* 130 F.2d 503, 505–506 (C.A.2 1942), legislative bodies, *e.g., Bethlehem Shipbuilding Corp. v. NLRB,* 114 F.2d 930, 937 (C.A.1 1940), and government agencies, *e.g., Moss Planing Mill Co.,* 103 N.L.R.B. 414, 418–419, enf'd, 206 F.2d 557 (C.A.4 1953). "The 74th Congress," this Court has noted, "knew well enough that labor's cause often is advanced on fronts other than collective bargaining and grievance settlement within the immediate employment context." *Eastex,* 437 U.S., at 565, 98 S.Ct. 2505.

Crucially important here, for over 75 years, the Board has held that the NLRA safeguards employees from employer interference when they pursue joint, collective, and class suits related to the terms and conditions of their employment. See, *e.g., Spandsco Oil and Royalty Co.,* 42 N.L.R.B. 942, 948–949 (1942) (three employees' joint filing of FLSA suit ranked as concerted activity protected by the NLRA); *Poultrymen's Service Corp.,* 41 N.L.R.B. 444, 460–463, and n. 28 (1942) (same with respect to employee's filing of FLSA suit on behalf of himself and others similarly situated), enf'd, 138 F.2d 204 (C.A.3 1943); *Sarkes Tarzian, Inc.,* 149 N.L.R.B. 147, 149, 153 (1964) (same with respect to employees' filing class libel suit); *United Parcel Service, Inc.,* 252 N.L.R.B. 1015, 1018 (1980) (same with respect to employee's filing class action regarding break times), enf'd, 677 F.2d 421 (C.A.6 1982); *Harco Trucking, LLC,* 344 N.L.R.B. 478, 478–479 (2005) (same with respect to employee's maintaining class action regarding wages). For decades, federal courts have endorsed the Board's view, comprehending that "the filing of a labor related civil action by a group of employees is ordinarily a concerted activity protected by § 7." *Leviton Mfg. Co. v. NLRB,* 486 F.2d 686, 689 (C.A.1 1973); see, *e.g., Brady v. National Football League,* 644 F.3d 661, 673 (C.A.8 2011) (similar). The Court pays scant heed to this longstanding line of decisions.

D

In face of the NLRA's text, history, purposes, and longstanding construction, the Court nevertheless concludes that collective proceedings do not fall within the scope of § 7. None of the Court's reasons for diminishing § 7 should carry the day.

1

The Court relies principally on the *ejusdem generis* canon. Observing that § 7's "other concerted activities" clause "appears at the end of a detailed list of activities," the Court says the clause should be read to "embrace" only activities "similar in nature" to those set forth first in the list, *ibid.* (internal quotation marks omitted), *i.e.,* " 'self-organization,' 'form[ing], join[ing], or assist[ing] labor organizations,' and 'bargain[ing] collectively,' " *ibid.* The Court concludes that § 7 should, therefore, be read to protect "things employees 'just do' for themselves." *Ibid.* (quoting *NLRB v. Alternative Entertainment, Inc.,* 858 F.3d 393, 415 (C.A.6 2017) (Sutton, J., concurring in part and dissenting in part); emphasis deleted). It is far from apparent why joining hands in litigation would not qualify as "things employees just do for themselves." In any event, there is no sound reason to employ the *ejusdem generis* canon to narrow § 7's protections in the manner the Court suggests.

The *ejusdem generis* canon may serve as a useful guide where it is doubtful Congress intended statutory words or phrases to have the broad scope their ordinary meaning conveys. See *Russell Motor Car Co. v. United States,* 261 U.S. 514, 519, 43 S.Ct. 428, 67 L.Ed. 778 (1923). Courts must take care, however, not to deploy the canon to undermine Congress' efforts to draft encompassing legislation. See *United States v. Powell,* 423 U.S. 87, 90, 96 S.Ct. 316, 46 L.Ed.2d 228 (1975) ("[W]e would be justified in narrowing the statute only if such a narrow reading was supported by evidence of congressional intent over and above the language of the statute."). Nothing suggests that Congress envisioned a cramped construction of the NLRA. Quite the opposite, Congress expressed an embracive purpose in enacting the legislation, *i.e.,* to "protec[t] the exercise by workers of full freedom of association." 29 U.S.C. § 151.

2

In search of a statutory hook to support its application of the *ejusdem generis* canon, the Court turns to the NLRA's "structure." Citing a handful of provisions that touch upon unionization, collective bargaining, picketing, and strikes, the Court asserts that the NLRA "establish [es] a regulatory regime" governing each of the activities protected by § 7. That regime, the Court says, offers "specific guidance" and "rules" regulating each protected activity. Observing that none of the NLRA's provisions explicitly regulates employees' resort to collective litigation, the Court insists that "it is hard to fathom why Congress would take such care to regulate all the other matters mentioned in [§ 7] yet remain mute about this matter alone—unless, of course, [§ 7] doesn't speak to class and collective action procedures in the first place." *Ibid.*

This argument is conspicuously flawed. When Congress enacted the NLRA in 1935, the only § 7 activity Congress addressed with any specificity was employees' selection of collective-bargaining representatives. See 49 Stat. 453. The Act did not offer "specific guidance" about employees' rights to "form, join, or assist labor organizations." Nor did it set forth "specific guidance" for any activity falling within § 7's "other concerted activities" clause. The only provision that touched upon an activity falling within that clause stated: "Nothing in this Act shall be construed so as to interfere with or impede or diminish in any way the right to strike." *Id.,* at 457. That provision hardly offered "specific guidance" regarding employees' right to strike.

Without much in the original Act to support its "structure" argument, the Court cites several provisions that Congress added later, in response to particular concerns. Compare 49 Stat. 449–457 with 61 Stat. 142–143 (1947) (adding § 8(d) to provide guidance regarding employees' and employers' collective-bargaining obligations); 61 Stat. 141–142 (amending § 8(a) and adding § 8(b) to proscribe specified labor organization practices); 73 Stat. 544 (1959) (adding § 8(b)(7) to place restrictions on labor organizations' right to picket employers). It is difficult to comprehend why Congress' later inclusion of specific guidance regarding some of the activities protected by § 7 sheds any light on Congress' initial conception of § 7's scope. But even if each of the provisions the Court cites had been included in the original Act, they still would provide little support for the Court's conclusion. For going on 80 years now, the Board and federal courts—including this one—have understood § 7 to protect numerous activities for which the Act provides no "specific" regulatory guidance.

3

[T]he Court maintains that the NLRA does not "even whispe[r]" about the "rules [that] should govern the adjudication of class or collective actions in court or arbitration." The employees here involved, of course, do not look to the NLRA for the procedures enabling them to vindicate their employment rights in arbitral or judicial forums. They assert that the Act establishes their right to act in concert using existing, generally available procedures, and to do so free from employer interference. The FLSA and the Federal Rules on joinder and class actions provide the procedures pursuant to which the employees may ally to pursue shared legal claims. Their employers cannot lawfully cut off their access to those procedures, they urge, without according them access to similar procedures in arbitral forums. See, *e.g.,* American Arbitration Assn., Supplementary Rules for Class Arbitrations (2011).

4

Further attempting to sow doubt about § 7's scope, the Court asserts that class and collective procedures were "hardly known when the NLRA was adopted in 1935." *Ante,* at 1624–1625. In particular, the Court notes, the FLSA's collective-litigation procedure postdated § 7 "by years" and Rule 23 "didn't create the modern class action until 1966." *Ibid.*

First, one may ask, is there any reason to suppose that Congress intended to protect employees' right to act in concert using only those procedures and forums available in 1935? Congress framed § 7 in broad terms, "entrust[ing]" the Board with "responsibility to adapt the Act to changing patterns of industrial life." *NLRB v. J. Weingarten, Inc.,* 420 U.S. 251, 266 (1975). With fidelity to Congress' aim, the Board and federal courts have recognized that the NLRA shields employees from employer interference when they, *e.g.,* join together to file complaints with administrative agencies, even if those agencies did not exist in 1935. See, *e.g., Wray Electric Contracting, Inc.,* 210 N.L.R.B. 757, 762 (1974) (the NLRA protects concerted filing of complaint with the Occupational Safety and Health Administration).

Moreover, the Court paints an ahistorical picture. As Judge Wood, writing for the Seventh Circuit, cogently explained, the FLSA's collective-litigation procedure and the modern class action were "not written on a clean slate." 823 F.3d 1147, 1154 (2016). By 1935, permissive joinder was scarcely uncommon in courts of equity. See 7 C. Wright, A. Miller, & M. Kane, Federal Practice and Procedure § 1651 (3d ed. 2001). Nor were representative and class suits novelties. Indeed, their origins trace back to medieval times. See S. Yeazell, From Medieval Group Litigation to the Modern Class Action 38 (1987). And beyond question, "[c]lass suits long have been a part of American jurisprudence." 7A Wright, *supra,* § 1751, at 12 (3d ed. 2005). It takes no imagination, then, to comprehend that Congress, when it enacted the NLRA, likely meant to protect employees' joining together to engage in collective litigation.

III

The inevitable result of today's decision will be the underenforcement of federal and state statutes designed to advance the well-being of vulnerable workers. See generally Jean R. Sternlight, *Disarming Employees: How American Employers Are Using Mandatory Arbitration To Deprive Workers of Legal Protections,* 80 Brooklyn L. Rev. 1309 (2015). The probable impact on wage and hours claims of the kind asserted in the cases now before the Court is all too evident. Violations of minimum-wage and overtime laws are widespread. See Ruan 1109–1111; A. Bernhardt et al., Broken Laws, Unprotected Workers: Violations of Employment and Labor Laws in America's Cities 11–16, 21–22 (2009).

If employers can stave off collective employment litigation aimed at obtaining redress for wage and hours infractions, the enforcement gap is almost certain to widen. Expenses entailed in mounting individual claims will often far outweigh potential recoveries. See *id.,* at 1184–1185 (because "the FLSA systematically tends to generate low-value claims," "mechanisms that facilitate the economics of claiming are required"); *Sutherland v. Ernst & Young LLP,* 768 F.Supp.2d 547, 552 (S.D.N.Y.2011) (finding that an employee utilizing Ernst & Young's arbitration program would likely have to spend $200,000 to recover only $1,867.02 in overtime pay and an equivalent amount in liquidated damages).

Fear of retaliation may also deter potential claimants from seeking redress alone. See, *e.g.,* Ruan 1119–1121; Bernhardt, *supra,* at 3, 24–25. Further inhibiting single-file claims is the slim relief obtainable, even of the injunctive kind. See *Califano v. Yamasaki,* 442 U.S. 682, 702, 99 S.Ct. 2545, 61 L.Ed.2d 176 (1979) ("[T]he scope of injunctive relief is dictated by the extent of the violation established."). The upshot: Employers, aware that employees will be disinclined to pursue small-value claims when confined to proceeding one-by-one, will no doubt perceive that the cost-benefit balance of underpaying workers tips heavily in favor of skirting legal obligations.

In stark contrast to today's decision, the Court has repeatedly recognized the centrality of group action to the effective enforcement of antidiscrimination statutes. With Court approbation, concerted legal actions have played a critical role in enforcing prohibitions against workplace discrimination based on race, sex, and other protected characteristics. See, *e.g., Griggs v. Duke Power Co.,* 401 U.S. 424, 91 S.Ct. 849, 28 L.Ed.2d 158 (1971). That reality, as just noted, holds true for enforcement of wage and hours laws.

I do not read the Court's opinion to place in jeopardy discrimination complaints asserting disparate-impact and pattern-or-practice claims that call for proof on a group-wide basis, see Brief for NAACP Legal Defense & Educational Fund, Inc., et al. as *Amici Curiae* 19–25, which some courts have concluded cannot be maintained by solo complainants, see, *e.g., Chin v. Port Auth. of N.Y. & N.J.,* 685 F.3d 135, 147 (C.A.2 2012) (pattern-or-practice method of proving race discrimination is unavailable in non-class actions).

I note, finally, that individual arbitration of employee complaints can give rise to anomalous results. Arbitration agreements often include provisions requiring that outcomes be kept confidential or barring arbitrators from giving prior proceedings precedential effect. As a result, arbitrators may render conflicting awards in cases involving similarly situated employees—even employees working for the same employer.

* * *

If these untoward consequences stemmed from legislative choices, I would be obliged to accede to them. But the edict that employees with wage and hours claims may seek relief only one-by-one does not come from Congress. It is the result of take-it-or-leave-it labor contracts harking back to the type called "yellow dog," and of the readiness of this Court to enforce those unbargained-for agreements. The FAA demands no such suppression of the right of workers to take concerted action for their "mutual aid or protection." Accordingly, I would reverse the judgment of the Fifth Circuit . . . and affirm the judgments of the Seventh and Ninth Circuits.

NOTES

1.   *Two ships passing in the night?* The contrasting styles of the majority and dissenting opinions are notable. The sheer breadth of the majority opinion is striking, and seems political and facile while the dissent emphasizes a more traditional approach to statutory interpretation, including the usual rule that a later enacted statute (NLRA) supersedes an earlier one (FAA) if there is a conflict, plus deference to the NLRB's longstanding view that concerted activity includes not only striking or picketing to improve wages but also filing collective actions. Do you agree? If so, what do you make of this? Is it possibly further evidence of the polarization of political views? Do you think the majority approach in *EPIC* is consistent with earlier U.S. Supreme Court opinions in *Washington Aluminum* or *Eastex*?

2.   *"Concerted Activity"—view it narrowly or broadly?* The majority opinion takes a quite narrow view of the phrase "concerted activities for the purpose of . . .other mutual aid or protection." The majority invokes *ejusdem generis,* an interpretation principle that the majority views as meaning that a later catch-all generic term, in this case "other mutual aid or protection," must be understood "to embrace only objects similar in nature to those objects enumerated by the preceding specific words." The dissent, however, cautions against using the principle of *ejusdem generis* to limit what Congress is trying to do, and points to the broad and general language used by Congress in the NLRA and its history when discussing worker rights. Which argument are you persuaded by? What are the implications of an *ejusdem generis* reading of the scope of Section 7?

3.   *Epic Systems* overturned the Board's expansive view of the phrase "concerted activities for the purpose of . . . other mutual aid and protection" adopted in *D.R. Horton, Inc.,* 357 N.L.R.B. 2277 (2012), and *Murphy Oil,* 361 N.L.R.B. 774 (2014), in which the Board maintained that NLRA Section 7 prohibited employer-required employee waivers of collective or class action litigation rights in favor of arbitration. For a good treatment of the *D.R. Horton* decision and an argument supporting its holding, see Charles A. Sullivan and Timothy P. Glynn, *Horton Hatches the Egg: Concerted Action Includes Concerted Dispute Resolution,* 64 Ala. L. Rev. 1013 (2013).

2. THE EFFECT OF EMPLOYER HANDBOOKS/ WORK RULES ON CONCERTED ACTIVITY

THE BOEING COMPANY
365 N.L.R.B. No. 154 (2017)

By CHAIRMAN MISCIMARRA and MEMBERS PEARCE, MCFERRAN, KAPLAN, and EMANUEL:

This case involves the legality of an employer policy, which is one of a multitude of work rules, policies and employee handbook provisions that have been reviewed by the Board using a test set forth in *Lutheran Heritage Village-Livonia*, 343 NLRB 646 (2004). In this case, the issue is whether Respondent's mere maintenance of a facially neutral rule is unlawful under the *Lutheran Heritage* "reasonably construe" standard, which is also sometimes called *Lutheran Heritage* "prong one" (because it is the first prong of a three-prong standard in *Lutheran Heritage*). Thus, in *Lutheran Heritage*, the Board stated:

> [O]ur inquiry into whether the maintenance of a challenged rule is unlawful begins with the issue of whether the rule explicitly restricts activities protected by Section 7. If it does, we will find the rule unlawful. If the rule does not explicitly restrict activity protected by Section 7, the violation is dependent upon a showing of one of the following: (1) *employees would reasonably construe the language to prohibit Section 7 activity*; (2) the rule was promulgated in response to union activity; or (3) the rule has been applied to restrict the exercise of Section 7 rights.

Id. at 646–647. Most of the cases decided under *Lutheran Heritage* have involved the *Lutheran Heritage* "reasonably construe" standard,[4] which the judge relied upon in the instant case. Specifically, the judge ruled that Respondent, The Boeing Company (Boeing), maintained a no-camera rule that constituted unlawful interference with the exercise of protected rights in violation of Section 8(a)(1) of the National Labor Relations Act (NLRA or Act).

Boeing designs and manufactures military and commercial aircraft at various facilities throughout the United States. The work undertaken at Boeing's facilities is highly sensitive; some of it is classified. Boeing's facilities are targets for espionage by competitors, foreign governments, and supporters of international terrorism, and Boeing faces a realistic threat of terrorist attack. Maintaining the security of its facilities and of the information housed therein is critical not only for Boeing's success as a

---

[4] For ease of reference, we refer hereafter to prong one of the *Lutheran Heritage* standard as "*Lutheran Heritage*." Also, we use the term "facially neutral" to describe policies, rules and handbook provisions that do not expressly restrict Sec. 7 activity, were not adopted in response to NLRA-protected activity, and have not been applied to restrict NLRA-protected activity.

business—particularly its eligibility to continue serving as a contractor to the federal government—but also for national security.

Boeing maintains a policy restricting the use of camera-enabled devices such as cell phones on its property. For convenience, we refer to this policy (which is contained in a more comprehensive policy Boeing calls "PRO-2783") as the "no-camera rule." Boeing's no-camera rule does not explicitly restrict activity protected by Section 7 of the Act, it was not adopted in response to NLRA-protected activity, and it has not been applied to restrict such activity. Nevertheless, applying prong one of the test set forth in *Lutheran Heritage*, the judge found that Boeing's maintenance of this rule violated Section 8(a)(1) of the Act. Based on *Lutheran Heritage*, the judge reasoned that maintenance of Boeing's no-camera rule was unlawful because employees "would reasonably construe" the rule to prohibit Section 7 activity.[6] In finding the no-camera rule unlawful, the judge gave no weight to Boeing's security needs for the rule.

The judge's decision in this case exposes fundamental problems with the Board's application of *Lutheran Heritage* when evaluating the maintenance of work rules, policies and employee handbook provisions. [W]e have decided to overrule the *Lutheran Heritage* "reasonably construe" standard. The Board will no longer find unlawful the mere maintenance of facially neutral employment policies, work rules and handbook provisions based on a single inquiry, which made legality turn on whether an employee "would reasonably construe" a rule to prohibit some type of potential Section 7 activity that might (or might not) occur in the future. In our view, multiple defects are inherent in the *Lutheran Heritage* test. . . .

Paradoxically, *Lutheran Heritage* is too simplistic at the same time it is too difficult to apply. The Board's responsibility is to discharge the "special function of applying the general provisions of the Act to the complexities of industrial life." Though well-intentioned, the *Lutheran Heritage* standard prevents the Board from giving meaningful consideration to the real-world "complexities" associated with many employment policies, work rules and handbook provisions. Moreover, *Lutheran Heritage* produced rampant confusion for employers, employees and unions. Indeed, the Board itself has struggled when attempting to apply *Lutheran Heritage*: since 2004, Board members have regularly disagreed with one another regarding the legality of particular rules or

---

[6] The judge additionally found that the Respondent engaged in unlawful surveillance when its security guards photographed employees engaged in union activity, and that it created an impression of surveillance when a security guard told employees that he had been directed to document all union activity and that he was taking photographs of "non-Boeing" activity. We agree with the judge, for the reasons stated in his decision, that the Respondent engaged in surveillance and created the impression of surveillance in violation of Sec. 8(a)(1) of the Act.

requirements, and in many cases, decisions by the Board (or a Board majority) have been overturned by the courts of appeals.[9]

These problems have been exacerbated by the zeal that has characterized the Board's application of the *Lutheran Heritage* "reasonably construe" test. Over the past decade and one-half, the Board has invalidated a large number of common-sense rules and requirements that most people would reasonably expect every employer to maintain. We do not believe that when Congress adopted the NLRA in 1935, it envisioned that an employer would violate federal law whenever employees were advised to "work harmoniously" or conduct themselves in a "positive and professional manner." Nevertheless, in *William Beaumont Hospital*, the Board majority found that it violated federal law for a hospital to state that nurses and doctors should foster "harmonious interactions and relationships," and Chairman (then-Member) Miscimarra stated in dissent:

> Nearly all employees in every workplace aspire to have "harmonious" dealings with their coworkers. Nobody can be surprised that a hospital, of all workplaces, would place a high value on "harmonious interactions and relationships." There is no evidence that the requirement of "harmonious" relationships actually discouraged or interfered with NLRA-protected activity in this case. Yet, in the world created by *Lutheran Heritage*, it is unlawful to state what virtually every employee desires and what virtually everyone understands the employer reasonably expects.

William Beaumont Hospital, supra, slip op. at 8. Under the standard we adopt today, when evaluating a facially neutral policy, rule or handbook provision that, when reasonably interpreted, would potentially interfere with the exercise of NLRA rights, the Board will evaluate two things: (i) the nature and extent of the potential impact on NLRA rights, *and* (ii)

---

[9]   See, e.g., *William Beaumont Hospital*, 363 NLRB No. 162 (2016) (Board majority, contrary to dissenting Member Miscimarra, invalidates rule prohibiting conduct that "impedes harmonious interactions and relationships"); *Whole Foods Market, Inc.*, 363 NLRB No. 87 (2015) (Board majority, contrary to dissenting Member Miscimarra, invalidates no-recording rule aimed at fostering employee free expression), enfd. mem. 691 Fed. Appx. 49 (2d Cir. 2017); *Triple Play Sports Bar & Grille*, 361 NLRB 308 (2014) (Board majority, contrary to dissenting Member Miscimarra, invalidates rule stating that social media use "may be violating the law and is subject to disciplinary action" if the employee engages in "inappropriate discussions about the company"), affd. sub nom. *Three D, LLC v. NLRB*, 629 Fed. Appx. 33 (2d Cir. 2015); *Fresh & Easy Neighborhood Market*, 361 NLRB 72 (2014) (Board majority, contrary to dissenting Member Johnson, invalidates rule requiring employees to "[k]eep customer and employee information secure"); *Flagstaff Medical Center*, 357 NLRB 659 (2011) (Board majority, contrary to dissenting Member Pearce, finds lawful an employer's no-camera rule in an acute-care hospital), petition for review granted in part and denied in part 715 F.3d 928 (D.C. Cir. 2013); *Hyundai America Shipping Agency, Inc.*, 357 NLRB 860 (2011), enf. denied in part 805 F.3d 309 (D.C. Cir. 2015) (court rejects Board's invalidation of rule stating "[v]oice your complaints directly to your immediate superior or to Human Resources through our 'open door' policy"); *Guardsmark, LLC*, 344 NLRB 809 (2005), enf. denied in relevant part 475 F.3d 369 (D.C. Cir. 2007) (court rejects Board's finding that a rule lawfully stated employees must not "fraternize on duty or off duty, date or become overly friendly with the client's employees or with co-employees").

legitimate justifications associated with the rule. We emphasize that *the Board* will conduct this evaluation, consistent with the Board's "duty to strike the *proper balance* between . . . asserted business justifications and the invasion of employee rights in light of the Act and its policy," focusing on the perspective of employees, which is consistent with Section 8(a)(1). As the result of this balancing, in this and future cases, the Board will delineate three categories of employment policies, rules and handbook provisions (hereinafter referred to as "rules"):

- *Category 1* will include rules that the Board designates as lawful to maintain, either because (i) the rule, when reasonably interpreted, does not prohibit or interfere with the exercise of NLRA rights; or (ii) the potential adverse impact on protected rights is outweighed by justifications associated with the rule. Examples of Category 1 rules are the no-camera requirement in this case, the "harmonious interactions and relationships" rule that was at issue in *William Beaumont Hospital*, and other rules requiring employees to abide by basic standards of civility.[15]

- *Category 2* will include rules that warrant individualized scrutiny in each case as to whether the rule would prohibit or interfere with NLRA rights, and if so, whether any adverse impact on NLRA-protected conduct is outweighed by legitimate justifications.

- *Category 3* will include rules that the Board will designate as *unlawful* to maintain because they would prohibit or limit NLRA-protected conduct, and the adverse impact on NLRA rights is not outweighed by justifications associated with the rule. An example

---

[15] Although the *maintenance* of Category 1 rules (and certain Category 2 rules) will be lawful, the *application* of such rules to employees who have engaged in NLRA-protected conduct may violate the Act, depending on the particular circumstances presented in a given case.

To the extent the Board in past cases has held that it violates the Act to maintain rules requiring employees to foster "harmonious interactions and relationships" or to maintain basic standards of civility in the workplace, those cases are hereby overruled. As then-Member Miscimarra observed in his dissent in *William Beaumont Hospital*, such rules reflect common-sense standards of conduct that advance substantial employee and employer interests, including the employer's legal responsibility to maintain a work environment free of unlawful harassment based on sex, race or other protected characteristics, its substantial interest in preventing workplace violence, and its interest in avoiding unnecessary conflict that interferes with patient care (in a hospital), productivity and other legitimate business goals; and nearly every employee would desire and expect his or her employer to foster harmony and civility in the workplace. We do not believe these types of employer requirements, when reasonably interpreted, would prohibit or interfere with the exercise of NLRA rights. However, even if basic civility requirements are viewed as potentially interfering with NLRA rights, we believe any adverse effect would be comparatively slight, because a broad range of activities protected by the NLRA are consistent with basic standards of harmony and civility; therefore, rules requiring workplace harmony and civility would have little if any adverse impact on these types of protected activities. Moreover, under the standard we announce today, when an employer lawfully maintains rules requiring employees to foster harmony and civility in the workplace, the *application* of such rules to employees who engage in NLRA-protected conduct may violate the Act, which the Board will determine based on the particular facts in each case.

of a Category 3 rule would be a rule that prohibits employees from discussing wages or benefits with one another.

The above three categories will represent a classification of *results* from the Board's application of the new test. The categories are not part of the test itself. The Board will determine, in future cases, what types of additional rules fall into which category. Although the legality of some rules will turn on the particular facts in a given case, we believe the standard adopted today will provide far greater clarity and certainty to employees, employers and unions. The Board's cumulative experience with certain types of rules may prompt the Board to re-designate particular types of rules from one category to another, although one can expect such circumstances to be relatively rare.

We emphasize that Category 1 consists of two subparts: (a) rules that are lawful because, when reasonably interpreted,[16] they would have no tendency to interfere with Section 7 rights and therefore no balancing of rights and justifications is warranted, and (b) rules that are lawful because, although they do have a reasonable tendency to interfere with Section 7 rights, the Board has determined that the risk of such interference is outweighed by the justifications associated with the rules.[17] Of course, as reflected in Categories 2 and 3, if a particular type of rule is determined to have a potential adverse impact on NLRA activity, the Board may conclude that maintenance of the rule is *unlawful*, either because individualized scrutiny reveals that the rule's potential adverse impact outweighs any justifications (Category 2), or because the type of rule at issue predictably has an adverse impact on Section 7 rights that outweighs any justifications (Category 3). Again, even when a rule's *maintenance* is deemed lawful, the Board will examine circumstances where the rule is *applied* to discipline employees who have engaged in NLRA-protected activity, and in such situations, the discipline may be found to violate the Act.

The balancing of employee rights and employer interests is not a new concept with respect to the Board's analysis of work rules. For example, in *Lafayette Park Hotel*, the Board expressly stated that "[r]esolution of the

---

[16] [M]ember Kaplan emphasizes this is an objective standard, and the reasonable interpretation of the rule is conducted from the perspective of a reasonable employee.

[17] Member Kaplan agrees with Chairman Miscimarra and Member Emanuel on the three categories described in the text. However, Member Kaplan would have preferred a structure in which Category 1's subparts would be separate, rather than being grouped into a single category.

Nonetheless, Chairman Miscimarra and Members Kaplan and Emanuel agree that in every future work-rules case, the Board will make the following distinctions when determining the legality of different types of rules: (i) rules that are generally lawful because, when reasonably interpreted, they do not prohibit or interfere with the exercise of NLRA rights; (ii) rules that are generally lawful even though they potentially interfere with the exercise of NLRA rights, but where this risk is outweighed by legitimate justifications; (iii) rules that warrant individualized scrutiny in each case; and (iv) rules that are generally unlawful because their potential interference with the exercise of protected rights outweighs any possible justifications. Under the three categories outlined in the text, groups "i" and "ii" will both be included in Category 1 (rules that the Board will find to be generally lawful).

issue presented by the contested rules of conduct involves 'working out an adjustment between the undisputed right of self-organization assured to employees under the Wagner Act and the equally undisputed right of employers to maintain discipline in their establishments. . . . Opportunity to organize and proper discipline are both essential elements in a balanced society.' " Since *Lutheran Heritage*, the Board has far too often failed to give adequate consideration and weight to employer interests in its analysis of work rules. Accordingly, we find that the Board must replace the *Lutheran Heritage* test with an analysis that will ensure a meaningful balancing of employee rights and employer interests.

Applying these standards to the instant case, we find below that the Respondent's justifications for Boeing's restrictions on the use of camera-enabled devices on Boeing property outweigh the rule's more limited adverse effect on the exercise of Section 7 rights. We therefore reverse the judge's finding that Boeing's maintenance of its no-camera rule violates Section 8(a)(1) of the Act.

II. DISCUSSION

D. *Application of the New Standard to Boeing's No-Camera Rule*

To determine the lawfulness of Boeing's no-camera rule under the standard we adopt today, the Board must determine whether the no-camera rule, when reasonably interpreted, would potentially interfere with the exercise of Section 7 rights, and if so, the Board must evaluate two things: (i) the nature and extent of the no-camera rule's adverse impact on Section 7 rights, *and* (ii) the legitimate business justifications associated with the no-camera rule. Based on our review of the record and our evaluation of the considerations described above, we find that the no-camera rule in some circumstances may potentially affect the exercise of Section 7 rights, but this adverse impact is comparatively slight. We also find that the adverse impact is outweighed by substantial and important justifications associated with Boeing's maintenance of the no-camera rule. Accordingly, we find that Boeing's maintenance of its no-camera rule does not constitute unlawful interference with protected rights in violation of Section 8(a)(1) of the Act. Although the justifications associated with Boeing's no-camera rule are especially compelling, we believe that no-camera rules, in general, fall into Category 1, types of rules that the Board will find lawful based on the considerations described above.

As stated above, the policy at issue here is Boeing's no-camera rule, which provides in relevant part as follows:

> Possession of the following camera-enabled devices is permitted on all company property and locations, except as restricted by government regulation, contract requirements or by increased local security requirements.

However, **use** of these devices to capture images or video is prohibited without a valid business need and an approved Camera Permit that has been reviewed and approved by Security:

5.   Personal Digital Assistants (PDAs)

6.   Cellular telephones and Blackberrys and iPod/MP3 devices

7.   Laptop or personal computers with web cameras for desktop video conferencing, including external webcams.

8.   Bar code scanners and bar code readers, or such devices for manufacturing, inventory, or other work, if those devices are capable of capturing images

Boeing's no-camera rule defines "business need" as "a determination made by the authorizing manager that images or video are needed for a contractual requirement, training, technical manuals, advertising, technical analysis, or other purpose that provides a positive benefit to the company."

Boeing Senior Security Manager James Harris furnished undisputed testimony concerning Boeing's justifications for maintaining its no-camera rule. His testimony establishes the following.

First, Boeing's no-camera rule is an integral component of Boeing's security protocols, which are necessary to maintain Boeing's accreditation as a federal contractor to perform classified work for the United States Government. These protocols involve layers of security, including the physical construction of the facilities themselves, a fenced perimeter, security officers, and background checks for personnel granted access to classified information. Boeing's rule regulating the use of camera-enabled devices is another of these layers of security. It furnishes a fail-safe to ensure that classified information will not be released outside of Boeing in the event that such information finds its way into a non-classified area.

Second, Boeing's no-camera rule plays a key role in ensuring that Boeing complies with its federally mandated duty to prevent the disclosure of export-controlled information or the exposure of export-controlled materials to unauthorized persons. "Export-controlled" materials include "sensitive equipment, software and technology," the export of which is controlled by the federal government "as a means to promote our national security and foreign policy objectives." For example, the export-control system "[p]revent[s] proliferation of weapons and technologies, including weapons of mass destruction, to problem end-users and supporters of international terrorism." Senior Security Manager Harris testified that the term *export* means "delivering information, technology or hardware to a non-U.S. person," and he added that "[a]n export can occur visually, orally or otherwise either within the United States or outside the United States."

In other words, export-controlled materials can be "delivered" visually, and therefore an "export" can occur when a "non-U.S. person" merely *sees* export-controlled materials. Boeing regulates the export of export-controlled materials in a variety of ways, including through the enforcement of standoff distances. Harris testified that a "standoff distance" is the distance from an object at which the eye "cannot see enough detail to constitute an export." However, *camera-enabled devices can defeat the purpose of a standoff distance.* Thus, Harris testified that even cell phones "are high enough resolution that if someone took a photograph even at the 25-foot standoff distance of an export-controlled item, that resolution could be refined and expanded to be able to get enough detail to determine what about it might be export controlled." Export-controlled information can be found at nearly every Boeing site in the Puget Sound region. Export violations may subject Boeing to fines of up to $1 million per incident, and they may result in Boeing being debarred from government contracts—not to mention the injury an export violation potentially may inflict on national security.

Third, Boeing's no-camera rule helps prevent the disclosure of Boeing's proprietary information, which Harris defined as "any nonpublic information that has potential economic value to Boeing," such as "manufacturing methods and processes" and "material usage." Proprietary information routinely may be found on the factory floor. Measures such as Boeing's no-camera rule to protect Boeing's proprietary information are critically important. Senior Security Manager Harris testified that Boeing "regularly receives reports" of "efforts" by "non-U.S. Government agencies" to "task visitors to . . . Boeing . . . with gaining specific kinds of manufacturing technologies, parts, processes, [and] material usage." Harris further testified concerning "documented circumstances" of "foreign powers . . . combing . . . through social media to gain knowledge about manufacturing techniques, manufacturing processes, and material usage that they do not currently have within their own countries in order to develop their own aircraft industries." Photographs or videos posted on social media websites "can be used as a tool to exploit their . . . mission."

Fourth, Boeing's no-camera rule limits the risk that employees' personally identifiable information will be released. Besides the invasion of employee privacy, photographs and videos that permit Boeing employees to be identified could also compromise proprietary information. For example, Harris testified that if a member of "the economic intelligence community"—i.e., an industrial spy—obtains a photograph that identifies someone as a Boeing employee, that photograph could potentially serve as a starting point to establish a seeming friendship for the ulterior purpose of eliciting proprietary information. In addition, if a photograph shows an employee's badge, that image could be used to create a counterfeit badge that an unauthorized person may use to gain entry to Boeing property.

Fifth, Boeing's no-camera rule limits the risk of Boeing becoming a target of terrorist attack. Harris testified that Boeing has "documented evidence" of surveillance by potentially hostile actors "to determine vulnerabilities" on Boeing property, and "[u]ncontrolled photography" could inadvertently disclose such vulnerabilities—such as "gaps in the fence line," "key utility entry points," "gas lines, hazardous chemical pipelines, [and] electrical substations."

The General Counsel sought to counter Boeing's claims regarding the justifications for maintaining the no-camera rule. For example, it is undisputed that Boeing conducts both public and VIP tours of some of its facilities, Boeing does not search tour participants for camera-enabled devices, and tour guides are not authorized to confiscate personal camera-enabled devices from individuals who have used them during a tour. However, Boeing's 777 Director of Manufacturing and Operations Jason Clark testified that tour participants are briefed before the tour begins regarding what is and is not allowed during the tour, and Boeing security personnel review tour participants' photos and video footage after the tour. The General Counsel sought to contest Clark's testimony by introducing the testimony of employee Shannon Moriarty. Moriarty testified that she participated in one VIP tour of Boeing's Everett, Washington facility. According to Moriarty, she was permitted to take photos during that tour, she was the last tour participant to leave, and at no time did Boeing personnel review her photos or anyone else's. Notwithstanding this evidence of a single instance when the practice of reviewing tour participants' photos may not have been followed, no evidence was introduced that disputed Clark's testimony that such reviews are standard practice. Moreover, the tour in which Moriarty participated was a VIP tour, and Senior Security Manager Harris testified that an effort is made to ensure that VIP tour participants in particular are not exposed to proprietary information.

Boeing occasionally holds "rollouts" of new products, at which time the large bay doors of the factory are open, and persons standing in proximity to the facility but off Boeing property are able to look inside the facility. During a rollout, however, Boeing ensures that sensitive information is not visible to such persons.

[T]he adverse impact of Boeing's no-camera rule on NLRA-protected activity is comparatively slight. The vast majority of images or videos blocked by the policy do not implicate any NLRA rights. Moreover, the Act only protects concerted activities that two or more employees engage in for the purpose of mutual aid or protection. Taking photographs to post on social media for the purpose of entertaining or impressing others, for example, certainly falls outside of the Act's protection. Additionally, in the instant case, there is no allegation that Boeing's no-camera rule has actually interfered with any type of Section 7 activity, nor is there any evidence that the rule prevented employees from engaging in protected activity.

We find that any adverse impact of Boeing's no-camera rule on the exercise of Section 7 rights is comparatively slight and is outweighed by substantial and important justifications associated with the no-camera rule's maintenance. Accordingly, we find that Boeing's maintenance of the no-camera rule did not constitute unlawful interference with protected rights in violation of Section 8(a)(1) of the Act.

MEMBER PEARCE, dissenting in part.

Overruling 13-year-old precedent, the majority today institutes a new standard for determining whether the maintenance of a challenged work rule, policy, or employee handbook provision is unlawful. Although characterized by the majority as a balancing test, its new standard is essentially a how-to manual for employers intent on stifling protected concerted activity before it begins. Overly protective of employer interests and under protective of employee rights, the majority's standard gives employers the green light to maintain rules that chill employees in the exercise of rights guaranteed by the National Labor Relations Act. Because the new standard is fundamentally at odds with the underlying purpose of the Act, I dissent.

II

I find particularly troubling the majority's designation of rules "requiring employees to abide by basic standards of civility" as always lawful to maintain (Category 1). First, no civility rules are involved in this case. By declaring civility rules always lawful, the majority goes far beyond the issue presented in this case and essentially provides an advisory opinion. The absence of any factual context or evidentiary record—not to mention argument from parties on both sides of the issue—renders its conclusion wholly abstract. It is well established that the Board does not give advisory opinions except on narrow jurisdictional questions. This is no more than "seat-of-the-pants" rulemaking without context.

Second, since early in the history of the Act, the Board and courts have interpreted Section 7 as protecting the right of employees to engage in robust debate, to complain to their employer and fellow employees, and to criticize their employer to government agencies and the public. Section 7 protection is not dependent on whether these activities are carried out in a courteous or civil manner. In other contexts, the Board and courts have repeatedly held that negative, disparaging, disrespectful, intemperate, and vulgar remarks uttered during the course of protected activities will not remove the activities from the Act's protection unless they are flagrant, violent, or extreme.

Our experience demonstrates, moreover, that the fear of reprisal that is instilled in employees by overbroad "civility rules" is well-founded. The cases in which employers have applied such rules to discipline or discharge employees for engaging in protected concerted activity are numerous. These cases confirm the tendency of employers to interpret overbroad and ambiguous civility rules to prohibit conduct that is clearly protected under the Act. In holding unlawful the promulgation and maintenance of such rules, therefore, the Board not only eliminates a clear restraint on Section 7 activity, it also discourages a second, independent violation—enforcement of such rules to punish employees for engaging in protected concerted activity.

[A partial dissent by MEMBER MCFERRAN is omitted]

NOTES

1.   On June 6, 2018, NLRB General Counsel Peter Robb issued a Memorandum (GC 18–04) "Handbook Rules Post-Boeing." The Memorandum explains how the regional offices will initially categorize many common workplace policies and provides illustrations of the policies it categorizes. Category 1 lawful policies include those prohibiting incivility and insubordination, unauthorized photography and recording, failure to cooperate, on-the-job conduct that adversely affects operations, disruptive behavior; disclosure of confidential, proprietary and customer information; defamation or misrepresentation; use of the employer's logos or other intellectual property; speaking for the employer without authorization; disloyalty, nepotism or self-enrichment. Category 2 policies include broad conflict-of-interest rules, broad confidentiality rules, rules prohibiting disparagement of the employer and regulating use of the employer's name, and rules restricting all contact with the media. Category 3 unlawful policies include restrictions on discussing wages, benefits or working conditions, and restrictions on joining outside organizations or restrictions on voting on matters concerning the employer.

2.   In In-N-Out Burger v. NLRB, 894 F.3d 707 (5th Cir. 2018), the U.S. Court of Appeals for the Fifth Circuit upheld a Board decision (365 N.L.R.B. No. 39 (2017)) finding In-N-Out Burger's company rule broadly prohibiting workers from "wearing any type of pin or stickers" unlawful under the NLRA. The rule was invoked by the company when employees in an Austin, Texas store began wearing buttons demonstrating solidarity with the "Fight for $15" campaign advocating for a $15 minimum wage among other things. The court agreed with the Board that In-N-Out's rule "restricts its employees' Section 7 rights and therefore is presumptively unlawful." In-N-Out argued that two sets of "special circumstances" served to justify the rule. First, In-N-Out maintained that its business plan fosters a particularized public image requiring the customer experience to be consistent from one store to another. Second, In-N-Out maintained the rule was required to maintain food safety. The court upheld the Board's decision in both cases, finding first that the public

image defense failed because In-N-Out did not have sufficient evidence showing a connection between the button rule and In-N-Out's interests in consistent menu, ownership structure, customer service, and a sparkling clean environment. The court also upheld the Board's view that In-N-Out's allowance of other buttons undercut the strength of its argument. Second, the court upheld the Board's view that the same food safety concerns should exist for all buttons, but only applied against "Fight for $15." How would In-N-Out Burger be analyzed now after the Board's Boeing decision? Does In-N-Out Burger's broad prohibition fall into Category 1, 2, or 3?

D. STRIKES

Section 7 of the NLRA protects concerted activity generally, but section 13 protects the strike specifically. Section 13, as it was originally written in the Wagner Act, stated that "Nothing in this act shall be construed so as either to interfere with or impede or diminish in any way the right to strike." The Taft-Hartley Act limited the right to strike in a number of ways, and amended section 13 to read: "Nothing in this Act, except as specifically provided herein, shall be construed so as either to interfere with or impede or diminish in any way the right to strike, or to affect the limitations or qualifications on that right."

The discussion of strikes that follows is divided into the three categories that labor law gives to concerted activity for mutual aid and protection: some is protected by section 7, some is unprotected, and some is not merely unprotected by section 7 but prohibited under section 8(b).

1. WHY PROTECT STRIKES?

To understand why federal labor law protects the right to strike, it is important to understand what prompts workers to strike and why strikes are difficult for workers and firms to endure. Some see strikes as irrational and believe they would not occur if both sides were rational and well informed. On this analysis, strikes occur when labor organizations and employers miscalculate each other's willingness to concede. On the other hand, as articulated by Mancur Olson in The Logic of Collective Action (1971), strikes are a collective good because they force employers to improve wages and working conditions, but generate a free rider problem because any individual worker wishes to avoid losing wages during the strike while hoping others will engage in the conduct that forces improvements. "All of the economic incentives affecting *individuals* are on the side of those workers who do not respect the picket lines." Yet strikes are not just an economic weapon; they are sometimes an expression of cultural and political self-determination.

Strikes are events of tremendous social, economic, and emotional intensity. As you consider the recent strikes described below, consider why the workers who participate should or should not be protected by law from being fired for participating in the strike.

Teachers Strikes of 2018. In the spring of 2018, tens of thousands of public school teachers in West Virginia, Oklahoma, Kentucky, Colorado, and Arizona went on strike, ultimately securing pay increases for teachers and other school staff and increases in funding for classrooms, books, and other school expenses. All states where teachers struck had seen years of steady declines in education funding until the strike, and striking teachers earned less than teachers in neighboring states and less in real dollars than teachers on average did in thirty years before. Striking teachers complained of shortages of qualified teachers because salaries are so low. Public employee strikes are illegal in all states where teachers struck (as of this writing), and in some states (including West Virginia, where the teachers' strike shut all public schools across the state for ten days), teachers have no legal right to bargain collectively. In some states the strike persisted after the teachers' union recommended ending it because the teachers did not trust the state to make good on the promises to increase school funding. In most states, the strikes ended only when the state enacted legislation to increase school funding.

In contrast, teacher strikes in jurisdictions in which teachers and school districts bargain collectively have tended to occur only when an elaborate process for resolving negotiating disputes has failed and only to the extent that law permits public employees to strike.

Texas teachers have objected to education funding cuts and declining teacher salaries but have not struck. Texas law provides that public employees who strike lose all rights they enjoy as public employees, including pension benefits and, in the case of teachers, their state teaching credential.

Fast Food Strikes. Beginning in New York City in late 2012 and spreading across many cities throughout 2013, employees of fast food outlets staged one-day strikes. Steven Greenhouse, *A Day's Strike Seeks to Raise Fast Food Pay*, NY Times (July 31, 2013); Steven Greenhouse, *In New Wave of Walkouts, Fast Food Strikers Gain Momentum*, NY Times (Aug. 29, 2013). These were the first organized strikes by fast food workers. Similar one-day strikes occurred on April 15 in subsequent years as part of the Fight for 15 campaign ("Fight 4 15"—get it?). The NLRB held these one-day strikes were protected concerted activity and ordered employees fired for participating in them reinstated. *See EYM King of Missouri, LLC*, 365 N.L.R.B. No. 16 (2017), enf'd sub nom. *NLRB v. EYM King of Missouri, LLC*, 726 Fed. Appx. 524 (8th Cir. 2018). The strikers articulated a variety of goals. Most prominent was to raise wages, either through a change of employer policy or through enactment of local living wage ordinances or amendment to the federal or state minimum wage laws. Other goals included publicizing the bad working conditions and low pay in fast food restaurants, the desire to form a union without retaliation, to protest erratic part-time work schedules that make it difficult for workers to arrange child care, attend school, or work a second job, or, in one case, to protest having to work without air conditioning. *See, e.g.,* Daily Labor Report (May 15, 2013) (describing May 15 Milwaukee fast food workers strike); Daily Labor Report (May 13, 2013) (describing May 10 Detroit fast food workers strike); Daily Labor Report (May 9, 2013) (describing May 8–9 St. Louis fast food workers strike). Some describe the strikes as being fundamentally about building solidarity for its own sake, and as a prelude to later engaging in more concerted activity to improve working conditions:

> "At first, I was nervous," said Chicago Subway employee Felix Mendez, who [planned to] be striking for the third time [on August 29, 2013]. Still, he told *Salon* he took the lead in getting all of his three co-workers to participate in the prior strikes, shutting down their store. "If we just sit back and do nothing about it," he recalled telling them, "we're never going to get what we want." Mendez said he makes $8.25 an hour after working at Subway for three years. "Before, I wasn't really too serious about anything . . ." said Mendez. "I have changed a whole lot since I've been part of this union."

Josh Eidelson, Largest Fast Food Strike Ever Today: 58 Cities Will be Affected, Salon.com (August 29, 2013).

Black Friday Strikes. As part of an effort to highlight what labor advocates call the high cost of low prices, workers at Walmart staged many short term walkouts and protests in 2012 and 2013. The strikes and protests publicized the company's low wages, erratic part-time work schedules, and hostility to unions. The largest protests were scheduled for the Friday after Thanksgiving, the busiest shopping day of the year known colloquially as Black Friday because it is the day on which retailers learn whether their sales for the year will put the company out of debt (out of red ink and into black). The striking workers did not demand union recognition and did not appear to expect the strikes to produce an immediate change in employer policies. Rather, judging from the statements of strikers and organizers, the strikes were about increasing public awareness of poor working conditions at low-cost retailers and about mobilizing workers to believe that they could eventually change their employers' policies if they stood together. Walmart filed unfair labor practice charges with the NLRB arguing that the one-day strikes violated the provision of section 8(b)(7), which prohibits strikes with the object of organizing a union or obtaining employer recognition of a union. (Section 8(b)(7) is covered in Chapter 6.) Steven Greenhouse, *Wal-Mart Plays Down Labor Protests at Its Stores*, NY Times (Nov. 23, 2012). Should the scope of section 7 and 13 protection for strikes differ depending on the motivations or aspirations of the strikers?

Days Without Immigrants. Beginning on May 1, 2006, and recurring on several May firsts in following years, immigrants' rights groups organized massive nationwide protest rallies called "A Day Without Immigrants." The purpose of the events, which included a rally and a march in major cities, was to show the importance of immigrant workers to the American economy by, among other things, illustrating what happens when immigrant workers withhold labor for a day. Dozens of workers around the country were fired for participating in the rally and failing to report to work.

Strikes in Hollywood. In the winter of 2007–2008, the Writers Guild of America, which represents motion picture and television writers, went on strike against the production companies that make films and TV shows. The principal bone of contention was the payment of royalties, also known as residuals, to writers for distribution of shows over the Internet. Writers are paid residuals every time a film or show for which they were the credited writer is shown on TV or in a theater. In a collective bargaining agreement in the 1980s, the writers did not manage to secure the same rights to payments for material rented in a DVD/video rental store, which proved to be a major loss of possible income as DVD rentals produced huge revenue for the studios and none for writers. The growth of the Internet as a medium for the dissemination of film and TV threatened the income of writers even more; many writers regarded forcing some sharing of revenues from the new media as a do-or-die issue. After a 14-week strike, the Writers Guild won a contract that promises writers residual payments for material streamed over the Internet and other digital media. The Directors Guild, a union that represents directors, won a similar (although slightly less generous) contract shortly before the WGA, and the Screen Actors Guild, which represents actors, eventually got a similar contract term. Edward Wyatt, *Screen Actors Approve New Contract*, N.Y. Times (June 9, 2002); Scott Collins, *Yes The Strike Was Worth It*, L.A. Times (Feb. 11, 2008); *Patrick Goldstein, In the Strike, the Studios Are Playing to Win*, L.A. Times (Dec. 11, 2007).

NOTES

1.   *Understanding why workers strike.* What prompted the workers in each of these situations to strike?

2.   *Alternatives to strikes.* What other strategies might the workers have adopted to gain improvements in working conditions? How should the availability of alternatives affect whether they should be entitled to return to their jobs after the strike?

3.   *Does law matter to what happened?* Strikes by public employees, including teachers, are not legally protected in West Virginia, Oklahoma, Kentucky, and many other states. Why did the government not seek to fire the striking teachers or get an injunction against the strike? As will be covered in greater detail in Chapter 6, under the NLRA's section 7 and 13 which protect the right to strike, striking employees cannot be fired but can be permanently

replaced. Consider the impact of those rules on the length of the strike, the significance of available replacement workers, the intransigence of the employees and their employers, the importance of community support for the strikers, and any other factors that explain the reasons for a strike, the length of the strike, and what law could or should do to change the use or the course of strikes.

4. *The changing nature of strikes.* To the extent that strikes are imagined as a way to exert leverage in negotiations, many question the utility of strikes today. Berendt, Moberg & Franklin, *The Labor Strike: Is it Still a Useful Economic Weapon for Unions?*, 35 J. Marshall L. Rev. 255 (2002); Paul Johnston, *Outflanking Power, Reframing Unionism: The Basic Strike of 1999–2001*, 28 Labor Studies J. No. 4 (2004). Some strikes do occur in the context of mature bargaining relationships, as in Hollywood. Strikes to secure a collective bargaining agreement or union recognition are far less common today than they were in the 1930s or 1940s. Many of the recent strikes described above had different goals, including seeking enactment of legislation, raising public awareness about poor working conditions, and building a sense of power and self-determination among striking workers.

2. EXCEPTIONS TO SECTION 7 PROTECTIONS FOR STRIKE ACTIVITY

The definition of the strike or other concerted activity that is protected under section 7 has not been given the widest possible interpretation by the Board and the courts. A variety of refusals to work, including strikes that do not involve vacating the employer's premises, slow-downs that do not involve a complete cessation of work, or intermittent work stoppages, are not deemed to be protected activity.

Some leading cases and examples of these forms of unprotected activity are discussed below.

a. Sit-Down Strikes and Slow-Downs

The statutory language does not compel the conclusion that only a full-blown and steady strike was protected by the Act. Here, as elsewhere in federal labor law, it helps to understand both the historical context and the unstated policy concerns animating the judicial interpretation.

In 1936, when the constitutionality and the future of the Wagner Act were still in doubt, a wave of sit-down strikes occurred in basic industry. The sit-down strike was a last-ditch weapon of the CIO unions and tended to be used when employers refused to recognize or bargain with a union and retaliated against workers. Most famously, a successful sit-down strike forced the formerly vigorously antiunion General Motors Corporation to recognize and bargain with the United Auto Workers. But sit-down strikes, slow-downs, and other forms of labor protest besides a walk-out followed by picketing have occurred in almost every sector of the economy. In the fall and winter of 1936 and 1937, as sit-down strikes in Detroit involved nearly 35,000 workers, female and male hotel and restaurant employees began to use the tactic. "[T]wenty-three year old [union] organizer [Myra] Wolfgang strode to the center of Detroit's main Woolworth store and blew her strike whistle, the union's prearranged signal for workers to sit down. After Woolworth capitulated, signing an agreement covering 1400 employees, the union toppled department stores, candy and soda shops and eateries of every description. Union inroads into the hotel sector began with a 'terrific uproar' at the Barlum Hotel: two days after serving the Woolworth strikers a victory dinner, the hotel's coffee shop waitresses occupied their own workplace. After union activists barricaded themselves inside other key hotels, the Detroit Hotel Association granted union recognition and raises of 10 to 15 percent." Dorothy Sue Cobble, Dishing It Out: Waitresses and their Unions in the Twentieth Century 97 (University of Illinois Press 1991).

Once the Supreme Court upheld the constitutionality of the Wagner Act, sit-down strikes declined in frequency. Nevertheless, they still occurred in the face of sustained employer resistance to unionism. One such case was *NLRB v. Fansteel Metallurgical Corp.*, 306 U.S. 240 (1939), which overturned a Board determination that sit-down strikers were entitled to reinstatement to their jobs upon the conclusion of the strike. The sit-down strikers were entirely peaceful and took pains to oil and maintain the machinery during their occupation of the building; indeed, one reason workers thought sit-down strikes would succeed was because employers would be reluctant to risk damage to the machinery by forcibly removing the workers from the plant. The Board in *Fansteel* found that the only damage to the factory occurred when the employer's agents and the police attempted to retake the building by force using tear-gas and other weapons. Nevertheless, because the workers' physical occupation of the plant was in defiance of a state court order, the Court held that the employer had cause to fire the striking employees.

As civil rights protesters demonstrated in the United States in the 1960s, and Lech Walesa and the Solidarity Movement showed in Poland later, sit-down strikes can be a powerful tool. Mass sit-ins and other occupations of employer property still occasionally occur in hard-fought organizing campaigns, such as in the United Farm Workers' successful effort to organize California agricultural workers in the 1960s and 1970s and the Service Employees International Union's successful Justice for Janitors campaign in the late 1980s, or a group of immigrant poultry workers in North Carolina in 1993 who repeatedly struck but did not leave their workplace to protest abusive supervisors, denial of bathroom breaks, unilateral wage cuts or work speed-ups, and other demeaning treatment. In many such sit-down strikes, a union organizer will explain that sit-down strikes and plant occupations are illegal and will advise the striking workers to leave the plant to go on strike. In others, the union will not cease to end the occupation and the employees will sometimes be arrested for trespass.

Many scholars have criticized the law and law-abiding union leaders for blunting union activism by insisting on compliance with the *Fansteel* rule. *See* Karl Klare, *Deradicalization of the Wagner Act and the Origins of Modern Legal Consciousness*, 1937–1941, 62 Minn. L. Rev. 265 (1978). Klare argues:

> [S]it-down strikes were essentially a reaction to the widespread and often violent refusal by employers to obey the law between 1935 and 1940. The historical record is clear that the sit-down strikes were an indispensable weapon with which workers stemmed the tide of employer resistance to unions and to the law. The sit-down strike was important not only because it was so effective tactically, but also because it minimized the risks of picket-line violence. The traditional strike separates the employees from the workplace and from each other. Typically striking workers come together only serially, on the picket line. In the sit-down, however, workers posed themselves as collectively capable of organizing the workplace. The logistics of the sit-down required the constant participation of all in decision-making and fostered a spirit of community, cooperation, and initiative. *Fansteel* condemned a tactic designed to transcend the disjunction between the union and its members; it bolstered the forces of union bureaucracy in the efforts to quell the spontaneity of the rank and file.

Sit-down strikes also have the advantage to workers of preventing the use of replacement workers and preventing violence against strikers.

The backdrop of property rights, which gives the employer a legal right to exclude workers from the workplace, made the legality of the sit-down strike an easy case for courts (though many labor activists and labor lawyers thought sit-down strikes were or should be legal). Slow-downs are a different case for there is no backdrop of law requiring employees to work at a pace dictated by management.

ELK LUMBER COMPANY
91 N.L.R.B. 333 (1950)

[The lumber manufactured at the employer's mill was loaded in railroad cars by carloaders, working in pairs. They were paid on a piecework basis and earned, on average, $2.71 an hour. A crew of two men could load two or three cars a day if the mill ran steadily, but because of frequent interruptions in its operation, they averaged only about a car and a half a day. As a result of changes in the plant, the method of loading changed so that car loaders could work more efficiently and load more cars. At the same time, the employer unilaterally cut the rate of pay to $1.52 ½ an hour. The car-loaders protested the speed-up of work and the simultaneous pay cut by agreeing to load one car a day, which they testified was the quota at other plants in the same area and which they thought "was a good day's work at a dollar and a half." The Board found they could have loaded more cars in a day and would have done so for more pay. During a discussion between the carloaders and the company vice president, one of the carloaders, "apparently speaking for and with the approval of the entire group that had engaged in the slowdown, suggested that the Respondent either return to the piecework rate of pay or increase the hourly rate, and made it clear that the men did not intend to increase their production unless they were given a corresponding increase in pay."]

Section 7 of the Act guarantees to employees the right to engage in concerted activities for the purpose of collective bargaining or other mutual aid or protection. However, both the Board and the courts have recognized that not every form of activity that falls within the letter of this provision is protected. The test is whether the particular activity involved is so indefensible as to warrant the employer in discharging the participating employees. Either an unlawful objective or the adoption of improper means of achieving it may deprive employees engaged in concerted activities of the protection of the Act.

Here, the objective of the carloaders' concerted activity—to induce the Respondent to increase their hourly rate of pay or to return to the piecework rate—was a lawful one. To achieve this objective, however, they adopted the plan of decreasing their production to the amount they considered adequate for the pay they were then receiving. In effect, this constituted a refusal on their part to accept the terms of employment set by their employer without engaging in a stoppage, but to continue rather to work on their own terms. The courts, in somewhat similar situations, have held that such conduct is justifiable cause for discharge.

[Here the Board quoted a Seventh Circuit decision finding an employer justified in firing employees who refused to work overtime on the ground that there is "no law or logic that gives the employee the right to work upon terms prescribed solely by him." The Board also quoted an Eighth Circuit case in which employees refused to process orders from another of their employer's plants where there was a strike. The Board quoted the Eighth Circuit's statements that "It was implied in the contract of hiring that these employees would do the work assigned to them in a careful and workmanlike manner," and that although employees have "the undoubted right to go on a strike and quit their employment, they could not continue to work and remain at their positions, accept the wages paid them, and at the same time select what part of their allotted tasks they cared to perform of their own volition, or refuse openly or secretly, to the employer's damage, to do other work."]

We believe that the principle of these decisions is applicable to the situation before us, and that, under the circumstances, the carloaders' conduct justified their discharge.

Furthermore, although the Respondent admittedly did not tell the carloaders how many cars a day they were expected to load, and, so far as the present record shows, did not warn them that they would be discharged if they did not increase their production, it is clear that the men knew that the rate they had adopted was not satisfactory. Despite this knowledge, they continued to load fewer cars a day than they could have loaded, or than they would have loaded for more money. Under these particular circumstances, we regard it as immaterial that the Respondent had given them no express order as to the amount of work required, or any warning that they would be discharged if they failed to meet the requirement.

NOTES

1.   *Sit-down strikes.* Through cases like *Fansteel,* courts and the Board have construed federal labor law to protect a right to a full strike that involves a complete cessation of work and a refusal to return to the employer's premises until the resolution of the dispute that prompted the strike. The law does not protect strikes that involve a refusal to vacate the work premises (as in *Fansteel*), slowdowns (as in *Elk Lumber*) or, as will be discussed below, what are known as intermittent or "quickie" strikes (that is, repeated short-term strikes punctuated by periods during which employees work). Property rights are said to justify the prohibition on sit-down strikes. What is the basis for refusing to protect slowdowns? Can you find the basis for the refusal to protect sit downs and slowdowns in the language of section 7 or 13?

2.   *A return to the means-ends doctrine of the 19th century?* As explained in Chapter 1, courts prior to the Wagner Act judged the permissibility of employees' concerted labor protest by inquiring whether the workers' goals were permissible, and, even if the goal was permissible, whether the means chosen to achieve it were permissible. Can you see a variation on that method of analysis in the treatment of sit-down strikes in *Fansteel*? In *Elk Lumber,* was the carloaders' goal for their slow-down acceptable? Was the means chosen to achieve that goal? How does the Board justify its decision? *See* James B. Atleson, Values and Assumptions in American Labor Law ch. 3 (University of Massachusetts Press, 1983) (tracing the similarity in reasoning from "unlawful means" test of *Vegelahn* through NLRB and court decisions finding sit-downs and slow-downs to be unprotected).

b.   Intermittent Strikes

Much of the law governing strikes assumes that they are used by labor organizations as a tactic to secure recognition of a union or a collective bargaining agreement. But, as we have seen in the examples discussed above, and in cases like *Washington Aluminum* and *City Disposal,* strikes are often not coordinated by labor organizations nor are they always planned with the goal of concluding only when the employer agrees to a contract or to recognize a union. Especially recently, workers have used short strikes, typically lasting only a single day, to achieve other goals or to express frustration over working conditions without a clear goal.

Although *Washington Aluminum* and *City Disposal* make clear that short strikes by both union and nonunion employees are protected, section 7 does not protect a series of repeated, short-term stoppages as part of a pattern of "quickie" strikes designed to "confuse" the employer and to cause it economic loss because it cannot operate and cannot replace the workers. *International Union, United Auto Workers v. Wisconsin Emp. Rels. Bd. (Briggs-Stratton)*, 336 U.S. 245 (1949). The *Briggs-Stratton* rule for intermittent strikes focuses on whether the short strikes are part of a plan to "harass" the employer and are a pattern. For example, when employees struck every weekend for four weeks pursuant to a plan to keep striking until a contract dispute was resolved, the Board found the strikes unprotected. *Honolulu Rapid Transit Co.*, 110 N.L.R.B. 1806 (1954). Similarly, employees were found to have been unprotected when "a great many of the employer's 200 offices walked off on different days instead of all at the same time; at many offices they returned to work after a short time and then walked out again after a day or two; and in some offices they again returned to work briefly and later quit anew a third time." *Pacific Telephone and Telegraph*, 107 N.L.R.B. 1547, 1548 (1954).

In an advice memorandum in 1999, the Board's General Counsel articulated a four-factor test to determine whether intermittent strikes are unprotected:

> (1) The occurrence of more than two separate strikes, or threats of repeated strikes; (2) the strikes are not responses to distinct employer actions or problems with working conditions, but rather part of a strategy to use a series of strikes in support of a single goal because this would be more crippling to the employer and/or would require less sacrifice by employees than a single prolonged work stoppage during which strikers could be replaced; (3) the union announces or otherwise states its intent to pursue a plan or strategy of intermittent strikes, or there is clear factual evidence of an orchestrated strategy to engage in intermittent strike activity, and (4) the strikes are of short duration and proximate in time.

University of Southern California, 31-CA-23538 (Apr. 27, 1999). In that case the GC found protected five short strikes, separated by five weeks, as part of a two-year HERE campaign to organize food outlets at USC.

Consider whether the fast-food strikes or the Black Friday Walmart strike are unprotected under the "intermittent" strike doctrine: (a) In the fast-food industry, the employer is typically not the large company (Burger King or McDonalds) but instead is a franchisee who may own only the single restaurant. Is a nationwide series of strikes against fast food franchise restaurants owned by dozens of different companies unprotected if any particular franchisee is only struck once or twice? (b) Walmart employees announce the intent to strike annually on Black Friday and perhaps one or two other busy shopping days, but each strike is several months distant from every other strike. (c) The strikers are protesting wage and personnel practices that are relatively uniform across the sector and that any individual franchisee may find it difficult to change because prices are dictated by the franchisor. (d) The strikers engage in one-day strikes because the employer has made it clear that it will hire permanent replacements for strikers (which the NLRA allows, see Chapter 6) and, therefore, the only way employees can strike without losing their jobs is by making the strike so short that the employer is unable to hire replacements. (e) The strikers insist their strikes are brief because the low-wage workers cannot afford to lose more than a day's pay and their goal is to not harass the employer but is instead to protest working conditions and to raise awareness about working conditions and to gain public support.

c.   Relation to Working Conditions

Consider the May Day immigrants' rights protests. Many workers who missed work to participate in the protests, or who walked off the job to join a protest, were fired. Were the discharges lawful? Would it matter whether the absences are proven to have caused economic harm to the employer? How can participating in the rally be distinguished from or analogized to participation in a general strike, such as those that occurred in major cities around the U.S. in 1934? The Board's General Counsel took the position in 2006 that leaving work to participate in the rallies was unprotected, *see, e.g., American Cable Co.,* 2007 Westlaw 4233177 (2007). It later modified its view and opined that participation in immigration and other political rallies would be protected under Section 7 because such participation is, like a strike, concerted activity for mutual aid and protection. *EZ Indus. Solutions,* 2017 Westlaw 8223257 (2017). An earlier General Counsel memorandum also opined that participation in the rallies is concerted activity for mutual aid and protection under section 7, and an employer would justified in discharging participating employees only if they apply neutral, nondiscriminatory attendance policies and/or if the work stoppage causes harm to the business. *See id.*; GC Memorandum 08–10 (2008).

d. What Is a Strike?

The illegality of public sector employee strikes and the absence of section 7 protection for slowdowns and intermittent strikes in the private sector sometimes leads workers to channel their protest or effort to exert bargaining power into alternative forms that do not clearly look like strikes. Should the following be deemed to be legal concerted activity or illegal strikes?

a. A concerted refusal by teachers to do any work except the instruction of students. Teachers refuse to do parent-teacher conferences (which are done during teachers' lunch-hours and after school), to supervise the playground during lunch or after school, or to chaperone field trips before or after school.

b. A concerted refusal by nurses to volunteer to work overtime or during their lunch break. *N.Y. State Nurses Ass'n*, 334 N.L.R.B. 798 (2001) (held to be a strike and was unprotected because nurses failed to give notice under § 8(g)); *St. Bernabas Hospital*, 334 N.L.R.B. 1000 (2001) (physicians' refusal to perform "on call" work was protected where work was "entirely voluntary"), *enf'd*, 46 Fed. Appx. 23 (2d Cir. 2002); *Honolulu Rapid Transit Co.*, 110 N.L.R.B. 1806 (1954) (refusal to perform mandatory overtime work is unprotected).

c. During a time when mechanics employed by a commercial airline were engaged in contract negotiations but had not called a strike, the mechanics became extremely scrupulous about following every required and suggested safety procedure before clearing planes for take-off. Every safety check was one that is officially required or recommended in the airline's operations manual, but it is extremely rare that every check would be done on every departure. Flight schedules are designed on the assumption that mechanics and pilots do not conduct every recommended safety check on every flight. As a consequence of the thoroughness with which pilots and mechanics were conducting safety checks, flights were significantly delayed in their departures, and customers complained vociferously. Assuming the rule for slowdowns is the same under the Railway Labor Act as under *Fansteel*, is the mechanics' and pilots' conduct protected? *See United Air Lines, Inc. v. Int'l Ass'n of Machinists*, 243 F.3d 349 (7th Cir. 2001); *United, Mechanics Dispute Raises Safety Worries*, USA Today (Feb. 22, 2001), p. 1B (reporting that although normally machinists write up safety issues that delay 3 percent of flights daily, during the contract dispute

machinists identified safety issues delaying 5 to 6 percent of
daily flights).

e. "Indefensible" Conduct

Even a full strike with picketing only on public property can be
unprotected because of its timing, as illustrated by the following case:

INTERNATIONAL PROTECTIVE SERVICES, INC.
339 N.L.R.B. 701 (2003)

CHAIRMAN BATTISTA and MEMBERS SCHAUMBER and WALSH:

The Respondent, International Protective Services, Inc., provided
security guard services for United States Government buildings in
Anchorage, Alaska, pursuant to a contract with the General Services
Administration (GSA). These buildings house the Federal courts, and
offices for the Federal Bureau of Investigation, U.S. Attorney,
Environmental Protection Agency, Internal Revenue Service, and other
Federal agencies. Heightened security measures had been instituted at the
Alaska Federal buildings and Federal buildings nationwide following the
bombing of the Federal building in Oklahoma City, Oklahoma.

The Respondent's security guards were stationed at the entrances to
certain of the Alaska Federal buildings. The guards carried firearms and
were required to be licensed to do so. The judge found that the Respondent's
contract with GSA mandated further "stringent" requirements for the
qualification and hiring of the security guards, including, inter alia, prior
"arrest authority" from law enforcement experience, and first aid
certification. The guards additionally received training in the operation of
an X-ray machine and magnetometer, which devices had been installed as
part of the increased security measures introduced after the Oklahoma
City bombing. The guards were required to screen entrants to the Federal
buildings, and their belongings, using these detection devices.

The Union, United Government Security Officers of America, Local 46,
was the collective-bargaining representative of the Respondent's security
guards at the Alaska Federal buildings. During the latter half of 1998 and
early 1999, the Respondent and the Union were unsuccessful in their
attempt to negotiate a collective-bargaining agreement. On March 10,
1999, the Union informed GSA that a strike was "imminent within the next
few weeks" and that the strike "will occur at the most opportune time" for
the Union. On March 12, GSA initiated a conference call with
representatives of the Union, Respondent, and [Federal Protective Service
(FPS), the law enforcement adjunct to GSA, which is responsible for
building security at the federal building] to discuss the safety of the Federal
buildings in the event of a strike. GSA representatives inquired of the
Union whether and when a strike would commence. The Union evaded

answering directly, indicating only that there "may or may not be a strike." GSA representatives emphasized to the Union that its overriding concern was to protect lives and property at the Federal buildings in the event of a strike. The judge found that the Union nevertheless "thwarted" the GSA's effort to "ascertain any details regarding the threatened strike."

On March 14, the Union conducted a strike vote authorizing Union President Charles Reed to conduct a strike "at an appropriate time suitable" to Reed. Reed testified that he was given authority to call a strike anytime over the next 2-month period. A strike threatened by Reed on March 23 was narrowly averted. Several security guards balked at striking at that time because of their security concerns. According to one guard, one of "the building[s] was very busy and there were fifty or more visiting military personnel in the building."

On the morning of April 21, the Union faxed a letter to the Respondent setting forth certain contract demands, and stating that the Union "must receive a signed & notarized affirmative response from you by 1100 hours, 04–21–99 Alaska time, to avoid the pending work stoppage." The Union commenced a strike at the Anchorage Federal buildings at approximately 12 noon on April 21.

According to the uncontradicted testimony of Joseph Sturrup of FPS, "GSA and FPS personnel were concerned about the possibility of a strike, particularly during the months of March and April," because the anniversary of the Oklahoma City Federal Building bombing was approaching, and "there were several other ominous anniversaries of infamous individuals in March and April . . . [T]his is the time when the majority of bomb threats are received." Thus, security at the Alaska Federal buildings is tightened during the months of March and April, and security guards are reminded to be sensitive to the increased security risk.

The general rule under the NLRA is that employees have the right to strike for the purpose of mutual aid and protection. The Act protects the right of employees to engage in concerted activities, including the right to strike without prior notice.

The right to strike is not without limitation, however. The Board has held concerted activity indefensible where employees fail to take reasonable precautions to protect the employer's plant, equipment, or products from foreseeable imminent danger due to sudden cessation of work.

[T]he test of whether the strike by the security guards lost the protection of the NLRA is not whether the Union gave the Respondent adequate notice of its strike, because such notice is not required under the NLRA. Nor is the test whether the Union's strike resulted in actual injury. Rather, the test of whether the strike by the security guards here lost the protection of the NLRA is whether they failed to take reasonable precautions to protect the employer's operations from such imminent danger as foreseeably would result from their sudden cessation of work.

The judge concluded that the Union's strike was not protected by the NLRA because it exposed the Federal buildings and their occupants to foreseeable danger. The judge based his conclusion on the Union's course of conduct beginning with its March 10 strike threat and culminating in its ultimate commencement of the strike on April 21. The judge found that the Union during this period evinced "total disregard" for the security of the Federal buildings by attempting "to capitalize on the element of surprise" and that the Union's April 21 strike was in fact "designed" to compromise the security of the Federal buildings and their occupants. We have carefully reviewed the record evidence and find that the judge's conclusion that the strike was not protected is fully supported by his key factual findings.

The judge commenced his analysis by examining the March 12 conference call concerning the importance of ensuring the safety of the Federal buildings in the event of a strike. The judge found that the Union responded to GSA's inquiries on this subject "with vitriolic invective and outrage at GSA's involvement in this matter." The judge further found that the Union destroyed a tape recording it had made of the conference call because it presented in explicit detail the "total disregard" evinced by the Union for the interest of GSA and the Respondent in maintaining security at the Federal buildings in the event of a strike. The record thus shows, in the words of the judge, that the Union "was not the least concerned about the Federal buildings or their occupants."

The judge next examined the strike threatened for March 23, which was narrowly averted. The judge found that three security guards at the FBI building had expressed unwillingness to strike on that date because of their belief that it would pose a major security risk, as the building was hosting a conference of some 50 law enforcement and military officials. The judge observed that Union President Reed failed to allay these guards' concern with assurances that they were not expected to leave their posts unguarded. Rather, the judge found that Reed angrily chastised the security guards, admonishing them that "you don't run fucking union business." The judge found further that Reed gave no instructions to guards that they were not to abandon their posts until relieved by replacements. The judge effectively credited testimony of a security guard that Union President Reed would schedule the strike at "the most inopportune time for [Respondent] and FPS . . . when FPS officers were not available" to fill in for striking guards. The judge thus found, and we agree, that "the Union, through Reed, who had been given sole discretion to call a strike at the most opportune time, was willing to compromise the security of the buildings and their occupants" in furtherance of the Union's agenda.

The record thus supports the judge's finding that on April 21 the Union was willing to compromise the security of the Federal buildings and their occupants by post abandonment. We accordingly agree with the judge that the Union failed to take reasonable precautions when exercising its right to strike to protect the Federal buildings and their occupants from such imminent danger as foreseeably would result from their sudden cessation of work.

The judge found further that, not only did the Union fail to take such reasonable precautions, the Union in fact affirmatively "attempted to capitalize on the element of surprise," knowing that it was very difficult to quickly assemble qualified replacement guards who were licensed to carry firearms, competent to operate X-ray machines and magnetometers, and in possession of the additional qualifications that GSA, FPS, and the Respondent were required to ensure. The judge found that indeed the Union's April 21 strike was "designed" to compromise the security of the Federal buildings and their occupants. We have reviewed the record evidence as a whole and agree with the judge's findings.

Because the Union failed to take reasonable precautions to protect the employer's operations from foreseeable imminent danger and essentially flouted the requirement to do so, we agree with the judge that the Union's strike was not protected by the NLRA, and that the Respondent thus did not violate the NLRA by terminating the employees who participated in the unprotected strike.

NOTES

1.   *Why prohibit strikes by security guards?* If the General Services Administration had not contracted out the security services to a private company, the employees would have been governed by the federal labor relations statute that prohibits strikes. What light, if any, should the contracting out shed on the permissibility of strikes by the guards?

2.   *What is the rule?* On the Board's reasoning, under what circumstances would it be acceptable for federal building security guards to strike?

3.   *The limits of the "indefensible" rule.* Under what other circumstances is a strike "indefensible"? Can the timing of a strike to cause maximum damage make the strike unlawful? Consider whether any of the following are "indefensible":

   a.   The union of newspaper writers and technical employees goes on strike the day before Election Day.

   b.   Airline employees call a strike the day before Thanksgiving.

   c.   Retail employees strike the two weeks before Christmas.

    d.   A group of laboratory employees with specialized skills go on strike when a project is half-way done, knowing that the employer will have difficulty replacing them and that without constant attention the project will be ruined, valuable equipment may be damaged, and, at a minimum, the employer will have to begin the project from scratch when the strike ends.

4. *Operating during a strike.* In deciding whether a strike is indefensible, what weight (if any) should the Board give to the difficulty the employer will have in operating during a strike? Since the whole point of a strike or lockout is to exert leverage by inflicting economic harm, how should the Board or the courts decide how much harm is too much? (This is the same issue that arose with respect to slow-downs, as noted above in connection with *Elk Lumber.*) The West Virginia teachers strike of 2018 shut down all schools in the state for two weeks. West Virginia, which like many states faces a teacher shortage, could not replace striking teachers. If such a strike were to occur in a state in which teacher strikes are not per se illegal, would the inability to replace striking teachers affect the legality of the strike? What if, unlike in West Virginia, the teachers did not take pains to help working parents make alternate child care arrangements for their children?

5. *If timing makes a strike indefensible, does it make a lockout indefensible?* Should the "indefensible" rule apply equally to employer lockouts timed to inflict maximum harm on employees? In professional sports, strikes are rare but lockouts are not, and lockouts always occur in the off-season so that the team owners do not lose revenue, seasons are not disrupted, and fans are not inconvenienced. Is there a reason to treat strikes and lockouts differently? Thus far, neither the NLRB nor any court has held a lockout unlawful simply because it was timed to maximize harm to labor and minimize harm to the employer, but as will be seen *infra* in Chapter 6, the idea that some harms are excessive in relation to the circumstances underlay the now-abandoned legal distinction between legal "defensive" and illegal "offensive" lockouts.

f.   Disloyalty

Section 10 of the Act describes the procedures and powers of the NLRB. One sentence in section 10(c) states: "No order of the Board shall require the reinstatement of any individual as an employee who has been suspended or discharged, or the payment to him of any back pay, if such individual was suspended or discharged for cause." This provision, added in the Taft-Hartley Act, has been interpreted in a series of cases not merely as a limitation on the remedial power of the Board, but as a limit on the kinds of concerted activities that are protected under Section 7. In particular, it has been interpreted to carve out from section 7 protections an exception for "disloyalty." In *NLRB v. Local Union No. 1229, Int'l Bhd. of Elec. Workers* (Jefferson Standard Broad.), 346 U.S. 464 (1953), *infra* p.

163, the Supreme Court upheld the discharge of ten technicians who had distributed handbills that read:

Is Charlotte a Second-Class City?

You might think so from the kind of Television programs being presented by the Jefferson Standard Broadcasting Co. over WBTV. Have you seen one of their television programs lately? Did you know that all the programs presented over WBTV are on film and may be from one day to five years old. There are no local programs presented by WBTV. You cannot receive the local baseball games, football games or other local events because WBTV does not have the proper equipment to make these pickups. Cities like New York, Boston, Philadelphia, Washington receive such programs nightly. Why doesn't the Jefferson Standard Broadcasting Company purchase the needed equipment to bring you the same type of programs enjoyed by other leading American cities? Could it be that they consider Charlotte a second-class community and only entitled to the pictures now being presented to them?

WBT Technicians

Quoting the language that § 10(c) deprives the Board of power to order reinstatement of an employee who has been suspended or discharged "for cause," the Court reasoned:

> There is no more elemental cause for discharge of an employee than disloyalty to his employer. The legal principle that insubordination, disobedience or disloyalty is adequate cause for discharge is plain enough. The difficulty arises in determining whether, in fact, the discharges are made because of such a separable cause or because of some other concerted activities engaged in for the purpose of collective bargaining or other mutual aid or protection which may not be adequate cause for discharge.

> Assuming that there had been no pending labor controversy, the conduct of the "WBT Technicians" unquestionably would have provided adequate cause for their disciplinary discharge within the meaning of § 10(c). Their attack related itself to no labor practice of the company. It made no reference to wages, hours or working conditions. The policies attacked were those of finance and public relations for which management, not technicians, must be responsible. The attack asked for no public sympathy or support. It was a continuing attack, initiated while off duty, upon the very interests which the attackers were being paid to conserve and develop. Nothing could be further from the purpose of the Act than to require an employer to finance such activities. Nothing would contribute less to the Act's declared purpose of promoting industrial peace and stability.

Look carefully at sections 7 and 10(c). Does § 10(c) make unprotected conduct that § 7 would otherwise protect? What statutory basis might there be for carving out other exceptions to the scope of § 7? In dissent, Justices Frankfurter, Black and Douglas faulted the majority's reading of the scope of section 10(c):

> The legislative history makes clear that Congress had no such purpose but was rather expressing approval of the construction of concerted activities adopted by the Board and the courts. Many of the legally recognized tactics and weapons of labor would readily be condemned for "disloyalty" were they employed between man and man in friendly personal relations.

> To suggest that all actions which in the absence of a labor controversy might be "cause"—or, to use the words commonly found in labor agreements, "just cause"—for discharge should be unprotected, even when such actions were undertaken as "concerted activities for the purpose of collective bargaining," is to misconstrue legislation designed to put labor on a fair footing with management. Furthermore, it would disregard the rough and tumble of strikes, in the course of which loose and even reckless language is properly discounted.

NOTES

1. *What made the leaflets disloyal?* Would the leaflets distributed by the WBT technicians have been protected if they had included a few sentences explaining that the poor quality programming was due to the station's unwillingness to spend more in labor costs to produce shows locally? What if the leaflets had simply said at the end "WBT is an unfair employer"?

2. *The disloyalty rule summarized.* Notwithstanding the breadth of the *Jefferson Standard* language, the Board generally finds only the following to be disloyal: (a) disparagement of the employer or its product not linked to a union-identified protest or strike; (b) knowingly untruthful product disparagement; (c) really outrageous rudeness; (d) advocating a consumer boycott of the employer's product not in the context of a labor dispute; (e) breaches of confidentiality. Even so, there is considerable uncertainty about the breadth of the disloyalty exception, as illustrated in the following cases:

> a. In *Endicott Interconnect Technologies v. NLRB,* 453 F.3d 532 (D.C. Cir. 2006), a company in a small town was sold and the management of the new company laid off 200 employees. An employee who was not laid off was quoted in the local newspaper as saying that layoffs of people with important knowledge left "gaping holes in this business" in areas of crucial technical knowledge. The same employee, responding to an anti-union post about the sale and layoff on a public blog sponsored by the local paper, wrote a post defending the benefits of union organization and added:

Hasn't there been enough divisiveness among the people working in this area? Isn't it about time we stood up for our jobs, our homes, our families and our way of life here? Do you want to sit by and watch this area go to hell and dissolve into a welfare town for people over 70? This business is being tanked by a group of people that have no good ability to manage. They will put it into the dirt just like the companies of the past.

The employee was fired and has filed an unfair labor practice charge. What result?

b.   Employees of Walmart are upset about the company's working conditions. Several of them active with the UFCW (which is trying to organize Walmart) publicly supported the boycott of Walmart and appeared at a rally at which they urged consumers to pressure Walmart and to shop instead at unionized retailers. They were fired for disloyalty. They have filed charges under §§ 8(b)(1) and 8(b)(3). What result? What if employees at a retailer that is not the subject of an organizing campaign wrote a letter to the editor of the local newspaper urging customers to boycott their store because of the employer's labor practices? Compare *New River Indus. v. NLRB*, 945 F.2d 1290 (4th Cir. 1991) (criticism of employer's policies is unprotected disloyalty) with *Reef Indus., Inc. v. NLRB*, 952 F.2d 830 (5th Cir. 1991) (criticism of employer's policies is protected; distinguishing *New River* on the grounds that there was no union involved, whereas at Reef Industries there had been a hotly-contested union election).

c.   To publicize a fast food employer's refusal to provide sick leave, employees start a social media campaign asking consumers to consider the possibility that they are eating a sandwich prepared by someone who has the flu. Their social media posts conclude by asking consumers to join the workers in pressuring the company to give employees paid sick days. Are the employees who instigated the campaign or worked on the social media posts protected by section 7? What if they just "liked" the post on Facebook?

g.   Picket Line Misconduct

While § 7 protects the right to strike and to picket, it does not protect the right to engage in destruction of property or other conduct that endangers the safety of persons or physical property. In addition, picketers may not enter or block access to private property. States retain the right to punish, by criminal law or the law of torts, such behavior as trespass or nuisance in the case of excessive noise or crowds. Employers have frequently resorted to state criminal, property, or tort law to seek relief against strike behavior that they have considered harmful. While in theory federal labor law preempts all state law regulating peaceful picketing that does not trespass or cause a nuisance or property damage, in practice state courts are often willing to enjoin such conduct, and it is then up to the union to seek through appeal to higher state courts to assert the federally protected right to picket. Because federal courts will in some circumstances abstain from resolving disputes that are the subject of ongoing state proceedings, *see, e.g., Younger v. Harris*, 401 U.S. 37 (1971) (federal courts may not enjoin ongoing state court criminal proceedings), and federal court abstention doctrine is notoriously confusing, it can be difficult for union lawyers to persuade a federal court to decide whether picketing is protected under federal law or prohibited under state law.

For these reasons, experienced labor lawyers know that the contours of state law and the attitudes of state law enforcement officers often matter a great deal in determining whether state courts or state officials will enjoin or criminally prosecute picketing. The following excerpt shows the importance of state law and state procedure regarding injunctions matters:

JUSTICE FOR JANITORS IN LOS ANGELES: LESSONS FROM THREE ROUNDS OF NEGOTIATIONS

Christopher Erickson, Catherine Fisk, Ruth Milkman, Daniel Mitchell & Kent Wong
40 British Journal of Industrial Relations 543 (2002)

In 1999 the California legislature enacted a statute restricting the ability of state courts to enjoin labour protest (Cal. Lab. Code § 1138.) Prior to the enactment of the new statute, employers . . . confronted with large, ebullient, and noisy protests of the sort used in the [Justice for Janitors ("JfJ")] campaign would seek a court order limiting the size, location and noise level of the protest. If a court issued such the injunction, any violation of the order would be punishable by contempt sanctions, which can be speedy, harsh, and devastating to the individual protesters and the union treasury.

SEIU Local 1877 and its lawyers believed that the new anti-injunction statute made a difference in how the courts responded to the strike and the related nightly protests. Building owners and their allies tried on five separate occasions to have a state court enjoin the protests; but each time the court rejected their request. This was because under the new law no state court may issue an injunction except after hearing testimony of witnesses in open court, with an opportunity for cross-examination. Under prior law, courts would have entertained and often granted requests for injunctions based only on sworn affidavits describing allegedly illegal protests and asserting threatened harm to business or property. Union lawyers explained in our interviews that cross-examination of employer witnesses was necessary to reveal that the harm allegedly caused by the protest was often exaggerated and that the protests did not pose any real threat to property.

Union lawyers also cited a second critical provision of the new law, namely that no state court may issue an injunction unless there is a showing that the police or other officers charged with protecting the complainant's property are unable or unwilling to do so. Union lawyers were able to show in court that Los Angeles police officers had been briefed and were prepared to deal with any illegal protests that might occur. As one union lawyer told us, the union and the police essentially agreed that the police got the streets and "we got the sidewalks."

The final feature of the new state law that made life easier for the union side was its restriction on the ability to hold a union responsible for the unlawful conduct of individual members. An often-successful management tactic is for an employer to obtain an injunction, wait for some picketers to violate the terms of the injunction, and then seek to hold the union officers in contempt of court for the violations. Penalties for contempt of court can include large fines that are payable out of the union treasury if it is shown that union officials were involved in, or approved of, the enjoined illegal activities. Contempt sanctions in the tens of millions of dollars have been awarded against unions in the past. *United Mine Workers v. Bagwell*, 512 U.S. 821 (1994). The threat of huge sanctions can be a significant disincentive to carry out an aggressive protest.

NOTES

1. *Why civil procedure matters.* List the aspects of civil procedure that made a difference in the ability of the employees to protest in the Justice for Janitors campaign. If you were to draft legislation regulating the procedure for issuing injunctions in labor disputes, which provisions would matter most to unions? Which would matter most to employers?

2. *Contempt sanctions.* In *United Mine Workers v. Bagwell*, 512 U.S. 821 (1994), a Virginia court imposed over $64 million in fines against the United Mine Workers union for contempt of an injunction in the context of a bitter strike against the Pittston Coal Company in the late 1980s and early 1990s. (The U.S. Supreme Court vacated the award on the ground that the fines were criminal rather than civil and therefore the judge erred in imposing them without a jury trial.) The strike—which was unsuccessful—was a turning point in the history of coal mining in Appalachia and a major loss for the mine workers. The story of the strike is told in the 1995 documentary film *Justice in the Coalfields.*

3. *Defining and proving picket line misconduct.* While picketing in hot weather, a striking newspaper employee carried a water pistol which he used to squirt himself and fellow picketers. A security guard with a video camera persisted in following the striker, who eventually squirted water at the camera lens and accidentally squirted the guard in the eye. The company deemed this serious misconduct and fired the striker, based on the security guard's report of pain from being squirted in the eye. Did the employer commit an unfair labor

practice? Would it matter if the employer believed, at the time it fired the employee, that the security guard had been injured by something more serious than a squirt gun filled with water? *See Detroit Newspaper Agency*, 342 N.L.R.B. No. 24 (2004) (Employer committed ULP; employer's good faith but erroneous belief that guard had been seriously injured is irrelevant).

4.   *Consequences of picket line misconduct.* Employees who engage in "serious misconduct" while on strike lose their right to reinstatement. *Clear Pine Mouldings*, 268 N.L.R.B. 1044 (1984). Serious misconduct includes assault, malicious destruction of property, or the use of egregiously profane, insulting, or humiliating language. Emotions often run high during a strike, and the emotions become even more intense when the employer hires permanent replacements. The Board has decided numerous cases trying to distinguish acceptable from unacceptable expressions of intense emotion on a picket line. In addition, state courts have adjudicated many cases involving torts and crimes committed by workers on picket lines.

CHAPTER 3

BOUNDARIES OF COLLECTIVE REPRESENTATION

■ ■ ■

A. INTRODUCTION

"We do the same work, but for second-class status—no health, no pension, no vacation, no stock. We're in the orange ghetto."

—Marcus Courtney, a Microsoft "perma-temp," referring to the orange ID cards that distinguish temporary workers from blue-carded full-time employees

A stark dilemma regarding freedom of association is faced by workers at temporary employment agencies, even at the high end of the economic ladder. These workers are defined as employees of the agency, not of the place where they work. Therefore, if they want to exercise the rights to organize and bargain collectively, they have to do so with other workers who are employed by the agency. Yet temporary agency employees have little contact or opportunity to communicate with each other because they are spread among different work sites. Meanwhile, those temporary agency workers who work for long periods at one place, often called "perma-temps," have none of the rights, benefits or protections afforded to regular employees, including the rights to form and join a union to deal with the employer.

A dramatic example of the temporary agency workers' dilemma can be found at the cutting edge of the new economy. Microsoft Corporation's elegant "campus" in Redmond, Wash., gives the appearance of a tranquil college setting. Graceful buildings are set among gentle slopes and winding brooks. Young people toss Frisbees and play softball on broad lawns and fields.

More than 20,000 workers are employed at Microsoft's Redmond campus and other nearby facilities. But 6,000 of them are not officially "employed" by Microsoft. Instead, they are employed by many temporary agencies supplying high-tech workers to Microsoft and other companies. Many have worked for several years at Microsoft. They have come to be known as "perma-temps": temporary employees working for long periods, often side-by-side in teams with regular, full-time employees (who are often referred to as "FTEs," or full-time equivalents).

Microsoft FTEs enjoy health insurance, pension plans, paid vacations, and share ownership in the company. Perma-temps have none of that. They

receive a generous hourly rate, usually $25 to $35 per hour, and nothing more. They have to pay $300 per month for family medical insurance. They often work fifty hours a week but are not entitled to overtime pay after forty hours because they are excluded from coverage under the Fair Labor Standards Act as highly skilled technical employees.

"It's an unbelievable erosion of what I expected from a company like Microsoft," said Marcus Courtney, a young Montanan who became a Microsoft perma-temp in 1996. "We do the same work, but for second-class status—no health, no pension, no vacation, no stock. We're in the orange ghetto," he said, referring to the orange ID cards that distinguish temporary employees from blue-carded FTEs.

"Here's a common situation—tell me how you would feel," said Jeff Nachtigal, another Microsoft perma-temp. "You work on a project for months in a team of ten people, five perma-temps and five FTEs. You do the same things. You become friends. You're all part of the same team. Then at the end of a project meeting, the FTEs plan a 'moral support' event paid for by Microsoft, a dinner at the nicest restaurant in town. But only for them. The rest of us just sit there."

"We needed to do something," said Courtney. He and other perma-temps formed the Washington Alliance of Technology Workers (WashTech) in early 1998, with help from the Communication Workers of America (CWA). The CWA is the union of AT & T workers and others in the high-technology sector.

WashTech is in the early stages of an effort to organize Microsoft perma-temps. "We've got a long way to go," Courtney concedes. "We're starting by establishing WashTech as a reliable source of information for high-tech workers in the area." Courtney said he told CWA organizers, "We have to do it differently here. The old-style union tactics of house visits and leaflets blasting management won't be enough."

But WashTech has a "Catch-22"-type problem. By defining perma-temps as contractors employed by various temporary agencies, Microsoft avoids being their employer for purposes of the National Labor Relations Act's protection of the right to organize. Meanwhile, the agencies tell temps that in order to form a union that management will deal with, they have to organize other employees of the agency, not just those working at Microsoft.

NOTES

1. *Common law employees?* Microsoft's perma-temp strategy was viewed with skepticism by not only WashTech but also the federal courts. In response, the company, as part of its effort to distinguish "permanent" from "temporary" workers (even though the two groups often performed identical work under identical conditions), started requiring some workers to sign a form agreement. This agreement purported to do at least three things: (1) classify

the signers as "Independent Contractor[s]," (2) state that nothing in the agreement created an "employer-employee relationship," and (3) make individual workers "responsible for all federal and state income taxes, withholding, social security, insurance, and other benefits." The effect was to deny "temporary" workers the same benefits, including participation in the company's Savings Plus Plan (SPP) and Employee Stock Purchase Plan (ESPP), which were granted to their "permanent" counterparts.

After Microsoft was pursued by the Internal Revenue Service, Donna Vizcaino and seven other plaintiffs brought suit demanding to be reclassified as common law employees so they could become eligible for these benefits. A three-judge panel of the Ninth Circuit sided with the plaintiffs, and eventually, an 11-judge en banc panel affirmed. *See Vizcaino v. Microsoft Corp.*, 97 F.3d 1187 (9th Cir. 1996), *aff'd*, 120 F.3d 1006 (9th Cir. 1997) (*en banc*). Despite this defeat, Microsoft and countless other companies continue to pursue the same strategy, or variations of it. Why? Is it because the economic benefits of violating the law outweigh the legal costs of complying with it? If you were legal counsel to a similarly-situated employer, and you believed the benefits of breaking the law outweighed the costs of getting caught, would you advise your client to violate the law?

2.   *To find success, look for the union label?* Wash Tech's efforts resulted in establishing it "as a reliable source of information for high-tech workers in the area," even though the group has never won a union election, gained recognition as the exclusive bargaining representative of anyone working for Microsoft, or negotiated a collective bargaining agreement. Instead, WashTech is more of a clearing house where workers can ask questions about their rights. Can this be called a successful organizing effort among "perma-temps"? It is possible to provide effective representation without forming a traditional union? *See, e.g.*, Danielle D. van Jaarsveld, *Overcoming Obstacles to Worker Representation: Insights for the Temporary Agency Workforce*, 50 N.Y.L. Sch. L. Rev. 355 (2005–06).

* * *

The National Labor Relations Act bestows rights only upon "employee[s]" and imposes obligations only upon "employer[s]." In effect, the terms are statutory boundaries. So this Chapter is organized around two key questions: Who is an "employee"? And who (or what) is the "employer"? The statutory boundaries indicated by these questions were drawn by Congress for the workplace of the 1930s, when America's dominant industry was manufacturing and her typical workplace was the shop floor. There was an established hierarchy between labor and management. It was relatively easy to distinguish between the people who did the work and the people for whom the work was done.

But the workplace for which these boundaries were drawn has been transformed. Today, America's dominant industries are services and information and her typical workplace is an office—although that office could be located in a car, coffee shop, or home, or even within earshot of a mobile telephone (if not inside a commercial building). As noted in Chapter 1, a revolution has restructured the way people work; due to a "flattening of hierarchies," more workers direct themselves. More people work outside a shared or designated physical space. And more people, especially knowledge workers, consider themselves to be self-directed professionals, not rank-and-file order-takers. In many industries, the traditional boundary between "employee" and "employer" has become blurred, or perhaps, irrelevant.

The people who do the work are different too. In contrast to the workforce of the New Deal era, which consisted mostly of white men with limited education who performed unskilled or semi-skilled labor, today's workforce is more ethnically and racially diverse, more female, and more educated. And low-wage immigrants—documented and otherwise—have become critical in many sectors of the economy, including the country's smaller, but still substantial, manufacturing base.

Moreover, the NLRA rules discussed here are not the only ways to grapple with the problem of who is covered. As appropriate, we will contrast the approaches of the Railway Labor Act, state public sector statutes, and international labor standards, which may approach the same coverage issues in very different ways.

All of this has had a profound impact on how we answer the most basic of labor law questions: who is covered by the NLRA? As you consider whether "perma-temp" workers at Microsoft are statutory employees, think about how your answer might affect the status of "salts," or workers paid by a union to join a company for the purpose of attempting to organize it; undocumented Latinos who toil in the manufacturing industries; drivers of big city trucks or taxi cabs; home health care providers; graduate students; and other types of workers commonly found in modern workplaces.

B. WHO IS AN "EMPLOYEE"?

Section 2(3) of the NLRA defines "employee" as follows:

The term "employee" shall include any employee, and shall not be limited to the employees of a particular employer, unless this subchapter explicitly states otherwise, and shall include any individual whose work has ceased as a consequence of, or in connection with, any current labor dispute or because of any unfair labor practice . . . but shall not include any individual employed as an agricultural laborer, or in the domestic service of any family or person at his home, or any individual employed by his parent or spouse, or any individual having the status of an independent contractor, or any individual employed as a supervisor, or any individual employed by an employer subject to the Railway Labor Act.

29 U.S.C. § 152(3).

The language in Section 2(3) of the Act was borrowed from Section 13(d) of the Norris LaGuardia Act, 29 U.S.C. § 113(d).

By its express terms, Section 2(3) is broad and unhelpfully self-referential. It defines "employee" as "any employee, and shall not be limited to the employees of a particular employer." Then it excludes from the definition of "employee" a short but substantial list of various categories of worker: individuals employed as agricultural laborers, domestic servants, certain close family members, independent contractors, supervisors, and workers for employers subject to the Railway Labor Act. The brevity of this list, however, has not prevented the Board and the courts from carving out more exclusions. The effect has been to narrow what otherwise is a broad statutory definition.

Perhaps the most significant exclusion from the definition of "employee" is the position of "supervisor." That is because, to the employee, his supervisor and his employer are effectively one and the same; they are "the boss." In the eyes of the law, a supervisor is the agent of the employer; therefore, it would pose a potential conflict of interest to treat a supervisor as both boss and subordinate at the same time. To avoid this potential conflict of interest, the NLRA recognizes only employee voices as entitled to the protections of the law, and denies such protections to supervisors. The complex task of determining who is a "supervisor" is reflected in Section 2(11) of the NLRA, which defines the term functionally: a supervisor is someone who carries out, or has the power to carry out, one or more of 12 enumerated supervisory functions. This book treats supervisors elsewhere, under the heading of who is an "employer" in Section C of this chapter, *infra* p. 300.

Other exclusions from NLRA coverage are accomplished both by statute and by custom or interpretation.

For example, over a million agricultural laborers are specifically excluded from coverage. To be considered agricultural, an employee's duties must form an integral part of ordinary farming operations, and such duties must be performed before the product can be marketed through normal channels. Employees engaged primarily in duties that serve to increase the value of already-marketable products do not fall within the exclusion. Under this interpretation, workers engaged in packing, processing, refining, and slaughtering have all found to be protected by the Act. *See, e.g., Holly Farms Corp. v. NLRB*, 517 U.S. 392 (1996); *Bayside Enters. Inc. v. NLRB*, 429 U.S. 298 (1977).

Instead, the labor-management relations of agricultural employees are governed by the laws of the individual states in which they work. Most of these states refer to common law principles, "little" Wagner or Norris-LaGuardia Acts, or both. *See, e.g., Bravo v. Dolsen Cos.*, 125 Wash.2d 745,

888 P.2d 147 (1995). At least four states—Arizona, California, Idaho, and Kansas—have passed agricultural labor relations statutes, which are patterned somewhat after the NLRA, in that they provide for employee elections and unfair labor practice proceedings. *See, e.g., Babbitt v. United Farm Workers*, 442 U.S. 289 (1979). California's Agricultural Labor Relations Act is one of the more comprehensive statutes. *See ALRB v. Superior Court*, 16 Cal.3d 392, 128 Cal. Rptr. 183, 546 P.2d 687, *appeal dismissed*, 429 U.S. 802 (1976).

Also specifically excluded are domestic employees: babysitters, butlers, cooks, home health care providers, maids, nannies, respite care workers, and others who work primarily in the home. But as noted in this Chapter, *infra* p. 240, a growing number of home health care workers in selected states are gaining collective bargaining rights with "employers of record" established by legislation.

From time to time, it is argued that particular categories of professional employees must be excluded from the Act because their work is too closely aligned with managerial prerogatives. Umpires in Major League Baseball were one such group, because they not only call balls and strikes, but also exercise power to remove unruly players and managers, suspend or cancel games due to the weather, and control other aspects of the work environment. The Board, however, rejected the argument. *See Am. League of Prof'l Baseball Clubs*, 180 N.L.R.B. 190 (1969).

Here in Section B of this chapter, we consider the status of some of the most potentially significant exclusions: (1) contingent workers, (2) union organizers; (3) apprentices, including graduate student teachers, trainees, and house staff; and (4) transborder workers, including undocumented, foreign, and multi-country workers. (As noted above, in Section C of this chapter, *infra* p. 300, we treat supervisors, who are also excluded, as part of the discussion of who is an "employer.")

1. CONTINGENT WORKERS

The NLRA was conceived and enacted long before terms such as "contingent worker" came into usage. Therefore, the statute defines neither what the term means nor what constitutes an attempt to exclude this type of worker from its protections. Yet it has become fashionable to use the term "contingent" to identify groups of workers who are to be denied the protected status of "employee" under Section 2(3), and for that matter, under a variety of other employment-related benefit and protection regimes.

According to the U.S. Bureau of Labor Statistics (BLS), a contingent worker is anyone who does not have "an explicit or implicit contract for ongoing employment." BLS, *Contingent and Alternative Employment Arrangements Summary* (Jun. 7, 2018), available at https://www.bls.gov/news.release/conemp.nr0.htm. BLS applies this definition in issuing its

Contingent Work Supplement, a periodic review of non-standard work arrangements. Relying on CWS data, as well as surveys conducted by the U.S. Census Bureau and other government agencies, the U.S. Government Accountability Office (GAO) has estimated the size of the contingent workforce as ranging from less than 5 percent to more than one-third of all American workers.[1] Government Accountability Office, *Contingent Workforce: Size, Characteristics, Earnings, and Benefits*, at 3 (Apr. 20, 2015) (letter to Sens. Patti Murray & Kirsten Gillibrand), available at https://www.gao.gov/assets/670/669899.pdf. The GAO has profiled the contingent workforce as follows:

> [C]ompared to standard full-time workers, core contingent workers are more likely to be younger, Hispanic, have no high school degree, and have low family income. These contingent workers are also more likely than standard workers to experience job instability, and to be less satisfied with their benefits and employment arrangements than standard full-time workers. Because contingent work can be unstable, or may afford fewer worker protections depending on a worker's particular employment arrangement, it tends to lead to lower earnings, fewer benefits, and a greater reliance on public assistance than standard work.

Id.

Some caution is called for in using the adjective "contingent" to describe people who may or may not be entitled to protection under the NLRA. Some workers who are commonly thought of as "contingent" are clearly protected by the statute; part-time employees are a case in point. *See, e.g.*, *The Pavilion at Crossing Pointe*, 344 N.L.R.B. 582 (2005). At least one scholar has argued that the use of value-laden legal metaphors such as "contingent" may be used as a smokescreen to manipulate the NLRA and other regulatory regimes to deny workers the protections of those regimes. *See, e.g.*, Catherine L. Fisk, *Knowledge Work: New Metaphors for the New Economy*, 80 Chi.-Kent L. Rev. 839 (2005).

That said, contingent work attracts attention because it is often, though not always, less attractive to workers than standard work arrangements. In the view of Professor David Weil, former Wage and Hour Administrator for the U.S. Department of Labor, the modern contingent workplace is "fissured": it is full of rock-like cracks that can deepen, spread,

---

[1]   Actually, the CWS distinguishes its estimate of the size of the "contingent" workforce from its estimates of the size of "alternative" work arrangements, such as arrangements affecting independent contractors, on-call workers, temporary help agency workers, and workers provided by contract firms. For example, in 2017, the CWS estimated the size of the "contingent" workforce at 3.8% percent of workers; in 2005, it had estimated the size of the same group at 4.1%. By contrast, for the same years, it estimated the size of the "independent contractor" workforce to be 6.9% and 7.4%, respectively. Surprisingly, both estimates dropped, but just slightly. *See* BLS, *Contingent and Alternative Employment Arrangements Summary* (Jun. 7, 2018), available at https://www.bls.gov/news.release/conemp.nr0.htm.

and split it apart. *See* David Weil, The Fissured Workplace: Why Work Became So Bad for So Many and What Can Be Done to Improve It 268 (2014). In the parlance of international law, "contingent" work is sometimes referred to as "precarious" work. For a comprehensive look at precarious work in Canada, the European Union, Israel, and other countries, see *Symposium—Precarious Work and Human Rights: Articles Presented at a Conference Held by the Minerva Center for Human Rights, Hebrew University of Jerusalem*, 34 Comp. Lab. L. & Pol'y J. 1 (2012).

What does contingent work look like? Recall the Microsoft "perma-temps." According to Dr. Richard Belous, the chief economist of the National Planning Association, it makes sense to distinguish the employment conditions of such "contingent" workers from those of "core" workers along at least four spectra:

Core Workers	Contingent Workers
Strong affiliation with employer	Weak affiliation with employer
Implicit long-term contract	No implicit long-term contract
Significant stakeholder in company	Insignificant stakeholder in company
Part of corporate family	Not part of corporate family

Richard S. Belous, *The Rise of the Contingent Workforce: The Key Challenges and Opportunities*, 52 Wash. & Lee L. Rev. 863, 865 (1995).

According to Professor Weil, who takes a broader view than the BLS or GAO, about 31% of the workforce is currently engaged in contingent employment. Although from 1995 to 2005 this number decreased from 32.1% to 30.1%, many categories of "fissured" work increased. For example, during the same period, the percentage of workers classified as independent contractors rose from 6.7% to 7.4% (from 8.3 million to 10.3 million workers). Moreover, the percentages of workers classified as day laborers and contract company workers grew by 36% and 26%, respectively, even though the workforce grew by just 13%. Weil, The Fissured Workplace, *supra*, at 272.

Similar trends in contingent work can be found in other major industrialized economies, at least as measured by part-time and temporary workforce statistics. From 1995 to 2011, the weighted average of part-time employment in nations affiliated with the Organization for Economic Cooperation and Development (OECD) rose from 11.6% to 16.5%. During the same period, the incidence of temporary employment rose from 10.6% to 12.0%. Growth in contingent work was particularly dramatic in Germany, France, Italy, and Canada. Weil, The Fissured Workplace, *supra*, at 273.

As noted above, contingent work arrangements offer substantial labor cost savings to employers, usually in the form of lower wages, eliminated fringe benefits, and increased flexibility in the deployment of workers. Moreover, at the macroeconomic level, these arrangements blunt the rise in labor costs during upswings in the business cycle. Many workers like the work arrangements too, especially if they are able to secure relatively high hourly pay or flexible work schedules. But contingent human resources systems generate serious costs too, and employers, workers, and society at large each bear some of those costs. According to Dr. Belous, some employers find it difficult to sustain long-term quality and productivity gains with contingent workers. Workers can discover that the risk of economic uncertainty has been shifted more to them, often in the form of having to pay for all of their own health care and pension coverage. And society at large finds it harder to enforce polices favoring equal employment opportunity and affirmative action. *See* Belous, The Rise of the Contingent Workforce, *supra*, at 875.

Of course, if the economics of contingent human resource systems did not pencil out, it is doubtful that employers would create them in the first place. And economics aside, establishing contingent work arrangements is not necessarily illegal or violative of workers' contractual rights. Even unionized employers enjoy considerable freedom to set up work systems of their choosing—a concept known as management rights. *See infra* Chapter 7-E.

Although contingent work arrangements are at least as old as the NLRA, the emerging economy of the Twenty-first Century seems to have accelerated their development. This emerging economy has been described as the "gig," "sharing," "App," and even the "stealing" economy. It includes such pioneering companies as Amazon and eBay; more recent entrants such as Airbnb, TaskRabbit, and Uber; and social media facilitators such as Facebook and LinkedIn. The economy in which these famous economic disrupters and their workers operate challenges the internal logic of both regulated industries and the legal regimes purporting to regulate them. Scholars have only begun to study the nature of this emerging economy, let alone figure out whether, why, or how to regulate it. *See, e.g.*, Orly Lobel, *The Law of the Platform*, 101 Minn. L. Rev. 87, 89–92 (2016); *see also* Jeremias Prassl, Humans as a Service: The Promise and Perils of Work in the Gig Economy (2018); Martin H. Malin, *A Framework for Thinking About Regulating Platforms*, Worklaw JOTWELL (Oct. 23, 2017), available at https://worklaw.jotwell.com/a-framework-for-thinking-about-regulating-platforms/.

Meanwhile, the task of interpreting and applying existing legal regimes remains, whether the contingent work in question is part of the old economy or the emerging one. To begin this task, we will examine the legal status of two types of workers who are generally regarded as "contingent": (a) independent contractors and (b) leased or subcontractors' employees.

a.   Independent Contractors

An independent contractor is somebody who works for herself instead of someone else. By excluding the independent contractor from its protections, the Act deems her to be an employer, not an employee. Although one image of the independent contractor depicts a robust, risk-taking entrepreneur, a different picture may show a vulnerable worker with minimal bargaining power who has little choice but to accept that the risks of finding and keeping work have been shifted completely onto her shoulders.

Over the years, three sets of tests have emerged for determining whether a worker is an employee or independent contractor under various workplace regulation schemes. Professor Kenneth Dau-Schmidt has summarized them as follows:

> The first general test commonly used to determine whether a person is an "employee" covered by some federal and state statutes is the "right-to-control test." *See* Restatement of Employment Law § 1.01 cmt. d (Am. Law Inst. 2015). This test was borrowed from common law tort agency doctrine designed to determine whether a principal sufficiently "controlled" the work of an agent so that the principal could reasonably be held liable for torts committed by that agent under the doctrine of "respondeat superior." To establish that a person is an "employee" under this test, the plaintiff has to show that the principal "controlled or had the right to control the manner and means of the agent's work." In making this determination, the court considers a list of factors concerning the relationship and the situation of the agent which include:

>> The skill required; the source of the instrumentalities and tools; the location of the work; the duration of the relationship between the parties; whether the hiring party has the right to assign additional projects to the hired party; the extent of the hired party's discretion over when and how long to work; the method of payment; the hired party's role in hiring and paying assistants; whether the work is part of the regular business of the hiring party; whether the hiring party is in business; the provision of employee benefits; and the tax treatment of the hired party. *Community for Creative Non-Violence v. Reid,* 490 U.S. 730, at 751–52 (1989); cited favorably in *Nationwide Mut. Ins. Co. v. Darden,* 503 U.S. 318, at 323 (1992).

The right-to-control test is a "totality of the circumstances" test in which none of the examined factors is necessary or controlling. If the agent is sufficiently outside of the principal's control, then he or she is an "independent contractor," not subject to the doctrine of respondeat superior or protective statutes that use this tort law definition of employee.

Despite its separate common law origin and purpose, the Supreme Court has stated that this is the default test for federal protective legislation where congress defines the term "employee" by merely referring again to the term employee in a circular fashion, without further elaboration. If the statute expressly exempts "independent contractors" that is also sometimes taken as an indication that the legislature intended the right-to-control test. The IRS has produced a "simplified" version of the right-to-control test which groups the considered factors into three aspects of the work relationship: "behavioral control," "financial control," and the "relationship of the parties." This formulation is commonly referred to as the "IRS Test," and it enjoys broad application among state administrative agencies. Federal statutes that use the right-to-control test include the NLRA, Title VII of the CRA, Americans with Disabilities Act (ADA), Age Discrimination in Employment Act (ADEA), ERISA, Occupational Safety and Health Act (OSHA); Worker Adjustment and Retraining Notification Act (WARN), Federal Unemployment Tax Act (FUTA), Federal Insurance Contributions Act (FICA) and Internal Revenue Code (IRC). State workers' compensation statutes commonly apply the right-to-control test.

The second general test commonly used to determine who is a covered "employee" under some federal and state statutes is the "economic realities test." This test was first developed in interpreting federal protective legislation to fulfill its purpose of protecting economically dependent workers. *See* Restatement of Employment Law § 1.01 cmt. d & e (Am. Law Inst. 2015). To establish that a person is an "employee" under this test, the plaintiff must show that under the "economic realities" of the situation, the agent is "economically dependent" on the principal so that it would fulfill the purposes of the legislation to include the agent as covered under the act. In determining economic dependence, the court considers a list of factors concerning the relationship and the situation of the agent that is generally very similar to the list of factors considered under the right-to-control test. Like the right-to-control test, the economic realities test is a "totality of the circumstances" test in which none of the examined factors is necessary or controlling.

The economic realities test is generally used where the definition of "employee" or "to employ" in the statute elaborates beyond a circular definition in a way that shows an intent at broad coverage, or where the legislative history shows evidence of such broad intent. For example, under the FLSA "to employ" is defined broadly as "to suffer or permit to work" and this expressed broad intent gives rise to application of the economic realities test.

The third general test commonly used to determine whether a worker is an "employee" covered by some state protective statutes is the "ABC test." Although this test was originally developed by Wisconsin in 1935, it has enjoyed a modern rebirth as more and more states have become dissatisfied with the vagueness and complexity of the right-to-control and economic realities tests and have adopted the ABC test to minimize misclassification problems. As formulated by Massachusetts, Mass. Gen. Laws Ann. ch. 149, § 148B(a)(1)–(3) (West 2014), under the ABC test, the agent is presumed to be a covered "employee" unless the principal can demonstrate three factors:

> (A) "the individual is free from direction and control," applicable both "under his contract for the performance of service and in fact,"
>
> (B) "the service is performed outside the usual course of business of the employer," and
>
> (C) the "individual is customarily engaged in an independently established trade, occupation, profession, or business of the same nature as that involved in the service performed."

The principal must prove all three factors to establish that the agent is an "independent contractor" outside of the coverage of the protective statute. Like the hybrid formulations of the economic realities test, the ABC test looks at both control and dependence in determining the agent's status as employee or independent contractor. Unlike the right-to-control test and the economic realities test, state legislatures and administrative agencies have been the primary movers for adoption of the ABC test, although courts have sometimes inferred application of the test to new statutes. The ABC test is commonly used in state Unemployment Insurance (UI) statutes, but has increasingly been applied to other state statutes.

Kenneth G. Dau-Schmidt, *The Problem of "Misclassification" or How to Define Who is an "Employee" Under Protective Legislation in the Information Age*, in The Cambridge Handbook of U.S. Labor Law: reviving

American Labor Law for a 21st Century Economy ___ (forthcoming 2018), available at https://papers.ssrn.com/sol3/papers.cfm?abstract_id=3143296.

In 2018, the adoption of the ABC test by California, see *Dynamex Operations West, Inc. v. Superior Court*, 4 Cal.5th 903 (2018), was heralded as a "bombshell" because it was thought to require hundreds of thousands of employers in that state—by some estimates the world's sixth largest economy—to reevaluate independent contractor relationships that arguably were lawful when they were created. *See* Jon Steingart, *Calif. Supreme Court Transforms Test for Who Is an Employee*, 86 U.S.L.W. (BBNA) 1547 (May 3, 2018). So far, California's application of the ABC test is limited to wage awards under its Labor Code, and not to workers' rights under other state statutes.

In this section, we study the independent contractor spectrum: on the high end, knowledge workers, such as the perma-temps at Microsoft, who want the same perquisites enjoyed by full-time employees; in the middle, package delivery truck drivers who are trying to organize a union; and on the low end, home health care workers, who are seeking to be paid more than the minimal wages offered by the state to assist elderly and infirm clients in their homes.

ROADWAY PACKAGE SYSTEM INC.
326 N.L.R.B. 842 (1998)

By CHAIRMAN GOULD and MEMBERS FOX, LIEBMAN, and BRAME:

Roadway, a Delaware corporation, operates a nationwide pickup and delivery system for small packages throughout the United States. This system currently is comprised of approximately 317 terminals and hub facilities [and 5,000 drivers]. The sole issue to be decided here is whether the drivers at Roadway's Ontario and Pomona terminals are employees under Section 2(3) of the Act or independent contractors not subject to the Board's jurisdiction.

The Ontario and Pomona drivers own or lease vans to perform their work for Roadway. Under the 1994 Agreement, the drivers may operate their vehicles for other commercial or personal purposes when not in the service of Roadway if they remove or mask all numbers, marks, logos, and insignia identifying Roadway. There is no evidence that the drivers use their vehicles for any commercial purpose other than hauling for Roadway.

Nearly all the drivers obtain either new vehicles through Bush Leasing or used vehicles from former drivers of Roadway.

Under the 1994 Agreement, the drivers may operate additional vehicles with Roadway's consent and may use additional "qualified persons" to operate the additional vehicles, pursuant to applicable laws and Roadway's safe driving standards that are attached to the agreement.

When the drivers signed the 1994 Agreement, they were granted a "proprietary interest" in their existing service areas. According to Roadway, this proprietary interest is manifested in the driver's contractual right to sell his service area or portions thereof, or to receive minimum compensation for customer accounts that are reassigned or removed from his service area.

According to Roadway, the concept of proprietary interest and the contractual right to sell service areas afford entrepreneurial opportunity for the drivers.

RELEVANT LEGAL PRINCIPLES

Roadway argues that the drivers are independent contractors. In support of its argument, Roadway emphasizes, inter alia, that the drivers control their own work schedules and other details of job performance; they are not subject to a disciplinary policy; and their compensation package is based on performance-related components. Roadway further asserts that the drivers are independent entrepreneurs because they have a significant proprietary interest in their service areas and they have experienced gains and losses in their businesses. Roadway notes that the drivers, like independent businessmen, receive no fringe benefits from it, and they are responsible for their own tax withholdings.

Section 2(3) of the Act, as amended by the 1947 Labor Management Relations Act (the Taft-Hartley Act), provides that the term "employee" shall not include "any individual having the status of independent contractor."

In *NLRB v. United Insurance Co.*, 390 U.S. 254 (1968), the Court upheld the Board's determination of employee status for the debit agents of the respondent insurance company. In doing so, the Court emphasized the following "decisive factors" present in that case:

> [T]he agents do not operate their own independent businesses, but perform functions that are an essential part of the company's normal operations; they need not have any prior training or experience, but are trained by company supervisory personnel; they do business in the company's name with considerable assistance and guidance from the company and its managerial personnel and ordinarily sell only the company's policies; the "Agent's Commission plan" that contains the terms and conditions under which they operate is promulgated and changed unilaterally by the company; the agents account to the company for the funds they collect under an elaborate and regular reporting procedure; the agents receive the benefits of the company's vacation plan and group insurance and pension fund; and the agents have a permanent working arrangement with the company

under which they may continue as long as their performance is satisfactory. 390 U.S. at 259–60.

For a long time, *United Insurance* has been the preeminent guidance to the lower courts and the Board on what standard should be applied in differentiating employee status from independent contractor status in the NLRA context. Recent Supreme Court precedent reinforces *United Insurance*'s observations about the appropriateness of using the common law of agency as the test for determining employee status. *See NLRB v. Town & Country Electric*, 516 U.S. 85 (1995).

The Supreme Court has clearly stated that "all of the incidents of the relationship must be assessed and weighed with no one factor being decisive." See *United Insurance*, 390 U.S. at 258. Thus, the common-law agency test encompasses a careful examination of all factors and not just those that involve a right of control.

APPLICATION OF AGENCY TEST FACTORS

We find that the dealings and arrangements between these drivers and Roadway, including those reflective of the changes made [recently], have many of the same characteristics of the employee-employer relationship presented in *United Insurance*. Reviewing the factors relied on by the Board in *Roadway I*, we see insignificant change pointing to independent contractor status.

The Ontario and Pomona drivers devote a substantial amount of their time, labor, and equipment to performing essential functions that allow Roadway to compete in the small package delivery market. "[T]he functions performed by the drivers . . . constitute a regular and essential part of the company's business operations." *NLRB v. Amber Delivery, supra*, 651 F.2d at 63 (citing Restatement (Second) of Agency, Section 220(h)). None of the drivers are required to have prior delivery training or experience. Those unfamiliar with Roadway's system can gain assistance and guidance from the new driver orientation meetings that are conducted by Roadway's personnel. While a few operate as incorporated businesses, all the Ontario and Pomona drivers do business in the name of Roadway. Wearing an "RPS-approved uniform," the drivers operate uniformly marked vehicles. In fact, the vehicles are custom designed by Roadway and produced to its specifications by Navistar. The vehicles are identical as to make, model, internal shelving, and rear door, differing only as to chassis and payload (three choices depending on the size of the driver's primary service area). All the vehicles clearly display Roadway's name, logo, and colors. Thus, the drivers' connection to and integration in Roadway's operations is highly visible and well publicized.

The drivers have a contractual right to use this customized truck in business activity outside their relationship with Roadway, though none of the Ontario and Pomona drivers (and only 3 out of Roadway's 5,000 drivers nationwide) have used their vehicles for other commercial purposes. This lack of pursuit of outside business activity appears to be less a reflection of entrepreneurial choice by the Ontario and Pomona drivers and more a matter of the obstacles created by their relationship with Roadway.

Roadway's drivers are prohibited under the 1994 Agreement from conducting outside business for other companies throughout the day. The drivers' commitment to Roadway continues through the evening hours when they must return their vehicles to the terminal to interface with Roadway's evening line-haul operations. Typically, most drivers then take their vehicles out of circulation. They leave their vehicles overnight at the terminal to take advantage of loading of the next day's assignments by Roadway's package handlers. As a consequence, their vehicles remain out of service during these off-work hours. Even if the drivers want to use their vehicles for other purposes during their off-work hours, there are several obvious built-in hindrances. First, the vehicles are not readily available. Second, before the driver can use his vehicle for other purposes, he must mask any marking reflecting Roadway's name or business. Every vehicle utilized by the driver has been dictated in detail—color, size, internal configuration including the internal shelving and door—by Roadway's operations. The vehicles are also not easily flexible or susceptible to modifications or adaptations to other types of use. Thus, these constraints on the drivers' use of their vehicles during their off-work hours "provide minimal play for entrepreneurial initiative and minimize the extent to which ownership of a truck gives its driver entrepreneurial independence." *Amber Delivery Service, supra* at 63. Roadway has simply shifted certain capital costs to the drivers without providing them with the independence to engage in entrepreneurial opportunities.

Truck ownership can suggest independent contractor status where, for example, an entrepreneur with a truck puts it to use in serving his or another business' customers. But the form of truck ownership here does not eliminate the Ontario and Pomona drivers' dependence on Roadway in acquiring their vehicles. Roadway's indirect control is further seen in that it requires the drivers to acquire and maintain their own specialty vans, and Roadway eases the drivers' burden through its arrangement and promotion of Navistar vans sold or leased through Bush Leasing. Although it does not directly participate in these van transfers, Roadway's involvement in these deals undoubtedly facilitates and ensures that a fleet of vehicles, built and maintained according to its specifications, is always readily available and recyclable among the drivers.

In addition to this vehicle assistance, the "business support package" helps ensure that the drivers' vehicles are properly maintained and covered by specific warranties. Roadway reminds the drivers that certain essential maintenance is needed by placing charts on the windows of the drivers' vehicles. The brochure to prospective drivers also advertises Roadway's

[handwritten margin note: Constraints on personal use of trucks]

maintenance "assistance" and further notes that "RPS provides warranty recovery assistance" to its drivers. The "business support package" also gives the drivers easy access to clean work uniforms. This assistance by Roadway points in the direction of finding employee status for the Ontario and Pomona drivers.

Other support for employee status can be found in Roadway's compensation package for the drivers. Here, Roadway establishes, regulates, and controls the rate of compensation and financial assistance to the drivers as well as the rates charged to customers. Generally speaking, there is little room for the drivers to influence their income through their own efforts or ingenuity. Whatever potential for entrepreneurial profit does exist, Roadway suppresses through a system of minimum and maximum number of packages and customer stops assigned to the drivers. For example, when a driver becomes busier and the number of packages or customer stops grows, his territory may be unilaterally reconfigured, and the extra packages or stops are reassigned if the driver has already attained the maximum level for his primary service area that has been already determined by Roadway. "[I]t is clear that, unlike the genuinely independent businessman, the drivers' earnings do not depend largely on their ability to exercise good business judgment, to follow sound management practices, and to be able to take financial risks in order to increase their profits."

The weekly settlement sheets supplied by Roadway show that the main components of the drivers' income are the van availability settlement, the temporary core zone settlement, and the piece-rate payments for packages delivered and picked up. The daily van availability settlement is virtually guaranteed income of $40 per day for the life of the driver's contract with Roadway. Because the 1994 Agreement requires the driver to make his vehicle available each weekday over a period ranging from 1 to 5 years, the driver must show up for work each day to fulfill his contract obligations. This is not a situation where "[e]ach driver can decide not to work on any particular day-a freedom that further links his compensation to his personal initiative and effort."

In a similar fashion, the temporary core zone settlement subsidizes the driver's income. With the 1994 Agreement, the driver receives this supplement until he reaches the "normal" range of pickups and deliveries for his service area. In this way, the temporary core zone settlement serves as an important safety net for the fledging driver to shield him from loss, and it guarantees an income level predetermined by Roadway, irrespective of the driver's personal initiative and effort in his service area.

CONCLUSION

Weighing all the incidents of their relationship with Roadway, we conclude that the Ontario and Pomona drivers are employees and not independent contractors. Accordingly, we find that these employees of

Roadway constitute an appropriate unit for the purposes of collective bargaining within the meaning of Section 9(b) of the Act.

NOTES

1.   *The Never Ending Saga.* The foregoing case can be thought of as the third chapter in a still-unfolding saga, which now stars shipping giant FedEx as corporate successor to Roadway's ground package delivery service. The saga affects at least 15,000 drivers in the company's Ground Division. Over the years, the story line has changed little: the company and its owners keep coming up with variations on a creative operating model that is designed to transform their workers into independent contractors, thereby blocking them from access to federal and state laws designed to protect employees.

The first and second chapters were written in *Roadway Package System (Roadway I)*, 288 N.L.R.B. 196 (1988), and *Roadway Package System (Roadway II)*, 292 N.L.R.B. 376 (1989), *enf'd*, 902 F.2d 34 (6th Cir. 1990). Those cases were initiated by the Teamsters Union as part of an effort to organize single-route package delivery drivers working out of Roadway's Louisville, Kentucky, and Redford, Michigan, territories. In those cases, the Board (twice) and the Sixth Circuit (once) found the drivers to be employees within the meaning of the Act. In response, Roadway tried again to characterize the drivers as independent contractors by adopting numerous changes in their terms and conditions of work. Once more, as we have seen, the Board found the drivers to be employees.

Meanwhile, FedEx succeeded Roadway and continued to defend the company's unique business structure.

Applying federal labor law, the NLRB certified the results of a representation election won by the Teamsters at FedEx's Wilmington, Massachusetts, facility. FedEx contested the results by refusing to bargain with the union. A company spokesman said: "Because the Teamsters do not have the best interest of our contractors in mind, we will continue to work with our contractors to protect their investments so they can run their businesses without third-party interference." Nora L. Macey, *Contractor Status of FedEx Ground Drivers Challenged*, 36 Lab. & Emp. L. No. 1, at p. 12 (Fall 2007). Later, the Board decided that FedEx had violated its duty to bargain under Section 8(a)(5). *FedEx Home Delivery*, 351 N.L.R.B. No. 16 (2007). The U.S. Court of Appeals for the District Columbia, however, granted the company's petition for review and vacated the Board's order. According to the majority, the presence in the record of the many of the same factors thought by the NLRB to indicate employee status actually indicated independent contractor status because they are "characteristics of entrepreneurial potential." *FedEx Home Delivery v. NLRB*, 563 F.3d 492, 498 (D.C. Cir. 2009).

On remand, the Board adhered to its earlier finding that the drivers were employees. Citing the Restatement (Second) of Agency, Chairman Pearce and Members Hirozawa and Schiffer reasoned that the entrepreneurial opportunity available to the drivers was only one factor among many to be considered, rather than the decisive factor, as the D.C. Circuit had suggested. In this case, such opportunities were "more theoretical than actual," because drivers were tied to both long shifts that prevented them from moonlighting for other delivery services, and vehicles that were "specifically tailored" for FedEx's operations. *FedEx Home Delivery*, 361 N.L.R.B. No. 55, slip op. at pp. 20–21 (2014). Member Johnson dissented. Member Miscimarra did not participate. On review, however, the D.C. Circuit granted the employer's petition for review and denied enforcement of the Board's order, but did not reach the merits. The court reasoned that, under the law-of-the-circuit doctrine, the NLRB was not permitted effectively to nullify a decision by a prior panel of the D.C. Circuit by asking a second panel to apply same law to same material facts involving same parties but give a different answer. *See Fed Ex Home Delivery v. NLRB*, 849 F.3d 1123 (D.C. Cir. 2017).

Outside the context of the NLRA, FedEx has faced class and mass action litigation all over the country challenging as misclassification its persistent attempts to treat its drivers as independent contractors.

For example, in California, in a case applying Section 2802 of the state's Labor Code, which requires employers to reimburse their employees for work-related expenditures, the California Court of Appeal affirmed a trial court's finding that FedEx drivers are employees who are entitled to such reimbursements. The court explained: "FedEx's control over every exquisite detail of the drivers' performance, including the color of their socks and the style of their hair, supports the trial court's conclusion that the drivers are employees, not independent contractors." *Estrada v. FedEx Ground Package Sys. Inc. (Estrada III)*, 154 Cal. App.4th 1, 11–12, 64 Cal. Rptr.3d 327, 336 (2007). In a "stunning countermove," FedEx announced that it would not renew any operating agreements for incumbent California drivers. Instead, under a "transition program," the company gave them three choices: (1) walk away from working for the company; (2) sign a release and accept a severance benefit; or (3) apply for a new type of operating agreement with new terms written by FedEx. Macey, *supra*, at p. 12.

In Massachusetts, applying the state's Independent Contractor Statute, which requires employers to pay wages without deducting for certain expenses, the First Circuit rejected FedEx's challenge that the statute was preempted by federal aviation law. *See Schwann v. FedEx Ground Package System, Inc.*, 813 F.3d 429 (1st Cir. 2016).

By 2005, 36 cases challenging FedEx's independent contractor designation of its drivers had been transferred to a single court, the U.S. District Court for the Northern District of Indiana, by the Judicial Panel on Multidistrict Litigation (MDL).[2] *In re FedEx Ground Package Sys. Inc., Emp't Practices Litig.*, 381 F. Supp. 2d 1380 (Jud. Panel Multi.-Dist. Lit. 2005). By 2008, over

---

[2]   MDL refers to a special procedure by which complex federal litigation can be transferred from multiple geographical areas of the country to a single federal district court for the purpose of speeding the handling of that litigation. The MDL Panel may order such a transfer when "civil actions involving one or more common questions of fact are pending in different districts." 28 U.S.C. § 1407(a).

50 cases had been transferred and were pending there. Plaintiffs claimed that they were employees, not independent contractors, who were entitled to protection under a variety of legal statutes, including the Family and Medical Leave Act (FMLA), Employee Retirement Income Security Act (ERISA), and federal and state disability and fair labor standards laws. A number of cases were certified to proceed as class actions. *See, e.g., In re FedEx Ground Package Sys. Inc., Employment Practices Litig.*, 273 F.R.D. 424 (N.D. Ind. 2008). In most of the appeals connected to this multidistrict litigation, the class of FedEx drivers in question has been found to consist of employees rather than independent contractors. *See, e.g., Craig v. FedEx Ground Package System Inc.*, 792 F.3d 818 (7th Cir. Jul. 8, 2015) (Kansas drivers); *Alexander v. FedEx Ground Package System Inc.*, 765 F.3d 981 (9th Cir. 2014) (California drivers); *Slayman v. FedEx Ground Package System Inc.*, 765 F.3d 1033 (9th Cir. 2014) (Oregon drivers); *see also, e.g., Carlson v. FedEx Ground Package Systems Inc.*, 787 F.3d 1313 (11th Cir. 2015) (reversing grant of summary judgment for company due to material factual dispute as to status of Florida drivers).

Even though it has lost more legal battles than it has won, FedEx keeps calling the drivers independent contractors because it so lucrative to do so. *See* Ben Rooney, *The FedEx Driver Who Sued and Won*, CNN Money (Nov. 21, 2014), available at http://money.cnn.com/2014/11/20/news/companies/fedex-driver-lawsuit/index.html. All of which raises the question: if employers refuse to accept the official outcomes of court or administrative agency decisions, what is the point of regulatory processes in the first place? Can anything be done to fix it?

2.   *Room to maneuver?* Among the many facts supporting the Board's original determination that Roadway drivers were employees rather than independent contractors was this observation:

> Roadway establishes, regulates, and controls the rate of compensation and financial assistance to the drivers as well as the rates charged to customers. Generally speaking, there is little room for the drivers to influence their income through their own efforts or ingenuity.

Can the essence of what it means to be an independent contractor—that is, to be one's own boss—be distilled into the notion that she determines her income by her "own efforts and ingenuity"? If so, should a finding that "there is little room for the drivers to influence their income" by dint of the same, be dispositive in concluding they are really employees and not independent contractors? Does the right of control test, as articulated by the Restatement (Second) of Agency, adequately account the importance of "efforts and ingenuity"? Recall the "perma-temps" at Microsoft. By this standard, how would you classify them?

3.   *Tell us what you want—what you really, really want.* FedEx, Roadway's successor, claims that most of its ground drivers prefer to work as independent contractors, notwithstanding how they are characterized by the Board or the federal courts. Indeed, there is some evidence that drivers, as a

breed, would rather think of themselves as rugged individualists than as employees serving a boss. The matter of what drivers really want is hotly debated by the plaintiffs, and especially, the Teamsters Union, which has sought to organize the drivers. What weight, if any, should be given to drivers' stated preferences in determining their legal status?

4. *Be careful what you wish for.* Like Fed Ex, many operators of container and cargo hauling services at major ports of entry—including the Ports of Los Angeles and Long Beach, California—have gone to great lengths to classify their drivers as independent contractors rather than employees, no matter what the drivers, their unions, or the governing agencies say. The grueling conditions under which these drivers work, and their poverty, are appalling. *See, e.g.*, Brett Murphy, *Rigged: Forced into Debt. Worked Past Exhaustion. Left with Nothing*, USA Today, Jun. 16, 2017, available at https://www.usatoday.com/pages/interactives/news/rigged-forced-into-debt-worked-past-exhaustion-left-with-nothing/.

Can the intentional misclassification of such workers itself constitute an unfair labor practice? Although the NLRB has yet to address this question, the Obama Era General Counsel weighed in by issuing an advice memorandum. *See Pac 9 Transportation Inc.*, Case No. 21-CA-150875 (Dec. 15, 2015) (finding such misclassification to violate Sections 8(a)(1) and (3)).

5. *Baby, you can drive your car.* Another type of driver—operators who use "apps" developed by Lyft, Uber, or other ride-hailing service to pick up fares with their own cars, or cars leased from the service—has become enmeshed in misclassification litigation too. In a series of class actions brought in major cities around the country, the key question is the same: whether such drivers are employees or independent contractors for purposes of the minimum wage and overtime protections of the FLSA.

In 2018, in the first case to grant summary judgment on the question, a federal district judge in Pennsylvania ruled that a class of drivers providing limousine service known as UberBLACK were independent contractors. The decision, which applied a six-factor version of the "economic realities" test, seemed to favor Uber's portrayal of the plaintiff-drivers as

> entrepreneurial business-owners who use UberBLACK as a means of acquiring trip requests, with their primary competition coming from other limousine-for-hire companies. Uber contends that Plaintiffs are not employees of Uber because Plaintiffs are not restricted from working for other companies, pay their own expenses (which are substantial), invest in their own companies, advertise and market for their own companies, engage workers for their own companies, work using UberBLACK as much or as little as they want, reject work from UberBLACK as much as they want, and use business acumen to attain their own profits (and losses). In Uber's view, UberBLACK is simply a source of "lead generation," like a "modern-day Yellow Pages," rather than an "employer" under the FLSA.

Razak v. Uber Technologies, Inc., 2018 WL 1744467 (E.D. Pa. Apr. 11, 2018), slip op. at 12.

What do you think? As a user or perhaps provider of ride-hailing services, do you think the driver is or should be treated as an employee? Why or why not?

6.   *The Canadian experience.* Not every jurisdiction considers an "independent contractor" to be ineligible for the labor law protections afforded to employees. For example, under the labor laws of Saskatchewan, Canada, the term "employee" includes "any person designated by the [province's labour relations] board as an employee for purposes of this Act notwithstanding that for the purpose of determining whether or not the person to whom he provides his services is vicariously liable for his acts or omissions he may be held to be an independent contractor." Saskatchewan Trade Union Act, 1978 Rev. Sask. Stat. § 2(f)(iii).

Does this mean there is such a thing as a "dependent" contractor? If not, should there be? How would you define the term? Would the perma-temps at Microsoft fit your definition of "dependent" contractors? For a discussion of scholarship proposing the creation of "dependent" contractor status in the U.S., see Kenneth G. Dau-Schmidt, *The Problem of "Misclassification" or How to Define who is an "Employee" Under Protective Legislation in the Information Age*, in The Cambridge Handbook of U.S. Labor Law: Reviving American Labor Law for a 21st Century Economy ___ (forthcoming 2018), available at https://papers.ssrn.com/sol3/papers.cfm?abstract_id=3143296.

HOME HEALTH CARE WORKERS GET ORGANIZED[3]

Stu Schneider
Dollars and Sense, pp. 25–27 (2003)

Thirteen thousand home care workers in Oregon voted overwhelmingly two years ago to join the Service Employees International Union (SEIU). The vote was the culmination of a four-year statewide campaign modeled on earlier efforts in Washington and California. "Twenty years of being unrecognized, underpaid, with no benefits, essentially an invisible workforce, has made many of us frustrated and searching for solutions," Herk Mertens, a home care worker from Waldport, Ore., told the Labor Research Association after the vote. "I honestly feel the union is the only way home care workers and our clients have the ability to be visible, to have a voice decision makers will hear, and to press for improvements in quality of care and working conditions."

Nationwide, 12 million people need long-term care services and support. Home care workers bathe, clean, and feed the frail elderly and individuals with physical disabilities. They assist their clients at the toilet and transfer them to bed. Their work is physically and emotionally

---

[3]   Reprinted by permission of *Dollars & Sense*, a progressive economics magazine www.dollarsandsense.org.

demanding, but essential in a society with an aging population. Their efforts enable home care consumers to live independently within their homes and communities.

Despite their importance, home care workers are among the most underpaid workers in the United States. Predominantly women of color, they typically earn minimum wage or just above. Too often they and their children remain mired in long-term poverty.

Home Care Workers' Legal Bind

Home care workers' economic plight is compounded by a legal bind. In many areas of the country, they are classified as independent contractors. Technically "self-employed," they have no outside employer (even though their pay often comes from federal or state funds like Medicaid). As a result, they get no employer-sponsored benefits or workers' compensation insurance, and they are responsible for paying both the employee and employer portions of their payroll taxes out of their own paltry paychecks. Moreover, federal antitrust law bans independent contractors from unionizing or bargaining collectively. In the eyes of the law, self-employed home care workers are not workers, but businesses. Any effort to join together and unionize, therefore, is viewed as "collusion."

This makes the recent west coast union victories all the more remarkable. In California, Oregon, and Washington, organized labor, in coalition with disabilities activists, senior citizens' lobbies, and community groups, forged a new three-step organizing strategy. In the process, these labor-community coalitions have transformed the structure of employment in the home health care sector.

California's Public Authority Model

The strategy was born in a 15-year struggle in California. In-Home Supportive Services (IHSS), the state's massive home care program, is the nation's largest and currently employs more than 202,000 workers. SEIU first attempted to organize these workers in the 1980s, but state courts created a roadblock. In 1990, the California Court of Appeal ruled that home care workers were employees of neither the State of California (which paid them) nor the local county where they worked (to whom they submitted their semi-monthly time sheets). *See SEIU Local 434 v. County of Los Angeles*, 225 Cal. App. 3d 761, 275 Cal. Rptr. 508 (1990). Home care worker Amanda Figueroa testified before the Los Angeles County Board of Supervisors in 2001 that the workers had been like "ping pong balls" tossed between the two governments, neither of which wanted to accept fiscal responsibility for wage increases or benefits coverage.

Following the court decision, SEIU realized it first had to establish an "employer of record." The union joined with consumer advocacy groups, including the California Senior Legislature, the California Foundation for Independent Living Centers, the Congress of California Seniors, and IHSS participants, to pursue public authority legislation. United under the slogan "Keep what works, fix what's wrong, and fund!" the coalition won passage in 1992 of a law that established county-level public authorities to oversee home health service delivery. The new law empowered counties to increase local control of IHSS, established mechanisms for consumer input into policy, and created an employer of record for workers. This in effect established a legal employment relationship between home care workers and the public authority for the purpose of collective bargaining, enabling SEIU to move forward with organizing drives. *See* Cal. Welf. & Inst. Code Ann. § 12301.6.

The public authority model initially spread across seven California counties, representing over 50% of the state's IHSS home care workers. Stakeholders—workers, clients, and the new authorities, along with statewide coalitions like the Public Interest Center on Long-Term Care and IHSS Agenda—kept public officials aware of the need for further improvements to the IHSS system. In 1999, SEIU Local 434B won the right to represent 74,000 home care workers in Los Angeles County. It was the biggest union victory, in terms of numbers of new members, since the 1940s. The same year, the public authorities joined activists to advocate successfully for additional legislation that mandated what had previously been optional: designating an employer of record for all IHSS workers and establishing consumer-majority advisory committees to oversee IHSS delivery issues. Faced with these new requirements, all 58 California counties have launched public authorities.

The 1999 legislation also mandated that California pay 65% of the wages and benefits of home care workers above a minimum threshold, so that total compensation could increase gradually to a maximum of $11.50 per hour over a four-year period (up from the minimum wage of $4.25 in 1991)—if counties funded the remaining 35%. While organized labor spearheaded this effort, these benefits could never have been won without assistance from consumers and the public authorities.

Economist Candace Howe evaluated the economic impact of the near doubling of IHSS workers' wages in San Francisco County. She found that IHSS jobs represent 8% of all low-wage jobs, 16% of low-wage jobs available to women, and 25% of all low-wage jobs available to immigrant women without English language proficiency. Her analysis suggests increasing wages for home care workers reduced San Francisco's overall poverty rate by about 16%.

Spreading the Model

In November 2000, Oregon voters approved a constitutional amendment creating a statewide quality home care commission modeled after California's reformed system. This entity became the employer of record for 13,000 independent contractors who assist nearly 20,000 long-term care consumers. *See* Ore. Rev. Stat. Ann. §§ 410.612, 410.614. "It was the first time ever that collective bargaining rights were extended through a ballot measure," SEIU Local 503 organizing director Steven Ward said.

In December 2001, independent contractors who were previously prohibited from collective bargaining voted—92% in favor—to join Local 503. In June 2003, after more than two years of negotiation, the state approved a contract with Local 503 that, for the first time in the program's history, offers home care workers paid health insurance, workers' compensation coverage, and paid vacation, while boosting wages by 70 cents per hour.

In November 2001, voters in the State of Washington passed ballot initiative 775 approving a statewide home care public authority to serve as the employer of record for 26,000 home care workers. *See* Rev. Code Wash. §§ 74.39A.230, 74.39A.270. Eighty-four percent of them supported the call to unionize. "Every state should be doing this," Karen Thompson, president of a sub-local union, said.

But one lesson from the Washington case is that in the current state fiscal environment, unionization does not always guarantee better pay. In Washington, any agreement between the union and the public authority board must be approved by the legislature and the governor. The statehouse passed a raise for home care workers, only to see it vetoed by Gov. Gary Locke in the name of a balanced budget.

Results

Still, the unionized public authority model has clearly brought gains. By serving as the employer of record for individuals previously considered independent contractors, public authorities in California, Oregon, and Washington allowed almost 300,000 home care workers to unionize and collectively bargain for higher compensation and other changes. While the financial gains have been small for some, for many others, pay and benefits improved dramatically.

Moreover, the election victories represent an area of growth for the labor movement. David Rolf, an organizer for SEIU Local 434B in Los Angeles County, told the New York Times after the vote: "It is a campaign where we reached out to low-income, women workers, workers of color, and immigrant workers. If you look at the demographic changes in Southern California, the labor movement has to figure out how to bring these workers in because they are the backbone of the new, low-wage service sector economy."

NOTES

1. *Further extensions.* California, Oregon, and Washington are not the only jurisdictions to extend collective bargaining rights to home health care workers by creating public authority employers of record. By 2006, Illinois had enacted such a statute, *see* Disabled Persons Rehabilitation Act, 20 Ill. Comp.

Stat. (Smith-Hurd) § 2405/3, and by 2013, Minnesota had done likewise, *see* Family Child Care Providers Representation Act, S.F. 778, *codified at* Minn. Stat. §§ 179A.50–179A.53.

In 2010, New York went in a somewhat different direction by enacting a package of reforms that both extended collective bargaining rights to all domestic workers without creating a public agency employer of record, and established minimum wage, overtime, and sexual harassment protections, *see* Domestic Workers' Bill of Rights, 2010 N.Y. Sess. Laws 1313 (McKinney), *codified at* N.Y. Exec. L. §§ 292, 296–b; N.Y. Lab. L. §§ 2, 160, 161, 170, 651; N.Y. Workers' Comp. L. § 201. In 2013, Hawaii did the same thing, *see* Domestic Workers' Bill of Rights, S.B. 535, *codified at* Haw. Rev. Stat. §§ 387–1, 387–3. Also in 2013, after revisiting the issue several times, California enacted a more limited statute granting overtime to personal attendants working in private homes, *see* Domestic Worker Bill of Rights, A.B. 241, *codified at* Cal. Lab. Code §§ 1450–1454.

In 2014, the U.S. Supreme Court decided an important case that called into question the financial viability of the public authority model embraced by California, Illinois, Minnesota, Oregon, Washington, and other states. By a vote of 5 to 4, the Court ruled that personal care assistants who are paid by the State of Illinois, but who are mostly supervised by the homecare recipients they serve, are not "full-fledged" public employees who could be compelled to pay their "fair share" of union dues. *Harris v. Quinn*, 134 S. Ct. 2618 (2014), discussed *infra* Chapter 8. The ruling made it more difficult for home health care workers' unions to finance their operations, including the organization and representation of such workers.

What is the practical reason for creating a public authority employer? Is it because the government is in a better position than the individual workers to spread the cost of employment risks, such as health benefits and unemployment insurance? Because public employees have political clout that elected officials ignore at their peril? What other reasons might there be?

2.   *America's next top model?* Recall the Microsoft perma-temps. Can the "public authority" model be extended to workers characterized as independent contractors in the private sector, or is it limited to workers whose wages are funded by public money? If it is not so limited, does this mean that insurance agents, gardeners, realtors, longshoremen, prize-fighters, and other workers who are usually considered "independent contractors" should have collective bargaining rights too? If it is limited, what other means of collective action are available to such workers? *See, e.g.,* Ruth Milkman, Joshua Bloom & Victor Narro, Working for Justice: The L.A. Model of Organizing and Advocacy (2010) (describing 11 Los Angeles-based organizing campaigns among low-wage workers such as day laborers, garment workers, car wash workers, security officers, taxi drivers, and hotel workers); *Janice Fine, Worker Centers: Organizing at the Edge of the Dream*, 50 N.Y.L. Sch. L. Rev. 417 (2005–2006) (describing 9 major workers' centers and their role in organizing immigrants seeking improved wages and working conditions); Christopher David Ruiz Cameron, *The Rakes of Wrath: Urban Agricultural Workers and the Struggle*

Against Los Angeles' Ban on Gas-Powered Leaf Blowers, 33 U.C. Davis L. Rev. 1087 (2000) (describing direct action and litigation strategy by residential gardeners, who challenged a city ordinance designed to curtail noise and air pollution by banning their use of gas-powered leaf blowers).

If the public authority model is limited to workers whose wages are funded by public money, how might day care, foster care, and respite care workers, who often toil for private operators providing services under government contracts, be able to take advantage of it?

3. *The home care industry: all in the family.* As reported by Stu Schneider, one study found that over 90% of all home care workers are women, one-third are African American, nearly one-fifth are Hispanic, and 20% are immigrants. The same study noted that one out of four home care workers is married with young children. According to the SEIU, of some 2 million paraprofessionals employed in the long-term care sector, 600,000 earn wages below the poverty line. In California, 77% of home care workers are women; half are between the ages of 41 and 60; and most work part-time. Almost 40% are relatives paid to care for parents, spouses, and other family members.

One scholar has described the hurdles facing domestic workers this way:

> Domestic workers have to struggle not only against the idea that the work they do is not really work (i.e., that it's just part of women's natural proclivities), and that its value in the labor market is limited, but also against deeply imbedded legal doctrine that treats the family home as a near-sacred forum into which there should be no governmental intrusion.

Donna E. Young, *The Constitutional Parameters of New York State's Domestic Workers Bill of Rights: Balancing the Rights of Workers and Employers*, 74 Alb. L. Rev. 1767, 1771 (2010–2011).

Do you agree? If so, how should this sentiment affect policy making in this area? Are there any policy concerns raised by extending collective bargaining rights to workers having such extensive family ties to their clients? Do these ties have any implications for demands that in-home working conditions, as opposed to wages and benefits, be changed?

4. *Don't know much about history?* Students (and practitioners) of the law sometimes forget that the evolution of present legal doctrine is rarely inevitable; any number of approaches might have been taken to tackle the problem. For example, the original definition of "employee" in the Wagner Act did not include an express exemption for "independent contractors." In interpreting this definition of employee, the Supreme Court applied the "economic realities test" which included anyone who, under the economic realities of the case, was a dependent worker who would benefit from collective bargaining so as to effectuate the purposes of the Act. Applying this test, the Board and the Supreme Court included as employees under the NLRA some workers who would be independent contractors under the common law agency test. *See NLRB v. Hearst Publ'ns, Inc.*, 322 U.S. 111 (1944) (holding that "newsboys"—who were generally grown men whom Hearst Publications had

solicited to purchase newspapers and resell them in newsstands or on streets—were employees of the paper under the NLRA). This extension of coverage of the NLRA to some independent contractors was so unpopular with business interests that Congress passed the Taft-Hartley Act amendments to Section 2(3) to exempt independent contractors from the NLRA—which specifically overruled *Hearst. See NLRB v. United Insurance Co.*, 390 U.S. 254 (1968). The "obvious purpose" of these amendments was to require the Board to apply common law agency principles in distinguishing between independent contractors and employees. *United Insurance*, 390 U.S. at 256.

As to the policy behind the Taft-Hartley Act amendments, do you agree with Congress' decision to exclude independent contractors, or should they still be considered employees entitled to the protections of the Act? Which approach better fulfills the Act's purpose of promoting equality in bargaining power? Is your answer influenced by the admitted difficulty of drawing lines between the very similar facts of different cases? Recall *Roadway Package System*, in which the drivers were held to be employees. Compare it with, for example, *Dial-A-Mattress Operating Corp.*, 326 N.L.R.B. 884 (1998), in which owner-operator drivers were held to be independent contractors. Would you draw the line in these cases any differently? The economic realities test is still used in defining who is an employee under several federal statutes, including the Fair Labor Standards Act. *See Secretary of Labor v. Lauritzen*, 835 F.2d 1529 (7th Cir. 1987). Is this test better for determining who should be covered by federal labor and employment statutes in the new age of contingent employment? Would it solve some of the current problems in determining who is an employee? What might the trade-offs be?

5. *Regulation vs. the market.* Is legislation the proper vehicle for addressing the human costs accompanying the growth of contingent work, or should the marketplace be left to its own devices? After all, substantial economic benefits must attach to contingent work arrangements, or producers of goods and services would not use them so widely. *See, e.g.*, Maria O'Brien Hylton, *The Case Against Regulating the Market for Contingent Employment*, 52 Wash. & Lee L. Rev. 849 (1995). Could the solution—if one is required—be as simple as expanding the definition of who counts as an "employee" under existing regulations, including Section 2(2) of the NLRA? *See e.g.*, Kenneth G. Dau-Schmidt, *The Labor Market Transformed: Adapting Labor and Employment Law to the Rise of the Contingent Workforce*, 52 Wash. & Lee L. Rev. 879 (1995).

b. Leased Employees and Subcontractors' Employees

Whereas independent contractors are contingent employees because they have chosen—willingly or not—to accept the shifting onto their shoulders of the risks associated with work, leased employees and subcontractors' employees are contingent because somebody else has unilaterally reallocated those risks for them. There are at least two ways to do this: by separating "core" from "non-core" employee functions, as contemplated by Dr. Belous, *supra* p. 226, or by subcontracting out parts of the job to third parties, such as non-union subsidiaries. The former arrangement is usually called employee "leasing"; the latter is called "subcontracting" or, if parts of the job are shipped to third parties overseas, "off shoring."

i. Leased Employees

The business of employee leasing has grown rapidly. By the mid-1990s, the largest employer in the United States was no longer General Motors, the automotive giant, but Manpower Inc., a temporary employment agency. *See* Patricia Schroeder, *Does the Growth in the Contingent Workforce Demand a Change in Federal Labor Policy?*, 52 Wash. & Lee L. Rev. 731, 731 (1995).

In a leased employee arrangement, the supplier company supplies or "leases" workers to the client or "user" company. Typically, the workers are carried on the payroll of the supplier company and directed in their day-to-day assignments by the client company, but there are many variations on this theme. In the years before employee leasing became so pervasive, the NLRB took the position that it was inappropriate for a bargaining unit to include workers of both the supplier company and the client company, even if they performed the same work, and even if some of them were conceded to be employed jointly by both companies. In essence, a worker could not be considered an "employee" of both the supplier and client companies absent the consent of both employers. *See Greenhoot Inc.*, 205 N.L.R.B. 250 (1973); *accord Lee Hospital*, 300 N.L.R.B. 947 (1990).

Four years later, the NLRB overruled *Sturgis* and reinstated the employer consent rule articulated in *Greenhoot* and *Lee Hospital. See Oakwood Care Center*, 343 N.L.R.B. 659 (2004). But twelve years after that, the Board overruled *Oakwood Care Center* and reinstated the rule articulated in *Sturgis*.

MILLER & ANDERSON, INC.
364 N.L.R.B. No. 39 (2016)

By CHAIRMAN PEARCE and MEMBERS MISCIMARRA, HIROZAWA, and McFERRAN:

DECISION ON REVIEW AND ORDER

I.   Introduction

The fundamental issue raised by the Petitioner's request for review is whether under the National Labor Relations Act the employees who work for a user employer—both those employees the user alone employs and those employees it jointly employs (along with a supplier employer)—must obtain employer consent if they wish to be represented for purposes of collective bargaining in a single unit, even if both groups of employees share a community of interest with one another under the Board's traditional test for determining appropriate units.

Anyone familiar with the Act's history might well wonder why employees must obtain the consent of their employers in order to bargain collectively. After all, Congress passed the Act to compel employers to recognize and bargain with the designated representatives of appropriate units of employees, even if the employers would prefer not to do so. But most recently in *Oakwood Care Center*, 343 N.L.R.B. 659 (2004), the Board held that bargaining units that combine employees who are solely employed by a user employer and employees who are jointly employed by that same user employer and an employer supplying employees to the user employer constitute multi-employer units, which are appropriate only with the consent of the parties. The *Oakwood* Board thereby overruled *M.B. Sturgis, Inc.*, 331 N.L.R.B. 1298 (2000), which had held that the Act permits such units without the consent of the user and supplier employers, provided the employees share a community of interest.

The Petitioner requests that the Board overturn *Oakwood* and return to the rule of *Sturgis* in its request for review of the Regional Director's administrative dismissal of its petition seeking to represent a unit of all sheet metal workers employed by Miller & Anderson, Inc. and/or Tradesmen International as either single employers or joint employers on all job sites in Franklin County, Pennsylvania.

We granted review to consider the important issue raised by the Petitioner.

After carefully considering the briefs of the parties and amici and the views of our dissenting colleague, we conclude that Sturgis is more consistent with our statutory charge. Accordingly, we overrule Oakwood and return to the holding of Sturgis. Employer consent is not necessary for units that combine jointly employed and solely employed employees of a single user employer. Instead, we will apply the traditional community of interest factors to decide if such units are appropriate. We also agree with the Sturgis Board's clarification that there is no statutory impediment to processing petitions that seek units composed only of the employees supplied to a single user, or that seek units of all the employees of a supplier employer and name only the supplier employer. We remand the case to the Regional Director for further proceedings consistent with this Decision.

III. Discussion

Section 9 of the Act speaks to the implementation of employees' right to bargain collectively through representatives of their own choosing. Section 9(a) thus provides that representatives "designated or selected for the purposes of collective bargaining by the majority of the employees in a unit appropriate for such purposes, shall be the exclusive representatives of all the employees in such unit for the purposes of collective bargaining in respect to rates of pay, wages, hours of employment, or other conditions of employment[.]" 29 U.S.C. § 159(a). And Section 9(b) relevantly provides that "[t]he Board shall decide in each case whether, in order to assure to employees the fullest freedom in exercising the rights guaranteed by this Act, the unit appropriate for the purposes of collective bargaining shall be the employer unit, craft unit, plant unit, or subdivision thereof[.]" 29 U.S.C. § 159(b). But neither Section, nor any other portion of Section 9 or the Act itself, explicitly addresses whether the Board may find appropriate a unit that combines employees solely employed by a user employer and employees jointly employed by that same user employer and a supplier employer.

That circumstance establishes two important foundations for our consideration of the employer-consent issue. First, the Act does not compel *Oakwood*'s holding that bargaining units combining solely employed and jointly employed employees are appropriate only with the consent of the user and supplier employers. Second, precisely because the Act does not dictate a particular rule, we may find that another rule is not only a permissible interpretation of the statute, but also that it better serves the purposes of the Act. For the reasons explained below, we find that the *Sturgis* rule, not requiring employer consent to units combining jointly employed and solely employed employees of a single user employer, meets both of those criteria.

A.   *Sturgis* Is Consistent With Section 9(b)

The "exact limits of the Board's powers" under Section 9 and "the precise meaning" of the term "employer unit" are not defined by the statute. Notably, however, the statutory definition of the terms "employer" and "employee" in Sections 2(2) and 2(3) of the Act are very broad, and, as described, Congress's "statutory command" to the Board, in deciding whether a particular bargaining unit is appropriate, is "to assure to employees the fullest freedom in exercising the rights guaranteed by th[e] Act[.]" *Gallenkamp Stores Co. v. NLRB*, 402 F.2d at 532 (quoting Section 9(b)). In that context, we are persuaded that a unit combining employees solely employed by a user employer and employees jointly employed by that same user employer and a supplier employer logically falls within the ambit of a 9(b) employer unit. All the employees in such a unit are performing work for the user employer and are employed within the meaning of the common law by the user employer. Thus, the user employer and the supplier employer are joint employers of the employees referred by the supplier to the user for the latter's use. The employees solely employed by the user employer likewise plainly perform work for the user employer and are employed by the user within the meaning of the common law. In sum, a *Sturgis* unit comprises employees who, working side by side, are part of a common enterprise.

The restrictive view that the *Oakwood* Board and our dissenting colleague place on Section 9(b) is based on the erroneous conception that bargaining in a *Sturgis* unit constitutes multi-employer bargaining, which requires the consent of all parties. However, in the traditional multi-employer bargaining situation, the employers are entirely independent businesses, with nothing in common except that they operate in the same industry. They are often in competition for work with each other, operate at separate locations on different work projects, and hire their own employees. Multi-employer bargaining units are created without regard for any preexisting community of interest among the employees of the various separate employers. In fact, the Board developed the consent requirement in such cases precisely because the employers at issue were physically and economically separate from each other, their operations were not intermingled, and their employees were not jointly controlled.

In multi-employer bargaining, the unrelated employers on their own initiative decide to join an employer association and bargain through a mutually selected agent to match union strength and to avoid the competitive disadvantages resulting from nonuniform contractual terms. As an agency relationship cannot be compelled, multi-employer bargaining is voluntary in nature; unions may not coerce employers into joining associations which negotiate labor contracts on behalf of their members. Indeed, by conceding that employer consent is not required when a petition names two employers and seeks a unit composed of the employees jointly employed by the two employers, *Oakwood* itself recognized that a bargaining unit involving more than one employer is not ipso facto a "multi-employer bargaining unit."

There plainly is a distinction of substance between a *Sturgis* unit and a multi-employer bargaining unit. Put simply, as shown, in a *Sturgis* unit, all of the employees are employed by the user employer. After all, the employees who are solely employed by the user employer share an employer (the user employer) with the contingent employees who are jointly employed by that same user employer and a supplier employer. Thus, a *Sturgis* unit fits comfortably within 9(b)'s sanctioning of an "employer unit." By contrast, although a multi-employer bargaining unit also involves more than one employer, there is no common user employer for all the employees in such a unit.

The legislative history relied on in *Oakwood*, 343 N.L.R.B. at 661, which indicates that "Congress included the phrase 'or subdivision thereof' [in Section 9(b)] to authorize other units 'not as broad as 'employer unit,' yet not necessarily coincident with the phrases 'craft unit' or 'plant unit,'" does not persuade us that a single user employer unit is inappropriate. That Congress sought to authorize the Board to find appropriate employer subunits hardly establishes that Congress sought to disallow units of employees of a user employer combined with employees who the user jointly employs with a supplier. Indeed, our dissenting colleague, like the Oakwood majority, cites no legislative history expressing disapproval of such units. The only concern expressed by either the Wagner Act Congress or the Taft-Hartley Congress with respect to bargaining units that included more than one employer was focused on industrywide or anticompetitive bargaining units and on multiple-worksite situations.

Tradesmen, several amici, and our dissenting colleague nevertheless contend that the Board is precluded from returning to Sturgis, relying on the following single phrase from Section 9(b) of the Act to support their argument:

> The Board shall decide in each case whether, in order to assure to employees the fullest freedom in exercising the rights guaranteed by this Act, the unit appropriate for the purposes of collective bargaining shall be the employer unit, craft unit, plant unit, or subdivision thereof[.]

29 U.S.C. § 159(b). Citing *Oakwood*, they reason that because the broadest permissible unit category listed in Section 9(b) is the "employer unit," with each of the other delineated types of appropriate units representing subgroups of the work force of an employer, "the text of the Act reflects that Congress has not authorized the Board to direct elections in units encompassing the employees of more than one employer." *Oakwood*, 343 N.L.R.B. at 661.

However, the proponents of this argument put more weight on those few words than they can reasonably carry. As we have explained, given the broad definition of "employer" and "employee" in Sections 2(2) and 2(3) of the Act, along with our statutory charge to afford employees "the fullest freedom" in exercising their right to bargain collectively, a combined unit of employees solely employed by a user employer and employees jointly employed by that same user employer and a supplier employer does not fall outside the ambit of a Section 9(b) "employer unit," because all work is performed for the user employer and all employees are employed, either solely, or jointly, by the user employer. And, as we explain below, finding such a unit to be appropriate is responsive to Section 9(b)'s statutory command and effectuates fundamental policies of the Act. Accordingly, we conclude that the Act does not preclude us from returning to *Sturgis*.

B.   Sturgis Effectuates Fundamental Policies of the Act that Oakwood Frustrates

Sturgis is manifestly more responsive than *Oakwood* to Section 9(b)'s "statutory command" to the Board, in deciding whether a petitioned-for bargaining unit is appropriate, " 'to assure to employees the fullest freedom in exercising the rights guaranteed' by th[e] Act[.]" *Gallenkamp Stores Co. v. NLRB*, 402 F.2d at 532 (quoting Section 9(b)). The Board has recognized that "[a] key aspect of the right to 'self-organization' is the right to draw the boundaries of that organization—to choose whom to include and whom to exclude." *Specialty Healthcare & Rehabilitation Center of Mobile,* 357 N.L.R.B. 934, 941 n.18 (2011), *aff'd sub. nom, Kindred Nursing Centers East, LLC v. NLRB,* 727 F.3d 552 (6th Cir. 2013). The *Sturgis* approach honors that principle because it does not require employees to obtain employer permission before they may organize in their desired unit. Nor does *Sturgis* mandate any particular bargaining unit for the contingent employees (who are jointly employed by a user employer and a supplier employer) and the employees solely employed by that same user employer.

In contrast, Oakwood denies employees in an otherwise appropriate unit full freedom of association. Requiring employees to obtain employer permission to organize in such a unit is surely not what Congress envisioned when it instructed the Board, in deciding whether a particular bargaining unit is appropriate, "to assure to employees the fullest freedom in exercising the rights guaranteed by th[e] Act." 29 U.S.C. § 159(b). In fact, by requiring employer consent to an otherwise appropriate bargaining unit desired by employees, *Oakwood* has upended the Section 9(b) mandate and allowed employers to shape their ideal bargaining unit, which is precisely the opposite of what Congress intended.

Oakwood also potentially limits the contingent employees' opportunity for workplace representation. Under Oakwood, the contingent employees cannot organize in the same unit as the employees solely employed by the user employer unless the user and supplier employers consent.

Sturgis is also more consistent with the premise upon which national labor policy is based, because it permits employees in an otherwise appropriate unit to pool their economic strength and act through a union freely chosen by the majority so that they can effectively bargain for improvements in their wages, hours and working conditions. *See NLRB v. Allis-Chalmers Manufacturing Co.,* 388 U.S. 175, 180 (1967) (our national labor policy "has been built on the premise that by pooling their economic strength and acting through a labor organization freely chosen by the majority, the employees of an appropriate unit have the most effective means of bargaining for improvements in wages, hours, and working conditions.").

The deleterious effects of the *Oakwood* rule requiring employer consent are all the more troubling because of changes in the American economy over the last several decades. In *Browning-Ferris Industries of California, Inc.,* 362 N.L.R.B. No. 186 (2015) (BFI II) [discussed *infra,* Chapter 3-C-5], we recently characterized these changes as follows:

> [T]he diversity of workplace arrangements in today's economy has significantly expanded. The procurement of employees through staffing and subcontracting arrangements, or contingent employment, has increased[.] The most recent Bureau of Labor Statistics survey from 2005 indicated that contingent

workers accounted for as much as 4.1 percent of all employment, or 5.7 million workers. Employment in the temporary help services industry, a subset of contingent work, grew from 1.1 million to 2.3 million workers from 1990 to 2008. As of August 2014, the number of workers employed through temporary agencies had climbed to a new high of 2.87 million, a 2 percent share of the nation's work force. Over the same period, temporary employment also expanded into a much wider range of occupations. A recent report projects that the number of jobs in the employment services industry, which includes employment placement agencies and temporary help services, will increase to almost 4 million by 2022, making it "one of the largest and fastest growing [industries] in terms of employment."

In *BFI II*, we concluded that given our "responsibility to adapt the Act to the changing patterns of industrial life," this change in the nature of the workforce was reason enough to revisit the Board's then current joint-employer standard. Just as was the case with respect to that standard, *Oakwood* imposes additional requirements that are disconnected from the reality of today's workforce and are not compelled by the Act. We correspondingly conclude that to fully protect employee rights, the Board should return to the standard articulated in Sturgis.

C. The Policy Arguments Advanced by Sturgis' Opponents Are Unpersuasive

Tradesmen, several amici, and our dissenting colleague also argue that returning to *Sturgis* would be unwise as a policy matter because it would hinder meaningful bargaining, threaten labor peace, and harm employee rights. They argue that this is so because *Sturgis* permits a bargaining structure that allegedly gives rise to significant conflicts both among the various employers and among the groups of employees participating in the process, thereby making agreement much less likely and increasing the chances for labor strife.

However, the specter of conflicts posited by *Sturgis'* opponents did not materialize during the many decades before Sturgis that the Board had "routinely found units of the employees of a single employer appropriate, regardless of whether some of those employees were jointly employed by other employers." *Sturgis*, 331 N.L.R.B. at 1302–07. And *Sturgis'* opponents do not demonstrate that those problems materialized in the years between Sturgis and *Oakwood*.

Nor are we persuaded by the other policy arguments opposing a return to *Sturgis*. For example, some amici argue that the Board would harm contingent workers and the economy as a whole if it were to return to *Sturgis*. They reason that if the Board were to overturn *Oakwood* and return to *Sturgis*, it would discourage employers from entering into, or maintaining, alternative staffing arrangements because user employers will wish to avoid the costs, uncertainty and inherent difficulties presented by the prospect of bargaining in *Sturgis* units. But this employer wish runs counter to the Act's stated policy of encouraging the practice of collective bargaining. In any event, *Sturgis* leaves employers free to enter into, or maintain, such arrangements. In other words, we have decided to return to *Sturgis*, not to prevent employers from entering into, or maintaining user-supplier arrangements, but rather to better effectuate the policies of the Act if the employees affected by such arrangements choose to exercise their Section 7 rights.

The Chamber of Commerce of the United States of America cautions that overturning *Oakwood* and returning to *Sturgis* would be bad for unions seeking to organize just the employees solely employed by the user employer, because "employers may use *Sturgis* as a weapon to dilute a union's support" and to preclude employees solely employed by a user employer "from being represented at all." The Chamber adds, "If the temporary [supplier] employees outnumber the employees solely employed by the user, this possibility may well become likely." In our view, rather than undermining the case for returning to *Sturgis*, the suggestion that employers might choose which positions to take regarding the inclusion of the supplier employees based solely on tactical considerations relating to the election, contradicts their claims that combined units hinder collective bargaining, foster labor strife, and undermine employee rights.

D.   Response to the Dissent

Our dissenting colleague offers both policy arguments and statutory arguments against a return to Sturgis, but, for reasons already suggested, we are not persuaded.

The dissent's contention that under *Sturgis*, an employer is required to bargain with respect to non-employees—in contravention of Section 8(a)(5)—is likewise mistaken. As explained above, in a *Sturgis* unit, each employer is obligated to bargain only over the employees with whom it has an employment relationship (and only with respect to such terms and conditions which it possesses the authority to control). Accordingly, no employer bargains regarding employees it does not employ, and so our colleague's use of the term "non-employer" bargaining is inaccurate.

Contrary to our dissenting colleague's suggestion, we are not, by returning to *Sturgis*, abdicating our responsibility to carefully review and make an appropriate bargaining unit determination in each case. As the *Sturgis* Board explained, "By our decision today, we do not suggest that every unit sought by a petitioner, which combines jointly employed and solely employed employees of a single user employer, will necessarily be found appropriate. As in the Board's pre-*Greenhoot* cases, application of our community of interest test may not always result in jointly employed employees being included in units with solely employed employees." *Sturgis*, 331 N.L.R.B. at 1305–06 (and cases cited therein).

IV. Conclusion

We hold today that *Sturgis* is more consistent with our statutory charge than *Oakwood*. Accordingly, we overrule *Oakwood* and return to the holding of *Sturgis*. Employer consent is not necessary for units that combine jointly employed and solely employed employees of a single user employer. Instead, we will apply the traditional community of interest factors to decide if such units are appropriate. We likewise agree with the Sturgis Board's sanctioning of units of the employees employed by a supplier employer, provided the units are otherwise appropriate.

ORDER

The Regional Director's administrative dismissal of the petition is reversed, and the petition is reinstated. The petition is remanded to the Regional Director for further action consistent with this Decision.

MEMBER MISCIMARRA, dissenting:

In Browning-Ferris Industries of California, Inc., 362 N.L.R.B. No. 186 (2015) (*BFI II*), the Board majority substantially expanded the circumstances when multiple entities would be deemed a joint employer of particular employees. Under *BFI II*, if two businesses have sufficient control over employment terms and conditions within an appropriate bargaining unit, then (i) both entities are jointly deemed the "employer," and (ii) if the union prevailed in an election, both business entities would be required to jointly engage in collective bargaining, with each entity negotiating "such terms and conditions which it possesses the authority to control." Former Member Johnson and I dissented in *BFI II*, based on our view that the expanded joint-employer standard was contrary to our statute and because it left employees, unions and employers "in a position where there can be no certainty or predictability regarding the identity of the 'employer.'" We were especially critical of the multiple-entity bargaining obligation described in *BFI II*, where each entity would be responsible for bargaining over some subjects and not others. In our view, this type of bargaining would "foster substantial bargaining instability by requiring the nonconsensual presence of too many entities with diverse and conflicting interests on the 'employer' side," and "even the commencement of good-faith bargaining may be delayed by disputes over whether the correct 'employer' parties are present."

In today's decision, my colleagues substantially enlarge the expanded joint-employer platform created by *BFI II* and require a more attenuated type of multi-employer/non-employer bargaining in a single unit when the multiple business entities do not even jointly employ all unit employees. Specifically, my colleagues hold that the Board may require two or more businesses to engage in multi-employer bargaining without their consent, even though one of the entities has no employment relationship with some of the unit employees, provided that other employees in the same unit are jointly employed by the employer entities. The latter determination (whether some individuals are jointly employed) will be governed by the expanded *BFI II* joint-employer standard.

My colleagues overrule *Oakwood Care Center*, 343 N.L.R.B. 659 (2004), and adopt standards governing multi-employer bargaining that have never previously existed, except for a 4-year period after the Board decided *M.B. Sturgis, Inc.*, 331 N.L.R.B. 1298 (2000). However, I do not agree that my colleagues today "return to the holding of *Sturgis*." It is true that *Sturgis* permitted the certification of multi-employer bargaining units, without consent, where some unit employees were jointly employed, and where other unit employees were employed only by one employer entity. However, throughout the 4-year period governed by *Sturgis* (and for many years before and after *Sturgis* was decided), the joint-employer landscape was circumscribed by well-known limiting principles that were repudiated, with considerable fanfare, in *BFI II*. Thus, my colleagues do not "return" to a legal regime that has ever existed. The Board and the courts have never previously applied the expansive joint-employer standards articulated in *Browning-Ferris* combined with the multi-employer/non-employer bargaining that will result from today's decision.

I respectfully dissent from the majority's approval of multi-employer/non-employer bargaining in the circumstances presented here.

NOTES

1. *Some perspective.* As Member Miscimarra suggested in his dissent, the practical implications of *Miller & Anderson* on who counts as an "employee" under Section 2(3) of the Act cannot fully be appreciated without reference to who counts as an "employer" under Section 2(2) of the Act as governed by the joint-employer doctrine, which the Board recently had modified in *Browning-Ferris*, 362 N.L.R.B. No. 186 (2015) (BFI II), discussed *infra* Chapter 3-C-5. In *Browning-Ferris*, the *Miller & Anderson* majority restated the joint-employer doctrine to hold that two or more entities are joint employers of a single work force if they are both employers within the meaning of the common law, and if they share or codetermine those matters governing the essential terms and conditions of employment. In the view of dissenting Member Miscimmara, who was joined by Member Johnson, the holding of *BFI II* was erroneous largely because leased employee arrangements are better understood as creating multi-employer bargaining units—which require the consent of all affected employers—than as joint employer units. Later, the Trump Board agreed with Member Miscimmara and overruled *BFI II*—although two months later it was forced to withdraw its opinion due to the conflict of interest of participating Member Emanuel, who had joined the overruling majority. *See Hy-Brand Industrial Contractors, Inc.*, 365 N.L.R.B. No. 156 (2017), *vacated*, 366 N.L.R.B. No. 26 (2018). Meanwhile, the *Miller & Anderson* majority embraced the opposite view. With whom do you agree?

2.   *Swing time.* The Board is often criticized for undertaking major policy shifts that seem to swing with the political views of the president who has managed to appoint a three-member majority. In *Miller & Anderson*, the policy implicated is a basic one treated throughout this chapter: who is considered to be a statutory "employee"—and equally important, who gets to decide? The holding of the case is two-fold. First, employer consent is not necessary for bargaining units that combine jointly employed and solely employed employees of a single user employer. Instead, the traditional community of interest factors will be applied to decide if such units are appropriate. Second, it is permissible to sanction bargaining units of the employees employed by a supplier employer, provided once again that those units are otherwise appropriate. This holding overturned *Oakwood*, which had overturned *Sturgis*, which had overturned *Lee Hospital*. In your opinion, where should the pendulum swing, and why should it stay there? Absent Congressional action to amend the Act—which has been rare since 1959—is there any way to avoid such pendulum swings? Would it be desirable to do so? Why or why not?

3.   *Speaking of Congressional (in)action.* Members of Congress often have targeted for reversal NLRB rulings with which they disagree (although the rate at which they have managed to pass reversal legislation, since 1959, is practically zero). *Miller & Anderson* and *Browning Ferris II* are examples of such targets, and an effort to reverse them is underway. *See* Tyron Richardson & Hassan A. Kanu, *Republican Lawmakers Plan Rollout of Joint Employer Legislation*, Bloomberg Law (Jul. 6, 2017), available at https://www.bna.com/republican-lawmakers-plan-n73014461289/.

Do you support this effort? Why or why not?

4.   *Going global.* The *Miller & Anderson* majority embraced much of the reasoning of the *Oakwood* dissenters, including the view of Member Liebman that *Oakwood* unduly limited the opportunities of the contingent workforce, which has continued to grow as the result of the relentless economic pressures imposed by globalization, to gain access to union representation. Of course, no reference to globalization can be found in the text of Section 2(3). Does this fact make such references to the policy implications of the Board's choices more or less persuasive?

5.   *Going, going, gone?* A longstanding but narrow exception to the rule that an election must be directed in an appropriate bargaining unit when a question of representation exists—whether or not the unit is a joint employer unit—is triggered when it is reasonably certain that an election will serve no purpose. So an election petition will be dismissed when cessation of the employer's operations is imminent, which can occur when the employer completely ceases to operate, sells its operations to another, or fundamentally changes the nature of its business. *See e.g., Hughes Aircraft Co.*, 308 N.L.R.B. 82, 83 (1992); *Martin Marietta Aluminum*, 214 N.L.R.B. 646, 646–47 (1974); *Cooper Int'l*, 205 N.L.R.B. 1057, 1057 (1973). Invoking this exception, can joint employers avoid a representation election merely by pointing to the fact the joint project giving rise to the election petition has ended, and they have no specific plans to work together on future projects? *See Retro Environmental*

Inc./Green Jobworks LLC, 364 N.L.R.B. No. 70 (2016) (holding answer to be no).

* * *

ii. Subcontractors' Employees

Whole industries are now built on the business model that the people who actually do the work are the "employees" of the downstream subcontractors or vendors that hire them, rather than the upstream contractors, wholesalers, and retailers for whom goods or services are eventually delivered, then marketed and sold to clients and consumers. That is, the "core" job functions relating to the production of goods or the delivery of services have been moved elsewhere, perhaps to an unseen vendor or labor supplier. Two prominent examples are the garment and janitorial services industries. In the former example, the people who actually sew the clothes work for a subcontractor who in turn works for a supplier who in turns works for a label that sells the clothes to the department store or mall boutique patronized by consumers. In the latter example, the people who actually vacuum the carpet in the law office are carried on the payroll of an agency that has a contract to clean the building with the building's manager, not the building's individual tenants, one of which is the law firm needing to have its carpets vacuumed in the first place. *See, e.g.*, Victor Narro, *Impact of Next Wave Organizing: Creative Corporate Strategies of the Los Angeles Workers Centers*, 50 N.Y.L. Sch. L. Rev. 465, 471–81 (2005). Agriculture, food service, non-durable goods manufacturing, and even tourism are some of the other industries in which this type of subcontracting is common.

The typical legal problem faced by workers in such industries—under both the NLRA and state and federal anti-discrimination, child labor, fair labor standards, and occupational safety laws—is that, despite widespread and highly-publicized abuses, "manufacturers feign ignorance of deplorable conditions," while the subcontractors who are prosecuted play the "shell game" of temporarily shutting down operations to avoid liability and reopening as new businesses—often using the same workers and equipment, if not the same location—to play the game anew. *See* Lora Jo Foo, The Vulnerable and Exploitable Immigrant Workforce and the Need for Strengthening Worker Protection Legislation, 103 Yale L.J 2179, 2188–89 (1994).

Take the following, not uncommon, example. Suppose seamstresses are sewing designer clothes for Acme Clothing. Acme is a sole proprietorship operated by Mr. Sweat, the operator of a small sewing shop. Acme's "factory" consists of a few sewing machines and little else. Mr. Sweat has a contract with Ecstasy, a designer label, which will pay him $3.00 per blouse to sew at least 5,000 blouses. Ecstasy, in turn, has a distribution contract with Needless Markups, an upscale department store chain, which will pay Ecstasy $10 per blouse. (In its stores, Needless Markups will sell each blouse for $30.) To maintain Acme's razor-thin profit margin—after all, fabric and materials have to be purchased, and the electric company must be paid to turn on the power that runs the sewing machines—Mr. Sweat pays seamstresses $1.50 per blouse. There is no overtime. Mr. Sweat also urges workers to sew as many blouses as possible, because the more volume he produces, the more money he will make. So he provides no regular bathroom or lunch breaks. If each seamstress can sew four blouses every 60 minutes, then she will earn the equivalent of $6.00 per hour, which is less than the minimum wage set by the Fair Labor Standards Act (FLSA). Suppose further that Sarah Kim, a recent immigrant from South Korea who is one of Mr. Sweat's seamstresses, files a complaint for unpaid wages, overtime and denial of break time with the U.S. Department of Labor. Assume the Labor Department is willing to expend its limited resources to pursue her claim. What will happen if Mr. Sweat, Ecstasy, and Needless Markups are each sued?

What is likely to happen is this: Mr. Sweat will close down Acme, move his sewing machines to a building a few blocks away, and reopen as Zenith Garment Co. Meanwhile, he will ignore the summons and complaint, and later, the default judgment entered against him. The judgment will remain unpaid, because Acme no longer exists and left behind no assets anyway. The Department might consider piercing the corporate veil by going after Mr. Sweat personally—a legal longshot that may be futile too, because Mr. Sweat will have hidden his assets under the names of trusted allies, such as family members.

Ecstasy and Needless Markups will successfully move for summary judgment on the theory that they cannot be held responsible for misconduct that they neither knew of, controlled, nor ratified. Needless Markups will offer the additional theory that it lacked privity with Acme. Indeed, Needless Markups will point to a clause in its contract with Ecstasy (and perhaps Ecstasy will point to a similar clause in its contract with Acme) that specifically prohibits the very violations of which Acme is accused.

Even if the Labor Department successfully obtains judgments against not only Acme, but also the deep-pocket, upstream, actors Ecstasy and Needless Markups, there is the question whether Sarah Kim, an undocumented immigrant, will be eligible for back-pay—assuming she can be found when the money comes in, months or years later.

Under these circumstances, the biggest problem may be the lack of voluntary compliance with the law. Owing to the many legal and practicable obstacles we have seen, most workers like Sarah Kim never file their claims in the first place.

The tangle of legal issues attending the upstream employer's use of subcontractors is limited neither to low-wage industries nor to the use of subcontractors to avoid collective bargaining obligations. If the subcontractor happens to be unionized, then the upstream employer may be tempted to reverse tactics. For example, in *CNN America Inc.*, 361 N.L.R.B. No. 47 (2014), CNN, the cable news network, replaced its unionized subcontractor, which provided audio and video technicians, with in-house nonunion technicians at its New York, N.Y., and Washington, D.C., bureaus. Chairman Pearce and Member Hirozawa found that CNN and the subcontractor were joint employers of the bargaining unit employees in both bureaus; that, as a joint employer, CNN was obligated to comply with the terms of the collective bargaining agreements between its subcontractor and the union; and that CNN's failure to do so violated Section 8(a)(5). The same majority also found that CNN violated Section 8(a)(3) by terminating its subcontract out of antiunion animus, thereby causing the discharge of the subcontractor's employees, and by failing to bargain with the union about both the decision to terminate the subcontract and the effects of that decision. Member Miscimarra dissented.

NOTES

1. *Getting organized.* Suppose that Sarah Kim tried to address her problems in a more systematic way by organizing a union that could collectively bargain with Mr. Sweat for better terms and conditions of employment—and was fired. What are the chances her firing was an unfair labor practice under the NLRA? What remedies would be appropriate? Should seamstresses have the right to bargain with Ecstasy or Needless Markups? Why or why not?

2. *The corporate food chain.* According to the figures discussed above, the sewing job earned Mr. Sweat at least $15,000, Ecstasy at least $50,000, and Needless Markups at least $150,000. In your judgment, what significance, if any, should these figures have in determining how best to address Ms. Kim's claim? By virtue of making more money, should either Ecstasy or Needless Markups be required to shoulder more responsibility for Acme's misbehavior? Or should their successful exercise of long-settled rights to adopt the corporate form and engage in a legitimate business pursuant to perfectly legal instruments be upheld? That is, just because Ms. Kim is the victim of injustice, does somebody have to pay? Or does the law countenance providing legal rights without necessarily providing effective remedies?

2. UNION ORGANIZERS

Union organizers—advocates of collective bargaining who seek to persuade a given workforce to form or join a labor organization—may be thought of as falling into two broad categories: paid professionals and amateur adherents. The prototypical professionals are outsiders. Their job is to help deliver what the amateurs want, and they are usually paid to do so by a union seeking to deliver such representation, sometimes by raising the workplace consciousness of other amateurs. They are on the payroll staff of that union. By contrast, the amateur adherents work on the inside.

They want improved wages and working conditions, not only for others, but also for themselves, and want to bring in the union to help deliver those benefits.

The status of professional organizers is addressed in *Lechmere Inc. v. NLRB*, 502 U.S. 527 (1992), a case treated more fully in Chapter 4, *infra* p. 461. Non-employee organizers, who were working for a union seeking to organize the employees of a retail store, sought to place handbills on the windshields of parked cars of store employees. The cars were parked in a private parking lot, from which the nonemployee organizers were barred as trespassers. The closest public property from which organizers might have sought to reach employees ran along a turnpike and was separated from the store's parking lot by a 46-foot-wide grassy strip. The union felt the public property was too far from store patrons to serve as an effective forum for handbilling and filed an unfair labor practice charge asserting the right to handbill in the parking lot. The Board and the First Circuit sided with the union, but the Supreme Court reversed:

> By its plain terms the NLRA confers rights only on employees, not on unions or their nonemployee organizers. In *NLRB v. Babcock & Wilcox Co.*, 351 U.S. 105 (1956), however, we recognized that insofar as the employees' "right of self-organization depends in some measure on [their] ability . . . to learn the advantages of self-organization from others," *id.* at 113, § 7 of the NLRA may, in certain limited circumstances, restrict an employer's right to exclude nonemployee union organizers from his property. It is the nature of those circumstances that we explore today. * * *
>
> In *Babcock*, we held that the Act drew a distinction "of substance," 351 U.S. at 113, between the union activities of employees and nonemployees. In cases involving employee activities, we noted with approval, the Board "balanced the conflicting interests of employees to receive information on self-organization on the company's property from fellow employees during nonworking time, with the employer's right to control the use of his property." *Id.* at 109–10. In cases involving nonemployee activities (like those at issue in Babcock itself), however, the Board was not permitted to engage in that same balancing (and we reversed the Board for having done so). By reversing the Board's interpretation of the statute for failing to distinguish between the organizing activities of employees and nonemployees, we were saying, in Chevron terms, that § 7 speaks to the issue of nonemployee access to an employer's property. Babcock's teaching is straightforward: § 7 simply does not protect nonemployee union organizers except in the rare case where "the inaccessibility of employees makes ineffective the reasonable attempts by nonemployees to

communicate with them through the usual channels," 351 U.S. at 112.

The threshold inquiry in this case, then, is whether the facts here justify application of Babcock's inaccessibility exception.

We cannot accept the Board's conclusion, because it "rest[s] on erroneous legal foundations," *Babcock*, 351 U.S. at 112. As we have explained, the exception to *Babcock*'s rule is a narrow one. It does not apply wherever nontrespassory access to employees may be cumbersome or less-than-ideally effective, but only where "the location of a plant and the living quarters of the employees place the employees beyond the reach of reasonable union efforts to communicate with them," 351 U.S. at 113 (emphasis added). Classic examples include logging camps, mining camps, and mountain resort hotels. *Babcock*'s exception was crafted precisely to protect the § 7 rights of those employees who, by virtue of their employment, are isolated from the ordinary flow of information that characterizes our society. The union's burden of establishing such isolation is, as we have explained, "a heavy one."

Lechmere, 502 U.S. at 532, 537–40.

NOTES

1.   As Justice Thomas notes for the majority, in *NLRB v. Babcock & Wilcox Co.*, 351 U.S. 105 (1956), a unanimous decision, "the Court held that the Act drew a distinction 'of substance,' 351 U.S. at 113, between the union activities of employees and nonemployees." In this case, the distinction meant the difference between being able to come onto the employer's property to place handbills on car windshields and displaying signs "from the public grassy strip adjoining Lechmere's parking lot," which was mostly ignored by passersby.

Can such a distinction be justified by the plain text of the statute? Professor Dannin argues that the answer is no. In striking a balance between access rights of workers and property rights of employers, the *Babcock* Court, which thought the task was to strike a balance between access rights of employees under Section 7 and the property rights of employers at common law, did not really address this question; the *Lechmere* Court did not address it either, because it was focused on analyzing whether the Board had properly read *Babcock*, rather than whether it had properly interpreted the statute per se. To decide *Lechmere* as it did, Professor Dannin contends, the Court had to invent a definition for the term "employees" that does not actually appear in Section 2(3):

> The Court said "employee" meant only the employees of a specific employer. This is the common meaning of the word, but the NLRA says exactly the opposite. The NLRA says that the term employee "shall include any employee, and shall not be limited to the employees

of a particular employer." This definition is intended to promote and protect worker solidarity across workplaces.

Ellen Dannin, Taking Back the Workers' Law: How to Fight the Assault on Labor Rights 13 (2006).

What do you think? Would it make a difference if one of the Wagner Act's principal drafters had unsuccessfully proposed a further amendment that would have made it clear that "union organizers" are covered by Section 2(3)? Apparently, that is what happened. See Memorandum by Philip Levy to Calvert Magruder (Apr. 17, 1935); *see also Marshall Field & Co. v. NLRB*, 200 F.2d 375 (7th Cir. 1952). What effect, if any, should the failure to add this amendment have on the construction of the statute?

2.   *The NLRA, the common law, and property rights.* According greater or lesser NLRA protection based on the distinction between employee and nonemployee status is well established and unlikely to be dislodged anytime soon. But if Professor Dannin is right, then even the Court's "nonemployee organizers" are really "employees" within the meaning of Act, because they are "employees" of somebody—in this case, the union attempting to organize the targeted employer. In the context of union organizing, this understanding would render obsolete common law notions about the employer's right, as a private property owner, to control access to the workplace by union organizers, including professionals. Agreeing with Professor Dannin, Professor Cameron argues that modifying common law notions of limited access to private property in the workplace is one of the basic points of the Act:

> Decisions like *Lechmere* undermine core labor rights by defining those rights more narrowly than the plain meaning of the statute. Majority opinions in these cases fail or refuse to recognize the transformative power of the NLRA, which was adopted to modify the application of free market principles to the workplace by granting workers access to the counterbalancing power of collective bargaining.

Christopher David Ruiz Cameron, *All Over But the Shouting? Some Thoughts on Amending the Wagner Act by Adjudication Rather Than Retirement*, 26 Berkeley J. of Empl. & Lab. L. 275, 278 (2005).

Is this just the wishful thinking of two academics? Or should the Board, and the Supreme Court, revisit the received interpretation of Section 2(3) in light of today's commonly-accepted cannons of statutory construction, including the plain meaning doctrine? Even if Professors Dannin and Cameron are right as a matter of statutory interpretation, is there something to be said for continuing to adhere to long-settled doctrine respecting the employee versus nonemployee distinction?

* * *

NLRB v. TOWN & COUNTRY ELECTRIC, INC.
516 U.S. 85 (1995)

JUSTICE BREYER delivered the opinion of the Court:

Can a worker be a company's "employee," within the terms of the National Labor Relations Act, 29 U.S.C. § 151 et seq., if, at the same time, a union pays that worker to help the union organize the company? We agree with the National Labor Relations Board that the answer is "yes."

I.

The relevant background is the following: Town & Country Electric, Inc., a nonunion electrical contractor, wanted to hire several licensed Minnesota electricians for construction work in Minnesota. Town & Country (through an employment agency) advertised for job applicants, but it refused to interview 10 of 11 union applicants (including two professional union staff) who responded to the advertisement. Its employment agency hired the one union applicant whom Town & Country interviewed, but he was dismissed after only a few days on the job.

The members of the International Brotherhood of Electrical Workers (Locals 292 and 343) (Union), filed a complaint with the National Labor Relations Board claiming that Town & Country and the employment agency had refused to interview (or retain) them because of their union membership. [The administrative law judge ruled in favor of the union, and the Board agreed. But the Eighth Circuit refused to enforce the Board's order.]

II.

The Act seeks to improve labor relations ("eliminate the causes of certain substantial obstructions to the free flow of commerce," 29 U.S.C. § 151 (1988 ed.)) in large part by granting specific sets of rights to employers and to employees. This case grows out of a controversy about rights that the Act grants to "employees," namely, rights "to self-organization, to form, join, or assist labor organizations, to bargain collectively . . . and to engage in other concerted activities for the purpose of collective bargaining or other mutual aid or protection." § 157. We granted certiorari to decide only that part of the controversy that focuses upon the meaning of the word "employee," a key term in the statute, since these rights belong only to those workers who qualify as "employees" as that term is defined in the Act. *See, e.g.*, § 158(a)(1) ("unfair labor practice" to "interfere with . . . employees in the exercise of the rights guaranteed in section 157 of this title") (emphasis added).

The relevant statutory language is found in Section 2(3):

The term "employee" shall include any employee, and shall not be limited to the employees of a particular employer, unless this subchapter explicitly states otherwise. . . . § 152(3).

We must specifically decide whether the Board may lawfully interpret this language to include company workers who are also paid union organizers.

We put the question in terms of the Board's lawful authority because this Court's decisions recognize that the Board often possesses a degree of legal leeway when it interprets its governing statute, particularly where Congress likely intended an understanding of labor relations to guide the Act's application. *See, e.g., Sure-Tan, Inc. v. NLRB*, 467 U.S. 883, 891 (1984) (interpretations of the Board will be upheld if "reasonably defensible"). *See also Chevron U.S.A. Inc. v. Natural Resources Defense Council, Inc.*, 467 U.S. 837, 842–43 (1984). We add, however, that the Board needs very little legal leeway here to convince us of the correctness of its decision.

Several strong general arguments favor the Board's position. For one thing, the Board's decision is consistent with the broad language of the Act itself—language that is broad enough to include those company workers whom a union also pays for organizing. The ordinary dictionary definition of "employee" includes any "person who works for another in return for financial or other compensation." American Heritage Dictionary 604 (3d ed.1992). *See also* Black's Law Dictionary 525 (6th ed.1990) (an employee is a "person in the service of another under any contract of hire, express or implied, oral or written, where the employer has the power or right to control and direct the employee in the material details of how the work is to be performed"). The phrasing of the Act seems to reiterate the breadth of the ordinary dictionary definition, for it says "[t]he term 'employee' shall include any employee." 29 U.S.C. § 152(3) (1988 ed.).

Of course, the Act's definition also contains a list of exceptions, for example, for independent contractors, agricultural laborers, domestic workers, and employees subject to the Railway Labor Act, 45 U.S.C. § 151 et seq.; but no exception applies here.

For another thing, the Board's broad, literal interpretation of the word "employee" is consistent with several of the Act's purposes, such as protecting "the right of employees to organize for mutual aid without employer interference," *Republic Aviation Corp. v. NLRB*, 324 U.S. 793, 798 (1945).

III.

Town & Country argues that application of common-law agency principles requires an interpretation of "employee" that excludes paid union organizers. It points to a section of the Restatement (Second) of Agency (dealing with respondeat superior liability for torts), which says:

> Since . . . the relation of master and servant is dependent upon the right of the master to control the conduct of the servant in the performance of the service, giving service to two masters at the

same time normally involves a breach of duty by the servant to one or both of them. . . . [A person] cannot be a servant of two masters in doing an act as to which an intent to serve one necessarily excludes an intent to serve the other.

Restatement (Second) of Agency § 226 comment a (1957). It argues that, when the paid union organizer serves the union—at least at certain times in certain ways—the organizer is acting adversely to the company. Indeed, it says, the organizer may stand ready to desert the company upon request by the union, in which case, the union, not the company, would have "the right . . . to control the conduct of the servant." Thus, it concludes, the worker must be the servant (i.e., the "employee") of the union alone. See *id.* § 1, and comment a ("agent" is one who agrees to act "subject to [a principal's] control").

As Town & Country correctly notes, in some cases, there may be a question about whether the Board's departure from the common law of agency with respect to particular questions and in a particular statutory context renders its interpretation unreasonable. But no such question is presented here since the Board's interpretation of the term "employee" is consistent with the common law.

Town & Country's common-law argument fails, quite simply, because, in our view, the Board correctly found that it lacks sufficient support in common law. The Restatement's hornbook rule (to which the quoted commentary is appended) says that a "person may be the servant of two masters . . . at one time as to one act, if the service to one does not involve abandonment of the service to the other." Restatement (Second) of Agency § 226 (1957).

The Board, in quoting this rule, concluded that service to the union for pay does not "involve abandonment of . . . service" to the company. 309 N.L.R.B. at 1254. And that conclusion seems correct. Common sense suggests that as a worker goes about his or her ordinary tasks during a working day, say, wiring sockets or laying cable, he or she is subject to the control of the company employer, whether or not the union also pays the worker. The company, the worker, the union, all would expect that to be so. And, that being so, that union and company interests or control might sometimes differ should make no difference. As Prof. Seavey pointed out many years ago, "[o]ne can be a servant of one person for some acts and the servant of another person for other acts, even when done at the same time," for example, where "a city detective, in search of clues, finds employment as a waiter and, while serving the meals, searches the customer's pockets." W. Seavey, Handbook of the Law of Agency § 85, at 146 (1964). The detective is the servant both "of the restaurateur" (as to the table waiting) and "of the city" (as to the pocket searching). *Id.* How does it differ from Prof. Seavey's example for the company to pay the worker for electrical work, and the union to pay him for organizing?

Moreover, union organizers may limit their organizing to nonwork hours. *See, e.g., Republic Aviation Corp. v. NLRB*, 324 U.S. 793 (1945); *Beth Israel Hosp. v. NLRB*, 437 U.S. 483 (1978). If so, union organizing, when done for pay but during nonwork hours, would seem equivalent to simple moonlighting, a practice wholly consistent with a company's control over its workers as to their assigned duties.

Town & Country's "abandonment" argument is yet weaker insofar as the activity that constitutes an "abandonment," *i.e.*, ordinary union organizing activity, is itself specifically protected by the Act. This is true even if a company perceives those protected activities as disloyal. After all, the employer has no legal right to require that, as part of his or her service to the company, a worker refrain from engaging in protected activity.

Neither are we convinced by the practical considerations that Town & Country adds to its agency law argument. The company refers to a Union resolution permitting members to work for nonunion firms, which, the company says, reflects a union effort to "salt" nonunion companies with union members seeking to organize them. Supported by amici curiae, it argues that "salts" might try to harm the company, perhaps quitting when the company needs them, perhaps disparaging the company to others, and perhaps even sabotaging the firm or its products. Therefore, the company concludes, Congress could not have meant paid union organizers to have been included as "employees" under the Act.

This practical argument suffers from several serious problems. For one thing, nothing in this record suggests that such acts of disloyalty were present, in kind or degree, to the point where the company might lose control over the worker's normal workplace tasks. Certainly the Union's resolution contains nothing that suggests, requires, encourages, or condones impermissible or unlawful activity. For another thing, the argument proves too much. If a paid union organizer might quit, leaving a company employer in the lurch, so too might an unpaid organizer, or a worker who has found a better job, or one whose family wants to move elsewhere. And if an overly zealous union organizer might hurt the company through unlawful acts, so might another unpaid zealot (who may know less about the law), or a dissatisfied worker (who may lack an outlet for his or her grievances). This does not mean they are not "employees."

Further, the law offers alternative remedies for Town & Country's concerns, short of excluding paid or unpaid union organizers from all protection under the Act. For example, a company disturbed by legal but undesirable activity, such as quitting without notice, can offer its employees fixed-term contracts, rather than hiring them "at will" as in the case before us; or it can negotiate with its workers for a notice period.

This is not to say that the law treats paid union organizers like other company employees in every labor law context. For instance, the Board states that, at least sometimes, a paid organizer may not share a sufficient "community of interest" with other employees (as to wages, hours, and working conditions) to warrant inclusion in the same bargaining unit. *See, e.g., NLRB v. Hendricks County Rural Elec. Membership Corp.*, 454 U.S. at 190 (some confidential workers, although "employees," may be excluded from bargaining unit). We need not decide this matter. We hold only that the Board's construction of the word "employee" is lawful; that term does not exclude paid union organizers.

NOTES

1.   *Solidarity forever?* Where do union organizers come from? They are not always professional "salts." An organizer may be an "insider" or employee of the targeted employer; a professional "outsider" employed by a union hoping to organize the targeted employer; or often, simply a volunteer, such as a union adherent who happens to work for the targeted employer's competitor. For examples of both "insider" and "outsider" organizers, see *Norma Rae* (20th Century Fox, 1979) (starring Best Actress Oscar winner Sally Field as "insider" mill worker Norma Rae and Ron Leibman and "outsider" professional organizer Ruben Warshawsky).

2.   *Duty of loyalty and conflict of interest.* Citing the Restatement (Second) of Agency § 226 comment a, the employer argued that recognizing "salts" as "employees" would compromise management's traditional prerogative to insist on the loyalty of its workforce. Did the Court dismiss this argument too hastily? Is having a duty to avoid taking positions adverse to those of the boss one of the essential attributes of being an "employee"? Even if this is so, does it prove too much, because there are always inherent conflicts between the owners and their managers on the one hand, and workers on the other? Is that why national labor policy favors allowing workers to choose collective representation? *See* Wagner Act § 1, 29 U.S.C. § 151 ("The inequality of bargaining power between employees who do not possess full freedom of association or actual liberty of contract, and employers who are organized in the corporate form or other forms of ownership association, substantially burdens and affects the flow of commerce. . . .").

3.   *Why the workforce can be peppered with "salts."* Justice Breyer gave at least two distinct, and arguably contradictory, reasons for reaching the conclusion that "salts" are "employees" entitled to the protection of the NLRA.

The first reason relates to the plain meaning of the language in Section 2(3), which says the term "employee" shall include "any employee, and shall not be limited to the employees of a particular employer." Judges relying on the plain meaning doctrine often consult dictionary definitions, as Justice Breyer did here.

The second reason relates to the ambiguity of Section 2(3), which unhelpfully uses the term "employee" as both the thing to be defined and the definition too. Justice Breyer assumed that such a tautological definition is not really a definition at all. Quoting with approval language from a prior decision, he reasoned that, when Congress does not more specifically define a term, such as "employee," courts interpreting the statute should conclude that Congress intended to describe "the conventional master-servant relationship as understood by common-law agency doctrine." Most lawyers trained in the nuances of the common law would no doubt agree. Do you? Would your answer change if you understood the NLRA as a well-planned assault on the common law "master-servant" relationship—an old-fashioned term that is not used in the Act? *See* William R. Corbett, *The Need for a Revitalized Common Law of the Workplace*, 69 Brooklyn L. Rev. 91, 98–99 (2003) (finding a place for updated common law principles in modern labor law).

4. *Deference to administrative agencies.* Justice Breyer gave a third reason for the result: deference to the expertise of an administrative agency. Here the NLRB had found that paid union organizers were "employees" entitled to the protections of the Act. As Justice Breyer noted, deference to the application of statutes by expert agencies entrusted with their enforcement is a longstanding principle of administrative law. *See Chevron USA Inc. v. Natural Resources Defense Council Inc.*, 467 U.S. 837, 842–43 (1984); *see, e.g., Sure-Tan, Inc. v. NLRB*, 467 U.S. 883, 891 (1984) (holding that Board's interpretations will be upheld if "reasonably defensible").

What do you suppose makes members of the National Labor Relations Board more expert in reading the NLRA than the courts charged with reviewing and enforcing their orders? Is it their education, training, or experience? Is it their recourse to experienced professional staff, including attorneys? Where do prospective Board members come from, anyway? How much deference to their views is too much, too little, or just right?

5. *Reconcilable differences?* Both *Lechmere*, which is excerpted *supra* p. 261 and discussed more fully *infra* p. 461 in Chapter 4, and *Town & Country* dealt with the rights of professional union organizers to reach an audience situated on the employer's private property. Can the results of these two cases be reconciled? Why or why not? How are your answers affected by the growth of cyberspace, when employees can be contacted virtually, without anyone physically having to enter the employer's private property?

3. APPRENTICES: GRADUATE STUDENTS, TRAINEES, AND HOUSE STAFF

A whole phalanx of workers-in-training may not be considered "employees" under the NLRA, even though they are engaged in substantial work—whether as university teachers, hospital house staff (including interns and residents), or even law externs. By any name, they are apprentices: learners who are also workers, because they are doing their learning on the job.

Anybody who is even casually familiar with the undergraduate curricula of major colleges and universities knows that graduate teaching assistants play central roles in delivering education, both inside and outside the classroom. They may attend and sometimes deliver professors' lectures; take lecture notes for students; teach small sections; meet with students during office hours; hold review or tutoring sessions; grade examinations and papers; and perform any number of duties that would be considered employment if they were undertaken by members of the tenured or tenure-track faculty. Modern academies of higher learning would find it difficult, if not impossible, to operate without them. *See, e.g.,* Grant M. Hayden, *The University Works Because We Do: Collective Bargaining Rights for Graduate Assistants*, 69 Ford. L. Rev. 1233 (2001).

For at least 25 years, however, the NLRB characterized graduate teaching assistants as "students" rather than "employees." *See, e.g., Leland Stanford Junior University*, 214 N.L.R.B. 621 (1974); *Adelphi University*, 195 N.L.R.B. 639 (1972); *see also* Martin H. Malin, Student Employees and Collective Bargaining, 69 Ky. L.J. 1 (1980) (discussing cases and noting that not all public sector jurisdictions agreed with NLRB's approach). In 2000, the Board reversed itself and declared these student workers could fill both roles—and therefore, in their capacity as employees, be entitled to engage in collective bargaining. *See New York Univ.*, 332 N.L.R.B. 1205 (2000). In 2004, the Bush Board changed course again and re-embraced the results and reasoning of *Leland Stanford Junior University* and *Adelphi University*. See *Brown University*, 342 N.L.R.B. 483 (2004). But in 2016, the Obama Board changed course yet again by overruling *Brown University*.

TRUSTEES OF COLUMBIA UNIVERSITY
364 N.L.R.B. No. 90 (2016)

By CHAIRMAN PEARCE and MEMBERS MISCIMARRA, HIROZAWA, and MCFERRAN:

The threshold question before us is whether students who perform services at a university in connection with their studies are statutory employees within the meaning of Section 2(3) of the Act. Here, after a hearing directed by the Board, the Regional Director applied *Brown University*, 342 N.L.R.B. 483 (2004), where the Board found that graduate student assistants were not employees within the meaning of Section 2(3), and dismissed a petition filed by the Graduate Workers of Columbia-GWC, UAW, which seeks to represent both graduate and undergraduate teaching assistants, as well as graduate research assistants.

We have decided to overrule *Brown University*, a sharply-divided decision, which itself overruled an earlier decision, *New York University*, 332 N.L.R.B. 1205 (2000) (NYU). We revisit *Brown University* not only because, in our view, the Board erred as to a matter of statutory interpretation, but also because of the nature and consequences of that error. That decision failed to acknowledge that the Act does not speak directly to the issue posed here, which calls on the Board to interpret the language of the statute in light of its policies. The *Brown University* decision, in turn, deprived an entire category of workers of the protections of the Act, without a convincing justification in either the statutory language or the policies of the Act.

Our starting point in determining whether student assistants are covered by the Act is the broad language of Section 2(3), which provides in relevant part that "[t]he term 'employee' shall include any employee," subject to certain exceptions—none of which address students employed by their universities. *Brown University* held that graduate assistants cannot be statutory employees because they "are primarily students and have a primarily educational, not economic, relationship with their university." We disagree. The Board has the statutory authority to treat student assistants as statutory employees, where they perform work, at the direction of the university, for which they are compensated. Statutory coverage is permitted by virtue of an employment relationship; it is not foreclosed by the existence of some other, additional relationship that the Act does not reach.

The unequivocal policy of the Act, in turn, is to "encourag[e] the practice and procedure of collective bargaining" and to "protect[ ] the exercise by workers of full freedom of association, self-organization, and designation of representatives of their own choosing." Given this policy, coupled with the very broad statutory definitions of both "employee" and "employer," it is appropriate to extend statutory coverage to students working for universities covered by the Act unless there are strong reasons not to do so. We are not persuaded by the Brown University Board's self-described "fundamental belief that the imposition [sic] of collective bargaining on graduate students would improperly intrude into the educational process and would be inconsistent with the purposes and policies of the Act." This "fundamental belief" is unsupported by legal authority, by empirical evidence, or by the Board's actual experience.

Thus, we hold today that student assistants who have a common-law employment relationship with their university are statutory employees under the Act. We will apply that standard to student assistants, including assistants engaged in research funded by external grants. Applying the new standard to the facts here, consistent with the Board's established approach in representation cases, we conclude (1) that all of the petitioned-for student-assistant classifications consist of statutory employees; (2) that the petitioned-for bargaining unit (comprising graduate students, terminal Master's degree students, and undergraduate students) is an appropriate unit; and (3) that none of the petitioned-for classifications consists of temporary employees who may not be included in the unit. Accordingly, we reverse the decision of the Regional Director and remand the proceedings to the Regional Director for further appropriate action.

I.   OVERVIEW OF PRECEDENT

A.   Board Precedent Prior to *Brown University*

The Board has exercised jurisdiction over private, nonprofit universities for more than 45 years. The Board first held that certain university graduate assistants were statutory employees in its 2000 decision in NYU. In NYU, the Board examined the statutory language of Section 2(3) and the common law agency doctrine of the conventional master-servant relationship, which establishes that such a "relationship exists when a servant performs services for another, under the other's control or right of control, and in return for payment." In so doing, the Board determined that "ample evidence exists to find that graduate assistants plainly and literally fall within the meaning of 'employee' as defined in Section 2(3)" and by the common law.

B.   *Brown University*

In *Brown University*, the majority described *NYU* as "wrongly decided," and invoked what it called the "underlying fundamental premise of the Act," *i.e.* that the Act is "designed to cover economic relationships." The Board further relied on its "longstanding rule" that the Board will decline to exercise its jurisdiction "over relationships that are 'primarily educational.'" In so deciding, the Brown University majority rejected *NYU*'s reliance on the existence of a common-law employment relationship between the graduate students and the university, stating that "[e]ven assuming arguendo" such a relationship existed, "it does not follow that [the graduate assistants] are employees within the meaning of the Act."

That issue was "not to be decided purely on the basis of older common-law concepts," but rather by determining "whether Congress intended to cover the individual in question." Disavowing the need for empirical analysis, the Brown University majority instead relied on what it perceived to be a fundamental tenet of the Act and a prerequisite to statutory coverage: a relationship that is primarily economic in character, regardless of whether it constitutes common-law employment.

We believe that the *NYU* Board and *Brown University* dissenters were correct in concluding that student assistants who perform work at the direction of their university for which they are compensated are statutory employees. That view better comports with the language of Section 2(3) of the Act and common-law agency principles, the clear policy of the Act, and the relevant empirical evidence.

II.   DISCUSSION

A.   The *Brown University* Board Erred

Where student assistants have an employment relationship with their university under the common law test—which they do here—this relationship is sufficient to establish that the student assistant is a Section

2(3) employee for all statutory purposes. We do not hold that the Board is required to find workers to be statutory employees whenever they are common-law employees, but only that the Board may and should find here that student assistants are statutory employees.

1.   Section 2(3)

Section 2(3) of the Act defines "employee" to "include any employee," subject to certain specified exceptions. The Supreme Court has observed that the "breadth of [Section] 2(3)'s definition is striking: the Act squarely applies to 'any employee.' " The "phrasing of the Act," the Court has pointed out, "seems to reiterate the breadth of the ordinary dictionary definition" of the term, a definition that "includes any 'person who works for another in return for financial or other compensation.' "

The Court has made clear, in turn, that the "task of defining the term "employee' is one that 'has been assigned primarily to the agency created by Congress to administer the Act,' " the Board.

None of the exceptions enumerated in Section 2(3) addresses students generally, student assistants in particular, or private university employees of any sort.

The Act does not offer a definition of the term "employee" itself. But it is well established that "when Congress uses the term 'employee' in a statute that does not define the term, courts interpreting the statute 'must infer, unless the statute otherwise dictates, that Congress means to incorporate the established meaning' " of the term, with reference to " 'common-law agency doctrine." Not surprisingly, then, the Supreme Court has endorsed the Board's determination that certain workers were statutory employees where that determination aligned with the common law of agency. Other federal courts have done so as well. In accordance with the statute's broad definition and with the Supreme Court's approval, the Board has interpreted the expansive language of Section 2(3) to cover, for example, paid union organizers (salts) employed by a company, undocumented aliens, and "confidential" employees, among other categories of workers.

The most notable instance in which apparent common-law employees were found not to be employees under the Act, in spite of the absence of an explicit statutory exclusion, is the exception that proves the rule. In *Bell Aerospace*, cited by the *Brown University* Board, the Supreme Court held that "managerial employees" were not covered by the Act because Congress had clearly implied their exclusion by the Act's design and purpose to facilitate fairness in collective bargaining. As the Court concluded, giving employee status to managers would be contrary to this purpose: it would place managers, who would be expected to be on the side of the employer in bargaining, and non-managerial employees in the same bargaining "camp," "eviscerat[ing] the traditional distinction between labor and management." The exclusion of managers rested on legislative history, along with the intrinsic purpose and structure of the Act. No legislative history supports excluding student assistants from statutory coverage, nor does the design of the Act itself.

2.   The *Brown University* Board Did Not Adequately Consider the Text of Section 2(3)

The fundamental error of the *Brown University* Board was to frame the issue of statutory coverage not in terms of the existence of an employment relationship, but rather on whether some other relationship between the employee and the employer is the primary one—a standard neither derived from the statutory text of Section 2(3) nor from the fundamental policy of the Act. Indeed, in spite of the Brown University Board's professed adherence to "Congressional policies," we can discern no such policies that speak to whether a common-law employee should be excluded from the Act because his or her employment relationship co-exists with an educational or other non-economic relationship.

We reject the *Brown University* Board's focus on whether student assistants have a "primarily educational" employment relationship with their universities. The Supreme Court has cautioned that "vague notions of a statute's 'basic purpose' are . . . inadequate to overcome the words of its text regarding the specific issue under consideration." The crucial statutory text here, of course, is the broad language of Section 2(3) defining "employee" and the language of Section 8(d) defining the duty to bargain collectively. It seems clear to us, then, that the Act's text supports the conclusion that student assistants who are common-law employees are covered by the Act, unless compelling statutory and policy considerations require an exception. As we explain next, the relevant considerations strongly favor statutory coverage.

B.   Asserting Jurisdiction over Student Assistants Promotes Goals of Federal Labor Policy

1.   Overview of Federal Labor Policy

Federal labor policy, in the words of Section 1 of the Act, is to "encourag[e] the practice and procedure of collective bargaining," and to protect workers' "full freedom" to express a choice for or against collective-bargaining representation. Permitting student assistants to choose whether they wish to engage in collective bargaining—not prohibiting it— would further the Act's policies.

The claims of the *Brown University* majority are almost entirely theoretical. The *Brown University* Board failed to demonstrate that collective bargaining between a university and its employed graduate students cannot coexist successfully with student-teacher relationships, with the educational process, and with the traditional goals of higher education. Labor law scholars have aptly criticized the *Brown University* decision as offering "no empirical support" for its claims, even though "those assertions are empirically testable."[58]

The National Labor Relations Act, as we have repeatedly emphasized, governs only the employee-employer relationship. For deciding the legal and policy issues in this case, then, it is not dispositive that student-teacher relationship involves different interests than the employee-employer relationship; that the educational process is individual, while collective bargaining is focused on the group; and that promoting equality of bargaining power is not an aim of higher education. Even conceded, all these points simply confirm that collective bargaining and education occupy different institutional spheres. In other words, a graduate student may be both a student and an employee; a university may be both the student's educator and employer. By permitting the Board to define the scope of mandatory bargaining over "wages, hours, and other terms and conditions of employment," the Act makes it entirely possible for these different roles to coexist—and for genuine academic freedom to be preserved.

2. Applying Act to Student Assistants Would Not Infringe Upon Academic Freedom

The Supreme Court has made clear that academic freedom, in the constitutional sense, involves freedom from government efforts "to control or direct the content of the speech engaged in by the university or those affiliated with it." No such effort is involved here. Neither the *Brown University* majority, nor the parties or amici in this case, have explained how the "right to speak freely in the classroom" (in the *Brown University* Board's phrase) would be infringed by collective bargaining over "terms and conditions of employment" for employed graduate students, as the Act envisions.

There is no compelling reason—in theory or in practice—to conclude that collective bargaining by student assistants cannot be viable or that it would seriously interfere with higher education.

Accordingly, we overrule *Brown University* and hold that student assistants who have a common-law employment relationship with their university are statutory employees entitled to the protections of the Act.

III. APPLICATION TO THIS CASE

For the reasons that follow, we conclude (1) that all of the petitioned-for student-assistant classifications consist of statutory employees; (2) that the petitioned-for bargaining unit (comprising graduate students, terminal Master's degree students, and undergraduate students) is an appropriate unit; and (3) that none of the petitioned-for classifications consists of

---

[58] Catherine L. Fisk & Deborah C. Malamud, *The NLRB in Administrative Exile: Problems with Its Structure and Function and Suggestions for Reform*, 58 Duke L. J. 2013, 2076–77 (2009).

temporary employees who must be excluded from the unit by virtue of the limited length of their employment.

A.   Statement of Facts

Columbia is a nonprofit postsecondary educational institution located in New York City. Columbia's major sources of annual revenue include tuition (net revenue of $940 million in 2015, nearly a quarter of operating revenue) and government contracts and grants ($750 million).

Graduate students at Columbia are selected by the faculty of the academic departments into which they are accepted on the basis of academic performance, as demonstrated by educational background and standardized test scores. In general, Ph.D. candidates spend five to nine years of study within their discipline, during which they take coursework, as well as prepare a doctoral thesis, that the candidates develop with guidance of faculty or in connection with their laboratory work. During their enrollment, candidates are subject to various academic requirements, including timely progress toward a thesis and proficiency in coursework. Most Ph.D. candidates are required to take on teaching duties for at least one semester as part of their academic requirements, although many departments require additional semesters of teaching as a condition for obtaining a degree.

Columbia fully funds most Ph.D. student assistants, typically providing tuition and a stipend, for at least their first 5 years of study. In most students' second through fourth year, taking on teaching or research duties is a condition for full receipt of such funding. For most Ph.D. candidates, the first and fifth years are funded without a condition of service. In students' sixth year and beyond, teaching-based support may be available. Research-based financial support, unlike teaching support, frequently comes in whole or in part from sources outside the University. Grants from government or other outside entities, generally to support a specified research task, often cover research assistants' financial awards. However, the University will make up any shortfall if outside grants provide a level of funding that falls below the standard graduate funding package.

Terminal Master's degree students (as opposed to those who earn the degree as an intermediate step toward earning a Ph.D.) typically earn their degrees in shorter time periods and do not prepare a thesis. They receive very little financial aid, although some take on teaching duties for which they receive compensation.

Instructional Officers include the specific classifications of Teaching Fellows and Teaching Assistants. Teaching Fellows are doctoral students in the Graduate School of Arts and Sciences, while Teaching Assistants may be either doctoral or Master's degree students and perform similar functions outside the Graduate School of Arts and Sciences. Teaching

Fellows and Teaching Assistants spend 15–20 hours a week undertaking a wide range of duties with respect to a course. Their duties may include grading papers and holding office hours, leading discussion or laboratory sessions, or assuming most or all the teaching responsibilities for a given course. Columbia maintains other, specialized teaching-assistant funding as well. Instructional officers who participate in the Teaching Scholars Program, a category that includes Ph.D. students who are somewhat advanced in their studies, teach courses that they have designed for undergraduates in their junior or senior years. Undergraduates serve in the Teaching Assistant III classification. They are responsible for grading homework and running laboratory or problem sections that are ancillary to large classes within the School of General Studies and Columbia College.

Research Officers generally participate in research funded by outside entities. The research grants specify the nature of the research and the duties of the individuals working on the grant. The revenue from the grant beyond the amounts allotted to research assistantships goes to Columbia's general operating expenses. Graduate Research Assistants in Ph.D. programs must both comply with the duties specified by the grant and simultaneously carry out research that they will ultimately present as part of their thesis. Departmental Research Assistants, by contrast, are Master's degree students and are appointed and funded by the University and provide research assistance to a particular department or school within the University.

Teaching and research occur with the guidance of a faculty member or under the direction of an academic department. In the teaching context, poor performance by an instructional officer is addressed through remedial training, although in one instance poor performance resulted in the University's removal of a student's teaching duties, and the cancellation of his stipend.

B.   Application of the Revised Section 2(3) Analysis

1.   Instructional Officers

Common-law employment, as noted above, generally requires that the employer have the right to control the employee's work, and that the work be performed in exchange for compensation. That is the case here.

The University directs and oversees student assistants' teaching activities. Indeed, the University possesses a significant interest in maintaining such control, as the student assistants' work advances a key business operation of the University: the education of undergraduate students. The record shows that teaching assistants who do not adequately perform their duties to the University's satisfaction are subject to corrective counseling or removal.

Instructional officers receive compensation in exchange for providing services to the University. Receipt of a full financial award is conditioned upon their performance of teaching duties. When they do not perform their assigned instructional duties, the record indicates they will not be paid. For instance, after one assistant, Longxi Zhao, was removed from his teaching assistantship, his stipend was cancelled. In his termination letter, the University indicated that, "[T]his termination is effective immediately. As a result, you will no longer receive a salary for this position." This letter, in connection with the explicit conditioning of awards on performance of teaching duties, demonstrates that the University offers student assistants stipends as consideration for fulfilling their duties to perform instructional services on the University's behalf.

Although the payments to Ph.D. student assistants may be standardized to match fellowship or other non-work based aid, these payments are not merely financial aid. Students are required to work as a condition of receiving this tuition assistance during semesters when they take on instructional duties, and such duties confer a financial benefit on Columbia to offset its costs of financial aid, even if it chooses to distribute the benefit in such a way that equalizes financial aid for both assistants and non-assistant students. Indeed, in semesters where a student assistant would normally be required to work as a condition of funding, he or she may opt not to work only if he or she finds a source of outside fellowship aid. Also, the stipend portion of the financial package given to assistants is generally treated as part of university payroll and is subject to W-2 reporting and I-9 employment verification requirements.

Teaching assistants frequently take on a role akin to that of faculty, the traditional purveyors of a university's instructional output. The teaching assistants conduct lectures, grade exams, and lead discussions. Significant portions of the overall teaching duties conducted by universities are conducted by student assistants. The delegation of the task of instructing undergraduates, one of a university's most important revenue-producing activities, certainly suggests that the student assistants' relationship to the University has a salient economic character.

We have no difficulty, then, in finding that all of the petitioned-for classifications here comprise statutory employees—with the possible exception of research assistants. That issue, as we explain next, is more complicated in light of Board precedent.

2.   Student Research Assistants

As indicated, Columbia argues that student research assistants have no common-law employment relationship with the University. It relies on *Leland Stanford*'s [214 N.L.R.B. 621 (1974)] determination that certain externally-funded research assistants were not employees. That holding was later applied by the *NYU* Board in finding that some research assistants in that case were not statutory employees, even as it reversed the overall exclusion of student assistants from the Act's protections. Applying our holding today regarding the employment status of student assistants, we find that core elements of the reasoning in *Leland Stanford* are no longer tenable. We further find that, under the common-law test discussed in our decision today, research assistants at Columbia are employees under the Act.

Leland Stanford, in many respects, focused upon the absence of the common-law features of employment of the externally-funded research assistants. It contrasted the research assistants with non-student, employee research associates who worked under the direction of their department, and it noted that the work performed by the externally-funded research assistants was largely done at the students' own discretion and for their own benefit. It also observed that these student research assistants could not be disciplined in a traditional sense. Their researcher status, and presumably their aid award, was not terminable based on a failure to meet any obligations of the grant, undermining a claim that the aid was compensation. However, the *Leland Stanford* decision arguably suggested that the mere fact that the performance of a task that advanced a student's personal educational goals could negate an employment relationship.

The premise of Columbia's argument concerning the status of its research assistants is that because their work simultaneously serves both their own educational interests along with the interests of the University, they are not employees under Leland Stanford. To the extent Columbia's characterization of *Leland Stanford* is correct, we have now overruled that decision. We have rejected an inquiry into whether an employment relationship is secondary to or coextensive with an educational relationship. For this reason, the fact that a research assistant's work might advance his own educational interests as well as the University's interests is not a barrier to finding statutory-employee status.

The research assistants here clearly fall into the category of common-law employees. The research of Columbia's student assistants, while advancing the assistants' doctoral theses, also meets research goals associated with grants from which the University receives substantial income. The research assistants here work under the direction of their departments to ensure that particular grant specifications are met. Indeed, another feature of such funding is that the University typically receives a benefit from the research assistant's work, as it receives a share of the grant as revenue, and it is relieved of any need to find other sources of funding for graduate students under a research grant; thus it has an incentive to ensure proper completion of the work in accordance with the grant. Further, a research assistant's aid package requires fulfillment of the duties defined in the grant, notwithstanding that the duties may also advance the assistant's thesis, and thus the award is compensation. Students, when working as research assistants, are not permitted to simply pursue their educational goals at their own discretion, subject only to the general requirement that they make academic progress, as they would be in semesters where they were under some form of financial aid other than a research grant.

The funding here is thus not akin to scholarship aid merely passed through the University by a grantor without specific expectations of the recipients. Because Columbia directs the student research assistants' work and the performance of defined tasks is a condition of the grant aid, we conclude that the research assistants in this case are employees under the Act.

C.   Student Assistants in the Petitioned-for Unit Share a Community of Interest

We now turn to the question of whether the petitioned-for unit is a unit appropriate for collective bargaining. Columbia argues that the petitioned-for unit is inappropriate because it groups undergraduate and Master's degree student assistants together in the same unit with Ph.D. assistants. According to Columbia, differences in pay and benefits, duties, and remunerative interests demonstrate the absence of a community of interest. We disagree.

* * *

ORDER

The Regional Director's Decision is reversed. The proceeding is remanded to the Regional Director for further appropriate action consistent with this Decision and Order.

MEMBER MISCIMARRA, dissenting:

In this case, my colleagues decide that college and university students are "employees" for purposes of collective bargaining under the National Labor Relations Act (NLRA or Act) when serving in a variety of academic assistant positions. No distinctions are drawn based on subject, department, whether the student must already possess a bachelor's or master's degree, whether a particular position has other minimum qualifications, whether graduation is conditioned on successful performance in the position, or whether different positions are differently remunerated. As a result of today's decision, all of these university student assistant positions are made part of a single, expansive, multi-faceted bargaining unit.

I believe the issues raised by the instant petition require more thoughtful consideration than the Board majority's decision gives them. In particular, my colleagues disregard a fundamental fact that should be the starting point when considering whether to apply the NLRA to university students. Full-time enrollment in a university usually involves one of the largest expenditures a student will make in his or her lifetime, and this expenditure is almost certainly the most important financial investment the student will ever make. Many variables affect whether a student will reap any return on such a significant financial investment, but three things are certain: (i) there is no guarantee that a student will graduate, and roughly 40 percent do not; (ii) college-related costs increase substantially the longer it takes a student to graduate, and roughly 60 percent of undergraduate students do not complete degree requirements within four years after they commence college; and (iii) when students do not graduate at all, there is likely to be no return on their investment in a college education.

I respect the views presented by my colleagues and by advocates on all sides regarding the issues in this case. However, Congress never intended that the NLRA and collective bargaining would be the means by which students and their families might attempt to exercise control over such an extraordinary expense. [F]or students enrolled in a college or university, their instruction-related positions do not turn the academic institution they attend into something that can fairly be characterized as a "workplace." For students, the least important consideration is whether they engage in collective bargaining regarding their service as research assistants, graduate assistants, preceptors, or fellows, which is an incidental aspect of their education. I believe winning in this context means fulfilling degree requirements, hopefully on time.

The Board has no jurisdiction over efforts to ensure that college and university students satisfy their postsecondary education requirements. However, Congress has certainly weighed in on the subject: an array of federal statutes and regulations apply to colleges and universities, administered by the U.S. Department of Education, led by the Secretary of Education. My colleagues disregard the Board's responsibility to accommodate this extensive regulatory framework. In addition, I believe collective bargaining and, especially, the potential resort to economic weapons protected by our statute fundamentally change the relationship between university students, including student assistants, and their professors and academic institutions. Moreover, I believe collective bargaining is likely to detract from the far more important goal of completing degree requirements in the allotted time, especially when one considers the potential consequences if students and/or universities resort to economic weapons against one another. I also believe that the Board's processes and procedures are poorly suited to deal with representation and unfair labor practice cases involving students. Add these up, and the sum total is uncertainty instead of clarity, and complexity instead of simplicity, with the risks and uncertainties associated with collective bargaining— including the risk of breakdown and resort to economic weapons— governing the single most important financial decision that students and their families will ever make.

I agree with former Member Brame, who stated that the Board resembles the "foolish repairman with one tool—a hammer—to whom every problem looks like a nail; we have one tool—collective bargaining— and thus every petitioning individual looks like someone's 'employee.'" *Boston Medical Center Corp.,* 330 N.L.R.B. 152, 182 (1999) (Member Brame, dissenting). Accordingly, I respectfully dissent.

I disagree with my colleagues' decision to apply the Act to college and university student assistants. In my view, this change is unsupported by our statute, and it is ill-advised based on substantial considerations, including those that far outweigh whether students can engage in collective bargaining over the terms and conditions of education-related positions while attempting to earn an undergraduate or graduate degree.

NOTES

1. *'Round and round and 'round she goes. Columbia University* represents the Board's fourth different answer in 45 years to this question: can graduate teaching assistants qualify as "employees" under the Act? For most of this period, the answer was no; now the answer is once again yes. Are you more persuaded by the "no" camp, which focuses on the tensions inherent in characterizing the academy as a workplace, or the "yes" camp, which focuses on the importance of adhering to the plain meaning of Section 2(3)? What do you make of warnings about the consequences, which management advocates consistently predict to be dire, but which employee advocates insist are harmless? *Compare, e.g.*, Noam Scheiber, *Grad Students Win Right to Unionize in an Ivy League Case*, N.Y. Times, Aug. 23, 2016 (citing workload as one of many potential bargaining issues with academic freedom implications that should be controlled entirely by the university) (remarks of Joseph Ambash, counsel to Brown University), available at https://www.nytimes.com/2016/08/24/business/graduate-students-clear-hurdle-in-effort-to-form-union.html, *with, e.g., id.* ("We don't observe bad effects on academic freedom, bad effects on faculty-student relationships,") (remarks of Prof. Paula Voos, co-author of study cited by NLRB).

2. Academic "production" in the modern American university is reminiscent of artisanal production, which is described in Chapter 1, *supra* p. 11. Yet the Board's approach seems to be all-or-nothing; academic workers must be either "employees" or "students," but implicitly, cannot be both. Do you suppose the drafters of the NLRA really meant to exclude either the artisans (*i.e.*, the professors) or the apprentices (*i.e.*, graduate teaching assistants) from coverage?

Not all jurisdictions have taken the all-or-nothing approach. A number of states that have adopted public sector labor relations statutes recognize dual status, which entitles an apprentice to the benefits of collective bargaining insofar as she is acting in her capacity as a working employee, but does not entitle her to the same insofar as she is acting as in her capacity as a student in training. For example, in California, graduate teaching assistants in public universities and interns and residents affiliated with public sector medical care facilities are treated as employees who are entitled to engage in collective bargaining. *See, e.g.*, Higher Education Employee Relations Act (HEERA), Cal. Gov't Code 3562(f); *compare, e.g., Association of Graduate Student Employees v. Regents of Univ. of Calif.*, 13 PERC ¶ 20,087 (1989) (holding graduate assistants not to be employees), *with Regents of Univ. of Calif.*, 22 PERC ¶ 29,084 (1998) (overruling earlier PERB decision).

3.   *You be the judge.* Not so long ago, you were enrolled in college or university courses that relied heavily on graduate teaching assistants. Did you think of them more as teachers or students like yourself? Do you agree with the Board's latest take on this subject? If not, what solution would you propose?

4.   *Are the doctors in?* The status of medical interns and residents has generally tracked that of graduate teaching assistants. For many years, the Board considered interns and residents to be students who were not entitled to collective bargaining rights. *See, e.g., St. Clare's Hosp.*, 229 N.L.R.B. 1000 (1977); *Cedars Sinai Medical Ctr.*, 223 N.L.R.B. 251 (1976). In 1999, however, the Board changed course and declared them to be employees who were so entitled. See *Boston Medical Ctr.*, 330 N.L.R.B. 152 (1999). After *Brown University*, there was a question whether *Boston Medical Center* remained good law—although so far the Board has left the decision untouched.

Should the interests of patients be relevant to whether medical house staff are deemed to be employees protected by the NLRA? If so, then are patients better or worse served when house staff have the right to unionize and bargain collectively?

5.   *Expansion of coverage to student apprentices and faculty at private schools.* Even before *Brown University*, the Obama Board, in *NYU II* and other cases, signaled its intention to resolve doubts about who should be considered an "employee" in Section 2(3) in favor of inclusion, at least with respect to student apprentices and faculty at private schools. For example, in *Pacific Lutheran University,* 361 N.L.R.B. No. 157 (2014), the non-tenure-track faculty of a college providing a religious educational environment nevertheless were held to be employees. Because they performed no religious function, these faculty members could be distinguished from parochial school teachers in cases such as *NLRB v. Catholic Bishop of Chicago*, 440 U.S. 490 (1979). Moreover, in *Chicago Mathematics & Science Academy Charter School Inc.*, 359 N.L.R.B. No. 41 (2012); *see also Pennsylvania Virtual Charter School*, 364 N.L.R.B. No. 87 (2016), a "charter school" operated by a private entity with whom a public school district had a contract was found to be an "employer" under Section 2(2) because it was not a political subdivision of the state under *NLRB v. Natural Gas Utility District of Hawkins County*, 402 U.S. 600 (1971), discussed *infra* Chapter 3-C-3. The effect of this decision was to expand Section 2(3) to many if not most charter school teachers.

Of course, the Trump Board may not agree with Obama Board precedents. Partly out of fear that *Columbia University* could be overturned by the Trump Board, four unions dedicated to organizing graduate students at private universities have formed a coalition to attempt to organize students outside the traditional processes of the NLRB. *See* Franczek Radelet, *A New Push to Organize Graduate Students at Private Colleges and Universities? Four Major Unions Announce a Coalition on Higher Ed Organizing*, JD Supra (Mar. 16, 2018), available at https://www.jdsupra.com/legalnews/a-new-push-to-organize-graduate-30679/.

6.   *Then the Board punted.* In *Northwestern University*, 362 N.L.R.B. No. 167 (2015), a much-anticipated case implicating the employment status of a unique group of student apprentices, the Regional Director directed an election among football players receiving student grant-in-scholarships at Northwestern University, a private institution operating a NCAA Division I athletic program. A vote was held and the ballots were impounded pending an answer to the big question: are these college athletes "employees" within the meaning of Section 2(3) of the Act? In the end, instead of answering this question, the NLRB declined to exercise its jurisdiction over the petitioning players or their putative employer. Taking its cue from briefs submitted by amici who urged it not to reach the merits, the Board unanimously agreed that a number of concerns counseled against the exercise of its jurisdiction. One concern was that it would not promote stable labor relations to subject only a handful of private universities operating top-tier football programs, such as Northwestern, to regulation under the NLRA, when the vast majority of public universities operating competing programs could not be subjected to the same regulation. (Recall that state employers and their political subdivisions fall outside the jurisdiction of the Act, see *infra* Chapter 3-C-3.) Another concern was that the nature of league sports and the NCAA's oversight role in Division I football would render individual team bargaining—as opposed to the multi-employer bargaining typically found in professional team sports—problematic.

Would you have reached the merits? If not, do you agree with the Board's reasoning? If so, would you have found the players to be "employees" having rights to choose union representation, or "students" lacking such rights? Do you think that, if the ballots had been counted, the players would vote for or against the union? Why? *See generally* Steven L. Willborn, *College Athletes as Employees: An Overflowing Quiver*, 69 U. MIAMI L. REV. 65 (2014) (identifying NLRA and other laws under which strong case could be made for treating student athletes as employees); Robert A. McCormick & Amy Christian McCormick, *The Myth of the Student-Athlete: The College Athlete as Employee*, 81 WASH. L. REV. 71 (2006) (recounting NCAA's campaign to label players as "student athletes" to avoid having them treated as employees).

In light of the Board's decision to punt, the legal battleground over compensation for exploiting the work of student athletes has shifted from whether to treat them as employees for labor relations purposes to whether they have a protectable intellectual property interest in the use of their names and likenesses. *See, e.g.*, *O'Bannon v. NCAA*, 7 F. Supp. 3d 955 (N.D. Cal. 2014), *aff'd in part and vacated in part*, 802 F.3d 1049 (9th Cir. 2015), *cert . denied*, 137 S. Ct. 277 (2016).

4. TRANSBORDER WORKERS

a. Undocumented Workers

As of 2015, it was estimated that 11.0 million undocumented people lived in the United States. After peaking at 12.2 million in 2007, this figure consistently has remained in the low 11 million range for six straight years. About half of this number are Mexican emigres. *See* Jeffrey S. Passel & D'Vera Cohn, *As Mexican Share Declined, U.S. Unauthorized Population Fell in 2015 Below Recession Level* (Apr. 25, 2017) (Pew Research Center report), available at http://www.pewresearch.org/fact-tank/2017/04/25/as-mexican-share-declined-u-s-unauthorized-immigrant-population-fell-in-2015-below-recession-level/. Undocumented immigrants play an indispensable role in the workforce; they constitute a huge fraction, if not a majority, of the workers found in many low-wage industries. *See* Catherine L. Fisk & Michael J. Wishnie, *The Story of Hoffman Plastic Compounds, Inc. v. NLRB*, in Labor Law Stories 399, 403 (Laura J. Cooper & Catherine L. Fisk, eds., 2005). It is not uncommon for a particular low-wage workforce to be populated by immigrant workers who are from certain ethnic or minority backgrounds. For example, Latino immigrants increasingly dominate agriculture, culinary service, domestic employment, health care, janitorial service, and poultry processing. *See* Christopher David Ruiz Cameron, *The Labyrinth of Solidarity: Why the Future of the American Labor Movement Depends on Latino Workers*, 53 U. Miami L. Rev. 1089, 1091–93 (1999). Although most Latino immigrants are legal residents, a substantial portion are undocumented and tend to be concentrated in low-wage work.

In theory, undocumented workers possess many of the same rights in the workplace that other workers do. For example, at least one court has held that undocumented workers remain "employees" under the Act, and therefore, are entitled to have their votes count in a representation election. *See Agri. Processors Co. v. NLRB*, 514 F.3d 1 (D.C. Cir. 2008) (requiring kosher meat wholesaler to bargain with victorious union). The NLRB's General Counsel has taken a similar position. *See* Memorandum to All Regional Directors, Officers-in-Charge and Resident Officers from Arthur F. Rosenfield at p. B-3 (July 19, 2002) (declaring employee's immigration status to be "irrelevant" in representation proceedings).

In practice, however, undocumented workers are often treated differently. For example, most workers discharged for engaging in activities protected by the NLRA are entitled to reinstatement and back pay to make them whole for their injuries. But in 1984, interpreting the old Immigration and Nationalization Act (INA), 8 U.S.C. § 1101 et seq., the Supreme Court held that undocumented workers must be denied the reinstatement remedy because giving it would conflict with the immigration laws. *See Sure-Tan Inc. v. NLRB*, 467 U.S. 883 (1984). In

2002, interpreting the after-enacted Immigration Reform and Control Act (IRCA), the Court addressed the availability of the back pay remedy.

HOFFMAN PLASTIC COMPOUNDS, INC. V. NLRB
535 U.S. 137 (2002)

CHIEF JUSTICE REHNQUIST delivered the opinion of the Court:

The National Labor Relations Board (Board) awarded backpay to an undocumented alien who has never been legally authorized to work in the United States. We hold that such relief is foreclosed by federal immigration policy, as expressed by Congress in the Immigration Reform and Control Act of 1986 (IRCA).

Petitioner Hoffman Plastic Compounds, Inc. (Hoffman), custom-formulates chemical compounds for businesses that manufacture pharmaceutical, construction, and household products. In May 1988, petitioner hired Jose Castro to operate various blending machines that "mix and cook" the particular formulas per customer order. Before being hired for this position, Castro presented documents that appeared to verify his authorization to work in the United States. In December 1988, the United Rubber, Cork, Linoleum, and Plastic Workers of America, AFL-CIO, began a union-organizing campaign at petitioner's production plant. Castro and several other employees supported the organizing campaign and distributed authorization cards to co-workers. In January 1989, Hoffman laid off Castro and other employees engaged in these organizing activities.

Three years later, in January 1992, respondent Board found that Hoffman unlawfully selected four employees, including Castro, for layoff "in order to rid itself of known union supporters" in violation of § 8(a)(3) of the National Labor Relations Act (NLRA). To remedy this violation, the Board ordered that Hoffman (1) cease and desist from further violations of the NLRA, (2) post a detailed notice to its employees regarding the remedial order, and (3) offer reinstatement and backpay to the four affected employees. Hoffman entered into a stipulation with the Board's General Counsel and agreed to abide by the Board's order.

In June 1993, the parties proceeded to a compliance hearing before an Administrative Law Judge (ALJ) to determine the amount of backpay owed to each discriminatee. On the final day of the hearing, Castro testified that he was born in Mexico and that he had never been legally admitted to, or authorized to work in, the United States. He admitted gaining employment with Hoffman only after tendering a birth certificate belonging to a friend who was born in Texas. He also admitted that he used this birth certificate to fraudulently obtain a California driver's license and a Social Security card, and to fraudulently obtain employment following his layoff by Hoffman. Neither Castro nor the Board's General Counsel offered any evidence that Castro had applied or intended to apply for legal authorization to work in the United States. Based on this testimony, the ALJ found the Board precluded from awarding Castro backpay or reinstatement as such relief would be contrary to *Sure-Tan, Inc. v. NLRB*, 467 U.S. 883 (1984), and in conflict with IRCA, which makes it unlawful for employers knowingly to hire undocumented workers or for employees to use fraudulent documents to establish employment eligibility.

In September 1998, four years after the ALJ's decision, and nine years after Castro was fired, the Board reversed with respect to backpay. The Board thus found that Castro was entitled to $66,951 of backpay, plus interest. It calculated this backpay award from the date of Castro's termination to the date Hoffman first learned of Castro's undocumented status, a period of 4 $\frac{1}{2}$ years. Dissenting Board Member [Hurtgen] would have affirmed the ALJ and denied Castro all backpay.

This case exemplifies the principle that the Board's discretion to select and fashion remedies for violations of the NLRA, though generally broad, is not unlimited.

Our decision in *Sure-Tan* set aside an award closely analogous to the award challenged here. There we confronted for the first time a potential conflict between the NLRA and federal immigration policy, as then expressed in the Immigration and Nationality Act (INA), 66 Stat. 163, as amended, 8 U.S.C. § 1101 et seq. Two companies had unlawfully reported alien-employees to the Immigration and Naturalization Service (INS) in retaliation for union activity. Rather than face INS sanction, the employees voluntarily departed to Mexico. The Board investigated and found the companies acted in violation of §§ 8(a)(1) and (3) of the NLRA. The Board's ensuing order directed the companies to reinstate the affected workers and pay them six months' backpay.

We affirmed the Board's determination that the NLRA applied to undocumented workers, reasoning that the immigration laws "as presently written" expressed only a " 'peripheral concern' " with the employment of illegal aliens. 467 U.S. at 892. With respect to the Board's selection of remedies, however, we found its authority limited by federal immigration policy. Thus, to avoid "a potential conflict with the INA," the Board's reinstatement order had to be conditioned upon proof of "the employees' legal reentry." Similarly, with respect to backpay, we stated: "[T]he employees must be deemed 'unavailable' for work (and the accrual of backpay therefore tolled) during any period when they were not lawfully entitled to be present and employed in the United States." *Id.* "[I]n light of the practical workings of the immigration laws," such remedial limitations were appropriate even if they led to "[t]he probable unavailability of the [NLRA's] more effective remedies." *Id.* at 904.

In 1986, two years after *Sure-Tan*, Congress enacted IRCA [the Immigration Reform and Control Act], a comprehensive scheme prohibiting the employment of illegal aliens in the United States. IRCA § 101(a)(1), 100 Stat. 3360, 8 U.S.C. § 1324a. As we have previously noted, IRCA "forcefully" made combating the employment of illegal aliens central to "[t]he policy of immigration law." *INS v. Nat'l Ctr. for Immigrants' Rights, Inc.*, 502 U.S. 183, 194, and n.8 (1991). It did so by establishing an extensive "employment verification system," § 1324a(a)(1), designed to deny employment to aliens who (a) are not lawfully present in the United States, or (b) are not lawfully authorized to work in the United States, § 1324a(h)(3).[3] This verification system is critical to the IRCA regime. To enforce it, IRCA mandates that employers verify the identity and eligibility of all new hires by examining specified documents before they begin work. § 1324a(b). If an alien applicant is unable to present the required documentation, the unauthorized alien cannot be hired. § 1324a(a)(1).

Similarly, if an employer unknowingly hires an unauthorized alien, or if the alien becomes unauthorized while employed, the employer is compelled to discharge the worker upon discovery of the worker's undocumented status. § 1324a(a)(2). Employers who violate IRCA are punished by civil fines, § 1324a(e)(4)(A), and may be subject to criminal prosecution, § 1324a(f)(1). IRCA also makes it a crime for an unauthorized alien to subvert the employer verification system by tendering fraudulent documents. § 1324c(a). It thus prohibits aliens from using or attempting to use "any forged, counterfeit, altered, or falsely made document" or "any document lawfully issued to or with respect to a person other than the possessor" for purposes of obtaining employment in the United States. §§ 1324c(a)(1)–(3). Aliens who use or attempt to use such documents are subject to fines and criminal prosecution. 18 U.S.C. § 1546(b). There is no dispute that Castro's use of false documents to obtain employment with Hoffman violated these provisions.

Under the IRCA regime, it is impossible for an undocumented alien to obtain employment in the United States without some party directly contravening explicit congressional policies. Either the undocumented alien tenders fraudulent identification, which subverts the cornerstone of IRCA's enforcement mechanism, or the employer knowingly hires the undocumented alien in direct contradiction of its IRCA obligations. The Board asks that we overlook this fact and allow it to award backpay to an illegal alien for years of work not performed, for wages that could not lawfully have been earned, and for a job obtained in the first instance by a criminal fraud. We find, however, that awarding backpay to illegal aliens runs counter to policies underlying IRCA, policies the Board has no

---

[3]   For an alien to be "authorized" to work in the United States, he or she must possess "a valid social security account number card," § 1324a(b)(C)(i), or "other documentation evidencing authorization of employment in the United States which the Attorney General finds, by regulation, to be acceptable for purposes of this section," § 1324a(b)(C)(ii). *See also* § 1324a(h)(3)(B) (defining "unauthorized alien" as any alien "[not] authorized to be so employed by this chapter or by the Attorney General"). Regulations implementing these provisions are set forth at 8 CFR § 274a (2001).

authority to enforce or administer. Therefore, as we have consistently held in like circumstances, the award lies beyond the bounds of the Board's remedial discretion.

The Board contends that awarding limited backpay to Castro "reasonably accommodates" IRCA, because, in the Board's view, such an award is not "inconsistent" with IRCA. Brief for Respondent 29–42. The Board argues that because the backpay period was closed as of the date Hoffman learned of Castro's illegal status, Hoffman could have employed Castro during the backpay period without violating IRCA. *Id.* at 37. What matters here, and what sinks the Board's claims, is that Congress has expressly made it criminally punishable for an alien to obtain employment with false documents. Far from "accommodating" IRCA, the Board's position, recognizing employer misconduct but discounting the misconduct of illegal alien employees, subverts it.

Indeed, awarding backpay in a case like this not only trivializes the immigration laws, it also condones and encourages future violations. The Board admits that had the INS detained Castro, or had Castro obeyed the law and departed to Mexico, Castro would have lost his right to backpay.

We therefore conclude that allowing the Board to award backpay to illegal aliens would unduly trench upon explicit statutory prohibitions critical to federal immigration policy, as expressed in IRCA.

Lack of authority to award backpay does not mean that the employer gets off scot-free. The Board here has already imposed other significant sanctions against Hoffman—sanctions Hoffman does not challenge. These include orders that Hoffman cease and desist its violations of the NLRA, and that it conspicuously post a notice to employees setting forth their rights under the NLRA and detailing its prior unfair practices. Hoffman will be subject to contempt proceedings should it fail to comply with these orders.

JUSTICE BREYER, with whom JUSTICES STEVENS, SOUTER, and GINSBURG join, dissenting:

I cannot agree that the backpay award before us "runs counter to," or "trenches upon," national immigration policy. As all the relevant agencies (including the Department of Justice) have told us, the National Labor Relations Board's limited backpay order will not interfere with the implementation of immigration policy. Rather, it reasonably helps to deter unlawful activity that both labor laws and immigration laws seek to prevent. Consequently, the order is lawful.

The Court does not deny that the employer in this case dismissed an employee for trying to organize a union—a crude and obvious violation of the labor laws. Nor can it deny that in such circumstances backpay awards serve critically important remedial purposes. Those purposes involve more than victim compensation; they also include deterrence, *i.e.*, discouraging employers from violating the Nation's labor laws.

Without the possibility of the deterrence that backpay provides, the Board can impose only future-oriented obligations upon law-violating employers—for it has no other weapons in its remedial arsenal. And in the absence of the backpay weapon, employers could conclude that they can violate the labor laws at least once with impunity. *See A.P.R.A. Fuel Oil Buyers Group, Inc.*, 320 N.L.R.B. 408, 415, n.38 (1995).

Where in the immigration laws can the Court find a "policy" that might warrant taking from the Board this critically important remedial power? Certainly not in any statutory language. The immigration statutes say that an employer may not knowingly employ an illegal alien, that an alien may not submit false documents, and that the employer must verify documentation. See 8 U.S.C. §§ 1324a(a)(1), 1324a(b); 18 U.S.C. § 1546(b)(1). They provide specific penalties, including criminal penalties, for violations. 8 U.S.C. §§ 1324a(e)(4), 1324a(f)(1). But the statutes' language itself does not explicitly state how a violation is to effect the enforcement of other laws, such as the labor laws. What is to happen, for example, when an employer hires, or an alien works, in violation of these provisions? Must the alien forfeit all pay earned? May the employer ignore the labor laws? More to the point, may the employer violate those laws with impunity, at least once—secure in the knowledge that the Board cannot assess a monetary penalty? The immigration statutes' language simply does not say.

To deny the Board the power to award backpay, however, might very well increase the strength of this magnetic force. That denial lowers the cost to the employer of an initial labor law violation (provided, of course, that the only victims are illegal aliens). It thereby increases the employer's incentive to find and to hire illegal-alien employees.

For these reasons, I respectfully dissent.

NOTES

1.   *Immigrant organizing.* Since the 1990s, undocumented immigrants have participated in a significant union and community organizing efforts across a wide spectrum of low-wage industries, including light manufacturing, as in *Hoffman Plastic Compounds*. Although some observers initially believed that undocumented workers would be more reluctant than citizens and "green card" holders to attempt unionization—due to the risks of deportation and other forms of retaliation by employers—others found that immigrant workers were willing to assume these risks:

> According to Peter Tovar, the NLRB Regional Attorney who handled the case, Castro had been considered a good, hard-working employee and he was not a leader of the union organizing drive. He was just in the wrong place at the wrong time. To the extent that he did actively

support the union, we can only speculate about his reasons. Scholars who studied union organizing campaigns in the 1980s and 1990s found little fear [among undocumented immigrants being organized]. Some workers said that if they were deported they would simply come back. Others said the possibility of INS raids seemed remote. Some Mexican and Central American immigrants had had positive experiences of unionism in their home countries and believed that, in contrast to the death threats leveled against union organizers by right-wing groups in Central America, in the U.S. the worst thing that could happen would be that they would lose a low-wage job, and be deported home to family.

Catherine L. Fisk & Michael J. Wishnie, *The Story of Hoffman Plastic Compounds, Inc. v. NLRB: Labor Rights Without Remedies for Undocumented Immigrants*, in Labor Law Stories 399, 409–10 (Laura J. Cooper & Catherine L. Fisk, eds., 2005).

2.   *"Salt" in the wound?* In *Town & Country*, the "salt" case discussed above, *supra* p. 264, the Court reasoned that "a broad, literal reading of the statute" (including the term "employee") "is consistent with cases in this Court" such as, say, *Sure-Tan, Inc. v. NLRB*, which held that undocumented aliens are "employees" who are protected by the Act. *See* 467 U.S. 883, 891–92 (1984). But *Sure-Tan* denied undocumented employees the remedy of reinstatement; *Hoffman* denied them the remedy of backpay as well. If the only remedies left, as Chief Justice Rehnquist notes, are the cease-and-desist order (violations of which are punishable by contempt) and the posting of a notice describing the employer's violation, can undocumented aliens truly be considered protected by the NLRA? If not, should anybody—besides undocumented workers themselves—be concerned? If they are breaking the law by entering and remaining in the U.S., is that sufficient justification for denying them the protections of the NLRA?

* * *

After *Hoffman*, many workers' advocates and scholars worried that the decision would lay the legal groundwork to preclude undocumented workers from enforcing their rights under other federal as well as state employment statutes. One of the co-authors of this casebook felt this was unlikely—a prediction that proved correct.

BORDERLINE DECISIONS: HOFFMAN PLASTICS COMPOUNDS, THE NEW BRACERO PROGRAM, AND THE SUPREME COURT'S ROLE IN MAKING FEDERAL LABOR POLICY

Christopher David Ruiz Cameron
51 UCLA L. Rev. 1, 4–7 (2003)

The *Hoffman* decision has been widely criticized, and rightly so. The decision, without apology to "the very persons who most need protection from exploitative employer practices"—as Justice Kennedy once described undocumented workers—creates in effect a new Bracero Program. [Between 1942 and 1964, an estimated 4.6 million Mexican nationals were temporarily admitted into this country under the old Bracero Program for the seemingly benign purpose of fortifying our agricultural labor pool; in reality, they were treated like indentured servants.] It authorizes the creation of an underclass of low-wage Latino immigrants who are promised workplace rights in theory, but not in practice.

Scholars and workers' advocates have focused on the disasters that *Hoffman* might portend for undocumented aliens asserting backpay claims under fair labor standards, employment discrimination, and other worker protection legislation. Although I share their concerns, I believe that over time *Hoffman* is unlikely to alter most of the substantive rights of undocumented workers in these nonlabor law areas, especially the rights of victims pursuing back wages for hours actually worked. The ill effects of *Hoffman* will be confined mostly to the ever-shrinking world of the NLRA, where undocumented aliens have long lived in the shadows. After all, *Hoffman* is the logical extension of the Court's 1984 decision in *Sure-Tan, Inc. v. NLRB*, which created a strong presumption that undocumented workers are not entitled to the equitable remedy of reinstatement that is usually awarded to victims of antiunion animus. The 1986 passage of IRCA, and especially, IRCA's declaration that the employment of undocumented persons is against the law, was practically invited by the *Sure-Tan* majority. Of the many things that might be said about *Hoffman*, surprising is hardly one of them.

To me, *Hoffman's* greatest evil lies in its not-so-subtle elevation of the Supreme Court over Congress as the final arbiter of federal labor policy. This promotion has been a long time in the making. Except for some narrow but significant changes made in 1984 [primarily, the enactment of Section 1113 of the Bankruptcy Code, which makes it more difficult for Chapter 11 debtor-employers to reject collective bargaining agreements in reorganization proceedings], Congress has enacted no substantive reforms of federal labor policy since [the Landrum-Griffin Act of] 1959. But the Supreme Court has. Seizing on purported conflicts between the NLRA and other federal legislation, the Court periodically has taken advantage of this repose to "enact" its own substantive policy choices. In selected cases, the Court has set up an apparent conflict between the NLRA and some other federal legislative scheme, then resolved that conflict by effectively abrogating federal labor policy in favor of federal "other" policy. Typically, the majority dresses its rationale in the clothing of true congressional intent, and dismisses as the ravings of an incompetent bureaucracy any views to the contrary expressed by the NLRB.

Hoffman, in creating a new Bracero Program, is but the most recent example of adjudication at the margins ordinarily separating labor law from other federal laws. The Court's opinions in such cases are "borderline decisions," not only because they involve false conflicts and dubious outcomes, but also because they have serious implications for people who work on the literal and metaphorical borders of our economy—people like the undocumented Latinos targeted in *Hoffman*.

NOTES

1. *Will Hoffman set precedent for other laws? Hoffman* generated a substantial amount of commentary. Most commentators, disagreeing with Professor Cameron, worried that the decision would preclude workers from vindicating their rights under other employment law regimes. *See, e.g.*, María Pabón López, *The Place of the Undocumented Worker in the United States Legal System after Hoffman Plastics Compounds: An Assessment and Comparison with Argentina's Legal System*, 15 Ind. Int'l & Comp. L. Rev. 301 (2005); María L. Ontiveros, *Immigrant Workers' Rights in a Post-Hoffman World— Organizing Around the Thirteenth Amendment*, 18 Geo. Immigr. L .J. 651 (2004); Ruben J. Garcia, *Ghost Workers in an Interconnected World: Going Beyond the Dichotomies of Domestic Immigration and Labor Laws*, 36 U. Mich. J. L. Ref. 737 (2003); Robert I. Correales, *Did Hoffman Plastic Compounds, Inc. Produce Disposable Workers?*, 14 Berkeley La Raza L.J. 103 (2003). One commentator raised fears about the effects a *Hoffman*-type decision even before *Hoffman* was actually decided. *See* Lori J. Nessel, *Undocumented Immigrants in the Workplace: The Fallacy of Labor Protection and the Need for Reform*, 36 Harv. C.R.–C.L. L. Rev. 345 (2001).

So far, however, Professor Cameron has proved to be correct; the lower federal and state courts have been reluctant to extend the reasoning of *Hoffman* to claims asserted under other employment law regimes. By 2009, there were

> at least forty-four reported decisions in which the [federal or state] court addressed the argument that *Hoffman* should limit the remedies or rights of undocumented workers for violations of state or federal employment laws, including employment discrimination, minimum wage, prevailing wage, unemployment compensation, workers' compensation, and workplace safety laws. (In some of these decisions, employers sought [unsuccessfully] to discover the immigration status of plaintiffs who were probably undocumented.) In all forty-four reported decisions, the court refused to follow, declined to extend, distinguished, or recognized the limits of, the holding in *Hoffman*.

Christopher David Ruiz Cameron, *The Borders of Collective Representation: Comparing the Rights of Undocumented Workers to Organize Under United States and International Labor Standards*, 44 USF L. Rev. 431, 540 (2009). More recent cases seem to be in accord. *See, e.g., Lucas v. Jerusalem Cafe, LLC*, 721 F.3d 927 (8th Cir. 2013) (upholding back pay for unpaid minimum wages and overtime under Fair Labor Standards Act because statute's broad definition includes aliens unauthorized to work).

Under the NLRA, however, *Hoffman*'s holding that the Board lacks remedial authority to award back pay to undocumented workers whose rights have been violated remains firmly in place. Even the Obama Board, led by two strong critics of *Hoffman*—Chairman Liebman and Member Pearce—has held that the case cannot be distinguished on the ground that the employer, rather than the employees involved, violated IRCA by failing to ask the seven employees in question for documentation when they were hired. *See Mezonos Maven Bakery, Inc.*, 357 N.L.R.B. No. 47 (2011).

2.   *The emergence of "immployment" law.* Notwithstanding the reluctance of the federal courts to scale back the non-NLRA employment rights of undocumented workers, in 2010 Arizona set in motion a wave of state-based efforts that were purportedly designed to ramp up enforcement of federal immigration laws by enacting the Support Our Law Enforcement and Safe Neighborhoods Act, S.B. 1070, as amended by H.B. 2162 ("S.B. 1070"), *codified at* Ariz. Rev. Stat. §§ 11–1051(B), 13–509, 13–2928(C), 13–3883(A)(5). Among other things, S.B. 1070 made it a misdemeanor for an alien to look for work, or otherwise be present in Arizona, without carrying the required federal documents. It also required state law enforcement officers to attempt to determine an individual's immigration status during a lawful stop, detention, or arrest when the officer has reasonable suspicion that the individual is undocumented. The latter provision became known as the "show your papers" rule. In 2011, five states—Alabama, Georgia, Indiana, South Carolina, and Utah—passed omnibus legislation patterned after S.B. 1070. *See* National Conference of State Legislatures, State Omnibus Immigration Legislation and Challenges (Aug. 27, 2012), reported at http://www.ncsl.org/research/immigration/omnibus-immigration-legislation.aspx. Critics, including labor leaders, attacked these laws on the grounds that they encouraged racial profiling—and were preempted anyway. In the end, the U.S. Supreme Court held most of S.B. 1070 to be preempted by federal immigration law, although it let stand the controversial "show your papers" rule. *Arizona v. United States*, 132 S. Ct. 2492 (2012).

Articulating a different type of preemption analysis, one scholar has argued that the preemptive force of the FLSA and Title VII of the Civil Rights Act of 1964 create a distinct—and supreme—sphere of federal "immployment" law that, under the Supremacy Clause, makes such restrictive state legislation unconstitutional. *See* Kati L. Griffith, *Discovering "Immployment" Law: The Constitutionality of Subfederal Immigration Regulation at Work*, 29 Yale L. & Pol'y Rev. 389 (2011); *see also* Keith Cunningham-Parmeter, Forced Federalism: States as Laboratories of Immigration Reform, 62 Hastings L.J. 1673 (2011) (challenging Justice Brandeis' oft-cited maxim that states can serve as valuable laboratories of democracy, at least with respect to regulation of undocumented immigrants).

3.   *Is a contract a contract?* Suppose an undocumented worker files a grievance alleging that she has been denied overtime at the higher pay rate

specified by the applicable collective bargaining agreement. Suppose further that the grievance goes to arbitration, where the employer defends on the ground that backpay is unavailable under *Hoffman*. Assuming the grievance is meritorious, should the arbitrator issue a backpay award? Would your answer be different if the same worker filed a grievance alleging that she had been discharged without just cause? In either case, if the arbitrator sustains the grievance and awards back pay, should the award be vacated as against public policy under Section 301 of the Taft-Hartley? *See Eastern Associated Coal Co. v. United Mine Workers of America, District 17,* 531 U.S. 57 (2000) (suggesting answer to be no).

4. *The Bracero Program.* By the mid-1960s, when the Bracero Program ended, the Civil Rights Era was in full swing. Activists, especially union organizers in the agricultural sector, viewed the program as inconsistent with the values that they were promoting, including equal rights for everyone. The *braceros* were Mexican immigrants. They were routinely paid as little as twenty cents an hour, subjected to hazardous working conditions, promised pensions they were never paid—and fired if they dared speak to union organizers. *See* Cameron, *Borderline Decisions, supra,* at 3. This happened despite guarantees of minimum wages and fair treatment. Growers got away with abuses because each *bracero* was bound by a government-supervised contract system to work on a single crop for a single employer; he was not free to shop around for better wages or working conditions with other employers. A *bracero* who was fired for any reason faced immediate deportation.

In light of this description, do you agree or disagree that *Hoffman* essentially creates a new Bracero Program? Does your answer depend on knowing that agricultural workers are specifically excluded from the definition of "employee" under the NLRA? Does this exclusion make sense to you? What policy reasons might support such an exclusion?

b. Foreign and Multi-Country Workers

International labor standards do not define who is an "employee," much less attempt to deny protections to workers based on their citizenship or nationality. If anything, international law transcends such boundaries by avoiding the term "employees" in favor of the broader term "workers." *See, e.g.,* International Labor Organisation (ILO) Convention No. 87 Concerning Freedom of Association and Protection of the Right to Organize, July 9, 1948, art. 2 ("Workers and employers, without distinction whatsoever, shall have the right to establish and, subject only to the rules of the organisation concerned, to join organisations of their own choosing without previous authorization.").

If, as many international scholars argue, labor rights are human rights, then the application of labor principles may be universal, without reference to national borders. *See, e.g.,* Clyde Summers, *The Battle in Seattle: Free Trade, Labor Rights and Societal Values,* 22 U. Pa. J. Int'l Econ. L. 61, 66–68 (2001). As a result, "the reasons for concluding international treatises on labour rights may thus be seen as primarily protective of employees, redressing the imbalance of their otherwise enfeebled status"—without regard in the literature to whose employees they really are. Janet Dine, *Human Rights and Company Law*, in Human Rights Standards and the Responsibility of Transnational Corporations 209, 209–12 (Michael K. Addo, ed., 1999).

WORKERS' FREEDOM OF ASSOCIATION IN THE UNITED STATES: THE GAP BETWEEN IDEALS AND PRACTICE
Lance Compa
Workers' Rights as Human Rights, pp. 23–41 (James A. Gross ed., 2003)

Freedom of association for workers has long been universally acknowledged as a fundamental right. A widely accepted body of international norms has established standards for workers' freedom of association covering the right to organize, the right to bargain collectively, and the right to strike.

Sources of international labor law on workers' freedom of association include human rights instruments developed by the United Nations and by regional human rights bodies, principles elaborated through worker, employer, and government representatives at the International Labor Organisation (ILO), and labor rights clauses in international trade agreements. The United States has acknowledged its international responsibility to honor workers' freedom of association by ratifying human rights instruments, in particular the International Covenant on Civil and Political Rights. It has also accepted obligations under ILO conventions on freedom of association and under the 1998 Declaration on Fundamental Principles and Rights at Work (DFPRW) [even though so far the U.S. has not ratified ILO Convention Nos. 87 and 98, discussed below].

Exclusion of Millions of Workers from Protection

International norms [of freedom of association] refer to the right of "every person" to form and join trade unions and to bargain collectively. Several of the cases examined for this report involved workers excluded from coverage by the NLRA, such as agricultural workers, domestic employees, and "independent" contractors who actually work in a dependent relationship with a single employer for years.

In all, millions of workers in the U.S. are excluded from coverage of laws that are supposed to protect [them]. Workers who fall under these exclusions can be summarily fired with impunity for seeking to form and join a union. Even where the employer does not fire them, workers' requests to bargain collectively can be ignored.

International Human Rights Instruments

The Universal Declaration of Human Rights (UDHR) (1948) states that "everyone has the right to freedom of peaceful assembly and association," and "everyone has the right to form and to join trade unions for the protection of his interests."

The International Covenant on Civil and Political Rights (ICCPR) (1966) declares: "Everyone shall have the right to freedom of association with others, including the right to form and join trade unions for the protection of his interests."

The International Covenant on Economic, Social, and Cultural Rights (ICESCR) (1966) obliges governments to "ensure the right of everyone to form trade unions and join the trade union of his choice . . . the right of unions to function freely . . . [and] the right to strike."

When the U.S. ratified the ICCPR in 1992, it took several reservations, understandings, and declarations sidestepping certain obligations in the covenant. But it took no reservations, understandings, or declarations with respect to Article 22 on the right to form and join trade unions, or to Article 2 requiring an "effective remedy" for rights violations.

Regional Instruments

The American Declaration of the Rights and Duties of Man (1948) states: "Every person has the right to assemble peaceably with others in a formal public meeting or an informal gathering, in connection with matters of common interest of any nature. Every person has the right to associate with others to promote, exercise and protect his legitimate interests of a political, economic, religious, social, cultural, professional, labor union or other nature."

The American Convention on Human Rights (1969) declares: "Everyone has the right to associate freely for ideological, religious, political, economic, labor, social, cultural, sports, or other purposes."

ILO Conventions

Over decades of painstaking treatment of allegations of violations of workers' rights, the ILO's Committee on Freedom of Association has elaborated authoritative guidelines for implementation of the right to organize, the right to bargain collectively, and the right to strike.

ILO Convention No. 87 on Freedom of Association and Protection of the Right to Organize says that "workers and employers, without distinction whatsoever, shall have the right to establish and, subject only to the rules of the organization concerned, to join organizations of their own choosing without previous authorization."

ILO Convention No. 98 declares that "workers shall enjoy adequate protection against acts of anti-union discrimination in respect of their employment. . . . Such protection shall apply more particularly in respect of acts calculated to (a) make the employment of a worker subject to the condition that he shall not join a union or shall relinquish union membership; (b) cause the dismissal of or otherwise prejudice a worker by reason of union membership or because of participation in union activities."

The ILO's Declaration of Fundamental Principles and Rights at Work (1998) says expressly: "All members, even if they have not ratified the Conventions in question, have an obligation arising from the very fact of membership in the Organization, to respect, to promote, and to realize, in good faith and in accordance with the [ILO] Constitution, the principles concerning the fundamental rights which are the subject of those Conventions, namely: (a) freedom of association and the effective recognition of the right to collective bargaining."

The North American Free Trade Agreement

The North American Free Trade Agreement (NAFTA) among the U.S., Canada, and Mexico brought with it a labor side agreement, the North American Agreement on Labor Cooperation (NAALC). Freedom of association and protection of the right to organize, the right to bargain collectively and protection of the right to strike are the first three "labor principles" of the NAALC.

Some provisions of U.S. law openly conflict with international standards on freedom of association. Millions of workers, including farm workers, household domestic workers, and low-level supervisors are expressly barred from the [NLRA's] protection of the right to organize. New forms of employment relationships have created millions of part-time, temporary, subcontracted, and otherwise "atypical" or "contingent" workers whose freedom of association is frustrated by the law's failure to adapt to changes in the economy.

NOTES

1.   *Workers of the world unite?* As noted above, the International Labor Organisation's Declaration of Fundamental Principles of Rights at Work (DFPRW) (1998) requires member nations, including the U.S., to honor the freedom of association protections guaranteed by ILO Convention Nos. 87 and 98, even if, like the U.S., they haven't expressly ratified those conventions. Following *Hoffman*, the American Federation of Labor and Congress of Industrial Organizations (AFL-CIO), together with the Confederación de Trabajadores de Mexico (CTM), filed with the International Labor Organisation's Committee on Freedom of Association (CFA) a complaint alleging that *Hoffman* violated the obligations of the United States under the DFPRW. In 2003, the CFA issued a report finding that eliminating the back pay remedy leaves the U.S. government with insufficient means for ensuring that undocumented workers are protected from anti-union discrimination. *See* International Labor Organisation, Committee on Freedom of Association, Complaints Against the Government of the United States Presented by the American Federation of Labor and Congress of Industrial Organizations (AFL-CIO) and the Confederation of Mexican Workers (CTM), Case No. 2227, Report

No. 332, ¶ 610 (Nov. 2003). The decision is binding on the U.S. by virtue of its having accepted obligations under the DFPRW.

A comparable convention, the American Convention on Human Rights (1969), declares: "Everyone has the right to associate freely for ideological, religious, political, economic, labor, social, cultural, sports, or other purposes." Concerned that *Hoffman* violated these principles, the Republic of Mexico, following a path similar to that taken by American and Mexican trade unionists before the ILO, filed a case with the Inter-American Court of Human Rights (IACHR). In 2003, the IACHR issued an opinion advising that, due to their irregular status, undocumented workers in the U.S. are frequently treated unfavorably compared to other workers. *See* Inter-American Court of Human Rights, Advisory Opinion OC–18/03, Juridical Condition and the Rights of the Undocumented Migrants, ¶ 136 (Sept. 17, 2003). The decision is not binding on the United States.

In general, the distinction made by *Hoffman* between documented employees, who are entitled to legal remedies, and undocumented employees, who are not so entitled, is unusual by international labor standards. (In the global arena, the corresponding terms would be "regular" and "irregular" workers.) In fact, according to one study of international labor law as codified in 18 separate instruments—including ILO Conventions Nos. 87 and 98, the DFPRW, and the IACHR, among others—the term "employee" is not to be found. Instead, rights are guaranteed to "everyone," "every person," or "workers." *See* Christopher David Ruiz Cameron, *The Borders of Collective Representation: Comparing the Rights of Undocumented Workers to Organize Under United States and International Labor Standards*, 44 USF L. Rev. 431, 438–39 (2009).

Do you agree with the ILO's Committee on Freedom of Association that the result in *Hoffman* places the U.S. in violation of international labor standards? Does it make sense to you that an international "convention" can be binding on a nation that has not ratified it? Does the IACHR's opinion, which advises that irregular workers are treated unfavorably compared to other workers, but is not binding on the U.S., better comport with your ideas about the application of precedent to a sovereign nation? In either case, if the decision turns out to be binding, what should the remedy be? As a matter of sound international or labor policy, should the U.S. honor such a result?

2. *Transborder regulations.* Professor Compa's article summarizes the wide range of international labor standards that reach the employment conditions of transborder workers. Yet the definition of "transborder" worker is rather fluid. It can include any of the following: foreign citizen workers laboring on U.S. soil for U.S. domestic companies, as in *Hoffman*; U.S citizen workers on U.S. soil laboring under the threat that the employer may send their jobs off shore to take advantage of lower labor costs there; U.S. citizen workers laboring abroad for U.S. companies; and U.S. citizen workers laboring on U.S. soil for foreign companies, to name but a few variations.

Which regulatory regime—U.S., foreign, international, or some combination thereof—protects these workers? What about foreign citizen workers laboring on U.S. soil for a transborder employer having operations both in the U.S. and abroad? Or the foreign citizen workers of such a company laboring outside the U.S.? *See, e.g., Morelli v. Cedel*, 141 F.3d 39 (2d. Cir. 1998) (holding that, under Sections 4(h)(2) and 11(f) of the Age Discrimination in Employment Act, 29 U.S.C. §§ 623(h)(2), 630(f), the first group is protected by the ADEA, partly because the second group counts for purposes of determining the statute's 20-employee jurisdictional minimum).

3. *The contingent workforce revisited.* In our prior discussion of contingent work, *supra* p. 224, we noted that, in the eyes of the NLRA and other statutes, an employer does not break the law merely by establishing and maintaining a contingent workforce. In many cases, the interests of employers, workers, and society at large are each served by such arrangements. Is Professor Compa arguing that, in the eyes of international labor standards, contingent work necessarily violates those standards? Why or why not?

4. *After NAFTA.* Siding with Professor Compa, organized labor spent years harshly criticizing NAFTA and the supposed protections of its labor side accord, NAALC, for excluding many workers from its labor protections and providing toothless remedies for workers that it did include. As this edition went to press, however, the Trump Administration announced completion of the United States-Mexico-Canada Agreement (USMCA), a trade pact purporting to replace NAFTA with a new text and 12 side letters touching on a variety of matters, including provisions requiring Mexico to make it easier for unions to organize workers. *See* Jim Tankersley, Trump Just Ripped Up Nafta. Here's What's in the New Trilateral Agreement, N.Y. Times, Oct. 1, 2018, at p. A8. But the details of this new trade deal remained to be seen.

C. WHO (OR WHAT) IS THE "EMPLOYER"?

Section 2(2) provides:

> The term "employer" includes any person acting as an agent of an employer, directly or indirectly, but shall not include the United States or any wholly owned Government corporation, or any Federal Reserve Bank, or any State or political subdivision thereof, or any person subject to the Railway Labor Act as amended from time to time, or any labor organization (other than when acting as an employer), or anyone acting in the capacity of officer or agent of such labor organization.

29 U.S.C. § 152(2). By implication, "employer" also includes at least one category of employee excluded by Section 2(3): "any individual employed as a supervisor." 29 U.S.C. § 152(3).

The blandness of this language masks the vigor with which parties often litigate the question of who is considered to be an "employer" under the NLRA. There are at least two reasons why these fights are so hotly contested.

First, as a practical matter, the stakes are high. At the beginning of this chapter, we met the perma-temps at Microsoft, *supra* p. 219. As their case demonstrates, a company that can avoid the label of "employer" is free to enter into working relationships left unregulated by most employment laws, including the NLRA. An entity that is not considered to be an "employer" is free to hire and fire, assign or reassign, promote or demote, and compensate or downsize, all without fear of either union intervention or unfair labor practice liability. The parties understand this and, accordingly, are willing to fight over the label.

Second, the laws of economics suggest such contests are inevitable. Take the question of who is a "supervisor," a question the NLRB and the Supreme Court have passed back and forth like a volleyball for almost two decades. In an economy based on the free flow of capital, there is an inherent conflict between the people who do the work and the people for whom the work is done. They are not the same folks; somebody has to be Me—and somebody else has to be The Boss of Me. According to Eric Hoffer, a longshoreman turned social commentator:

> To the eternal workingman, management is substantially the same whether it is made up of profit-seekers, idealists, technicians, or bureaucrats. The allegiance of the manager is to the task and its results. However noble his motives he cannot help viewing the workers as a means to an end. He will always try to get the utmost out of them; and it matters not whether he does it for the sake of profit, for a holy cause, or for the sheer principle of efficiency.

> One need not view management as an enemy or feel self-righteous about doing an honest day's work to realize that things are likely to get tough when management can take the worker for granted; when it can plan and operate without having to worry about what the worker will say or do.

Eric Hoffer, *The Workingman Looks at The Boss*, Harper's, Mar. 1954, in Charles Craypo, The Economics of Collective Bargaining: Case Studies in the Private Sector 1 (1986).

Thus the Act presumes a hierarchical, adversarial economic relationship between workers on the one hand and management on the other. As we have already seen, this presumption is increasingly at odds with the flatter hierarchies of the modern American workplace—a fact that makes it more difficult to draw the boundaries of collective representation. *See, e.g.*, Catherine L. Fisk, *Supervisors in a World of Flat Hierarchies.* 64 Hast. L. J. 1403, 1404, 1420 (2013).

Like Section 2(3), which defines the term "employee," Section 2(2) defines the term "employer" in part by carving out from its coverage certain actors. Among these are railroad and airline employers whose labor relations are already regulated by the Railway Labor Act (RLA), 45 U.S.C. §§ 151–188. Under the RLA, there is no adjudicatory agency equivalent to the NLRB, but the National Mediation Board is established to regulate the conditions under which the parties may be released from negotiations to use strikes, lockouts, and other economic weapons. *See* RLA § 5, First, 45 U.S.C. § 155, First.

The commercial operations of American Indian tribes are generally excluded from coverage due to the doctrine of tribal sovereign immunity. *See Fort Apache Timber Co.*, 226 N.L.R.B. 503 (1976). But recently the Board ruled, and at least one circuit court of appeals has agreed, that the Act reaches on-reservation Indian gaming casinos, at least when they employ many non-Indians and cater mainly to non-Indians. *See San Manuel Indian Bingo & Casino*, 341 N.L.R.B. 1055 (2004), *enf'd*, 475 F.3d 1306 (D.C. Cir. 2007).

Asserting a discretionary power reserved in Section 14(c)(1), the Board has declined to exercise jurisdiction over any employer or industry involved in a labor dispute having an effect on commerce that is "not sufficiently substantial." 29 U.S.C. § 164(c). For example, owners and operators of tracks in the horse racing industry have been excluded under this power. *See Walter A. Kelley*, 139 N.L.R.B. 744 (1962). The core operations of religious institutions, including the employment of teachers in elementary and secondary schools, arguably could be excluded under this power, but the Supreme Court has seen fit instead to exclude them by interpreting the statute narrowly to avoid constitutional problems under the First Amendment's free exercise clause. See *NLRB v. Catholic Bishop of Chicago*, 440 U.S. 490 (1979).

Pursuant to Section 14(c)(1), the Board has established the following minimum standards for exercising jurisdiction over employers:

Type of employer	Annual gross volume
Retail	$500,000 or more
Non-retail	Over $50,000 outflow/inflow
Channels of interstate commerce	$50,000 or more
Public utilities	$250,000 or more
Transit systems (non-taxi)	$50,000 or more
Communications	$100,000 or more
National defense	Substantial impact on commerce

Health care institutions   At least $250,000

Law firms   At least $250,000

NLRB, Jurisdictional Standards, available at https://www.nlrb.gov/rights-we-protect/jurisdictional-standards.

This section treats five types of workers or entities who may or may not be treated as the "employer," sometimes on the ground their interests are more closely aligned with management than labor, sometimes for separate policy reasons: (1) supervisors, (2) managerial and confidential employees, (3) workers for public sector entities, (4) workers for multiple entities that actually constitute a single employer (the "single employer" doctrine), (5) joint employers, and (6) workers for transborder employers.

1. SUPERVISORS

Section 2(11) of the Act defines a "supervisor" as

[A]ny individual having the authority, in the interest of the employer, to hire, transfer, suspend, lay off, recall, promote, discharge, assign, reward, or discipline other employees, or responsibly to direct them, or to adjust their grievances, or effectively to recommend such action, if in connection with the foregoing the exercise of such authority is not of a merely routine or clerical nature, but requires the use of independent judgment.

29 U.S.C. § 152(11).

In theory, the determination of who is a supervisor would seem to be a simple matter. A "supervisor" is someone who (a) holds authority in the employer's interest, (b) exercises, or has power to effectively recommend action as to, one or more of the Section 2(11) functions—hire, transfer, suspend, lay off, recall, promote, discharge, assign, reward, discipline, direct work, or adjust grievances—and (c) uses independent judgment in so doing. In practice, the Board and the courts have much difficulty identifying which workers are true supervisors. No matter how the question is decided, either labor or management is bound to be unhappy with the result.

In *NLRB v. Kentucky River Cmty. Care Inc.*, 532 U.S. 706 (2001), the Supreme Court, for the second time in a decade, took issue with the NLRB's long-running efforts to determine who is a "supervisor," and therefore, excluded as part of management from the Act's protections. After holding that certain nurses did not exercise "independent judgment" when they relied on their ordinary professional or technical judgment to direct less skilled employees, the Court remanded with instructions that the Board establish clear standards for interpreting not only the term "independent judgment," but also the terms "assign" and "responsibly to direct" as found in the list of Section 2(11) supervisory functions.

After mulling things over for almost half a decade, the Board finally delivered its response in a trio of cases: *Oakwood Healthcare Inc.*, 348 N.L.R.B. 686 (2006); *Beverly Enters.-Minn. Inc. (Golden Crest Healthcare Center)*, 348 N.L.R.B. 727 (2006); *Croft Metals Inc.*, 348 N.L.R.B. 717 (2006). The first case, perhaps the most influential of the trio, is reprinted here.

IN RE OAKWOOD HEALTHCARE, INC.

348 N.L.R.B. 686 (2006)

By CHAIRMAN BATTISTA and MEMBERS LIEBMAN, SCHAUMBER, KIRSANOW, and WALSH:

I.   FACTS

The Employer has approximately 181 staff RNs [registered nurses] who provide direct care to patients in 10 patient care units at Oakwood Heritage Hospital, an acute care hospital with 257 licensed beds. The patient care units are behavioral health, emergency room, intensive care, intermediate care, medical/surgical east, medical/surgical west, operating room, pain clinic, post-anesthesia care/recovery, and rehabilitation. The RNs report to the on-site nursing manager, clinical managers, clinical supervisors, and assistant clinical managers—all stipulated supervisors. In providing patient care, RNs follow the doctors' orders and perform tasks such as administering medications, running blood tests, taking vital signs, observing patients, and processing admissions and discharges. RNs may direct less-skilled employees to perform tasks such as feeding, bathing, and walking patients. RNs may also direct employees to perform tests that are ordered by doctors for their patients.

Many RNs at the hospital serve as charge nurses. Charge nurses are responsible for overseeing their patient care units, and they assign other RNs, licensed practical nurses (LPNs), nursing assistants, technicians, and paramedics to patients on their shifts. Charge nurses also monitor the patients in the unit, meet with doctors and the patients' family members, and follow up on unusual incidents. Charge nurses may also take on their own patient load, but those who do assume patient loads will sometimes, but not always, take less than a full complement of patients. When serving as charge nurses, RNs receive an additional $1.50 per hour.

Twelve RNs at the hospital serve permanently as charge nurses on every shift they work, while other RNs take turns rotating into the charge nurse position. In the patient care units of the hospital employing permanent charge nurses, other RNs may serve as charge nurses on the permanent charge nurses' days off or during their vacations. Depending on the patient care unit and the work shift, the rotation of the charge nurse position may be worked out by the RNs among themselves, or it may be set by higher-level managers. The frequency and regularity with which a particular RN will serve as a "rotating" charge nurse depends on several factors (i.e., the size of the patient care unit in which the RN works, the number of other RNs who serve as rotating charge nurses in that unit, and whether the unit has any permanent charge nurses). However, some RNs do not serve as either rotating or permanent charge nurses at the hospital. Most individuals who fit in this category are either new employees at the hospital or those who work in the operating room or pain clinic units. There are also a handful of RNs at the hospital who choose not to serve as charge nurses.

The Petitioner, joined by several amici, would include all the charge nurses in the RN unit. The Employer, joined by other amici, seeks to exclude the permanent and the rotating charge nurses from the unit on the basis that they are supervisors within the meaning of Section 2(11) because they use independent judgment in assigning and responsibly directing employees.[11] The Acting Regional Director found that none of the charge nurses are 2(11) supervisors and directed an election in the RN unit including them.

II.   LEGAL PRINCIPLES

A.   Introduction

[I]ndividuals are statutory supervisors if (1) they hold the authority to engage in any 1 of the 12 supervisory functions (e.g., "assign" and "responsibly to direct") listed in Section 2(11); (2) their "exercise of such authority is not of a merely routine or clerical nature, but requires the use of independent judgment;" and (3) their authority is held "in the interest of the employer." Supervisory status may be shown if the putative supervisor has the authority either to perform a supervisory function or to effectively recommend the same. The burden to prove supervisory authority is on the party asserting it.

Both the drafters of the original amendment and Senator Ralph E. Flanders, who proposed adding the term "responsibly to direct" to the definition of supervisor, agreed that the definition sought to distinguish two classes of workers: true supervisors vested with "genuine management prerogatives," and employees such as "straw bosses, lead men, and set-up men" who are protected by the Act even though they perform "minor supervisory duties." *NLRB v. Bell Aerospace Co.*, 416 U.S. 267, 280–81 (1974) (quoting S. Rep. No. 105, 80th Cong., 1st Sess., 4 (1947)).[15] Thus, the dividing line between these two classes of workers, for purposes of Section 2(11), is whether the putative supervisor exercises "genuine management

---

[11]   The employer also argues that the charge nurses have the authority to adjust grievances within the meaning of Sec. 2(11). We adopt the Acting Regional Director's finding that no evidence of such authority exists.

[15]   Senate Rep. No. 105 stated that the committee took "great care" that employees excluded from the coverage of the Act "be truly supervisory." NLRB, Legislative History of the Labor Management Relations Act of 1947, 410.

prerogatives." Those prerogatives are specifically identified as the 12 supervisory functions listed in Section 2(11) of the Act. If the individual has authority to exercise (or effectively recommend the exercise of) at least one of those functions, 2(11) supervisory status exists, provided that the authority is held in the interest of the employer and is exercised neither routinely nor in a clerical fashion but with independent judgment.

Whether an individual possesses a 2(11) supervisory function has not always been readily discernible by either the Board or reviewing courts. Indeed, in applying Section 2(11), the Supreme Court has recognized that "[p]hrases [used by Congress] such as 'independent judgment' and 'responsibly to direct' are ambiguous." *NLRB v. Healthcare & Retirement Corp.*, 511 U.S. 571, 579 (1994).

In interpreting those statutory terms, we do not, as the dissent maintains, blindly adopt "dictionary-driven" definitions. Rather, we begin our analysis with a first principle of statutory interpretation that "in all cases involving statutory construction, our starting point must be the language employed in Congress . . . and we assume that the legislative purpose is expressed by the ordinary meaning of the words used." *INS v. Phinpathya*, 464 U.S. 183, 189 (1984). Thus, we eschew a results-driven approach and we start, as we must, with the words of the statute. We do not, as the dissent contends, ignore potential "real-world" consequences of our interpretations. Rather, we simply decline to engage in an analysis that seems to take as its objective a narrowing of the scope of supervisory status and to reason backward from there, relying primarily on selective excerpts from legislative history.

B.   Assign and Responsibly to Direct

Possession of the authority to engage in (or effectively recommend) any one of the 12 supervisory functions listed in Section 2(11) is necessary to establish supervisory status. Since the Act delineates 12 separate functions, and since canons of statutory interpretation caution us to eschew a construction that would result in redundancy, we start from the premise that [there are] distinct meanings to "assign" and "responsibly to direct."

1.   Assign

The ordinary meaning of the term "assign" is "to appoint to a post or duty." Webster's Third New International Dictionary 132 (1981). Because this function shares with other 2(11) functions—i.e., hire, transfer, suspension, layoff, recall, promotion, discharge, reward or discipline—the common trait of affecting a term or condition of employment, we construe the term "assign" to refer to the act of designating an employee to a place (such as a location, department, or wing), appointing an employee to a time (such as a shift or overtime period), or giving significant overall duties, *i.e.*, tasks, to an employee. That is, the place, time, and work of an employee are part of his/her terms and conditions of employment. In the health care setting, the term "assign" encompasses the charge nurses' responsibility to assign nurses and aides to particular patients. It follows that the decision or effective recommendation to affect one of these—place, time, or overall tasks—can be a supervisory function.

The assignment of an employee to a certain department (e.g., housewares) or to a certain shift (e.g., night) or to certain significant overall tasks (e.g., restocking shelves) would generally qualify as "assign" within our construction. However, choosing the order in which the employee will perform discrete tasks within those assignments (e.g., restocking toasters before coffeemakers) would not be indicative of exercising the authority to "assign." To illustrate our point in the health care setting, if a charge nurse designates an LPN to be the person who will regularly administer medications to a patient or a group of patients, the giving of that overall duty to the LPN is an assignment. On the other hand, the charge nurse's ordering an LPN to immediately give a sedative to a particular patient does not constitute an assignment. In sum, to "assign" for purposes of Section 2(11) refers to the charge nurse's designation of significant overall duties to an employee, not to the charge nurse's ad hoc instruction that the employee perform a discrete task.

2.   Responsibly to Direct

We now address the term "responsibly to direct." The phrase "responsibly to direct" was added to Section 2(11) after the other supervisory functions of Section 2(11) already had been enumerated in the proposed legislation. Senator Flanders, who made the proposal to add "responsibly to direct" to Section 2(11), explained that the phrase was not meant to include minor supervisory functions performed by lead employees, straw bosses, and set-up men. Rather, the addition was designed to ensure that the statutory exemption of Section 2(11) encompassed those individuals who exercise basic supervision but lack the authority or opportunity to carry out any of the other statutory supervisory functions (e.g., where promotional, disciplinary and similar functions are handled by a centralized human resources department). Senator Flanders was concerned that the person on the shop floor would not be considered a supervisor even if that person directly oversaw the work being done and would be held responsible if the work were done badly or not at all. Consequently, the authority "responsibly to direct" is not limited to department heads as the dissent suggests. The "department head" may be a person between the personnel manager and the rank and file employee, but he or she is not necessarily the only person between the manager and the employee. If a person on the shop floor has "men under him," and if that person decides "what job shall be undertaken next or who shall do it," that person is a supervisor, provided that the direction is both "responsible" (as explained below) and carried out with independent judgment. In addition, as the statute provides and Senator Flanders himself recognized, the person who effectively recommends action is also a supervisor.

Since the enactment of Senator Flanders' amendment, the Board rarely has sought to define the parameters of the term "responsibly to direct." In *Providence Hospital*, 120 N.L.R.B. 717 (1996),[29] the Board majority summarized past efforts on the part of several courts of appeals, namely the First, Fifth, Sixth, Seventh, and Ninth Circuits, to ascertain the limits of this term. The Board majority in *Providence Hospital* concluded that these courts endorsed, for the most part, an accountability definition for the word "responsibly" that was consistent with the ordinary meaning of the word. The majority cited to the Fifth Circuit's interpretation, which is set forth in *NLRB v. KDFW-TV Inc.*, 790 F.2d 1273, 1278 (5th Cir. 1986), as follows: "To be responsible is to be answerable for the discharge of a duty or obligation."

The majority in *Providence Hospital*, however, found it unnecessary to pass on the courts' accountability definition. We have decided to adopt that definition. We agree with the circuit courts that have considered the issue and find that for direction to be "responsible," the person directing and performing the oversight of the employee must be accountable for the performance of the task by the other, such that some adverse consequence may befall the one providing the oversight if the tasks performed by the employee are not performed properly. This interpretation of "responsibly to direct" is consistent with post-*Kentucky River* Board decisions that considered an accountability element for "responsibly to direct."

Thus, to establish accountability for purposes of responsible direction, it must be shown that the employer delegated to the putative supervisor the authority to direct the work and the authority to take corrective action, if necessary. It also must be shown that there is a prospect of adverse consequences for the putative supervisor if he/she does not take these steps.

C.   Independent Judgment

In *Kentucky River*, the Supreme Court took issue with the Board's interpretation of "independent judgment" to exclude the exercise of "ordinary professional or technical judgment in directing less skilled employees to deliver services." That is, in the Board's then-extant view, even if the Section 2(11) function is exercised with a substantial degree of discretion, there was no independent judgment if the judgment was of a particular kind, namely, "ordinary professional or technical judgment in directing less-skilled employees to deliver services." While recognizing that the Board has the discretion to resolve ambiguities in the Act, the Supreme Court found that the Board had improperly inserted "a startling categorical

---

[29]   To the extent that *Providence Hospital* is inconsistent with any aspect of our decision in this case, *Providence Hospital* and those cases relying on it are overruled.

exclusion into statutory text that does not suggest its existence." The Court held that it is the degree of discretion involved in making the decision, not the kind of discretion exercised—whether professional, technical, or otherwise—that determines the existence of "independent judgment" under Section 2(11). *Id.* We are guided by these admonitions.

Consistent with the Court's *Kentucky River* decision, we adopt an interpretation of the term "independent judgment" that applies irrespective of the Section 2(11) supervisory function implicated, and without regard to whether the judgment is exercised using professional or technical expertise. In short, professional or technical judgments involving the use of independent judgment are supervisory if they involve one of the 12 supervisory functions of Section 2(11). Thus, for example, a registered nurse who makes the "professional judgment" that a catheter needs to be changed may be performing a supervisory function when he/she responsibly directs a nursing assistant in the performance of that work. Whether the registered nurse is a 2(11) supervisor will depend on whether his or her responsible direction is performed with the degree of discretion required to reflect independent judgment.

To ascertain the contours of "independent judgment," we turn first to the ordinary meaning of the term. "Independent" means "not subject to control by others." Webster's Third New International Dictionary 1148 (1981). "Judgment" means "the action of judging; the mental or intellectual process of forming an opinion or evaluation by discerning and comparing." Webster's Third New International Dictionary 1223 (1981). Thus, as a starting point, to exercise "independent judgment" an individual must at minimum act, or effectively recommend action, free of the control of others and form an opinion or evaluation by discerning and comparing data. Although we start with the "ordinary meaning of the words used," we also consider the Act as a whole, its legislative history, policy considerations, and judicial precedent. Here, we must interpret "independent judgment" in light of the contrasting statutory language, "not of a merely routine or clerical nature." It may happen that an individual's assignment or responsible direction of another will be based on independent judgment within the dictionary definitions of those terms, but still not rise above the merely routine or clerical.

In our view, and that of the Supreme Court, actions form a spectrum between the extremes of completely free actions and completely controlled ones, and the degree of independence necessary to constitute a judgment as "independent" under the Act lies somewhere in between these extremes. As the Court indicated in *Kentucky River, supra* at 713–14, there are, at one end of the spectrum, situations where there are detailed instructions for the actor to follow. At the other end, there are other situations where the actor is wholly free from constraints. In determining the meaning of the term "independent judgment" under Section 2(11), the Board must assess the degree of discretion exercised by the putative supervisor.

Consistent with the Court's view, we find that a judgment is not independent if it is dictated or controlled by detailed instructions, whether set forth in company policies or rules, the verbal instructions of a higher authority, or in the provisions of a collective-bargaining agreement. Thus, for example, a decision to staff a shift with a certain number of nurses would not involve independent judgment if it is determined by a fixed nurse-to-patient ratio. Similarly, if a collective-bargaining agreement required that only seniority be followed in making an assignment, that act of assignment would not be supervisory.[42]

On the other hand, the mere existence of company policies does not eliminate independent judgment from decision-making if the policies allow for discretionary choices. Thus a registered nurse, when exercising his/her authority to recommend a person for hire, may be called upon to assess the applicants' experience, ability, attitude, and character references, among other factors. If so, the nurse's hiring recommendations likely involve the exercise of independent judgment. Similarly, if the registered nurse weighs the individualized condition and needs of a patient against the skills or special training of available nursing personnel, the nurse's assignment involves the exercise of independent judgment.

As Senator Flanders remarked, the supervisor determines "who shall do [the job]" and in making that determination the supervisor makes "[a] personal judgment based on personal experience, training, and ability." As stated above, Section 2(11) contrasts "independent judgment" with actions that are "of a merely routine or clerical nature." Thus, the statute itself provides a baseline for the degree of discretion required to render the exercise of any of the enumerated functions of 2(11) supervisory. If there is only one obvious and self-evident choice (for example, assigning the one available nurse fluent in American Sign Language (ASL) to a patient dependent upon ASL for communicating), or if the assignment is made solely on the basis of equalizing workloads, then the assignment is routine or clerical in nature and does not implicate independent judgment, even if it is made free of the control of others and involves forming an opinion or evaluation by discerning and comparing data. By contrast, if the hospital has a policy that details how a charge nurse should respond in an emergency, but the charge nurse has the discretion to determine when an emergency exists or the authority to deviate from that policy based on the charge nurse's assessment of the particular circumstances, those

---

[42]   We do not suggest, however, that so long as detailed instructions do not dictate or control specific action, that it necessarily follows that the requisite degree of independence for Sec. 2(11) purposes will have been established. There may be instances where instructions do not strictly dictate a sequence of actions, but nonetheless constrain the exercise of discretion below the statutory threshold.

deviations, if material, would involve the exercise of independent judgment.

The dissent portends that our analysis in assessing supervisory status under Section 2(11) may exclude "most professionals" from coverage under the Act. We disagree. A charge nurse is not automatically a "supervisor" because of his or her exercise of professional, technical, or experienced judgment as a professional employee. And it is equally true that his or her professional status does not prevent the charge nurse from having statutory supervisory status if he or she exercises independent judgment in assigning employees work or responsibly directing them in their work. To hold otherwise would come dangerously close to recommitting the very error the Supreme Court corrected in *Kentucky River*.

D.   Persons Who Are Supervisors Part of the Time

Where an individual is engaged a part of the time as a supervisor and the rest of the time as a unit employee, the legal standard for a supervisory determination is whether the individual spends a regular and substantial portion of his/her work time performing supervisory functions. Under the Board's standard, "regular" means according to a pattern or schedule, as opposed to sporadic substitution. The Board has not adopted a strict numerical definition of substantiality and has found supervisory status where the individuals have served in a supervisory role for at least 10–15% of their total work time. We find no reason to depart from this established precedent.

III. THE CASE AT BAR

It is well established that the "burden of proving supervisory status rests on the party asserting that such status exists." The party seeking to prove supervisory status must establish it by a preponderance of the evidence. *Dean & Deluca*, 338 N.L.R.B. 1046, 1047 (2003); *Bethany Medical Center*, 328 N.L.R.B. 1094, 1103 (1999).

As discussed below, we find that the Employer has failed to establish that its charge nurses possess the authority "responsibly to direct" employees within the meaning of Section 2(11). However, we also find that the Employer has adduced evidence sufficient to establish that certain of its permanent charge nurses are supervisors based on their delegated authority to assign employees using independent judgment. Finally, we find that the Employer has failed to establish that its rotating charge nurses, as opposed to the 12 permanent charge nurses we find to be supervisors, spend a regular and substantial portion of their work time performing supervisory functions. Consequently, we exclude only the 12 permanent charge nurses from the unit.

A.   Responsible Direction

The Employer alleges that its charge nurses responsibly direct nursing staff by directing them to perform certain tasks. As part of their duties, the charge nurses are responsible for checking the crash cart, taking an inventory of narcotics, and providing statistical information to Heritage's administrative staff for their shifts. The charge nurses may undertake these tasks themselves or delegate them to another staff member working that shift. The delegation of these charge-nurse specific tasks is the sole basis for the Employer's claim that the charge nurses responsibly direct the nursing staff. We find that the Employer failed to carry its burden of proving that the charge nurses responsibly direct the nursing staff within the meaning of Section 2(11). As explained above, to constitute "responsible" direction the person performing the oversight must be held accountable for the performance of the task, and must have some authority to correct any errors made. The Employer has not demonstrated that the charge nurses meet this accountability standard. The record reveals no evidence that the charge nurses must take corrective action if other staff members fail to adequately check the crash cart, take the narcotics inventory, or provide the statistical information to management. There is no indication that the charge nurses are subject to discipline or lower evaluations if other staff members fail to adequately perform these charge nurse-specific tasks. Instead, the Employer points to an instance in which it disciplined a charge nurse for failing to make fair assignments. This evidence, however, shows that the charge nurses are accountable for their own performance or lack thereof, not the performance of others, and consequently is insufficient to establish responsible direction.

B.   Assignment

The record establishes that charge nurses assign nursing personnel to patients. At the beginning of each shift, and as new patients are admitted thereafter, the charge nurses for each patient care unit (except the emergency room) assign the staff working the unit to the patients that they will care for over the duration of the shift.

In the emergency room, the process of assigning work operates differently. There, the charge nurses have primary responsibilities to "triage" the incoming patients and keep the other patient care units in the hospital informed about possible admissions from the emergency room. The charge nurses do not assign nursing personnel to patients in this department. Rather, the charge nurses assign employees to geographic areas within the emergency room. In making these assignments, the charge nurses do not take into account employee skill or the nature or severity of the patient's condition. After these initial assignments, the employees then rotate geographical locations within the emergency room among themselves on a periodic basis.

The charge nurses' assignment of patients to other staff and assignment of nurses to specific geographic locations within the emergency room fall within our definition of "assign" for purposes of Section 2(11). In patient care units other than the emergency room, the actions of the charge nurses involve assigning nurses to patients in rooms and "giving significant overall tasks to an employee." The charge nurses in the emergency room designate employees to a particular place. The charge nurses' assignments determine what will be the required work for an employee during the shift, thereby having a material effect on the employee's terms and conditions of employment. Unlike the case of Senator Flanders' "straw bosses, leadmen, and set-up men," the charge nurse's duties of assignment are not "incidental" to the charge nurse's own nursing duties. The charge nurse has his or her own patients, but independently of that, he or she will assign other nursing personnel to other patients.

Having found that the charge nurses hold the authority to engage in one of the supervisory functions of Section 2(11), our next step is to determine whether the charge nurses exercise independent judgment in making these assignments.

C.   Independent Judgment

The charge nurses at the hospital make their assignments by choosing between or among the members of the staff available on each shift. In addition to the charge nurse, there are two to six RNs on each shift, depending on the time of day and the unit, and many of the units also have licensed practical nurses or other licensed staff working each shift. In the health care context, choosing among the available staff frequently requires a meaningful exercise of discretion. Matching a nurse with a patient may have life and death consequences. Nurses are professionals, not widgets, and may possess different levels of training and specialized skills. Similarly, patients are not identical and may require highly particularized care. A charge nurse's analysis of an available nurse's skill set and level of proficiency at performing certain tasks, and her application of that analysis in matching that nurse to the condition and needs of a particular patient, involves a degree of discretion markedly different than the assignment decisions exercised by most leadmen. As discussed below, the record evidence establishes that a number of the Employer's charge nurses exercise independent judgment in assigning other staff to patients and therefore possess supervisory authority under Section 2(11) of the Act.

Therefore, we find that the Employer failed to demonstrate that the charge nurses in the emergency room unit exercise independent judgment in making patient care assignments. Because, as discussed above, the exercise of independent judgment is a necessary element of establishing supervisory status, we find that the Employer has failed to prove that the charge nurses in the emergency room are supervisors, despite the parties' stipulation. We shall include the emergency room charge nurses in the unit.

D. "Rotating" Charge Nurses

We find that the Employer has carried its burden of proof with respect to the 12 permanent charge nurses that are assigned to the following 5 units: behavioral health, intensive care, intermediate care, medical/surgical east, and medical/surgical west. The Employer offered uncontradicted testimony that the permanent charge nurses in those units serve in that capacity on every shift they work. Indeed, the permanent charge nurses do not really fit the definition of a "rotating" supervisor. They serve full-time as supervisors on a regular basis. Accordingly, we shall exclude these individuals from the unit.

In contrast, the Employer has failed to demonstrate regularity for the "rotating" charge nurses assigned to behavioral health, intensive care, intermediate care, medical/surgical east, medical/surgical west, post-anesthesia care/recovery, and rehabilitation units. The Employer offered only superficial evidence as to the regularity with which these 112 nonpermanent or "rotating" charge nurses serve in the charge nurse role. The record reveals that none of the units involved have an established pattern or predictable schedule for when and how often RNs take turns in working as charge nurses. In those units where the RNs decide among themselves who will serve as charge nurses, the record does not demonstrate any pattern for these selections. In those units where the managers are in charge of making assignments, the managers likewise do not use any particular system or order for assigning charge nurses.

In the absence of a sufficient showing of regularity for assigning the "rotating" charge nurses, we need not decide whether these RNs possess the "rotating" charge nurse duties for a "substantial" part of their work time. Accordingly, we shall include in the unit, as nonsupervisors, the 112 RNs who are not permanent charge nurses but rather irregularly rotate through the charge nurse position at the hospital.

CONCLUSION

Our dissenting colleagues predict that our definitions will "create a new class of workers" who are excluded from the Act but do not exercise "genuine prerogatives of management." We anticipate no such sea change in the law, and will continue to assess each case on its individual merits. Accordingly, we shall remand this case to the Regional Director for further processing in accordance with this decision.

MEMBERS LIEBMAN and WALSH, dissenting in part and concurring in part in the result:

Today's decision threatens to create a new class of workers under Federal labor law: workers who have neither the genuine prerogatives of management, nor the statutory rights of ordinary employees. Into that category may fall most professionals (among many other workers), who by 2012 could number almost 34 million, accounting for 23.3% of the work force. Most professionals have some supervisory responsibilities in the sense of directing another's work—the lawyer his secretary, the teacher his teacher's aide, the doctor his nurses, the registered nurse her nurse's aide, and so on.

If the National Labor Relations Act required this result—if Congress intended to define supervisors in a way that swept in large numbers of professionals and other workers without true managerial prerogatives— then the Board would be duty bound to apply the statute that way. But that is not the case. The language of the Act, its structure, and its legislative history all point to significantly narrower interpretations of the ambiguous statutory terms "assign . . . other employees" and "responsibly to direct them" than the majority adopts.

This case involves the interpretation of three terms incorporated in Section 2(11) of the Act, the statutory definition of a "supervisor": (1) "assign . . . other employees;" (2) "responsibly to direct them [other employees];" and (3) "independent judgment." There would seem to be no dispute that these terms are ambiguous and thus open to interpretation, as the Supreme Court has observed. Where statutory language is ambiguous, it is not enough to consult the dictionary. *Dolan v. U.S. Postal Serv.*, 546 U.S. 481, 486 (2006).

In this case, a narrow focus on dictionary definitions of individual words in isolation leads the majority astray. If we read the whole statutory text, consider the context and purpose of the National Labor Relations Act, and consult authoritative legislative history, then the majority's statutory interpretation is revealed as untenable. Despite its claim to the contrary, the majority proceeds as if the "ordinary meaning of the words used" in Section 2(11) can dictate a choice among potential alternative interpretations. But where the words of a statute are ambiguous, the text alone cannot tell us which interpretation is best and why. The majority never offers a clear and carefully reasoned explanation of its choices.

Certainly, we are constrained by the decisions in *Kentucky River* and *Health Care & Retirement*. But the Court did not dictate the largely dictionary-driven approach taken by the majority. Nor did it hold that the Board may not be guided by the structure of the Act as a whole, by its legislative history, or by policy concerns.

The majority fails to take account of the Act's explicit recognition that professionals, and certain persons who perform work under the supervision of professionals, may be statutory employees—a factor that surely weighs against a broad interpretation of supervisory functions as defined in the statute, given the general oversight that professionals typically exercise over less-skilled employees. The definitive report of the Senate Committee on Labor and Public Welfare explained that:

> A recent development which probably more than any other single factor has upset any real balance of power in the collective-bargaining process has been the successful efforts of labor organizations to invoke the Wagner Act for covering personnel, traditionally regarded as part of management, into organizations composed of or subservient to the unions of the very men they were hired to supervise.

> In drawing an amendment to meet this situation, the committee has not been unmindful of the fact that certain employees with minor supervisory duties have problems which may justify their inclusion in that act. It therefore distinguished between straw bosses, leadmen, set-up men, and other minor supervisory employees, on the one hand, and the supervisor vested with such genuine management prerogatives as the right to hire or fire, discipline, or make effective recommendations with respect to such action.

> It is natural to expect that unless this Congress takes action, management will be deprived of the undivided loyalty of its foremen.

S. Rep. No. 105, 80th Cong., 1st Sess. 4–5 (1947), reprinted in National Labor Relations Board, Legislative History of the Labor Management Relations Act, 1947 at 410–11 (1985).

The legislative history explains that Congress "exercised great care, desiring that the employees . . . excluded from the coverage of the act be truly supervisory." Legislative History, *supra* at 425 (Senate Report No. 105) (emphasis added). The Board must be sensitive, then, to the distinction between "minor supervisory employees" (persons Congress intended to treat as employees) and the equivalent of "foremen" (persons Congress intended to exclude from statutory coverage).

Our disagreement with the majority on the interpretation of "assign" focuses on the treatment of task assignments made to employees, which we view as a quintessential function of the minor supervisors whom Congress clearly did not intend to cover in Section 2(11). As to responsible direction, we differ principally concerning the scope and scale of the authority required to satisfy the statutory test. In our view, the phrase "responsibly to direct" was intended to reach persons who were effectively in charge of a department-level work unit, even if they did not engage in the other supervisory functions identified in Section 2(11). Our differences with the majority might seem arcane and insignificant. But the real-world consequences of the competing interpretations, in terms of who is (and is not) a statutory supervisor, could prove dramatic.

The consequences of today's decision, among the most important in the Board's history, will take time to play out. The result could come as a rude shock to nurses and other workers who for decades have been effectively protected by the National Labor Relations Act, but who now may find themselves treated, for labor-law purposes, as members of management, with no right to pursue collective bargaining or engage in other concerted activity in the workplace. Indeed, supervisors may be conscripted into an employer's anti-union campaign, while their pro-union activity is now strictly limited. The majority's decision thus denies the protection of the Act to yet another group of workers, while strengthening the ability of employers to resist the unionization of other employees. Accordingly, we dissent.

NOTES

1.   *Oakwood's definitions. Oakwood Health Care* addressed the Supreme Court's remand directive by issuing the following definitions of "independent judgment," "assign," and "responsibly to direct":

- "Independent judgment" is determined by the *degree* of discretion involved, not the type (e.g., professional, technical, or other expertise). An individual who is "engaged part of the time as a supervisor and the rest of the time as a unit employee" will be considered a supervisor if she spends "a regular and substantial portion" of her work time performing supervisor functions. "Regular" means "according to a pattern or schedule, as opposed to sporadic substitution." Thus the rotating charge nurses at issue were deemed not to be supervisors.

- "Assign" means "the act of designating an employee to a *place* (such as a location, department, or wing), appointing an employee to a *time* (such as a shift or overtime period), or giving *significant overall duties, i.e., tasks,* to an employee" (emphasis added). In a healthcare setting, this includes the charge nurses' responsibility to assign other nurses and aides to particular patients.

- "Responsibly to direct" means deciding what job will be undertaken next or who will do it, provided that the individual making that decision is "accountable for the performance of the task by the other, such that some adverse consequence may befall the one providing the oversight if the tasks . . . are not performed properly."

Applying these standards, the Board found that rotating charge nurses were not supervisors, but some of the permanent charge nurses were. Applying the same standards in *Croft Metals Inc.*, 348 N.L.R.B. 717 (2006), one of the two companion cases, the Board found that the 25 to 30 lead persons working at the employer's manufacturing facility were not supervisors either. Do these results clear up the confusion as to who is a "supervisor"?

2.   *Before and after.* Before the *Oakwood* trio was decided, economists sympathetic to organized labor were predicting that an unfavorable ruling could strip collective bargaining rights from as many as 8 million employees by re-labeling them as "supervisors." *Speakers Say Broad Ruling of 'Supervisor' Would Deprive Millions of Representation,* 75 U.S.L.W. (BNA) 2186, 2187 (2006) (analysis by Economic Policy Institute).

Predictably, after the *Oakwood* trio was decided, at least one labor leader called it "devastating" because it "welcomes employers to strip millions of workers of their right to have a union by reclassifying them as 'supervisors' in name only"; another said it provides "a road map for excluding workers from a union" and gives employers "a blueprint to make workers supervisors." *Long-Awaited Ruling on Supervisors Prompts Flood of Reaction from Unions, Management,* 75 U.S.L.W. (BNA) 2205, 2205 (2006) (remarks of AFL-CIO President John Sweeney and AFT Healthcare Chief Candice Owley, respectively). In dissent, Member Liebman observed that by 2012, the number of affected supervisor-employees could be as high as 34 million.

But a management spokesman said critics were "overstating the breadth of the ruling"; a former NLRB member said, "This isn't the tsunami predicted by organized labor, but it does indicate isolated thunderstorms" *id.* (remarks of National Chamber Litigation Center Director Stephan A. Bokat and ex-Member John Radabaugh, respectively).

3.   *Truth "or" consequences?* The real problem for organized labor may lie not in the Board's interpretation of the Act, but in the language it has to work with. Recall that Section 2(11) defines "supervisor" as any individual having the authority, in the interest of the employer, to do at least one of 13 things: "hire, transfer, suspend, lay off, recall, promote, discharge, assign, reward, **or** discipline other employees, *or* responsibly to direct them, **or** to adjust their grievances, *or* effectively to recommend such action" (emphases supplied). The use of the disjunctive term "or" means that a worker has only to do one of these 13 things to become a supervisor, and thereby lose her protection as an "employee" under the NLRA. This is why Professor Dennis Nolan calls "or" the most important two-letter word in the entire Act. Do you agree?

4.   *Power trip?* Does the *Oakwood* trio put organized labor in the awkward position of arguing that the people it wishes to represent should not be promoted? Does your answer depend on whether somebody called a "supervisor" wields real power in the workplace, as opposed merely to wearing a title?

5.   *International labor standards.* Could an expanded definition of who is a "supervisor" violate international labor standards? The AFL-CIO thought so. About a month after the Board issued its decisions in the *Oakwood* cases, the labor federation filed a complaint asking the International Labor Organisation's Committee on Freedom of Association to find the U.S. in violation of core labor principles, including the right to form and join unions guaranteed by ILO Convention No. 87 and 98. The ILO's Committee on

Freedom of Association addressed the complaint by expressing concern that the *Oakwood* cases "could give rise to an expansive interpretation [of supervisor] which would exclude large numbers of workers from workers' rights" and would "appear to give rise to an overly wide definition of supervisory staff that would go beyond freedom of association principles." International Labor Organisation, Committee on Freedom of Association, Complaints Against the Government of the United States Presented by the American Federation of Labor and Congress of Industrial Organizations (AFL-CIO), Case No. 2524, Report No. 349, ¶ 854 (Mar. 2008). It also requested the U.S. Government to take necessary steps to limit the interpretation of supervisor to "to those workers genuinely representing the interests of employers," and asked to be kept informed about developments. *Id.* ¶¶ 856–857. The decision is binding on the U.S. by virtue of its having accepted obligations under the DFPRW. Do you agree with the approach taken by the Committee on Freedom of Association?

6.   *Supervisors' unions.* The Act does not forbid supervisors from forming or joining unions, but effectively says that, if they do so, they will not enjoy its protections. See NLRA § 14(a), 29 U.S.C. § 164(a). This is not necessarily so under other labor relations regimes. For example, the Railway Labor Act (RLA) does not specifically exclude supervisors from its protections, but does protect "employees or subordinate officials." *See* RLA § 201, 45 U.S.C. § 181; *compare, e.g., Dorsey v. United Parcel Serv.*, 195 F.3d 814 (6th Cir. 1999) (holding assistant chief pilots to be "subordinate officials" entitled to bring discriminatory discharge claims), *with, e.g., Robinson v. Pan Am. World Airways Inc.*, 597 F. Supp. 1063 (S.D.N.Y. 1984) (rejecting such finding); *see also Carnival Air Lines Inc.*, 24 N.M.B. 256 (1997) (classifying in-flight supervisors as "employees or subordinate officials"). Supervisors also tend to be protected under state law public sector and European private sector regimes. *See, e.g.,* Paula B. Voos, *Expanding Voice for Professional and Managerial Employees*, in Proceedings of the 58th Annual Labor and Employment Research Association, *available at* http://lerachapters.org/OJS/ojs-2.4.4-1/index.php/PFL/article/view/494. Nevertheless, a number of unions operating in NLRA-governed industries are highly successful, even though most of the workers they represent are true "supervisors" within the meaning of Section 2(11). For example, the Directors Guild of America Inc., which represents film and television directors, first and second assistant directors, and other production supervisors, comes immediately to mind. In the entertainment industry, the DGA wields power sufficient not only to command respect at the bargaining table, but also to discourage film and TV producers from challenging the standing of DGA members to invoke the protections of the NLRA in proceedings before the Board. *See, e.g., Directors Guild of Am., Inc. (Association of Motion Picture & Television Producers, Inc.)*, 198 N.L.R.B. 707 (1972) (rejecting producers' objection that DGA was not a labor organization on ground some of its members, here second assistant directors, were supervisors). Interestingly, many DGA members hold dual supervisor-employee status simultaneously on the same productions because they are also members of the Writers Guild of America Inc., which is a union composed

mainly of non-supervisors, although some "show runners"—who hire and fire writers—do wield supervisory authority. *See, e.g., American Broad. Cos. v. Writers Guild of Am., West, Inc.*, 437 U.S. 411 (1978).

* * *

The list of 13 supervisorial actions in Section 2(11) includes "discipline [of] other employees or . . . [the authority] effectively to recommend such action." When it comes to telling whether a putative supervisor is empowered to discipline or effectively recommend discipline of other employees, some cases are closer than others. For example, in *Veolia Transportation Services, Inc.*, 363 N.L.R.B. No. 188 (2016), the Board voted 2 to 1 to overturn the Regional Director's determination that road supervisors and lead road supervisors of a transportation services company—who drove around observing in the field the performance of passenger van operators to ensure their compliance with the policies and procedures of both the company and a local public transit agency—were statutory supervisors. The reason: evidence of their authority to discipline or effectively to recommend discipline of the operators was inconclusive.

According to the record, road and lead road supervisors filled out road observation reports (RORs), on which they would check boxes to indicate whether an operator performed satisfactorily or unsatisfactorily when arriving at an intersection, approaching a railroad crossing, backing up, and conducting certain pre- and post-trip actions; investigated accidents and completed accident "kits," for which they would indicate whether an accident was preventable (i.e., the operator's fault) or not; and held operators out of service if there was reason to test for the presence of drugs or alcohol.

Two road supervisors, Brian Jackson and Thomas Holtz, testified about their role in the disciplinary process. When road supervisors observe operators violating company or agency policies and procedures, they counsel the offending operator. A road supervisor can decide whether to memorialize a counseling by writing and submitting an ROR. Both Jackson and Holtz stated that they would consider factors like the experience level of the operator and the severity of the misconduct in deciding whether to memorialize a counseling in writing. Both men specified that they would, however, memorialize a counseling if they witnessed an operator repeating behavior for which that operator has already been counseled.

But the evidence of what happened next was mixed. For example, there was evidence of only one specific incident in which an ROR ever had been completed. Neither Holtz nor Jackson could testify based on personal knowledge what happened after an ROR was submitted. Neither of them testified that he had ever held an operator out of service or escorted one off the job after finding reasonable suspicion to test for drugs or alcohol. And although the operators were covered by two separate collective bargaining agreements, it was unclear which agreement, and which system of progressive discipline, was applied by Holtz or Jackson in any particular case.

In addition, Holtz testified that he never had recommend discipline while working for this company. By contrast, Jackson testified that he had recommended discipline more than 25 times in the past year, and claimed that his recommendations are "usually" followed. But he also conceded that that his recommendations may not be followed due to "other variables." Jackson did not indicate if these recommendations were contained in RORs or made by some other means. Jackson also testified that discipline is handled on a case-by-case basis and is "a collective effort sometimes."

Based on this record, Chairman Pearce, joined by Member Hirozawa, found that the evidence was "too vague, limited, and conflicting" to establish the role that the road supervisors actually played in the company's system of progressive discipline, or that such system was consistently applied. Member Miscimarra dissented.

2. MANAGERIAL AND CONFIDENTIAL EMPLOYEES

The differences between supervisory employees on the one hand and managerial or confidential employees on the other hand are not always clear. But there is one similarity that is clear: each is considered to be too closely aligned with the boss to enjoy the protections of the Act. To permit managerial and confidential workers to exercise Section 7 rights would pose a conflict of loyalties, if not interests. Thus such workers are considered to be employers, or proxies of the employer, rather than rank-and-file employees. As labor economist Charles Craypo explains:

> Workers and managers never see things in quite the same way. A worker for someone else is more interested in the job than in the final product. The manager has the opposite interest. At every turn their priorities differ. A slower work pace is lost production for the employer. Higher wages are cost increases for the firm. Job security for labor means less control over the workplace for capital. Managers often persuade workers that together they are a team and that their interests ultimately coincide, but labor history shows that sooner or later events convince the workers otherwise.

Charles Craypo, The Economics of Collective Bargaining: Case Studies in the Private Sector 1–2 (1986).

The academic workplace illustrates how hotly contested the managerial employee exception can be. The main pressure point is faculty governance—a principle whose pedigree is traced to the medieval European tradition that a college or university is a "community of scholars." In the scholarly community, in a manner reminiscent of the artisans discussed in Chapter 1, faculty both direct production (by developing, selecting and managing the curriculum) and undertake production (by teaching the curriculum).

The importance of this dual role is captured by the saying, "The faculty is the school, the school is the faculty." The principle of faculty governance is so firmly rooted in American higher education that it prompted one professor publicly to correct the then-president of his institution, one Dwight D. Eisenhower, whose White House years still lay ahead of him. According to Columbia University lore, at a ceremony honoring Professor Isidore Rabi, who had helped develop the atomic bomb and later won a Nobel Prize, Eisenhower remarked that it was always good to see an employee of the university be recognized. Professor Rabi interrupted: "Excuse me, sir, but the faculty are not employees of the university. The faculty *are* the university!"

NLRB v. YESHIVA UNIVERSITY
444 U.S. 672 (1980)

JUSTICE POWELL delivered the opinion of the Court:

Supervisors and managerial employees are excluded from the categories of employees entitled to the benefits of collective bargaining under the National Labor Relations Act. The question presented is whether the full-time faculty of Yeshiva University fall within those exclusions.

I.

Yeshiva is a private university which conducts a broad range of arts and sciences programs at its five undergraduate and eight graduate schools in New York City. On October 30, 1974, the Yeshiva University Faculty Association (Union) filed a representation petition with the National Labor Relations Board (Board). The Union sought certification as bargaining agent for the full-time faculty members at 10 of the 13 schools. The University opposed the petition on the ground that all of its faculty members are managerial or supervisory personnel and hence not employees within the meaning of the Act.

The evidence at the hearings showed that a central administrative hierarchy serves all of the University's schools. Ultimate authority is vested in a Board of Trustees, whose members (other than the President) hold no administrative positions at the University. The President sits on the Board of Trustees and serves as chief executive officer, assisted by four Vice Presidents who oversee, respectively, medical affairs and science, student affairs, business affairs, and academic affairs. An Executive Council of Deans and administrators makes recommendations to the President on a wide variety of matters.

The individual schools within the University are substantially autonomous. Each is headed by a Dean or Director, and faculty members at each school meet formally and informally to discuss and decide matters of institutional and professional concern. At four schools, formal meetings are convened regularly pursuant to written bylaws. The remaining faculties meet when convened by the Dean or Director. Most of the schools also have faculty committees concerned with special areas of educational policy. Faculty welfare committees negotiate with administrators concerning salary and conditions of employment. Through these meetings and committees, the faculty at each school effectively determine its curriculum, grading system, admission and matriculation standards, academic calendars, and course schedules.[4]

Faculty power at Yeshiva's schools extends beyond strictly academic concerns. The faculty at each school make recommendations to the Dean or Director in every case of faculty hiring, tenure, sabbaticals, termination and promotion. Although the final decision is reached by the central administration on the advice of the Dean or Director, the overwhelming majority of faculty recommendations are implemented.[5] Even when financial problems in the early 1970's restricted Yeshiva's budget, faculty recommendations still largely controlled personnel decisions made within the constraints imposed by the administration. Indeed, the faculty of one school recently drew up new and binding policies expanding their own role in these matters. In addition, some faculties make final decisions regarding the admission, expulsion, and graduation of individual students. Others have decided questions involving teaching loads, student absence policies, tuition and enrollment levels, and in one case the location of a school.

II.

The Union won the election and was certified by the Board. The University refused to bargain, reasserting its view that the faculty are managerial. In the subsequent unfair labor practice proceeding, the Board refused to reconsider its holding in the representation proceeding and ordered the University to bargain with the Union. When the University still refused to sit down at the negotiating table, the Board sought enforcement in the Court of Appeals for the Second Circuit, which denied the petition. We granted certiorari, and now affirm.

---

[4]   For example, the Deans at Yeshiva and Erna Michael Colleges regard faculty actions as binding. Administrators testified that no academic initiative of either faculty had been vetoed since at least 1968. When the Stern College faculty disagreed with the Dean's decision to delete the education major, the major was reinstituted. The Director of the Teacher's Institute for Women testified that "the faculty is the school," while the Director of the James Striar School described his position as the "executive arm of the faculty," which had overruled him on occasion. All decisions regarding academic matters at the Yeshiva Program and Bernard Revel are made by faculty consensus.

[5]   One Dean estimated that 98% of faculty hiring recommendations were ultimately given effect. Others could not recall an instance when a faculty recommendation had been overruled.

III.

There is no evidence that Congress has considered whether a university faculty may organize for collective bargaining under the Act. Indeed, when the Wagner and Taft-Hartley Acts were approved, it was thought that congressional power did not extend to university faculties because they were employed by nonprofit institutions which did not "affect commerce."

The Act was intended to accommodate the type of management-employee relations that prevail in the pyramidal hierarchies of private industry. In contrast, authority in the typical "mature" private university is divided between a central administration and one or more collegial bodies. This system of "shared authority" evolved from the medieval model of collegial decisionmaking in which guilds of scholars were responsible only to themselves. At early universities, the faculty were the school. Although faculties have been subject to external control in the United States since colonial times, traditions of collegiality continue to play a significant role at many universities, including Yeshiva. For these reasons, the Board has recognized that principles developed for use in the industrial setting cannot be "imposed blindly on the academic world." The Board reasoned that faculty members are "professional employees" within the meaning of § 2(12) of the Act and therefore are entitled to the benefits of collective bargaining.

Yeshiva does not contend that its faculty are not professionals under the statute. But professionals, like other employees, may be exempted from coverage under the Act's exclusion for "supervisors" who use independent judgment in overseeing other employees in the interest of the employer, or under the judicially implied exclusion for "managerial employees" who are involved in developing and enforcing employer policy.

IV.

Managerial employees are defined as those who "formulate and effectuate management policies by expressing and making operative the decisions of their employer." These employees are "much higher in the managerial structure" than those explicitly mentioned by Congress, which "regarded [them] as so clearly outside the Act that no specific exclusionary provision was thought necessary." Managerial employees must exercise discretion within, or even independently of, established employer policy and must be aligned with management. Although the Board has established no firm criteria for determining when an employee is so aligned, normally an employee may be excluded as managerial only if he represents management interests by taking or recommending discretionary actions that effectively control or implement employer policy.

V.

The controlling consideration in this case is that the faculty of Yeshiva University exercise authority which in any other context unquestionably would be managerial. Their authority in academic matters is absolute. They decide what courses will be offered, when they will be scheduled, and to whom they will be taught. They debate and determine teaching methods, grading policies, and matriculation standards. They effectively decide which students will be admitted, retained, and graduated. On occasion their views have determined the size of the student body, the tuition to be charged, and the location of a school. When one considers the function of a university, it is difficult to imagine decisions more managerial than these. To the extent the industrial analogy applies, the faculty determines within each school the product to be produced, the terms upon which it will be offered, and the customers who will be served.

The record shows that faculty members at Yeshiva also play a predominant role in faculty hiring, tenure, sabbaticals, termination and promotion. These decisions clearly have both managerial and supervisory characteristics. Since we do not reach the question of supervisory status, we need not rely primarily on these features of faculty authority.

There may be some tension between the Act's exclusion of managerial employees and its inclusion of professionals, since most professionals in managerial positions continue to draw on their special skills and training. But we have been directed to no authority suggesting that that tension can be resolved by reference to the "independent professional judgment" criterion proposed in this case.[24] Outside the university context, the Board routinely has applied the managerial and supervisory exclusions to professionals in executive positions without inquiring whether their decisions were based on management policy rather than professional expertise.

Moreover, the Board's approach would undermine the goal it purports to serve: To ensure that employees who exercise discretionary authority on behalf of the employer will not divide their loyalty between employer and union. In fact, the faculty's professional interests—as applied to governance at a university like Yeshiva—cannot be separated from those of the institution.

The "business" of a university is education, and its vitality ultimately must depend on academic policies that largely are formulated and

---

[24] The Board has cited no case directly applying an "independent professional judgment" standard. On the related question of accountability for implementation of management policies, it cites only *NLRB v. Fullerton Publ'g Co.*, 283 F.2d 545, 550 (9th Cir. 1960), which held that a news editor "responsibly directed" his department so as to fall within the definition of a supervisor, 29 U.S.C. § 152(11). The court looked in part to accountability in rejecting the claim that the editor merely relayed assignments and thus was not "responsible" for directing employees as required by the statute. The case did not involve the managerial exclusion and has no application to the issues before us.

generally are implemented by faculty governance decisions. Faculty members enhance their own standing and fulfill their professional mission by ensuring that the university's objectives are met. But there can be no doubt that the quest for academic excellence and institutional distinction is a "policy" to which the administration expects the faculty to adhere, whether it be defined as a professional or an institutional goal. It is fruitless to ask whether an employee is "expected to conform" to one goal or another when the two are essentially the same.

The problem of divided loyalty is particularly acute for a university like Yeshiva, which depends on the professional judgment of its faculty to formulate and apply crucial policies constrained only by necessarily general institutional goals. The university requires faculty participation in governance because professional expertise is indispensable to the formulation and implementation of academic policy. The large measure of independence enjoyed by faculty members can only increase the danger that divided loyalty will lead to those harms that the Board traditionally has sought to prevent.

There may be institutions of higher learning unlike Yeshiva where the faculty are entirely or predominantly nonmanagerial. There also may be faculty members at Yeshiva and like universities who properly could be included in a bargaining unit. It may be that a rational line could be drawn between tenured and untenured faculty members, depending upon how a faculty is structured and operates. But we express no opinion on these questions, for it is clear that the unit approved by the Board was far too broad.

Affirmed.

JUSTICE BRENNAN, with whom JUSTICES WHITE, MARSHALL, and BLACKMUN join, dissenting:

Unlike the purely hierarchical decisionmaking structure that prevails in the typical industrial organization, the bureaucratic foundation of most "mature" universities is characterized by dual authority systems. The primary decisional network is hierarchical in nature: authority is lodged in the administration, and a formal chain of command runs from a lay governing board down through university officers to individual faculty members and students. At the same time, there exists a parallel professional network, in which formal mechanisms have been created to bring the expertise of the faculty into the decisionmaking process.

What the Board realized—and what the Court fails to apprehend—is that whatever influence the faculty wields in university decisionmaking is attributable solely to its collective expertise as professional educators, and not to any managerial or supervisory prerogatives. Although the administration may look to the faculty for advice on matters of professional and academic concern, the faculty offers its recommendations in order to serve its own independent interest in creating the most effective environment for learning, teaching, and scholarship. The University always retains the ultimate decisionmaking authority, and the administration gives what weight and import to the faculty's collective judgment as it chooses and deems consistent with its own perception of the institution's needs and objectives.

Moreover, insofar as faculty members are given some say in more traditional managerial decisions such as the hiring and promotion of other personnel, such discretion does not constitute an adequate basis for the conferral of managerial or supervisory status. Indeed, in the typical industrial context, it is not uncommon for the employees' union to be given the exclusive right to recommend personnel to the employer, and these hiring-hall agreements have been upheld even where the union requires a worker to pass a union-administered skills test as a condition of referral.

Yeshiva's faculty is not accountable to the administration in its governance function, nor is any individual faculty member subject to personal sanction or control based on the administration's assessment of the worth of his recommendations. Unlike industrial supervisors and managers, university professors are not hired to "make operative" the policies and decisions of their employer. Nor are they retained on the condition that their interests will correspond to those of the university administration. Indeed, the notion that a faculty member's professional competence could depend on his undivided loyalty to management is antithetical to the whole concept of academic freedom. Faculty members are judged by their employer on the quality of their teaching and scholarship, not on the compatibility of their advice with administration policy.

It is no answer to say, as does the Court, that Yeshiva's faculty and administration are one and the same because their interests tend to coincide. The mere coincidence of interests on many issues has never been thought to abrogate the right to collective bargaining on those topics as to which that coincidence is absent. Ultimately, the performance of an employee's duties will always further the interests of the employer, for in no institution do the interests of labor and management totally diverge. Both desire to maintain stable and profitable operations, and both are committed to creating the best possible product within existing financial constraints. Differences of opinion and emphasis may develop, however, on exactly how to devote the institution's resources to achieve those goals. When these disagreements surface, the national labor laws contemplate their resolution through the peaceful process of collective bargaining. And in this regard, Yeshiva University stands on the same footing as any other employer.

Moreover, the congruence of interests in this case ought not to be exaggerated. The very fact that Yeshiva's faculty has voted for the Union to serve as its representative in future negotiations with the administration indicates that the faculty does not perceive its interests to be aligned with those of management. Indeed, on the precise topics which are specified as mandatory subjects of collective bargaining-wages, hours, and other terms and conditions of employment, the interests of teacher and administrator are often diametrically opposed.

Finally, the Court's perception of the Yeshiva faculty's status is distorted by the rose-colored lens through which it views the governance structure of the modern-day university. The Court's conclusion that the faculty's professional interests are indistinguishable from those of the administration is bottomed on an idealized model of collegial decisionmaking that is a vestige of the great medieval university. But the university of today bears little resemblance to the "community of scholars" of yesteryear. Education has become "big business," and the task of operating the university enterprise has been transferred from the faculty to an autonomous administration, which faces the same pressures to cut costs and increase efficiencies that confront any large industrial organization. The past decade of budgetary cutbacks, declining enrollments, reductions in faculty appointments, curtailment of academic programs, and increasing calls for accountability to alumni and other special interest groups has only added to the erosion of the faculty's role in the institution's decision-making process.

Today's decision threatens to eliminate much of the administration's incentive to resolve its disputes with the faculty through open discussion and mutual agreement. By its overbroad and unwarranted interpretation of the managerial exclusion, the Court denies the faculty the protections of the NLRA and, in so doing, removes whatever deterrent value the Act's availability may offer against unreasonable administrative conduct.

NOTES

1. *Managerial employees.* Unlike the term "supervisor," the term "managerial" employee is not defined in the Act. The decision to equate a managerial employee with the term "employer" under Sections 2(2) and 2(11), rather than with the term "employee" under Section 2(3), was dictated by judicial interpretation, not statutory language. *See, e.g., NLRB v. Bell Aerospace Corp.*, 416 U.S. 267 (1974). Applying *Yeshiva*, the NLRB has held that faculty who had no say in the governance of a medical school negotiated themselves out of statutory protection by entering into a collective bargaining agreement that conferred on the faculty "almost plenary authority" over academic and some nonacademic matters, *College of Osteopathic Medicine & Surgery*, 265 N.L.R.B. 295, 297 (1982), but has also held that the faculty of a private school for kindergarten through grade 12 were not managers because their "considerable discretion" did not extend beyond "the routine performance of the tasks to which they have been assigned," *Wordsworth Academy*, 262 N.L.R.B. 438, 443 (1982).

As noted above, *supra* p. 302, Section 14(c)(1) gives the Board the discretion not to exercise jurisdiction when an employer's effect on commerce is "not sufficiently substantial." How broadly or narrowly should the NLRB exercise this discretion? In a particular case, should it resolve doubts about substantiality in favor or against coverage?

2. *Conflict of interest.* According to the *Yeshiva* majority, the managerial employee exclusion had to be created to avoid "the problem of divided loyalty": the inherent conflicts of interest that would arise if a professor could join a union and bargain with the administration like any other "employee," even though such professor is also helping to set policy for the "employer," like any supervisor. The problem, Justice Powell says, "is particularly acute for a university like Yeshiva, which depends on the professional judgment of its faculty to formulate and apply crucial policies constrained only by necessarily general institutional goals."

Over the years, Justice Powell's explanation has been much debated by academics. On the one hand, it has struck many professors—including the authors of this textbook—as missing the mark. Most professors would consider themselves labor rather than management. Faculties and administrators often sharply disagree over academic policies great and small, and if no compromise is reached, then the administration usually has the final say. In support of this view, Justice Brennan wrote: "Faculty members are judged by their employer on the quality of their teaching and scholarship, not on the compatibility of their advice with administration policy." On the other hand, most administrators—including plenty of law school deans—would point out how rare it is for administrators to hire or promote a professor who has been voted down by the faculty. That is, the full faculty often retain the power "effectively to recommend" whether a colleague will be hired or promoted. In the plain language of Section 2(11), is this not enough to transform them into supervisors? Managerial employees? After the *Oakwood* trio, must the administrators win the argument? Would your opinion be different if you knew that many states explicitly grant the faculty of public universities the right to form and join labor organizations, and to bargain collectively with the administration? *See, e.g.,* California, Cal. Gov't Code § 3563(e) (employees of Regents of University of California and California State University, and Hastings College of Law); Hawaii, Haw. Rev. Stat. § 89–6(7) (faculty of the University of Hawaii and community college system); Illinois, 5 Ill. Comp. Stat. (Smith-Hurd) § 2(b) (part-time and full-time "academic employees" of community colleges and state universities).

3. *It's not just academic.* What implications does this *Yeshiva* have for the definition of who or what is the "employer" in workplaces outside the university setting? In dissent, Justice Brennan observed: "Unlike the purely hierarchical decisionmaking structure that prevails in the typical industrial organization, the bureaucratic foundation of most 'mature' universities is characterized by dual authority systems." Drawing on a tradition that dates to the medieval times, the typical university administration, Brennan noted, must share certain decisionmaking responsibilities with the faculty.

Could Brennan be describing the twenty-first century, high-performance workplace, where flattened hierarchies and dual authority systems are more common? Or could he be describing the artisanal workplace, discussed in Chapter 1, *infra* p. 11?

4.   *WashTech revisited.* Recall the perma-temps at Microsoft, discussed at the beginning of this Chapter, *supra* p. 11. Might they be reclassified as managerial or confidential employees, and on that basis, denied the protections of the NLRA? Why or why not?

5.   *Read all about it.* In *Republican Co.*, 361 N.L.R.B. 93 (2014), the Board offered the following examples of who may be considered a managerial employee of a newspaper, and therefore, excludable from the bargaining unit. As to the editorial page editor, he was considered to be a managerial employee due to his discretionary role in formulating, determining, and effectuating the newspaper's editorial policies, even though the publisher had the final say about what those policies would be and how they would be expressed. As to the assistant classified adverting manager and the production manager, however, neither was considered to be truly managerial, because the employer did not carry its burden of proving that either one performed any managerial function, such as hiring or effectively recommending the hiring of employees.

Does this clarify who should be considered a managerial employee?

* * *

Like managerial employees discussed above, confidential employees are neither defined nor discussed by the Act, either for exclusion from the "employee" category under Section 2(3) or for inclusion in the "employer" category under Section 2(2). Yet under longstanding precedent, the NLRB considers both to be too closely aligned with management to enjoy the full protections of the statute.

For some years, the Board was confronted with arguments that workers possessing or using confidential business information should not have any Section 7 rights. Instead, the agency chose a narrower path: denial of such rights is appropriate when such workers have access to the employer's confidential labor relations information. The term "confidential" embraces "only those employees who assist and act in a confidential capacity to persons who exercise 'managerial' functions in the field of labor relations." *Ford Motor Co.*, 66 N.L.R.B. 1317, 1322 (1946). Fitting this definition are human resources employees having advance information about the employer's position on contract negotiations, the disposition of grievances, and similar subjects. The Supreme Court has agreed with this approach. See *NLRB v. Hendricks County Rural Elec. Membership Corp.*, 454 U.S. 170 (1981).

3.   PUBLIC SECTOR EMPLOYERS

In what is probably the most significant carve-out from the Act's coverage of employers, Section 2(2) specifically excludes "the United States or any wholly owned Government corporation, or any Federal Reserve Bank, or any State or political subdivision thereof." 29 U.S.C. § 152(2). This means that as many as 20 million employees of federal, state, county, and municipal governments—about 15% of the total U.S. workforce—are denied the protections of the NLRA. Of these, about 3 million are civilian employees who work for federal agencies in Washington, D.C., and throughout the country; about 17 million are the employees of state and local governments, including agencies that employ workers in the courts, education, transportation and highway safety, police and fire protection, and sanitation.

Most state public sector employers, however, are covered by specific statutes granting their employees the right to form and join unions and engage in collective bargaining, often with the important caveat that the right to strike is curtailed or eliminated. These statutes tend to be modeled on the NLRA. Before the 1960s, few states had passed such statutes, but by the 1980s, the situation had changed so dramatically that the union density rate in the public sector had surpassed that in the private sector. And by 2009, for the first time ever, the total number of unionized public sector workers was higher than the total number of unionized private sector workers. *See* Steven Greenhouse, *Most U.S. Union Members Are Working for Government, New Data Shows*, N.Y. Times, Jan. 22, 2010, at p. B10. In 2012, the U.S. Bureau of Labor Statistics reported that, of the country's 14.3 million unionized workers, 7.3 million worked in the public sector (at a union density rate of 35.9%) and 7.0 million worked in the private sector (at a union density rate of 6.6%).

In general, federal public sector employers are covered by the Civil Service Reform Act (CSRA), 92 Stat. 111, 5 U.S.C. §§ 7101–7135. The statute creates the Federal Labor Relations Authority (FLRA), which is modeled on the NLRB. But federal employee unions are forbidden "to call, or participate in, a strike, work stoppage, or slowdown, or picketing of an agency in a labor-management dispute if such picketing interferes with an agency's operations." 5 U.S.C. § 7116(b)(7)(A). Other modifications of traditional NLRA rights are codified in the CSRA.

In a leading case, the Supreme Court defined "any State or political subdivision thereof" under Section 2(2)'s to mean an entity that is either (1) created directly by the state so as to constitute a department or administrative arm of the government or (2) administered by individuals who are responsible to public officials or to the general electorate. *See NLRB v. Natural Gas Utility District of Hawkins County*, 402 U.S. 600, 604–05 (1971).

In recent years, the NLRB has begun to apply *Hawkins* to the phenomenon of charter schools.

PENNSYLVANIA VIRTUAL CHARTER SCHOOL
364 N.L.R.B. No. 87 (2016)

DECISION ON REVIEW AND ORDER

By CHAIRMAN PEARCE and MEMBERS MISCIMARRA, HIROZAWA, and MCFERRAN:

The issues in this case are whether the Board has jurisdiction over a nonprofit corporation that operates a charter school in Pennsylvania, and, if so, whether we should nevertheless decline to assert that jurisdiction as a matter of our discretion. We answer those questions yes and no, respectively. We find that the Pennsylvania Virtual Charter School (PVCS or the School) is not exempt from our jurisdiction as a political subdivision of the Commonwealth of Pennsylvania within the meaning of Section 2(2) of the National Labor Relations Act. Nor are there persuasive reasons for the Board to exercise its discretion to decline to assert jurisdiction in this case. We explain these conclusions below.

On January 5, 2015, the PA Virtual School Education Association, PSEA/NEA (the Union), filed a petition seeking to represent a unit of approximately 83 full-time and part-time kindergarten through grade 12 teachers and academic support staff at PVCS. PVCS opposed the petition, contending, under *Chicago Mathematics & Science Academy*, that it is a political subdivision of the Commonwealth of Pennsylvania. On February 11, 2015, after a hearing, the Regional Director applied *NLRB v. Natural Gas Utility District of Hawkins County*, 402 U.S. 600 (1971), and found that the School is not a political subdivision: he found that the School was neither created directly by the state so as to constitute a department or administrative arm of the government nor is it administered by individuals who are responsible to public officials or the general electorate. PVCS sought review of the Regional Director's decision.

Our decision today is based on the facts of this case, which involves the operation of a cyber charter school in the Commonwealth of Pennsylvania established under the Pennsylvania Charter School Law. We are not announcing a bright-line rule asserting jurisdiction over charter schools nationwide.

Facts

Pennsylvania Charter School Law

The Pennsylvania Public School Code includes the Charter School Law (CSL), which was enacted in 1997 and provides the framework for the establishment and operation of charter schools, including cyber charter schools providing remote instruction in Pennsylvania. The CSL defines a "Cyber Charter School" as:

> [A]n independent public school established and operated under a charter from the [Pennsylvania] Department of Education and in which the school uses technology in order to provide a significant portion of its curriculum and to deliver a significant portion of instruction to its students through the Internet or other electronic means. A cyber charter school must be organized as a public, nonprofit corporation. A charter may not be granted for a for-profit entity.

A cyber charter school in Pennsylvania may be established by individuals, by an organization such as a nonsectarian college or museum, or by a corporation or association. 24 P.S. § 17–1717–A(a). Cyber charter schools must admit any eligible student residing in Pennsylvania. 24 P.S. § 17–1724–A(a). Charter schools do not charge tuition, but receive most of their operating funds from public sources, primarily the students' home school districts. 24 P.S. § 17–1725–A.

Pennsylvania charter schools are exempt from certain state laws and regulations that otherwise pertain to public schools under the Public School Law, but are required to comply with the statutes and regulations specified in the CSL. *See* 24 P.S. § 17–1715–A.

The CSL provides that a charter school's board of trustees shall have the authority to decide matters related to the operation of the school, including budgeting, curriculum, and operating procedures consistent with the school's charter. The trustees also have the authority to employ the school's professional and nonprofessional employees, and establish their terms and conditions for employment. 24 P.S. § 17–1716–A(a) & 17–1724–A(a). The CSL further authorizes the trustees to appoint a chief executive officer or other administrator to oversee and manage the operation of the charter school. Under the CSL, a charter school's trustees and administrators are "public officials" for purposes of state ethics and financial disclosure laws. 24 P.S. § 17–1715–A(11), (12).

A charter school must submit an annual report to the Department of Education so the latter may review the school's performance on various standardized tests and other performance indicators to assure compliance and operation consistent with the school's charter and the CSL. 24 P.S. § 17–1728–A. The Department of Education has ongoing access to all records, instructional materials, and student and staff records of each charter school. The CSL provides that a charter may be revoked or not renewed by the Department of Education if the school's financial or education obligations are not or cannot be met, or if the school commits a material violation of its charter agreement. 24 P.S. § 17–1729–A.

The Pennsylvania Virtual Charter School

PVCS operates a public cyber charter school that provides educational services over the internet to approximately 3,000 students who reside within Pennsylvania. PVCS was founded in 2001 when several individuals, known as "the Founding Board" or "the Founding Coalition," organized and submitted a charter application to the Norristown Area School District.

On about January 16, 2001, the Founding Board incorporated PVCS as a Pennsylvania nonprofit corporation to operate for educational purposes. On February 12, 2001, the school district approved the application and entered into a Charter School Agreement with the School, which the parties understood to "constitute a charter within the meaning of the CSL." The charter agreement set forth the parties' rights and responsibilities, including the school district's access to the School's records to ensure compliance with the charter and the CSL, and the school district's commitment to provide consulting and administrative support to facilitate the funding for the School. The charter was issued for a 5-year term.

Pursuant to Act 88, the Department of Education renewed the School's charter in 2006 and again in 2011. The current charter expires June 20, 2016. The record includes the School's 2010 renewal application.

PVCS' bylaws, last amended September 26, 2011, set forth the operating rules for the board of trustees—the School's governing board. Pursuant to its bylaws, PVCS' current six-member board of trustees decides all matters related to the School's operations, including setting the curriculum; hiring, firing, and disciplining employees; and setting wages for all staff. The board may consist of a minimum of five and a maximum of nine members, who serve 5-year terms with no term limits. Under the bylaws, the board also appoints and removes its own members, by majority vote of the trustees. PVCS employs a chief executive officer and a chief financial officer. Both the CEO and CFO were appointed by and report directly to the board of trustees. The board also has the authority to remove the CEO and CFO.

The board is responsible for ensuring that the School is operated in compliance with the charter application and all applicable laws, and ensuring that the School remains financially viable. PVCS' board sets wages for the School's staff; hires, fires, and disciplines its employees; and establishes and maintains all policies and procedures related to employment. The board determines the School's curriculum, which cannot be changed without the board's approval and must be in compliance with the state's established standards. The board also approves and ratifies all contracts, authorizes all expenditures, and adopts the School's annual budget, which is prepared by the CFO in consultation with the board's Planning and Budget Committee.

The School's operating budget is funded almost entirely (97 percent) by the school districts where the students reside, which transmit a set percentage of their annual per capita student cost to PVCS. The remaining funding (3 percent) comes from federal programs such as No Child Left Behind and the Individuals with Disabilities Education Act.

Analysis

Section 2(2) of the National Labor Relations Act provides that the term "employer" shall not include any state or political subdivision thereof. The term "political subdivision" is not defined in the Act. In *Hawkins County*, however, the Supreme Court observed that the legislative history revealed that Congress enacted Section 2(2):

> to except from Board cognizance the labor relations of federal, state, and municipal governments, since governmental employees did not usually enjoy the right to strike. In light of that purpose, the Board . . . has limited the exemption for political subdivisions to entities that are either (1) created directly by the state, so as to constitute departments or administrative arms of government, or (2) administered by individuals who are responsible to public officials or to the general electorate.

402 U.S. at 604–05 (footnotes omitted).

Consistent with that understanding, the Board has held that "[t]he plain language of Section 2(2) 'exempts only government entities or wholly owned government corporations from its coverage—not private entities acting as contractors for the government.'" *Research Foundation of the City Univ. of New York*, 337 NLRB 965, 968 (2002), quoting *Aramark Corp. v. NLRB*, 179 F.3d 872, 878 (10th Cir. 1999). Applying these principles, we agree with the Regional Director and find that PVCS is not a political subdivision of the Commonwealth of Pennsylvania under either prong of the Hawkins County test.

PVCS was Not "Created Directly by the State"

In order to determine whether an entity is a political subdivision under the first prong of the *Hawkins County* test, the Board determines first whether the entity was created directly by the state, such as by a government entity, legislative act, or public official. If it was, the Board then considers whether the entity was created so as to constitute a department or administrative arm of the government. Both of these subparts need to be met for the employer to be exempt from the Act. We find that PVCS fails the first prong of the *Hawkins County* test because it was created by private individuals and not by a government entity, special legislative act, or public official. Moreover, PVCS was not created to be an administrative arm of the government.

The Board has routinely found employing entities to be exempt political subdivisions where they were created by legislation or statute in order to discharge a state function. The Board has also found the first prong of *Hawkins County* satisfied where the employing entity was created by an act of the judiciary, rather than the legislature. In contrast, the Board has consistently held that entities created by private individuals as nonprofit corporations are not exempt under the first prong of *Hawkins County*. Furthermore, an entity is not exempt simply because it receives public funding or operates pursuant to a contract with a governmental entity, as does PVCS. The Board routinely asserts jurisdiction over private employers that have agreements with government entities to provide services. As the Board stated in Research Foundation, *supra* at 968, the "plain language" of Section 2(2) does not exempt private entities acting as government contractors from the Board's jurisdiction. Further, "[t]he creation of the Employer by private individuals as a private corporation, without any state enabling action or intent, clearly leaves the Employer outside the ambit of the Section 2(2) exemption."

Applying these principles here, we find that PVCS does not share the "key characteristic of political subdivision status" with those entities that the Board has found to be exempt. That is, PVCS was not created directly by any Commonwealth of Pennsylvania government entity, special statute, legislation, or public official, but instead by private individuals as a nonprofit corporation.

Here, the School was founded in 2001, when a group of private individuals, known as "the Founding Board" or "the Founding Coalition," organized and filed a comprehensive application for a charter from the Norristown Area School District. After applying for the initial charter, the Founding Board filed for nonprofit corporate status with the Pennsylvania Department of State. Thereafter, the charter was signed by the board of trustees and the school district. There is no evidence that the school district amended any part of the School's charter, or rejected the initial board of trustees. Thus, the Regional Director correctly concluded under the CSL and Board precedent that neither the school district nor any state agency initially created the School; rather, it was created by private individuals. No doubt many private entities would not exist but for the public contracts they carry out; they nevertheless are not 'administrative arms of the government.'"). Nor, as the Regional Director correctly observed, is the Department of Education's involvement in the subsequent renewals of the School's charter significant. It does not change the fact that the School was established by private individuals.

It is therefore unnecessary to examine whether PVCS is an administrative arm or department of the government. See *Regional Medical Center at Memphis*, 343 NLRB at 358 (upon finding that employer was not created by the State, Board stated that employer could be exempt under *Hawkins County* only under second prong analysis *i.e.*, "only if officials who are responsible to public officials or to the general electorate administer it. Nevertheless, we find that PVCS fails this element of the prong one test, as well. To begin, we do not find merit in PVCS' reliance on the CSL's characterization of cyber charter schools as "independent public schools" or charter administrators as "public officials" to argue that PVCS is an administrative arm of the government. It is federal, not state, law that governs the determination of whether an entity created under state law is a political subdivision within the meaning of Section 2(2) of the Act. H*awkins County*, 402 U.S. at 602–603. While state determinations about whether an entity is a political subdivision are "worthy of careful consideration," these determinations do not control. The record supports the Regional Director's conclusion that "the [School] is a corporate entity which holds a charter to function as an independent public school, in a manner more akin to a subcontractor than a department of government."

Moreover, the School's governing body—its board of trustees—was established under the School's own charter. The trustees are appointed by other trustees, for a 5-year term, and are not subject to any term limits. In contrast, public school board members are elected by the voters in the school district for terms of 4 years. Under the CSL, the board oversees the day-to-day operations of the School, acts autonomously, and has the authority to decide all matters related to the operation of the School, consistent with the School's charter and applicable law. The CSL states that the board shall determine the level of compensation and all terms and conditions of employment of the staff. Additionally, matters such as quorum and regularity of meetings are within the discretion of the School's board of trustees, but are legislated for public schools.

The School's argument that the Department of Education's ability to revoke charters gives it more power over charter schools than it does over public schools is also unavailing. The power to revoke a charter is analogous to a state's decision to cease subcontracting work to a private employer that fails to satisfy the state's standards. It does not convert the contractor into a state entity.

PVCS Is Not Administered by Individuals Who Are Responsible to Public Officials or the General Electorate

Under the second *Hawkins County* prong, an entity will be deemed a political subdivision if it is "administered by individuals who are responsible to public officials or to the general electorate." In making this determination, the Board examines whether those individuals are appointed by or subject to removal procedures applicable to public officials . . . ." In some cases, the Board has also considered whether additional factors demonstrate a responsibility to public officials or the electorate. Here, for the reasons that follow, we find it dispositive that none of PVCS' governing board members are appointed by or subject to removal by any public official. Hence, no further inquiry is required.

Here, we draw on the reasoning of the decision in *Charter School Administration Services*, 353 N.L.R.B. 394 (2008) (CSAS), finding that a private, for-profit corporation that managed and operated charter schools was not a political subdivision of the State of Michigan. *CSAS* found that the members of CSAS's governing board were not responsible to public officials or the general electorate inasmuch as they were neither appointed, nor subject to removal, by public officials. *Id.* at 397–398. We are persuaded by that reasoning and adopt it here.

We summarize the principles that the CSAS Board applied: in determining whether an entity is administered by individuals who are responsible to public officials or the general electorate, the "relevant inquiry" is whether a majority of the individuals who administer the entity—the governing board and executive officers—are appointed by and subject to removal by public officials. The Board examines whether the composition, selection, and removal of the members of an employer's governing board are determined by law, or solely by the employer's governing documents.

Where the appointment and removal of a majority of an entity's governing board members is controlled by private individuals—as opposed to public officials—the entity is subject to the Board's jurisdiction. *See, e.g.*, *Research Foundation, supra* (no exemption where employer's bylaws, not state law, defined appointment and removal of members of the board of directors); *St. Paul Ramsey Medical Center*, 291 N.L.R.B. 755 (1988) (medical center not a political subdivision because there was no requirement that board of directors be public officials or appointed and removed by public officials); *Truman Medical Center v. NLRB*, 641 F.2d 570 (8th Cir. 1981) (hospital's governing body was self-perpetuating board of directors, majority of whom were not appointed by or subject to removal by public officials).

The Board's "sole focus" in *CSAS* was on the composition of the employer's board of directors and to whom those board members were accountable. The members of CSAS' board of directors were elected by the employer's shareholders, who could remove a director for or without cause. Furthermore, CSAS' corporate officers were elected or appointed by, and subject to removal by, the board of directors. No person involved in running CSAS' corporate enterprise—not its board of directors, executive board, or administrative staff—was appointed by or subject to removal by any public official, and there was no indication that the board of directors or corporate officers had any "direct personal accountability to public officials or the general electorate."20 The CSAS Board concluded:

We find no merit in PVCS' arguments that the trustees themselves are "public officials" under the CSL and that the board of trustees are accountable to the Pennsylvania Secretary of Education, a public official, merely because the Secretary has oversight and authority to renew the School's charter. First, as discussed earlier, CSL's "public officials" designation alone fails to establish that trustees and administrators are in fact public officials for the purposes of the National Labor Relations Act, when the evidence demonstrates that PVCS' board was created and governed by its internal bylaws (the first board was selected by the private citizens comprising the Founding Coalition) and is a self-perpetuating entity.

Second, that the School is subject to oversight and regulation by the Secretary of Education is insufficient to find that the School is accountable to a public official. Critically, nothing in the bylaws allows the Secretary of Education or any other public official to elect or remove a trustee.

The Board Should Not Decline to Assert Jurisdiction over PVCS

In the alternative, PVCS argues that even if the Board has statutory jurisdiction over PVCS, the Board should nonetheless decline to assert jurisdiction over cyber charter schools. PVCS points out that there are only 14 cyber charter schools in Pennsylvania and asserts, on that basis, that they only have a de minimis impact on interstate commerce. Further, PVCS argues that if the Board exercises jurisdiction, it would effectively supplant state control over its own public education system and the state's ability to regulate labor relations at those schools. We reject those arguments.

Under Section 14(c)(1) of the Act, the Board may "in its discretion . . . decline to assert jurisdiction over any labor dispute involving any class or category of employers, where, in the opinion of the Board, the effect of such labor dispute on commerce is not sufficiently substantial to warrant the exercise of its jurisdiction." But Section 14(c) of the Act manifests a congressional policy favoring the assertion of discretionary jurisdiction where "the Board finds that the operations of a class of employers exercise a substantial effect on commerce." *Cornell University*, 183 N.L.R.B. 329, 332 (1970). The Board has not hesitated to assert jurisdiction over nonprofit corporations and other entities merely because they perform work for state or local governments. *See, e.g., Boys & Girls Aid Society*, 224 N.L.R.B. 1614 (1976); *St. Aloysius Home*, 224 N.L.R.B. 1344 (1976).

Although PVCS suggests that the Board not exercise jurisdiction because cyber charter schools do not "exercise substantial effect on commerce," PVCS alone serves about 3,000 students and its operating budget is in the millions of dollars each year. And it is but one of 14 cyber charter schools in Pennsylvania. All of those schools employ teachers and staff and purchase products and services in the private sector economy. Accordingly, we reject PVCS' claim that Pennsylvania's cyber charter schools do not substantially affect commerce.

PVCS' further argument, that the Board's assertion of jurisdiction would supplant state control, is merely another way of asserting that PVCS is a state school. But it is not. Pennsylvania law does not mandate the establishment of charter schools as a means of fulfilling "the state's obligation to provide public education"; rather, it permits others to establish them as an alternative to the public schools. The Commonwealth having made that choice, PVCS is subject to the same federal regulation as are other private employers.

Our dissenting colleague goes a step further than PVCS, arguing that the Board should decline to exercise jurisdiction over all charter schools under Section 14(c)(1), because, assertedly, charter schools have an insubstantial effect on interstate commerce and the exercise of jurisdiction would lead to instability and confusion. We do not find those policy arguments persuasive.

NOTES

1.   Like so many questions in this Chapter, the question in this case was close, and could have gone the other way. Here the question was whether the charter school was a "political subdivision" exempt from the reach of the NLRA. In light of Section 2(2)'s substantial carve-out of federal and state public sector employers from the Act, should doubts about the NLRA's coverage be resolved, as they were here, against finding such coverage? Why or why not?

2.   *Public sector collective bargaining in perspective.* Historically, the states were reluctant to step into the gap created by the NLRA and grant collective bargaining rights to public sector employees. The reasons for this were founded on several fears, which are discussed in Chapter 1, *supra* pp. 79–80. One fear was that elected government officials, if not the voters themselves, would be subject to unique political pressures to pay more in wages and benefits to employees represented by public sector unions than they would have to pay in a free private sector labor market. Many public sector unions are respected for their ability to turn out large numbers of voters, who may swing the outcome, especially in local elections. Another fear was that employees performing essential public services would paralyze the community if they went on strike or engaged in other concerted activities in support of their demands. *See generally* Harry H. Wellington & Ralph K. Winter, The Unions and the Cities (1971). For a comprehensive look at the development and growth of public sector labor relations law, see Martin H. Malin, Ann C. Hodges & Joseph E. Slater, Pubic Sector Employment Cases and Materials (3d ed. 2016). For thoughtful consideration of public sector unionism in both the U.S. and Canada, France, Germany, Greece, Italy, and Japan, see *Symposium—Public Sector Collective Bargaining and the Distortion of Democracy: Do Public Sector Unions Have "Too Much" Power?,* 34 Comp. Lab. L. & Pol'y J. 245 (2013).

In 2011, based partly on the fears described above, public sector workers became the focus of anger across the country as state and local officials, casting a wary eye toward the costs of wage and benefit packages that had been negotiated by labor, dealt with shrunken revenues by cutting spending without raising taxes—and taking on public employee unions. Republican-dominated legislatures from Ohio in the North to Alabama in the South and Arizona in the West to Maine in the East pushed new laws designed to curb the power of unions representing government workers.

Nowhere was this push stronger than in Wisconsin, where Governor Scott Walker signed Act 10, which effectively stripped most state workers of their right to engage in collective bargaining by, among other things, requiring annual recertification of bargaining representatives, eliminating fair share agreements, and prohibiting municipalities from collecting agency fees. (Ironically, in 1959, Wisconsin had been the first state to pass legislation granting collective bargaining rights to such workers.) The move sparked weeks of daily protests by up to 100,000 people in Madison, the state's capital. It also sparked a hotly-contested attempt to recall Walker and several legal challenges to the legislation. Walker beat the recall effort, and to date, all legal challenges to Act 10. *See Wisconsin ex rel. Ozanne v. Fitzgerald*, 334 Wisc. 2d 70 (2011) (rejecting state open meeting law challenge); *Wisconsin Education Association Council v. Walker*, 705 F.3d 640 (7th Cir. 2013) (rejecting federal equal protection challenge); *Madison Teachers, Inc. v. Walker*, 358 Wisc. 2d 1 (2014) (rejecting freedom of association challenge).

In 2017, following the example set by Wisconsin, Iowa enacted similar legislation. *See* H.F. 291, 2017 Ia. Acts, *codified at* Ia. Code § 20.6.(5).

How do you feel about collective bargaining by public sector employees? Does it make any difference that historically the wages of public sector workers tend to be lower than those of their private sector counterparts, or that, as quid pro quo, public sector employees increasingly demand more generous medical, pension, and other benefits than private sector workers? Do you share the concerns of elected officials in financially-strapped municipalities that taxpayers can no longer afford to pay for these benefits, and should be able to abrogate the collective bargaining agreements (often called MOUs, or memoranda of understanding) to balance their books? *See, e.g., In re County of Orange*, 179 Bank. 177 (Bankr. C.D. Cal. 1995). The Orange County, California, bankruptcy is discussed in Chapter 9, *infra* p. 1186.

4. MULTIPLE ENTITIES OR SINGLE ENTITY? THE SINGLE EMPLOYER AND ALTER EGO DOCTRINES

A common means by which a unionized employer may attempt to avoid its legal obligations is by taking the position that it should not be considered the employer at all. It may establish a non-union entity through which business can be conducted, and workers can be hired, without the restrictions on wages, benefits, and working conditions that ordinarily would be imposed on its unionized counterpart by either the NLRA or a collective bargaining agreement. This tactic, which is sometimes called "double-breasting," is especially common in the construction and coal mining industries. But it can appear in many other industries, especially those for which production is undertaken on a project-by-project or seasonal basis, such as motion picture and television production. *See, e.g., NBC, Inc.*, Case No. 2-CA-37396, 2007 WL 700894 (2007) (reporting administrative law judge's finding that NBC broadcasting network and MSNBC cable network constitute a single employer).

In the classic double breasting case, a unionized subcontractor wishes to bid on jobs for which the general contractor or owner permits nonunion subcontractors to bid as well. The problem is that if the unionized subcontractor's bid is based on the prevailing rates for labor set by the collective bargaining agreement, the bidder risks losing out to non-union competitors with lower labor cost structures. To be more competitive, the unionized subcontractor may establish a nonunion alter ego to do its bidding. This nonunion entity may be either a separate corporation or a wholly-owned subsidiary of a parent holding company. And it may or may not draw on the same administrative structure, workforce, operating assets, and other resources of the unionized counterpart.

Although not explicitly characterized as illegal under the NLRA, double-breasting is sometimes challenged by the affected union as a "sham" operation designed to siphon away bargaining unit work from unionized employees. In such a case, the basic legal inquiry is whether the nonunion affiliate was created for legitimate business purposes or solely as a vehicle to escape bargaining obligations. But as the cases below demonstrate, this inquiry is often complicated by the application of corporate law doctrines. *See* Ben Marsh, *Corporate Shell Games: Use of The Corporate Form To Evade Bargaining Obligations*, 2 U. Pa. J. Lab. & Emp. L. 543 (2000).

Two similar but distinct labor law doctrines constitute the principal legal weapons used to attack alleged double breasting operations: the "single employer" doctrine and the "alter ego" doctrine. Under both doctrines, it is argued that the unionized entity and its nonunion counterpart are really one integrated entity that is answerable under law and by contract for the same obligations. A "single employer" relationship is said to exist where two ostensibly separate entities are actually part of a single integrated enterprise. By contrast, an "alter ego" status often involves an effort to avoid a collective bargaining obligation through a sham transaction. Each doctrine is discussed in turn.

a.   The Single Employer Doctrine

To decide whether nominally separate union and nonunion entities are truly a single integrated employer, the Board undertakes a two-step analysis. The first step is to look for indicia of four factors: interrelated operations, common management, common ownership, and centralized control of labor relations. Of these, the last—centralized control of labor relations—is the most important. It must be ascertained whether comparable arrangements would have been reached in an arms-length relationship among nonintegrated companies. The second step is to determine whether the two entities constitute an appropriate bargaining unit. (The standard is the "community of interest" test, which is discussed in Chapter 4, *infra* p. 521.) The Supreme Court has approved this two-step analysis, but with an important caveat: due to the Board's exclusive role in determining the appropriate bargaining unit, the determination whether the "community of interest" test is met must be made in the first instance by the NLRB, not by the federal courts. *See South Prairie Construction Co. v. Local No. 627, International Union of Operating Engineers*, 425 U.S. 800 (1976) (*per curiam*).

The single employer doctrine may be invoked in response to a number of situations in which double breasting is suspected, such as satisfying the sums affecting interstate commerce necessary to support NLRA jurisdiction, *see Radio & Television Technicians Local 1264 v. Broadcast Serv. of Mobile, Inc.*, 380 U.S. 255 (1965); asserting coverage over work for which union jurisdiction is promised by collective bargaining agreement, *see, e.g., Communication Workers of Am. v. United States West Direct*, 847 F.2d 1475 (10th Cir. 1988); collecting unpaid pension and benefit fund contributions for work performed by employees of the nonunion entity, *see, e.g., Carpenters Local 1846 v. Pratt-Farnsworth, Inc.*, 690 F.2d 489 (5th Cir. 1982); and obtaining information related to the unionized employer's statutory duty to bargain, *see, e.g., Dodger Theatricals Holdings, Inc.*, 347 N.L.R.B. 953 (2006).

The following case is an example of how the Board implements its two-step analysis in a manner that is consistent with *South Prairie Construction*.

MERCY HOSPITAL OF BUFFALO
336 N.L.R.B. 1282 (2001)

By CHAIRMAN HURTGEN and MEMBERS LIEBMAN and WALSH:

The issues presented in this case arise from the formation of Southtowns Catholic MRI, Inc. [Southtowns] as a joint venture by Respondent Mercy Hospital (the Respondent), and Our Lady of Victory Hospital. Southtowns was created for the purpose of providing magnetic resonance imaging (MRI) diagnostic health care services. Following the formation of Southtowns, the Respondent ceased providing MRI services at its Western New York Medical Park satellite facility (the Medical Park) and began referring patients to Southtowns. The transfer of MRI services from the Medical Park to Southtowns resulted in the elimination of two MRI technologist positions from the unit of Respondent's employees represented by the Union.

Findings of Fact

The Respondent operates an acute care hospital and various satellite facilities. It is one of five hospitals in Western New York owned by the Catholic Health System[, which also includes] Our Lady of Victory Hospital.

Since September 26, 1991, the Union has represented a unit of the Respondent's service, technical, and clerical employees (STC unit) at Mercy Hospital and numerous satellite facilities. The Respondent's recognition of the Union has been embodied in successive collective-bargaining agreements.

In January 1995, the Respondent acquired a radiological services practice in West Seneca, New York, in a complex known as the Medical Park. Since that time, it has provided radiological, physical therapy, occupational therapy, and some laboratory services at the Medical Park. Prior to the formation of Southtowns, all MRIs ordered by doctors at the Respondent took place at the Medical Park, unless otherwise specified by the doctor. The Union represents the service, technical, and clerical employees of the Respondent at the Medical Park, including MRI technologists.

In 1997, the Respondent, Our Lady of Victory Hospital, and Abbott Radiology began discussing the formation of a joint venture to purchase and operate a new, state-of-the-art MRI machine, capable of performing magnetic resonance angiograms (MRAs). At that time, the three entities were operating separate MRIs, none of which were capable of performing MRAs.

As a result of the discussions between the Respondent, Abbott Radiology, and Our Lady of Victory, two new companies were formed: MRI Associates, L.L.C., and Southtowns. MRI Associates is owned 25 percent by the Respondent, 25 percent by Our Lady of Victory, and 50 percent by Abbott. Southtowns is owned 50 percent by the Respondent and 50 percent by Our Lady of Victory.

MRI Associates constructed a new building on property leased from the Respondent at the Mercy Ambulatory Care Center (the MACC) in Orchard Park, New York. MRI Associates then purchased and installed a new MRI machine in the building. Southtowns leases the building and the MRI from MRI Associates.

The intent of the Respondent was for Southtowns to manage and operate the new MRI after obtaining the necessary New York licenses. However, since the MRI began operating in May 1998, it has been managed and operated by Abbott Radiology, through its wholly owned subsidiary, Orchard Park MRI, P.C. All employees providing MRI services at the Southtowns are employed by Orchard Park.

By memorandum dated July 22, 1998, the Respondent instructed the Staff at Mercy Hospital to schedule all MRIs and MRAs at Southtowns, unless otherwise specified by the patient's doctor. Subsequently, the Respondent stopped referring patients to the Medical Park for MRI procedures.

By letter dated October 13, 1998, the Respondent informed the Union that it was discontinuing MRI services at the Medical Park effective December 1, 1998. The discontinuation of MRI services at the Medical Park resulted in the elimination of two full-time MRI technologist positions within the STC unit.

On October 26, 1998, the Union filed a grievance over the elimination of the MRI technologist positions and the Respondent's failure to apply the terms of its collective-bargaining agreement with the Union to the employees providing MRI services at the Southtowns facility. On October 27, 1998, the Union filed the charge in this matter.

I. ANALYSIS

A. *Single-Employer Relationship and Failure to Apply Agreement*

The judge found that the Respondent and Southtowns, along with Southtowns Associates MRI, Abbott Radiology, and Orchard Park MRI-are so interrelated as to constitute what he characterized as "one ball of wax," with no separate corporate identity. He therefore found that the Respondent and Southtowns are a single employer and that the Respondent violated Section 8(a)(5) and (1) by failing to apply its collective-bargaining agreement with the Union to the employees performing MRI services at Southtowns facility. For the reasons explained below, we disagree.

A single-employer relationship exists when two or more employing entities are in reality a single-integrated enterprise. Four criteria determine whether a single-employer relationship exists: (1) common ownership; (2) common management; (3) functional interrelation of operations; and (4) centralized control of labor relations. *Broadcast [Employees NABET Local 1264 v. Broadcast Service of Mobile*, 380 U.S. 255 (1965).] It is well established that not all of these criteria need to be present to establish single-employer status. Single-employer status ultimately depends on "all the circumstances of a case" and is characterized by the absence of an "arm's-length relationship found among unintegrated companies." The Board has generally held that the most critical factor is centralized control over labor relations. Common ownership, while significant, is not determinative in the absence of centralized control over labor relations. Applying this standard to the facts before us, we find, contrary to the judge, that the Respondent and Southtowns do not constitute a single employer.

B.   Common Ownership

Because Southtowns is owned 50 percent by the Respondent and 50 percent by Our Lady of Victory Hospital, and the Respondent and Our Lady of Victory Hospital are in turn wholly owned by the Catholic Health System, some degree of common ownership is present. Common ownership alone, however, does not establish a single-employer relationship. A single-employer relationship will be found only if one of the entities exercises actual or active control over the day-to-day operations or labor relations of the other. The record is clear that each of the entities involved in this case retains operational independence.

C.   Common Management

The judge found common management based on the following: James Connolly was president and chief operating officer of both the Respondent and Southtowns until February 1999. In February 1999, Connolly was succeeded by John Davanzo at the Respondent, but Connolly remained as president of Southtowns. Both Connolly and Davanzo were on the board of directors for Southtowns. Further, the board of directors for the Respondent and Our Lady of Victory, who jointly own Southtowns, are identical.

We find that the factors relied on by the judge are insufficient to establish common management. During the time that Connolly was President of both Southtowns and the Respondent, Southtowns was not legally able to operate the MRI at the MACC, because it had not obtained the necessary licenses from the State of New York. Therefore, it was impossible for the Respondent to exercise control over the day-to-day operations of Southtowns through Connolly, because Southtowns had no relevant employee operations to control during that period. By the time Southtowns received its license to operate an MRI in September 1999, the Respondent and Southtowns had separate presidents. Further, although there is some overlap of directors—i.e., Connolly is a member of the board of directors of both entities—the fact that each entity has its own president with responsibility for the day-to-day operations of the companies precludes a finding of common management based on the existence of common directors.

Similarly, we find that the fact the board of directors of the Respondent and Our Lady of Victory are identical does not evince the necessary overlap of shared operations necessary to find single employer status between those two entities, in the absence of evidence that they also have common officers in control of their day-to-day operating decisions.

D.   Centralized Control Over Labor Relations

The judge found evidence of common control over labor relations in the role played by Martin Oscadal at the Respondent and Southtowns. From 1993 to March 1999, Oscadal was vice president for human resources for both the Catholic Health System and the Respondent. According to Oscadal, as the human resources official for the Respondent, he was "responsible for all the human resource functions, which would have been: recruitment, employee labor relations, compensation benefits; . . . employee health and workmen's compensation."

At the time of the hearing in October 1999, Oscadal was no longer the Respondent's vice president. Instead, since March 1999, he was the human resource official for the Catholic Health System, with responsibility for the facilities under the umbrella of that system, including Southtowns. As the human resources official for the Catholic Health System, Oscadal was primarily responsible for recruitment and training. Significantly, he testified that he had no responsibility for labor relations, compensation, or benefits. Moreover, although the Catholic Health System includes Southtowns, the undisputed evidence is that Southtowns does not have any employees. The employees who staff the new MRI at the MACC site are employed by Orchard Park, a wholly owned subsidiary of Abbott Radiology. Neither Abbott Radiology nor Orchard Park are part of the Catholic Health System, and thus neither operates under the authority of Oscadal as human resources official for the Catholic Health System. Indeed, the undisputed testimony of Oscadal establishes the Respondent does not have any employees at the new MRI facility; the Respondent does not have any supervisory authority or other relationship with the employees of Orchard Park at the new MRI facility; no personnel policies of the Respondent, or of the Catholic Health System, are applied to the employees at the new MRI facility; and neither the Respondent nor the Catholic Health System controls or is involved in the labor relations or the terms and conditions of employment of those employees.

Ordinarily, Oscadal's testimony would be sufficient to defeat a single-employer finding. However, the judge discredited Oscadal's testimony because he found it to be partial and inconsistent with documentary evidence. For instance, the judge found Oscadal's testimony inconsistent with his February 5, 1999 letter to the Union, which stated that the employees providing the MRI services at the new MRI site are employed by Abbott Radiology, that the Respondent had no legal ownership or interest in Abbott Radiology, and that *eventually the employees providing the MRI services at the MACC site would be employed by Southtowns.* (Emphasis added.)

The judge also cited several documents which he described as establishing, contrary to Oscadal's testimony, that Abbott Radiology, Orchard Park, Southtowns, Mercy Hospital, and the Catholic Health System are so interrelated as to be functionally dependent on each other. First, he cited the newsletter "Bridge" published by the Catholic Health Systems, which stated, "Two Catholic Health Systems hospitals have partnered with Abbott Radiology" on the MRI project. Second, the judge cited an internal memorandum stating that the MRI at the MACC is owned by "Our Lady of Victory, Mercy, and Southtowns Radiology." Third, the judge cited an equipment lease between MRI Associates and Orchard Park, signed by Noel Chiantella on behalf of Orchard Park, which shows that Orchard Park was the "lessee" of the MRI equipment owned by MRI Associates. Fourth, he cited a lease agreement, dated March 20, 1998, between MRI Associates and Orchard Park, signed by Connolly on behalf of the former and Chiantella on behalf of the latter. Fifth, the judge cited two documents titled, "Continuing Guaranty," in which Chiantella signs the first on behalf of Orchard Park, and the second for himself, each as guarantor for a loan by MRI Associates as the borrower. Finally, the judge cited a certificate of MRI Associate, L.L.C., which states that it is in good standing in the State of New York. The certificate is signed by Dr. Noel Chiantella, Dr. Mary L. Turkiewicz, and Dr. James Connolly, as members of the limited liability corporation. Chiantella and Turkiewicz are physicians of Abbott Radiology. Connolly is the president of Mercy Hospital.

While the Board attaches great weight to an administrative law judge's credibility findings based on demeanor, it may proceed to an independent evaluation of a witnesses' credibility when the administrative law judge has based his credibility findings on factors other than demeanor. We have carefully examined the documentary evidence on which the judge based his credibility findings. Contrary to the judge, we find nothing in the documentary evidence which is inconsistent with Oscadal's testimony. We therefore conclude that the judge's refusal to credit Oscadal's testimony was in error. Accordingly, we reverse the judge's credibility findings in this regard.

Based on the above, we find that the General Counsel has failed to demonstrate common control over labor relations between the Respondent and Southtowns.

E.   Functional Interrelation of Operations

The judge found evidence of interrelated operations in MRI Associates' lease of property from the Respondent, and in Southtowns's lease from MRI Associates of the building housing the MRI. The judge found additional evidence of interrelation of operations in the fact that the Respondent was able to close its own MRI facility at the Medical Park as a result of the opening of the Southtowns facility. The judge found further evidence of an interrelationship in the Respondent's furnishing, through unit employees, linen and garbage service at the Southtowns site; in the Respondent's loan of an oxygen valve to the new MRI; and in the employment of Virginia Buranich, one of the Respondent's former MRI technologists, at the new site.

Contrary to the judge, we do not find significant the Respondent's lease of land to MRI Associates or MRI Associates' lease of the building to

Southtowns. Those arrangements are pursuant to written agreements which provide for full reimbursement. In the absence of any indication that the agreements are not arm's length, we do not find that these mutually convenient arrangements detract from the corporate independence of the entities. Similarly, regarding the Respondent's decision to close its own MRI facility and use the Southtowns facility in its stead, we find that the Respondent and Southtowns have an arm's-length customer-supplier relationship that does not detract from their separate corporate identities. The other evidence of interrelation which the judge cited—combined linen and garbage services, the loan of an oxygen valve, and the employment by Southtowns of a former employee of the Respondent—is not sufficient to show the degree of interrelatedness necessary to find single employer status.

In summary, based on our examination of the four criteria of single-employer status, we find that the record does not substantiate the judge's characterization of the two entities at issue here. Although there is some degree of common ownership, in that the Respondent is one of two 50 percent owners of Southtowns, the other three factors, including the "critical" factor of centralized control of labor relations, are absent. Based on this record, we find that the Respondent and Southtowns are not a single employer. We therefore dismiss the allegation that the Respondent violated Sections 8(a)(5) and (1) by failing to apply its collective-bargaining agreement with the Union to the employees of Orchard Park performing MRI services at the Southtowns facility.

NOTES

1. *The single employer doctrine.* The "single employer" rubric "normally applies . . . to situations in which ongoing, nominally distinct businesses are alleged to be one and the same in terms of common control over labor relations, integration of operations, common management and common ownership." *Gilroy Sheet Metal*, 280 N.L.R.B. 1075 (1986). Even if it is determined that the examined firms constitute a single employer, union representation and the collective bargaining agreement will not be extended to cover the nonunion employees unless the two groups of employees are found to constitute an appropriate bargaining unit. If the groups of employees are found to constitute two separate bargaining units, then, consistent with Section 7 and *South Prairie Construction*, a separate determination must be made as to employee representation in the nonunion unit.

Recall the "perma-temps" who work at Microsoft, *supra* p. 219. Assume that, as part of WashTech's organizing drive among orange-carded perma-temps and blue-carded full-time workers, it is first determined that the controlling criteria of "interrelation of operations, common management, centralized control of labor relations and common ownership," *Radio & Television Broad. Technicians Local Union 1264 v. Broadcast Service*, 380 U.S. 255, 256 (1965), are satisfied. Shouldn't we be able to assume that a bargaining unit combining the two groups is also appropriate? Why or why not? For more about determining the appropriate bargaining unit, see Chapter 4, *infra* p. 521.

2.   *Labor relations, front and center.* The most important factor in the single employer test is whether the entities are organized with centralized labor relations. Why should this be so? Isn't the effect of this test merely to encourage the union-avoiding employer to hire two human resources managers instead of one? Could a single economic entity have multiple centers of labor relations management? Indeed, many modern corporations undertake operations with decentralized labor relations that are conducted with more or less independence at each geographic site. For a critique of the single employer doctrine, see Stephen F. Befort, *Labor Law and the Double-Breasted Employer: A Critique of the Single Employer and Alter Ego Doctrines and a Proposed Reformulation*, 1987 Wisc. L. Rev. 67.

3.   *Mercy, mercy me?* If Mercy Hospital and Southtowns do not constitute a single economic entity, then must they be considered economic competitors? After all, don't they share an economic interest? Why would Mercy Hospital send patients to Southtowns if it didn't have an economic interest in that outcome?

b.   The Alter Ego Doctrine

As noted above, an "alter ego" status often involves an effort to avoid a collective bargaining obligation through a sham transaction. In deciding whether a nonunion company is the alter ego of a unionized employer, the NLRB will often look to factors that bear similarities to those analyzed under the single employer doctrine, such as whether the two entities have substantially identical management, business purpose, operation, equipment, customers, supervision, and ownership. *See, e.g.,* Carpenters *Union Local No. 1846 v. Pratt-Farnsworth Inc.*, 690 F.2d 489, 507 (5th Cir. 1982). But the focus of the alter ego doctrine, unlike that of single employer doctrine, is on the existence of the unionized employer's disguised continuance as a nonunion entity, or its attempt to avoid the obligations of collective bargaining agreement through a technical change in operations. *Id.* at 508. The following case illustrates how this may occur.

MICHAEL'S PAINTING, INC. & PAINTING L.A., INC.
337 N.L.R.B. 860 (2002), *enf'd*, 85 Fed. Appx. 614 (9th Cir. 2004)

By CHAIRMAN HURTGEN and MEMBERS LIEBMAN and BARTLETT:

The Board has considered the decision and the record in light of the exceptions and briefs and has decided to affirm the judge's rulings, findings, and conclusions and to adopt the recommended Order as modified and set forth in full below.

JAY R. POLLACK, ADMINISTRATIVE LAW JUDGE:

The complaint alleges that Respondent Painting L.A., Inc. (L.A.) is an alter ego of Respondent Michael's Painting, Inc. (Michael's). The complaint further alleges that Respondent violated the Act by discharging or laying off employees, and conditioning employment on production of immigration documents in retaliation for the employees' union activities. Moreover, the complaint alleges that Respondents unlawfully interrogated employees, took picket signs away from employees, and threatened to close its business. Finally the complaint alleges that a bargaining order is the proper remedy for Respondents' egregious conduct. Respondents deny that Respondent L.A. is an alter ego of Respondent Michael's and Respondents deny the commission of any unfair labor practices.

A. Facts

Respondent Michael's was a painting contractor in Van Nuys, California. The only officers, stockholders, and directors of the corporation were Michael Abikasis and his wife, Laurie Abikasis.

During January and February 1998, the Union held a series of meetings for the employees of Respondent Michael's. The Union officials discussed union benefits and also questioned whether Respondents were paid the prevailing wages required by certain of its subcontracts on government jobs. At these meetings, union authorization cards were distributed and signed.

On March 27, employees of Michael's Painting accompanied by agents of the Union began picketing Michael's Painting's jobsite in Santa Monica, California. Employees Alejandro Duenas, Jose Lainez, Guadalupe Salazar, Jose Salazar, Martin Salas, and Saul Romero, participated in the picketing which took place during the employees' lunch break. The signs protested the alleged failure to pay prevailing wages. Respondent Michael's supervisor, Vicente Cheverria, took picket signs away from Lainez and Jose Salazar. After the employees had returned to work, Cheverria questioned the employees as to whether they joined or supported the Union. The employees answered that they supported the Union. Respondent had 12 employees on its payroll at this time.

On the afternoon of March 27, employees also picketed at the offices of Respondent Michael's with signs protesting the alleged failure to pay prevailing wages. The signs stated, "We need a Union," "Michael's Painting is unfair," "Michael's fired me for asking for the legal wage," and "Michael's Painting doesn't pay prevailing wages." Union Business Agent Alexander Lopez told Laurie Abikasis that he had signed union authorization cards from Respondents' employees. Lopez read the names of the employees to [Ms.] Abikasis. Laurie Abikasis told Lopez that she didn't have anything to do with Respondent Michael's. Lopez answered that she owned 51 percent of the Company. Laurie Abikasis told Lopez to return Monday, March 30, to speak with Michael Abikasis, and Lopez agreed to do so. That same afternoon, Laurie Abikasis questioned employee Alejandro Duenas about his union sentiments. Laurie Abikasis also told employee Carlos Vega not to talk to the people picketing.

The picketing moved to the Abikasis' residence during the evening of March 27. Laurie Abikasis told the employees that Respondent did not want the Union and did not need the Union. She also said that she and her husband would close the Company rather than become a union shop. Laurie Abikasis said she could not afford to be Union; she would go broke if she became a union shop, and that the union agents were parasites.

On Monday, March 30, Laurie Abikasis told each of the employees that their paychecks could not be released unless the employees first provided a green card, social security number, or driver's license. Laurie told Duenas that his social security number was not valid and if he did not bring a valid green card, social security card, or driver's license, he could no longer work for Respondent Michael's.

Prior to this dispute, Respondent was indifferent towards immigration documents. Cheverria had told job applicants that they could present fake immigration documents, it made no difference to Respondent Michael's. Further, prior to this dispute, Respondent Michael's only requested immigration documents at the time of an employee's hire. There was no follow-up. However, on the afternoon of March 30, Laurie and Michael Abikasis told five employees that they could not receive their paychecks absent valid documentation. The employees were eventually paid that afternoon.

The next day, on March 31, Respondent Painting L.A. was incorporated. When Lainez, Duenas, Romero, Martin Vega, and Carlos Vega reported for work, Michael Abikasis turned them away. Abikasis said, "There is no more work for you guys. It's finito." The employees did not work for Respondent Michael's again. On April 2, the board of directors of Respondent L.A. (Laurie Abikasis) approved the purchase of the assets and vehicles of Respondent Michael's. On April 15, Michael's Painting accepted an offer from Painting L.A. for Respondent L.A. to perform warranty work on Respondent Michael's outstanding jobs. On May 8, acting through an escrow agent, Respondent Michael's sold its assets to Respondent L.A. in return for the cancellation of an allegedly preexisting obligation to Painting L.A.

Laurie Abikasis is the sole shareholder, director and officer of Respondent L.A. However, Respondent L.A.'s employee rules instruct employees that their work must be satisfactory to Michael Abikasis. Michael Abikasis made hiring, firing, and wage determinations for Respondent L.A. Further Michael Abikasis visited jobsites and gave work directions to employees and foremen. Michael Abikasis was the contact person for Respondent L.A.'s customers.

[During April, Lainez sought work from Respondent Painting L.A. Lainez had worked for Respondent Michael's for 3 years. Laurie and Michael Abikasis questioned Lainez regarding his union authorization card and the cards of other employees. Lainez answered these questions in writing, desiring to obtain employment with Respondents. However, Lainez was never called back to work.]

Respondent L.A.'s payroll records show that it did not employ any employees until June, when it employed 10 employees. Three of these employees had been employed by Respondent Michael's on March 27, but did not engage in the picketing. The only other employee of Respondent's Michael's who did not engage in the picketing was later hired as a supervisor by Respondent L.A. Respondent L.A. did not employ the other eight employees on Respondent Michael's payroll on March 27.

Respondents contend that Respondent Michael's ceased doing business and Respondent L.A. commenced its painting business solely because of the troubles Respondent Michael's was having in obtaining liability insurance. Respondent Michael's liability insurance was set to expire on March 1, 1998. Due to over 10 claims for product defects against the Company, the company was facing significant increased costs for insurance premiums. Laurie Abikasis and Respondent Michael's insurance agent concluded that the only way to obtain affordable insurance for the business was to obtain insurance under the name of Painting L.A. Since Painting L.A. did not have a loss history, Painting L.A. was able to obtain insurance at a premium agreeable to Laurie Abikasis. Based on these facts, I conclude that even in the absence of the union activities described above, Respondents would have commenced business as Painting L.A. on April 1, 1998.

The parties stipulated that the following employees of Respondents, constitute an appropriate collective-bargaining unit: All painters employed by Michael's Painting at its Van Nuys, California facility excluding office clerical workers, guards, and supervisors as defined in the Act. The General Counsel alleges that on March 27, the Union had obtained signed authorization cards from a majority of the employees in the unit. The General Counsel offered 18 authorization cards to establish a card majority prior to March 27, 1998. I find that by March 27, 1998, the Union had 18 valid authorization cards in a bargaining unit consisting of 34 employees.

B. Conclusions

1. Alter ego

The complaint alleges that Respondent Painting L.A. is an alter ego of Respondent Michael's Painting. The criteria the Board looks to in deciding alter ego status are substantially identical management, business purposes, operation, equipment, customers, supervision, and ownership. See *Merchants Iron & Steel Corp.*, 321 N.L.R.B. 360 (1996).

In *Perma Coatings*, 293 N.L.R.B. 803, 804 (1989), the Board stated:

> While it is true that a sincere motivation for operation of a new corporation does not preclude finding alter ego status, the absence of union animus nevertheless generally militates against finding a "disguised continuance" of the predecessor. The Board in *Perma Coatings*, *supra*, found no alter ego where there was no substantial commonality of ownership and no evidence of antiunion animus.

As stated above, I find that Laurie and Michael Abikasis established Respondent L.A. to continue operating their painting business without the substantially higher insurance premiums that would have been charged Respondent Michael's. There can be no doubt that Respondent L.A. continued the business of Respondent Michael's with the identical management, business purposes, operation, equipment, customers, supervision, and ownership. The only change in the business was the name. Just 4 days prior to the name change, Respondents were faced with the unwanted demands of the employees for higher wages and union representation.

From the record evidence it is apparent that Respondents used the formation of Respondent L.A. to rid itself of the eight employees who had picketed Respondent Michael's in support of the claims for higher wages and union recognition. I find that there is strong evidence of union animus. The evidence reveals that Respondents firmly believed that the costs of the Union's demands would put Respondents out of business. Laurie Abikasis threatened to close the business rather than become a union shop. Michael Abikasis admitted that as long as the employees supported the Union, he would not assign them work. There was no lawful reason why Respondents had to discharge the employees after the name of the business was changed to Painting L.A. for insurance reasons.

All the indicia for the finding of an alter ego are present in this case. The fact that Respondents changed the name of the business to avoid higher insurance premiums should not allow Respondents to avoid its obligations to the employees and the Union under the Act.

[Judge Pollack went on to find that the employer committed several violations of the NLRA in that: (1) union animus was a substantial and motivating factor in the discharge of the five employees, Duenas, Romero, Lainez, Carlos Vega, and Martin Vega, in violation of Section 8(a)(3); (2) union animus was a substantial and motivating factor in the demands for additional documentation of legal immigration in violation of Section 8(a)(1); (3) confiscation of employee picket signs interfered with protected activity in violation of Section 8(a)(1); (4) Laurie Abikasis' statements that Respondents would close the business rather than become a union shop were coercive of employees' Section 7 rights in violation of Section 8(a)(1); and (5) the questioning of Lainez by Michael and Laurie Abikasis about the circumstances under which he and the other employees signed their union authorization cards constituted coercive interrogation in violation of Section 8(a)(1).]

The Remedy

Having found that Respondents engaged in unfair labor practices, I shall recommend that they be ordered to cease and desist therefrom and take certain affirmative action to effectuate the policies of the Act.

I shall recommend that Respondents offer Jose Lainez, Alejandro Duenas, Carlos Vega, Martin Vega, and Saul Romero full and immediate reinstatement to the positions they would have held, but for their unlawful terminations. Further, Respondents shall be directed to make whole Jose Lainez, Alejandro Duenas, Carlos Vega, Martin Vega, and Saul Romero for any and all loss of earnings and other rights, benefits, and privileges of employment they may have suffered by reason of Respondents' discrimination against them, with interest. Respondents shall be required, upon request, to recognize and bargain collectively with Southern California Painters and Allied Trades, District Council No. 36, Affiliated with International Brotherhood of Painters and Allied Trades, AFL-CIO, as the exclusive collective-bargaining representative from March 27, 1998, with respect to the painters employed by Respondents, regarding wages, hours, and other terms and conditions of employment and, if an understanding is reached, embody the understanding in a signed agreement.

NOTES

1. *Alter egos.* In determining whether an open shop is the "alter ego" of a union shop, the Board considers whether there is "substantially identical management, business purpose, operation, equipment, customers, and supervision, as well as ownership" and a "purpose to evade responsibilities under the Act." *Advance Electric*, 268 N.L.R.B. 1001 (1984). No single criterion is controlling. What result do you get if you apply the alter-ego doctrine to the facts of *Mercy Hospital, supra*, at p. 343? Do you get the same result as the Board did under the single-employer doctrine? What are the differences in the two tests? Is there a reason for having two tests? What criteria should the Board and courts consider in deciding whether to enforce collective bargaining responsibilities against a related business entity?

2. *Of alter egos, single employers, joint employers, corporate veils, and their friends (or "allies").* At least five distinct legal tests have been developed by the NLRB to determine whether and to what extent nominally separate legal entities are actually a single entity, and should be treated as such, under the NLRA. In addition to the single employer and alter ego doctrines, there are the "joint employer," "piercing the corporate veil," and the "ally" doctrines. *See* Grant Crandall, Sarah J. Starrett & Douglas L. Parker, *Hiding Behind The Corporate Veil: Employer Abuse Of The Corporate Form to Avoid or Deny*

Workers' Collectively Bargained and Statutory Rights, 100 W. Va. L. Rev. 537 (1998). Are five different doctrines needed to serve this purpose?

Under the Obama Board, the joint employer theory seemed to be receiving renewed attention. Following nationwide protests demanding that Burger King, McDonald's, Wendy's, and other name-brand fast food companies require their franchisees to pay employees a "living wage" in excess of the minimum wage—$15 per hour is the amount most commonly demanded—a number of employees were disciplined or discharged for taking part in the protests. Regarding the largest company, McDonald's USA LLC, the General Counsel responded by issuing consolidated complaints naming the franchisor, its franchisees, or both, as respondents on the theory that they were joint employers. As of December 2014, the General Counsel had issued 13 such complaints raising 78 separate charges filed across the country. Since November 2012, the General Counsel had received a total of 291 charges, some of which were resolved but many of which remained under investigation. *See* Office of Public Affairs, *NLRB Office of the General Counsel Issues Consolidated Complaints Against McDonald's Franchisees and their Franchisor McDonald's*, USA, LLC as Joint Employers (Dec. 19, 2014), available at https://www.nlrb.gov/news-outreach/news-story/nlrb-office-general-counsel-issues-consolidated-complaints-against. Of course, it remains to be seen whether the Board, and the courts, will agree with the General Counsel. With the change of administration, however, the new General Counsel changed direction and made plans to settle these cases. *See* Office of Public Affairs, *Proposed Settlement Agreements Presented McDonald's USA LLC, et al.*, Mar. 20, 2018, available at https://www.nlrb.gov/news-outreach/news-story/proposed-settlement-agreements-presented-mcdonald%E2%80%99s-usa-llc-et-al.

3.   *Arsenals and old lace.* The facts of *Michael's Painting* provided the Board with an opportunity to fire practically the entire arsenal of make-whole remedies authorized by the Act: the cease and desist order, reinstatement, backpay, and the bargaining order. And yet many have criticized these remedies as inadequate to ensure that employers will comply with their obligations. *See, e.g.*, Michael Weiner, *Can the NLRB Deter Unfair Labor Practices? Reassessing the Punitive-Remedial Distinction in Labor Law Enforcement*, 52 UCLA L. Rev. 1579 (2005); Robert M. Worster III, *If It's Hardly Worth Doing, It's Hardly Worth Doing Right: How the NLRA's Goals are Defeated Through Inadequate Remedies*, 38 U. Rich. L. Rev. 1073 (2004). Do you agree that such remedies do not adequately deter employer misconduct? If so, should fines or punitive damages be imposed? Why or why not? Would the Act have to be amended to add such remedies?

5. JOINT EMPLOYERS

As noted above, *supra* Chapter 3-B-1-b-i, the procurement of employees through staffing and subcontracting arrangements—a subset of contingent employment known as the temporary help services or employee leasing industry—is widespread, although the perception that such arrangements have undergone substantial expansion is likely misplaced.

According to the BLS, a temporary help agency worker is anyone "who [is] paid by a temporary help agency, whether or not [her] job is temporary." BLS, *Contingent and Alternative Employment Arrangements Summary* (Jun. 7, 2018), available at https://www.bls.gov/news.release/conemp.nr0. htm. In 2017, the CWS reported that 0.9% of the workforce, or 1.4 million people, worked in this capacity. *Id.* By contrast, in 2005, the CWS reported that the same percentage of the workforce, or 1.2 million people, worked for a temporary help agency. The modest increase suggests this type of contingent work arrangement is substantial but expanding modestly. See BLS, *Contingent and Alternative Work Arrangements*, at 5 (Jul. 27, 2005), available at https://www.bls.gov/news.release/archives/conemp_07272005. pdf.

In much of the temporary help services industry, a supplier company supplies or "leases" workers to the client or "user" company. Typically, the workers are carried on the payroll of the supplier company and directed in their day-to-day assignments by the client company, but there are many variations on this theme.

Even as the diversity of workplace arrangements in the U.S. economy has expanded, however, the Board's view of what constitutes employment under these circumstances has narrowed. An important example can be found in the Board's interpretation and application of the joint employer doctrine.

Under the joint employer doctrine, two or more entities are considered to be the joint employers of a single workforce if certain conditions are met.

In 1982, the U.S. Court of Appeals for the Third Circuit, in an influential opinion, enforced an NLRB decision holding that joint employment exists if two conditions are met: first, the putative employers are "employers" as defined by the common law; and second, they "share or codetermine those matters governing the essential terms and conditions of employment." *NLRB v. Browning-Ferris Industries of Pennsylvania, Inc.*, 691 F.2d 1117, 1123 (3d Cir. 1982), *enf'g* 259 N.L.R.B. 148 (1981) (*BFI I*). But starting in 1984, the Board articulated new conditions that made it harder to support a joint employer finding. The most significant of these new conditions was the requirement that a putative joint employer not only *possess* the authority to control employees' terms and conditions of employment but also *exercise* that authority. *See, e.g., TLI, Inc.*, 271 N.L.R.B. 798 (1984), *enf'd mem.* 772 F.2d 894 (3d Cir. 1985); *Laerco Transportation*, 269 N.L.R.B. 324 (1984).

In 2015, however, the Obama Board changed direction, and in *BFI II*, re-embraced *BFI I* and overruled *TLI, Laerco*, and their progeny. Although *BFI II* is reprinted here, its reasoning and result are under reconsideration by the Trump Board. In fact, in late 2017, the Trump Board issued a decision overturning *BFI II*, only to withdraw it two months later, when it came to light that participating Member William Emanuel, who had joined the overruling majority, had a conflict of interest. *See Hy-Brand Industrial Contractors, Inc.*, 365 N.L.R.B. No. 156 (2017), *vacated*, 366 N.L.R.B. No. 26 (2018). So *BFI II* remains the law—for now.

BROWNING-FERRIS INDUSTRIES OF CALIFORNIA, INC. (*BFI II*)
362 N.L.R.B. No. 186 (2015)

By CHAIRMAN PEARCE and MEMBERS MISCIMARRA, HIROZAWA, JOHNSON, and MCFERRAN:

DECISION ON REVIEW AND DIRECTION OF ELECTION

In this case, we consider whether the Board should adhere to its current standard for assessing joint-employer status under the National Labor Relations Act or whether that standard should be revised to better effectuate the purposes of the Act, in the current economic landscape.

The issue in this case is whether BFI Newby Island Recyclery (BFI), and Leadpoint Business Services (Leadpoint) are joint employers of the sorters, screen cleaners, and housekeepers whom the Union petitioned to represent. The Regional Director issued a Decision and Direction of Election finding that Leadpoint is the sole employer of the petitioned-for employees. The Union filed a timely request for review of that decision.

The current standard, as reflected in Board decisions such as *TLI, Inc.*, 271 N.L.R.B. 798 (1984), *enf'd mem.* 772 F.2d 894 (3d Cir. 1985), and *Laerco Transportation*, 269 N.L.R.B. 324 (1984), is *NLRB v. Browning-Ferris Industries of Pennsylvania, Inc.*, 691 F.2d 1117 (3d Cir. 1982), *enforcing* 259 N.L.R.B. 148 (1981) (*BFI I*), which endorsed the Board's then-longstanding standard. But, as we will explain, the Board, without explanation, has since imposed additional requirements for finding joint-employer status, which have no clear basis in the Third Circuit's decision, in the common law, or in the text or policies of the Act. The Board has never articulated how these additional requirements are compelled by the Act or by the common-law definition of the employment relationship. They appear inconsistent with prior case law that has not been expressly overruled.

Moreover, these additional requirements—which serve to significantly and unjustifiably narrow the circumstances where a joint-employment relationship can be found—leave the Board's joint-employment jurisprudence increasingly out of step with changing economic circumstances, particularly the recent dramatic growth in contingent employment relationships. This disconnect potentially undermines the core protections of the Act for the employees impacted by these economic changes.

Today, we restate the Board's joint-employer standard to reaffirm the standard articulated by the Third Circuit in the *BFI I* decision. Under this standard, the Board may find that two or more statutory employers are joint employers of the same statutory employees if they "share or codetermine those matters governing the essential terms and conditions of employment." In determining whether a putative joint employer meets this standard, the initial inquiry is whether there is a common-law employment relationship with the employees in question. If this common-law employment relationship exists, the inquiry then turns to whether the putative joint employer possesses sufficient control over employees' essential terms and conditions of employment to permit meaningful collective bargaining.

Central to both of these inquiries is the existence, extent, and object of the putative joint employer's control. Consistent with earlier Board decisions, as well as the common law, we will examine how control is manifested in a particular employment relationship. We reject those limiting requirements that the Board has imposed—without foundation in the statute or common law—after *BFI I*. We will no longer require that a joint employer not only possess the authority to control employees' terms and conditions of employment, but also exercise that authority. Reserved authority to control terms and conditions of employment, even if not exercised, is clearly relevant to the joint-employment inquiry. As the Supreme Court has observed, the question is whether one statutory employer "possesse[s] sufficient control over the work of the employees to qualify as a joint employer with" another employer. Nor will we require that, to be relevant to the joint-employer inquiry, a statutory employer's control must be exercised directly and immediately. If otherwise sufficient, control exercised indirectly—such as through an intermediary—may establish joint-employer status.

The Board's established presumption in representation cases like this one is to apply a new rule retroactively. Applying the restated joint-employer standard here, we reverse the Regional Director and find that the Union established that BFI and Leadpoint are joint employers of the employees in the petitioned-for unit.

I.   Facts

A.   Overview

BFI owns and operates the Newby Island recycling facility, which receives approximately 1,200 tons per day of mixed materials, mixed waste, and mixed recyclables. The essential part of its operation is the sorting of these materials into separate commodities that are sold to other businesses at the end of the recycling process. BFI solely employs approximately 60 employees, including loader operators, equipment operators, forklift operators, and spotters. Most of these BFI employees work outside the facility, where they move materials and prepare them to be sorted inside the facility. These BFI employees are part of an existing separate bargaining unit that is represented by the Union.

The interior of the facility houses four conveyor belts, called material streams. Each stream carries a different category of materials into the facility: residential mixed recyclables, commercial mixed recyclables, dry waste process, and wet waste process. Workers provided to BFI by Leadpoint stand on platforms beside the streams and sort through the material as it passes; depending on where they are stationed, workers remove from the stream either recyclable materials or prohibited materials. Other material is automatically sorted when it passes through screens that are positioned near the conveyor belts.

As indicated, BFI, the user firm, contracts with Leadpoint, the supplier firm, to provide the workers who manually sort the material on the streams (sorters), clean the screens on the sorting equipment and clear jams (screen cleaners), and clean the facility (housekeepers).

The Union seeks to represent approximately 240 full-time, part-time, and on-call sorters, screen cleaners, and housekeepers who work at the facility. The relationship between BFI and Leadpoint is governed by a temporary labor services agreement (Agreement), which took effect in October 2009, and remains effective indefinitely. It can be terminated by either party at will with 30 days' notice. The Agreement states that Leadpoint is the sole employer of the personnel it supplies, and that nothing in the Agreement shall be construed as creating an employment relationship between BFI and the personnel that Leadpoint supplies.

B.   Management Structure

BFI and Leadpoint employ separate supervisors and lead workers at the facility. BFI Operations Manager Paul Keck oversees the material recovery facility and supervises the BFI employees. BFI Division Manager Carl Mennie oversees the recycling and compost operations and reports to Keck. Shift Supervisors Augustine Ortiz and John Sutter supervise BFI employees at the site, including the control room operator. They also spend a percentage of each workday in the material stream areas, monitoring the operation and productivity of the streams. Ortiz testified that part of his job is to ensure the productivity of the streams.

Leadpoint employs Acting On-Site Manager Vincent Haas, three shift supervisors, and seven line leads who work with the Leadpoint sorters. Haas oversees Leadpoint operations at the facility and reports to the Leadpoint corporate office in Arizona. The shift supervisors, who report to Haas, create the sorters' schedules, oversee the material streams, and coach the line leads. The line leads work on the floor with the sorters and are Leadpoint's first-line supervisors. Frank Ramirez, Leadpoint's CEO and President, visits the facility two or three times per quarter to evaluate whether Leadpoint is meeting BFI's expectations and goals; he also meets with BFI and Leadpoint managers, and addresses any problems.

BFI and Leadpoint maintain separate human resource departments. BFI does not have an HR manager onsite. Leadpoint has an onsite HR manager who operates in a trailer (marked with the Leadpoint logo) outside the facility. Leadpoint employees use the BFI break rooms, bathrooms, and parking lot.

C.   Hiring

The Agreement between BFI and Leadpoint provides that Leadpoint will recruit, interview, test, select, and hire personnel to perform work for BFI. BFI Managers Keck and Mennie, and Shift Supervisors Ortiz and Sutter testified that they are not involved in Leadpoint's hiring procedure and have no input into Leadpoint's hiring decisions. However, as to hiring, the Agreement requires Leadpoint to ensure that its personnel "have the appropriate qualifications (including certification and training) consistent with all applicable laws and instructions from [BFI], to perform the general duties of the assigned position." BFI also has the right to request that personnel supplied by Leadpoint "meet or exceed [BFI's] own standard selection procedures and tests."

The Agreement also requires Leadpoint to make "reasonable efforts" not to refer workers who were previously employed by BFI and were deemed ineligible for rehire. Under the Agreement, Leadpoint must ask workers if they were previously employed by BFI and verify with BFI that all workers provided are eligible to work with BFI. If Leadpoint inadvertently refers an ineligible worker, it must immediately cease referring her, upon notification by BFI.

D.   Discipline and Termination

Although the Agreement provides that Leadpoint has sole responsibility to counsel, discipline, review, evaluate, and terminate personnel who are assigned to BFI, it also grants BFI the authority to "reject any Personnel, and . . . discontinue the use of any personnel for any or no reason."

BFI Managers Keck and Mennie, and Shift Supervisors Ortiz and Sutter testified that they have never been involved in any disciplinary decisions for Leadpoint employees. However, the record includes evidence of two incidents where discipline of Leadpoint employees was prompted by BFI action. In a June 2013 email from BFI Operations Manager Keck to Leadpoint CEO Ramirez, Keck stated that he observed two Leadpoint employees passing a pint of whiskey at the jobsite. Keck then contacted Leadpoint Manager Haas, who immediately sent the two employees for alcohol and drug screening. Ramirez testified that, in response to Keck's email "request[ing] [the employees'] immediate dismissal," Leadpoint investigated the complaint and terminated one employee and reassigned the other.

E.   Wages and Benefits

The Agreement includes a rate schedule that requires BFI to compensate Leadpoint for each worker's wage plus a specified percentage mark-up; the mark-up varies based on whether the work is performed during regular hours or as overtime. Although the Agreement provides that Leadpoint "solely determines the pay rates paid to its Personnel," it may not, without BFI's approval, "pay a pay rate in excess of the pay rate for full-time employees of [BFI] who perform similar tasks." Mennie testified that Leadpoint has never made such a request. Leadpoint issues paychecks to employees and maintains their payroll records.

The record includes a Rate Schedule Addendum between BFI and Leadpoint executed in response to a minimum wage increase from $8.75 to $10 by the City of San Jose. Pursuant to the Addendum, the parties agreed that BFI would pay a higher hourly rate for the services of Leadpoint employees after the minimum wage increase took effect.

Leadpoint employees are required to sign a benefits waiver stating they are eligible only for benefits offered by Leadpoint and are not eligible to participate in any benefit plan offered by BFI. Leadpoint provides employees with paid time-off and three paid holidays after they have worked for 2,000 hours, and the option to purchase medical, life, and disability insurance.

F.   Scheduling and Hours

BFI establishes the facility's schedule of working hours. It operates three set shifts on weekdays: 4 a.m. to 1:00 p.m., 2:00 p.m. to 11:30 p.m., and 10:30 p.m. to 7:00 a.m. Leadpoint is responsible for providing employees to cover all three shifts. Although Leadpoint alone schedules which employees will work each shift, Leadpoint has no input on shift schedules. Keck testified that any modification in shift times would require modifying the facility's hours of operation and the work schedules for all BFI employees.

BFI will keep a stream running into overtime if it determines that the material on a specific stream cannot be processed by the end of a shift. A BFI manager will normally convey this decision to a Leadpoint shift supervisor; Leadpoint, in turn, determines which employees will stay on the stream to complete the overtime work.

BFI also dictates when the streams stop running so that Leadpoint employees can take breaks. Keck has instructed Leadpoint employees to spend 5 minutes gathering the debris around their stations before breaking. Although Keck asserted that this assignment would not affect the length of breaks, sorter Andrew Mendez testified that, as a practical matter, the clean-up requirement has cut into employees' break time.

G.   Work Processes

BFI determines which material streams will run each day and provides Leadpoint with a target headcount of workers needed. BFI also dictates the number of Leadpoint laborers to be assigned to each material stream, but Leadpoint assigns specific Leadpoint employees to specific posts. The record includes an email from Keck to Haas directing Haas to reduce the number of sorters on a specific line by two per shift. The email detailed what positions sorters should occupy on the stream, what materials should be prioritized, and whether a right-handed or left-handed sorter was preferred. The email concluded by stating "[t]his staffing change is effective Monday, August 5, 2013." Ramirez testified that the sorters occupy set work stations along each stream and that BFI dictates the location of these stations. During a shift, BFI might direct Leadpoint supervisors to move employees to another stream in response to processing demands.

BFI managers set productivity standards for the material streams. BFI Division Manager Mennie testified that BFI tracks the tons per hour processed on each stream, the proportion of running time to downtime on each stream, and various quality standards. BFI has sole authority to set the speed of the material streams based on its ongoing assessment of the optimal speed at which materials can be sorted most efficiently.

H.   Training and Safety

When Leadpoint employees begin working at the facility, they receive an orientation and job training from Leadpoint supervisors. Periodically, they also receive substantive training and counseling from BFI managers.

As to safety, the Agreement mandates that Leadpoint require its employees to comply with BFI's safety policies, procedures, and training requirements. For all employees working in positions deemed safety-sensitive by BFI, Leadpoint must obtain a written acknowledgement that they have read, understand, and agree to comply with BFI's safety policy. BFI also "reserves the right to enforce the Safety Policy provided to [Leadpoint] personnel."

II.   The Regional Director's Findings

The Regional Director, applying *TLI*, found that BFI is not a joint-employer of the Leadpoint employees because it does not "share or codetermine [with Leadpoint] those matters governing the essential terms and conditions of employment" of the sorters, screen cleaners, or housekeepers.

* * *

V. Revisiting the Joint-Employer Standard

As the Board's view of what constitutes joint employment under the Act has narrowed, the diversity of workplace arrangements in today's economy has significantly expanded. The procurement of employees through staffing and subcontracting arrangements, or contingent employment, has increased steadily since *TLI* was decided. The most recent Bureau of Labor Statistics survey from 2005 indicated that contingent workers accounted for as much as 4.1 percent of all employment, or 5.7 million workers. Employment in the temporary help services industry, a subset of contingent work, grew from 1.1 million to 2.3 million workers from 1990 to 2008. As of August 2014, the number of workers employed through temporary agencies had climbed to a new high of 2.87 million, a 2 percent share of the nation's work force. Over the same period, temporary employment also expanded into a much wider range of occupations. A recent report projects that the number of jobs in the employment services industry, which includes employment placement agencies and temporary help services, will increase to almost 4 million by 2022, making it "one of the largest and fastest growing [industries] in terms of employment."

This development is reason enough to revisit the Board's current joint-employer standard.

We begin with the obvious proposition that in order to find that a statutory employer (i.e., an employer subject to the National Labor Relations Act) that has a duty to bargain with a union representing a particular group of statutory employees, the Act requires the existence of an employment relationship between the employer and the employees. Section 2(3) of the Act provides that the "term 'employee' . . . shall not be limited to the employees of a particular employer, unless the Act explicitly states otherwise." Section 9(c) authorizes the Board to process a representation petition when it alleges that "employees . . . wish to be represented for collective bargaining . . . and their employer declines to recognize their representative." Section 8(a)(5), in turn, makes it an unfair labor practice for an employer "to refuse to bargain collectively with the representatives of his employees."

In determining whether an employment relationship exists for purposes of the Act, the Board must follow the common-law agency test. The Supreme Court has made this clear in connection with Section 2(3) of the Act and its exclusion of "any individual having the status of an independent contractor" from the Act's otherwise broad definition of statutory employees. In determining whether a common-law employment relationship exists in cases arising under Federal statutes like the Act, the Court has regularly looked to the Restatement (Second) of Agency (1958) for guidance. Section 220(1) of the Restatement (Second) provides that a "servant is a person employed to perform services in the affairs of another and who with respect to the physical conduct in the performance of the services is subject to the other's control or right to control."

The core of the Board's current joint-employer standard—with its focus on whether the putative joint employer "share(s) or codetermine(s) those matters governing the essential terms and conditions of employment"—is firmly grounded in the concept of control that is central to the common-law definition of an employment relationship. The Act surely permits the Board to adopt that formulation. No federal court has suggested otherwise, and the Third Circuit in *BFI I*, of course, has endorsed this aspect of the standard.

Under common-law principles, the right to control is probative of an employment relationship—whether or not that right is exercised. Sections 2(2) and 220(1) of the Restatement (Second) of Agency make this plain, in referring to a master as someone who "controls or has the right to control" another and to a servant as "subject to the [employer's] control or right to control" (emphasis added). In setting forth the test for distinguishing between employees and independent contractors, Restatement (Second) Section 220(2), considers (among other factors) the "extent of control which, by the agreement, the master may exercise over the details of the work" (emphasis added). The Board's joint-employer decisions requiring the exercise of control impermissibly ignore this principle.

Where a user employer reserves a contractual right (emphasis added) to set a specific term or condition of employment for a supplier employer's workers, it retains the ultimate authority to ensure that the term in question is administered in accordance with its preferences. Where a user has reserved authority, we assume that it has rationally chosen to do so, in its own interest. There is no unfairness, then, in holding that legal consequences may follow from this choice.

VI. The Restated Joint-Employer Standard

We return to the traditional test used by the Board (and endorsed by the Third Circuit in *BFI I*): The Board may find that two or more entities are joint employers of a single work force if they are both employers within the meaning of the common law, and if they share or codetermine those matters governing the essential terms and conditions of employment. In evaluating the allocation and exercise of control in the workplace, we will consider the various ways in which joint employers may "share" control over terms and conditions of employment or "codetermine" them, as the Board and the courts have done in the past.

We adhere to the Board's inclusive approach in defining "essential terms and conditions of employment." The Board's current joint-employer standard refers to "matters relating to the employment relationship such as hiring, firing, discipline, supervision, and direction" a nonexhaustive list of bargaining subjects. Essential terms indisputably include wages and hours, as reflected in the Act itself. Other examples of control over mandatory terms and conditions of employment found probative by the Board include dictating the number of workers to be supplied; controlling scheduling, seniority, and overtime; and assigning work and determining the manner and method of work performance. This approach has generally been endorsed by the Federal courts of appeals.

Also consistent with the Board's traditional approach, we reaffirm that the common-law concept of control informs the Board's joint-employer standard. But we will no longer require that a joint employer not only possess the authority to control employees' terms and conditions of employment, but must also exercise that authority, and do so directly, immediately, and not in a "limited and routine" manner. Accordingly, we overrule *Laerco*, *TLI*, *A&M Property*, and *Airborne Express*, and other Board decisions, to the extent that they are inconsistent with our decision today. The right to control, in the common-law sense, is probative of joint-employer status, as is the actual exercise of control, whether direct or indirect.

Our dissenting colleagues accuse us of articulating a test "with no limiting principle" that "removes all limitations on what kind or degree of control over essential terms and conditions of employment may be sufficient to warrant a joint-employer finding." This is simply not the case. The dissent ignores the limitations that are inherent to the common law, particularly those set forth in the Restatement provisions enumerated above. Instead, the dissent suggests that, under the revised joint-employer test, a homeowner who hires a plumber or a lender who sets the homeowner's financing terms may each be deemed a statutory employer. But by any common-law analysis, these parties will not exercise, or have the right to exercise, the requisite control over the details of employees' work to forge common-law employment relationships. It should therefore come as no surprise that the annals of Board precedent contain no cases that implicate the consumer services purchased by unsuspecting homeowners or lenders.

The dissent is particularly pointed in its criticism of our assignment of probative weight to a putative employer's indirect control over employees; it contends that "anyone contracting for services, master or not, inevitably will exert and/or reserve some measure of indirect control by defining the parameters of the result desired to ensure he or she gets the benefit of his or her bargain." We see no reason why this obvious control of employees by BFI should be discounted merely because it was exercised via the supplier rather than directly.

VII. Response to Dissent's Arguments Regarding the Common Law

Notwithstanding the strong basis in common law for the standard we adopt, our dissenting colleagues assert repeatedly that the Board is not applying common law but instead reverting to the "economic realities" test that was once applied by the Supreme Court in *NLRB v. Hearst Publications*, 322 U.S. 111 (1944). In *Hearst*, the Court interpreted the Act to include "employees (who) are at times brought into an economic relationship with employers who are not their employers"; to "reject conventional limitations" in defining an employee or employer; and to intend that those definitions be applied "broadly . . . by underlying economic facts." Our dissenting colleagues also assert that while the *Hearst* standard would include indirect control over terms of employment within the definition of joint employer, common law does not.

Both of these assertions are incorrect. As we have already made clear, our revised standard considers—as does common law—only an entity's control over terms of employment, not the wider universe of all "underlying economic facts" that surround an employment relationship. Moreover, courts applying the "economic realities" test for an employer under the Fair Labor Standards Act and the Agricultural Workers Protection Act (AWPA) have recognized that although that test is significantly more expansive than the common-law test, indirect control over terms of employment is clearly a factor in the common-law test.

VIII.   Application of the Restated Test

With the above principles in mind, we evaluate here whether BFI constitutes a joint employer under the Act. As always, the burden of proving joint-employer status rests with the party asserting that relationship. Having assessed all of the relevant record evidence, we conclude that the Union has met its burden of establishing that BFI is a statutory joint employer of the sorters, screen cleaners, and housekeepers at issue. The facts demonstrate that it shares or codetermines those matters governing the essential terms and conditions of employment for the Leadpoint employees. In many relevant respects, its right to control is indisputable. Moreover, it has exercised that control, both directly and indirectly.

IX. The Implications of Today's Decision

Our colleagues' long and hyperbolic dissent persistently mischaracterizes the standard we adopt today and grossly exaggerates its consequences, but makes no real effort to address the difficult issue presented here: how best to "encourag[e] the practice and procedure of collective bargaining" (in the Act's words) when otherwise bargainable terms and conditions of employment are under the control of more than one statutory employer. Instead, the dissent puts the preservation of the current status quo far ahead of any cognizable statutory policy. Our colleagues never adequately explain why the Board should adhere to an approach that they essentially concede is not compelled by the common law and that demonstrably fails to fully advance the goals of the Act.

The law-school-exam hypothetical of doomsday scenarios that they predict will result from today's decision is likewise based on an exaggeration of the challenges that can sometimes arise when multiple employers are required to engage in collective bargaining. The potential for these types of challenges to arise has existed for as long as the Board has recognized the joint-employer concept. Nonetheless, employers and unions have long managed to navigate these challenges, and the predicted disasters have not come to pass.

It is not the goal of joint-employer law to guarantee the freedom of employers to insulate themselves from their legal responsibility to workers, while maintaining control of the workplace. Such an approach has no basis in the Act or in federal labor policy.

DIRECTION

It is directed that the Regional Director for Region 32 shall, within 14 days of this Decision on Review and Direction, open and count the impounded ballots cast by the employees in the petitioned-for unit, prepare and serve on the parties a tally of ballots, and thereafter issue the appropriate certification.

MEMBERS MISCIMARRA and JOHNSON, dissenting:

Today, in the most sweeping of recent major decisions, the Board majority rewrites the decades-old test for determining who the "employer" is. More specifically, the majority redefines and expands the test that makes two separate and independent entities a "joint employer" of certain employees. This change will subject countless entities to unprecedented new joint-bargaining obligations that most do not even know they have, to potential joint liability for unfair labor practices and breaches of collective-bargaining agreements, and to economic protest activity, including what have heretofore been unlawful secondary strikes, boycotts, and picketing.

Our colleagues are driven by a desire to ensure that the prospect of collective bargaining is not foreclosed by business relationships that allegedly deny employees' right to bargain with employers that share control over essential terms and conditions of their employment. However well-intentioned they may be, there are five major problems with this objective.

First, no bargaining table is big enough to seat all of the entities that will be potential joint employers under the majority's new standards. In this regard, we believe the majority's new test impermissibly exceeds our statutory authority.

Second, the majority's rationale for overhauling the Act's "employer" definition—to protect bargaining from limitations resulting from third-party relationships that indirectly control employment issues—relies in substantial part on the notion that these relationships are unique in our modern economy and represent a radical departure from simpler times when labor negotiations were unaffected by the direct employer's commercial dealings with other entities. However, such an economy has not existed in this country for more than 200 years. Many forms of subcontracting, outsourcing, and temporary or contingent employment date back to long before the 1935 passage of the Act. Congress was obviously aware of the existence of these third-party intermediary business relationships in 1935 [and thereafter].

Third, courts have afforded the Board deference in this context merely as to the Board's ability to make factual distinctions when applying the common-law agency standard. However, our colleagues mistakenly interpret this as a grant of authority to modify the agency standard itself. This type of change is clearly within the province of Congress, not the Board.

Fourth, the majority abandons a longstanding test that provided certainty and predictability, and replaces it with an ambiguous standard that will impose unprecedented bargaining obligations on multiple entities in a wide variety of business relationships, even if this is based solely on a never-exercised "right" to exercise "indirect" control over what a Board majority may later characterize as "essential" employment terms. This new test leaves employees, unions, and employers in a position where there can be no certainty or predictability regarding the identity of the "employer."

Fifth, to the extent the majority seeks to correct a perceived inequality of bargaining leverage resulting from complex business relationships. [But] the inequality targeted by the new "joint-employer" test is a fixture of our economy—business entities have diverse relationships with different interests and leverage that varies in their dealings with one another. The Board needs a clear congressional [mandate]—and none exists here— before undertaking an attempt to reshape this aspect of economic reality. The Act does not redress imbalances of power between employers, even if those imbalances have some derivative effect on employees.

For all of these reasons, we dissent.

The number of contractual relationships now potentially encompassed within the majority's new standard appears to be virtually unlimited:

- Insurance companies that require employers to take certain actions with employees in order to comply with policy requirements for safety, security, health, etc.

- Franchisors.

- Banks or other lenders whose financing terms may require certain performance measurements.

- Any company that negotiates specific quality or product requirements.

- Any company that grants access to its facilities for a contractor to perform services there, and then continuously regulates the contractor's access to the property for the duration of the contract.

- Any company that is concerned about the quality of the contracted services.

- Consumers or small businesses who dictate times, manner, and some methods of performance of contractors.

Our colleagues make this sweeping change in the law without any substantive discussion whatsoever of significant adverse consequences.

Consider the following [hypothetical], which depicts a single cleaning company named "CleanCo," which has cleaning contracts with three clients. CleanCo employees work at each client's facilities in circumstances similar to the instant case, and CleanCo periodically adds future clients.

Assuming circumstances like those presented here, the majority would find that CleanCo and Client A are a "joint employer" at the Client A location; CleanCo and Client B are a "joint employer" at the Client B location; and CleanCo and Client C are a "joint employer" at the Client C location. Such a situation—involving a single vendor and only three clients, each with only one location—creates all of the following problems under the majority's test:

1.   Union Organizing Directed at CleanCo. CleanCo employees are currently unrepresented and a union seeks to organize them, this gives rise to the following issues and problems:

- What Bargaining Unit(s)? Although CleanCo directly controls all traditional indicia of employer status, the new majority test establishes that three different entities—Clients A, B, and C—have distinct "employer" relationships with discrete and potentially overlapping groups of different CleanCo employees. It is unclear whether a single bargaining unit consisting of all CleanCo employees could be considered appropriate, given the distinct role that the new majority test requires each client to play in bargaining.

- What "Employer" Participates in NLRB Election Proceedings? If the union files a representation petition with the Board, the Act requires the Board to afford "due notice" and to conduct an "appropriate hearing" for the "employer." Currently, the Board has no means of identifying—much less providing "due notice" and affording the right of participation to—"employer" entities like Clients A, B, and C, even though they would inherit bargaining obligations if CleanCo employees select the union.

- Who Does the Bargaining? If the union wins an election involving all CleanCo employees, the majority test would require participation in bargaining by CleanCo and Clients A, B, and C. Here, the majority test provides that each party "will be required to bargain only with respect to such terms and conditions which it possesses the authority to control" (emphasis added). However, because the majority's standard is so broad—spanning "direct control," "indirect control" and the "right to control" (even if never exercised in fact)—nobody could ever reasonably know who is responsible for bargaining what.

- CleanCo "Confidential" Information—Forced Disclosure to Clients. The most contentious issue between CleanCo and Clients A, B, and C is likely to involve the amounts charged by CleanCo, which predictably could vary substantially between Clients A, B, and C, depending on their respective leverage, the need for CleanCo's services, the duration of their respective client contracts (i.e., whether short-term or long-term), and other factors. If a union successfully organizes all CleanCo employees, the resulting bargaining— since the majority test requires participation by Clients A, B, and C—will almost certainly require the disclosure of sensitive CleanCo financial information to Clients A, B, and C, which is likely to enmesh the parties in an array of disagreements with one another, separate from the bargaining between the union and the "employer" entities.

2.   Union Organizing Directed at Client(s). If two different unions, rather than targeting CleanCo, engage in organizing directed at Client A and Client B, respectively, with Client C remaining nonunion, this gives rise to additional issues and problems:

- All of the Above Issues/Problems. If the CleanCo employees at Client A are organized by one union, and if the CleanCo employees at Client B are organized by a different union, then the majority test would make CleanCo and Client A the "joint employer" of the CleanCo/Client A employees, and CleanCo and Client B the "joint employer" of the CleanCo/Client B employees. In both cases, the "joint employer" status would give rise to all of the above problems and issues, in addition to those described below.

- Strikes and Picketing—"Neutral" Secondary Boycott Protection Eliminated. Sections 8(b)(4) and 8(e) of the Act protect neutral parties from being subjected to "secondary" picketing and other threats, coercion and restraint that have an object of forcing one employer to cease doing business with another. Therefore, if the CleanCo/Client A and CleanCo/Client B employees were involved in a labor dispute, under the Board's traditional joint-employer standard Clients A and B (as non-employers) would be neutral parties protected from "secondary" union activity. Under the majority's standard, however, Clients A and B would be employers right along with CleanCo and thus subject to picketing.

The Board is not Congress. It can only exercise the authority Congress has given it. In this instance, our colleagues have announced a new test of joint-employer status based on policy and economic interests that Congress has expressly prohibited the Board from considering. That alone is reason enough why the new test should not stand.

Accordingly, we respectfully dissent.

NOTES

1.   *Some perspective.* The practical implications of *BFI II* on who counts as a joint "employer" under Section 2(2) of the Act cannot fully be appreciated without reference to who counts as an "employee" under Section 2(3), which the Board later modified in *Miller & Anderson Inc.*, 364 N.L.R.B. No. 39 (2016), discussed *supra* Chapter 3-B-1-b-i. In *Miller & Anderson*, the same majority from *BFI II* answered the questions of who is considered to be a statutory "employee"—and equally important, who gets to decide—in a leased employment arrangement as follows. First, employer consent is not necessary for bargaining units that combine jointly employed and solely employed employees of a single user employer. Instead, the traditional community of interest factors will be applied to decide if such units are appropriate. Second, it is permissible to sanction bargaining units of the employees employed by a supplier employer, provided once again that those units are otherwise appropriate.

2.   *Back to school.* The dissent raised a number of concerns about the potential effects of the holding in *BFI II*. What were these concerns? The majority characterized these concerns as "law-school-exam hypothetical . . . doomsday scenarios." Do you agree, or did the dissent have some legitimate points? Which ones were they?

3.   *Speaking of Congressional (in)action.* In dissent, Members Miscimarra and Johnson reminded us, "The Board is not Congress." Famously, Congress has declined to pass any major amendments to the NLRA since 1959. As noted above, that hasn't stopped members of Congress from trying; legislation to overturn both *Miller & Anderson* and *Browning Ferris II* is pending. *See* Tyron Richardson & Hassan A. Kanu, *Republican Lawmakers Plan Rollout of Joint Employer Legislation*, Bloomberg Law (Jul. 6, 2017), available at https://www.bna.com/republican-lawmakers-plan-n73014461289/.

4. *Speaking of the dissent.* In their "CleanCo" hypothetical, Members Miscimarra and Johnson analyzed a number of problems that they asserted would arise from the majority's approach. Do you agree? What evidence supports your answer? What evidence, if any, can be gathered from the application of *BFI II* since its issuance? Note: In 2018, the Trump Board gave notice of pending rulemaking, and invited comment, on the joint employer question. *See* Office of Public Affairs, Invites Briefs on Joint Employment Standard, https://www.nlrb.gov/news-outreach/news-story/nlrb-invites-briefs-joint-employment-standard.

6.   TRANSBORDER EMPLOYERS

A dilemma faced by workers contemplating unionization in the globalized economy is the pressure on employers to remain competitive by reducing labor costs. Often this is accomplished by restructuring businesses to gain access to, or perhaps to exploit, low-wage workers in other countries. This pressure may be manifested by the employer's threat to move—either by sending the workers' jobs overseas, or by transforming itself into an overseas employer. Either way, the result is the same: high-wage jobs disappear from U.S. soil and reappear as low-wage jobs elsewhere. Although occasionally the NLRB may reach across our border to require a runaway employer to relocate back to the U.S., *see, e.g., Aguayo ex rel. NLRB v. Quadrtech Corp.*, 129 F. Supp. 2d 1273 (C.D. Cal. 2000), such remedies are quite rare, reserved for the most blatant violations of the NLRA for which alternative remedies are lacking.

There are many variations on the problem of transborder employers seeking to escape the reach of American authorities and employment regulations. In recent years, overseas workers have put increased pressure on transborder employers by pursuing them in U.S. courts under federal and state laws, with mixed results. *Compare, e.g., Doe v. Unocal Corp.*, 110 F. Supp. 2d 1294, 1308–10 (C.D. Cal. 2000) (U.S. company building pipeline in Myanmar entitled to dismissal of employees' forced labor claim under federal Alien Tort Claims Act), *with, e.g., Roe III v. Unocal Corp.* (Cal. Super. Ct. 2001), reported in 2001 Daily Lab. Rep. (BNA) No. 170, at p. A-10 (denying dismissal as to similar claim brought under California Constitution and statutes). More recently, however, the U.S. Supreme Court has cast substantial doubt on the viability of such claims, at least when pursued under the Alien Tort Claims (ATS) Act. *See Kiobel v. Royal Dutch Petroleum Co.*, 569 U.S. 108 (2013) (declining to permit ATS claims against foreign corporation alleged to have committed relevant acts outside U.S.); *accord Jesner v. Arab Bank, PLC*, 138 S. Ct. 1386 (2018) (declining to permit ATS claims against foreign corporations, regardless where relevant acts were committed).

In another variation, the overseas employees of an overseas company that is in turn the subsidiary of a U.S. parent may attempt to pierce the corporate veil to enforce an overseas collective bargaining agreement in federal court—but not necessarily succeed in doing so.

LABOR UNION OF PICO KOREA, LTD. V. PICO PRODUCTS, INC.
968 F.2d 191 (2d Cir.), cert. denied, 506 U.S. 985 (1992)

CARDAMONE, CIRCUIT JUDGE:

This appeal questions the territorial scope of § 301 of the Labor Management Relations Act which provides that suits for violations of labor contracts may be brought in federal court without regard to the citizenship of the parties if the employees work in an industry affecting commerce between a foreign country and a state. A rigid and literal reading of this provision might permit the instant action to lie. But since the extraterritorial application of our laws is not favored because such may readily lead to inadvertent clashes with the laws of other nations, we cannot presume Congress intended a Korean labor contract to come within § 301's compass.

Plaintiffs, citizens and domiciliaries of South Korea, are former employees of Pico Korea, Ltd. (Korea), a South Korean corporation with its principal place of business in Seoul. The labor union that served as plaintiffs' bargaining representative is a duly formed trade union under the laws of South Korea. Korea's American connection is that it was a wholly-owned subsidiary of Pico Macom, Inc. (Macom), a Delaware corporation with its principal place of business in California. Macom is, in turn, a wholly-owned subsidiary of defendant Pico Products, Inc., a New York corporation with its principal place of business in New York. Viewing this vertical corporate structure from the other direction, Pico Products owns Macom, which in turn owned Korea.

The facts are not in dispute. Korea was incorporated in 1985 to manufacture electronic components, all of which its parent Macom purchased except for a small amount sold to other customers at Macom's direction. In April 1988 Korea experienced cash shortages, and the parent company had to advance working capital. In June 1988 the companies' workers formed a labor union. A collective bargaining agreement was signed on November 15, 1988 with their employer. James D. O'Connell signed the agreement on Korea's behalf as president. From 1986 through February 1989 O'Connell served as the executive vice-president and director of Pico Products and as a member of the Board of Directors of Macom. He was the only person serving as a director of all three corporations.

Because Korea's problems—increasing labor costs, low productivity and lack of operating capital—had an adverse impact on both Macom and Pico Products, a meeting of Pico Products' Board of Directors was held on

February 23, 1989 to discuss these developments. The meeting resulted in a resolution directing Macom immediately to cease providing additional working capital to Korea. The effect of this action, not unanticipated, was that Korea went out of business.

Plaintiffs instituted the present action asserting, inter alia, claims for breach of contract or, alternatively, tortious interference with advantageous contractual relationships. The essence of plaintiffs' complaint is that the shutdown of Korea did not conform to the provisions of the labor agreement. Plaintiffs predicated jurisdiction under § 301 of the Labor Management Relations Act (LMRA), 29 U.S.C. § 185. The district court held federal question jurisdiction was lacking because § 301 was "passed . . . with respect to United States workers, not workers in a foreign country." Nonetheless, the action proceeded based on diversity of citizenship. The parties stipulated that New York (as opposed to South Korean) law applied.

After a bench trial, the district judge concluded that although "Pico Korea lacked autonomy over all but the most basic daily operations," piercing the corporate veil to hold Pico Products liable under the terms of the labor contract was not warranted because "there [was] insufficient proof to conclude that this control was within the hands of the defendant." The district court held plaintiffs had failed—as was required to hold Pico Products liable—"to pierce two corporate veils, not one." With respect to plaintiffs' tortious interference claim, the district court believed that though there was a valid and binding contract between plaintiffs and Korea—of which defendant was aware and the breach of which defendant induced—liability could not attach because "Pico Products' action in inducing the breach of the contract was not malicious, but rather was motivated by justifiable concerns."

Plaintiffs insist on appeal that federal law—under which they believe it is generally easier to pierce a corporate veil—should have been applied to determine the propriety of holding Pico Products liable as Korea's alter ego. We disagree and affirm the judgment in favor of defendant Pico Products on plaintiffs' state law claims substantially for the reasons stated by the district judge. Hence the merits of defendant's cross-appeal need not be reached. We write in this case because the issue of § 301's territorial scope presents a novel question.

DISCUSSION

As in all matters of statutory construction, we start with the statute itself. Section 301 provides in pertinent part that:

> [s]uits for violation of contracts between an employer and a labor organization representing employees in an industry affecting commerce . . . may be brought in any district court of the United States having jurisdiction of the parties, without respect to the

amount in controversy or without regard to the citizenship of the parties. 29 U.S.C. § 185(a). Federal courts have undertaken under this statute to develop a federal common law for the interpretation and enforcement of collective bargaining agreements, thus "requiring issues raised in suits of a kind covered by § 301 to be decided according to the precepts of federal labor policy."

Local 174, Teamsters, Chauffeurs, Warehousemen & Helpers of Am. v. Lucas Flour Co., 369 U.S. 95 (1962).

The question presented is whether Congress planned that the sort of labor contract at issue was to be "covered by" § 301.

Congress is presumed, as one might expect, to be concerned with domestic conditions first, and for that reason laws generally apply only in those geographical areas or territories subject to the legislative control of the United States, absent Congress' clearly expressed affirmative aim to the contrary. *See Foley Bros., Inc. v. Filardo*, 336 U.S. 281 (1949). Plaintiffs carry the burden of demonstrating a Congressional purpose to overcome the presumption against extraterritorial application. *See EEOC v. Arabian Am. Oil Co.*, 499 U.S. 244 (1991) (superseded by Pub. L. No. 102–166 (1991)). They attempt to meet this burden in two ways.

The first derives from the statute's language "without regard to the citizenship of the parties." According to plaintiffs, the plain meaning of this language is clear: § 301 and federal law govern the resolution of this suit irrespective of the fact that plaintiffs are citizens of South Korea. This argument is misplaced because the issue is not plaintiffs' citizenship, but rather whether the labor agreement at issue is of the type Congress planned on having § 301 control. Merely because § 301 grants federal jurisdiction without regard to the citizenship of the parties does not mean federal jurisdiction exists without consideration of the nature of the collective bargaining agreement at issue. The phrase "without regard to the citizenship of the parties" simply establishes federal question jurisdiction and does not overcome the broad presumption against extraterritorial application of federal law. In other words, when it is triggered § 301 provides federal question jurisdiction. The question before us is the threshold one: was § 301 triggered in this case?

Determining whether § 301 has application brings us to plaintiffs' second attempt to overcome the presumption in favor of territorial limitation. It is their contention that the only limitation on § 301's applicability is that the industry in which employees covered by the collective bargaining agreement work must be one "affecting commerce." And, plaintiffs continue, the term "commerce" is defined for purposes of § 301 to include trade "between any foreign country and any State." 29 U.S.C. § 152(6); *see id.* § 142(1), (3). We assume the activities of Pico Korea, though the issue was not addressed by the district court, affect commerce within the meaning of § 301. According to plaintiffs, this conclusion should end the inquiry, for the statute's language is clear and must control.

We agree that Congress has authority under the commerce clause to make the instant labor contract subject to § 301. See *Arabian American*, 111 S. Ct. at 1230. Yet it remains to be decided whether when Congress enacted § 301 it meant to exercise the full limits of its power. In the present instance Supreme Court precedent suggests otherwise. The Supreme Court has held that the Eight Hour Law—requiring that contracts to which the United States is a party compensate laborers at time and a half for work in excess of eight hours, *see* 40 U.S.C. §§ 324, 325a, repealed by Pub. L. No. 87–581 (1962), 40 U.S.C. §§ 328–30—does not apply to contracts performed in foreign countries. *See Foley Bros.*, 336 U.S. at 284–85. That law, like § 301, made no distinction between alien and citizen labor. The Court took this to indicate that the statute was intended to apply only where the labor conditions of both citizen and alien employees are a probable concern of Congress. "Such places do not include foreign countries." The Court specifically rejected the assertion that because the statute said "every contract" it encompassed the contract at issue, holding that the presumption against extraterritorial application had not been overcome.

Similarly, *Benz v. Compania Naviera Hidalgo*, 353 U.S. 138 (1957), held that the LMRA did not govern a dispute stemming from the picketing of a foreign ship operated entirely by foreign seamen under foreign articles while the vessel was temporarily in an American port. Although Congress could have decided to regulate the matter in light of the fact that the vessel was in the territorial waters of the United States, the Supreme Court ruled that the Congressional scheme did not contemplate such a sweep because the LMRA "is concerned with industrial strife between American employers and employees."

In the case at bar, the employees of Pico Korea are citizens and domiciliaries of South Korea, doing work in South Korea, for a South Korean company. The fact that Pico Korea is a wholly-owned subsidiary of a United States corporation does not change the character of this labor dispute into one over which Congress can be presumed to have intended § 301 to control.

Nor does the fact that the work performed by Pico Korea's employees may "affect commerce" within the meaning of § 301 suffice to demonstrate a contrary congressional aim. *See Arabian American*, 111 S. Ct. at 1231–32 ("boilerplate language" concerning reach of statute enacted under Congress' power to regulate commerce does not overcome presumption against extraterritoriality). *See also Juneau Spruce*, 342 U.S. at 242 (though § 301 enacted partially to limit obstacles to suit in federal court, jurisdiction nonetheless may be limited by territorial considerations).

In the present "global economy" ever-expanding trade makes it increasingly possible that foreign industry might affect commerce "between

[a] foreign country and any State." But to construe § 301 as governing collective bargaining agreements in such an industry "would inevitably lead to embarrassment in foreign affairs and be entirely infeasible in actual practice." That the dispute in this case does not focus on the interpretation, per se, of the labor contract is not relevant. For were we to accept jurisdiction under § 301 merely for the purpose of deciding whether Pico Products is liable for the agreement's breach under federal labor law, it would lead to federal courts being called upon to determine if agreements such as this were in fact breached. Such a result would conflict with "[t]he general and almost universal rule . . . that the character of an act as lawful or unlawful must be determined wholly by the law of the country where the act is done." *N.Y. Cent. R.R. v. Chisholm*, 268 U.S. 29, 31 (1925) (Federal Employers' Liability Act does not govern in damages action brought on behalf of United States citizen employed by United States railroad injured in Canada).

If Congress wants federal courts to enforce collective bargaining agreements between foreign workers and foreign corporations doing work in foreign countries according to the body of labor law developed pursuant to § 301, such legislative purpose must be made unmistakably clear. The statute evinces no such purpose. The subject collective bargaining agreement therefore is not governed by § 301.

Hence, whether Pico Products is liable as Pico Korea's alter ego is not to be determined according to the precepts of federal labor law. From this it follows that plaintiffs' suit for tortious interference with the labor agreement also is not governed by federal law.

CONCLUSION

The judgment appealed from accordingly is affirmed.

NOTES

1.   *Walk softly, and carry a little stick?* Unlike the executive branch, the judicial branch historically has been reluctant to approve the extraterritorial application of U.S. law, including federal labor and employment laws. *See, e.g., McCulloch v. Sociedad Nacional de Marineros de Honduras*, 372 U.S. 10 (1963) (NLRA does not govern competing unions' claims to represent alien crews of ships owned by foreign subsidiaries of U.S. corporation that make regular trips between American and foreign ports transporting parent's products). *But see International Longshoremen's Local 1416 v. Ariadne Shipping Co.*, 397 U.S. 195 (1970) (NLRA applies to dispute over picketing to protest wages paid by foreign vessels to American sailors working in American ports). *See also, e.g., Keller Found./Case Found. v. Tracy*, 696 F.3d 835 (9th Cir. 2012) (rejecting argument under Longshore and Harbor Workers' Compensation Act (LHWCA) by U.S.-based construction firm as to claim by employee who sought compensation for cumulative injuries suffered in foreign territorial waters,

including Indonesia and Singapore, during work for firm over course of career), *cert. denied*, 81 U.S.L.W. (BNA) 3503 (2013).

The year before *Pico Products* was decided, the Supreme Court held that the employment discrimination provisions of Title VII of the Civil Rights Act of 1964 did not reach a U.S. corporation that was allegedly violating the statute in Saudi Arabia against an American citizen employed there. *See EEOC v. Arabian Am. Oil Co. (ARAMCO)*, 499 U.S. 244 (1991). Shortly thereafter, as part of the Civil Rights Act of 1991, Pub. L. No. 102–166, § 109(b) (1991), Congress overruled the result in *ARAMCO*.

2.   *Plain meaning vs. inevitable embarrassment?* After conceding that a "rigid and literal reading of this provision might permit the instant action to lie," Judge Cardamone went on to explain why "we cannot presume Congress intended a Korean labor contract to come within § 301's compass," and therefore, why the action must be dismissed: permitting plaintiffs to proceed "would inevitably lead to embarrassment in foreign affairs and be entirely infeasible in actual practice." Who (or what) would have been so embarrassed? Why would permitting the plaintiffs to proceed be "entirely infeasible in actual practice"? What would have been the effect of permitting plaintiffs to proceed? Would liability for Korea's apparent failures have automatically attached to either Pico Products or Macom? Or would something more have to be proved first?

To many, Judge Cardamone's reasoning would seem to violate modern canons of statutory interpretation, which favor giving effect to the plain meaning of the words enacted by Congress, irrespective of the policy implications. What do you think? Do you agree that a decision favoring the plaintiffs would harm our foreign policy? Should it have made any difference that Congress, as the Second Circuit concedes, has the power to give § 301 the territorial reach sought by the plaintiffs? Do you agree that the burden was on the plaintiffs, rather than the employer, to show that Congress had "unmistakably" exercised such power?

3.   *The law of unintended consequences: imports and exports.* What affect might transborder claims litigation have on the practices of domestic and foreign lawyers who represent workers and employers? *See, e.g.*, Susan Bisom-Rapp, *Exceeding Our Boundaries: Transnational Employment Law Practice and the Export of American Lawyering Styles to the Global Worksite*, 25 Comp. Lab. L. & Pol. J. 257, 258–62 (2004) (describing rise of transnational employment practice and potential influence of U.S. management-side firms such on non-U.S. attorneys, and vice versa).

CHAPTER 4

ESTABLISHING COLLECTIVE REPRESENTATION

■ ■ ■

A. INTRODUCTION

"Enderby shouldn't have many work rules, but the rules we do have—like no company e-mail for personal messages—should be enforced to the letter."

—Steve Workman, Enderby's Chief Executive Officer

Enderby, Inc., the company we met at the beginning of Chapter 2, is based in Eugene, Ore., where it manufactures LCD and LED ultra high definition television sets, PC tablets, and other electronic accessories and devices. Like many electronics manufacturers, the company was very successful during the 1980s. But since the 1990s, increased foreign competition has cut substantially into profits (although Enderby remains profitable). The Programmers Union, which is affiliated with the AFL-CIO, seeks to organize the company's 50 software programmers employed at the Eugene facility. In addition to the programmers, Enderby employs assemblers, distribution workers, and business office clerical employees. It has a second facility in Tulsa, Oklahoma, where it employs a similar complement of workers.

Although the Programmers Union has yet to establish itself as the recognized collective bargaining representative of Enderby's workforce, the company has created three "work teams" to which programmers may be elected by their colleagues: the productivity team, the bonus team, and the troubleshooting team. The company created these work teams for two reasons: first, to generate ideas about how to improve the company's productivity, bonus structure, and software programming capacity; and second, to show employees that they do not need the Programmers Union to have a voice in the workplace. For example, members of the bonus team meet once a month on company property, sometime during the work day, to discuss and make recommendations about the formula to be used in distributing the annual year-end bonus. The meeting is chaired by an assistant to Workman. The assistant takes notes and provides information about the total amount available for bonuses, but does not express any opinion about the merits of recommendations by team members. Workman himself reserves the right unilaterally to award compensation and set bonus policy, but so far, he has followed every recommendation made by the bonus team.

Enderby rents office space on the fifth floor of a 10-story building in High Tech Park, a nine-acre, privately owned complex. (High Tech Park is a modern suburban mixed use space, with retail and housing facilities in close proximity.) Enderby's programmers work long, irregular hours. They arrive to work in their office cubicles sometime between 7:00 am and 12:00 noon, and leave sometime between 5:00 pm and 2:00 am, depending on work load. They eat lunch and dinner at odd hours too, usually while sitting at their work stations.

E-mail is by far the most common method of communication among Enderby's programmers. They use it to exchange information and advice about a wide range of work-related matters, including the troubleshooting of problems related to the software used in the TV sets. Occasionally, programmers use e-mail to offer opinions about company management. Programmers also use e-mail to announce office-related events, such as company softball games, but not personal news, such as birthday parties or wedding showers. A company rule prohibits use of the e-mail system to send personal messages.

One afternoon, Penny, an employee sympathetic to the Programmers Union, sent to all programmers an e-mail message urging support for the union. She asked them to sign an "electronic" union authorization card, which was attached to the message. Each card stated: "I want the Programmers Union to represent me in negotiating terms and conditions of employment with Enderby." The message was sent from her Enderby office personal computer. Inadvertently, Penny also sent the message to Steve Workman, the company's chief executive officer. Workman likes to say, "Enderby shouldn't have many work rules, but the rules we do have—like no company e-mail for personal messages—should be enforced to the letter." After reading Penny's message, Workman promptly fired her for breaking the rule.

For several weeks after being fired, Penny and two professional union organizers stood alongside one of the 14 roads leading into and out of High Tech Park, and attempted to distribute leaflets to passersby, most of whom were driving automobiles and did not slow down to take the leaflets. The leaflets said: "Tell Enderby employees to sign authorization cards!" Meanwhile, the Programmers Union counted the "electronic" authorization cards that were signed and sent back by employees who responded to Penny's e-mail. The Union is now contemplating making a demand that Enderby recognize it as the programmers' exclusive bargaining representative.

NOTES

1.   This version of the Enderby problem raises several threshold issues relating to the establishment of collective representation that are treated in this Chapter. One set of issues relates to whether the "work teams" are actually employer-dominated labor organizations—sometimes called "company unions"—that enable programmers to "deal with" the company over bonuses and other terms of employment in violation of Section 8(a)(2). Three other issues relate to regulation of the employer's private property: employee access to and use of employer e-mail systems to send messages exercising their Section 7 rights; retaliation against employees for exercising those rights in violation of an employer rule regulating use of its communications equipment; and access by employee versus non-employee organizers to the employer's customers and workforce.

As to the set of Section 8(a)(2) issues that are addressed in the next section of this Chapter, what is the legal significance of the fact that Enderby, rather than an independent group of workers, created the work teams? Do the work teams discuss employment terms, such as compensation and safety, or do they discuss carpools, social activities, and other ancillary matters? Are they controlled by the employer, or independently run by employees? Are they merely advisory in nature, or do they actually exercise management powers by determining employment terms? If advisory, then *Electromation, infra* p. 387, suggests that they would be held to be illegitimate; if the exercising management powers, then *Crown Cork & Seal, infra* p. 398, suggests that they would be held to be legitimate. Which facts can be used to characterize the bonus team as the former versus the latter?

One of the motivating factors behind creating the work teams was to generate ideas about how to improve the company's productivity, bonus structure, and software programming capacity. These would seem to be good things. But the typical remedy for violating Section 8(a)(2) is disestablishment of the work team. What policies of the Act would be served by outlawing the bonus team and other work teams created by Enderby? What policies would be undermined? Could anything be done to resolve this tension? Would your answer change if you recalled the early history of the labor movement, during which employers often sought to undermine employees' free choice in the selection of their bargaining representatives by setting up "company unions" instead?

2.   *Wait a minute, Mr. E-Postman.* Suppose that, shortly after Penny's firing, Workman calls a meeting of all programmers to discuss Enderby's no-personal-e-mails policy. During the meeting, Workman warns everyone that violators will meet the same fate as Penny. Does Workman have the right to call such a meeting? To issue such a warning? Why or why not?

Suppose then that, after several weeks of effort by Penny and the two professional organizers, the Programmers Union succeeded in handing out only a few leaflets, and failed to get a single authorization card beyond the few it had collected before Penny was fired. The main problem was that the three organizers could not gain access to speak to Enderby employees. Should the organizers be able to enter Enderby's office on the fifth floor of the office building in High Tech Park and speak to employees onsite? Why would the union prefer this approach? If organizers are not allowed to enter the office, what about the lobby of the building? Or the area just outside the door to the lobby? Should all three organizers have the same right of access, or does Penny have a stronger case, because she is a former employee who was fired under possibly illegal circumstances?

Then there is the matter of Penny's e-mail message. Was Enderby justified in punishing her for violating company policy? Would it make a difference if Quincy, another programmer, had sent an e-mail inviting employees to his bachelor party, but was not disciplined?

Now suppose something else altogether: despite the difficulties, Penny and her cohorts got signed authorization cards from 26 of the company's 50 programmers. The Programmers Union then demanded that Enderby recognize it as the exclusive representative of all programmers and enter into negotiations for a collective bargaining agreement. Workman refused on the ground the signatures may have been forged. If the union offers to have a neutral third party verify the signatures, should Enderby be required to recognize the union because there is demonstrated majority support? Would a secret ballot election be better? For whom?

3. *The NLRA in cyberspace.* A major concern about the NLRB's supervision of the NLRA representation system has been raised by observers who say that it lags behind the technological times. Barely two decades into the Internet Age, the NLRB, in 2012, finally decided its first case dealing with employees' use of Facebook and other social media, *Hispanics United of Buffalo, supra* p. 166. Only five years before that, in 2007, the Board issued its first major pronouncement on employees' right of access to an employer's e-mail system in *Register Guard, infra* p. 485. How and when may employers restrict employees' use of company e-mail or instant messaging systems? Does the internet eliminate the need for distinguishing between access by employee and nonemployee organizers? What about the work time use of personal devices, such as iPads, iPhones, Androids, and other picture-taking devices, by employees? Should the rules be different if the modern workplace is no longer a "place," because employees do not report to or meet in a central location? Some labor scholars have attempted to offer frameworks for adapting the NLRA to the electronic workplace. *See, e.g.,* Jeffrey M. Hirsch, *The Silicon Bullet: Will the Internet Kill the NLRA?,* 76 Geo. Wash. L. Rev. 262 (2008).

4. *Appropriate bargaining units.* The Enderby problem assumes that all 50 programmers share a "community of interest" that makes it appropriate for them to be treated as a single bargaining unit for purposes of representation, irrespective of their particular duties or location. The bargaining unit is the entity that gains representational rights that may be certified by the NLRB. If all 50 programmers share a community of interest, then all of them must be represented by the Programmers Union, so long as a simple majority of them

choose such representation. Later in this Chapter, we will study the law governing when a bargaining unit is "appropriate."

* * *

The NLRA offers at least three distinct routes to union representation: by a Board certification election, held among employees in a bargaining unit in which there is a question concerning representation; by bargaining order, as issued by the NLRB against a recalcitrant employer; and by the employer's voluntary recognition of a union presenting evidence of majority support among employees. Although it is sometimes forgotten that voluntary recognition is a common, time-honored path to representation, the election is probably the method most commonly associated in the public mind with the establishment of labor organizations in the workplace. The 1979 film "Norma Rae," starring Oscar-winning actress Sally Field, depicts the prototypical election, in which there is a hard-fought, political-style campaign, followed by a secret ballot vote in which employees choose whether they want a union to represent them.

But hypothetical cases like Enderby and real ones like *Gissel Packing* and *Exchange Parts* have fueled a sense among workers' rights advocates that the traditional union election actually thwarts—rather than promotes—employee free choice. They believe the election, as supervised by the NLRB, places too many stumbling blocks in the path of employees who might otherwise choose union representation. These include restrictive access for unions wishing to convince employees of the benefits of representation; employer campaign "speech" that threatens or coerces employees in the exercise of their voting rights; delays in vindicating the rights of employees who have been fired or coerced in violation of their Section 7 rights; and inadequate remedies for those violations.

In this chapter, Part B covers the threshold issue of what defines a labor organization or labor union. Part C addresses the regulation of union access to employees on employer property. Part D examines the regulation of campaign speech by employers. Part E surveys the regulation of other behavior that tends to coerce employees in their exercise of section 7 rights. Part F examines employee protection against discrimination with regard to hire, tenure, and other terms and conditions of employment. Finally, Part G outlines the traditional and non-traditional roads to union representation.

B. DEFINITION OF LABOR ORGANIZATION

Generally, we know that a labor union is a recognized group of employees that is more or less formally organized to negotiate with an employer over the terms and conditions of employment. We also know that some of the NLRA's basic protections apply even to employees who do not belong to a union if they are engaged in concerted activity. We may also suspect—as confirmed by other sections of this Chapter—that the Act protects workers engaged in fledgling efforts to organize a union, even if no such organization has yet been formed. So what *is* a union, and how can it be distinguished from protected but less formal efforts by workers to combine their separate voices into one voice? This section attempts to answer that question, and to shed light on the Act's mechanisms to foster workers' collective efforts.

To preserve employee freedom of choice, the NLRA casts a wide net, protecting even very nascent acts of collective activity by employees. It does this by safeguarding "labor organizations," which it defines broadly, and not confining its scope to the more formal entities we commonly refer to as labor "unions." The breadth of the definition of what constitutes a labor organization also serves to prevent the employer from both interfering with employee efforts early in the organizing process and from displacing independent employee organizations by setting up employer-dominated entities—commonly referred to as "company unions"—that can act as barriers to bona fide organizing efforts.

1. EMPLOYER DOMINATION, SUPPORT, AND INTERFERENCE

Sec. 2. [§ 152.] When used in this Act [subchapter]—

(3) The term "employee" shall include any employee, and shall not be limited to the employees of a particular employer, unless the Act [this subchapter] explicitly states otherwise, and shall include any individual whose work has ceased as a consequence of, or in connection with, any current labor dispute or because of any unfair labor practice, and who has not obtained any other regular and substantially equivalent employment, but shall not include any individual employed as an agricultural laborer, or in the domestic service of any family or person at his home, or any individual employed by his parent or spouse, or any individual having the status of an independent contractor, or any individual employed as a supervisor, or any individual employed by an employer subject to the Railway Labor Act [45 U.S.C. § 151 et seq.], as amended from time to time, or by any other person who is not an employer as herein defined.

(5) The term "labor organization" means any organization of any kind, or any agency or employee representation committee or plan, in which employees participate and which exists for the purpose, in whole or in part, of dealing with employers concerning grievances, labor disputes, wages, rates of pay, hours of employment, or conditions of work.

Sec. 8. [§ 158.](a) It shall be an unfair labor practice for an employer—

(2) to dominate or interfere with the formation or administration of any labor organization or contribute financial or other support to it: *Provided*, That subject to rules and regulations made and published by the Board pursuant to section 6 [section 156 of this title], an employer shall not be prohibited from permitting employees to confer with him during working hours without loss of time or pay. . . .

Section 8(a)(2) was promulgated as part of the original Wagner Act in order to address the issue of the "company union." These unions, which had become popular prior to 1935, were typically dominated by employers who controlled every aspect of their formation, organization, and mission. Congress knew that the existence of these types of unions would interfere with employee free choice as well as the institution of employee voice in the workplace. *See* Robert Gorman & Matthew Finkin, Basic Text on Labor Law, § 9.1, 257–58 (2d ed. 2004). Section 8(a)(2) is powerful legislation in that it defines labor organization so broadly as to capture any form of employer domination irrespective of the employer's good or bad intentions. *Scienter* is not required to make out a Section 8(a)(2) violation; the only requirement being the mere existence of a labor organization with certain employer involvement. The section was dormant for decades until the advent in the mid-1980s of management styles associated with large Japanese companies—such as consensus decision-making and "total quality management"—that sought to involve workers more meaningfully in the operation of the firm. In the cases that follow, the Board had to determine whether and when these efforts run afoul of the Act. In *Electromation*, it said yes; in *Crown Cork & Seal*, it said no.

ELECTROMATION, INC.
309 N.L.R.B. 990 (1992)

CHAIRMAN STEPHENS and MEMBERS DEVANEY, OVIATT, and RAUDABAUGH:

This case presents the issue of whether "Action Committees" composed, in part, of the Respondent's employees constitute a labor organization within the meaning of Section 2(5) of the Act. In the notice of hearing of May 14, 1991, the Board framed the pertinent issue[ ] as follows:

(1) At what point does an employee committee lose its protection as a communication device and become a labor organization?

For the reasons below, we find that the Action Committees were not simply "communication devices" but instead constituted a labor organization within the meaning of Section 2(5) of the Act.

I.

The Respondent is engaged in the manufacture of electrical components and related products. It employs approximately 200 employees. These employees were not represented by any labor organization at the time of the events described herein.

In late 1988 the Respondent concluded that it was experiencing unacceptable financial losses. It decided to cut expenses by altering the existing employee attendance bonus policy and, in lieu of a wage increase for 1989, distributed year-end lump-sum payments based on length of service. Shortly after these changes were announced, the Respondent became aware that employees were displeased with the reduction in benefits. In early January 1989, the Respondent received a petition signed by 68 employees expressing displeasure with the new attendance policy. Upon receipt of this petition, the Respondent's president, John Howard, met with the Respondent's supervisors to discuss the petition and the employees' complaints. At this meeting, the Respondent decided to meet directly with employees to discuss their problems. Thereafter, on January 11, the Respondent met with a selected group of eight employees and discussed with them a number of issues, including wages, bonuses, incentive pay, attendance programs, and leave policy.

After the January 11 meeting, President Howard again met with his supervisors and concluded that the Respondent had serious problems with its employees. Howard testified that it was decided at that time that "it was very unlikely that further unilateral management action to resolve these problems was going to come anywhere near making everybody happy . . . and we thought that the best course of action would be to involve the employees in coming up with solutions to these issues." Howard testified further that management came up with the idea of "action committees" as a method to involve employees.

The Respondent next met with the same group of eight employees on January 18. Howard explained to the assembled group that management had distilled the employees' complaints into five categories. Howard testified that he proposed the creation of Action Committees that "would meet and try to come up with ways to resolve these problems; and that if they came up with solutions that . . . we believed were within budget concerns and they generally felt would be acceptable to the employees, that we would implement these suggestions or proposals." Howard testified further that the reaction of the assembled employees to the concept of action committees was "not positive." Howard explained to the employees that because "the business was in trouble financially . . . we couldn't just put things back the way they were . . . we don't have better ideas at this point other than to sit down and work with you on them." According to Howard, as the meeting went on, the employees "began to understand that

that was far better than leaving things as they were, and that we weren't going to just unilaterally make changes. And so they accepted it." Howard agreed that employees would not be selected at random for the committees based on seniority and that, instead, sign-up sheets would be posted.

After the Action Committees were organized, the Respondent posted a notice to all employees announcing the members of each Committee and the dates of the initial Committee meetings. The Action Committees were designated as (1) Absenteeism/Infractions, (2) No Smoking Policy, (3) Communication Network, (4) Pay Progression for Premium Positions, and (5) Attendance Bonus Program.

The Action Committees began meeting in late January and early February. The Respondent's coordinator of the Action Committees, Dickey, testified that management expected that employee members on the Committees would "kind of talk back and forth" with the other employees in the plant, get their ideas, and that, indeed, the purpose of the Respondent's postings was to ensure that "anyone [who] wanted to know what was going on, they could go to these people" on the Action Committees. Other management representatives, as well as Dickey, participated in the Action Committees' meetings, which were scheduled to meet on a weekly basis in a conference room on the Respondent's premises. The Respondent paid employees for their time spent participating and supplied necessary materials. Dickey's role in the meetings was to facilitate the discussions.

On February 13, the Union made a demand to the Respondent for recognition. There is no evidence that the Respondent was aware of organizing efforts by the Union until this time. On about February 21, Howard informed Dickey of the recognition demand and, at the next scheduled meeting of each Action Committee, Dickey informed the members that the Respondent could no longer participate but that the employees could continue to meet if they so desired. The Absenteeism/Infraction and the Communication Network Committees each decided to continue their meetings on company premises; the Pay Progression Committee disbanded; and the Attendance Bonus Committee decided to write up a proposal they had discussed previously and not to meet again. The Attendance Bonus Committee's proposal was one of two proposals that the employees had developed concerning attendance bonuses. The first one, developed at the committee's second or third meeting, was pronounced unacceptable by the Respondent's controller, a member of that committee, because it was too costly. Thereafter the employees devised a second proposal, which the controller deemed fiscally sound. The proposal was not presented to President Howard because the Union's campaign to secure recognition had intervened.

On March 15, Howard informed employees that "due to the Union's campaign, the Company would be unable to participate in the committee meetings and could not continue to work with the committees until after the election," which was to be held on March 31.

On the foregoing evidence, the judge found that the Action Committees constituted a labor organization within the meaning of Section 2(5). He noted that employees, supervisors, and managerial personnel served as committee members and that their discussions concerned conditions of employment.

In its exceptions and brief, the Respondent contends that the Action Committees were not statutory labor organizations and did not interfere with employee free choice. It notes that no proposals from any committee were ever implemented, that the committees were formed in the absence of knowledge of any union activity, and that they followed a tradition of similar employer-employee meetings.

II.

Section 2(5) of the Act defines a "labor organization" as follows:

> The term "labor organization" means any organization of any kind, or any agency or employee representation committee or plan, in which employees participate and which exists for the purpose, in whole or in part, of dealing with employers concerning grievances, labor disputes, wages, rates of pay, hours of employment, or conditions of work.

Whenever we are attempting to determine the application of the statute to particular facts, we must first determine whether the statutory language standing alone answers the question. Here, we cannot properly limit our analysis to the statutory language because the terms are not all self-defining. For example, although the "Action Committees" are committees in which "employees participate," the parties have raised questions about the meaning of "representation" in the phrase "employee representation committee." We therefore seek guidance from the legislative history to discern what kind of activity Congress intended to prohibit when it made it an unfair labor practice for an employer to "dominate or interfere with the formation or administration of any labor organization" or to contribute support to it.

The legislative history reveals that the provisions outlawing company dominated labor organizations were a critical part of the Wagner Act's purpose of eliminating industrial strife through the encouragement of collective bargaining. Early in his opening remarks Senator Wagner stated:

> Genuine collective bargaining is the only way to attain equality of bargaining power. . . . The greatest obstacles to collective bargaining are employer-dominated unions, which have

multiplied with amazing rapidity since the enactment of [the National Industrial Recovery Act]. Such a union makes a sham of equal bargaining power. . . . [O]nly representatives who are not subservient to the employer with whom they deal can act freely in the interest of employees. For these reasons the very first step toward genuine collective bargaining is the abolition of the employer dominated union as an agency for dealing with grievances, labor disputes, wages, rates, or hours of employment.

Because of the Wagner Act's purpose to eliminate employer dominated unions, the term "labor organization" was defined broadly. Indeed, even though the original Senate Bill (S.2976) broadly defined "labor organization" as "any organization, labor union, association, corporation, or society of any kind in which employees participate to any degree whatsoever and which exists for the purpose . . . of dealing with employers concerning grievances, labor disputes, wages, rates of pay, or hours of employment, or conditions of work", the Wagner Act, as finally enacted, expanded the initial part of the definition in order to encompass common forms of company dominated unions that had arisen following passage of the National Industrial Recovery Act. Professor Edwin E. Witte was influential in securing the enacted broader definition of "labor organization." Professor Witte expressed concern whether the legislation as introduced would include the most prevalent form of company-dominated union, the employee representation committee, which Professor Witte described as "the loose organization if you can call it an organization, that has no members, no dues, that is merely a method of electing representatives." Senator Wagner's explanation of the revised definition reveals that the revision's purpose was to include this form of dominated labor organization within the statutory definition:

> It has been argued frequently by employers as well as by protagonists of the bill last year that an employee representation plan or committee arrangement is not a labor organization or a union but simply a method of contact between employers and employees. But the act is entitled to prescribe its own definitions of labor organizations, for its own purposes, and it is clear that unless these plans, etc., are included in the definition, whether they merely "deal" or "adjust," or exist for the purpose of collective bargaining, most of the activity of employers in connection therewith which we are seeking to outlaw would fall outside the scope of the act. The act would thus be entirely nullified. If, as employers insist, such "plans," etc., are lawful representatives of employees, then employer activity relative to them should clearly be included.

With respect to employer conduct that was to come within the ambit of Section 8(a)(2) itself, it is noteworthy that the original Senate bill

(S.2926) made it an unfair labor practice for an employer to "initiate, participate in, supervise, or influence the formation, rules, and other policies of a labor organization." After considering testimony that certain unaffiliated employee organizations confined to representing employees on a single employer basis often operated in an amicable and cooperative atmosphere, the Senate sponsors modified Section 8(a)(2) specifically to permit employees to confer with their employer during working hours without loss of time or pay. In this regard it is also noteworthy that the modified version contained in S.1958 substituted the term "to dominate or interfere with the formation or administration" for the terms "initiate, participate in, supervise, or influence." Thus, Congress concluded that ridding collective bargaining of employer-dominated organizations, the formation and administration of which had been fatally tainted by employer "domination" or "interference," would advance the Wagner Act's goal of eliminating industrial strife. That conclusion was based on the nation's experience under the NIRA, recounted by witnesses at the Senate hearings, that employer interference in setting up or running employee "representation" groups actually robbed employees of the freedom to choose their own representatives. Senator Wagner here made a distinction, important for this inquiry, between interference and minimal conduct—"merely suggesting to his employees that they organize a union or committee"—that the nation's experience had shown did not rob employees of their right to a representative of their own choosing. In sum, Congress brought within its definition of "labor organization" a broad range of employee groups, and it sought to ensure that such groups were free to act independently of employers in representing employee interests.

III.

Although Section 8(a)(2) does not define the specific acts that may constitute domination, a labor organization that is the creation of management, whose structure and function are essentially determined by management, and whose continued existence depends on the fiat of management, is one whose formation or administration has been dominated under Section 8(a)(2). In such an instance, actual domination has been established by virtue of the employer's specific acts of creating the organization itself and determining its structure and function. However, when the formulation and structure of the organization is determined by employees, domination is not established, even if the employer has the potential ability to influence the structure of effectiveness of the organization. Thus, the Board's cases following [NLRB v.] Cabot Carbon [Co., 360 U.S. 203 (1959)] reflect the view that when the impetus behind the formation of an organization of employees emanates from an employer and the organization has no effective existence independent of the employer's active involvement, a finding of domination is appropriate if the purpose of the organization is to deal with the employer concerning conditions of employment.

As noted previously, Board precedent and decisions of the Supreme Court indicate that the presence of antiunion motive is not critical to finding an 8(a)(2) violation. We also see no basis in the statutory language, the legislative history, or decisions apart from [*NLRB v.*] *Scott & Fetzer*[, 691 F.2d 288 (6th Cir. 1982)] to require a finding that the employees believe their organization to be a labor union. Instead, our inquiry is two-fold. First, we inquire whether the entity that is the object of the employer's allegedly unlawful conduct satisfies the definitional elements of Section 2(5) as to (1) employee participation, (2) a purpose to deal with employers, (3) concerning itself with conditions of employment or other statutory subjects, and (4) if an "employee representation committee or plan" is involved, evidence that the committee is in some way representing the employees. Second, if the organization satisfies those criteria, we consider whether the employer has engaged in any of the three forms of conduct proscribed by Section 8(a)(2).

Of course, Section 2(5) literally requires us to inquire into the "purpose" of the employee entity at issue because we must determine whether it exists "for the purpose of dealing" with conditions of employment. But "purpose" is different from motive; and the "purpose" to which the statute directs inquiry does not necessarily entail subjective hostility towards unions. Purpose is a matter of what the organization is set up to do, and that may be shown by what the organization actually does. If a purpose is to deal with an employer concerning conditions of employment, the Section 2(5) definition has been met regardless of whether the employer has created it, or fostered its creation, in order to avoid unionization or whether employees view that organization as equivalent to a union.

IV.

Applying these principles to the facts of this case, we find, in agreement with the judge, that the Action Committees constitute a labor organization within the meaning of Section 2(5) of the Act; and that the Respondent dominated it, and assisted it, i.e., contributed support, within the meaning of Section 8(a)(2).

First, there is no dispute that employees participated in the Action Committees. Second, we find that the activities of the committees constituted dealing with an employer. Third, we find that the subject matter of that dealing—which included the treatment of employee absenteeism and employee remuneration in the form of bonuses and other monetary incentives—concerned conditions of employment. Fourth, we find that the employees acted in a representational capacity within the meaning of Section 2(5). Taken as a whole, the evidence underlying these findings shows that the Action Committees were created for, and actually served, the purpose of dealing with the Respondent about conditions of employment.

As discussed in section I, the Action Committees were created in direct response to the employees' disaffection concerning changes in conditions of employment that the Respondent unilaterally implemented in late 1988. These changes resulted in a petition that employees presented to the Respondent. President Howard testified that after a January 11 meeting with a group of employees selected by management, he realized that the Respondent had serious problems with the employees and that "it was very unlikely that further unilateral management action to resolve these problems" would succeed. Accordingly, the Action Committees were created in order to achieve a bilateral solution to these problems. Employees on the Action Committees, according to Howard, were to meet with their management counterparts and, "try to come up with ways to resolve these problems." Howard also explained what would happen to any solutions that came out of the Action Committees. Howard testified that if the Committee's solutions satisfied the Respondent's budgetary concerns, "we would implement those suggestions or proposals."

The evidence thus overwhelmingly demonstrates that a purpose of the Action Committees, indeed their only purpose, was to address employees' disaffection concerning conditions of employment through the creation of a bilateral process involving employees and management in order to reach bilateral solutions on the basis of employee-initiated proposals. This is the essence of "dealing with" within the meaning of Section 2(5).

It is also clear that the Respondent contemplated that employee-members of the Action Committees would act on behalf of other employees. Thus, after talking "back and forth" with their fellow employees, members were to get ideas from other employees regarding the subjects of their committees for the purpose of reaching solutions that would satisfy the employees as a whole. This could occur only if the proposals presented by the employee-members were in line with the desires of other employees. In these circumstances, we find that employee-members of the Action Committees acted in a representational capacity and that the Action Committees were an "employee representation committee or plan" as set forth in Section 2(5).

There can also be no doubt that the Respondent's conduct vis à vis the Action Committees constituted "domination" in their formation and administration. It was the Respondent's idea to create the Action Committees. When it presented the idea to employees on January 18, the reaction, as the Respondent's President Howard admitted, was "not positive." Howard then informed employees that management would not "just unilaterally make changes" to satisfy employees' complaints. As a result, employees essentially were presented with the Hobson's choice of accepting the status quo, which they disliked, or undertaking a bilateral "exchange of ideas" within the framework of the Action Committees, as presented by the Respondent. The Respondent drafted the written purposes and goals of the Action Committees which defined and limited the subject matter to be covered by each Committee, determined how many members would compose a committee and that an employee could serve on only one committee, and appointed management representatives to the Committees to facilitate discussions. Finally, much of the evidence supporting the domination finding also supports a finding of unlawful contribution of support. In particular, the Respondent permitted the employees to carry out the committee activities on paid time within a structure that the Respondent itself created.

On these facts, we find that the Action Committees were the creation of the Respondent and that the impetus for their continued existence rested with the Respondent and not with the employees. Accordingly, the Respondent dominated the Action Committees in their formation and administration and unlawfully supported them.

We also agree with the judge that the Respondent did not effectively disestablish the Action Committees upon receipt of the union's bargaining demand. Thus, some of the Committees continued to meet and President Howard, in his speech to employees on March 15, implied that the Respondent would be involved with the Action Committees "after the election."

In sum, this case presents a situation in which an employer alters conditions of employment and, as a result, is confronted with a work force that is discontented with its new employment environment. The employer responds to that discontent by devising and imposing on the employees an organized Committee mechanism composed of managers and employees instructed to "represent" fellow employees. The purpose of the Action Committees was, as the record demonstrates, not to enable management and employees to cooperate to improve "quality" or "efficiency," but to create in employees the impression that their disagreements with management had been resolved bilaterally. By creating the Action Committees the Respondent imposed on employees its own unilateral form of bargaining or dealing and thereby violated Section 8(a)(2) and (1) as alleged.

MEMBER OVIATT, concurring:

American companies, their employees, and labor unions representing those employees are at present confronted with diverse competitive forces requiring an array of different responses if those companies are to remain competitive in the world economy. To the extent present laws are interpreted to apply restrictions and roadblocks to companies' ability to perform more efficiently and to respond promptly to competitive conditions, the more difficult will be the common task of achieving or retaining equality. This is a time of testing for the American and world economies and we must proceed with caution when we address the legality of innovative employee involvement programs directed to improving efficiency and productivity. I view the violations found here as clear cut, however. Accordingly, I join in the majority opinion, but I do so as much for what the opinion does not condemn as an unfair labor practice as for what it does find to be a violation of Section 8(a)(2) and (1). Thus, I write separately to stress the wide range of lawful activities which I view as untouched by this decision.

In my view, the critical question in most cases of alleged violations of Section 8(a)(2) through domination or support of an entity that includes employees among its membership is whether the entity is created with any purpose to deal with "grievances, labor disputes, wages, rates of pay, hours of employment, or conditions of work" as set forth in the Section 2(5) definition of "labor organization." In this case, I have no doubt that the subject matter of the Action Committees falls comfortably within the definition. The Committee's purpose was to address and find solutions for issues related to absenteeism, pay progression, attendance bonuses, and no-smoking policies. These are plainly among the subject matters about which labor organizations traditionally bargain since they involve "wages" or "conditions of work."

There is, however, an important area of industrial relations where committees and groups of employees and managerial personnel act together with the purpose of communicating, addressing and solving problems in the workplace that do not implicate the matters identified in Section 2(5). Among the employee-participation groups that may be established by management are so-called "quality circles" whose purpose is to use employee expertise by having the group examine certain operational problems such as labor efficiency and material waste. *See Beaver, Are Worker Participation Plans "Labor Organizations" Within the Meaning of Section 2(5)? A Proposed Framework of Analysis*, [36] Lab. L. J. 226 (1985). Other such committees have been dubbed "quality-of work-life programs." These involve management's attempt to draw on the creativity of its employees by including them in decisions that affect their work lives. These decisions may go beyond improvements in productivity and efficiency to include issues involving worker self-fulfillment and self-enhancement. *See,* Fulmer and Coleman, *Do Quality-of Work-Life Programs Violate Section 8(a)(2)?*, 35 Lab. L. J. 675 (1984). Others of these programs stress joint problem-solving structures that engage management and employees in finding ways of improving operating functions. *See,* Lee, *Collective Bargaining and Employee Participation: An Anomalous Interpretation of the National Labor Relations Act*, 38 Lab. L. J. 206, 207 (1987). And then there are employee-management committees that are established by a company with the purpose of creating better communications between employer and employee by exploring employee attitudes, communicating certain information to employees, and making management more aware of employee problems. See Beaver, *supra*.

Certainly, I find nothing in today's decision that should be read as a condemnation of cooperative programs and committees of the type I have outlined above. The statute does not forbid direct communication between the employer and its employees to address and solve significant productivity and efficiency problems in the workplace. In my view, committees and groups dealing with these subjects alone plainly fall outside the Section 2(5) definition of "labor organization" since they are not concerned with grievances, labor disputes, wages, rates of pay, hours of employment or conditions of work. Indeed, in this age of increased global competition I consider it of critical importance that management and employees be able, indeed, are encouraged, to engage in cooperative endeavors to improve production methods and product quality.

MEMBER DEVANEY, concurring:

I agree that the Respondent violated Section 8(a)(2) and (1) by "dominating or supporting" the Action Committees, which were "labor organizations" under Section 2(5). I write separately in response to concerns, raised by the parties and *amici* on both sides of the issue, over the lawfulness under Section 8(a)(2) of contemporary employee participation programs.

Like my colleagues, I acknowledge that a genuine "employee participation program" is not before the Board today, and, in agreeing that the Respondent violated Section 8(a)(2), I do not pass on the status of any other arrangement. It is my position, however, notwithstanding the concerns of some *amici*, that legislative history, binding judicial precedent, and Board precedent provide significant latitude to employers seeking to involve employees in the workplace. In my view, Section 8(a)(2) prohibits a specific form of employer conduct. It is not a broad-based ban on employee/employer communications. Thus, adjudication of the dealings between an employer and an employee organization must begin with an understanding of exactly what harms to Section 7 rights Section 8(a)(2) was intended to prevent and a targeting of Section 8(a)(2) enforcement at exactly those harms.

I base these conclusions on the following observations. First a "pure" employee participation plan was not before Congress in 1935 and has never been before the Supreme Court. Second, the legislative history of the Wagner Act, although replete with expressions of outright alarm over the development of employer-dominated sham "unions," shows virtually no concern over employer-initiated programs concerned with efficiency, quality, productivity, or other essentially managerial issues. Third, Board law itself has also recognized that employer-supported "committees" may take forms that are lawful under Section 8(a)(2). Based on the above, I would answer the question, posed by one *amicus*, thus: Section 8(a)(2) should not create obstacles for employers wishing to implement employee involvement programs—as long as those programs do not impair the right of employees to free choice of a bargaining representative.

[A concurring opinion by Member Raudabaugh advocating a reinterpretation of Section 8(a)(2) is omitted.]

CROWN, CORK & SEAL CO.
334 N.L.R.B. 699 (2001)

CHAIRMAN HURTGEN and MEMBERS LIEBMAN, TRUESDALE, and WALSH:

The relevant facts can be summarized as follows: The Respondent employs approximately 150 employees at its aluminum can manufacturing plant in Sugar Land, Texas. Ever since the plant opened in 1984, a system of employee management has been utilized known as the "Socio-Tech System." The central purpose of the Socio-Tech System is to delegate to employees substantial authority to operate the plant through their participation on numerous standing and temporary teams, committees, and boards (collectively committees). There was no union organizational activity occurring at the time the Socio-Tech System was adopted or at the time of the events in issue here. The seven committees discussed below are alleged to be employer-dominated labor organizations. All seven committees make decisions by a process of discussion and consensus. If a member of a committee cannot join in a consensus, he abstains on the issue. The management members of a committee have no greater authority than other committee members.

A.   The Four Production Teams

Production Teams A, B, C, and D are self-managed work groups that lie at the heart of the Socio-Tech System. Every employee in the plant participates on one of these teams. Each team is made up of 33 members: 1 team leader (a member of management) and 32 "production technicians" (production and maintenance employees).

Crediting the testimony of the plant manager, Rich De Young, the judge found that the four production teams "decide and do" on a wide variety of workplace issues, "including production, quality, training, attendance, safety, maintenance, and discipline short of suspension or discharge." For example, the teams have the authority to stop the production lines without management approval. With respect to quality issues, De Young testified that if team members working in the shipping area were concerned that scratched cans may have been shipped to a customer, "they're empowered to call up the customer and stop that delivery and turn it around." Regarding training, the teams have the authority to decide which members are given formal and informal training. The production teams administer the plant's absentee program, deciding whether to grant a team member's request for time off and whether an absence is excused or unexcused. With respect to safety, the production teams have the authority to investigate accidents and correct safety-related problems. For example, Plant Manager De Young testified that production teams would correct the problem of a piece of machinery "eating people's fingers" by building and installing a guard without further review by anyone else in the plant. Teams take this kind of action "time and time again."

The production teams decide what disciplinary action to take against a team member failing to meet team norms with respect to performance or behavior. The team can counsel the member and, if necessary, require the member to enter into a "social contract." A "social contract" can be verbal or written and is designed to modify the member's behavior. If the social contract does not have the desired effect and the team believes that suspension or discharge is warranted, the decision is in the form of a recommendation to the Organizational Review Board discussed below.

B.   The Organizational Review Board; the Advancement
Certification Board; and the Safety Committee

These three committees exist at one administrative level above the production teams. Each one has about a dozen members, including two members from each of the four teams and some members of management. Many of the decisions made by these three committees are reviewed by the Management Team composed of 15 members of management. The plant manager is above the Management Team. He has the ultimate authority to review all decisions made by the three committees.

Under the Socio-Tech System, the Organizational Review Board (ORB) is charged with monitoring plant policies to insure that they are administered consistently among the four teams. The ORB also suggests modifications to plant norms, including hours, layoff procedures, smoking policies, vacations, and all terms and conditions of employment. Decisions of the ORB are in the form of recommendations forwarded to the Management Team or the plant manager. Plant Manager De Young testified that he could not recall a single instance when he over-ruled the ORB. "I just haven't done it." Further, De Young testified that decisions of the ORB often have been implemented by the time they reach him:

> So, usually, by the time the decision is made, everybody in the plant has discussed it so often, it's common knowledge. So, usually, by the time it finally gets to the ORB and the

Management Team and I see it, it's something that's been implemented and it's, you know, done.

In addition, the ORB reviews production team recommendations to suspend or discipline a team member. Again, the record shows that the plant manager gives great weight to the recommendation of the ORB. In a case involving an employee who urinated on a plant building, De Young was faced with conflicting disciplinary recommendations from the ORB and the Management Team. Rejecting the Management Team's discharge recommendation, De Young approved ORB's suspension recommendation.

Like the other committees, the ORB must operate within established parameters. The record indicates that one of the roles of management is to ensure that the committees do not exceed their delegated authority. For example, when the ORB recommended a layoff procedure that contained a provision for seniority, the Management Team returned the matter to the ORB with the following comment: "We do not have seniority in this plant." The final version of the layoff policy did not include seniority as an independent factor.

The Socio-Tech System delegates to the Advancement Certification Board (ACB) the authority to administer the Respondent's "Pay for Acquired Skills Program." The ACB certifies that employees have advanced to higher skill levels and recommends pay increases to the plant manager. De Young has never overruled a recommendation of the ACB.

The Socio-Tech System delegates to the Safety Committee the authority to review production team accident reports and consider the best methods to ensure a safe workplace. The plant manager has never overruled a recommendation of the Safety Committee. In fact, De Young indicated that he would defer to the Safety Committee on an issue even if he did not agree with it. Thus, when asked what he would do if the Safety Committee wanted more anti-slide grit on the floors and his examination of the area showed no deficit of the grit, De Young testified:

> I mean, you know, if I went back to the Safety Committee and they felt like that wasn't sufficient grit even though I thought it was, I would have more installed because they work there, I don't.

II. ANALYSIS

By its terms, Section 8(a)(2) provides that it is an unfair labor practice for an employer to dominate or support "any labor organization." Consequently, before a violation of Section 8(a)(2) can be found, the entity involved must be a statutory "labor organization."

One of the required elements for "labor organization" status under Section 2(5) is that the entity "exists for the purpose, in whole or in part, of *dealing with* employers concerning grievances, labor disputes, wages, rates of pay, hours of employment, or conditions of work." (Emphasis added.) The

Board has explained that "dealing with" contemplates "a bilateral mechanism involving proposals from the employee committee concerning the subjects listed in Section 2(5), coupled with real or apparent consideration of those proposals by management." *Electromation, Inc.*, 309 N.L.R.B. 990, 995 fn. 21 (1992), *enf'd*, 35 F.3d 1148 (7th Cir. 1994). "That 'bilateral mechanism' ordinarily entails a pattern or practice in which a group of employees, over time, makes proposals to management, [and] management responds to these proposals by acceptance or rejection by word or deed. . . ." *E. I. du Pont & Co.*, 311 N.L.R.B. 893, 894 (1993).

Keeler Brass Co., 317 N.L.R.B. 1110 (1995), illustrates the concept of "dealing." In that case, an employee grievance committee decided that the company's decision to discharge an employee under its "no-call, no-show" policy was too harsh. The committee recommended that the employee be rehired and that the policy be reexamined. The company considered the committee's proposal, changed the no-call, no-show policy, but decided that the discharge was justified by past practice. The grievance committee then heard additional testimony on the past-practice issue, reversed itself, and denied the grievance. On these facts, the Board found that statutory "dealing" was present with respect to the discharge grievance and the no-call, no-show policy because the committee and the company "went back and forth explaining themselves until an acceptable result was achieved." *Id.* at 1114.

By contrast, the element of "dealing" was absent in *Gen. Foods Corp.*, 231 N.L.R.B. 1232 (1977). That case involved a "job enrichment program" designed "to enlarge the powers and responsibilities of all its rank-and-file employees and to give them certain powers or controls over their job situations which are normally not assigned to manual laborers." *Id.* at 1232–1233. Employees were divided into four teams. Acting by consensus, the teams made job assignments to individual team members, assigned job rotations, and scheduled overtime. Individual team members also served on ad hoc committees that interviewed job applicants, made safety inspections of the plant, and, within certain limits, set starting and quitting times.

The *General Foods* Board found that "these are managerial functions being flatly delegated to employees and do not involve any dealing with the employer on a group basis within the meaning of Section 2(5), however expansively that term is applied." *Id.* at 1235. The decision continued as follows:

> While the employer could withdraw the powers delegated to employees to perform these functions on its behalf, the withdrawal of authority would be wholly unilateral on its part just as was Respondent's original delegation. There was no dealing between employer and employee (or employee group) involved in

these matters. These functions were just other assignments of job duties, albeit duties not normally granted to rank-and-file personnel. [*Id.*]

In its subsequent *Electromation* decision, the Board cited *General Foods* for the proposition that there is no "dealing" if the organization's "purpose is limited to performing essentially a managerial" function. 309 N.L.R.B. at 995.

With these principles in mind, we now turn to the issue before us of whether the seven committees exist for the purpose of "dealing with" the Respondent.

The Respondent and the *amicus* assert that the facts of the instant case resemble those of *General Foods*. We agree. As in *General Foods*, management has delegated to the committees in issue the authority to operate the plant within certain parameters. This is the essence of the Socio-Tech System. As the judge recognized, the Socio-Tech System represents a significant variation on the traditional plant organizational structure where authority is delegated to descending levels of managers who make decisions on an individual basis. Under the Socio-Tech System, authority is delegated to descending levels of committees which make decisions by consensus.

Nevertheless, the two systems have an important element in common and that is that at each level the authority being exercised is unquestionably managerial. With respect to the four production teams, Plant Manager De Young testified, the judge found, and we agree, that the authority they exercise is comparable to that of the front-line supervisor in the traditional plant setting. Similarly, given De Young's credited testimony that he has rarely, if ever, overruled one of the recommendations of the ORB, the ACB, or the Safety Committee, it cannot be doubted that each committee exercises as a group authority that in the traditional plant setting would be considered to be supervisory. Therefore, we conclude that the rationale of *General Foods* applies here and that the seven committees are not labor organizations because their purpose is to perform essentially managerial functions, and thus they do not "deal with" the Respondent within the meaning of Section 2(5) of the Act.

In contending otherwise, the General Counsel maintains that because none of the seven committees possess authority that is final and absolute, "dealing" must necessarily be occurring when their recommendations are passed on to the Management Team and the plant manager. Like the judge, we reject this contention. Few, if any, supervisors in a conventional plant possess authority that is final and absolute. At the Respondent's facility, just as in a more traditional plant, one level of management (e.g., the ORB), acting within its sphere of delegated authority, forwards for review its recommendations to a higher level of authority (e.g., the plant manager).

But it would not be accurate to characterize that exchange as "dealing" within the meaning of Section 2(5) of the Act. Rather, what is occurring in the Respondent's facility is the familiar process of a managerial recommendation making its way up the chain of command. Higher-management review of a recommendation made by lower management cannot be equated to the "dealing" between an employer and a representative of its employees contemplated by the statute. Indeed, it is the fact that the interaction is occurring between two management bodies that distinguishes this case from cases such as *Keeler Brass* and persuades us that the statutory element of dealing is absent.

In sum, the record establishes that the seven committees in issue do not "deal with" management within the meaning of Section 2(5). Rather, the evidence shows that, within their delegated spheres of authority, the seven committees are management. For this reason, we affirm the judge's findings that the seven committees are not statutory labor organizations and that, consequently, the Respondent has not violated Section 8(a)(2) of the Act.

NOTES

1.   One of the key reasons for the outcome in *Electromation* is that intent, or *scienter*, is not an element of proof in establishing a violation Section 8(a)(2). One can imagine that if there had been an intent element, the Wagner Act's goals would have taken much longer to accomplish as company union litigation would have surely been extended over disputes about intent. In *Bernhard Altmann*, *infra* p. 410, the Supreme Court made clear that intent is not a factor in Section 8(a)(2) cases:

> The petitioner, while taking no issue with the fact of its minority status on the critical date, maintains that both Bernhard-Altmann's and its own good-faith beliefs in petitioner's majority status are a complete defense. To countenance such an excuse would place in permissibly careless employer and union hands the power to completely frustrate employee realization of the premise of the Act—that its prohibitions will go far to assure freedom of choice and majority rule in employee selection of representatives. We find nothing in the statutory language prescribing *scienter* as an element of the unfair labor practices here involved. . . . More need not be shown, for, even if mistakenly, the employees' rights have been invaded. It follows that prohibited conduct cannot be excused by a showing of good faith. 366 U.S. 731, 738–39 (1961).

Should the intent requirement be read back into the statute, now that unions are established, and now that most Section 8(a)(2) charges seem to be directed at workplace productivity committees? How you answer may depend on whether you think that even well-intentioned employer efforts to create committees with control over labor relations can stand in the way of effective union organizing and an independent union. To better understand the tension between Section 8(a)(2) and employer participation committees, see Robert Moberly, *The Story of Electromation: Are Employee Participation Programs a Competitive Necessity or a Wolf in Sheep's Clothing?*, in Labor Law Stories 315 (Laura J. Cooper & Catherine L. Fisk, eds., 2005).

2. *Work teams vs. advisory committees.* Employers may create "advisory committees" to help improve plant operations. The employer can provide space for the meeting, hold meetings during work time and pay the employees who attend the meeting. But the main purpose of the advisory committee cannot be the discussion and proposal of terms and conditions of employment. In *Stabilus Inc.*, 355 N.L.R.B. 836 (2010), the employer drafted a document called "operating structure and guidelines" (OSG) that created committees and established operational committee topics: operations, safety, quality, productivity, training, scheduling, preventive maintenance, overtime, supplies, and staffing. The document provided that no member had veto power and decisions were to be by consensus, but that any member could select a discussion topic that would be prioritized by the facilitator, a human resources representative. Further, each committee had the authority to directly implement a course of action "subject to budgetary or financial restraints." The Board, in a case in which it found a number of violations of the Act, upheld an ALJ decision that the advisory committees were not labor organizations because they did not "deal with" the employer regarding terms and conditions of employment. Although many issues were raised in the committees, some even related to working conditions, the ALJ found, and the Board agreed, that the primary focus of the committees was not terms and conditions of employment. *Id.*

3. *Just deal with it—or don't.* The requirement that the employee committee must "deal with" the employer in order to violate Section 8(a)(2) has proved to be the thorniest of the required elements. As the Board states in *Electromation*, the heart of the "dealing with" requirement is "creation of a bilateral process involving employees and management in order to reach bilateral solutions on the basis of employee-initiated proposals." In addition, those proposals must receive "real or apparent consideration by management." Thus, in *Crown, Cork & Seal*, the Board found that there was no "dealing with" where management authority was effectively delegated to a group of employees. Critical to the Board's decision in *Crown, Cork & Seal* was its finding that the Plant Manager was effectively a "rubber stamp" for the decisions of the Plant's Safety Committee. Does the fact that a manager has not exercised authority in the past necessarily mean that she will not do so in the future? If she does later, can the 8(a)(2) charge be revived? In *Crown, Cork and Seal*, the Board found that the committees were not labor organizations because they were not "dealing with" the employer. Instead, the committees were exercising management functions that had been delegated to them. Are the committee members employees or are they now managers, excluded from the Act's protections?

By contrast, in *DaNite Sign Co.*, 356 N.L.R.B. 975 (2011), the employer implemented a "moving forward team" (MFT) whose purpose was to facilitate employee consultation with the employer about terms and conditions of employment. The employees were selected by the employer and gave input on merit wage increases, health insurance, and the content of a survey regarding compensation. Although there were no actual back and forth dealings between the MFT and the employer, the Board found that the MFT was a labor organization, inferring that the purpose of the MFT was to advise the employer of consensus employee sentiment on these matters and decide whether to accept or reject it.

Management-created committees that operate more like a "suggestion box" have been found by the Board not to be labor organizations because they are missing the "dealing with" component required. For example, in *EFCO Corp.*, 327 N.L.R.B. 372 (1998), the Board failed to find that an employee suggestion screening committee was a labor organization because it merely performed a "clerical or ministerial function" facilitating the employer's consideration of suggestions made by employees even though the committee screened suggestions for the employer to consider. Recently, however, in *T-Mobile USA, Inc.*, 2017 WL 1230099 (2017), a Board ALJ found that the company's T-Voice program, intended to "identify, assess, and resolve" complaints by Customer Service Representatives, was a labor organization because "T-Voice did not just screen [complaints or suggestions.] The T-Voice representatives participated in focus groups about the issues, which is beyond the screening of suggestions, and implies a bilateral mechanism, beyond brainstorming, to address [complaints or suggestions." *Id.*

4. *Chapter 3 revisited: Who's an "employee"?* As explained in *Electromation,* in order to violate Section 8(a)(2), those involved in the committee or group must be employees as defined by the Act. The Act's definition has been applied expansively in determining who constitutes an employee for purposes of the Act's coverage. *See, e.g., Sahara Datsun, Inc. v. NLRB,* 811 F.2d 1317 (9th Cir. 1987) (group of automobile sales representatives constitutes labor organization, even though it holds few meetings and has no formal structure); *Am. River Touring Ass'n,* 246 N.L.R.B. 935 (1979) (whitewater canoe guides are employees); *N. Am. Soccer League,* 236 N.L.R.B. 1317 (1978) (professional soccer players are employees). Nonetheless, those expressly excluded from the definition of employee (e.g., independent contractors, supervisors, managerial employees) have been held not to qualify as employees, meaning that employer domination of those workers cannot constitute a violation of § 8(a)(2). *See North Am. Van Lines, Inc. v. NLRB,* 869 F.2d 596 (D.C. Cir. 1989).

5. *A slap on the wrist?* As *Electromation* shows, when the Board finds employer domination, it orders the labor organization disestablished. If the Board disestablishes an employer-dominated committee, should it also wipe out whatever the committee has accomplished? If it does, can it blame this loss on the union or union adherent who filed the Section 8(a)(2) charge in the first place? Is there any legal disincentive for an employer who wishes to create a

dominated labor organization, or is the remedy just a slap on the wrist? *See Planned Bldg. Servs., Inc.*, 347 N.L.R.B. 670 (2006), *overruled by Pressroom Cleaners*, 361 N.L.R.B. 643 (2014) ("slap on the wrist" remedy of allowing successor employer to present evidence about what would have happened in bargaining is inconsistent with longstanding Board doctrine resistant to speculation about possible results of bargaining, presents successor employer with extraordinary option not available in other "refusal to bargain" situations, and prolongs litigation while discouraging bargaining); *Dairyland USA Corp.*, 347 N.L.R.B. 310 (2006).

6.   *The Somali Workers' Case revisited.* Consider the case of the Somali workers at the beginning of Chapter 2, *supra* p. 113. Could Enderby's Human Resources Director create a committee of workers, including the Somalis, to address and make suggestions about accommodations for prayer and improved promotion processes? Could the committee make suggestions directly to management? What if Enderby empowered the committee by delegation to make its own decisions and implement them? What if the committee were asked to look at ways to improve productivity by streamlining and making the prayer break more efficient? After *Electromation*, would any of these violate section 8(a)(2)? After *Crown Cork & Seal*?

7.   *No domination? What about assistance and interference?* In addition to prohibiting employer domination of labor organizations, section 8(a)(2) has been read to forbid employer assistance or interference with unions and labor organizations as entities. Sometimes referred to as "minor" domination, assistance or interference is distinguished from domination by degree, meaning that domination tends to irrevocably undermine the independence of a union while assistance or interference can be remedied by eliminating employer intrusion, resulting in a functioning independent entity. The failure of any of the three-prongs of the domination test, set out above in *Electromation*, will usually result in a finding of interference or assistance rather than domination. *See Bernhard-Altmann*, above (although employer recognized minority union as exclusive representative there were no allegations of employer control over the union); *Spiegel Trucking Co.*, 225 N.L.R.B. 178 (1976) (although employer took an active role in forming a labor organization, no evidence that employer controlled the group after formation).

Assistance or interference violations run the gamut from supervisor involvement with a union to bargaining with a union before it has established majority status to providing financial assistance to the union or coercively enforcing dues check-off provisions. With respect to employer support of a union, the trickiest questions involve types of assistance like allowing the use of company property or allowing activities to take place on company time. These are handled by the NLRB on a case by case basis. *See Coamo Knitting Mills, Inc.*, 150 N.L.R.B. 579 (1964). As a practical matter, the key difference between a finding of domination versus one of assistance or interference is the remedy. For domination, the NLRB typically requires disestablishment of the union or labor organization while assistance or interference violations may only require that the employer cease from supporting and/or recognizing the union. *See Wells Enterprises,* 365 N.L.R.B. No. 7 (2016) (NLRB reversed ALJ who had ordered employer to cease recognizing a union, but limiting 8(a)(2) violation remedy to rescission of employer's illegal sales commission agreement with the union).

A particularly difficult issue has been employer involvement in campaigns involving contending unions. For many years, the Board and the courts required employers to remain neutral in situations involving contending unions or risk violating section 8(a)(2). *See Midwest Piping & Supply Co.,* 63 N.L.R.B. 1060 (1945); *Shea Chem. Corp.,* 121 N.L.R.B. 1027 (1958). But in 1982 the Board changed course and allowed an employer to recognize, and even bargain with, an incumbent union, in certain circumstances. In *RCA del Caribe, Inc.,* 262 N.L.R.B. 963 (1982), the employer recognized and continued bargaining with an incumbent union despite the filing of a valid election petition by a rival union. The Board held that promoting the stability of the existing bargaining relationship favored continuing the status quo until the Board determined the results of the election. In *Bruckner Nursing Home,* 262 N.L.R.B. 955 (1982), a companion case to *RCA del Caribe,* there was no incumbent union, but the Board held that, in the absence of a valid election petition, an employer does not violate section 8(a)(2) by recognizing or even bargaining with a union that represents a majority of its employees. Once a valid election petition is filed by any union (where there is no incumbent union), however, the employer must cease recognizing any rival unions.

2. EXCLUSIVE REPRESENTATION AND MAJORITY RULE

a. The Issue of Minority Unions

THE BLUE EAGLE AT WORK: RECLAIMING DEMOCRATIC RIGHTS IN THE AMERICAN WORKPLACE[1]

Charles J. Morris
Introduction 1–4 (2005)

Almost all ancient peoples believed the Earth to be flat. And almost all Americans involved in employment relations believe that a minority union has no right to engage in collective bargaining, even where no majority union has yet been designated. But come with me on a journey of legal discovery—or rather rediscovery—and we shall learn that this conventional wisdom is an illusion without foundation and that what will appear to be a new world of labor relations lies beyond. Historically, however, this new legal landscape will be no more new than the new world that Columbus found, but the prospect for change in American labor relations, as with the rediscovery of America, will indeed be new.

---

[1]   Reprinted from Charlie Morris, The Blue Eagle at Work: Reclaiming Democratic Rights in the American Workplace. Copyright © 2005 by Cornell University. Used by permission of the publisher Cornell University Press.

My personal journey of rediscovery began in the year 2001 when a friend, Peter Zschiesche, director of the San Diego Employee Rights Center, called my attention to the plight of seventeen immigrant workers for whom he had filed an unfair labor practice charge. These were young men who had been employed at Hi Tech Honeycomb, Inc., a southern California aerospace subcontracting company. Reacting to their low wages and abysmal working conditions, on the morning of February 10, 1999—without labor-union assistance—they organized themselves into an informal peer group and staged a brief walkout to protest those conditions. The company owner refused to meet with them as a group to discuss their grievances and swiftly retaliated by firing all of them. In response to Zschiesche's request, I provided those workers with pro bono legal representation before the Regional Director and the General Counsel of the National Labor Relations Board (NLRB, or Board). While engaged in such representation, I began to analyze the multiple legal issues posed by their situation and to delve into the labor and legislative history that affected those issues. After lengthy study that continued far beyond the final action in the NLRB case, I was able to confidently reconfirm—contrary to conventional wisdom—that in workplaces where there is not yet a majority/exclusive representative, collective bargaining on behalf of the members of a minority labor union is a protected right fully guaranteed by the National Labor Relations Act (NLRA, Wagner Act, or Act).

My attention to the iconoclastic thesis that I am here presenting was prompted earlier—in 1990—when I read Professor Clyde Summers's article, *Unions Without Majority—A Black Hole*, in which he made an observation that had not appeared in the legal literature since 1936, to wit, that the plain words of the Act "would seem to require an employer, in the absence of a majority union, to bargain collectively with a non-majority union for its own members"; and he noted various historical features to support that observation. He suggested, however, that "it may be too late to open this question." Writing separately in 1993, Professors Alan Hyde and Matthew Finkin, although not disagreeing with Summers's premise, contended that because of the passage of time legislative action would be required to reaffirm this true meaning of the law. Rejecting that pessimistic appraisal, I wrote in 1994 that although "the role of the minority union should be reaffirmed and reinvigorated . . . amending the Act is not essential to the confirmation of the existence of the rights of minority unions"; nevertheless, I then conceded that amendments, or perhaps the issuance of administrative rules, would be desirable to emphasize and clarify those rights. And so the matter rested—at least for me—until my interest was aroused again by the peremptory firing of those seventeen immigrant workers. Subsequent research that I initiated on their behalf produced considerable new evidence and substantiated that the present law is clear and sufficient, that amendments to the Act—which in any event would be unobtainable in the foreseeable future—are unnecessary and would serve no useful purpose.

What happened to those seventeen workers was a disgrace to American democracy. Those young men, who were of Vietnamese, Cambodian, and Philippine origin and new to America, apparently trusted that this was a land of opportunity where they could improve their lot through hard work and cooperation with others. Lacking the usual fear that traditional American employees typically display toward organizational activity in the workplace, they boldly decided to join together to confront their employer about their grievances. The company, which employed about fifty production workers, manufactured honeycombs (filters made of welded metal that resemble beehive honeycombs) for jet engines. Despite the low wages, which were only slightly above minimum wage for most of the group, the employees' job tasks required considerable skill and attention. The group's chief complaints were that they had been promised wage increases that were either long delayed or never delivered; they had been denied such basic safety protections as gloves (for handling hazardous fluid) and safety goggles and face masks when needed; some of them had been promised promotions which never materialized; some had often been denied rest breaks; and some had suffered verbal abuse from the owner himself.

Operating on the premise that "enough is enough," these aggrieved workers organized and signed a petition for presentation to their employer through a spokesperson whom they had democratically selected. He then asked management for a meeting on behalf of the group, but when that was not promptly forthcoming the aggrieved employees shut down their machines and quietly walked out. Soon after, they gathered at a meeting in a public park near where they lived, and later that day they returned to the factory to renew their request for a group meeting with management to discuss their complaints. The owner denied their request, insisting that the company would not meet with them as a group and would only see them individually. Preferring to maintain their group solidarity, the employees refused to meet alone, whereupon management immediately advised them that they had all forfeited their jobs. They were thus terminated for having engaged in concerted activity that was intended to improve their wages and working conditions through a civilized process of jointly discussing their grievances with management—that is, through a rudimentary form of collective bargaining. Federal law unequivocally states that they "have the right . . . to bargain collectively through representatives of their own choosing. . . ." The Hi Tech owner admitted to one of his supervisors that the reason "he did not want them together as a group [was] because he felt that they would back each other up if he offered something to one employee." This seemed to fly in the face of the congressional intent behind the Act that was meant to create "some equality of bargaining power."

Out of desperation—for they had families to feed—several of the men broke ranks. Later that afternoon, assuming they had no alternative, a few met individually with management, and some were rehired shortly thereafter. A few others were selectively rehired during the next several months. The remainder sought other employment or left the area. Hi Tech Honeycomb had thus effectively squelched this fledgling effort by a group of its employees to achieve self-organization in their new American workplace.

Previous to my being made aware of the happenings at Hi Tech, the NLRB Regional Director had issued a complaint against the company and the case was set for hearing, for the discharges were clearly in violation of well-settled law (although the employer could have obtained the same result legally by replacing—instead of discharging—the striking employees'). However, it had not occurred to the Regional Director to seek an order requiring the employer to meet and bargain with the employee group, which was really the key issue. I tried, unsuccessfully, to achieve that objective with an amendment to the complaint, citing as a separate unfair labor practice the company's refusal to meet with the employees as a group. The General Counsel declined to consider such an amendment because the case had already been set for hearing and apparently a settlement was deemed likely. In fact, over my objection, the employer eagerly settled the case for 80 percent of lost back wages, a belated offer of reinstatement (a year and a half had elapsed since the discharges), and the posting of an effectively meaningless notice. Thus, for a total payment of only $26,000 for all lost wages, the company was able to relish its success in crushing the organizational efforts of seventeen courageous but naive employees.

INTERNATIONAL LADIES' GARMENT WORKERS' UNION (BERNHARD-ALTMANN TEXAS CORP.) V. NLRB
366 U.S. 731 (1961)

JUSTICE CLARK delivered the opinion of the Court:

We are asked to decide in this case whether it was an unfair labor practice for both an employer and a union to enter into an agreement under which the employer recognized the union as exclusive bargaining representative of certain of his employees, although in fact only a minority of those employees had authorized the union to represent their interests. The Board found that by extending such recognition, even though done in the good-faith belief that the union had the consent of a majority of employees in the appropriate bargaining unit, the employer interfered with the organizational rights of his employees in violation of § 8(a)(1) of the National Labor Relations Act and that such recognition also constituted unlawful support to a labor organization in violation of § 8(a)(2). In addition, the Board found that the union violated § 8(b)(1)(A) by its acceptance of exclusive bargaining authority at a time when in fact it did not have the support of a majority of the employees, and this in spite of its bona fide belief that it did. Accordingly, the Board ordered the unfair labor practices discontinued and directed the holding of a representation election. The Court of Appeals, by a divided vote, granted enforcement. We granted certiorari. We agree with the Board and the Court of Appeals that such extension and acceptance of recognition constitute unfair labor practices, and that the remedy provided was appropriate.

In October 1956 the petitioner union initiated an organizational campaign at Bernhard-Altmann Texas Corporation's knitwear manufacturing plant in San Antonio, Texas. No other labor organization was similarly engaged at that time. During the course of that campaign, on July 29, 1957, certain of the company's Topping Department employees went on strike in protest against a wage reduction. That dispute was in no way related to the union campaign, however, and the organizational efforts were continued during the strike. Some of the striking employees had signed authorization cards solicited by the union during its drive, and, while the strike was in progress, the union entered upon a course of negotiations with the employer. As a result of those negotiations, on August 30, 1957, the employer and union signed a "memorandum of understanding." In that memorandum the company recognized the union as exclusive bargaining representative of "all production and shipping employees." The union representative asserted that the union's comparison of the employee authorization cards in its possession with the number of eligible employees [that] representatives of the company furnished it indicated that the union had in fact secured such cards from a majority of employees in the unit. Neither employer nor union made any effort at that time to check the cards in the union's possession against the employee roll, or otherwise, to ascertain with any degree of certainty that the union's assertion, later found by the Board to be erroneous, was founded on fact rather than upon good-faith assumption. The agreement, containing no union security provisions, called for the ending of the strike and for certain improved wages and conditions of employment. It also provided that a "formal agreement containing these terms" would "be promptly drafted . . . and signed by both parties within the next two weeks."

Thereafter, on October 10, 1957, a formal collective bargaining agreement, embodying the terms of the August 30 memorandum, was signed by the parties. The bargaining unit description set out in the formal contract, although more specific, conformed to that contained in the prior memorandum. It is not disputed that as of execution of the formal contract the union in fact represented a clear majority of employees in the appropriate unit. In upholding the complaints filed against the employer and union by the General Counsel, the Board decided that the employer's good-faith belief that the union in fact represented a majority of employees in the unit on the critical date of the memorandum of understanding was not a defense, "particularly where, as here, the Company made no effort to check the authorization cards against its payroll records." Noting that the union was "actively seeking recognition at the time such recognition was granted," and that "the Union was [not] the passive recipient of an unsolicited gift bestowed by the Company," the Board found that the union's execution of the August 30 agreement was a "direct deprivation" of the nonconsenting majority employees' organizational and bargaining rights. Accordingly, the Board ordered the employer to withhold all recognition from the union and to cease giving effect to agreements entered into with the union; the union was ordered to cease acting as bargaining representative of any of the employees until such time as a Board-conducted election demonstrated its majority status, and to refrain from seeking to enforce the agreements previously entered. The Court of Appeals found it difficult to "conceive of a clearer restraint on the employees' right of self-organization than for their employer to enter into a collective-bargaining agreement with a minority of the employees."

At the outset, we reject as without relevance to our decision the fact that, as of the execution date of the formal agreement on October 10, petitioner represented a majority of the employees. As the Court of Appeals indicated, the recognition of the minority union on August 30, 1957, was "a fait accompli depriving the majority of the employees of their guaranteed right to choose their own representative." It is, therefore, of no consequence that petitioner may have acquired by October 10 the necessary majority if, during the interim, it was acting unlawfully. Indeed, such acquisition of majority status itself might indicate that the recognition secured by the August 30 agreement afforded petitioner a deceptive cloak of authority with which to persuasively elicit additional employee support.

Lastly, the violation which the Board found was the grant by the employer of exclusive representation status to a minority union, as distinguished from an employer's bargaining with a minority union for its members only. Therefore, the exclusive representation provision is the vice in the agreement, and discussion of "collective bargaining," as distinguished from "exclusive recognition," is pointless. Moreover, the insistence that we hold the agreement valid and enforceable as to those employees who consented to it must be rejected. On the facts shown, the agreement must fail in its entirety. It was obtained under the erroneous claim of majority representation. Perhaps the employer would not have entered into it if he had known the facts. Quite apart from other conceivable situations, the unlawful genesis of this agreement precludes its partial validity.

The petitioner, while taking no issue with the fact of its minority status on the critical date, maintains that both Bernhard-Altmann's and its own good-faith beliefs in petitioner's majority status are a complete defense. To countenance such an excuse would place in permissibly careless employer and union hands the power to completely frustrate employee realization of the premise of the Act—that its prohibitions will go far to assure freedom of choice and majority rule in employee selection of representatives. We find nothing in the statutory language prescribing *scienter* as an element of the unfair labor practices here involved. The act made unlawful by § 8(a)(2) is employer support of a minority union. Here that support is an accomplished fact. More need not be shown, for, even if mistakenly, the employees' rights have been invaded. It follows that prohibited conduct cannot be excused by a showing of good faith.

This conclusion, while giving the employee only the protection assured him by the Act, places no particular hardship on the employer or the union. It merely requires that recognition be withheld until the Board-conducted election results in majority selection of a representative. The Board's order here, as we might infer from the employer's failure to resist its enforcement, would apparently result in similarly slight hardship upon it. We do not share petitioner's apprehension that holding such conduct unlawful will somehow induce a breakdown, or seriously impede the progress of collective bargaining. If an employer takes reasonable steps to verify union claims, themselves advanced only after careful estimate— precisely what Bernhard-Altmann and petitioner failed to do here—he can readily ascertain their validity and obviate a Board election. We fail to see any onerous burden involved in requiring responsible negotiators to be careful, by cross-checking, for example, well-analyzed employer records with union listings or authorization cards. Individual and collective employee rights may not be trampled upon merely because it is inconvenient to avoid doing so. Moreover, no penalty is attached to the violation. Assuming that an employer in good faith accepts or rejects a union claim of majority status, the validity of his decision may be tested in an unfair labor practice proceeding. If he is found to have erred in extending or withholding recognition, he is subject only to a remedial order requiring him to conform his conduct to the norms set out in the Act, as was the case here. No further penalty results. We believe the Board's remedial order is the proper one in such cases.

JUSTICE DOUGLAS, with whom JUSTICE BLACK concurs, dissenting in part:

I agree that, under the statutory scheme, a minority union does not have the standing to bargain for all employees. That principle of representative government extends only to the majority. But where there is no majority union, I see no reason why the minority union should be disabled from bargaining for the minority of the members who have joined it. Yet the order of the Board, now approved, enjoins petitioner union from acting as the exclusive bargaining representative "of any of the employees," and it enjoins the employer from recognizing the union as the representative of "any of its employees."

I think the Court is correct insofar as it sets aside the exclusive recognition clause in the contract. I think it is incorrect in setting aside the entire contract. First, that agreement secured valuable benefits for the union's members regarding wages and hours, work standards and distribution, discharge and discipline, holidays, vacations, health and welfare fund, and other matters. Since there was no duly selected representative for all the employees authorized in accordance with the Act, it certainly was the right of the employee union members to designate the union or any other appropriate person to make this contract they desired. To hold the contract void as to the union's voluntary members seems to me to go beyond the competency of the Board under the Act and to be unsupported by any principle of contract law. Certainly there is no principle of justice or fairness with which I am familiar that requires these employees to be stripped of the benefits they acquired by the good-faith bargaining of their designated agent. Such a deprivation gives no protection to the majority who were not members of the union and arbitrarily takes from the union members their contract rights.

Second, the result of today's decision is to enjoin the employer from dealing with the union as the representative of its own members in any manner, whether in relation to grievances or otherwise, until it is certified as a majority union. A case for complete disestablishment of the union cannot be sustained under our decisions. While the power of the Board is broad, it is "not limitless." Thus a distinction has been taken between remedies in situations where a union has been dominated by the employer and where unions have been assisted but not dominated.

NOTES

1.   *For members only?* Justices Douglas and Black, partly dissenting in *Bernhard-Altmann*, maintain that a minority union, one that represents only its members, and not the bargaining unit or even the majority, in a given workplace, should be allowed. Although the Board's references are to very early cases and the minority union concept has been lost in the US for some time, a number of unions and labor law scholars, embracing arguments put forth by Professor Charles Morris, *supra* p. 407, have asked the NLRB to issue rules allowing an employer to bargain with a minority union when no majority union exists. Of course, the minority union could not be the exclusive representative of all employees; instead, it would bargain with the employer as to the terms of employment applied to members of the minority union only. In sum, the argument is that the NLRA does not outlaw such bargaining; *Bernhard-Altmann* only prohibits recognition of a minority union as the *exclusive* representative of the entire work unit. To this end, in 2007, seven unions filed a rulemaking petition on members-only minority unions. *See* Petition of United

Steel, Paper and Forestry, Rubber, Manufacturing, Energy, Allied Industrial and Service Workers International Union, AFL-CIO, and Other Labor Organizations, as "Interested Persons" Under 29 U.S.C. § 2(1), 29 C.F.R. § 102.124, 5 U.S.C. § 551(2), and 5 U.S.C. § 553(3), *In re Rulemaking Regarding Members-Only Minority-Union Collective Bargaining* (Aug. 14, 2007), http://www.laborrelationstoday.com/uploads/file/PetitionRequesting RulemakingMinorityUnion.pdf. In 2008, the Change to Win coalition did likewise. *See* Petition of Change to Win, *In re Rulemaking Regarding Members-Only Minority-Union Collective Bargaining* (Jan. 4, 2008), http://op.bna.com/ dlrcases.nsf/id/smgk–7amt9z/$File/ctwpetition.pdf. In 2010, the NLRB received amicus briefs on the subject from various labor law professors (including some co-authors of this text) led by Professor Morris.

Professor Morris and the rulemaking petition present some interesting technical questions. Must the statute be read so that the exclusivity principle codified in section 9 explicitly limits the duty to bargain codified in section 8(a)(5) only to those unions selected by a majority? Or can the statute be read to allow members-only bargaining unless there is a certification under section 9? Which side has the better argument? Notwithstanding your answer, what weight should the Board and reviewing courts give to the longstanding practice of allowing collective bargaining based solely on the exclusivity principle? In the absence of statutory amendment, should the Board should be permitted to innovate—by rulemaking or otherwise—in this area? Is your answer affected by the fact that every major amendment to the NLRA has been either rejected or filibustered for five decades? Should the Board have greater or lesser authority than other independent agencies to change its practices through interpretation rather than waiting for Congress to amend the statute?

To date, the NLRB has neither adopted nor rejected members-only collective bargaining. However, on August 26, 2011, it did deny the two petitions noted above. According to the Board:

> After careful consideration, we have decided to deny the above petitions, without passing on the merits of the arguments set out therein. Our decision is based on our judgment respecting the most effective allocation of the Board's limited resources. The petitions call for a significant reinterpretation of the National Labor Relations Act, and would require the dedication of substantial Board resources to study the issues raised by the petitions and the significant legal and policy considerations presented thereby. We have determined that the resources that would be required to address the petitions are better allocated to the adjudication of cases and to the rulemaking proceedings currently in progress at the Board.

The order was signed by Chairman Liebman and Members Becker, Pearce, and Hayes, with the notation that Member Hayes questioned the Board's authority to promulgate the proposed rule, although he agreed that "the Board's limited resources are better allocated to case adjudication." Presumably, the Board's refusal to act now would allow the issue to be considered without prejudice in the future. For more in depth discussion of this issue, see Catherine Fisk & Xenia Tashlitsky, *Imagine a World Where Employers Are Required to Bargain with Minority Unions: Thoughts on the Arguments for and Against Members-Only Bargaining*, 27 ABA J. Lab. & Emp. Law 1 (2011); Catherine Fisk & Benjamin Sachs, *Restoring Equity in Right-to-Work Law*, 4 U. C. Irvine L. Rev. 857 (2014) (arguing among several approaches that in states where right to work laws prevent unions from collecting dues from nonmembers, but requires unions to still represent them, states should relax the requirement of exclusive representation and allow members-only bargaining).

2.   The International Labor Organization (ILO), of which the United States is a member, and which is affiliated with the United Nations, sets international labor standards. It has clearly determined that, as a matter of international labor policy, minority unions should have the right to bargain with employers when there is no majority union. As the its Freedom of Association Committee has stated:

> Problems may arise when the law stipulates that a trade union must receive the support of 50 per cent of the members of a bargaining unit to be recognized as a bargaining agent: a majority union which fails to secure this absolute majority is thus denied the possibility of bargaining. The Committee considers that under such a system, if no union covers more than 50 per cent of the workers, collective bargaining rights should be granted to all the unions in this unit, at least on behalf of its own members.

Freedom of Association and Collective Bargaining: International Labour Conference 81st Session, 1994 (Geneva: International Labour Office, 1994) at ¶ 241. For a more detailed discussion of U.S. labor law obligations under international labor standards see *infra* ch. 8-C.

3.   *Is exclusive representation constitutional?* In a recent public sector case related to minority bargaining in the context of individual rights, workers filed a lawsuit against the SEIU challenging the exclusivity principle for domestic and healthcare workers as an affront to First Amendment freedom of association. *See Hill v. SEIU Healthcare*, 850 F.3d 861 (7th Cir. 2017) ("As the First Circuit explained in *D'Agostino* [*v. Baker (2016)*] in assessing a substantially similar state program, exclusive bargaining representation does not rise to the level [constitutional concern], as providers 'are not compelled to act as public bearers of an ideological message they disagree with[,] . . . accept an undesired member of any association they may belong to, . . . [or] modify the expressive message of any public conduct they may choose to engage in.' 812 F.3d at 244(internal citations omitted). We agree with this reasoning; the [Illinois public sector law]'s exclusive-bargaining provision does not create associations like those the Supreme Court has found to be constitutionally problematic." *Id.* at 865). Since the U.S. Supreme Court has found that public sector laws mandating or allowing compelled payment of union dues are unconstitutional as a violation of the free speech guarantee of the Constitution

(see *Janus v. AFSCME Council 31*, 138 S. Ct. 2448 (2018) will the right to association likewise be implicated by an exclusive representation requirement?

4.   *Prehire agreements in the construction industry.* A corollary to the holding in *Bernhard-Altmann* that an employer violates section 8(a)(2) when it recognizes a minority union, is the rule that employers also violate section 8(a)(2) if they recognize a union before they have hired a representative complement of their workforce, even if the union has majority support at the time of recognition. In the construction industry only, Section 8(f) allows the employer to execute with a minority union a collective bargaining agreement before it has hired a single employee and the agreement may require union membership within seven (as opposed to 30) days as a condition of employment. 29 U.S.C. § 158(f)). The exception for the construction industry was carved out because of the very short duration of most construction industry jobs. But the execution of a prehire agreement does not mean that a union has achieved majority status, nor will it serve as a bar to any union election under Section 9. *See generally John Deklewa & Sons*, 282 N.L.R.B. 1375 (1987), *enf'd*, 843 F.2d 770 (3d Cir.), *cert. denied*, 488 U.S. 889 (1988). As a matter of law, the NLRB and the courts have also recognized in limited circumstances an employer's recognition of a union in advance of the opening of a future facility so long as the agreement conditions such recognition on the union's achieving majority status in fact once the facility opens. *See, e.g., Kroger Co.*, 219 N.L.R.B. 388 (1978); NLRB General Counsel Advice Memorandum: GM-UAW Saturn Project, 122 L.R.R.M. (BNA) 1187 (1978). The lawfulness of these arrangements stems from the employer's duty to bargain with an incumbent union over the "effects" of an employer decision related to the business that has potential adverse consequences for unit employees. The GM-UAW prehire agreement was also allowed by the NLRB on a one-time basis because of the innovative aspect of an employer/union project regarding a new business venture.

b.   Exclusive Representation and Its Obligations

Section 9 of the Act provides:

> Representatives designated or selected for the purposes of collective bargaining by the majority of the employees in a unit appropriate for such purposes, shall be the exclusive representatives of all the employees in such unit for the purposes of collective bargaining in respect to rates of pay, wages, hours of employment, or other conditions of employment: *Provided*, That any individual employee or a group of employees shall have the right at any time to present grievances to their employer and to have such grievances adjusted, without the intervention of the bargaining representative, as long as the adjustment is not inconsistent with the terms of a collective-bargaining contract or agreement then in effect: *Provided further*, That the bargaining

representative has been given opportunity to be present at such adjustment. 29 U.S.C. § 159.

Exclusiveness of representation is one of the unique hallmarks of American labor law. Once a union is selected by a majority of employees in a bargaining unit, the union becomes the exclusive representative for all of the employees in the unit. A collective bargaining agreement negotiated by an exclusive representative supersedes any individual contracts held by the employees in the unit to the extent that they are inconsistent with the group labor contract. An independent agreement, if it exists, cannot contradict, lessen, and in many situations, even add to the provisions of the collective bargaining agreement. This is because the very purpose of collective bargaining is to allow individual workers to benefit from the coherence and collective strength of the group. As the Court made plain in the leading case of *J. I. Case*:

> Individual contracts, no matter what the circumstances that justify their execution or what their terms, may not be availed of to defeat or delay the procedures prescribed by the National Labor Relations Act looking to collective bargaining, nor to exclude the contracting employee from a duly ascertained bargaining unit; nor may they be used to forestall bargaining or to limit or condition the terms of the collective agreement. . . . We cannot except individual contracts generally from the operation of collective ones because some may be more individually advantageous. Individual contracts cannot subtract from collective ones, and whether under some circumstances they may add to them in matters covered by the collective bargain, we leave to be determined by appropriate forums under the laws of contracts applicable, and to the Labor Board if they constitute unfair labor practices. *J. I. Case Co. v. NLRB*, 321 U.S. 332, 337, 339 (1944).

Although individual contracts are to be viewed with suspicion, the very purpose of sanctioning collective bargaining was to allow individual workers to benefit from the strength of the collective. However, there are exceptions. As the Court acknowledged:

> Of course, where there is great variation in circumstances of employment or capacity of employees, it is possible for the collective bargain to prescribe only minimum rates or maximum hours or expressly to leave certain areas open to individual bargaining. . . . It also is urged that such individual contracts may embody matters that are not necessarily included within the statutory scope of collective bargaining, such as stock purchase, group insurance, hospitalization, or medical attention. We know of nothing to prevent the employee's, because he is an employee, making any contract provided it is not inconsistent with a

collective agreement or does not amount to or result from or is not part of an unfair labor practice. But in so doing the employer may not incidentally exact or obtain any diminution of his own obligation or any increase of those of employees in the matters covered by collective agreement. *Id.* at 338–39.

The most common examples of "variation in circumstances of employment or capacity of employees" are in the professional sports and entertainment industries. In those industries, collective bargaining agreements typically set minimum salaries, leaving each individual athlete or artist to negotiate his or her own pay in excess of the minimum. Why are individual agreements the norm in these industries but not in others? And why do unions in these industries remain strong compared to those in other industries?

The Court in *J. I. Case* mentioned the potential destructiveness of individual deals and side agreements. As the Court explained:

> [A]dvantages to individuals may prove as disruptive of industrial peace as disadvantages. They are a fruitful way of interfering with organization and choice of representatives; increased compensation, if individually deserved, is often earned at the cost of breaking down some other standard thought to be for the welfare of the group, and always creates the suspicion of being paid at the long-range expense of the group as a whole. *Id.*

A similar principle of exclusivity is found in the railway and airline industries, which are governed by the Railway Labor Act. 45 U.S.C. §§ 151–188. *See Order of R.R. Telegraphers v. Railway Express Agency*, 321 U.S. 342 (1944) (holding individual agreements cannot supersede contracts collectively bargained by union representative).

Tension may arise between the principle of exclusivity, which unites employees behind a single voice, and a wide variety of federal and state legal rights enjoyed by individual employees, who are usually free to assert those rights by raising—if they so choose—a cacophony of voices. In the following case, such tension arises in the context of claims of discrimination asserted by African American employees. The twist is that the relevant anti-discrimination law has been incorporated into the collective bargaining agreement, which the union must enforce by invoking the contract's grievance and arbitration procedures, rather than by undertaking picketing and other group action.

EMPORIUM CAPWELL CO. v. WESTERN ADDITION COMMUNITY ORG.

420 U.S. 50 (1975)

JUSTICE MARSHALL delivered the opinion of the Court:

This litigation presents the question whether, in light of the national policy against racial discrimination in employment, the National Labor Relations Act protects concerted activity by a group of minority employees to bargain with their employer over issues of employment discrimination. The National Labor Relations Board held that the employees could not circumvent their elected representative to engage in such bargaining. The Court of Appeals for the District of Columbia Circuit reversed and remanded, holding that in certain circumstances the activity would be protected. We now reverse.

I

The Emporium Capwell Co. (Company) operates a department store in San Francisco. At all times relevant to this litigation it was a party to the collective-bargaining agreement negotiated by the San Francisco Retailer's Council, of which it was a member, and the Department Store Employees Union (Union) which represented all stock and marking area employees of the Company. The agreement, in which the Union was recognized as the sole collective-bargaining agency for all covered employees, prohibited employment discrimination by reason of race, color, creed, national origin, age, or sex, as well as union activity. It had a no-strike or lockout clause, and it established grievance and arbitration machinery for processing any claimed violation of the contract, including a violation of the antidiscrimination clause.

On April 3, 1968, a group of Company employees covered by the agreement met with the secretary-treasurer of the Union, Walter Johnson, to present a list of grievances including a claim that the Company was discriminating on the basis of race in making assignments and promotions. The Union official agreed to take certain of the grievances and to investigate the charge of racial discrimination. He appointed an investigating committee and prepared a report on the employees' grievances, which he submitted to the Retailer's Council and which the Council in turn referred to the Company. The report described "the possibility of racial discrimination" as perhaps the most important issue raised by the employees and termed the situation at the Company as potentially explosive if corrective action were not taken. It offered as an example of the problem the Company's failure to promote a Negro stock employee regarded by other employees as an outstanding candidate but a victim of racial discrimination.

Shortly after receiving the report, the Company's labor relations director met with Union representatives and agreed to "look into the matter" of discrimination and see what needed to be done. Apparently unsatisfied with these representations, the Union held a meeting in September attended by Union officials, Company employees, and representatives of the California Fair Employment Practices Committee (FEPC) and the local antipoverty agency. The secretary-treasurer of the Union announced that the Union had concluded that the Company was discriminating, and that it would process every such grievance through to arbitration if necessary. Testimony about the Company's practices was taken and transcribed by a court reporter, and the next day the Union notified the Company of its formal charge and demanded that the joint union-management Adjustment Board be convened "to hear the entire case."

At the September meeting some of the Company's employees had expressed their view that the contract procedures were inadequate to handle a systemic grievance of this sort; they suggested that the Union instead begin picketing the store in protest. Johnson explained that the collective agreement bound the Union to its processes and expressed his view that successful grievants would be helping not only themselves but all others who might be the victims of invidious discrimination as well. The FEPC and antipoverty agency representatives offered the same advice. Nonetheless, when the Adjustment Board meeting convened on October 16, James Joseph Hollins, Tom Hawkins, and two other employees whose testimony the Union had intended to elicit refused to participate in the grievance procedure. Instead, Hollins read a statement objecting to reliance on correction of individual inequities as an approach to the problem of discrimination at the store and demanding that the president of the Company meet with the four protestants to work out a broader agreement for dealing with the issue as they saw it. The four employees then walked out of the hearing.

Hollins attempted to discuss the question of racial discrimination with the Company president shortly after the incidents of October 16. The president refused to be drawn into such a discussion but suggested to Hollins that he see the personnel director about the matter. Hollins, who had spoken to the personnel director before, made no effort to do so again. Rather, he and Hawkins and several other dissident employees held a press conference on October 22 at which they denounced the store's employment policy as racist, reiterated their desire to deal directly with "the top management" of the Company over minority employment conditions, and announced their intention to picket and institute a boycott of the store. On Saturday, November 2, Hollins, Hawkins, and at least two other employees picketed the store throughout the day and distributed at the entrance handbills urging consumers not to patronize the store. Johnson encountered the picketing employees, again urged them to rely on the grievance process, and warned that they might be fired for their activities. The pickets, however, were not dissuaded, and they continued to press their demand to deal directly with the Company president.

On November 7, Hollins and Hawkins were given written warnings that a repetition of the picketing or public statements about the Company could lead to their discharge. When the conduct was repeated the following Saturday, the two employees were fired.

Western Addition Community Organization (hereinafter respondent), a local civil rights association of which Hollins and Hawkins were members, filed a charge against the Company with the National Labor Relations Board. The Board's General Counsel subsequently issued a complaint alleging that in discharging the two the Company had violated § 8(a)(1) of the National Labor Relations Act. After a hearing, the NLRB Trial Examiner found that the discharged employees had believed in good faith that the Company was discriminating against minority employees, and that they had resorted to concerted activity on the basis of that belief. He concluded, however, that their activity was not protected by § 7 of the Act and that their discharges did not, therefore, violate § 8(a)(1).

The Board, after oral argument, adopted the findings and conclusions of its Trial Examiner and dismissed the complaint. Among the findings adopted by the Board was that the discharged employees' course of conduct "was no mere presentation of a grievance but nothing short of a demand that the [Company] bargain with the picketing employees for the entire group of minority employees."

The Board concluded that protection of such an attempt to bargain would undermine the statutory system of bargaining through an exclusive, elected representative, impede elected unions' efforts at bettering the working conditions of minority employees, "and place on the Employer an unreasonable burden of attempting to placate self-designated representatives of minority groups while abiding by the terms of a valid bargaining agreement and attempting in good faith to meet whatever demands the bargaining representative put forth under that agreement."

On respondent's petition for review the Court of Appeals reversed and remanded. The court was of the view that concerted activity directed against racial discrimination enjoys a "unique status" by virtue of the national labor policy against discrimination, as expressed in both the NLRA, *see United Packinghouse Workers v. NLRB*, and Title VII of the Civil Rights Act of 1964, and that the Board had not adequately taken account of the necessity to accommodate the exclusive bargaining principle of the NLRA to the national policy of protecting action taken in opposition to discrimination from employer retaliation. The court recognized that protection of the minority-group concerted activity involved in this case would interfere to some extent with the orderly collective-bargaining process, but it considered the disruptive effect on that process to be outweighed where protection of minority activity is necessary to full and immediate realization of the policy against discrimination. In formulating a standard for distinguishing between protected and unprotected activity, the majority held that the "Board should inquire, in cases such as this, whether the union was actually remedying the discrimination to the fullest extent possible, by the most expedient and efficacious means. Where the union's efforts fall short of this high standard, the minority group's concerted activities cannot lose [their] section 7 protection." Accordingly, the court remanded the case for the Board to make this determination and, if it found in favor of the employees, to consider whether their particular tactics were so disloyal to their employer as to deprive them of § 7 protection under our decision in *NLRB v. Electrical Workers*.

II

A

Section 7 affirmatively guarantees employees the most basic rights of industrial self-determination, "the right to self-organization, to form, join, or assist labor organizations, to bargain collectively through representatives of their own choosing, and to engage in other concerted activities for the purpose of collective bargaining or other mutual aid or protection," as well as the right to refrain from these activities. These are, for the most part, collective rights, rights to act in concert with one's fellow employees; they are protected not for their own sake but as an instrument of the national labor policy of minimizing industrial strife "by encouraging the practice and procedure of collective bargaining." 29 U.S.C. § 151.

Central to the policy of fostering collective bargaining, where the employees elect that course, is the principle of majority rule. If the majority of a unit chooses union representation, the NLRA permits it to bargain with its employer to make union membership a condition of employment, thereby imposing its choice upon the minority. 29 U.S.C. §§ 157, 158(a)(3). In establishing a regime of majority rule, Congress sought to secure to all members of the unit the benefits of their collective strength and bargaining power, in full awareness that the superior strength of some individuals or groups might be subordinated to the interest of the majority. As a result, "[the] complete satisfaction of all who are represented is hardly to be expected.".

The Court most recently had occasion to re-examine the underpinnings of the majoritarian principle in *NLRB v. Allis-Chalmers Mfg. Co.*, 388 U.S. 175 (1967). In that case employees in two local unions had struck their common employer to enforce their bargaining demands for a new contract. In each local at least the two-thirds majority required by the constitution of the international union had voted for the strike, but some members nonetheless crossed the picket lines and continued to work. When the union later tried and fined these members, the employer charged that it had violated § 8(b)(1)(A) by restraining or coercing the employees in the exercise of their § 7 right to refrain from concerted activities. In holding that the unions had not committed an unfair labor practice by disciplining the dissident members, we approached the literal language of § 8(b)(1)(A) with an eye to the policy within which it must be read:

> National labor policy has been built on the premise that by pooling their economic strength and acting through a labor organization freely chosen by the majority, the employees of an appropriate unit have the most effective means of bargaining for improvements in wages, hours, and working conditions. The policy therefore extinguishes the individual employee's power to order his own relations with his employer and creates a power vested in the chosen representative to act in the interests of all employees. "Congress has seen fit to clothe the bargaining representative with powers comparable to those possessed by a legislative body both to create and restrict the rights of those whom it represents. . . ." *Steele v. Louisville & N. R. Co.*, 323 U.S. 192, 202. Thus only the union may contract the employee's terms and conditions of employment, and provisions for processing his grievances; the union may even bargain away his right to strike during the contract term. . . .

388 U.S., at 180 (footnotes omitted).

In vesting the representatives of the majority with this broad power Congress did not, of course, authorize a tyranny of the majority over minority interests. First, it confined the exercise of these powers to the context of a "unit appropriate for the purposes of collective bargaining," i.e., a group of employees with a sufficient commonality of circumstances to ensure against the submergence of a minority with distinctively different interests in the terms and conditions of their employment. Second, it undertook in the 1959 Landrum-Griffin amendments, 73 Stat. 519, to assure that minority voices are heard as they are in the functioning of a democratic institution. Third, we have held, by the very nature of the exclusive bargaining representative's status as representative of all unit employees, Congress implicitly imposed upon it a duty fairly and in good faith to represent the interests of minorities within the unit. *Vaca v. Sipes*, supra; *Wallace Corp. v. NLRB*; cf. *Steele v. Louisville & N. R. Co.* And the Board has taken the position that a union's refusal to process grievances against racial discrimination, in violation of that duty, is an unfair labor practice. *Hughes Tool Co.; see Miranda Fuel Co.* Indeed, the Board has ordered a union implicated by a collective-bargaining agreement in discrimination with an employer to propose specific contractual provisions to prohibit racial discrimination.

Against this background of long and consistent adherence to the principle of exclusive representation tempered by safeguards for the protection of minority interests, respondent urges this Court to fashion a limited exception to that principle: employees who seek to bargain separately with their employer as to the elimination of racially discriminatory employment practices peculiarly affecting them, should be free from the constraints of the exclusivity principle of § 9(a). Essentially because established procedures under Title VII or, as in this case, a grievance machinery, are too time consuming, the national labor policy against discrimination requires this exception, respondent argues, and its adoption would not unduly compromise the legitimate interests of either unions or employers.

Plainly, national labor policy embodies the principles of nondiscrimination as a matter of highest priority, and it is a commonplace that we must construe the NLRA in light of the broad national labor policy of which it is a part. These general principles do not aid respondent, however, as it is far from clear that separate bargaining is necessary to help eliminate discrimination. Indeed, as the facts of this litigation demonstrate, the proposed remedy might have just the opposite effect. The collective-bargaining agreement involved here prohibited without qualification all manner of invidious discrimination and made any claimed violation a grievable issue. The grievance procedure is directed precisely at determining whether discrimination has occurred. That orderly determination, if affirmative, could lead to an arbitral award enforceable in court. Nor is there any reason to believe that the processing of grievances is inherently limited to the correction of individual cases of discrimination. Quite apart from the essentially contractual question of whether the Union could grieve against a "pattern or practice" it deems inconsistent with the nondiscrimination clause of the contract, one would hardly expect an employer to continue in effect an employment practice that routinely results in adverse arbitral decisions.

The decision by a handful of employees to bypass the grievance procedure in favor of attempting to bargain with their employer, by contrast, may or may not be predicated upon the actual existence of discrimination. An employer confronted with bargaining demands from each of several minority groups would not necessarily, or even probably, be able to agree to remedial steps satisfactory to all at once. Competing claims on the employer's ability to accommodate each group's demands, e. g., for reassignments and promotions to a limited number of positions, could only set one group against the other even if it is not the employer's intention to divide and overcome them. Having divided themselves, the minority employees will not be in position to advance their cause unless it be by recourse seriatim to economic coercion, which can only have the effect of further dividing them along racial or other lines. Nor is the situation materially different where, as apparently happened here, self-designated representatives purport to speak for all groups that might consider themselves to be victims of discrimination. Even if in actual bargaining the various groups did not perceive their interests as divergent and further subdivide themselves, the employer would be bound to bargain with them in a field largely pre-empted by the current collective-bargaining agreement with the elected bargaining representative. In this instance we do not know precisely what form the demands advanced by Hollins, Hawkins, et al. would take, but the nature of the grievance that motivated them indicates that the demands would have included the transfer of some minority employees to sales areas in which higher commissions were paid. Yet the collective-bargaining agreement provided that no employee would be transferred from a higher-paying to a lower-paying classification except by consent or in the course of a layoff or reduction in force. The potential for conflict between the minority and other employees in this situation is manifest. With each group able to enforce its conflicting demands—the incumbent employees by resort to contractual processes and the minority employees by economic coercion—the probability of strife and deadlock, is high; the likelihood of making headway against discriminatory practices would be minimal.

What has been said here in evaluating respondent's claim that the policy against discrimination requires § 7 protection for concerted efforts at minority bargaining has obvious implications for the related claim that legitimate employer and union interests would not be unduly compromised thereby. The court below minimized the impact on the Union in this case by noting that it was not working at cross-purposes with the dissidents, and that indeed it could not do so consistent with its duty of fair representation and perhaps its obligations under Title VII. As to the Company, its obligations under Title VII are cited for the proposition that it could have no legitimate objection to bargaining with the dissidents in order to achieve full compliance with that law.

This argument confuses the employees' substantive right to be free of racial discrimination with the procedures available under the NLRA for securing these rights. Whether they are thought to depend upon Title VII or have an independent source in the NLRA, they cannot be pursued at the expense of the orderly collective-bargaining process contemplated by the NLRA. The elimination of discrimination and its vestiges is an appropriate subject of bargaining, and an employer may have no objection to incorporating into a collective agreement the substance of his obligation not to discriminate in personnel decisions; the Company here has done as much, making any claimed dereliction a matter subject to the grievance-arbitration machinery as well as to the processes of Title VII. But that does not mean that an employer may not have strong and legitimate objections to bargaining on several fronts over the implementation of the right to be free of discrimination for some of the reasons set forth above. Similarly, while a union cannot lawfully bargain for the establishment or continuation of discriminatory practices, it has a legitimate interest in presenting a united front on this as on other issues and in not seeing its strength dissipated and its stature denigrated by subgroups within the unit separately pursuing what they see as separate interests. When union and employer are not responsive to their legal obligations, the bargain they have struck must yield pro tanto to the law, whether by means of conciliation through the offices of the [Equal Employment Opportunity Commission], or by means of federal-court enforcement at the instance of either that agency or the party claiming to be aggrieved.

Accordingly, we think neither aspect of respondent's contention in support of a right to short-circuit orderly, established processes for eliminating discrimination in employment is well-founded. The policy of industrial self-determination as expressed in § 7 does not require fragmentation of the bargaining unit along racial or other lines in order to consist with the national labor policy against discrimination. And in the face of such fragmentation, whatever its effect on discriminatory practices, the bargaining process that the principle of exclusive representation is meant to lubricate could not endure unhampered.

Reversed.

JUSTICE DOUGLAS, dissenting:

The Court's opinion makes these Union members—and others similarly situated—prisoners of the Union. The law, I think, was designed to prevent that tragic consequence. Hence, I dissent.

The Board has held that the employees were unprotected because they sought to confront the employer outside the grievance process, which was under Union control. The Court upholds the Board, on the view that this result is commanded by the principle of "exclusive representation" embodied in § 9 of the NLRA. But in the area of racial discrimination the Union is hardly in a position to demand exclusive control, for the employee's right to nondiscriminatory treatment does not depend upon Union demand but is based on the law. We held in *Alexander v. Gardner-Denver Co.* that a union may not circumscribe an employee's opportunity to seek relief under Title VII. We said there that Title VII "concerns not majoritarian processes, but an individual's right to equal employment opportunities. Title VII's strictures are absolute and represent a congressional command that each employee be free from discriminatory practices." The law should facilitate the involvement of unions in the quest for racial equality in employment, but it should not make the individual a prisoner of the union. While employees may reasonably be required to approach the union first, as a kind of "exhaustion" requirement before resorting to economic protest, cf. *NLRB v. Tanner Motor Livery*, they should not be under continued inhibition when it becomes apparent that the union response is inadequate. The Court of Appeals held that the employees should be protected from discharge unless the Board found on remand that the Union had been prosecuting their complaints "to the fullest extent possible, by the most expedient and efficacious means." I would not disturb this standard. Union conduct can be oppressive even if not made in bad faith. The inertia of weak-kneed, docile union leadership can be as devastating to the cause of racial equality as aggressive subversion. Continued submission by employees to such a regime should not be demanded.

I would affirm the judgment below.

NOTES

1.   In *Emporium Capwell*, the union clearly stated the course of action it would take: process any complaints of discrimination against minority employees by pursuing them as grievances—to arbitration, if necessary—under the collective bargaining agreement. This stated action was in direct conflict with the decision of dissident workers to protest alleged discrimination by picketing the store, handbilling customers, and demanding to bargain directly with the company president. Thus the dissidents' actions tended to undermine the collective bargaining process, including the position of the union as the exclusive representative of all employees. But what if the dissidents had picketed before the union decided and announced its course of action? *See NLRB v. Chelsea Labs., Inc.,* 825 F.2d 680 (2d Cir. 1987) (request to meet and other conduct intended to pave way for new union local and not destructive of old union, which employees voted to decertify, protected by Section 7). What if the workers had walked out without union approval but had not undertaken to negotiate with the employer? *See East Chicago Rehab. Center, Inc. v. NLRB,* 710 F.2d 397 (7th Cir. 1983) (short walk-out by workers protected by section 7 since workers expressed no dissatisfaction with the union and no desire to take negotiations into their own hands but were only expressing anger at employer's unilateral change in work rules).

2.   *Attitude adjustment?* Recall the main proviso to Section 9(a):

> *Provided,* That any individual employee or a group of employees shall have the right at any time to present grievances to their employer and to have such grievances adjusted, without the intervention of the bargaining representative, as long as the adjustment is not inconsistent with the terms of a collective-bargaining contract or agreement then in effect. . . . 29 U.S.C. § 159(a).

Now imagine that all the dissidents in *Emporium Capwell* were doing could be characterized as presenting and demanding the adjustment of grievances without the intervention of their union. Was this an illegal attempt to bargain, or was it protected activity under the main proviso to Section 9(a)? What if African American employees had filed grievances and picketed, but not distributed handbills to customers or demanded direct bargaining with the company's president. Would this have made a difference? Why? What if they had successfully persuaded the employer to offer special promotional opportunities or pay raises only to minority employees? Would such an agreement be enforceable under *JI Case*?

3. *Majority rules.* Section 9(a) of the NLRA provides that representatives designated by a majority of employees in a bargaining unit shall be the exclusive representative of all the employees in such unit. This notion of exclusivity of representation is uniquely American. Do you agree with Justice Marshall in the majority opinion that exclusivity ultimately serves unions by giving elected representatives greater leverage, and therefore more power in negotiating with management? Or does exclusivity come at too high a price to individual freedom? *See* George Schatzki, *Should Exclusivity Be Abolished?*, 123 U. Pa. L. Rev. 897 (1975); Matthew Finkin, *The Road Not Taken: Some Thoughts on Nonmajority Employee Representation*, 69 Chi.-Kent L. Rev. 195 (1993).

4. *Let's make a (direct) deal.* Note that exclusivity prohibits not only the making of individual contracts (when inconsistent with the applicable collective bargaining agreement), but also direct dealing between the employer and the individual employee or groups of individual employees. In opposing a union organizing campaign, the typical employer may decry the prohibition on direct dealing ("If you elect the union, you'll lose the ability to talk to me directly. Your supervisor won't be able to give you the afternoon off to take care of a sick child, and the union will have the right to sit in on every meeting with your supervisor and to learn confidential information about you, your health, and your family situation."). Once the union has been voted in, however, the same employer may be less resistant to dealing directly with employees when it would serve the employer's interests to do so. For example, a hotel whose employees were facing a decertification election wrote to each employee in the bargaining unit promising that, if they voted to decertify the union, the hotel would not reduce their wages, benefits, or paid vacation. The union filed an 8(a)(5) charge alleging that this was illegal direct dealing. What result?

5. *Any volunteers?* Tennessee amended its public sector statute governing collective negotiations with teachers to abolish exclusive representation in 2011. *See* Tennessee Professional Educators Collaborative Conferencing Act of 2011 (PECCA), Tenn. Code Ann. §§ 49–5–601 to 49–5–613 (2017). Under a new provision, if at least 15% of the professional employees (i.e., teachers) submit a written request for "collaborative conferencing" between October 1 and November 1, then the school board must appoint a committee consisting of equal numbers of board members and professional employees to conduct a confidential poll of employees. The poll must ask whether the employees wish to undertake collaborative conferencing with the board of education and provide options of "yes" and "no" responses. For employees who vote "yes," the poll must also ask which professional organization they wish to represent them in collaborative conferencing. One of the options must be "unaffiliated." For employees who vote "no," the poll must

offer the same options as the employees who vote "yes," plus the option "none of the above," which is to be selected if they vote to opt out of collaborative conferencing even if a majority vote for it. If a majority votes for collaborative conferencing, then the school board must appoint a committee consisting of seven to 11 representatives. The employees are entitled to seat the same number of representatives on the committee. Each organization that received at least 15% of the votes is entitled to seat the number of representative proportionate to the percentage of votes it received. If the option of "unaffiliated" receives at least 15% of the votes, then it is entitled to seat a proportionate number of representatives too. The joint school board-employee committee that conducted the election is charged with selecting the representative(s) of the "unaffiliated" employees. For each constituency, the term of representation is three years. At the end of the term, the process begins anew, with another poll conducted by a joint school board-employee committee. *See* Tenn. Code Ann. § 49–5–605.

What do you think of this approach to the idea of exclusive representation and to collective negotiation? Will it benefit or burden employees to create more bargaining options, but reduce their collective strength? Could this approach be a model for the private sector?

C. REGULATION OF ACCESS

At common law, the employer as property owner alone decided who was permitted to come onto its property and what they could say or do once they got there. Traditionally, the workplace was literally a parcel of real estate—perhaps a farm, factory, or shop—over which the employer exercised the power of a territorial sovereign and the employee assumed the status of a subject. In terms such as "master" and "servant," the common law codified the superiority of the employer and the subordination of the employee. This relationship ran to all things in the employer's dominion, including the job. The general common law rule, at least in America, was—and many ways, remains—that an employment relationship that was not for a specified duration was terminable at will. In the common law world, the job was a type of property, but it was property belonging to the master rather than the servant.

The Wagner Act can be understood as a rejection of much of the common law of master and servant. According to one scholar, the statute's author, Senator Robert Wagner, "wanted to convert the relation of master and servant into an equal and cooperative partnership that planted a sense of power, individuality, freedom, and security in the hearts of men and make them the people they were meant to be." Ellen Dannin, Taking Back the Workers' Law: How to Fight the Assault on Labor Rights 28 (2006). Hence Section 1, paragraph 3 of the Act, 29 U.S.C § 151, para. 3, speaks of "encouraging practices fundamental to the friendly adjustment of industrial disputes" and "restoring equality of bargaining power between employers and employees"—goals that would remain beyond reach if management retained the unchecked power it enjoyed at common law to exclude union organizers from its premises or to condition the job on the worker's forswearing collective action.

The NLRA makes inroads on employer common law property rights in at least two ways. First, a pair of provisions regulate the employer's control over access to its property, speech and behavior: Section 8(a)(1) prohibits employer interference, restraint and coercion of employee exercise of rights protected by Section 7; Section 8(a)(3) prohibits employer discrimination to encourage or discourage membership in a labor organization. Second, the NLRB has imposed special regulations that apply to the employer when a representation election is pending. To preserve a non-coercive environment, the NLRB requires something rarely, if ever, required in democratic politics outside the workplace: waging the campaign under what have come to be known as "laboratory conditions." These conditions must not "create[ ] an atmosphere calculated to prevent the free and untrammeled choice" by employees. As early as 1948, the Board announced this requirement:

> In election proceedings, it is the Board's function to provide a laboratory in which an experiment may be conducted, under conditions as nearly ideal as possible, to determine the uninhibited desires of the employees. It is our duty to establish those conditions; it is also our duty to determine whether they have been fulfilled. When, in the rare extreme case, the standard drops too low, because of our fault or that of others, the requisite laboratory conditions are not present and the experiment must be conducted over again.

General Shoe Corp., 77 N.L.R.B. 124, 126–27 (1948), *enf'd*, 192 F.2d 504 (6th Cir. 1951), *cert. denied*, 343 U.S. 904 (1952). Unlike findings of unfair labor practices which support orders of affirmative relief, breaches of laboratory conditions result only in voiding the tainted election and holding a rerun election.

In this section, we will explore how the Act has modified or amended the common law respecting two types of access: (1) access by employee organizers to coworkers on and off the employer's property, and (2) access by nonemployee organizers to workers on or near the employer's property. We will also explore how the NLRB and the courts have attempted to balance competing notions of workplace property interests and who "owns" them.

1. EMPLOYEE ACCESS TO COWORKERS

Employees are not considered trespassers when they report to work on the employer's property, because they are licensed by the employer to be there. At common law, however, the employer exercised absolute control over the scope of the license it gave to such individuals. An employer could, and did, restrict employees' activities by prohibiting them from soliciting others while on the property. An employee who violated the restriction exceeded the scope of the license and was considered a trespasser who was subject to removal from the premises. *See* Cynthia L. Estlund, *Labor, Property and Sovereignty After Lechmere*, 46 Stan. L. Rev. 305 (1994).

Early in the history of the NLRA, the Supreme Court recognized that the Act's prohibitions on interference, restraint, or coercion of Section 7 rights modified this common law rule. In *Republic Aviation Corp. v. NLRB*, 324 U.S. 793 (1945), the employer had a rule prohibiting all solicitation on its property. The employer enforced the rule across the board. Nevertheless, the Court held that termination of an employee for soliciting coworkers to join a union and for wearing union buttons violated Section 8(a)(1). The Court upheld the Board's presumption that no-solicitation rules are illegal as applied to workers soliciting coworkers during nonworking time, such as breaks and the periods before or after work shifts. It also upheld the presumption that prohibitions on wearing union buttons or other insignia in the workplace are illegal. The employer could rebut the presumption by showing that special circumstances, such as potential interference with regular operations on the selling floors of retail stores, or in the patient care areas of health care facilities, warranted restrictions on solicitation or the wearing of insignia to protect a valid business interest. Questions of special circumstances frequently involve fine line drawing. For example, in *Washington State Nurses Ass'n v. NLRB*, 526 F.3d 577 (9th Cir. 2008), a hospital allowed nurses to wear a variety of union buttons in nonpatient care areas but prohibited one button which read, "RNs Demand Safe Staffing," anywhere that the nurses might encounter patients or family members. The NLRB upheld the ban on the ground that the hospital's concern that the button might upset patients or family members established special circumstances. Reversing, the Ninth Circuit held that the concern was speculative and not supported by any evidence in the record.

Republic Aviation involved a traditional industrial workplace where the employer owned the factory and employed the people who worked there. Modern, multi-use workplaces, with their interrelated employment and business relationships, can be much more complex. Consider the following cases arising out of litigation involving the New York New York Hotel and Casino in Las Vegas, Nev.: *New York New York Hotel, LLC* (NYNY I), 334 N.L.R.B. 762 (2001), *enf. denied*, 313 F.3d 585 (D.C. Cir 2002); *New York New York, LLC* (NYNY II), 334 N.L.R.B. 772 (2001), *enf. denied*, 313 F.3d 585 (D.C. Cir 2002); *New York New York, LLC* (NYNY III), 356 N.L.R.B. 907 (2011), *enf. granted*, 676 F.3d 193 (D.C. Cir. 2012), *cert. denied*, 133 S. Ct. 1580 (2013).

NEW YORK NEW YORK HOTEL (I)

334 N.L.R.B. 762 (2001), *enf. denied*, 313 F.3d 585 (D.C. Cir. 2002)

By CHAIRMAN HURTGEN and MEMBERS LIEBMAN and TRUESDALE:

The Respondent owns and operates a hotel and casino facility in Las Vegas, Nevada. The Union represents a bargaining unit of certain of the Respondent's employees. Ark Las Vegas Restaurant Corporation (Ark) operates several restaurants and eateries within the casino. At the time of the events in this case, the Union was attempting to organize Ark's employees and to obtain recognition from Ark.

On July 9, 1997, three off-duty Ark employees went to the "porte cochere" (the area just outside the main entrance to the casino), where they stood on the sidewalk and attempted to distribute handbills to customers as they entered the facility. The handbills bore an area standards message, stating that Ark paid its employees less than unionized workers and urging customers to tell Ark to sign a union contract. The handbills expressly disclaimed any dispute with the Respondent. Shortly after the handbillers appeared, they were informed by managers of the Respondent that they were trespassing on the Respondent's property and that they were not allowed to solicit or distribute handbills there. When the handbillers refused to leave, the Respondent called the police, who issued trespass citations to the handbillers and escorted them off the premises.

The [administrative law] judge found that the Respondent violated Section 8(a)(1) of the Act by prohibiting the handbilling. In reaching that conclusion, the judge found that, as employees of Ark, the handbillers enjoyed the right to use the nonwork areas of the Respondent's premises to distribute handbills to customers entering or leaving. We agree. As the judge observed, the Board has held that employees of a subcontractor of a property owner who work regularly and exclusively on the owner's property are rightfully on that property pursuant to the employment relationship, even when off duty. By contrast, individuals who do not work regularly and exclusively on the employer's property, such as nonemployee union organizers, may be treated as trespassers, and are entitled to access to the premises only if they have no reasonable nontrespassory means to communicate their message.

A clear distinction exists between the Ark employees, who work regularly and exclusively in the Respondent's facility, and taxi and limousine drivers and other delivery personnel who visit that facility intermittently in the course of their employment. Contrary to the Respondent, nothing in this decision or in those on which it is based suggests that the Respondent would be required to allow individuals [such as taxi and limousine drivers] to solicit or distribute handbills on its property.

Accordingly, such off-duty employees may engage in protected solicitation and distribution in nonwork areas of the owner's property unless the owner can show that prohibiting that sort of activity is necessary to maintain production and discipline.

The judge also found that the porte-cochere was a nonwork area, despite the fact that some of the Respondent's employees work there. We agree with that finding for the reasons set forth in his decision. We note also that in *Santa Fe Hotel & Casino*, 331 N.L.R.B. 723 (2000), which issued after the judge rendered his decision, the Board came to the same conclusion. The Board found that the main function of the employer's hotel/casino was to lodge people and allow them to gamble, and that the work of bellmen, valet parking attendants and security, maintenance, and gardening personnel around entrances to the employer's facility was incidental to that function. Were it to hold such areas to be "work areas" from which off-duty employee handbillers could be excluded, the Board reasoned, employees would be effectively denied the right to distribute literature anywhere at the facility. Accordingly, the Board held that those areas were not work areas. The same reasoning applies here.

The Respondent contends that the judge erred in failing to find that its expulsion of the handbillers was justified in the interest of maintaining production and discipline. In this regard, the Respondent argues that the ban was necessary to ensure proper service to its guests and for the safety and security of its guests, employees, and property. We find no merit in this exception. As the judge found, the handbilling did not adversely affect either the customers' ability to enter or leave the facility or the Respondent's employees' ability to perform their customary work in the porte-cochere area. He also found, and we agree, that the handbilling of customers has no inherent tendency to interfere significantly with any of those activities. We therefore find that the Respondent has not shown that its ban on handbilling is necessary to maintain production and discipline.

NOTES

1.   The D.C. Circuit denied enforcement of the Board's order in *NYNY I*, above, and remanded the case, due largely to the NLRB's failure to answer a key question: "Does the fact that the Ark employees work on NYNY's premises give them *Republic Aviation* rights throughout all of the nonwork areas of the hotel and casino?" *See New York New York LLC v. NLRB*, 313 F.3d 585, 590 (D.C. Cir. 2002). As discussed below, *infra* p. 436, that question eventually would be answered "yes," with some nuances, in *New York New York LLC (NYNY III)*, 356 N.L.R.B. 907 (2011), *enf'd*, 676 F.3d 193 (D.C. Cir. 2012), *cert. denied*, 133 S. Ct. 1580 (2013).

2.   *Déjà vu all over again?* Shortly after distributing the handbills discussed above, off-duty employees once again distributed handbills at the New York New York Hotel (this time inside the casino but outside two Ark-

owned restaurants, America and Gonzalez y Gonzalez); once again they were cited by the police and escorted from the premises; and once again the NLRB determined that the hotel had committed unfair labor practices. But in *NYNY II*, the hotel defended in part on the ground that the areas inside the casino, but outside the two restaurants, were work areas subject to regulation. A majority of the Board, speaking through, Members Liebman and Truesdale, disagreed:

> [The hotel] is primarily in the business of providing people with hotel and gambling facilities. The areas in front of America and Gonzalez y Gonzalez are not gambling or lodging areas. They are passageways through which employees, guests of the facility, and the public pass from one area of the facility to another. As the judge found, cleaning and maintenance personnel work in those areas, but that is the same kind of work that the Board in *Santa Fe Hotel* found to be incidental to the facility's main function of providing gambling and lodging facilities. Numerous employees pass through those areas in the course of their work (for example, bellmen transporting guests' luggage from the entrances to their hotel rooms), but it would be a rare portion of such a facility which no employees used in that fashion. As the Board found in *Santa Fe Hotel*, to hold that such passageways constitute work areas would effectively deny employees the right to engage in protected distribution anywhere on the Respondent's property. *NYNY II*, 334 N.L.R.B. 772, 774 (2001).

Chairman Hurtgen dissented. Although he agreed that the areas near the porte cochere and Gonzalez y Gonzalez were nonwork areas, he argued that America was different:

> The area outside the America restaurant was a work area. This is so because of the proximity of slot machines to the space in question. A row of slot machines was stationed approximately 27 feet directly across from the entrance to America, with additional slot machines immediately to the right of those slot machines. These additional slot machines surround a structure in the middle of the casino floor that houses a service bar and public restrooms. Employees involved in the hotel's gaming operations are among those who work in these areas in front of and adjacent to the entrance of America. These include change persons from the Respondent's Slot Operations department. These employees circulate throughout the area in carts resembling miniature New York taxi cabs, sell change to customers, convert cash into coins for customers to play the machines, and convert large bills into smaller denominations.

> Slot floor employees also refill slot machines, pay customers who win jackpots, and perform minor slot machine repairs. They also circulate around the area to ensure the orderly use of the machines and also to ensure that no minors are playing the machines in the area. Slot technicians perform major slot machine repairs. There are also other

employees of the casino whose daily job responsibilities require them to work with or near the slot machines. I cannot agree with my colleagues' description of these areas as mere "passageways" for employees and guests when they pass from one area of the casino to another. They are, in a very real sense, employee work stations. *Id.* at 775–76 (2001) (Hurtgen, Chairman, dissenting).

3. *Law and litter(ature).* The employees did more than solicit; they distributed literature. Does an employer have a legitimate concern that literature distribution could cause a problem with litter? If so, how should that concern be factored into the balancing of competing rights and interests? *See Stoddard-Quirk Mfg. Co.,* 138 N.L.R.B. 615 (1962) (holding that litter concern justifies prohibiting literature distribution in working areas).

4. *Unions and waivers.* May a union waive the employees' rights to solicit their coworkers on employer property? In *NLRB v. Magnavox Co.,* 415 U.S. 322 (1974), the Supreme Court held that a union may not waive in the collective bargaining agreement employees' rights under Section 7 to solicit and distribute literature on employer property supporting or opposing the incumbent union. Would a provision in the collective bargaining agreement prohibiting employees from soliciting coworkers during paid coffees breaks but allowing it during unpaid lunch breaks be lawful? *See NLRB v. United Techs. Corp.,* 706 F.2d 1254 (2d Cir. 1983) (rejecting Board's position that contractual prohibition on solicitation during paid nonworking time is discriminatory).

* * *

In 2002, the U.S. Court of Appeals for the District of Columbia Circuit granted the employer's petition for review and denied enforcement of the Board's orders in both *NYNY I* and *NYNY II. See* 313 F.3d 585 (D.C. Cir. 2002). On remand, the NLRB was directed squarely to address the question it had avoided below: whether the employees of a contractor working on property under another employer's control are "employees" possessing Section 7 rights within the meaning of the Act. The question was important, because the Supreme Court had never addressed it either. *Id.* at 588, 590. Over eight years later, in 2011, the Board finally did so in *New York New York III.*

NEW YORK NEW YORK HOTEL (III)
356 N.L.R.B. 907 (2011), *enf'd,* 676 F.3d 193 (D.C. Cir. 2012), *cert. denied,* 133 S. Ct. 1580 (2013)

By CHAIRMAN LIEBMAN and MEMBERS BECKER and PEARCE:

These cases require us to revisit issues arising when the off-duty employees of an onsite contractor seek access to the premises of the property owner to distribute handbills in support of their organizing efforts.

Today, we adopt an access standard that reflects the specific status of such workers as statutorily protected employees exercising their own rights under the National Labor Relations Act, but not employees of the property owner. We reject both the view that these workers enjoy precisely the same access rights as the employees of the property owner (under *Republic Aviation*) and the view that the property owner may deny access to these workers except in the limited circumstances when even "nonemployee" union organizers must be permitted on the property (under *Lechmere* and *Babcock & Wilcox*). Instead, we strike an accommodation between the contractor employees' rights under federal labor law and the property owner's state-law property rights and legitimate managerial interests. The Supreme Court instructed us to seek such an accommodation in *Hudgens v. NLRB*, 424 U.S. 507, 521 (1976) (holding that the "accommodation between employees' rights and employers' property rights . . . must be obtained with as little destruction of one as is consistent with the maintenance of the other"). We conclude that such an accommodation is possible.

FACTS

Ark has contracted to provide food service to NYNY's guests and customers in three sit-down restaurants and a food court consisting of 10 fast food outlets as well as through banquet catering and room service. Ark also provides food service to employees of NYNY and of its contractors (including Ark's own employees) in NYNY's Employee Dining Room. Ark's is a large operation, employing approximately 900 people and operating 7 days per week, 24 hours per day within the hotel.

In 1997, Ark employees working on NYNY's premises initiated a campaign to obtain representation by the Union, which already represented NYNY's employees. Among other actions in pursuit of representation, on three occasions in July 1997 and April 1998, off-duty Ark employees entered onto NYNY's property (i.e., their regular worksite) to distribute handbills to Ark's and NYNY's customers. The handbills described Ark's lack of a union contract as "unfair" and compared the wages and benefits of the nonunion Ark employees to the wages and benefits of unionized employees doing comparable work at other hotels and casinos on the Las Vegas Strip. The handbills requested that customers tell Ark's managers that Ark should "recognize and negotiate a fair contract with its workers." The handbills distributed by Ark employees in July 1997 (but not those distributed in April 1998) expressly disclaimed any dispute with NYNY.

The handbills were distributed at three access points—at NYNY's porte-cochere (the covered sidewalk and driveway just outside NYNY's main entrance) and directly in front of two Ark-operated restaurants within the hotel, America and Gonzales y Gonzales. On all three occasions, the Ark employees refused NYNY's requests that they leave the property. NYNY summoned the Las Vegas police, who issued trespassing citations to the employees and escorted them off the property. These incidents resulted in the unfair labor practice charges at issue here, which allege that NYNY violated Section 8(a)(1) by prohibiting the Ark employees from distributing handbills on its premises.

ANALYSIS

The narrow issue in this case is whether NYNY violated Section 8(a)(1) of the Act when it prohibited off-duty Ark employees from distributing handbills to customers of Ark and NYNY at three locations on NYNY's property. We must address the broader legal and policy questions raised by the factual pattern here, which encompasses two circumstances that pull in opposite directions: the Ark employees were *not* employees of NYNY, but they *were* regularly employed on NYNY's property by its contractor.

A.

As a preliminary point, it is clear that the undisputed lack of an employment relationship between the Ark employees and NYNY is not dispositive here. The Act clearly regulates the relationship between an employer (such as NYNY) and employees of other employers (such as the employees of Ark). The Act contains not only a broad definition of the term "employee," but one whose breadth is aimed directly at the question at issue. The Act provides that

> [t]he term "employee" shall include any employee, and *shall not be limited to the employees of a particular employer,* unless the Act explicitly states otherwise.

Section 2(3), 29 U.S.C. § 152(3) (emphasis added).

The precise terms of the Act's prohibitions also make clear that an employer's action toward the employees of other employers can constitute an unfair labor practice. The prohibition at issue in this case, contained in Section 8(a)(1), provides that it is an unfair labor practice for an employer "to interfere with, restrain, or coerce employees in the exercise of the rights guaranteed in section 7." The prohibition is not limited to interference with the rights of *his* employees. In contrast, the prohibition in Section 8(a)(5) is so limited, providing that it is an unfair labor practice for an employer "to refuse to bargain collectively with the representatives of *his* employees" (emphasis added.) Finally, further evidence of Congress' clear intent regarding this issue is found in the Act's definition of the statutory term "labor dispute" to include "any controversy concerning . . . the association or representation of persons in negotiating, fixing, maintaining, changing, or seeking to arrange terms or conditions of employment, regardless of whether the disputants stand in the proximate relation of employer and employee."

In each of these ways, Congress made clear in the text of the Act that the term "employee" does not refer to a relationship between individual workers and a single employer and, specifically, that the prohibition contained in Section 8(a)(1) of the Act extends to actions by employers affecting employees of other employers. As the Supreme Court explained:

> This was not fortuitous phrasing. It had reference to the controversies engendered by constructions placed upon the Clayton Act and kindred state legislation in relation to the functions of workers' organizations and the desire not to repeat those controversies. . . . The broad definition of "employee," "unless the Act explicitly states otherwise," as well as the definition of "labor dispute" in § 2(9), expressed the conviction of Congress "that disputes may arise regardless of whether the disputants stand in the proximate relation of employer and employee." *Phelps Dodge Corp. v. NLRB*, 313 U.S. 177, 192 (1941).

Based on these clear textual indications of Congress' intent, the Board as well as the courts have held in a wide variety of contexts that "an employer under Section 2(3) of the Act may violate Section 8(a) not only with respect to its own employees but also by actions affecting employees who do not stand in such an immediate employer/employee relationship." *International Shipping Assn.*, 297 N.L.R.B. 1059, 1059 (1990).

The Ark employees, then, are statutorily protected employees, and NYNY is a covered employer that can, under certain circumstances, be held to violate the Ark employees' statutory rights, even though the Ark employees are not employees of NYNY.

We seek to establish an access standard that reflects the specific status of the Ark employees as protected employees who are not employees of the property owner, but who are regularly employed on the property. Neither *Lechmere* nor *Republic Aviation* involved this category of persons. Neither case, in the court's words, "yields [a] definitive answer" here.

Our answer is reached by analyzing the statutory rights of such workers and the property rights and managerial interests of the property owner, seeking an accommodation between the two. In employing this form of analysis, we are guided by the Supreme Court's observation that

> [u]nder the [National Labor Relations] Act, the task of the Board, subject to review by the courts, is to resolve conflicts between § 7 rights and private property rights, "and to seek a proper accommodation between the two."

After *Lechmere,* the Board—with the approval of both the Sixth Circuit and the District of Columbia Circuit, the latter in a decision that came after the remand decision here—has employed such an analysis in cases analogous to this one involving the access rights of off-duty employees of the employer/property owner who are employed at locations separate from where they seek access. *See Hillhaven Highland House,* 336 N.L.R.B. 646 (2001) (establishing test governing access rights of offsite employees), *enforced, First Healthcare Corp. v. NLRB,* 344 F.3d 523 (6th Cir. 2003); *ITT Industries, Inc. v. NLRB,* 413 F.3d 64 (D.C. Cir. 2005) (affirming Board test adopted in *Hillhaven*).

In seeking the proper accommodation here, we thus do not write on a blank slate. Under *Republic Aviation,* it is well established that an employer that operates on property it owns ordinarily violates the Act if it bars its employees from distributing union literature during their nonwork time in nonwork areas of its property. Moreover, such an employer's off-duty employees have a presumptive right to return to their work site and gain access to exterior, nonwork areas for purposes of otherwise protected solicitation under *Tri-County Medical Center,* 222 N.L.R.B. 1089 (1976), and *Nashville Plastic Products,* 313 N.L.R.B. 462 (1993). Finally, the employer's off-duty employees who are employed at another location presumptively have the same rights as off-duty employees who work at the location at issue. *Hillhaven Highland House.* Under these precedents, as the court of appeals recognized, if NYNY had barred its own employees from engaging in the expressive activity engaged in by the Ark employees in the same locations, it would have violated the Act. In conducting the analysis here, then, we ask whether the relevant rights and interests are different in this case because the employees are not employees of the property owner (even though they are regularly employed on the property) and, if so, how that affects the proper accommodation.

B.

We turn now to a closer, more practical examination of the Section 7 rights involved in this case and the property rights and managerial interests with which they must be accommodated. As we will explain, the balance here tips in favor of finding that NYNY unlawfully excluded the off-duty Ark employees from its property.

We begin by considering the Ark employees' rights and interests in relation to the specific activity they engaged in on NYNY's property. As part of a campaign to win union representation for themselves, the Ark employees distributed handbills to Ark's and NYNY's customers, seeking their support in getting Ark to "recognize and negotiate a fair contract with its workers."

Indeed, the Ark employees were not "outsiders," in contrast to the union organizers in *Babcock & Wilcox* and *Lechmere.* This distinction is relevant in considering both the weight of the employees' rights and the extent to which their exercise interferes with the owner's rights and interests (as discussed below). The Ark employees were regularly employed on NYNY's property by the company's contractor. The hotel and casino complex was their workplace. They worked not only inside Ark's restaurants but throughout the premises, providing room service, carrying supplies, and servicing and patronizing NYNY's employee cafeteria. As the Supreme Court has observed, the workplace is the "one place where employees clearly share common interests and where they traditionally seek to persuade fellow workers in matters affecting their union organizational life and other matters related to their status as employees." *Eastex,* 437 U.S. at 574. It seems unlikely, as a practical matter, that Ark employees would view the limits of Ark's leasehold as setting the boundaries for engaging in Section 7 activity at work. Yet NYNY's argument—which would have the Board treat Ark employees no differently from union organizers—suggests that the hotel could bar an Ark employee from handing a union card to a fellow employee in the hotel's parking lot, as they walked together through the hotel to the restaurant, or as they sat together at lunch in NYNY's employee cafeteria.

[N]either the circuit nor the Board has ever drawn a substantive distinction between solicitation of fellow employees and solicitation of nonemployees. *Stanford Hospital & Clinics v. NLRB,* 325 F.3d 334, 343 (D.C. Cir. 2003); *see also Santa Fe Hotel & Casino,* 331 N.L.R.B. 723, 728–29 (2000) (holding that employer unlawfully prohibited off-duty employees from handbilling customers at entrances to hotel and casino, seeking support in persuading employer to bargain for first contract).

Indeed, in the context of this case, the intended audience of the Ark employees is a factor that strengthens, rather than weakens, their statutory claim to access, certainly with respect to the areas in front of the Ark-operated restaurants. At those locations, Ark employees were uniquely able to identify and communicate with the relevant subset of NYNY customers—those considering whether to patronize an Ark restaurant—with minimal difficulty and expense. *See Scott Hudgens,* 230 N.L.R.B. at 416 (explaining that intended audience of picketers, potential customers of store, "became established as such only when individual shoppers decided to enter the store"). For this reason, the location of the expressive activity here—the very threshold of the employees' own workplace—has been a central site of protected Section 7 activity since the passage of the Act. Wholly excluding the Ark handbillers from these uniquely effective locations would place a serious burden on the exercise of their Section 7 rights to communicate with the relevant members of the public.

In sum, we find that the statutorily-recognized interests of the Ark employees, as implicated here, are much more closely aligned to those of NYNY's own employees (who, under our law, would have been entitled to the access sought) than they are to the interests of the union organizers at issue in *Lechmere* and *Babcock & Wilcox.* As we have explained, despite their lack of an employment relationship with NYNY, the Ark employees are statutorily protected employees, who were exercising their own Section 7 rights of self-organization, not rights derived from those of other employees. They were not strangers or outsiders to NYNY's property; rather, they worked there regularly, for an employer with a close economic relationship to NYNY. Finally, they sought access to locations that were uniquely suited to the effective exercise of their statutory rights.

We turn now to a consideration of NYNY's interests in denying off-duty Ark employees access to portions of its property outside Ark's leasehold for purposes of distributing literature. Most fundamentally, there is no question that—countervailing considerations of federal labor law aside—NYNY, as the property owner, had a right to exclude the Ark employees. "[O]ne of the essential sticks in the bundle of property rights is the right to exclude others." *PruneYard Shopping Center v. Robins,* 447 U.S. 74, 82 (1980). Any rule derived from federal labor law that requires a property owner to permit unwanted access to his property for a nonconsensual purpose necessarily impinges on the right to exclude. We must, and do, give weight to that fact. As a corollary, it also seems clear that, purely from the perspective of state property law, the Ark employees were trespassers at the moment they began to distribute handbills. Whatever their status as NYNY's invitees at other times and for other purposes, there is no suggestion that the off-duty Ark employees had an invitation from NYNY that privileged them to distribute handbills to the public in the locations involved here. This fact, too, must be taken into account, although it cannot be dispositive consistent with the well-established principle that state law property rights sometimes must yield to the imperatives of federal labor law.

Apart from its state law property right to exclude, NYNY also has a legitimate interest in preventing interference with the use of its property. Whether that interest is deemed a property right or a "management interest," perhaps ultimately derived from property ownership, it is entitled to appropriate weight. Indeed, even under *Republic Aviation,* an employer can impose restrictions on its own employees' solicitation and distribution if the restrictions are shown to be necessary to maintain production and discipline. *See Beth Israel Hospital v. NLRB,* 437 U.S. 483, 492–493 (1978); *Republic Aviation,* 324 U.S. at 803 n.10. On the records here, however, the judges found, and we agree, that the Ark employees' handbilling did *not* interfere with operations or discipline at NYNY's complex. The handbilling did not adversely affect the ability of customers to enter, leave, or fully use the facility or the ability of Ark or NYNY employees to perform their work, and it was not a violation of any rule that NYNY attempts to defend as necessary to ensure operations or discipline.

We must nevertheless consider the fact that the Ark employees had no employment relationship with NYNY and ask whether that fact might justify a prophylactic rule limiting their access, despite the lack of any disruption or misconduct in this case.

Given the voluntary and mutually beneficial arrangement between NYNY and Ark, NYNY reasonably could have anticipated that Ark employees would seek access to its property for Section 7 activity (access that, under existing law, NYNY would have been compelled to grant to its own employees), and NYNY was free to negotiate contractual terms with Ark sufficient to protect its interests in relation to Ark's employees. In fact, NYNY's contract with Ark did exactly that, requiring Ark to make all reasonable efforts to ensure that Ark employees abide by any reasonable rules and regulations as New York New York] may, from time to time, reasonably adopt for the safety, care and cleanliness of [Ark's premises, or the Hotel or for the preservation of good order thereon or to assure the operation of a first-class resort hotel facility.

NYNY's contract with Ark also imposed specific requirements on the contractor in relation to its employees, including that they be subject to drug testing. Furthermore, NYNY's control over Ark's employees, through its relationship with Ark, extended specifically to their off-duty, on-premises conduct, for example, to barring them from wearing their uniforms and entering the bars inside the hotel.

Even absent the express contractual commitment on the part of Ark to use its employment authority to enforce NYNY's rules and so protect against disruption of the hotel's operations, NYNY and Ark share an economic interest in ensuring that Ark employees do nothing that might interfere with the operations of the hotel. NYNY is simply wrong, then, when it argues that "there existed no means for NYNY to regulate or control the infringement on its private property other than through reliance on state trespass laws."

NYNY's ability to protect its operational and property interests in relation to its contractors' employees is the rule, not the exception. The Board's case law reflects long and extensive experience with contractual relationships between employer/contractors and property owners. Our experience suggests that such a relationship ordinarily permits the property owner to quickly and effectively intervene, both through the employer and directly, to prevent any inappropriate conduct by the employer's employees on the owner's property. As the judge found in one case affirmed by the Board, "[a]n employer receiving contracted labor services will of necessity exercise sufficient control over the operations of . . . the contractor at its facility so that it will be in a position to take action to prevent disruption of its own operations." *Southern California Gas Co.,* 302 N.L.R.B. 456, 461 (1991). Property owners often give directions to employees of contractors through the contractors' onsite managers and supervisors. Contractor employees, then, are ordinarily deterred from engaging in misconduct not only by the presence of their own employer on site (whose managers and supervisors are just as likely as those of the owner to immediately respond to any disruptive behavior), but also by the property owner's ability to direct the employer's managers and supervisors to take action. In specific instances, such as when they observe misconduct, property owners themselves often direct contractors' employees without the mediation of the contractor/employer's agents. Finally, property owners can exercise their authority to direct contractors to remove employees from the premises and not permit them to return. Such exclusion by the owner may result in the contractor terminating the employee. The owner need not even make a request of the contractor, in many instances, as the contractor has every incentive not to permit its employees to interfere with the owner's operations and thereby jeopardize its contract.

These cases support our conclusion that property owners ordinarily are able to protect their property and operational interests, in relation to employees of contractors working on their premises, without resort to state trespass law. Like these property owners, NYNY is very differently situated with respect to Ark employees seeking access to its property than were the property owners in *Lechmere* and *Babcock & Wilcox* faced with union organizers who sought access to their property.

C.

The Board's task is thus to find an accommodation between the Ark employees' Section 7 interests and NYNY's property rights and managerial interests as we have analyzed them. Careful consideration of the questions asked by the court of appeals, and of our own case law and experience, leads us to conclude that the property owner generally has the legal right and practical ability to fully protect its interests through its contractual and working relationship with the contractor (as this case illustrates), but the contractors' employees have no parallel ability to protect their statutory rights and legitimate interests in and around their workplace without our intervention.

Nevertheless, our decision is a relatively narrow one. We address only the situation where, as here, a property owner seeks to exclude, from nonworking areas open to the public, the off-duty employees of a contractor who are regularly employed on the property in work integral to the owner's business, who seek to engage in organizational handbilling directed at potential customers of the employer and the property owner.

We conclude that the property owner may lawfully exclude such employees only where the owner is able to demonstrate that their activity significantly interferes with his use of the property or where exclusion is justified by another legitimate business reason, including, but not limited to, the need to maintain production and discipline (as those terms have come to be defined in the Board's case law). Thus, any justification for exclusion that would be available to an employer of the employees who sought to engage in Section 7 activity on the employer's property would also potentially be available to the nonemployer property owner, as would any justification derived from the property owner's interests in the efficient and productive use of the property. The standard we adopt today is thus analogous to that adopted in *Hillhaven Highland House,* which was enforced by the District of Columbia Circuit.

We leave open the possibility that in some instances property owners will be able to demonstrate that they have a legitimate interest in imposing reasonable, nondiscriminatory, narrowly-tailored restrictions on the access of contractors' off-duty employees, greater than those lawfully imposed on its own employees. We express no view today, however, on precisely which unique restrictions on contractor employees' access might be lawful, although they will be evaluated consistent with the accommodation of interests we have engaged in here. Such determinations are best made on a case-by-case basis.

In adopting this test, we decline to condition access to the property on a showing by the off-duty employees (or by the General Counsel on their behalf) that they lack a reasonable alternative means, however defined, of communicating with their intended audience.

As a general matter, the test we adopt today seeks to place the Ark employees and similarly situated, protected employees at a point on the spectrum of accommodation between Section 7 rights and property rights that reflects the similarities and differences between them and other access seekers considered in the Supreme Court's and our prior jurisprudence, as well as the similarities and differences between NYNY and other property owners who wish to exclude the protected employees from their property. As in *Hillhaven Highland House,* we have sought a nuanced resolution of the legal issue presented to us, rather than simply fitting the Ark employees into some preexisting category.

E.

Applying the test adopted here, we conclude that NYNY violated Section 8(a)(1) by excluding the handbilling Ark employees from its property. NYNY has not demonstrated that the handbilling significantly interfered with its use of the property or that exclusion was justified by some other legitimate business reason, such as the need to maintain operations or discipline. Because NYNY had no preexisting restrictions on access applicable to the Ark employees, we need not consider what, if any, restrictions short of a blanket prohibition on distribution NYNY lawfully might have imposed.

MEMBER HAYES, dissenting in part:

In determining that the Respondent violated the Act by excluding employees of food concessionaire Ark Las Vegas Restaurants from soliciting customer support for their organizational campaign in the interior of Respondent's hotel and casino complex, [my colleagues] apply a test that artificially equates the Section 7 rights of a contractor's employees with those of the property owner's employees, pays only lip service to the owner's property interests, and gives no consideration to the critical factor of alternative means of communication.

The majority's purported balancing test affords as much, if not more, protection to the efforts of Ark employees to engage in union organizational activity on the Respondent's premises as the Respondent's own employees would have. Applying what I believe to be the correct test, and in the absence of a sufficient record regarding the existence of less intrusive reasonable alternative means of communication, I would find that the Respondent acted unlawfully only when it excluded Ark handbillers from the nonwork porte-cochere area outside the main entrance to the hotel and casino complex.

The inevitable result of the majority's analysis represents no real accommodation of competing interests. There will be no case-by-case balancing. The contractor employees' rights to engage in organizational activity will trump the property owner's rights every time, subject only to the suggested possibility that in some future case a property owner may be able to justify the imposition of "reasonable, non-discriminatory, narrowly-tailored restrictions on the access of contractors' employees, greater than those lawfully imposed on its own employees."

In my view, the appropriate balancing test must be drawn from the *Babcock* framework, inasmuch as it involves nonemployees of the property owner. The fact that they work regularly and exclusively for their employer on the property of another should be considered in that test, but it cannot elevate those nonemployees to equal standing with the property owner's own employees vis-à-vis the assertion of Section 7 rights, nor can it abnegate the owner's exclusionary property rights. In this particular case, I would find based on the existing record that the Respondent has failed to prove the availability of reasonable nontrespassory means for Ark handbillers to communicate their message. I therefore conclude that the Respondent unlawfully excluded Ark employees from engaging in minimally intrusive handbilling activity on the Respondent's property in the porte-cochere area. In a future case with different facts, particularly as to reasonable nontrespassory alternative means of communication, I would not require that a property owner's rights should yield at all.

NOTES

1. *The access question.* This case presents a question that is increasingly common in entertainment centers, shopping malls, and other multi-use facilities: when and where must off-duty employees of an onsite contractor have access to the premises of the property owner to distribute handbills in support of their organizing efforts? The challenge in such cases is to strike the proper balance between the right to access sought by workers and the right to exclude sought by property owners. In attempting to strike that balance, the majority leaned toward characterizing the access sought by Ark employees as akin to that of employees of the property owner under *Republic Aviation*; the dissent leaned toward characterizing the right to exclude as akin to that of property owners dealing with trespassers under *Lechmere* (*infra*, p. 461). Who do you think got it right, and why?

2. *On-duty vs. off-duty.* The *NYNY* litigation is but a complex variation on a standard tension raised by the NLRA: although the employer retains the general rights associated with owning or possessing private property, there are limits to its power to deny premises access to employees, including off-duty employees. Under established Board law, a rule restricting access by off-duty employees is valid only if it (1) limits access solely with respect to the interior of the plant and other working areas, (2) is clearly disseminated to all employees, and (3) applies to off-duty employees seeking access to the plant for any purpose, not just union organizing activity. *See Tri-County Med. Ctr.*, 222 N.L.R.B. 1089 (1976). For example, in *J.W. Marriott at Los Angeles L.A. Live*, 359 N.L.R.B. 392 (2012), Members Block and Griffin, over the dissent of Member Hayes, found that a hotel owner's rule prohibiting employee access to the "interior areas" of the hotel "property" for more than 15 minutes before the start or after the end of the shift, without the employer's prior approval, violates Section 8(a)(1). According to the majority, such a rule unreasonably tends to "chill" concerted activities. *Accord Sodexo America LLC*, 358 N.L.R.B. 668 (2012); *St. John's Health Center*, 357 N.L.R.B. 2078 (2011).

3. *Forgive us our trespassers?* The *NYNY* employee solicitors were off duty. They appeared on the property at a time that they had not been invited to be there by their employer. Did that make them trespassers? The NLRB has held that off-duty employees are entitled to access to exterior gates, parking lots, and other nonworking areas of employer's property, unless a contrary rule is uniformly enforced and justified by business necessity. *See, e.g., St. Luke's Hospital*, 300 N.L.R.B. 836 (1990). Did the owner of the hotel and casino complex have such a business necessity?

Owners of multi-use facilities may assert their property rights by summoning the police to remove or arrest handbillers as trespassers. Such assertions are often met by the filing of unfair labor practice charges. Invoking the right to petition the government for redress of grievances—here, that handbillers are illegally on private property and should be removed or arrested by the authorities—may an employer defend against a ULP charge on First Amendment grounds? *See Venetian Casino Resort LLC*, 357 N.L.R.B. 1725

(2011), *order vacated Venetian Casino Resort, L.L.C. v. NLRB*, 793 F.3d 85 (D.C.Cir. 2015). Judge Kavanagh held that calling the police was direct petition to government for redress of grievances, and thus was protected from liability under the NLRA for unfair labor practices by virtue of the *Noerr-Pennington* doctrine, and NLRB would be required on remand to determine whether employer's attempt to summon police officers to enforce state trespass law was a sham petition not entitled to protection under the doctrine.

4.   *What stays in Vegas?* The Board expressly reserved judgment as to whether Ark employees would be entitled to access to "all other or, indeed, any other nonwork areas" of the hotel. Even a casual visitor to Las Vegas knows that slot machines and card tables are positioned directly in the path of every hotel guest as soon as she enters the building. Nearly every pathway to a lobby, front, desk, elevator bank, or connected building passes through a casino area. Are these pathways work areas or nonwork areas? Should employees be permitted to pass out handbills to guests or other workers who use them?

5.   *California dreaming?* Of course, a state that so chooses is free to modify its common law trespass rules to grant union organizers more generous access to an employer's private property. *Cf., e.g., Ralphs Grocery Co. v. UFCW Local 8*, 55 Cal. 4th 1083 (2012) (holding that, although private sidewalk in front of customer entrance to retail store in shopping center is not public forum for expressive activity, including picketing, substantive and procedural protections of certain California statutes nevertheless protect peaceful union picketing on private sidewalk outside targeted retail store during labor dispute, which cannot be enjoined as trespass).

6.   *Justice delayed.* The events giving rise to this litigation first occurred in 1997. Fourteen years and three agency decisions later, the Board finally issued a decision, and two years after that, it withstood review in the appellate courts. Does such a lengthy delay make sense to you? What role, if any, should the passage of time play in the analysis of Board members and judges who are trying to determine if employees' section 7 rights were violated? Can you think of any reforms that could reduce such delays?

* * *

In the problem that opened this chapter, Enderby terminated Penny for sending an e-mail message urging her coworkers to support the Programmers' Union. Had she been terminated for urging such support in an off-duty face-to-face discussion with coworkers, Enderby surely would have violated the NLRA. Should the same approach to face-to-face communication on the employer's premises apply to electronic communication over the employer's e-mail network? Should it matter that the employer tolerates employee use of the e-mail system for personal communications?

In 2007, these issues were considered by the Bush Board in *Register Guard*, 351 N.L.R.B. 1110 (2007), *remanded in part*, 571 F.3d 53 (D.C. Cir. 2009), which voted 3 to 2 to hold that an employer does not violate section

8(a)(1) by prohibiting the use of its e-mail system for all "non-job-related solicitations," although it left open the possibility that some forms of discriminatory enforcement of such a prohibition could run afoul of Section 8(a)(3).

In 2014, however, the Obama Board voted 3 to 2 vote to overturn *Register Guard*—a decision that the Trump Board is expected to revisit.

PURPLE COMMUNICATIONS INC.
361 N.L.R.B. 1050 (2014)

CHAIRMAN PEARCE and MEMBERS MISCIMARRA, HIROZAWA, JOHNSON, and SCHIFFER:

At issue in this case is the right of employees under Section 7 of the National Labor Relations Act to effectively communicate with one another at work regarding self-organization and other terms and conditions of employment. The workplace is "uniquely appropriate" and "the natural gathering place" for such communications, and the use of email as a common form of workplace communication has expanded dramatically in recent years. Consistent with the purposes and policies of the Act and our obligation to accommodate the competing rights of employers and employees, we decide today that employee use of email for statutorily protected communications on nonworking time must presumptively be permitted by employers who have chosen to give employees access to their email systems. We therefore overrule the Board's divided 2007 decision in *Register Guard* to the extent it holds that employees can have no statutory right to use their employer's email systems for Section 7 purposes.[4] We believe, as scholars have pointed out,[5] that the *Register Guard* analysis was clearly incorrect. The consequences of that error are too serious to permit it to stand. By focusing too much on employers' property rights and too little on the importance of email as a means of workplace communication, the Board failed to adequately protect employees' rights under the Act and

---

[4]   The Respondent maintained an electronic communications policy limiting employee use of its email and other electronic systems to "business purposes only" and "specifically prohibit[ing]" certain uses by employees. Acknowledging that the Respondent's policy comports with current law, the General Counsel and the Charging Party ask the Board to overrule *Register Guard* and find that the Respondent's policy violates the Act.

[5]   *See, e.g.*, Jeffrey M. Hirsch, *Communication Breakdown: Reviving the Role of Discourse in the Regulation of Employee Collective Action*, 44 U.C. Davis L. Rev. 1091, 1151 (2011) ("[T]he regulation of workplace discourse has become so far adrift that the NLRB now views email as an affront to employer interests, rather than a low-cost, effective means for employees to exercise their right to collective action."); William R. Corbett, *Awakening Rip Van Winkle: Has the National Labor Relations Act Reached a Turning Point?*, 9 Nev. L.J. 247, 252 (2009) (*Register Guard* "elevated employers' property interests over employees' rights, and interpreted the NLRA in a restrictive way that threatens to make it irrelevant and obsolescent"); Christine Neylon O'Brien, *Employees On Guard: Employer Policies Restrict NLRA Protected Concerted Activities On E-Mail*, 88 Ore. L. Rev. 195, 222 (2009) (*Register Guard's* "overemphasis on the employer's property interests at the expense of the employees' section 7 rights undermines the credibility of the majority opinion.

abdicated its responsibility "to adapt the Act to the changing patterns of industrial life."

Our decision is carefully limited. In accordance with longstanding Board and Supreme Court precedent, it seeks to accommodate employees' Section 7 rights to communicate and the legitimate interests of their employers. First, it applies only to employees who have already been granted access to the employer's email system in the course of their work and does not require employers to provide such access. Second, an employer may justify a total ban on nonwork use of email, including Section 7 use on nonworking time, by demonstrating that special circumstances make the ban necessary to maintain production or discipline. Absent justification for a total ban, the employer may apply uniform and consistently enforced controls over its email system to the extent such controls are necessary to maintain production and discipline. Finally, we do not address email access by nonemployees, nor do we address any other type of electronic communications systems, as neither issue is raised in this case.

FACTS

The Respondent provides sign-language interpretation services. Its employees, known as video relay interpreters, provide two-way, real-time interpretation of telephone communications between deaf or hard-of-hearing individuals and hearing individuals. The interpreters work at 16 call centers that process calls on a nationwide, around-the-clock, "first come, first served" basis.

Since June 2012, the Respondent has maintained an employee handbook that contains its electronic communications policy. That policy states:

Internet, Intranet, Voicemail, and Electronic Communication Policy

Computers, laptops, internet access, voicemail, electronic mail (email), Blackberry, cellular telephones and/or other Company equipment is provided and maintained by the [sic] Purple to facilitate Company business. All information and messages stored, sent, and received on these systems are the sole and exclusive property of the Company, regardless of the author or recipient. All such equipment and access should be used for business purposes only.

* * *

Prohibited Activities

Employees are strictly prohibited from using the computer, internet, voicemail and email systems, and other Company equipment in connection with any of the following activities:

* * *

    2.   Engaging in activities on behalf of organizations or persons with no professional or business affiliation with the Company.

* * *

    5.   Sending uninvited email of a personal nature.

The Respondent assigns its interpreters individual email accounts on its email system, and they use those accounts every day that they are at work. They are able to access their company email accounts on the computers at their workstations, as well as on computers in the call centers' break areas and on their personal computers and smartphones. The interpreters have access to the internet on the break-area computers but very limited access at their workstations. The record is sparse regarding the extent to which the interpreters have used the Respondent's email for nonbusiness purposes or have been disciplined for a violation of the electronic communications policy.

In the fall of 2012, the Charging Party [Communication Workers of America, AFL-CIO] filed petitions to represent the interpreters that resulted in Board elections at seven of the Respondent's call centers. The Charging Party filed objections to the results at the Respondent's Corona and Long Beach facilities, including an objection asserting that the electronic communications policy interfered with the interpreters' freedom of choice in the election. The Charging Party also filed an unfair labor practice charge regarding the policy, leading to the issuance of the complaint allegation now before us.

DISCUSSION

In *Register Guard*, the Board, over the dissent of two Members, held that an employer may completely prohibit employees from using the employer's email system for Section 7 purposes, even if they are otherwise permitted access to the system, without demonstrating any business justification, so long as the employer's ban is not applied discriminatorily. The twin premises of that decision were that email systems are the equivalent of other employer communications-related equipment, including bulletin boards, copy machines, public address systems, and telephones, and that employers are free under the Act to ban any nonwork use of such equipment by employees. We conclude that the *Register Guard* majority's analysis was incorrect in several significant respects. First, we find that the *Register Guard* decision undervalued employees' core Section 7 right to communicate in the workplace about their terms and conditions of employment, while giving too much weight to employers' property rights. Second, the *Register Guard* majority inexplicably failed to perceive the importance of email as a means by which employees engage in protected communications, an importance that has increased dramatically during the 7 years since *Register Guard* issued. Finally, the *Register Guard* majority mistakenly placed more weight on the Board's equipment decisions than those precedents can bear. For those reasons, we overrule *Register Guard*'s holding that, under ordinary circumstances, even employees who have been given access to their employer's email system have no right to use it for Section 7 purposes.

Instead, we adopt a presumption that employees who have been given access to the employer's email system in the course of their work are entitled to use the system to engage in statutorily protected discussions about their terms and conditions of employment while on nonworking time, absent a showing by the employer of special circumstances that justify specific restrictions.

A.   Centrality of Workplace Communication to Section 7 Rights

The necessity of communication among employees as a foundation for the exercise of their Section 7 rights can hardly be overstated.

Employees' exercise of their Section 7 rights "necessarily encompasses the right effectively to communicate with one another regarding self-organization at the jobsite." The workplace is "a particularly appropriate place for [employees to exercise their Section 7 rights], because it is the one place where [employees] clearly share common interests and where they traditionally seek to persuade fellow workers in matters affecting their union organizational life and other matters related to their status as employees." *Eastex, Inc. v. NLRB*, 437 U.S. at 574 (internal quotations omitted). Employees' need to share information and opinions is particularly acute in the context of an initial organizing campaign, like the one that was occurring in this case. And, as the Supreme Court has repeatedly recognized, "the place of work is a place uniquely appropriate for dissemination of views" about such matters. *NLRB v. Magnavox Co. of Tennessee*, 415 U.S. 322, 325 (1974).

B.   Nature and Common Use of Business Email

There is little dispute that email has become a critical means of communication, about both work-related and other issues, in a wide range of employment settings. Indeed, even the *Register Guard* majority acknowledged that "e-mail has, of course, had a substantial impact on how people communicate, both at and away from the workplace." 351 N.L.R.B. at 1116. The *Register Guard* dissent noted that, according to a 2004 survey, over 81 percent of employees spent an hour or more on email during a typical workday, with about 10 percent spending at least 4 hours. *Id.* at 1125 (citing American Management Association, 2004 Workplace E-Mail and Instant Messaging Survey (2004)). The same survey found that about 86 percent of employees sent and received nonbusiness-related email at work.

An April 2014 report found that "[e]mail remains the most pervasive form of communication in the business world" and predicted that work-related email traffic will continue to increase. Not coincidentally, the increased use of email has been paralleled by dramatic increases in transmission speed and server capacity, along with similarly dramatic decreases in email's costs.

Some personal use of employer email systems is common and, most often, is accepted by employers. The Supreme Court recently acknowledged, in a case involving an employee's use of his work pager for personal texts, that "[m]any employers expect or at least tolerate personal use of [electronic communications] equipment by employees because it often increases worker efficiency." *City of Ontario v. Quon*, 560 U.S. 746, 759 (2010).

In addition, the number and percentage of employees who telework is increasing dramatically, resulting in more employees who interact largely via technology rather than face to face.

C. Board's "Equipment" Precedents

We agree with the *Register Guard* dissenters that email's flexibility and capacity make competing demands on its use considerably less of an issue than with earlier forms of communications equipment the Board has addressed. Employee email use will rarely interfere with others' use of the email system or add significant incremental usage costs, particularly in light of the enormous increases in transmission speed and server capacity. In contrast, bulletin boards have a finite amount of space for postings to convey information to employees. Copy machines—even current, high-speed models—process print jobs sequentially and can become backed up by heavy use. Public address systems, obviously, can convey only one message at a time. Given their vastly greater speed and capacity, email systems function as an ongoing and interactive means of employee communication in a way that other, older types of equipment clearly cannot.

General principles of property law also militate against a rule that employers may lawfully ban employee use of employer equipment for Section 7 purposes on nonworking time, regardless of the circumstances. Black-letter property law protects real property rights more absolutely than personal property rights. Since 1945, the Supreme Court has held that, when employees seek to engage in Section 7 activity on their employer's land, even against the owner's wishes, the owner's property rights may have to yield to some extent to accommodate the employees' Section 7 rights. Logically, the same must be true of the owner's property rights with regard to its equipment; if anything, an owner's rights regarding its personal property would seem relatively weaker as against competing Section 7 rights.

D.   Adoption of a New Analytical Framework

We agree with the General Counsel, the Charging Party, and others who maintain that *Republic Aviation* should be our starting point.

In *Republic Aviation*, the Board considered an employer policy banning all oral solicitation at any time on company property. At the time, the face-to-face oral communication at issue in the case was the norm, and both the Board and the Supreme Court naturally focused on conversation as the primary form of solicitation. In earlier cases, the Board had reasoned that an employer may make reasonable rules governing employee conduct on working time, but nonworking time "is an employee's time to use as he wishes without unreasonable restraint, although the employee is on company property." *Republic Aviation*, 324 U.S. at 803 fn. 10. And the Board had adopted a presumption that a ban on oral solicitation on employees' nonworking time was "an unreasonable impediment to self-organization," and that an employer wishing to restrict such activity must demonstrate "that special circumstances made the rule necessary in order to maintain production or discipline." *Id.* at 804 fn. 10. The Supreme Court approved the presumption as a legitimate accommodation of the employer's and the employees' rights and affirmed the Board's application of the presumption in *Republic Aviation. Id.* at 804.

For nearly 70 years, the Board has applied *Republic Aviation* to assess employee rights to engage in Section 7 activity on their employer's premises, i.e., real property. As the Court instructed, the Board has sought to accommodate the employees' Section 7 rights and the employers' property and management rights, consistent with the Court's recognition that "the locus of [the] accommodation [between the legitimate interests of employers and employees] may fall at differing points along the spectrum depending on the nature and strength of the respective § 7 rights and private property rights asserted in any given context."

We recognize that significant differences exist between an employer-owned email system, like that at issue here, and an employer's bricks-and-mortar facility and the land on which it is located, which were involved in *Republic Aviation* and many subsequent cases. Indeed, an email system is substantially different from any sort of property that the Board has previously considered, other than in *Register Guard* itself. Accordingly, we apply Republic Aviation and related precedents by analogy in some but not all respects. We also find it unnecessary to characterize email systems as work areas or nonwork areas. In the vast majority of cases, an employer's email system will amount to a mixed-use area, in which the work-area restrictions permitted on literature distribution generally will not apply.

Further, because our decision today applies only to employees who already have access to their employer's email system for work purposes, the right to use that system for Section 7 communications does not turn on the unavailability of traditional face-to-face discussion. Nor does it turn on the current availability of alternative communication options using personal electronic devices and other electronic media—e.g., Facebook, Twitter, YouTube, blogging, or personal email accounts—that the Respondent, its supporting amici, and our dissenting colleagues emphasize.

Our decision today is a limited one. We address only email systems, not any other electronic communications systems, because only email systems are at issue in this case. Our decision encompasses email use by employees only; we do not find that nonemployees have rights to access an employer's email system. Nor do we require an employer to grant employees access to its email system, where it has not chosen to do so. The presumption that we apply is expressly limited to nonworking time. And, although we will presume that an employer that has granted such access for work purposes must allow access for Section 7 purposes as well, we permit the employer to rebut the presumption by showing that special circumstances make the presumption inappropriate in its workplace. Further, we do not prevent an employer from establishing uniform and consistently enforced restrictions, such as prohibiting large attachments or audio/video segments, if the employer can demonstrate that they would interfere with the email system's efficient functioning.

Our decision does not prevent employers from continuing, as many already do, to monitor their computers and email systems for legitimate management reasons, such as ensuring productivity and preventing email use for purposes of harassment or other activities that could give rise to employer liability.

E.   Retroactivity and Application to This Case

Finally, after careful consideration, we find it appropriate to apply our new policy retroactively. In determining whether the retroactive application of a Board decision will cause manifest injustice, the Board balances three factors: (1) the reliance of the parties on preexisting law; (2) the effect of retroactivity on accomplishment of the purposes of the Act; and (3) any particular injustice arising from retroactive application.

Balancing the factors considered above, we find that applying today's decision to this case and others currently pending, consistent with our usual practice, would not cause manifest injustice. As stated, however, we will remand this aspect of this case to the administrative law judge for further proceedings consistent with this decision, including allowing the parties to introduce evidence relevant to a determination of the lawfulness of the Respondent's electronic communications policy.

F. Conclusion

The *Register Guard* dissenters viewed the decision as confirming that the Board was "the Rip Van Winkle of administrative agencies," by "fail[ing] to recognize that e-mail ha[d] revolutionized communication both within and outside the workplace" and by unreasonably contending "that an e-mail system is a piece of communications equipment to be treated just as the law treats bulletin boards, telephones, and pieces of scrap paper." *Register Guard*, 351 N.L.R.B. at 1121 (dissenting opinion). In overruling *Register Guard*, we seek to make "[n]ational labor policy . . . responsive to the enormous technological changes that are taking place in our society."

We recognize that those technological changes are continuing; indeed, they are accelerating. Today's decision cannot resolve all the questions that will arise as a result of our recognizing the right of employees to use their employers' email systems for protected communications on nonworking time, let alone as a result of the still more advanced electronic communications systems now in existence and yet to come. We are, nonetheless, unwilling to avoid those questions by closing our eyes to the importance of electronic means of communication to employees' exercise of their rights under the Act.

MEMBER MISCIMARRA, dissenting:

When evaluating rights and obligations under the National Labor Relations Act, several principles are suggested by our long history, supplemented by guidance and occasional rebukes by the courts. The Supreme Court has held that the validity of any presumptions developed by the Board "depends upon the rationality between what is proved and what is inferred." Presumptions are not favored as an alternative to clear standards, based on the need to give employees, unions, and employers reasonable "certainty beforehand" regarding what they may and may not do. Especially when changing existing law, the Board should first endeavor to do no harm: we should be vigilant to avoid doing violence to undisputed, decades-old principles that are clear, widely understood, and easy to apply. And more directly relevant to the issue in this case, when the Board evaluates any conflict between protected employee conduct and employer property rights, we must strive to accommodate the two "with as little destruction of one as is consistent with the maintenance of the other."

The majority gives employees a statutory right to use employer email systems for nonbusiness purposes, such as communicating with other employees about union organizing and other matters in circumstances that trigger NLRA protection. I believe the right created by the majority represents an unfortunate and ill-advised departure from all of the above principles. Accordingly, for four reasons, I dissent from these newly created standards.

First, the majority decision improperly presumes that limiting an employer's email system to business purposes constitutes "an unreasonable impediment to self-organization." Given the current state of electronic communications, there is no rational basis for such a presumption. National uprisings have resulted from the use of social media sites like Facebook and Twitter, for example, even when governments have used force to prevent such activities. Also, unlike single-purpose business email systems, other electronic communication platforms such as social media sites, text messaging, and email services such as Gmail and Yahoo!Mail undergo near-constant development and expansion. Accordingly, these public forms of electronic communication have features that are more effective, more user-friendly, and more conducive to facilitating concerted activities than employer email systems. Indeed, employees now have more opportunities to conduct concerted activities relating to their employment than at any other time in human history (which, of course, makes the Act's history of nearly 80 years pale by comparison). These facts—and certainly the record currently before the Board in this case—render implausible any suggestion that employees are unreasonably prevented from engaging in NLRA-protected communications absent a statutory right to conduct such activities on the employer's business email system.

Second, the majority has come full circle from the Board's finding—a mere 20 years ago—that employers can violate the Act by providing "pencils," "paper," "telephones," and a "calculator" for employees to use during "paid time." The majority now effectively requires employers to give many employees the Board-mandated use of computer systems and related equipment requiring investments ranging into the millions of dollars. Even if one could identify a colorable need for employees to use an employer's business email system to engage in union organizing and other concerted activities, I believe the majority's creation of such an employee right impermissibly fails to accommodate the substantial employer property rights associated with its computer resources, which typically involve substantial acquisition and maintenance costs. The majority implies that, once an employer grants employees access to its email system for any purpose, the employer's property right in its email system becomes irrelevant. In my view, Republic Aviation—the very decision upon which the majority principally relies—demonstrates the incorrectness of such a position. Moreover, the majority's balancing fails to recognize the many ways in which the Board-mandated use of employer email systems for NLRA-protected communications will cause other problems, as described more fully below.

Third, the majority's new statutory right adversely affects a significant number of other legal requirements, including many imposed by the Act. These problems include difficult questions regarding the Act's prohibition of employer surveillance of protected activities; the ever-increasing need for employers to carefully monitor email systems for unauthorized usage and security intrusions; and the need to search and retrieve emails for a host of reasons, including workplace investigations, subpoenas, and litigation-related discovery requests (mostly having nothing to do with NLRA-protected activities). And this new right will wreak havoc on the enforcement of one of the oldest, clearest, most easily applied of the Board's standards—"working time is for work." The majority's new right—combined with the nature of email and computer usage in most workplaces—will make it all but impossible to determine whether or what communications violate lawful restrictions against solicitation during working time. The resulting confusion will be out of all proportion to whatever benefit the new standard might yield for NLRA-protected concerted activities.

Fourth, the majority today replaces a longstanding rule that was easily understood. In its place, the majority substitutes (i) a presumption giving all employees the right to engage in Section 7 activities using employer email systems to which they otherwise have access, and (ii) unspecified "special circumstances" that, if proven by the employer in after-the-fact Board litigation, will mean employees did not have the majority's presumed statutory "use-of-email" right.

I credit my colleagues for recognizing the reality that many constraints preclude giving employees unqualified access to employer email systems. Although the majority's new standards are well intentioned, they are terribly suited to govern this very important area, which can quickly involve thousands of electronic communications even in small workplaces; where the debilitating impact on productivity and discipline will likely become clear only after the fact; and where virtually nobody will really understand—in real time—whether or when particular communications are protected. Many employees will undoubtedly exercise this new right to use their employer's email system to send what they believe are protected nonbusiness communications, only to learn, afterwards, that they face lawful discipline or discharge either because their communications did not constitute Section 7 activity, or the employee's use of email violated a lawful business-only requirement based on the "special circumstances" exceptions created today by the Board majority. For similar reasons, unions and employers are likely to have great difficulty advising employees whether or when they can engage in nonbusiness uses of the employer email systems.

[The dissenting opinion of MEMBER JOHNSON is omitted.]

NOTES

1. *A wake-up call for Rip Van Winkle?* Citing Chairman Liebman's dissent in *Register Guard*, the majority in *Purple Communications* seemed

eager to suggest that the NLRB no longer be considered the "Rip Van Winkle" of federal agencies. Who got it right: the majority in *Register Guard* or the majority in *Purple*? Do you agree with *Purple* that *Register Guard* placed too much emphasis on employers' property rights and too little on the importance of email as a means of workplace communication, and thereby abdicated its responsibility "to adapt the Act to the changing patterns of industrial life"? Why or why not? How does *Purple* affect your view of whether the NLRA modifies the employer's common law right to control its private property?

2. *Statutory rights and statutory wrongs.* In dissent, Member Miscimarra wrote that the majority gave employees "a statutory right to use employer email systems for nonbusiness purposes." Is this what *Purple* does, or is there a more subtle interpretation of the holding? If so, what would it be? By Member Miscimarra's reasoning, does the Board—or for that matter, any federal agency or court—create a new "statutory right" every time it clarifies or reinterprets the law by overturning prior precedent?

3. *The law of unintended consequences.* In dissent, Member Miscimarra warned of the unintended consequences that could flow from adopting the presumption that employees enjoy a Section 7 right to use the employer's email system. For example, he argued that this standard is "terribly suited to govern this very important area, which can quickly involve thousands of electronic communications even in small workplaces," and "where the debilitating impact on productivity and discipline will likely become clear only after the fact." Are unintended consequences part of the price to be paid for the adoption of any new rule or standard? If so, what role, if any, should knowing this play in fashioning the rule or standard in the first place?

4. *Blog, blog, blog.* Like e-mail, web logs created for the internet—"blogs"—are an important forum in which workers can overcome their physical isolation from each other and communicate in the modern work "place." One pair of scholars argues that employees' blogging, especially when conducted off duty, is the modern equivalent of meeting for a chat at the union hall, and should be similarly protected as concerted activity. They would not only reinterpret the NLRA to recognize this development, but also reinterpret state common law, as well as adopt new legislation, to protect blogging as a form of off-duty conduct beyond the reach of employer sanctions. As to the latter, they note that some states have passed laws protecting the private lives of off-duty employees to smoke, notwithstanding workplace policies against smoking. *See* Rafael Gely & Leonard Bierman, *Social Isolation and American Workers: Employee Blogging and Legal Reform*, 20 Harv. J.L. & Tech. 287 (2007).

Is the reasoning of the *Purple* majority consistent with this view? What about the reasoning of the dissent?

5. *Discriminatory enforcement: The Case of the Girl Scout Cookies.* *Register Guard* was harshly-criticized for taking a twentieth century view of the twenty-first century workplace, but perhaps its real significance lay in its less-noticed change in the Board's approach to determining whether and when an employer has violated the law by discriminatorily enforcing its no-access

rules. As discussed in this chapter, *infra* p. 461, it is long-settled law that an employer may exclude as trespassers all nonemployee organizers, and promulgate rules prohibiting them from gaining access to employees or soliciting them on employer property. But there is an important exception: an employer may lose its right to exclude by discriminatorily granting access to some nonemployees while denying it to union representatives.

In the classic case of illegal access discrimination, management promulgates a "strict" no-access, no-distribution policy, yet occasionally grants access to nonemployees who are soliciting for a recognized charity (such as the Girl Scouts, the Salvation Army, or the United Way) while denying access to nonemployee union organizers. The remedy the Board usually orders for such selective enforcement is to grant access after all to nonemployee union organizers. The rationale is that an employer may not arbitrarily pick and choose to whom it will apply the sanctity of private property rights; either everybody must be excluded, or nobody can be. Courts have divided over the Board's view that such selective enforcement of such no-access, no-solicitation, or no-distribution policies is discriminatory. Compare, *e.g.*, *Four B Corp. v. NLRB*, 163 F.3d 1177 (10th Cir. 1998) (finding discrimination in selective enforcement favoring Salvation Army and Cub Scouts) and *Lucile Salter Packard Children's Hosp. v. NLRB*, 97 F.3d 583 (D.C. Cir. 1996) (finding discrimination in selective enforcement allowing literature distribution by credit union, insurance company, social services provider, and medical textbook publishers, but not union) with, *e.g.*, *Salmon Run Shopping Center v. NLRB*, 534 F.3d 108 (2d Cir. 2008) (finding no discrimination in selective enforcement allowing solicitation and distribution of messages deemed by shopping center to be beneficial to the mall, but not allowing distribution by union of literature protesting tenant's use of contractor paying below area standards) and *Cleveland Real Estate Partners v. NLRB*, 95 F.3d 457 (6th Cir. 1996) (finding no discrimination in selective enforcement allowing solicitations by Girl Scouts, Knights of Columbus, and children selling candy).

Register Guard suggested that a more conservative majority of the Board would no longer consider it discriminatory for an employer to grant access to troopers selling Girl Scout cookies while denying access to nonemployee organizers soliciting workers to join a union. It reasoned that, to be unlawful, "discrimination must be along Section 7 lines"—meaning the "unequal treatment of equals." For example, an employer would violate the Act "if it permitted employees to use e-mail to solicit for one union but not another, or if it permitted solicitation by antiunion employees but not by prounion employees." But permitting charities to have access and denying it to union adherents doesn't count as discrimination.

Purple's more liberal majority rejected this view, but there is little to prevent the Trump Board from re-embracing it.

Which definition of discrimination do you favor? Recall the case of Enderby, Inc. Would a company rule that granted representatives of the Red Cross or the Salvation Army to solicit donations, but not professional organizers from the Programmers Union, access to the lobby of the company's building in High Tech Park, be discriminatory? If not, why not? Does it matter that national labor policy favors giving employees access to information about their Section 7 rights, but there is no such policy about giving them access to information about supporting well-known charities? If so, what should the remedy be?

6. *Getting one's kicks—on Route 86.* E-mail systems connect to the internet via a router which can be programmed to block a variety of messages. Would an employer violate Section 8(a)(1) if it programmed the router to block all e-mail messages coming from e-mail addresses associated with the union seeking to organize its workers? What if it programmed the router to block all e-mails coming from ".org" e-mail addresses?

2. ACCESS BY NONEMPLOYEE ORGANIZERS

In the problem presented at the beginning of this chapter, Enderby's offices were on the fifth floor of a ten-story building in a large, privately owned complex. Two union organizers stood along one of the roads leading into and out of the complex and attempted to distribute leaflets to passing motorists who generally did not slow down to receive the leaflets. It is likely that this leafleting campaign would have been more effective if it could have been carried out in front of the entrance to the building housing Enderby's offices, but that area was privately owned.

Since *NLRB v. Babcock & Wilcox Co.*, 351 U.S. 105 (1956), the NLRA has been understood as conferring access rights in favor of employee organizers and imposing restrictions on such rights against nonemployee organizers. But *Babcock* recognized that insofar as the employees' right of self-organization "depends in some measure on [their] ability . . . to learn the advantages of self-organization from others," Section 7 "may, in certain limited circumstances, restrict an employer's right to exclude nonemployee union organizers from his property." The nature of those circumstances is explored in the following case.

LECHMERE, INC. V. NLRB
502 U.S. 527 (1992)

JUSTICE THOMAS delivered the opinion of the Court:

This case stems from the efforts of Local 919 of the United Food and Commercial Workers Union to organize employees at a retail store in Newington, Conn., owned and operated by petitioner Lechmere, Inc. The store is located in the Lechmere Shopping Plaza, which occupies a roughly rectangular tract measuring approximately 880 feet from north to south and 740 feet from east to west. Lechmere's store is situated at the Plaza's south end, with the main parking lot to its north. A strip of 13 smaller "satellite stores" not owned by Lechmere runs along the west side of the

Plaza, facing the parking lot. To the Plaza's east (where the main entrance is located) runs the Berlin Turnpike, a four-lane divided highway. The parking lot, however, does not abut the Turnpike; they are separated by a 46-foot-wide grassy strip, broken only by the Plaza's entrance. The parking lot is owned jointly by Lechmere and the developer of the satellite stores. The grassy strip is public property (except for a 4-foot-wide band adjoining the parking lot, which belongs to Lechmere).

The union began its campaign to organize the store's 200 employees, none of whom was represented by a union. After a full-page advertisement in a local newspaper drew little response, nonemployee union organizers entered Lechmere's parking lot and began placing handbills on the windshields of cars parked in a corner of the lot used mostly by employees. Lechmere's manager immediately confronted the organizers, informed them that Lechmere prohibited solicitation or handbill distribution of any kind on its property, and asked them to leave. They did so, and Lechmere personnel removed the handbills. The union organizers renewed this handbilling effort in the parking lot on several subsequent occasions; each time they were asked to leave and the handbills were removed. The organizers then relocated to the public grassy strip, from where they attempted to pass out handbills to cars entering the lot during hours (before opening and after closing) when the drivers were assumed to be primarily store employees. For one month, the union organizers returned daily to the grassy strip to picket Lechmere; after that, they picketed intermittently for another six months. They also recorded the license plate numbers of cars parked in the employee parking area; with the cooperation of the Connecticut Department of Motor Vehicles, they thus secured the names and addresses of some 41 nonsupervisory employees (roughly 20% of the store's total). The union sent four mailings to these employees; it also made some attempts to contact them by phone or home visits. These mailings and visits resulted in one signed union authorization card.

Jean Country, 291 N.L.R.B. 11 (1988), represents the Board's latest attempt to implement the rights guaranteed by § 7. It sets forth a three-factor balancing test: "[I]n all access cases our essential concern will be (1) the degree of impairment of the Section 7 right if access should be denied, as it balances against (2) the degree of impairment of the private property right if access should be granted. We view the consideration of (3) the availability of reasonably effective alternative means as especially significant in this balancing process." 291 N.L.R.B. at 14.

Citing its role "as the agency with responsibility for implementing national labor policy," the Board maintains in this case that *Jean Country* is a reasonable interpretation of the NLRA entitled to judicial deference. It is certainly true, and we have long recognized, that the Board has the "special function of applying the general provisions of the Act to the complexities of industrial life." Like other administrative agencies, the

NLRB is entitled to judicial deference when it interprets an ambiguous provision of a statute that it administers.

Before we reach any issue of deference to the Board, however, we must first determine whether *Jean Country*—at least as applied to nonemployee organizational trespassing—is consistent with our past interpretation of § 7. "Once we have determined a statute's clear meaning, we adhere to that determination under the doctrine of *stare decisis,* and we judge an agency's later interpretation of the statute against our prior determination of the statute's meaning."

In *Babcock,* we held that the Act drew a distinction "of substance," 351 U.S. at 113, between the union activities of employees and nonemployees. In cases involving *employee* activities, we noted with approval, the Board "balanced the conflicting interests of employees to receive information on self-organization on the company's property from fellow employees during nonworking time, with the employer's right to control the use of his property." *Id.* at 109–10. In cases involving *nonemployee* activities (like those at issue in *Babcock* itself), however, the Board was not permitted to engage in that same balancing (and we reversed the Board for having done so). By reversing the Board's interpretation of the statute for failing to distinguish between the organizing activities of employees and nonemployees, we were saying that § 7 speaks to the issue of nonemployee access to an employer's property. *Babcock's* teaching is straightforward: § 7 simply does not protect nonemployee union organizers *except* in the rare case where "the inaccessibility of employees makes ineffective the reasonable attempts by nonemployees to communicate with them through the usual channels," 351 U.S. at 112. Our reference to "reasonable" attempts was nothing more than a commonsense recognition that unions need not engage in extraordinary feats to communicate with inaccessible employees—*not* an endorsement of the view (which we expressly rejected) that the Act protects "reasonable" trespasses. Where reasonable alternative means of access exist, § 7's guarantees do not authorize trespasses by nonemployee organizers, *even* "under . . . reasonable regulations" established by the Board.

Jean Country, which applies broadly to "all access cases," misapprehends this critical point. So long as nonemployee union organizers have reasonable access to employees outside an employer's property, the requisite accommodation has taken place. It is *only* where such access is infeasible that it becomes necessary and proper to take the accommodation inquiry to a second level, balancing the employees' and employers' rights. At least as applied to nonemployees, *Jean Country* impermissibly conflates these two stages of the inquiry—thereby significantly eroding *Babcock's* general rule that "an employer may validly post his property against nonemployee distribution of union literature," 351 U.S. at 11. We reaffirm that general rule today, and reject the Board's attempt to recast it as a multifactor balancing test.

The threshold inquiry in this case, then, is whether the facts here justify application of *Babcock*'s inaccessibility exception.

We cannot accept the Board's conclusion, because it "rest[s] on erroneous legal foundations," *Babcock*, 351 U.S. at 112. As we have explained, the exception to *Babcock*'s rule is a narrow one. It does not apply wherever nontrespassory access to employees may be cumbersome or less-than-ideally effective, but only where "the location of a plant and the living quarters of the employees place the employees beyond the reach of reasonable union efforts to communicate with them," 351 U.S. at 113. Classic examples include logging camps, mining camps, and mountain resort hotels. *Babcock*'s exception was crafted precisely to protect the § 7 rights of those employees who, by virtue of their employment, are isolated from the ordinary flow of information that characterizes our society. The union's burden of establishing such isolation is, as we have explained, "a heavy one."

The Board's conclusion in this case that the union had no reasonable means short of trespass to make Lechmere's employees aware of its organizational efforts is based on a misunderstanding of the limited scope of this exception. Because the employees do not reside on Lechmere's property, they are presumptively not "beyond the reach," of the union's message. Although the employees live in a large metropolitan area (Greater Hartford), that fact does not in itself render them "inaccessible" in the sense contemplated by *Babcock*. Their accessibility is suggested by the union's success in contacting a substantial percentage of them directly, via mailings, phone calls, and home visits. Such direct contact, of course, is not a necessary element of "reasonably effective" communication; signs or advertising also may suffice. In this case, the union tried advertising in local newspapers; the Board said that this was not reasonably effective because it was expensive and might not reach the employees. Whatever the merits of that conclusion, other alternative means of communication were readily available. Thus, signs (displayed, for example, from the public grassy strip adjoining Lechmere's parking lot) would have informed the employees about the union's organizational efforts. (Indeed, union organizers picketed the shopping center's main entrance for months as employees came and went every day.) Access to employees, not success in winning them over, is the critical issue—although success, or lack thereof, may be relevant in determining whether reasonable access exists. Because the union in this case failed to establish the existence of any "unique obstacles" that frustrated access to Lechmere's employees, the Board erred in concluding that Lechmere committed an unfair labor practice by barring the nonemployee organizers from its property.

[The dissenting opinions of JUSTICE WHITE, with whom JUSTICE BLACKMUN joined, and JUSTICE STEVENS, are omitted.]

NOTES

1.   As Justice Thomas notes for the majority, in *NLRB v. Babcock & Wilcox Co.*, 351 U.S. 105 (1956), "the Court held that the Act drew a distinction 'of substance' between the union activities of employees and nonemployees." In this case, the distinction meant the difference between being able to come onto the employer's property to speak directly to employees or to place handbills on their car windshields, which might actually be read by employees, and displaying signs "from the public grassy strip adjoining Lechmere's parking lot," which were mostly ignored by passersby.

Recall from the discussion of who counts as an "employee" in Chapter 3, *supra* p. 222, that the *Lechmere* Court did not consider the organizers to be employees because they were not employed by the employer that was the target of the organizing. This meant that they had no rights to solicit the Lechmere employees on the employer's property; the only rights at issue were those of the Lechmere employees to learn about the union, i.e., to receive the message that the organizers sought to communicate. If the Lechmere employees could receive that message through other means of communication, then the employer's prohibiting the organizers from coming onto its property did not interfere with the Lechmere employees' rights. Does such a distinction appear in the text of the statute? Professor Dannin says the answer is clearly no. To decide the case as it did, she argues, the Court had to invent a definition for the term "employees" that does not actually appear in Section 2(3):

> The Court said "employees" meant only the employees of a specific employer. This is the common meaning of the word, but the NLRA says exactly the opposite. The NLRA says that the term employee "shall include any employee, and shall not be limited to the employees of a particular employer." This definition is intended to promote and protect worker solidarity across workplaces.

Ellen Dannin, Taking Back the Workers' Law: How to Fight the Assault on Labor Rights 13 (2006). One of the Wagner Act's principal drafters, Philip Levy, proposed a further amendment that would have made it clear that "union organizers" are covered by the definition of employee in Section 2(3). *See* Memorandum by Philip Levy to Calvert Magruder, Apr. 17, 1935, *cited in* Archibald Cox, Derek Curtis Bok, Robert A. Gorman & Matthew W. Finkin, Labor Law: Cases and Materials 142 (15th ed. 2011); *see also Marshall Field & Co. v. NLRB*, 200 F.2d 375 (7th Cir. 1952). What effect, if any, should the failure to add this amendment have on the construction of the statute?

2.   *The NLRA, the common law, and property rights.* If Professor Dannin is right, then even the Court's "nonemployee organizers" are really "employees" within the meaning of Act, because they are "employees" of somebody—in this case, the union attempting to organize the targeted employer. In the context of union organizing, this would render obsolete common law notions about the

employer's right, as a private property owner, to control access to the workplace by non-invitees, including professional union organizers. Agreeing with Professor Dannin, Professor Cameron argues that overthrowing common law notions of private property in the workplace is perhaps the whole point of the Act:

> Decisions like *Lechmere* undermine core labor rights by defining those rights more narrowly than the plain meaning of the statute. Majority opinions in these cases fail or refuse to recognize the transformative power of the NLRA, which was adopted to modify the application of free market principles to the workplace by granting workers access to the counterbalancing power of collective bargaining.

Christopher David Ruiz Cameron, *All Over But the Shouting? Some Thoughts About Amending the Wagner Act by Adjudication Rather Than Retirement*, 26 Berkeley J. of Emp. & Lab. L. 275, 278 (2005). For a discussion of how the Court has effectively limited access and other rights granted by the NLRA, and replaced them with Lochner-era common law principles, see James Gray Pope, *How American Workers Lost the Right to Strike, and Other Tales*, 103 Mich. L. Rev. 518 (2004).

3.   *A Penny for your thoughts.* Recall Penny, the prounion programmer at Enderby, Inc. After being fired for violating the company's rule banning use of the e-mail system for personal messages, she and two professional union organizers tried to distribute leaflets urging employees to sign authorization cards. They stood alongside one of the 14 roads leading into and out of High Tech Park, the privately-owned, nine-acre, mixed-use suburban complex where Enderby maintains its offices. But most of the passersby were driving automobiles, and did not slow down to take the leaflets. Is it an unfair labor practice for the owners of High Tech Park (or Enderby itself) to bar the trio from access to the grounds of High Tech Park? From the parking lot where Enderby employees park their cars? From the lobby of the 10-story building in High Tech Park where Enderby maintains its office? From the fifth floor where Enderby is headquartered? If Penny had not been fired, would your answer be different as to her in any of these situations?

4.   *The importance of state law. Lechmere* states that an employer need not tolerate trespassing on its property except in very limited circumstances. What if state law does not regard the union organizer's solicitations on the employer's property as a trespass? For example, in California, shopping centers may not categorically exclude non-commercial solicitors from their property. *See PruneYard Shopping Ctr. v. Robins*, 447 U.S. 74 (1980). Does a shopping center in California violate the NLRA if it prohibits union organizers from soliciting on its property? *See Bristol Farms, Inc.*, 311 N.L.R.B. 437 (1993) (holding yes); Jeffrey M. Hirsch, *Taking State Property Rights out of Federal Labor Law*, 47 B.C.L. Rev. 891 (2006).

5.   *The lunch counter cases.* A retail store has a cafeteria that is open to the public. A union organizer enters the cafeteria, purchases a meal, sits at a

table and speaks to employees who are on their lunch breaks about the benefits of union organization. May the employer bar the organizer from the cafeteria? *See Montgomery Ward & Co. v. NLRB*, 692 F.2d 1115 (7th Cir. 1982) (upholding Board finding of violation for such exclusion). In *Farm Fresh, Inc.*, 326 N.L.R.B. 997 (1998), however, the Board overruled *Montgomery Ward*, reasoning that the decision was inconsistent with *Lechmere*. On appeal, the D.C. Circuit held that the Board's finding that Farm Fresh had ejected union organizers from its snack bar because they were violating its no-solicitation rule was not supported by substantial evidence. Rather, the court found, the record established that the organizers were ejected because they had outstanding trespass warrants against them. The court remanded the case to the Board for reconsideration. *United Food & Commercial Workers Local 400 v. NLRB*, 222 F.3d 1030 (D.C. Cir. 2000). On remand, the Board vacated its prior overruling of *Montgomery Ward* and dismissed the unfair labor practice charge on the ground that Farm Fresh had ejected the organizers because of prior trespass warrants pending against them. *Farm Fresh, Inc.*, 332 N.L.R.B. 1424 (2000).

6. *Lechmere in the public sector.* Should *Lechmere* apply to state public sector labor relations laws governing employers whose property is publicly owned? In *Palatine Community Consolidated School District No. 15*, 18 Pub. Emp. Rptr. Ill. ¶ 1043 (Ill. Educ. Lab. Rel. Bd. 2002), the Illinois Educational Labor Relations Board (IELRB) held *Lechmere* inapplicable under the Illinois Educational Labor Relations Act. Instead, the IELRB found more relevant the distinction drawn in the Supreme Court's First Amendment jurisprudence between public forums and nonpublic forums. It held that a public educational employer could not exclude union organizers from areas controlled by the employer that are considered public forums.

* * *

Lechmere recognizes that employer property rights may have to yield to employee Section 7 rights in cases where the employees are beyond the reach of reasonable means of communication. Such cases typically involve employees who reside on the employer's property. *See, e.g., Nabors Alaska Drilling, Inc. v. NLRB*, 190 F.3d 1008 (9th Cir. 1999) (employees resided in camps at remote Alaska oil drilling sites and on off shore drilling platforms). Modern technology, however, enables employment of workforces that are widely dispersed. In some cases, the employees may report for duty and work virtually, via computer terminal, rather than physically, from a central location. The effects on access by nonemployee organizers due to such dispersal are explored in the following case.

TECHNOLOGY SERVICE SOLUTIONS (I)
332 N.L.R.B. 1096 (2000)

CHAIRMAN TRUESDALE and MEMBERS FOX and HURTGEN:

The Respondent installs, services, and repairs computer systems nationwide. Its employees who perform computer installation, maintenance, and service work are called customer service representatives (CSRs). In its south-central region, covering Colorado, New Mexico, Oklahoma, Kansas, Missouri, Arkansas, and parts of Nebraska and Wyoming, the Respondent employs 236 CSRs. The Respondent's headquarters for the region is located in Englewood, Colorado, a Denver suburb. CSRs are geographically dispersed and do not report to work at any one location. Rather, they typically work out of their homes or vehicles and spend most of their time at customers' locations.

Starting in late 1994 and continuing into 1995, the Union, at the request of a CSR and with his assistance, attempted to organize the Respondent's CSRs in the State of Colorado. Although the CSRs were scattered throughout the State and, to some extent, worked separately from each other, the Union, with diligent effort, obtained enough signed authorization cards to establish a showing of interest supporting its representation petition. Following a hearing, the Regional Director issued a Decision and Direction of Election finding that the CSRs in each of the Respondent's two territories within Colorado constituted an appropriate bargaining unit. The Respondent provided the Union with the *Excelsior* list containing the names and addresses of the 63 CSRs in the two units [as required by *Excelsior Underwear*, 156 N.L.R.B. 1236 (1966)]. A mail-ballot election was held in each unit, but the ballots were impounded, as the Respondent filed a request for review of the Regional Director's decision, which the Board granted. In its unpublished Decision on Review and Order, the Board found that the bargaining units established by the Regional Director [for the 63 Colorado CSRs only] were not appropriate and that the only appropriate unit was one covering all the Respondent's 236 CSRs in its south-central region.

On July 25, the Union sent a letter to the Respondent contending that, due to the Respondent's centralized organization and wireless dispatch system, the Union lacked access to the Respondent's CSRs in the south-central region, and this lack of access interfered with and restrained the CSRs in the exercise of their Section 7 rights. Therefore, the Union requested that the Respondent provide it with the names and addresses of all CSRs in the south-central region. On July 31, the Respondent denied the Union's request.

In contending that the Respondent's denial of the Union's request to provide it with the CSRs' names and addresses violated the Act, the General Counsel invokes by analogy the inaccessibility exception to the general rule, set forth in *Lechmere*, that an employer may lawfully prohibit nonemployee union representatives from trespassing on its property to engage in organizational activity. The inaccessibility exception to this rule requires that an employer must allow such trespass in rare instances when "the location of the plant and the living quarters of the employees place the employees beyond the reach of reasonable union efforts to communicate with them." The General Counsel contends that, due to the Respondent's operational structure, the unit employees are so widely dispersed over a large area and so isolated from each other that they are effectively beyond the reach of reasonable union efforts to communicate with them. Therefore, according to the General Counsel, the Respondent was obligated to grant the Union's request for a list of the employees' names and addresses, as providing such a list would be less intrusive than allowing nonemployee union representatives to enter onto private property.

We find, based on the credited testimony, that the General Counsel simply fell short of proving his contention that the Union had no reasonable means of communicating with the bargaining unit employees unless the Respondent provided it with their names and addresses. The judge found that, after the Board's earlier ruling that the appropriate unit included CSRs in all the Respondent's south-central region, the Union, despite its possession of the *Excelsior* list, failed to contact any of the 63 Colorado CSRs other than Phillips to inquire whether they could put the Union in touch with any of the unit CSRs outside Colorado. Many of the CSRs were former IBM Corporation employees, some of whom knew each other from their employment at IBM. Additionally, Colorado CSRs occasionally met CSRs from elsewhere in the Respondent's south-central region at training sessions conducted by the Respondent. Consequently, there was reason to believe that some Colorado CSRs would know or at least possess names and addresses or telephone numbers of unit CSRs outside of Colorado. In any event, the Union failed to explore this possibility.

Additionally, although the Union had come in contact with two New Mexico CSRs during its organizing efforts in Colorado, it failed to contact them again after the unit was expanded to include New Mexico (among other States). In failing to inquire of the CSRs whose names and addresses it did possess whether they could help the Union identify and contact unit CSRs outside of Colorado, the Union failed to pursue an obvious possible means for it to reach the non-Colorado unit employees. Indeed, the Union's earlier success in identifying and contacting a sufficient number of CSRs to obtain a showing of interest for its desired Colorado unit was accomplished, in large measure, through information provided by CSRs. Consequently, as the Union did not attempt to use this obvious possible means, the General Counsel was unable to demonstrate, as a factual matter, that the Union had no reasonable means to communicate with bargaining unit employees outside of Colorado.

Under existing case law, an employer has no obligation to provide the names and addresses of its employees to a union that wishes to organize them. Unless ordered as an unfair labor practices remedy, an employer's provision of its employees' names and addresses to a union is required only when, following the union's filing of an election petition accompanied by a sufficient showing of interest, the Board directs an election or approves the parties' consent-election agreement under *Excelsior Underwear*. Nevertheless, in the present case, even though no election had been directed or agreed to, the General Counsel alleged that the Respondent violated the Act by denying the Union's request for the Respondent's employees' names and addresses "where there was no reasonable alternative means for the Union to communicate with the Unit employees." By using this language, the General Counsel invoked the Supreme Court's decision in *Lechmere, Inc. v. NLRB*, 502 U.S. 527 (1992), and its precursor, *NLRB v. Babcock & Wilcox Co.*, 351 U.S. 105 (1956), which generally permit an employer to bar non-employee union organizers from trespassing on its property unless there is no reasonable alternative means for the union to communicate its organizational message to the employer's employees.

We find application of *Lechmere*'s "no reasonable alternative means" standard to be appropriate here. Indeed, application of a lesser standard, under which the Respondent would be required to supply a list of its employees' names and addresses to the Union even when it is not shown that the Union lacks a reasonable means to communicate with the employees, would tend to undermine the careful balance drawn by the Board's *Excelsior* decision, which, as discussed above, requires employers to provide such a list only after an election has been directed or agreed to.

In its effort to organize the desired Colorado unit, the Union asked unit CSRs with whom it had come in contact to supply the names, addresses, and telephone numbers of other Colorado CSRs. Once the unit was expanded to include all the Respondent's south-central region, however, the Union declined to further employ this technique. That is, the Union failed to ask the CSRs who it knew to supply the names, addresses, and telephone numbers of unit CSRs outside of Colorado. As the Board has previously held, where, as here, a union has "achieved a fair measure of success in communicating with the [employees by using certain methods] in the past . . . it is particularly necessary for a showing to be made that, in the organizing campaign at issue here, these methods were attempted or that they would have been futile. Given the Union's success in Colorado in asking CSRs with whom it had come in contact to supply the names, addresses, and telephone numbers of other unit CSRs, it is hardly a subjective approach for us to require that the General Counsel show that the Union attempted to employ this previously used method in contacting unit CSRs outside of Colorado or that such an attempt would have been futile. Further, absent an effort to use this technique to identify and communicate with unit CSRs outside of Colorado, we can hardly presume that such an effort, if attempted, would have been futile.

Accordingly, on this basis, we adopt the judge's dismissal of the complaint allegation that the Respondent's failure to provide the names and addresses of the unit employees violated Section 8(a)(1).

MEMBER FOX, dissenting in part:

I do not agree with my colleagues' application of *Lechmere Inc. v. NLRB,* 502 U.S. 527 (1992), to the issue of whether the Respondent violated Section 8(a)(1) by refusing to provide the Union with a list of names and addresses of bargaining unit employees, nor do I agree with their conclusion.

At the outset, it is worth noting how it came to be that the Union undertook to organize the bargaining unit at issue here. The Union initially sought to represent a unit of customer service representatives (CSRs) in the State of Colorado. Following a hearing, the Regional Director directed elections in two separate units, which he found to be appropriate, encompassing organizational groups within Colorado (and small portions of south-central Wyoming, western Nebraska and northeastern New Mexico). The Board subsequently reversed the Regional Director, agreeing with the Respondent that the only appropriate unit was one covering all the Respondent's 236 CSRs in its south-central region (covering Colorado, New Mexico, Oklahoma, Kansas, Missouri, Arkansas, and parts of Nebraska and Wyoming). Thus, the unit determined to be appropriate was not that sought initially by the Union and was substantially expanded in size and scope by the Board at the request of the Respondent, to include people scattered over eight different States who share no geographically centralized place of work.

In my view, the unique characteristics of the bargaining unit in this case present circumstances in which Respondent's refusal to provide the Union with a list of names and addresses of bargaining unit employees unjustifiably interferes with Section 7 organizational rights. The bargaining unit includes individuals who, for the most part, work alone without a commonly shared workplace, who are geographically dispersed over the expanse of eight States, who have little or no knowledge of, contact with, or ways to communicate with their coworkers, and who are largely unknown to union organizers who might seek to inform them of the advantages of organization. In other words, the structural isolation imposed on these individual employees who comprise the bargaining unit in this case greatly restricts both "the right of employees to organize for mutual aid without employer interference."

Historically, more typical employment settings have consisted of a commonly shared workplace or, at least, a location at which the employees gather on some regular basis. These more typical employment settings, by their structure, foster opportunities for the exercise of the employees' organizational rights. The collective gathering of employees found in more typical employment settings, by their structure, also allows nonemployee union organizers to attempt multiple methods of identifying and communicating with employees about the advantages of organization.

Consequently, when dealing with more typical employment settings, the Board has not required an employer to provide a list of the names and addresses of bargaining unit employees prior to the time an employer is required to file an *Excelsior* list.

The structure of the bargaining unit in the present case, however, is an outgrowth of the ongoing changes in the American work force and the continuing creation of new and varied forms of workplaces in response to advances achieved by American business and technology. The unique characteristics of this bargaining unit, which largely isolate these employees and restrict them from exercising their organizational rights, call for a different result. Under these circumstances, allowing an employer to refuse to provide a union with a list of names and addresses of bargaining unit employees is unjustified, particularly in light of the fundamental organizational rights which are at risk.

Most of the "usual channels" that nonemployee union organizers historically have attempted to use to communicate with employees about the advantages of organization, however, would be wholly ineffective in reaching the employees of this bargaining unit. This is because the usual channels of communication either rely on a model of a commonly shared workplace for reaching otherwise unidentified employees—such as distributing leaflets by hand near their place of employment, talking with them on nearby streets, placing signs on nearby public property, advertising in local newspapers, or recording license plate numbers of cars parked in nearby parking lots—or they are applicable only if the union already knows the names, addresses, or telephone numbers of employees—such as mailing literature to employees, talking with them over the telephone, or driving to their homes and talking with them there.

Here, there is no commonly shared workplace or other place that the employees regularly gather, nor are the names, addresses, or telephone numbers of the 173 non-Colorado CSRs known to the Union. Therefore, few, if any, of the usual channels are available under the facts of this case, and accordingly the Union's reasonable attempts to identify and communicate with the bargaining unit employees through the usual channels of communication will necessarily be ineffective within the meaning of *Lechmere*.

Accordingly, I dissent from that portion of the majority opinion, which misapplies the *Lechmere* balancing test to this case.

NOTES

1. *Traditional vs. electronic workplaces.* To Professors Malin and Perritt, the facts of the *Technology Services Solutions* raise important questions about the regulation of union organizing in the electronic workplace that reach far beyond the problem of fashioning an appropriate remedy for the violation of workers' rights. Writing before either *Register Guard* or *Purple* was decided, they anticipated the argument that, whereas person-to-person solicitation in the traditional workplace lends itself to stringent rules confining it to nonworking time, electronic solicitation in the modern workplace does not, due to the *de minimus* disruption it is likely to cause. The recipient of an email message can control when she will actually read the message, which can be postponed until her break or after work. As they put it:

> In physical workplaces, the solicitor and the target of the solicitation usually are in the same place at the same time. The solicitation takes place in a discrete transaction which has a beginning and an end. Solicitations in electronic workplaces do not share these characteristics. The solicitor may be anywhere and the target of the solicitation may receive and read the solicitor's message minutes, hours, or even days after it is sent.

> Access rules developed in traditional workplaces center on discrete physical boundaries and discrete separations between working and nonworking time. E-mail and related electronic technologies blur these boundaries. Employees who work all or part of their time from their homes tend to integrate home and work in a manner directly contrary to the strong home-work boundary found in traditional industrial settings. Remote access to the job also blurs the distinction between working and nonworking time. The blurring of these distinctions strongly suggests that employer solicitation of employees at their homes does not carry with it the same level of intimidation that such home solicitation carries in traditional workplaces. Electronic workplace home solicitations by employers should not be considered per se coercive. Rather, the NLRB should scrutinize them on a case-by-case basis, inquiring into whether the solicitation differs materially from other communications sent by the employer to, or accessed by the employee at, the employee's home. The burden should be on the General Counsel to demonstrate the coercive nature of the home solicitation.

* * *

> Consequently, there is no reason to assume that the electronic solicitation of employees necessarily causes more than a *de minimus* disruption of the workplace. In many respects, the sending of electronic solicitations to employees in the workplace resembles the distribution of leaflets to employees as they enter the workplace. The employee may choose to read the leaflet during working time or may

reserve it until break or other nonworking time. The possibility that the employee may decide to read the leaflet on the job does not justify the employer in prohibiting the leaflet's distribution.

Martin H. Malin & Henry H. Perritt, Jr., *The National Labor Relations Act in Cyberspace*, 49 U. Kan. L. Rev. 1, 48, 52–53 (2000).

2.   *Lechmere, Schmechmere.* In *Technology Service Solutions I*, the unfair labor practice charged was the employer's refusal to provide the union with a list of employee names and addresses. Does such a complaint seek to impose on the employer a duty to aid the union's organizing drive, as opposed to a duty to refrain from interfering with the organizing drive? Should the Board have dismissed the charge on this basis alone, without ever considering the applicability of *Lechmere*?

3.   *Whose property?* May an employer claim to have a property right to its employees' names and home addresses? If not, why should *Lechmere* even apply to this case? Is not *Lechmere* premised on the employer's property right to exclude trespassers?

4.   *Throwing a "brick" at Windows?* In a portion of the decision not reproduced above, the Board found the employer liable for unfair labor practices that were independent of the denial of the list of names and addresses. In *Technology Service Solutions II*, 334 N.L.R.B. 116 (2001), a proceeding to determine the proper remedy for those unfair labor practices, the Board ordered the posting of a notice notifying the employees of the violations. For years, the time-honored method of giving such notice was to post a piece of paper in a common workplace area, such as the bulletin board of the break room or cafeteria. Because TSS had no such common area, the NLRB ordered that letters be sent to each affected employee. But it rejected the General Counsel's request that e-mail notice also be sent to each employee via his or her "brick," or personal computer terminal. Does the remedy make sense?

3.   ACCESS AND LABORATORY CONDITIONS

In some circumstances, the Board's "laboratory conditions" doctrine, as articulated in *General Shoe Corp.*, 77 N.L.R.B. 124, 126–27 (1948), *enf'd*, 192 F.2d 504 (6th Cir. 1951), *cert. denied*, 343 U.S. 904 (1952), discussed *supra* Chapter 4-C-2-b, imposes stricter regulation than is found under Section 8(a)(1). For example, the Board—with apparent Supreme Court approval—has held that an employer may require employees to attend meetings at which anti-union presentations are made. *See NLRB v. United Steelworkers (Nutone, Inc.)*, 357 U.S. 357 (1958). But if "captive audience" meetings are held or speeches are given within 24 hours of a representation election, they are presumed to taint the required laboratory conditions and may cause the Board to void the results of an election lost by the union. *See Peerless Plywood Co.*, 107 N.L.R.B. 427 (1953).

As noted in *Technology Service Solutions*, when an election is ordered, an employer must share its eligible voter list. *See Excelsior Underwear*,

Inc., 156 N.L.R.B. 1236 (1966). The *Excelsior* list is supposed to be an accurate and complete list of first and last names and addresses of all persons eligible to vote in a representation election, and must be filed by the employer with the Regional Director, who then turns it over to the union.

The eligible voters whose names must appear on an *Excelsior* list are all the employees in the bargaining unit and on employer's most recent payroll, including: economic strikers; ULP strikers; permanent replacements; probationary employees (whose duties are substantially similar to those of regular employees and who have reasonable expectation of continued employment); employees on sick leave or other limited leave; "salts"; laid-off employees who have a reasonable expectation of recall; and regular part-time employees, *see, e.g., The Pavilion at Crossing Pointe*, 344 N.L.R.B. 582 (2005) (employee who violated employer's general part-time rule by failing to work 4 or more hours per week in quarter preceding eligibility date nonetheless qualified as laid-off employee with reasonable expectation of recall).

But noneligible voters whose names need not appear on the *Excelsior* are several, including: employees who have quit; employees who have been discharged for cause; or employees whose Section 8(a)(3) charges for discriminatory discharge remain pending. This last exclusion is notable because it may encourage employers to violate the Act by firing pesky employee-organizers. *See, e.g.*, Paul C. Weiler, *Promises to Keep: Securing Workers' Rights to Self-Organization Under the NLRA*, 96 Harv. L. Rev. 1769, 1781 (1983) (estimating odds that a union supporter will be fired for exercising rights guaranteed by NLRA at 1 in 20, and noting effect of such firing on other potential supporters). The list must be produced within seven days of either the direction of an election or approval of a consent election agreement. The employer's list must be in substantial compliance or the Board may set aside the election. *See Pole-Litus, Ltd.*, 229 N.L.R.B. 196 (1977).

And then there is the matter of e-mail. For the better part of a decade, the Board debated whether to expand the contact information on the *Excelsior* list to include employees' e-mail addresses. In 2007, in *Trustees of Columbia University*, 350 N.L.R.B. 574 (2007), the NLRB declined to do so by a vote of 2 to 1. The majority reasoned that, in the absence of a full record and briefing by amici, it was not in a position to weigh all the ramifications of making such a ruling. But in 2014, after twice undertaking rulemaking procedures—which included the solicitation of extensive comments from the public—the Board issued a new final rule streamlining its representation case ("R Case") procedures. Among other things, this rule requires that employees' e-mail addresses, as well as personal telephone numbers, be provided as a matter of course if available to the employer. See 29 C.F.R. §§ 102.62(d), 102.67(*l*) (2017); *NLRB Issues Final Rule to*

Modernize Representation Case Procedures (December 12, 2014), www.nlrb. gov/news-outreach/news-story/nlrb-issues-final-rule-modernize-represent ation-case-procedures, discussed *infra* Chapter 4-G-2.

D. REGULATION OF SPEECH

Section 8(a)(1)'s prohibition on employer interference, restraint or coercion of employees' section 7 rights regulates both what employers may say during a union organizing campaign, and how they may say it. This provision must be reconciled with section 8(c)(1), which provides:

> The expressing of any views, argument, or opinion, or the dissemination thereof, whether in written, printed, graphic, or visual form, shall not constitute or be evidence of an unfair labor practice under any provision of this Act, if such expression contains no threat of reprisal or force or promise of benefit. 29 U.S.C. § 158(c)(1).

The key phrase in Section 8(c)(1) is the qualifier "if such expression contains no threat of reprisal or force or promise of benefit." Thus the Act attempts to draw a fine line between protected employer free speech and impermissible employer coercion, as illustrated by the following case.

NLRB v. GISSEL PACKING CO.
395 U.S. 575 (1969)

CHIEF JUSTICE WARREN delivered the opinion of the Court:

When petitioner's president first learned of the Union's drive in July, he talked with all of his employees in an effort to dissuade them from joining a union. He particularly emphasized the results of the long 1952 strike, which he claimed "almost put our company out of business," and expressed worry that the employees were forgetting the "lessons of the past." He emphasized, secondly, that the Company was still on "thin ice" financially, that the Union's "only weapon is to strike," and that a strike "could lead to the closing of the plant," since the parent company had ample manufacturing facilities elsewhere. He noted, thirdly, that because of their age and the limited usefulness of their skills outside their craft, the employees might not be able to find re-employment if they lost their jobs as a result of a strike. Finally, he warned those who did not believe that the plant could go out of business to "look around Holyoke and see a lot of them out of business." The president sent letters to the same effect to the employees in early November, emphasizing that the parent company had no reason to stay in Massachusetts if profits went down.

During the two or three weeks immediately prior to the election on December 9, the president sent the employees a pamphlet captioned: "Do you want another 13-week strike?" stating, inter alia, that: "We have no doubt that the Teamsters Union can again close the Wire Weaving Department and the entire plant by a strike. We have no hopes that the Teamsters Union Bosses will not call a strike. The Teamsters Union is a strike happy outfit." Similar communications followed in late November, including one stressing the Teamsters' "hoodlum control." Two days before the election, the Company sent out another pamphlet that was entitled "Let's Look at the Record," and that purported to be an obituary of companies in the Holyoke-Springfield, Mass., area that had allegedly gone out of business because of union demands, eliminating some 3,500 jobs; the first page carried a large cartoon showing the preparation of a grave for the Sinclair Company and other headstones containing the names of other plants allegedly victimized by the unions. Finally, on the day before the election, the president made another personal appeal to his employees to reject the Union. He repeated that the Company's financial condition was precarious; that a possible strike would jeopardize the continued operation of the plant; and that age and lack of education would make re-employment difficult. The Union lost the election 7–6, and then filed both objections to the election and unfair labor practice charges which were consolidated for hearing before the trial examiner.

The Board agreed with the trial examiner that the president's communications with his employees, when considered as a whole, "reasonably tended to convey to the employees the belief or impression that selection of the Union in the forthcoming election could lead (the Company) to close its plant, or to the transfer of the weaving production, with the resultant loss of jobs to the wire weavers." Thus, the Board found that under the "totality of the circumstances" petitioner's activities constituted a violation of § 8(a)(1) of the Act.

[W]e note that an employer's free speech right to communicate his views to his employees is firmly established and cannot be infringed by a union or the Board. Thus, § 8(c) merely implements the First Amendment by requiring that the expression of "any views, argument, or opinion" shall not be evidence of an unfair labor practice, so long as such expression contains "no threat of reprisal or force or promise of benefit" in violation of § 8(a)(1). Section 8(a)(1), in turn, prohibits interference, restraint or coercion of employees in the exercise of their right to self-organization.

Any assessment of the precise scope of employer expression, of course, must be made in the context of its labor relations setting. Thus, an employer's rights cannot outweigh the equal rights of the employees to associate freely, as those rights are embodied in § 7 and protected by § 8(a)(1) and the proviso to § 8(c). And any balancing of those rights must take into account the economic dependence of the employees on their employers, and the necessary tendency of the former, because of that relationship, to pick up intended implications of the latter that might be more readily dismissed by a more disinterested ear. Stating these obvious principles is but another way of recognizing that what is basically at stake is the establishment of a nonpermanent, limited relationship between the employer, his economically dependent employee and his union agent, not the election of legislators or the enactment of legislation whereby that relationship is ultimately defined and where the independent voter may be freer to listen more objectively and employers as a class freer to talk.

Within this framework, we must reject the Company's challenge to the decision below and the findings of the Board on which it was based. [A]n employer is free to communicate to his employees any of his general views about unionism or any of his specific views about a particular union, so long as the communications do not contain a "threat of reprisal or force or promise of benefit." He may even make a prediction as to the precise effects he believes unionization will have on his company. In such a case, however, the prediction must be carefully phrased on the basis of objective fact to convey an employer's belief as to demonstrably probable consequences beyond his control or to convey a management decision already arrived at to close the plant in case of unionization. If there is any implication that an employer may or may not take action solely on his own initiative for reasons unrelated to economic necessities and known only to him, the statement is no longer a reasonable prediction based on available facts but a threat of retaliation based on misrepresentation and coercion, and as such without the protection of the First Amendment. We therefore agree with the court below that "(c)onveyance of the employer's belief, even though sincere, that unionization will or may result in the closing of the plant is not a statement of fact unless, which is most improbable, the eventuality of closing is capable of proof." As stated elsewhere, an employer is free only to tell what he reasonably believes will be the likely economic consequences of unionization that are outside his control, and not "threats of economic reprisal to be taken solely on his own volition."

Equally valid was the finding by the court and the Board that petitioner's statements and communications were not cast as a prediction of "demonstrable economic consequences," but rather as a threat of retaliatory action. The Board found that petitioner's speeches, pamphlets, leaflets, and letters conveyed the following message: that the company was in a precarious financial condition; that the "strike-happy" union would in all likelihood have to obtain its potentially unreasonable demands by striking, the probable result of which would be a plant shutdown, as the past history of labor relations in the area indicated; and that the employees in such a case would have great difficulty finding employment elsewhere. In carrying out its duty to focus on the question, "[W]hat did the speaker intend and the listener understand?," the Board could reasonably conclude that the intended and understood import of that message was not to predict that unionization would inevitably cause the plant to close but to threaten to throw employees out of work regardless of the economic realities. In this connection, we need go no further than to point out (1) that petitioner had no support for its basic assumption that the union, which had not yet even presented any demands, would have to strike to be heard, and that it admitted at the hearing that it had no basis for attributing other plant closings in the area to unionism; and (2) that the Board has often found that employees, who are particularly sensitive to rumors of plant closings, take such hints as coercive threats rather than honest forecasts.

Petitioner argues that the line between so-called permitted predictions and proscribed threats is too vague to stand up under traditional First Amendment analysis and that the Board's discretion to curtail free speech rights is correspondingly too uncontrolled. It is true that a reviewing court must recognize the Board's competence in the first instance to judge the impact of utterances made in the context of the employer-employee relationship. But an employer, who has control over that relationship and therefore knows it best, cannot be heard to complain that he is without an adequate guide for his behavior. He can easily make his views known without engaging in "brinkmanship" when it becomes all too easy to "overstep and tumble (over) the brink." At the least he can avoid coercive speech simply by avoiding conscious overstatements he has reason to believe will mislead his employees.

NOTES

1. *Line drawing.* How fine a line should be drawn between free speech and coercive speech where the underlying substantive message is the same? Is it legal to say, "You can avoid a lot of trouble if you just refuse to sign that authorization card"? What about, "If a union comes here, bargaining will start from scratch"? *See, e.g., Shaw's Supermarkets, Inc.*, 289 N.L.R.B. 844 (1988) (finding context of statement to be threatening and issuing cease-and-desist order), *enf. denied*, 884 F.2d 34 (1st Cir. 1989). Should a line be drawn between these statements and the truthful message that unionization can result in lower wages and benefits? *See S. Monterey County Hosp.*, 348 N.L.R.B. 327 (2006) (finding no threat or coercion in such statement).

2. *Monkey business.* A manager tells employees in a factory that he can teach monkeys to weld, the painters could all be replaced within ten minutes, union people are stupid, and union supporters are just being used by union bosses who live it up on members' dues. Do such statements violate Section 8(a)(1) or are they protected by Section 8(c)? *See Trailmobile Trailer, LLC*, 343 N.L.R.B. 95 (2004) (declining to hold such "flip and intemperate" remarks by themselves to be unlawful but finding ULP on other grounds). Should it matter if the manager adds that wages will continue to be set by management, union or no union? *See Trane Co.*, 137 N.L.R.B. 1506 (1962) (finding laboratory conditions to be tainted and ordering re-run election). What if the manager says, "You should know that in collective bargaining you can lose what you have now"? *See Wild Oats Markts., Inc.*, 344 N.L.R.B. 717 (2005) (finding such statement to be protected expression and refusing to order re-run election).

Can the Board draw meaningful distinctions between lawful expressions of opinion and unlawful statements of fact, such as misstatements of the employees' legal rights? Does the employer have right to say that union organizing is futile?

3. *Misrepresentations.* Factual misrepresentations made by employers or unions during representation campaigns implicate the preservation of the required laboratory conditions rather than coercion. The NLRB rules regarding speech in this area have flip-flopped many times, particularly regarding the use of forged documents as a type of campaign literature.

As to factual misrepresentations, two views have held sway.

On the one hand is the view that workplace elections occur in an environment that is less free for employee voters than a general election for citizen voters, yielding a regulatory, paternalistic view that misrepresentations should be policed. In *Hollywood Ceramics*, 140 N.L.R.B. 221 (1962), the Board announced that elections may be set aside when the prevailing party misrepresents facts in a way that "involves a substantial departure from the truth, at a time which prevents the other party or parties from making an effective reply" resulting in the misrepresentation "hav[ing] a significant impact on the election." *Id.* at 224.

On the other hand is the view that employees are generally sophisticated enough to understand that campaign propaganda should not be taken seriously, and that the NLRB should not get bogged down in the role of election police. In *Shopping Kart Food Market, Inc.*, 228 N.L.R.B. 1311 (1977), the Board overruled *Hollywood Ceramics* and explained that it would no longer probe into the truth or falsity of representation election campaign statements. *Id.* at 1313. Less than two years later, in *General Knit of Calif., Inc.*, 239 N.L.R.B. 619 (1978), the Board overruled itself again and reinstated *Hollywood Ceramics*. But four years later, in *Midland Nat'l Life Ins.Co.*, 263 N.L.R.B. 127 (1982), the Board changed course once again; it reversed *General Knit* (and hence, *Hollywood Ceramics*) and reinstated the hands-off rule of *Shopping Kart*.

As to forged documents, in general, these have been treated more seriously, especially when the forgeries are official Board documents. The most common type of forgery is an official-looking NLRB election ballot that has been marked to suggest a vote for one of the parties. In *Midland Nat'l Life Ins.*, the Board explained that it would continue to intervene in elections where either forged documents were not recognizable as propaganda or the forged documents suggested a Board endorsement of one of the parties to the election. Since *Midland Nat'l Life*, however, the NLRB has relaxed its view of what it might consider an actionable alteration on several occasions. For example, in *SDC Investments*, 274 N.L.R.B. 556 (1985), the Board stated that the key inquiry was not the fact of the forgery, but whether the altering party was clearly identifiable on the face of the document. If so, then there is no violation. In 1990, however, the Board indicated yet another shift, maintaining that even where there is no indication of the altering party on the face of the document, if the circumstances surrounding the distribution of the document identify the altering party then there is no violation. *See 3 Day Blinds*, 299 N.L.R.B. 110 (1990). But in 1993, the Board yet again shifted position when it decided to start putting a disclaimer in its Notice of Election documents stating that the NLRB has not been involved in any defacement or alteration and does not endorse either party in an election. *See Kwik Care v. NLRB*, 82 F.3d 1122 (D.C. Cir. 1996); *Irvington Nursing Care Servs.*, 312 N.L.R.B. 594 (1993). The Board's current approach in most cases is to let the Notice of Election document speak for itself.

4. *The "captive audience" speech.* In light of the above rules governing employer speech, would the following "captive audience" speech, delivered by Enderby CEO Steve Workman a few days before the election, conform to laboratory conditions?

VOTE NO-UNION

The NLRB election will be held here at Enderby on January 30. You will be asked to vote for the Programmers Union or to vote for No-Union. I will abide by the results of the election, but it is important for you to know that while the Union has vigorously campaigned and said critical things about management, you stand to lose if you vote for the Union. A Union victory can result in SERIOUS HARM.

To get your vote, the Union is making lots of promises. That's because promises are all a Union can make. Promises can't put food on your table or send your kids to college. Only the Company can put money in your pay envelope. Remember this when it comes time to vote.

Our competitors who have been organized by the Union in this region uniformly have a wage scale BELOW that which exists here. If the Union wins the election, the Company will bargain with the Union as required by law, but the law gives the Company the right to bargain hard and to insist on the reduction of certain economic benefits which you now have.

If tough bargaining takes place, the Union can extract concessions only by calling a strike. If you join the strike—and just you try not to!—you and your family will lose your earnings (which cannot be replaced by unemployment benefits because you will have chosen voluntarily to leave work) and the law permits me to hire another worker to replace you permanently. You will lose all of the benefits that come with length of service at Enderby.

Should the Union insist that the Company take action which will result in higher prices, we have expressly been informed by our two principal clients that that they will immediately cease purchasing our programming services. If they did this, just think how many jobs would be discontinued!

Another way a union can harm our business is by striking. If we were struck, every account of any substance would desert us like a sinking ship. There would be a cutback in production, and perhaps a closing of our doors.

The choice on January 30 is yours and yours alone. Your future may depend on it. Vote to continue our happy working relationship. Vote NO-UNION.

Assume that all the facts stated in this speech are true, except that the wage scales at competing companies organized by the Programmers Union are higher, not lower, than those at Enderby. The Programmers Union lost the election by two votes. Should a re-run election be called? If not, why not? If so, on what grounds? Would your answer be different if the union had lost by 20 votes rather than two? *Compare, e.g., DTR Indus. Inc. v. NLRB*, 39 F.3d 106 (6th Cir. 1994) (refusing to enforce *Gissel* order after union lost election by one vote—despite management's prediction that union victory would cause loss of up to 50% of business—on ground Board lacked substantial evidence to show fair election could not be held), *and NLRB v. Village IX Inc.*, 723 F.2d 1360 (7th Cir. 1983) (refusing to enforce *Gissel* order after union lost election by 16 votes, despite employer's commission of numerous ULPs), *with, e.g., Larson Tool & Stamping Co.*, 296 N.L.R.B. 895 (1989) (ordering re-run of election union lost by eight votes after management issued Enderby-type pre-election statement found to constitute threat of job loss); *see also Dal-Tex Optical Co.*, 137 N.L.R.B. 1782 (1962) (setting aside election union lost by five votes after president gave speeches threatening reprisal and refusal to bargain).

5.   *Racial prejudice.* From time to time, the Board has been asked to overturn election results when antiunion election propaganda by employers or local community groups made sweeping appeals to racist sentiment. *See, e.g., Universal Mfg. Co.*, 156 N.L.R.B. 1459 (1966) (setting aside election lost by union on ground employer had made irrelevant racist appeals, including statement critical of Teamsters Union for donating $25,000 to Dr. Martin Luther King Jr.); *Sewell Mfg. Co.*, 138 N.L.R.B. 66 (1962) (setting aside election lost by union on similar ground, including circulation of letter warning about "race mixing" with photograph of white union officer dancing with African American woman). In such cases, the Board has been cautious to explain that civil rights is a legitimate subject for debate in union election campaigns, but that when propaganda exacerbates racial feelings by "irrelevant, inflammatory appeals" which in addition are not factually correct, the laboratory conditions are tainted.

E. REGULATION OF OTHER TYPES OF COERCION

1. GRANT OR WITHDRAWAL OF BENEFITS

NLRB v. EXCHANGE PARTS CO.

375 U.S. 405 (1964)

JUSTICE HARLAN delivered the opinion of the Court:

This case presents a question concerning the limitations which § 8(a)(1) of the NLRA places on the right of an employer to confer economic benefits on his employees shortly before a representation election. The precise issue is whether that section prohibits the conferral of such benefits, without more, where the employer's purpose is to affect the outcome of the election.

The respondent, Exchange Parts Company, is engaged in the business of rebuilding automobile parts in Fort Worth, Texas. Prior to November 1959 its employees were not represented by a union. On November 9, 1959, the International Brotherhood of Boilermakers, Iron Shipbuilders, Blacksmiths, Forgers and Helpers, AFL-CIO, advised Exchange Parts that the union was conducting an organizational campaign at the plant and that a majority of the employees had designated the union as their bargaining representative. On November 16 the union petitioned for a representation election. The Board conducted a hearing on December 29, and on February 19, 1960, issued an order directing that an election be held. The election was held on March 18, 1960.

At two meetings on November 4 and 5, 1959, C.V. McDonald, the Vice-President and General Manager of Exchange Parts, announced to the employees that their "floating holiday" in 1959 would fall on December 26 and that there would be an additional "floating holiday" in 1960. On February 25, six days after the Board issued its election order, Exchange Parts held a dinner for employees at which Vice-President McDonald told the employees that they could decide whether the extra day of vacation in 1960 would be a "floating holiday" or would be taken on their birthdays. The employees voted for the latter. McDonald also referred to the forthcoming representation election as one in which the employees would "determine whether [they] wished to hand over their right to speak and act for themselves." He stated that the union had distorted some of the facts and pointed out the benefits obtained by the employees without a union. He urged all the employees to vote in the election.

On March 4 Exchange Parts sent its employees a letter which spoke of "the Empty Promises of the Union" and "the fact that it is the Company that puts things in your envelope." After mentioning a number of benefits, the letter said: "The Union can't put any of those things in your envelope—

only the Company can do that." Further on, the letter stated: "[I]t didn't take a Union to get any of those things and it won't take a Union to get additional improvements in the future." Accompanying the letter was a detailed statement of the benefits granted by the company since 1949 and an estimate of the monetary value of such benefits to the employees. Included in the statement of benefits for 1960 were the birthday holiday, a new system for computing overtime during holiday weeks which had the effect of increasing wages for those weeks, and a new vacation schedule which enabled employees to extend their vacations by sandwiching them between two weekends. Although Exchange Parts asserts that the policy behind the latter two benefits was established earlier, it is clear that the letter of March 4 was the first general announcement of the changes to the employees. In the ensuing election the union lost.

The Board found that the announcement of the birthday holiday and the grant and announcement of overtime and vacation benefits were arranged by Exchange Parts with the intention of inducing the employees to vote against the union. It found that this conduct violated § 8(a)(1).

[But] the Court of Appeals rejected the finding [and] denied enforcement of the Board's order. It believed that it was not an unfair labor practice under § 8(a)(1) for an employer to grant benefits to its employees in these circumstances.

We think the Court of Appeals was mistaken. We have no doubt that [§ 8(a)(1)] prohibits not only intrusive threats and promises but also conduct immediately favorable to employees which is undertaken with the express purpose of impinging upon their freedom of choice for or against unionization and is reasonably calculated to have that effect. The danger inherent in well-timed increases in benefits is the suggestion of a fist inside the velvet glove. Employees are not likely to miss the inference that the source of benefits now conferred is also the source from which future benefits must flow and which may dry up if it is not obliged. The danger may be diminished if, as in this case, the benefits are conferred permanently and unconditionally. But the absence of conditions or threats pertaining to the particular benefits conferred would be of controlling significance only if it could be presumed that no question of additional benefits or renegotiation of existing benefits would arise in the future; and, of course, no such presumption is tenable.

It is true that in most cases of this kind the increase in benefits could be regarded as "one part of an overall program of interference and restraint by the employer," and that in this case the questioned conduct stood in isolation. Other unlawful conduct may often be an indication of the motive behind a grant of benefits while an election is pending, and to that extent it is relevant to the legality of the grant; but when as here the motive is otherwise established, an employer is not free to violate § 8(a)(1) by conferring benefits simply because it refrains from other, more obvious violations. The beneficence of an employer is likely to be ephemeral if prompted by a threat of unionization which is subsequently removed. Insulating the right of collective organization from calculated good will of this sort deprives employees of little that has lasting value.

NOTES

1. *Of fists inside velvet gloves.* *Exchange Parts* is often cited for this turn of phrase by Justice Harlan: "The danger inherent in well-timed increases in benefits is the suggestion of a fist inside the velvet glove. Employees are not likely to miss the inference that the source of benefits now conferred is also the source from which future benefits must flow and which may dry up if it is not obliged." Justice Harlan relied in part on *Medo Photo Supply Corp. v. NLRB*, 321 U.S. 678, 686 (1944), where the Court had said: "The action of employees with respect to the choice of their bargaining agents may be induced by favors bestowed by the employer as well as by his threats or domination." In *Medo Photo*, there was already a designated bargaining agent and the offer of "favors" came in response to the employees' own suggestion that they would leave the union if such favors were bestowed. Nevertheless, Justice Harlan reasoned, "the principles which dictated the result there are fully applicable here."

Is there any difference between blandishments offered to persuade employees to kick out an incumbent representative, as opposed to turning down representation in the first place? Between offering better pay or benefits, as opposed to threatening to lower them?

2. *Enderby revisited.* Recall the union organizing drive at Enderby, Inc. Suppose the company had offered to increase pay or benefits to programmers in hopes of undermining union support. Would it pervert the purposes of the NLRA to punish the employer for instituting the very terms and conditions of employment that a union might seek to negotiate if it ever got a chance to sit at the bargaining table? Might the message to employees be this: if you can improve your benefits merely by threatening to organize a union, imagine what you could get if you actually organize one? Note that, generally speaking, the Board allows employees to keep unilateral improvements in wages or working conditions, even if they are later found to be "a fist inside the velvet glove." Does knowing this affect your answer?

3. *Is timing everything?* Generally, the NLRB infers that unilaterally conferring benefits during a representation campaign is for the purpose of influencing the outcome of the election, unless the employer offers another credible explanation. *See, e.g., Register Guard,* 344 N.L.R.B. 1142 (2005). Under what circumstances might an employer carry its burden? *See, e.g., Delchamps, Inc. v. NLRB,* 588 F.2d 476 (5th Cir. 1979) (employer initiated wage survey of its competitors before union organizing drive began and, based on survey results, raised wages across the board at all 44 of its stores while union was organizing at 15 of the stores); *Hampton Inn NY-JFK Airport,* 348

N.L.R.B. 16 (2006) (employer unaware of union organizing campaign at the time it announced a wage increase); *Automated Prods., Inc.*, 242 N.L.R.B. 424 (1979) (shortly before union organizing campaign, employer advised employees that they could expect higher than usual pay raises due to company's expansion; company raised wages and converted from a merit-based pay system to a longevity-based system due to need to hire large numbers of additional workers because of such expansion).

4.   *Ask and ye shall receive?* Should an employer be able to react to an organizing campaign by asking employees what their concerns are? Should it matter if the solicitation of grievances is conducted by a method that existed before organizing began, or by a new or enhanced method? *See, e.g., TNT Logistics of N. Am., Inc.*, 345 N.L.R.B. 290 (2005) (supervisor inquiries of employees, "What would make things better?" consistent with existing open door policy and supervisors questioning subordinates); *DTR Indus., Inc.*, 311 N.L.R.B. 833 (1993) (instituting new employee suggestion box and toll free employee hot line after union organizing campaign began was unlawful solicitation of grievances and implied promise to remedy them), *enf'd in pertinent part*, 39 F.3d 106 (6th Cir. 1994).

5.   *Raffles and prizes.* Suppose Workman, Enderby's CEO, held a "Vote No Raffle," at which prizes in the form of free laptop computers were awarded by random drawing to Enderby employees. Is the chance to win such a prize "the promise of a benefit" outlawed by *Exchange Parts*? Would it make a difference if the raffle were held on the day of the certification election? *See Atlantic Limousine Inc.*, 331 N.L.R.B. 1025, 1029 (2000), which bars election-day raffles under the following conditions:

> [When] (1) eligibility to participate in the raffle or win prizes is in any way tied to voting in the election or being at the election site on election day or (2) the raffle is conducted at any time during a period beginning 24 hours before the scheduled opening of the polls and ending with the closing of the polls. The term "conducting a raffle" includes the following: (1) announcing a raffle; (2) distributing raffle tickets; (3) identifying the raffle winners; and (4) awarding the raffle prizes.

6.   *Employer vs. union speech.* Should the same rules apply to unions? In *Smith Co.*, 192 N.L.R.B. 1098, 1101 (1971), the Board opined that union promises to gain benefits controlled by the employer "are easily recognized by employees to be dependent on contingencies beyond the Union's control and do not carry with them the same degree of finality as if uttered by an employer who has it within his power to implement promises or benefits." But in *NLRB v. Savair Mfg. Co.*, 414 U.S. 270 (1973), the Supreme Court held that a union's offer to waive initiation fees for any employee joining prior to the election tainted laboratory conditions and called for throwing out an election that the union had won. The Court suggested, however, that an offer to waive initiation fees that extended after the election would not be objectionable. What might justify the distinction?

2. INTERROGATION AND POLLING

Interrogation of employees as to their affiliation with or participation in union activity is unlawful if, considered in light of all the circumstances, it would reasonably tend to coerce them. *See Rossmore House*, 269 N.L.R.B. 1176 (1984), *review denied, Hotel Employees & Restaurant Employees Local 11 v. NLRB*, 760 F.2d 1006 (9th Cir. 1985). To determine whether interrogation is coercive, the Board used to examine at least four factors: the time and place of interrogation; the personnel involved in the interrogation; the nature of the information sought; and the employer's known preferences about unionization. *See Charlotte Union Bus Station, Inc.*, 135 N.L.R.B. 228 (1962); *see also Lorben v. NLRB*, 345 F.2d 346 (2d Cir. 1965). Over the years, the number and order of these factors has been refined. Today the Board considers the following in determining whether questioning of this nature is unlawful:

1. The background, i.e., is there is a history of employer hostility and discrimination?

2. The nature of the information sought, e.g., did the questioner appear to be seeking information on which to base taking action against individual employees?

3. The identity of the questioner, i.e., how high was he/she in the company hierarchy?

4. The place and method of interrogation, e.g., was the employee called from work to the boss's office? Was there an atmosphere of unnatural formality?

5. The truthfulness of the employee's reply.

Phillips 66 (Sweeny Refinery), 360 N.L.R.B. 125, 128 (2014). When relevant, the Board also considers the nature of the relationship between the supervisor and the employee; a preexisting hostile relationship could suggest that the questioning was coercive. *See, e.g., Intertape Polymer Corp.*, 360 N.L.R.B. 957, 958 (2014). In any event, these factors are not to be "mechanically applied." *Sunnyvale Med. Clinic*, 277 N.L.R.B. 1217, 1218 (1985).

Polling employees to determine the extent of support for union representation is permissible if the following conditions are satisfied: the polling must be conducted by secret ballot; the purpose of polling is to determine the union's claim of majority support; employees must have been notified of such purpose; adequate assurances against reprisals have been given; and the employer has not created a coercive atmosphere or committed unfair labor practices. *See Struksnes Constr. Co.*, 165 N.L.R.B. 1062 (1967).

The potential for coercion in questioning workers about their union sympathies can pose a serious problem for an employer who is gathering evidence from employees in order to prepare for proceedings before the NLRB or other tribunals. Here too the Board has established the conditions that must be satisfied: the purpose of the questioning must be communicated to the employees being questioned; assurances against reprisals must be given; employee participation must be voluntary; the questioning must be free from anti-union animus; the questioning must not be coercive in nature; the questions must be relevant to the issues in litigation; the subjective state of mind of the employees questioned must not be probed; and the questions must not otherwise interfere with Section 7 rights. *See Johnnie's Poultry Co.*, 146 N.L.R.B. 770 (1964), *enf. denied on other grounds*, 344 F.2d 617 (8th Cir. 1965).

3. SURVEILLANCE

Surveillance of employees who are engaged in protected activities in the open and on or near the employer's premises is lawful. *See, e.g., Roadway Package Sys.*, 302 N.L.R.B. 961 (1991); *Southwire Co.*, 277 N.L.R.B. 377 (1985), *enf'd*, 820 F.2d 453 (D.C. Cir. 1987); *Porta Sys. Corp.*, 238 N.L.R.B. 192 (1978), *enf'd*, 625 F.2d 399 (2d Cir. 1980). For example, a supervisor's conspicuous observation of employees who openly meet with a union organizer within 100 feet of the employer's property, and under an expressway, is not unlawful, if the employees do not attempt to conceal their activities. *See Basic Metal & Salvage Co.*, 322 N.L.R.B. 462 (1996). But conspicuous surveillance that causes intimidation of employees, or otherwise interferes with their protected activities, may be unlawful. *See Carry Cos. of Ill.*, 311 N.L.R.B. 1058 (1993), *enf'd*, 30 F.3d 922 (7th Cir. 1994).

Surveillance by means of videorecording or photographing employees, however, deserves special mention, because the Board has set a "lower threshold" for finding such surveillance unlawful under Section 8(a)(1). *Allie-Kiski Med. Ctr.*, 339 N.L.R.B. 361, 365 (2003). Although the employer has the right to maintain security measures necessary to further legitimate business interests during union activity, videorecording and photographing such activity can be justified only if the surveillance serves a legitimate security objective, *see National Steel & Shipbuilding Co.*, 324 N.L.R.B. 499 (1997), *enf'd*, 156 F.3d 1268 (D.C. Cir. 1998), or if the employer can demonstrate a reasonable basis to believe that misconduct would occur, see *NLRB v. Colonial Haven Nursing Home*, 542 F.2d 691 (7th Cir. 1976).

In responding to a union organizing campaign, an employer may engage in the tactic of soliciting employees to participate in recorded interviews in which they may be asked to express antiunion views. Is this a form of surveillance? Can an employee voluntarily consent to such recording, and would such consent preclude a finding of coercion or interference? The following case considers these questions.

ALLEGHENY LUDLUM CORP. V. NLRB

301 F.3d 167 (3d Cir. 2002)

SLOVITER, CIRCUIT JUDGE:

Allegheny Ludlum is a manufacturer of specialty steel products in Western Pennsylvania. In July 1994, the United Steelworkers of America ("the Union"), who already represented Allegheny Ludlum's production employees, began organizing to represent its salaried, nonexempt employees. On October 4, 1994, the Union filed an election petition with the NLRB and an election was scheduled for December 2, 1994. Prior to the election, Allegheny Ludlum campaigned vigorously against the Union, employing outside consultants to formulate an anti-union campaign strategy.

In mid-November, Allegheny Ludlum began production of a videotape for use in its antiunion campaign, seeking to persuade its salaried employees to vote against the Union. Allegheny Ludlum's Manager of Communication Services, Mark Ziemianski, personally supervised the filming by an outside camera crew. The filming occurred on the premises of the company over a period of three days. On the first day, November 14, 1994, Ziemianski, accompanied by the camera crew, approached several employees at their desks and asked them if they would consent to be videotaped. Those who agreed were instructed to sit at their desks, turn to the camera, smile, and wave.

Although some employees filmed that day were given advance written notice explaining that the video would be used in the company's election campaign and that they could decline to participate, others were given no notice until after they were filmed. The notice explained that anyone who did not wish to appear in the video could contact one of two company managers to be edited out of the video. James Goralka, one of the employees who had been filmed before seeing the notice, called Joyce Kurcina, one of the two managers listed on the notice, and asked that he and several of his co-workers be edited out of the video. Kurcina instructed him to contact Ziemianski who then informed Goralka that it would be "no problem" to remove them from the tape but that Goralka needed to put the request in writing listing the employees' names who did not wish to appear in the video. Goralka complied and he and the listed co-workers were deleted from the video.

The filming continued on November 15 and 16. Unlike the first day, Ziemianski prepared two written notices that were distributed to employees in advance, either by handing them out when the film crew entered work areas or by interoffice mail. One notice stated:

Please be advised that a film crew will be in and around your work areas filming footage for an upcoming video presentation that the company will use to present the facts about the current election campaign involving the Steelworkers. If you prefer not to be used in footage, please advise either Director of Employee Relations Joyce Kurcina or Human Relations Counsel Steve Spolar as soon as possible. We will be happy to accommodate your request.

The other notice was identical in all material respects except that it instructed employees to "advise the video crew," rather than Kurcina or Spolar, if they did not want to appear in the video. Ultimately, the company filmed approximately eighty employees, or 17% of the voting unit. Roughly thirty employees provided Ziemianski with written requests to be excluded from the video. Others declined to appear when approached by the film crew or simply left the work area when the film crew was present. In addition, a number of employees complained to the Union about the filming and the Union contacted Allegheny Ludlum to express its concern that the taping was coercive. The filming continued and eventually the employees were required to watch the finished video during business hours.

The completed video contained testimony by employees expressing their satisfaction with the status quo, their dissatisfaction with union representation at prior employers or in different units of Allegheny Ludlum, and their discontent with the Union's representation in particular. Several employees noted that unionized segments of Allegheny Ludlum had experienced layoffs, while a narrator noted that nonunion employees had experienced no layoffs since 1980. The video concluded with footage of employees waving at the camera, accompanied by upbeat music containing such lyrics as "Allegheny Ludlum is you and me," and stating reasons to vote against union representation.

In the election, held on December 2, 1994, the votes against union representation exceeded the votes in favor, 237 to 225.

From its prior cases, the Board devised the standard that an employer may lawfully solicit employees to appear in a campaign video provided the employer meets the following five requirements:

1.   The solicitation is in the form of a general announcement which discloses that the purpose of the filming is to use the employee's picture in a campaign video, and includes assurances that participation is voluntary, that nonparticipation will not result in reprisals, and that participation will not result in rewards or benefits.

2.   Employees are not pressured into making the decision in the presence of a supervisor.

3. There is no other coercive conduct connected with the employer's announcement such as threats of reprisal or grants or promises of benefits to employees who participate in the video.

4. The employer has not created a coercive atmosphere by engaging in serious or pervasive unfair labor practices or other comparable coercive conduct.

5. The employer does not exceed the legitimate purpose of soliciting consent by seeking information concerning union matters or otherwise interfering with the statutory rights of employees.

In applying these requirements to the instant case, the Board found that Allegheny Ludlum violated section 8(a)(1) "by approaching individual employees and asking them to consent to be filmed for the purpose of a campaign videotape, and by requiring employees to register an objection with an agent of [Allegheny Ludlum] in order to avoid being including in its campaign videotape."

This case closely resembles those cases in which the Board found an unlawful poll because the employees were forced to make an observable choice about their union sympathies, [such as when] supervisors hand out anti-union hats to employees, [which forces] employees to make an observable choice. Thus, the Board did not err in considering this case under its "polling" precedents.

Allegheny Ludlum contends that the five-factor test is unduly burdensome because it effectively eliminates an employer's ability to videotape employees in the workplace during an election campaign. This contention considerably overstates the prohibition. As the Board's decision clearly states, an employer may make a general announcement regarding its desire to videotape employees for use in a campaign video and subsequently videotape anyone who comes forward, as long as it makes the necessary assurances. These guidelines do not make it "virtually impossible for an employer to videotape its employees in the workplace during the campaign effort" as Allegheny Ludlum contends, nor has Allegheny Ludlum shown why a general announcement is "simply not an effective means" for securing participants. Rather, the Board's requirements allow an employer to videotape its employees, while at the same time barring the employer from placing an employee in the position of having to express openly a willingness or unwillingness to appear in an anti-union video. The Board's decision is consistent with the purposes of the NLRA and reasonably balances the rights created under sections 8(a)(1) and 8(c). Thus, we defer to the Board's accommodation of the competing interests.

NOTES

1.   Review the five factors governing the proper solicitation of employees to participate in making antiunion video recordings articulated by the Board and cited with approval by the Second Circuit in *Allegheny Ludlum*. Is taking into account these five factors sufficient to protect employees from having to make an "observable choice" about the merits of unionization? Should the same factors apply to union as opposed to employer solicitation of such video recording? *See Pepsi-Cola Bottling Co.*, 289 N.L.R.B. 736 (1988), *overruled, Randell Warehouse of Ariz., Inc.*, 328 N.L.R.B. 1034 (1999), *overruled on remand*, 347 N.L.R.B. 591 (2006).

2.   Suppose that you serve as management counsel to Enderby, Inc. Penny, the union adherent, has just been fired for violating the company's e-mail policy. Steve Workman, the chief executive officer, now wants to send to each employee a confidential e-mail message soliciting participation in making an antiunion video, and promising a handsome bonus to every employee who discreetly replied "yes" to the message. His message would say: "There is absolutely no pressure on you to participate in this project." Would you advise him that it is permissible to send the message? Would it constitute interference, restraint, or coercion? Are the *Allegheny Ludlum* factors met? Or is it "a fist inside the velvet glove" masquerading as the promise of benefit?

3.   The notion that employees are actually affected by the things management says during an organizing campaign has come under assault by a handful of respected labor scholars. The central finding of one much-debated study, now over 40 years old, based on an examination of 31 elections and interviews with over 1,000 employees, was that unlawful campaigning has no greater effect on employee voting behavior in union representation elections than lawful campaigning does. The authors recommended that the NLRB should not attempt to distinguish between lawful and unlawful campaigning; that the results of an election, once conducted, should be final; that speech should be wholly free; and that the Board should neither set aside elections nor find unfair labor practices based on oral or written communications by employers or unions. *See* Julius G. Getman, Stephen B. Goldberg & H.J. Herman, Union Representation Elections: Law and Reality 139–53 (1976).

Both the empirical work and conclusions of Getman, et al., drew sharp criticism in subsequent studies made in the 1980s. *See, e.g.*, Paul C. Weiler, *Promises to Keep: Securing Workers' Rights to Self-Organization Under the NLRA*, 96 Harv. L. Rev. 1769, 1781–86 (1983) (contending their data actually support conclusion employees are coerced by employer campaign threats); *see also* William T. Dickens, *The Effect of Company Campaigns on Certification Elections: Law and Reality Once Again*, 36 Indus. & Lab. Rel. Rev. 560 (1983).

Should the speech of employers, employees, or unions be deregulated during organizing drives? Why or why not?

F. PROTECTION AGAINST DISCRIMINATION

The central purpose of Section 8(a)(3)'s protection against discrimination to encourage or discourage union activity is to ensure that a worker's job is not used as leverage in any struggle between management and labor over union representation. The idea behind the protection is to preserve worker jobs even in the face of advocacy by the worker. *See Radio Officers v. NLRB*, 347 U.S. 17, 40 (1954). Of course, the policy behind the Act protects worker jobs as well when the employer and the union would work together to encourage union activity. The only exception carved into the statute by Congress involves the requirement of payment of union dues and fees, more fully explored in Chapter 8. To ensure robust protection, the scope of Section 8(a)(3) must necessarily be broad, protecting job applicants and employees and extending beyond jobs to also include benefits and other terms and conditions of employment. Not surprisingly, since much discrimination is not overt, the central challenge for this part of the statute is how to determine that discrimination has indeed taken place. The following cases set out and examine the mechanisms created to prove violations against individuals and the collective.

NLRB v. Transportation Management Corp.
462 U.S. 393 (1983)

Affirmative defense

Justice White delivered the opinion of the Court:

The National Labor Relations Act (NLRA or Act) makes unlawful the discharge of a worker because of union activity, but employers retain the right to discharge workers for any number of other reasons unrelated to the employee's union activities. When the General Counsel of the National Labor Relations Board (Board) files a complaint alleging that an employee was discharged because of his union activities, the employer may assert legitimate motives for his decision. In *Wright Line*, 251 N.L.R.B. 1083 (1980), the Board reformulated the allocation of the burden of proof in such cases. It determined that the General Counsel carried the burden of persuading the Board that an antiunion animus contributed to the employer's decision to discharge an employee, a burden that does not shift, but that the employer, even if it failed to meet or neutralize the General Counsel's showing, could avoid the finding that it violated the statute by demonstrating by a preponderance of the evidence that the worker would have been fired even if he had not been involved with the union. The question presented in this case is whether the burden placed on the employer in *Wright Line* is consistent with §§ 8(a)(1) and 8(a)(3), as well as with § 10(c) of the NLRA, which provides that the Board must find an unfair labor practice by a "preponderance of the testimony."

Prior to his discharge, Sam Santillo was a bus driver for respondent Transportation Management Corp. On March 19, 1979, Santillo talked to officials of the Teamsters Union about organizing the drivers who worked with him. Over the next four days Santillo discussed with his fellow drivers the possibility of joining the Teamsters and distributed authorization cards. On the night of March 23, George Patterson, who supervised Santillo and the other drivers, told one of the drivers that he had heard of Santillo's activities. Patterson referred to Santillo as two-faced, and promised to get even with him.

Later that evening Patterson talked to Ed West, who was also a bus driver for respondent. Patterson asked, "What's with Sam and the Union?" Patterson said that he took Santillo's actions personally, recounted several favors he had done for Santillo, and added that he would remember Santillo's activities when Santillo again asked for a favor. On Monday, March 26, Santillo was discharged. Patterson told Santillo that he was being fired for leaving his keys in the bus and taking unauthorized breaks.

Santillo filed a complaint with the Board alleging that he had been discharged because of his union activities, contrary to §§ 8(a)(1) and 8(a)(3) of the NLRA. The General Counsel issued a complaint. The Administrative Law Judge (ALJ) determined by a preponderance of the evidence that Patterson clearly had an antiunion animus and that Santillo's discharge was motivated by a desire to discourage union activities. The ALJ also found that the asserted reasons for the discharge could not withstand scrutiny. Patterson's disapproval of Santillo's practice of leaving his keys in the bus was clearly a pretext, for Patterson had not known about Santillo's practice until after he had decided to discharge Santillo; moreover, the practice of leaving keys in buses was commonplace among respondent's employees. Respondent identified two types of unauthorized breaks, coffee breaks and stops at home. With respect to both coffee breaks and stopping at home, the ALJ found that Santillo was never cautioned or admonished about such behavior, and that the employer had not followed its customary practice of issuing three written warnings before discharging a driver. The ALJ also found that the taking of coffee breaks during working hours was normal practice, and that respondent tolerated the practice unless the breaks interfered with the driver's performance of his duties. In any event, said the ALJ, respondent had never taken any adverse personnel action against an employee because of such behavior. While acknowledging that Santillo had engaged in some unsatisfactory conduct, the ALJ was not persuaded that Santillo would have been fired had it not been for his union activities.

The Board affirmed, adopting with some clarification the ALJ's findings and conclusions and expressly applying its *Wright Line* decision. It stated that respondent had failed to carry its burden of persuading the Board that the discharge would have taken place had Santillo not engaged in activity protected by the Act. The Court of Appeals for the First Circuit, relying on its previous decision rejecting the Board's *Wright Line* test,

NLRB v. *Wright Line*, 662 F.2d 899 (1981), refused to enforce the Board's order and remanded for consideration of whether the General Counsel had proved by a preponderance of the evidence that Santillo would not have been fired had it not been for his union activities. We now reverse.

Employees of an employer covered by the NLRA have the right to form, join, or assist labor organizations. It is an unfair labor practice to interfere with, restrain, or coerce the exercise of those rights, or by discrimination in hire or tenure "to encourage or discourage membership in any labor organization." Under these provisions it is undisputed that if the employer fires an employee for having engaged in union activities and has no other basis for the discharge, or if the reasons that he proffers are pretextual, the employer commits an unfair labor practice. He does not violate the NLRA, however, if any antiunion animus that he might have entertained did not contribute at all to an otherwise lawful discharge for good cause. Soon after the passage of the Act, the Board held that it was an unfair labor practice for an employer to discharge a worker where antiunion animus actually contributed to the discharge decision. In its Third Annual Report, the Board stated: "Where the employer has discharged an employee for two or more reasons, and one of them is union affiliation or activity, the Board has found a violation [of § 8(a)(3)]." 3 NLRB Ann. Rep. 70 (1938). In the following year in *Dow Chemical Co.*, [13 N.L.R.B. 993 (1939)] the Board stated that a violation could be found where the employer acted out of antiunion bias "whether or not the [employer] may have had some other motive . . . and without regard to whether or not the [employer's] asserted motive was lawful." This construction of the Act—that to establish an unfair labor practice the General Counsel need show by a preponderance of the evidence only that a discharge is in any way motivated by a desire to frustrate union activity—was plainly rational and acceptable. The Board has adhered to that construction of the Act since that time.

At the same time, there were [federal court] decisions indicating that the presence of an antiunion motivation in a discharge case was not the end of the matter. An employer could escape the consequences of a violation by proving that without regard to the impermissible motivation, the employer would have taken the same action for wholly permissible reasons.

The Courts of Appeals were not entirely satisfied with the Board's approach to dual-motive cases. The Board's *Wright Line* decision in 1980 was an attempt to restate its analysis in a way more acceptable to the Courts of Appeals. The Board held that the General Counsel of course had the burden of proving that the employee's conduct protected by § 7 was a substantial or a motivating factor in the discharge. Even if this was the case, and the employer failed to rebut it, the employer could avoid being held in violation of §§ 8(a)(1) and 8(a)(3) by proving by a preponderance of the evidence that the discharge rested on the employee's unprotected conduct as well and that the employee would have lost his job in any event.

It thus became clear, if it was not clear before, that proof that the discharge would have occurred in any event and for valid reasons amounted to an affirmative defense on which the employer carried the burden of proof by a preponderance of the evidence. "The shifting burden merely requires the employer to make out what is actually an affirmative defense. . . ." *Wright Line*, 251 N.L.R.B. at 1088, n. 11.

As we understand the Board's decisions, they have consistently held that the unfair labor practice consists of a discharge or other adverse action that is based in whole or in part on antiunion animus—or as the Board now puts it, that the employee's protected conduct was a substantial or motivating factor in the adverse action. The General Counsel has the burden of proving these elements under § 10(c). But the Board's construction of the statute permits an employer to avoid being adjudicated a violator by showing what his actions would have been regardless of his forbidden motivation. It extends to the employer what the Board considers to be an affirmative defense but does not change or add to the elements of the unfair labor practice that the General Counsel has the burden of proving under § 10(c). We assume that the Board could reasonably have construed the Act in the manner insisted on by the Court of Appeals. We also assume that the Board might have considered a showing by the employer that the adverse action would have occurred in any event as not obviating a violation adjudication but as going only to the permissible remedy, in which event the burden of proof could surely have been put on the employer. The Board has instead chosen to recognize, as it insists it has done for many years, what it designates as an affirmative defense that the employer has the burden of sustaining. We are unprepared to hold that this is an impermissible construction of the Act. "[The] Board's construction here, while it may not be required by the Act, is at least permissible under it . . .," and in these circumstances its position is entitled to deference.

The Board's allocation of the burden of proof is clearly reasonable in this context, for the reason stated in *NLRB* v. *Remington Rand, Inc.*, 94 F.2d 862, 872 [(2d Cir. 1938)], a case on which the Board relied when it began taking the position that the burden of persuasion could be shifted. The employer is a wrongdoer; he has acted out of a motive that is declared illegitimate by the statute. It is fair that he bear the risk that the influence of legal and illegal motives cannot be separated, because he knowingly created the risk and because the risk was created not by innocent activity but by his own wrongdoing.

For these reasons, we conclude that the Court of Appeals erred in refusing to enforce the Board's orders, which rested on the Board's *Wright Line* decision.

The Board was justified in this case in concluding that Santillo would not have been discharged had the employer not considered his efforts to

establish a union. At least two of the transgressions that purportedly would
have in any event prompted Santillo's discharge were commonplace, and
yet no transgressor had ever before received any kind of discipline.
Moreover, the employer departed from its usual practice in dealing with
rules infractions; indeed, not only did the employer not warn Santillo that
his actions would result in being subjected to discipline, it also never even
expressed its disapproval of his conduct. In addition, Patterson, the person
who made the initial decision to discharge Santillo, was obviously upset
with Santillo for engaging in such protected activity. It is thus clear that
the Board's finding that Santillo would not have been fired if the employer
had not had an antiunion animus was "supported by substantial evidence
on the record considered as a whole."

NOTES

1.   There are two evidentiary frameworks used to prove Section 8(a)(3)
violations: the "pretext" (single motivation) and the mixed motive (dual
motivation) framework. By far the most commonly used today is the mixed
motive framework, probably because the General Counsel tends to proceed
with complaints in the stronger cases and can meet the initial burden causing
the full burden to shift to the employer. In the typical pretext case, once the
General Counsel has made out a prima facie case of employer discrimination
against employee section 7 activities, the employer then attempts to show that
either the General Counsel's case is flawed by rebutting the General Counsel's
evidence, or showing that the real reason for the employer's action is a
legitimate one. In these cases, credibility is attacked as each side tries to show
theirs is the true account of what happened. By contrast, in the mixed motive
case, based on the strength of the evidence against the employer that an
unlawful motivation played a part in the action against the employee, the full
burden shifts and the employer must then show, by a preponderance of the
evidence, that the action would have been taken despite the unlawful
motivation, for legitimate reasons. *See Holo-Krome Co. v. NLRB,* 954 F.2d 108,
110 (2d Cir. 1992).

2.   Section 10(c) of the NLRA states that (1) an employer may only be
found to violate Section 8(a)(3) based upon "preponderance of the testimony
taken," and (2) employers may always terminate an employee "for cause."
These burden of proof and for cause requirements have been incorporated into
the existing frameworks, pretext and mixed motive, for determining whether
the employer has discriminated in violation of Section 8(a)(3).

3.   *The requirement of intent.* While Section 8(a)(1) and 8(a)(2) violations
can be established without showing antiunion animus, Section 8(a)(3)
violations mostly carry the requirement of intentional action by the employer.
Of course, intent can be proved circumstantially, as is typically the case.

The relevance of the motivation of the employer in such discrimination
has been consistently recognized under both § 8(a)(3) and its predecessor. In
the first case to reach the Court under the National Labor Relations Act, *NLRB*

v. Jones & Laughlin Steel Corp., 301 U.S. 1 (1937), which upheld the constitutionality of the Act, the Court said with respect to limitations placed upon employers' right to discharge by that section that "the [employer's] true purpose is the subject of investigation with full opportunity to show the facts." In another case the same day the Court found the employer's "real motive" to be decisive and stated that "the act permits a discharge for any reason other than union activity or agitation for collective bargaining with employees." Courts of Appeals have uniformly applied this criterion, and writers in the field of labor law emphasize the importance of the employer's motivation to a finding of violation of this section. That Congress intended the employer's purpose in discriminating to be controlling is clear. The Senate Report on the Wagner Act said: "Of course nothing in the bill prevents an employer from discharging a man for incompetence; from advancing him for special aptitude; or from demoting him for failure to perform." Senator Wagner spoke of § 8(3), the predecessor to § 8(a)(3), as reaching "those very cases where the employer is strong enough to impress his will without the aid of the law."

But it is also clear that specific evidence of intent to encourage or discourage is not an indispensable element of proof of violation of § 8(a)(3). Both the Board and the courts have recognized that proof of certain types of discrimination satisfies the intent requirement. This recognition that specific proof of intent is unnecessary where employer conduct inherently encourages or discourages union membership is but an application of the common-law rule that a person is held to intend the foreseeable consequences of his conduct. Thus an employer's protestation that it did not intend to encourage or discourage must be unavailing where a natural consequence of its action was such encouragement or discouragement. Concluding that encouragement or discouragement will result, it is presumed that such consequence was intended. In such circumstances intent to encourage is sufficiently established. *Radio Officers v. NLRB,* 347 U.S. 17, 43–45 (1954).

4. *The section 8(a)(3) prima facie case.* As *Wright Line* and *Transportation Management* suggest, the mixed motive case is one where the General Counsel can show *ab initio*, through either direct or circumstantial evidence, that a *substantial* or *motivating* factor in the employer's discrimination against an employee or employees was to interfere with Section 7 rights. To do so, the General Counsel will attempt to marshal the following evidence: (1) employer knowledge of employee Section 7 activities, (2) suspect timing of employer action, (3) excellence of employee work record, (4) extremity of discipline, (5) circumstances of employer action tending to show antiunion animus, and (6) evidence of history of union hostility. For a relatively recent NLRB discussion of this type of evidence, see *Lucky Cab Co.,* 360 N.L.R.B. 271 (2014). If the General Counsel succeeds in showing that discrimination against Section 7 activities was a substantial or motivating factor in the employer action, the burden of persuasion shifts to the employer to show that the employer action would have been taken regardless of antiunion animus, the equivalent of showing that the action was "for cause," by a preponderance of the testimony taken.

5.   *The mixed-motive case and the requirements of section 10(c)*. These were addressed by the *Transportation Management* Court in footnote 6, which stated:

> The language of the NLRA requiring that the Board act on a preponderance of the testimony taken was added by the LMRA, 61 Stat. 136, in 1947. A closely related provision directed that no order of the Board reinstate or compensate any employee who was fired for cause. Section 10(c) places the burden on the General Counsel only to prove the unfair labor practice, not to disprove an affirmative defense. Furthermore, it is clear from the legislative history of the LMRA that the drafters of § 10(c) were not thinking of the mixed-motive case. Their discussions reflected the assumption that discharges were either "for cause" or punishment for protected activity. Read fairly, the legislative history does not indicate whether, in mixed-motive cases, the employer or the General Counsel has the burden of proof on the issue of what would have happened if the employer had not been influenced by his unlawful motives; on that point the legislative history is silent.
>
> The "for cause" proviso was not meant to apply to cases in which both legitimate and illegitimate causes contributed to the discharge. The amendment was sparked by a concern over the Board's perceived practice of inferring from the fact that someone was active in a union that he was fired because of antiunion animus even though the worker had been guilty of gross misconduct. The House Report explained the change in the following terms:
>
> "A third change forbids the Board to reinstate an individual unless the weight of the evidence shows that the individual was not suspended or discharged for cause. In the past, the Board, admitting that an employee was guilty of gross misconduct, nevertheless frequently reinstated him, 'inferring' that, because he was a member or an official of a union, this, not his misconduct, was *the* reason for his discharge." H.R. Rep. No. 245, at 42 (1947) (emphasis added).
>
> The proviso was thus a reaction to the Board's readiness to infer antiunion animus from the fact that the discharged person was active in the union, and thus has little to do with the situation in which the Board has soundly concluded that the employer had an antiunion animus and that such feelings played a role in a worker's discharge. 462 U.S. 393, 401 n.6 (1983).

6.   Consider again the hypothetical problem at the beginning of the Chapter. Recall that Penny, an employee sympathetic to the Programmers' Union, was terminated by Workman, Enderby's CEO, immediately after sending an e-mail message advocating support for the union. Penny, of course, maintains that she was fired because of the substance of her communication, a clear violation of Section 8(a)(3). Workman, on the other hand, maintains that nothing could be further from the truth. He states that, in fact, Penny was

fired for violating a strictly enforced company work rule against personal e-mail messages, and argues that the NLRA expressly protects an employer's right to terminate employees for work-related reasons. As an attorney, how do you begin to marshal evidence to determine who is right? Does the problem state facts sufficient to allow Penny to go forward on a mixed motive rationale? In other words, is the fact of a firing immediately after the sending of a pro-union message enough to show that a motivating factor in the employer's decision was union activity? Can the timing of the discharge and the substance of the message alone be enough to meet the employee's prima facie burden? What about the employer? Are there sufficient facts in the problem to show that the employer would have fired Penny regardless of the fact that her message was pro-union? If not, what other kind of evidence would be helpful?

TOWN & COUNTRY ELECTRIC V. NLRB

106 F.3d 816 (8th Cir. 1997)

WOLLMAN, CIRCUIT JUDGE:

This matter returns to us on remand from the Supreme Court. We deny the petition for review and enforce the Board's order.

Town & Country received the contract for the International Falls job in early September 1989 and was to start work on September 11. Town & Country learned that Minnesota law required it to have one Minnesota-licensed electrician on the job for every two unlicensed electricians. Because Town & Country had no Minnesota-licensed electricians on its staff, it retained Ameristaff, a temporary personnel service, to recruit Minnesota-licensed electricians. Any electricians hired would be carried as Ameristaff's employees but would be subject to Town & Country's plenary authority and control.

Ameristaff placed ads in a Minneapolis newspaper on September 3 and planned to conduct interviews at a Minneapolis hotel on September 7. Ron Sager, human resources manager for Town & Country, made it clear to Ameristaff before the ad was placed that Town & Country needed more than one electrician and that applicants had to be willing to work a nonunion job. As part of the screening process, Ameristaff's receptionist asked potential applicants whether they preferred to work union or nonunion and if they preferred union work, whether they would work a nonunion job. Ameristaff ultimately set up interviews for seven applicants.

Sager, along with Town & Country project manager Dennis Defferding and Ameristaff president Steven Buelow, flew from Town & Country's headquarters in Appleton, Wisconsin, to Minneapolis on September 7. They did not arrive at the hotel until 11 a.m. because their flight was delayed. When they arrived, only one applicant with a scheduled interview was waiting. Also waiting were approximately one dozen members of Local 292 of the International Brotherhood of Electrical Workers. Local 292 officials had learned of the ads and encouraged their unemployed members to apply and, if hired, organize the jobsite.

The applicants accompanied the company officials to the interview rooms. Sager described Town & Country and explained its employee benefits plans. The applicants then filled out applications while Sager and Defferding began interviews in another room. They first interviewed a union member who did not have an appointment and then the sole applicant who had scheduled an interview. Neither was offered a position. Buelow told Sager that none of the remaining applicants had appointments for interviews. Sager asked how those present had known about the interviews. Buelow responded by showing Sager several applications and stating, "I think they're union." Buelow returned to the other room and told the eleven remaining applicants that the job was nonunion. The applicants generally replied that they were interested in any work available.

Sager decided to return to Appleton without interviewing anyone else, allegedly because he had to attend an important meeting that afternoon. He announced to the remaining applicants that no further interviews would be conducted and requested that they leave. One of the union members, Malcolm Hansen, protested that he had called Ameristaff that morning and scheduled an interview. After confirming that this was true, Sager agreed to interview Hansen. He refused to interview anyone else and threatened to call hotel security if the remaining union members did not leave.

The administrative law judge (ALJ) concluded that the General Counsel had established a prima facie case that Town & Country had discriminatorily refused to consider for hire the ten applicants it had refused to interview. The ALJ rejected Town & Country's defenses largely on the basis of his determination that Sager's proffered reasons for his decision to immediately end the interviews were implausible and not credible. The ALJ concluded that Town & Country had violated section 8(a)(3) because it failed to establish that it would not have interviewed and considered for hire the ten remaining applicants in the absence of their union membership. The Board affirmed the ALJ's findings and agreed with the ALJ's conclusions.

Our standard of review affords great deference to the Board's affirmation of the ALJ's findings. We will enforce the Board's order if the Board has correctly applied the law and its factual findings are supported by substantial evidence on the record as a whole, even if we might have reached a different decision had the matter been before us de novo. Credibility determinations are for the ALJ to make.

[W]e conclude that the Board's findings are supported by substantial evidence, and we agree with the Board's conclusion that Town & Country violated sections 8(a)(1) and (a)(3) with respect to the ten applicants it refused to interview and consider for hire. On Thursday, September 7, Town & Country did not have a single licensed electrician for a job that started the next Tuesday, September 11. When Sager, Buelow, and Defferding arrived at the hotel, they were pleased with the size of the turnout even though it was larger than the number of scheduled appointments. Sager made his decision to interview only those applicants with appointments, effectively terminating the interviews, only after Buelow told him that the remaining applicants were union members. Sager testified that he suspected that Town & Country was being harassed or set up. The ALJ's decision to discredit Sager's various explanations for why he decided to terminate the interviews is not so lacking in evidentiary support as to require us to set it aside.

Sager interviewed and hired Hansen for the International Falls job, knowing that Hansen was a union member. Although Hansen was technically an Ameristaff employee, Town & Country retained sole discretion regarding his supervision and discharge.

Hansen reported to the jobsite on Monday, September 11. The five-man crew (Supervisor Rod Smithback, Mike Grow, Randy Reinders, Tom Steiner, and Hansen) began work Tuesday, September 12. Hansen hinted about his union membership that day. During a morning break the following day he openly announced that he was a union member and was there to organize for the union. Smithback and Sager repeatedly told Hansen not to talk about the union, whether at work or at the cabin where the crew was staying. Grow, Reinders, and Steiner repeatedly told Hansen they were not interested in joining the union and complained to Smithback about Hansen's talking and pressure. Smithback told Hansen he was not interested in joining the union and asked Hansen what it would take for Hansen to drop his union membership and "come over" to Town & Country's side. With tensions already high, a confrontation occurred at lunch on September 14 between Hansen and other crew members about Hansen's organizing pressure.

On September 14, Sager informed Buelow that because state law prevented Town & Country from using Ameristaff's temporary personnel on the jobsite, it could no longer use Hansen to meet the state requirements unless it directly hired him, which it did not intend to do. After this conversation, Buelow discharged Hansen that afternoon. Hansen called Sager to ask if Town & Country would hire him directly onto its payroll, to which Sager responded, "Absolutely not."

The ALJ found that the General Counsel made a prima facie case that Town & Country's decision not to retain Hansen was motivated by Hansen's union activity. Town & Country offered the defenses that Hansen was a poor worker who failed to meet productivity standards and failed to perform in a craftsmanlike manner. The ALJ discredited these defenses, characterizing Town & Country's case as "shifting, replete with contradiction," its witnesses as "biased," and its defense as "structured upon a composite of lies." The ALJ concluded that Town & Country's decision to not retain Hansen was based upon Hansen's union activities, in violation of sections 8(a)(1) and (a)(3).

The record supports the ALJ's rejection of Town & Country's defenses. At the time of Hansen's termination, the only objective complaint Smithback documented was Hansen's lack of productivity. Town & Country's allegations that Hansen's work was not of craftsmanlike quality and that Hansen misused and abused Town & Country's tools were not documented during Hansen's tenure, and the ALJ found that they were post-hoc justifications. Sager admitted at the hearing that Hansen's alleged violation of safety rules was not a factor in the decision to terminate him. Town & Country claimed it would have discharged Hansen earlier in the week due to his lack of productivity except that it needed his Minnesota license. The ALJ found, however, that at the time of Hansen's discharge, Town & Country needed at least two licensed electricians at the jobsite, did not have a replacement for Hansen, and risked not being able to work without having a licensed electrician.

Town & Country stated that one factor in its decision not to retain Hansen was the crew's low morale and the disharmony Hansen was causing. We agree with the ALJ that the evidence clearly showed that the disharmony was due to Hansen's organizing activities. Furthermore, while the disharmony set the stage for the noontime confrontation that occurred on September 14, the confrontation was directly the product of Hansen's organizing activities on nonworking time, which was protected activity. The ALJ found that this was the event that sealed Town & Country's decision not to retain Hansen, a finding that supports the inference of improper motivation.

Although Hansen may not have been a model employee, Town & Country failed to establish that it decided to discharge Hansen on the basis of his level of productivity. [I]t is the employer's burden of proving by a preponderance of the evidence "that it would have discharged [the employee] even in the absence of his union activities." We conclude that substantial evidence supports the ALJ's conclusion that Town & Country's failure to retain Hansen was motivated by Hansen's protected union activities.

NOTES

1.   Is *Town & Country* a pretext case or a mixed motive case? The early focus on whether the employer's reasons were truthful seems to suggest a single motive case focused on which party is telling the truth. However, the General Counsel's prima facie case is strong and most likely sufficient to show from the beginning that an unlawful motivation, discrimination against union

activities, was behind the employer's discharge decision. Also, the court concludes by suggesting the employer did not meet its burden of proving by a preponderance of the evidence "that it would have discharged [the employee] even in the absence of his union activities," a clear indication the court considers the case to be mixed motive. For a similar case decided before the application of the mixed motive framework, but involving a poor worker fired when it became clear he favored a union other than the management-controlled union put in place by the company, see *Edward G. Budd Mfg. Co. v. NLRB*, 138 F.2d 86 (3d Cir. 1943).

2.   As the *Town & Country* cases show, union organizers may apply for jobs with an employer in order to organize from within. An issue that has arisen from this strategy involves how cases of discrimination in employment regarding these "salts" should be handled within the framework of Section 8(a)(3). Early on, the controversy was framed as a remedial one—should damages be awarded to someone who has no real intention to work for the employer, and even if the answer is yes, what if the salt is not qualified for the position or what if there are no positions available? The NLRB tackled these questions in *FES (Division of Thermo Power)*, 331 N.L.R.B. 9 (2000). There, the NLRB established the prima facie burdens, consistent with *Transportation Management* and *Wright Line*, for the General Counsel in refusal to consider for employment and in refusal to hire cases involving salts. However, in 2007, the NLRB modified the *FES* framework by requiring as part of a prima facie case that the General Counsel prove that the applicant is genuinely interested in working for the employer. *See Toering Electric Co.*, 351 N.L.R.B. 225 (2007). Nevertheless, the Board has consistently found union organizers employed or seeking employment by an employer to be "employees" under the Act whether or not they are paid by a union also. *See, e.g., Braun Electric Co.*, 324 N.L.R.B. 1 (1997). For a more detailed discussion of salts and their employment rights under the NLRA, see Pamela A. Howlett, *"Salt" in the Wound? Making a Case and Formulating a Remedy When an Employer Refuses to Hire Union Organizers,* 81 Wash. U. L. Q. 201 (2003).

3.   *Effectiveness of remedies under the NLRA.* Many scholars have criticized the remedies available under the Act for violations of Section 8(a)(3) as insufficient to deter employer termination or discipline of union advocates in organizing campaigns. *See* Wilma B. Liebman, *Decline and Disenchantment: Reflections on the Aging of the National Labor Relations Board*, 28 Berkeley J. Emp. & Lab. L. 584–586 (2007) (the Board is reticent to use even the limited remedies it has at its disposal); Paul C. Weiler, *Promises to Keep: Securing Workers' Rights to Self Organization under the NLRA*, 96 Harv. L. Rev. 1769 (1983) (detailing the various doctrines limiting backpay awards (average award only $2,000), the ineffectiveness of the reinstatement remedy (studies show only about 40% of employees reinstated actually go back to their job), and the overall impact of NLRB delay in assuring an effective remedial response); William B. Gould IV, Agenda for Reform: The Future of Employment Relationships and the Law 158–162, 165–167 (1993).

4. *NLRA protection against retaliation.* Section 8(a)(4) of the NLRA prohibits discharge or discrimination in terms and conditions of employment against a worker "because he has filed charges or given testimony under this Act." The language of the statute, though stated in narrow terms, has generally been interpreted broadly by the Board. For example, a worker need not actually file a charge to be protected, nor does he actually have to testify if he was terminated merely for agreeing to testify. *See, e.g., NLRB v. Scrivener*, 405 U.S. 117 (1972); *Operating Engineers, Local 39*, 346 N.L.R.B. 336 (2006); *Belle Knitting Mills, Inc.*, 331 N.L.R.B. 80 (2000); *First Nat'l Bank & Trust*, 209 N.L.R.B. 95 (1974). Recent decisions under Section 8(a)(4) have focused on the discharge of undocumented workers who have been involved in or assisted with Board proceedings or Board-conducted elections. Compare *Concrete Form Walls, Inc.*, 346 N.L.R.B. 831 (2006) (Board rejected employer's defense that it was complying with immigration law, IRCA, where real reason was undocumented workers' participation in union election), with *International Baking Co. & Earthgrains*, 348 N.L.R.B. 1133 (2006) (employer did not violate NLRA where undocumented status was discovered in normal work permit review process).

* * *

At times, an employer may not simply resist unionization by acting against individual employees. Employer action against a group of employees may more effectively serve an employer's needs by increasing the stakes of a unionization effort. For example, a reduction in force of several workers is generally likely to have more of a chilling effect on unionization than a firing of any individual worker, with the possible exception of firing the leading union advocate. Moreover, opportunities for acting against the collective, such as by a reduction in force, may present themselves more readily in the normal ebb and flow of decisions about a business as a whole. At the same time, the employer's ability to manage its business was meant to be preserved, not endangered, by the NLRA. Business decisions involving the allocation of capital, such as business closing and relocation, subcontracting, sales of the business or just asset sales pose particular challenges for the Act.

To deal with collective infringements of Section 8(a)(3), imagine that the workforce status quo ante is a "playing field" in which capital and labor may vie for loyalty and leverage. We know by now, of course, that both labor and capital are allowed to join together collectively in an enterprise. We know too that labor has certain rights guaranteed by Section 7 of the NLRA and that businesses have certain property interests that the Act respects. There are times, however, when these clash, and any resolution requires a balancing of these interests.

TEXTILE WORKERS UNION OF AMERICA V.
DARLINGTON MFG. CO.
380 U.S. 263 (1965)

JUSTICE HARLAN delivered the opinion of the Court:

Darlington Manufacturing Company was a South Carolina corporation operating one textile mill. A majority of Darlington's stock was held by Deering Milliken, a New York "selling house" marketing textiles produced by others. Deering Milliken in turn was controlled by Roger Milliken, president of Darlington, and by other members of the Milliken family. The National Labor Relations Board found that the Milliken family, through Deering Milliken, operated 17 textile manufacturers, including Darlington, whose products, manufactured in 27 different mills, were marketed through Deering Milliken.

In March 1956 petitioner Textile Workers Union initiated an organizational campaign at Darlington which the company resisted vigorously in various ways, including threats to close the mill if the union won a representation election.[3] On September 6, 1956, the union won an election by a narrow margin. When Roger Milliken was advised of the union victory, he decided to call a meeting of the Darlington board of directors to consider closing the mill. Mr. Milliken testified before the Labor Board:

> "I felt that as a result of the campaign that had been conducted and the promises and statements made in these letters that had been distributed [favoring unionization], that if before we had had some hope, possible hope of achieving competitive [costs] . . . by taking advantage of new machinery that was being put in, that this hope had diminished as a result of the election because a majority of the employees had voted in favor of the union. . . ."

The board of directors met on September 12 and voted to liquidate the corporation, action which was approved by the stockholders on October 17. The plant ceased operations entirely in November, and all plant machinery and equipment were sold piecemeal at auction in December.

The union filed charges with the Labor Board claiming that Darlington had violated §§ 8(a)(1) and (3) of the National Labor Relations Act by closing its plant, and § 8(a)(5) by refusing to bargain with the union after the election. The Board, by a divided vote, found that Darlington had been closed because of the antiunion animus of Roger Milliken, and held that to be a violation of § 8(a)(3). The Board also found Darlington to be part of a

---

[3]	The Board found that Darlington had interrogated employees and threatened to close the mill if the union won the election. After the decision to liquidate was made, Darlington employees were told that the decision to close was caused by the election, and they were encouraged to sign a petition disavowing the union. These practices were held to violate § 8(a)(1) of the National Labor Relations Act, and that part of the Board decision is not challenged here.

single integrated employer group controlled by the Milliken family through Deering Milliken; therefore Deering Milliken could be held liable for the unfair labor practices of Darlington. Alternatively, since Darlington was a part of the Deering Milliken enterprise, Deering Milliken had violated the Act by closing part of its business for a discriminatory purpose. The Board ordered back pay for all Darlington employees until they obtained substantially equivalent work or were put on preferential hiring lists at the other Deering Milliken mills. Respondent Deering Milliken was ordered to bargain with the union in regard to details of compliance with the Board order.

On review, the Court of Appeals, sitting *en banc*, set aside the order and denied enforcement by a divided vote. The Court of Appeals held that even accepting *arguendo* the Board's determination that Deering Milliken had the status of a single employer, a company has the absolute right to close out a part or all of its business regardless of antiunion motives. The court therefore did not review the Board's finding that Deering Milliken was a single integrated employer. We granted certiorari to consider the important questions involved. We hold that so far as the Labor Relations Act is concerned, an employer has the absolute right to terminate his entire business for any reason he pleases, but disagree with the Court of Appeals that such right includes the ability to close part of a business no matter what the reason. We conclude that the cause must be remanded to the Board for further proceedings.

Preliminarily it should be observed that both petitioners argue that the Darlington closing violated § 8(a)(1) as well as § 8(a)(3) of the Act. We think, however, that the Board was correct in treating the closing only under § 8(a)(3). Section 8(a)(1) provides that it is an unfair labor practice for an employer "to interfere with, restrain, or coerce employees in the exercise of" § 7 rights. Naturally, certain business decisions will, to some degree, interfere with concerted activities by employees. But it is only when the interference with § 7 rights outweighs the business justification for the employer's action that § 8(a)(1) is violated. A violation of § 8(a)(1) alone therefore presupposes an act which is unlawful even absent a discriminatory motive. Whatever may be the limits of § 8(a)(1), some employer decisions are so peculiarly matters of management prerogative that they would never constitute violations of § 8(a)(1), whether or not they involved sound business judgment, unless they also violated § 8(a)(3). Thus it is not questioned in this case that an employer has the right to terminate his business, whatever the impact of such action on concerted activities, if the decision to close is motivated by other than discriminatory reasons. But such action, if discriminatorily motivated, is encompassed within the literal language of § 8(a)(3). We therefore deal with the Darlington closing under that section.

We consider first the argument, advanced by the petitioner union but not by the Board, and rejected by the Court of Appeals, that an employer may not go completely out of business without running afoul of the Labor Relations Act if such action is prompted by a desire to avoid unionization. Given the Board's findings on the issue of motive, acceptance of this contention would carry the day for the Board's conclusion that the closing of this plant was an unfair labor practice, even on the assumption that Darlington is to be regarded as an independent unrelated employer. A proposition that a single businessman cannot choose to go out of business if he wants to would represent such a startling innovation that it should not be entertained without the clearest manifestation of legislative intent or unequivocal judicial precedent so construing the Labor Relations Act. We find neither.

So far as legislative manifestation is concerned, it is sufficient to say that there is not the slightest indication in the history of the Wagner Act or of the Taft-Hartley Act that Congress envisaged any such result under either statute.

The courts of appeals have generally assumed that a complete cessation of business will remove an employer from future coverage by the Act. Thus the Court of Appeals said in these cases: "The Act 'does not compel a person to become or remain an employee. It does not compel one to become or remain an employer. Either may withdraw from that status with immunity, so long as the obligations of any employment contract have been met.' "

The AFL-CIO suggests in its *amicus* brief that Darlington's action was similar to a discriminatory lockout, which is prohibited " 'because designed to frustrate organizational efforts, to destroy or undermine bargaining representation, or to evade the duty to bargain.' " One of the purposes of the Labor Relations Act is to prohibit the discriminatory use of economic weapons in an effort to obtain future benefits. The discriminatory lockout designed to destroy a union, like a "runaway shop," is a lever which has been used to discourage collective employee activities in the future. But a complete liquidation of a business yields no such future benefit for the employer, if the termination is bona fide. It may be motivated more by spite against the union than by business reasons, but it is not the type of discrimination which is prohibited by the Act. The personal satisfaction that such an employer may derive from standing on his beliefs and the mere possibility that other employers will follow his example are surely too remote to be considered dangers at which the labor statutes were aimed. Although employees may be prohibited from engaging in a strike under certain conditions, no one would consider it a violation of the Act for the same employees to quit their employment *en masse*, even if motivated by a desire to ruin the employer. The very permanence of such action would negate any future economic benefit to the employees. The employer's right to go out of business is no different.

We are not presented here with the case of a "runaway shop," whereby Darlington would transfer its work to another plant or open a new plant in another locality to replace its closed plant. Nor are we concerned with a shutdown where the employees, by renouncing the union, could cause the plant to reopen. Such cases would involve discriminatory employer action for the purpose of obtaining some benefit from the employees in the future.[19] We hold here only that when an employer closes his entire business, even if the liquidation is motivated by vindictiveness toward the union, such action is not an unfair labor practice.[20]

While we thus agree with the Court of Appeals that viewing Darlington as an independent employer the liquidation of its business was not an unfair labor practice, we cannot accept the lower court's view that the same conclusion necessarily follows if Darlington is regarded as an integral part of the Deering Milliken enterprise.

The closing of an entire business, even though discriminatory, ends the employer-employee relationship; the force of such a closing is entirely spent as to that business when termination of the enterprise takes place. On the other hand, a discriminatory partial closing may have repercussions on what remains of the business, affording employer leverage for

---

[19]   All of the cases to which we have been cited involved closings found to have been motivated, at least in part, by the expectation of achieving future benefits. The two cases which are urged as indistinguishable from *Darlington* are *Labor Board* v. *Savoy Laundry*, 327 F.2d 370, and *Labor Board* v. *Missouri Transit Co.*, 250 F.2d 261. In *Savoy Laundry* the employer operated one laundry plant where he processed both retail laundry pickups and wholesale laundering. Once the laundry was marked, all of it was processed together. After some of the employees organized, the employer discontinued most of the wholesale service, and thereafter discharged some of his employees. There was no separate wholesale department, and the discriminatory motive was obviously to discourage unionization in the entire plant. *Missouri Transit* presents a similar situation. A bus company operated an interstate line and an intrastate shuttle service connecting a military base with the interstate terminal. When the union attempted to organize all of the drivers, the shuttle service was sold and the shuttle drivers were discharged. Although the two services were treated as separate departments, it is clear from the facts of the case that the union was attempting to organize all of the drivers, and the discriminatory motive of the employer was to discourage unionization in the interstate service as well as the shuttle service.

[20]   Nothing we have said in this opinion would justify an employer's interfering with employee organizational activities by threatening to close his plant, as distinguished from announcing a decision to close already reached by the board of directors or other management authority empowered to make such a decision. We recognize that this safeguard does not wholly remove the possibility that our holding may result in some deterrent effect on organizational activities independent of that arising from the closing itself. An employer may be encouraged to make a definitive decision to close on the theory that its mere announcement before a representation election will discourage the employees from voting for the union, and thus his decision may not have to be implemented. Such a possibility is not likely to occur, however, except in a marginal business; a solidly successful employer is not apt to hazard the possibility that the employees will call his bluff by voting to organize. We see no practical way of eliminating this possible consequence of our holding short of allowing the Board to order an employer who chooses so to gamble with his employees not to carry out his announced intention to close. We do not consider the matter of sufficient significance in the overall labor-management relations picture to require or justify a decision different from the one we have made.

discouraging the free exercise of § 7 rights among remaining employees of much the same kind as that found to exist in the "runaway shop" and "temporary closing" cases. Moreover, a possible remedy open to the Board in such a case, like the remedies available in the "runaway shop" and "temporary closing" cases, is to order reinstatement of the discharged employees in the other parts of the business. No such remedy is available when an entire business has been terminated. By analogy to those cases involving a continuing enterprise we are constrained to hold, in disagreement with the Court of Appeals, that a partial closing is an unfair labor practice under § 8(a)(3) if motivated by a purpose to chill unionism in any of the remaining plants of the single employer and if the employer may reasonably have foreseen that such closing would likely have that effect.

While we have spoken in terms of a "partial closing" in the context of the Board's finding that Darlington was part of a larger single enterprise controlled by the Milliken family, we do not mean to suggest that an organizational integration of plants or corporations is a necessary prerequisite to the establishment of such a violation of § 8(a)(3). If the persons exercising control over a plant that is being closed for antiunion reasons (1) have an interest in another business, whether or not affiliated with or engaged in the same line of commercial activity as the closed plant, of sufficient substantiality to give promise of their reaping a benefit from the discouragement of unionization in that business; (2) act to close their plant with the purpose of producing such a result; and (3) occupy a relationship to the other business which makes it realistically foreseeable that its employees will fear that such business will also be closed down if they persist in organizational activities, we think that an unfair labor practice has been made out.

Although the Board's single employer finding necessarily embraced findings as to Roger Milliken and the Milliken family which, if sustained by the Court of Appeals, would satisfy the elements of "interest" and "relationship" with respect to other parts of the Deering Milliken enterprise, that and the other Board findings fall short of establishing the factors of "purpose" and "effect" which are vital requisites of the general principles that govern a case of this kind.

Thus, the Board's findings as to the purpose and foreseeable effect of the Darlington closing pertained *only* to its impact on the Darlington employees. No findings were made as to the purpose and effect of the closing with respect to the employees in the other plants comprising the Deering Milliken group. It does not suffice to establish the unfair labor practice charged here to argue that the Darlington closing necessarily had an adverse impact upon unionization in such other plants. We have heretofore observed that employer action which has a foreseeable consequence of discouraging concerted activities generally does not amount to a violation of § 8(a)(3) in the absence of a showing of motivation which is aimed at achieving the prohibited effect. In an area which trenches so closely upon otherwise legitimate employer prerogatives, we consider the absence of Board findings on this score a fatal defect in its decision. The Court of Appeals for its part did not deal with the question of purpose and effect at all, since it concluded that an employer's right to close down his entire business because of distaste for unionism, also embraced a partial closing so motivated.

Apart from this, the Board's holding should not be accepted or rejected without court review of its single employer finding, judged, however, in accordance with the general principles set forth above. Review of that finding, which the lower court found unnecessary on its view of the cause, now becomes necessary in light of our holding in this part of our opinion, and is a task that devolves upon the Court of Appeals in the first instance.

In these circumstances, we think the proper disposition of this cause is to require that it be remanded to the Board so as to afford the Board the opportunity to make further findings on the issue of purpose and effect.

— Remand to Board

NOTES

1. On remand, the Board held that Roger Milliken had indeed violated the law under the Supreme Court's new test. The Board found Milliken's many antiunion speeches to private and government groups, as well as Milliken's mailing of a publication about the Darlington case to managers at Deering Milliken's other mills and advising them to mount public relations campaigns against unionization were sufficient to show a "foreseeable" effect to "chill" unionization elsewhere. *See Darlington Mfg. Co.,* 165 N.L.R.B. 1074 (1967), *enf'd,* 397 F.2d 760 (4th Cir.), *cert. denied* 393 U.S. 1023 (1968).

2. Once it is determined that an employer has acted for an improper purpose, meaning it has discriminated against Section 7 rights, the focus of inquiry should turn to those affected: in *Darlington,* the workers who have been terminated in retaliation for unionization. The *Darlington* test, by contrast, measures whether a partial closing is unlawful by asking about the effect on workers at other sites with respect to possible future unionization. The *Darlington* decision has been called "bizarre" and "puzzling," primarily because the Supreme Court's test for a violation in the case of a partial closing is seemingly pulled out of the air and has no close relationship to the concerns of the Act or Section 8(a)(3). *See* James Atleson, Values and Assumptions in American Labor Law 136–140 (1983); Clyde Summers, *Labor Law in the Supreme Court: 1964 Term,* 75 Yale L. J. 59, 64–67 (1965). Why do you suppose the Court did this? What is the effect of the Court's changed focus? What about the proposition that a business should be allowed to shut down simply because a union won an election? Should it be unquestioned that an employer may close up shop for any reason? See Karl Klare, *Teaching Local 1330—Reflections on Critical Legal Pedagogy,* 7 Unbound: Harv. J. Legal Left 81, 111 (2011) (questioning the Court's assumption that the law protects an employer from

allows emp-r to close down biz but if they do that it's no econom-c benefit it's hurtful

liability for going out of business entirely in order to avoid dealing with a union).

3.   Refer back to the scenario at the beginning of the Chapter. Assume that instead of firing Penny the Programmer, Workman agreed to meet with the local business agent for the Programmers' Union. At that meeting, the business agent showed Workman data that the prevailing wage for unionized programmers across the country was a full $10 an hour more than what Enderby was paying. The business agent also told Workman that if Enderby did not agree to pay the union rate there would be a strike that would effectively close down Enderby's Oregon facility. The business agent told Workman, "Trust me, if we come in, you'll pay the higher rate—no one has ever been able to resist us." The business agent also informed Workman that any other company facilities would soon be organized as well, consistent with the union business model. He indicated that once he organized a part of a company, the rest of the company soon followed. After the meeting, Enderby announced that it was closing its operations in Eugene, Oregon, and instead would subcontract its programming work to other companies and also increase the programming workload of existing Enderby programmers located in Tulsa, Oklahoma. Has Enderby violated the law? What if Workman explains that he "doesn't have anything against the union. It's simply all a matter of cost. Enderby just cannot pay the union rate. Rather than take a strike we just had to figure some other things out."? Is Workman more sympathetic than Roger Milliken? What if Workman is right that the increased cost would literally break the company? See NLRB v. Adkins Transfer Co., 226 F.2d 324 (6th Cir. 1955).

4.   For a more recent case, consider the actions of The Boeing Company, in the news for the better part of 2010. Using the evidentiary framework set forth in Wright Line and Transportation Management above, the General Counsel would need to show, through direct or circumstantial evidence that a substantial motivating factor in Boeing's decision to move assembly of its new Dreamliner aircraft from Washington state, where the company has longstanding production lines, to South Carolina was to interfere with employees' section 7 rights. If successful, the burden of persuasion would shift to Boeing to show that the move to South Carolina would have occurred regardless of antiunion animus.

The NLRB General Counsel could establish a prima facie case: (1) Boeing had knowledge of Section 7 activities. Boeing has a long-established collective bargaining relationship with the union and, following a strike that ended in November 2008, had a collective bargaining agreement in place through September 8, 2012. Boeing referenced Section 7 strike activity in its press statement. (2) Boeing's timing was suspect. It appears that negotiations to locate the production in Washington were ongoing, however, shortly after the South Carolina employees decertified and a 20-year 'no strike' agreement for the Washington workers failed, Boeing announced that production of the new line would be moved to South Carolina. (3) There is nothing to show any problems in the unionized employees' work record other than the frequency of strikes. (4) Moving a substantial amount of production to South Carolina is extreme in that it would take work away from unionized employees. Of course, Boeing would argue that it was not moving anything, that the *Dreamliner* represented a new production line. (5) The circumstances of Boeing's actions could be argued to show antiunion animus. In addition to the direct statements by Boeing officials, Boeing's CEO also announced that duplication and inefficiencies caused by the move to South Carolina would be more than overcome by avoiding strikes every three or four years. On the other hand, Boeing could argue that the new Dreamliner production line was not a relocation of work, but a new line. Boeing attempted to negotiate a no-strike pledge, but failed. Boeing could argue it had nothing against the union, but went to South Carolina with the new line when the union would not agree. (6) Finally there had been a long history of management hostility toward the union over strikes. Two strikes over the past three years had cost Boeing billions of dollars and added to a backlog on its assembly line.

After much negative media attention and severe questioning by conservative politicians, the Board's General Counsel issued a complaint against Boeing on April 20, 2011. For details related to the complaint, see *Boeing Co.*, 2011 WL 2597601 (Jun. 30, 2011) (denying motion to dismiss complaint). The NLRB asserted, *inter alia*, that Boeing officials' statements showed anti-union animus and discouraged membership in the Union in violation of Section 8(a)(3) of the Act. Boeing contested the claim, stating that the South Carolina production line is a *new* line, not a transferred one, and that no Washington state Boeing jobs were adversely affected. The NLRB's complaint came with criticism from Senators who claimed that not allowing companies to open new sites in right-to-work states, such as South Carolina, would push business overseas. In June 2011, the Board granted employee intervenors leave to file briefs on the matter after the Board ALJ had earlier granted sixteen state attorneys general leave to write amicus curiae briefs regarding the Boeing case. *Boeing Co.*, 2011 WL 2451725 (2011). In July 2011, the multi-million dollar South Carolina plant, the size of ten football fields, began production and the workers had already rebuked efforts of the Machinists to organize the workforce.

The Boeing case was ultimately settled in December 2011 after unprecedented involvement by Congress in the investigatory details of the case. The Board approved the union's request to withdraw the ULP charge after reaching a settlement under which it entered into a new four-year collective bargaining agreement with Boeing and obtained commitments that the company would build a new line of 737 MAX aircraft in Washington state. *See* Office of Public Affairs, NLRB Acting General Counsel Announces Closing of Boeing Case, Dec. 9, 2011, http://www.nlrb.gov/news-outreach/news-story/ nlrb-acting-general-counsel-announces-close-boeing-case; *see also* Julius Getman, *Boeing, the IAM, and the National Labor Relations Board: Why U.S. Labor Law is Failing*, 98 Minn. L. Rev. 1651 (2014); Julius Getman, *The Boeing Case: Creating Outrage Out of Very Little*, 27 ABA J. Lab. & Emp. Law 99 (2011).

An interesting question arising in the *Boeing* case involved the possible remedy in case of violation. Several of these had been discussed in the context of settlement talks between Boeing and the NLRB. Boeing argued that with its substantial investment in South Carolina it could hardly return production to Washington. Alternative possibilities included a Boeing agreement to return foreign production to the U.S., a promise to locate future production in Washington state (in exchange for an IAM "no-strike" pledge), or a Boeing agreement to "card check" recognition at the South Carolina plant. What does the *Darlington* case suggest about what the remedy should be? Is this the kind of case that should now be decided under a *Transportation Management* "mixed motive" analysis? *See Verizon,* 350 N.L.R.B. 542 (2007); *Manhattan Day School,* 346 N.L.R.B. 992 (2006). Who should prevail, though, if the employer's primary economic argument is potential strike delays? Doesn't that make the employer's rationale one of complete anti-union motivation? Wasn't this the basic issue, although less directly stated, in the *Adkins Transfer* case above?

G. ROUTES TO UNION RECOGNITION

As mentioned at the beginning of this Chapter, there are three routes to recognition that are sanctioned within the legal framework of the National Labor Relations Act: (1) representation election (union prevails by majority vote in an NLRB-conducted election); (2) bargaining order (the NLRB orders the employer to bargain with the union after the Board has determined that substantial employer unfair labor practices interfered with employee free choice either in advance of or during an election); and (3) lawful voluntary recognition (an employer agrees to recognize a union after it has shown, typically by signed authorization cards or an employer poll, that the union has the support of a majority of employees in a unit appropriate for representation at an employer's workplace). Each route involves the determination of some preliminary issues, including the appropriateness of the bargaining unit.

1. APPROPRIATE BARGAINING UNITS

In the problem that opened this chapter, the Programmer's Union was considering demanding recognition based on having received authorization cards from 26 of Enderby's 50 programmers at the Eugene facility. Enderby, however, might argue that the appropriate grouping for recognition also includes the assemblers, engineers and business office clericals. Alternatively, it may argue that the Programmer's Union's strength should be judged against all of its programmers, including those employed in its Tulsa facility. These arguments raise questions of what grouping of Enderby employees constitutes an appropriate bargaining unit. Depending on how that unit is defined, the Programmer's Union may or may not have majority support.

As the Enderby problem illustrates, the discussion about the bargaining unit often begins with the group that the potential representative has identified as the unit of employees that it desires to represent. Fortunately, by statute the NLRB does not have to determine which group of employees in a given workplace would be the best for bargaining, but only whether the petitioned-for group would be satisfactory or "appropriate." The question is often strategic. An employer, for example, may believe that the union is seeking a particular unit because that unit gives it the best chance at prevailing in an election. As a result, an employer that is resistant to the union effort may urge a different "appropriate" unit. Often, the employer will argue for a larger unit believing that it will be harder for the union to organize more workers. The employer, however, may be taking a risk with that particular strategy because if the union is successful in the larger unit there will be a larger union, presumably with more leverage against the employer.

The original Wagner Act directed the NLRB to "decide in each case whether, in order to assure to employees the fullest freedom in exercising the rights guaranteed by this Act [subchapter], the unit appropriate for the purposes of collective bargaining shall be the employer unit, craft unit, plant unit, or subdivision thereof." The Board took the mandate to assure to employees the fullest freedom in exercising their statutory rights seriously and often determined bargaining units to be appropriate because they reflected the extent of the union's support. *See, e.g., Garden State Hosiery Co.*, 74 N.L.R.B. 318 (1947). Congress reacted against this approach by providing, in the Taft-Hartley Act, that "the extent to which the employees have organized shall not be controlling." Beyond these two provisions, the statute offers only minimal express guidance. It provides in § 9(b)(1) that professional employees may not be combined in the same unit as non-professionals unless the professionals consent in a secret ballot election, in § 9(b)(2) that a unit of craft employees may not be deemed inappropriate solely because a different unit was previously determined by the Board unless a majority of the craft employees vote against separate representation, and in § 9(b)(3) that guards may not be combined with other employees and may not be represented by a union that admits employees other than guards to membership or that is affiliated with such an organization.

In 1974, when Congress extended the NLRB's jurisdiction to include not-for-profit health care institutions, no special provisions for hospital bargaining units were added to the Act. However, the House and Senate committee reports cautioned against the undue proliferation of bargaining units in health care institutions. After considerable litigation over the composition of hospital bargaining units, the Board promulgated regulations defining such units, which were challenged in the following case.

AMERICAN HOSPITAL ASS'N V. NLRB
499 U.S. 606 (1991)

JUSTICE STEVENS delivered the opinion of the Court:

For the first time since the National Labor Relations Board (Board or NLRB) was established in 1935, the Board has promulgated a substantive rule defining the employee units appropriate for collective bargaining in a particular line of commerce. The rule is applicable to acute care hospitals and provides, with three exceptions, that eight, and only eight, units shall be appropriate in any such hospital. The three exceptions are for cases that present extraordinary circumstances, cases in which nonconforming units already exist, and cases in which labor organizations seek to combine two or more of the eight specified units. The extraordinary circumstances exception applies automatically to hospitals in which the eight-unit rule will produce a unit of five or fewer employees. *See* 29 C.F.R. § 103.30 (1990).

Petitioner American Hospital Association first [makes] a general challenge to the Board's rulemaking authority in connection with bargaining unit determinations based on the terms of the National Labor Relations Act as originally enacted in 1935. In § 1 of the NLRA Congress made the legislative finding that the "inequality of bargaining power" between unorganized employees and corporate employers had adversely affected commerce and declared it to be the policy of the United States to mitigate or eliminate those adverse effects "by encouraging the practice and procedure of collective bargaining and by protecting the exercise by workers of full freedom of association, self-organization, and designation of representatives of their own choosing, for the purpose of negotiating the terms and conditions of their employment or other mutual aid or protection." The central purpose of the Act was to protect and facilitate employees' opportunity to organize unions to represent them in collective-bargaining negotiations.

Petitioner argues that § 9(b) provides such a limitation because this section requires the Board to determine the appropriate bargaining unit "in each case." We are not persuaded.

Section 6 granted the Board the "authority from time to time to make, amend, and rescind . . . such rules and regulations as may be necessary to carry out the provisions" of the Act. This grant was unquestionably sufficient to authorize the rule at issue in this case unless limited by some other provision in the Act.

Section 9(a) of the Act provides that the representative "designated or selected for the purposes of collective bargaining by the majority of the employees in a unit appropriate for such purposes" shall be the exclusive bargaining representative for all the employees in that unit. This section, read in light of the policy of the Act, implies that the initiative in selecting an appropriate unit resides with the employees. Moreover, the language suggests that employees may seek to organize "a unit" that is "appropriate"—not necessarily *the* single most appropriate unit. Thus, one union might seek to represent all of the employees in a particular plant, those in a particular craft, or perhaps just a portion thereof.

Given the obvious potential for disagreement concerning the appropriateness of the unit selected by the union seeking recognition by the employer—disagreements that might involve rival unions claiming jurisdiction over contested segments of the work force as well as disagreements between management and labor—§ 9(b) authorizes the Board to decide whether the designated unit is appropriate. Section 9(b) provides:

> The Board shall decide *in each case* whether, in order to insure to employees the full benefit of their right to self-organization and to collective bargaining, and otherwise to effectuate the policies of this Act, the unit appropriate for the purposes of collective bargaining shall be the employer unit, craft unit, plant unit, or subdivision thereof.

(Emphasis added.) Petitioner reads the emphasized phrase as a limitation on the Board's rulemaking powers. Although the contours of the restriction that petitioner ascribes to the phrase are murky, petitioner's reading of the language would prevent the Board from imposing any industry-wide rule delineating the appropriate bargaining units. We believe petitioner's reading is inconsistent with the natural meaning of the language read in the context of the statute as a whole.

The more natural reading of these three words is simply to indicate that whenever there is a disagreement about the appropriateness of a unit, the Board shall resolve the dispute. Under this reading, the words "in each case" are synonymous with "whenever necessary" or "in any case in which there is a dispute." Congress chose not to enact a general rule that would require plant unions, craft unions, or industry-wide unions for every employer in every line of commerce, but also chose not to leave the decision up to employees or employers alone. Instead, the decision "in each case" in which a dispute arises is to be made by the Board.

In resolving such a dispute, the Board's decision is presumably to be guided not simply by the basic policy of the Act but also by the rules that the Board develops to circumscribe and to guide its discretion either in the process of case-by-case adjudication or by the exercise of its rulemaking authority. The requirement that the Board exercise its discretion in every disputed case cannot fairly or logically be read to command the Board to exercise standardless discretion in each case.

Even petitioner acknowledges that "the Board could adopt rules establishing general principles to guide the required case-by-case bargaining unit determinations." Petitioner further acknowledges that the Board has created many such rules in the half-century during which it has adjudicated bargaining unit disputes. Petitioner contends, however, that a rule delineating the appropriate bargaining unit for an entire industry is qualitatively different from these prior rules, which at most established rebuttable presumptions that certain units would be considered appropriate in certain circumstances.

We simply cannot find in the three words "in each case" any basis for the fine distinction that petitioner would have us draw. Contrary to petitioner's contention, the Board's rule is not an irrebuttable presumption; instead, it contains an exception for "extraordinary circumstances." Even if the rule did establish an irrebuttable presumption, it would not differ significantly from the prior rules adopted by the Board. As with its prior rules, the Board must still apply the rule "in each case." For example, the Board must decide in each case, among a host of other issues, whether a given facility is properly classified as an acute care hospital and whether particular employees are properly placed in particular units.

NOTE

The rule at issue established the following eight bargaining units: (1) registered nurses, (2) physicians, (3) all other professionals, (4) technical employees, (5) skilled maintenance employees, (6) clerical employees, (7) guards, and (8) all other nonprofessional employees. The Court held that the rule was not arbitrary or capricious, observing that the Board enjoys broad discretion in fashioning bargaining units. It also rejected the American Hospitals Association's argument that the rule was inconsistent with the admonition in the House and Senate committee reports against undue proliferation of bargaining units in health care institutions. The Court regarded the statements in the legislative history as mere cautions to the Board that if it did not give appropriate consideration to this concern, Congress might respond legislatively.

* * *

The Programmers Union at Enderby sought representation in a bargaining unit limited to programmers at the Eugene facility. It probably did so because that was where its support lay. It had no support among programmers at the Tulsa facility and may not have even attempted to organize them. If the NLRB limits the bargaining unit to the Eugene facility, would it be violating the statutory admonition that extent of organization may not be the determining factor?

On the other hand, Enderby may advocate a bargaining unit that combines the Eugene and Tulsa facilities because such a unit would be much more difficult to organize. Enderby may also have central policies, including uniform fringe benefits, a uniform employee manual and a uniform discipline system that apply to both facilities. It would not want to carve out the Eugene programmers for separate treatment through collective bargaining. If it has to bargain with a union, it may prefer to bargain one contract for all of its programmers. If the NLRB combines the Eugene and Tulsa facilities into a single unit, it may doom the union's organizing campaign. In so doing, would it be violating the statutory mandate to assure employees their fullest freedom to exercise their rights? As the following case illustrates, the stakes in determining whether a unit encompasses a single or multiple locations are often quite high.

FRIENDLY ICE CREAM CORP. V. NLRB
705 F.2d 570 (1st Cir. 1983)

BOWNES, CIRCUIT JUDGE:

Friendly, a Massachusetts corporation, owns and operates a chain of 605 restaurants in sixteen states. The eastern region of the chain is headquartered in Wilbraham, Massachusetts. Executive personnel at Wilbraham formulate standard policies applicable to all restaurants in the chain, covering such matters as: menus, pricing, food preparation, formulas, interior and exterior decor, employee uniforms, maintenance, marketing, advertising, purchasing, inventory, cash accounting, security, hours of operation and personnel. The eastern region is divided into twelve divisions, each supervised by a Division Manager. Division I, covering portions of eastern and southern Massachusetts, is further subdivided into nine districts. Each district comprises from four to nine restaurants, for a total of sixty-five restaurants within Division I. A District Manager supervises the operations of the restaurants within each district, and reports to the Division Manager.

The store involved in this proceeding, the Weymouth restaurant, is part of a district comprised of eight restaurants. The restaurant employs approximately twenty-four part-time and three full-time employees. The supervisory hierarchy of the Weymouth restaurant begins with the Shift Supervisor, who acts as the Store Manager's delegate when she or he is not present. The Store Manager, who works between fifty and fifty-five hours per week, bears overall responsibility for the day-to-day operation of the restaurant. The Store Manager is supervised by the District Manager, who regularly visits the eight restaurants within the district. While at a restaurant, the District Manager checks the supplies, sales, service, cleanliness and employees. Estimates of the frequency of the District Manager's visits range from one to three times per week, and estimates of the length of the visits range from fifteen minutes to several hours. The District Manager reports to the Division Manager, located in Braintree, Massachusetts, who visits the Weymouth restaurant about once a month.

On April 5, 1979, the Union filed a representation petition seeking certification as the collective bargaining representative of specified employees at the Weymouth restaurant. Friendly did not dispute the composition of this unit, but argued that the scope of the unit was inappropriate because it covered only a single restaurant within the chain. Friendly argued that the most appropriate unit would be one encompassing all of its restaurants in the United States. Four alternative units were also proposed: a unit composed of all restaurants within the Boston Standard Metropolitan Statistical Area; all restaurants within Division I; all restaurants within a county; or a cluster of restaurants within a defined geographical area.

The Board's Regional Office held a comprehensive fourteen-day representation hearing at which both parties presented exhaustive testimony, exhibits and arguments concerning the appropriate scope of the bargaining unit. On May 30, 1980, the Regional Director determined that the petitioned-for single store unit was appropriate and directed that an election be held. Friendly's request for review of this decision was denied by the Board on the ground that it raised no substantial issues warranting review.

On September 30, 1981, the Union was certified as the exclusive bargaining representative of the employees at the Weymouth restaurant.

In October 1981, the Union requested collective bargaining, was refused, and filed an unfair labor practice charge. The Regional Director issued a complaint alleging that Friendly had refused to bargain with the Union in violation of Sections 8(a)(5) and 8(a)(1) of the Act. While Friendly acknowledged its refusal to bargain, it raised as an affirmative defense the invalidity of the Board's certification of the Union.[3] The Board . . . issued an order requiring Friendly to cease and desist from interfering with its employees' collective bargaining rights. The company was ordered to bargain collectively with the Union and to post copies of an appropriate remedial notice. Friendly now petitions for review of the Board's order, alleging that [the Weymouth store is an inappropriate unit for bargaining]. The Board cross-petitions for enforcement of its order.

Primary responsibility for determining the appropriateness of a collective bargaining unit has been vested in the Board. Because this is an area requiring expertise, the Board is given extraordinarily broad discretionary power, subject only to the statutory direction that the chosen unit "assure to employees the fullest freedom in exercising the rights guaranteed by [the Act]."

---

[3] Under present law, an employer cannot obtain direct review of the Board's unit determination. Instead, it must refuse to bargain and then raise the issue of the unit's appropriateness in the subsequent unfair labor practice proceedings. *Pac. Sw. Airlines v. NLRB*, 587 F.2d 1032, 1035 n.3 (9th Cir. 1978).

The Board is not required to select the most appropriate unit in a particular factual setting; it need only select *an* appropriate unit from the range of units appropriate under the circumstances. An employer seeking to challenge the Board's unit determination cannot merely point to a more appropriate unit. Rather, the burden of proof is on the employer to show that the Board's unit is clearly inappropriate. It follows that the Board's unit determinations are rarely disturbed.

In making a unit determination, the Board's primary duty is to effect the Act's overriding policy of assuring employees the fullest freedom in exercising their right to bargain collectively. At the same time, the Board must "respect the interest of an integrated multi-unit employer in maintaining enterprise-wide labor relations." Accordingly, the Board must grant some minimum consideration to the employer's interest in avoiding the disruptive effects of piecemeal unionization. An employer with a central labor policy can be expected to prefer a bargaining unit which corresponds to the company's internal organization. While an employer's interest in bargaining with the most convenient possible unit should be accommodated when feasible, the Board is free to grant greater weight to the employees' interest in being represented by a representative of their own choosing. The Act expressly dictates that employee freedom of choice must be paramount in any unit determination. Thus, this factor of employee freedom can legitimately tip the balance in determining which of two equally appropriate units should be preferred.

The critical consideration in determining the appropriateness of a proposed unit is whether the employees comprising the unit share a "community of interest." In determining whether the requisite community of interest exists, the Board considers several criteria, no single factor alone being determinative. The factors include:

(a) geographic proximity of the stores in relation to each other;

(b) level of employee interchange between various stores;

(c) degree of autonomy exercised by the local store manager, especially with respect to labor relations;

(d) extent of union organization;

(e) history of collective bargaining;

(f) desires of the affected employees;

(g) employer's organizational framework;

(h) similarity in skills, employee benefits, wages and hours of work.

In weighing these factors and determining what group of employees constitutes an appropriate unit, the Board is not bound to follow any rigid rule laid down by the law or prior decisions. Since each unit determination is dependent upon factual variations, the Board is free to decide each case on an ad hoc basis. The Board has, however, developed certain administrative policies which guide it in making unit determinations. When considering the appropriateness of a single store bargaining unit in a multistore retail operation, the Board is aided by its policy that a single store is "presumptively an appropriate unit for bargaining."[4] This rebuttable presumption is consistent with the Act, has a rational foundation, and reflects the Board's expertise. Thus, in an appropriate case, the Board is entitled to invoke this presumption

We have recently upheld the Board determination that a single store constitutes an appropriate unit for collective bargaining. In *NLRB v. Living & Learning Ctrs., Inc.*, 652 F.2d 209 (1st Cir. 1981), the Board had ordered a representation election to be held at one day care center which was part of a twenty-nine unit chain operating in Massachusetts. While each center had a director who could hire, fire, schedule vacations and resolve work-related disputes, the director was bound by central management's specification of curriculum, wages and benefits. In reviewing the Board's unit determination, we acknowledged the high "degree of the Employer's control of personnel policies and the extent of integration of the Massachusetts centers." *Id.* at 212. Yet, we felt that these factors were insufficient to overcome the presumptive appropriateness of the single center unit. As we explained: "It [one center] immediately seems to be *an* appropriate unit because there is apt to be a bond of interest among all the persons employed by the same employer in connection with the same enterprise at the same locus." *Id.* at 213 (emphasis in original).

Friendly alleges three major flaws in the Board's determination that the employees of the Weymouth restaurant constituted an appropriate bargaining unit. First, Friendly alleges that there was not substantial evidence to support the Board's finding that the Store Manager of the Weymouth restaurant possessed autonomy in employee relations matters. This argument is coupled with Friendly's contention that the Board committed an error of law in not affording consideration to the role of the District Manager. Second, Friendly alleges that the Board committed an

---

[4]   The Board's unit determinations in the area of multistore retail operations have fluctuated widely. Throughout the 1950's the Board insisted that a collective bargaining unit "should embrace all employees within the categories sought who perform their work within the Employer's administrative division or [geographic] area." *Safeway Stores, Inc.*, 96 N.L.R.B. 998, 1000 (1951) (footnote omitted). In light of its increasing experience, the Board in 1962 rejected this view, replacing it with a policy which found single store units to be "presumptively appropriate unless it be established that the single plant has been effectively merged into a more comprehensive unit so as to have lost its individual identity." *Frisch's Big Boy Ill-Mar, Inc.*, 147 N.L.R.B. 551, n.1 (1964) (citations omitted), *enforcement denied*, 356 F.2d 895 (7th Cir. 1966). While several Board decisions have found a single store unit to be inappropriate under the circumstances, *see, e.g., Kirlin's Inc.*, 227 N.L.R.B. 1220 (1977); *Gray Drug Stores, Inc.*, 197 N.L.R.B. 924 (1972); *Twenty-First Century Restaurant Corp.*, 192 N.L.R.B. 881 (1971); *Waiakamilo Corp.*, 192 N.L.R.B. 878 (1971), the Board still adheres to its presumption of appropriateness. *See, e.g., Walgreen Co.*, 198 N.L.R.B. 1138 (1972).

error of law in not considering the degree of employee interchange among ninety-nine Friendly restaurants specified by the company. Third, Friendly finds another error of law in the Board's refusal to consider evidence showing the geographic proximity of Friendly restaurants within a circle, centered at the Weymouth store, with a radius of twenty miles. We address the three alleged errors in order.

Autonomy of the Store Manager

The administration of the Friendly chain is a casebook study in centralized control. Like most retail chains, Friendly relies upon uniform policies which regulate practically every aspect of the individual stores' operations. But the company's determination of the most efficient form of organization cannot be ascribed controlling significance in matters of unit determination. Otherwise, "an employer, by centralizing all matters of labor policy, [could] prevent the NLRB from selecting as appropriate a unit of smaller dimensions than the employer's whole enterprise even though that smaller unit was the one which in light of all the relevant factors the NLRB determined would be appropriate under [the Act]." *NLRB v. Living and Learning Centers, Inc.*, 652 F.2d at 215.

In the context of a retail chain operation, one of the most weighty factors in determining the appropriateness of a single store unit is the degree of control vested in the local store manager. Such control does not specifically refer to the local manager's freedom to establish prices, decor or menus—though control of these decisions might be indicative of the level of integration of the employer's business. Rather, the Board considers as significant the local manager's effective control of those areas "which most directly affect the restaurant's employees." Here, the Board reasonably found that the Weymouth Store Manager exercised significant, albeit limited, authority in those matters which most directly affect the Weymouth employees.

Employee Interchange

At the representation hearing which preceded the election, the hearing examiner accepted extensive testimony as to the number and type of employee transfers within the Friendly chain. In its Direction of Election of May 30, 1980, the Board recited the transfer statistics for the Weymouth restaurant during 1978: thirty-four temporary transfers (many of which lasted only for one six-hour shift) and three permanent transfers. Not mentioned by the Board was evidence, introduced by Friendly, that during the same one-year period, there had been 1,329 transfers involving ninety-nine restaurants identified by the employer. Friendly alleges that this failure to mention explicitly the interchange data for the ninety-nine restaurant grouping was an error of law. We disagree.

The Board, in its final decision, was not required to allude to every piece of evidence which the parties had chosen to present. Rather, the

Board had only to consider that evidence in the record which was relevant to the issue before it; *i.e.*, assessing the appropriateness of the Weymouth bargaining unit. Evidence of interchange between the Weymouth restaurant and other restaurants within the chain was germane to this determination, and was considered by the Board. Evidence as to employee interchanges not involving the Weymouth restaurant, however, did not bear directly on the issue of the appropriateness of the Weymouth unit. Such evidence went to the question of whether a ninety-nine restaurant unit was a more appropriate collective bargaining unit—an issue which the Board was not required to address.

Geographic Proximity

Looking at the evidence pertaining to the number of Friendly restaurants within a fifteen-mile circle, the Board could reasonably determine that the geographic proximity of these restaurants did not destroy the community of interest which existed among the Weymouth employees. The Board was not required to look further and analyze the number of restaurants contained within a twenty-mile circle. Friendly has indicated no reason why evidence pertaining to a fifteen-mile circle is insufficient as a matter of law, whereas evidence pertaining to a twenty-mile circle would suffice. Without specifying the smallest geographic area which the Board must consider in making its assessment of geographic proximity, we find that the Board committed no error of law in failing to consider that area beyond a fifteen-mile circle.

In sum, the Board's determination that the employees at the Weymouth restaurant constituted an appropriate bargaining unit was within its discretion and supported by substantial evidence in the record.

NOTES

1.   As discussed in the principal case, the NLRB presumes that a single-location bargaining unit is appropriate and places the burden on the party, typically the employer, seeking a multi-location unit to show otherwise. On which facts did Friendly Ice Cream rely in its attempt to meet its burden? Why was its showing insufficient?

2.   Although the NLRB applies its single location presumption to most industries, it presumes that a system-wide unit is the only appropriate unit for public utilities. The Board reasons that "the public utility industry is characterized by a high degree of interdependence of its various segments and that the public has an immediate and direct interest in the uninterrupted maintenance of the essential services that the public utility industry alone can adequately provide." *Baltimore Gas & Elec. Co.*, 206 N.L.R.B. 199, 201 (1973).

3.   Alyeska Pipeline Service Co., a consortium of several oil companies, operates the Trans Alaska Pipeline, which transports oil from the North Slope of Alaska to the Valdez Marine Terminal (VMT) where it is loaded onto ships.

Along the way, some of the oil is diverted to three refineries which refine it into petroleum products, such as gasoline, diesel fuel, jet fuel, and heating oil, which are distributed locally. Alyeska employs 163 technicians at the VMT and another 165 at seven pumping stations along the 800 miles of pipeline. The pumping station technicians are flown by the company to the remote station locations for their workweeks, where they reside in company provided housing and eat in company provided dining facilities. The VMT technicians reside in the Valdez area and are responsible for their own housing, food and transportation. A union has filed a representation petition in a unit limited to the VMT technicians. Is such a unit appropriate? *See Alyeska Pipeline Service Co.*, 348 N.L.R.B. 779 (2006) (holding 2–1 that only a system-wide unit was appropriate).

4.   The NLRB's single location presumption is relatively anomalous in United States labor law. The Railway Labor Act does not use the term "bargaining unit," but instead speaks of representation in a "craft or class." Under the RLA, bargaining units are established on a system-wide basis. RLA § 2, Fourth; *see American Airlines*, 19 N.M.B. 113, 126 (1991). In the public sector, most states reject the NLRB's approach of selecting an appropriate bargaining unit and, instead, limit representation to the most appropriate unit. This is often the largest appropriate unit. *See* Andrea S. Knapp, *Anatomy of a Public Sector Bargaining Unit*, 35 Case W. Reserve L. Rev. 395 (1985).

* * *

In *Specialty HealthCare & Rehabilitation Ctr. of Mobile*, 357 N.L.R.B. 934 (2011), *enf'd sub nom. Kindred Nursing Ctrs. E., LLC v. NLRB*, 727 F.3d 552 (6th Cir. 2013), the NLRB purported to clarify its approach to determining appropriate bargaining units. In the context of determining whether certified nursing assistants formed an appropriate bargaining unit in a skilled nursing home, the Board declared:

> When the proposed unit describes employees readily identifiable as a group and when consideration of the traditional factors demonstrates that the employees share a community of interest, both the Board and courts of appeals have necessarily required a heightened showing to demonstrate that the proposed unit is nevertheless inappropriate because it does not include additional employees. Although different words have been used to describe this heightened showing, in essence, a showing that the included and excluded employees share an overwhelming community of interest has been required.

Id. The Board thus adopted a two-prong approach in evaluating the bargaining unit specified in a union's representation petition. First, the Board would ask whether the employees in the proposed unit share a readily identifiable community of interests. If they did, the Board would then ask whether the party seeking a larger unit has met its burden to establish that the additional employees share an overwhelming community of interests with the employees in the petitioned-for unit. However, in 2017, the Board overruled its decision in *Specialty Healthcare* in the following case.

PCC STRUCTURALS, INC.
365 N.L.R.B. No. 160 (2017)

CHAIRMAN MISCIMARRA and MEMBERS PEARCE, MCFERRAN, KAPLAN, EMANUEL:

Today, we clarify the correct standard for determining whether a proposed bargaining unit constitutes an appropriate unit for collective bargaining when the employer contends that the smallest appropriate unit must include additional employees. In so doing, and for the reasons explained below, we overrule the Board's decision in *Specialty Healthcare & Rehabilitation Center of Mobile*, 357 NLRB 934 (2011) (*Specialty Healthcare*), enfd. sub nom. *Kindred Nursing Centers East, LLC v. NLRB*, 727 F.3d 552 (6th Cir. 2013), and we reinstate the traditional community-of interest standard as articulated in, e.g., *United Operations, Inc.*, 338 NLRB 123 (2002).[3]

Background

The Employer manufactures steel, superalloy, and titanium castings for use in jet aircraft engines, airframes, industrial gas turbine engines, medical prosthetic devices, and other industry markets. The Employer's operation in the Portland, Oregon area consists of three "profit and loss centers" located within approximately a 5-mile radius of one another. Petitioner and Employer agree that these three centers comprise the entire Portland operation. As described by the Regional Director, the manufacturing process is the same at all three facilities. That process involves two stages. The first or "front end" stage involves creation of the casting. In this stage, production employees create a wax mold of the customer's product, "invest" the mold by alternately dipping it into a slurry and into sand until a hard ceramic shell is formed around the wax, and then melt the wax away to leave the empty ceramic shell, into which liquid metal is poured to create the casting. The second stage (sometimes referred to as "back end") involves inspecting and reworking the casting. The employees in the petitioned-for unit are welders who work in the "back end" stage of the production process, primarily repairing defects in the metal castings. The exception is the one rework specialist/crucible repair employee, who appears to work in the "front end" or casting portion of the manufacturing process. To determine the appropriateness of the

---

[3]   Additionally, for the reasons stated by former Member Hayes in his dissenting opinion in *Specialty Healthcare*, we reinstate the standard established in *Park Manor Care Center*, 305 NLRB 872 (1991), for determining appropriate bargaining units in nonacute healthcare facilities. See *Specialty Healthcare*, 357 NLRB at 948–950 (Member Hayes, dissenting).

petitioned-for unit, the Regional Director applied the standard set forth in *Specialty Healthcare*. As a Board majority explained its standard in that decision, when a union seeks to represent a unit of employees "who are readily identifiable as a group (based on job classifications, departments, functions, work locations, skills, or similar factors), and the Board finds that the employees in the group share a community of interest after considering the traditional criteria, the Board will find the petitioned-for unit to be an appropriate unit" for bargaining. *Specialty Healthcare*, 357 N.L.R.B. at 945–946. If the petitioned-for unit is deemed appropriate, the burden shifts to the proponent of a larger unit (typically the employer) to demonstrate that the additional employees the proponent seeks to include "share 'an overwhelming community of interest' " with the petitioned-for employees, "such that there 'is no legitimate basis upon which to exclude certain employees from' " the petitioned-for unit because the traditional community-of-interest factors " 'overlap almost completely." *Id.* at 944 (quoting *Blue Man Vegas, LLC v. NLRB*, 529 F.3d 417, 422 (D.C. Cir. 2008)).

Applying the foregoing standard, the Regional Director first concluded that the employees in the petitioned-for unit are readily identifiable as a group on the basis that the employees in the proposed unit are welders in related job classifications who repair manufacturing defects in metal castings.

The Regional Director further concluded that the petitioned-for rework welders and rework specialists share a community of interest amongst themselves under the traditional criteria. In this regard, however, he found that two factors weigh against a community-of-interest finding. First, the unit sought by the Petitioner does not conform to an administrative grouping or department within the Employer's organizational structure, and the employees in the proposed unit are scattered throughout numerous departments in the Portland operation. Second, the petitioned-for employees do not share common supervision. Rather, employees with a variety of job titles report to each production supervisor, and no production supervisor oversees only the petitioned-for employees. Thus, rework welders and rework specialists testified that their immediate supervisors "also supervise rework grinders, visual dimensional inspectors, x-ray shooters and readers, and florescent penetrant inspectors."

Notwithstanding these two factors adverse to the proposed unit, the Regional Director found that a number of factors favor a finding that the petitioned-for employees share a community of interest with one another, including shared skills, training, certification requirements, and in-house training requirements. He also found that the petitioned-for rework welders and rework specialists are functionally integrated amongst themselves because they all perform the same work: repairing defects in metal castings. As for employee contact, the Regional Director found that rework welders and rework specialists work either in open-air chambers or in booths, and the booths are adjacent to one another. While evidence of temporary interchange with employees outside the proposed unit was inconclusive, and such interchange appears minimal, the Regional Director found permanent interchange within the petitioned-for unit in that all rework specialists were previously rework welders. The Regional Director also based his community-of-interest finding on evidence that the petitioned-for employees share many of the same terms and conditions of employment, even though all production employees share the same terms and conditions. Thus, all production employees, including the petitioned-for employees, work similar hours, are paid on the same wage scale, receive the same benefits, are subject to the same employee handbook and work rules, wear similar attire and protective gear (steel-toed shoes, safety glasses and hearing protection), work under the same safety requirements, and participate in ongoing training regarding harassment, safety, and other matters.

Turning to the second step of the *Specialty Healthcare* analysis, the Regional Director rejected the Employer's contention that the rest of the production and maintenance employees share an "overwhelming community of interest" with the petitioned-for employees and must therefore be included in the unit. He acknowledged that functional integration weighs in favor of finding an overwhelming community of interest between the petitioned-for employees and the rest of the production employees: rework welders and rework specialists function as part of an integrated production process, repairing defects identified by other employees and working in "rework teams" that include employees in other job classifications. He also recognized that the petitioned-for unit does not track departmental lines and the employees therein are not separately supervised. But he concluded that the Employer did not carry its burden to establish that the smallest appropriate unit is a wall-to-wall production and maintenance unit. In this regard, he determined that shared terms and conditions of employment constituted a neutral factor: on one hand, all of the Employer's production and maintenance employees are subject to the same policies and rules, work similar hours, are paid under the same wage structure, receive the same benefits, and wear the same attire and protective equipment; on the other hand, the welders are paid at the high end of the pay scale, and they use distinctive welding and metalwork equipment. Further, the Regional Director found that the welders' distinct qualifications and training, their performance of distinct job duties, their limited contact with other employees, and the lack of significant interchange across proposed-unit lines all weigh against a finding that the petitioned-for employees share an overwhelming community of interest with the remainder of the production and maintenance employees.

In its request for review, the Employer contends that *Specialty Healthcare* was wrongly decided. Alternatively, the Employer argues that even under the *Specialty Healthcare* standard, the petitioned-for employees are not a readily identifiable group, and they share an overwhelming community of interest with the remainder of the production and maintenance employees. In arguing that the Board should overrule *Specialty Healthcare,* the Employer contends that in *Specialty Healthcare,* the Board effectively abdicated its duty to determine an appropriate unit on a case-by-case basis as required by Section 9(b) of the Act; that it gave controlling weight to the extent of union organizing in making unit determinations; that the *Specialty Healthcare* standard results in the proliferation of fractured bargaining units because it ignores the importance of shared interests among petitioned-for and excluded employees; and that it does not adequately consider the Section 7 rights of excluded employees.

Discussion

B.   The Board's Traditional Community-of-Interest Test is
an Appropriate Framework for Unit Determinations

[T]he Board traditionally has determined, in each case in which unit appropriateness is questioned, whether the employees in a petitioned-for group share a community of interest sufficiently distinct from the interests of employees excluded from the petitioned-for group to warrant a finding that the proposed group constitutes a separate appropriate unit. Throughout nearly all of its history, when making this determination, the Board applied a multi-factor test that requires the Board to assess

> whether the employees are organized into a separate department; have distinct skills and training; have distinct job functions and perform distinct work, including inquiry into the amount and type of job overlap between classifications; are functionally integrated with the Employer's other employees; have frequent contact with other employees; interchange with other employees; have distinct terms and conditions of employment; and are separately supervised.

United Operations, Inc., 338 N.L.R.B. 123, 123 (2002). Thus, in *Wheeling Island Gaming,* 355 N.L.R.B. 642 (2010), where the Board applied its traditional community-of-interest test, the Board indicated that it never addresses, solely and in isolation, the question whether the employees in the unit sought have interests in common with one another. Numerous groups of employees fairly can be said to possess employment conditions or interests "in common." Our inquiry—though perhaps not articulated in every case—necessarily proceeds to a further determination whether the interests of the group sought are *sufficiently distinct* from those of other employees to warrant the establishment of a separate unit.

The required assessment of whether the sought-after employees' interests are sufficiently distinct from those of employees excluded from the petitioned-for group provides some assurance that extent of organizing will not be determinative, consistent with Section 9(c)(5); it ensures that bargaining units will not be arbitrary, irrational, or "fractured"—that is, composed of a gerrymandered grouping of employees whose interests are insufficiently distinct from those of other employees to constitute that grouping a separate appropriate unit; and it ensures that the Section 7 rights of excluded employees who share a substantial (but less than "overwhelming") community of interests with the sought-after group are taken into consideration.

C.   The Specialty Healthcare Standard Improperly Detracts
from the Board's Statutory Responsibility to Make
Appropriate Bargaining Unit Determinations

The Board majority in *Specialty Healthcare* described its decision as a mere clarification of preexisting standards for determining appropriate bargaining units. However, we believe the majority in *Specialty Healthcare* substantially *changed* the applicable standards. Indeed, the Board majority itself in *Specialty Healthcare* referred to the decision as implementing "changes in the law." In any event, it is not essential to our decision today to determine whether *Specialty Healthcare* changed or merely clarified then-existing standards. Regardless of how they are characterized, the Board majority in *Specialty Healthcare* did three things that have affected the Board's bargaining-unit determinations since *Specialty Healthcare* was decided. First, in *Specialty Healthcare*, the majority overruled *Park Manor Care Center*, *supra*, which set forth the standard for determining appropriate bargaining units in non-acute healthcare facilities.

Second, the majority in *Specialty Healthcare* established that the "traditional community-of-interest approach" would thereafter apply to unit determinations in such facilities rather than the so-called "pragmatic" test described in *Park Manor*. 357 NLRB at 937–941. Third and most significantly, although the majority in *Specialty Healthcare* nominally was considering unit questions specific to non-acute healthcare facilities, the *Specialty Healthcare* decision applied to *all* workplaces (except acute care hospitals) whenever a party argues that a petitioned-for unit improperly excludes certain employees. Although the majority purported to apply the traditional community-of-interests standard as exemplified in *Wheeling Island Gaming*, 357 NLRB at 944–946, the *Specialty Healthcare* standard discounts—or eliminates altogether—any assessment of whether shared interests among employees *within* the petitioned-for unit are sufficiently distinct from the interests of *excluded* employees to warrant a finding that the smaller petitioned-for unit is appropriate. This aspect of *Specialty Healthcare* is obvious from the majority test itself, under which, if the petitioned-for employees are deemed readily identifiable as a group and share a community of interests among themselves, this inward-looking inquiry is controlling, *regardless* of the interests of excluded employees, except for the rare instance where it can be proven that the excluded employees share an "overwhelming" community of interests with employees in the petitioned-for unit. As noted previously, we believe this aspect of *Specialty Healthcare* undermines fulfillment of the Board's responsibility to "assure" to employees "in each case" their "fullest freedom" in the exercise of Section 7 rights, as stated in Section 9(b) of the Act. Moreover, by extinguishing scrutiny of the interests that excluded employees have in common with those in the petitioned-for unit except in the rare case where the employer can satisfy its burden of proving that excluded employees share an "overwhelming" community of interests with employees in the proposed unit, *Specialty Healthcare* created a regime under which the petitioned-for unit is controlling in all but narrow and highly unusual circumstances.

In these respects, *Specialty Healthcare* detracts from what Congress contemplated when it added mandatory language to Section 9(b) directing the Board to determine the appropriate bargaining unit "in each case" and mandating that the Board's unit determinations guarantee to employees the "fullest freedom" in exercising their Section 7 rights. Most importantly, the enumeration of potential unit configurations in Section 9(b) demonstrates, inescapably, that Congress intended that the Board "in each case" would carefully consider the interests of *all* employees. This is evident from the fact that the types of bargaining units mentioned in Section 9(b), to be evaluated by the Board in each case, include "the *employer unit*, craft unit, plant unit, *or subdivision thereof.*" In contrast with this language, *Specialty Healthcare* gives all-but-conclusive deference to every petitioned-for "subdivision" unit, without attaching *any* weight to the interests of excluded employees in potential "employer," "craft," "plant," or alternative "subdivision" units, unless the employer proves the existence of "overwhelming" interests shared between petitioned-for employees and those outside the petitioned-for "subdivision." The discrepancy between what Section 9(b) requires, on the one hand, and what *Specialty Healthcare* precludes, on the other, is reinforced by Section 9(c)(5), added to the Act in 1947, where Congress expressly states that "[i]n determining whether a unit is appropriate . . . the extent to which the employees have organized shall not be controlling." We believe *Specialty Healthcare* effectively makes the extent of union organizing "controlling," or at the very least gives far greater weight to that factor than statutory policy warrants, because under the *Specialty Healthcare* standard, the petitioned-for unit is deemed appropriate in all but rare cases. Section 9(b) and 9(c)(5), considered together, leave no doubt that Congress expected *the Board* to give careful consideration to the interests of all employees when making unit determinations, and Congress did not intend that the Board would summarily reject arguments, in all but the most unusual circumstances, that the petitioned-for unit fails to appropriately accommodate the Section 7 interests of employees outside the "subdivision" specified in the election petition.

Having reviewed the *Specialty Healthcare* decision in light of the Act's policies and the Board's subsequent applications of the "overwhelming community of interest" standard, we conclude that the standard adopted in *Specialty Healthcare* is fundamentally flawed. We find there are sound policy reasons for returning to the traditional community-of-interest standard that the Board has applied throughout most of its history, which permits the Board to evaluate the interests of all employees—both those within and those outside the petitioned-for unit—without regard to whether these groups share an "overwhelming" community of interests. In making this finding, we especially rely on the following considerations.

First, we agree with the view expressed by Chairman (then-Member) Miscimarra in his dissent in *Macy's, Inc.*, that *Specialty Healthcare* constituted an unwarranted departure from the standards that have long governed the Board's appropriate-bargaining-unit determinations. Despite reciting the traditional test and claiming that it was merely clarifying that test, the majority in *Specialty Healthcare* clearly held that "[w]hen the petitioned-for unit contains employees readily identified as a group who share a community of interest" *among themselves*, an employer opposing this unit as inappropriate because it excludes certain employees bears the next-to-impossible burden of proving that "employees inside and outside [the] proposed unit share an overwhelming community of interest." It is *the Board's* responsibility to determine unit appropriateness based on a careful examination of the community of interests of employees both within *and* outside the proposed unit. The Board reaffirmed this approach in *Wheeling Island Gaming*, in which it recognized that the Board's task is to examine "whether the interests of the group sought are *sufficiently distinct* from those of other [excluded] employees to warrant establishment of a separate unit." ... We reject as implausible the *Specialty Healthcare* majority's statement that they were merely restating and clarifying the Board's traditional test. Yet, as indicated above, we need not conclusively determine whether *Specialty Healthcare* changed or merely clarified the Board's traditional community-of-interest standard governing appropriate-unit determinations. We merely hold that when it is asserted that the smallest appropriate unit must include employees excluded from the petitioned-for unit, the Board will no longer be constrained by the extraordinary deference that *Specialty Healthcare* affords to the petitioned-for unit. Rather, applying the Board's traditional community-of-interest factors, the Board will determine whether the petitioned-for employees share a community of interest sufficiently distinct from employees excluded from the proposed unit to warrant a separate appropriate unit; and the Board may find that the exclusion of certain employees renders the petitioned-for unit inappropriate even when excluded employees do not share an "overwhelming" community of interest with employees in the petitioned-for unit.

Second, although the Board in *Specialty Healthcare* stated that its decision was "not intended to disturb" rules developed by the Board regarding particular industries, subsequent decisions have demonstrated that petitioned-for units are deemed controlling under *Specialty Healthcare* even when a broader unit is clearly compelled by industry standards. Thus, in *Macy's*, supra, a Board majority, over then-Member Miscimarra's dissent, found appropriate a unit limited to employees in the store's cosmetics and fragrances department—one of 11 sales departments in Macy's Saugus, Massachusetts store—notwithstanding the Board's longstanding rule that favors storewide units in the retail industry. In *DPI Secuprint*, 362 NLRB No. 172 (2015), the Board majority, over then-Member Johnson's dissent, found appropriate a unit consisting of prepress, digital press, offset bindery, digital bindery, and shipping and receiving employees—excluding the press operators and feeder-tenders at the heart of the employer's functionally integrated production process—even though the smaller unit contravened the Board's "traditional" rule that press and prepress employees should ordinarily be included in the same "lithographic unit." As this history shows, the *Specialty Healthcare* "overwhelming community of interest" standard has effectively superseded the Board's traditional industry-specific rules governing appropriate unit determinations, despite the *Specialty Healthcare* majority's claim to the contrary.

Third, we find that Sections 9(b) and 9(c)(5), considered together, strongly favor applying the traditional community-of-interest standard when making bargaining unit determinations, without giving the petitioned-for unit an artificial supremacy that substantially limits the Board's discretion when discharging its statutory duty to determine unit appropriateness. In short, the Board's role "in each case" should be to undertake a broader and more refined analysis, and to play a more active role, when determining whether or not a proposed unit is "appropriate" than is allowed under the *Specialty Healthcare* standard.

Fourth, applying the historical community-of-interest standard rather than the "overwhelming" community-of-interest requirement will ensure that the Board does not unduly limit its focus to the Section 7 rights of employees in the petitioned-for unit, while disregarding or discounting the Section 7 rights of excluded employees except in the rare case when excluded employees share "overwhelming" interests (i.e., interests that "overlap almost completely") with petitioned-for employees. All statutory employees have Section 7 rights, including employees that have been excluded from the petitioned-for unit. And the two core principles at the heart of Section 9(a)—the principles of exclusive representation and majority rule—require bargaining-unit determinations that protect the Section 7 rights of all employees. Henceforth, the Board's determination of unit appropriateness will consider the Section 7 rights of employees *excluded* from the proposed unit *and* those included in that unit, regardless of whether there are "overwhelming" interests between the two groups. We believe this corrects the imbalance created by *Specialty Healthcare*, which makes "the relationship between petitioned-for unit employees and excluded coworkers irrelevant in all but the most exceptional circumstances." Even if *Specialty Healthcare* permits the Board to consider the interests of employees excluded from the petitioned-for unit, we believe the overwhelming community-of-interest standard unduly limits the Board's discretion when evaluating unit appropriateness, and nothing in the Act imposes such a requirement on the Board. Thus, we find that considering the interests of excluded employees along with those in the petitioned-for unit, without the "overwhelming" community-of-interest requirement, better effectuates the policies and purposes of the Act, which requires the Board to "assure to employees the fullest freedom in exercising the rights guaranteed by [the] Act." . . .

Finally, although the Board overrules *Specialty Healthcare* and will no longer apply the "overwhelming community of interests" standard when determining whether an appropriate bargaining unit must include employees excluded from the petitioned-for unit, the Board retains the discretion—after engaging in an appropriate review of employee community of interests—to *approve* the unit described in the petition, provided that the unit's appropriateness is supported by the record and that the petitioned-for unit will help to assure employees their fullest freedom in exercising rights protected by the Act. Nothing in today's decision disfavors the unit configuration sought by a petitioner or described in a representation petition filed with the Board. Rather, we merely require that the Board undertake an examination of unit appropriateness " 'in each case' in which a dispute arises" over that issue, taking into consideration the interests of employees both within and outside the petitioned-for unit, in light of the policies and purposes of the Act.

E.   Response to the Dissent

Most of our dissenting colleagues' objections have been effectively addressed above. However, some of their contentions warrant the following observations.

[O]ur dissenting colleagues greatly exaggerate today's ruling by asserting that abandoning *Specialty Healthcare* represents a "radical new approach," nor are they correct that the Board is departing from the principle that a proposed unit need only be *an* appropriate unit and need not be *the most* appropriate unit. As stated previously, nothing in today's decision provides for the Board to reject an appropriate petitioned-for bargaining unit on the basis that a larger unit is *more* appropriate. Our decision merely underscores that the Act requires the Board "in each case" to decide *whether* the petitioned-for unit is appropriate. When evaluating unit appropriateness, as the Act requires, the Board will consider different unit configurations identified in the statute (i.e., "the employer unit, craft unit, plant unit, or subdivision thereof"), and nothing in today's decision precludes the possibility that, in a given case, multiple potential bargaining units may be appropriate. We merely hold that, when a petitioned-for unit excludes certain employees, the Board will consider the possibility that excluded employees must be part of an appropriate unit, without regard to whether or not an "overwhelming" community of interests exists between the petitioned-for employees and those excluded from the unit.

MEMBERS PEARCE and MCFERRAN, dissenting:

It is a foundational principle of United States labor law that, when workers are seeking to organize and select a collective-bargaining representative, and have petitioned the Board to direct an election to that end, the role of the Board in overseeing this process should be conducted with the paramount goal of ensuring that employees have "the fullest freedom in exercising the rights guaranteed by" the Act. Thus, as numerous courts of appeals have acknowledged, the "initiative in selecting an appropriate unit [for bargaining] resides with the employees." *FedEx Freight, Inc. v. NLRB*, 816 F.3d 515, 523 (8th Cir. 2016), quoting *American Hospital Assn. v. NLRB*, 499 U.S. 606, 610 (1991). When workers seeking a representative have selected a bargaining unit in which they seek to organize, the role of the Board in reviewing that selection is to determine whether the selected unit is an appropriate one under the statute not the unit the Board would prefer, or the unit the employer would prefer. Part of ensuring workers the "fullest freedom" in exercising their right to organize is acknowledging that they can, and should—within the reasonable boundaries that the statute delineates—be able to associate with the coworkers with whom they determine that they share common goals and interests.

With these principles in mind, this case should present no difficult issues for the Board. The Union has filed a petition to represent a bargaining unit of 102 welders at an advanced manufacturing plant in the Portland, Oregon area. The welders are a group of highly-skilled, highly-paid employees performing a distinct function. These workers have gone through specialized training and certifications unique to their positions. They do not significantly interchange with other employees, but instead perform distinct work that no other employees are qualified to do. They are readily identifiable as a group and represent two clearly delineated job classifications within the Employer's organizational structure. The 102 workers in this unit would constitute a significantly larger-than-average bargaining unit when compared to other recently certified units.

Despite these largely uncontested facts, the Employer objected to the proposed unit, claiming that the *only* appropriate unit in which these workers should be able to choose a representative would have to include all 2,565 employees who work in production and maintenance at the petitioned-for facilities. The Regional Director correctly rejected the Employer's contention, and directed an election among the welders. The workers voted 54 to 38 for the Union, and the Employer sought review of the Regional Director's decision with the Board.

The Regional Director's decision was unquestionably correct—these 102 workers clearly share a community of interest under any standard ever applied by the Board. Nonetheless, the majority nullifies the Direction of Election for the unit of welders and orders the Regional Director to reconsider, under more favorable terms, the Employer's argument that welders should not be able to bargain collectively unless they can win sufficient support from all 2565 production and maintenance employees. Instead of performing its statutory duty to affirm these workers' choice to organize in an appropriate unit and allowing them to commence the collective-bargaining process with their employer, the Board's newly-constituted majority seizes on this otherwise straightforward case as a jumping off point to overturn a standard that has been upheld by every one of the eight federal appellate courts to consider it. The newly-constituted Board majority makes sweeping and unwarranted changes to the Board's approach in assessing the appropriateness of bargaining units when an employer asserts that the unit sought by the petitioning union must include additional employees. Without notice, full briefing, and public participation, and in a case involving a manifestly appropriate unit, the majority overturns *Specialty Healthcare & Rehabilitation Center of Mobile*, 357 NLRB 934 (2011). In its place, the majority adopts an arbitrary new approach that will frustrate the National Labor Relations Act's policies of ensuring that employees enjoy "the fullest freedom in exercising" their right to self-organization and of expeditiously resolving questions of representation. The majority's new approach will bog down the Board and the parties in an administrative quagmire—a result that the majority apparently intends.

The majority's rejection of the *Specialty Healthcare* framework reflects a failure to engage in the sort of reasoned decision-making demanded of the Board and other administrative agencies. First, the majority follows a flawed process. It seizes on a case that does not fairly present the issues that the majority decides—including, most obviously, the resurrection of a standard once applied only in non-acute healthcare facilities (a far cry from the workplace involved here). And, in a sharp break with established practice, the majority completely excludes the public from participating in this case involving the reversal of significant Board precedent.

Second, in discarding the Board's judicially-approved approach, the majority relies on arguments that have been specifically rejected by the federal courts—including the remarkable assertion that the *Specialty Healthcare* framework is contrary to the National Labor Relations Act. The majority mistakenly insists that the Board cannot retain *Specialty Healthcare* and then adopts a new standard that is inferior to *Specialty Healthcare* in every important respect, including consistency with the statute.

As reflected by its favorable reception in the federal courts, the *Specialty Healthcare* framework—itself based on an earlier decision of the U.S. Court of Appeals for the District of Columbia Circuit—represented a major improvement to the Board's approach in this area. It brought greater clarity and predictability to unit determinations, while vindicating the goals of federal labor law. There is simply no justifiable reason—certainly not a change in the Board's membership alone—to reverse course and abandon a doctrine that has been so widely accepted and praised. . . .

NOTES

1.   On remand in *PCC Structurals,* a Board ALJ found that the original unit of welders petitioned-for by the union was appropriate under the traditional community of interest test required by the Board in *PCC Structurals. See PCC Structurals, Inc. II,* Case No. 19-RC-202188 (May 4, 2018) (supplemental decision) ("I find that the record establishes that the petitioned-for welders constitute a craft unit that shares a community of interest sufficiently distinct from excluded employees under the standard set forth in *PCC Structurals.*").

2.   *A separate rule for security guards.* Under § 9(b)(3), the Board cannot certify a union as the representative of a bargaining unit containing security guards "if such organization admits to membership, or is affiliated directly or indirectly with an organization which admits to membership employees other than guards." In addition, the Board cannot certify a bargaining unit that contains both guards and nonguards. The purpose of § 9(b)(3) was to ensure that during strikes or labor unrest the employer "would have a core of plant-protection employees who would enforce the employer's rules for the protection of his property and persons thereon without being confronted with a division of loyalty between the employer and dissatisfied fellow union members." *McDonnell Aircraft Corp.,* 109 N.L.R.B. 967 (1954). The § 9(b)(3) prohibition on mixed guard and nonguard units and unions applies only to the Board's certification processes. As with professional employees, an employer and union may voluntarily establish a mixed unit.

A major contemporary organizing campaign by the SEIU involves organizing security guards in commercial office buildings where the SEIU represents janitorial employees. Security guards, like janitors, generally work for subcontractors, not directly for the building owner or property manager. Like janitors, they are often poorly paid and have no benefits and little job security. The job of security guard in commercial office buildings was, for a few decades before now, a labor market niche that tended to be occupied by African-American male employees. Recently, an increasing number of security guards are Latinas or other recent immigrants.

What are the reasons for the SEIU's security guards campaign? Why might building owners or property managers, or the companies that contract with them to provide security guards, be interested in the question whether the guards join a union in general, or the SEIU in particular? Why might security guards prefer to join the union that represents other employees in a commercial office building rather than another union? In assessing the desirability or legality of security guards in non-guard unions, how should the possibility of conflicting loyalties during a strike be weighed against the other concerns shared by janitorial and security staff in a building?

3.   *Multi-employer bargaining units.* It is often advantageous for multiple employers to group together for purposes of collective bargaining. Such action conserves resources for all parties, as the union need negotiate only a single collective bargaining agreement and the employers are able to pool their resources for negotiation. Such action also ensures that all employers will be governed by the same wages and working conditions, eliminating the possibility that one competitor will secure a labor cost advantage over the others. For multi-employer bargaining to occur, the union and all employers involved must consent. Once negotiations have begun, however, a party may withdraw from the arrangement only with the agreement of all other parties or by showing special circumstances. In *Charles D. Bonanno Linen Service v. NLRB,* 454 U.S. 404 (1982), the Supreme Court agreed with the NLRB that a bargaining impasse was not a special circumstance justifying withdrawal from a multi-employer unit.

2.   REPRESENTATION ELECTIONS

The National Labor Relations Board's certification process begins when a union (or group of employees) or an employer files an election petition with a Regional Office of the NLRB.[2] The Regional Office immediately investigates to determine whether there is a legitimate "question concerning representation" ("QCR"). There is a QCR if no barriers, either procedural or substantive, exist for the conduct of an election. The following are the typical barriers addressed by the Regional Office.

Substantial Showing of Interest: The Regional Office first determines whether there is a "substantial" showing of interest among employees to

---

[2]   In 1961, the NLRB, pursuant to the 1959 amendments to the NLRA, delegated much of its power in election cases to NLRB Regional Directors. The Board's review of RD [decertification] election decisions is discretionary and limited.

invoke the NLRB's election resources. Accordingly, a union or employee-filed petition (RC petition) must be accompanied by a showing of proof (typically by authorization or union membership cards) that at least 30% of employees in an appropriate unit support the representative named in the petition. Another union may intervene so long as it can show support of at least 10% of employees in roughly the same unit. An employer petition (RM petition) need not be accompanied by any showing of employee support, but can only be filed after a demand for recognition by a union or group of employees.

Jurisdiction: After determining sufficient interest, the Regional Office determines whether the Board has jurisdiction over the employer named in the petition. The employer may be within the jurisdiction of the National Mediation Board if it is sufficiently aligned with an airline or railroad employer. Or, if the employer is agricultural, there may be no federal labor jurisdiction at all. The more common jurisdictional issues involve small employers. Although the Board's jurisdiction is co-extensive with the Commerce Clause, the Board has self-imposed limits on jurisdiction (to preserve resources). As discussed *infra* ch. 3, *supra* p. 302, the most general of these concern the Board's inflow and outflow requirements requiring that businesses either buy or sell sufficient dollar amounts across state lines to trigger NLRB concern.

Appropriate Bargaining Unit: As explained above, a bargaining unit is a group of employees who come together for the purpose of unionizing and then collectively bargaining with an employer. The NLRA requires the NLRB in Section 9 to ensure that in each case the bargaining unit sought is one that is appropriate for bargaining purposes.

Bars to Election: To avoid the problem of constant union elections in any given workplace, the NLRA and the NLRB, through interpretation of the statute and its own power of adjudication, have developed various doctrines relating to an appropriate spacing of election activity. These are:

<u>Lawful Voluntary Recognition Bar</u>: As discussed in section 4, the NLRB provides limited election protection for a union that has been voluntarily recognized by an employer. In cases of voluntary recognition, the union will have a "reasonable period of time" to bargain with the employer without fear of a rival union petition. The length of the lawful voluntary recognition bar was expressly left open by the NLRB in *Dana Corp.*, 351 N.L.R.B. 434 (2007), but was addressed by the Board when it reversed *Dana Corp.* in *Lamons Gasket*. There the Board said:

> Drawing on the Board's decision in *Lee Lumber & Building Material Corp.*, 334 NLRB 399 (2001), we define a reasonable period of bargaining, during which the recognition bar will apply, to be no less than 6 months after the parties' first bargaining session and no more than 1 year. In determining whether a

reasonable period has elapsed in a given case, we will apply the multifactor test of *Lee Lumber* and impose the burden of proof on the General Counsel to show that further bargaining should be required.

Id. The *Lee Lumber* test requires the following factors to be considered in extending a "reasonable period" beyond 6 months:

> (1) whether the parties are bargaining for an initial contract; (2) the complexity of the issues being negotiated and of the parties' bargaining processes; (3) the amount of time elapsed since bargaining commenced and the number of bargaining sessions; (4) the amount of progress made in negotiations and how near the parties are to concluding an agreement; and (5) whether the parties are at impasse.

Lee Lumber, 334 N.L.R.B. 399, 402 (2001).

Election Bar: The election bar is statutory. Section 9(c)(3) states that, "[n]o election shall be directed in any bargaining unit . . . within which in the preceding twelve month period, a valid election shall have been held." During the last 60 days prior to expiration of the one-year period of the bar, an election petition may be filed so long as the election itself does not take place within the one year bar period. The election bar applies only to valid elections and therefore does not preclude a Board mandated re-run election.

Certification Bar: The NLRB, to promote stability in collective bargaining relations between unions and employers, requires that a certified union's status must remain unquestioned for one year, absent unusual circumstances. The Supreme Court upheld the NLRB's certification bar rule in *Brooks v. NLRB,* 348 U.S. 96 (1954). Unusual circumstances include a schism within the union or its defunctness and a radical change in the size of the unit over a short period. Moreover, the NLRB has expanded the doctrine to include an extension of majority status beyond one year when the employer's failure to bargain in good faith results in lost bargaining time to the union. *See Mar-Jac Poultry Co.,* 136 N.L.R.B. 785 (1962).

Contract Bar: The NLRB, to promote stability in collective bargaining relations between unions and employers, has required that a current and legitimate collective bargaining agreement ("contract") will bar a certification election. To serve as an effective bar, however, a contract must: (1) be binding on the parties, including being written and properly executed by the parties, (2) be of a definite duration, although a fixed duration agreement will not bar an election for more than 3 years, and (3) contain substantive terms and conditions of employment that are lawful and consistent with the purposes of the NLRA. *See* National Labor Relations Board, Thirty Seventh Annual Report 52 (1972). However, it should be noted that a party seeking an election need not wait the entire 3-year term before filing an election petition with the Board. A petition may be filed not more than 90 nor less than 60 days before the end of the 3-year term (90 to 120 days in the health care industry).

Blocking Charges: The Board will not hold an election in cases where there are substantial pending unfair labor practices affecting the bargaining unit. These are referred to as "blocking charges" because they block the holding of the election. The election will be held once the charges are resolved or if the party that would be affected adversely by the alleged unfair labor practices agrees to go forward with the election even though the charges remain pending.

Voluntary Election Agreement: Once the Board is satisfied that the prerequisites for an election are met, it will seek to go forward with the consent of the parties for an election agreement, which obviates the need for a representation hearing. There are two types of voluntary election agreements: (1) Agreement for consent election: waives the right to a representation hearing at all stages, and gives the Regional Director the authority to resolve all election issues (*e.g.*, challenged ballots, voter eligibility). In addition, this kind of agreement makes it very hard to challenge Regional Director decisions by giving the NLRB only very limited, "arbitrary and capricious," review power. (2) Stipulation for certification upon consent election ("stip"): The "stip" is the most common type of consent election agreement. Under it, the parties waive their right to a pre-election, but not a post-election, representation hearing. Also, the Board, not the Regional Director, makes final decisions on election issues. However, in 2005, the Board introduced a new agreement possibility, one in which the parties leave unit and voter eligibility issues unresolved up front, but agree to have all issues, pre and post-election resolved by the Regional Director, not the Board. *See* 29 C.F.R. § 102.62.

The elements of a voluntary election agreement typically include: the date of election, generally 4 weeks after "informal" election conference (payday is preferred to optimize voter turnout); the place of the election (generally, the employer's premises); the time of the election (based on work schedules; up to 100 employees per hour can vote); the bargaining unit (parties may agree, so long as they avoid conflict with NLRA and established NLRB policy); and voter eligibility (based on specific payroll period).

The Representation Hearing: With no voluntary election agreement, the parties proceed to a representation hearing. The purpose of the representation hearing is to create a full record of pertinent facts to permit the Regional Director and NLRB to rule on disputed issues (e.g., proper inclusion or exclusion of purported supervisors and managerial employees, appropriate bargaining unit, etc.). The structure is set up to be investigative and non-adversarial: witnesses are examined and cross-examined under oath, rules of evidence are not controlling, and the use of stipulations is encouraged (parties, jurisdiction, uncontested job classifications, etc.). The hearing is held before a hearing officer (usually on NLRB attorney or field examiner), and parties may have counsel present. Closing argument or written post-hearing briefs (due in seven days) are allowed.

After the hearing, the hearing officer submits a report summarizing the issues and the evidence. If the Regional Director finds a question concerning representation (QCR), he or she issues a decision and direction of election, with the election to follow within 30 days. If the Regional Director finds no QCR, he or she issues a Decision and Order dismissing the election petition. An appeal of the Regional Director's decision must be filed with the General Counsel within 14 days of service of decision. *See* 29 C.F.R. § 102.67(b). Appeals are granted only for compelling reasons, including: substantial questions of law or policy or departure from established NLRB precedent, clearly erroneous and prejudicial factual determination by Regional Director, prejudicial error in the conduct of the hearing, or compelling reasons to reconsider an important NLRB policy or rule. *See* 29 C.F.R. § 102.67(c)(1)–(4).

If an appeal is granted, there is generally no stay of election, unless the Board so orders. If an appeal request remains pending on election day, ballots that might be affected are segregated, impounded, and remain unopened pending disposition. *See* 29 C.F.R. § 102.67(b). A statement opposing a request for review may be filed by any party, and if a review request is granted, parties may file additional briefs within 14 days of the order granting review. A denial of review amounts to approval of the Regional Director's decision.

Conducting the Election: An NLRB agent oversees the conduct of the election. The parties are entitled to an equal number of observers. Any observer or Board agent may challenge the eligibility of any voter. The ballots of challenged voters are segregated and impounded and are opened only after the challenges are resolved. Voting is in-person by secret ballot but the Regional Director has discretion to direct that a mail ballot be used, typically where employees are scattered over large distances or widely-variable shifts.

When the polls close, the Board agent may seek to resolve ballot challenges through agreement of the observers. The non-challenged votes are tallied. If the remaining challenged ballots could affect the outcome of the election, the challenges are investigated and, if substantial factual issues remain, a hearing is held. If a union received a majority of the votes cast, it is certified as exclusive bargaining representative. If there are more than two choices on the ballot and no choice received a majority, a run-off is held between the top two vote-getters.

Within seven days following the counting of the ballots, any party may file objections to the election. Objections allege that the election outcome was tainted by a breach of laboratory conditions which may but need not constitute an unfair labor practice. The objecting party must submit evidence in support of the objections within seven days of its filing. If the evidence would establish a prima facie case, the Regional Director conducts a hearing on the objections. If objections are sustained, a rerun election is ordered. If objections are overruled, the election results are certified.

Judicial Review: In contrast to unfair labor practice cases, the Supreme Court determined very early on that NLRB decisions in representation cases ("R" cases) are not "final" orders, meaning judicial review is unavailable. *See AFL v. NLRB*, 308 U.S. 401 (1940). As a result, challenges to Board representation decisions are limited and strained. An employer may challenge a Board decision on an issue regarding representation (e.g., bargaining unit determination or jurisdiction) by refusing to bargain with the union and then raising the representation issue in defense of its unfair labor practice. After all, it could hardly be contested that the unfair labor practice can only be found if the union is properly certified. This type of unfair labor practice is known as a "technical" 8(a)(5) and is more or less tolerated since it is one of the only ways for an employer to air its representation grievance in federal court.

There is another, rarely used avenue for review of NLRB representation decisions. In *Leedom v. Kyne*, 358 U.S. 184 (1958), the Supreme Court took up a challenge of a Board decision to bypass an express statutory mandate by refusing to first hold an election among professional employees before proceeding to an election in the broader, mixed unit of professionals and nonprofessionals. *See* § 9(b)(2). The Supreme Court maintained that it was not reviewing the case under the NLRA's provisions, but rather a statutory challenge of the NLRB for overstepping its explicit delegated authority. For more on *Leedom*, see Note, *Leedom v. Kyne and the Implementation of a National Labor Policy*, 1981 Duke L.J. 853.

On December 12, 2014, the NLRB issued its Final Rule on Modernizing Case Representation Procedures ("Final Rule"),. *See NLRB Issues Final Rule to Modernize Representation Case Procedures* (December 12, 2014), www.nlrb.gov/news-outreach/news-story/nlrb-issues-final-rule-modernize-representation-case-procedures. According to the NLRB,

> The National Labor Relations Board has adopted a final rule amending its representation-case procedures to modernize and streamline the process for resolving representation disputes. The

rule will be published in the Federal Register on December 15, and will take effect on April 14, 2015.

Of the final rule, Chairman Pearce said, "I am heartened that the Board has chosen to enact amendments that will modernize the representation case process and fulfill the promise of the National Labor Relations Act. Simplifying and streamlining the process will result in improvements for all parties. With these changes, the Board strives to ensure that its representation process remains a model of fairness and efficiency for all." The final rule was approved by Board Chairman Mark Gaston Pearce and Members Kent Y. Hirozawa and Nancy Schiffer. Board Members Philip A. Miscimarra and Harry I. Johnson III dissented. The rule includes detailed explanations regarding the rule's impact on current procedures and the views of the majority and dissenting members.

Comparison of Old/New Procedures. The following table provides a side-by-side comparison of old and new representation case procedures:

NLRB Comparison of the Old and New Election Procedures	
Old procedures	**New procedures**
Parties cannot electronically file election petitions. Parties and NLRB regional offices do not electronically transmit certain representation case documents.	Election petitions, election notices and voter lists can be transmitted electronically. NLRB regional offices can deliver notices and documents electronically, rather than by mail.
The parties and prospective voters receive limited information.	Parties will receive a more detailed description of the Agency's representation case procedures, as well as a Statement of Position form, when served with the petition. The Statement of Position will help parties identify the issues they may want to raise at the pre-election hearing. A Notice of Petition for Election, which will be served with the Notice of Hearing, will provide employees and the employer with information about the petition and their rights and obligations. The Notice of Election will provide prospective voters with more detailed information about the voting process.
The parties cannot predict when a pre- or post-election hearing will be held because practices vary by Region.	The Regional Director will generally set a pre-election hearing to begin 8 days after a hearing notice is served and a post-election hearing 21 days after the tally of ballots.
There is no mechanism for requiring parties to identify issues in dispute.	Non petitioning parties are required to identify any issues they have with the petition, in their Statements of Positions,

	generally one business day before the pre-election hearing opens. The petitioner will be required to respond to any issue raised by the non-petitioning parties in their Statements of Positions at the beginning of the hearing. Litigation inconsistent with these positions will generally not be allowed.
The employer is not required to share a list of prospective voters with the NLRB's regional office or the other parties until after the regional director directs an election or approves an election agreement.	As part of its Statement of Position, the employer must provide a list of prospective voters with their job classifications, shifts and work locations, to the NLRB's regional office and the other parties, generally one business day before the pre-election hearing opens. This will help the parties narrow the issues in dispute at the hearing or enter into an election agreement.
Parties may insist on litigating voter eligibility and inclusion issues that do not have to be resolved in order to determine whether an election should be held.	The purpose of the pre-election hearing is clearly defined and parties will generally litigate only those issues that are necessary to determine whether it is appropriate to conduct an election. Litigation of a small number of eligibility and inclusion issues that do not have to be decided before the election may be deferred to the post-election stage. Those issues will often be mooted by the election results.
Parties may file a brief within 7 days of the closing of the pre-election hearing, with permissive extensions of 14 days or more.	Parties will be provided with an opportunity to argue orally before the close of the hearing and written briefs will be allowed only if the regional director determines they are necessary.
Parties waive their right to challenge the regional director's pre-election decision if they do not file a request for review before the election. This requires parties to appeal issues that may be rendered moot by the election results.	Parties may wait to see whether the election results have made the need to file a request for review of the regional director's pre-election decision unnecessary and they do not waive their right to seek review of that decision if they decide to file their request after the election.
Elections are delayed 25–30 days to allow the Board to consider any request for review of the regional director's decision that may be filed. This is so even though such requests are rarely filed, even more rarely granted and almost never result in a stay of the election.	There will be no automatic stay of an election.

The Board is required to review every aspect of most post-election disputes, regardless of whether any party has objected to it.	The Board is not required to review aspects of post-election regional decisions as to which no party has raised an issue, and may deny review consistent with the discretion it has long exercised in reviewing pre-election rulings.
The voter list provided to non-employer parties to enable them to communicate with voters about the election includes only names and home addresses. The employer must submit the list within 7 days of the approval of an election agreement or the regional director's decision directing an election.	The voter list will also include personal phone numbers and email addresses (if available to the employer). The employer must submit the list within 2 business days of the regional director's approval of an election agreement or decision directing an election.
(available at: https://www.nlrb.gov/news-outreach/fact-sheets/nlrb-representation-case-procedures-fact-sheet)	

The United States Court of Appeals for the Fifth Circuit upheld the NLRB's new election rules in a comprehensive facial challenge by the Associated Builders and Contractors of Texas (ABC) and the National Federation of Independent Businesses/Texas. *See Associated Builders and Contractors of Texas v. NLRB,* 826 F.3d 215 (5th Cir. 2016). ABC argued that the NLRB improperly made sweeping changes departing from the plain meaning and legislative history of the NLRA, and that the Board exceeded its statutory authority in doing so. In a twenty page opinion, the court analyzed each rule, concluding each time that the Board neither exceeded the scope of its authority nor acted in an arbitrary and capricious manner. The court did emphasize the high burden faced by ABC in such a facial challenge, that ABC to invalidate rules on their face would have to show "that no set of circumstances exists under which the [Rule] would be valid." *Id.* at 220.

3. BARGAINING ORDERS

Although the representation election is the traditional route to recognition, a union may also gain recognition as exclusive bargaining representative through unfair labor practice proceedings. The following cases explore the circumstances under which the NLRB will order an employer to bargain with a union as a remedy in an unfair labor practice case.

NLRB v. GISSEL PACKING CO.

395 U.S. 575 (1969)

CHIEF JUSTICE WARREN delivered the opinion of the Court:

These cases involve the extent of an employer's duty under the National Labor Relations Act to recognize a union that bases its claim to representative status solely on the possession of union authorization cards, and the steps an employer may take, particularly with regard to the scope and content of statements he may make, in legitimately resisting such card-based recognition.

[T]he National Labor Relations Board contends that we should approve its interpretation and administration of the duties and obligations imposed by the Act in authorization card cases. The Board argues (1) that unions have never been limited under § 9(c) of either the Wagner Act or the 1947 amendments to certified elections as the sole route to attaining representative status. Unions may, the Board contends, impose a duty to bargain on the employer under § 8(a)(5) by reliance on other evidence of majority employee support, such as authorization cards. The Board contends (2) that the cards themselves, when solicited in accordance with Board standards which adequately insure against union misrepresentation, are sufficiently reliable indicators of employee desires to support a bargaining order against an employer who refuses to recognize a card majority in violation of § 8(a)(5). The Board argues (3) that a bargaining order is the appropriate remedy for the § 8(a)(5) violation, where the employer commits other unfair labor practices that tend to undermine union support and render a fair election improbable.

Relying on these three assertions, the Board asks us to approve its current practice, which is briefly as follows. When confronted by a recognition demand based on possession of cards allegedly signed by a majority of his employees, an employer need not grant recognition immediately, but may, unless he has knowledge independently of the cards that the union has a majority, decline the union's request and insist on an election, either by requesting the union to file an election petition or by filing such a petition himself under § 9(c)(1)(B).

The Union argues here that an employer's right to insist on an election in the absence of unfair labor practices should be more circumscribed, and a union's right to rely on cards correspondingly more expanded, than the Board would have us rule. The Union's contention is that an employer, when confronted with a card-based bargaining demand, can insist on an election only by filing the election petition himself immediately under § 9(c)(1)(B) and not by insisting that the Union file the election petition, whereby the election can be subjected to considerable delay. If the employer does not himself petition for an election, the Union argues, he must recognize the Union regardless of his good or bad faith and regardless of his other unfair labor practices, and should be ordered to bargain if the cards were in fact validly obtained. And if this Court should continue to utilize the good faith doubt rule, the Union contends that at the least we should put the burden on the employer to make an affirmative showing of his reasons for entertaining such doubt.

Because the employers' refusal to bargain in each of these cases was accompanied by independent unfair labor practices which tend to preclude the holding of a fair election, we need not decide whether a bargaining order is ever appropriate in cases where there is no interference with the election processes.

The first issue facing us is whether a union can establish a bargaining obligation by means other than a Board election and whether the validity of alternate routes to majority status, such as cards, was affected by the 1947 Taft-Hartley amendments. The most commonly traveled route for a union to obtain recognition as the exclusive bargaining representative of an unorganized group of employees is through the Board's election and certification procedures under § 9(c) of the Act; it is also, from the Board's point of view, the preferred route. A union is not limited to a Board election, however, for, in addition to § 9, the present Act provides in § 8(a)(5), as did the Wagner Act in § 8(5), that "it shall be an unfair labor practice for an employer . . . to refuse to bargain collectively with the representatives of his employees, subject to the provisions of section 9(a)." Since § 9(a), in both the Wagner Act and the present Act, refers to the representative as the one "designated or selected" by a majority of the employees without specifying precisely how that representative is to be chosen, it was early recognized that an employer had a duty to bargain whenever the union representative presented "convincing evidence of majority support." Almost from the inception of the Act, then, it was recognized that a union did not have to be certified as the winner of a Board election to invoke a bargaining obligation; it could establish majority status by other means under the unfair labor practice provision of § 8(a)(5)—by showing convincing support, for instance, by a union-called strike or strike vote, or, as here, by possession of cards signed by a majority of the employees authorizing the union to represent them for collective bargaining purposes.

An early version of the bill in the House would have amended § 8(5) of the Wagner Act to permit the Board to find a refusal-to-bargain violation only where an employer had failed to bargain with a union "currently recognized by the employer or certified as such [through an election] under section 9." H.R. Rep. 3020 at § 8(a)(5) (1947). The proposed change, which would have eliminated the use of cards, was rejected in Conference (H.R. Conf. Rep. No. 510, at 41 (1947)), however, and we cannot make a similar change in the Act simply because, as the employers assert, Congress did not expressly approve the use of cards in rejecting the House amendment. Nor can we accept the conclusion that the change was wrought when

Congress amended § 9(c) to make election the sole basis for *certification* by eliminating the phrase "any other suitable method to ascertain such representatives," under which the Board had occasionally used cards as a certification basis. A certified union has the benefit of numerous special privileges which are not accorded unions recognized voluntarily or under a bargaining order and which, Congress could determine, should not be dispensed unless a union has survived the crucible of a secret ballot election.

The employers rely finally on the addition to § 9(c) of subparagraph (B), which allows an employer to petition for an election whenever "one or more individuals or labor organizations have presented to him a claim to be recognized as the representative defined in section 9(a)." That provision was not added, as the employers assert, to give them an absolute right to an election at any time; rather, it was intended, as the legislative history indicates, to allow them, after being asked to bargain, to test out their doubts as to a union's majority in a secret election which they would then presumably not cause to be set aside by illegal antiunion activity. We agree with the Board's assertion here that there is no suggestion that Congress intended § 9(c)(1)(B) to relieve any employer of his § 8(a)(5) bargaining obligation where, without good faith, he engaged in unfair labor practices disruptive of the Board's election machinery. And we agree that the policies reflected in § 9(c)(1)(B) fully support the Board's present administration of the Act; for an employer can insist on a secret ballot election, unless, in the words of the Board, he engages "in contemporaneous unfair labor practices likely to destroy the union's majority and seriously impede the election."

In short, we hold that the 1947 amendments did not restrict an employer's duty to bargain under § 8(a)(5) solely to those unions whose representative status is certified after a Board election.

We next consider the question whether authorization cards are such inherently unreliable indicators of employee desires that, whatever the validity of other alternate routes to representative status, the cards themselves may never be used to determine a union's majority and to support an order to bargain. In this context, the employers urge us to take the step the 1947 amendments and their legislative history indicate Congress did not take, namely, to rule out completely the use of cards in the bargaining arena. [T]he employers argue, at the very least we should overrule the *Cumberland Shoe* doctrine and establish stricter controls over the solicitation of the cards by union representatives.[18]

---

[18] In dealing with the reliability of cards, we should re-emphasize what issues we are not confronting. As pointed out above, we are not here faced with a situation where an employer, with "good" or "bad" subjective motivation, has rejected a card-based bargaining request without good reason and has insisted that the Union go to an election while at the same time refraining from committing unfair labor practices that would tend to disturb the "laboratory conditions" of that election. We thus need not decide whether, absent election interference by an employer's unfair labor practices, he may obtain an election only if he petitions for one himself; whether, if he does

The objections to the use of cards boil down to two contentions: (1) that, as contrasted with the election procedure, the cards cannot accurately reflect an employee's wishes, either because an employer has not had a chance to present his views and thus a chance to insure that the employee choice was an informed one, or because the choice was the result of group pressures and not individual decision made in the privacy of a voting booth; and (2) that quite apart from the election comparison, the cards are too often obtained through misrepresentation and coercion which compound the cards' inherent inferiority to the election process. Neither contention is persuasive, and each proves too much. The Board itself has recognized, and continues to do so here, that secret elections are generally the most satisfactory—indeed the preferred—method of ascertaining whether a union has majority support. The acknowledged superiority of the election process, however, does not mean that cards are thereby rendered totally invalid, for where an employer engages in conduct disruptive of the election process, cards may be the most effective—perhaps the only—way of assuring employee choice. As for misrepresentation, in any specific case of alleged irregularity in the solicitation of the cards, the proper course is to apply the Board's customary standards (to be discussed more fully below) and rule that there was no majority if the standards were not satisfied. It does not follow that because there are some instances of irregularity, the cards can never be used; otherwise, an employer could put off his bargaining obligation indefinitely through continuing interference with elections.

That the cards, though admittedly inferior to the election process, can adequately reflect employee sentiment when that process has been impeded, needs no extended discussion, for the employers' contentions cannot withstand close examination. The employers argue that their employees cannot make an informed choice because the card drive will be over before the employer has had a chance to present his side of the unionization issues. Normally, however, the union will inform the employer of its organization drive early in order to subject the employer to the unfair labor practice provisions of the Act; the union must be able to show the employer's awareness of the drive in order to prove that his contemporaneous conduct constituted unfair labor practices on which a bargaining order can be based if the drive is ultimately successful. Thus, in all of the cases here but the Charleston campaign in *Heck's* the employer, whether informed by the union or not, was aware of the union's organizing

---

not, he must bargain with a card majority if the Union chooses not to seek an election; and whether, in the latter situation, he is bound by the Board's ultimate determination of the card results regardless of his earlier good faith doubts, or whether he can still insist on a Union-sought election if he makes an affirmative showing of his positive reasons for believing there is a representation dispute. In short, a union's right to rely on cards as a freely interchangeable substitute for elections where there has been no election interference is not put in issue here; we need only decide whether the cards are reliable enough to support a bargaining order where a fair election probably could not have been held, or where an election that was held was in fact set aside.

drive almost at the outset and began its antiunion campaign at that time; and even in the *Heck's* Charleston case, where the recognition demand came about a week after the solicitation began, the employer was able to deliver a speech before the union obtained a majority. Further, the employers argue that without a secret ballot an employee may, in a card drive, succumb to group pressures or sign simply to get the union "off his back" and then be unable to change his mind as he would be free to do once inside a voting booth. But the same pressures are likely to be equally present in an election, for election cases arise most often with small bargaining units where virtually every voter's sentiments can be carefully and individually canvassed. And no voter, of course, can change his mind after casting a ballot in an election even though he may think better of his choice shortly thereafter.

The employers' second complaint, that the cards are too often obtained through misrepresentation and coercion, must be rejected also in view of the Board's present rules for controlling card solicitation, which we view as adequate to the task where the cards involved state their purpose clearly and unambiguously on their face. We would be closing our eyes to obvious difficulties, of course, if we did not recognize that there have been abuses, primarily arising out of misrepresentations by union organizers as to whether the effect of signing a card was to designate the union to represent the employee for collective bargaining purposes or merely to authorize it to seek an election to determine that issue. And we would be equally blind if we did not recognize that various courts of appeals and commentators have differed significantly as to the effectiveness of the Board's *Cumberland Shoe* doctrine to cure such abuses.

Thus, even where the cards are unambiguous on their face, both the Second Circuit (*NLRB* v. *S. E. Nichols Co.*, 380 F.2d 438 (1967)) and the Fifth Circuit (*Engineers & Fabricators, Inc.* v. *NLRB*, 376 F.2d 482 (1967)) have joined the Fourth Circuit below in rejecting the Board's rule that the cards will be counted unless the solicitor's statements amounted under the circumstances to an assurance that the cards would be used only for an election, or for no other purpose than an election. And even those circuits which have adopted the Board's approach have criticized the Board for tending too often to apply the *Cumberland* rule too mechanically, declining occasionally to uphold the Board's application of its own rule in a given case. Among those which reject the *Cumberland* rule, the Fifth Circuit agrees with the Second Circuit (*see S. E. Nichols Co., supra*), that a card will be vitiated if an employee was left with the impression that he would be able to resolve any lingering doubts and make a final decision in an election, and further requires that the Board probe the subjective intent of each signer, an inquiry expressly avoided by *Cumberland*. Where the cards are ambiguous on their face, the Fifth Circuit, joined by the Eighth Circuit departs still further from the Board rule. And there is a conflict among those courts which otherwise follow the Board as to single-purpose cards (compare *NLRB* v. *Lenz Co.*, 396 F.2d 905, 908 (6th Cir. 1968), with *NLRB* v. *C. J. Glasgow Co.*, 356 F.2d 476, 478 (7th Cir. 1966)).

We need make no decision as to the conflicting approaches used with regard to dual-purpose cards, for in each of the five organization campaigns in the four cases before us the cards used were single-purpose cards, stating clearly and unambiguously on their face that the signer designated the union as his representative. And even the view forcefully voiced by the Fourth Circuit below that unambiguous cards as well present too many opportunities for misrepresentation comes before us somewhat weakened in view of the fact that there were no allegations of irregularities in four of those five campaigns (*Gissel*, the two *Heck's* campaigns, and *Sinclair*). Only in *General Steel* did the employer challenge the cards on the basis of misrepresentations. There, the trial examiner, after hearing testimony from over 100 employees and applying the traditional Board approach, concluded that "all of these employees not only intended, but were fully aware, that they were thereby designating the Union as their representative." Thus, the sole question before us, raised in only one of the four cases here, is whether the *Cumberland Shoe* doctrine is an adequate rule under the Act for assuring employee free choice.

In resolving the conflict among the circuits in favor of approving the Board's *Cumberland* rule, we think it sufficient to point out that employees should be bound by the clear language of what they sign unless that language is deliberately and clearly canceled by a union adherent with words calculated to direct the signer to disregard and forget the language above his signature. There is nothing inconsistent in handing an employee a card that says the signer authorizes the union to represent him and then telling him that the card will probably be used first to get an election. Elections have been, after all, and will continue to be, held in the vast majority of cases; the union will still have to have the signatures of 30% of the employees when an employer rejects a bargaining demand and insists that the union seek an election. We cannot agree with the employers here that employees as a rule are too unsophisticated to be bound by what they sign unless expressly told that their act of signing represents something else. In addition to approving the use of cards, of course, Congress has expressly authorized reliance on employee signatures alone in other areas of labor relations, even where criminal sanctions hang in the balance, and we should not act hastily in disregarding congressional judgments that employees can be counted on to take responsibility for their acts.[27]

---

[27] In explaining and reaffirming the *Cumberland Shoe* doctrine in the context of unambiguous cards, the Board stated: 'Thus the fact that employees are told in the course of solicitation that an election is contemplated, or that a purpose of the card is to make an election possible, provides in our view insufficient basis in itself for vitiating unambiguously worded authorization cards on the theory of misrepresentation. A different situation is presented, of course, where union organizers solicit cards on the explicit or indirectly expressed representation

The employers argue as a final reason for rejecting the use of the cards that they are faced with a Hobson's choice under current Board rules and will almost inevitably come out the loser. They contend that if they do not make an immediate, personal investigation into possible solicitation irregularities to determine whether in fact the union represents an uncoerced majority, they will have unlawfully refused to bargain for failure to have a good faith doubt of the union's majority; and if they do make such an investigation, their efforts at polling and interrogation will constitute an unfair labor practice in violation of § 8(a)(1) and they will again be ordered to bargain. As we have pointed out, however, an employer is not obligated to accept a card check as proof of majority status, under the Board's current practice, and he is not required to justify his insistence on an election by making his own investigation of employee sentiment and showing affirmative reasons for doubting the majority status. If he does make an investigation, the Board's recent cases indicate that reasonable polling in this regard will not always be termed violative of § 8 (a)(1) if conducted in accordance with the requirements set out in *Struksnes Constr. Co.*, 165 N.L.R.B. 1062 (1967). And even if an employer's limited interrogation is found violative of the Act, it might not be serious enough to call for a bargaining order. As noted above, the Board has emphasized that not "any employer conduct found violative of Section 8(a)(1) of the Act, regardless of its nature or gravity, will necessarily support a refusal-to-bargain finding."

Remaining before us is the propriety of a bargaining order as a remedy for a § 8(a)(5) refusal to bargain where an employer has committed independent unfair labor practices which have made the holding of a fair election unlikely or which have in fact undermined a union's majority and caused an election to be set aside. We have long held that the Board is not limited to a cease-and-desist order in such cases, but has the authority to issue a bargaining order without first requiring the union to show that it has been able to maintain its majority status. *See NLRB* v. *Katz*, 369 U.S. 736, 748, n.16 (1962); *NLRB* v. *P. Lorillard Co.*, 314 U.S. 512 (1942). And we have held that the Board has the same authority even where it is clear that the union, which once had possession of cards from a majority of the employees, represents only a minority when the bargaining order is entered. *Franks Bros. Co. v. NLRB*, 321 U.S. 702 (1944). We see no reason now to withdraw this authority from the Board. If the Board could enter

---

that they will use such cards only for an election and subsequently seek to use them for a different purpose. * * *' The Board stated further in a footnote: 'The foregoing does not of course imply that a finding of misrepresentation is confined to situations where employees are expressly told *in haec verba* that the 'sole' or 'only' purpose of the cards is to obtain an election. The Board has never suggested such a mechanistic application of the foregoing principles, as some have contended. The Board looks to substance rather than to form. It is not the use or nonuse of certain key or 'magic' words that is controlling, but whether or not the totality of circumstances surrounding the card solicitation is such, as to add up to an assurance to the card signer that his card will be used for no purpose other than to help get an election.' " *Levi Strauss & Co.*, 172 N.L.R.B. 732, 733 (1968).

only a cease-and-desist order and direct an election or a rerun, it would in effect be rewarding the employer and allowing him "to profit from [his] own wrongful refusal to bargain," while at the same time severely curtailing the employees' right freely to determine whether they desire a representative. The employer could continue to delay or disrupt the election processes and put off indefinitely his obligation to bargain;[30] and any election held under these circumstances would not be likely to demonstrate the employees' true, undistorted desires.[31]

The employers argue that the Board has ample remedies, over and above the cease-and-desist order, to control employer misconduct. The Board can, they assert, direct the companies to mail notices to employees, to read notices to employees during plant time and to give the union access to employees during working time at the plant, or it can seek a court injunctive order under § 10(j) as a last resort. In view of the Board's power, they conclude, the bargaining order is an unnecessarily harsh remedy that needlessly prejudices employees' § 7 rights solely for the purpose of punishing or restraining an employer. Such an argument ignores that a bargaining order is designed as much to remedy past election damage as it is to deter future misconduct. If an employer has succeeded in undermining a union's strength and destroying the laboratory conditions necessary for a fair election, he may see no need to violate a cease-and-desist order by further unlawful activity. The damage will have been done, and perhaps the only fair way to effectuate employee rights is to re-establish the conditions as they existed before the employer's unlawful campaign.[33]

---

[30]   The Board indicates here that its records show that in the period between January and June 1968, the median time between the filing of an unfair labor practice charge and a Board decision in a contested case was 388 days. But the employer can do more than just put off his bargaining obligation by seeking to slow down the Board's administrative processes. He can also affect the outcome of a rerun election by delaying tactics, for figures show that the longer the time between a tainted election and a rerun, the less are the union's chances of reversing the outcome of the first election. See n. 31, *infra.*

[31]   A study of 20,153 elections held between 1960 and 1962 shows that in the 267 cases where rerun elections were held over 30% were won by the party who caused the election to be set aside. *See* Pollitt, *NLRB Re-Run Elections: A Study,* 41 N.C.L. Rev. 209, 212 (1963). The study shows further that certain unfair labor practices are more effective to destroy election conditions for a longer period of time than others. For instance, in cases involving threats to close or transfer plant operations, the union won the rerun only 29% of the time, while threats to eliminate benefits or refuse to deal with the union if elected seemed less irremediable with the union winning the rerun 75% of the time. *Id.,* at 215–216. Finally, time appears to be a factor. The figures suggest that if a rerun is held too soon after the election before the effects of the unfair labor practices have worn off, or too long after the election when interest in the union may have waned, the chances for a changed result occurring are not as good as they are if the rerun is held sometime in between those periods. Thus, the study showed that if the rerun is held within 30 days of the election or over nine months after, the chances that a different result will occur are only one in five; when the rerun is held within 30–60 days after the election, the chances for a changed result are two in five. *Id.,* at 221.

[33]   It has been pointed out that employee rights are affected whether or not a bargaining order is entered, for those who desire representation may not be protected by an inadequate rerun election, and those who oppose collective bargaining may be prejudiced by a bargaining order if in fact the union would have lost an election absent employer coercion. Any effect will be minimal at best, however, for there "is every reason for the union to negotiate a contract that will satisfy the

There is, after all, nothing permanent in a bargaining order, and if, after the effects of the employer's acts have worn off, the employees clearly desire to disavow the union, they can do so by filing a representation petition. For, as we pointed out long ago, in finding that a bargaining order involved no "injustice to employees who may wish to substitute for the particular union some other . . . arrangement," a bargaining relationship "once rightfully established must be permitted to exist and function for a reasonable period in which it can be given a fair chance to succeed," after which the "Board may, . . . upon a proper showing, take steps in recognition of changed situations which might make appropriate changed bargaining relationships." *Frank Bros., supra,* at 705–706.

Before considering whether the bargaining orders were appropriately entered in these cases, we should summarize the factors that go into such a determination. Despite our reversal of the Fourth Circuit below in Nos. 573 and 691 on all major issues, the actual area of disagreement between our position here and that of the Fourth Circuit is not large as a practical matter. While refusing to validate the general use of a bargaining order in reliance on cards, the Fourth Circuit nevertheless left open the possibility of imposing a bargaining order, without need of inquiry into majority status on the basis of cards or otherwise, in "exceptional" cases marked by "outrageous" and "pervasive" unfair labor practices. Such an order would be an appropriate remedy for those practices, the court noted, if they are of "such a nature that their coercive effects cannot be eliminated by the application of traditional remedies, with the result that a fair and reliable election cannot be had." The Board itself, we should add, has long had a similar policy of issuing a bargaining order, in the absence of a § 8(a)(5) violation or even a bargaining demand, when that was the only available, effective remedy for substantial unfair labor practices.

The only effect of our holding here is to approve the Board's use of the bargaining order in less extraordinary cases marked by less pervasive practices which nonetheless still have the tendency to undermine majority strength and impede the election processes. The Board's authority to issue such an order on a lesser showing of employer misconduct is appropriate, we should reemphasize, where there is also a showing that at one point the union had a majority; in such a case, of course, effectuating ascertainable employee free choice becomes as important a goal as deterring employer misbehavior. In fashioning a remedy in the exercise of its discretion, then, the Board can properly take into consideration the extensiveness of an employer's unfair practices in terms of their past effect on election conditions and the likelihood of their recurrence in the future. If the Board

---

majority, for the union will surely realize that it must win the support of the employees, in the face of a hostile employer, in order to survive the threat of a decertification election after a year has passed." Bok, *The Regulation of Campaign Tactics in Representation Elections Under the National Labor Relations Act*, 78 Harv. L. Rev. 38, 135 (1964).

finds that the possibility of erasing the effects of past practices and of ensuring a fair election (or a fair rerun) by the use of traditional remedies, though present, is slight and that employee sentiment once expressed through cards would, on balance, be better protected by a bargaining order, then such an order should issue.

We emphasize that under the Board's remedial power there is still a third category of minor or less extensive unfair labor practices, which, because of their minimal impact on the election machinery, will not sustain a bargaining order. There is, the Board says, no *per se* rule that the commission of any unfair practice will automatically result in a § 8(a)(5) violation and the issuance of an order to bargain.

With these considerations in mind, we turn to an examination of the orders in these cases. In *Sinclair*, No. 585, the Board made a finding, left undisturbed by the First Circuit, that the employer's threats of reprisal were so coercive that, even in the absence of a § 8(a)(5) violation, a bargaining order would have been necessary to repair the unlawful effect of those threats. The Board therefore did not have to make the determination called for in the intermediate situation above that the risks that a fair rerun election might not be possible were too great to disregard the desires of the employees already expressed through the cards.

In the [other] cases from the Fourth Circuit, on the other hand, the Board did not make a similar finding that a bargaining order would have been necessary in the absence of an unlawful refusal to bargain. Nor did it make a finding that, even though traditional remedies might be able to ensure a fair election, there was insufficient indication that an election (or a rerun in *General Steel*) would definitely be a more reliable test of the employees' desires than the card count taken before the unfair labor practices occurred. The employees argue that such findings would not be warranted, and the court below ruled in *General Steel* that available remedies short of a bargaining order could guarantee a fair election. We think it possible that the requisite findings were implicit in the Board's decisions below to issue bargaining orders (and to set aside the election in *General Steel*); and we think it clearly inappropriate for the court below to make any contrary finding on its own. Because the Board's current practice at the time required it to phrase its findings in terms of an employer's good or bad faith doubts, however, the precise analysis the Board now puts forth was not employed below, and we therefore remand these cases for proper findings.

NOTES

1.   The *Gissel* Court approved of NLRB bargaining orders in cases in which the union has achieved majority support by authorization cards and in which the employer has committed substantial unfair labor practices. Not surprisingly, much of the case law since *Gissel* has focused on defining the

nature of the unfair labor practices that can result in a bargaining order. There are certain "hallmark" violations that usually rise to the level of supporting a bargaining order, including: closure of, or a threat to close, a plant; discharge or demotion of union advocates; and the grant of extraordinary benefits to employees. *See, e.g., NLRB v. Jamaica Towing, Inc.*, 632 F.2d 208, 212 (2d Cir. 1980); *California Gas Transport, Inc.*, 347 N.L.R.B. 1314 (2006), *enf'd*, 507 F.3d 847 (5th Cir. 2007); *but see Cast-Matie Corp. d/b/a/ Intermet Stevensville*, 350 N.L.R.B. 1349 (2007) (denying bargaining order despite threats of plant closing and job losses where hallmark violations affected only two of 79 employees and were made by a low level manager).

2.   Should the effects of the employer's unfair labor practices be evaluated at the time of their commission or at the time of the Board's decision? The Board generally evaluates the effects at the time of commission, *see, e.g., Intersweet, Inc.*, 321 N.L.R.B. 1 (1996), *enf'd*, 125 F.3d 1064 (7th Cir. 1997), but some circuits have held that the effects must also be evaluated at the time the order is issued, particularly where there has been substantial turnover of employees or the managers who committed the unfair labor practices have left the employer. *See, e.g., Overnite Transp. Co. v. NLRB*, 280 F.3d 417 (4th Cir. 2002).

3.   The courts of appeals have differed in the degree to which they will defer to the NLRB's judgments in *Gissel* bargaining order cases. Some require the Board to give detailed analyses of why its traditional remedies will not allow for the holding of a fair election. Others are more deferential to the Board's judgments. For commentary from management and union perspectives, see Gil A. Abramson, *The Uncertain Fate of* Gissel *Bargaining Orders in the Circuit Courts of Appeal*, 18 Lab. Law. 121 (2002); Peter J. Leff, *Failing to Give the Board Its Due: The Lack of Deference Afforded by the Appellate Courts in Gissel Bargaining Order Cases*, 18 Lab. Law. 93 (2002).

4.   *Nonmajority bargaining orders*. Can the Board issue a *Gissel* bargaining order without any showing that a union has ever achieved majority support among employees? In *Gissel* dictum, the Supreme Court hypothesized that there may be times when an employer's "pervasive" and "outrageous" unfair labor practices would prevent a union from ever even collecting a majority of authorization cards among employees. In those cases, the Act may require a bargaining order. The NLRB has never been comfortable with the idea of issuing a bargaining order where majority support has not been achieved by the union and did not even attempt to do so until 1982. Perhaps emboldened by a Third Circuit decision in 1979 remanding a non-majority case back to the Board for a bargaining order to help effectuate the goal of the Act to "further the majority preference of all employees" and to deter employers from attempting to defeat card majorities by committing serious unfair labor practices, *see United Dairy Farmers Co-op. v. NLRB*, 633 F.2d 1054 (3d Cir. 1980), the NLRB issued a bargaining order in *Conair Corp.*, 261 N.L.R.B. 1189 (1982), only to be rebuffed by the D.C. Circuit on appeal, which, without clear intention from Congress, was unwilling to sustain a Board-issued bargaining order without the union ever having achieved majority support. *Conair Corp.*

v. NLRB, 721 F.2d 1355, 1383 (D.C. Cir. 1983). In 1984, in *Gourmet Foods*, 270 N.L.R.B. 578, 583 (1984), the Board overruled *Conair Corp.*, stating:

> As is apparent from this review, the majority rule principle has been the focus for Board opponents of non-majority bargaining orders. In contrast, the imposition of non-majority bargaining orders as the only effective remedy for "pervasive" and "outrageous" unfair labor practices has been the focus for Board proponents. Our own review of the statute, its legislative history, Board and court precedent, and legal commentary have convinced us that the majority rule principle is such an integral part of the Act's current substance and procedure that it must be adhered to in fashioning a remedy, even in the most "exceptional" cases. We view the principle as a direct limitation on the Board's existing statutory remedial authority as well as a policy that would render improper exercise of any remedial authority to grant non-majority bargaining orders which the Board might possess.

The Board's continuing reluctance to issue non-majority bargaining orders is perhaps best demonstrated by its 2004 decision in *First Legal Support Services*, 342 N.L.R.B. 350 (2004). There, the employer committed outrageous and pervasive unfair labor practices (category I *Gissel* violation). Despite this, the union was able to procure valid authorization cards from 50% of the unit employees. An additional card was successfully contested by the employer, resulting in a failure of the union to achieve a majority. The Board, invoking its *Gourmet Foods* precedent, refused even to consider issuing a bargaining order. 342 N.L.R.B. at 351. According to Member Liebman in dissent,

> With due respect to my colleagues, it is wishful thinking to conclude that the Board's traditional remedies, even supplemented with a broad cease-and-desist order, are adequate to permit a fair election. By its egregious misconduct, the Respondent demonstrated its intolerance for its employees' Section 7 rights—not to mention its disregard for the Board. Apparently still not satisfied that the employees got the message, the Respondent threatened that their organizing effort was futile: even if the "NLRB issues an order, for compliance . . . they bring that order to us and we say 'fuck your order.'" The Respondent thereby laid bare its determination to frustrate any attempt by its employees to exercise their statutory rights. It is clear to me that the extraordinary relief is necessary to counter the lingering coercive effects of this misconduct.

Id. at 352 (Member Liebman, dissenting in part).

5.   Even in cases where *Gissel* bargaining orders are issued when the union has at one point achieved majority support, the bargaining orders have not been very effective. Professor Paul Weiler has emphasized the dubious kind of victory that a Board-imposed *Gissel* bargaining order represents. "The bargaining order," he states, "has been issued because the employer's behavior is thought to have so thoroughly cowed the employees that they cannot express their true desires about collective bargaining even within the secrecy of the

voting booth. But all the order can do is license the union to bring negotiations to the point at which its leadership must ask those same employees to put their jobs on the line by going on strike." Paul C. Weiler, *Promises to Keep: Securing Workers' Rights to Self Organization Under the NLRA*, 96 Harv. L. Rev. 1769, 1795 (1983). In a survey of bargaining orders issued by the Board between 1978 and 1982, for example, only about 20% resulted in collective bargaining agreements, and in only a woeful 10% of cases was the union able to maintain its representative status. *See* Terry Bethel & Catherine Melfi, *The Failure of* Gissel *Bargaining Orders*, 14 Hofstra Lab. L.J. 423, 437–38 (1997). The authors conclude:

> The *Gissel* Bargaining order extracts significant costs and provides relatively few rewards. As the Board's most drastic remedial step, the *Gissel* order is an abject failure. Employers who are determined to remain non-union have a reasonably good chance of doing so. Although the cost may have some deterrent effect on some employers, that provides little relief for the employees whose employers have used the process to defeat the union. Ironically, then, the most the Board can claim for its most vaunted remedy is the possibility of just the kind of effect it eschews. It provides some punishment, but even that is scant deterrent to employers willing to pay the price.

Id. a 451–52; *see also* James J. Brudney, *A Famous Victory: Collective Bargaining Protections and the Statutory Aging Process*, 74 N.C.L. Rev. 939 (1996), arguing that the Board has, over the years, modified its more aggressive approach to remedial bargaining orders, upheld in *Gissel,* because of consistent appellate court determinations disfavoring such orders as too great an impingement on individual freedom of choice and discounting the importance of stability in collective bargaining.

An issue left open by the Court in *Gissel* was whether an employer, faced with a demand for recognition based on signed authorization cards, could lawfully refuse the demand even if it did not file a representation petition to contest the union's claim of majority support. The unions in *Gissel* had argued that the employer could not, but, because of the presence of substantial unfair labor practices committed by the employers, the Court found it unnecessary to reach that issue. The Court was again presented with the issue in the following case.

LINDEN LUMBER V. NLRB
419 U.S. 301 (1974)

JUSTICE DOUGLAS delivered the opinion of the Court:

[R]espondent union obtained authorization cards from a majority of petitioner's employees and demanded that it be recognized as the collective-bargaining representative of those employees. Linden said it doubted the union's claimed majority status and suggested the union petition the Board for an election. The union filed such a petition with the

Board but later withdrew it when Linden declined to enter a consent election agreement or abide by an election, on the ground that respondent union's organizational campaign had been improperly assisted by company supervisors. Respondent union thereupon renewed its demand for collective bargaining; and again Linden declined, saying that the union's claimed membership had been improperly influenced by supervisors. Thereupon respondent union struck for recognition as the bargaining representative and shortly filed a charge of unfair labor practice against Linden based on its refusal to bargain.

There is no charge that Linden engaged in an unfair labor practice apart from its refusal to bargain. The Board held that Linden should not be guilty of an unfair labor practice solely on the basis "of its refusal to accept evidence of majority status other than the results of a Board election." 190 N.L.R.B. 718, 721 (1971).

In *Gissel* we held that an employer who engages in "unfair" labor practices " 'likely to destroy the union's majority and seriously impede the election' " may not insist that before it bargains the union get a secret ballot election. There were no such unfair labor practices here, nor had the employer in either case agreed to a voluntary settlement of the dispute and then reneged. [W]e reserved in *Gissel* the questions "whether, absent election interference by an employer's unfair labor practices, he may obtain an election only if he petitions for one himself; whether, if he does not, he must bargain with a card majority if the Union chooses not to seek an election; and whether, in the latter situation, he is bound by the Board's ultimate determination of the card results regardless of his earlier good faith doubts, or whether he can still insist on a Union-sought election if he makes an affirmative showing of his positive reasons for believing there is a representation dispute."

We recognized in *Gissel* that while the election process had acknowledged superiority in ascertaining whether a union has majority support, cards may "adequately reflect employee sentiment."

Generalizations are difficult; and it is urged by the unions that only the precise facts should dispose of concrete cases. As we said, however, in *Gissel*, the Board had largely abandoned its earlier test that the employer's refusal to bargain was warranted, if he had a good-faith doubt that the union represented a majority. A different approach was indicated. We said:

> [An] employer is not obligated to accept a card check as proof of majority status, under the Board's current practice, and he is not required to justify his insistence on an election by making his own investigation of employee sentiment and showing affirmative reasons for doubting the majority status. *See Aaron Brothers*, 158 N.L.R.B. 1077, 1078. If he does make an investigation, the Board's recent cases indicate that reasonable polling in this regard will

not always be termed violative of § 8(a)(1) if conducted in accordance with the requirements set out in *Struksnes Construction Co.*, 165 N.L.R.B. [1062] (1967). And even if an employer's limited interrogation is found violative of the Act, it might not be serious enough to call for a bargaining order. As noted above, the Board has emphasized that not "any employer conduct found violative of Section 8(a)(1) of the Act, regardless of its nature or gravity, will necessarily support a refusal-to-bargain finding," *Aaron Brothers, supra*, at 1079.

395 U.S., at 609–610.

In the present case[ ] the Board found that the employer[ ] "should not be found guilty of a violation of Section 8(a)(5) solely upon the basis of [its] refusal to accept evidence of majority status other than the results of a Board election." The question whether the employer[ ] had good reasons or poor reasons was not deemed relevant to the inquiry. The Court of Appeals concluded that if the employer had doubts as to a union's majority status, it could and should test out its doubts by petitioning for an election. It said:

> While we have indicated that cards alone, or recognitional strikes and ambiguous utterances of the employer, do not necessarily provide such "convincing evidence of majority support" so as to require a bargaining order, they certainly create a sufficient probability of majority support as to require an employer asserting a doubt of majority status to resolve the possibility through a petition for an election, if he is to avoid both any duty to bargain and any inquiry into the actuality of his doubt.

487 F.2d, at 1111.

To take the Board's position is not to say that authorization cards are wholly unreliable as an indication of employee support of the union. An employer concededly may have valid objections to recognizing a union on that basis. His objection to cards may, of course, mask his opposition to unions. On the other hand he may have rational, good-faith grounds for distrusting authorization cards in a given situation. He may be convinced that the fact that a majority of the employees strike and picket does not necessarily establish that they desire the particular union as their representative. Fear may indeed prevent some from crossing a picket line; or sympathy for strikers, not the desire to have the particular union in the saddle, may influence others. These factors make difficult an examination of the employer's motive to ascertain whether it was in good faith. To enter that domain is to reject the approval by *Gissel* of the retreat which the Board took from its "good faith" inquiries.

The union which is faced with an unwilling employer has two alternative remedies under the Board's decision in the instant cases. It can file for an election; or it can press unfair labor practice charges against the employer under *Gissel*. The latter alternative promises to consume much time. In *Linden* the time between filing the charge and the Board's ruling was about 4 $1/2$ years. The Board's experience indicates that the median time in a contested case is 388 days. *Gissel*, 395 U.S., at 611 n. 30. On the other hand the median time between the filing of the petition for an election and the decision of the Regional Director is about 45 days. In terms of getting on with the problems of inaugurating regimes of industrial peace, the policy of encouraging secret elections under the Act is favored. The question remains—should the burden be on the union to ask for an election or should it be the responsibility of the employer?

The Court of Appeals concluded that since Congress in 1947 authorized employers to file their own representation petitions by enacting § 9(c)(1)(B), the burden was on them. But the history of that provision indicates it was aimed at eliminating the discrimination against employers which had previously existed under the Board's prior rules, permitting employers to petition for an election only when confronted with claims by two or more unions. There is no suggestion that Congress wanted to place the burden of getting a secret election on the employer.

> Today an employer is faced with this situation. A man comes into his office and says, "I represent your employees. Sign this agreement, or we strike tomorrow." Such instances have occurred all over the United States. The employer has no way in which to determine whether this man really does represent his employees or does not. The bill gives him the right to go to the Board under those circumstances, and say, "I want an election. I want to know who is the bargaining agent for my employees." 93 Cong. Rec. 3838 (1947) (remarks of Senator Taft).

Our problem is not one of picking favorites but of trying to find the congressional purpose by examining the statutory and administrative interpretations that incline one way or another. Large issues ride on who takes the initiative. A common issue is, what should be the representative unit?

Section 9(c)(1)(B) visualizes an employer faced with a claim by individuals or unions "to be recognized as the representative defined in § 9(a)." That question of representation is raised only by a claim that the applicant represents a majority of employees, "in a unit appropriate for such purposes." § 9(a). If there is a significant discrepancy between the unit which the employer wants and the unit for which the union asked recognition, the Board will dismiss the employer's petition. In that event the union, if it desired the smaller unit, would have to file its own petition, leaving the employer free to contest the appropriateness of that unit. The Court of Appeals thought that if the employer were required to petition the Board for an election, the litigable issues would be reduced. The recurring conflict over what should be the appropriate bargaining unit, coupled with the fact that if the employer asks for a unit which the union opposes his election petition is dismissed, is answer enough.

The Board has at least some expertise in these matters and its judgment is that an employer's petition for an election, though permissible, is not the required course. It points out in its brief here that an employer wanting to gain delay can draw a petition to elicit protests by the union, and the thought that an employer petition would obviate litigation over the sufficiency of the union's showing of interest is in its purview apparently not well taken. A union petition to be sure must be backed by a 30% showing of employee interest. But the sufficiency of such a showing is not litigable by the parties.

In light of the statutory scheme and the practical administrative procedural questions involved, we cannot say that the Board's decision that the union should go forward and ask for an election on the employer's refusal to recognize the authorization cards was arbitrary and capricious or an abuse of discretion.

In sum, we sustain the Board in holding that, unless an employer has engaged in an unfair labor practice that impairs the electoral process,[10] a union with authorization cards purporting to represent a majority of the employees, which is refused recognition, has the burden of taking the next step in invoking the Board's election procedure.

[The dissenting opinion of JUSTICE STEWART, joined by JUSTICES WHITE, MARSHALL and POWELL, is omitted.]

NOTES

1.   As discussed in *Gissel*, at one time the NLRB held that an employer faced with a union demand for recognition supported by authorization cards signed by a majority of the employees was required to recognize the union unless it filed a representation petition or otherwise had good faith doubts of the union's claim of majority support. By the time the Court decided *Gissel*, the NLRB had abandoned this position. In light of the Court's decision in *Linden Lumber*, is the NLRB free to revert back to its pre-*Gissel* position?

2.   Consider footnote 10 at the very end of the *Linden Lumber* case. Is the court suggesting that if an employer agrees to be bound by a card check, it may not disavow that pledge later? Or is the court saying that in card cases in which the employer has agreed in advance to be bound by the results of a card check that it might well be the employer who must proceed to the Board if he

---

[10]   We do not reach the question whether the same result obtains if the employer breaches his agreement to permit majority status to be determined by means other than a Board election. *See Snow & Sons*, 134 N. L. R. B. 709 (1961), enf'd, 308 F.2d 687 (CA9 1962). In the instant cases the Board said that the employers and the unions "never voluntarily agreed upon any mutually acceptable and legally permissible means, other than a Board-conducted election, for resolving the issue of union majority status." 190 N.L.R.B., at 721; *see* 198 N.L.R.B., at 998.

would prefer an election? Does the note suggest that agreements between employers and unions regarding recognition might be followed and enforced even if they contradict the default election policy of the NLRA? If not any of these, why would the Court go to all the trouble of suggesting that there might be a different analysis in cases of an agreement about recognition procedure between the union and the employer? Note that the Board has recognized the validity of collective bargaining clauses in which an employer agrees to waive the right to an election in after-acquired facilities. *See Houston Div. of the Kroger Co.*, 219 N.L.R.B. 388 (1975).

3.   If an employer, through polling or interrogating employees, learns that a majority wish to be represented by the union, may the employer continue to refuse the union's demand for recognition? Should it matter whether the polling or interrogation occurred before or after the union demanded recognition? *See Sullivan Elec. Co. v. NLRB*, 479 F.2d 1270 (6th Cir. 1973); *Tenn. Shell Co.*, 212 N.L.R.B. 193 (1974), *aff'd mem. sub nom. United Mine Workers v. NLRB*, 515 F.2d 1018 (D.C. Cir. 1975).

4.   The Operating Engineers union secured signed authorization cards of the nine drillers and helpers employed by Terracon, a national engineering consulting firm, at its Naperville, Illinois facility. A union organizer and union attorney met with the employer's Naperville office manager, showed him the cards and demanded recognition. The manager confirmed that all employees had signed cards but declined to sign a recognition agreement. They then discussed employee demands for better winter clothing and shoes, additional time to inspect equipment and better hazardous material training. The manager responded favorably to those demands and suggested that the organizer and attorney return later when the regional manager would be present. They did and in a meeting with the regional manager that lasted an hour, the regional manager reviewed the cards and confirmed that all employees had signed, characterized the issues of winter clothing, HazMat training and equipment inspection time as "peanuts," discussed the union's apprenticeship program and benefit plans and told the organizer and attorney that the company could not afford to pay union wage scale and if forced to do so would subcontract its drilling work. After the meeting, the union wrote the regional manager confirming that negotiations had begun with tentative agreements to provide better winter clothing and HazMat training. The regional manager retained counsel who responded characterizing the meeting as a "courtesy call" and denying that there had been recognition or negotiations. As counsel for the union, how should you proceed? *See Int'l Union of Operating Eng'rs Local 150 v. NLRB*, 361 F.3d 395 (7th Cir. 2004).

5.   *Mandating card check recognition.* Several states have mandated card check recognition for public sector employees. New York was the first state to provide for certification based on a showing of majority support without an election. The New York PERB rules implementing the statute provide, "If the choice available to the employees in a negotiating unit is limited to the selection or rejection of a single employee organization . . . the employee organization involved will be certified without an election if a majority of the

employees within the unit have indicated their choice by the execution of dues deduction authorization cards which are current, or by individual designation cards which have been executed within six months prior to the date of the director's decision recommending certification without an election." NYPERB Rules § 201.9(g). The rules require that a union seeking certification without an election submit a sworn declaration of authenticity attesting on personal knowledge or inquiries that the affiant has made that the cards were signed by the individuals whose names appear on them on the dates specified, that they are in fact current members of the union, and that inquiry was made as to whether they were included in any existing negotiation unit. *Id.* § 201.4(d).

In 2003, Illinois became the second state to mandate card check certification. Two agencies administer the Illinois public sector collective bargaining statutes: the Illinois Educational Labor Relations Board (IELRB) has jurisdiction over employers and employees in public education and the Illinois Labor Relations Board (ILRB) has jurisdiction over the rest of the public sector. The IELRB regulations are found at 80 Ill. Adm. Code § 1110.105, and the ILRB regulations are found at 80 Ill. Adm. Code § 1210.100(b). Both provide that the union may file a "majority interest petition," accompanied by its evidence of majority status based on "dues deduction authorizations or other evidence submitted in support of a designation of representative without an election." Both provide for posting a notice and both require the employer to supply to the Board a list of employees in the bargaining unit and handwriting exemplars for those employees. Pursuant to statute, both Boards' regulations provide that a majority interest petition may be defeated by a showing by clear and convincing evidence that the showing of interest was procured by fraud or coercion, in which case a representation election is conducted. Both provide that if issues concerning the appropriateness of the bargaining unit or the inclusion of specific employees would affect the determination of majority status they are resolved by holding a hearing, but if the issues would not affect the outcome, they are resolved through the Boards' unit clarification procedures. The IELRB regulations allow a party to petition to intervene but the ILRB's regulations do not. Instead, the ILRB regulations allow a competing union to file a representation petition supported by a 30% showing of interest. The IELRB regulations provide that a party may allege that dues deduction authorizations or other evidence of majority support were changed, altered, withdrawn or withheld as a result of employer fraud, coercion or unfair labor practice and if the allegations are proven and it is proven that absent the fraud, coercion or unfair labor practice the union would have had majority support, the Board certifies the union as exclusive representative. The ILRB regulations do not have a comparable provision.

New Jersey (2005), Oregon (2007), and Massachusetts (2007) all now have mandatory card check laws. Several states, including California, Connecticut, Kansas, Maryland, North Dakota, and Oklahoma, allow card check recognition for some types of employees, but not others. *See generally* Rafael Gely &

Timothy Chandler, *Organizing Principles: The Significance of Card Check Laws,* 30 St. Louis Univ. Pub. L. Rev. 475 (2011).

4. VOLUNTARY RECOGNITION AND OTHER METHODS OUTSIDE THE NLRA'S PROCESSES

A substantial segment of the labor movement regards the NLRA's processes as unduly favoring management. Many unions object to the restrictions the NLRA allows employers to impose on union access to employees, to the types of anti-union campaigns that the Act allows employers to run and to the representation election process, which they believe takes too long and gives employers the opportunity to coerce employees into rejecting union representation. A number of these unions have negotiated agreements with employers that by-pass the statutory regime. Often these agreements provide that the union will have greater access to the employees on employer property, the employer will remain neutral during the union's organizing campaign, and the employer will recognize the union if a majority of its employees sign authorization cards. Sometimes the agreements go so far as to establish a framework for negotiating the first contract following recognition or even providing various terms that such an agreement will contain.

Often employers enter into these so called "neutrality and card check recognition" agreements as part of the collective bargaining contracts covering the already-unionized segments of their workforces. However, where the union does not currently represent any of the employer's employees, its ability to gain a neutrality and card check agreement will often depend on the type of economic pressure it is able to bring to bear on the employer.

a. Recognitional/Organizational Picketing

A union may choose to engage in picketing rather than file for a representation election for a number of strategic reasons. One of the main reasons today would be to compel an employer voluntarily to recognize the union. Even if the employer will not voluntarily recognize the union, it may file for an expedited election, allowed under § 8(b)(7), in order to stop the picketing. Since a lengthy run-up to an election generally disfavors unions, the expedited election process may be preferable. Other types of picketing, however, like informational or area standards picketing, also discussed below, do not necessarily have a recognitional goal. Distinguishing these different types of picketing is key to determining the appropriate remedial implications. *See* Lee Modjeska, *Recognition Picketing under the NLRA,* 35 Fla. L. Rev. 633 (1983). Section 8(b)(7) of the Act provides:

> It shall be an unfair labor practice for a labor organization or its agents—

(7) to picket or cause to be picketed, or threaten to picket or cause to be picketed, any employer where an object thereof is forcing or requiring an employer to recognize or bargain with a labor organization as the representative of his employees, or forcing or requiring the employees of an employer to accept or select such labor organization as their collective-bargaining representative, unless such labor organization is currently certified as the representative of such employees:

(A) where the employer has lawfully recognized in accordance with this Act [subchapter] any other labor organization and a question concerning representation may not appropriately be raised under section 9(c) of this Act [section 159(c) of this title],

(B) where within the preceding twelve months a valid election under section 9(c) of this Act [section 159(c) of this title] has been conducted, or

(C) where such picketing has been conducted without a petition under section 9(c)[section 159(c) of this title] being filed within a reasonable period of time not to exceed thirty days from the commencement of such picketing: *Provided*, That when such a petition has been filed the Board shall forthwith, without regard to the provisions of section 9(c)(1) [section 159(c)(1) of this title] or the absence of a showing of a substantial interest on the part of the labor organization, direct an election in such unit as the Board finds to be appropriate and shall certify the results thereof: *Provided further*, That nothing in this subparagraph (C) shall be construed to prohibit any picketing or other publicity for the purpose of truthfully advising the public (including consumers) that an employer does not employ members of, or have a contract with, a labor organization, unless an effect of such picketing is to induce any individual employed by any other person in the course of his employment, not to pick up, deliver or transport any goods or not to perform any services.

Nothing in this paragraph (7) shall be construed to permit any act which would otherwise be an unfair labor practice under this section 8(b) [this subsection].

Section 8(b)(7) was added to the NLRA by the Landrum-Griffin Act of 1959. It was styled as a congressional response to abusive "blackmail picketing." However, it was the subject of intense lobbying on all sides which resulted in very dense, convoluted language.

Think of a section 8(b)(7) violation as having four elements:

- *Picketing or the threat of picketing*. For most people, the term "picketing" conjures up visions of people patrolling carrying signs, but the Act does not expressly define the term. The Board and the courts have held that the crucial characteristic of picketing is not patrolling or the carrying of signs but the element of confrontation. *See, e.g., NLRB v. United Furniture Workers of America*, 337 F.2d 936 (2d Cir. 1964).

- *By a labor organization other than one certified as exclusive bargaining representative.* Recall the definition of "labor organization" in Section 2(5). To be a labor organization, the entity must be one in which employees participate. Thus, a union of supervisors may engage in recognitional picketing because supervisors are not employees and their union is not a labor organization. Of course, because they are not employees, picketing supervisors also are not protected by Sections 7 and 8(a).

- *With an object of forcing the employer to recognize the union or the employees to select the union as collective bargaining representative.* Only picketing with the prohibited object is prohibited by section 8(b)(7). A frequently litigated issue is whether picketing to protest an employer's failure to pay "area standards," i.e., to provide wages and benefits equivalent to that provided by unionized employers, is picketing for the proscribed object. It may be argued that picketing which seeks to raise the targeted employer's wages or benefits is attempting to attain something usually obtained through collective bargaining and therefore has a recognitional object. However, a union has an interest independent of recognition in protesting "substandard" employers—protecting the wages and benefits being paid by unionized employers from competitors with lower labor costs. Consequently, true area standards picketing is not prohibited by section 8(b)(7). *See Houston Bldg. & Constr. Trades Council (Claude Everet Const.),* 136 N.L.R.B. 321 (1962). The Board polices area standards cases closely. It has held that the union has the burden to investigate whether the targeted employer is in fact paying below area standards. *See, e.g., Teamsters Local 544 (Better Homes Deliveries),* 274 N.L.R.B. 164 (1985). Typically, a union will notify a targeted employer that it is paying below area standards, ask the employer what wages and benefits it is paying, and advise the employer that, unless the employer furnishes the information and meets area standards, picketing will begin. The notice will also affirmatively disclaim any recognitional object. Where, however, the union goes beyond seeking the targeted employer's payment of current area standards, its picketing will be deemed recognitional. *See, e.g., Centralia Bldg. & Constr. Trades Council (Pac. Sign & Steel Bldg. Co.)*, 155 N.L.R.B. 803 (1965) (finding Section 8(b)(7) violation where union wanted employer to agree to pay area standards currently and in the future), *enf'd*, 363 F.2d 699 (D.C. Cir. 1966).

- *Satisfies either subsection (A), (B), or (C).* Subsections (A) and (B) are relatively straightforward. Subsection (A) applies where the employer has lawfully recognized an incumbent union and a QCR cannot be raised, typically because an existing contract bars a representation petition. Subsection (B) applies whenever there has been a valid NLRB-conducted election within the prior 12 months

Subsection (C) applies when there has not been a recent election and there is no incumbent union. Note that under Subsection (C), the union may engage in recognitional picketing as long as it limits the picketing to a reasonable time not to exceed 30 days. The union may picket beyond 30 days, as long as a representation petition is filed, but if such a petition is filed, there may be an expedited election, with no concern for the union's showing of interest and no representation hearing. Thus, section 8(b)(7)(C) is designed to allow recognitional picketing for a limited period of time while channeling the representation dispute to a quick resolution. If the union wins the election, it becomes exclusive bargaining representative and may continue to picket. If the union loses the election, further picketing is barred by Section 8(b)(7)(B). While this approach to the issue of recognitional picketing seems straightforward, as the next case illustrates, it can become complicated quickly.

INTERNATIONAL HOD CARRIERS, LOCAL 840 (BLINNE CONSTRUCTION)
135 N.L.R.B. 1153 (1962)

MEMBERS RODGERS, LEEDOM, and FANNING:

Before proceeding to determine the application of Section 8(b)(7)(C) to the facts of the instant case, it is essential to note the interplay of the several subsections of Section 8(b)(7), of which subparagraph (C) is only a constituent part.

The section as a whole, as is apparent from its opening phrases, prescribes limitations only on picketing for an object of "recognition" or "bargaining" (both of which terms will hereinafter be subsumed under the single term "recognition") or for an object of organization. Picketing for other objects is not proscribed by this section. Moreover, not all picketing for recognition or organization is proscribed. A "currently certified" union may picket for recognition or organization of employees for whom it is certified. And even a union which is not certified is barred from recognition or organization picketing only in three general areas. The first area, defined in subparagraph (A) of Section 8(b)(7), relates to situations where another union has been lawfully recognized and a question concerning representation cannot appropriately be raised.[5] The second area, defined in subparagraph (B), relates to situations where, within the preceding 12 months, a "valid election" has been held.

The intent of subparagraphs (A) and (B) is fairly clear. Congress concluded that where a union has been lawfully recognized and a question concerning representation cannot appropriately be raised, or where the employees within the preceding 12 months have made known their views concerning representation, both the employer and employees are entitled to immunity from recognition or organization picketing for prescribed periods.

Congress did not stop there, however. Deeply concerned with other abuses, most particularly "blackmail" picketing, Congress concluded that it would be salutary to impose even further limitations on picketing for recognition or organization. Accordingly, subparagraph (C) provides that even where such picketing is not barred by the provisions of (A) or (B) so that picketing for recognition or organization would otherwise be permissible, such picketing is limited to a reasonable period not to exceed 30 days unless a representation petition is filed prior to the expiration of that period. Absent the filing of such a timely petition, continuation of the picketing beyond the reasonable period becomes an unfair labor practice. On the other hand, the filing of a timely petition stays the limitation and picketing may continue pending the processing of the petition. Even here, however, Congress by the addition of the first proviso to subparagraph (C) made it possible to foreshorten the period of permissible picketing by directing the holding of an expedited election pursuant to the representation petition.

The expedited election procedure is applicable, of course, only in a Section 8(b)(7)(C) proceeding, i.e., where an 8(b)(7)(C) unfair labor practice charge has been filed. Congress rejected efforts to amend the provisions of Section 9(c) of the Act so as to dispense generally with preelection hearings. Thus, in the absence of an 8(b)(7)(C) unfair labor practice charge, a union will not be enabled to obtain an expedited election by the mere device of engaging in recognition or organization picketing and filing a representation petition. And on the other hand, a picketing union which files a representation petition pursuant to the mandate of Section 8(b)(7)

---

[5]   It will be noted, of course, that subparagraph (A) represents a substantial enlargement upon the prohibition already embodied in Section 8(b)(4)(C) of the Taft-Hartley Act which merely insulates certified unions from proscribed "raiding" by rival labor organizations. Subparagraph (A) affords protection to lawfully recognized unions which do not have certified status, and also incorporates, in effect, the Board's contract-bar rules relating to the existence of a question concerning representation.

(C) and to avoid its sanctions will not be propelled into an expedited election, which it may not desire, merely because it has filed such a petition. In both the above situations, the normal representation procedures are applicable; the showing of a substantial interest will be required, and the preelection hearing directed in Section 9(c)(1) will be held.

This, in our considered judgment, puts the expedited election procedure prescribed in the first proviso to subparagraph (C) in its proper and intended focus. That procedure was devised to shield aggrieved employers and employees from the adverse effects of prolonged recognition or organization picketing. Absent such a grievance, it was not designed either to benefit or to handicap picketing activity.

Subparagraphs (B) and (C) serve different purposes. But it is especially significant to note their interrelationship. Congress was particularly concerned, even where picketing for recognition or organization was otherwise permissible, that the question concerning representation which gave rise to the picketing be resolved as quickly as possible. It was for this reason that it provided for the filing of a petition pursuant to which the Board could direct an expedited election in which the employees could freely indicate their desires as to representation. If, in the free exercise of their choice, they designate the picketing union as their bargaining representative, that union will be certified and it will by the express terms of Section 8(b)(7) be exonerated from the strictures of that section. If, conversely, the employees reject the picketing union, that union will be barred from picketing for 12 months thereafter under the provisions of subparagraph (B).

The scheme which Congress thus devised represents what that legislative body deemed a practical accommodation between the right of a union to engage in legitimate picketing for recognition or organization and abuse of that right. One caveat must be noted in that regard. The congressional scheme is, perforce, based on the premise that the election to be conducted under the first proviso to subparagraph (C) represents the free and uncoerced choice of the employee electorate. Absent such a free and uncoerced choice, the underlying question concerning representation is not resolved and, more particularly, subparagraph (B) which turns on the holding of a "valid election" does not become operative.

There remains to be considered only the second proviso to subparagraph (C). In sum, that proviso removes the time limitation imposed upon, and preserves the legality of, recognition or organization picketing falling within the ambit of subparagraph (C), where that picketing merely advises the public that an employer does not employ members of, or have a contract with, a union unless an effect of such picketing is to halt pickups or deliveries, or the performance of services.

Needless to add, picketing which meets the requirements of the proviso also renders the expedited election procedure inapplicable.

Except for the final clause in Section 8(b)(7) which provides that nothing in that section shall be construed to permit any act otherwise proscribed under Section 8(b) of the Act, the foregoing sums up the limitations imposed upon recognition or organization picketing by the Landrum-Griffin amendments. However, at the risk of laboring the obvious, it is important to note that structurally, as well as grammatically, subparagraphs (A), (B), and (C) are subordinate to and controlled by the opening phrases of Section 8(b)(7). In other words, the thrust of all the Section 8(b)(7) provisions is only upon picketing for an object of recognition or organization, and not upon picketing for other objects. Similarly, both structurally and grammatically, the two provisos in subparagraph (C) appertain only to the situation defined in the principal clause of that subparagraph.

Having outlined, in concededly broad strokes, the statutory framework of Section 8(b)(7) and particularly subparagraph (C) thereof, we may appropriately turn to a consideration of the instant case which presents issues going to the heart of that legislation.

The relevant facts may be briefly stated. On February 2, 1960, all three common laborers employed by Blinne at the Fort Leonard Wood jobsite signed cards designating the Union to represent them for purposes of collective bargaining. The next day the Union demanded that Blinne recognize the Union as the bargaining agent for the three laborers. Blinne not only refused recognition but told the Union it would transfer one of the laborers, Wann, in order to destroy the Union's majority. Blinne carried out this threat and transferred Wann 5 days later, on February 8. Following this refusal to recognize the Union and the transfer of Wann the Union started picketing at Fort Wood. The picketing, which began on February 8, immediately following the transfer of Wann, had three announced objectives: (1) recognition of the Union; (2) payment of the Davis-Bacon scale of wages; and (3) protest against Blinne's unfair labor practices in refusing to recognize the Union and in threatening to transfer and transferring Wann.

The picketing continued, with interruptions due to bad weather, until at least March 11, 1960, a period of more than 30 days from the date the picketing commenced. The picketing was peaceful, only one picket was on duty, and the picket sign he carried read "C. A. Blinne Construction Company, unfair." The three laborers on the job (one was the replacement for Wann) struck when the picketing started.

The Union, of course, was not the certified bargaining representative of the employees. Moreover, no representation petition was filed during the more than 30 days in which picketing was taking place. On March 1, however, about 3 weeks after the picketing commenced and well within the statutory 30-day period, the Union filed unfair labor practice charges against Blinne, alleging violations of Section 8(a)(1), (2), (3), and (5). On March 22, the Regional Director dismissed the 8(a)(2) and (5) charges, whereupon the Union forthwith filed a representation petition under Section 9(c) of the Act. Subsequently, on April 20, the Regional Director approved a unilateral settlement agreement with Blinne with respect to the Section 8(a)(1) and (3) charges which had not been dismissed. In the settlement agreement, Blinne neither admitted nor denied that it had committed unfair labor practices.

The Trial Examiner found on the basis of the evidence in the record that the Union represented all the employees in what he "assumed" in the absence of adequate evidence to be an appropriate unit. He found further that Blinne "not only rejected the principle of collective bargaining but was willing to and did engage in further unfair labor practices to insure that his obligations under the statute would not be met." Notwithstanding that, in this frame of reference, "the equities . . . so obviously rest with the picketing union," the Trial Examiner "reluctantly" concluded that Section 8(b)(7) deprived employees of rights considered fundamental under other provisions of the Act. Accordingly, he found that Respondent Union had violated Section 8(b)(7)(C) of the Act and entered a cease-and-desist order framed in the language of that provision.

In our view, the Trial Examiner has set up a false dichotomy. We do not believe that Section 8(b)(7) denies, or that Congress intended it to deny, fundamental rights theretofore guaranteed by the Act and still embodied in its provisions. We believe rather that the Trial Examiner's dilemma arose from his misconception of the structure of Section 8(b)(7), its operational interrelationship with the other provisions of the Act, and settled decisional law thereunder. Moreover, as we shall also point out, we believe the Trial Examiner made certain factual assumptions not warranted by the evidence.

Respondent, urging the self-evident proposition that a statute should be read as a whole, argues that Section 8(b)(7)(C) was not designed to prohibit picketing for recognition by a union enjoying majority status in an appropriate unit. Such picketing is for a lawful purpose inasmuch as Sections 8(a)(5) and 9(a) of the Act specifically impose upon an employer the duty to recognize and bargain with a union which enjoys that status. Accordingly, Respondent contends, absent express language requiring such a result, Section 8(b)(7)(C) should not be read in derogation of the duty so imposed.

There is grave doubt that the argument here made is apposite in this case. But, assuming its relevance, we find it to be without merit. To be sure, the legislative history is replete with references that Congress in framing the 1959 amendments was primarily concerned with "blackmail" picketing where the picketing union represented none or few of the employees whose allegiance it sought. Legislative references susceptible to an interpretation that Congress was concerned with the evils of majority picketing are sparse. Yet it cannot be gainsaid that Section 8(b)(7) by its explicit language exempts only "currently certified" unions from its proscriptions. Cautious as we should be to avoid a mechanical reading of statutory terms in involved legislative enactments, it is difficult to avoid giving the quoted words, essentially words of art, their natural construction. Moreover, such a construction is consonant with the underlying statutory scheme which is to resolve disputed issues of majority status, whenever possible, by the machinery of a Board election. Absent unfair labor practices or preelection misconduct warranting the setting aside of the election, majority unions will presumably not be prejudiced by such resolution. On the other hand, the admitted difficulties of determining majority status without such an election are obviated by this construction.

Congress was presumably aware of these considerations. In any event, there would seem to be here no valid considerations requiring that Congress be assumed to have intended a broader exemption than the one it actually afforded.

We turn now to the issue whether employer unfair labor practices are a defense to an 8(b)(7)(C) violation. As set forth in the original Decision and Order, the Union argues that Blinne was engaged in unfair labor practices within the meaning of Section 8(a)(1) and (3) of the Act; that it filed appropriate unfair labor practice charges against Blinne within a reasonable period of time after the commencement of the picketing; that it filed a representation petition as soon as the 8(a)(2) and (5) allegations of the charges were dismissed; that the 8(a)(1) and (3) allegations were in effect sustained and a settlement agreement was subsequently entered into with the approval of the Board; and that, therefore, this sequence of events should satisfy the requirements of Section 8(b)(7)(C).

The majority of the Board in the original Decision and Order rejected this argument. Pointing out that the representation petition was concededly filed more than 30 days after the commencement of the picketing, the majority concluded that the clear terms of Section 8(b)(7)(C) had been violated.

The majority also addressed itself specifically to the Union's contention that Section 8(b)(7)(C) could not have been intended by Congress to apply where an employer unfair labor practice had occurred. Its opinion alludes to the fact that the then Senator, now President, Kennedy had proposed statutory language to the effect that any employer unfair labor practice would be a defense to a charge of an 8(b)(7) violation both with respect to an application to the courts for a temporary restraining order and with respect to the unfair labor practice proceeding itself. The majority noted that the Congress did not adopt this proposal but instead limited itself merely to the insertion of a proviso in Section 10(*l*) prohibiting the application for a restraining order under Section 8(b)(7)(C) if there was reason to believe that a Section 8(a)(2) violation existed. Accordingly, the majority concluded that Congress had specifically rejected the very contention which Respondent urged.

The dissenting member in the original Decision and Order took sharp issue with the majority. In his view, the majority failed to "look to the provisions of the whole law and its object and policy" [citing *Mastro Plastics Corp.* v. *NLRB*, 350 U.S. 270, 285 (1956)]. Conceding that Section 8(b)(7)(C) in terms outlawed recognition picketing for more than 30 days unless a representation petition was filed, he emphasized that the cited section also provided for an expedited election if such a petition was filed. The purpose of the election is to obtain a free and uncoerced expression of the employees' desires as to their representation. Where unfair labor practices have taken place, however, such a free and uncoerced expression is precluded and the filing of a representation petition would be a futility. Indeed, consistent Board practice, presumably known to Congress, is to stay representation proceedings and elections thereunder until the effect of existing unremedied unfair labor practices is dissipated. Accordingly, the dissenting member concluded that the failure of a picketing union to file a timely petition in the face of employer unfair labor practices should not be made the basis for a finding of a violation under Section 8(b)(7)(C) of the Act.

The dissenting opinion likewise did not find the majority's reliance upon the proviso to Section 10(*l*) persuasive. On the basis of the relevant legislative history, the dissent concluded that this proviso was intended merely to implement Section 8(b)(7)(A) of the Act, that is, to insure that a union which was the beneficiary of a "sweetheart agreement" with an employer could not derive the benefit of injunctive relief that would otherwise be accorded by virtue of the provisions of subparagraph (A).

In retrospect, both the majority and dissenting opinions are not without logic or respectable foundation. Certainly, the narrow proviso embodied in Section 10(*l*), and the failure to embrace a proposal that would exempt recognition and organization picketing from the Section 8(b)(7)(C) bar where employer unfair labor practices had been committed, suggest that Congress was reluctant to grant such an exemption. Conversely, as the dissenting opinion argues, to hold that employer unfair labor practices sufficient to affect the results of an election are irrelevant in an 8(b)(7)(C) context seems incongruous and inconsistent with the overall scheme of the Act.

Fortified by the advantages of hindsight and added deliberation as to the ramifications of the majority and minority opinions, we are now of the view that neither opinion affords a complete answer to the question here presented. It seems fair to say that Congress was unwilling to write an exemption into Section 8(b)(7)(C) dispensing with the necessity for filing a representation petition wherever employer unfair labor practices were alleged. The fact that the bill as ultimately enacted by the Congress did not contain the amendment to Section 10(*l*) which the Senate had adopted in S. 1555 cogently establishes that this reluctance was not due to oversight. On the other hand, it strains credulity to believe that Congress proposed to make the rights of union and employees turn upon the results of an election which, because of the existence of unremedied unfair labor practices, is unlikely to reflect the true wishes of the employees.

In our view, therefore, Congress intended that, except to the limited extent set forth in the first proviso, the Board in 8(b)(7)(C) cases follow the tried and familiar procedures it typically follows in representation cases where unfair labor practice charges are filed. That procedure, as already set forth, is to hold the representation case in abeyance and refrain from holding an election pending the resolution of the unfair labor practice charges. Thus, the fears that the statutory requirement for filing a timely petition will compel a union which has been the victim of unfair labor practices to undergo a coerced election are groundless. No action will be taken on that petition while unfair labor practice charges are pending, and until a valid election is held pursuant to that petition, the union's right to picket under the statutory scheme is unimpaired.

On the other side of the coin, it may safely be assumed that groundless unfair labor practice charges in this area, because of the statutory priority accorded Section 8(b)(7) violations, will be quickly dismissed. Following such dismissal an election can be directed forthwith upon the subsisting petition, thereby effectuating the congressional purpose. Moreover, the fact that a timely petition is on file will protect the innocent union, which through a mistake of fact or law has filed a groundless unfair labor practice charge, from a finding of an 8(b)(7)(C) violation. Thus, the policy of the entire Act is effectuated and all rights guaranteed by its several provisions are appropriately safeguarded.

The facts of the instant case may be utilized to demonstrate the practical operation of the legislative scheme. Here the union had filed unfair labor practice charges alleging violations by the employer of Section 8(a)(1), (2), (3), and (5) of the Act. General Counsel found the allegations of 8(a)(2) and (5) violations groundless. Hence had these allegations stood alone and had a timely petition been on file, an election could have been directed forthwith and the underlying question concerning representation out of which the picketing arose could have been resolved pursuant to the statutory scheme. The failure to file a timely petition frustrated that scheme.

On the other hand, the Section 8(a)(1) and (3) charges were found meritorious. Under these circumstances, and again consistent with uniform practice, no election would have been directed notwithstanding the currency of a timely petition; the petition would be held in abeyance pending a satisfactory resolution of the unfair labor practice charges. The aggrieved union's right to picket would not be abated in the interim and the sole prejudice to the employer would be the delay engendered by its own unfair labor practices. The absence of a timely petition, however, precludes disposition of the underlying question concerning representation which thus remains unresolved even after the Section 8(a)(1) and (3) charges are satisfactorily disposed of. Accordingly, to condone the refusal to file a timely petition in such situations would be to condone the flouting of a legislative judgment. Moreover, and most important, to impose a lesser requirement would fly in the face of the public interest which prompted that judgment.

Because we read Section 8(b)(7)(C) as requiring in the instant case the filing of a timely petition and because such a petition was admittedly not filed until more than 30 days after the commencement of the picketing, we find that Respondent violated Section 8(b)(7)(C) of the Act.

NOTES

1.   It is helpful to understanding the case to set out a timeline of events. Notice that the picketing went on beyond 30 days after the union filed unfair labor practice charges but before it filed a representation petition. Although the picketing literally violated section 8(b)(7)(C), the union offered two defenses. What were they and why did the Board reject them?

2.   *Unfair labor practices and their impact on section 8(b)(7)(C).* As indicated in *Blinne*, even if the employer commits unfair labor practices, the union must file an election petition with the NLRB within 30 days of the beginning of picketing. However, so long as a petition is filed, the union may continue picketing beyond the 30 days allowed by Section 8(b)(7)(C) until the unfair labor practices have been resolved. But if the employer seeks an expedited election, the union could face an election with unfair labor practice charges pending. How did the Board resolve this dilemma?

3.   *Notice and comment.* Notice the Board's comment that "[t]he expedited election procedure is applicable, of course, only in a Section 8(b)(7)(C) proceeding, i.e., where an 8(b)(7)(C) unfair labor practice charge has been filed." In other words, a union may not obtain an expedited election by picketing and filing a representation petition. The expedited election is granted only if the employer files an 8(b)(7)(C) charge. The charge, in effect, serves as the employer's request for an expedited election. As counsel for an employer that has been subjected to recognitional picketing, consider the strategic issues

you face. If the union has also filed a representation petition, the employer's options are to file an 8(b)(7)(C) charge and gain an expedited election, in which case it will not have much time to campaign, or let the election run its normal course but continue to endure the picketing until the election has been held. If the union has not filed a representation petition, the employer's options are to file its own representation petition and obtain an expedited election or endure the picketing while waiting to see if the union will wait to file its representation petition on the 29th day of picketing, and be able to continue picketing through the election campaign. In either scenario, the employer must consider the possibility that the union will block the holding of the expedited election, at least for a few days, by filing unfair labor practice charges.

4.   *Section 8(b)(7)(C)'s publicity proviso.* Recognitional or organizational picketing may continue beyond 30 days *without* the filing of an election petition if the picketing complies with the requirements of 8(b)(7)(C)'s publicity proviso. Under the proviso's requirements, informational picketing may continue beyond 30 days without filing an election petition despite a recognitional or organizational purpose if: (1) the picketing is addressed to the public, (2) it is truthful, and (3) it does not have the effect of inducing stoppage of deliveries to the employer. *See Smitley d/b/a Crown Cafeteria v. NLRB,* 327 F.2d 351 (9th Cir. 1964). Most proviso picketing uses the words of the proviso itself, is addressed to the public (not workers or delivery people), and occurs at public entrances during times when the business is open to consumers. To measure the effect on deliveries, the Board will look at the overall impact of delivery stoppage on the business, not merely the number of delivery refusals. *See Retail Clerks Local 324 (Barker Bros.),* 138 N.L.R.B. 478 (1962), *aff'd,* 328 F.2d 431 (9th Cir. 1964).

5.   *Enderby revisited.* Suppose that instead of distributing leaflets after Penny was fired, the union set up two pickets alongside one of the roads leading into High Tech Park. The picket signs simply said, "Enderby Unfair." Is it obvious that the picketing is recognitional? How do we know its purpose? If you were representing the employer, Enderby, how would you respond to the picketing? Would it be best simply to leave the picketers alone? If you were representing the union, what risks of recognitional picketing would you point out to the union? Would you advise the union to try a different type of picketing, or not to picket at all?

6.   *Do not patronize?* Assume that a union set up pickets at the consumer entrances to a new Apple Computer store that it is interested in organizing, but that the union has not requested recognition and that the pickets are for the explicit purpose of advising the public. The picket signs say, "APPLE STORE NONUNION—PLEASE DO NOT PATRONIZE. LOCAL UNION #7." Assume also that to insure that the purpose of their picketing was not misunderstood and that deliveries of merchandise or the performance of services would not be halted by reason of the picketing, the union took the following steps: (1) e-mails were sent to the president of the Joint Teamsters Council indicating where the picket lines were being established and requesting that the Teamster Locals be advised that the purpose was *not* to

stop deliveries; (2) the union placed advertisements in the local newspapers advising the public that the purpose of the picket lines was only to advertise that the retail stores were nonunion in their selling operation and urging labor organizations not to stop deliveries or services at these stores; and (3) the pickets were explicitly instructed not to picket at delivery entrances and not to interfere with the public or with the drivers making deliveries. Assume the pickets complied with these instructions, but that on three occasions deliveries were in fact hindered when individual delivery people refused to cross the lines. On two of those occasions deliveries were not made at all and on one occasion, deliveries were delayed. Is the picketing an unfair labor practice under 8(b)(7)(C)? *See Retail Clerks Local 324 (Barker Bros.)*, 138 N.L.R.B. 478 (1962), *enf'd*, 328 F.2d 431 (9th Cir. 1964).

7. *What happens to an employee who participates in picketing?* Employees engaging in picketing which violates Section 8(b)(7)(C) of the NLRA are not required to be reinstated by the employer and are not entitled to any other remedy. *Exec. Mgmt. Servs.*, 355 NLRB 185 (2010). Both the courts and the Board have recognized that employee picketing that is not prohibited by the Act is considered protected by the Act, meaning that the employer cannot take retaliatory action. *Civil Serv. Emp. Ass'n. v. NLRB*, 569 F.3d 88, 92 (2d Cir. 2009). However, the effect would presumably be different depending on the object of the picketing. For example, unfair labor practice strikers who make unconditional offers to return to work are entitled to immediate reinstatement to their former positions whether or not replacements for them have been hired. *Grinnell Fire Protections Sys. Co.*, 335 NLRB 473, 475 (2001). Presuming this principle applies to picketing employees in addition to striking employees, then the consequences to an employee are determined by the motive behind the picketing.

* * *

A critical decision for a union seeking to represent a group of employees is when to make a demand for recognition by the employer. Too late, and the employer has a chance to marshal its resources for resistance and work on diluting employee resolve for representation. Too early, and the employer may attempt to get a quick election while the union is still building support. Section 8(b)(7)(C) presents a potential pitfall here. The following case discusses the possibilities.

NEW OTANI HOTEL & GARDEN
331 N.L.R.B. 1078 (2001)

MEMBERS FOX, LIEBMAN, and HURTGEN:

On August 26, 1997, the New Otani Hotel & Garden (the Employer) filed a petition for an election, based on the activities (detailed below) of Local 11 of the Hotel Employees and Restaurant Employees (the Union).

The Employer operates a hotel in downtown Los Angeles. The Employer asserts that the Union has been engaging in efforts to organize the employees at its hotel for 4 years, and that an election is therefore mandated due to the Union's present demand for recognition. The Employer relies primarily on the Union's picketing/boycott of the hotel and the Union's repeated requests that the Employer sign a neutrality/card check agreement. With regard to the Union's picketing, the Employer asserts that the Union's placards and leaflets evidence a recognitional object. The Union's placards read: "New Otani Hotel is non-union and does not have a contract with HERE Local 11. Please boycott." Similarly, the Employer refers to and provides copies of Union press releases and other documents, including a publicly-disseminated document advising that the nonunion New Otani hotel "has substandard working conditions when compared with Union hotels in downtown L.A." and urging consumers not to patronize the hotel.[2] In further support of its contention that the Union's underlying objective is recognitional, the Employer asserts that the Union sought to "punish" the Employer with an economic boycott until it would have no choice but to recognize the Union.

The Board has consistently construed Section 9(c)(1)(B) as requiring evidence of a *present* demand for recognition as the majority representative of an employer's employees before the employer's petition will be processed. The starting point is the language of the statute. Section 9(c)(1) provides in relevant part that where a petition is filed:

> (B) by an employer, alleging that one or more labor organizations have presented to him a claim to be recognized as the representative defined in section 9(a) . . . the Board shall [process the petition].

Section 9(a) provides in relevant part:

> Representatives designated or selected for the purposes of collective bargaining by the majority of the employees in a unit appropriate for such purposes, shall be the exclusive representatives of all the employees in such unit for the purposes of collective bargaining in respect to rates of pay, wages, hours of employment, or other conditions of employment.

Literally, the words of the statute dictate that "absent a claim by someone for recognition as the majority-supported representative of the employees, an employer is not entitled to an election under Section 9(c)(1)(B)."

As discussed in full in *Windee's Metal Industries, Inc.*, 309 N.L.R.B. 1074, 1074–1075 (1992), when Congress enacted Section 9(c)(1)(B) as part

---

[2] This document additionally alleges that after workers at the New Otani began an organizing effort, management responded with a "vicious and illegal anti-union campaign" and, as a consequence, the employees and Union were seeking a pledge from the Employer that it would not threaten the employees or interfere with their organizing campaign.

of the Taft-Hartley Act of 1947, it recognized that there was a potential for abuse in giving employers expanded rights to petition for an election, in that employers might file petitions early in organizational campaigns in an effort to obtain a vote rejecting the union before the union had a reasonable opportunity to organize. The legislative history shows that Congress therefore included the language limiting employer petitions to cases in which the union has presented a "claim to be recognized as the representative defined in section 9(a)," and that Congress understood this language to mean that employers could ask for an election only after a union had sought recognition as the majority representative of the employees. *Id.* (citing legislative history). As the Board explained in *Albuquerque Insulation,*

> The Section 9(c)(1)(B) requirement that an employer may secure an election *only if* a claim is made by a party that it is the majority representative of the employees was placed in the statute to prevent an employer from precipitating a premature vote before a union has the opportunity to organize. Thus, the Act contemplates that a union which is not presently majority representative may decide when or whether to test its strength in an election by its decision as to when or whether to request recognition or itself petition for an election. This is important because, under Section 9(c)(3) and Section 8(b)(7)(B), a Board-conducted election has the effect of barring any further election or recognitional picketing for a full year. Until the union makes such a move, it is free to organize without the imposition of an election. . . . Once the union seeks recognition as majority representative, the election process—with its potential risks and rewards—may be invoked by either side. But, until that time, an employer may not attempt to short-circuit the process or immunize itself from recognitional picketing by obtaining a premature election.

Albuquerque Insulation, 256 N.L.R.B. at 63 (emphasis added).

The mere fact that the union is engaged in activities which it hopes will enable it *eventually* to obtain recognition by the employer is not evidence of a present demand for recognition such as would support the processing of an employer petition. In accordance with that principle, the Board has consistently held that informational picketing as defined in the second proviso to Section 8(b)(7)(C) of the Act—that is, picketing that truthfully advises the public, including consumers, that an employer does not employ members of, or have a contract with, a union—does not, without more, establish that the union has made a claim to be recognized as required by Section 9(c)(1)(B), even assuming that the union is interested in organizing the employees and in ultimately representing them. The Board has also made clear that picketing for the purpose of putting pressure on the employer to conform its wage and benefit practices with area standards does not constitute a demand for recognition that would support a petition under Section 9(c)(1)(B). Only if informational or area standards picketing occurs in conjunction with other actions or statements establishing that the union's real object is to obtain immediate recognition as the employee's representative will the Board find that the union's conduct is tantamount to a present demand for recognition. Such other actions or statements might include a demand by the union for a contract or a statement by the union that picketing would cease if the employer would agree to negotiate and sign an agreement.

Applying these principles to this case, we agree with the Regional Director that the Union has not engaged in any conduct which demonstrates a present demand for recognition as the majority representative of the Employer's employees. Dismissal of the Employer's election petition is therefore warranted.

It is, of course, undisputed that the Union's campaign has an overall organizational objective with the eventual goal of obtaining recognition as the employees' representative. As we have discussed, however, the law is clear that the existence of such objectives does not mean that the union is making an immediate "claim to be recognized" as the employees' representative within the meaning of Section 9(c)(1)(B). Here, there is no evidence to indicate that the Union at any time conveyed to the Employer any claim, written or oral, that it represented its employees or that it was seeking immediate recognition or a contract. Rather, in a letter from the Union's president to the Employer's general manager requesting that the Employer accept a neutrality agreement, the Union president specifically disclaimed any immediate recognitional objective, stating: "Please understand that I am not asking you to recognize Local 11 as your employees' bargaining representative, nor am I asking you to negotiate a collective bargaining agreement with our union." Although the Employer contends to the contrary, there is nothing in the record to indicate that the Union has engaged in conduct inconsistent with that disclaimer, or that the Union has otherwise conveyed to the Employer that it did not in fact mean what it said. The only picketing engaged in by the Union was informational picketing as defined in the second proviso to Section 8(b)(7)(C). The statements made on the Union's placards, advising the public that the Employer does not have a contract with the Union and requesting a boycott, were limited to language that is expressly sanctioned under that proviso. As discussed above, under well-established precedent, such picketing does not constitute evidence of a present demand for recognition that would support the processing of a petition under Section 9(c)(1)(B).

Neither is there anything in the content of the handbills distributed by the Union that would demonstrate an immediate recognitional object. The allegation in the handbills that working conditions at the hotel are substandard when compared with union hotels is not, as noted above, evidence of such an object, nor does the fact that the handbills accused the Employer of engaging in unlawful conduct in response to the union organizing campaign demonstrate such an object.

Finally, we reject the Employer's contention that the Union's repeated requests that it sign a neutrality/card check agreement evince a present demand for recognition. Under such an agreement, the Employer would pledge not to campaign against the Union during an organizing campaign and to recognize the Union upon proof that a majority of workers have signed authorization cards. The Employer provides numerous examples of such requests in the form of letters to Employer management from the Union, letters to Employer management from various third-party groups and community leaders, and statements addressed to the public. The Employer asserts that based on the Union's continuing organizing efforts, the economic boycott (and associated pressure from third-party community leaders), and the above documents, it is evident that the Union is requesting recognition through a card-check procedure. In its opposition, the Union maintains that its attempts to secure a neutrality agreement are concerned with future campaign conduct, and that "[a] card-check as the hypothetical end of a neutral campaign does not support a present demand for recognition."

We agree with the Regional Director's conclusion that "the instant circumstances do not raise a claim by the Union that it represents a majority of the employees in the appropriate unit." The Union's repeated requests that the Employer sign a neutrality/card check agreement necessarily contemplate an organizing drive during which the Employer would pledge not to express any opinion on whether its employees should choose the Union as their bargaining representative or to interfere with employees' organizational activities. As such, the Union's requests do not constitute a *present* demand for recognition. In all of the examples of such requests submitted by the Employer, the language utilized by the Union is conditional; for example, a Union press release provides that "under [the card check] process, which is endorsed by the NLRB, *if* a majority of the workers sign union cards, the hotel *would recognize* the union based on their signatures" (emphasis added). Our dissenting colleague mischaracterizes the Union's request for a neutrality/card check agreement as a straight demand for immediate recognition upon a card check. As we have indicated, the Union in this instance merely requested—in conjunction with its request for a neutrality agreement—that the Employer agree to a card check procedure, in lieu of a Board election, at some point *in the future*. Our colleague also fails to distinguish between an organizational objective (contemplating a future claim for recognition) and a recognitional objective (making a present claim for recognition). This, explained in *Albuquerque Insulation Contractor*, is a critical distinction, necessary to prevent an employer from precipitating a premature election and thus interrupting employee efforts to organize for at least the Section 9(c)(3) year.

Moreover, as noted above, the letter from the Union president to the Employer's general manager requesting that the Employer accept a neutrality agreement specifically contains a disclaimer stating that the Union is not asking the Employer to recognize or negotiate an agreement with the Union. Although the Employer correctly asserts that the Board will disregard self-serving union disclaimers, there is no evidence in this instance that the Union acted inconsistently with its position. Thus, we similarly are not convinced that the Union's requests for a neutrality/card check agreement in conjunction with the Union's picketing and boycott, are sufficient to establish a present demand for recognition.

[A dissent by Member Hurtgen is omitted.]

NOTES

1.   Notice the strategic issues involved. Why didn't the employer file an 8(b)(7)(C) charge? Might its strategy have been different if the union picketed by the hotel's loading dock as well as by its public entrances? What constitutes a demand for recognition? A request for a neutrality agreement certainly suggests an organizational objective, but what if the card campaign proves to be unsuccessful? Shouldn't the union be able to withdraw and refuse to go forward with a request for recognition? Do you agree with the Board that a neutrality agreement request should be accompanied by a disclaimer from the union that it is not presently requesting recognition? Is a disclaimer necessary?

2.   It is important to note that over a strong dissent the Bush Board voted in 2006 to revisit the issue of whether some circumstances involving picketing to compel a card check agreement by an employer might not together constitute a present demand for recognition allowing an employer to request an expedited election. *See Marriott Hartford Downtown Hotel*, 347 N.L.R.B. 865 (2006). The Obama Board never addressed this issue.

b.   Lawful Voluntary Recognition

Perhaps the most efficient way to decide whether a majority of employees supports a union is to have supporters sign authorization cards. Not surprisingly, this has become the method most favored by unions. Recognition of unions by authorization cards has been allowed since passage of the Wagner Act in 1935, and, until the Act was amended to favor Board-run elections in 1947, a union could be certified by the NLRB based on a card check. After 1947, and until the decision in *Gissel*, there had been some question raised by employers about the general reliability of authorization cards and therefore their attendant legality as a method of showing majority support. Nonetheless, authorization cards had been upheld by the NLRB so long as they unambiguously showed that the signer favored the union as representative and the signer was not told, despite the wording, that the card would be used *solely* to get an election. *See Cumberland Shoe Corp.*, 144 N.L.R.B. 1268 (1963). In *Gissel*, the Supreme Court approved that view.

NEUTRALITY AGREEMENTS AND CARD CHECK RECOGNITION: PROSPECTS FOR CHANGING PARADIGMS

James J. Brudney
90 Iowa L. Rev. 819 (2005)

The past decade has witnessed a growing challenge by organized labor to the validity of the election paradigm as a preferred approach in ascertaining which "representatives of their own choosing" employees want. A central component of unions' challenge is their success in negotiating agreements that provide for employers to remain neutral during an upcoming union organizing campaign. These neutrality agreements generally include language specifying that the employer will not exercise its right to demand a Board-supervised election, but will instead recognize the union as exclusive representative, and participate in collective bargaining, if a majority of its employees sign valid authorization cards.

Neutrality agreements combined with card check recognition provide a distinct mechanism enabling employees to select representatives for purposes of collective bargaining. This approach to union organizing has partially displaced Board-supervised elections, and has become the principal strategy pursued by many labor organizations. Its non-electoral focus has attracted increased attention from labor law scholars, generated resistance from segments of the business community, and sparked controversy in Congress. Legislation has been proposed to ban the new organizing technique, and supporters of that legislative effort invoke the election paradigm as the sole method appropriate for implementing employees' freedom to choose their representatives.

A labor organizing campaign typically begins when a union is contacted by employees who for any number of reasons feel unfairly treated in their work environment. In the course of its campaign, the union distributes authorization cards, providing supportive employees with the chance to designate the union as their bargaining representative. If the union has received card support from a majority of employees at the establishment, it ordinarily will request that the employer recognize the union and enter into a collective bargaining relationship. The employer may lawfully accede to this request (provided there is in fact uncoerced majority support for the union). Employers, however, usually decline the union's request and exercise their right to demand a representation election, in which they will urge their employees to vote against unionization; the election is thus a contest challenging the union's assertion that it enjoys majority support. After an employer refuses a request for recognition, the union files a petition with the NLRB in order to schedule the election in which it can demonstrate its majority status.

Starting in the late 1970s, individual employers and unions began negotiating agreements that modified this traditional approach by providing for employers to remain neutral in future organizing campaigns. A 1976 letter agreement between General Motors and the United Auto Workers specified that "General Motors management will neither discourage nor encourage the Union's efforts in organizing production and maintenance employees traditionally represented by the Union elsewhere in General Motors, but will observe a posture of neutrality in these matters." Other early neutrality agreement language conditioned an employer's neutral stance on "responsible" union behavior, pledging that management would remain neutral in future organizing campaigns "providing the Union conducts itself in a manner which neither demeans the Corporation as an Organization nor its representatives as individuals."

By the late 1990s, as unions bargained for neutrality protection with greater frequency, these agreements had become a central component of the labor movement's organizing strategy. In an important empirical study, Professors Adrienne Eaton and Jill Kriesky collected and analyzed 132 neutrality agreements negotiated by twenty-three different national unions; approximately 80% of the agreements they examined were bargained during the 1990s. One-half of the neutrality agreements covered employees in the service sector, with the majority of these negotiated in the hospitality, gaming, and telecommunication areas. Within the manufacturing sector, most agreements were in the auto and steel industries.

Not surprisingly, Professors Eaton and Kriesky found considerable variation in the substantive aspects of these agreements. Certain core provisions, however, were present in the vast majority of settings. Almost all agreements included an explicit employer commitment to neutrality (93%), and some two-thirds of the agreements (65%) included both a statement of neutrality and a provision to recognize union majority status through card check procedures. Notably, card check provisions (with and even without neutrality statements) were associated with a substantial reduction in the numbers of employers running anti-union campaigns, and card check arrangements also reduced the intensity of such campaigns. The diminished levels of employer opposition presumably relate to unions' ability to recruit majority support in a shorter time span through authorization cards than under election arrangements and also to unions' ability to reach large numbers of workers before employers can begin to generate pressure against the organizing effort.

The Eaton and Kriesky study reported certain other common features that were typically included in these bargained-for organizing agreements.

Some two-thirds of the agreements called for union access to the employer's physical property, thereby contracting around the access restrictions established in 1992 by the Supreme Court. Nearly four-fifths of the agreements imposed certain limits on the union's behavior—most often the union agreed not to attack management during its campaign, but agreements also provided for organizing to occur during a specified period of time or for unions to notify management in advance of their intention to initiate a particular organizing campaign. Finally, more than 90% of the agreements called for some form of dispute resolution, most often arbitration, to address differences about unit determination or allegations of non-neutral conduct by one of the parties.

Organized labor's increased reliance on neutrality agreements plus card check does not mean that unions have forsaken the NLRB elections process. While the annual number of representation elections declined by roughly 50% during the early 1980s, election usage remained relatively constant at slightly under 3500 per year between 1983 and 1998. Since 1998, however, the number of Board elections has declined again by close to 30%. Strikingly, as union organizing activity has increased, the annual number of Board representation elections has reached its lowest level since the 1940s.

To be sure, unions in recent times have enjoyed higher win rates when seeking to organize through elections. The union win rate in NLRB representation elections has climbed steadily from 47.7% in 1996 to 57.8% in 2003, its highest level since the late 1960s. This period of success corresponds to the 1995 arrival of John J. Sweeney as the new president of the American Federation of Labor-Congress of Industrial Organizations ("AFL-CIO"). Sweeney prevailed in a contested campaign after promising to focus more aggressively on organizing efforts, and both the AFL-CIO and its affiliates have committed substantial additional resources to organizing since 1995. Comments from prominent management attorneys suggest that union organizers have become more sophisticated and effective in their use of traditional techniques during election campaigns, including direct worker contact and strategic targeting of employers within a given industry. Unions also are using some less traditional techniques in these campaigns, such as forging partnerships with religious organizations and community groups, and researching target companies as part of corporate campaigns that appeal to stockholders, board members, and institutional lenders.

At the same time, however, the proliferation of neutrality agreements that include card check provisions is part of a larger commitment on the part of unions to modify the NLRB election-based approach to organizing. The AFL-CIO has reported organizing nearly three million workers in the six years from 1998 to 2003; less than one-fifth of these newly organized employees were added through the formerly pre-eminent Board elections process. Some of the recent organizing success involves public sector employees, and some is attributable to other contractually based approaches, such as accretions of previously unrepresented or newly acquired facilities that build on existing bargaining units, or negotiated elections supervised by a third party distinct from the NLRB. Still, neutrality combined with card check has become a major weapon in the arsenal of organized labor. The Service Employees, Needle Trades Workers, Hotel and Restaurant Workers, and Autoworkers report that a plurality or majority of newly organized members have come in through contractual arrangements rather than traditional Board supervised election campaigns. For these and other unions, neutrality plus card check accounts for more new recruits than NLRB election victories.

The labor movement's growing interest in organizing outside the framework of representation elections has special relevance with respect to entities that employ larger numbers of workers. It has long been true that unions' election win rates fall as the size of the contested unit rises, and as a result, unions' overall win rate before the NLRB can be somewhat deceptive. From 1999–2003, unions won nearly 60% of the more than 9000 representation elections that involved units of fewer than fifty employees, but prevailed in only 42% of the 2200 elections involving 100–499 employees and in a mere 37% of some 260 elections in which units of more than 500 workers were at stake. Many successes in neutrality plus card check arrangements have involved larger units, often with more than 500 employees, and some unions may be targeting these larger units for their new approach.

The Eaton and Kriesky findings suggest a link between what provisions are included in a neutrality agreement and the ultimate success of union organizing efforts. Organizing campaigns that featured an employer neutrality statement without providing for card check resulted in recognition for the union 46% of the time. By contrast, organizing campaigns in which the parties agreed to both employer neutrality and card check ended with union recognition 78% of the time.

There are notable recent instances where organizing under a neutrality and card check arrangement has produced no union gains. Still, the 78% success rate reported by Eaton and Kriesky is well above the union win rate in Board elections since 1996 and is almost twice the level of union success in elections involving mid-size and larger units of 100 or more employees. Moreover, and importantly, the rate of achieving a first contract following recognition approached 100% in the nearly 200 successful organizing campaigns monitored by Eaton and Kriesky. That degree of achievement far exceeds the roughly 60% success rate associated with first contracts following NLRB election victories by unions.

NOTES

1.   Why would an employer opposed to unionization voluntarily recognize a union? Some reasons are: 1) the employer is already dealing with the union elsewhere, 2) the employer feels it will eventually become unionized and the union seeking recognition is better than any number of potential alternative unions, or 3) the employer fears recognitional picketing.

2.   In the past, unions would sometimes simply send an employer a package of authorization cards from a majority of employees in the bargaining unit accompanied by a request to voluntarily recognize the union. As a result, management attorneys typically now advise employers early on to simply turn over any union or anonymous letters or packages to them even though the *Gissel* case strongly suggests the choice about a certification election is theirs.

3.   *The mechanics of a card check.* Recall the *Bernard-Altman* case earlier in this chapter. An employer that voluntarily recognizes a union that does not have majority support at the time of recognition violates section 8(a)(2). Consequently, the parties typically agree to have a neutral third party conduct a card check. The employer will provide the third party with a list of employees in the bargaining unit and samples of their signatures, such as from their W-4 forms or signed receipts of the employee handbook or work rules. The union will provide the cards. The third party will check the signatures on the cards against the examples provided by the employer and will then count the number of cards and determine whether a majority of employees on the list provided by the employer signed cards. The third party's certification provides very strong evidence to rebut any potential 8(a)(2) charge. Consider the "electronic cards" that Penny Programmer gathered from coworkers in the problem that opened this chapter. Would they be sufficiently reliable indicators of employee support to justify voluntary recognition and survive an 8(a)(2) challenge?

4.   *State laws banning card checks.* In 2010, Arizona, South Carolina, South Dakota, and Utah passed state constitutional amendments requiring secret ballot elections, thereby closing the voluntary recognition pathway. In January 2011, the NLRB threatened legal action against these states, and in May of 2011 filed a suit against Arizona to overturn its amendment on the basis that it is preempted by federal law. As the complaint stated, "[t]he NLRA permits but does not require secret ballot elections for the designation, selection, or authorization of a collective bargaining representative where, for example, employees successfully petition their employer to voluntarily recognize their designated representative on the basis of reliable evidence of majority support." See *NLRB Initiates Litigation Against the State of Arizona on Amendment Limiting Method for Choosing Union Representation*, www.nlrb.gov (May 6, 2011). On September 5, 2012, in *NLRB v. State of Arizona and Save Our Secret Ballot,* Judge Frederick J. Martone of the U.S. District Court for the District of Arizona rejected the Board's federal preemption challenge. The court held that since the provision had not yet been applied in a case or controversy, the NLRB's lawsuit was premature. *See NLRB*

v. State, 2012 WL 3848400 (D. Ariz. 2012). For a prediction of the ultimate outcome of these challenges, see Ryan Walters, *Provoking Preemption: Why State Laws Protecting the Right to a Union Secret Election are Preempted by the NLRA,* 52 Santa Clara L. Rev. 1031 (2012).

If an employer voluntarily recognizes a union, should the union be protected from rival union election or decertification petitions for a "reasonable period of time" while it attempts to negotiate a contract with the employer? In 2007, the Board abruptly changed its long-standing practice in the following case.

DANA CORP.
351 N.L.R.B. 434 (2007)

CHAIRMAN BATTISTA, and MEMBERS SCHAUMBER and KIRSANOW:

Metaldyne Corporation and Dana Corporation (the Employers) independently entered into separate neutrality and card-check agreements with the [UAW]. Subsequently, the Employers recognized the Union upon a showing of majority support of the respective unit employees. Shortly after the Employers' recognition of the Union (22 days for the Metaldyne unit and 34 days for the Dana unit), employees in each unit filed a petition seeking a decertification election. The Metaldyne petitions were supported by over 50 percent of the unit employees, while the Dana petition was supported by over 35 percent of the unit employees. The Regional Director for Region 6 and the Regional Director for Region 8 dismissed the Metaldyne and Dana petitions, respectively, based on an application of the Board's recognition-bar doctrine. According to this doctrine, an employer's voluntary recognition of a union, in good faith and based on a demonstrated majority status, immediately bars an election petition filed by an employee or a rival union for a reasonable period of time. A collective-bargaining agreement executed during this insulated period generally bars Board elections for up to 3 years of the new contract's term. The Board granted review to re-examine its recognition-bar doctrine.

Our inquiry here requires us to strike the proper balance between two important but often competing interests under the National Labor Relations Act: "protecting employee freedom of choice on the one hand, and promoting stability of bargaining relationships on the other." In striking that balance here, we find that the immediate post-recognition imposition of an election bar does not give sufficient weight to the protection of the statutory rights of affected employees to exercise their choice on collective-bargaining representation through the preferred method of a Board-conducted election.

In order to achieve a "finer balance" of interests that better protects employees' free choice, we herein modify the Board's recognition-bar doctrine and hold that no election bar will be imposed after a card-based recognition unless (1) employees in the bargaining unit receive notice of the recognition and of their right, within 45 days of the notice, to file a decertification petition or to support the filing of a petition by a rival union, and (2) 45 days pass from the date of notice without the filing of a valid petition. If a valid petition supported by 30 percent or more of the unit employees is filed within 45 days of the notice, the petition will be processed. The requisite showing of interest in support of a petition may include employee signatures obtained before as well as after the recognition. These principles will govern regardless of whether a card-check and/or neutrality agreement preceded the union's recognition.

Modifications of the recognition bar cannot be fully effective without also addressing the election-bar status of contracts executed within the 45-day notice period, or contracts executed without employees having been given the newly-required notice of voluntary recognition. Consequently, we make parallel modifications to current contract-bar rules as well such that a collective-bargaining agreement executed on or after the date of voluntary recognition will not bar a decertification or rival union petition unless notice of recognition has been given and 45 days have passed without a valid petition being filed.

We do not question the legality of voluntary recognition agreements based on a union's showing of majority support. Voluntary recognition itself predates the National Labor Relations Act and is undisputedly lawful under it. We also do not address the legality of card-check and/or neutrality agreements preceding recognition. [T]he issue before us is limited to deciding whether an employer's voluntary recognition of a union based on a presumably valid majority showing—usually consisting of signed authorization cards—should bar a decertification or rival union election petition for some period of time thereafter.

The Board announced the recognition-bar doctrine in *Keller Plastics Eastern, Inc.,* 157 N.L.R.B. 583 (1966). This was an unfair labor practice case in which the complaint alleged that the respondent employer unlawfully executed a collective-bargaining agreement with a minority union. It was stipulated that the employer had lawfully recognized the union based on its majority representative status, but the union no longer retained majority support when the parties executed their contract a month later. The Board dismissed the complaint, reasoning that,

> like situations involving certifications, Board orders, and settlement agreements, the parties must be afforded a reasonable time to bargain and to execute the contracts resulting from such bargaining. Such negotiations can succeed, however, and the policies of the Act can thereby be effectuated, only if the parties can normally rely on the continuing representative status of the lawfully recognized union for a reasonable period of time.

Soon after *Keller Plastics,* the Board relied on the recognition-bar doctrine in holding that a respondent employer unlawfully withdrew its voluntary recognition of a union based on the filing of a decertification petition approximately two and a half months after the recognition agreement. *Universal Gear Services Corp.,* 157 N.L.R.B. 1169 (1966), *enfd.* 394 F.2d 396 (6th Cir. 1968). Then, in *Sound Contractors,* 162 N.L.R.B. 364 (1966), the Board said that the recognition-bar doctrine would apply in representation cases to bar the filing of election petitions for a reasonable time after voluntary recognition. Although the Board permitted the processing of a petition in *Sound Contractors* because the rival union filing it was engaged in organizing the employer's employees at the time the incumbent was recognized, the Board has since broadly applied the recognition bar and dismissed petitions in circumstances that raise serious questions whether employee free choice was given adequate weight. While Section 9 of the Act permits the exercise of employee free choice concerning union representation through the voluntary recognition process, this does not require that Board policy in representation case proceedings must treat the majority card showings the same as the choice expressed in Board elections. On the contrary, both the Board and courts have long recognized that the freedom of choice guaranteed employees by Section 7 is better realized by a secret election than a card check. "[S]ecret elections are generally the most satisfactory—indeed the preferred—method of ascertaining whether a union has majority support."

MEMBERS LIEBMAN and WALSH, dissenting in part, but concurring in the result:

As the majority recognizes, the Board's task in these cases is to balance the Act's twin interests in promoting stable bargaining relationships and employee free choice. But the appropriate balance was struck 40 years ago, in *Keller Plastics,* and nothing in the majority's decision justifies its radical departure from that well-settled, judicially approved precedent. The voluntary recognition bar, as consistently applied for the past four decades, promotes both interests: it honors the free choice already exercised by a majority of unit employees, while promoting stable bargaining relationships. By contrast, the majority's decision subverts both interests: it subjects the will of the majority to that of a 30 percent minority, and destabilizes nascent bargaining relationships. In addition, the majority's view fails to give sufficient weight to the role of voluntary recognition in national labor policy and to the efficacy of existing unfair labor practice sanctions to remedy the problems the majority claims to see. Accordingly, we dissent.

LAMONS GASKET CO.

357 N.L.R.B. 739 (2011)

By CHAIRMAN LIEBMAN and MEMBERS BECKER, PEARCE, and HAYES:

"[A] bargaining relationship once rightfully established must be permitted to exist and function for a reasonable period in which it can be given a fair chance to succeed." *Franks Bros. Co. v. NLRB*, 321 U.S. 702, 705, 64 S. Ct. 817, 88 L. Ed. 1020 (1944). Consistent with that principle, it was settled Board law from 1966 to 2007 that an employer's voluntary recognition of a union, based on a showing of uncoerced majority support for representation, barred the processing of an election petition for a reasonable period of time, in order to permit the employees' chosen representative to serve in that capacity and seek to negotiate a collective-bargaining agreement with the employer. The "recognition bar" applied only after "good-faith recognition of a union by the employer based on an unassisted and uncoerced showing of interest from a majority of unit employees." *Smith's Food & Drug Centers, Inc.*, 320 NLRB 844, 846 (1996). During that 41-year period, no member of the Board dissented from the application of the recognition bar under circumstances such as those existing in this case and its application was uniformly sustained in the courts of appeals.

Four years ago, in *Dana Corp.*, 351 NLRB 434 (2007), a sharply divided Board rejected this longstanding principle, established in *Keller Plastics Eastern*, 157 NLRB 583 (1966), in favor of a "modified" recognition bar, under which a minority of employees are permitted immediately to challenge the freely expressed will of the majority. *Dana* established a 45-day "window period" after voluntary recognition during which employees may file a decertification petition supported by a 30-percent showing of interest. *Dana* further required that, in order to start the running of the 45-day window period after voluntary recognition, employers must post an official Board notice informing employees of their newly created right to seek an election within the 45-day period to oust the lawfully recognized union. Id. at 441–443. Wholly absent from the majority decision in *Dana* was any empirical evidence supporting the majority's suspicion that the showing of majority support that must underlie any voluntary recognition is not freely given or is otherwise invalid in a significant number of cases, or that the existing statutory mechanisms for preventing coercion in the solicitation of support and recognition based on coerced support are inadequate.

We granted review to consider the experiences of employers, employees, unions, and the Board under *Dana*. Based on our consideration of the record and the briefs of the parties and amici, as well as of publicly available data concerning the Board's processing of cases arising under *Dana*, we find that the approach taken in *Dana* was flawed, factually, legally, and as a matter of policy. Accordingly, we overrule *Dana* and return to the previously well-established rule barring an election petition for a reasonable period of time after voluntary recognition of a representative designated by a majority of employees. We also define, for the first time, the benchmarks for determining a "reasonable period of time."

I.   FACTS

On July 13, 2003, Lamons Gasket (the Employer) and the United Steel, Paper and Forestry, Rubber, Manufacturing, Energy, Allied Industrial and Service Workers International Union (the Union) entered into an agreement detailing the conditions under which the Employer would voluntarily recognize the Union as the representative of its employees at several facilities, including the facility in Houston, Texas. The agreement provided, inter alia, that the Employer would voluntarily recognize the Union upon presentation of proof of majority support for representation by the Union in the form of authorization cards signed by employees. On November 5, 2009, after presentation of signed cards from a majority of the unit employees to an arbitrator and the arbitrator's verification of the majority, the Employer voluntarily recognized the Union as the exclusive representative of a unit of production, maintenance, and warehouse employees at the Houston facility. As required by *Dana*, the Employer notified the Board's Region 16 that it had recognized the Union, and the Region transmitted a notice to the Employer to post in its facility notifying employees of the recognition and of their right to seek a decertification election within 45 days.

On November 23, the Employer posted the notice. On December 9, Michael E. Lopez (the Petitioner) filed a timely petition for a decertification election, supported by a showing of interest among at least 30 percent of the employees in the unit. On January 20, 2010, the Employer and the Union began bargaining for an initial collective-bargaining agreement. On July 21, the Regional Director issued a Decision and Direction of Election, finding that *Dana* was controlling and that the "voluntary recognition and the timely filed decertification petition raise a question [concerning representation]." The Union filed a request for review.

The Employer and the Union reached a collective-bargaining agreement on August 8. On August 26, the decertification election was held and the ballots were impounded because of the pending request for review. On August 27, the Board granted the Union's request for review and solicited briefs from the parties and amici.

III.   DISCUSSION

Congress has expressly recognized the legality of employers' voluntary recognition of their employees' freely chosen representative, as well as the place of such voluntary recognition in the statutory system of workplace representation. Nevertheless, the extraordinary process established in

Dana was, fundamentally, grounded on a suspicion that the employee choice which must precede any voluntary recognition is often not free and uncoerced, despite the law's requirement that it be so. The evidence now before us as a result of administering the *Dana* decision during the past 4 years demonstrates that the suspicion underlying the decision was unfounded. Without an adequate foundation, *Dana* thus imposed an extraordinary notice requirement, informing employees only of their right to reconsider their choice to be represented, under a statute commanding that the Board remain strictly neutral in relation to that choice. The decision in *Dana* thus undermined employees' free choice by subjecting it to official question and by refusing to honor it for a significant period of time, without sound justification. *Dana* was thus an unwarranted departure from the principle that "a bargaining relationship once rightfully established must be permitted to exist and function for a reasonable period in which it can be given a fair chance to succeed." *Franks Bros.*, 321 U.S. at 705. Prior to *Dana* and *MV Transportation*, 337 NLRB 770 (2002), which we also overrule today, the Board uniformly implemented that principle in a variety of contexts. The statutory policies that underlie the bars interposed in those contexts extend to voluntary recognition. For these reasons, as fully explained below, we conclude that *Dana* has been shown to be unnecessary and, in fact, to disserve the purposes of the Act.

A.   Congress Has Expressly Recognized Employers' Voluntary Recognition of Their Employees' Freely Chosen Representative as a Lawful Element of the System of Representation Created by the NLRA

Federal labor law not only permits, but expressly recognizes two paths employees may travel to obtain representation for the purpose of collective bargaining with their employer. As the Supreme Court observed, a "Board election is not the only method by which an employer may satisfy itself as to the union's majority status." *United Mine Workers v. Arkansas Oak Flooring Co.*, 351 U.S. 62, 72 fn. 8, 76 S. Ct. 559, 100 L. Ed. 941 (1956). In fact, as the *Dana* majority acknowledged, "Voluntary recognition itself predates the National Labor Relations Act and is undisputedly lawful under it." 351 NLRB at 436.

Voluntary recognition must be based on evidence of majority support for representation. Absent majority support, voluntary recognition is unlawful. *Ladies' Garment Workers' v. NLRB (Bernhard-Altmann)*, 366 U.S. 731, 81 S. Ct. 1603, 6 L. Ed. 2d 762 (1961). Voluntary recognition based on support that was induced by either union or employer coercion is unlawful, as is the coercion.

The evidence of majority support that must underlie voluntary recognition may take many forms. The *Dana* majority referred to voluntary recognition as "card-based recognition," 351 NLRB at 434, but that is an inaccurate or, at least, a drastically underinclusive characterization. Voluntary recognition may be, and has been, based on evidence of majority support as informal as employees walking into the owner's office and stating they wish to be represented by a union, . . . and as formal as a secret-ballot election conducted by a third party such as the American Arbitration Association. . . .

Clear evidence of Congress' intentions concerning the relationship between voluntary recognition and Board-supervised elections is contained in Section 9(c)(1)(A)(i) of the Act. In that section, Congress provided that employees could file a petition for an election, alleging that a substantial number of employees wish to be represented and "that their employer declines to recognize their representative." That language makes unmistakably clear that Congress recognized the practice of voluntary recognition and strongly suggests that Congress believed Board-supervised elections were necessary only when an employer had declined to recognize its employees' chosen representative.

Congress was well aware of the practice of voluntary recognition when it adopted the Act in 1935, because the practice long predated the Act. That is significant because Congress not only expressly recognized the practice in Section 9(c)(1)(A)(i), but also gave no indication anywhere in the Act that it intended to supplant that process with or subordinate it to Board-supervised elections. Importantly, Section 8(a)(5) of the Act requires an employer to bargain collectively with "the representatives of his employees," but does not specify that such representatives must be chosen in a Board-supervised election. Rather, Section 8(a)(5) states that the employer's obligation to bargain with its employees' representative is "subject to the provisions of section 9(a)." Section 9(a) similarly does not limit the exclusive representative of employees to representatives chosen in a Board-supervised election. Rather, Section 9(a) provides that "[r]epresentatives *designated or selected* for the purposes of collective bargaining by the majority of the employees" shall be the exclusive collective-bargaining representatives (emphasis supplied). In enacting the Taft-Hartley amendments in 1947, Congress considered, but rejected, an amendment to Section 8(a)(5) that would have permitted the Board to find that an employer had unlawfully refused to bargain only with "a union 'currently recognized by the employer or certified as such [through an election] under section 9.' " *NLRB v. Gissel Packing Co.*, 395 U.S. 575, 598, 89 S. Ct. 1918, 23 L. Ed. 2d 547 (1969) (citing H.R. Conf. Rep. No. 510, 80th Cong., 1st Sess., 41 (1947)). The purpose of the rejected amendment was to prevent the Board from issuing a bargaining order in favor of a union that had been *neither* voluntarily recognized nor selected in a Board-supervised election. Significantly, the proposed amendment did not so much as question the practice of voluntary recognition, but, in fact, equated voluntary recognition with certification after an election.

As the legislative history of the Taft-Hartley amendments demonstrates, voluntary recognition is not simply permitted under the Act, but its grant imposes statutory duties on the part of both the employer and the union, which have for over 75 years been enforced by the Board. "Once voluntary recognition has been granted to a majority union," the Board explained in *Brown & Connolly, Inc.*, supra, 237 NLRB at 275, "the Union becomes [the] exclusive collective-bargaining representative of the employees, and withdrawal or reneging from the commitment to recognize before a reasonable time for bargaining has elapsed violates the employer's bargaining obligation." In other words, voluntary recognition, no less than certification, creates a legally recognized and enforceable relationship between the employer and the recognized representative.

To be sure, the Act provides that the Board can *certify* a representative, with the attendant legal advantages thereof (including a 12-month bar) only after a Board-supervised election. Nevertheless, far from being the suspect and underground process the *Dana* majority characterized it to be, voluntary recognition has been woven into the very fabric of the Act since its inception and has, until the decision in *Dana*, been understood to be a legitimate means of giving effect to the uncoerced choice of a majority of employees. . . .

B. Experience Has Demonstrated that the Dana Procedures Are Unnecessary

In the 41 years between *Keller Plastics* and *Dana*, although individual Board members occasionally disagreed over the application of the recognition bar in particular cases, no Board Member challenged the existence of the bar itself. During those 41 years, there were no changes in the language of the Act or in its interpretation that would support limiting application of the recognition bar. As the majority in *Dana* essentially conceded when it granted review, the only change was the perception that unions were increasingly seeking voluntary recognition and doing so successfully.

Without some reason to think that Board doctrine was failing to promote statutory policies, the increased use of a recognition method that predates the Act itself and is not only lawful, but woven expressly into the Act's representation procedures, was a dubious basis for reexamining precedent. Yet, *Dana* did that and more: through adjudication, the *Dana* Board created an entirely new category of representation case and new filing and notice-posting requirements.

Four years ago, when *Dana* was decided, the majority stated, "There is good reason to question whether card signings . . . accurately reflect employees' true choice concerning union representation." *Dana*, 351 NLRB at 439. The majority cited no empirical evidence for that sweeping statement. Now, however, we have considerable empirical evidence, and it establishes that the *Dana* majority's assertion was wrong.

As of May 13, 2011, the Board had received 1,333 requests for *Dana* notices. In those cases, 102 election petitions were subsequently filed and 62 elections were held. In 17 of those elections, the employees voted against continued representation by the voluntarily recognized union, including 2 instances in which a petitioning union was selected over the recognized union and 1 instance in which the petition was withdrawn after objections were filed. Thus, employees decertified the voluntarily recognized union under the *Dana* procedures in only 1.2 percent of the total cases in which *Dana* notices were requested. Those statistics demonstrate that, contrary to the *Dana* majority's assumption, the proof of majority support that underlay the voluntary recognition during the past 4 years was a highly reliable measure of employee sentiment.

The Petitioner and supporting amici argue that the percentage of cases in which the recognized union was rejected is not insignificant. But whenever voters are given a chance to revisit their choice—whether that choice was expressed in an election or by signing cards—some individuals will likely change their minds. There is no reason to think that the same small degree of "buyer's remorse" would not occur after a secret-ballot election-and, in fact, it has. *Brooks v. NLRB*, 348 U.S. 96, 97, 75 S. Ct. 176, 99 L. Ed. 125 (1954), illustrates that very point. In *Brooks*, the union won a Board election by a vote of 8 to 5, but a week later, the employees presented the employer with a petition signed by nine employees stating that they no longer wanted union representation. The Court nevertheless held that the employer could not question the certified union's majority status for a period of 1 year. See also *Gissel*, supra, 395 U.S. at 604 (recognizing that a voter "may think better of his choice" shortly after an election). Thus, the fact that in a small percentage of cases, a vote held a month or two after a majority of employees have expressed their desire to be represented produces a contrary result says little about the validity of those employees' initial choice to vote yes or sign a card.

The *Dana* decision itself has produced the data that was absent from the majority's opinion, and that data demonstrates that the empirical assumption underlying the decision was erroneous. As the Supreme Court has explained, the "constant process of trial and error . . . differentiates perhaps more than anything else the administrative from the judicial process." *NLRB v. J. Weingarten, Inc.*, 420 U.S. 251, 265, 95 S. Ct. 959, 43 L. Ed. 2d 171 (1975), quoting *NLRB v. Seven-Up Bottling Co. of Miami*, 344 U.S. 344, 349, 73 S. Ct. 287, 97 L. Ed. 377 (1953). The "process of trial and error" has been followed here, and it supports overruling *Dana*.

C. Dana *Compromises the Neutrality of the Board and Undermines the Purposes of the Act*

Although *Dana* rhetorically aimed for a "finer balance" of interests, the procedures it created to achieve that balance actually placed the Board's thumb decidedly on one side of what should be a neutral scale. *Dana* subjected the majority's choice to an extraordinary, mandatory notice informing employees of their right to seek a decertification election—a notice that casts doubt on the majority's choice by suggesting that voluntary recognition is inherently suspect. The "Act is wholly neutral when it comes to [employees'] basic choice" of whether to be represented, *NLRB v. Savair Mfg. Co.*, 414 U.S. 270, 278, 94 S. Ct. 495, 38 L. Ed. 2d 495 (1973), but the notice scheme established in *Dana* is not.

Setting to one side the remedial notices that the Board requires be posted after an employer or labor organization violates the Act and the balanced notice informing employees about the details of an upcoming election, after *Dana*, the Board required that employees be notified of only two of their many rights under Section 7: (1) their right not to join and to limit their financial support of their lawfully chosen representative; and (2) their newly created right to file a petition seeking to decertify their recently chosen and lawfully, voluntarily recognized representative. Moreover, the Board required that an official Board notice be posted *only* for the latter purpose. This notice scheme is starkly at odds with both the express terms of Section 7, which vest in employees the right "to form, join, or assist labor organizations" and the right "to refrain from any or all such activities," as well as with the Board's statutory role as an impartial "referee" administrating Federal labor law. *H.K. Porter Co. v. NLRB*, 397 U.S. 99, 108, 90 S. Ct. 821, 25 L. Ed. 2d 146 (1970).

In no other context does the Board require that employees be given notice of their right to change their minds about a recent exercise of statutory rights. For example, when an employer withdraws recognition from employees' representative based on objective, but non-electoral evidence that the majority of employees no longer desire to be represented, the Board does not require that the employer post notice of employees' right to file a petition for an election to compel the employer to once again recognize the representative. This is the case even when the choice may have future consequences employees may not be fully aware of. Using the same example, when an employer withdraws recognition, the Board does not require that the employer post a notice informing employees that if they do not file a petition for an election to compel the employer to once again recognize the representative, the employer will be free to unilaterally change their terms and conditions of employment.

The *Dana* notice, understood in context, clearly suggests to employees that the Board considers their choice to be represented suspect and signals to employees that their choice should be reconsidered through the filing of a petition. Such administrative action is not appropriate under the Act.

D. The Statutory Policies Underlying the Board's System of Bars Extend to Voluntary Recognition

As we noted above, the Supreme Court recognized more than half a century ago that "a bargaining relationship once rightfully established must be permitted to exist and function for a reasonable period in which it can be given a fair chance to succeed." *Franks Bros.*, supra, 321 U.S. at 705. Underlying that principle is the recognition that "[a] union should be given ample time for carrying out its mandate on behalf of its members, and should not be under exigent pressure to produce hothouse results or be turned out." *Brooks*, supra, 348 U.S. at 100. Taken together, the *Franks* and *Brooks* decisions provided the underlying foundations for the "general Board policy of protecting validly established bargaining relationships during their embryonic stages." *NLRB v. Cayuga Crushed Stone, Inc.*, 474 F.2d 1380, 1384 fn. 5 (2d Cir. 1973).

In accordance with the logic of *Franks* and *Brooks*, the Board, with court approval, gradually developed a coherent body of jurisprudence—of which the recognition bar was but one element prior to *Dana*—barring election petitions or other challenges to a union's representative status for a reasonable period after a legally recognized and enforceable bargaining relationship was established. Such bars applied in the following circumstances.

First, after a duty to bargain is imposed on an employer as a result of Board certification after an election, a petition for a new election is barred for a period of 1 year, as is withdrawal of recognition by the employer. The former result is compelled by the Act and the latter is the result of Board precedent. . . .

Second, the Board precludes any challenge to the union's representative status for a reasonable period of time after the Board has issued a bargaining order against an employer as a remedy for unfair labor practices or when the employer has unlawfully withdrawn recognition or wholly refused to bargain. . . .

Third, prior to *Dana*, the Board precluded any challenge to a union's representative status for a reasonable period of time after an employer voluntarily recognized the union based on a showing of majority support outside a Board-supervised election. . . .

Finally, prior to *MV Transportation*, which we also overrule today, when a new employer assumed an operation and the conditions for successorship were satisfied so that the new employer also assumed a legally enforceable duty to recognize and bargain with a union that represented its predecessor's employees, the Board barred any challenge to the union's representative status for a similar reasonable period of time. *St. Elizabeth Manor, Inc.*, 329 NLRB 341 (1999).

Although the decisions cited above arose in different contexts— certification following a Board-supervised election, remedial bargaining orders, voluntary recognition, and successorship—they share the same animating principle: that a newly created bargaining relationship should be given a reasonable chance to succeed before being subject to challenge. "The common thread running through these decisions is that when a bargaining relationship has been initially established, or has been restored after being broken, it must be given a reasonable time to work and a fair chance to succeed." . . . The recognition bar was thus not an anomaly.

In *Keller Plastics*, *supra*, the Board applied the principles found in *Franks* and *Brooks* to hold that a legally enforceable bargaining relationship born out of voluntary recognition was also entitled to be insulated for a reasonable period of time from challenge to the union's majority status. The Board held that the parties' "negotiations can succeed . . . and the policies of the Act can thereby be effectuated, only if the parties can normally rely on the continuing representative status of the lawfully recognized union for a reasonable period of time." 157 NLRB at 587. In *Keller*, the Board held that an employer could not withdraw recognition, even if it had a good-faith doubt about the union's continued majority support, for a reasonable period of time. In *Sound Contractors*, supra, 162 NLRB 364, the Board extended *Keller Plastics* to representation cases, holding that a petition seeking to challenge the recognized union's status is barred for a reasonable period of time following the recognition. Id. at 365. Between *Keller Plastics* and *Dana*, the Board, repeatedly and without dissent, applied the recognition bar in cases like this one. The appellate courts also uniformly and repeatedly endorsed the recognition bar, relying on the Supreme Court's decisions in *Franks* and *Brooks* in doing so.

Dana did not wholly eliminate the recognition bar. Rather, it provides for a suspension of the bar pending confirmation of the employees' original, uncoerced choice through either a Board-supervised decertification election or a failure of at least 30 percent of employees to support a petition for such an election following what amounts to an official Board invitation to file such a petition. *Dana's* holding thus rests on the notion that the policy underlying the system of bars does not extend to voluntary recognition based on an uncoerced showing of majority support for representation, unless that majority support is confirmed by either an election or a form of knowing waiver of the right to request an election. That notion was erroneous.

The *Dana* majority focused narrowly on a comparison of the moment an employee signs an authorization card with the moment an employee marks a ballot and drops it in the ballot box. But the important policy choice at issue here requires a broader focus, considering the place of employees' choice in the statutory scheme and the existing means of protecting the integrity of the procedures used to register employees' choice. First, and most importantly, we must consider the purpose of the employees' choice and its place in the statutory scheme. Employees are choosing whether to be represented "for the purpose of collective bargaining" with their employer. In deciding whether to insulate the uncoerced choice of employees to be represented for that statutorily protected purpose for a reasonable period of time, it is surely relevant that their employer, the party that will sit on the other side of the table in bargaining with their chosen representative, has voluntarily agreed to recognize the employees' representative and engage in such bargaining. In other words, both the statutory protection of employees' choice concerning representation and the provision of a government-supervised, but non-exclusive means of making that choice—the Board-supervised election—are merely elements in a Federally sanctioned system of private ordering. "The object of th[e] Act," the Supreme Court observed in *H.K. Porter*, supra, 397 U.S. at 103, "was not to allow governmental regulation of the terms and conditions of employment, but rather to insure that employers and their employees could work together to establish mutually satisfactory conditions." This congressional "solicitude for the collective-bargaining process," the Board recognized in *International Paper Co.*, 319 NLRB 1253, 1270 (1995), enf. denied on other grounds, 115 F.3d 1045, 325 U.S. App. D.C. 142 (D.C.Cir. 1997), "reflects a recognition that the process and the promotion of an autonomous relationship between the parties is the fundamental construct of the National Labor Relations Act." We believe that the fact that the parties to the congressionally created system of private ordering have entered into it voluntarily is highly relevant to the policy question of whether we should bar any challenge to employees' representative in that system for a reasonable period of time. This is because imposition of such a bar following voluntary recognition is more likely to advance the statutory purpose of preventing "industrial strife or unrest" and "encouraging the practice and procedure of collective bargaining." Sec. 1. We find this to be true both as a matter of logic and experience. Indeed, we find statutory support for this position both in the terms of Section 9(c)(1)(A)(i) discussed above and in section 1 where Congress made express the statutory aim of "encouraging practices fundamental to the friendly adjustment of industrial disputes." The simple fact is that bargaining after voluntary recognition is more likely to achieve the underlying "purpose" of the statutory "promotion of collective bargaining as a method of defusing and channeling conflict between labor and management." *First National Maint. Corp. v. NLRB*, 452 U.S. 666, 674, 101 S. Ct. 2573, 69 L. Ed. 2d 318 (1981). "The establishment of a successful collective-bargaining relationship is best accomplished by the parties themselves—the employer, the union, and the unit employees." *Smith Food & Drug*, supra, 320 NLRB at 847 (Chairman Gould, concurring).

Second, the policy choice before us requires consideration not simply of the means through which individual employees register their choice (signing an authorization card versus marking a ballot), but also of the rules used to aggregate those choices. In this regard, a more demanding standard is imposed on voluntary recognition than on certification following a Board-supervised election. In the latter, the ordinary rule universally used in elections for political office governs, i.e., a majority of the votes cast determines the outcome. *RCA Mfg. Co.*, 2 NLRB 159, 177–178 (1936). In order for voluntary recognition to be lawful, however, it must be based on a showing that a majority of *all* employees in the unit wish to be represented. See *Bernhard-Altmann*, supra, 366 U.S. at 734 fn. 4, 737–738. In fiscal year 2010, turnout in Board-supervised elections was 80.7 percent. In other words, on average, the choice of only 40 percent plus one of employees in a unit could bind all of their coworkers for a period of at least 12 months after an election while it took at least 50 percent to obtain representation pursuant to voluntary recognition.

Third, the policy choice before us requires consideration of both the contents of the rules preventing coercion of employees' choice and their enforcement mechanisms. In this regard, an employee who believes that a voluntarily recognized union lacks majority support, or that such support was not voluntary, is not without recourse. As pointed out in the dissent in *Dana*, recognition of a minority union violates Section 8(a)(2) and 8(b)(1)(A), and the remedy is to order the employer not to recognize or bargain with the union, and the union not to accept recognition, until the union is certified by the Board following a Board-supervised election. See *Bernhard-Altmann*, supra, 366 U.S. 731; *Dairyland USA Corp.*, 347 NLRB 310, 313–314 (2006), enfd. 273 Fed. Appx. 40 (2d Cir. 2008). If an employer that has violated Section 8(a)(2) by recognizing a union absent uncoerced majority support subsequently enters into a contract with the union and deducts dues or fees pursuant to a union-security clause, it is jointly and severally liable along with the union to repay such deductions. See, e.g., *Dairyland*, supra, 347 NLRB at 314. Coercion by an employer or a union during the organizing campaign violates Section 8(a)(1) and 8(b)(1)(A). Significantly, anyone—including any employee—may file an unfair labor practice charge alleging such conduct. The Board's General Counsel then investigates and, if probable cause is found, prosecutes. Moreover, employees have 6 months following any unlawful coercion or improper recognition to file a charge, while objections to conduct affecting the results of an election must be filed within 7 days of the tally. See Sec. 102.69(a) of the Board's Rules. The majority in *Dana* did not explain why these existing safeguards, which, in critical respects, are more protective of freedom of choice than those used in Board-supervised elections, are inadequate to insure that voluntary recognition truly rests on employees' free choice. For these reasons, we conclude that the policies underlying the Board's system of bars extend to a new collective-bargaining relationship lawfully established by voluntary recognition without the imposition of the extraordinary procedures created by *Dana*.

Dana characterized its modifications of the recognition bar as the result of a balance of free choice and stability in bargaining relationships. See 351 NLRB at 434. However, the modifications have proved unnecessary to protect free choice and thus unnecessarily undermine the Act's purpose of encouraging collective bargaining with employees' freely chosen representative. As the dissent in *Dana* observed, "Although the parties will technically have an obligation to bargain upon recognition, the knowledge that an election petition may be filed gives the employer little incentive to devote time and attention to bargaining during the first 45 days following recognition." 351 NLRB at 447. Our experience under *Dana* makes clear that this period of uncertainty ordinarily extends beyond the 45 days expected by the dissent. Our records reveal that the average time between an employer informing the Regional Office of voluntary recognition and the employer posting the *Dana* notice is 18.7 days. Adding the 45 days the window for filing a petition must remain open, this means that meaningful bargaining is likely to be delayed at least 63 days, not including the time between recognition and when the employer informs the Regional Office that recognition has been granted. If an employer refused to agree on dates for bargaining to begin for that length of time, we likely would find a failure to bargain in good faith. Yet *Dana* virtually guarantees such a delay in serious bargaining and the resulting undermining of the "nascent relationship between the employer and the lawfully recognized union." *Smith's Food*, supra, 320 NLRB at 845–846. The lengthy period of uncertainty created by *Dana* thus unnecessarily interferes with the bargaining process, rendering successful collective bargaining less likely.

The potential for uncertainty and delay in serious bargaining created by *Dana* actually disserves the very employee free choice the majority sought to protect, because employees who support the union do so because they want meaningful representation as soon as practicable. The recognition bar "effectuates rather than impedes employee free choice." *Smith's Food & Drug*, supra, 320 NLRB at 848 (Chairman Gould, concurring). This is because, "[w]hen employees execute authorization cards during a union organizing drive, their hope is to obtain union representation as soon as possible. The Board provides no benefit to these employees by delaying the implementation of their designation in order to reconfirm through an election the desires they have already expressed." Id.

E.   A Return To Formerly Settled Law Is Warranted

Dana represented a major change in Board law, one that was based on the majority's suspicion of voluntary recognition—suspicion that, based on the empirical evidence acquired since 2007, we conclude was unwarranted. We therefore overrule *Dana* and return to the previously settled rule that an employer's voluntary recognition of a union, based on a showing of the union's majority status, bars an election petition for a reasonable period of time.

As in *UGL-UNICCO*, supra, also decided today, which defined the reasonable period of bargaining during which the "successor bar" will apply, we alter the rule of *Keller Plastics* in one respect. Drawing on the Board's decision in *Lee Lumber & Building Material Corp.*, 334 NLRB 399 (2001), we define a reasonable period of bargaining, during which the recognition bar will apply, to be no less than 6 months after the parties' first bargaining session and no more than 1 year. In determining whether a reasonable period has elapsed in a given case, we will apply the multifactor test of *Lee Lumber* and impose the burden of proof on the General Counsel to show that further bargaining should be required.

While we overrule *Dana*, we have made no changes to established law regarding secret-ballot elections. An election remains the only way for a union to obtain Board certification and its attendant benefits. Neither the pre-*Dana* law nor the law after today equates the processes of voluntary recognition and certification following a Board-supervised election. We merely restore settled law on the recognition bar, from which *Dana* was a brief and unwarranted detour. Our decision reflects important values: fidelity to congressional purpose, the neutrality of the Board, and the consistency and coherence of Board doctrine. Each of these obligations strongly supports overruling *Dana* and we do so today. Our dissenting colleague repeatedly asserts that our decision reflects "ideological bias." We will not respond in kind because the statutory, doctrinal and policy grounds for our decision are fully set forth above. The rule that we return to today was adopted by the Board in 1966 and was repeatedly reaffirmed by Board Members appointed by Republican and Democratic Presidents during the subsequent 41 years until it was reversed in *Dana*. Not-withstanding the dissent's heated rhetoric, we take some comfort in aligning ourselves with this long line of distinguished public servants.

We will apply this new rule retroactively in all pending cases, except those in which an election was held and the ballots have been opened and counted, consistent with the Board's established approach in representation proceedings.

MEMBER HAYES, dissenting:

Today, my colleagues overrule *Dana Corp.* in this case and *MV Transportation* in *UGL-UNICCO*. Thus, they restore an immediate bar to a secret ballot election in all voluntary recognition and successorship situations. Such a bar will preclude employees or rival unions from filing Board election petitions for a minimum of 6 months and for a maximum of 4 years. Theirs is a purely ideological policy choice, lacking any real empirical support and uninformed by agency expertise. They have failed to provide any reasoned explanation why the policies they advocate are preferable to the reasonable policies established in the precedent they now overrule. As such, their holdings are not entitled to deference and should be put to strict scrutiny upon judicial review.

I.

To begin, the majority mischaracterizes *Dana* as an assault on voluntary recognition. On the contrary, the *Dana* decision was not intended to interfere with the establishment of collective-bargaining relationships through voluntary recognition, and, as discussed below, it has not been shown to have had such an effect. *Dana* focused on if and when an election bar and corollary contract bar should apply in the wake of lawful voluntary recognition.

Notably, *Dana* addressed only the filing of employee and rival union petitions during the 45-day open period. None of the decisions by the courts of appeals cited by the majority represents an express endorsement of a discretionary recognition bar to such petitions. Consistent with *Keller Plastics*, an unfair labor practice case, they enforce Board orders against *employers* for unilaterally withdrawing recognition from a union. These decisions are based on the equitable premise that the employers waived the right to insist on an election by voluntarily recognizing the union and must therefore bargain for a reasonable period of time without challenge to the union's majority status. None of these cases states that the Board must have a corresponding immediate bar against *employee* or *rival union* election petitions, particularly if there are substantial justifications for delaying the imposition of a bar for a short while to better protect employee free choice.

II.

In granting review of *Dana*, the majority plainly sought empirical evidence in order to legitimize a purely ideological reversal of policy. Unfortunately, the majority's invitation for parties and amici to provide external empirical evidence of experience under *Dana* yielded a goose egg. Only five respondents sought to overturn *Dana*, and only two of them supported their arguments for doing so with the barest of anecdotal evidence. Thus, the only real empirical evidence of experience, and the only evidence to which my colleagues refer, is the Board's own statistical compilation. As summarized by the majority, these statistics show that as of May 13, 2011, the Board had received 1,333 requests for *Dana* notices. In those cases, 102 election petitions were subsequently filed and 62 elections were held. In 17 of those elections, the employees voted against continued representation by the voluntarily recognized union, including two instances in which a petitioning union was selected over the recognized union and one instance in which the petition was withdrawn after objections were filed.

In the majority's view, these statistics show both that the alleged premise in *Dana* about the reliability of cards was faulty and that, in any event, the *Dana* process is unnecessary. I disagree. The statistics show that in one of every four elections held, an employee majority voted against representation by the incumbent recognized union. While that 25-percent rejection rate is below the recent annual rejection rate for all decertification elections, it is nevertheless substantial and supports the need for retention of a notice requirement and brief open period.

As for the 1231 cases in which *Dana* notices were requested, but no petitions were filed, we know *nothing* about the reasons for this outcome. To be more specific, we do not know anything about the reliability of the proof of the majority support that underlay voluntary recognition in each of these cases, nor do we know the reasons why no petition was filed. It is plausible that in many instances, even if a certain number of card signings or other showing of support did not accurately reflect the views of some employees, there remained a majority favoring representation by the recognized union. This is particularly likely where the parties have an agreement requiring the union to make a supermajority showing in order to gain recognition. It is also possible that in some cases a majority of employees would have voted against the recognized union in an election but, in spite of the Board notice, felt that the choice on union representation was a fait accompli. The majority holding in a different *Dana* case, overturning well-established precedent, that an employer and union can negotiate substantive terms and conditions of employment even prior to majority-based recognition will no doubt encourage this perception. Yet another possibility is that employees in a particular case may have been inclined to petition for an election but were persuaded by the results of collective-bargaining not to do so. This, of course, is an outcome that *Dana* facilitates by requiring that the usual Section 8(d) bargaining obligation should apply during the open period for filing.

In sum, here is what we really know from the *Dana* experience: (1) *Dana* has served the intended purpose of assuring employee free choice in those cases where the choice made in the preferred Board electoral process contradicted the showing on which voluntary recognition was granted; (2) in those cases where the recognized union's majority status was affirmed in a *Dana* election, the union gained the additional benefits of 9(a) certification, including a 1-year bar to further electoral challenge; (3) there is no substantial evidence that *Dana* has had any discernible impact on the number of union voluntary recognition campaigns, or on the success rate of such campaigns; and (4) there is no substantial evidence that *Dana* has had any discernible impact on the negotiation of bargaining agreements during the open period or on the rate at which agreements are reached after voluntary recognition.

The majority's solicitation of empirical evidence with respect to the *Dana* experience was ostensibly based on the premise that such information was necessary to decide whether or not to adhere to the modified recognition bar policy established there. That premise has been exposed as false. We have received no meaningful information from external sources. Our own statistics confirm *Dana's* benefits and reveal no negatives in the effectuation of statutory goals. Yet the majority concludes that *Dana* must be overruled.

IV.

My colleagues are concerned with policies of adherence to longstanding precedent, employee free choice, and labor relations stability only when those policies further unionization, which they believe in good faith must be the paradigm for the American work force. If a decades-old recognition bar policy serves this aim, then it is unassailable regardless of a dramatic, empirically established change in union organizational tactics that impacts the statutorily preferred practice of resolving questions concerning representation through a Board election. If not, then longstanding election policies may be sua sponte reviewed for elimination. If employee free choice means a vote for unionization, it must be nurtured like a newborn babe. If not, it should be suspected and exposed to immediate challenge. If labor relations stability means the establishment or maintenance of a collective-bargaining relationship, then a wall of legal protections should be erected to that end. If labor relations stability means the neutral continuation of a status quo in which over 90 percent of the private work force is unrepresented, then lines must be radically redrawn to change the status quo. In any event, labor relations stability clearly does not mean consistency and coherence in the interpretation and application of Federal labor relations law in order to facilitate the ability of employees, unions and employers to order their relationships.

The notice and open period requirements promulgated in *Dana* did represent an attempt to balance competing statutory interests. Empirical evidence of *Dana's* application in the past four years indicates that it has served its purpose without adverse impact on voluntary recognition. I dissent from its overruling.

NOTES

1.   Neutrality and card check agreements typically provide for enforcement in arbitration, and courts have upheld their enforceability. What if the employer, in apparent violation of a neutrality and card check agreement,

files a representation petition with the Board? In *Shaw's Supermarkets*, 343 N.L.R.B. 963 (2004), the employer and union had an after acquired stores clause in their collective bargaining agreement which provided that the employer would recognize the union and apply the contract when a majority of employees in a new store authorized the union to represent them. The regional director dismissed the employer's representation petition because it contravened the agreement. The Board reversed and remanded to the regional director to consider such issues as whether the clause covered the bargaining unit at issue, whether the employer waived its right to file a representation petition, and whether such a waiver was contrary to public policy. What if a union grieves the employer's violation and demands arbitration? How should an arbitrator handle the NLRA issues? For a discussion of this complicated area, see Laura Cooper, *Privatizing Labor Law: Neutrality, Card Check Agreements and the Role of the Arbitrator*, 83 Ind. L.J. 1589 (2008). For examples of arbitration awards, see *Alden North Shore*, 120 Lab. Arb. (BNA) 1469 (2004) (Malin, Arb.); *Dana Corp.*, 76 Lab. Arb. (BNA) 125 (1981) (Mittenthal, Arb.).

2.   In *Lamons Gasket*, both majority and dissent refer to the issue presented by neutrality agreements involving premature recognition of, and bargaining with, a union before it receives majority support by workers, a potential section 8(a)(2) violation. This is the *Majestic Weaving* doctrine. *See Majestic Weaving*, 147 N.L.R.B. 869 (1964), *enf. denied* 355 F.2d 854 (2d Cir. 1966). The doctrine is implicated in the following case involving Dana Corp.

DANA CORP. (II)
356 N.L.R.B. 256 (2010)

CHAIRMAN LIEBMAN and MEMBER PEARCE:

Respondents Dana Corporation and International Union, United Automobile, Aerospace, and Agricultural Implement Workers of America (UAW), AFL-CIO—two parties with a long history of collective bargaining—entered into a Letter of Agreement (LOA or Agreement) setting forth ground rules for additional union organizing, procedures for voluntary recognition upon proof of majority support, and substantive issues that collective bargaining would address if and when Dana recognized the UAW at an unorganized facility. The issues before us are whether, in entering into and maintaining the LOA, Dana rendered unlawful support to the UAW in violation of Section 8(a)(1) and (2) the Act, and whether the UAW accepted that support in violation of Section 8(b)(1)(A). We conclude that the Agreement was lawful, and we therefore dismiss the complaint.

II.   FACTS

Dana manufactures automotive parts at about 90 facilities throughout the United States, Canada, and as many as 30 other countries. Dana and the UAW have a longstanding bargaining relationship: the UAW represents Dana's employees in nine bargaining units at various locations covering 2200 to 2300 employees in total.

This case arose at Dana's St. Johns, Michigan facility, where Dana employs about 305 unrepresented employees and where, in early 2002, the UAW began an organizing campaign. On August 6, 2003, Dana and the UAW entered into the LOA, which set forth a framework to govern their relationship in the future, in the event that a majority of the St. Johns employees chose to designate the UAW as their exclusive collective-bargaining representative. The LOA's introductory statement of purpose recognized "that dramatic changes in the domestic automotive market ha[ve] created new quality, productivity and competitiveness challenges for the automotive component supplier." It further stated that Dana and the UAW believed that "these challenges will be more effectively met through a partnership that is more positive, non-adversarial and with constructive attitudes toward each other." The introductory statement continued:

> Employee freedom to choose is a paramount concern of Dana as well as the UAW. We both believe that membership in a union is a matter of personal choice and acknowledge that if a majority of employees wish to be represented by a union, Dana will recognize that choice. The Union and the Company will not allow anyone to be intimidated or coerced into a decision on this important matter. The parties are also committed to an expeditious procedure for determining majority status.

The LOA then set forth ground rules for both parties that would be applicable in any organizing campaign the UAW might undertake at an unorganized Dana facility. Dana agreed to inform employees that it was "totally neutral regarding the issue of representation by the Union" and that it has "a constructive and positive relationship with the UAW and that a National Partnership Agreement with the UAW exists in which both parties are committed to the success and growth" of Dana. Dana agreed to provide the UAW, upon request, with a list of the names and addresses of employees in any facility covered by the agreement and to permit the UAW to meet with employees in nonwork areas. The parties made a no-strike/no-lockout commitment, effective at a given facility when the UAW requested an employee list for the facility and continuing until a first contract was negotiated or any contract-related dispute was resolved.

Dana agreed to recognize and bargain with the UAW upon proof of majority status, to be determined by a card check by a neutral third party. The LOA specified that Dana "may not recognize the Union as the exclusive representative of employees in the absence of a showing" of majority status.

In addition, the LOA set forth certain principles that would inform future bargaining on particular topics, if and when the UAW was recognized. For instance, regarding healthcare, article 4.2.1 of the LOA stated that "the Union commits that in no event will bargaining between the parties erode current solutions and concepts in place or scheduled to be implemented January 1, 2004, at Dana's operations which include premium sharing, deductibles, and out-of-pocket maximums." Article 4.2.2 specified that the minimum duration of any collective-bargaining agreement between Dana and the UAW would be 4 years, and that the parties would discuss contract durations of up to 5 years. Article 4.2.4 provided as follows:

> The parties agree that in labor agreements bargained pursuant to this Letter, the following conditions must be included for the facility to have a reasonable opportunity to succeed and grow.
>
> • Healthcare costs that reflect the competitive reality of the supplier industry and product(s) involved
>
> • Minimum classifications
>
> • Team-based approaches
>
> • The importance of attendance to productivity and quality
>
> • Dana's idea program (two ideas per person per month and 80% implementation)
>
> • Continuous improvement
>
> • Flexible Compensation
>
> • Mandatory overtime when necessary (after qualified volunteers) to support the customer.

The LOA also specified steps that the parties would take if they were unable to reach a final agreement. Article 4.2 provided that, after 5 months, the parties would submit unresolved issues to a joint UAW/Dana committee. If 6 months were to pass without a contract, the parties would submit unresolved issues to a neutral for interest arbitration, and the neutral would select either Dana's final offer or the UAW's.

In early December 2003, the UAW requested a list of the employees working at the St. Johns facility, pursuant to the LOA. Thereafter, the three individual Charging Parties, who are Dana employees at the St. Johns facility, filed unfair labor practice charges. On September 30, 2004, the General Counsel issued a complaint alleging that, by "entering into" and "maintain[ing]" the LOA, Dana rendered unlawful assistance to the UAW in violation of Section 8(a)(2) and (1) of the Act and the UAW restrained and coerced employees in the exercise of their Section 7 rights in violation of Section 8(b)(1)(A).

III. THE [ADMINISTRATIVE LAW] JUDGE'S DECISION

[The Administrative Law Judge] observed that an employer violates Section 8(a)(2) when it recognizes a minority union as the exclusive bargaining representative, and that a union violates Section 8(b)(1)(A) when it accepts such recognition. *Bernhard-Altmann.* The judge concluded, however, that Dana had not granted recognition here.

The judge rejected the argument that the LOA constituted a collective-bargaining agreement from which recognition could be inferred. He found that the LOA "touch[ed] upon" some terms and conditions of employment, but was "a far cry from a collective-bargaining agreement." The judge reasoned that the lack of recognition and the absence of a collective-bargaining agreement distinguished this case from *Majestic Weaving,* 147 NLRB 869 (1964), *enf. denied* 355 F.2d 854 (2d Cir. 1966). In that case, the Board held that an employer violated Section 8(a)(1) and (2) by negotiating a complete collective-bargaining agreement, the signing of which was conditioned on the union's achieving majority status.

Accordingly, the judge dismissed the complaint.

V. DISCUSSION

We agree with the judge, for the reasons stated below, that the complaint should be dismissed on the merits. We decline the General Counsel's invitation to extend the Board's decision in *Majestic Weaving* to reach the facts of this case. Neither *Majestic Weaving* nor *Bernhard-Altmann* requires us to find a violation here, and such a finding would contravene fundamental policies embodied in the Act. We leave for another day the adoption of a general standard for regulating prerecognition negotiations between unions and employer. As the Supreme Court has observed, there are issues of labor law where the " 'nature of the problem, as revealed by unfolding variant situations,' requires 'an evolutionary process for its rational response, not a quick, definitive formula as a comprehensive answer.' " *Eastex, Inc. v. NLRB,* 437 U.S. 556, 575 (1978), quoting *Electrical Workers v. NLRB,* 366 U.S. 667, 674 (1961).

A.

Section 8(a)(2) of the Act prohibits an employer from "dominat[ing] or interfer[ing] with the formation or administration of any labor organization or contribut[ing] financial or other support to it." The primary legislative purpose of Section 8(a)(2) "was to eradicate company unionism, a practice whereby employers would establish and control in-house labor organizations in order to prevent organization by autonomous unions." 1 Higgins, *Developing Labor Law* 418–419 (5th ed. 2006). In the words of the Act's chief sponsor, Senator Robert Wagner:

> Genuine collective bargaining is the only way to attain equality of bargaining power. . . . The greatest obstacles to collective

bargaining are employer-dominated unions, which have multiplied with amazing rapidity. . . .

1 Leg. Hist. 15 (NLRA 1935).[9]

Section 8(a)(2) is grounded in the notion that foisting a union on unconsenting employees and thus impeding employees from pursuing representation by outside unions are incompatible with "genuine collective bargaining." It is in this context that the statutory prohibition on "financial or other support" to unions must be understood.

Although it is clear that an employer may not render unlawful support, "it is also clear—and the Board has so held with court approval—that a certain amount of employer cooperation with the efforts of a union to organize is insufficient to constitute unlawful assistance." *Steak and Brew of Huntington*, 205 NLRB 1025, 1031 (1973). "The quantum of employer cooperation which surpasses the line and becomes unlawful support is not susceptible to precise measurement. Each case must stand or fall on its own particular facts." Id. at 1031.

The Board and courts have long recognized that various types of agreements and understandings between employers and unrecognized unions fall within the framework of permissible cooperation. Notably, employers and unions may enter into "members-only" agreements, which establish terms and conditions of employment only for those employees who are members of the union. See *Consolidated Edison Co. v. NLRB*, 305 U.S. 197, 237, 59 S. Ct. 206, 83 L. Ed. 126 (1938). In that decision, the Supreme Court reasoned that such agreements could be beneficial to interstate and foreign commerce by protecting against disruptions caused by industrial strife. Id.

An employer is also permitted to express to employees a desire to enter into a bargaining relationship with a particular union and, essentially, to inform employees that it will enter into a bargaining agreement upon proof of majority support. *Coamo Knitting Mills*, 150 NLRB 579 (1964).

Outside the Section 8(a)(2) context, the Board and courts have also considered and enforced agreements between employers and unrecognized unions. For example, an employer may agree that it will voluntarily recognize a union in the future if the union demonstrates majority support by means other than an election, including signed authorization cards. See, e.g., *Snow & Sons*, 134 NLRB 709, 710 (1961) (employer bound by agreement to honor results of card check), *enfd.* 308 F.2d 687 (9th Cir. 1962); *Hotel & Restaurant Employees Local 217 v. J.P. Morgan Hotel*, 996

---

[9]   Company unions proliferated in the years following passage of Sec. 7(a) of the National Industrial Recovery Act (the precursor to Sec. 7 of the National Labor Relations Act), and "a consensus opinion was that the primary motive in many cases was to forestall union organization." Kaufman, *Accomplishments and Shortcomings of Nonunion Employee Representation in the Pre-Wagner Act Years: A Reassessment*, Nonunion Employee Representation 25 (2000).

F.2d 561 (2d Cir. 1993) (enforcing card-check and neutrality agreement pursuant to Sec. 301 of Labor-Management Relations Act). The courts have rejected arguments that card-check/neutrality agreements between unions and employers violate Section 302 of the Taft-Hartley Act, which (with certain exceptions) prohibits employers from providing a "thing of value" to unions.

B.

Although the law permits certain forms of cooperation between employers and minority or unrecognized unions, an employer crosses the line between cooperation and support, and violates Section 8(a)(2) when it recognizes a minority union as the exclusive bargaining representative. This is the principle reflected in the Supreme Court's decision in *Bernhard-Altmann*, supra.

The Supreme Court held that the employer violated Section 8(a)(2) by recognizing a minority union as the exclusive bargaining representative (even though the employer believed in good faith that the union had majority support) and that the union violated Section 8(b)(1)(A) by accepting recognition. In the Court's view, it was irrelevant that the union had majority support at the time the collective-bargaining agreement was executed, because the employer's prior recognition of the union, when it did not have majority support, was "a *fait accompli* depriving the majority of the employees of their guaranteed right to choose their own representative." 366 U.S. at 736 (quoting the lower court's decision, 280 F.2d 616, 621, 108 U.S. App. D.C. 68 (D.C. Cir. 1960)). The Court reasoned that the union's later acquisition of majority status "itself might indicate that the recognition secured by the [MOU] afforded [the union] a deceptive cloak of authority with which to persuasively elicit additional employee support." Id.

Three years after *Bernhard-Altmann*, and relying entirely on the Supreme Court's decision, the Board held in *Majestic Weaving*, supra, that an employer violated Section 8(a)(2) in similar circumstances. 147 NLRB at 860–861. In *Majestic Weaving*, the Teamsters Union, which did not represent employees at any of Majestic's facilities, requested recognition at one facility where Majestic was still in the process of hiring employees. Majestic orally agreed to negotiate a contract, "conditioning the actual signing with [the Teamsters] on the latter achieving a majority at the 'conclusion' of negotiations." The parties then negotiated a collective-bargaining agreement; prior to signing it, the Teamsters presented Majestic with authorization cards signed by a majority of the unit employees. Another union, the Textile Workers, then began an organizing campaign at the facility, ultimately securing authorization cards from a majority of the employees and demanding recognition. Majestic refused that demand, asserting that it had already recognized the Teamsters.

The Board found that Majestic had unlawfully assisted the Teamsters by facilitating the solicitation of authorization cards by a company supervisor and had unlawfully recognized the Teamsters. The Board observed that:

> In the *Bernhard-Altmann* case an interim agreement . . . was the vehicle for prematurely granting a union exclusive bargaining status which was found objectionable; in this case contract negotiation following an *oral recognition agreement* was the method. We see no difference between the two in the effect upon employee rights. 147 NLRB at 860 (emphasis added).

The Board accordingly ruled that Majestic's recognition of the Teamsters and negotiation of a collective-bargaining agreement with the union before it had achieved majority support violated Section 8(a)(2) of the Act. Id. at 860–861.

C.

The General Counsel and the Charging Parties argue that *Majestic Weaving* creates a per se rule that negotiation with a union "over substantive terms and conditions of employment" is unlawful if it occurs before the union has attained majority support. Such negotiations, they contend, grant the union "privileged" status in the eyes of employees and present the sort of "fait accompli" prohibited by *Majestic Weaving*, because "give and take negotiations" resulting in an agreement like the one involved here amount to "tacit recognition" of the union.

We reject this broad reading of *Majestic Weaving*. Neither *Majestic Weaving*, nor the decision on which it rests, *Bernhard-Altmann*, compels a finding that the conduct at issue here violated Section 8(a)(2). Adopting the prohibition urged by the General Counsel and the Charging Parties, in turn, would not advance the policies of the Act as a whole. Rather, it would create an unnecessary obstacle to legitimate collective bargaining without genuinely promoting employee free choice.1.

There are obvious and significant distinctions between this case and *Majestic Weaving*. *Majestic Weaving* involved an initial, oral grant of exclusive recognition by the employer to the union. That recognition was followed by the negotiation of a complete collective-bargaining agreement, which was consummated except for the ministerial act of execution by the parties. The union's showing of majority support not only came after the complete agreement was reached, but it depended on the solicitation of authorization cards by a supervisor, as facilitated by the employer itself.

Here, the LOA did no more than create a framework for future collective bargaining, if (as specified in the agreement) the UAW were first able to provide proof of majority status by means of a card-check conducted by a neutral third party. The LOA did not contain an exclusive-representation provision (the "vice" of the agreement in *Bernhard-Altmann*). Indeed, the LOA expressly prohibited Dana from recognizing the UAW without a showing of majority support. Only the negotiation of the LOA, and no other conduct, is alleged to be an unfair labor practice interfering with employee free choice.

The crux of the General Counsel's position is that the negotiation of the LOA itself precluded a truly free choice. That position has no real support in *Majestic Weaving* or *Bernhard-Altmann*. In those cases, a premature grant of exclusive recognition by the employer gave the union, in the Supreme Court's words, a "deceptive cloak of authority" as it sought employee support. But neither the negotiation of the LOA nor the Agreement itself can be equated with a grant of exclusive recognition as that concept has been long understood in our law.

That the LOA set forth certain principles that would inform future bargaining on particular topics—bargaining contingent on a showing of majority support, as verified by a neutral third party—is not enough to constitute exclusive recognition. The UAW did not purport to speak for a majority of Dana's employees, nor was it treated as if it did. On the contrary, the LOA unmistakably disclaimed exclusive recognition by setting forth the process by which such status could be achieved. Nothing in the LOA affected employees' existing terms and conditions of employment or obligated Dana to alter them. Any potential effect on employees would have required substantial negotiations, following recognition pursuant to the terms of the Agreement. Nothing in the Agreement, its context, or the parties' conduct would reasonably have led employees to believe that recognition of the UAW was a foregone conclusion or, by the same token, that rejection of UAW representation by employees was futile.

The General Counsel's position is rooted in the assumption that any employer conduct having the potential to enhance an unrecognized union's status in the employees' eyes is unlawful. But that is contrary to our law. For example, as shown above in Section A, an employer may negotiate nonexclusive "members-only" agreements, may agree to remain neutral in an organizing campaign, may agree to voluntarily recognize the union upon proof of majority support, and may state its preference for unionization. In each of those scenarios, the employer's cooperation with the union could enhance the union's prestige, yet none of them is unlawful.

All of the decisions relied upon by the General Counsel for the proposition that negotiation of the LOA amounted to "tacit recognition" are easily distinguishable. None involves a situation where recognition is attacked as unlawful under Section 8(a)(2). Rather, they involve employers that reviewed a union's proffered evidence of majority support and either began bargaining or agreed to bargain, but later denied that a legally binding recognition had occurred. Plainly, those circumstances are not present here. The UAW has not claimed majority status, let alone presented proof to Dana, and neither the UAW nor Dana claims that recognition has taken place.

In this case, the UAW and Dana stayed well within the boundaries of what the Act permits. The LOA was reached at arm's length, in a context free of unfair labor practices. It disclaimed any recognition of the union as exclusive bargaining representative, and it created, on its face, a lawful mechanism for determining if and when the union had achieved majority support. The LOA had no immediate effect on employees' terms and conditions of employment, and even its potential future effect was both limited and contingent on substantial future negotiations. As its statement of purpose makes clear, the LOA was an attempt to directly address certain challenges of the contemporary workplace. Considering the LOA as a whole, we find nothing that presents UAW representation as a fait accompli or that otherwise constitutes unlawful support of the UAW. Indeed, according to the General Counsel, employees here had no difficulty in rejecting the UAW's representation.

3.

Our dissenting colleague asserts that we "effectively overrule *Majestic Weaving*, at least in substantial part." But this claim, like the General Counsel's position here, is predicated on a sweeping interpretation of *Majestic Weaving*, grounded in a different view of labor relations policy. That policy view is the basis for our colleague's insistence that "[t]here are no meaningful factual or legal distinctions between" this case and *Majestic Weaving*. We have read *Majestic Weaving* carefully, and we have explained why we regard that case as, indeed, distinct both factually and legally from this one. It is appropriate, of course, for the Board both to interpret its own decisions and, where the language of the Act itself does not settle a question of labor law, to apply its own policy views.

The dissent's reading of *Majestic Weaving* rests on two aspects of that decision: a provision in the Board's order and the overruling of an earlier Board decision, *Julius Resnick*. . . . Neither point compels the conclusion that the dissent reaches. The order in *Majestic Weaving* prohibited the employer from, among other things, "negotiating a contract with any labor organization which does not represent a majority of its employees in the appropriate unit." 147 NLRB at 862. That remedial provision was tailored to the violations found, which involved the oral recognition of a minority union, followed by the negotiation of a complete collective-bargaining agreement—the type of "contract" to which the order refers. The overruling of *Julius Resnick*, in turn, did not somehow broaden the holding of *Majestic Weaving* itself. [T]he conduct in *Julius Resnick* was comparable to the conduct found unlawful in *Bernhard-Altmann* and *Majestic Weaving* itself, and distinct from what is involved here.

In short, the Board's precedent does not—despite our colleague's claim—compel the categorical conclusion that an employer violates Section 8(a)(2) whenever it "negotiates terms and conditions of employment with a union before a majority of unit employees affected by these actions has designated the union as their bargaining representative." That broad legal rule is stated nowhere in our case law. Nor does the dissent offer persuasive policy reasons for adopting such a rule today.

The essential premise of the dissent is that employees, made aware of an agreement like the one at issue here, "could reasonably believe they had no choice but to agree to [union] representation." Our colleague offers no evidence in support of this hypothesis—and the evidence here certainly tends to refute it: a majority of the employees subsequently rejected the UAW. Where, as in this case, an agreement expressly requires a showing of majority support, as determined by a neutral third party, before the union can be recognized, and where no unfair labor practices have been committed, it is hard to believe that a reasonable employee—a rational actor presumed by federal labor law to be capable of exercising free choice—would feel compelled to sign a union-authorization card simply because the agreement prospectively addresses some substantive terms and conditions of employment. If anything, such an agreement tends to promote an informed choice by employees. They presumably will reject the union if they conclude (or suspect) that it has agreed to a bad deal or that it is otherwise compromised by the agreement from representing them effectively.

VI. CONCLUSION

Accordingly, we find that Dana, by entering into the LOA, did not cross the line from lawful cooperation with the UAW to unlawful support of it. Likewise, the UAW has not accepted unlawful support from Dana.

MEMBER HAYES, dissenting.

In *Majestic Weaving Co.*, 147 NLRB 859 (1964), *enf. denied* 355 F.2d 854 (2d Cir. 1966), the Board found that an employer violated the Act when it negotiated a complete collective-bargaining agreement with a minority union. In the present case, the Respondent Dana negotiated substantive contract provisions in a Letter of Agreement (LOA) with minority union Respondent UAW. There are no meaningful factual or legal distinctions between the two cases. By dismissing the complaint, my colleagues effectively overrule *Majestic Weaving*, at least in substantial part. . . . My colleagues' approach threatens to reinstate the very practice that those statutory provisions were meant to prohibit, i.e., the establishment of collective-bargaining relationships based on self-interested union-employer agreements that preempt employee choice and input as to their representation and desired terms and conditions of employment. By statutory definition, this practice does not further genuine industrial peace.

We do not write on a clean slate here. It is well established that an employer unlawfully supports a union by recognizing it as the exclusive bargaining representative of employees among whom it does not have majority support. *Bernhard-Altmann*, 366 U.S. at 738. A bargaining agreement executed between the parties after premature recognition is unenforceable even if the union has achieved majority support in the interim. Id. at 736–737. This is so because "such acquisition of majority status itself might indicate that the recognition secured by the . . . agreement afforded [the union] a deceptive cloak of authority with which to persuasively elicit additional employee support." Id. at 736.

However, premature recognition is *not* a prerequisite for finding unlawful support in dealings between an employer and a minority union. In *Majestic Weaving*, 147 NLRB at 860, the Board held that an employer unlawfully assisted a union by negotiating a bargaining agreement with it even though the parties did not execute the agreement until after the union had secured majority support. The Board in *Majestic Weaving* also found implied oral recognition of the Teamsters local, 147 NLRB at 860, in spite of the facts recited in the trial examiner's decision showing that the employer never stated that it was recognizing the union, id. at 866–867. However, the Board's order in *Majestic Weaving* contains separate injunctive paragraphs, one requiring the employer to cease and desist from recognizing a minority union and the other requiring the employer to cease and desist from giving assistance and support to the Teamsters, "and *negotiating a contract* with any labor organization which does not represent a majority of its employees in the appropriate unit." (Emphasis added.) Most significantly, the Board overruled a prior case, *Julius Resnick*, 86 NLRB 38 (1949), "to the extent that it holds that an employer and a union may agree to terms of a contract before the union has organized the employees concerned, so long as the union has majority representation when the contract is executed." Id. at 864 fn. 4. There was no need to overrule this case if the finding of unlawful assistance in *Majestic Weaving* turned on the fact of recognition of a minority union, as opposed to negotiating a contract with one.

Thus, our precedent supports the proposition, which I would reaffirm and apply here, that premature recognition is not a prerequisite to finding unlawful employer assistance of a minority union. In sum, it is clear that an employer violates Section 8(a)(2) and (1) if it either recognizes a union or negotiates terms and conditions of employment with a union before a majority of unit employees affected by these actions has designated the union as their bargaining representative, and a union violates Section 8(b)(1)(A) by accepting recognition or entering into such an agreement.

This is so even when the recognition or the negotiations are conditioned on the union's subsequently obtaining majority employee support. In either instance, the employer has provided the minority union with "a deceptive cloak of authority with which to persuasively elicit additional employee support," thereby interfering with employee free choice.

The Respondents agreed to substantive terms and conditions of employment for unrepresented employees covering important bargaining subjects, such as those set forth in article 4.2.4: attendance, classifications, compensation, healthcare, mandatory overtime, team-based work schemes, and work incentives. Furthermore, in advance of any card majority authorizing the UAW to act on behalf of the St. Johns employees, the Respondents mutually agreed that the items of article 4.2.4 *had to be included* in any prospective future collective-bargaining agreement covering these employees.

The LOA was a contract. It did more than establish a purely procedural framework for potential future bargaining. By virtue of the LOA, the parties significantly limited the parameters for negotiation of a number of substantive issues. The LOA mandated a contract term of 4–5 years, foreclosed erosion of Dana's current healthcare cost initiatives, and included contract provisions for 8 bargaining subjects, interest arbitration after 6 months of negotiations, and a waiver of strike rights in advance of any final contract. Whether or not there would have to be more bargaining, the Respondents' conclusion of the LOA impermissibly signaled that the UAW already had a say in the determination of substantive terms and conditions of employment for Dana's St. Johns employees, among whom the UAW did not yet have majority support, giving the UAW " 'a marked advantage over any other in securing the adherence of employees.' "

My colleagues also emphasize that unions and employers might further benefit from knowing in advance of executing a voluntary recognition agreement what the substantive terms of a contract between them would be. I agree. However, the legality of negotiating such terms must turn on the statutory rights of employees, not on the commercial interests of unions and employers. To hold otherwise is to encourage the escalation of top-down organizing, by which unions organize employers first and employees last. Employers already enter into voluntary recognition agreements for a variety of reasons, including the financial savings from avoiding economic warfare and the potential benefits of support from the union when dealing with governmental entities or seeking to enter new markets. They are not likely to be deterred from acting on these self-interests simply because they cannot also determine in advance the precise labor costs of operating with a unionized work force.

By contrast, employees who are aware that their employer has already agreed with a union on contract terms applicable to them may be substantially deterred from exercising their right to decide whether they want to be represented by that union, by another union, or by no union. They would reasonably view the determination of the representation question as a fait accompli. The situation is arguably even worse in the context of the LOA here, whose substantive terms were not disclosed to employees. In such circumstances, employees could reasonably believe they had no choice but to agree to representation by the UAW without even knowing whether they approved or disapproved of the contract terms that union had negotiated for them.

My colleagues emphasize the statutory purpose of achieving industrial peace to justify overruling (or what they characterize as distinguishing) Majestic Weaving. They essentially reason that (a) the process of voluntary recognition of a "legitimate" union always serves that purpose and (b) the process cannot be fully effective unless parties are permitted to negotiate substantive terms and conditions of employment in advance of majority-based recognition. Of course, they readily admit that employer recognition of dominated company unions does not serve industrial peace. It was to prevent such a practice that Section 8(a)(2) was enacted.

For all the above reasons, I find that the Respondents' execution and maintenance of the LOA was unlawful. My colleagues' decision to permit substantive contract negotiations as long as the union is not formally recognized as a bargaining representative is contrary to the holding and rationale of *Majestic Weaving* . . ., which they lack the power to overrule. Instead, my colleagues facilitate the preemptive practice of top-down organizing of employers by unions, thereby subordinating the statutory rights of employees to the commercial self-interests of the contracting parties. This is a practice that Section 8(a)(2) and (1) and Section 8(b)(1)(A) of the Act were designed to prohibit in the interests of industrial peace. Accordingly, I would reverse the judge and find violations as alleged.

CHAPTER 5

COLLECTIVE BARGAINING

■ ■ ■

A. INTRODUCTION

The Congress Plaza Hotel is an 850-room hotel in downtown Chicago. It was built in 1893 to house visitors to the World Columbian Exposition. It is not part of any chain. Until the mid-1990s, the Congress Plaza was part of a multi-employer bargaining unit that negotiated with Hotel Employees and Restaurant Employees (HERE), Local 1. After leaving the multi-employer group, the Congress Plaza continued to agree with HERE Local 1 to contracts modeled on the multi-employer contract. The last such contract expired on December 31, 2002.

In September 2002, HERE reached agreement with the multi-employer group on a new contract that provided substantial increases in wages and benefits. For example, it raised the housekeeper wage rate from $8.83 per hour to $10.00 per hour and provided for further increases totaling 37% over the following four years. Congress Plaza refused to agree to similar terms. Instead, it insisted on a 7% wage cut, reducing housekeeper wage rates to $8.22 per hour, and refused to agree to increased contributions to the union's health and welfare fund that the fund trustees advised were necessary to maintain the hotel's participation. The health and welfare fund provided health insurance to the employees.

Negotiations continued after the contract expired, but in May 2003, the Congress Plaza rejected a union request to seek mediation from the Federal Mediation and Conciliation Service (FMCS). On May 14, 2003, the hotel unilaterally implemented its proposals, including the wage cuts. The union filed unfair labor practice charges accusing the hotel of bargaining in bad faith and, on June 15, 2003, struck the hotel. The hotel continued to operate, using supervisors, employees who crossed the union's picket lines and workers supplied by temporary help agencies.

The union's unfair labor practice charges were settled when the hotel agreed to rescind the wage cuts. Ironically, the beneficiaries of this agreement were the employees who were crossing the picket lines to work. In late summer 2006, when the strike was more than three years old, HERE Local 1 reached agreements on new contracts with the other unionized hotels in Chicago which, among other things, raised housekeeper wages to $13.20 per hour. Housekeeper wages at the Congress Plaza remained frozen at $8.83 per hour.

623

On May 30, 2013, two weeks shy of the strike's tenth anniversary, the union made an unconditional offer to return to work. Local 1's president stated, "The decision to end the Congress strike was a hard one, but it is the right time for the Union and the strikers to move on. The boycott has effectively dramatically reduced the hotel's business. The hotel treats their workers and customers equally poor and the community knows it. There is no more to do there." Strikers who returned to their jobs did so at the wage rates in effect when the contract expired in 2003.

Collective bargaining statutes reflect a policy determination that favors a privately ordered workplace over one controlled by direct government mandates specifying terms and conditions of employment. The collective bargaining process is the means by which an employer and its employees, acting through their exclusive bargaining representative, establish their private law of the workplace. The National Labor Relations Act, like most other labor relations acts, imposes on employers and unions a duty to bargain in good faith. Section 8(d) of the NLRA defines the duty as:

> [T]he performance of the mutual obligation of the employer and the representative of the employees to meet at reasonable times and confer in good faith with respect to wages, hours and other terms and conditions of employment, or the negotiation of an agreement, or any question arising thereunder, and the execution of a written contract incorporating any agreement reached if requested by either party, but such obligation does not compel either party to agree to a proposal or require the making of a concession.

Bargaining occurs in the context of the governing statute's structure and procedures, which can have a major impact on the results of collective negotiations. As the Congress Plaza-HERE negotiations demonstrate, the NLRA takes a laissez faire approach to collective bargaining. Section 8(d) merely requires that a party seeking to terminate or modify a collective bargaining agreement serve notice to that effect sixty days prior to the agreement's expiration date and notify the Federal Mediation and Conciliation Service (FMCS) within thirty days if no agreement has been reached. FMCS may mediate but only if the parties jointly request its assistance. Thus, the Congress Plaza was able to block mediation by refusing to join HERE in a request to FMCS.

As will be developed in detail later in this chapter, under the NLRA, parties are required to maintain the status quo with respect to wages, hours and terms and conditions of employment until they have bargained to the point of impasse. However, the NLRA has no mechanism for a party to petition the NLRB or any other agency to determine whether negotiations have hit impasse. Instead, the Congress Plaza's actions are typical. The employer declares that negotiations have reached impasse and unilaterally implements its position. The union may respond by filing unfair labor practice charges alleging that the parties were not at impasse or that the impasse was tainted by the employer's bad faith bargaining. The union may also respond by engaging in a job action. HERE did both, filing charges and going on strike. The Congress Plaza was determined to resist the strike. As a result, both sides became locked in a war of attrition.

In contrast, under the Railway Labor Act, the government is a much more active intervener in the parties' negotiations. The RLA requires that a party seeking to modify a collective bargaining agreement serve at least thirty days' notice to that effect on the other party. A request for mediation from only one party, which may come at any time, results in the National Mediation Board's (NMB's) involvement in the negotiations. If the parties' negotiations have ceased and neither party has requested NMB mediation within ten days following the end of negotiations, the parties are free to resort to self-help, but in practice one party always requests NMB intervention. Once the NMB becomes involved, the parties must maintain the status quo while the NMB attempts mediation. If the NMB concludes that further mediation would be fruitless, it offers the parties arbitration. If at least one party rejects the offer of arbitration, a thirty-day "cooling off" period begins to run during which the parties must continue the status quo. Upon expiration of the thirty-day period, the parties may resort to self-help. However, if the NMB determines that the dispute "threaten[s] substantially to interrupt interstate commerce to a degree such as to deprive any section of the country of essential transportation service," it so notifies the President who may appoint an Emergency Board to investigate the dispute. Such a Presidential Emergency Board (PEB) must investigate and make its report within thirty days of its appointment. The parties must maintain the status quo for at least thirty days after the PEB issues its report.

If the Congress Plaza negotiations had taken place under the RLA, the employer could not have thwarted the union's request for federal mediation. The employer also could not have simply declared impasse, unilaterally reduced wages and dared the union to strike and file charges. Instead, the employer would have had to participate in mediation until the mediator concluded further efforts would be fruitless. Even then, the employer could not have unilaterally implemented its position until expiration of a 30-day cooling off period. As will be seen later in this chapter, the ability to keep the parties in mediation and preclude the union from striking and the employer from making unilateral changes gives the mediator considerable power to pressure the parties to reach agreement. Operation of the RLA can be vividly seen in the negotiations between United Airlines and the union representing its mechanics in the period that ultimately led to United's filing for bankruptcy.

District Lodge 141-M of the International Association of Machinists and Aerospace Workers (IAMAW) represented United Airline's mechanics and utility workers. The contract between Lodge 141 and United provided that it could not be amended until July 12, 2000. In December 1999, the parties began negotiations on proposals for changes to the agreement.

United had a banner year in 1999 when it had a profit of $5.3 billion. In 2000, as the economy slowed, United experienced a reduction in profits to $2.6 billion. As of September 2000, the parties had not reached agreement and they entered mediation with the NMB. They still had not reached agreement when the terrorist attacks of September 11, 2001 dealt United a devastating blow that eventually landed it in bankruptcy. United was losing $15 million per day.

Lodge 141-M sought wage increases of 15 and 18 percent for utility workers and machinists respectively retroactive to July 12, 2000, an additional 6 percent increase retroactive to July 12, 2001, and 3.5 percent increases in the following three years. United sought a wage freeze until such time as it returned to profitability.

On November 19, 2001, the NMB concluded that further mediation would not be fruitful and offered the parties arbitration. United accepted the offer but the IAMAW rejected it, triggering the thirty-day cooling off period. On December 12, 2001, with no agreement in sight, the NMB notified the President that the dispute threatened to interrupt essential transportation services and on December 20, 2001, the President created Presidential Emergency Board No. 236 (PEB 236). PEB 236 filed its report on January 19, 2002.

PEB 236 recognized that without labor cost concessions, United likely would be unable to avoid bankruptcy. However, PEB 236 also recognized that the pilots and flight attendants had reached agreements with United prior to September 11, 2001, that provided them with industry-leading compensation packages. PEB 236 reasoned that the machinists and utility workers should not bear the brunt of United's financial difficulties. The Board recommended substantial increases in wages and further recommended that following the signing of the collective bargaining agreement, IAMAW agree to participate in a financial recovery plan in which all domestic United employees would participate proportionately and fairly, i.e. on comparable terms. Under the Board's recommendation, IAMAW would be bound to the same concessions that the other unions would agree to without a further ratification vote of its membership. The Board also recommended that much of the wage increase be retroactive but that the retroactive pay be paid to the employees in eight installments, beginning in April 2003, so as not to further tax United's cash flow.

The release of PEB 236's report began another thirty-day cooling off period during which the parties had to continue the status quo. At the end of that period United announced that it would accept the recommended settlement and the union leadership agreed to submit it for a membership ratification vote and take no formal position on it. On February 12, 2002, the membership voted 68% to 32% to reject the PEB recommended settlement. Members reportedly objected to the deferral of retroactive pay and to being automatically bound to concessions proportionate to those that might be agreed to by the other unions.

United and the IAMAW returned to negotiations. On February 18, 2002, they agreed that any future concessions would be subject to membership ratification, advanced the beginning of the payout of retroactive pay to December 2002 and raised pensions and the amount of license fees that United would pay for its machinists. On March 5, 2002, the union membership voted to ratify the agreement.

United then began the process of negotiating concessions with the pilots and flight attendants unions as well as with the IAMAW. United reached tentative agreement first with the pilots and then with the flight attendants. In late November it reached a tentative agreement with the IAMAW which provided for $800 million in wage and benefit cuts for ramp workers and customer service agents, who IAMAW also represented and $700 million in cuts for machinists and utility workers. The ramp workers and customer service agents ratified the agreement but the machinists and utility workers voted to reject it. The union leadership and United then modified the agreement slightly, providing for employee input in selecting vacation days that they would take without pay and agreement to work on grievances over supervision. The IAMAW scheduled a ratification vote for December 5, 2002, but cancelled the vote when the Air Transportation Stabilization Board rejected United's application for federal loan guarantees. United filed for bankruptcy on December 9, 2002.

NOTES

1. The United negotiations proceeded very differently than they might have gone had they been governed by the NLRA. When the September 11, 2001, terrorist attacks hit, United was in the midst of a process of negotiating wage increases with the IAMAW. The nature of the RLA process caused United to have to continue to resolve negotiations over wage increases even while losing $15 million per day and seeking a federal loan guarantee that would enable it to avoid bankruptcy. That process was not completed until March 2002 and then the process began anew, this time on wage and benefit concessions. United could not declare impasse and unilaterally reduce wages. It had to maintain the status quo, continuing to pay at an industry-leading wage rate while it lost tens of millions of dollar per day. Eventually, United ran out of time as its application for federal loan guarantees was rejected and it filed for bankruptcy.

2. As an employer advocate would you prefer to negotiate under the NLRA or the RLA? As a union advocate, which statute would you prefer? Does

your answer to these questions depend on the relative bargaining power of your client vis-à-vis the other party?

3.   United Parcel Service and DHL Express are considered package delivery services and are covered by the NLRA. Federal Express is considered a freight airline and is covered by the RLA. The United States Postal Service is covered by the Postal Reorganization Act of 1974. It is generally covered by the NLRA except that strikes by its employees are illegal and matters that cannot be resolved in collective bargaining are submitted to an arbitrator for resolution. These four entities compete against each other in package delivery services, particularly overnight deliveries. Do any of them gain a competitive advantage from the labor relations statute that governs them?

B. MODELS OF THE COLLECTIVE BARGAINING PROCESS

As seen in the introduction, the NLRA and RLA have different approaches to the collective bargaining process. The NLRA approach is relatively laissez faire, with government involvement usually reserved for when the parties jointly request it and with an expectation that the parties' abilities to resort to economic warfare and their desire to avoid such showdowns will lead to agreement. The RLA relies much more heavily on government supervision of the bargaining process through mediation and mediator control over whether and when the parties may resort to economic weapons.

A third model exists in the public sector. Most states prohibit public employee strikes and all prohibit strikes by law enforcement personnel and firefighters. Many states provide that employees who lack the right to strike may compel their employers to arbitrate issues that the parties are unable to resolve at the bargaining table. This process is called "interest arbitration." Others provide for "factfinding," where a neutral adjudicator conducts a hearing and issues non-binding recommendations for settlement, akin to a PEB under the RLA. A few jurisdictions allow at least some employees to strike but all that do so require that they first resort to mediation and, in some states, to factfinding before there can be a lawful strike. These models are explored below.

1. THE NATIONAL LABOR RELATIONS ACT

NLRB v. INSURANCE AGENTS INTERNATIONAL UNION
361 U.S. 477 (1960)

JUSTICE BRENNAN delivered the opinion of the Court:

This case presents an important question whether the Board may find that a union, which confers with an employer with the desire of reaching agreement on contract terms, has nevertheless refused to bargain collectively solely and simply because during the negotiations it seeks to put economic pressure on the employer to yield to its bargaining demands by sponsoring on-the-job conduct designed to interfere with the carrying on of the employer's business.

Since 1949 the respondent Insurance Agents' International Union and the Prudential Insurance Company of America have negotiated collective bargaining agreements covering district agents employed by Prudential in 35 States and the District of Columbia. In January 1956 Prudential and the union began the negotiation of a new contract to replace an agreement expiring in the following March. Bargaining was carried on continuously for six months before the terms of the new contract were agreed upon on July 17, 1956. It is not questioned that, if it stood alone, the record of negotiations would establish that the union conferred in good faith for the purpose and with the desire of reaching agreement with Prudential on a contract.

However, in April 1956, Prudential filed a § 8(b)(3) charge of refusal to bargain collectively against the union. The charge was based upon actions of the union and its members outside the conference room, occurring after the old contract expired in March. The union had announced in February that if agreement on the terms of the new contract was not reached when the old contract expired, the union members would then participate in a "Work Without a Contract" program—which meant that they would engage in certain planned, concerted on-the-job activities designed to harass the company.

It was developed in the evidence that the union's harassing tactics involved activities by the member agents such as these: refusal for a time to solicit new business, and refusal (after the writing of new business was resumed) to comply with the company's reporting procedures; refusal to participate in the company's "May Policyholders' Month Campaign"; reporting late at district offices the days the agents were scheduled to attend them, and refusing to perform customary duties at the offices, instead engaging there in "sit-in-mornings," "doing what comes naturally" and leaving at noon as a group; absenting themselves from special business conferences arranged by the company; picketing and distributing leaflets outside the various offices of the company on specified days and hours as directed by the union; distributing leaflets each day to policyholders and others and soliciting policyholders' signatures on petitions directed to the company; and presenting the signed policyholders' petitions to the company at its home office while simultaneously engaging in mass demonstrations there.

The hearing examiner's analysis of the congressional design in enacting the statutory duty to bargain led him to conclude that the Board was not authorized to find that such economically harassing activities constituted a § 8(b)(3) violation. The Board's opinion answers flatly "We do not agree" and proceeds to say "the Respondent's reliance upon harassing tactics during the course of negotiations for the avowed purpose of compelling the Company to capitulate to its terms is the antithesis of reasoned discussion it was duty-bound to follow. Indeed, it clearly revealed an unwillingness to submit its demands to the consideration of the bargaining table where argument, persuasion, and the free interchange of views could take place. In such circumstances, the fact that the Respondent continued to confer with the Company and was desirous of concluding an agreement does not alone establish that it fulfilled its obligation to bargain in good faith." Accordingly, as is said in the Board's brief, "The issue here . . . comes down to whether the Board is authorized under the Act to hold that such tactics, which the Act does not specifically forbid but Section 7 does not protect, support a finding of a failure to bargain in good faith as required by Section 8(b)(3)."

First. The bill which became the Wagner Act included no provision specifically imposing a duty on either party to bargain collectively. Senator Wagner thought that the bill required bargaining in good faith without such a provision. However, the Senate Committee in charge of the bill concluded that it was desirable to include a provision making it an unfair labor practice for an employer to refuse to bargain collectively in order to assure that the Act would achieve its primary objective of requiring an employer to recognize a union selected by his employees as their representative.

However, the nature of the duty to bargain in good faith thus imposed upon employers by § 8(5) of the original Act was not sweepingly conceived. The Chairman of the Senate Committee declared: "When the employees have chosen their organization, when they have selected their representatives, all the bill proposes to do is to escort them to the door of their employer and say, 'Here they are, the legal representatives of your employees.' What happens behind those doors is not inquired into, and the bill does not seek to inquire into it."

The limitation implied by the last sentence has not been in practice maintained—practically, it could hardly have been—but the underlying purpose of the remark has remained the most basic purpose of the statutory provision. That purpose is the making effective of the duty of management to extend recognition to the union; the duty of management to bargain in good faith is essentially a corollary of its duty to recognize the union. Decisions under this provision reflect this. For example, an employer's unilateral wage increase during the bargaining processes tends to subvert the union's position as the representative of the employees in matters of this nature, and hence has been condemned as a practice violative of this statutory provision. And as suggested, the requirement of collective bargaining, although so premised, necessarily led beyond the door of, and into, the conference room. The first annual report of the Board declared: "Collective bargaining is something more than the mere meeting of an employer with the representatives of his employees; the essential thing is rather the serious intent to adjust differences and to reach an acceptable common ground. . . . The Board has repeatedly asserted that good faith on the part of the employer is an essential ingredient of collective bargaining." This standard had early judicial approval. Collective bargaining, then, is not simply an occasion for purely formal meetings between management and labor, while each maintains an attitude of "take it or leave it"; it presupposes a desire to reach ultimate agreement, to enter into a collective bargaining contract. This was the sort of recognition that Congress, in the Wagner Act, wanted extended to labor unions; recognition as the bargaining agent of the employees in a process that looked to the ordering of the parties' industrial relationship through the formation of a contract.

But at the same time, Congress was generally not concerned with the substantive terms on which the parties contracted. Obviously there is tension between the principle that the parties need not contract on any specific terms and a practical enforcement of the principle that they are bound to deal with each other in a serious attempt to resolve differences and reach a common ground. And in fact criticism of the Board's application of the "good-faith" test arose from the belief that it was forcing employers to yield to union demands if they were to avoid a successful charge of unfair labor practice. Thus, in 1947 in Congress the fear was expressed that the Board had "gone very far, in the guise of determining whether or not employers had bargained in good faith, in setting itself up as the judge of what concessions an employer must make and of the proposals and counterproposals that he may or may not make." H.R. Rep. No. 245, p. 19. Since the Board was not viewed by Congress as an agency which should exercise its powers to arbitrate the parties' substantive solutions of the issues in their bargaining, a check on this apprehended trend was provided by writing the good-faith test of bargaining into § 8(d) of the Act.

The same problems as to whether positions taken at the bargaining table violate the good-faith test continue to arise under the Act as amended. But it remains clear that § 8(d) was an attempt by Congress to prevent the Board from controlling the settling of the terms of collective bargaining agreements

Second. At the same time as it was statutorily defining the duty to bargain collectively, Congress, by adding § 8(b)(3) of the Act through the Taft-Hartley amendments, imposed that duty on labor organizations. Unions obviously are formed for the very purpose of bargaining collectively; but the legislative history makes it plain that Congress was wary of the position of some unions, and wanted to ensure that they would approach the bargaining table with the same attitude of willingness to reach an agreement as had been enjoined on management earlier. It intended to prevent employee representatives from putting forth the same "take it or leave it" attitude that had been condemned in management. 93 Cong.Rec. 4135, 4363, 5005.

Third. It is apparent from the legislative history of the whole Act that the policy of Congress is to impose a mutual duty upon the parties to confer in good faith with a desire to reach agreement, in the belief that such an approach from both sides of the table promotes the over-all design of achieving industrial peace. Discussion conducted under that standard of good faith may narrow the issues, making the real demands of the parties clearer to each other, and perhaps to themselves, and may encourage an attitude of settlement through give and take. The mainstream of cases before the Board and in the courts reviewing its orders, under the provisions fixing the duty to bargain collectively, is concerned with insuring that the parties approach the bargaining table with this attitude. But apart from this essential standard of conduct, Congress intended that the parties should have wide latitude in their negotiations, unrestricted by any governmental power to regulate the substantive solution of their differences.

We believe that the Board's approach in this case—unless it can be defended, in terms of § 8(b)(3), as resting on some unique character of the union tactics involved here—must be taken as proceeding from an erroneous view of collective bargaining. It must be realized that collective bargaining, under a system where the Government does not attempt to control the results of negotiations, cannot be equated with an academic collective search for truth—or even with what might be thought to be the ideal of one. The presence of economic weapons in reserve, and their actual exercise on occasion by the parties, is part and parcel of the system that the Wagner and Taft-Hartley Acts have recognized. Abstract logical analysis might find inconsistency between the command of the statute to negotiate toward an agreement in good faith and the legitimacy of the use of economic weapons, frequently having the most serious effect upon individual workers and productive enterprises, to induce one party to come to the terms desired by the other. But the truth of the matter is that at the present statutory stage of our national labor relations policy, the two factors—necessity for good-faith bargaining between parties, and the availability of economic pressure devices to each to make the other party incline to agree on one's terms—exist side by side. One writer recognizes this by describing economic force as "a prime motive power for agreements in free collective bargaining." Doubtless one factor influences the other; there may be less need to apply economic pressure if the areas of controversy have been defined through discussion; and at the same time, negotiation positions are apt to be weak or strong in accordance with the degree of economic power the parties possess. A close student of our national labor relations laws writes: "Collective bargaining is curiously ambivalent even today. In one aspect collective bargaining is a brute contest of economic power somewhat masked by polite manners and voluminous statistics. As the relation matures, Lilliputian bonds control the opposing concentrations of economic power; they lack legal sanctions but are nonetheless effective to contain the use of power. Initially it may be only fear of the economic consequences of disagreement that turns the parties to facts, reason, a sense of responsibility, a responsiveness to government and public opinion, and moral principle; but in time these forces generate their own compulsions, and negotiating a contract approaches the ideal of informed persuasion." Archibald Cox, The Duty to Bargain in Good Faith, 71 Harv. L. Rev. 1401, 1409 (1958).

For similar reasons, we think the Board's approach involves an intrusion into the substantive aspects of the bargaining process—again, unless there is some specific warrant for its condemnation of the precise tactics involved here. The scope of § 8(b)(3) and the limitations on Board power which were the design of § 8(d) are exceeded, we hold, by inferring a lack of good faith not from any deficiencies of the union's performance at the bargaining table by reason of its attempted use of economic pressure, but solely and simply because tactics designed to exert economic pressure were employed during the course of the good-faith negotiations. Thus the Board in the guise of determining good or bad faith in negotiations could regulate what economic weapons a party might summon to its aid. And if the Board could regulate the choice of economic weapons that may be used as part of collective bargaining, it would be in a position to exercise considerable influence upon the substantive terms on which the parties contract. Our labor policy is not presently erected on a foundation of government control of the results of negotiations. Nor does it contain a charter for the National Labor Relations Board to act at large in equalizing disparities of bargaining power between employer and union.

Fourth. The use of economic pressure, as we have indicated, is of itself not at all inconsistent with the duty of bargaining in good faith. The Board freely (and we think correctly) conceded here that a "total" strike called by the union would not have subjected it to sanctions under § 8(b)(3), at least if it were called after the old contract, with its no-strike clause, had expired.

(a) The Board contends that the distinction between a total strike and the conduct at bar is that a total strike is a concerted activity protected against employer interference by §§ 7 and 8(a)(1) of the Act, while the activity at bar is not a protected concerted activity. We may agree *arguendo* with the Board that the employee conduct here was not a protected concerted activity. On this assumption the employer could have discharged or taken other appropriate disciplinary action against the employees participating in these "slow-down," "sit-in," and arguably unprotected disloyal tactics. But surely that a union activity is not protected against disciplinary action does not mean that it constitutes a refusal to bargain in good faith. The reason why the ordinary economic strike is not evidence of a failure to bargain in good faith is not that it constitutes a protected activity but that, as we have developed, there is simply no inconsistency between the application of economic pressure and good-faith collective bargaining. There is little logic in assuming that because Congress was willing to allow employers to use self-help against union tactics, if they were willing to face the economic consequences of its use, it also impliedly declared these tactics unlawful as a matter of federal law. Our problem remains that of construing § 8(b)(3)'s terms, and we do not see how the availability of self-help to the employer has anything to do with the matter.

(b) The Board contends that because an orthodox "total" strike is "traditional" its use must be taken as being consistent with § 8(b)(3); but since the tactics here are not "traditional" or "normal," they need not be so viewed. Further, the Board cites what it conceives to be the public's moral condemnation of the sort of employee tactics involved here. But again we cannot see how these distinctions can be made under a statute which simply enjoins a duty to bargain in good faith. Again, these are relevant arguments when the question is the scope of the concerted activities given affirmative protection by the Act. But as we have developed, the use of economic pressure by the parties to a labor dispute is not a grudging exception to some policy of completely academic discussion enjoined by the Act; it is part and parcel of the process of collective bargaining. On this basis, we fail to see the relevance of whether the practice in question is time-honored or whether its exercise is generally supported by public opinion. It may be that the tactics used here deserve condemnation, but this would not justify attempting to pour that condemnation into a vessel not designed to hold it. The same may be said for the Board's contention that these activities, as opposed to a 'normal' strike, are inconsistent with § 8(b)(3) because they offer maximum pressure on the employer at minimum economic cost to the union. One may doubt whether this was so here, but the matter does not turn on that. Surely it cannot be said that the only economic weapons consistent with good-faith bargaining are those which minimize the pressure on the other party or maximize the disadvantage to the party using them. The catalog of union and employer weapons that might thus fall under ban would be most extensive.[28]

Fifth. These distinctions essayed by the Board here, and the lack of relationship to the statutory standard inherent in them, confirm us in our

---

[28] There is a suggestion in the Board's opinion that it regarded the union tactics as a unilateral setting of the terms and conditions of employment and hence also on this basis violative of § 8(b)(3), just as an employer's unilateral setting of employment terms during collective bargaining may amount to a breach of its duty to bargain collectively. It seems baseless to us. There was no indication that the practices that the union was engaging in were designed to be permanent conditions of work. They were rather means to another end. The question whether union conduct could be treated, analogously to employer conduct, as unilaterally establishing working conditions, in a manner violative of the duty to bargain collectively, might be raised for example by the case of a union, anxious to secure a reduction of the working day from eight to seven hours, which instructed its members, during the negotiation process, to quit work an hour early daily. But this situation is not presented here, and we leave the question open.

conclusion that the judgment of the Court of Appeals, setting aside the order of the Board, must be affirmed. For they make clear to us that when the Board moves in this area, with only § 8(b)(3) for support, it is functioning as an arbiter of the sort of economic weapons the parties can use in seeking to gain acceptance of their bargaining demands. It has sought to introduce some standard of properly 'balanced' bargaining power, or some new distinction of justifiable and unjustifiable, proper and 'abusive' economic weapons into the collective bargaining duty imposed by the Act. The Board's assertion of power under § 8(b)(3) allows it to sit in judgment upon every economic weapon the parties to a labor contract negotiation employ, judging it on the very general standard of that section, not drafted with reference to specific forms of economic pressure. We have expressed our belief that this amounts to the Board's entrance into the substantive aspects of the bargaining process to an extent Congress has not countenanced.

[The separate opinion of JUSTICE FRANKFURTER, joined by JUSTICES HARLAN and WHITTAKER, has been omitted.]

NOTES

1.   In footnote 28, the Court distinguished the union's tactics from a unilateral setting of terms and conditions of employment. Under what circumstances, if any, might a union be found to have unilaterally implemented its preferred employment terms? Consider *Cutler v. NLRB,* 395 F.2d 287 (2d Cir. 1968). The American Federation of Musicians (AFM) negotiated collective bargaining agreements with purchasers of musical services for standing engagements, i.e., engagements that are to last longer than one week. Shorter engagements were considered single engagements. AFM's bylaws had for many years established minimum wages for AFM members employed in single engagements and AFM enforced the bylaws by fining or expelling members who worked for less than the specified minimum. Cutler, an orchestra leader who for many years hired AFM members on an as needed basis for single engagements, always paid the AFM minimum wage scale. AFM unilaterally amended its bylaws increasing the minimum wage scale for single engagements by $1.50 per hour and requiring that employers contribute at least $1.00 per hour per musician to an AFM-administered welfare plan. Cutler demanded that AFM bargain with respect to the musicians that Cutler employed on single engagements. AFM met with Cutler several times to negotiate a collective bargaining agreement but insisted that the minimum wage rates and welfare plan contributions set in its bylaws established a floor and refused to consider any proposals by Cutler that were lower than those rates. The court held that AFM did not violate section 8(b)(3). It observed that the wage rates could not become the rates Cutler paid his employees unless Cutler agreed to them. It recognized that as a practical matter, Cutler had no choice but to agree but attributed this situation to the union's superior bargaining power. The court opined that the situation did not

fall within the circumstances that the Court reserved in footnote 28 of *Insurance Agents*.

2.   The Associated Home Builders (AHB) is a multiemployer organization that has a collective bargaining agreement with the Carpenters Union. The agreement does not specify productivity standards, AHB has found that its carpenters average laying 7 ½ squares of wood shingles per week. AHB members have dismissed slower carpenters and refused to hire slower carpenters for new projects. This has caused many carpenters to complain to the union. In response to those complaints, the union adopted a resolution that no member may install more than six squares of wood shingles in any week and has threatened to fine any members who exceed the production ceiling. Has the union violated section 8(b)(3)? See *Associated Home Builders of Greater East Bay, Inc. v. NLRB*, 352 F.2d 745 (9th Cir. 1965) (holding that the union unilaterally changed a term and condition of employment in violation of the NLRA).

NLRB v. KATZ
369 U.S. 736 (1962)

JUSTICE BRENNAN delivered the opinion of the Court:

Is it a violation of the duty "to bargain collectively" imposed by § 8(a)(5) of the National Labor Relations Act for an employer, without first consulting a union with which it is carrying on bona fide contract negotiations, to institute changes regarding matters which are subjects of mandatory bargaining under § 8(d) and which are in fact under discussion? The National Labor Relations Board answered the question affirmatively in this case, in a decision which expressly disclaimed any finding that the totality of the respondents' conduct manifested bad faith in the pending negotiations. A divided panel of the Court of Appeals for the Second Circuit denied enforcement of the Board's cease-and-desist order.

The respondents are partners engaged in steel fabricating under the firm name of Williamsburg Steel Products Company. Following a consent election in a unit consisting of all technical employees at the company's plant, the Board, on July 5, 1956, certified as their collective bargaining representative Local 66 of the Architectural and Engineering Guild, American Federation of Technical Engineers, AFL-CIO. The Board simultaneously certified the union as representative of similar units at five other companies which, with the respondent company, were members of the Hollow Metal Door & Buck Association. The certifications related to separate units at the several plants and did not purport to establish a multi-employer bargaining unit.

The first meeting between the company and the union took place on August 30, 1956. On this occasion, as at the ten other conferences held between October 2, 1956, and May 13, 1957, all six companies were in attendance and represented by the same counsel. It is undisputed that the subject of merit increases was raised at the August 30, 1956, meeting although there is an unresolved conflict as to whether an agreement was reached on joint participation by the company and the union in merit reviews, or whether the subject was simply mentioned and put off for discussion at a later date. It is also clear that proposals concerning sick leave were made. Several meetings were held during October and one in November, at which merit raises and sick leave were each discussed on at least two occasions. It appears, however, that little progress was made.

On December 5, a meeting was held at the New York State Mediation Board attended by a mediator of that agency, who was at that time mediating a contract negotiation between the union and Aetna Steel Products Corporation, a member of the Association bargaining separately from the others; and a decision was reached to recess the negotiations involved here pending the results of the Aetna negotiation. When the mediator called the next meeting on March 29, 1957, the completed Aetna contract was introduced into the discussion. At a resumption of bargaining on April 4, the company, along with the other employers, offered a three-year agreement with certain initial and prospective automatic wage increases. The offer was rejected. Further meetings with the mediator on April 11, May 1, and May 13, 1957, produced no agreement, and no further meetings were held.

Meanwhile, on April 16, 1957, the union had filed the charge upon which the General Counsel's complaint later issued. The complaint's charge of unfair labor practices particularly referred to three acts by the company: unilaterally granting numerous merit increases in October 1956 and January 1957; unilaterally announcing a change in sick-leave policy in March 1957; and unilaterally instituting a new system of automatic wage increases during April 1957. [T]he company defended that the Board could not hinge a conclusion that § 8(a)(5) had been violated on unilateral actions alone, without making a finding of the employer's subjective bad faith at the bargaining table; and that the unilateral actions were merely evidence relevant to the issue of subjective good faith. This argument prevailed in the Court of Appeals.

The duty "to bargain collectively" enjoined by § 8(a)(5) is defined by § 8(d) as the duty to "meet . . . and confer in good faith with respect to wages, hours, and other terms and conditions of employment." Clearly, the duty thus defined may be violated without a general failure of subjective good faith; for there is no occasion to consider the issue of good faith if a party has refused even to negotiate in fact—"to meet . . . and confer"—about any of the mandatory subjects. A refusal to negotiate in fact as to any subject which is within § 8(d), and about which the union seeks to negotiate, violates § 8(a)(5) though the employer has every desire to reach agreement with the union upon an over-all collective agreement and earnestly and in all good faith bargains to that end. We hold that an employer's unilateral change in conditions of employment under negotiation is similarly a violation of § 8(a)(5), for it is a circumvention of the duty to negotiate which frustrates the objectives of § 8(a)(5) much as does a flat refusal.

The unilateral actions of the respondent illustrate the policy and practical considerations which support our conclusion.

We consider first the matter of sick leave. A sick-leave plan had been in effect since May 1956, under which employees were allowed ten paid sick-leave days annually and could accumulate half the unused days, or up to five days each year. Changes in the plan were sought and proposals and counterproposals had come up at three bargaining conferences. In March 1957, the company, without first notifying or consulting the union, announced changes in the plan, which reduced from ten to five the number of paid sick-leave days per year, but allowed accumulation of twice the unused days, thus increasing to ten the number of days which might be carried over. This action plainly frustrated the statutory objective of establishing working conditions through bargaining. Some employees might view the change to be a diminution of benefits. Others, more interested in accumulating sick-leave days, might regard the change as an improvement. If one view or the other clearly prevailed among the employees, the unilateral action might well mean that the employer had either uselessly dissipated trading material or aggravated the sick-leave issue. On the other hand, if the employees were more evenly divided on the merits of the company's changes, the union negotiators, beset by conflicting factions, might be led to adopt a protective vagueness on the issue of sick leave, which also would inhibit the useful discussion contemplated by Congress in imposing the specific obligation to bargain collectively.

Other considerations appear from consideration of the respondents' unilateral action in increasing wages. At the April 4, 1957, meeting the employers offered, and the union rejected, a three-year contract with an immediate across-the-board increase of $7.50 per week, to be followed at the end of the first year and again at the end of the second by further increases of $5 for employees earning less than $90 at those times. Shortly thereafter, without having advised or consulted with the union, the company announced a new system of automatic wage increases whereby there would be an increase of $5 every three months up to $74.99 per week; an increase of $5 every six months between $75 and $90 per week; and a merit review every six months for employees earning over $90 per week. It is clear at a glance that the automatic wage increase system which was instituted unilaterally was considerably more generous than that which had shortly theretofore been offered to and rejected by the union. Such action conclusively manifested bad faith in the negotiations. And so would have violated § 8(a)(5) even on the Court of Appeals' interpretation, though no additional evidence of bad faith appeared. An employer is not required to lead with his best offer; he is free to bargain. But even after an impasse *Essentially, this* is reached he has no license to grant wage increases greater than any he *move circumvented* has ever offered the union at the bargaining table, for such action is *the bargain & clearly* necessarily inconsistent with a sincere desire to conclude an agreement *sought to force out* with the union. *or undercut the Union.*

The respondents' third unilateral action related to merit increases, which are also a subject of mandatory bargaining. The matter of merit increases had been raised at three of the conferences during 1956 but no final understanding had been reached. In January 1957, the company, without notice to the union, granted merit increases to 20 employees out of the approximately 50 in the unit, the increases ranging between $2 and $10. This action too must be viewed as tantamount to an outright refusal to negotiate on that subject, and therefore as a violation of § 8(a)(5), unless the fact that the January raises were in line with the company's long-standing practice of granting quarterly or semiannual merit reviews—in effect, were a mere continuation of the status quo—differentiates them from the wage increases and the changes in the sick-leave plan. We do not think it does. Whatever might be the case as to so-called 'merit raises' which are in fact simply automatic increases to which the employer has already committed himself, the raises here in question were in no sense automatic, but were informed by a large measure of discretion. There simply is no way in such case for a union to know whether or not there has been a substantial departure from past practice, and therefore the union may properly insist that the company negotiate as to the procedures and criteria for determining such increases.

It is apparent from what we have said why we see nothing in *Insurance Agents* contrary to the Board's decision. The union in that case had not in any way whatever foreclosed discussion of any issue, by unilateral actions or otherwise. The conduct complained of consisted of partial-strike tactics designed to put pressure on the employer to come to terms with the union negotiators. We held that Congress had not, in § 8(b)(3), the counterpart of § 8(a)(5), empowered the Board to pass judgment on the legitimacy of any particular economic weapon used in support of genuine negotiations. But *Basis for proper* the Board is authorized to order the cessation of behavior which is in effect *Board finding* a refusal to negotiate, or which directly obstructs or inhibits the actual *power.* process of discussion, or which reflects a cast of mind against reaching agreement. Unilateral action by an employer without prior discussion with the union does amount to a refusal to negotiate about the affected conditions of employment under negotiation, and must of necessity obstruct bargaining, contrary to the congressional policy. It will often disclose an unwillingness to agree with the union. It will rarely be justified by any reason of substance. It follows that the Board may hold such unilateral action to be an unfair labor practice in violation of § 8(a)(5), without also finding the employer guilty of over-all subjective bad faith. While we do not foreclose the possibility that there might be circumstances

Board retains discretion NoT to take action or to approve/excuse such unilateral action.

which the Board could or should accept as excusing or justifying unilateral action, no such case is presented here.

The judgment of the Court of Appeals is reversed and the case is remanded with direction to the court to enforce the Board's order.

NOTES

1.   Consider the three issues on which the employer made unilateral changes: sick leave, automatic wage increases and merit increases. Why was each a violation of section 8(a)(5)?

2.   What are the terms and conditions of employment that may not be changed without first bargaining to impasse? Are the wages and benefits paid to each employee frozen until the matter has been bargained to impasse or may the employer change wages and benefits in accordance with prior practices? Is an employer obligated to change wages and benefits in accordance with prior practices?

In *Wilkes-Barre Hosp. Co. v. NLRB*, 857 F.3d 364 (D.C. Cir. 2017), the court enforced the Board's finding that the employer violated section 8(a)(5) when it refused to continue to pay longevity increases following expiration of the collective bargaining agreement. The contract covering the employer's nurses provided that a nurse's minimum wage rate was determined by the nurse's experience level, with employees grouped as follows: 0–2 years, 3–4 years, 5–9 years, 10–14 years, 15–19 years, 20–24 years, and 25 or more years. Under the contract, employees received longevity-based increases on January 27 following the employee's qualifying anniversary date. After the contract expired, the employer refused to pay the longevity increases. The court agreed with the Board that the longevity payments were part of the status quo that the employer was required to maintain following contract expiration until bargaining had reached impasse or agreement.

In contrast, in *Finley Hospital*, 362 N.L.R.B. No. 102 (2015), the parties entered into their first contract following NLRB certification of the union as exclusive bargaining representative for a bargaining unit of nurses. The one-year contract provided that for the duration of the contact, each employee would receive a 3% pay increase on his or her anniversary date. When the contract expired, the parties were still in negotiations for a successor. The employer, without notice to the union, notified all employees that, in light of the expiration of the collective bargaining agreement, the 3% anniversary raises would cease. The NLRB, by vote of 2—1, held that the employer violated section 8(a)(5) by unilaterally changing a term and condition of employment without bargaining to impasse. The Board majority reasoned that, although the employer's contractual obligation to pay the raises expired with the contract, its statutory obligation to refrain from unilateral changes prior to bargaining to impasse continued unless the employer could show that the union clearly and unmistakably waived the right to maintenance of the status quo. The Board majority found no such clear and unmistakable waiver in the contractual provision that the raises would be paid for the duration of the contract. Member Johnson dissented. He viewed the contract as providing a one year commitment for a single wage increase to each employee and concluded that the employer acted properly to maintain the status quo during negotiations by keeping wages at the rates that were in effect on the last day of the contract.

But, in *Finley Hosp. v. NLRB*, 827 F.3d 720 (8th Cir. 2016), the Eighth Circuit, also by a vote of 2–1, reversed. The majority agreed with Member Johnson. It wrote, "Article 20.3 of the CBA, the raise-providing provision, states that it applies only "for the duration of this Agreement." That phrase, or a slight variation of that phrase, is used three times in Article 20.3, and the parties knew that the CBA expired in one year. The generally prevailing meaning of that phrase, in light of all the circumstances, is that each nurse gets one 3% raise on one date during the year that the CBA is in effect. Thus, the plain language of the CBA does not, as the Board states, provide for periodic wage increases or annual raises; rather, the language sets forth a straight forward, singular pay increase on a particular day during the one-year contract."

Dissenting Judge Murphy agreed with the Board majority. He wrote, "[T]he union proved its prima facie case since the nurse pay raise provision was a mandatory subject of bargaining, and an express term of the CBA. The pay raise provision defined the status quo despite the clauses limiting it to the "duration of" the CBA because the agreement's expiration was extended by law until the parties reached an impasse or a new agreement. Since the hospital failed to pay nurse raises after the expiration of the CBA, but before an impasse or a new agreement, the union proved its prima facie case. The duration clauses in the pay raise provision are only relevant to the hospital's affirmative defense of waiver." Judge Murphy opined that because the pay raise provision did not state that the raises would terminate upon expiration of the contract, the hospital failed to prove that the union waived its statutory right to maintenance of the status quo until a new agreement or impasse.

In *Wilkes-Barre* and *Findley*, the wage increases were automatic. What if changes in wages or benefits involve the exercise of employer discretion. Collective bargaining agreements often provide that the employees will receive the same health insurance benefits as non-bargaining unit employees. Employers typically make changes in the health insurance plan in advance of annual open enrollment periods. If the open enrollment period takes place after the most recent collective bargaining agreement expired and the parties are still negotiating a successor agreement, may the employer apply the changes to bargaining unit employees? The Board has often changed its position with respect to this question. Two recent decisions illustrate the different approaches. In *E.I. DuPont de Nemours*, 364 N.L.R.B. No. 113 (2016), the Board, by a 3–1 vote, held that the employer violated section 8(a)(5) by making changes to its health care plan and applying those changes to bargaining unit employees while negotiations for a successor contract were underway. The Board majority reasoned that, because the changes were not automatic, unlike longevity-based wage increases, the employer's exercise of substantial discretion in making the changes constituted a deviation from the status quo and could only be accomplished after bargaining to impasse. In *Raytheon Network Centric Sys.*, 365 N.L.R.B. No. 161 (2017), the Board by a 3–2 vote, overruled *DuPont*. The Board reasoned that where the employer had a long-established practice of making annual changes to its healthcare plan and applying those changes to bargaining unit as well as non-bargaining unit employees, the employer's practice was part of the status quo and the employer did not violate section 8(a)(5) when it applied the plan changes going into the open enrollment period even though the parties were still negotiating a successor collective bargaining agreement.

Employer discretion also was a factor in *Total Security Mgmt. Ill. 1, LLC*, 364 N.L.R.B. No. 106 (2016). The Board, by a 3–1 vote, held that an employer, while negotiating a first contract with an exclusive representative, has a duty to bargain before discharging or suspending a bargaining unit employee where the discipline was imposed pursuant to the employer's existing discipline policy but the policy allowed for the exercise of employer discretion in imposing discipline. The Board reasoned, "The imposition of discipline on individual employees alters their terms or conditions of employment and implicates the duty to bargain if it is not controlled by pre-existing nondiscretionary employer policies or practices." But the Board held that the employer need bargain only over those matters on which it exercised discretion, such as the length of a suspension where particular misconduct resulted in suspension but the employer exercised discretion over the length. The Board further held that the employer need not await an overall impasse in bargaining before imposing discipline, but may impose the discipline after initially bargaining subject to a continuing duty to bargain over the possibility of rescinding it. The Board also held that the employer need not bargain before imposing discipline in cases of exigent circumstances, such as where the employer has a good faith, reasonable belief that the employee's continued presence at the workplace presents an imminent danger to the employer's business or personnel. Member Miscimarra dissented, arguing that discretionary discipline was part of the status quo that the employer was maintaining while negotiations were underway.

3.   *What is impasse?* In *Taft Broadcasting Co.*, 163 N.L.R.B. 475, 478 (1967), the Board set forth the factors it considers in determining whether the parties were at impasse when the employer unilaterally changed terms and conditions of employment:

> Whether a bargaining impasse exists is a matter of judgment. The bargaining history, the good faith of the parties in negotiations, the length of the negotiations, the importance of the issue or issues as to which there is disagreement, the contemporaneous understanding of the parties as to the state of negotiations are all relevant factors to be considered in deciding whether an impasse in bargaining existed.

See generally Ellen J. Dannin, *Legislative Intent and Impasse Resolution Under the National Labor Relations Act: Does Law Matter?*, 15 Hofstra Lab. & Emp. L.J. 11 (1997). Note that the test is very fact-specific and is applied in an unfair labor practice proceeding long after the events that a party, usually the employer, argues reflected impasse. A skillful negotiator can gain bargaining power by manipulating the negotiations so that the other party is not sure whether impasse has been reached, or more precisely whether the NLRB will months later find that impasse was reached, and therefore deter the other party from implementing unilaterally. This tactic can be particularly effective where the employer is seeking concessions from the union.

For example, in *Mike-sell's Potatoe Chip Co. v. NLRB,* 807 F.3d 318 (D.C. Cir. 2015), the employer had lost about $5.5 million over four years. The employer sought concessions with respect to the commission structure and commission rate paid to employees, health insurance and pension contributions. Three days before the existing collective bargaining agreement was scheduled to expire, the union expressed a willingness to accept the employer's proposed changes to commission structure but requested an increase in commission rate and agreed to increased employee contributions to health insurance. When the parties recessed negotiations, the employer suggested meeting two days later but union representatives had scheduling conflicts and advised that they would get back to the employer with alternate dates. Two days later, the employer presented the union what it termed its final offer and the following day implemented it. The court recognized the employer's precarious position. "[I]f an employer, such as Petitioner, facing financial difficulty wishes relief from existing collective bargaining costs and therefore puts into place significantly diminished compensation, its risk is considerable because the Board, if it finds a violation of 8(a)(5) (no impasse existed), will order extensive back compensation, as it did in this case." *Id.* at 324. The court opined, "If an employer remains firm in collective bargaining as to one or more essential issues and credibly declares a last offer *in the negotiations,* a last offer that is consistent with and follows logically from its negotiating position, a union's failure to agree creates an impasse. A union official's denial that an impasse exists, combined with a new negotiating proposal that does not meet the employer's position, does not rebut an impasse." *Id.* But, the court found no impasse existed when the employer unilaterally implemented what it had termed its final offer. The court noted that in their last bargaining session, the union acquiesced in the employer's commission structure and exchanged proposals on commission rates and the employer did not reject the union's counterproposals on health insurance. It characterized the final offer and implementation as "abrupt," and concluded that the employer "had not displayed the requisite firmness on the key issues in negotiations . . ." *Id.* at 235.

4. *Does impasse relate to a particular issue or the contract as a whole?* The employer and union are negotiating for a successor collective bargaining agreement as the prior contract has expired. One of the employer's proposals has been to move from a weekly payroll to a biweekly payroll system. Each time the employer has raised this proposal the union has responded that it is categorically opposed because the members would be up in arms if they were not paid weekly. The parties have made progress in negotiations on other issues, although they have not reached agreement. The employer is anxious to

implement its change to a biweekly payroll system and the union has remained adamant in its opposition. May the employer unilaterally implement the change? *Compare Duffy Tool & Stamping, LLC v. NLRB*, 233 F.3d 995 (7th Cir. 2000); *Vincent Indus. Plastics, Inc. v. NLRB*, 209 F.3d 727 (D.C. Cir. 2000); *Visiting Nurse Servs. of W. Mass. v. NLRB*, 177 F.3d 52 (1st Cir. 1999); *NLRB v. Cent. Plumbing Co.*, 492 F.2d 1252 (6th Cir. 1974) (all holding that employer may not act unilaterally on an issue on which it has reached impasse when it has not reached impasse in negotiations as a whole) *with Winn-Dixie Stores, Inc. v. NLRB*, 567 F.2d 1343 (5th Cir. 1978); *A. H. Belo Corp. v. NLRB*, 411 F.2d 959 (5th Cir. 1969) (allowing issue-by-issue impasse and unilateral action). *See also CalMat Co.*, 331 N.L.R.B. 1084 (2000) (impasse on a single critical issue can lead to an overall breakdown in negotiations).

5. In the Congress Plaza Hotel dispute discussed earlier, the employer refused to increase its contributions to the union pension and health and welfare plans despite notice that increased contributions were necessary to maintain participation beyond December 31, 2002. The employer continued to make contributions at the 2002 rate, even after the union went on strike. The plan trustees notified the employer that coverage for its employees would terminate on December 31, 2003, unless the employer reached a new contract with the union providing for the new minimum contributions. On December 31, 2003, the union plans terminated coverage for all Congress Plaza employees. Effective January 1, 2004, the employer placed all employees in the bargaining unit in its health insurance plan. It did so with no prior consultation with the union. Did the employer violate section 8(a)(5)?

6. Is it possible for an employer to violate section 8(a)(5) by unilaterally implementing a proposal after reaching impasse? What if the employer's proposal called for all increases in pay to be based on merit as determined by the employer, with no objective standards specified and with the employer's decisions not being subject to any review involving the union? In *McClatchy Newspapers, Inc. v. NLRB*, 131 F.3d 1026 (D.C. Cir. 1997), the court held that implementation of such a proposal, even at impasse, is inconsistent with good faith negotiations because it completely cuts the union out of negotiating wages.

2. RAILWAY LABOR ACT

As the introductory discussion of the United Airlines negotiations illustrates, the RLA provides for a more active government role in supervising negotiations than does the NLRA. Thus, only one party need request mediation for the NMB to get involved, and mediation continues, with a corresponding duty on the parties to maintain the status quo, until the NMB decides that further mediation would be fruitless. To what extent should a party frustrated with the NMB's handling of negotiations be able to resort to the courts for relief? Consider the following case.

AMERICAN TRAIN DISPATCHERS DEPT., BROTHERHOOD OF LOCOMOTIVE ENGINEERS V. FORT SMITH RY. CO.

121 F.3d 267 (7th Cir. 1997)

CUDAHY, CIRCUIT JUDGE:

A strike by even a small part of our nation's railroad workers could bring much of interstate commerce to a halt and disrupt the daily lives of millions of Americans. This risk of disruption brought about the enactment of the Railway Labor Act, 45 U.S.C. § 151 *et seq.* (RLA or Act). The Act's main purpose is to "avoid any interruption to commerce or to the operation of any carrier engaged therein." 45 U.S.C. § 151a. The RLA works not by controlling the types of independent action employers and unions can take after bargaining has failed (*e.g.,* strikes, lockouts). Instead, the RLA strives to prevent interruptions of interstate commerce by creating a mediation structure which requires the parties to "exert every reasonable effort to make and maintain agreements . . . and to settle all disputes . . . to avoid any interruption to commerce." 45 U.S.C. § 152, First. The obligation that parties "exert every reasonable effort" has been described as the "heart" of the RLA. *Bhd of R.R. Trainmen v. Jacksonville Terminal Co.*, 394 U.S. 369, 377–78 (1969). The obligation is a legal one, given shape by the National Mediation Board's (NMB) recommendations and "enforceable by whatever appropriate means might be developed on a case-by-case basis." *Chi. & N.W.R.R. Co. v. United Transp. Union,* 402 U.S. 570, 577 (1971). The NMB is free to "experiment[ ] with any mediation device that can fairly be said to be designed to settle a dispute without a strike and does not independently offend other laws." *Int'l Ass'n of Machinists v. Nat'l Mediation Bd.,* 930 F.2d 45, 48 (D.C. Cir. 1991). Any party to a dispute may invoke the NMB when the dispute concerns changes in rates of pay, rules or working conditions; the NMB may also proffer its services without a request from a party. 45 U.S.C. § 155, First.

Here, the Brotherhood of Locomotive Engineers (BLE), representing the locomotive engineers, conductor/brakemen and carmen employed by Fort Smith Railroad Co. (Railroad), invoked the NMB on March 28, 1995. At that point, negotiations had been ongoing since October 11, 1994. The NMB assigned Robert Martin to perform mediation, and sessions were held on May 2, August 15 and November 8 of 1995 and on January 30, 1996. All of these sessions were held at the Railroad's headquarters in Peoria, Illinois. On February 8, 1996, Stephen Crable, the NMB's Chief of Staff wrote the following letter to the parties:

> Mediator Robert B. Martin will resume mediation involving the Fort Smith Railroad Company and the BLE-ATDA Division, Case Nos. A-12715, A-12716 and A-12717, at the NMB's office in Washington, DC, at 10:00 a.m. on February 28 and 29, 1996. Please advise who will represent you and provide local telephone and fax numbers.

In immediate response the Railroad wrote: "we cannot agree to a meeting in Washington, D.C. We are, however, agreeable to meeting on February 28, or March 1 (Tuesdays and Thursdays are bad days for us), at a 'neutral' site. I have proposed Springfield, Illinois, since that is where Mr. Martin is located. . . . [W]e would also agree to St. Louis." The NMB acceded to the Railroad's objections and held the mediation session in St. Louis on February 28, 1996. Unfortunately, that session, like those before it, failed to result in a resolution.

The next mediation session was again scheduled to take place in Washington D.C., on April 24 and 25, 1996. And again, the Railroad objected to the site:

> [W]e do not feel that Washington, D.C. is an appropriate site. FSR's office is in Peoria, Illinois, and its operations are in Fort Smith, Arkansas. Washington is a very long way from both of those places.
>
> Secondly, FSR presented its final offer to the Union during our recent bargaining session in St. Louis. My notes indicate that Mr. Volz said he was not going to recommend the contract. . . .
>
> You indicated to me this morning that you felt the Union was rejecting the proposal. Assuming that the union is unwilling to accept our final proposal, because it does not include seniority, I think we all agreed in St. Louis that these negotiations are at impasse. . . . Another bargaining session is not likely to be productive at this time.
>
> In summary, FSR believes these negotiations are at impasse, and, in any event, FSR is not agreeable to holding any negotiating sessions in Washington, D.C.

This letter obviously had an effect on the Union since only six days later it offered to drop its demands for seniority, overtime and the length of the agreement term. The Railroad, however, rejected the Union's offer, objecting to the yearly salary increase, bereavement leave and back pay. The Railroad reiterated its request that Robert Martin declare an impasse and release the parties from mediation. A last communication from the NMB read as follows:

> This is to advise you that mediation sessions scheduled for April 24 and 25, 1996, at the NMB offices, Washington, DC have been canceled because of carrier refusal to attend. Consistent with the Board's obligation under the Railway Labor Act to make its best efforts to assist the parties in making agreements, the mediator has determined that convening the parties in Washington, DC will further this purpose. Please advise me by no later than April 25, 1996 of four consecutive days in April or May in which you will be available to meet with mediator Martin.

No change in the parties' positions regarding the place to meet was forthcoming.

The Union sought both a temporary and a permanent injunction enjoining the Railroad from refusing to negotiate when and where the NMB recommended. The district court granted both injunctions after a consolidated hearing and trial. The Railroad now appeals.

Both the preliminary and the permanent injunction turn on one issue: whether the Railroad violated the RLA by refusing to attend the NMB-called negotiation sessions in Washington, D.C. The parties' obligation to "exert every reasonable effort" is given shape by the recommendations of the NMB. 45 U.S.C. § 152, First. As noted, the NMB acts as a referee. "The Mediation Board makes no 'order' . . . The function of the Board under § 2, Ninth is more the function of a referee. To this decision of the referee Congress has added a command enforceable by judicial decree. But the 'command' is that 'of the statute, not of the Board.' " *Switchmen's Union of N. Am. v. Nat'l Mediation Bd.*, 320 U.S. 297 (1943) (interpreting the Board's power to determine Union representation). The issue here is whether a procedural determination by the Board (here involving the location for meeting) is enforceable in court. In this connection, our authority to review the actions of the NMB is "extraordinarily limited." *Local 808 v. Nat'l Mediation Bd.*, 888 F.2d 1428, 1433 (D.C. Cir. 1989); *Prof'l Cabin Crew Ass'n v. Nat'l Mediation Bd.*, 872 F.2d 456, 459 (D.C. Cir. 1989). We will intervene in the activities of the NMB only upon a showing of "patent official bad faith." *Int'l Ass'n of Machinists*, 930 F.2d at 48 (citing *Local 808, Bldg. Maint. Serv. & R.R. Workers v. Nat'l Mediation Bd.*, 888 F.2d 1428, 1434 (D.C. Cir. 1990)). But while our jurisdiction to review Board decisions is limited, our jurisdiction to enforce provisions of the Act is not. *See Air Line Pilots Ass'n Int'l v. Transamerica Airlines, Inc.*, 817 F.2d 510, 513 (9th Cir. 1987). And, of course, we do not closely examine what might be the Board's rationale for the sort of procedural decision made here. The D.C. Circuit has emphasized the deference to be accorded by courts to the NMB:

> The members of the Mediation Board are no more to be called to the courthouse to explain their undisclosed reasons for action than the members of a legislature. The Mediation Board is entitled to as strong a presumption as the legislature, that if any state of facts might be supposed that would support its action, those facts must be presumed to exist. . . .

> It may well be that the likelihood of successful mediation is marginal. That success of settlement may lie in the realm of possibility, rather than confident prediction, does not negative the good faith and validity of the Board's effort. The legislature provided procedures purposefully drawn out, and the Board's process may draw on them even to the point that the parties deem "almost interminable."

Int'l Ass'n of Machinists v. Nat'l Mediation Bd., 425 F.2d 527, 540–41 (D.C. Cir.1970). Whatever the NMB's reasons for choosing Washington, D.C., we find no evidence of "patent official bad faith." *Int'l Ass'n of Machinists*, 930 F.2d at 48. Nor does the choice of Washington, D.C. put attendance at the meeting beyond the Railroad's obligation to exert every reasonable effort. The Board is allowed to employ coercive techniques to bring the parties to conciliation. See *Id.* at 47.

If the Railroad could refuse to attend mediation sessions called by the NMB on the basis of location, the Railroad could in effect refuse to continue negotiating. The NMB's primary resource, the ability to force continuing negotiations almost interminably, would be thwarted. We therefore affirm the district court's grant of a permanent injunction.

NOTES

1.   Consider how the negotiations would have proceeded under the NLRA. When the railroad rejected the union's offer in late April, the railroad likely would have implemented its offer unilaterally, daring the union to strike or file unfair labor practice charges. Instead, the NMB mediator rejected the railroad's request that he declare the parties at impasse and ordered the parties to meet in Washington, DC. Perhaps the mediator believed that bringing the parties to the nation's capital might change the tone of the negotiations. Perhaps he was determined to harass the railroad and otherwise pressure it into making concessions to the union to reach agreement. Why should one individual, the NMB mediator, have such power over the parties, when the Supreme Court has expressly stated that the NLRB lacks such power?

2.   What are the relative advantages and disadvantages of the NLRA and RLA models? Can the different treatment of collective bargaining negotiations with railroads and airlines be justified? If so, what rationales can you give for treating the rest of the private sector differently?

3.   THE PUBLIC SECTOR

As previously noted, most jurisdictions in the public sector prohibit strikes. Jurisdictions that provide for interest arbitration generally do not allow parties to make unilateral changes. They must await the outcome of the arbitration procedure which will determine the wages, hours and terms and conditions of employment. Jurisdictions that provide for non-binding factfinding also do not allow parties to make unilateral changes while those proceedings are being used. However, they typically allow unilateral changes after the proceedings have been exhausted and impasse has been reached. *See, e.g., Mountain Valley Educ. Ass'n v. Me. Sch. Admin. Dist. No. 43*, 655 A.2d 348 (Me. 1995).

In the few jurisdictions in which public employees have a right to strike, the right is circumscribed in ways that it is not under the NLRA.

All such jurisdictions require the parties resort to mediation before a lawful strike may occur and some require factfinding and a rejection of the factfinder's recommendations as a prerequisite to a strike. Should such jurisdictions follow the NLRA model of allowing employers to make unilateral changes after exhausting statutorily-required impasse procedures or should the employer's flexibility be circumscribed as well? Consider the following case.

PHILADELPHIA HOUSING AUTHORITY V. PENNSYLVANIA LABOR RELATIONS BOARD

620 A.2d 594 (Penn. Cmmw. Ct. 1993)

DOYLE, JUDGE:

The most recent collective bargaining agreement between PHA [Philadelphia Housing Authority] and the Union expired on March 31, 1990. The parties agreed to extend the contract for thirty days. During the period from March 15, 1990 to June 1, 1990 the parties participated in approximately nine bargaining sessions and also had five meetings with a state mediator. Tentative agreements were reached on some issues during this time period; however, all tentative agreements were conditional upon a complete and final agreement.

On June 1, 1990 PHA made a final offer to the Union. The offer contained all tentative agreements previously agreed upon including, *inter alia,* a provision pertaining to medical insurance. Under this provision, to be effective August 1, 1990, only two HMO plans would have been made available free of charge to Union members; this represented a reduction from four plans previously available to employees on a no cost basis. On June 3, 1990 the Union, at one of its meetings, rejected the entire proposal.

Approximately six weeks later, on July 10, 1990, the Union submitted a counterproposal to PHA. Its counterproposal contained substantial differences from PHA's final offer including wage increases and a suggestion that the collective bargaining agreement be limited to one year in duration rather than three as proposed by the PHA. The Union's counterproposal did not express any objection, however, to the reduction of no-cost HMO's from four to two. That same day PHA rejected the Union's counterproposal. Soon thereafter counsel for PHA wrote separately to the state mediator, on July 12, 1990, and to counsel for the Union, on July 17, 1990, stating the fact that negotiations had been at an impasse for several weeks. He also advised counsel for the Union that PHA would, over the ensuing several weeks, implement its June 1, 1990 proposal including the pension, wage and medical insurance provisions. As of August 1, 1990 PHA did so, while the Union members continued to work.

The Union filed an unfair labor practice charge with the Board alleging that PHA had breached its statutory obligation to bargain in good faith by unilaterally implementing its final offer. The hearing examiner found that the parties had bargained in good faith and that an impasse had been reached. Ultimately, the hearing examiner determined that because the parties had reached an impasse and the HMO provision had been tentatively agreed upon by both sides as early as March 28, 1990, the implementation of the final offer did not violate Section 1201 of PERA.

On November 12, 1991, the [Pennsylvania Labor Relations] Board upheld the hearing examiner's findings including the finding that an impasse existed at the time PHA implemented its final offer, but it rejected the hearing examiner's legal conclusion that there had been no unfair labor practice under Section 1201 of PERA. In so doing the Board opined that the hearing examiner's reliance on federal law was misplaced in this instance because of the important distinctions between public and private sector law. The Board explained its view that *two* preconditions must exist before an employer bound by PERA may implement a unilateral action: an impasse *and* cessation of work.

Thereafter, PHA appealed to the Court of Common Pleas of Philadelphia County which disagreed with the Board's legal conclusions opining that Pennsylvania case law did not *compel* the result reached by the Board, and, looking to federal law and the law of other states as persuasive, the lower court reversed the Board. The Board's appeal to this Court followed.

The General Assembly of the Commonwealth of Pennsylvania declares that it is the public policy of this Commonwealth and the purpose of this act to promote orderly and constructive relationships between all public employers and their employees subject, however, to the paramount right of the citizens of this Commonwealth to keep inviolate the guarantees for their health, safety and welfare. Unresolved disputes between the public employer and its employees are injurious to the public and the General Assembly is therefore aware that adequate means must be established for minimizing them and providing for their resolution.

Initially, we recognize that the purpose of a collective bargaining agreement in private-sector federal law is to assist employees in counteracting an employer's almost complete control over employment concerns. This purpose is very different from that espoused in PERA. Consequently, in private-sector federal law a strike is recognized as a legitimate and powerful economic weapon available to employees. Its sanctity has been expressly preserved by the National Labor Relations Act. A strike is not precluded during the course of contract negotiations, nor is it viewed as inconsistent with such negotiations. But it *is* under Section 1002 of PERA, 43 P.S. § 1101.1002.

Under the National Labor Relations Act, strikes are part and parcel of the collective bargaining process. The unilateral implementation of an employer policy during negotiations (which can be viewed as employer's economic weapon) however, is generally prohibited in private-sector federal law, because it is viewed as inconsistent with good faith negotiation. *NLRB. v. Katz.* Thus, absent an impasse (*i.e.,* deadlock) in which the duty to bargain temporarily terminates, unilateral implementation is not permitted. To summarize then, in a private sector labor market, labor's right to strike is jealously guarded and virtually unfettered while management's corresponding right to unilaterally change contract terms is curtailed only moderately, *i.e.,* permitted only after impasse. Thus, there is an effort to afford the parties some balance in the economic weapons available to them.

In contrast to the private sector endorsement of strikes, however, public sector law in Pennsylvania has traditionally not recognized such a right. While PERA now recognizes such a right for most public employees, the right to strike is much more circumscribed than under federal law. Strikes can be implemented only when statutorily prescribed impasse procedures are exhausted, *see* 43 P.S. §§ 1101.1002, 1101.1003, and can be enjoined where they create a "clear and present danger or threat to the health, safety or welfare of the public." 43 P.S. § 1101.1003. Thus, the right to strike under PERA is far more limited than under federal private sector law.

When one recognizes that the employer's counter-balancing economic weapon, a unilateral implementation, is circumscribed in situations where a *broad* right to strike is recognized, how much more cogently should it follow that it should be no less circumscribed where strike rights are much more limited. And that brings us to the question now facing us. Is the use of such an employer weapon where a statutory impasse has been reached, but no strike has ensued, a violation of Section 1201 of PERA?

As all parties and amici agree (or concede) there is no express authority in PERA for unilateral implementation after an impasse has occurred. And, we believe that to infer that such a major substantive provision exists in the "penumbra" of PERA would be the height of judicial legislation. Consequently, if public employers feel they need more economic weapons in their arsenal, it is to the legislature that they must turn.

[I]t would not serve the legislature's declared goal of promoting orderly and constructive relationships between public employers and their employees through good faith collective bargaining to allow a public employer to implement its final offer when the employees in the unit have not disrupted the continuation of public services by striking. Unilateral action by an employer during a period of no contract while employees continue to work serves to polarize the process and would encourage strikes by employees who otherwise may wish to continue working under the terms of the expired agreement while negotiations continue.

Good faith negotiation would be seriously jeopardized by permitting the employer to implement its bargaining position after a few face-to-face bargaining sessions and the requisite number of mediation sessions with the mediator. The employer's unilateral achievement of its bargaining position effectively relieves pressure on it to arrive at a mutually agreed resolution of the bargaining impasse. It is the tension created by the need to find common ground between the parties which is at the core of the process. Relieving that tension greatly removes the incentive of a party to bargain with a sincere desire to reach agreement.

Accordingly, we reverse the order of the Court of Common Pleas and reinstate the Board's order.

JUDGE COLLINS, dissenting:

[T]he ramifications of the instant opinion create a precedent that compels municipal corporations or authorities to continue to operate indefinitely under expired labor agreements regardless of the financial impossibility of doing so. To compel any municipality to maintain financial commitments in perpetuity in the face of a declining population or a shrinking tax base or any other adverse circumstance, creates a precedent in this Commonwealth which is most dangerous and is contrary to the public interest.

As the majority acknowledges, PERA limits public employees' right to strike in recognition of the negative impact on the public when government services are not forthcoming. This limitation on the right to strike, however, does more than simply protect the public; it achieves a tenuous balance in bargaining power between the public sector employer and public employees. The majority's decision weakens PERA's limitation on public employees' right to strike and accordingly threatens the delicate balance of bargaining power between employer and employee in the public sector.

I would affirm the opinion of the trial court in the instant matter.

NOTES

1.   The NLRA allows employers to make unilateral changes after reaching impasse, effectively daring the union to strike. The majority does not want to allow a public employer to do the same. Is this good public policy?

2.   The dissent raises concern that a public employer seeking concessions in response to a decline in tax revenues will not be able to place any pressure on the union if it cannot implement unilaterally. Should the courts recognize some type of "compelling need" exception to the majority's rule that the employer may not make unilateral changes except in response to a work stoppage?

3.   A collective bargaining agreement between AFSCME District 33 and the City of Philadelphia expired June 30, 2009. The parties began negotiations for a new contract on April 30, 2009. After almost four years of negotiations without reaching agreement, the city filed a petition in the Pennsylvania Court of Common Pleas on February 4, 2013, seeking declaratory and injunctive

relief, alleging that the parties were at impasse and that negotiations had been stymied because the decision in *Philadelphia Housing Auth.* had empowered the union to maintain the status quo indefinitely. The following day, the city filed a petition in the Pennsylvania Supreme Court seeking extraordinary relief by having the court assert jurisdiction over the case immediately. The court denied the petition for extraordinary relief, but Chief Justice Castille dissented, echoing the concerns raised in Judge Collins' dissent. *City of Philadelphia v. AFSCME District 33*, 68 A.3d 323 (Pa. 2013).

C. DETERMINING GOOD FAITH: THE PROBLEM OF SURFACE BARGAINING

1. SURFACE BARGAINING UNDER THE NLRA

Recall the HERE-Congress Plaza Hotel dispute at the beginning of this chapter. Whereas in prior years, the Congress Plaza agreed to a contract that mirrored the terms contained in HERE's contract with the multi-employer group, in 2002, it not only refused to agree to the pay raises in the multi-employer contract but insisted on a wage cut. The union charged the Congress Plaza with bargaining in bad faith. Section 8(d) of the NLRA imposes on both parties an obligation to "confer in good faith" but stipulates that the obligation does not require the making of concessions. How might HERE's charges against the Congress Plaza be adjudicated?

There is general agreement that a party which goes through the motions of negotiations with no intent of reaching agreement breaches the obligation of good faith. Such a party is said to be engaging in "surface bargaining." Occasionally, there will be direct evidence that a party lacks the intent of ever reaching agreement. *See, e.g., U.S. Ecology Corp.*, 331 N.L.R.B. 223 (2001), *enf'd*, 26 Fed. Appx. 435 (6th Cir. 2001) (evidence that plant manager and employee relations manager stated there would be no contract no matter what the union did to force the union to strike and "bust itself."). Sometimes, bad faith may be inferred from a party's dilatory tactics with respect to questions of where and when to meet or other procedural matters. *See, e.g., Teamsters Local 122 (Busch & Co.)*, 334 N.L.R.B. 1190 (2001) (union stalling tactics in effort to pressure employer to sell operation to a more union-friendly employer violated § 8(b)(3)); *Health Care Servs. Group., Inc.*, 331 N.L.R.B. 333 (2000) (employer stalling tactics including failing to show up for scheduled bargaining sessions evidenced bad faith). But in the more common situation, such evidence is lacking. May bad faith be inferred from the content of bargaining proposals?

NLRB v. AMERICAN NATIONAL INSURANCE CO.

343 U.S. 395 (1952)

CHIEF JUSTICE VINSON delivered the opinion of the Court:

This case arises out of a complaint that respondent refused to bargain collectively with the representatives of its employees as required under the National Labor Relations Act.

The Office Employees International Union A.F. of L., Local No. 27, certified by the National Labor Relations Board as the exclusive bargaining representative of respondent's office employees, requested a meeting with respondent for the purpose of negotiating an agreement governing employment relations. At the first meetings, beginning on November 30, 1948, the Union submitted a proposed contract covering wages, hours, promotions, vacations and other provisions commonly found in collective bargaining agreements, including a clause establishing a procedure for settling grievances arising under the contract by successive appeals to management with ultimate resort to an arbitrator.

On January 10, 1949, following a recess for study of the Union's contract proposals, respondent objected to the provisions calling for unlimited arbitration. To meet this objection, respondent proposed a so-called management functions clause listing matters such as promotions, discipline and work scheduling as the responsibility of management and excluding such matters from arbitration. The Union's representative took the position "as soon as (he) heard (the proposed clause)" that the Union would not agree to such a clause so long as it covered matters subject to the duty to bargain collectively under the Labor Act.

Several further bargaining sessions were held without reaching agreement on the Union's proposal or respondent's counterproposal to unlimited arbitration. As a result, the management functions clause was "by-passed" for bargaining on other terms of the Union's contract proposal. On January 17, 1949, respondent stated in writing its agreement with some of the terms proposed by the Union and, where there was disagreement, respondent offered counter-proposals, including a clause entitled "Functions and Prerogatives of Management" along the lines suggested at the meeting of January 10th. The Union objected to the portion of the clause providing:

> The right to select and hire, to promote to a better position, to discharge, demote or discipline for cause, and to maintain discipline and efficiency of employees and to determine the schedules of work is recognized by both union and company as the proper responsibility and prerogative of management to be held and exercised by the company, and while it is agreed that an employee feeling himself to have been aggrieved by any decision of the company in respect to such matters, or the union in his

behalf, shall have the right to have such decision reviewed by top management officials of the company under the grievance machinery hereinafter set forth, it is further agreed that the final decision of the company made by such top management officials shall not be further reviewable by arbitration.

At this stage of the negotiations, the National Labor Relations Board filed a complaint against respondent based on the Union's charge that respondent had refused to bargain as required by the Labor Act and was thereby guilty of interfering with the rights of its employees guaranteed by Section 7 of the Act and of unfair labor practices under Sections 8(a)(1) and 8(a)(5) of the Act. While the proceeding was pending, negotiations between the Union and respondent continued with the management functions clause remaining an obstacle to agreement. During the negotiations, respondent established new night shifts and introduced a new system of lunch hours without consulting the Union.

On May 19, 1949, a Union representative offered a second contract proposal which included a management functions clause containing much of the language found in respondent's second counterproposal, quoted above, with the vital difference that questions arising under the Union's proposed clause would be subject to arbitration as in the case of other grievances. Finally, on January 13, 1950, after the Trial Examiner had issued his report but before decision by the Board, an agreement between the Union and respondent was signed. The agreement contained a management functions clause that rendered nonarbitrable matters of discipline, work schedules and other matters covered by the clause. The subject of promotions and demotions was deleted from the clause and made the subject of a special clause establishing a union-management committee to pass upon promotion matters.

While these negotiations were in progress, the Board's Trial Examiner conducted hearings on the Union's complaint. The Examiner held that respondent had a right to bargain for inclusion of a management functions clause in a contract. However, upon review of the entire negotiations, including respondent's unilateral action in changing working conditions during the bargaining, the Examiner found that from and after November 30, 1948, respondent had refused to bargain in a good faith effort to reach agreement. The Examiner recommended that respondent be ordered in general terms to bargain collectively with the Union.

The Board agreed with the Trial Examiner that respondent had not bargained in a good faith effort to reach an agreement with the Union. But the Board rejected the Examiner's views on an employer's right to bargain for a management functions clause and held that respondent's action in bargaining for inclusion of any such clause "constituted, quite (apart from) Respondent's demonstrated bad faith, per se violations of Section 8(a)(5) and (1)." Accordingly, the Board not only ordered respondent in general terms to bargain collectively with the Union, but also included in its order a paragraph designed to prohibit bargaining for any management functions clause covering a condition of employment.

On respondent's petition for review and the Board's cross-petition for enforcement, the Court of Appeals for the Fifth Circuit agreed with the Trial Examiner's view that the Act does not preclude an employer from bargaining for inclusion of any management functions clause in a labor agreement. The Court of Appeals further found that the evidence does not support the view that respondent failed to bargain collectively in good faith by reason of its bargaining for a management functions clause. As a result, enforcement of the portion of the Board's order directed to the management functions clause was denied.

First. The National Labor Relations Act is designed to promote industrial peace by encouraging the making of voluntary agreements governing relations between unions and employers. The Act does not compel any agreement whatsoever between employees and employers. Nor does the Act regulate the substantive terms governing wages, hours and working conditions which are incorporated in an agreement. The theory of the Act is that the making of voluntary labor agreements is encouraged by protecting employees' rights to organize for collective bargaining and by imposing on labor and management the mutual obligation to bargain collectively.

[I]t is now apparent from the statute itself that the Act does not encourage a party to engage in fruitless marathon discussions at the expense of frank statement and support of his position. And it is equally clear that the Board may not, either directly or indirectly, compel concessions or otherwise sit in judgment upon the substantive terms of collective bargaining agreements.

Second. The Board offers in support of the portion of its order before this Court a theory quite apart from the test of good faith bargaining prescribed in Section 8(d) of the Act, a theory that respondent's bargaining for a management functions clause as a counterproposal to the Union's demand for unlimited arbitration was, 'per se,' a violation of the Act.

Counsel for the Board do not contend that a management functions clause covering some conditions of employment is an illegal contract term. As a matter of fact, a review of typical contract clauses collected for convenience in drafting labor agreements shows that management functions clauses similar in essential detail to the clause proposed by respondent have been included in contracts negotiated by national unions with many employers. The National War Labor Board, empowered during the last war "(t)o decide the dispute, and provide by order the wages and hours and all other terms and conditions (customarily included in collective-bargaining agreements)," ordered management functions clauses included in a number of agreements. Several such clauses ordered by the

War Labor Board provided for arbitration in case of union dissatisfaction with the exercise of management functions, while others, as in the clause proposed by respondent in this case, provided that management decisions would be final. Without intimating any opinion as to the form of management functions clause proposed by respondent in this case or the desirability of including any such clause in a labor agreement, it is manifest that bargaining for management functions clauses is common collective bargaining practice.

If the Board is correct, an employer violates the Act by bargaining for a management functions clause touching any condition of employment without regard to the traditions of bargaining in the particular industry or such other evidence of good faith as the fact in this case that respondent's clause was offered as a counterproposal to the Union's demand for unlimited arbitration. The Board's argument is a technical one for it is conceded that respondent would not be guilty of an unfair labor practice if, instead of proposing a clause that removed some matters from arbitration, it simply refused in good faith to agree to the Union proposal for unlimited arbitration. The argument starts with a finding, not challenged by the court below or by respondent, that at least some of the matters covered by the management functions clause proposed by respondent are "conditions of employment" which are appropriate subjects of collective bargaining under Sections 8(a)(5), 8(d) and 9(a) of the Act. The Board considers that employer bargaining for a clause under which management retains initial responsibility for work scheduling, a "condition of employment," for the duration of the contract is an unfair labor practice because it is "in derogation of" employees' statutory rights to bargain collectively as to conditions of employment.

Conceding that there is nothing unlawful in including a management functions clause in a labor agreement, the Board would permit an employer to "propose" such a clause. But the Board would forbid bargaining for any such clause when the Union declines to accept the proposal, even where the clause is offered as a counterproposal to a Union demand for unlimited arbitration. Ignoring the nature of the Union's demand in this case, the Board takes the position that employers subject to the Act must agree to include in any labor agreement provisions establishing fixed standards for work schedules or any other condition of employment. An employer would be permitted to bargain as to the content of the standard so long as he agrees to freeze a standard into a contract. Bargaining for more flexible treatment of such matters would be denied employers even though the result may be contrary to common collective bargaining practice in the industry. The Board was not empowered so to disrupt collective bargaining practices. On the contrary, the term "bargain collectively" as used in the Act "has been considered to absorb and give statutory approval to the philosophy of bargaining as worked out in the labor movement in the United States." Congress provided expressly that the Board should not pass upon the desirability of the substantive terms of labor agreements. Whether a contract should contain a clause fixing standards for such matters as work scheduling or should provide for more flexible treatment of such matters is an issue for determination across the bargaining table, not by the Board. If the latter approach is agreed upon, the extent of union and management participation in the administration of such matters is itself a condition of employment to be settled by bargaining.

Accordingly, we reject the Board's holding that bargaining for the management functions clause proposed by respondent was, per se, an unfair labor practice. Any fears the Board may entertain that use of management functions clauses will lead to evasion of an employer's duty to bargain collectively as to "rates of pay, wages, hours and conditions of employment" do not justify condemning all bargaining for management functions clauses covering any "condition of employment" as per se violations of the Act. The duty to bargain collectively is to be enforced by application of the good faith bargaining standards of Section 8(d) to the facts of each case rather than by prohibiting all employers in every industry from bargaining for management functions clauses altogether.

[The dissenting opinion of JUSTICE MINTON, joined by JUSTICES BLACK and DOUGLAS, has been omitted.]

NOTES

1.   If the company insisted on the broad management functions clause with management functions exempt from arbitration recognizing that the union would never agree to it, would the company have violated section 8(a)(5)? What if the company decided to insist on the clause because such insistence would guarantee that no agreement would ever be reached? Is there a difference between these two propositions? If so, how can one tell into which category a particular case falls?

2.   What is the relevance of the frequency of management functions clauses found in other collective bargaining agreements and in the awards of the War Labor Board? Would the Court have reached a different result if such clauses were rare in other contracts? What if such clauses were nonexistent in other contracts?

3.   In the model of collective bargaining that underlies the Court's opinion, what is the union to do if it does not want to agree to the management functions clause on which the employer insists? Why do you think the union did not take such action in the instant case?

HARDESTY COMPANY, INC. DBA
MID-CONTINENT CONCRETE

336 N.L.R.B. 258 (2001), *enf'd*, 308 F.3d 859 (8th Cir. 2002)

By CHAIRMAN HURTGEN and MEMBERS LIEBMAN and TRUESDALE:

The judge found, and we agree, that on or about October 13, 1995, and continuing thereafter, the Respondent engaged in surface bargaining in violation of Section 8(a)(5) of the Act.

Section 8(d) of the Act requires "the employer to meet at reasonable times with the representative of its employees and confer in good faith with respect to wages, hours and other terms and conditions of employment. This obligation does not compel either party to agree to a proposal or to make a concession." Nonetheless, the Act is predicated on the notion that the parties must have a sincere desire to enter into "good faith negotiation with an intent to settle differences and arrive at an agreement." Therefore, "mere pretense at negotiations with a completely closed mind and without a spirit of cooperation does not satisfy the requirements of the Act." A violation may be found where the employer will only reach an agreement on its own terms and none other.

In determining whether the Respondent bargained in bad faith, we look to the "totality of the Respondent's conduct," both at and away from the bargaining table. Relevant factors include: unreasonable bargaining demands, delaying tactics, efforts to bypass the bargaining representative, failure to provide relevant information, and unlawful conduct away from the bargaining table.

From its first proposal forward, the Respondent called for a substantial reduction in extant wages and benefits, particularly economic benefits. Prior to the advent of the Union as the employees' exclusive representative, the employees had received paid overtime after 40 hours, 7 days' vacation, a companywide insurance plan to which the employees made monthly contributions, and 401(k) and bonus load plans. In addition, employees were entitled to a 1-week vacation after 1 year and 2-week vacation after 2 years. Under the Respondent's initial proposals, the employees would lose paid overtime, resulting in a substantial loss of income. The Respondent also changed the employee's insurance coverage, such that the employees were required to pay higher premiums and received less coverage and proposed the elimination of the 401(k) and bonus load plans.

With respect to its vacation proposal, the Respondent engaged in regressive bargaining. On November 29, 1995, the Respondent proposed a 1-week vacation after 1 year of employment and 2 weeks' vacation after 2 years. Under the proposal that the Respondent advanced on February 5, 1996, however, the employees were required to work a minimum of 1540 hours per year or 38-1/2 (40 hours) weeks before they would be entitled to any vacation time, and they would not receive a second weeks' vacation until they worked 3 years, rather than 2.

Where the proponent of a regressive proposal fails to provide an explanation for it, or the reason appears dubious, the Board may weigh that factor in determining whether there has been bad-faith bargaining. As the Board stated in *John Asquaga's Nuggett*, 298 N.L.R.B. 524, 527 (1990), *enfd. in pertinent part sub nom. Sparks Nugget v. NLRB*, 968 F.2d 991 (9th Cir. 1992), "refusal[s] to budge from an initial bargaining position, [refusals] to offer explanations for one's bargaining proposals (beyond conclusional statements that that is what a party wants), and [refusals] to make any efforts at compromise in order to reach [a] common ground" can constitute evidence of bad-faith bargaining.

The Respondent failed to provide a legitimate explanation to justify the significant differences between the proposals that it advanced in negotiations and the status quo prior to negotiations. The record shows that, in bargaining, the Respondent did not attempt to justify its economic proposals. Even when it attempted to do so after-the-fact on brief by asserting that the Fort Smith/Van Buren facility was Mid-Continent Concrete's least profitable facility, no evidence was presented to support this claim. Belying this contention is the statement by the Respondent's general manager, Bill Lincks, that, had employees not elected the union they would be earning $10 an hour, a wage rate higher than the status quo prior to bargaining. When the Respondent insisted on eliminating paid overtime, a benefit accounting for a significant portion of the employees' wages, its only explanation was its unsubstantiated claim that it was considering this practice on a companywide basis. The Respondent, however, provided no evidence that it considered or implemented a no-overtime policy at any of its other facilities. In contrast, the Respondent also proposed maintaining current wage rates for unit employees despite the contemporaneous grant of wage increases to the Respondent's other nonunion facilities. The Respondent also refused, without explanation, the Union's proposal of accumulating vacation on a pro rata basis, and the Respondent proposed elimination of the 401(k) and bonus load plans.

The Respondent was similarly unwilling to compromise on, or provide explanations for, its noneconomic proposals. The Respondent's management-rights clause would allow the Respondent to assign all unit work to employees outside the unit. The Respondent's explanation was that it wanted the ability to subcontract work, including bargaining unit work when it believed that it would be beneficial to do so. The examples the Respondent gave where the subcontracting clause would be of use concerned nonbargaining unit work (e.g., equipment repair which unit employees were untrained to perform), yet the language of the provision was much broader than what the Respondent claimed was its intended use. Viewing, as did the judge, the "totality of the circumstances," we find that the Respondent's lack of an explanation and justification for these proposals, its intransigence, and its failure to make concessions support a finding that the Respondent intended to avoid reaching an agreement.

Further evidence of bad faith can be found in the orchestrated, almost staged, manner of the negotiation. Unexplained concessions can be considered a tool to disguise and conceal a party's strategy of surface bargaining. The Respondent's negotiating style was to put forward a harsh bargaining proposal, stand by the proposal, then as the negotiations dragged on, concede no more than the status quo, and stall the negotiations by refusing or delaying its response to any additional proposals. Negotiations were held approximately once a month, and the negotiating sessions did not increase in frequency even as the parties' differences narrowed. The Respondent put forward several unsubstantiated proposals, and then later retreated from them, with no explanation. Additionally, as the negotiations progressed, the Respondent, in a uniform manner, appeared to slow down and drag out the negotiations. An example is its vacation proposals. Prior to February 12 the parties had agreed to a number of noneconomic proposals. On February 12, roughly 6 months into the negotiations, the Respondent submitted a regressive vacation proposal. The Respondent withdrew a proposal that would have left vacation at the status quo and substituted a proposal that included a provision that entitled the employees to 2 weeks' vacation only after 3 years' employment. No reason was advanced for why the Respondent altered its proposal. Later, the Respondent made a concession in giving up its demand for 2 weeks' vacation only after 3 years. There was no indication that Respondent's concession was in exchange for anything. Backing off on part of the proposal enabled the Respondent to claim it had made concessions while still allowing the Respondent to stall the negotiations. The Respondent also compromised on the elimination of the 401(k) and bonus load plan for no apparent reason (i.e., there was no tradeoff). By April, the Respondent's chief negotiator indicated that, although it had new proposals, it was instructed not to present them. By July, the Respondent was delaying its responses to the Union's proposals, particularly the September 5 proposal which represented a significant movement toward the Respondent's position.

In addition, the 8(a)(1) statements of one of the Respondent's supervisors provide a roadmap to the Respondent's bargaining strategy. Thus, in October 1995, Supervisor Bill Lincks, in response to employee Chris Poole's statement of approval over the Respondent's perceived willingness to negotiate at the onset of bargaining, replied that "the Union would be there one year." In April 1996, Gary Lincks told employee Paul Cook that "within a year the whole thing would be over with and they'd probably have a new vote." Bill Lincks also told employee J.R. Cook that he was going to "appoint [him] supervisor, that way [he] won't be able to vote next time." When questioned as to when the next vote would take place, Bill Lincks replied: "the same time it did last year," with implied reference to the conclusion of the certification year. Also in April 1996, Gary Lincks told employee Wesley Smith that "it would be to the Company's benefit not to enter into a contract with the Union, the main reason being it would cost them money and that they would and could wait until all the Union's supporters were gone then they'd have everything their own way." Wesley Smith was also told that "it wouldn't do us any good to negotiate with the Company because they'll just wait . . . till the next election." On September 5, 1996, Bill Lincks asked employee Poole whether he was needed at what would prove to be the final bargaining session. When Poole responded that he was needed, Links replied that "he didn't know why they needed both of you (i.e., Poole and Paul Cook) all here. You are going to accomplish the same thing you've always accomplished which is absolutely zero." These statements clearly indicate that the Respondent intended to drag out the negotiations until a year had passed and then request a new vote to rid itself of the Union. The statements also inform the employees that bargaining is futile and that they would be better off without the Union because, as Bill Lincks told Poole, "if they hadn't joined [they would] have done had $10 an hour and done had new trucks."

Thus, the Respondent's conduct both at and away from the bargaining table clearly demonstrates that it intended to frustrate negotiations, and prevent the successful negotiation of a bargaining agreement. Accordingly, we find that the Respondent violated Section 8(a)(5) of the Act by engaging in surface bargaining.

CHAIRMAN HURTGEN, concurring in part:

I agree with my colleagues that the Respondent has engaged in bad-faith bargaining in violation of Section 8(a)(5) and has committed other violations of Section 8(a)(1) and (5). Unlike my colleagues, however, in finding that the Respondent did not bargain in good faith, I rely principally on statements by Respondent's agents. In these statements, the Respondent vowed to end the bargaining relationship after the certification year had expired, threatened to insure a union loss in a new election by appointing prounion bargaining unit employees to supervisory positions, told employees that they would have higher wages and new trucks if they reject union representation, and predicted that the Union would accomplish "absolutely zero" in negotiations. In my view these statements are sufficiently tied to the Respondent's position in bargaining as to reflect the Respondent's intent to avoid reaching an agreement. I would not, however, rely on the fact that the Respondent made initial proposals which, if accepted, would have resulted in the employees receiving lower pay and fewer benefits than they had received before the advent of the Union. Under Section 8(d), neither party is required to make concessions. A union can ask for more than the status quo, and the employer can offer less.

NOTES

1.   If the employer's supervisors had not made the various statements recounted in the opinion, would the Board majority have still found surface bargaining? Would such a finding be consistent with *American National Insurance*? Even without the express statements from the supervisors, could the Board infer that the employer had no intention of ever reaching agreement with the union but rather intended to wait out the certification year and then seek to have the union decertified?

2.   If as a remedy, the Board orders the employer to cease and desist its refusal to bargain in good faith, what must the employer do to comply with the order? Is this consistent with section 8(d)'s provision that the duty to bargain does not require the making of concessions?

3.   In *American National Insurance*, the answer to the union's complaint of the employer's insistence on an extremely one-sided management functions clause was to either accept the proposal or exert economic pressure on the employer to force it to modify its demands. Why not simply say to the union in *Hardesty* that if it finds the employer's proposals to be so one-sided, its remedy is not to seek help from the NLRB but rather it should exert economic pressure to force the employer to modify its position?

4.   The negotiations in *Hardesty* were for a first contract following certification and recognition of the union as exclusive bargaining representative. Should the Board scrutinize bargaining proposals and bargaining table conduct more closely when the parties are bargaining for a first contract than when they are bargaining for successor contracts? Should it matter whether the employer actively campaigned against union representation? Should it matter whether the employer committed unfair labor practices during the representation campaign?

5.   The Board's obligation to police the parties' good faith in negotiations coupled with the admonition that it is not to police the substance of their proposals forces it to walk a very fine line in surface bargaining cases. How the Board walks that line is frequently the subject of judicial scrutiny. For example, in *NLRB v. A-1 King Size Sandwiches, Inc.*, 732 F.2d 872 (11th Cir. 1984), the court upheld a Board finding of bad faith bargaining. The parties had held 18 bargaining sessions over 11 months. They reached agreement on a recognition clause; plant visitation by Union representatives; the number, rights and duties of union stewards; the Union's use of a bulletin board; pay for jury duty; leaves of absence; and a grievance and arbitration procedure. Among other provisions, the employer insisted that it have absolute authority to determine wages, to discipline, discharge and lay off employees and to remove work from the bargaining unit; and insisted on a "zipper clause" whereby the union would waive the right to bargain over all issues for the duration of the contract. The employer refused union proposals for a nondiscrimination clause and for dues check-off and insisted on a very broad no strike clause. The court regarded the employer as insisting on retaining absolute control over every meaningful issue concerning the employees. In

contrast, in *Chevron Oil Co. v. NLRB*, 442 F.2d 1067 (5th Cir. 1971), the court reversed an NLRB finding of bad faith bargaining even though the employer had insisted on broad management rights and no strike clauses and opposed arbitration of grievances.

6.   Questions of surface bargaining, i.e., subjective good faith of one of the parties (typically the employer) arise primarily in situations where the union has been too weak to pressure the employer into reevaluating its position. The unfair labor practice charge may be filed because the union believes it is too weak to strike or because the union has struck, the employer has replaced the strikers and the union is seeking to have the strike determined to be an unfair labor practice strike. As we will see in Chapter 6, an employer need not discharge permanent replacements to reinstate returning economic strikers but must reinstate returning unfair labor practice strikers even if it means discharging replacements. Thus, the real issue in many surface bargaining cases is the status of a union's strike or strike threat and its vulnerability to permanent replacement. Is this context relevant to determining how closely a labor board should be able to police subjective good faith? *See* Martin H. Malin, *Afterword: Labor Law Reform—Waiting for Congress?*, 69 Chi-Kent L. Rev. 277 (1994).

7.   The extremes to which employer proposals must go before they will support a finding of bad faith surface bargaining make it feasible for a skilled employer negotiator facing a weak union to present proposals that the union will be unable to accept but that are not likely to support an inference of surface bargaining. In a first contract situation, such an employer may try to wait the union out and ultimately obtain its decertification. In two highly-regarded articles dealing with labor law reform, Professor Weiler reported that a union recognized following a *Gissel* bargaining order had only a 37% chance of successfully negotiating a first contract and only a 10% chance of negotiating a successor contract. Paul Weiler, *Promises to Keep: Securing Worker's Rights to Self-organization under the NLRA*, 96 Harv. L. Rev. 1769, 1795 n. 94 (1983). Even unions recognized following NLRB elections faced substantial risks that they would be unable to negotiate first contracts. They succeeded 63% of the time. Paul Weiler, *Striking A New Balance: Freedom of Contract and the Prospects for Union Representation*, 98 Harv. L. Rev. 351, 353–55 & tbl. 1 (1984). Professor Weiler concluded:

> [I]t is the current interpretation of the statutory commitment to free collective bargaining that is in large part responsible for the inability of workers to translate their choice in favor of union representation into a first agreement—a milestone that may be more important to the establishment of an enduring bargaining relationship than is legal certification. For those who believe, as I do, in the importance of ensuring workers a collective voice in the conditions of their employment, these considerations compel a searching reexamination of a legal regime that seems more and more to frustrate rather than to facilitate the achievement of the original aims of the NLRA.

Id. at 363. Do you agree?

2. SURFACE BARGAINING AND THE RLA

How would the situation in *Hardesty* have been handled under the Railway Labor Act? Under cases such as *American Train Dispatchers Division v. Ft. Smith Ry,* the NMB mediator has almost absolute control over the negotiations. In *Ft. Smith*, the employer clearly wanted to declare impasse, wait out the 30-day cooling off period, unilaterally implement its proposals and dare the union to strike. It may well have expected that the union would look weak regardless of whether it struck, and ultimately would be decertified. But, the mediator can prevent this from happening by simply refusing to release the parties from mediation. The mediator can, by requiring the employer to attend sessions at inconvenient times and inconvenient places, pressure the employer to modify its position to one more likely to be accepted by the union. Is this model preferable to the NLRA approach?

3. SURFACE BARGAINING IN THE PUBLIC SECTOR

In the public sector in a state where the ultimate impasse resolution procedure is interest arbitration surface bargaining may actually be expected. In traditional interest arbitration, the arbitrator may select the final offer of either party or may award a resolution between the two offers. Parties frequently present final offers that are more extreme than what the parties would be willing to take in settlement, believing that they must give the arbitrator room to devise an award between the two final offers. Some states use a procedure called "final offer package" interest arbitration, where the arbitrator must select the entire final offer of one of the parties. In final offer package arbitration, there is considerable pressure on the parties to present the most reasonable positions they find acceptable. Otherwise, they increase the risk that the arbitrator will award the other party's final offer. Consequently, final offer package interest arbitration greatly reduces the risk of surface bargaining

In states whose final impasse resolution procedure is non-binding factfinding, the risk of surface bargaining arguably is elevated because the employer can reject the factfinder's recommendation, force an impasse and unilaterally implement its position. Consequently, some public sector jurisdictions exercise greater vigilance than the NLRB in policing subjective good faith in negotiations. For an example, *see Oakland Community College*, 15 Mi. P.E.R. ¶ 33006 (Mich. Emp. Rel. Comm'n 2001).

D. INTERPRETING "GOOD FAITH" AS OBJECTIVE RULES OF CONDUCT

1. THE DUTY TO SUPPLY INFORMATION UNDER THE NLRA

The preceding section focused on the difficulties in policing subjective good faith in collective bargaining. In light of those difficulties, some have suggested that courts and labor boards should interpret the requirement of good faith objectively to establish rules of conduct which will be easier to police. The duty to refrain from making unilateral changes prior to impasse is one such objective rule of conduct. A second objective rule, the duty to furnish information, evolved out of an effort to police subjective good faith. In *NLRB v. Truitt Mfg. Co.*, 351 U.S. 149 (1956), the union demanded a pay raise of 10 cents per hour. The employer refused, stating that any raise in excess of 2 ½ cents per hour would bankrupt the company. The union demanded access to the company's financial books and records but the company refused. The union then demanded that the company produce whatever financial evidence served as the basis for its claim of inability to grant the pay raise but the company refused. The NLRB found that the company failed to bargain in good faith and the Supreme Court agreed. The Court reasoned:

> Good-faith bargaining necessarily requires that claims made by either bargainer should be honest claims. This is true about an asserted inability to pay an increase in wages. If such an argument is important enough to present in the give and take of bargaining, it is important enough to require some sort of proof of its accuracy. And it would certainly not be farfetched for a trier of fact to reach the conclusion that bargaining lacks good faith when an employer mechanically repeats a claim of inability to pay without making the slightest effort to substantiate the claim. Such has been the holding of the Labor Board since shortly after the passage of the Wagner Act. In *Pioneer Pearl Button Co.*, decided in 1936, where the employer's representative relied on the company's asserted "poor financial condition," the Board said: "He did no more than take refuge in the assertion that the respondent's financial condition was poor; he refused either to prove his statement, or to permit independent verification. This is not collective bargaining." 1 N.L.R.B. 837, 842–843. This was the position of the Board when the Taft-Hartley Act was passed in 1947 and has been its position ever since. We agree with the Board that a refusal to attempt to substantiate a claim of inability to pay increased wages may support a finding of a failure to bargain in good faith.

Id. at 152–53. In *NLRB v. Acme Industrial Co.*, 385 U.S. 432 (1967), the Court extended *Truitt* to union requests for information necessary for it to administer the collective bargaining agreement. The Court again addressed that duty in the following case.

DETROIT EDISON CO. V. NLRB
440 U.S. 301 (1979)

JUSTICE STEWART delivered the opinion of the Court:

The duty to bargain collectively, imposed upon an employer by § 8(a)(5) of the National Labor Relations Act includes a duty to provide relevant information needed by a labor union for the proper performance of its duties as the employees' bargaining representative. In this case an employer was brought before the National Labor Relations Board to answer a complaint that it had violated this statutory duty when it refused to disclose certain information about employee aptitude tests requested by a union in order to prepare for arbitration of a grievance. The employer supplied the union with much of the information requested, but refused to disclose three items: the actual test questions, the actual employee answer sheets, and the scores linked with the names of the employees who received them. The Board, concluding that all the items requested were relevant to the grievance and would be useful to the union in processing it, ordered the employer to turn over all of the materials directly to the union, subject to certain restrictions on the union's use of the information. A divided Court of Appeals for the Sixth Circuit ordered enforcement of the Board's order without modification.

The petitioner, Detroit Edison Co. (hereinafter Company), is a public utility engaged in the generation and distribution of electric power in Michigan. Since about 1943, the Utility Workers Union of America, Local 223, AFL-CIO (Union) has represented certain of the Company's employees. At the time of the hearing in this case, one of the units represented by the Union was a unit of operating and maintenance employees at the Company's plant in Monroe, Mich. The Union was certified as the exclusive bargaining agent for employees in that unit in 1971, and it was agreed that these employees would be covered by a pre-existing collective-bargaining agreement, one of the provisions of which specified that promotions within a given unit were to be based on seniority "whenever reasonable qualifications and abilities of the employees being considered are not significantly different." Management decisions to bypass employees with greater seniority were subject to the collective agreement's grievance machinery, including ultimate arbitration, whenever a claim was made that the bypass had been arbitrary or discriminatory.

The aptitude tests at issue were used by the Company to screen applicants for the job classification of "Instrument Man B." An Instrument

Man is responsible for installing, maintaining, repairing, calibrating, testing, and adjusting the powerplant instrumentation. The position of Instrument Man B, although at the lowest starting grade under the contract and usually requiring on-the-job training, was regarded by the Company as a critical job because it involved activities vital to the operation of the plant.

The Company has used aptitude tests as a means of predicting job performance since the late 1920's or early 1930's. In the late 1950's, the Company first began to use a set of standardized tests (test battery) as a predictor of performance on the Instrument Man B job.

In the late 1960's, the technical engineers responsible for the Company's instrumentation department complained that the test battery was not an accurate screening device. The Company's industrial psychologists, accordingly, performed a revalidation study of the tests. As a result, [one] [t]est was dropped, and the scoring system was changed. Instead of the former three-tier system, two scores were possible under the revised battery: "not recommended" and "acceptable." The gross test score required for an "acceptable" rating was raised to 10.3, a figure somewhat lower than the former score required for a "recommended" but higher than the "acceptable" score used previously.

The Company administered the tests to applicants with the express commitment that each applicant's test score would remain confidential. Tests and test scores were kept in the offices of the Company's industrial psychologists who, as members of the American Psychological Association, deemed themselves ethically bound not to disclose test information to unauthorized persons. Under this policy, the Company's psychologists did not reveal the tests or report actual test numerical scores to management or to employee representatives. The psychologists would, however, if an individual examinee so requested, review the test questions and answers with that individual.

The present dispute had its beginnings in 1971 when the Company invited bids from employees to fill six Instrument Man B openings at the Monroe plant. Ten Monroe unit employees applied. None received a score designated as "acceptable," and all were on that basis rejected. The jobs were eventually filled by applicants from outside the Monroe plant bargaining unit.

The Union filed a grievance on behalf of the Monroe applicants, claiming that the new testing procedure was unfair and that the Company had bypassed senior employees in violation of the collective-bargaining agreement. The grievance was rejected by the Company at all levels, and the Union took it to arbitration. In preparation for the arbitration, the Union requested the Company to turn over various materials related to the Instrument Man B testing program. The Company furnished the Union with copies of test-validation studies performed by its industrial psychologists and with a report by an outside consultant on the Company's entire testing program. It refused, however, to release the actual test battery, the applicants' test papers, and their scores, maintaining that complete confidentiality of these materials was necessary in order to insure the future integrity of the tests and to protect the privacy interests of the examinees.

The Union then filed with the Board the unfair labor practice charge involved in this case. The charge alleged that the information withheld by the Company was relevant and necessary to the arbitration of the grievance, "including the ascertainment of promotion criteria, the veracity of the scoring and grading of the examination and the testing procedures, and the job relatedness of the test(s) to the Instrument Man B classification."

After filing the unfair labor practice charge, the Union asked the arbitrator to order the Company to furnish the materials at issue. He declined on the ground that he was without authority to do so. In view of the pendency of the charges before the Board, the parties proceeded with the arbitration on the express understanding that the Union could reopen the case should it ultimately prevail in its claims. During the course of the arbitration, however, the Company did disclose the raw scores of those who had taken the test, with the names of the examinees deleted. In addition, it provided the Union with sample questions indicative of the types of questions appearing on the test battery and with detailed information about its scoring procedures. It also offered to turn over the scores of any employee who would sign a waiver releasing the Company psychologist from his pledge of confidentiality. The Union declined to seek such releases.

The arbitrator's decision found that the Company was free under the collective agreement to establish minimum reasonable qualifications for the job of Instrument Man and to use aptitude tests as a measure of those qualifications; that the Instrument Man B test battery was a reliable and fair test in the sense that its administration and scoring had been standardized; and that the test had a "high degree of validity" as a predictor of performance in the job classification for which it was developed. He concluded that the 10.3 score created a "presumption of significant difference under the contract." He also expressed the view that the Union's position in the arbitration had not been impaired because of lack of access to the actual test battery.

Several months later the Board issued a complaint based on the Union's unfair labor practice charge. At the outset of the hearing before the Administrative Law Judge, the Company offered to turn over the test battery and answer sheets to an industrial psychologist selected by the Union for an independent evaluation, stating that disclosure to an intermediary obligated to preserve test secrecy would satisfy its concern that direct disclosure to the Union would inevitably result in dissemination of the questions. The Union rejected this compromise.

The Administrative Law Judge found that notwithstanding the conceded statistical validity of the test battery, the tests and scores would be of probable relevant help to the Union in the performance of its duties as collective-bargaining agent. He reasoned that the Union, having had no access to the tests, had been "deprived of any occasion to check the tests for built-in bias, or discriminatory tendency, or any opportunity to argue that the tests or the test questions are not well suited to protect the employees' rights, or to check the accuracy of the scoring." The Company's claim that employees' privacy might be abused by disclosure to the Union of the scores he rejected as insubstantial. Accordingly, he recommended that the Company be ordered to turn over the test scores directly to the Union. He did, however, accept the Company's suggestion that the test battery and answer sheets be disclosed to an expert intermediary. Disclosure of these materials to lay Union representatives, he reasoned, would not be likely to produce constructive results, since the tests could be properly analyzed only by professionals. The Union was to be given "the right to see and study the tests," and to use the information therein "to the extent necessary to process and arbitrate the grievances," but not to disclose the information to third parties other than the arbitrator.

The Company specifically requested the Board "to adopt that part of the order which requires that tests be turned over to a qualified psychologist," but excepted to the requirement that the employee-linked scores be given to the Union. It contended that the only reason asserted by the Union in support of its request for the scores—to check their arithmetical accuracy—was not sufficient to overcome the principle of confidentiality that underlay its psychological testing program. The Union filed a cross exception to the requirement that it select a psychologist, arguing that it should not be forced to "employ an outsider for what is normal grievance and Labor-Management work."

The Board, and the Court of Appeals for the Sixth Circuit in its decision enforcing the Board's order, ordered the Company to turn over all the material directly to the Union. They concluded that the Union should be able to determine for itself whether it needed a psychologist to interpret the test battery and answer sheets. Both recognized the Company's interest in maintaining the security of the tests, but both reasoned that appropriate restrictions on the Union's use of the materials would protect this interest. Neither was receptive to the Company's claim that employee privacy and the professional obligations of the Company's industrial psychologists should outweigh the Union request for the employee-linked scores.

Two issues are presented on this record. The first concerns the Board's choice of a remedy for the Company's failure to disclose copies of the test battery and answer sheets. The second, and related, question concerns the propriety of the Board's conclusion that the Company committed an unfair labor practice when it refused to disclose, without a written consent from the individual employees, the test scores linked with the employee names.

We turn first to the question whether the Board abused its remedial discretion when it ordered the Company to deliver directly to the Union the copies of the test battery and answer sheets. The Company urges that disclosure directly to the Union would carry with it a substantial risk that the test questions would be disseminated. Since it spent considerable time and money validating the Instrument Man B tests and since its tests depend for reliability upon the Examinee's lack of advance preparation, it contends that the harm of dissemination would not be trivial. The future validity of the tests is tied to secrecy, and disclosure to employees would not only threaten the Company's investment but would also leave the Company with no valid means of measuring employee aptitude.

In his brief on behalf of the Board, the Solicitor General has acknowledged the existence of a strong public policy against disclosure of employment aptitude tests and, at least in the context of civil service testing, has conceded that "[g]overnmental recruitment would be seriously disputed and public confidence eroded if the integrity of . . . tests were compromised." Indeed, he has also acknowledged that the United States Civil Service Commission "has been zealous to guard against undue disclosure and has successfully contended for protective orders which limit exposure of the tests to attorneys and professional psychologists with restrictions on copying or disseminating test materials." He urges, however, that the Board's order can be justified on the grounds that the Union's institutional interests militate against improper disclosure, and that the specific protective provisions in the Board's order will safeguard the integrity of the tests. He emphasizes the deference generally accorded to "the considered judgment of the Board, charged by Congress with special responsibility for effectuating labor policy." We do not find these justifications persuasive.

A union's bare assertion that it needs information to process a grievance does not automatically oblige the employer to supply all the information in the manner requested. The duty to supply information under § 8(a)(5) turns upon "the circumstances of the particular case," *NLRB v. Truitt Mfg. Co*, 351 U.S. at 153, and much the same may be said for the type of disclosure that will satisfy that duty. Throughout this proceeding, the reasonableness of the Company's concern for test secrecy has been essentially conceded. The finding by the Board that this concern did not outweigh the Union's interest in exploring the fairness of the Company's criteria for promotion did not carry with it any suggestion that the concern itself was not legitimate and substantial. Indeed, on this record—which has established the Company's freedom under the collective contract to use aptitude tests as a criterion for promotion, the empirical validity of the tests, and the relationship between secrecy and test validity—the strength of the Company's concern has been abundantly demonstrated. The Board has cited no principle of national labor policy to warrant a remedy that would unnecessarily disserve this interest, and we are unable to identify one.

It is obvious that the remedy selected by the Board does not adequately protect the security of the tests. The restrictions barring the Union from taking any action that might cause the tests to fall into the hands of employees who have taken or are likely to take them are only as effective as the sanctions available to enforce them. In this instance, there is substantial doubt whether the Union would be subject to a contempt citation were it to ignore the restrictions. It was not a party to the enforcement proceeding in the Court of Appeals, and the scope of an enforcement order under § 10(e) is limited by Fed. R. Civ. P. 65(d) making an injunction binding only "upon the parties to the action . . . and upon those persons in active concert or participation with them. . . ." *See Regal Knitwear Co. v. NLRB*, 324 U.S 9. The Union, of course, did participate actively in the Board proceedings, but it is debatable whether that would be enough to satisfy the requirement of the Rule. Further, the Board's regulations contemplate a contempt sanction only against a respondent, 29 C.F.R. §§ 101.9, 101.14 & 101.15 (1978), and the initiation of contempt proceedings is entirely within the discretion of the Board's General Counsel. Effective sanctions at the Board level are similarly problematic. To be sure, the Board's General Counsel could theoretically bring a separate unfair labor practice charge against the Union, but he could also in his unreviewable discretion refuse to issue such a complaint. Moreover, the Union clearly would not be accountable in either contempt or unfair labor practice proceedings for the most realistic vice inherent in the Board's remedy—the danger of inadvertent leaks.

We are mindful that the Board is granted broad discretion in devising remedies to undo the effects of violations of the Act, and of the principle that in the area of federal labor law "the relation of remedy to policy is peculiarly a matter for administrative competence." Nonetheless, the rule of deference to the Board's choice of remedy does not constitute a blank check for arbitrary action. The role that Congress in § 10(e) has entrusted to the courts in reviewing the Board's petitions for enforcement of its orders is not that of passive conduit. The Board in this case having identified no justification for a remedy granting such scant protection to the Company's undisputed and important interests in test secrecy, we hold that the Board abused its discretion in ordering the Company to turn over the test battery and answer sheets directly to the Union.

The dispute over Union access to the actual scores received by named employees is in a somewhat different procedural posture, since the

Company did on this issue preserve its objections to the basic finding that it had violated its duty under § 8(a)(5) when it refused disclosure. The Company argues that even if the scores were relevant to the Union's grievance (which it vigorously disputes), the Union's need for the information was not sufficiently weighty to require breach of the promise of confidentiality to the examinees, breach of its industrial psychologists' code of professional ethics, and potential embarrassment and harassment of at least some of the examinees. The Board responds that this information does satisfy the appropriate standard of "relevance," *see NLRB v. Acme Industrial Co.*, 385 U.S. 432, and that the Company having "unilaterally" chosen to make a promise of confidentiality to the examinees, cannot rely on that promise to defend against a request for relevant information. The professional obligations of the Company's psychologists, it argues, must give way to paramount federal law. Finally, it dismisses as speculative the contention that employees with low scores might be embarrassed or harassed.

We may accept for the sake of this discussion the finding that the employee scores were of potential relevance to the Union's grievance, as well as the position of the Board that the federal statutory duty to disclose relevant information cannot be defeated by the ethical standards of a private group. Nevertheless we agree with the Company that its willingness to disclose these scores only upon receipt of consents from the examinees satisfied its statutory obligations under § 8(a)(5).

The Board's position appears to rest on the proposition that union interests in arguably relevant information must always predominate over all other interests, however, legitimate. But such an absolute rule has never been established, and we decline to adopt such a rule here. There are situations in which an employer's conditional offer to disclose may be warranted. This we believe is one.

The sensitivity of any human being to disclosure of information that may be taken to bear on his or her basic competence is sufficiently well known to be an appropriate subject of judicial notice. There is nothing in this record to suggest that the Company promised the examinees that their scores would remain confidential in order to further parochial concerns or to frustrate subsequent Union attempts to process employee grievances. And it has not been suggested at any point in this proceeding that the Company's unilateral promise of confidentiality was in itself violative of the terms of the collective-bargaining agreement. Indeed, the Company presented evidence that disclosure of individual scores had in the past resulted in the harassment of some lower scoring examinees who had, as a result, left the Company.

Under these circumstances, any possible impairment of the function of the Union in processing the grievances of employees is more than justified by the interests served in conditioning the disclosure of the test scores upon the consent of the very employees whose grievance is being processed. The burden on the Union in this instance is minimal. The Company's interest in preserving employee confidence in the testing program is well founded.

In light of the sensitive nature of testing information, the minimal burden that compliance with the Company's offer would have placed on the Union, and the total absence of evidence that the Company had fabricated concern for employee confidentiality only to frustrate the Union in the discharge of its responsibilities, we are unable to sustain the Board in its conclusion that the Company, in resisting an unconsented—to disclosure of individual test results, violated the statutory obligation to bargain in good faith. *See NLRB v. Truitt Mfg. Co.*, 351 U.S. 149. Accordingly, we hold that the order requiring the Company unconditionally to disclose the employee scores to the Union was erroneous.

[The opinions of JUSTICE STEVENS concurring in part and dissenting in part, and JUSTICE WHITE dissenting have been omitted.]

NOTES

1.   Was there any question that Detroit Edison's refusal to furnish the test questions and test scores by employee name was undertaken in subjective good faith? If not, why didn't the Court stop there and hold that the company did not violate section 8(a)(5)? How does the Court's analysis differ from its analysis in *Truitt*?

2.   In light of your answer to question 1, revisit *Truitt*. Can the result in *Truitt* be explained in terms of the Court's analysis in *Detroit Edison*?

3.   In *A T & T Services, Inc.*, 366 N.L.R.B. No. 48 (2018), the Board held that the employer violated section 8(a)(5) when it refused to provide the union with the name, work location, job title, seniority date and test result for all employees taking the employer's Technical Mechanical Tests. Employees who passed the tests were guaranteed protection against layoffs. The employer was willing to furnish a list of all test scores with the names of test takers redacted but with two names unredacted each quarter. The employer argued that redacting the test takers' names was necessary to preserve test integrity by preventing the union from interviewing the test takers to reconstruct the test. The Board found the employer's concern for test integrity speculative and distinguished *Detroit Edison* on the ground that unlike the employer in *Detroit Edison*, the employer in the instant case had not given test takers assurances that their scores would be kept confidential.

4.   When a union requests information concerning employees in the bargaining unit, the request is presumed to be relevant to the union's carrying out its responsibilities as exclusive bargaining representative. The burden is on the employer to rebut the presumption or otherwise show why disclosure is not appropriate. However, when the union requests information concerning persons outside the bargaining unit, the union has the burden of demonstrating relevance. In *New York & Presbyterian Hospital v. NLRB*, 649

F.3d 723 (D.C. Cir. 2011), the court enforced the Board's order that the employer, a hospital affiliated with Columbia University, provide the union with the names, dates of hire or termination, job duties, departments or areas of work, shifts and whether they were full or part time, for all nurse practitioners performing services at the hospital who were employed by Columbia. Although the individuals were not employees of the hospital, and thus were not in the bargaining unit represented by the union, the court agreed with the Board that the information was relevant to the union's investigation as to whether the Columbia employees were performing bargaining unit work in violation of the union's contract with the hospital. The court also observed that, although an employer is not required to provide information that it does not have, it is required to provide whatever relevant information it does have and the employer had much of the requested information because of its role in accrediting the nurse practitioners to work in the hospital.

5.   Assume that negotiations for a new agreement have broken down, the union has gone on strike and the employer has hired replacement workers to continue operating. If the union demands a list of replacements' names and addresses, must the employer comply? See JHP & Assocs. v. NLRB, 360 F.3d 904 (8th Cir. 2004) (holding employer had a duty to provide names of replacements but not their home addresses and telephone numbers unless union established it had no other means of contacting them); Chi. Tribune Co. v. NLRB, 79 F.3d 604 (7th Cir. 1996) (holding union entitled to names but not home addresses of replacements in light of other means by which union could contact replacements and history of violence by union against replacements); Chi. Tribune Co. v. NLRB, 965 F.2d 244 (7th Cir. 1992) (holding that company was not required to provide union with names of replacement workers where there had been incidents of death threats, windows shot out and the firebombing of a supervisor's garage and company had offered alternative methods of meeting union's legitimate needs for list of names); Georgetown Assocs., 235 N.L.R.B. 485 (1978) (finding employer violated 8(a)(5) by refusing union request for names and home addresses of replacements because information was presumptively relevant to union's duties as exclusive bargaining representative and information was not available from any alternative source).

6.   When investigating an incident of possible employee misconduct, employers often take written statements from witnesses who are often coworkers of the employee under investigation. If after concluding the investigation the employer disciplines one or more employees, the union often asks for copies of the witness statements. In Anheuser-Busch, Inc., 237 N.L.R.MB. 982 (1978), the Board held that the section 8(a)(5) duty to disclose does not obligate an employer to disclose witness statements taken under a promise of confidentiality. However, in Piedmont Gardens, 362 N.L.R.B. No. 139 (2015), by a 3–2 vote, the Board overruled Anhueser-Busch and held that employer refusals to provide witness statements would no longer be per se lawful and would instead be judged under the Detroit Edison balancing test. The Board majority reasoned that the new rule more appropriately takes into account the employees' and union's interests in disclosure and rejected the

suggestion that disclosure to the union will likely lead to harassment of the persons who gave the statements. The Board held that it would balance legitimate employer confidentiality concerns against union need to access on a case-by-case basis. The dissenters argued that the risk of harassment was sufficient to justify the per se rule of *Anheuser-Busch* and that the rule was necessary to facilitate employer investigations because witnesses will be reluctant to provide statements if the employer cannot guarantee them confidentiality.

7. Should the duty to furnish information be applied to unions under section 8(b)(3)? If so, under what circumstances? *See, e.g., Teamsters Local 500 (Acme Markets),* 340 N.L.R.B. 251 (2003); *Printing and Graphic Communications Local 13 (Oakland Press Co.),* 233 N.L.R.B. 994 (1977), *aff'd,* 598 F.2d 267 (D.C. Cir. 1979).

* * *

SDBC Holdings, Inc. v. NLRB, **711 F.3d 281 (2d Cir. 2013).** StellaD'oro Biscuit Co., a manufacturer of baked goods in the Bronx, N.Y., was acquired by Brynwood Partners, a private equity firm, with a view to improving the company's financial condition over five to ten years and selling it at a profit. During negotiations for a new contract, the company demanded concessions, stated that the company was losing $1.5 million per year, that the firm had invested $3 million in new equipment and was willing to fund continued losses in the short term but that if it could not turn the company around to make a profit it would take its "toy," i.e., its financial subsidies, and go home, closing the plant. The company negotiators told the union bargaining team that the employees' choices were to have jobs at lower pay or have no jobs at all.

The company allowed the union's negotiators to inspect the company's balance sheet from the prior year and invited the union to send its attorneys and accountants to the company's lawyer's office to inspect the balance sheet and take notes. A divided NLRB held that the company's refusal to provide the union with a copy of the balance sheet breached its duty to bargain in good faith. The court of appeals reversed, holding that the company had no duty to give the union access to its financial records because the company had not claimed an inability to pay. The court reasoned:

> Contrary to the decision of the Board majority, the record is clear that StellaD'oro's bargaining position was based on its unwillingness, and not its inability, to meet the Union's contract demands. StellaD'oro's parent company, Brynwood, had invested $3.1 million in StellaD'oro to introduce automated packaging equipment immediately before bargaining began—a fact that StellaD'oro pointed out during the course of its discussions with the Union. Brynwood also expressed its willingness during bargaining to expend an additional $6 million to extricate

StellaD'oro from the Union's pension plan, thus evidencing at the bargaining table itself that StellaD'oro had access to substantial capital from its parent owner. As the Board majority determined, moreover, StellaD'oro's chief negotiator expressly informed the Union during bargaining that Brynwood, an investment firm that "purchases companies with the aim of improving their financial condition and then selling them at a profit in 5 to 10 years," was "prepared to fund losses." And Hartong, a Brynwood partner, explicitly told the Union Committee that Brynwood's desire was "to invest in the operation and make it profitable." Given such evidence, we agree with [dissenting] Member Schaumber that StellaD'oro "plainly was not contending that it lacked funds to meet the Union's contract demands." Rather, its position was that it would not meet such demands "if the wage scales and labor costs were not restructured to help achieve profitability."

The NLRB acknowledges that StellaD'oro never expressly pled an inability to pay. The Board majority nevertheless concluded that StellaD'oro impliedly did so, because its negotiators made clear that StellaD'oro was losing money and would be cut off from Brynwood's supply of cash if the Union did not grant the sought-after concessions. The Board majority relied principally on the testimony of Union representatives Alston and Filippou to the effect that [Company lawyer] Jacoby and Hartong asserted throughout the negotiations that the Company was "not going to be able to survive," "might have to close the business" and was a "bleeding, distressed asset-losing proposition." These statements, however, must be viewed in context, for *Truitt* instructs that we should not find inability to pay "in every case in which economic inability is raised as an argument." And while Jacoby and Hartong unsurprisingly stressed StellaD'oro's financial difficulties, they repeatedly characterized their bargaining position in terms of what Brynwood was willing to do with its investment, not what StellaD'oro itself could or could not afford. Thus, in the words of one official, Brynwood made clear that it would "take [its] toy and . . . leave" unless it got concessions. And when pressed by Filippou, Hartong acknowledged that selling StellaD'oro off immediately to turn a profit was an option, but he reiterated that though "we could do that at any time . . . it's not the option that we prefer. The option we prefer is to try to improve the company's financial condition, return it to profitable condition." These are statements of unwillingness to pay, not inability to pay, and the record simply does not support the majority's conclusion to the contrary.

NOTES

1.   Did Brentwood place StellaD'oro's financial condition at issue in the negotiations? If so, why make its duty to provide the union with its financial statement turn on whether its claim was an inability to pay or an unwillingness to pay?

2.   Note that the company was willing to allow the union to inspect its financial statement but the Board required that the company provide the union with its own copy. Under what circumstances, if any, should allowing inspection but not providing a copy fulfill a party's duty to bargain in good faith? Under what circumstances, if any, should if not fulfill the duty?

3.   If an employer claims that it cannot meet union demands because doing so will make it impossible for the employer to compete, may the union compel the employer to disclose financial and other information which formed the basis for the employer's analysis? *See, e.g., Conagra, Inc. v. NLRB,* 117 F.3d 1435 (D.C. Cir. 1997) (excellent discussion of the history of this issue in the Board and the courts).

In *Wayron, LLC,* 364 N.L.R.B. No. 60 (2016), the employer, a metal fabricator, insisted in negotiations for a new collective bargaining agreement that labor costs be reduced from $30.51 per hour to $24.00 per hour. The employer had laid off most of its workforce and told the union that it had very little work because its labor costs made it impossible to compete against non-union shops. Employer representatives expressly disclaimed saying that they were unable to pay wages and benefits in the existing contract but said that the company was unable to provide jobs if it was not competitive. The union requested access for its auditor to the employer's financial records and the employer refused, again saying that it was not claiming inability to pay existing wages and benefits but rather that it was unable to compete and was seeking reduced costs to continue to secure work.

The Board majority held that the employer violated section 8(a)(5) in refusing the union's request for access to its financial records. The Board observed that the employer had told the union that it had lost money in each of the past three years and was "out of reserves" and "into debt," and needed cost reductions in a "short term fashion" to be able to acquire a new line of credit. The majority concluded:

> It is, of course, an entirely unsurprising proposition that competitive disadvantage, if continued at length, may eventually lead to inability to pay—especially when the business is losing money and lacks financial resources to cover its loses. Here, we find that the facts and circumstances establish that the Respondent, despite its surface characterizations to the contrary, was asserting that it could not pay, during the life of the contract being negotiated, the existing (or higher) levels of compensation that the Unions sought.

Member Miscimarra dissented. He argued that the employer continuously disclaimed any claim of inability to pay existing wages and benefits. He observed that the employer told the union that its landlord had agreed to reduce its rent and that the union needed to "get on board" so that the employer could renegotiate its line of credit and that although the employer said it would be in financial trouble if it did not reach agreement with the bank it did not say it would be unable to meet payroll. Emphasizing that the employer's "unvarying message" was that it was not claiming an inability to pay but rather an inability to compete and that one of the union's negotiators demanded access to the employer's financial records based on its claim of inability to compete, Member Miscimarra would have found that the denial of access did not violate the NLRA.

4.   In what ways does the duty to furnish information facilitate collective bargaining? Professor Dau-Schmidt has hypothesized a scenario where each party individually does better if it is intransigent in negotiations than if it is cooperative but both parties do better if they both are cooperative. He suggests that requiring the employer to supply the union with relevant information enables the parties to see mutually beneficial cooperative solutions and engenders trust on both sides. He critiques the decisions that limited the employer duty to furnish financial information to situations where the employer claims an inability to pay. Kenneth G. Dau-Schmidt, *A Bargaining Analysis of American Labor Law and the Search for Bargaining Equity and Industrial Peace*, 81 Mich. L. Rev. 419 (1992). Are there any downsides to a broader duty to disclose?

2. INFORMATION DISCLOSURE UNDER THE RLA AND IN THE PUBLIC SECTOR

In *Pacific Fruit Express Joint Protective Board v. Union Pacific Express Co.*, 826 F.2d 920 (9th Cir. 1987), the court declined to apply the duty to provide information under the Railway Labor Act. The court reasoned:

> [W]e think the extensive judicial intervention that court-ordered disclosure would require is inconsistent with the history and principles of the Railway Labor Act. The Act "was the product of agreement between the carriers and the unions, based on extensive negotiation and compromise as well as decades of experience with railroad labor legislation." *Air Line Pilots Ass'n v. Tex. Int'l Airlines, Inc.*, 656 F.2d 16, 19 (2d Cir. 1981). Congress intended the parties to work out disputes themselves, with a minimum of judicial intervention. *Pacific Fruit*'s interpretation of Section 2 First would place the courts at the heart of the bargaining process whenever either side in a railway labor dispute sought information about the other. We think Congress intended otherwise.

> Finally, we think it is significant that the Railway Labor Act created no administrative board comparable to the National Labor Relations Board (NLRB). When the NLRA requires a party

to disclose information, the courts' role in the process is limited to reviewing NLRB disclosure orders under a deferential standard. Under the union's interpretation of the Railway Labor Act, on the other hand, the courts would be solely responsible for administering and enforcing prearbitration disclosure. In the absence of clear evidence to the contrary, we are reluctant to assume that Congress intended to impose such a duty on the courts.

Id. at 923. *But see Int'l Fed'n of Flight Attendants v. Trans World Airlines, Inc.*, 716 F. Supp. 1003, 1020–21 (W.D. Mo. 1988), *aff'd on other grounds*, 878 F.2d 254 (8th Cir. 1989).

Availability of information in the public sector may be broader in some respects and narrower in others. Much information which a union in the private sector must request from an employer and may not be entitled to receive is publicly available in the public sector. The information may be available in published form, either in print or electronically on the employer's website, or it may be obtainable via a Freedom of Information Act request. For example, a union negotiating in the public sector typically has ready access to such information as the employer's budget, its revenue and sources of revenue, its expenditure in other areas, and the salaries and benefits of all employees, not just those in the bargaining unit.

On the other hand, information disclosure may be restricted by statutes that do not apply to the private sector. For example, in *Dep't of Defense v. FLRA*, 510 U.S. 487 (1994), the Supreme Court held that the Privacy Act amendment to the Freedom of Information Act, 5 U.S.C. § 552, prohibited the disclosure of the home addresses of bargaining unit employees by a federal agency to the employees' exclusive bargaining representative.

3. OTHER PER SE VIOLATIONS UNDER THE NLRA

The NLRB and the courts have interpreted the NLRA's duty to bargain in good faith to prescribe other objective conduct. It is a violation of section 8(a)(5) or 8(b)(3) for a party to refuse to reduce an agreement to writing. In *NLRB v. Auciello Iron Works*, 517 U.S. 781 (1996), the union unconditionally orally accepted an employer's offer. Subsequent to the union's acceptance, the employer withdrew recognition, claiming a good faith doubt as to the union's continuing majority status, and refused to execute a written contract. The Supreme Court held that the employer's refusal to execute a written contract violated section 8(a)(5), and that the contract barred the employer's withdrawal of recognition because under the contract bar rule no question concerning representation could be raised.

Refusals to meet at reasonable times or conditioning meeting on improper demands also breach the duty to bargain in good faith. *See, e.g., Caribe Supply Co.*, 313 N.L.R.B. 877 (1994). Similarly, a union violates section 8(b)(3) when it unreasonably delays submitting a tentative agreement to a ratification vote or obstructs the ratification vote. *See NLRB v. Teamsters Local 662* (W. S. Darley & Co.), 368 F.3d 741 (7th Cir. 2004). As discussed in Chapter 4, an employer violates section 8(a)(5) by bypassing the union and dealing directly with the employees.

MERCY HEALTH PARTNERS
358 N.L.R.B. 566 (2012)

CHAIRMAN PEARCE and MEMBERS HAYES and BLOCK:

I.

The Respondent, a regional healthcare provider, operated multiple hospitals in Michigan, including the two at issue in this case—Hackley and Mercy. Each hospital was responsible for performing pre-registration work for its own patients. The Union represented the Hackley-based pre-registration employees as part of a larger Hackley unit; Mercy's pre-registration employees were unrepresented.

The Respondent was also one of 19 subsidiaries of Trinity Health, a national healthcare provider. Until 2008, Trinity was a passive holding company. That year, it decided to transition to being an active parent company by assuming direct responsibility for, among other things, its subsidiaries' pre-registration work.

On November 23, 2009, the Respondent's Director of Labor Relations, Robin Belcourt, along with several other supervisors, met with five employees who performed pre-registration work at Hackley. She notified them that, as part of Trinity's transition, their positions would be relocated to Mercy. Belcourt further informed the employees that, pursuant to the collective-bargaining agreement between the Respondent and the Union, they would have 72 hours to decide whether to accept layoff or to "bump" a less senior unit employee. She also gave them 72 hours to decide whether to accept one of the newly created positions at Mercy. Belcourt informed them that the positions at Mercy were nonunion, but would have nearly the same wages and benefits as their positions at Hackley. All five employees (four at that time and one a few days later) accepted Belcourt's offer to transfer to Mercy. Belcourt also distributed letters to the five employees in which she summarized the above information. In that letter, Belcourt advised employees that, if they had any questions, they could consult with their labor relations manager or their union representative.

This relocation announcement likely did not come as a surprise to the employees. A couple of weeks before the November 23 meeting, a Hackley pre-registration employee learned from her colleague at Mercy that the Respondent was preparing an office for them at Mercy. Later, when confronted, her supervisor confirmed the rumor, but asked that she not tell a lot of people, particularly the union steward, because the Respondent had not yet formally announced the relocation. Despite her supervisor's request, the employee alerted the union steward.

Immediately following the November 23 announcement to employees, Belcourt formally notified the Union that the Respondent had decided to relocate unit work from Hackley to Mercy and that it had given employees notice of their rights under the collective-bargaining agreement. The Respondent informed the Union that the relocation of work would be completed by December 7. Later that day, the Union demanded effects bargaining. The parties engaged in effects bargaining on December 7.

II.

A.

Direct dealing "involves dealing with employees (bypassing the Union) about a mandatory subject of bargaining." The Board will therefore find a direct dealing violation when (1) the employer communicated directly with union-represented employees; (2) the discussion was for the purpose of establishing or changing wages, hours, and terms and conditions of employment or undercutting the union's role in bargaining; and (3) such communication was made to the exclusion of the union.

B.

Bypassing the Union and dealing directly with the employees is precisely what the Respondent did here. Without seeking the approval of the Union, Belcourt met directly with unit employees to inform them of the decision to relocate unit work. She then presented them with three offers— they could stay at Hackley by bumping a less senior unit employee, transfer to Mercy, or accept layoff. One of those offers, the option to transfer (which is a mandatory subject of bargaining in its own right), and the condition attached to that offer, acceptance within 72 hours, had not previously been presented to the Union. By that point, Belcourt had plainly crossed the line from discussing the relocation decision to discussing the effects of that decision on unit employees. Thus, while excluding the Union, the Respondent discussed a mandatory subject of bargaining directly with unit employees at the November 23 meeting.

Moreover, the Respondent's conduct suggests that it intended to undercut the Union's role as bargaining agent. After a unit employee heard rumors of the upcoming relocation, she confronted her supervisor, who, after confirming the rumor, asked her not to tell the union steward. As our dissenting colleague observes, the Respondent suggested in its letter to the employees that they could ask questions of the Union. But that option was of little practical benefit because, as a result of the Respondent's own actions, the Union had no more information than did the employees themselves.

[T]he Respondent offered employees three options, one of which it had not previously presented to the Union, and received responses to the options from all but two of the employees, and all before informing the Union. It then allowed the employees to choose the option they preferred. The Respondent also requested that its employee not inform the union steward of the decision to relocate. As discussed, that evidence indicates that the Respondent was primarily interested in resolving effects issues with its employees rather than with their Union.

Accordingly, we find that the Respondent dealt directly with union-represented employees in violation of Section 8(a)(5) and (1) of the Act.

MEMBER HAYES dissenting in part:

I dissent from my colleagues' decision to reverse the judge and find that the Respondent violated 8(a)(5) by dealing directly with Hackley unit employees about the option of transferring to nonunit positions at Mercy.

I agree with the [administrative law] judge that the Respondent lawfully offered the Hackley unit employees a predetermined transfer option, in addition to the contractual bumping and layoff options previously negotiated with the Union. The judge correctly relied on precedent holding that the mere presentation of a predetermined employment term does not constitute proscribed dealing with unit employees about the establishment of, or changes in, their terms and conditions of employment. Further, there is negligible support for their claim that the Respondent intended to undermine the Union's representative status, much less that it had this effect. On the contrary, I find it significant that there is no allegation that the Respondent failed to fulfill its statutory obligation to engage in bargaining about the effects of its relocation decision. In fact, the parties did engage in effects bargaining subsequent to the presentation of the transfer option, and the Union did not seek to discuss this option. Particularly in these circumstances, I would find that the judge correctly applied Board law in finding no unlawful direct dealing.

NOTES

1. Note that one of the three Board members who decided this case, Sharon Block, was serving by a recess appointment that the Supreme Court later held was unconstitutional. Chairman Pearce and Member Hayes were properly nominated by the President and confirmed by the Senate.

2. Which of the opinions is more persuasive? How might the employer's interaction with the employees have undermined the union's status as exclusive representative? Why might Member Hayes have characterized this as negligible?

3. What remedy might the Board issue for this violation?

4. The union that represents a company's employees is a loose-knit informal group with no constitution or bylaws, dues or formal officers. The

individual who negotiated the current contract no longer works for the company. Although the contract does not expire for another six months, the company just learned that it must have a new contract in place in three months to meet a demand of its only customer. The company has contact information for the former employee who negotiated the current contract but is not sure how to proceed. What advice do you give the company? *See Alan Ritchey, Inc.*, 346 N.L.R.B. 241 (2006) (company polled employees as to whether they wanted the former employee to continue to represent them; Board majority found no unfair labor practice under the circumstances; dissent maintained that company was obligated to continue to deal with the individual who negotiated the prior contract until informed otherwise).

5.   You represent an employer whose employees are on strike. Your client believes that many of the strikers are dissatisfied with the hard line taken by the union at the bargaining table. Your client has asked the union to transmit its most recent offer to the employees for a vote but the union negotiators have refused to do so. Your client believes the negotiators are holding out on certain issues that are important to them personally but are not of interest to the majority of the bargaining unit. Your client has asked if there is anything it may do to communicate its position to the striking employees. How will you advise your client? Compare *United Techs. Corp.*, 274 N.L.R.B. 609 (1985) (holding it lawful for employer to publicize offer for three year contract while union was willing to negotiate only on two year reopener, and to urge employees to encourage union officials to consider the three year offer) with *Obie Pac., Inc.*, 196 N.L.R.B. 458 (1972) (holding it illegal for employer to poll employees concerning their view of a clause in the contract that employer was trying to change).

6.   One of the most notorious examples of an employer illegally bypassing the union and dealing directly with employees was General Electric's strategy in the late 1950s and early 1960s known as "Boulwarism," after its vice president Lemuel Boulware. The Second Circuit Court of Appeals described the strategy in *NLRB v. Gen. Electric Co.*, 418 F.2d 736, 740–41 (2d Cir. 1969):

> GE began by soliciting comments from its local management personnel on the desires of the work force, and the type and level of benefits that they expected. These were then translated into specific proposals, and their cost and effectiveness researched, in order to formulate a 'product' that would be attractive to the employees, and within the Company's means. The last step was the most important, most innovative, and most often criticized. GE took its 'product'—now a series of fully-formed bargaining proposals—and 'sold' it to its employees and the general public. Through a veritable avalanche of publicity, reaching awesome proportions prior to and during negotiations, GE sought to tell its side of the issues to its employees. It described its proposals as a 'fair, firm offer,' characteristic of its desire to 'do right voluntarily,' without the need for any union pressure or strike. In negotiations, GE announced that it would have

nothing to do with the 'blood-and-threat-and-thunder' approach, in which each side presented patently unreasonable demands, and finally chose a middle ground that both knew would be the probable outcome even before the beginning of the bargaining. The Company believed that such tactics diminished the company's credibility in the eyes of its employees, and at the same time appeared to give the union credit for wringing from the Company what it had been willing to offer all along. Henceforth GE would hold nothing back when it made its offer to the Union; it would take all the facts into consideration, and make that offer it thought right under all the circumstances. Though willing to accept Union suggestions based on facts the Company might have overlooked, once the basic outlines of the proposal had been set, the mere fact that the Union disagreed would be no ground for change. When GE said firm, it meant firm, and it denounced the traditional give and take of the so-called auction bargaining as 'flea bitten eastern type of cunning and dishonest but pointless haggling.'

By a 2–1 vote, the Second Circuit upheld the Board's finding that G.E.'s approach to negotiations violated § 8(a)(5). As explained by concurring Judge Waterman:

> What makes these practices unfair is GE's 'widely publicized stance of unbending firmness,' that is, GE's communications to its employees that firmness was one of the company's independent policies. Two distinct evils derive from such publicity. First, publicity regarding firmness tends to make the company seal itself into its original position in such a way that, even if it wished to change that position at a later date, its pride and reputation for truthfulness are so at stake that it cannot do so. Second, publicity regarding firmness fixes in the minds of employees the idea that the company has set itself up as their representative and therefore that the union is superfluous. Doubtless these evils exist to some extent whenever a company makes, and stands by, a firm fair offer even when there is no company publicity of the kind here involved. However, it seems clear that publicity tends to amplify these undesirable tendencies to the point that, in a case such as this one, the amplification can well be construed to have been activated by a company motive not to bargain in good faith.

E. THE EFFECT OF A STRIKE ON THE DUTY TO BARGAIN

The duty to bargain does not require a party to engage in "fruitless marathon discussions." *NLRB v. Am. Nat'l Ins. Co.*, 343 U.S. 395, 405 (1952). The economic pressure of a strike, however, may motivate parties to reconsider their positions and a strike does not license a party to avoid its obligation to bargain under all circumstances. For example, in *NLRB v.*

U.S. Cold Storage Corp., 203 F.2d 924 (5th Cir. 1953), the union struck, the employer replaced several strikers and advised the union that it should submit further proposals in writing. The union submitted a proposed contract which reduced its wage demands and asked to meet to resume negotiations. The employer rejected the union's proposal and refused to meet on the ground that all areas of substantial disagreement had been discussed thoroughly and that it saw no reason to meet. The employer invited the union to submit a revised proposal in writing. The union asked the employer to meet in person two more times but the employer refused. The court upheld the Board's finding that the employer violated section 8(a)(5). The court stated:

> Enforcement of the obligation to bargain collectively is crucial to the statutory scheme and it will not do for respondent to say that it was relieved of the duty to bargain collectively because prestrike bargaining had resulted in an impasse and future negotiations during the strike would have been futile. The Board recognized that the duty to meet does not mean that parties must engage in futile bargaining in the face of a genuine impasse. Its decision was based on the assumption that the impasse which existed before the strike was broken by the strike and by the change in circumstances that developed subsequent thereto.

Id. at 928.

Should the onset of economic warfare affect the objective rules of conduct developed under the duty to bargain in good faith? Recall note 5, p. 675 above, concerning whether an employer who hires replacements during a strike is required to furnish the union with the replacements' names and addresses. Should the employer be required to bargain with the union about the decision to hire replacements, whether the replacements will be temporary or permanent, or the terms on which replacements will be hired? Should the employer be required to bargain with the striking union over the decision to subcontract struck work? Should it matter whether the subcontracting will be temporary or permanent? *See Land Air Delivery, Inc. v. NLRB*, 862 F.2d 354 (D.C. Cir. 1980) (holding employer obligated to bargain decision to permanently subcontract bargaining unit work, distinguishing the decision to subcontract from the decision to hire permanent replacements).

F. THE DUTY TO BARGAIN DURING THE TERM OF A CONTRACT

UAW v. NLRB

765 F.2d 175 (D.C. Cir. 1985)

EDWARDS, CIRCUIT JUDGE:

I. BACKGROUND

A. *Factual Background*

The basic facts of this case were stipulated by the parties. Illinois Coil Spring Company, a manufacturer of automobile parts, was, at the dates germane to this case, composed of three divisions—Holly Spring, McHenry Spring and Milwaukee Spring. UAW represented the Milwaukee Spring employees at the time of the alleged unfair labor practices. The relevant collective bargaining agreement between Milwaukee Spring and the UAW, effective from April 1, 1980, to March 31, 1983, contained specific wage and benefits provisions, a union recognition clause, a management rights clause, an arbitration clause and an "entire agreement" or "zipper" clause. The contract did not, however, include a work preservation clause—that is, a provision requiring bargaining unit work to remain at the Milwaukee facility for the duration of the agreement. The McHenry Spring employees were not represented by a union.

On January 26, 1982, Milwaukee Spring first approached the Union seeking midterm contract concessions. On that date, the Company asked the UAW to forgo a wage increase scheduled for April 1, and to consent to other modifications. On March 12, Milwaukee Spring informed the Union that the Company's financial position had deteriorated since January, principally due to the loss of a major contract. In order to obtain relief from the comparatively higher labor costs under the union contract at Milwaukee Spring, the Company subsequently proposed relocating its Milwaukee assembly operations to the nonunion McHenry plant. The Company characterized this relocation decision as tentative, and indicated a willingness to consider any proposals or suggestions offered by the Union.

The parties engaged in substantial bargaining over the proposed relocation, but were unable to agree on the core issue of wages. Essentially, the employees voted to reject the terms under which the Company would agree to retain assembly operations at the Milwaukee facility, which included the cancellation of the scheduled wage increase, a reduction in the base wage rate for all employees, and the elimination of an incentive program for assembly operators. The employees also rejected any further consideration of contract concessions. The Company then announced its decision to transfer the assembly operations to the McHenry facility.

B. *Procedural History*

On April 8, the UAW filed an unfair labor practice charge with the NLRB. The parties stipulated that the "relocation decision is economically motivated and is not the result of union animus" and that the "failure to provide an adequate return on investment prompted the decision to relocate . . ., not an inability to pay the contractual wage rates." They also stipulated that Milwaukee Spring had bargained to impasse with the UAW over the move.

In its initial Decision and Order in *Milwaukee Spring I,* the Board held that the Company's unilateral decision to transfer its assembly operations and the layoff of unit employees during the term of the collective bargaining agreement constituted a midterm contract modification within the meaning of section 8(d) and, thus, violated sections 8(a)(1), (3), and (5) of the Act. As relief, the Board ordered the Company to cease the transfer and attendant layoffs, restore any work that had been moved, reinstate any employees who had been laid off due to the relocation, and compensate any such employees for losses suffered as a consequence. The Company sought review of the Board's decision in the United States Court of Appeals for the Seventh Circuit. While the case was pending in the Seventh Circuit, the NLRB filed a motion to remand the case to the Board for further consideration, which the court granted.

On remand, in *Milwaukee Spring II,* the Board reversed its earlier decision and dismissed the complaint. The Board first noted that section 8(d) requires an employer to obtain the consent of a union bargaining agent before implementing changes that will modify the terms and conditions contained in an existing collective bargaining agreement. Consequently, the Board reasoned, before it could find a violation of section 8(d) in this case, it must identify a specific term "contained in" the contract that was modified by the Company's decision to relocate. It found no explicit work preservation clause and held that neither the wage and benefit provisions nor the union recognition clause gave rise to an implied agreement to preserve bargaining unit work at the Milwaukee plant for the duration of the contract. The Board expressly found that no other term in the contract restricted the Company's decision-making regarding relocation. Therefore, the NLRB concluded that Milwaukee Spring's decision to relocate did not modify the contract in contravention of sections 8(d) and 8(a)(5). The Board also held that, because the parties stipulated that the Company had bargained to impasse over the relocation, the Company had not violated section 8(a)(5) of the Act.

II. DISCUSSION

A. General Principles Regarding the Duty to Bargain During the Term of an Agreement

The duty of management and labor to negotiate in good faith over mandatory subjects of bargaining, imposed by section 8(a)(5) and defined in section 8(d) of the Act, persists even after a collective bargaining agreement is reached. During the term of a contract, however, the scope of the duty to bargain over a particular mandatory subject depends upon whether that subject is "contained in" the contract.

Where a mandatory subject is not contained in the contract, an employer must bargain in good faith to impasse with union representatives; if no agreement is reached, the employer may unilaterally implement its bargaining proposal with respect to the matter not contained in the agreement. Where a mandatory subject is contained in the contract, however, section 8(d) further limits an employer's actions. That section provides that "no party to [the] contract shall terminate or modify [it], unless the party desiring [the] termination or modification . . . (4) continues in full force and effect, without resorting to strike or lock-out, all the terms and conditions of the existing contract . . . until its expiration date." The statute also states that neither party shall be "requir[ed] . . . to discuss or agree to any modification of the terms and conditions contained in a contract for a fixed period, if such modification is to become effective under the provisions of the contract." Thus, it is well understood that section 8(d) prohibits an employer from altering contractual terms concerning mandatory subjects of bargaining during the life of a collective bargaining agreement without the consent of the union.

A mandatory subject of bargaining may be brought into the "contained in" category, and therefore within the provisions of section 8(d), either through explicit reference, such as a wage provision, or through a general waiver of the duty to bargain, such as a zipper clause. Generally speaking, a zipper clause has the effect of incorporating all possible topics of bargaining—both those actually discussed and those neither discussed nor contemplated during bargaining—into the contract. As a result, with the inclusion of a zipper clause, section 8(d)'s "contained in" requirements are brought into play with regard to all mandatory subjects of bargaining; neither party may require the other to bargain over any mandatory subject, nor unilaterally implement a change in the status quo concerning a mandatory subject, even after bargaining to impasse.

B. Application of the "Contained In" Requirements of Section 8(d)

The wage concession issue is straightforward and simple. Wages are indisputably a mandatory subject of bargaining and, as it was explicitly addressed by the collective bargaining agreement between Milwaukee

Spring and the UAW, section 8(d) limitations on midterm modifications apply. The record offers no evidence that the UAW was in any way "required" to bargain over the proposed wage concessions. Instead, there is every indication that the Union participated in the negotiations voluntarily, and chose, as was its right under section 8(d), to reject the Company's proposal. Furthermore, as the Board found, the Company implemented no change in the wage structure. Thus, section 8(d) was not violated by Milwaukee Spring's actions concerning the requested modification of wages.

The Board's and the parties' treatment of the relocation decision obscures somewhat the threshold issue whether it was "contained in" the contract. Nevertheless, we think it is clear from the Company's assertions, the Union's concessions, and the Board's treatment of the relocation decision, that the Board proceeded on the theory that the subject of relocation was "contained in" the collective bargaining agreement. Specifically, the Board seems to have determined that the Company's right to make relocation decisions stemmed either from the management rights clause or from implied management reserved rights. In either case, it is undisputed that the Company acted consistently with the contract in deciding to relocate, and thus did not modify the agreement in violation of section 8(d).

First, the Company insists that it "bargained for and secured a management rights clause[24] that permit[ted it] to determine what work would be conducted at its Milwaukee Spring plant" and that this clause "constituted unequivocal waiver by the Union of any bargaining right it otherwise might have had regarding the relocation decision." On appeal, the Union does not challenge this interpretation of the agreement.

Second, the Union does not contest the Company's right to make the relocation decision under the contract. Nor does it argue here that Milwaukee Spring in any way modified or violated the contract. In effect, the UAW concedes the Company's contractual right to make that decision. This tacit concession is not surprising in light of the breadth of the management rights clause. If the UAW had believed that the management rights clause did not grant Milwaukee Spring the right to make relocation decisions, the Union would have argued to the Board that the zipper

---

[24] The management rights clause reads as follows:

Except as expressly limited by the other Articles of this Agreement, the Company shall have the exclusive right to manage the plant and business and direct the working forces.

These rights include, but are not limited to, the right to plan, direct and control operations, to determine the operations or services to be performed in or at the plant or by the employees of the Company, to establish and maintain production and quality standards, to schedule the working hours, to hire, promote, demote, and transfer, to suspend, discipline or discharge for just cause or to relieve employees because of lack of work or for other legitimate reasons, to introduce new and improved methods, materials or facilities, or to change existing methods, materials or facilities.

clause[27] prohibited the Company from unilaterally implementing the relocation decision, even after bargaining to impasse.

Finally, the Board expressly found that "no . . . term in the contract restrict[ed Milwaukee Spring's] decision-making regarding relocation." This means that, given the presence of the zipper clause in the parties' contract, the Board implicitly decided either that the management rights clause gave the Company the right to make relocation decisions or that, based on a reserved management rights theory, such a right is inferable from the contract. Essentially, then, the Board determined that, in deciding to relocate, Milwaukee Spring acted consistently with the contract, and thus did not violate section 8(d).

It could be argued that the Board treated the relocation decision as a subject that was not "contained in" the contract, and thus decided that, since the parties stipulated that they bargained in good faith to impasse, the Company did not violate section 8(d) by then deciding to relocate. Given the zipper clause, we do not believe this characterization of the Board's analysis to be viable. If relocation is a mandatory subject and it was found either *not* to be contained in the management rights clause or *not* to be an implied management reserved right, the zipper clause would have prevented the Company from unilaterally deciding to relocate the assembly operation during the term of the contract, even after bargaining to impasse. Although a zipper clause may waive the obligation to bargain over all mandatory subjects during the term of an agreement, it surely does not waive the union's right to object to an employer's taking unilateral action with respect to such subjects. Thus, if an employer is not acting on a claim of right under the contract, or pursuant to a reserved management right inferable from the contract, it may not institute changes with respect to mandatory subjects without the consent of the union. Since the Union did not pursue this line of analysis, and did not rely on the zipper clause to oppose the relocation decision, it is clear that the UAW assumed that the Company acted pursuant to a right under the agreement.

C. *The Union Claims Regarding "Economic Pressure"*

The Union urges upon this court the theory that, while neither the Company's request for midterm contract concessions nor its decision to relocate may offend section 8(d) when taken in isolation, the combination of the two somehow violates that section of the Act. According to the UAW, section 8(d)'s provisions that neither party to a collective bargaining agreement is "requir[ed] . . . to discuss or agree to any modification of the terms and conditions contained in a contract for a fixed period, if such

---

[27] The zipper clause contained in the contract was a typical one, in which each party waives the right, and each agrees that the other shall not be obligated, to bargain collectively with respect to any subject or matter referred to or covered in this Agreement, or with respect to any subject or matter not specifically referred to or covered in this Agreement, even though such subject or matter may not have been within the knowledge or contemplation of either or both of the parties at the time they negotiated or signed this Agreement.

modification is to become effective before such terms and conditions can be reopened under the provisions of the contract," and that an employer may not force its employees to accede to midterm modifications by locking them out, should be construed together to proscribe the use of *any* economic pressure to obtain contract concessions during the life of an agreement. Specifically, the Union argues here that section 8(d) prohibits an employer from coupling a request for midterm contract concessions with a statement of intention to exercise a right under the contract—in this instance, a right to relocate for economic reasons—if the Union does not find the proposed modification acceptable.

The Union's theory is untenable. First, we cannot see how two rights can make a wrong. Second, we can find no support for the UAW's proposition that section 8(d) condemns any midterm behavior by one party to a contract that results in the other party feeling "economic pressure" to bargain over modifications. The plain language of the statute proscribes only lockouts and strikes. Nothing in the rest of section 8(d), nor the Act's legislative history, persuades us that the Union's expansive reading of section 8(d)(4) is correct. Furthermore, the Union has been unable to cite any precedents to support its thesis that "an employer or a union that uses economic pressure in the mid-term of a contract to force bargaining over or agreement on such a modification commits an unfair labor practice."

In the absence of antiunion animus, it is lawful—and indeed common in this era of concession bargaining—for one party to a collective bargaining agreement to propose, midterm, the trade of a right it has under the contract for a modification of the agreement. The Union was under no compulsion to discuss wage concessions; it did so because it made sense in the context of the parties' bargaining relationship. This sort of ongoing flexibility in labor-management relations is crucial. The freedom to suggest exchanges of rights permits parties to adapt their relationship to unanticipated events or changed circumstances during the lifetime of a contract, thus keeping the collective bargaining process vital and responsive to both sides' needs.

III. CONCLUSION

Given that Milwaukee Spring acted without antiunion animus for purely economic reasons and fulfilled any statutory obligation to bargain that it might have had, we hold that the Company did not violate section 8(d) of the Act, either by offering to exchange its right to relocate for a midterm modification of the contract or by deciding to relocate when the Union rejected its modification proposals. The decision of the NLRB is *Affirmed.*

NOTES

1.   How does the duty to bargain during the term of a contract differ from the duty to bargain for an initial or successor contract?

2. If the contract had not had the zipper clause, would the case have been decided differently? Could the Board or court have found a waiver based on the management rights clause alone?

3. When the Board first decided the case, it held that the company had violated section 8(a)(5). While the company's appeal was pending, a change in Board personnel prompted the Board to have the case remanded and it then reversed itself. If the original Board decision had proceeded through appellate review, would it likely have been enforced?

4. What if instead of relocating the work to its nonunion plant, the company had unilaterally required employees to undergo unannounced drug testing? Would its failure to bargain that decision with the union have violated section 8(a)(5)? Would it matter whether the contract contained the zipper clause? *See Johnson Bateman Co.*, 295 N.L.R.B. 180 (1989) (holding general management rights clause not a clear and unmistakable waiver of right to bargain drug testing); *but see Chi. Tribune Co. v. NLRB*, 974 F.2d 933 (7th Cir. 1991) (holding no violation in unilaterally imposing drug and alcohol testing standards where management rights clause gave employer right to issue reasonable rules related to employee conduct).

5. Assume that prior to the union's certification, the employer had provided group medical insurance with employees paying one-half of the premiums. The employer had no pension or retirement savings plan. During negotiations, the parties discussed health insurance and a union demand that the employer pay the full premium costs. The employer rejected the proposal but the parties agreed to changes in plan benefits and costs, although no changes were incorporated into the written contract. The parties never discussed pension or retirement savings plans. The parties agreed on a three-year contract with a wage reopener after 18 months. The union demanded negotiations pursuant to the wage reopener. It also demanded negotiations over a pension plan and over changes in allocation of premiums for health insurance. May the employer restrict mid-term negotiations to wages? *See Jacobs Mfg. Co.*, 94 N.L.R.B. 1214 (1951), *enf'd*, 196 F.2d 680 (2d Cir. 1952).

6. *Duty to Bargain Mid-term in Other Models.* Contracts under the Railway Labor Act never expire. Rather, they define the status quo which both parties are obligated to maintain until the statute's provisions for resolving major disputes, including mediation by the NMB, are exhausted. A party seeking to modify all or part of a contract begins the process by serving notice to that effect on the other party. Thus, a party could serve notice of intent to modify a contract shortly after agreement on the contract was reached. A practice has developed, however, whereby the parties agree to moratoria on such notices for specified periods of time. For example, as discussed at the beginning of this chapter, the contract between United Airlines and the IAMAW did not become "amendable" until July 12, 2000.

Midterm bargaining in the public sector is governed by state law or, in the case of federal government employees, by the Federal Service Labor Management Relations Statute. Are there any special considerations where a unit of government is the employer that argue against requiring midterm bargaining? *See Nat'l Fed'n of Fed. Employees v. Dep't of Interior*, 526 U.S. 86 (1999) (rejecting government's arguments that a duty to bargain mid-term would give unions an incentive to hold back certain issues in end-term bargaining so that they could take those issues to a separate interest arbitration proceeding).

G. SUBJECTS OF BARGAINING

1. THE NLRA

Section 8(d) defines the duty to bargain in good faith as applicable to "wages, hours and other terms and conditions of employment." The statute contains no further express definition concerning what the parties are required to bargain about. In *NLRB v. Wooster Div., Borg-Warner Corp.*, 356 U.S. 342 (1958), the Supreme Court divided subjects of bargaining into two categories: mandatory and permissive. The NLRB, in that case, had certified the international union as the exclusive bargaining representative. The employer demanded to substitute the local union as exclusive bargaining representative. The employer also demanded that the union agree not to strike without first submitting the employer's last offer for a vote of all employees and affording the employer 72 hours to provide a new proposal in the event of employee rejection. The Court held that although it was permissible for the parties to bargain about the employer's demands, the demands fell outside the boundaries of wages, hours and other terms and conditions of employment, the subjects it characterized as mandatory subjects of bargaining. The Court ruled that insistence to impasse on permissive subjects violated section 8(a)(5).

Although insistence to impasse on a permissive subject of bargaining violates the duty to bargain in good faith, absent a contractual restriction, a party is free to make unilateral changes in permissive subjects and has no duty to furnish information with respect to permissive subjects. An employer may bypass the union and deal directly with employees with respect to permissive subjects. The consequences of labeling a subject as mandatory or permissive sometimes drive the decision as to which label to apply.

The Board and courts have recognized a third category: prohibited subjects of bargaining. Prohibited subjects are any proposals for provisions that are illegal. These include proposals to discriminate on the basis of race, gender or other protected status and proposals that violate the NLRA, such as proposals for closed shops and for hot cargo agreements. Insisting on such proposals in negotiations, even prior to impasse, is prohibited and if such proposals are included in a contract they are unenforceable.

The line between mandatory and permissive subjects can be particularly difficult to draw with respect to decisions about business structure that directly and substantially affect the employees. There is agreement that employers have a duty to bargain about the impact of those decisions on the employees but there is considerable dispute over whether they are obligated to bargain about the decisions themselves.

For example, consider an employer that operates a customer service call center whose employees are represented by a union. Several of the employer's competitors have moved their call centers to low wage countries. This employer has decided not to do that because of reports that competitors' customers have been complaining about inability to understand the accented speech of foreign call center employees. Instead, the employer has decided to dismantle its physical call center and sell the building. It will require its employees to work from their homes after it installs special phone lines and computers that will route service calls to employees as they become available. Must the employer bargain about this decision with the union?

In the following two cases, the Supreme Court addressed these types of decisions. The cases should be read together.

FIBREBOARD PAPER PRODUCTS CORP. V. NLRB
379 U.S. 203 (1964)

CHIEF JUSTICE WARREN delivered the opinion of the Court:

Petitioner, Fibreboard Paper Products Corporation (the Company), has a manufacturing plant in Emeryville, California. Since 1937 the East Bay Union Machinists, Local 1304, United Steelworkers of America, AFL-CIO (the Union) has been the exclusive bargaining representative for a unit of the Company's maintenance employees.

The Company, concerned with the high cost of its maintenance operation, had undertaken a study of the possibility of effecting cost savings by engaging an independent contractor to do the maintenance work. At the July 27, [1959] meeting, the Company informed the Union that it had determined that substantial savings could be effected by contracting out the work upon expiration of its collective bargaining agreements with the various labor organizations representing its maintenance employees. The Company delivered to the Union representatives a letter which stated in pertinent part:

> For some time we have been seriously considering the question of letting out our Emeryville maintenance work to an independent contractor, and have now reached a definite decision to do so effective August 1, 1959.

> In these circumstances, we are sure you will realize that negotiation of a new contract would be pointless. However, if you have any questions, we will be glad to discuss them with you.

After some discussion of the Company's right to enter a contract with a third party to do the work then being performed by employees in the bargaining unit, the meeting concluded with the understanding that the parties would meet again on July 30.

By July 30, the Company had selected Fluor Maintenance, Inc., to do the maintenance work. Fluor had assured the Company that maintenance costs could be curtailed by reducing the work force, decreasing fringe benefits and overtime payments, and by preplanning and scheduling the services to be performed. The contract provided that the Company would pay Fluor the costs of the operation plus a fixed fee of $2,250 per month.

At the July 30 meeting, the Company's representative, in explaining the decision to contract out the maintenance work, remarked that during bargaining negotiations in previous years the Company had endeavored to point out through the use of charts and statistical information "just how expensive and costly our maintenance work was and how it was creating quite a terrific burden upon the Emeryville plant." He further stated that unions representing other Company employees "had joined hands with management in an effort to bring about an economical and efficient operation," but "we had not been able to attain that in our discussions with this particular Local."

The Union filed unfair labor practice charges against the Company, alleging violations of §§ 8(a)(1), 8(a)(3) and 8(a)(5). The Board ordered the Company to reinstitute the maintenance operation previously performed by the employees represented by the Union, to reinstate the employees to their former or substantially equivalent positions with back pay computed from the date of the Board's supplemental decision, and to fulfill its statutory obligation to bargain.

[W]e are concerned here only with whether the subject upon which the employer allegedly refused to bargain—contracting out of plant maintenance work previously performed by employees in the bargaining unit, which the employees were capable of continuing to perform—is covered by the phrase "terms and conditions of employment" within the meaning of § 8(d).

The subject matter of the present dispute is well within the literal meaning of the phrase "terms and conditions of employment." A stipulation with respect to the contracting out of work performed by members of the bargaining unit might appropriately be called a "condition of employment." The words even more plainly cover termination of employment which, as the facts of this case indicate, necessarily results from the contracting out of work performed by members of the established bargaining unit.

The inclusion of "contracting out" within the statutory scope of collective bargaining also seems well designed to effectuate the purposes of the National Labor Relations Act. One of the primary purposes of the Act is to promote the peaceful settlement of industrial disputes by subjecting labor-management controversies to the mediatory influence of negotiation. The Act was framed with an awareness that refusals to confer and negotiate had been one of the most prolific causes of industrial strife. To hold, as the Board has done, that contracting out is a mandatory subject of collective bargaining would promote the fundamental purpose of the Act by bringing a problem of vital concern to labor and management within the framework established by Congress as most conducive to industrial peace.

The conclusion that "contracting out" is a statutory subject of collective bargaining is further reinforced by industrial practices in this country. While not determinative, it is appropriate to look to industrial bargaining practices in appraising the propriety of including a particular subject within the scope of mandatory bargaining. Industrial experience is not only reflective of the interests of labor and management in the subject matter but is also indicative of the amenability of such subjects to the collective bargaining process. Experience illustrates that contracting out in one form or another has been brought, widely and successfully, within the collective bargaining framework. Provisions relating to contracting out exist in numerous collective bargaining agreements, and "(c)ontracting out work is the basis of many grievances; and that type of claim is grist in the mills of the arbitrators."

The facts of the present case illustrate the propriety of submitting the dispute to collective negotiation. The Company's decision to contract out the maintenance work did not alter the Company's basic operation. The maintenance work still had to be performed in the plant. No capital investment was contemplated; the Company merely replaced existing employees with those of an independent contractor to do the same work under similar conditions of employment. Therefore, to require the employer to bargain about the matter would not significantly abridge his freedom to manage the business.

The Company was concerned with the high cost of its maintenance operation. It was induced to contract out the work by assurances from independent contractors that economies could be derived by reducing the work force, decreasing fringe benefits, and eliminating overtime payments. These have long been regarded as matters peculiarly suitable for resolution within the collective bargaining framework, and industrial experience demonstrates that collective negotiation has been highly successful in achieving peaceful accommodation of the conflicting interests. Yet, it is contended that when an employer can effect cost savings in these respects by contracting the work out, there is no need to attempt to achieve similar economies through negotiation with existing employees or to provide them with an opportunity to negotiate a mutually acceptable alternative. The short answer is that, although it is not possible to say whether a satisfactory solution could be reached, national labor policy is founded upon the congressional determination that the chances are good enough to warrant subjecting such issues to the process of collective negotiation.

While "the Act does not encourage a party to engage in fruitless marathon discussions at the expense of frank statement and support of his position," *NLRB v. Am. Nat'l Ins. Co.*, 343 U.S. 395, it at least demands that the issue be submitted to the mediatory influence of collective negotiations. As the Court of Appeals pointed out, "(i)t is not necessary that it be likely or probable that the union will yield or supply a feasible solution but rather that the union be afforded an opportunity to meet management's legitimate complaints that its maintenance was unduly costly."

We are thus not expanding the scope of mandatory bargaining to hold, as we do now, that the type of "contracting out" involved in this case—the replacement of employees in the existing bargaining unit with those of an independent contractor to do the same work under similar conditions of employment—is a statutory subject of collective bargaining under § 8(d). Our decision need not and does not encompass other forms of "contracting out" or "subcontracting" which arise daily in our complex economy.

JUSTICE STEWART, with whom JUSTICE DOUGLAS and JUSTICE HARLAN join, concurring:

The question posed is whether the particular decision sought to be made unilaterally by the employer in this case is a subject of mandatory collective bargaining within the statutory phrase "terms and conditions of employment." That is all the Court decides.

It is important to note that the words of the statute are words of limitation. The National Labor Relations Act does not say that the employer and employees are bound to confer upon any subject which interests either of them; the specification of wages, hours, and other terms and conditions of employment defines a limited category of issues subject to compulsory bargaining.

The phrase "conditions of employment" is no doubt susceptible of diverse interpretations. At the extreme, the phrase could be construed to apply to any subject which is insisted upon as a prerequisite for continued employment. Such an interpretation, which would in effect place the compulsion of the Board behind any and all bargaining demands, would be contrary to the intent of Congress, as reflected in this legislative history. Yet there are passages in the Court's opinion today which suggest just such an expansive interpretation, for the Court's opinion seems to imply that any issue which may reasonably divide an employer and his employees must be the subject of compulsory collective bargaining.

While employment security has thus properly been recognized in various circumstances as a condition of employment, it surely does not follow that every decision which may affect job security is a subject of compulsory collective bargaining. Many decisions made by management affect the job security of employees. Decisions concerning the volume and kind of advertising expenditures, product design, the manner of financing, and sales, all may bear upon the security of the workers' jobs. Yet it is hardly conceivable that such decisions so involve "conditions of employment" that they must be negotiated with the employees' bargaining representative.

In many of these areas the impact of a particular management decision upon job security may be extremely indirect and uncertain, and this alone may be sufficient reason to conclude that such decisions are not "with respect to . . . conditions of employment." Yet there are other areas where decisions by management may quite clearly imperil job security, or indeed terminate employment entirely. An enterprise may decide to invest in labor-saving machinery. Another may resolve to liquidate its assets and go out of business. Nothing the Court holds today should be understood as imposing a duty to bargain collectively regarding such managerial decisions, which lie at the core of entrepreneurial control. Decisions concerning the commitment of investment capital and the basic scope of the enterprise are not in themselves primarily about conditions of employment, though the effect of the decision may be necessarily to terminate employment. If, as I think clear, the purpose of § 8(d) is to describe a limited area subject to the duty of collective bargaining, those management decisions which are fundamental to the basic direction of a corporate enterprise or which impinge only indirectly upon employment security should be excluded from that area.

Applying these concepts to the case at hand, I do not believe that an employer's subcontracting practices are, as a general matter, in themselves conditions of employment. Upon any definition of the statutory terms short of the most expansive, such practices are not conditions—tangible or intangible—of any person's employment. The question remains whether this particular kind of subcontracting decision comes within the employer's duty to bargain. On the facts of this case, I join the Court's judgment, because all that is involved is the substitution of one group of workers for another to perform the same task in the same plant under the ultimate control of the same employer. The question whether the employer may discharge one group of workers and substitute another for them is closely analogous to many other situations within the traditional framework of collective bargaining. Compulsory retirement, layoffs according to seniority, assignment of work among potentially eligible groups within the plant—all involve similar questions of discharge and work assignment, and all have been recognized as subjects of compulsory collective bargaining.

Analytically, this case is not far from that which would be presented if the employer had merely discharged all its employees and replaced them with other workers willing to work on the same job in the same plant without the various fringe benefits so costly to the company. While such a situation might well be considered a § 8(a)(3) violation upon a finding that the employer discriminated against the discharged employees because of their union affiliation, it would be equally possible to regard the employer's action as a unilateral act frustrating negotiation on the underlying questions of work scheduling and remuneration, and so an evasion of its duty to bargain on these questions, which are concededly subject to compulsory collective bargaining. Similarly, had the employer in this case chosen to bargain with the union about the proposed subcontract, negotiations would have inevitably turned to the underlying questions of cost, which prompted the subcontracting. Insofar as the employer frustrated collective bargaining with respect to these concededly bargaining issues by its unilateral act of subcontracting this work, it can properly be found to have violated its statutory duty under § 8(a)(5).

This kind of subcontracting falls short of such larger entrepreneurial questions as what shall be produced, how capital shall be invested in fixed assets, or what the basic scope of the enterprise shall be. In my view, the Court's decision in this case has nothing to do with whether any aspects of those larger issues could under any circumstances be considered subjects of compulsory collective bargaining under the present law.

FIRST NATIONAL MAINTENANCE CORP. V. NLRB
452 U.S. 666 (1981)

JUSTICE BLACKMUN delivered the opinion of the Court:

Must an employer, under its duty to bargain in good faith "with respect to wages, hours, and other terms and conditions of employment," negotiate with the certified representative of its employees over its decision to close a part of its business? In this case, the National Labor Relations Board (Board) imposed such a duty on petitioner with respect to its decision to terminate a contract with a customer, and the United States Court of Appeals, although differing over the appropriate rationale, enforced its order.

Petitioner, First National Maintenance Corporation (FNM), is a New York corporation engaged in the business of providing housekeeping, cleaning, maintenance, and related services for commercial customers in the New York City area. It supplies each of its customers, at the customer's premises, contracted-for labor force and supervision in return for reimbursement of its labor costs (gross salaries, FICA and FUTA taxes, and insurance) and payment of a set fee. It contracts for and hires personnel separately for each customer, and it does not transfer employees between locations.

During the spring of 1977, petitioner was performing maintenance work for the Greenpark Care Center, a nursing home in Brooklyn. Its written agreement dated April 28, 1976, with Greenpark specified that

Greenpark would pay petitioner weekly "the sum of five hundred dollars plus the gross weekly payroll and fringe benefits." Its weekly fee, however, had been reduced to $250 effective November 1, 1976. On June 30, by telephone, it asked that its weekly fee be restored at the $500 figure and, on July 6, it informed Greenpark in writing that it would discontinue its operations there on August 1 unless the increase were granted. By telegram on July 25, petitioner gave final notice of termination.

While FNM was experiencing these difficulties, District 1199, National Union of Hospital and Health Care Employees, Retail, Wholesale and Department Store Union, AFL-CIO (union), was conducting an organization campaign among petitioner's Greenpark employees. On March 31, 1977, at a Board-conducted election, a majority of the employees selected the union as their bargaining agent. On July 12, the union's vice president, Edward Wecker, wrote petitioner, notifying it of the certification and of the union's right to bargain, and stating: "We look forward to meeting with you or your representative for that purpose. Please advise when it will be convenient." Petitioner neither responded nor sought to consult with the union.

On July 28, petitioner notified its Greenpark employees that they would be discharged three days later. Wecker immediately telephoned petitioner's secretary-treasurer, Leonard Marsh, to request a delay for the purpose of bargaining. Marsh refused the offer to bargain and told Wecker that the termination of the Greenpark operation was purely a matter of money, and final, and that the 30 days' notice provision of the Greenpark contract made staying on beyond August 1 prohibitively expensive. With nothing but perfunctory further discussion, petitioner on July 31 discontinued its Greenpark operation and discharged the employees.

II

Although parties are free to bargain about any legal subject, Congress has limited the mandate or duty to bargain to matters of "wages, hours, and other terms and conditions of employment." Congress deliberately left the words "wages, hours, and other terms and conditions of employment" without further definition, for it did not intend to deprive the Board of the power further to define those terms in light of specific industrial practices.

Nonetheless, in establishing what issues must be submitted to the process of bargaining, Congress had no expectation that the elected union representative would become an equal partner in the running of the business enterprise in which the union's members are employed. Despite the deliberate open-endedness of the statutory language, there is an undeniable limit to the subjects about which bargaining must take place.

Some management decisions, such as choice of advertising and promotion, product type and design, and financing arrangements, have only an indirect and attenuated impact on the employment relationship.

See Fibreboard, 379 U.S., at 223 (Stewart, J., concurring). Other management decisions, such as the order of succession of layoffs and recalls, production quotas, and work rules, are almost exclusively "an aspect of the relationship" between employer and employee. The present case concerns a third type of management decision, one that had a direct impact on employment, since jobs were inexorably eliminated by the termination, but had as its focus only the economic profitability of the contract with Greenpark, a concern under these facts wholly apart from the employment relationship. This decision, involving a change in the scope and direction of the enterprise, is akin to the decision whether to be in business at all, "not in [itself] primarily about conditions of employment, though the effect of the decision may be necessarily to terminate employment." *Fibreboard*, 379 U.S., at 223 (Stewart, J., concurring). *Cf. Textile Workers v. Darlington Co.*, 380 U.S. 263, 268 (1965) ("an employer has the absolute right to terminate his entire business for any reason he pleases"). At the same time, this decision touches on a matter of central and pressing concern to the union and its member employees: the possibility of continued employment and the retention of the employees' very jobs.

The concept of mandatory bargaining is premised on the belief that collective discussions backed by the parties' economic weapons will result in decisions that are better for both management and labor and for society as a whole. This will be true, however, only if the subject proposed for discussion is amenable to resolution through the bargaining process. Management must be free from the constraints of the bargaining process to the extent essential for the running of a profitable business. It also must have some degree of certainty beforehand as to when it may proceed to reach decisions without fear of later evaluations labeling its conduct an unfair labor practice. Congress did not explicitly state what issues of mutual concern to union and management it intended to exclude from mandatory bargaining. Nonetheless, in view of an employer's need for unencumbered decision-making, bargaining over management decisions that have a substantial impact on the continued availability of employment should be required only if the benefit, for labor-management relations and the collective-bargaining process, outweighs the burden placed on the conduct of the business.

The Court in *Fibreboard* implicitly engaged in this analysis with regard to a decision to subcontract for maintenance work previously done by unit employees. Holding the employer's decision a subject of mandatory bargaining, the Court relied not only on the "literal meaning" of the statutory words, but also reasoned:

> The Company's decision to contract out the maintenance work did not alter the Company's basic operation. The maintenance work still had to be performed in the plant. No capital investment was

contemplated; the Company merely replaced existing employees with those of an independent contractor to do the same work under similar conditions of employment. Therefore, to require the employer to bargain about the matter would not significantly abridge his freedom to manage the business. 379 U.S. at 213.

The Court also emphasized that a desire to reduce labor costs, which it considered a matter "peculiarly suitable for resolution within the collective bargaining framework," *id.* at 214, was at the base of the employer's decision to subcontract.

The prevalence of bargaining over "contracting out" as a matter of industrial practice generally was taken as further proof of the "amenability of such subjects to the collective bargaining process." *Id.* at 211.

With this approach in mind, we turn to the specific issue at hand: an economically motivated decision to shut down part of a business.

III

A

A union's interest in participating in the decision to close a particular facility or part of an employer's operations springs from its legitimate concern over job security. The Court has observed: "The words of [§ 8(d)] . . . plainly cover termination of employment which . . . necessarily results" from closing an operation. *Fibreboard*, 379 U.S. at 210. The union's practical purpose in participating, however, will be largely uniform: it will seek to delay or halt the closing. No doubt it will be impelled, in seeking these ends, to offer concessions, information, and alternatives that might be helpful to management or forestall or prevent the termination of jobs.[19] It is unlikely, however, that requiring bargaining over the decision itself, as well as its effects, will augment this flow of information and suggestions. There is no dispute that the union must be given a significant opportunity to bargain about these matters of job security as part of the "effects" bargaining mandated by § 8 (a)(5). And, under § 8(a)(5), bargaining over the effects of a decision must be conducted in a meaningful manner and at a meaningful time, and the Board may impose sanctions to insure its adequacy. A union, by pursuing such bargaining rights, may achieve valuable concessions from an employer engaged in a partial closing. It also may secure in contract negotiations provisions implementing rights to notice, information, and fair bargaining.

Moreover, the union's legitimate interest in fair dealing is protected by § 8(a)(3), which prohibits partial closings motivated by antiunion animus, when done to gain an unfair advantage. Under § 8(a)(3) the Board may inquire into the motivations behind a partial closing. An employer

---

[19] We are aware of past instances where unions have aided employers in saving failing businesses by lending technical assistance, reducing wages and benefits or increasing production, and even loaning part of earned wages to forestall closures.

may not simply shut down part of its business and mask its desire to weaken and circumvent the union by labeling its decision "purely economic."

Thus, although the union has a natural concern that a partial closing decision not be hastily or unnecessarily entered into, it has some control over the effects of the decision and indirectly may ensure that the decision itself is deliberately considered. It also has direct protection against a partial closing decision that is motivated by an intent to harm a union.

Management's interest in whether it should discuss a decision of this kind is much more complex and varies with the particular circumstances. If labor costs are an important factor in a failing operation and the decision to close, management will have an incentive to confer voluntarily with the union to seek concessions that may make continuing the business profitable. At other times, management may have great need for speed, flexibility, and secrecy in meeting business opportunities and exigencies. It may face significant tax or securities consequences that hinge on confidentiality, the timing of a plant closing, or a reorganization of the corporate structure. The publicity incident to the normal process of bargaining may injure the possibility of a successful transition or increase the economic damage to the business. The employer also may have no feasible alternative to the closing, and even good-faith bargaining over it may both be futile and cause the employer additional loss.

There is an important difference, also, between permitted bargaining and mandated bargaining. Labeling this type of decision mandatory could afford a union a powerful tool for achieving delay, a power that might be used to thwart management's intentions in a manner unrelated to any feasible solution the union might propose. In addition, many of the cases before the Board have involved, as this one did, not simply a refusal to bargain over the decision, but a refusal to bargain at all, often coupled with other unfair labor practices. In these cases, the employer's action gave the Board reason to order remedial relief apart from access to the decision-making process. It is not clear that a union would be equally dissatisfied if an employer performed all its bargaining obligations apart from the additional remedy sought here.

While evidence of current labor practice is only an indication of what is feasible through collective bargaining, and not a binding guide, the evidence supports the apparent imbalance weighing against mandatory bargaining. We note that provisions giving unions a right to participate in the decision-making process concerning alteration of the scope of an enterprise appear to be relatively rare. Provisions concerning notice and "effects" bargaining are more prevalent.

An employer would have difficulty determining beforehand whether it was faced with a situation requiring bargaining or one that involved economic necessity sufficiently compelling to obviate the duty to bargain.

If it should decide to risk not bargaining, it might be faced ultimately with harsh remedies forcing it to pay large amounts of backpay to employees who likely would have been discharged regardless of bargaining, or even to consider reopening a failing operation. If the employer intended to try to fulfill a court's direction to bargain, it would have difficulty determining exactly at what stage of its deliberations the duty to bargain would arise and what amount of bargaining would suffice before it could implement its decision. If an employer engaged in some discussion, but did not yield to the union's demands, the Board might conclude that the employer had engaged in "surface bargaining," a violation of its good faith. A union, too, would have difficulty determining the limits of its prerogatives, whether and when it could use its economic powers to try to alter an employer's decision, or whether, in doing so, it would trigger sanctions from the Board.

We conclude that the harm likely to be done to an employer's need to operate freely in deciding whether to shut down part of its business purely for economic reasons outweighs the incremental benefit that might be gained through the union's participation in making the decision,[22] and we hold that the decision itself is *not* part of § 8(d)'s "terms and conditions," over which Congress has mandated bargaining.

B

In order to illustrate the limits of our holding, we turn again to the specific facts of this case. First, we note that when petitioner decided to terminate its Greenpark contract, it had no intention to replace the discharged employees or to move that operation elsewhere. Petitioner's sole purpose was to reduce its economic loss, and the union made no claim of antiunion animus. In addition, petitioner's dispute with Greenpark was solely over the size of the management fee Greenpark was willing to pay. The union had no control or authority over that fee. The most that the union could have offered would have been advice and concessions that Greenpark, the third party upon whom rested the success or failure of the contract, had no duty even to consider. These facts in particular distinguish this case from the subcontracting issue presented in *Fibreboard*. Further, the union was not selected as the bargaining representative or certified until well after petitioner's economic difficulties at Greenpark had begun. We thus are not faced with an employer's abrogation of ongoing negotiations or an existing bargaining agreement. Finally, while petitioner's business enterprise did not involve the investment of large amounts of capital in single locations, we do not believe that the absence of "significant investment or withdrawal of capital," is crucial. The decision to halt work at this specific location represented a significant change in

---

[22]   In this opinion we of course intimate no view as to other types of management decisions, such as plant relocations, sales, other kinds of subcontracting, automation, etc., which are to be considered on their particular facts.

petitioner's operations, a change not unlike opening a new line of business or going out of business entirely.

[The dissenting opinion of JUSTICE BRENNAN, joined by JUSTICE MARSHALL, is omitted.]

NOTES

1.   Consider the facts of *Fibreboard* and *First National Maintenance*. Can the two decisions be reconciled on their facts?

2.   Consider the rationales of the two decisions. Can the rationales be reconciled?

3.   Note that both decisions expressly disclaim deciding whether other types of management decisions are mandatory subjects of bargaining. In light of these decisions, how would you advise the employer seeking to eliminate its physical call center and require call center employees to work from their homes described at the beginning of this section? Is that employer obligated to bargain about the decision?

4.   Even where the decision is a permissive, rather than mandatory, subject of bargaining, the employer is still obligated to bargain about the effects of the decision on the employees' wages, hours and working conditions. To fulfill its duty, the employer must give the union notice and an opportunity to bargain sufficiently in advance of implementation of the decision to allow for effective bargaining. Whether the employer has fulfilled its duty has been the subject of considerable controversy. For example, in *Comau, Inc.*, 364 N.L.R.B. No. 48 (2016), the employer designed assembly line and robotic equipment for the auto industry. It was a wholly-owned subsidiary of Fiat. On November 30, 2011, Fiat notified the employer that it was to close temporarily one of its facilities, represented by the union involved, and move the work to two other facilitates, one of which was represented by another union and one of which was non-union. On December 1, the employer notified the union of the temporary shut down and that the employees would be temporarily transferred to the other two facilities effective December 5. The employer also began moving equipment out of the plant. The union requested a meeting which was held on December 2 or 3 and at which the employer granted a request from two employees present at the meeting who had been assigned to the other two plants to switch their assignments. The Board majority found that the employer breached its duty to engage in effects bargaining because the notice it gave the union was not sufficiently in advance of the decision's implementation and effectively presented the union with a fait accompli. The dissent would have found no breach because the employer notified the union of the decision the day after it found out about it and the parties did meet and agree to change the assignments of two employees and the union raised no other effects issues at the meeting.

* * *

The Court in *Fibreboard* seemed to employ a presumption favoring bargaining, observing that the decision was amenable to resolution at the bargaining table and dismissed concerns about intrusion on employer entrepreneurial rights because the employer continued in the same business and was not required to reach agreement with the union, only to bargain. The Court in *First National Maintenance* began by expressing the need to free the employer up from the burdens and uncertainties of bargaining over business decisions and thereby employed a presumption against bargaining overcome only when the benefits of bargaining outweigh the burdens on employer decision-making. The Court dismissed union and worker concerns finding them sufficiently protected by section 8(a)(3)'s prohibition on partial closings motivated by anti-union animus and on the incentive for the employer to voluntarily discuss the decision with the union if the union has something to offer. In both cases, the Court expressly stated that it was not deciding whether other types of decisions were mandatory subjects.

Even characterizing *Fibreboard* and *First National Maintenance* as holding that decisions to subcontract are mandatory subjects while decisions to go partially out of business are not can be problematic. Consider *Bob's Big Boy Family Restaurants*, 264 N.L.R.B. 1369 (1982). The employer processed a number of food items for distribution to its restaurants, including frozen breaded shrimp. Problems with the escalating price of raw shrimp and inconsistent quality leading to poor portion control led the employer to terminate its shrimp processing employees, sell some of its equipment and return rented equipment to the lessor and purchase frozen breaded shrimp from an outside supplier. The Board divided 3 to 2 over whether the decision was a mandatory subject. The majority characterized it as a decision to subcontract shrimp processing governed by *Fibreboard*, while the dissent characterized it as a decision to go out of the shrimp processing business governed by *First National Maintenance*. The more fundamental dispute between the majority and dissent, however, concerned their views of the union's role at the bargaining table. The majority reasoned that the decision turned on production costs and quality control, two matters it viewed as traditionally and appropriately discussed in bargaining. The dissent urged that the union could not affect the escalating price of raw shrimp or its uneven quality and therefore had no role to play in bargaining.

The narrowest view of the union's rule in bargaining decisions came from a Board plurality in *Otis Elevator Co.*, 269 N.L.R.B. 891 (1984). There, two of the four Board members who decided the case (there was one Board vacancy at the time) opined that a decision need be bargained only where it turned on labor costs. In other words, to the plurality, the only union role to consider was that of offering concessions in wages, benefits and working conditions that could save employee jobs.

DUBUQUE PACKING CO.

303 N.L.R.B. 386 (1991), *enf'd*, 1 F.3d 24 (D.C. Cir. 1993)

CHAIRMAN STEVENS and MEMBERS CRACRAFT, DEVANEY, OVIATT and RAUDABAUGH:

The most difficult issue before us is the general one of what standard to apply in determining whether an employer's decision to relocate bargaining unit work is a mandatory subject of bargaining. The more specific question presented is whether the Respondent violated Sections 8(a)(5) and (1) of the Act by failing to bargain in good faith with the Union over the Respondent's decision to relocate its hog kill and cut operations from its home plant in Dubuque, Iowa, to a new plant in Rochelle, Illinois. For the reasons set forth below, we have decided to adopt a new test for determining whether bargaining is required over a relocation decision, to overrule our original Decision and Order in this case, and to find that the Respondent violated the Act.

The Respondent has been engaged in the business of meat slaughtering, processing, and packing at several facilities nationwide, including a facility in Dubuque, Iowa. Employees at the Dubuque facility were represented by the United Food and Commercial Workers International Union, AFL-CIO, Local No. 150A (the Union) for many years until October 15, 1982, when the plant closed. Prior to the closing approximately 2000 employees worked at the Dubuque plant, 1900 of whom were represented by the Union. The Respondent and the Union were parties to numerous successive collective-bargaining agreements. The parties' last two collective-bargaining agreements, which were in effect during periods material herein, were effective from September 1, 1976, to September 1, 1979, and from September 1, 1979, to September 1, 1982. The latter agreement was extended to September 1, 1983.

Beginning in 1977, the Respondent's Dubuque plant began posting a loss. Losses at the plant became increasingly severe in the late 1970s and early 1980s. As a result of the waning profitability of its operations in Dubuque, the Respondent began encountering financial problems with its lenders and approached the Union about obtaining relief from its collective-bargaining agreements in order to continue operations. The events which gave rise to the instant proceeding occurred in the context of the Respondent's requests for midterm concessions and centered on the Respondent's actions with respect to the hog kill and cut departments.

In 1978, the union membership voted to accept an increase in incentive standards in order to help alleviate the Respondent's financial situation. In 1979 and 1980, the Respondent's financial problems continued to mount. In June 1980, the Respondent notified the Union of its decision to close the beef kill and related departments effective December 12, 1980.

In 1980, the hog kill and cut departments also became the focus of discussions between the parties. The Respondent argued that in order to remain competitive, top productivity per man hour would have to be obtained. In August 1980, the parties agreed to modify the contract to eliminate all incentive pay and require that employees continue to meet the production standards they had been achieving. In return, the Respondent agreed that it would not seek further concessions for the remainder of the contract's term. This agreement saved the Respondent approximately $5 million annually.

In December 1980, the Respondent's request for a $5 million loan for modernization of the Dubuque plant was rejected. In January 1981, the lead bank called the Respondent's $10 million loan and advised of its intention to terminate the Respondent's $45 million line of credit. In response, the Respondent instituted several cost-savings measures and sought alternative sources of credit. In March 1981, the Respondent successfully repaid the $10 million loan.

Also in March 1981, the Respondent pressed the Union for further concessions, specifically an increase in the hog kill "chain speed" (the number of animals slaughtered per hour). When the Union rejected this proposal, the Respondent announced on March 31, 1981, that the hog kill and cut departments would be closed in 6 months. The Union did not request bargaining over the partial closure decision.

In early June 1981, the Respondent proposed that if the employees agreed by July 1 to a wage freeze, the hog kill and cut operations would continue for the balance of the contract term. Later, the Respondent added that the employees could also participate in a profit-sharing plan if they would agree to a wage freeze. These proposals were rejected by the union membership on June 9, 1981.

On June 10, 1981, after learning of the union membership's rejection of the wage freeze/profit-sharing plan, the Respondent issued a press release confirming that the hog kill and cut departments would be discontinued and for the first time announcing that the Respondent had an alternate plan to relocate these operations. Until the time of this announcement, the Respondent had spoken only in terms of closing these operations, not relocating them. On June 16, 1981, the Respondent successfully negotiated a new $50 million line of credit. However, the lenders could withdraw from this arrangement at will.

On June 23, 1981, in response to the Respondent's announcement that a decision to relocate had been made, the Union requested extensive corporate wide information substantiating the need for concessions. The Union also scheduled another vote on the wage freeze/profit-sharing plan on June 28, 1981.

On June 24, 1981, the Respondent advised the union membership that a vote for the Respondent's wage freeze/profit-sharing plan would save the hog kill and cut departments. Nevertheless, on June 28, 1981, the membership voted to reject the Respondent's proposals.

With respect to the Union's information request, the Respondent objected on the grounds of relevancy and confidentiality. The Respondent's letter in response to the Union's request stated: "Your request for this information appears to be related to a desire to negotiate with the Company as to its decision to close part of its operations." The Respondent denied that it had any obligation to bargain over what it characterized as a decision to close part of its business.

On July 1, 1981, the Respondent notified the Union that the decision to close the hog kill and cut departments was irrevocable.

On July 10 and 11, 1981, the Respondent announced that it had purchased the Rochelle, Illinois plant as a replacement for the hog kill and cut departments in Dubuque. The Rochelle plant opened on October 1, 1981, and the hog kill and cut departments in Dubuque closed on October 3, 1981.

Negotiations over the potential relocation of processing operations were conducted from July through October 1981. During these negotiations, when the Union requested bargaining over the hog kill and cut departments, the Respondent responded that the hog kill and cut departments were closed and there was no duty to bargain over the closure.

In early 1982, the Respondent lost its financing. On October 15, 1982, the Dubuque and Rochelle plants were closed and sold.

In addressing the question of whether a decision to relocate unit work is a mandatory subject of bargaining giving rise to an obligation to bargain, we are guided by the principles set forth in *First National Maintenance*. Initially, we note that the decision to relocate falls within the third category of management decisions described in *First National Maintenance* (decisions which have a direct impact on employment but have as their focus the economic profitability of the employing enterprise). Such decisions are neither clearly covered by nor clearly excluded from Section 8(d)'s "terms and conditions of employment" over which Congress has mandated bargaining. It is therefore the Board's task to determine whether a relocation decision is a mandatory subject of bargaining or whether it should be considered as within the ambit of an employer's "retained freedom to manage its affairs unrelated to employment."

In our experience, the circumstances surrounding decisions to relocate vary significantly. In some instances, a relocation decision would be a fruitful subject of labor-management negotiations, while in others it would not. For this reason, it is not feasible to categorize all decisions to relocate as mandatory or nonmandatory subjects of bargaining.

In formulating a new analysis for relocation decisions, we are mindful of the Court's concern in *First National Maintenance* that an employer "must have some degree of certainty beforehand as to when it may proceed to reach decisions without fear of later evaluations labeling its conduct an unfair labor practice." Accordingly, we have endeavored to develop a test that provides guidance and predictability to the parties.

In analyzing a decision to relocate unit work, we pay close attention to the crucial inquiry posed by the Court in *First National Maintenance*: Will requiring bargaining over the decision advance the neutral purposes of the Act? In *First National Maintenance*, the Court plainly believed that no such result would obtain, while in *Fibreboard* the Court reached the opposite conclusion. In harmonizing the different results reached in the two cases, there are at least three important points to consider.

First, in *First National Maintenance*, the employer "had no intention to replace the discharged employees or to move that operation elsewhere." In contrast, *Fibreboard* involved the "replace[ment] [of] existing employees with those of an independent contractor."

Second, in *First National Maintenance*, the Court was confronted with a decision changing the scope and direction of the enterprise "akin to the decision whether to be in business at all." In *Fibreboard*, the employer's decision "did not alter the Company's basic operation."

Third, in *First National Maintenance*, the employer's decision was based "solely [on] the size of the management fee [the nursing home] was willing to pay." In *Fibreboard*, "a desire to reduce labor costs . . . was at the base of the employer's decision to subcontract."

Measured by these three considerations, a decision to relocate unit work case is more closely analogous to the subcontracting decision found mandatory in *Fibreboard* than the partial closing decision found nonmandatory in *First National Maintenance*. We will examine each of these considerations in turn.

First, unlike the employer in *First National Maintenance*, an employer relocating unit work does intend "to replace the discharged employees [and] to move th[e] operation elsewhere." In this respect, a relocation decision is similar to the *Fibreboard* subcontracting decision described by Justice Stewart in his concurrence as "the substitution of one group of workers for another to perform the same task. . . ."

Second, a relocation decision is not "akin to the decision whether to be in business at all." A decision to relocate presupposes that the employer intends to continue in business with the unanswered question being where the business entity will be in operation as opposed to whether it will be in operation. A decision to conduct business at one location rather than another, standing alone, does not generally involve a "managerial decision [lying] at the core of entrepreneurial control . . . concerning . . . the basic scope of the enterprise." Without more, the fact that an employer may relocate work does not alter the employer's basic operation: the employer is producing the same product for the same customers under essentially the same working conditions.

Third, as the facts of this case and others illustrate, and unlike the situation in *First National Maintenance*, a union may have substantial "control or authority" over the basis for the employer's decision to relocate. Often this is due to the very nature of a relocation decision. Because a relocation decision, like the *Fibreboard* subcontracting decision, involves the replacement of one group of employees with another, it logically follows that the differential in the labor costs of the two groups may be of considerable importance to the employer. The union representing the incumbent workers has the ability to vary that differential and thereby influence the employer's decision. Thus, the decision to relocate is susceptible to resolution through collective bargaining.

Based on the foregoing considerations, we announce the following test for determining whether the employer's decision is a mandatory subject of bargaining. Initially, the burden is on the General Counsel to establish that the employer's decision involved a relocation of unit work unaccompanied by a basic change in the nature of the employer's operation. If the General Counsel successfully carries his burden in this regard, he will have established prima facie that the employer's relocation decision is a mandatory subject of bargaining. At this juncture, the employer may produce evidence rebutting the prima facie case by establishing that the work performed at the new location varies significantly from the work performed at the former plant, establishing that the work performed at the former plant is to be discontinued entirely and not moved to the new location, or establishing that the employer's decision involves a change in the scope and direction of the enterprise. Alternatively, the employer may proffer a defense to show by a preponderance of the evidence: (1) that labor costs (direct and/or indirect) were not a factor in the decision or (2) that even if labor costs were a factor in the decision, the union could not have offered labor cost concessions that could have changed the employer's decision to relocate.

The first prong of the employer's burden is self-explanatory: If the employer shows that labor costs were irrelevant to the decision to relocate unit work, bargaining over the decision will not be required because the decision would not be amenable to resolution through the bargaining process.

Under the second prong, an employer would have no bargaining obligation if it showed that, although labor costs were a consideration in the decision to relocate unit work, it would not remain at the present plant because, for example, the costs for modernization of equipment or environmental controls were greater than any labor cost concessions the union could offer. On the other hand, an employer would have a bargaining obligation if the union could and would offer concessions that approximate, meet, or exceed the anticipated costs or benefits that prompted the relocation decision, since the decision then would be amenable to resolution through the bargaining process.

As an evidentiary matter, an employer might establish that it has no decision bargaining obligation, even without discussing the union's position on concessions, if the wage and benefit costs of the unit employees were already so low that it was clear on the basis of those figures alone that the employees could not make up the difference. In any event, an employer would enhance its chances of establishing this defense by describing its reasons for relocating to the union, fully explaining the underlying cost or benefit considerations, and asking whether the union could offer labor cost reductions that would enable the employer to meet its profit objectives.

Perhaps the most significant differences between the analytical framework we adopt today and those set forth in *Otis Elevator* concern the definition and allocation of the parties' respective burdens. We believe our proposed analysis more clearly apprises the parties of their obligations at the bargaining table and in litigation. Further, we believe that we are warranted in placing on the employer the burden of adducing evidence as to its motivation for the relocation decision because it alone, more often than not, is the party in possession of the relevant information. Finally, we believe that our test is most responsive to the central purposes for which the Act was created: promoting labor peace through collective bargaining over those matters suitable for negotiation where there is a general duty to recognize and bargain with a labor organization.

If, under our analysis, the relocation decision is a mandatory subject of bargaining, the employer's obligation will be the usual one of negotiating to agreement or a bona fide impasse. However, we recognize that there may be circumstances under which a relocation decision must be made or implemented expeditiously. If such circumstances are established, the Board will take them into account in determining whether a bargaining impasse has been reached on the relocation question. Accordingly, the extent of the employer's obligation to notify the union and give it an opportunity to bargain will be governed by traditional 8(a)(5) criteria, taking into account any special or emergency circumstances as well as the exigencies of each case.

[The Board went on to analyze the record and concluded that the General Counsel established a prima facie case that the relocation was a mandatory subject and the company failed to rebut the prima facie case.]

NOTES

1.   The D.C. Circuit enforced the Board's order but modified the employer's defense from proving that the union could not have offered cost

concessions that would have changed the decision (a defense of impossibility) to proving that the union would not have offered such concessions (a defense of futility). *United Food & Commercial Workers Local 150 v. NLRB*, 1 F.3d 24 (D.C. Cir. 1993). Of what practical significance in the difference between the two versions of the defense?

2.   How does the Board that decided *Dubuque* view the scope of the union's role in negotiating with respect to decisions such as the relocation of bargaining unit work? How would the Board that decided *Dubuque* have decided *Bob's Big Boy*, discussed on page 86, following *First National Maintenance*?

3.   Does the approach in *Dubuque* adequately account for the Court's concern in *First National Maintenance* that employers should be freed from the uncertainties of the bargaining process to run their businesses? After *Dubuque*, need employers worry about taking action only to have been found later to have committed unfair labor practices?

4.   Does the approach in *Dubuque* shed further light on the question posed on page 695, whether an employer's decision to terminate its call center and have all employees work from home is a mandatory subject of bargaining?

5.   Your client provides various services to the steel industry, including patching the inside of furnaces by applying its proprietary material on the furnace walls. You client regards the composition of the material and the application process as trade secrets. The union represents a bargaining unit of employees who apply the material. Your client wants to require every employee involved in the application process to sign an agreement not to disclose anything about the material or its application and not to work for an entity that competes with your client for a period of 12 months following termination of employment. Must your client bargain about this with the union? *See Minteq Int'l. Inc. v. NLRB*, 855 F.3d 329 (D.C. Cir. 2017) (holding that a covenant not to compete is a mandatory subject of bargaining). Some engineers are organizing collectively around the issue of covenants not to compete. They have created the Employee Association to Renegotiate Noncompetes (EARN) which they characterize as a "pop-up union." Their approach is for tech workers to organize a union for the purpose of getting their employer to eliminate covenants not to compete and, upon accomplishing that purpose, dissolve the union. *See* Helen Horrwitz, *Kevin Johnson: Abolishing Noncompetes One Company at a Time*, IEEE—USA Insight (Sept. 20, 2017), https://insight.ieeeusa.org/articles/kevin-johnson-abolishing-noncompetes-one-company-at-a-time/.

* * *

Allied Chemical & Alkali Workers Local 1 v. Pittsburgh Plate Glass Division, **404 U.S. 157 (1971).** The collective bargaining agreement provided that retirees could participate in the group health insurance plan and that the employer would contribute a specified amount per month to the costs of the premiums. After Medicare was enacted, the employer wrote to each retiree offering to pay the retiree's costs of supplemental Medicare if the retiree withdrew from the health insurance plan. The NLRB found that, in doing so, the employer violated section 8(a)(5), but the Sixth Circuit reversed. In an opinion by Justice Brennan, the Supreme Court affirmed the Sixth Circuit. The court reasoned:

> In this cause we hold that the Board's decision is not supported by the law. The Act, after all, as § 1 makes clear, is concerned with the disruption to commerce that arises from interference with the organization and collective-bargaining rights of "workers"—not those who have retired from the work force. The inequality of bargaining power that Congress sought to remedy was that of the "working" man, and the labor disputes that it ordered to be subjected to collective bargaining were those of employers and their active employees. Nowhere in the history of the National Labor Relations Act is there any evidence that retired workers are to be considered as within the ambit of the collective-bargaining obligations of the statute.

> The ordinary meaning of "employee" does not include retired workers; retired employees have ceased to work for another for hire.

> In addition to holding that pensioners are not "employees" within the meaning of the collective-bargaining obligations of the Act, we hold that they were not and could not be "employees" included in the bargaining unit. The unit determined by the Board to be appropriate was composed of "employees of the Employer's plant . . . working on hourly rates, including group leaders who work on hourly rates of pay. . . ." Apart from whether retirees could be considered "employees" within this language, they obviously were not employees "working" or "who work" on hourly rates of pay. Although those terms may include persons on temporary or limited absence from work, such as employees on military duty, it would utterly destroy the function of language to read them as embracing those whose work has ceased with no expectation of return.

> In any event, retirees could not properly be joined with the active employees in the unit that the Union represents. Here, even if, as the Board found, active and retired employees have a common concern in assuring that the latter's benefits remain adequate, they plainly do not share a community of interests broad enough to justify inclusion of the retirees in the bargaining unit. Pensioners' interests extend only to retirement benefits, to the exclusion of wage rates, hours, working conditions, and all other terms of active employment. Incorporation of such a limited-purpose constituency in the bargaining unit would create the potential for severe internal conflicts that would impair the unit's

ability to function and would disrupt the processes of collective bargaining. Moreover, the risk cannot be overlooked that union representatives on occasion might see fit to bargain for improved wages or other conditions favoring active employees at the expense of retirees' benefits.

NOTES

1.   Why did the Court not defer to the Board's expertise in interpreting the term "employees," or in deciding that even if retirees were not employees, their health insurance vitally affected employees in the bargaining unit?

2.   Existing employees may frequently be family members, friends or at least long-time coworkers of the retirees. If so, won't they wish to rise to the defense of retirees who are facing reductions in their benefits? What does the Court's reasoning imply about the Court's view of worker solidarity?

3.   An employer has decided to require all job applicants to submit a urine specimen which will be tested for drugs. Must the employer first negotiate this decision with the union representing the bargaining unit in which applicants are seeking jobs? *See Star Tribune*, 295 N.L.R.B. 543 (1989) (rejecting argument that testing applicants vitally affected incumbent employees).

4.   Benefits for existing, as opposed to future, retirees are a permissive subject of bargaining. What happens if the parties bargain about them? The answer depends on whether the benefits were vested. Vesting means that the employees were promised that the benefits would never be changed even after expiration of the contract. Vesting, in turn, depends on the language of the contract that provided for the benefits. If the benefits were not vested, the employer may change them unilaterally. Legally, the employer's decision to bargain with the union prior to changing the benefits is irrelevant. *See, e.g., Senn v. Union Dominion Indus., Inc.*, 951 F.2d 806 (7th Cir. 1992). However, if the benefits were vested then the employer may not change them, even if the union agrees to the change. For example, in *Paperworkers Local 1020 v. Muskegon Paper Box Co.*, 704 F. Supp. 744 (W.D. Mich. 1988), the union and employer negotiated a plant closing agreement which, among other things, terminated retiree benefits. The union then sued the employer on behalf of the retirees for breach of the former collective bargaining agreement which had established the retiree benefits. The court granted the union's motion for summary judgment on the ground that the benefits under the former contract had vested and the union lacked authority to bargain them away in the plant closing agreement. Do you think the decision would have been the same if the Court in *Pittsburgh Plate Glass* had held that retiree benefits were a mandatory subject of bargaining? The determination of whether retiree benefits have vested is considered in greater detail in Chapter 7.

2. RAILWAY LABOR ACT

In *Order of Railroad Telegraphers v. Chicago & North Western Railway Co.*, 362 U.S. 330 (1960), the Supreme Court held that a railroad's decision to close little-used stations was a mandatory subject of bargaining because the closures would put the agents assigned to those stations out of work. The Court rejected the employer's argument that the closures were the exercise of a managerial right over which it need not bargain. In *Pittsburgh & Lake Erie Railroad v. Railway Labor Executives Ass'n*, 491 U.S. 490 (1989), the Court refused to extend *Railroad Telegraphers* to mandate bargaining over a railroad's decision to sell all of its assets to another company. The Court instead applied its NLRA precedent, particularly *Darlington*, to hold that the employer had an absolute right to go out of business. The Court acknowledged, however, that there is an "enlarged scope of mandatory bargaining" under the RLA. What policy concerns account for this? What other limits, if any, might apply to this enlarged scope of mandatory bargaining?

3. THE PUBLIC SECTOR

In the public sector, limits on the scope of mandatory bargaining do not result from concerns with allowing a private party to run its business as it deems necessary. Rather, they result from concerns that collective bargaining can be anti-democratic. In holding that economically motivated layoffs, clearly a mandatory subject of bargaining in the private sector, were not mandatorily bargainable under the Wisconsin Municipal Employment Relations Act, the Wisconsin Supreme Court opined:

> The residents of Brookfield through their elected representatives on the city council requested city budget reductions. Unquestionably, fewer firefighters will reduce the level and quality of services provided, but this is a policy decision by a community favoring a lower municipal tax base. Ch. 62 does not expressly prohibit the topic of economically motivated lay offs from becoming a permissive subject of collective bargaining, but the decision to discuss the topic at a bargaining table is a choice to be made by the electorate as expressed through its designated representatives and department heads.

> In municipal employment relations the bargaining table is not the appropriate forum for the formulation or management of public policy. Where a decision is essentially concerned with public policy choices, no group should act as an exclusive representative; discussions should be open; and public policy should be shaped through the regular political process. Essential control over the management of [a] school district's affairs must be left with the school board, the body elected to be responsible for those affairs under state law.

City of Brookfield v. Wisconsin Employment Relations Comm'n, 87 Wis. 2d 819, 832, 275 N.W.2d 723, 729–30 (1979).

Some jurisdictions extend this rationale to the point of not recognizing permissive subjects of bargaining. They hold that all subjects must be mandatory or prohibited. These jurisdictions want to prevent public employers from trading off permissive subject to gain concessions on mandatory subjects. *See, e.g., Montgomery County Educ. Ass'n v. Bd. of Ed.*, 311 Md. 303, 534 A.2d 980 (1987) (holding that school calendar and job reclassification decisions are prohibited subjects of bargaining); *Dunnellen Bd. of Educ. v. Dunnellen Educ. Ass'n*, 64 N.J. 17, 311 A.2d 737 (1973) (holding that decision to consolidate two positions was a prohibited subject of bargaining); *Aberdeen Educ. Ass'n v. Aberdeen Bd. of Educ.*, 88 S.D. 127, 215 N.W.2d 837 (1974) (holding a variety of subjects including class size and teacher planning periods to be prohibited subjects of bargaining). Courts in many jurisdictions have held subjects that would clearly be mandatorily bargainable under the private sector were not mandatory subjects in the public sector. These include such matters as class size, subcontracting, no smoking policies and drug testing. For further discussion *see* Martin H. Malin, Ann C. Hodges & Joseph E. Slater, *Public Sector Employment: Cases and Materials* ch. 7 (West 3d ed. 2016).

H. BARGAINING REMEDIES

H. K. PORTER CO. v. NLRB
397 U.S. 99 (1970)

JUSTICE BLACK delivered the opinion of the Court:

After an election respondent United Steelworkers Union was, on October 5, 1961, certified by the National Labor Relations Board as the bargaining agent for certain employees at the Danville, Virginia, plant of the petitioner, H. K. Porter Co. Thereafter negotiations commenced for a collective-bargaining agreement. Since that time the controversy has seesawed between the Board, the Court of Appeals for the District of Columbia Circuit, and this Court. This delay of over eight years is not because the case is exceedingly complex, but appears to have occurred chiefly because of the skill of the company's negotiators in taking advantage of every opportunity for delay in an act more noticeable for its generality than for its precise prescriptions. The entire lengthy dispute mainly revolves around the union's desire to have the company agree to "check off" the dues owed to the union by its members, that is, to deduct those dues periodically from the company's wage payments to the employees. The record shows, as the Board found, that the company's objection to a checkoff was not due to any general principle or policy against making deductions from employees' wages. The company does deduct charges for things like insurance, taxes, and contributions to charities, and at some other plants it has a check-off arrangement for union dues. The evidence shows, and the court below found, that the company's objection was not because of inconvenience, but solely on the ground that the company was "not going to aid and comfort the union." Efforts by the union to obtain some kind of compromise on the check-off request were all met with the same staccato response to the effect that the collection of union dues was the "union's business" and the company was not going to provide any assistance. Based on this and other evidence the Board found, and the Court of Appeals approved the finding, that the refusal of the company to bargain about the check-off was not made in good faith, but was done solely to frustrate the making of any collective-bargaining agreement.

In the course of that opinion, the Court of Appeals intimated that the Board conceivably might have required petitioner to agree to a check-off provision as a remedy for the prior bad-faith bargaining, although the order enforced at that time did not contain any such provision. In the ensuing negotiations the company offered to discuss alternative arrangements for collecting the union's dues, but the union insisted that the company was required to agree to the check-off proposal without modification. Because of this disagreement over the proper interpretation of the court's opinion, the union, in February 1967, filed a motion for clarification of the 1966 opinion. The motion was denied by the court on March 22, 1967, in an order suggesting that contempt proceedings by the Board would be the proper avenue for testing the employer's compliance with the original order. A request for the institution of such proceedings was made by the union, and, in June 1967, the Regional Director of the Board declined to prosecute a contempt charge, finding that the employer had "satisfactorily complied with the affirmative requirements of the Order." The union then filed in the Court of Appeals a motion for reconsideration of the earlier motion to clarify the 1966 opinion. The court granted that motion and issued a new opinion in which it held that in certain circumstances a "check-off may be imposed as a remedy for bad faith bargaining." The case was then remanded to the Board and on July 3, 1968, the Board issued a supplemental order requiring the petitioner to "(g)rant to the Union a contract clause providing for the check-off of union dues." The Court of Appeals affirmed this order.

The object of [the Wagner] Act was not to allow governmental regulation of the terms and conditions of employment, but rather to ensure that employers and their employees could work together to establish mutually satisfactory conditions. The basic theme of the Act was that through collective bargaining the passions, arguments, and struggles of prior years would be channeled into constructive, open discussions leading, it was hoped, to mutual agreement. But it was recognized from the beginning that agreement might in some cases be impossible, and it was never intended that the Government would in such cases step in, become a party to the negotiations and impose its own views of a desirable settlement.

Recognizing the fundamental principle "that the National Labor Relations Act is grounded on the premise of freedom of contract," the Court of Appeals in this case concluded that nevertheless in the circumstances presented here the Board could properly compel the employer to agree to a proposed check-off clause. The Board had found that the refusal was based on a desire to frustrate agreement and not on any legitimate business reason. On the basis of that finding the Court of Appeals approved the further finding that the employer had not bargained in good faith, and the validity of that finding is not now before us. Where the record thus revealed repeated refusals by the employer to bargain in good faith on this issue, the Court of Appeals concluded that ordering agreement to the check-off clause "may be the only means of assuring the Board, and the court, that (the employer) no longer harbors an illegal intent."

In reaching this conclusion the Court of Appeals held that § 8(d) did not forbid the Board from compelling agreement. That court felt that "(s)ection 8(d) defines collective bargaining and relates to a determination of whether a . . . violation has occurred and not to the scope of the remedy which may be necessary to cure violations which have already occurred." We may agree with the Court of Appeals that as a matter of strict, literal interpretation that section refers only to deciding when a violation has occurred, but we do not agree that that observation justifies the conclusion that the remedial powers of the Board are not also limited by the same considerations that led Congress to enact § 8(d). It is implicit in the entire structure of the Act that the Board acts to oversee and referee the process of collective bargaining, leaving the results of the contest to the bargaining strengths of the parties. It would be anomalous indeed to hold that while § 8(d) prohibits the Board from relying on a refusal to agree as the sole evidence of bad-faith bargaining, the Act permits the Board to compel agreement in that same dispute. The Board's remedial powers under § 10 of the Act are broad, but they are limited to carrying out the policies of the Act itself. One of these fundamental policies is freedom of contract. While the parties' freedom of contract is not absolute under the Act, allowing the Board to compel agreement when the parties themselves are unable to agree would violate the fundamental premise on which the Act is based— private bargaining under governmental supervision of the procedure alone, without any official compulsion over the actual terms of the contract.

In reaching its decision the Court of Appeals relied extensively on the equally important policy of the Act that workers' rights to collective bargaining are to be secured. In this case the court apparently felt that the employer was trying effectively to destroy the union by refusing to agree to what the union may have considered its most important demand. Perhaps the court, fearing that the parties might resort to economic combat, was also trying to maintain the industrial peace that the Act is designed to further. But the Act as presently drawn does not contemplate that unions will always be secure and able to achieve agreement even when their economic position is weak, or that strikes and lockouts will never result from a bargaining impasse. It cannot be said that the Act forbids an employer or a union to rely ultimately on its economic strength to try to secure what it cannot obtain through bargaining. It may well be true, as the Court of Appeals felt, that the present remedial powers of the Board are insufficiently broad to cope with important labor problems. But it is the job of Congress, not the Board or the courts, to decide when and if it is necessary to allow governmental review of proposals for collective-bargaining agreements and compulsory submission to one side's demands. The present Act does not envision such a process.

The judgment is reversed and the case is remanded to the Court of Appeals for further action consistent with this opinion.

NOTES

1.   If the purpose of a remedy is to place the parties in the position they would have occupied had the violation not occurred and the NLRB, exercising its expert judgment, finds that if the employer had bargained in good faith the parties would have agreed on a dues check-off, why is the Board prohibited from ordering the dues check-off? Is it that the Court lacks confidence in the Board's conclusion? Is it that the conclusion is inherently speculative and therefore may not form the basis for a remedy? Is there an overriding policy concern?

2.   If the NLRB may not order a party to agree to a term it finds the party would have agreed to had the party bargained in good faith, what remedies, beyond a cease and desist order, may it award? May it award compensatory damages to make a party whole for the violation? *See Int'l Union of Elec., Radio & Mach. Workers v. NLRB*, 426 F.2d 1243 (D.C. Cir. 1970); *Tidee Prods., Inc.*, 194 N.L.R.B. 1234 (1972), enf'd, 502 F.2d 349 (D.C. Cir. 1974); *Ex-Cell-O Corp.*, 185 N.L.R.B. 107 (1970), aff'd, 449 F.2d 1058 (D.C. Cir. 1971). May the Board order the offending party to pay the other party's negotiating expenses and to pay the General Counsel's and the other party's attorney fees? *See Unbelievable, Inc. v. NLRB*, 118 F.3d 795 (D.C. Cir. 1997); *Teamsters Local 122* (August A. Busch & Co.), 334 N.L.R.B. 1190 (2001).

3.   In *Ex-Cell-O Corp.*, 185 N.L.R.B. 107 (1970), the Board, by a 3–2 vote, held that it would not award a compensatory remedy where an employer refused to bargain as a means of obtaining judicial review of a Board decision in an underlying representation case. The trial examiner had recommended that the Board order the employer to compensate the employees for the difference between the wages and working conditions under which they labored and those which they would have received had the employer bargained and reached agreement with the union on a contract. The Board majority considered a determination of what would have resulted had the employer

bargained to be highly speculative and the recommended remedy to be tantamount to imposing an agreement on the parties, and therefore in conflict with *H.K. Porter*.

4.   *Remedies in First Contract Situations.* When the parties are negotiating their first collective bargaining agreement, the relationship is especially fragile and the temptation is considerable for the employer to stall negotiations until the union's presumption of majority support becomes rebuttable and then withdraw recognition or otherwise seek to oust the union. The NLRB General Counsel has identified certain unfair labor practices that have a "high impact" on first contract negotiations. These are: refusals to bargain or overall bad faith tantamount to a repudiation of the bargaining relationship; refusals to meet at reasonable times or other tactics that delay negotiation; unilateral changes; and discriminatory discharges of union supporters. In such cases, the General Counsel will seek remedies beyond the traditional cease and desist order, including: imposing a specific schedule for bargaining such as a requirement that the parties meet a minimum number of days or hours per week; requiring periodic reports to the Board on bargaining progress; a minimum six-month extension of the certification year; and reimbursement to the charging party of its bargaining expenses. NLRBGC Memo 07–98 (May 29, 2007). Where these additional remedies are sought, the General Counsel will also seek preliminary injunctive relief under section 10(j). *See* NRLBGC Memo 08–09 (July 1, 2008).

MUNICIPALITY OF METROPOLITAN SEATTLE V. PUBLIC EMPLOYMENT RELATIONS COMMISSION
826 P.2d 158 (Wash. 1992)

JUSTICE ANDERSON delivered the opinion of the court:

The question raised by this appeal is whether the Public Employment Relations Commission (PERC) has authority to order "interest" arbitration as part of an unfair labor practice remedy. We hold that, in limited circumstances, it does.

The PERC order challenged in this action requires the employer, Municipality of Metropolitan Seattle (Metro), to participate in interest arbitration if collective bargaining between Metro and the International Federation of Professional and Technical Engineers, Local 17, AFL-CIO (Local 17) does not result in a collective bargaining agreement. "Interest" (or contract) arbitration differs from the more familiar "grievance" arbitration. Grievance arbitration requires the employer and union to submit unresolved disputes regarding the interpretation or application of an existing collective bargaining contract to an objective arbitrator. Interest arbitration, on the other hand, occurs only at a point where an impasse has been reached in new contract negotiations. At that point, the unresolved items of the new collective bargaining agreement are submitted to an arbitrator who then decides the terms of the future collective bargaining contract.

This case concerns five employees who, until April 1984, worked as clerical employees for the City of Seattle's commuter pool. The city employees were represented by their exclusive bargaining agent, Local 17. In 1982 or 1983, Metro, a public transit authority serving the greater Seattle area, began negotiating with the City of Seattle for a transfer of the City's commuter pool program to Metro. The plan involved the transfer of approximately 29 employees, including the five clerical employees who were members of Local 17. The statute authorizing such transfers places certain obligations, including the duty to collectively bargain with existing unions, upon any metropolitan corporation which acquires an existing transportation system.

The five commuter pool employees were transferred to Metro in early April 1984. In the years from the date of that transfer to the present time, Metro has refused to recognize Local 17 as the appropriate bargaining unit for the transferred employees. During those years, Metro has also refused to bargain with the union, despite court and PERC orders to do so. [Portions of the court's opinion detailing the history of Metro's attempts to avoid bargaining through legal actions, including a petition for "unit clarification" are omitted.]

In February 1985, Local 17 filed the unfair labor practice complaint that resulted in the appeal before us. Local 17's complaint alleged a refusal to bargain on the part of Metro. Although the hearing on the unfair labor practice complaint was held in early November 1986, the decision was not issued until January 1988. The delay was due to PERC's decision to hold the matter in abeyance until a decision was reached by the King County Superior Court in Metro's unit clarification action. In the unfair labor practice case, Metro argued that it had changed its operations to such an extent that the commuter pool which was transferred from the City was no longer intact and thus no longer existed as a separate bargaining unit. The PERC hearing examiner found this argument to be "frivolous" in light of settled law requiring that the "effects" of such significant changes in working conditions must be bargained before being implemented. The hearing examiner noted that during the pendency of the action, and after the previous unit clarification petition had been dismissed, Metro had filed yet another petition with PERC asking that its bargaining obligations toward Local 17 be terminated. The hearing examiner found:

> METRO has attempted at every turn to evade its bargaining obligations. It is evident that METRO has not given up the fight, and that it is still not prepared to fulfill its bargaining obligations towards Local 17. . . . METRO will likely continue to put up one defense after another in an ongoing attempt to defeat having a bargaining relationship with Local 17. . . . METRO has asserted,

and continues to assert, inherently frivolous defenses in an ongoing effort to subvert and avoid its bargaining obligations towards Local 17.

The hearing examiner then crafted the order which is now before us on Metro's challenge. The order requires Metro to restore the status quo with respect to the five commuter pool employees and to make those employees whole. Based on a finding of bad faith on the part of Metro, it requires Metro to pay the union's reasonable attorneys' fees and costs. It orders Metro to post notices with respect to the unfair labor practice and orders that Metro [bargain with the Union in good faith] and, if no agreement is reached through bilateral negotiations within sixty (60) days after Local 17 has requested to bargain, either party may request the Public Employment Commission Relations [sic] to provide the services of a mediator to assist the parties. If no agreement is reached by using the mediation process, and the Executive Director, on the request of either of the parties and the recommendation of the assigned mediator, concludes that the parties are at impasse following a reasonable period of negotiations, shall submit the remaining issues to interest arbitration using the procedures of 41.56.450, *et seq*, and the standards for firefighters. The decision of the neutral arbitration panel shall be final and binding upon both the parties.

This case presents a conflict between the need to preserve the integrity of the collective bargaining process on the one hand, and, on the other, the genuine need to remedy flagrant abuses of that process in situations where employees are unable, through legal means or by use of traditional economic weapons, to remedy the situation themselves. The Public Employees' Collective Bargaining Act, Wash. Rev. Code Ann. § 41.56, was enacted in 1967, in order to promote the continued improvement of the relationship between public employers and their employees by providing a uniform basis for implementing the right of public employees to join labor organizations of their own choosing and to be represented by such organizations in matters concerning their employment relations with public employers. The Act requires public employers, including municipal corporations such as Metro, to participate in collective bargaining with the exclusive bargaining representatives of its employees. Collective bargaining is defined by the Act as the performance of the mutual obligations of the public employer and the exclusive bargaining representative to meet at reasonable times, to confer and negotiate in good faith, and to execute a written agreement with respect to grievance procedures and collective negotiations on personnel matters, including wages, hours and working conditions, which may be peculiar to an appropriate bargaining unit of such public employer, except that by such obligation neither party shall be compelled to agree to a proposal or be required to make a concession unless otherwise provided in this chapter. Wash. Rev. Code Ann. § 41.56.030(4).

Employers have traditionally not been compelled to agree or to accept the terms of a collective bargaining contract to which they do not agree. Resolution of bargaining impasses has thus depended on the economic pressures that the employer and employees could bring to bear upon one another. Where those economic pressures can be limited or prohibited or where their usefulness is questionable, other—more peaceful—methods of resolving contract impasses may be advantageous. While interest arbitration is generally a voluntary process both this court and the Legislature have given limited approval to the use of compulsory interest arbitration to resolve collective bargaining impasses in the public employment arena. Wash. Rev. Code Ann. § 41.56.450 requires interest arbitration between law enforcement and firefighter unions and their employers when contract negotiations and mediation have failed to produce a contract. In *Green River Comm'ty Coll. v. Higher Educ. Pers. Bd.*, 95 Wash. 2d 108, 622 P.2d 826 (1980), *modified on reconsideration*, 95 Wash. 2d 962, 633 P.2d 1324 (1981), this court approved a regulation promulgated by the Higher Education Personnel Board (HEP Board) that permitted either a college or its employee union to submit unresolved collective bargaining issues to the HEP Board for compulsory resolution through interest arbitration. Heretofore we have not determined whether PERC has the power to order interest arbitration as a remedy for an unfair labor practice.

An agency has only those powers which are expressly granted or which are necessarily implied from statutory grants of authority. PERC derives its power from Wash. Rev. Code Ann. § 41.58, the statute that creates the Commission, and from Wash. Rev. Code Ann. § 41.56, the Public Employees' Collective Bargaining Act. The creation of the Commission was intended to achieve more efficient and expert administration of public labor relations administration and to thereby ensure the public of quality public services. Wash. Rev. Code Ann. § 41.58.005. In addition to other duties, PERC is empowered and directed to prevent any unfair labor practice and to issue appropriate remedial orders. Wash. Rev. Code Ann. § 41.56.160.

When interpreting the Public Employees' Collective Bargaining Act, we will liberally construe the Act in order to accomplish its purpose. The purpose of the Act "is to provide public employees with the right to join and be represented by labor organizations of their own choosing, and to provide for a uniform basis for implementing that right." With that purpose in mind, we interpret the statutory phrase "appropriate remedial orders" to be those necessary to effectuate the purposes of the collective bargaining statute and to make PERC's lawful orders effective. The authority granted PERC by the remedial provision of the statute has been interpreted to be broad enough to authorize an award of attorney fees when such an award "is necessary to make the order effective and if the defense to the unfair labor practice is frivolous or meritless." In *State ex rel. Wash. Fed'n of State Employees v. Bd. of Trs.*, 93 Wash. 2d 60, 605 P.2d 1252 (1980), this court stated that the HEP Board's determination as to remedies under the Public Employees' Collective Bargaining Act should be accorded considerable judicial deference, and noted that the "relation of remedy to policy is peculiarly a matter of administrative competence." PERC's expertise in resolving labor disputes also has been judicially recognized and accorded deference. PERC thus has authority to issue appropriate orders that it, in its expertise, believes are consistent with the purposes of the Act, and that are necessary to make its orders effective unless such orders are otherwise unlawful.

Metro argues that because the Legislature did not include transit workers within the interest arbitration provisions of the statute, it intended that those workers not participate in interest arbitration. This argument ignores the impact of *Green River Comm'ty Coll. v. Higher Educ. Pers. Bd.,* 95 Wash. 2d 108, 622 P.2d 826 (1980), *modified on reconsideration,* 95 Wash. 2d 962, 633 P.2d 1324 (1981). Many of the arguments here presented by Metro were considered in *Green River,* where this court rejected those arguments and ruled that the HEP Board, through its regulatory powers, could require all public colleges and their employees to participate in interest arbitration, if collective bargaining and contract mediation failed. This court found such a regulation to be consistent with the intent and purpose of the law governing collective bargaining between public colleges and their employees.

The *Green River* court distinguished significant federal precedent that is now relied on by Metro. In *Green River,* this court declined to follow *H.K. Porter Co. v. NLRB,* 397 U.S. 99 (1970), a United States Supreme Court case that held the NLRB did not have authority to require a particular provision be included in a collective bargaining agreement.

This court, in distinguishing *H.K. Porter Co.,* stated that reliance on NLRA precedents in the present context is inappropriate. The NLRA regulates labor relations only in the private sector. The Act specifically guarantees employees the right to strike. Private sector bargaining and public sector bargaining are radically different, as both parties agree. *Green River* supports the union's and PERC's position that interest arbitration need not be specifically permitted or required by statute in order for it to be lawful.

Metro also argues that compelled interest arbitration is contrary to traditional collective bargaining principles and to the philosophy behind collective bargaining. When faced with a situation such as that which exists here, there is little that a union can legally do to enforce the collective bargaining rights of its members. For 7 years Metro has been involved in litigation over the representation rights of these five employees. Court orders and financial sanctions have had no effect on Metro. The employer's delays and legal maneuvering have, in fact, resulted in a prolonged period in which the employees have not had an opportunity to negotiate the terms and conditions of their employment. During this time Metro accomplished the disbursement of the employees represented by Local 17 so that the bargaining unit became unidentifiable. This disbursement of employees throughout other bargaining units was the reason for PERC's order requiring a return to the status quo. The conflict here thus arises because the employer in this case has been able to use the law to avoid its clear obligation to collectively bargain with the union and now, when ordered to participate in interest arbitration, claims that such an order is violative of the philosophy behind collective bargaining. In this case PERC specifically found that the remedy of interest arbitration, upon impasse, was necessary to make its order to bargain effective. In the very limited circumstances presented by the facts of this case, such an order is not contrary to collective bargaining principles. Instead, it serves as an impetus to successfully negotiate an agreement.

NOTES

1.   How would you define the "limited circumstances" which justified the imposition of interest arbitration as a remedy in this case? Under what other circumstances, if any, would such a remedy be justified? Would it be appropriate under a system which calls for non-binding factfinding?

2.   The court assumed that the remedy was inconsistent with the rationale of *H.K. Porter*. If the NLRB were to issue a comparable remedy, would it survive judicial review?

3.   Why would the PERC use interest arbitration as a remedy rather than directly mandate a remedy? Should the union have to wait even longer for a final resolution? Or can the arbitration process offer benefits the PERC process cannot?

CHAPTER 6

ECONOMIC WEAPONS

∎ ∎ ∎

A. INTRODUCTION

After three decades of sporadic local successes in organizing, telephone workers finally created a national federation of unions throughout the telephone business in 1938 after the enactment of the National Labor Relations Act in 1935 protected the right to unionize. A major national strike in 1947 and AT&T's consolidation of the telephone industry under the banner of the Bell System eventually enabled the Communications Workers of America and the International Brotherhood of Electrical Workers to secure middle-class wages, health and disability insurance, and pensions for telephone workers nationwide. But the stability of this arrangement was challenged in the 1990s by changing technology and by the determination of company management to reduce labor costs through use of non-union labor in the growing wireless side of the telecommunications business.

For more than six weeks in spring 2016, roughly 36,000 Verizon workers in the northeastern United States went on strike. The strikers were from the wireline (as opposed to wireless) side of the business, which included the declining landline telephone business but also the profitable state-of-the-art broadband internet, voice, and video service to subscribers. Verizon insisted that the future of telecommunications is in wireless, which was growing rapidly and was extremely profitable. For the striking workers, the big picture was whether Verizon would dis-invest in its unionized wireline (landline and fiber optic broadband) business in order to grow its wireless business. Most Verizon Wireless workers are non-union, and their wages and benefits are much lower than those of unionized wireline workers. The union and some independent analysts believed that broadband expansion would benefit communities by improving their access to telecommunications technologies and information, would benefit workers by protecting and creating good jobs, and would be profitable for the company. The union appealed to federal, state, and local legislators and the Federal Communications Commission (F.C.C.), which regulates the telecommunications industry, to pressure Verizon to invest in broadband. The union also asked sympathetic government officials to pressure the company to negotiate fairly with the union over wages, benefits, and job elimination. One independent analyst said, "The purposes of the strike are to build public support for the workers and to put pressure on the politicians and the regulators to put pressure on Verizon." Another described the strategy as involving, in part, building awareness of the F.C.C.'s lack of "an effective policy to build out broadband in the U.S.," which, he said, "has not provided the appropriate incentives" to encourage private investment in the infrastructure of the information superhighway.

One of the major points of contention in the strike was whether Verizon should be able to increase the contracting out of customer service and sales jobs to low-wage, non-union call centers. The strikers said the strike was about preserving and expanding middle class jobs. Some analysts pointed to studies showing that outsourcing service work to low-wage, non-union call center contractors does not save as much money in the long term as some consultants insist because of high worker turnover, the cost of managing the outsource contracting process, and increased customer dissatisfaction. Verizon, for its part, maintained that it needed to cut costs and increase flexibility in managing its workforce, and it insisted that the future of the company is in wireless, not in broadband. The head of Verizon's consumer and mass business unit was quoted in the New York Times as saying that expansion of broadband would mean a lot of "great high-paying work" but that "it doesn't matter whether they're a contractor or an employee."

The strike grew especially acrimonious two weeks in, when Verizon discontinued health benefits for striking workers. There were boisterous picket lines in major northeast cities and public relations campaigns by the unions as well as Verizon, each trying to convince the public and public officials that they were the true protectors of the public interest. The Obama Administration Secretary of Labor and the Director of the Federal Mediation and Conciliation Service both began to broker talks to break the stalemate.

The contract that settled the strike was claimed as a victory by Verizon and by the unions. Workers would get an 11 percent pay increase over four years as well as modest bonuses and profit-sharing. The company abandoned plans to reduce pension and sickness and disability benefits. The contract preserved a provision from prior contracts requiring that between 50 and 80 percent of customer calls be answered by unionized workers in-house, and Verizon committed to create over 1000 unionized call center jobs to accommodate new demand and to reduce closings of unionized call centers. The union contracts covered about 65 workers at Verizon Wireless stores; this was the first time that Verizon retail wireless workers had been included in a union contract. The union hoped this would be an entering wedge in gaining union protection for retail wireless workers. However, the company won the right to eliminate some jobs, won more flexibility in routing customer service calls within the company, and won substantial health care costs savings. In explaining why the union won as much as it did from the strike, analysts were quoted in the New York Times as saying that it is rare for a strike in the telecommunications industry to have an economic effect, as opposed to a public relations impact, but that

Verizon may have underestimated the unions' ability to hold out for as long as they did. Verizon reported that the strike caused a decline in installations which hurt its financial performance for the quarter. Although companies typically rely on managers to replace skilled striking workers, Verizon apparently did not have enough managers or others with the skills to replace the striking workers.

The readings that follow shed light on the legal constraints that would affect the choices of companies, workers, and their lawyers, in this scenario.

Labor relations are inevitably governed by the use of economic force. In times of labor scarcity, workers use their market power to negotiate for advantageous working conditions, and in times of labor surplus, employers do the same. Although worker strikes and employer lockouts have a long and storied tradition in American labor law, and strikes are specifically protected under section 13 of the NLRA, they are neither the only nor the most significant form of economic force in the contemporary workplace. Both labor and employers seek market strength by the strategic use of information: advertising (in the case of firms) and boycotts or consumer appeals (in the case of labor). Economic power associated with the deliberate control of the supply of work or jobs and the control of information are inevitable, but they can be harmful to workers, firms, consumers, and the public at large. Legislatures and courts therefore regulate the strategic use of labor market power, just as they regulate other forms of market power.

Strikes and boycotts are sometimes more than just a bargaining tactic. Political scientists and sociologists see strikes as an expression of a desire for cultural and political self-determination. In "If the Workers Took a Notion": The Right to Strike and American Political Development 12 (Cornell University Press 2005), Josiah Bartlett Lambert offers the theory that strikes are expressive activities in which groups of workers participate in democratic community-building:

> Strikes . . . are more than instruments in the collective bargaining process; they are also expressive activities through which groups of workers voice their grievances and proclaim their allegiances. They are a form of protest, an expression of defiance, and one of the most powerful ways for wage earners to say they will not accept arbitrary treatment and work. Strikes also give wage earners a voice in the firm and thus serve to extend democracy and justice into economic institutions.

A contemporary example of the symbolic and expressive nature of strikes occurred on January 29, 2017, when New York taxi drivers serving New York's Kennedy International Airport struck for one hour in solidarity with immigrants who were being turned away from the United States under President Donald Trump's newly-announced ban on immigration from predominantly Muslim countries. In a social media post, the New York

Taxi Workers Alliance said: "We cannot be silent. We go to work to welcome people to a land that once welcomed us. We will not be divided." The Alliance said taxi workers had decided to strike because New York taxi drivers are "largely Muslim, a workforce that's almost universally immigrant and a working-class movement that is rooted in the defense of the oppressed." As illustrated by the New York taxi drivers, Lambert notes that strikes have long served as a form of cultural expression:

> Traditionally, strikes involved extremely rich symbolic displays. During the nineteenth century, strikers would don the traditional garb of their craft and display the symbols emblematic of their trades as they paraded through the streets, calling others to walk out. Strikes have prompted a tradition of folk music, as strikers expressed their grievances and allegiances in song. Picketers display placards publicizing their grievances and often exhibit religious symbols. Mass strike rallies have frequently attracted the most famous orators of the day.

As discussed in Chapter 1, until the enactment of the Norris La-Guardia Act in 1932 and the NLRA in 1935, both federal and state courts regarded strikes and boycotts as unlawful and issued injunctions against them under state common law and federal antitrust law. The NLRA was premised on the idea that law should not dictate substantive working conditions but instead should create a process by which the parties would negotiate their own terms and would use the economic weapons of strikes, lockouts, and boycotts, within certain bounds, to secure favorable terms. Large numbers of strikes in the aftermath of World War II prompted Congress to rethink the Wagner Act's tolerance of the use of economic weapons. The Taft-Hartley Act of 1947 provided for judicial enforcement of collective bargaining agreements so that voluntary arbitration, strikes, or lockouts would not be the only weapons. Taft-Hartley also restricted some types of union tactics, particularly the secondary boycott and picketing for union recognition.

Employer intransigence about union organizing and about unions' contract demands appeared to intensify in the recessionary economy of the 1970s and in the face of declines in American manufacturing and basic industry. The symbolic turning point at which strikes to extract better wages and working conditions became highly risky was in 1981 when federal air traffic controllers struck in defiance of a federal statute prohibiting government employee strikes. Although air traffic controllers in the past had struck without suffering discipline, President Reagan fired them, which emboldened other employers to permanently replace employees engaged in legal strikes. The strike quickly became a foolhardy and potentially disastrous strategy as the use of permanent replacements grew common. For example, a strike at a Hormel meat packing plant in Austin, Minnesota in the bitter winter of 1985–1986 failed when Hormel, the major employer in the small mid-western town, permanently replaced most of the striking employees and drastically cut wages, thus transforming forever the town and the middle-class way of life that had been built around the unionized jobs. Similarly, in the late 1980s, the failure of a strike against the Pittston Coal Company's drastic cut in health care benefits marked a major turning point in coal mining as a way of life in Appalachia.

By the early 1990s, new waves of immigrant workers entered the U.S. willing to work for much less than native-born workers. At the same time, employers increasingly used replacement workers to operate during a strike. Peter Cramton, *et al.*, *The Use of Replacement Workers in Union Contract Negotiations: The U.S. Experience*, 1980–1989, 17 J. Lab. Econ. 667 (1998). Immigration, the use of replacement workers, and the ability of employers to move production overseas drastically changed the bargaining power of unions. Unions doubted whether the strike had any future. Still, there were some notable strike successes. A strike at UPS in the mid-1990s prompted the company to scale back its plans to substitute part-time for full-time work. But the successes were few, and strikes declined in significance. Indeed, lockouts may be now more common than strikes, at least in cases involving negotiating disputes in mature collective bargaining relationships. According to data compiled by the federal Bureau of Labor Statistics, time lost due to work stoppages has declined steadily since the 1950s. It has stayed below one-tenth of one percent of working hours since 2001. In 2016, the annual total number of major work stoppages—which includes both strikes and lockouts—was 15, up from five in 2009, the year which recorded the lowest number since the U.S. Bureau of Labor Statistics began compiling data in 1947 on the amount of working time lost to work stoppages. News Release, U.S. Bureau of Labor Statistics, Work Stoppages Summary (2017), https://www.bls.gov/news.release/wkstp.nr0.htm; News Release, U.S. Bureau of Labor Statistics, Work Stoppages Involving 1000 or More Workers, 1947–2016 (Table 1) (2017), https://www.bls.gov/news.release/wkstp.t01.htm.

Nevertheless, the spring of 2018 saw a major strike wave among public school teachers in six states (West Virginia, Oklahoma, Kentucky, Arizona, North Carolina, and Colorado). The West Virginia teachers strike shut all the state's schools for ten days, and in other states the strikes were widespread though not quite as long. The strikes featured marches across the state and huge rallies in the state capitol, along with well-publicized efforts of teachers to ensure that families whose students depend on free school lunches were fed and cared for during the strike. The six states prohibit public employee strikes, and most prohibit teacher collective bargaining. All had seen steady and severe declines in school funding. These strikes were not part of a collective bargaining process, but rather were described by strike leaders as desperate move to force the legislature and the voters to consider the dire situation of the public schools and the hidden costs of education funding cuts, including low pay of teachers. In most of these states the teachers earned less in real dollars than teachers had thirty years before, and less than teachers in neighboring states. There are shortages of qualified teachers in these states, which meant not only that some teachers were teaching subjects or grades for which they were not certified, but also that the striking teachers could not easily be replaced. In some states, the strike persisted after the teachers' union recommended ending it because the teachers did not trust the state to make good on the promises to increase school funding.

Even as strikes declined, other forms of economic protest have grown in significance. Dismayed by weak and slow remedies under the NLRA, as well as by employer noncompliance with minimum wage, workplace safety, and other federal and state protective labor legislation, worker advocates tend to think that appeals to the public to support workers with their wallets in the form of boycotts and other tactics, which may or may not involve picketing, are more effective than strikes or filing legal claims. For example, activists concerned about low wages paid to workers harvesting tomatoes sold to fast food companies did not use strikes to seek wage improvements but instead launched consumer boycotts and coordinated efforts to get businesses that use large quantities of tomatoes to do business only with growers and suppliers that agree to ensure that farmworkers are paid a decent wage. An early phase of this effort, which was launched by the Coalition of Immokalee Workers, pressured Taco Bell by mobilizing students to get universities to remove Taco Bell from college campuses. (The Fair Food Program created by the Coalition of Immokalee Workers and other forms of consumer-focused campaigns will be covered later in this chapter and in detail in Chapter 8.)

In some cases, short strikes have recently played a part in some public- and consumer-oriented campaigns. The Fight for 15 campaign (which was most active 2012–2015) used one-day strikes along with rallies, protests, and social media to raise consumer awareness of poor working conditions in the fast food industry. Although the Fight for 15 campaign originally began by demanding a $15 hourly wage and effective protection for the right to join a union, the campaign's greatest success was in securing the enactment of $15 (or somewhat lower) local minimum wage laws in cities and some states across the country. The fast food strikes were short in part because low-wage workers cannot afford to do without wages for days or weeks on end and in part to deprive businesses of the practical ability to hire permanent replacements. Moreover, when companies illegally fire striking workers, legal remedies are unavailable for undocumented workers both as a matter of law under the Supreme Court's interpretation of the NLRA in *Hoffman Plastics,* and as a matter of practical reality under other laws because filing a charge might trigger an immigration raid. Consumer boycotts and other economic weapons are now seen not as an alternative to enforcement of substantive legal rights but instead as necessary to obtain enforcement.

The rise of brief and targeted walk-outs means that work stoppages today may be more like swarming bees than trench warfare. Charles Heckscher, *Organizations, Movements, and Networks*, 50 N.Y.L. Sch. L. Rev. 313 (2005); John Arquilla & David Ronfeldt, Swarming and the Future of Conflict (2000) http://www.rand.org/pubs/documented_briefings/ DB311.html. Moreover, strikes and grassroots activism are used not merely to resolve bargaining disputes in existing relationships, or to urge an employer to recognize a union, but also to persuade employers to agree to remain neutral in organizing campaigns and to agree to union recognition based on a showing of signed union authorization cards (what is known as "organizing outside the Act"). And as the percentage of the American workforce belonging to unions has steadily declined, the use of economic force by worker groups other than unions became a much more significant part of the legal landscape, prompting a change in strategy by firms and their advocates and by employees and their advocates. Worker centers, which today perform significant legal and political advocacy on low-wage work, use protest and boycotts to publicize employer violations of law and to organize grassroots support for legal change. César F. Rosado Marzán, Worker Centers and the Moral Economy: Disrupting Through Brokerage, Prestige, and Moral Framing, 2017 U. Chi. Legal F. 409; Janice Fine, Worker Centers: Organizing Communities at the Edge of the Dream (Cornell University Press 2006). Worker centers are also covered in detail in Chapter 8.

Strikes and other worker protest, especially among low-wage workers, now tend to be brief, to occur as a mobilizing strategy, political advocacy, and as an improvisational expression of solidarity, rather than as a bargaining tactic. *See* Michael M. Oswalt, *Improvisational Unionism*, 104 Cal. L. Rev. 597 (2016). The goals of this kind of contemporary worker activism often include appeals to state and local governments to enact or enforce laws combatting poor working conditions. The results of these protests have not, as yet, included unionization of workplaces of the activist workers. They have, however, produced changes in state and local law and employer policies regarding minimum wages, schedules, and safety and other protections for workers. *See* Kate Andrias, *The New Labor Law*, 126 Yale L.J. 2, 58 (2016) (describing worker social movements as a new form of unionism that "rejects the old regime's commitment to the employer-employee dyad and to a system of private ordering" in favor of a system addressing "basic standards of employment at the sectoral level and [that] positions unions as social actors empowered to advance the interests of workers generally").

NOTES

1.   If you were a labor activist, how might you challenge the problem of low wages and the evident ability of industries that had long been unionized to cut wages?

2.   If you were counsel to the unions representing Verizon workers, or to unions, worker centers, and other groups helping the tomato workers or fast food workers, what advice might you give about strategies to challenge poor working conditions? How do the nature of the workforce and the nature of the industry affect the legal protections the workers have? What about the New York taxi drivers, who mainly work as independent contractors and therefore have no federal labor law right to unionize? What role might immigration status play in the risks to workers of engaging in high-profile activism or work stoppages?

3.   If you were counsel to the firms, what advice would you give about anticipating activism by employees?

B. CONSTITUTIONAL PROTECTIONS FOR STRIKES AND PROTEST

1. DUE PROCESS PROTECTIONS FOR EMPLOYERS

In the late nineteenth century, state and federal courts, including the United States Supreme Court, understood the federal and many state constitutions to grant protections for businesses against the perceived threat of activism by workers agitating to improve working conditions. Most famously, in *Lochner v. New York,* 198 U.S. 45 (1905), the Supreme Court found that a law regulating working conditions of bakers violated the due process rights of employers and workers to contract upon whatever terms the market would bear. In *Adair v. United States*, 208 U.S. 161 (1908), and *Coppage v. Kansas,* 236 U.S. 1 (1915), the Court declared unconstitutional federal and state laws prohibiting employers from requiring employees not to join unions on the ground that such laws interfered with the constitutional right of freedom of contract protected by the due process clause. In *Truax v. Corrigan*, 257 U.S. 312 (1921), the Court decided that a state law prohibiting state courts from issuing injunctions in labor disputes violated the due process and equal protection clauses of the Fourteenth Amendment. The substantive due process protections for businesses to be free from worker activism did not survive the reorientation of the Supreme Court in 1937 when the Court abandoned the substantive due process and property rights jurisprudence that invalidated economic legislation. With the demise of *Lochner* jurisprudence, the Due Process clause ceased to be a major restriction on federal and state regulation of work relationships. Other provisions of the constitution gained greater significance; in the field of union-management relationships, the First Amendment gained in importance.

2. FIRST AMENDMENT PROTECTIONS FOR WORKERS

A large retailer sells clothes produced in sweatshop conditions. A member of the labor union trying to organize the workers employed by a subcontractor who makes clothes sold by the retailer walks back and forth in front of the store holding up a sign on a stick advising customers of the sweatshop problem and the connection to the store's low prices and urging a boycott of the store. A store employee walks next to her, holding up a sign of identical size urging customers to shop at the store and advertising its low prices. A member of Students Against Sweatshops walks next to both of them with a sign identical to the union picketer's sign.

The unionist's message is an illegal call for a secondary boycott if she has a picket sign and walks back and forth; it is a protected consumer appeal if she stands still and distributes leaflets. The store's message is legal regardless of the size of the sign and the movement of the person carrying it so long as it truthfully states the prices. And the student's behavior (again, regardless of the size of the sign or the patrolling) is almost certainly legal, even if it contains factual inaccuracies, because it is political speech entitled to the highest level of First Amendment protection. *See* James Gray Pope, *The First Amendment, the Thirteenth Amendment, and the Right to Organize in the Twenty-First Century*, 51 Rutgers L. Rev. 941, 950 (1999). To understand why labor union speech receives less First Amendment protection than that of other activists, it is necessary to explain the historical development of the jurisprudence of labor speech.

At the time that federal labor law was developing, there were fewer constitutional protections for speech and assembly than there are today. The First Amendment protections for freedom of speech and assembly were not held to apply to states until 1925 and 1937, respectively. First Amendment protection was not given until the 1960s and 1970s for the full array of speech and expressive conduct that is today constitutionally protected. With no constitutional protection available, prior to the Wagner Act there was no legal right to engage in labor protest, and state courts routinely enjoined it (as federal courts had prior to the enactment of the Norris LaGuardia Act). William E. Forbath, Law and the Shaping of the American Labor Movement (1991); Victoria E. Hattam, Labor Visions and State Power: The Origins of Business Unionism in the United States (1993). During times of upheaval about working conditions, especially the strike wave that followed the lifting of World War II era wage and price controls, courts found labor protest to be especially threatening to public order. For these reasons, as you will see in the cases that follow, the Supreme Court has largely deferred to what it has described as Congress' careful balancing of the competing policies in regulating labor protest. The high water mark for constitutional protection of labor speech was *Thornhill v. Alabama* (1940), excerpted below, but it was soon followed by retrenchment in *Teamsters v. Vogt* (1957), also excerpted below. The statutory restrictions on picketing and boycotts that are contained in section 8(b) apply only to labor organizations and their agents, not to non-labor speakers. These restrictions would likely be deemed unconstitutional if ordinary First Amendment rules for content-based discrimination in speech applied, but the Supreme Court has largely upheld them. As will be seen in the cases that follow, the Court has generally not tried to reconcile its treatment of labor cases with other kinds of free speech cases but has instead emphasized Congress' strong interest in regulating labor speech, and has deemed the comprehensiveness and complexity of legislation to be reasons for the Court to avoid declaring unconstitutional the aspects of it that restrict speech.

Many contemporary protests about working conditions are not conducted exclusively or even primarily by labor unions and their members. The constitutional protection for speech is more robust when the speaker is not a labor union or its agents. The likely explanation for the difference is the time when the issues reached the Supreme Court. Until the early 1960s, the Supreme Court treated civil rights picketing and protest under the same statutory and constitutional rules it applied to labor picketing and protest. Civil rights picketers protesting race discrimination in employment were protected against federal injunctions by the Norris-LaGuardia Act in 1937, just as labor picketers were. *See New Negro Alliance v. Sanitary Grocery,* 303 U.S. 552 (1938). And, later, when the Supreme Court had largely eliminated First Amendment protection for labor protest, the Court upheld a state court injunction against picketing protesting race discrimination in employment. *Hughes v. Superior Court,* 339 U.S. 460 (1950). But then, in 1963, the Court reversed breach of the peace convictions of civil rights protesters who had engaged in peaceful mass picketing, *Edwards v. South Carolina,* 372 U.S. 229 (1963). Thereafter it became increasingly clear that the Supreme Court would give constitutional protection to civil rights picketing that it had long denied to labor picketing. In a series of cases, including *Chicago v. Mosley* (1972) and *NAACP v. Claiborne Hardware* (1982) (both of which are excerpted below), the Supreme Court granted First Amendment protection to civil rights picketing and calls for boycotts over working conditions, including secondary boycotts. The different legal protections given to labor protest as compared to civil rights protest causes confusion today because many contemporary protests about working conditions are not conducted solely by unions. Even when unions are involved, the activists often direct their speech to the public. In assessing the legality of contemporary labor protests, many of which involve civil rights organizations, worker centers, community groups, and religious organizations in addition to or instead of unions, a lawyer needs to be attentive to the different levels of constitutional protection.

a. Picketing

THORNHILL V. ALABAMA
310 U.S. 88 (1940)

JUSTICE MURPHY delivered the opinion of the Court:

Petitioner, Byron Thornhill, was convicted in the Circuit Court of Tuscaloosa County, Alabama, of the violation of § 3448 of the State Code of 1923. [Section 3448 made it a misdemeanor to "go near to or loiter about" or to "picket" "the premises or place of business of any other person, firm, corporation, or association . . . for the purpose, or with the intent of influencing, or inducing other persons not to trade with, buy from, sell to, have business dealings with, or be employed by such persons, firm, corporation, or association." The statute specifically exempted efforts to "solicit trade or business for a competitive business." Thornhill was sentenced to 73 days in prison.]

It appears that petitioner on the morning of his arrest was seen "in company with six or eight other men" "on the picket line" at the plant of the Brown Wood Preserving Company. Some weeks previously a strike order had been issued by a Union, apparently affiliated with the American Federation of Labor, which had as members all but four of the approximately one hundred employees of the plant. Since that time a picket line with two picket posts of six to eight men each had been maintained around the plant twenty-four hours a day.

The Company scheduled a day for the plant to resume operations. One of the witnesses, Clarence Simpson, who was not a member of the Union, on reporting to the plant on the day indicated, was approached by petitioner who told him that "they were on strike and did not want anybody to go up there to work." None of the other employees said anything to Simpson, who testified: "Neither Mr. Thornhill nor any other employee threatened me on the occasion testified to. Mr. Thornhill approached me in a peaceful manner, and did not put me in fear; he did not appear to be mad." "I then turned and went back to the house, and did not go to work." The other witness, J. M. Walden, testified: "At the time Mr. Thornhill and Clarence Simpson were talking to each other, there was no one else present, and I heard no harsh words and saw nothing threatening in the manner of either man." For engaging in some or all of these activities, petitioner was arrested, charged, and convicted as described.

The freedom of speech and of the press, which are secured by the First Amendment against abridgment by the United States, are among the fundamental personal rights and liberties which are secured to all persons by the Fourteenth Amendment against abridgment by a State.

The safeguarding of these rights to the ends that men may speak as they think on matters vital to them and that falsehoods may be exposed through the processes of education and discussion is essential to free government. Those who won our independence had confidence in the power of free and fearless reasoning and communication of ideas to discover and spread political and economic truth. Noxious doctrines in those fields may be refuted and their evil averted by the courageous exercise of the right of free discussion. Abridgment of freedom of speech and of the press, however, impairs those opportunities for public education that are essential to effective exercise of the power of correcting error through the processes of popular government.

Section 3448 has been applied by the state courts so as to prohibit a single individual from walking slowly and peacefully back and forth on the public sidewalk in front of the premises of an employer, without speaking to anyone, carrying a sign or placard on a staff above his head stating only the fact that the employer did not employ union men affiliated with the American Federation of Labor; the purpose of the described activity was concededly to advise customers and prospective customers of the relationship existing between the employer and its employees and thereby to induce such customers not to patronize the employer. The statute as thus authoritatively construed and applied leaves room for no exceptions based upon either the number of persons engaged in the proscribed activity, the peaceful character of their demeanor, the nature of their dispute with an employer, or the restrained character and the accurateness of the terminology used in notifying the public of the facts of the dispute.

The freedom of speech and of the press guaranteed by the Constitution embraces at the least the liberty to discuss publicly and truthfully all matters of public concern without previous restraint or fear of subsequent punishment. The exigencies of the colonial period and the efforts to secure freedom from oppressive administration developed a broadened conception of these liberties as adequate to supply the public need for information and education with respect to the significant issues of the times. Freedom of discussion, if it would fulfill its historic function in this nation, must embrace all issues about which information is needed or appropriate to enable the members of society to cope with the exigencies of their period.

In the circumstances of our times the dissemination of information concerning the facts of a labor dispute must be regarded as within that area of free discussion that is guaranteed by the Constitution. It is recognized now that satisfactory hours and wages and working conditions in industry and a bargaining position which makes these possible have an importance which is not less than the interests of those in the business or industry directly concerned. The health of the present generation and of those as yet unborn may depend on these matters, and the practices in a single factory may have economic repercussions upon a whole region and affect widespread systems of marketing. The merest glance at state and federal legislation on the subject demonstrates the force of the argument that labor relations are not matters of mere local or private concern. Free discussion concerning the conditions in industry and the causes of labor disputes appears to us indispensable to the effective and intelligent use of the processes of popular government to shape the destiny of modern industrial society. The issues raised by regulations, such as are challenged here, infringing upon the right of employees effectively to inform the public of the facts of a labor dispute are part of this larger problem.

The range of activities proscribed by § 3448, whether characterized as picketing or loitering or otherwise, embraces nearly every practicable, effective means whereby those interested—including the employees directly affected—may enlighten the public on the nature and causes of a labor dispute. The safeguarding of these means is essential to the securing of an informed and educated public opinion with respect to a matter which is of public concern. It may be that effective exercise of the means of advancing public knowledge may persuade some of those reached to refrain from entering into advantageous relations with the business establishment which is the scene of the dispute. Every expression of opinion on matters that are important has the potentiality of inducing action in the interests of one rather than another group in society. But the group in power at any moment may not impose penal sanctions on peaceful and truthful discussion of matters of public interest merely on a showing that others may thereby be persuaded to take action inconsistent with its interests.

The State urges that the purpose of the challenged statute is the protection of the community from the violence and breaches of the peace, which, it asserts, are the concomitants of picketing. The power and the duty of the State to take adequate steps to preserve the peace and to protect the privacy, the lives, and the property of its residents cannot be doubted. But no clear and present danger of destruction of life or property, or invasion of the right of privacy, or breach of the peace can be thought to be inherent in the activities of every person who approaches the premises of an employer and publicizes the facts of a labor dispute involving the latter. We are not now concerned with picketing *en masse* or otherwise conducted which might occasion such imminent and aggravated danger to these interests as to justify a statute narrowly drawn to cover the precise situation giving rise to the danger.

NOTES

1.   *Is picketing speech?* In what respect is picketing "speech"? In what respect is it not? Under what circumstances is conduct other than speech sufficiently expressive that it should be treated as speech? Consider hand gestures, wearing symbolic clothing or jewelry, or engaging in behavior such as ritual burning of objects such as draft cards and crosses.

2.   *Should picketing be protected under the First Amendment?* Why should picketing be treated as speech protected by the First Amendment? Why

should it not be protected? How should courts balance workers' interests in conveying their message against the harms that labor protest can cause to employers business interests? What are the interests of the government in regulating picketing?

3. *The First Amendment in action.* Consider the problem involving Verizon or the account of the Fight for 15 campaign that began this chapter. How would the strategy of the unions or the employers be affected if legislation and the constitution did not protect the right of striking workers to picket? What are the arguments for and against allowing employers to call upon the police to help customers and workers to ignore picketing by striking workers and their allies?

INTERNATIONAL BROTHERHOOD OF TEAMSTERS V. VOGT
354 U.S. 284 (1957)

JUSTICE FRANKFURTER delivered the opinion of the Court:

Respondent owns and operates a gravel pit in Oconomowoc, Wisconsin, where it employs 15 to 20 men. Petitioner unions sought unsuccessfully to induce some of respondent's employees to join the unions and commenced to picket the entrance to respondent's place of business with signs reading, "The men on this job are not 100% affiliated with the A. F. L." In consequence, drivers of several trucking companies refused to deliver and haul goods to and from respondent's plant, causing substantial damage to respondent. Respondent thereupon sought an injunction to restrain the picketing.

The trial court held that by virtue of Wis. Stat. § 103.535, prohibiting picketing in the absence of a "labor dispute," the petitioners must be enjoined from maintaining any pickets near respondent's place of business, from displaying at any place near respondent's place of business signs indicating that there was a labor dispute between respondent and its employees or between respondent and any of the petitioners, and from inducing others to decline to transport goods to and from respondent's business establishment.

It is not too surprising that the response of States—legislative and judicial—to use of the injunction in labor controversies should have given rise to a series of adjudications in this Court relating to the limitations on state action contained in the provisions of the Due Process Clause of the Fourteenth Amendment. It is also not too surprising that examination of these adjudications should disclose an evolving, not a static, course of decision.

The series begins with *Truax v. Corrigan,* 257 U.S. 312 (1921), in which a closely divided Court found it to be violative of the Equal Protection Clause—not of the Due Process Clause—for a State to deny use of the injunction in the special class of cases arising out of labor conflicts. The considerations that underlay that case soon had to yield, through legislation and later through litigation, to the persuasiveness of undermining facts. Thus, to remedy the abusive use of the injunction in the federal courts (*see* Frankfurter & Greene, The Labor Injunction), the Norris-LaGuardia Act, withdrew, subject to qualifications, jurisdiction from the federal courts to issue injunctions in labor disputes to prohibit certain acts. Its example was widely followed by state enactments.

[Later], the Court made sweeping pronouncements about the right to picket in holding unconstitutional a statute that had been applied to ban all picketing, with "no exceptions based upon either the number of persons engaged in the proscribed activity, the peaceful character of their demeanor, the nature of their dispute with an employer, or the restrained character and the accurateness of the terminology used in notifying the public of the facts of the dispute." *Thornhill v. Alabama.* As the statute dealt at large with all picketing, so the Court broadly assimilated peaceful picketing in general to freedom of speech, and as such protected against abridgment by the Fourteenth Amendment.

These principles were applied by the Court in *A. F. of L.* v. *Swing,* 312 U.S. 321 (1941), to hold unconstitutional an injunction against peaceful picketing, based on a State's common-law policy against picketing when there was no immediate dispute between employer and employee. On the same day, however, the Court upheld a generalized injunction against picketing where there had been violence because "it could justifiably be concluded that the momentum of fear generated by past violence would survive even though future picketing might be wholly peaceful." *Milk Wagon Drivers Union v. Meadowmoor Dairies,* 312 U.S. 287, 294 (1941).

Soon, however, the Court came to realize that the broad pronouncements, but not the specific holding, of *Thornhill* had to yield to the impact of facts unforeseen, or at least not sufficiently appreciated. Cases reached the Court in which a State had designed a remedy to meet a specific situation or to accomplish a particular social policy. These cases made manifest that picketing, even though "peaceful," involved more than just communication of ideas and could not be immune from all state regulation. "Picketing by an organized group is more than free speech, since it involves patrol of a particular locality and since the very presence of a picket line may induce action of one kind or another, quite irrespective of the nature of the ideas which are being disseminated." *Bakery Drivers Local v. Wohl,* 315 U.S. 769, 776 (1942) (concurring opinion); *see Carpenters Union v. Ritter's Cafe,* 315 U.S. 722, 725–728 (1942).

These latter two cases required the Court to review a choice made by two States between the competing interests of unions, employers, their employees, and the public at large. In the *Ritter's Cafe* case, Texas had enjoined as a violation of its antitrust law picketing of a restaurant by unions to bring pressure on its owner with respect to the use of nonunion labor by a contractor of the restaurant owner in the construction of a building having nothing to do with the restaurant. The Court held that Texas could, consistent with the Fourteenth Amendment, insulate from the dispute a neutral establishment that industrially had no connection with it. This type of picketing certainly involved little, if any, "communication."

The implied reassessments of the broad language of the *Thornhill* case were finally generalized in a series of cases sustaining injunctions against peaceful picketing, even when arising in the course of a labor controversy, when such picketing was counter to valid state policy in a domain open to state regulation. The decisive reconsideration came in *Giboney v. Empire Storage & Ice Co.,* 336 U.S. 490 (1949). A union, seeking to organize peddlers, picketed a wholesale dealer to induce it to refrain from selling to nonunion peddlers. The state courts, finding that such an agreement would constitute a conspiracy in restraint of trade in violation of the state antitrust laws, enjoined the picketing. This Court affirmed unanimously.

The Court concluded that it was "clear that appellants were doing more than exercising a right of free speech or press. . . . They were exercising their economic power together with that of their allies to compel Empire to abide by union rather than by state regulation of trade." The following Term, [i]n *Hughes v. Superior Court*, 339 U.S. 460 (1950), the Court held that the Fourteenth Amendment did not bar use of the injunction to prohibit picketing of a place of business solely to secure compliance with a demand that its employees be hired in percentage to the racial origin of its customers. "We cannot construe the Due Process Clause as precluding California from securing respect for its policy against involuntary employment on racial lines by prohibiting systematic picketing that would subvert such policy." The Court also found it immaterial that the state policy had been expressed by the judiciary rather than by the legislature.

The series of cases following *Thornhill* and *Swing* demonstrate that the policy of Wisconsin enforced by the prohibition of this picketing is a valid one. In this case, the circumstances set forth in the opinion of the Wisconsin Supreme Court afford a rational basis for the inference it drew concerning the purpose of the picketing. No question was raised here concerning the breadth of the injunction, but of course its terms must be read in the light of the opinion of the Wisconsin Supreme Court, which justified it on the ground that the picketing was for the purpose of coercing the employer to coerce his employees.

JUSTICE DOUGLAS, with whom the CHIEF JUSTICE and JUSTICE BLACK concur, dissenting:

The Court has now come full circle. In *Thornhill v. Alabama,* we struck down a state ban on picketing on the ground that "the dissemination of information concerning the facts of a labor dispute must be regarded as within that area of free discussion that is guaranteed by the Constitution."

Less than one year later, we held that the First Amendment protected organizational picketing on a factual record which cannot be distinguished from the one now before us. *A. F. of L.* v. *Swing*. Of course, we have always recognized that picketing has aspects which make it more than speech. *Bakery Drivers Local v. Wohl*. That difference underlies our decision in *Giboney v. Empire Storage & Ice Co.* There, picketing was an essential part of "a single and integrated course of conduct, which was in violation of Missouri's valid law." We emphasized that "there was clear danger, imminent and immediate, that unless restrained, appellants would succeed in making [the state] policy a dead letter. . . ." Speech there was enjoined because it was an inseparable part of conduct which the State constitutionally could and did regulate.

But where, as here, there is no rioting, no mass picketing, no violence, no disorder, no fisticuffs, no coercion—indeed nothing but speech—the principles announced in *Thornhill* and *Swing* should give the advocacy of one side of a dispute First Amendment protection.

NOTES

1. *Why retreat from* Thornhill? Justice Frankfurter refers to "facts unforeseen, or at least not sufficiently appreciated" as a basis for distinguishing *Thornhill*. What facts might those be?

2. *Signal picketing.* The opinion articulates the notion that picketing is not just speech but instead a signal: "Picketing by an organized group is more than free speech, since it involves patrol of a particular locality and since the very presence of a picket line may induce action of one kind or another, quite irrespective of the nature of the ideas which are being disseminated." This is the basis for the Court's refusal to give labor picketing the strict scrutiny accorded under the First Amendment to other forms of speech, including other forms of picketing. Is patrolling a form of conduct that communicates like speech? Does the fact that labor picketing is a "signal" mean it is not speech? At whom is the signal directed? How does picketing induce action "irrespective of the ideas" that it communicates?

3. *Peddlers and the gig-economy.* In *Giboney v. Empire Storage & Ice Co.*, 336 U.S. 490 (1949), discussed in *Vogt*, workers who had been employed as delivery drivers were outsourced because their employers decided that it would be cheaper to shift to the drivers the cost of maintaining the delivery trucks and the risks of slack demand for their services. The employee drivers in *Giboney* and similar cases thus became independent contractors or sole proprietors of small businesses who delivered things like bakery products and ice from producers to restaurants and grocery stores. When they unionized and organized picket lines and boycotts to persuade businesses to pay the union wage and not to deal with low-wage non-union drivers, the companies argued that their picketing and boycotts were not legitimate labor protest but were instead conspiracies in restraint of trade in violation of state antitrust law. The Supreme Court agreed, and upheld a state court injunction against the

picketing and boycott. The same arguments are made today about efforts of app-based drivers for hire (Uber and Lyft) or delivery drivers (Postmates, UberEats) to raise their pay through concerted action. If independent contractor drivers called for a boycott, how should courts distinguish between constitutionally-protected labor protest and constitutionally-proscribable regulation of anti-competitive activity by small businesses? *See* Jeffrey M. Hirsch & Joseph A. Seiner, *A Modern Union for the Modern Economy*, 86 Fordham L. Rev. 1727 (2018); V.B. Dubal, *The Drive to Precarity: A Political History of Work, Regulation, & Labor Advocacy in San Francisco's Taxi & Uber Economies*, 38 Berk. J. Emp. & Lab. L. 73 (2017).

* * *

Not long after Congress (in the Taft-Hartley Act in 1947 and the Landrum-Griffin Act in 1959) began to sharply limit labor picketing and the Supreme Court retreated from *Thornhill* and upheld both federal and state laws limiting labor picketing, civil rights organizations began to use picketing, boycotts, sit-ins, marches, and other forms of protest to challenge racism in employment and places of public accommodation. The Court's analysis of civil rights protest differed markedly from its analysis of labor protest, even when both of them focused on employers.

In *Police Department of the City of Chicago v. Mosley*, 408 U.S. 92 (1972), the Supreme Court invalidated a city ordinance that prohibited picketing within 150 feet of a school during school hours. Earl Mosley had peacefully picketed the school with a sign that read "Jones High School practices black discrimination." The Court found the ordinance to violate the equal protection clause of the Fourteenth Amendment because it contained an exception allowing picketing "of any school involved in a labor dispute." The Court explained:

> The central problem with Chicago's ordinance is that it describes permissible picketing in terms of its subject matter. But, above all else, the First Amendment means that government has no power to restrict expression because of its message, its ideas, its subject matter, or its content. To permit the continued building of our politics and culture, and to assure self-fulfillment for each individual, our people are guaranteed the right to express any thought, free from government censorship. The essence of this forbidden censorship is content control. Any restriction on expressive activity because of its content would completely undercut the profound national commitment to the principle that debate on public issues should be uninhibited, robust, and wide-open. This is not to say that all picketing must always be allowed. We have continually recognized that reasonable time, place and manner regulations of picketing may be necessary to further significant governmental interests. Similarly, under an equal protection analysis, there may be sufficient regulatory interests

justifying selective exclusions or distinctions among pickets. Conflicting demands on the same place may compel the State to make choices among potential users and uses. And the State may have a legitimate interest in prohibiting some picketing to protect public order. But these justifications for selective exclusions from a public forum must be carefully scrutinized. Because picketing plainly involves expressive conduct within the protection of the First Amendment, *see, e. g., Thornhill v. Alabama,* discriminations among pickets must be tailored to serve a substantial governmental interest.

The Court did not find a substantial government interest to be established based on the city's argument that non-labor picketing is more prone to produce violence than labor picketing. It said that predictions about imminent disruption from picketing should be made "on an individualized basis, not by means of broad classifications, especially those based on subject matter."

NOTES

1.   *Political picketing and labor picketing.* What arguments can you make for giving Mosley's picketing more or less constitutional protection than that of the workers in *Thornhill* or in *Vogt*? Should you emphasize the content of the speech? The identity of the speaker? The likely impact of the speech on its target audience? In what respects is the picketing in *Vogt* more of a signal, and therefore potentially more harmful, than the picketing in *Mosley*?

2.   *Federal preemption.* As you will see, cases subsequent to *Vogt* have held that federal regulation of labor picketing preempts state law, so the Wisconsin law at issue in *Vogt* would now be preempted insofar as it applies to workers covered by the NLRA. Picketing designed to persuade an employer to recognize a union or to persuade employees to join a union is now covered by § 8(b)(7)(C), covered in Chapter 4.

3.   *First Amendment protection for labor picketing.* Under modern First Amendment jurisprudence, although some laws restricting picketing would be upheld as reasonable time, place, and manner restrictions, laws that prohibit labor picketing would run afoul of many rules: they are content-based and often discriminate based on viewpoint (by proscribing speech that seeks to deter people from dealing with certain businesses but not speech that encourages it). In *Reed v. Town of Gilbert,* 135 S. Ct. 2218 (2015), the Supreme Court struck down a city ordinance that limited the use of outdoor signs advertising temporary events. The unanimous Court stressed that the ordinance was unconstitutional because it discriminated among signs based on their content and was not narrowly tailored to serve a compelling governmental interest. Can the NLRA's restrictions on picketing in sections 8(b)(4) and 8(b)(7) (covered in detail later in this chapter) be upheld in light of *Reed*? *See* Catherine L. Fisk, *A Progressive Labor Vision of the First Amendment,* 118 Columbia L. Rev. ___ (2018) (arguing that, under recent Supreme Court

precedent, labor picketing and secondary boycotts are speech protected by the First Amendment and that labor law prohibitions on them are not narrowly tailored to serve a compelling government interest); *but see* NLRB v. Int'l Ass'n of Bridge and Ironworkers, Local 443, 891 F.3d 1182 (9th Cir. 2018) (per curiam) (summarily rejecting First Amendment challenge to an injunction against secondary picketing, holding that recent cases do not undermine earlier Supreme Court authority upholding section 8(b)(4)).

4.　*More First Amendment developments.* NLRA restrictions on picketing are also quite vague and overbroad. In *McCullen v. Coakley*, 134 S. Ct. 2518 (2014), the Supreme Court struck down a state statute which made it a crime to knowingly stand outside clinics that provide abortion services; the statute's aim was to impose a buffer zone to protect patients and staff from harassment. The majority found that although the statute was not content-based, as in *Mosley*, it was not narrowly tailored because it significantly restricted sidewalk anti-abortion speech more than necessary to protect the safety of patients, and protecting them from hearing unwelcome speech was not a legitimate government interest. In *Schenck v. Pro-Choice Network*, 519 U.S. 357 (1997), the Supreme Court invalidated a state law providing for a floating buffer zone restricting speech around family planning clinics because the zone where picketing was prohibited was broader than necessary to protect the right to enter the clinic. As you consider the contours of the NLRA's restrictions on picketing, consider whether *Reed, McCullen,* and *Schenck* suggest that if the NLRA were challenged today its speech restrictions on both labor and management speech might be unconstitutionally overbroad. *See* Catherine L. Fisk & Jessica Rutter, *Labor Protest Under the New First Amendment*, 36 Berkeley J. Lab & Emp. L. 277 (2015). What are the arguments for or against upholding the speech restrictions notwithstanding these problems?

5.　*Identifying labor picketing.* The relaxed First Amendment protection for labor picketing requires analysis of two things: What is *labor* picketing? What is *picketing*? What, besides walking around carrying a sign, is comparable to picketing? Can any of the following be constitutionally banned if they are engaged in on a public walkway adjacent to a large retail business? Later in this chapter we will consider whether and when the NLRA prohibits these forms of speech and conduct; for now focus on whether the NLRA can constitutionally prohibit them.

　　a.　**Leaflets.** Union members distribute leaflets protesting the employer's unfair labor practices. *See Edward J. DeBartolo Corp. v. Fla. Gulf Coast Bldg. & Constr. Trades Council*, 485 U.S. 568 (1988) (suggesting that leaflets are constitutionally protected speech), excerpted below at p. 851.

　　b.　**Banners.** Union members hold up banners calling the business exploitative without patrolling. *See Overstreet v. United Bhd. of Carpenters*, 409 F.3d 1199 (9th Cir. 2004) (signs and banner are protected speech) (see p. 855); *United Bhd. of Carpenters, Local Union No. 1506 (Eliason & Knuth)*, 355 NLRB No. 159 (2010) (display of banner is not picketing or coercive) (see p. 854). *But* *see Verizon New England, Inc.*, 362 NLRB no. 24 (2015) (informational signs placed inside employee vehicles on company property constituted picketing).

c. **The Rat.** The colloquial term "rat" among unionized construction workers refers to a nonunion employer or nonunion workers. In labor disputes all over the country, particularly those involving the construction trades, labor activists have begun using pictures of rats, people dressed up in rat costumes, inflatable balloons in the shape of rats, and other references to rats. Courts reached conflicting results on which uses of rat language, costumes, and images were permissible, but the NLRB concluded that rat displays are not picketing or coercive and therefore do not violate the NLRA. *Sheet Metal Workers Int'l Ass'n, Local Union 15,* 356 NLRB No. 162 (2011). *See Tucker v. Fairfield*, 398 F.3d 457 (6th Cir. 2005) (12-foot tall rat balloon was protected speech and could not be enjoined under a city ordinance that prohibits establishing a "structure" on a public right of way); *San Antonio Comm. Hosp. v. S. Calif. Dist of Carpenters*, 125 F.3d 1230 (9th Cir. 1997) (display of sign at a hospital saying "This building is full of rats" and explaining in smaller letters the colloquial meaning of "rat" was defamatory and therefore not protected speech). Should all rat references be constitutional? Would it matter whether the rat display is a construction site or a hospital? Should it matter whether the rat appears menacing or humorous?

6. *Offensive speech.* Speech on a picket line often gets heated, as picketers call those who cross "scabs" and accuse the employer of "exploitation" and worse. Although the NLRB and courts have generally tolerated name-calling and harsh language on the picket line, there are some limits. For example, should racist or sexist epithets directed at those crossing the picket line be allowed? What if an employee crossing the picket line every day filed a sexual harassment suit against the union on the grounds that the daily barrage of comments constituted severe and pervasive harassment on the basis of sex? Should ordinary rules of defamation ("there are rats in this restaurant") or racial or sexual harassment apply in the context of picket line speech? If not, what other rule should apply? *See Cooper Tire & Rubber Co. v. NLRB*, 866 F.3d 885 (8th Cir. 2017) (ordering reinstatement of picketing employee who made a comment about watermelon and fried chicken as a van carrying African American replacement workers crossed the picket line); *NMC Finishing v. NLRB*, 101 F.3d 528 (8th Cir. 1996) (upholding firing of picketing employee who followed individual female replacement worker with a sign accusing her, by name, of performing fellatio).

Should offensive or arguably threatening comments made on social media during the course of a strike be deemed unprotected by section 7, or an unfair labor practice under section 8(b), if the same speech would be treated differently if uttered on a picket line? In *Weigand v. NLRB*, 783 F.3d 889 (D.C.

Cir. 2015), the court upheld the NLRB's determination that Facebook comments made during a strike were not a ULP because the Facebook page was accessible only by union members and were not made by a union agent. Why should it matter whether the person who posts on social media is a union agent? Should it matter whether the union disavowed the comments?

7. *The role of state tort and criminal law.* The tort and criminal law of many states prohibits workers from using violence or intimidation in conducting protests, including in picketing. Among the prohibited conduct is actual or threatened physical violence or property damage, mass protests, trespass, and blocking ingress or egress from private property. Such conduct is prohibited under state law even if it is part of otherwise permissible picketing. The contours of state law, particularly the procedural requirements for obtaining injunctions or arrests for illegal picketing, are enormously significant in actual labor protest. *See* Christopher L. Erickson, Catherine L. Fisk, Ruth Milkman, Daniel J.B. Mitchell & Kent Wong, *Justice for Janitors in Los Angeles: Lessons from Three Rounds of Negotiations*, 40 British J. Indus. Rel. 543 (2002).

In *Fechko Excavating, Inc. v. Ohio Valley & S.*, 2009 Ohio 5155, 2009 WL 3119723 (2009) an employer sued employees for defamation for accusing the employer of cheating on stone bedding specifications and bringing down the industry standards. The appellate court affirmed the dismissal of Fechko's defamation claims because the union made the heated statements in the context of a labor dispute in order to inform the public and local government members that the company was a non-union employer. In *Overhill Farms, Inc. v. Lopez*, 190 Cal. App. 4th 1248, 1252 (2010), an employer brought a defamation action against employees who accused the company of harboring racist opinions and engaging in mass layoffs for racist and ageist reasons. The appellate court agreed that Overhill had borne its burden of showing a probability of winning on defamation and held that, unlike a general statement accusing a person of racism, a charge of racially motivated employment termination was a provably false fact.

8. *New First Amendment challenges to differential treatment of labor picketing.* The contrast between the lax First Amendment protection for labor protest and the higher level of protection for civil rights and political protest has recently become controversial. Because of the extensive federal regulation of labor picketing and the lax constitutional protection for it, many state statutes regulating picketing explicitly exempt labor picketing in order to avoid federal preemption challenges. *Chicago v. Mosley* is an example of such a law. In a few recent cases, state courts have held that the differential treatment of labor picketing in state law violates the First Amendment, relying on *Mosley*. In *State v. Borowski*, 231 Ore. App. 511, 516 (2009), a court invalidated a state's standards for agricultural protests because the statute exempted from various criminal penalties only labor protesters who engaged in picketing. In another case the California Supreme Court rejected the argument that state laws regulating the issuance of injunctions in labor disputes (so-called "little Norris-LaGuardia Acts") are unconstitutional because they create a different rule for

injunctions in labor disputes than in other disputes. *Ralphs Grocery Co. v. United Food and Commercial Workers Union Local 8*, 290 P.3d 1116 (Cal. 2012).

b. Boycotts

NATIONAL ASSOCIATION FOR THE ADVANCEMENT OF COLORED PEOPLE V. CLAIBORNE HARDWARE CO.
458 U.S. 886 (1982)

JUSTICE STEVENS delivered the opinion of the Court:

In March 1966, black citizens of Port Gibson, Miss., and other areas of Claiborne County presented white elected officials with a list of particularized demands for racial equality and integration. The complainants did not receive a satisfactory response and, at a local National Association for the Advancement of Colored People (NAACP) meeting at the First Baptist Church, several hundred black persons voted to place a boycott on white merchants in the area. On October 31, 1969, several of the merchants filed suit in state court to recover losses caused by the boycott and to enjoin future boycott activity.

[C]ertain practices generally used to encourage support for the boycott were uniformly peaceful and orderly. The few marches associated with the boycott were carefully controlled by black leaders. Pickets used to advertise the boycott were often small children. The police made no arrests—and no complaints are recorded—in connection with the picketing and occasional demonstrations supporting the boycott.

One form of "discipline" of black persons who violated the boycott appears to have been employed with some regularity. Individuals stood outside of boycotted stores and identified those who traded with the merchants. Some of these "store watchers" were members of a group known as the "Black Hats" or the "Deacons." The names of persons who violated the boycott were read at meetings of the Claiborne County NAACP and published in a mimeographed paper entitled the "Black Times." As stated by the chancellor, those persons "were branded as traitors to the black cause, called demeaning names, and socially ostracized for merely trading with whites."

Each of these elements of the boycott is a form of speech or conduct that is ordinarily entitled to protection under the First and Fourteenth Amendments. The black citizens named as defendants in this action banded together and collectively expressed their dissatisfaction with a social structure that had denied them rights to equal treatment and respect. There are, of course, some activities, legal if engaged in by one, yet illegal if performed in concert with others, but political expression is not one of them.

Of course, the petitioners in this case did more than assemble peaceably and discuss among themselves their grievances against governmental and business policy. Other elements of the boycott, however, also involved activities ordinarily safeguarded by the First Amendment.

Speech itself also was used to further the aims of the boycott. Nonparticipants repeatedly were urged to join the common cause, both through public address and through personal solicitation. These elements of the boycott involve speech in its most direct form. In addition, names of boycott violators were read aloud at meetings at the First Baptist Church and published in a local black newspaper. Petitioners admittedly sought to persuade others to join the boycott through social pressure and the "threat" of social ostracism. Speech does not lose its protected character, however, simply because it may embarrass others or coerce them into action.

The claim that the expressions were intended to exercise a coercive impact on respondent does not remove them from the reach of the First Amendment. Petitioners plainly intended to influence respondent's conduct by their activities; this is not fundamentally different from the function of a newspaper. Petitioners were engaged openly and vigorously in making the public aware of respondent's real estate practices. Those practices were offensive to them, as the views and practices of petitioners are no doubt offensive to others. But so long as the means are peaceful, the communication need not meet standards of acceptability.

The presence of protected activity, however, does not end the relevant constitutional inquiry. Governmental regulation that has an incidental effect on First Amendment freedoms may be justified in certain narrowly defined instances. A nonviolent and totally voluntary boycott may have a disruptive effect on local economic conditions. This Court has recognized the strong governmental interest in certain forms of economic regulation, even though such regulation may have an incidental effect on rights of speech and association. The right of business entities to "associate" to suppress competition may be curtailed. Unfair trade practices may be restricted. Secondary boycotts and picketing by labor unions may be prohibited, as part of "Congress' striking of the delicate balance between union freedom of expression and the ability of neutral employers, employees, and consumers to remain free from coerced participation in industrial strife."

It is not disputed that a major purpose of the boycott in this case was to influence governmental action. [T]he petitioners certainly foresaw—and directly intended—that the merchants would sustain economic injury as a result of their campaign. Unlike [boycotts that the Supreme Court had previously held to violate federal antitrust law], however, the purpose of petitioners' campaign was not to destroy legitimate competition. Petitioners sought to vindicate rights of equality and of freedom that lie at the heart of the Fourteenth Amendment itself. The right of the States to regulate economic activity could not justify a complete prohibition against a nonviolent, politically motivated boycott designed to force governmental and economic change and to effectuate rights guaranteed by the Constitution itself.

The First Amendment does not protect violence. Although the extent and significance of the violence in this case are vigorously disputed by the parties, there is no question that acts of violence occurred. No federal rule of law restricts a State from imposing tort liability for business losses that are caused by violence and by threats of violence. When such conduct occurs in the context of constitutionally protected activity, however, precision of regulation is demanded.

Respondents argue that liability may be imposed on individuals who were either "store watchers" or members of the "Black Hats." There is nothing unlawful in standing outside a store and recording names. Similarly, there is nothing unlawful in wearing black hats, although such apparel may cause apprehension in others. [M]ere association with either group—absent a specific intent to further an unlawful aim embraced by that group—is an insufficient predicate for liability. At the same time, the evidence does support the conclusion that some members of each of these groups engaged in violence or threats of violence. Unquestionably, these individuals may be held responsible for the injuries that they caused; a judgment tailored to the consequences of their unlawful conduct may be sustained.

It is clear that "fighting words"—those that provoke immediate violence—are not protected by the First Amendment. *Chaplinsky v. N. H.* Similarly, words that create an immediate panic are not entitled to constitutional protection. *Schenck v. U.S.* This Court has made clear, however, that mere *advocacy* of the use of force or violence does not remove speech from the protection of the First Amendment. In *Brandenburg v. Ohio,* we reversed the conviction of a Ku Klux Klan leader for threatening "revengeance" if the "suppression" of the white race continued; we relied on "the principle that the constitutional guarantees of free speech and free press do not permit a State to forbid or proscribe advocacy of the use of force or of law violation except where such advocacy is directed to inciting or producing imminent lawless action and is likely to incite or produce such action."

[The Court then considered whether the NAACP could be held liable for acts of violence and vandalism based on speeches given at NAACP meetings by Charles Evers.] The emotionally charged rhetoric of Charles Evers' speeches did not transcend the bounds of protected speech set forth in *Brandenburg.* The lengthy addresses generally contained an impassioned plea for black citizens to unify, to support and respect each other, and to realize the political and economic power available to them. In the course of those pleas, strong language was used. If that language had been followed by acts of violence, a substantial question would be presented whether Evers could be held liable for the consequences of that unlawful conduct. In this case, however the acts of violence identified in 1966 occurred weeks or months after the April 1, 1966, speech; the chancellor made no finding of any violence after the challenged 1966 speech. Strong and effective extemporaneous rhetoric cannot be nicely channeled in purely dulcet phrases. An advocate must be free to stimulate his audience with spontaneous and emotional appeals for unity and action in a common cause. When such appeals do not incite lawless action, they must be regarded as protected speech. To rule otherwise would ignore the "profound national commitment" that "debate on public issues should be uninhibited, robust, and wide-open." *N.Y. Times v. Sullivan.*

To impose liability [upon the NAACP] without a finding that the NAACP authorized—either actually or apparently—or ratified unlawful conduct would impermissibly burden the rights of political association that are protected by the First Amendment.

NOTES

1. *Is more speech the remedy for harmful speech?* It is often said the First Amendment protects speech because the best remedy for allegedly harmful speech is more speech. Would more speech remedy the harm caused by the NAACP boycotts?

2. *Boycott as a signal?* Did the speech or conduct of the NAACP and the store watchers have a signaling effect? Do you suppose the effect was comparable to the signaling effect of the picket line in *Vogt* or the picketer in *Mosley?*

3. *The practical significance of organizational liability.* Why might those harmed by the NAACP boycott want to hold the NAACP liable? What are the advantages and disadvantages of holding an organization liable for harms caused by its members?

4. *Authorization of violence.* The Court suggests in the final paragraph that the NAACP could be held liable if it "actually or apparently" authorized the violence. How would you prove that?

5. *Using RICO to stop labor protests.* A novel litigation strategy has emerged in which employers that are targets of union publicity campaigns sue unions, individual union members, and members of community and religious groups allied with unions, under the federal Racketeer Influenced and Corrupt Organizations Act (RICO), 18 U.S.C. § 1962, which prohibits extortion. RICO was originally intended to create federal authority to prosecute the Mafia by criminalizing conduct—including extortion, bribery, and certain types of fraud—that were common Mafia tactics. RICO also includes civil penalties for certain conduct, thus enabling private persons injured by the prohibited conduct to sue for damages. The breadth and vagueness of the civil and criminal provisions of RICO have spawned creative efforts to apply RICO to

actors other than those having any connection to the Mafia. Controversy has arisen about civil RICO suits in which employers sue workers and unions on the theory that the workers' publicity campaign against the employers' labor, safety, and environmental record—which takes the form of picketing company premises and officials, lobbying local governments, calling for consumer boycotts, conducting community meetings, and issuing press releases—is an effort to extort voluntary recognition of the union from the company by scaring the company's customers. Some courts have held that RICO may not be used to challenge comprehensive campaigns or ordinary union organizing. *See, e.g., Cook-Illinois Corp. v. Teamsters' Local 777*, 2012 WL 1655976 (N.D. Ill., May 2012); *Cintas Corp. v. Unite Here*, 601 F. Supp. 2d 571 (S.D.N.Y.), aff'd, 355 F. App'x 508 (2d Cir. 2009); *Wackenhut Corp. v. SEIU*, 593 F. Supp. 2d 1289 (S.D. Fla. 2009). At least one other court has suggested that some forms of employee activity may be extortion within the meaning of RICO. *See, e.g., Smithfield Foods, Inc. v. Commercial Workers Int'l*, 593 F. Supp. 2d 840 (E.D. Va. 2008) (denying union's motion to dismiss RICO claims); Adam Liptak, *A Corporate View of Mafia Tactics: Protesting, Lobbying, and Citing Upton Sinclair*, N.Y. Times (Feb. 5, 2008). *See generally* James J. Brudney, *Collateral Conflict: Employer Claims of RICO Extortion Against Union Comprehensive Campaigns*, 83 S. Cal. L. Rev. 731 (2010).

What tactical advantages does a RICO suit offer to a firm that is the target of a union campaign? (Consider the cost and burden of litigation.) Should the union lawyers defend on the grounds that the conduct is protected by the First Amendment or not covered at all by RICO?

INTERNATIONAL LONGSHOREMEN'S ASSOCIATION V. ALLIED INTERNATIONAL, INC.

456 U.S. 212 (1982)

JUSTICE POWELL delivered the opinion of the Court:

On January 9, 1980, Thomas Gleason, president of the International Longshoremen's Association (ILA), ordered ILA members to stop handling cargoes arriving from or destined for the Soviet Union. Gleason took this action to protest the Russian invasion of Afghanistan. In obedience to the order, longshoremen up and down the east and gulf coasts refused to service ships carrying Russian cargoes.

Respondent Allied International, Inc. (Allied), is an American company that imports Russian wood products for resale in the United States. Allied contracts with Waterman Steamship Lines (Waterman), an American corporation operating ships of United States registry, for shipment of the wood from Leningrad to ports on the east and gulf coasts of the United States. Waterman, in turn, employs the stevedoring company of John T. Clark & Son of Boston, Inc. (Clark), to unload its ships docking in Boston. Under the terms of the collective-bargaining agreement between ILA Local 799 and the Boston Shipping Association, of which Clark is a member, Clark obtains its longshoring employees through the union hiring hall.

As a result of the boycott, Allied's shipments were disrupted completely. Ultimately, Allied was forced to renegotiate its Russian contracts, substantially reducing its purchases and jeopardizing its ability to supply its own customers.

The secondary boycott provisions in § 8(b)(4)(B) prohibit a union from inducing employees to refuse to handle goods with the object of forcing any person to cease doing business with any other person. By its terms the statutory prohibition applies to the undisputed facts of this case. The ILA has no dispute with Allied, Waterman, or Clark. It does not seek any labor objective from these employers. Its sole complaint is with the foreign and military policy of the Soviet Union. As understandable and even commendable as the ILA's ultimate objectives may be, the certain effect of its action is to impose a heavy burden on neutral employers. And it is just such a burden, as well as widening of industrial strife, that the secondary boycott provisions were designed to prevent.

Nor can it be argued that the ILA's action was outside of the prohibition on secondary boycotts because its object was not to halt business between Allied, Clark, and Waterman with respect to Russian goods, but simply to free ILA members from the morally repugnant duty of handling Russian goods. Such an argument misses the point. Undoubtedly many secondary boycotts have the object of freeing employees from handling goods from an objectionable source. Nonetheless, when a purely secondary boycott "reasonably can be expected to threaten neutral parties with ruin or substantial loss," *NLRB v. Retail Store Employees*, 447 U.S. 607, 614 (1980), the pressure on secondary parties must be viewed as at least one of the objects of the boycott or the statutory prohibition would be rendered meaningless. The union must take responsibility for the "foreseeable consequences" of its conduct. Here the union was fully aware of the losses it was inflicting upon Allied. It is undisputed that Allied officials endeavored to persuade ILA leaders to allow it to fulfill its Russian contracts. On the basis of the record before it, the Court of Appeals correctly concluded that Allied had alleged a violation of § 8(b)(4).

Neither is it a defense to the application of § 8(b)(4) that the reason for the ILA boycott was not a labor dispute with a primary employer but a political dispute with a foreign nation. Section 8(b)(4) contains no such limitation. The prohibition was drafted broadly to protect neutral parties, "the helpless victims of quarrels that do not concern them at all." H. R. Rep. No. 245, 23 (1947). Despite criticism from President Truman as well as from some legislators that the secondary boycott provision was too sweeping, the Congress refused to narrow its scope.

We would create a large and undefinable exception to the statute if we accepted the argument that "political" boycotts are exempt from the secondary boycott provision. The distinction between labor and political objectives would be difficult to draw in many cases. In the absence of any limiting language in the statute or legislative history, we find no reason to conclude that Congress intended such a potentially expansive exception to a statutory provision purposefully drafted in broadest terms.

Application of § 8(b)(4) to the ILA's activity in this case will not infringe upon the First Amendment rights of the ILA and its members. We have consistently rejected the claim that secondary picketing by labor unions in violation of § 8(b)(4) is protected activity under the First Amendment. It would seem even clearer that conduct designed not to communicate but to coerce merits still less consideration under the First Amendment. The labor laws reflect a careful balancing of interests. There are many ways in which a union and its individual members may express their opposition to Russian foreign policy without infringing upon the rights of others.

NOTES

1. *Reconciling* Allied International *and* Claiborne. The last paragraph of the opinion as reprinted above contains the entire discussion of the First Amendment. The Court did not attempt to distinguish *NAACP v. Claiborne Hardware.* Can you? Both decisions were unanimous and both were decided in the same Term of the Supreme Court. What might explain the different results?

2. *Distinguishing expression from coercion.* If the UFCW local that represented the grocery employees in the problem that began this chapter called for a consumer boycott of the grocery stores, would its conduct be protected under *Claiborne* or prohibited under *Allied International*? What if the UFCW extended its boycott to other stores owned by the same corporation that owns the Ralphs chain of stores? What if it extended the boycott to Ralphs' major suppliers?

3. *When is a boycott expressive and when is it just anticompetitive?* A group of lawyers appointed by the court to provide legal representation for indigent criminal defendants refused to accept any new cases until the legislature, which sets the fees for court-appointed lawyers, increased the hourly rate. Was the lawyers' refusal to work constitutionally protected? In *FTC v. Superior Court Trial Lawyers Association,* 493 U.S. 411 (1990), the Supreme Court held that the protest was a price-fixing agreement prohibited by the federal antitrust law and rejected the lawyers' contention that the conduct was protected by the First Amendment under *Claiborne Hardware.* Conceding that, as in *Claiborne,* the lawyers' protest was about vindicating constitutional rights (in this case, the Sixth Amendment right to effective assistance of counsel in criminal cases), the Court nevertheless reasoned "no matter how altruistic the motives of respondents may have been, it is undisputed that their immediate objective was to increase the price that they would be paid for their services. Such an economic boycott is well within the

category" of activity that may be punished. "Those who joined the *Claiborne Hardware* boycott sought no special advantage for themselves. . . . They sought only the equal respect and equal treatment to which they were constitutionally entitled. They struggled to change a social order that had consistently treated them as second class citizens. . . . Equality and freedom are preconditions of the free market, and not commodities to be haggled over within it. The same cannot be said of attorney's fees." Gary Minda, in *The Law and Metaphor of Boycott*, 41 Buff. L. Rev. 807 (1993), suggests that the legal treatment of boycotts depends on whether judges emphasize the harms of coercion as compared to the benefits of free expression, or a motive of self-interest as opposed to a motive of protesting political or moral injustice. Are these appropriate distinctions for courts to draw? Are they helpful in predicting the legality of future boycotts?

4. *Distinguishing labor boycotts from political boycotts.* The line between political boycotts, which enjoy full First Amendment protection, and labor boycotts, which are illegal, is difficult to draw. Consider the following two examples:

(a) An organization originally founded by college students, Students Against Sweatshops (SAS), organizes a boycott of clothing with certain labels to protest the use of child labor and sweatshop conditions in Southeast Asia where the clothes are manufactured. The labor union representing garment workers, UNITE, joins the boycott and both SAS and UNITE use the publicity of the successful boycott to publicize sweatshops in the United States as well. UNITE and SAS distribute leaflets on college campuses and outside of stores selling the clothes. In addition, the two organizations take out paid advertisements in newspapers detailing the labor law violations at both the factories in Southeast Asia and in the United States. The manufacturer sues them under state law for defamation and interference with contractual relations, and also sues UNITE under the federal labor law prohibiting secondary boycotts. The defendants move to dismiss on the grounds of the First Amendment. What result? *See* Liza Featherstone, Students Against Sweatshops (Verso 2002).

(b) Workers of Florida tomato processing plants called a boycott to protest poor working conditions and their employer's refusal to recognize a union. A very large purchaser of the tomatoes is the company that supplied tomatoes to Taco Bell, a nationwide chain of fast food restaurants. The workers called for a boycott of Taco Bell to publicize their plight. They also appropriated the icon of Taco Bell's famous advertising campaign, a talking, sombrero-wearing Chihuahua dog, and began to urge supporters to wear T-shirts and use bumper stickers with the dog with a red circle and a slash over it—the universal sign for "no"—as a way of publicizing their call for a boycott of Taco Bell. Is the boycott constitutionally protected under

Allied International? Would it or should it matter whether the labor union or an immigrants' rights group organized the boycott?

c.   Other Regulation of Labor Protest

Regardless of the degree of constitutional protection for picketing and protest speech, the location of the protesters matters. If protesters are standing on public property, the First Amendment and federal labor law are the primary determinants of the permissibility of their speech. If they are on private property, however, the property owner or tenant may have state law property rights to exclude them, even if their speech would otherwise be constitutionally protected. The advent of the shopping mall, resort hotel, and office or industrial park poses a problem for labor protesters. For a time, it appeared that the Supreme Court would protect the right of workers to protest on private property when the property operated essentially as a public space. In *Marsh v. Alabama*, 326 U.S. 501 (1946), a Jehovah's Witness was convicted of criminal trespass for distributing literature on a sidewalk in Chickasaw, Alabama, which was wholly owned by the Gulf Shipbuilding Corporation. The Supreme Court overturned the conviction on the ground that if Chickasaw had "belonged not to a private but to a municipal corporation," the First Amendment would have protected the speech. The company town principle was extended to shopping centers in *Amalgamated Food Employees Union Local 590 v. Logan Valley Plaza, Inc.*, 391 U.S. 308 (1968), which involved union picketing immediately outside one store in a large shopping mall. The Court explained that "the shopping center here is clearly the functional equivalent of the business district of Chicasaw," and held that the First Amendment protected the picketing. The Supreme Court overruled *Logan Valley Plaza* in *Hudgens v. NLRB*, 424 U.S. 507 (1976), which involved labor picketing at a single store that was one of 60 in a large enclosed mall. The Court emphasized that a mall, unlike a company town, does not involve an entity operating with "all of the attributes of a state-created municipality and the exercise by that enterprise of semi-official municipal functions as a delegate of the state." A large shopping center, the Court held, is not "the functional equivalent of a municipality." Therefore, it has the rights of a private property owner to exclude anyone it deems as a trespasser, subject to the limits of the National Labor Relations Act.

As we will see later in this chapter when we study the nuances of the NLRA's prohibitions of picketing, handbilling, and other forms of labor speech and protest, section 8(b)(4) of the NLRA broadly prohibits picketing and other forms of "coercion" directed at anyone other than the employer with whom the picketing employees have a labor dispute. Labor disputes involving businesses in a mall or in other privately-owned but shared space like office parks raise the risk that a protest about the working conditions or labor practices of one store in a mall may affect customers of other stores or may affect the mall as a whole. In *Edward J. DeBartolo Corp. v. Florida*

Gulf Coast Bldg. & Construction Trades Council, 485 U.S. 568 (1988), excerpted below at p. 851, the Court suggested that the NLRA could not constitutionally be interpreted as banning peaceful handbilling on public property at a mall even if the handbilling persuaded some prospective shoppers to decline to do business with mall stores not involved in the labor dispute. The Court avoided the constitutional question by construing the statute not to prohibit such handbilling.

C. STATUTORY PROTECTIONS FOR EMPLOYEE PROTEST

1. STRIKES

a. The Right to Strike

As we saw above in Chapter 2, section 7 of the NLRA protects concerted activity generally, and section 13 protects the strike specifically. The Taft-Hartley Act limited the right to strike in a number of ways, and amended section 13 to read: "Nothing in this Act, except as specifically provided herein, shall be construed so as either to interfere with or impede or diminish in any way the right to strike, or to affect the limitations or qualifications on that right."

We have seen a number of instances of strikes, ranging from spontaneous and short-lived refusals to work, as in the example of the Somali workers in the problem at the beginning of Chapter 2 and the spontaneous refusal to work in a bitterly cold factory in *NLRB v. Washington Aluminum Co.,* 370 U.S. 9 (1962), which is excerpted in Chapter 2. Recall that in *Washington Aluminum,* the Court held that the group of workers who walked out of work were engaged in concerted activity protected under section 7 of the NLRA even though they were not unionized and did not present a specific demand to management in connection with their walk-out. We dealt at length above in Chapter 2 with the contours of section 7. In this chapter, we focus mainly on the limits of section 7 protection for strikes.

b. Exceptions to Statutory Protections for Strikes

The definition of the strike or other concerted activity that is protected under section 7 has not been given the widest possible interpretation by the Board and the courts. A variety of refusals to work, including strikes that do not involve vacating the employer's premises, slow-downs that do not involve a complete cessation of work, or intermittent work stoppages, are not deemed to be protected activity. Each of these is covered in detail in Chapter 2 or elsewhere in this book; the following list is merely a summary:

(1) Activity inconsistent with exclusivity, which includes efforts by a minority to bargain for their own working conditions (see *Emporium Capwell,* covered in Chapter 4).

(2) Sit-down strikes and slow-downs (see *Fansteel,* covered in Chapter 2).

(3) "Indefensible" or "unprotected" conduct (see *Elk Lumber* and *International Protective Services* covered in Chapter 2.D.2), including "harassing tactics" (as in *Insurance Agents*, covered in Chapters 2 and 5).

(4) Disloyalty (as in *Jefferson Standard Broadcasting*, covered in Chapter 2).

(5) Violence or trespass while picketing (covered in Chapter 2).

(6) Strikes in violation of the collective bargaining agreement. This category encompasses economic strikes during the term of a CBA with a no-strike clause, but not unfair labor practice strikes unless the CBA waives the right to engage in an unfair labor practice strike (see *Mastro Plastics* below). Two forms of strike occur during the term of a CBA: a "wildcat" strike, which is semi-spontaneous, usually led by a group of workers in response to a particularly objectionable management action, and not officially sanctioned by the union; and a "sympathy" strike, which is where one or more workers strike in sympathy with another group of workers, or refuse to cross a picket line established by others.

(7) Strikes and lockouts over non-mandatory subjects of bargaining are unprotected and are also a violation of the duty to bargain under § 8(a)(5) and § 8(b)(3) (covered in Chapter 5).

(8) Although there is no general obligation under the NLRA to give notice of an intent to strike, and a union is free to strike as soon as a collective bargaining agreement containing a no strike clause expires, there are obligations to give notice in the following circumstances:

   a. Under the Railway Labor Act

   b. In the health care industry, under section 8(g). In *Civil Serv. Employees Ass'n v. NLRB*, 569 F.3d 88, 89, 94 (2d Cir. 2009), the NLRB had concluded that employees who picketed without following the 8(g) notice requirements were unprotected and subject to discharge, but the court of appeals disagreed. The court held that although *unions* are subject to sanctions for striking or picketing without observing the 8(g) notice requirements,

employees were subject to sanctions only if they strike
and not if they picket (unless the employees were union
agents).

c.   Most public sector employees are prohibited by law from
striking. However, those who are allowed to strike are
typically required to give notice and also to engage in
some form of ADR before resorting to a strike

c.   The Effect of a No-Strike Clause

A union can waive some of the section 7 rights of its members. In
particular, a no-strike clause in a collective bargaining agreement waives
the right to strike, and a strike conducted in violation of a no-strike clause
is therefore unprotected. In *Mastro Plastics Corp. v. NLRB,* 350 U.S. 270
(1956), the Supreme Court held that a no-strike clause in a collective
bargaining agreement waived only the right to engage in "economic"
strikes, and not the right to engage in strikes to protest the employer's
unfair labor practices. The collective bargaining agreement contained a
standard no-strike clause in which the union promised "there shall be no
interference of any kind with the operations of the Employers, or any
interruptions or slackening of production of work by any of its members.
The union further agrees to refrain from engaging in any strike or work
stoppage during the term of this agreement." Shortly before the agreement
expired, the employer fired a union supporter and provided assistance to
an insurgent union seeking to oust the incumbent union. The incumbent
union called a strike, which the NLRB found to have been a protest of the
employer's unfair labor practices (the firing and the assistance to the
insurgent union) rather than in support of the union's bargaining demands.
The employer fired the striking employees. The Supreme Court held that
the no strike clause should be interpreted to apply only to strikes in support
of bargaining demands or to enforce the collective bargaining agreement,
not to a strike to protest the employer's unfair labor practices. "Whatever
may be said of the legality of such a waiver when explicitly stated, there is
no adequate basis for implying its existence without a more compelling
expression of it than appears in" this contract.

The Board has also determined that a general no strike clause does
waive the right to strike over "non-serious" unfair labor practices that can
be redressed through the grievance machinery established by the collective
bargaining agreement. *Arlan's Dep't Store,* 133 N.L.R.B. 802 (1961).

d.   Sympathy Strikes

Employees on strike sometimes picket not only at their own place of
business but may picket other work locations. Employees sometimes like
to form common cause with striking employees at other firms by refusing
to cross their picket lines or refusing to do work that the struck employer

has transferred to their employer. Strikes during negotiations for collective bargaining agreements for janitors in the 1990s and 2000s featured short strikes by janitors working for the same multinational building service firms in other cities—so during a strike by Los Angeles janitors, janitors in Houston and other cities struck. What is the goal of such sympathy strikes? Should the goal matter in assessing its legality?

When employees picket as part of a protected strike against their employer, both they and the employees of other employers who refuse to cross their picket line face a possibility of discharge or other discipline—the picketers for inducing employees of a neutral employer not to perform work and the employees of the other employer for refusing to work. It is important to sort out their rights. "Sympathy strike" is a term used loosely to describe a number of different kinds of activism, including:

(a) Striking employees establish roving picket lines at their employer's other locations to inform employees, customers or suppliers at the other location about a labor dispute involving the same company.

(b) Employees respect a picket line at their own worksite established by employees in a different bargaining unit.

(c) Employees respect a picket line established by employees of other employers at a shared worksite.

(d) A delivery employee refuses to cross a picket line established by employees of another employer at the other employer's worksite where the employee is scheduled to make a pick-up or delivery.

Depending on the circumstances, either maintaining or observing these picket lines may be protected or unprotected by section 7, or illegal under section 8.

Ordinarily, employees who refuse to cross a picket line at their own employer's place of business are treated as engaged in the same kind of strike as the picketing employees. If the picketers are engaged in a protected strike, so is the employee who refuses to cross. If the picketers are engaged in an unprotected or an illegal strike, so is the employee who refuses to cross. The rules are different, however, if the worksite is shared by many employers (such as a construction site). An employee of an employer who is not in a labor dispute who refuses to cross a picket line at a shared worksite is usually deemed to be engaged in an unlawful secondary boycott (and the picketers who induced the employee not to cross are likewise engaged in an illegal effort to induce a secondary boycott). If an employee refuses to cross a picket line at somewhere *other than* her own employer's place of business (e.g., a delivery truck driver refuses to cross a picket line to make a delivery to a customer), the rights of the employee are determined by his or her collective bargaining agreement. While some collective bargaining agreements expressly address the rights of employees to honor picket lines other than at their own workplace, when a CBA contains just a general no-strike clause, the Board has to decide whether or when it prohibits sympathy strikes. As the membership of the Board has changed over the years, so have the rules on this issue. For a long time, the Board held that a general no strike clause did not waive the right to honor a picket line. Only a no-strike clause containing "clear and unmistakable" language waiving the right to observe a picket line would waive the right. *Operating Eng'rs Local 18 (Davis-McKee)*, 238 N.L.R.B. 652 (1978). Then in *Indianapolis Power & Light Co.*, 273 N.L.R.B. 1715 (1985), the Board reversed itself and held that a no strike clause waives the right to observe a picket line unless either the contract language or extrinsic evidence of the bargaining history or past practice shows that the parties intended to allow sympathy strikes. The Board further modified this standard in *Indianapolis Power & Light II,* 291 N.L.R.B. No. 145 (1988) by finding that a union did not clearly and unmistakably waive the right to engage in sympathy strikes where there is conflicting evidence as to whether the parties intended a no strike clause to waive that right. Even a clear contractual waiver of the right to engage in a sympathy strike does not waive the right to honor any picket line that is protesting a severe unfair labor practice.

Even if a collective bargaining agreement has not waived the right to observe a picket line, under some circumstances an employer may discipline an employee for refusing to cross it, such as where the employer needs the employee to cross the picket line. There is substantial uncertainty in the law as to what an employer must show in order to justify firing an employee who refuses to cross a picket line.

ELECTRONIC DATA SYSTEMS CORPORATION
331 N.L.R.B. 343 (2000)

The Respondent [Electronic Data Systems ("EDS")] provides communication services to Xerox Corporation (Xerox) and contracts with service vendors to resolve various technical problems for Xerox. Charging Party Eaton worked as a service representative in the Respondent's customer support centers (CSC) and was responsible for taking calls from Xerox employees and customers concerning computer problems. [Eaton and other EDS employees were not represented by a union.] When these problems involve a telephone or a system line, CSC employees transfer these types of issues to the Respondent's network operations center (NOC), whose sole function is to resolve circuit problems for Xerox customers. The service vendor responsible for maintaining circuits and telephone lines for the Xerox account is Rochester Telephone Company. The Respondent's NOC employees interact daily with Rochester Telephone, sometimes as many as 12 times each day, to resolve problems for Xerox.

On the afternoon of January 31, 1996, Eaton spoke with her husband, who was an employee of Rochester Telephone, and learned that Rochester Telephone employees might shortly go on strike. Later that afternoon, Eaton sent two computer e-mail messages to her fellow employees[1] and then had direct conversations with several NOC employees regarding the situation at Rochester Telephone. The credited testimony establishes that in these conversations Eaton told NOC employees not to call, refer service requests to, or interact with Rochester Telephone. Thereafter, the Respondent discharged Eaton for soliciting the Respondent's NOC employees to refrain from dispatching calls to the Respondent's vendor, Rochester Telephone, and for sending a message containing physical threats to anyone crossing picket lines.

The judge found that Eaton's actions were not concerted and bore no "legitimate relationship to the interests of employees, either her fellow EDS employees or the Unionized employees of [Rochester Telephone]." It is well settled, however, that "employees' conduct on behalf of the employees of another employer who are engaged in protected concerted activity is itself protected concerted activity." *Office Depot, Inc.*, 330 N.L.R.B. 640, 642 (2000). Thus, Eaton's e-mail solicitation of fellow employees to support the striking Rochester Telephone employees was clearly concerted activity. Because she went further, however, and asked other employees not to call or refer service requests to Rochester Telephone, we agree with the judge that Eaton solicited the Respondent's NOC employees to stop performing an important portion of their jobs— referring telephone service and circuit problems of Xerox customers to Rochester Telephone—and that this amounted to the solicitation of an intermittent, partial work stoppage by the NOC employees. Thus, Eaton essentially sought to convince the NOC employees to stay on the job and perform a portion of their usual duties, but to ignore the several daily dispatches that pertained to telephone and systems problems normally referred to Rochester Telephone.

It is well established that a partial refusal to work, in contrast to a complete work stoppage, is unprotected activity because it constitutes an attempt by employees to set their own terms and conditions of employment while remaining on the job. When the form of conduct at issue, as here, is unprotected, it logically follows that the solicitation or inducement of such conduct also is unprotected.[2] Accordingly, in these circumstances, we find that the Respondent's discharge of Eaton did not violate the Act.

---

[1]   Eaton's initial e-mail message was sent to NOC employees and stated that "Local 1170 will be on strike as (of) 12:01 tonight. Please help support them in their effort against Rochester Telephone." Eaton's second e-mail message was sent to CSC employees and stated that "Local 1170 will be on strike from Rochester Telephone as of 12:01 tonight. Please be aware that anyone or any person crossing their picket line will suffer the consequences. Local 1170 will be fighting for their jobs."

[2]   The present case is distinguishable from a one-time refusal to work mandatory overtime, which is protected because it is not an attempt to determine unilaterally employees' own conditions

NOTES

1. *What is a sympathy strike?* If an EDS employee was sent to the Rochester Telephone facility to work and she refused to cross the picket line, could she be fired?

2. *Should EDS be overruled? If so, how?* The outcome in the EDS case was quite controversial. As with many controversial NLRB decisions, it might be a candidate for overruling by a future Board. Can you construct the argument to reach a conclusion other than the one reached by the Board in *EDS*?

3. *How to read a no strike clause.* Suppose Eaton and her coworkers had been represented by a union and had a collective bargaining agreement with a standard no-strike clause providing that there shall be no "strike, picketing, slow-down, or other curtailment of work or interference with the operation of the Company's business." If Eaton were disciplined and filed a grievance, should an arbitrator interpret the no-strike clause to cover what Eaton did?

4. *Who has the right to refuse to cross a picket line?* A college student who works part time for a temporary staffing agency reports to a new job assignment as an office assistant at a bakery and discovers that the bakery workers are on strike and picketing. The student refuses to cross the picket line and calls into the temp agency office immediately to report that she cannot cross the picket line. She is fired and files a section 8(a)(1) charge. What result? *See Bus. Servs. by Manpower*, 272 N.L.R.B. 827 (1984) (employer violated § 8(a)(1)), *enforcement denied* 784 F.2d 442 (2d Cir. 1986) (employer did not violate § 8(a)(1) because it needed employee to cross picket line and employee's § 7 rights were "weak" by comparison). Would it matter whether the college student was a union member? What if she had been assigned to do work that would have been done by the striking workers, as opposed to clerical work when the clerical workers were not on strike?

e. Special Statutory Limitations on Strikes

Section 8(d) requires that any party seeking to terminate or modify an existing collective bargaining agreement give written notice to the other party to the contract at least sixty days prior to the expiration date of the contract, must notify the Federal Mediation and Conciliation Service (FMCS) at least 30 days later of the existence of any bargaining dispute, and must not resort to a strike or a lockout for 60 days after giving the notice or intent to terminate or modify the contract. Beyond the obligation to give 60 days notice of the intent to seek modification of a contract, there is no general obligation to give notice of the intent to strike, subject to the rules about "indefensible conduct." *See* Chapter 2.D.2.c.

---

of employment. *Sawyer of Napa*, 300 N.L.R.B. 131, 137 (1990). Nor is the present case akin to the refusal of a delivery driver to cross a picket line, a traditional form of permissible support, but which may subject the driver to replacement in the interest of balancing an employee's protected activity with an employer's efficient operation of its business.

In addition, Congress determined that the disruption caused by work stoppages merits particular protection in industries where disruption would cause extraordinary harm to the public:

Health Care. Section 8(g) requires a union to give ten days prior notice to the employer and to the FMCS before "engaging in any strike, picketing, or other concerted refusal to work at any health care institution." In *Civil Serv. Employees Ass'n v. NLRB*, 569 F.3d 88, 89 (2d Cir. 2009), the NLRB had concluded that employees who picketed for collective bargaining purposes without following the § 8(g) notice requirements were exposed to discharge, notwithstanding the protections of § 7, but the court of appeals disagreed. While *unions* are subject to sanctions for striking or picketing without observing the § 8(g) notice requirements, *employees* are subject to sanctions only in cases of strikes and not in cases of picketing.

Railways and Airlines. As we saw in Chapter 5, the Railway Labor Act provides for resolution of negotiating disputes through mediation processes and arbitration. The use of economic weapons is allowed only for some disputes and only after statutory dispute resolution processes have failed. In the case of "major" disputes (those concerning an "intended change in agreements affecting rates of pay, rules, or working conditions") the parties must give notice of the dispute and then submit to the negotiation process. During the negotiations, either party may request the National Mediation Board to mediate. If negotiation fails, and mediation is either not requested, not offered, or unsuccessful, the parties are allowed to resort to self help, including economic weapons. If and when the NMB determines that mediation will be unsuccessful, the Board offers binding arbitration to the parties. If both parties accept arbitration, the dispute is subjected to binding interest arbitration. If either party rejects arbitration, neither party may resort to self-help for 30 days. The final step for resolution of some major disputes is the appointment of a Presidential Emergency Board when the NMB determines that the dispute threatens "substantially to interrupt interstate commerce to a degree such as to deprive any section of the country of essential transportation service." If the President decides not to create an Emergency Board, the parties may resort to self help at the end of the cooling off period. If the President appoints an Emergency Board, it conducts an investigation and makes a report to the President. The report is not binding on the parties, although on occasion Congress has enacted special legislation to make the report binding in the case of particular disputes. The submission of the report to the President begins the final 30-day cooling off period, after which the parties can resort to self-help. "Minor" disputes (those "arising out of grievances or out of the interpretation or application of agreements") are resolved through negotiation and grievance processes and, if that fails, are committed to the exclusive jurisdiction of the appropriate system board for final and binding arbitration. The Supreme Court held in *Railroad Trainmen v. Chicago River & Indiana Railroad*, 353 U.S. 30 (1957), that because minor disputes are subject to the compulsory dispute resolution procedures of the RLA, courts are empowered to enjoin strikes that are designed to evade those procedures.

National Emergency Provisions. In reaction to the post-World War II strike wave, the new Republican majority in Congress made labor unrest a major theme and included in the Taft-Hartley Act a provision authorizing the United States to seek an injunction against work stoppages that caused a national emergency.

> Simply outlawing such strikes would be ineffective without providing some alternative way to resolve the underlying issues. The primary alternative to tolerating those strikes was compulsory arbitration, but ... compulsory arbitration was anathema not only to the unions who had opposed the Republicans but also to the business interests that had supported them. The remaining option was a package of delaying actions that would combine mediation with public and political pressure to encourage settlements.

Dennis R. Nolan, "We Didn't Have Time to Train the Monkeys": The 2002 Presidential Board of Inquiry on the Work Stoppage in the West Coast Ports, Proceedings of the National Academy of Arbitrators (2004). The National Emergency process involves appointment of a Board of Inquiry, the production of a report by the Board, the seeking of an injunction which may last only 80 days, conciliation by the Federal Mediation and Conciliation Services, another report by the Board of Inquiry, and the dissolution of the injunction. The National Emergency provisions were invoked with some regularity in the 1950s and 1960s, but had not been invoked since a failed 1976 attempt by President Carter to secure an injunction until President Bush obtained an injunction against a work stoppage in the West Coast ports in 2002. Professor Nolan, describing what he regards as his futile involvement in the Presidential Board of Inquiry in the 2002 West Coast Ports lockout that is the subject of the following case, says "There is almost universal agreement among affected employees and unions, and among academics who have studied the matter, that the Taft-Hartley Act's emergency provisions are at best ineffective and quite likely counter-productive." *Id.* Why might that be?

Section 208 of the Taft-Hartley Act provides that a district court may enjoin any strike or lockout:

> Upon receiving a report from a board of inquiry the President may direct the Attorney General to petition any district court of the United States having jurisdiction of the parties to enjoin such strike or lockout or the continuing thereof, and if the court finds that such threatened or actual strike or lockout—

    (i)   affects an entire industry or a substantial part thereof engaged in trade, commerce, transportation, transmission, or communication among the several States or with foreign nations, or engaged in the production of goods for commerce; and

    (ii)   if permitted to occur or to continue, will imperil the national health or safety,

it shall have jurisdiction to enjoin any such strike or lockout, or the continuing thereof, and to make such other orders as may be appropriate.

Globalization, particularly the growth of imports from China, has led to a huge increase in the quantity and value of goods imported via ship through the major U.S. ports. The industries in which work stoppages are likely to be declared a national emergency are, therefore, no longer basic manufacturing (such as steel), but rather transportation. It is thus no surprise that the lockout which closed down the 29 West Coast ports in 2002 was declared by President Bush to be a national emergency and litigation over the scope of the national emergency provisions arose out of that lockout.

In *United States v. Pacific Maritime Association*, 229 F. Supp. 2d 1008 (N.D. Cal. 2002), the court enjoined the lockout under the national emergency provisions. The court also decided, although the issue was not raised by the parties, that it had the authority to enjoin future strikes by the longshore workers as well as the ongoing lockout by employers. Noting that the west coast ports handled over half of the nation's containerized imports and exports, and that many industries were dependent on the ports, the court found that the lockout would imperil the national health. Importantly, the court also found that the lockout would jeopardize national security. Quoting an affidavit of the Secretary of Defense submitted by the employers, the court explained that the Defense Department depends on civilian shipping to supply its operations and "sudden, unforeseen developments in world events may at any time demand that additional ocean shipping capacity be made immediately available for military needs. The cumulative effect of delays, or lack of sufficient shipping capacity when needed, would adversely affect our ability to deliver military cargo to overseas destinations as required, and jeopardize the defense effort and the Global War on Terrorism." Therefore, the court concluded, "at a time when our nation is at war with international terrorists and when our national defense system must be fully prepared, the sustained closure of West Coast ports would imperil the national safety." No court has ever found a national emergency to exist justifying an injunction against a work stoppage based solely on the harm to the economy.

NOTES

1.   *What is a national emergency?* Would there be a national emergency without the so-called global war on terror? Is interruption of commerce sufficient?

2.   *Are the national emergency provisions more likely to constrain unions or employers?* An unusual feature of the litigation was that the employer association was seeking an injunction against its own lockout. One might wonder why, if the employers found themselves inconvenienced by their lockout, the solution wasn't simply for them to end the lockout and allow their workers to return to work. The answer is that the Pacific Maritime Association believed the International Longshore and Warehouse Union, which represents west coast port workers, had been engaged in a slowdown. As you learned in Chapter 2, slowdowns are unprotected under federal labor law. *See Elk Lumber,* 91 N.L.R.B. 333 (1950). Why didn't the employers fire the workers participating in the slowdown? Should the employer association's tactic, prompted as it was by its inability to replace the West Coast Port workforce, render the situation a national emergency? Is there another way to prevent powerful unions with a high degree of solidarity from abusing their power?

f.   Work Stoppages in the Public Sector

Employees of the federal government and of the governments of many states and localities are specifically prohibited from striking. Strikes are prohibited both because government employee services are sometimes considered more essential than private sector service (e.g., police officers), and also because the predominant source of public employer revenue is from taxes which are not affected by a labor stoppage. A public sector strike is a political weapon that is used to pressure public officials to modify their bargaining position, or to illustrate to the legislature the need for more generous appropriations for the affected public services.

Although most states and the federal government prohibit some or all public employee strikes, the punishments for striking vary from criminal prosecution (rare) to loss of all benefits of government employment, including a pension (as in Texas), to relatively toothless rules that make it difficult to enjoin them.

One state that allows some public employees to strike is California. In *County Sanitation District v. SEIU Local 660,* 38 Cal.3d 564 (1985), the California Supreme Court canvassed the reasons traditionally offered for prohibiting public employee strikes and found them wanting. The court therefore concluded that "strikes by public employees are not unlawful at common law unless or until it is clearly demonstrated that such a strike creates a substantial and imminent threat to the health and safety of the public." What kind of showing should be necessary to establish that a strike poses "a substantial and imminent threat to the health and safety of the public"? Consider this question in the context of a strike by (a) sanitation workers; (b) school teachers; (c) city bus and subway drivers; and (d) clerical employees of government agencies.

Even states that allow some public employees to strike generally prohibit strikes by public safety workers, including police officers and firefighters.

Defining a Strike. Prohibiting a strike will not necessarily prevent employees from venting their frustrations over negotiating by engaging in various forms of interruptions of work. States that prohibit strikes have had to decide whether a number of behaviors count as a strike and are therefore subject to the statutorily authorized remedies for unlawful work stoppages (e.g., workplace discipline of employees, fines against the union, an injunction, or criminal prosecution). Consider the following:

1. *Blue flu.* During contract negotiations, police officers report an unusually high number of illnesses and stay home on sick leave. The police force has difficulty staffing all shifts on account of the large number of absences. The officers who call in sick are using only the number of sick days allowed by their employer and otherwise follow all requirements for taking of sick leave. How would you prove that this is a "strike"? What remedy would be most effective in stopping it? Assuming an injunction is an available remedy, how would you craft an injunction to prevent this? Can employers discipline employees for promoting a slow-down among public sector workers? Three police union members urged other officers to write fewer tickets in order to place the county under pressure through loss of revenue. *Douglas v. Dekalb County*, 308 F. App'x 396, 397, 399 (11th Cir. 2009). The appellate court affirmed the police department's power to discipline the officers because a Georgia statute barred public employees from promoting strikes, which included slow-downs.

2. *Work to Rule.* During contract negotiations, school bus drivers refuse to drive any bus that fails to meet applicable safety standards. Approximately 50 percent of the bus fleet fails to meet standards, but bus drivers have not previously insisted on adherence to the standards. *Local 252, Transport Workers Union v. New York State PERB*, 448 N.E.2d 116 (N.Y. 1983).

3. *Refusal to Work Overtime.* Police officers refuse to sign up to work overtime during the annual city festival held over Labor Day weekend. In past years, plenty of officers volunteered to work at the festival, but during contract negotiations this year, no officers volunteered. In deciding whether this is an illegal strike, or what remedy to order if it is, would it matter whether the city had some mechanism to order officers to

work overtime? *Appeal of City of Manchester*, 741 A.2d 70 (N.H. 1999) (finding no illegal strike and declining to issue an injunction; noting the city invoked its right to order officers to work overtime); *New York Nurses Ass'n*, 334 NLRB 798 (2001) (nurses' concerted refusal to work overtime is a strike and is unprotected because nurses failed to give advance notice required under § 8(g)).

4.   *Refusing to Do Certain Aspects of Job.* During contract negotiations, a teachers' union urged its members to decline (1) to complete student progress reports and report cards; (2) to attend after-school meetings and activities; (3) to supervise students except in the classroom; (4) to complete attendance records; (5) to administer standardized tests; or (6) to work more than eight hours in a day, which meant that teachers stopped (a) taking papers home to grade, (b) taking students on long field trips, (c) scheduling parent-teacher conferences in the late afternoon or early evening, which they previously had done to accommodate working parents, and (d) supervising school clubs that met in the morning before school. Are all or any of these a strike? Would it matter which are "required" and which are "volunteer" parts of a job? If it does matter, how do you determine which is required? *Los Angeles Unified School Dist. v. United Teachers of Los Angeles*, 14 P.E.R. Cal. P21082 (Cal. PERB 1990); Amit R. Paley, Calvert Teachers Keep Eye on Clock; Job Action Restricts Work to 7.5 Hours, Wash. Post, Sep. 19, 2004, at T03; Nancy Trejos, "Work to Rule" Protest Disrupts Student Clubs; Teachers Absent after School, Wash. Post, Mar. 25, 2001, at SME.1. (Southern Maryland Extra).

Remedies for Unlawful Strikes. Where a strike is illegal, remedies vary widely: (1) Injunctions are sometimes available, although when the strike is something less than a full-scale walk-out (e.g., work to rule or a sick out), it is often difficult to craft and enforce the injunction. (2) Damages against the union are occasionally available. (3) A union may be decertified, as occurred with the Professional Air Traffic Controllers Union after the 1981 PATCO strike. Discipline of striking employees is sometimes available, ranging from loss of pay to summary dismissal. (4) In one case a court imposed a fine on a teachers' union that ignored a state employment relations board's order to rescind a strike vote. *Commonwealth Empl. Rels. Bd. v. Boston Teachers Union*, 74 Mass. App. Ct. 500, 503 (2009). As was illustrated in the wave of teachers' strikes in the spring of 2018, even illegal strikes may sometimes achieve gains for workers when they have strong public support, making discipline of striking employees a political liability, and when it is impossible to replace striking workers.

Alternatives to Strikes. A strike, of course, is a means to an end: resolution of negotiating disputes (at least in an established bargaining relationship). If striking is not allowed, there needs to be some method of resolving the bargaining dispute. As discussed in Chapter 5, most jurisdictions that ban strikes provide for one or more alternative means of resolving negotiating disputes. An alternative used in almost every jurisdiction is mediation, in which a neutral third party (such as the Federal Mediation and Conciliation Service) helps the parties reach agreement. Another alternative is fact-finding, where a body is appointed to examine the parties' situation and make recommendations about the causes and possible resolution of the negotiating dispute. Fact-finding is commonly used to settle public sector negotiating disputes. A third alternative is interest arbitration, in which a respected neutral (or panel of arbitrators) is empowered to resolve the dispute for the parties. This, too, is common in state public sector labor laws and has been proposed as a reform to the NLRA. It exists but has rarely been used in California's Agricultural Labor Relations Act.

2. LEGAL REGULATION OF EFFORTS TO ENCOURAGE OR DISCOURAGE SOLIDARITY

Strikes and other forms of labor protest rely entirely on the solidarity of workers. A great deal of the law regulating strikes and lockouts addresses the efforts of labor and management to encourage or discourage solidarity. This section first examines the legality of the various tactics management has tried to discourage employees from commencing or joining a strike, and then the legality of tactics unions have developed to discourage employees from abandoning a strike.

a. Management Tactics: Replacing Striking Workers

Although the right to strike is protected under the NLRA, the scope of protection is quite narrow. *Mackay Radio* held it is a right not to be fired, not a right to keep one's job.

NLRB v. MACKAY RADIO & TELEGRAPH CO.
304 U.S. 333 (1938)

JUSTICE ROBERTS delivered the opinion of the Court:

The respondent, a California corporation, is engaged in the transmission and receipt of telegraph, radio, cable, and other messages between points in California and points in other states and foreign countries. It maintains an office in San Francisco for the transaction of its business wherein it employs upwards of sixty supervisors, operators and clerks, many of whom are members of Local No. 3 of the American Radio Telegraphists Association, a national labor organization. At midnight

Friday, October 4, 1935, all the men there employed went on strike. The respondent, in order to maintain service, brought employees from its Los Angeles office and others from the New York and Chicago offices of the parent company to fill the strikers' places.

Although none of the San Francisco strikers returned to work Saturday, Sunday, or Monday, the strike proved unsuccessful in other parts of the country and, by Monday evening, October 7th, a number of the men became convinced that it would fail and that they had better return to work before their places were filled with new employees. [A company official told the striking workers] that the men might return to work in their former positions but that, as the company had promised eleven men brought to San Francisco they might remain if they so desired, the supervisor would have to handle the return of the striking employees in such fashion as not to displace any of the new men who desired to continue in San Francisco. Tuesday morning, October 8th, six of the eleven in question took their places and resumed their work without challenge. It turned out that only five of the new men brought to San Francisco desired to stay.

Five strikers who were prominent in the activities of the union and in connection with the strike reported at the office at various times between Tuesday and Thursday. Each of them was told that he would have to fill out an application for employment; that the roll of employees was complete, and that his application would be considered in connection with any vacancy that might thereafter occur.

The strikers remained employees under section 2(3) of the act, which provides: "The term 'employee' shall include . . . any individual whose work has ceased as a consequence of, or in connection with, any current labor dispute or because of any unfair labor practice, and who has not obtained any other regular and substantially equivalent employment." Within this definition the strikers remained employees for the purpose of the act and were protected against the unfair labor practices denounced by it.

There is no evidence and no finding that the respondent was guilty of any unfair labor practice in connection with the negotiations in New York. On the contrary, it affirmatively appears that the respondent was negotiating with the authorized representatives of the union. Nor was it an unfair labor practice to replace the striking employees with others in an effort to carry on the business. Although section 13 of the Act provides, "Nothing in this Act (chapter) shall be construed so as to interfere with or impede or diminish in any way the right to strike," it does not follow that an employer, guilty of no act denounced by the statute, has lost the right to protect and continue his business by supplying places left vacant by strikers. And he is not bound to discharge those hired to fill the places of strikers, upon the election of the latter to resume their employment, in order to create places for them. The assurance by respondent to those who accepted employment during the strike that if they so desired their places might be permanent was not an unfair labor practice, nor was it such to reinstate only so many of the strikers as there were vacant places to be filled. But the claim put forward is that the unfair labor practice indulged by the respondent was discrimination in reinstating striking employees by keeping out certain of them for the sole reason that they had been active in the union. As we have said, the strikers retained, under the act, the status of employees. Any such discrimination in putting them back to work is, therefore, prohibited by section 8.

[S]ix of the eleven strikers listed for separate treatment who reported for work early Tuesday morning, or within the next day or so, were permitted to go back to work and were not compelled to await the approval of their applications. It appears that all of the men who had been on strike signed applications for re-employment shortly after their resumption of work. The Board found, and we cannot say that its finding is unsupported, that, in taking back six of the eleven men and excluding five who were active union men, the respondent's officials discriminated against the latter on account of their union activities and that the excuse given that they did not apply until after the quota was full was an afterthought and not the true reason for the discrimination against them. As we have said, the respondent was not bound to displace men hired to take the strikers' places in order to provide positions for them. It might have refused reinstatement on the grounds of skill or ability, but the Board found that it did not do so. It might have resorted to any one of a number of methods of determining which of its striking employees would have to wait because five men had taken permanent positions during the strike, but it is found that the preparation and use of the list, and the action taken by respondent, was with the purpose to discriminate against those most active in the union.

NOTES

1.   *The most influential dictum in labor law.* What was the issue before the Court in *Mackay*? Why did the Court issue dictum on the legality of hiring permanent replacements? The NLRB's lawyer conceded in oral argument that an employer could permanently replace striking workers. Why do you suppose the lawyer made that concession? Why did the Court deem it unnecessary to consider whether the employer should have to justify its decision to offer permanent rather that temporary employment to replacement workers? Professor James Pope surmises that the lawyer and the Court were responding to concerns that empowering the Board to order employers to employ strikers would violate the employers' Fifth Amendment liberty of contract rights to refuse to deal with employees who had harmed their business. *See* James Gray Pope, *How American Workers Lost the Right to Strike, and Other Tales,* 103 Mich. L. Rev. 518, 533–34 (2004).

2. *Why allow replacements for strikers?* If you were reasoning from first principles, how would you decide whether the NLRA would allow the hiring of replacement workers, and, if so whether they could be permanent or temporary?

3. *Legal rights and personnel policy.* If you were advising management in a labor dispute, what would you suggest about the wisdom of hiring replacement workers, as opposed to curtailing operations or operating using supervisors? If your client wanted to hire replacement workers, what advice would you give about whether or to whom the employer should describe the replacements as "permanent" or "temporary"?

A NOTE ON THE USE OF PERMANENT REPLACEMENTS

From 1938 until 1980, it was rare for companies to permanently replace striking workers. Reasons for the reluctance were several. Hiring striker replacements made strikers extremely angry which tended to galvanize support for the strike and prolong it rather than shorten it. Replacement workers made it harder to settle strikes, as the negotiating dispute would then have another contentious issue: the fate of the replacement workers and the returning strikers. Relations between the returned strikers and any retained replacement workers were likely to be hostile for months or years after the end of the strike.

That changed in the recessionary and deindustrializing economy of the early 1980s. Companies used permanent replacements to break unions in a number of high-profile fights, beginning with President Reagan's firing of hundreds of striking air traffic controllers in 1981. *See* Herbert Northrup, *The Rise and Demise of PATCO*, 37 Indus. & Lab. Rel. Rev. 167 (1984). Two years later, another high-profile strike was broken at Phelps Dodge's copper refinery in Arizona and the workforce was deunionized. *See* Jonathan Rosenblum, Copper Crucible: How the Arizona Miners' Strike of 1983 Recast Labor Management Relations in America (ILR Press 1998). Then in 1985–86, the use of replacement workers at the Hormel meat packing plant in Austin, Minnesota resulted in hundreds of strikers losing their jobs. Most had to leave their homes to seek work elsewhere, as Hormel was the major employer in the town. *See* Peter Rachleff, Hard-Pressed in the Heartland: the Hormel Strike and the Future of the Labor Movement (South End Press, 1993). Just a year later, the devastating total replacement of the unionized workforce by the International Paper Company at its plant in Jay, Maine in 1987–88 seemed to sound the death knell of the strike. *See* Julius Getman, The Betrayal of Local 14 (ILR Press 1998). It appeared that no amount of worker militance was enough to stop a determined employer from exploiting its legal rights to eliminate unions by demanding huge wage concessions, thus precipitating a strike, and then permanently replacing its entire union workforce and breaking the union.

There are important differences between firing strikers (which is prohibited) and permanently replacing them (which *Mackay Radio* permits). First, strikers do not lose their jobs until replacements are in fact hired. Until replacements have been hired, an employer may not tell a striking employee that he or she has been replaced or decline to reinstate a striker who makes an unqualified offer to return to work. Second, permanently replaced strikers retain the right to vote in union elections for one year from the date the strike commences. If the strikers were fired they would no longer be employees and thus no longer entitled to vote. Third, permanently replaced strikers have a qualified right to reinstatement to their job when vacancies become available under the NLRB's decision in *Laidlaw Corp.*, 171 N.L.R.B. 1366 (1968). To obtain reinstatement under *Laidlaw*, the striker must make an unconditional offer to return to work and must not have "abandoned the employ of [the employer] for substantial and equivalent employment." *Id.* Once the strikers make such an offer, it is "incumbent on [the employer] to seek them out as positions [are] vacated." *Id.* An employer can decline to reinstate strikers if it can show a "business justification" for refusing to do so, such as that the vacant jobs require skills that the strikers do not possess. Strikers entitled to reinstatement must be reinstated with full seniority, but they may not use their seniority to get their preferred job or shift assignment.

Recently, courts have expanded the hiring of permanent replacements from its status under *Mackay*—a weapon that was not prohibited by the NLRA—into a right affirmatively protected against federal or state infringement. After Hormel broke the UFCW strike in Austin, Minnesota by hiring permanent replacement workers in 1986, the Minnesota state legislature enacted a law banning the use of permanent replacements. Employers promptly filed suit and the Eighth Circuit declared that federal labor law preempted the state striker replacement law. *Employers Ass'n v. United Steelworkers*, 32 F.3d 1297 (8th Cir. 1994). Labor advocates then turned their attention to the federal government, and President Clinton issued an Executive Order banning the use of permanent replacement by government contractors. Employers again filed suit, and the D.C. Circuit held that the NLRA preempted the Executive Order on the grounds that the use of permanent replacements is a right affirmatively guaranteed under the NLRA. *Chamber of Commerce v. Reich*, 74 F.3d 1322 (D.C. Cir. 1996).

Mackay allows replacement of workers in a so-called "economic strike," that is, one that was to protest the employer's economic demands. In *Mastro Plastics Corp. v. NLRB,* 350 U.S. 270 (1956), the Supreme Court held that employees who are striking to protest the employer's unfair labor practice (so-called "unfair labor practice strikers") may not be permanently replaced. Why should ULP strikers be entitled to greater protection than economic strikers? Although *Mastro Plastics* involved a strike during the term of a collective bargaining agreement, it has been interpreted to prohibit permanent replacement of workers engaged in a strike protesting an unfair labor practice even if the collective bargaining agreement has expired. Unfair labor practice strikers may be temporarily replaced, but upon the cessation of the strike and the strikers' unconditional offer to return to work, the employer must take the strikers back regardless of the existence of replacement workers or of the subcontracting out of the work the strikers formerly performed. It is up to the employer, of course, to decide whether to terminate the replacements or to find other work for them.

In *Belknap v. Hale,* 463 U.S. 491 (1983), an employer had promised replacement workers that they would be permanent, but subsequently terminated them to make way for reinstated strikers. The replacement workers filed state law claims for misrepresentation and breach of contract. The employer argued that the state law claims were preempted by the federal labor law "right" to hire permanent replacements. The Supreme Court disagreed and held the state claims could proceed:

> Arguments that entertaining suits by innocent third parties for breach of contract or for misrepresentation will "burden" the employer's right to hire permanent replacements are no more than arguments that "this is war," that "anything goes," and that promises of permanent employment that under federal law the employer is free to keep, if it so chooses, are essentially meaningless. It is one thing to hold that the federal law intended to leave the employer and the union free to use their economic weapons against one another, but is quite another to hold that either the employer or the union is also free to injure innocent third parties without regard to the normal rules of law governing those relationships. We cannot agree with the dissent that Congress intended such a lawless regime.

> The argument that entertaining suits like this will interfere with the asserted policy of the federal law favoring settlement of labor disputes fares no better. This is just another way of asserting that the employer need not answer for its repeated assurances of permanent employment or for its otherwise actionable misrepresentations to secure permanent replacements. We do not think that the normal contractual rights and other usual legal interests of the replacements can be so easily disposed of by broad-brush assertions that no legal rights may accrue to them during a strike because the federal law has privileged the "permanent" hiring of replacements and encourages settlement.

The difference of rights between economic and unfair labor practice strikers is enormously significant. It creates obvious incentives for dispute over the characterization of the motivation of a strike, which not surprisingly has produced a body of Board decisions on how to identify the motivation for a strike. The problem is further complicated by NLRB cases holding that an economic strike can be "converted" to an unfair labor practice strike if the employer commits an unfair labor practice during the course of the strike that the employees can prove *prolonged* the strike. Any employees who are replaced after the date on which the economic strike was proven to have been converted to an unfair labor practice strike are entitled to their jobs back, regardless of the hiring of replacements, upon an unconditional offer to return to work. The distinction between economic and ULP strikers requires the Board to engage in a counterfactual inquiry based on the totality of the circumstances in which it must be decided whether it was a ULP or an economic demand that precipitated a strike and, in the case of conversion, at what point the strikers would have abandoned a strike but for the commission of unfair labor practices. In the 1994 strike by professional baseball players, Major League Baseball's plan to play a season with the use of replacement players was thwarted by the Board's determination that the strike had converted to an unfair labor practice strike before the date on which any replacement players were hired. The story of the Board's response to the strike, as told by Stanford Law professor (and lifelong Red Sox fan) William B. Gould, who was Chair of the NLRB during the relevant years, appears in William B. Gould, Labored Relations (MIT Press 2002).

Sophisticated negotiators are aware of the greater rights of unfair labor practice strikers. Unions will be especially alert to any employer unfair labor practices before or during a strike in order to prevent an employer from permanently replacing employees. Conversely, employers who otherwise might be unconcerned about NLRB remedies for unfair labor practices might be very concerned about the possibility of having to reinstate strikers. This is particularly true when the employer had anticipated hiring permanent replacements, waiting out the strike for the one year that the strikers would be eligible to vote in a union election, and then seeking to decertify the union with the votes of the permanent replacements.

NOTES

1.   *The effect of the law on bargaining.* The ULP that an employer is most likely to commit during a strike is a failure to bargain, which usually occurs when the employer unilaterally implements its last offer without having reached impasse. Given that, what strategy would you expect a union to use in negotiations during a strike?

2.   *Distinguishing firing from permanent replacement.* As noted above, it is an unfair labor practice for an employer to tell striking employees that they have been permanently replaced before replacements have been hired or to threaten to fire them if they do not abandon the strike. It is, however, permissible under *Mackay* for an employer to permanently replace striking workers, and to announce the intention to do so. How can an employer encourage employees to abandon a strike by advising them of its right and intention to hire permanent replacements without committing an unfair labor practice by threatening to fire the strikers?

3.   *Employer motive.* Hiring permanent replacements is legal if the employer does so to carry on its business during the strike but illegal if the employer does so for an "independent unlawful purpose." An unlawful purpose includes seeking employees who will be willing to cross a picket line in the event of a future strike or to "teach the strikers and the Union a lesson" so as to avoid future strikes. *American Baptist Homes*, 364 N.L.R.B. no. 13 (2016). In the absence of evidence of such an unlawful purpose, could the Board find hiring permanent replacements to be unlawful if it found that it was unnecessary to hire permanent replacements to carry on the business? In other words, what evidence should be necessary (if any) to show hiring permanent

replacements was a legal tactic to protect a business against the harms of a strike as opposed to an illegal infringement of the right to strike?

* * *

Particularly in times of labor shortage or in the case of highly skilled labor, firms may not find it easy to replace striking employees or may wish to offer inducements beyond the threat of job loss to persuade workers to abandon the strike. In the following two cases, the Board and the Court addressed the question of whether an employer unlawfully interferes with the right to strike by offering inducements to strikers to abandon the strike and return to work.

NLRB v. Erie Resistor Corp., 373 U.S. 221 (1963). The company announced during a strike that replacement workers and anyone who abandoned the strike would have twenty years added to the length of a worker's actual service for purposes of future layoffs and recalls, which were determined on a seniority basis. The super-seniority would give replacement workers protection against seasonal or other downturns in work, and would impose all the costs of layoffs on strikers. After the announcement, a substantial number of strikers returned to work and the union called off the strike shortly thereafter. Although many of the hold-out strikers were reinstated, when the company laid off a large number of employees some months later, many of those laid off were strikers who had held out and therefore had not received super-seniority. The employer defended against the unfair labor practice charge by asserting that it had granted super-seniority to keep its plant operating rather than to harm the union or the strike. The Board held that the grant of super-seniority was an unfair labor practice regardless of the employer's motivation and determined that specific evidence of the employer's antiunion motivation was not necessary. The Supreme Court agreed, stating that granting super-seniority was conduct "inherently destructive" of section 7 rights and thus did not require specific proof of discriminatory intent. Noting the "relevance and importance of showing the employer's intent or motive to discriminate or to interfere with union rights" in some cases, the Court stated that "specific evidence of such subjective intent is not an indispensable element of proof of violation. Some conduct may by its very nature contain the implications of the required intent; the natural foreseeable consequences of certain action may warrant the inference." The Court, following the reasoning of the Board, found the super-seniority plan unlawful in a way that permanently replacing striking workers was not, for five reasons. The Court explained:

> (1) Super-seniority affects the tenure of all strikers whereas permanent replacement, proper under *Mackay,* affects only those who are, in actuality, replaced. It is one thing to say that a striker is subject to loss of his job at the strike's end but quite another to hold that in addition to the threat of replacement, all strikers will

at best return to their jobs with seniority inferior to that of the replacements and of those who left the strike.

(2) A super-seniority award necessarily operates to the detriment of those who participated in the strike as compared to non-strikers.

(3) Super-seniority made available to striking bargaining unit employees as well as to new employees is in effect offering individual benefits to the strikers to induce them to abandon the strike.

(4) Extending the benefits of super-seniority to striking bargaining unit employees as well as to new replacements deals a crippling blow to the strike effort. At one stroke, those with low seniority have the opportunity to obtain the job security which ordinarily only long years of service can bring, while conversely, the accumulated seniority of the older employees is seriously diluted. This combination of threat and promise could be expected to undermine the strikers' mutual interest and place the entire strike effort in jeopardy.

(5) Super-seniority renders future bargaining difficult, if not impossible, for the collective bargaining representative. Unlike the replacement granted in *Mackay* which ceases to be an issue once the strike is over, the plan here creates a cleavage in the plant continuing long after the strike is ended.

NLRB v. Great Dane Trailers, Inc., 388 U.S. 26 (1967). During a strike in which the employer continued operations with replacements and others, the employer offered to pay vacation pay on the terms provided in the expired collective bargaining agreement to replacement workers and those who abandoned the strike by a specified date. Shortly before, the company had rejected a request from the strikers for their accrued vacation pay on the grounds that the agreement had expired. The company insisted that the payment to the replacement workers was simply a new "policy" rather than compliance with the expired agreement. The Board found the different treatment was discrimination against the strikers prohibited by section 8(a)(3), but the Court of Appeals found no evidence of any anti-union sentiment. The Supreme Court upheld the Board's determination of an unfair labor practice and established a test for determining whether evidence of specific discriminatory intent was necessary:

First, if it can reasonably be concluded that the employer's discriminatory conduct was "inherently destructive" of important employee rights, no proof of antiunion motivation is needed, and the Board can find an unfair labor practice even if the employer introduces evidence that the conduct was motivated by business considerations. Second, if the adverse effect of the discriminatory conduct on employee rights is "comparatively slight," an antiunion motivation must be proved to sustain the charge *if* the employer has come forward with evidence of legitimate and substantial business justifications for the conduct.

Noting that the company had failed to introduce any evidence of a legitimate motive for its discrimination in paying vacation pay, the Court concluded it was unnecessary to decide whether the vacation pay scheme was "inherently destructive" or was, instead, the sort of thing that would have a "comparatively slight" effect on section 7 rights.

Restated, the rule after *Great Dane* is as follows. (1) If the employer does not provide a legitimate and substantial justification for discrimination against strikers, it violates section 8(a)(3). (2) If the employer does provide such a justification but its treatment of strikers is nevertheless "inherently destructive" of section 7 rights, it violates section 8(a)(3). (3) If the employer provides a legitimate and substantial justification and the discrimination against strikers has only a "comparatively slight" effect on section 7 rights, the employer does not violate section 8(a)(3) unless anti-union motivation can be proven.

NOTES

1.   *Why seniority matters.* In many unionized workplaces, unions have negotiated for seniority to be a principal determinant of compensation and job advancement. Unions prefer seniority (which is an objective measure) to other measures (like merit) because it is not susceptible to manipulation by supervisors. Unions and employers both favor rewards for seniority in times of labor scarcity because it induces loyalty to the firm and gives employees a sense of optimism about their future. Seniority rules are important to most workers, but they are more institutionalized and less subject to unilateral change in unionized workplaces. Given the enormous importance of seniority to compensation, to an employee's ability to get favorable shift or job assignments, and to job security in times of labor force reduction, can you see why the employer in *Erie Resistor* thought an offer of super-seniority was an effective device to recruit strike breakers and why the Supreme Court thought it was so problematic?

2.   *Identifying the principles underlying the rules.* What principle does the Court use in *Erie Resistor* and in *Great Dane* to decide which economic weapons are permissible and which are impermissible? Are you persuaded by the Court's distinction between permanent replacements (allowed under *Mackay*) and granting super-seniority to permanent replacements (not allowed under *Erie Resistor*)? Can you reconcile *Erie Resistor* and *Mackay*? What criteria should the Board use—other than the Board Members' own sense of which tactics are productive of industrial peace and which are not, or which give one side excessive power and which do not—to distinguish tactics that are illegal and those that are not?

3. *The means-ends test again?* Notice the similarity between the distinctions among economic weapons and the doctrine of "indefensible" strikes discussed above at pp. 200–215. Both bodies of law invite policy judgments about appropriate behavior and a desirable balance of bargaining power.

4. *Who should make policy judgments?* What deference, if any, should a court give to the Board's judgment that particular weapons are unacceptable? Is this an area in which courts should defer to agency expertise? If so, how should courts assess whether the NLRB's judgment is based on expertise as opposed to the policy preferences of the current Board members?

5. *Proving anti-union motive.* How would the Board's general counsel prove the discriminatory intent required to establish a § 8(a)(3) violation in the preferential treatment of replacement workers?

* * *

When a striker is reinstated to a job after termination of a strike, he or she must be reinstated with full seniority. In the case that follows, the Court considers whether returning strikers can use their greater seniority to bump replacement workers from more desirable jobs. In the airline industry, in which many employees much prefer to fly some routes rather than others, the question whether returning strikers can displace less senior replacements is of great practical significance.

TRANS WORLD AIRLINES, INC. V. INDEPENDENT FEDERATION OF FLIGHT ATTENDANTS
489 U.S. 426 (1988)

JUSTICE O'CONNOR delivered the opinion of the Court:

We decide today whether, at the end of a strike, an employer is required by the Railway Labor Act to displace employees who worked during the strike in order to reinstate striking employees with greater seniority.

In March 1984, Trans World Airlines, Inc. (TWA), and the Independent Federation of Flight Attendants (IFFA or Union) began negotiations on a new collective bargaining agreement to replace their prior agreement due to expire on July 31, 1984. The existing collective bargaining agreement created a complex system of bidding the general effect of which was to insure that those flight attendants with the greatest seniority would have the best opportunity to obtain their preferred job assignments, flight schedules, and bases of operation as vacancies appeared, and to insure that senior flight attendants would be least affected by the periodic furloughs endemic to the airline industry.

[After two years of fruitless negotiations, the Union went out on strike.]

TWA continued its operations during the 72-day strike by utilizing approximately 1,280 flight attendants who either did not strike or returned to work before the end of the strike and by hiring and fully training approximately 2,350 new flight attendants, some 1,220 of whom were hired during the first few days of the strike. On May 17, 1986, the Union made an unconditional offer to TWA on behalf of the approximately 5,000 flight attendants who had remained on strike to return to work. TWA accepted the offer but refused the Union's May 27th demand that TWA displace those prestrike employees who were working as of May 17th ("crossover" employees). Accordingly, TWA initially recalled only the 197 most senior full-term strikers to fill available job and domicile vacancies. By the terms of a poststrike arbitral agreement, these strikers and all subsequently reinstated full-term strikers returned to work as vacancies arose and with precisely the seniority they would have had if no strike had occurred. In May 1988, more than 1,100 full-term strikers had been reinstated with full seniority.

In an effort to reinstate all the full-term strikers by displacing the newly hired flight attendants and less senior crossover employees, the Union . . . filed the instant action contending that, even assuming the strike was economic, the full-term strikers were entitled to reinstatement either under the terms of the prestrike collective bargaining agreement or under the RLA itself.

TWA argues that it would be completely anomalous to hold that full-term strikers may displace junior crossovers when, as the Union has conceded, they may not displace newly hired permanent replacements under either statute. The Union, by contrast, argues that the rule of *Mackay Radio* is inapplicable to junior crossovers because of differences between the RLA and the NLRA and because, even under the NLRA, junior crossovers would be treated differently from newly hired permanent replacements.

The Union does not and cannot contend that reinstated full-term strikers have less seniority relative to new hires and junior crossovers than they would have had if they had not remained on strike. It is clear that reinstated full-term strikers lost no seniority either in absolute or relative terms. Thus, unlike the situation in *Erie Resistor*, any future reductions in force at TWA will permit reinstated full-term strikers to displace junior flight attendants exactly as would have been the case in the absence of any strike. Similarly, should any vacancies develop in desirable job assignments or domiciles, reinstated full-term strikers who have bid on those vacancies will maintain their priority over junior flight attendants, whether they are new hires, crossovers, or full-term strikers. In the same vein, periodic bids on job scheduling will find senior reinstated full-term strikers maintaining their priority over all their junior colleagues. In short, once reinstated, the seniority of full-term strikers is in no way affected by their decision to strike.

Nevertheless, IFFA argues that TWA's refusal to displace junior crossovers will create a "cleavage" between junior crossovers and reinstated full-term strikers at TWA long after the strike is ended. This is the case because desirable job assignments and domiciles that would have been occupied by the most senior flight attendants had there been no strike will continue to be held by those who did not see the strike through to its conclusion. For example, the senior full-term striker who worked in the Los Angeles domicile before the strike may have been replaced by a junior crossover. As poststrike vacancies develop in TWA's work force, permitting reinstatement of full-term strikers, they are not likely to occur in the most desirable domiciles. Thus, it is unlikely that the senior full-term striker would be reinstated back to her preferred domicile. Resentful rifts among employees will also persist after the strike, the Union argues, because TWA's prestrike assurance of nondisplacement to junior crossovers, unlike the same assurance to new hires, set up a competition *among* those individuals who participated in the original decision to strike, and thereby undermined the group's ability to take the collective action that it is the very purpose of the [RLA] to protect.

We reject this effort to expand *Erie Resistor*. Both the RLA and the NLRA protect an employee's right to choose not to strike and, thereby, protect employees' rights to the benefit of their individual decisions not to strike. Accordingly, in virtually every strike situation there will be some employees who disagree with their union's decision to strike and who cannot be required to abide by that decision. It is the inevitable effect of an employer's use of the economic weapons available during a period of self-help that these differences will be exacerbated and that poststrike resentments may be created. Thus, for example, the employer's right to hire permanent replacements in order to continue operations will inevitably also have the effect of dividing striking employees between those who, fearful of permanently losing their jobs, return to work and those who remain stalwart in the strike. In such a situation, apart from the "pressure on the strikers *as a group* to abandon the strike," to which the dissent refers, a "competition" may arise *among* the striking employees to return to work in order to avoid being displaced by a permanent replacement. Similarly, employee awareness that an employer may decide to transfer working employees to necessary positions previously occupied by more senior striking employees will isolate employees fearful of losing those positions and employees coveting those positions from employees more committed to the strike. Conversely, a policy such as TWA employed here, in creating the incentive for individual strikers to return to work, also "puts pressure on the strikers *as a group* to abandon the strike," in the same manner that the hiring of permanent replacements does.

None of these scenarios, however, present the prospect of a continuing diminution of seniority upon reinstatement at the end of the strike that was central to our decision in *Erie Resistor*. All that has occurred is that the employer has filled vacancies created by striking employees. Some of these vacancies will be filled by newly hired employees, others by doubtless more experienced and therefore more needed employees who either refused to strike or abandoned the strike. The dissent's observation that, "at the conclusion of the strike," discrimination in the filling of "available positions" based on union activity is impermissible is beside the point. The positions occupied by newly hired replacements, employees who refused to strike, and employees who abandoned the strike are simply not "available positions" to be filled. As noted above, those positions that were available at the conclusion of the strike were filled "according to some principle, such as seniority, that is neutral. . . ." That the prospect of a reduction in available positions may divide employees and create incentives among them to remain at work or abandon a strike before its conclusion is a secondary effect fairly within the arsenal of economic weapons available to employers during a period of self-help.

To distinguish crossovers from new hires in the manner IFFA proposes would have the effect of penalizing those who decided not to strike in order to benefit those who did. Because permanent replacements need not be discharged at the conclusion of a strike in which the union has been unsuccessful, a certain number of prestrike employees will find themselves without work. We see no reason why those employees who chose not to gamble on the success of the strike should suffer the consequences when the gamble proves unsuccessful. Requiring junior crossovers, who cannot themselves displace the newly hired permanent replacements, and "who rank lowest in seniority," to be displaced by more senior full-term strikers is precisely to visit the consequences of the lost gamble on those who refused to take the risk. While the employer and union in many circumstances may reach a back-to-work agreement that would displace crossovers and new hires or an employer may unilaterally decide to permit such displacement, nothing in the NLRA or the federal common law we have developed under that statute requires such a result. That such agreements are typically one mark of a successful strike is yet another indication that crossovers opted not to gamble; if the strike was successful the advantage gained by declining to strike disappears.

JUSTICE BRENNAN, with whom JUSTICE MARSHALL joins, dissenting:

In the first place, refusing to discriminate in favor of crossovers is not to visit the consequences of the lost strike on "those who refused to take the risk," but rather on those who rank lowest in seniority. Whether a given flight attendant chose to take the risk of the strike or not is wholly immaterial. Rather—as is virtually universally the case when work-force reductions are necessary for whatever reason in a unionized enterprise—it is the most junior employees, whether strikers or crossovers, who are most vulnerable. This is precisely the point of seniority.

More fundamental, I fear, is the legal mistake inherent in the Court's objection to "penalizing those who decided not to strike in order to benefit those who did." The Court, of course, does precisely the opposite: it allows TWA to single out for penalty precisely those employees who were faithful to the strike until the end, in order to benefit those who abandoned it. What is unarticulated is the Court's basis for choosing one position over the other. If indeed one group or the other is to be "penalized," what basis does the Court have for determining that it should be those who remained on strike rather than those who returned to work? I see none, unless it is perhaps an unarticulated hostility toward strikes. In any case the NLRA *does* provide a basis for resolving this question. It requires simply that in making poststrike reinstatements an employer may not discriminate among its employees on account of their union activity. That, in fact, is the *holding* of *NLRB v. Mackay Radio*—the more familiar teaching as to the employer's right to hire permanent replacements having been dictum. If an employer may not discriminate—in either direction—on the basis of the employee's strike activity, then it follows that the employer must make decisions about which employees to reinstate on the basis of some neutral criterion, such as seniority. That is precisely what the Union asks.

We have recognized only a narrow exception to the general principle prohibiting discrimination against employees for exercising their right to strike. Since *Mackay Radio* it has been accepted that an employer may hire "permanent replacements" in order to maintain operations during a strike, and that these replacements need not be displaced to make room for returning strikers. The question here is whether the *Mackay* exception should be expanded to cover the present case, involving as it does members of the striking bargaining unit who have crossed the picket lines, rather than new hires from outside the bargaining unit. Despite the superficial similarity between the two situations, strong reasons counsel against applying the *Mackay* rule to crossover employees.

The employer's promise to members of the bargaining unit that they will not be displaced at the end of a strike if they cross the picket lines addresses a far different incentive to the bargaining-unit members than does the employer's promise of permanence to new hires. The employer's threat to hire permanent replacements from outside the existing work force puts pressure on the strikers *as a group* to abandon the strike before their positions are filled by others. But the employer's promise to members of the striking bargaining unit that if they abandon the strike (or refuse to join it at the outset) they will retain their jobs at strike's end in preference to more senior workers who remain on strike produces an additional dynamic: now there is also an incentive for *individual* workers to seek to save (or improve) their own positions at the expense of other members of the striking bargaining unit. We have previously observed that offers of "individual benefits to the strikers to induce them to abandon the strike . . . could be expected to undermine the strikers' mutual interest and place the entire strike effort in jeopardy." *NLRB v. Erie Resistor Corp.* Such a "divide and conquer" tactic thus "strike[s] a fundamental blow to union . . . activity and the collective bargaining process itself."

In *Erie Resistor* we found the employer's offer of superseniority to new hires and crossovers to be "inherently destructive" of the right to strike and therefore in contravention of §§ 8(a)(1) and 8(a)(3) of the NLRA. In my view the same conclusion should apply here. Beyond its specific holding outlawing superseniority, I read *Erie Resistor* to stand for the principle that there are certain tools an employer may not use, even in the interest of continued operations during a strike, and that the permissibility of discriminatory measures taken for that purpose must be evaluated by weighing the "necessity" of the employer's action (*i. e.,* its interest in maintaining operations during the strike) against its prejudice to the employees' right to strike. It seems clear to me that in this case the result of such an analysis should be to forbid the employer to give preferential treatment to crossovers, because of the destructive impact of such an action on the strikers' mutual interest. Thus, when an employer recalls workers to fill the available positions at the conclusion of a strike, it may not discriminate against either the strikers or the crossovers. Rather it must proceed according to some principle, such as seniority, that is neutral as between them.[6] That TWA failed to do.

Similarly, the Court's concluding statement that "the decision to guarantee to crossovers the same protections lawfully applied to new hires was a simple decision to apply the pre-existing seniority terms of the collective bargaining agreement uniformly to all *working* employees," again assumes what must be proved. If "working" refers to the poststrike period, which employees are working and which are not is a function of the employer's decision to give preference to the crossovers; if instead it refers to the period prior to the strike's end, the question remains whether the employer may make poststrike employment decisions on the basis of which employees were "working" during the strike.

[The dissenting opinion of JUSTICE BLACKMUN is omitted.]

NOTES

1. *Understanding the impact of the Court's rule.* TWA's policy caused some immediate hardships for striking workers and other longer-term harms. For example, during the strike, TWA allowed a re-bidding of routes for all

---

[6] While there might be circumstances in which some neutral principle other than seniority might be acceptable as a basis for recalls (*e. g.,* the employer's need for particular skills), seniority is so well established in labor relations as the basis for such decisions that exceptions should be rare. In any case, TWA has made no pretense that its discriminatory recalls are justified by some other neutral principle.

nonstriking employees and excluded the striking flight attendants from the bidding. Since shifts and routes were determined by seniority, an employee who had worked for years to earn a good shift or to fly desirable routes might find herself suddenly demoted to a much less desirable position. The policy also caused longer-term harms, as the length of time it would take for an employee to get her old position back would depend on the amount of turnover and also on whether the airline expanded or contracted its routes and schedules.

2.   *Is the "inherent destructiveness" of a policy about strikers always a function of the labor market or is some other principle at stake?* Given that the severity and duration of the harm suffered by the strikers was a function of the labor market, is the Court's distinction of *Erie Resistor* persuasive? Should the rights of strikers depend on the circumstances of whether the strike occurs during a period of job growth or contraction? Do they inevitably depend on whether the labor market enables the employer to recruit permanent replacements?

3.   *Is there a principled distinction between* Erie Resistor *and* TWA? Once a court or the Board concludes that some advantages accruing to employees who cross a picket line are of the employer's doing (as in *Erie Resistor* and *Great Dane*) and others are due to the employees' decision to strike (as in *TWA*), what is the most principled way to distinguish between legal and the illegal tactics to encourage employees to abandon a strike?

4.   *State laws regulating the use of striker replacements are preempted.* By design, strikes interrupt the operations of a struck business and cause inconvenience to customers. Governments in some states have attempted to protect workers from being permanently replaced. For example, after the devastating strike at the Hormel meat plant in Austin, Minnesota resulted in the permanent replacement of hundreds of striking workers, the Minnesota legislature prohibited the hiring of permanent replacements in some circumstances. The legislation was held to be preempted. *Employers Ass'n v. United Steelworkers*, 32 F.3d 1297 (8th Cir. 1994). Governments in other states have entered the fray on the side of the employer, believing that the employer's right to hire replacements workers is inadequate to protect the public interest and that laws ensuring continuous work are necessary. The NLRA has been held to preempt most such legislation. For example, in *Cannon v. Edgar*, 33 F.3d 880 (7th Cir. 1994), the court held preempted an Illinois law providing for a reserve pool of cemetery workers to provide burial services in case of a strike.

b.   Union Tactics in the Battle for Solidarity

Given that the NLRA has been construed to create an employer right to hire replacement workers, unions face challenges in maintaining solidarity during a strike. One way unions discourage their members from crossing a picket line is by disciplining them for doing so. Both employers and dissident union members have challenged such union rules.

In *NLRB v. Allis-Chalmers*, 388 U.S. 175 (1967), the Court upheld the power of a union to fine members for crossing a picket line. A lower court had held that the discipline coerced employees in violation of § 8(b)(1)(A), but the Supreme Court disagreed:

> Integral to federal labor policy has been the power in the chosen union to protect against erosion of its status under that policy through reasonable discipline of members who violate rules and regulations governing membership. That power is particularly vital when the members engage in strikes. The economic strike against the employer is the ultimate weapon in labor's arsenal for achieving agreement upon its terms, and the power to fine or expel strikebreakers is essential if the union is to be an effective bargaining agent.
>
> [The Court then canvassed both the legislative history of the Taft-Hartley addition of section 8(b)(1)(A) and the legislative history of the 1959 Landrum Griffin Act's further refinements of section 8(b).] To say that Congress meant in 1947 by the § 7 amendments and § 8(b)(1)(A) to strip unions of the power to fine members for strikebreaking, however lawful the strike vote, and however fair the disciplinary procedures and penalty, is to say that Congress preceded the Landrum-Griffin amendments with an even more pervasive regulation of the internal affairs of unions. It is also to attribute to Congress an intent at war with the understanding of the union-membership relation which has been at the heart of its effort "to fashion a coherent labor policy" and which has been a predicate underlying action by this Court and the state courts. More importantly, it is to say that Congress limited unions in the powers necessary to the discharge of their role as exclusive statutory bargaining agents by impairing the usefulness of labor's cherished strike weapon. It is no answer that the proviso to § 8(b)(1)(A) preserves to the union the power to expel the offending member. Where the union is strong and membership therefore valuable, to require expulsion of the member visits a far more severe penalty upon the member than a reasonable fine. Where the union is weak, and membership therefore of little value, the union faced with further depletion of its ranks may have no real choice except to condone the member's disobedience. Yet it is just such weak unions for which the power to execute union decisions taken for the benefit of all employees is most critical to effective discharge of its statutory function.
>
> The 1959 Landrum-Griffin amendments, thought to be the first comprehensive regulation by Congress of the conduct of internal union affairs, also negate the reach given § 8(b)(1)(A) by the majority en banc below. In 1959 Congress did seek to protect union members in their relationship to the union by adopting measures to insure the provision of democratic processes in the

conduct of union affairs and procedural due process to members subjected to discipline. Indeed, that Congress expressly recognized that a union member may be "fined, suspended, expelled, or otherwise disciplined," and enacted only procedural requirements to be observed. Moreover, Congress added a proviso to the guarantee of freedom of speech and assembly disclaiming any intent "to impair the right of a labor organization to adopt and enforce reasonable rules as to the responsibility of every member toward the organization as an institution." 29 U.S.C. § 411(a)(2).

The requirements of adherence to democratic principles, fair procedures and freedom of speech apply to the election of union officials and extend into all aspects of union affairs. In the present case the procedures followed for calling the strikes and disciplining the recalcitrant members fully comported with these requirements, and were in every way fair and democratic. Whether § 8(b)(1)(A) proscribes arbitrary imposition of fines, or punishment for disobedience of a fiat of a union leader, are matters not presented by this case.

After *Allis-Chalmers*, a union member who wished to cross a picket line without facing discipline under union rules could do so only if he or she resigned membership in the union. Some unions therefore tried to limit the ability of members to resign during a strike. In *Pattern Makers' League v. NLRB,* 473 U.S. 95 (1985), the Court invalidated union rules restricting resignation during strikes. (The case is excerpted *infra* in Chapter 8.) During the course of a lengthy strike, several union members resigned from the union, crossed a picket line, and returned to work. After the strike settled, the union attempted to fine the workers in an amount equal to what they had earned during the strike. The employer filed unfair labor practice charges on behalf of the employees against the union. The Court upheld the Board's determination that restrictions on the right to resign restrained or coerced employees in violation of § 8(b)(1)(A). The Court discerned in the federal labor law a policy that union membership must be voluntary and deduced from that both that an employer rule adversely affecting employees based on their union membership or a union rule attempting to restrict employees' choice of membership violated the NLRA.

There is a proviso in § 8(b)(1)(A) that nothing in it shall "impair the right of a labor organization to prescribe its own rules with respect to the acquisition or retention of membership therein." The majority of the Court rejected the argument that the proviso allowed restrictions on the right to resign because it saw no limiting principle that would distinguish when a union could prevent members from resigning and when it could not: "An absolute restriction on resignations would enhance a union's collective-bargaining power, as would a rule that prohibited resignations during the life of the collective-bargaining agreement. In short, there is no limiting principle."

NOTES

1.   *The rights of employees against the union.* In both *Allis-Chalmers* and *Pattern Makers*, and, as you will see in Chapter 8, in many other cases addressing the rights of dissident employees against the union, it was the employer or employer association that litigated the case on behalf of the dissident workers. Employer groups, including the National Right to Work Committee, have been influential in advocating the development of the law protecting the rights of employees against unions. Why do employers advocate the rights of nonunion workers or dissident union-represented workers?

2.   *The significance of being a supervisor.* Under § 8(b)(1)(B), can a union fine a supervisor who is also a union member for crossing a picket line or performing struck work? Does it depend on whether the supervisor is an "employee" protected by the NLRA?

3.   *Is ostracism unlawful?* Does a union violate § 8(b)(1)(A) by encouraging members to shun or ostracize former union members who cross a picket line? What can a union do to persuade its members to honor a strike or otherwise to maintain solidarity?

4.   *What does the union owe to striker replacements?* Does a union violate § 8(b)(1)(A) by persuading an employer to terminate replacement workers at the conclusion of a strike, or to displace cross-overs to allow those who stayed with the strike to resume their old jobs? Would an employer violate § 8(a)(3) by displacing replacement workers or cross-overs to make way for returning strikers at the end of the strike?

5.   *Deference to the Board.* In *Pattern Makers,* the Court deferred to the Board's determination that the union's rule violated § 8(b)(1)(A) and was not saved by the proviso. If the Board had reached the contrary conclusion, would the Court have been obligated to defer to it?

6.   *Advising a union about how to handle dissidents.* If a strike appears to be controversial (or weak) enough that a significant number of employees may choose not to participate in it, what should a union consider before deciding to take actions against its dissenting members? If the union is unduly harsh on its dissenting members, who do you suppose will be the most vigorous advocates of a subsequent effort to decertify the union?

A NOTE ON CORPORATE SOCIAL RESPONSIBILITY CAMPAIGNS

As we have seen, there are many limitations on the statutory protections for the right to strike. Depending on the surplus of labor, employers have a number of weapons (both legal and illegal) to fight a strike. Both law and practical concerns limit a union's ability to force employees to stick with a strike when the going gets tough. Not surprisingly, many unions have all but abandoned the strike in organizing campaigns, in efforts to secure a first collective bargaining agreement, or even in negotiations for a renewed collective bargaining agreement. In the contemporary workplace, unions seek leverage through a variety of other forms of protest that have come to be known loosely as a "corporate campaign," a "comprehensive campaign," or a "worker-driven corporate social responsibility campaign," which includes the external pressure from consumers along with efforts to generate workforce activism and to use legal tactics within the workplace to exert leverage. The basic idea of such a campaign is to identify political and economic vulnerabilities of the target employer and to apply pressure at those points.

The modern worker-driven corporate social responsibility campaign emerged in the 1980s in reaction to the weak protections of the NLRA for strikes. Strikes were perceived to be both too expensive for unions and too risky for workers. Workers sought other ways to exert social, political, and financial pressure on the firm. Originally, these campaigns were used primarily during contract negotiations to pressure financial backers of the employer to discourage employer resistance to the union's bargaining demands. Now such campaigns are an integral part of many organizing campaigns. The law and practice of these campaigns is covered in Chapter 8.

D. EMPLOYER WEAPONS

1. LOCKOUTS

In addition to the ability to replace striking workers under *Mackay Radio*, employers have other weapons that the Board and the Court have held to be permissible under the NLRA. One of the most potent is the lockout, which enables the employer to enhance its bargaining power by prohibiting employees from working and thus earning money.

Historically, the Board regarded some lockouts as a permissible defense to a threatened strike, and others as an impermissible effort to gain offensive advantage in negotiations. An "offensive" lockout, which is one initiated without the employer having any reason to believe a strike was likely, was deemed an unfair labor practice because it coerced employees based on their exercise of § 7 rights to bargain collectively. A "defensive" lockout, in which an employer locks out employees in anticipation of an imminent strike, was permissible in three circumstances. One was when the union was conducting "whipsaw" strikes of multiple employers in the same industry. Whipsaw strikes are successive (not simultaneous) strikes against businesses that compete against each other; they are an advantageous tactic because each individual employer is afraid to lose its customers to its competitors. A defensive lockout was also permissible when the union was engaged in a pattern of "quickie strikes." Finally, a defensive lockout was permissible when the union timed a strike for the employer's peak sales or service period in a seasonal industry in order to inflict the most harm.

The distinction between offensive and defensive lockouts was significantly eroded by the Supreme Court in *American Ship Building Co. v. NLRB*, 380 U.S. 300 (1965), in which the Supreme Court held that a lockout was not an unfair labor practice. American Ship Building operated shipyards on the Great Lakes. The work was concentrated in the winter months when the freezing of the Great Lakes renders shipping impossible. When the collective bargaining agreement expired in August, the company laid off most of its employees and shut the shipyards down. The Board found that the lockout violated sections 8(a)(1) and 8(a)(3). Although the work could be described as seasonal, the Board found that this lockout was "offensive"—intended to pressure the union in negotiations rather than to protect the employer's business. The Supreme Court rejected the distinction and upheld the lockout.

> No one would deny that an employer is free to shut down his enterprise temporarily for reasons of renovation or lack of profitable work unrelated to his collective bargaining situation. Similarly, we put to one side cases where the Board has concluded on the basis of substantial evidence that the employer has used a lockout as a means to injure a labor organization or to evade his duty to bargain collectively. [The Court also rejected the Board's position that the lockout] "punishes employees for the presentation of and adherence to demands made by their bargaining representatives and so coerces them in the exercise of their right to bargain collectively." [T]here is no indication, either as a general matter or in this specific case, that the lockout will necessarily destroy the unions' capacity for effective and responsible representation. The unions here involved have vigorously represented the employees since 1952, and there is nothing to show that their ability to do so has been impaired by the lockout. Nor is the lockout one of those acts which are demonstrably so destructive of collective bargaining that the Board need not inquire into employer motivation, as might be the case, for example, if an employer permanently discharged his unionized staff and replaced them with employees known to be possessed of a violent antiunion animus. *NLRB v. Erie Resistor Corp.* The lockout may well dissuade employees from adhering to the position which they initially adopted in the bargaining, but the right to bargain collectively does not entail any "right" to insist on one's position free from economic disadvantage.

The Court also rejected the Board's conclusion that the lockout interfered with the right to strike.

> It is true that recognition of the lockout deprives the union of exclusive control of the timing and duration of work stoppages calculated to influence the result of collective bargaining

negotiations, but there is nothing in the statute which would imply that the right to strike carries with it the right exclusively to determine the timing and duration of all work stoppages. The right to strike as commonly understood is the right to cease work—nothing more. No doubt a union's bargaining power would be enhanced if it possessed not only the simple right to strike but also the power exclusively to determine when work stoppages should occur, but the Act's provisions are not indefinitely elastic, content-free forms to be shaped in whatever manner the Board might think best conforms to the proper balance of bargaining power.

Finally, the Court rejected the Board's conclusion that a lockout violated section 8(a)(3):

It has long been established that a finding of violation under this section will normally turn on the employer's motivation. But we have consistently construed the section to leave unscathed a wide range of employer actions taken to serve legitimate business interests in some significant fashion, even though the act committed may tend to discourage union membership. *See, e.g., NLRB v. Mackay Radio & Telegraph Co.*, 304 U.S. 333 (1938). [T]his lockout does not fall into that category of cases arising under § 8(a)(3) in which the Board may truncate its inquiry into employer motivation. The purpose and effect of the lockout were only to bring pressure upon the union to modify its demands. Similarly, it does not appear that the natural tendency of the lockout is severely to discourage union membership while serving no significant employer interest. It is true that the employees suffered economic disadvantage because of their union's insistence on demands unacceptable to the employer, but this is also true of many steps which an employer may take during a bargaining conflict, and the existence of an arguable possibility that someone may feel himself discouraged in his union membership or discriminated against by reason of that membership cannot suffice to label them violations of § 8(a)(3) absent some unlawful intention. The employer's permanent replacement of strikers, his unilateral imposition of terms, or his simple refusal to make a concession which would terminate a strike—all impose economic disadvantage during a bargaining conflict, but none is necessarily a violation of § 8(a)(3).

The Board has justified its ruling in this case and its general approach to the legality of lockouts on the basis of its special competence to weigh the competing interests of employers and employees and to accommodate these interests according to its expert judgment. The Board has reasonably concluded that the availability of such a weapon would so substantially tip the scales in the employer's favor as to defeat the Congressional purpose of placing employees on a par with their adversary at the bargaining table. To buttress its decision as to the balance struck in this particular case, the Board points out that the employer has been given other weapons to counterbalance the employees' power of strike. The employer may permanently replace workers who have gone out on strike, or, by stockpiling and subcontracting, maintain his commercial operations while the strikers bear the economic brunt of the work stoppage. Similarly, the employer can institute unilaterally the working conditions which he desires once his contract with the union has expired. Given these economic weapons, it is argued, the employer has been adequately equipped with tools of economic self-help. [W]e think that the Board construes its functions too expansively when it claims general authority to define national labor policy by balancing the competing interests of labor and management. Sections 8(a)(1) and (3) do not give the Board a general authority to assess the relative economic power of the adversaries in the bargaining process and to deny weapons to one party or the other because of its assessment of that party's bargaining power. In this case the Board has, in essence, denied the use of the bargaining lockout to the employer because of its conviction that use of this device would give the employer "too much power." In so doing, the Board has stretched §§ 8(a)(1) and (3) far beyond their functions of protecting the rights of employee organization and collective bargaining.

NOTES

1.   *The offensive-defensive distinction.* Was the lockout in *American Ship Building* offensive or defensive? Does the difficulty of distinguishing between them suggest why the distinction ultimately faded from significance?

2.   *Are lockouts the equivalent of strikes?* Should lockouts be more or less favored by law than strikes? What reasons exist for treating them differently than strikes?

3.   *The "indefensible" principle again.* Recall from Chapter 2 the "indefensible" exception to section 7 protection, which declares that strikes timed to inflict maximal harm on an employer might be unprotected. Can you see how the old "offensive-defensive" distinction among lockouts resembled the "indefensible" exception? Now that the Court has largely abandoned the distinction, might a union be able to argue that a lockout timed to inflict maximal harm on workers is "indefensible" and therefore an unfair labor practice?

4.   *Lockouts in professional sports.* The most highly publicized lockouts (or threatened lockouts) in recent times are those in major professional sports, including the 161-day lockout of players in 2011 that shortened the 2011–2012

National Basketball Association season, and the 18-week lockout of players in 2011 in the National Football League. (Both lockouts ended when the players and owners reached new collective bargaining agreements.) The NFL locked out referees in 2012 and used replacement officials for a number of games; the debatable calls by inexperienced officials caused considerable consternation among players and fans. And the National Hockey League player lockout in 2012–2013 reduced the regular season from a normal 82 games to 48 and nearly resulted in cancellation of the entire season. Why did or might the owners in these sports resort to lockouts when the players or referees did not strike? Why do lockouts typically commence in the off-season?

In both football and basketball, the players voted to decertify their union and filed antitrust claims against the owners alleging that the lockout and the related refusal to draft new players was an unlawful conspiracy in restraint of trade. The significance of the decertification of the union was to remove the exemption from antitrust liability that employers enjoy when their employees are unionized; absent the antitrust exemption, both the employers and the unions might be prohibited from colluding to set terms of compensation. In both instances, the owners defended on the ground that the disbanding of the union was a sham. In *Brady v. NFL*, 644 F.3d 661 (8th Cir. 2011), the court of appeals held that the Norris-LaGuardia Act prohibited the issuance of an injunction against the NFL lockout and declined to address the question whether the disbanding of the union rendered the owners subject to antitrust liability for colluding to lock out the players. Among the major legal issues arising out of the lockouts are those concerning the owners' efforts to protect their own revenue stream from television and other sources. For example, the NFL owners negotiated a TV broadcast contract that pays them millions of dollars even if no games are played, and NFL players insist that the revenue should be shared with them. What labor regulation, if any, should govern what employers can do to remain profitable during a lockout? This labor dispute is discussed in detail in Chapter 9.

5. *Time to reassess the law of lockouts?* Two scholars have argued that fifty years of empirical evidence on the effects of the offensive bargaining lockout shows that the NLRB should revisit *American Ship Building*'s underlying principles and limit the circumstances under which lockouts are lawful. Douglas E. Ray & Christopher David Ruiz Cameron, *Revisiting the Offensive Bargaining Lockout on the Fiftieth Anniversary of American Ship Building Company v. NLRB*, 31 ABA J. Lab. & Emp. L. 326 (2016). The authors propose that a lockout in support of a bargaining position be allowed only if: (a) the lockout supports a good faith bargaining position; (b) the parties have bargained to impasse; (c) the employer is forbidden to use temporary replacements during the lockout. A lockout that fails to adhere to these three rules, the authors argue, should be deemed to be inherently destructive of workers' section 7 rights. Do you agree with their proposal? Why or why not?

2. PARTIAL LOCKOUTS

Once the Supreme Court made it clear that the old offensive-defensive distinction was irrelevant to the legality of lockouts, the question remained whether it was still relevant to determining whether or how an employer could continue to operate its business during the lockout. May an employer lock out some but not all of its employees? Is an employer that locks out its employees free to resort to all the tactics employers use to survive strikes, including the subcontracting out of work and temporarily or permanently replacing its employees? May the employer selectively lock out only those employees who are inessential to its operations? If an employer may lock out its employees and permanently replace them, is that a weapon that would allow any employer to get rid of its unionized employees? The following opinions, a decision of the Board and of the court of appeals in the same case illustrate different points of view in this rapidly changing area of law.

MIDWEST GENERATION
343 N.L.R.B. 69 (2004)

By CHAIRMAN BATTISTA and MEMBERS SCHAUMBER and WALSH:

On June 28, 2001 the Union commenced an economic strike in support of its bargaining position. The entire bargaining unit—approximately 1150 employees—participated in the strike as of its commencement, with the exception of approximately 8 bargaining unit members who continued working (nonstrikers).

During the course of the economic strike, the Respondent maintained operations using supervisory personnel, contractors, and some temporary replacement employees. The Respondent did not use permanent replacements during the strike, or during its subsequent lockout.

Some bargaining unit employees returned to work for the Respondent during the strike. From June 28 to August 31, approximately 47 striking employees individually offered to return to work, and Respondent accepted them back (these employees are hereafter referred to as crossover employees).

As of August 31, the Respondent and the Union had not reached agreement on the terms of a new collective-bargaining agreement, and were still engaged in bargaining for a new contract. By letter dated August 31, the Union notified the Respondent that it was terminating the strike, and made an unconditional offer to return to work on behalf of all strikers.

The parties held a bargaining session on September 4. The Respondent advised the Union that it was evaluating the Union's offer to return to work, and had not yet reached any decision. By letter dated September 6, the Respondent declined the Union's offer to return to work, and instituted a lockout of all those individuals on strike as of the date of the offer (August 31). The Respondent's September 6 letter notified the Union that it "will not allow striking employees to return to work until a new contract is agreed to and ratified by your membership." The letter stated that "[t]hose employees who had already returned to work, or were scheduled to return to work, prior to Friday, August 31, 2001 will be allowed to continue to work."

Many bargaining unit employees sought to return to work after the lockout commenced. The Respondent informed them they could not return until a new contract was agreed to and ratified by the union membership.

On October 16, the bargaining unit ratified the Respondent's September 21 contract proposal. On October 22, the Respondent ended the lockout, and all locked out employees who opted to do so returned to work.

The evidence here clearly establishes that the Respondent's lockout was for the purpose of applying economic pressure in support of its legitimate bargaining proposals. [T]he lockout here, brought in support of the Respondent's legitimate bargaining position, cannot be considered inherently destructive of employee rights under *Great Dane*. Accordingly, we shall treat the Respondent's lockout as having a "comparatively slight" impact on employee rights and apply the second *Great Dane* test to determine the lockout's legality. "[I]f the action is deemed to have only a comparatively slight impact on employee rights, an affirmative showing of antiunion motivation must be made to sustain a violation under the second test of *Great Dane*, if the employer has first come forward with evidence of a legitimate and substantial business justification for its conduct."

The Respondent has justified the partial nature of its lockout. The Respondent explains that the lockout applied only to employees who were actively participating in the strike on August 31 in support of the Union's bargaining demands, in order to pressure them to abandon those demands.

[I]t is settled that the Board recognizes the legality of partial lockouts when justified by operational needs and without regard to union membership status.

First, there is no dispute that the partial nature of the lockout was unrelated to union affiliation; the parties have stipulated that the Respondent accepted bargaining unit employees back to work without regard to membership status in the Union. Second, there can be no dispute that the Respondent sought to effectively continue operations during the lockout, as it had while successfully weathering the strike. Of course, there can be no more fundamental employer interest than the continuation of business operations. The Respondent lawfully used supervisory personnel, contractors, and temporary employees to maintain operations during the strike—as well as the crossovers and the nonstrikers—and continued to do so during the lockout. It is self-evident that the Respondent's retention of the crossover employees and non-strikers during the lockout augmented its effort to maintain continued production. The Respondent's retention of these employees during the lockout was fully consistent with its lawful use of temporary replacements and others to maintain operations during the lockout.

Notwithstanding our finding that that the lockout as implemented served a legitimate business interest, a violation of Section 8(a)(1) and (3) may still be found if the evidence warrants an inference that the Respondent's use of the lockout was motivated by antiunion animus. We have carefully searched the record and find no evidence that the lockout was motivated by antiunion animus.

The parties have stipulated that the Respondent bargained in good faith throughout the negotiations. The Respondent further fully complied with an information request made by the Union. The General Counsel does not allege any violations of the Act by the Respondent other than the partial lockout itself. With regard to the lockout, the parties have stipulated that the Respondent accepted crossover employees back to work without regard to their membership status in the Union.

[U]nder *Great Dane*, "discrimination" can be lawful if there is a legitimate and substantial justification for it. In our view, there was such a justification. That justification was to place economic pressure on the Union and the employees to accept the Respondent's bargaining position. Concededly, the lockout was not a total one. But that does not remove the justification. The non-strikers and crossovers had decided that they did not wish to suffer the loss of pay associated with a strike. It makes no difference whether they did so because they no longer shared the Union's goals or because they simply could not afford to go without a paycheck. The significant point is that it was no longer necessary for the Respondent to place additional pressure upon them in order for Respondent to achieve its bargaining goals, for these employees had already eschewed the strike weapon during the strike. To be sure, the Respondent could have locked them out as well. However, there is nothing in the law that requires an employer to use the maximum economic pressure. If the employer believes that lesser pressure will suffice, he can use that lesser pressure.

At bottom, the issue here is whether the distinction made by the Respondent (nonstrikers and crossovers vs. those who stayed on strike) was for the purpose of punishing the latter *or* was for the purpose of winning the economic battle. We believe that the General Counsel has not shown the former.

The main argument of the General Counsel and the Union is that the timing of the lockout demonstrates animus. As discussed above, they contend that the Respondent purposefully delayed implementing the lockout from August 31 until September 6 to allow the six cross-over employees who had offered to return to work before August 31 to be reinstated and processed onto the payroll before the start of the lockout. We find no meaningful evidentiary support for this contention, however.

[The dissenting opinion of MEMBER WALSH is omitted.]

The Board's decision in *Midwest Generation* was reviewed by the Seventh Circuit:

LOCAL 15, INTERNATIONAL BROTHERHOOD OF ELECTRICAL WORKERS v. NLRB (MIDWEST GENERATION)

429 F.3d 651 (7th Cir. 2005)

FLAUM, CHIEF JUDGE:

No evidence that the sixty-one non-participants and crossovers were necessary to maintain operations during the strike was submitted. Employees who returned to work were not questioned concerning their status in the Union and Midwest did not encourage or assist any employee in resigning from the Union.

The issue is whether Midwest has shown that its lockout had any business justification that was neither frivolous nor based upon an impermissible violation of section 7 rights.

Midwest offered no proof that its operational needs justified the partial lockout. Indeed, the record indicates that Midwest's operational needs were being "successfully maintained . . . through the efforts of supervisory personnel, contractors, and some temporary replacement employees." [The court then distinguished cases that had allowed partial lockouts to avert "repeated work stoppages," to avoid "public hazards," or to allow certain employees to work to prevent explosions of "enormous kilns that operate at 2700 degrees Fahrenheit and take between twelve hours and three days to shut down."]

The facts of this case further belie the operational needs justification. First, Midwest's own claims demonstrate that it successfully maintained operations throughout the strike without the use of crossover employees or non-strikers. Midwest does not argue that the lockout was based upon operational needs, but rather states its intent to pressure the employees to abandon their demands. Second, the last six crossover employees did not even start work until after the August 31 unconditional offer to return to work, which demonstrates that these employees were unnecessary for continued operation. Third, early in the strike Midwest was able to maintain operations with only eight of the approximately 1,150 employees who were members of the bargaining unit. The claim that these eight employees and/or the last six crossovers, together representing less than 2% of the total bargaining unit, were so vital to the maintenance of business operations that it was necessary for Midwest to violate employees' section 7 rights stretches the bounds of credulity.

Simply put, to justify a partial lockout on the basis of operational need, an employer must provide a reasonable basis for finding some employees necessary to continue operations and others unnecessary.

Throughout the course of this litigation, Midwest contended that it allowed the non-strikers and crossovers to return to work because they "had removed themselves from the Union's economic action," making it unnecessary to pressure them into abandoning the Union's bargaining position. This allegation rests on the proposition that "working for a struck employer may, without more, be equated with abandonment of the Union's bargaining demands." This assumption is fatally flawed. There can be several reasons why an employee might choose to cross a picket line. Abandonment of the Union's bargaining demands is merely one possible explanation, standing alongside individual financial motivations, personal relationships with employers, indifference, an attempt to impress management, etc. Midwest has failed to offer any direct correlation between employees' non-participation in a strike and lack of support for the Union's demands.

Midwest claims that it was unnecessary to lock out the crossovers and non-strikers because they had taken "affirmative action in derogation of the Union's bargaining position." Any business justification that relies upon workers having "removed themselves from the Union's economic action," or argues that by returning to their jobs, workers had abandoned their demands cannot carry the day in this case. When Midwest announced the selective lockout, all of the employees in the bargaining unit had removed themselves from the economic strike by offering to return to work. The only distinction between employees was whether an individual worker had made his or her offer to return as part of the Union's action or individually.

Midwest argues that an employee who has returned to work no longer demonstrates a commitment to the Union's position. Therefore, no economic pressure against such an employee is required. What Midwest fails to note is that at the time of the lockout, all employees had offered to return to work.

There is no evidence in the record indicating why individual employees chose not to participate in the strike. It is unclear and unknown whether non-strikers and crossovers voted for or against Midwest's collective bargaining agreement proposals. Nothing has been presented to distinguish the motivation of those who offered to return to work before August 31 and those who offered to return to work after August 31.

The Board also justified the use of a partial lockout on the basis that "there is nothing in the law that requires an employer to use maximum economic pressure." While this statement is a truism, it does not address the relevant question before the Board. The burden remains upon the employer to prove that it had a legitimate and substantial basis for its actions. In this case, the Board appears to find sufficient any reason presented by Midwest without evidence of a "legitimate and substantial" basis for distinguishing between those employees it locked out and those it did not.

While we find no foundation for the assumption that those employees who crossed the picket line were not supporters of the Union's position, assuming *arguendo* that Midwest could irrefutably prove that crossovers and non-strikers had abandoned the Union's bargaining position, it still could not discriminate on this basis.

An employer may not discriminate against certain employees merely because it anticipates that they will honor a picket line or otherwise engage in protected activity. An employer's discriminatory lockout on the basis of a protected activity is unlawful even when it is supportive of an employer's bargaining position. The *American Ship Building* rule does not give the employer license to pick and choose among its employees and suspend those whose protected picket line activities are most damaging to it. The mere selection of such an employee from among all those in the unit for suspension is per se discriminatory.

The Board in this case appears to launch a new approach with no discernible parameters. If employers were free to exercise economic penalties selectively against those employees whom they believe economic coercion would be most effective, an employer could take discriminatory actions that have traditionally been barred. Under the Board's analysis, an employer could choose to lock out only union leaders or only employees it believes voted against a proposed contract. This type of discrimination cannot be a legitimate and substantial business justification for a partial lockout.

Not only has Midwest failed to put forth a legitimate and substantial business justification, but in its attempts to justify the partial lockout it has given further support to the Union's claim that the lockout was used in a retributive fashion to discourage employees from exercising their section 7 right to strike.

In the context of collective bargaining negotiations, nearly all employer actions are attempts to win an economic battle. Merely because retribution against strikers may be effective does not make such actions legitimate and substantial. The fact that employers have acted with the best judgment as to the interests of their business has not been deemed an absolute defense to an unfair labor practice charge.

By acting only against those who had exercised their section 7 right to strike, Midwest appears to have demonstrated an anti-union animus. The *only* distinction between the two groups of employees at the time of the lockout was their participation in Union activities. Discriminating in a way that has a natural tendency to discourage participation in concerted union activities is a violation of section 8(a)(3) of the National Labor Relations Act.

The Board argued in its brief to this Court that employees could have avoided " 'punishment' by simply agreeing to the Company's bargaining demands." Following this logic, a partial lockout would be valid provided any offer, no matter what the terms, was made to the employees. The fact that employees could avoid partial lockouts by agreeing to employer demands would in effect validate all partial lockouts. Undoubtedly, this would render ineffective the requirement of a legitimate and substantial business justification for discriminatory employer action and would be in derogation of nearly four decades of employee protection.

NOTES

1.   *The strategy of using a partial versus complete lockout.* Why did Midwest Generation use a partial rather than a complete lockout?

2.   *Facts, law, or policy?* Is the difference between the Board and the court of appeals in the *Midwest Generation* proceedings one of fact or about differing views of the most desirable legal rule? Should the court have granted deference to the Board's interpretation of the statute?

3.   *When is a partial lockout permissible?* Under the court of appeals' rule, what would an employer have to show in order to prove its partial lockout was permissible? What constitutes a legitimate reason? What kind of evidence would be necessary to prove anti-union animus? In the last paragraph of the opinion above, the court criticizes the Board's rule on the grounds that "it would in effect validate all partial lockouts." What would be wrong—as a matter of statutory interpretation and as a matter of policy—with allowing all partial lockouts?

3.   REPLACEMENT WORKERS DURING LOCKOUTS

One of the most controversial recent issues has been whether an employer is allowed to lock out its employees and then hire either temporary or permanent replacements. Before considering the details of the law, consider the practical effect of allowing the use of replacement workers during a lockout. Why might an employer hire replacements when locking out some of its employees? Why might the employer want to lock out and replace as many workers as possible? And why would the employer particularly want to make the replacements permanent?

In the case of defensive lockouts, where the work was either seasonal or an employer in a multi-employer bargaining unit locked out its employees when the union struck another employer in the same unit, the Board had held that temporary replacement of locked out workers was permissible. But in the case of offensive lockouts, initiated by the employer for the sole purpose of pressuring the union in negotiations, the Board had long held that both the lockout and the use of temporary replacements were unfair labor practices. After the Supreme Court signaled the permissibility of offensive lockouts in *American Ship Building,* the Board still adhered to its view that the use of replacement workers was illegal. And the courts of appeals agreed. *Inland Trucking Co. v. NLRB,* 440 F.2d 562 (7th Cir. 1971). Then, in *Harter Equipment, Inc.,* 280 N.L.R.B. 597 (1986), a divided Board changed its mind and upheld the legality of temporary replacements during an offensive lockout. The courts of appeals accepted the Board's new view, both on a petition for review in the *Harter Equipment* case, *Local 825 Int'l Union of Operating Engineers v. NLRB,* 829 F.2d 458 (3d Cir. 1987), and in other cases, *International Brotherhood of Boilermakers v. NLRB,* 858 F.2d 756 (D.C. Cir. 1988). Thus it appears that the original distinction between defensive and offensive lockouts has vanished with respect to temporary replacements during lockouts: employers may use them regardless of the nature of the lockout.

The use of permanent replacements during a lockout is a different question. As noted in the case that follows, when the D.C. Circuit upheld the use of temporary replacements during a lockout, it remarked that permanently replacing locked out workers "might too easily become a device for union busting." *Int'l Bhd. of Boilermakers,* 858 F.2d at 769 (quoting Bernard D. Meltzer, *The Lockout Cases*, 1965 Sup. Ct. Rev. 87, 104). The Board has stated that hiring or threatening to hire permanent replacements during a lockout is an unfair labor practice. *Harborlite Corp.,* 357 N.L.R.B. No. 151 (2011); *Ancor Concepts, Inc.,* 323 N.L.R.B. 742 (1999).

The question then arose whether an employer could either temporarily or permanently subcontract out work during an offensive lockout. The Board had previously allowed temporary subcontracting during a lockout only upon a showing of business necessity. *Elliott River Tours,* 246 N.L.R.B. 935 (1979). In *Land Air Delivery v. NLRB,* 862 F.2d 354 (D.C. Cir. 1988), the court upheld the Board's determination that an employer committed an unfair labor practice by permanently contracting out bargaining unit work during a strike without notifying and bargaining with a union. In the following case, the court considered the use of permanent subcontracting during a lockout.

INTERNATIONAL PAPER CO. V. NLRB
115 F.3d 1045 (D.C. Cir. 1997)

KAREN LECRAFT HENDERSON, CIRCUIT JUDGE:

This case involves a labor dispute at IP's paper mill in Mobile, Alabama, where production and maintenance employees are jointly represented by the United Paperworkers International Union (UPIU) and the International Brotherhood of Electrical Workers. IP and the Unions were parties to a collective bargaining agreement in force at the Mobile plant until January 31, 1987. In early January 1987, IP and the Unions began negotiating for a new contract. During the next few weeks the parties met frequently but were unable to reach an agreement. On February 20, IP presented its "best and final" offer and stated its intention to lockout employees if its offer was not accepted. The Unions rejected IP's offer and on March 7, IP unilaterally implemented its proposal.

On March 21, in order to prevent a coordinated strike by the UPIU at several other IP facilities, IP locked out 915 production and 285 maintenance employees at the Mobile mill. Before the lockout IP had entered into a contract with BE&K Construction Company (BE&K) to provide temporary maintenance workers in the event of a work stoppage. Once the lockout began, IP continued to operate the Mobile mill with supervisors and workers from other mills and with BE&K workers providing maintenance.

During the lockout IP found that it was saving money by using BE&K workers to perform its maintenance work. Accordingly IP requested BE&K to submit a proposal for a permanent subcontract of the mill's maintenance work. After receiving BE&K's proposal IP concluded that it could ultimately save $7.2 million per year by permanently subcontracting maintenance work.

On August 11, 1987, with the lockout still in effect, IP implemented a permanent subcontract with BE&K to perform IP's maintenance work after fulfilling its bargaining obligations on the issue. Under the terms of the subcontract either party could terminate the agreement on 30 days' notice. If IP terminated the contract within 3 years without cause, it was required to pay BE&K a fee of $250,000. The Unions were aware of the terms of the permanent subcontract because a copy of the contract was provided to them. Before executing the contract IP sent a letter to BE&K confirming that the end of the lockout would constitute cause to terminate the permanent subcontract without penalty. The Unions were not aware of the letter.

Over the next nine months the parties continued to negotiate but were unable to reach an agreement. On May 3, 1988, upon hearing that the Board's General Counsel intended to issue a complaint alleging that IP's implementation of the permanent subcontract was unlawful, IP canceled the subcontract and re-executed the agreement with BE&K to provide temporary maintenance work during the remainder of the lockout. IP also withdrew its permanent subcontracting proposal from the bargaining table. The parties nonetheless could not reach agreement and the lockout continued for an additional five months. In October 1988 the parties finally reached an agreement and the lockout ended. While the Unions agreed to allow IP to subcontract, IP agreed to retain enough of its maintenance employees to perform maintenance work at the Mobile mill without subcontracting.

The Board found that IP had violated section 8(a)(3) of the Act by implementing a permanent subcontract for maintenance work during the lockout at the Mobile mill.

An employer does not violate section 8(a)(3) every time it acts in a manner that may affect union activity. Rather, an employer's action violates section 8(a)(3) only if it acts specifically with the intent or purpose of encouraging or discouraging union membership. This does not mean, however, that a violation of the Act cannot be established absent direct evidence of unlawful motivation. Employer conduct may so tend to discourage union activity that an unlawful purpose will be inferred. This conduct is divided into two categories—"inherently destructive" and "comparatively slight"—depending on the potential effect of the employer's conduct on union activity. *NLRB v. Great Dane Trailers, Inc.,* 388 U.S. 26 (1967).

An employer that engages in inherently destructive conduct may overcome the inference of unlawful intent with sufficient evidence of a legitimate and substantial business justification. We have, however, described the employer's burden in justifying inherently destructive conduct as "heavy . . . if not impossible." *Int'l Bhd. of Boilermakers, Local 88 v. NLRB,* 858 F.2d 756, 763 (D.C. Cir. 1988). Here the Board found that IP's implementation of the permanent subcontract was inherently destructive of employee rights and that IP had failed to meet the heavy burden of establishing a business justification to overcome the inference of unlawful motive.

We begin our analysis by isolating the narrow sliver of IP's conduct that is alleged to be unlawful. The lockout itself did not violate the Act. *See Am. Ship Bldg.* Likewise, IP's temporary subcontract during the lockout did not violate the Act. *See Boilermakers,* 858 F.2d at 769. Permanent subcontracting of bargaining unit work is a mandatory subject of collective bargaining. *See Fibreboard Paper.* Therefore, IP's *proposal* to implement the permanent subcontract when the lockout ended was also lawful. Finally, because subcontracting is a mandatory subject of bargaining, IP would have been free to implement its permanent subcontract proposal (at least once the lockout ended) after bargaining to impasse. In short, under both Supreme Court and circuit precedent, it would have been entirely lawful for IP to lockout its employees, implement a temporary subcontract, propose a permanent subcontract during the lockout and implement the permanent subcontract the day after the lockout ended (assuming impasse had been reached). We conclude that IP's implementation of the permanent subcontract while the lockout was in progress but only after having fulfilled its bargaining obligations on the issue produced too minimal an effect to place IP's conduct in the inherently destructive category.

Whether employer conduct is inherently destructive of employee rights turns upon the distinction between substance and process in collective bargaining. Or, to use the *Boilermakers* formulation, employees are guaranteed the "right to bargain, not [the] right to *a* bargain." In *Boilermakers* the court assessed two potential collective bargaining process concerns when an employer hires *temporary* replacements during a lockout—creating cleavage among employees and producing a belief in employees that bargaining collectively is futile—and concluded that the collective bargaining process concerns did not in fact render the employer's conduct inherently destructive. Today we conclude the same two concerns do not make IP's action in this case—hiring *permanent* replacements during a lockout—inherently destructive.

The Unions contend that IP's implementation of the permanent subcontract caused a cleavage problem because it meant that IP's production employees would have to work with BE&K maintenance workers. The cleavage concern the *Boilermakers* court addressed, however, involved division among employees. Here, assuming subcontractors remained after the lockout, there would be no divide *among employees* because the subcontractors would not be employees. The distinction is an important one. The goal of our inquiry is to maintain the integrity of the collective bargaining process and cleavage among employees has an adverse effect on the bargaining process if there is division *within* a bargaining unit. To the extent the members of a bargaining unit work at cross-purposes it is less likely they can present a united front and bargain collectively with an employer. That is not a concern here because the subcontracted maintenance workers would not be bargaining together with the production employees in the future. Accordingly, we conclude that IP's implementation of the permanent subcontract during the lockout did not create employee divisiveness adversely affecting the process of collective bargaining.

Boilermakers identified a second factor that could affect the collective bargaining process—fostering the belief in employees that collective bargaining is futile. The Unions contend and the Board found that IP's implementation of the subcontract made employees believe collective bargaining was futile because IP's conduct sent the message that the consequence of collective bargaining was that employees would lose their jobs. We disagree. They could have received the same message from the lawful *proposal* to permanently subcontract or from a lawful subcontract implemented *outside* the lockout context. Implementation during lockout is not so different from a proposal during lockout or implementation outside lockout to produce the prohibited employee futility resulting from inherently destructive employer conduct. Employees may believe that the collective bargaining process has extracted concessions from the employer that have made the employer's labor costs high enough to increase the likelihood the employer will subcontract. But that risk is omnipresent for employees who engage in collective bargaining.

In its decision the Board examined two additional factors purportedly relevant to the determination whether IP's conduct was inherently destructive. First, the Board looked to the "severity of the harm to employees' Section 7 rights." The Board concluded that the criterion supported a finding of inherently destructive employer conduct because the permanent subcontract would have permanently put the maintenance workers (or production workers with less seniority who were bumped) out of work, the "most severe penalty unit maintenance employees could have suffered." 319 N.L.R.B. at 1270. The same result would have occurred, however, had IP implemented the permanent subcontract (after bargaining to impasse) outside the lockout context—a lawful action. The severity criterion, then, does not support a finding that implementation of the permanent subcontract was inherently destructive. Second, the Board looked to the "temporal impact of the employer's conduct." *Id.* at 1269. The Board distinguished an employer's attempt to pressure union members to accept a particular proposal, which is not indicative of inherently destructive conduct, from employer action that "creates visible and continuing obstacles to the future exercise of employee rights," which, according to the Board, is indicative of inherently destructive behavior. In concluding that IP's implementation of the permanent subcontract would present an obstacle to the *future* exercise of employee rights, the Board assumed that the continuing presence of the BE&K workers after the lockout ended would inhibit future collective bargaining. This is the same cleavage concern we have rejected because it shows, at most, simply that implementation of the permanent subcontract could affect the bargain, as opposed to the process of collective bargaining between the parties.

[The court then distinguished *Erie Resistor* and *Great Dane* on the grounds that in both, "the employer treated employees *within* a bargaining unit differently depending upon the degree of their union activity."]

By contrast IP did not distinguish among the members of the bargaining unit. The maintenance workers perhaps had the most to lose— not based on their union activity but because those were the positions IP subcontracted. In other words there was no correlation between degree of union activity and negative consequences to union activists.

In *NLRB v. Mackay Radio & Telegraph Co.*, the Supreme Court held that an employer may hire permanent replacements for striking workers without violating the Act because the employer has "the right to protect and continue his business by supplying places left vacant by strikers." We believe that an employer's implementation of a permanent subcontract during a lockout is sufficiently analogous to the replacement of workers during a strike to fall within *Mackay*. There are important pragmatic reasons for treating the strike and lockout cases the same. It may be within an employer's power to provoke a strike by insisting on terms unacceptable to its employees. Because *Mackay* allows permanent replacements during a strike, a contrary rule in the lockout scenario could provide an employer the incentive to provoke a strike in order to accomplish what could not be accomplished by locking out employees. Provocation would be undesirable because such tactics might poison the atmosphere more than a candid resort to a lockout and might also create bargaining gaps that might otherwise be avoided in the bargaining process. The requirement of good faith bargaining under the Act does provide some constraint on an employer's ability to adopt this strategy. *See, e.g., Land Air Delivery, Inc. v. NLRB*, 862 F.2d 354, 357–58 (D.C. Cir. 1988) (employer has duty to bargain before implementing permanent subcontract because "permanent subcontract diminishes the bargaining unit by the scope of the subcontract"). Nevertheless, an employer might attempt to provoke a strike while going to the edge of what counts as good faith bargaining. As we stated in *Boilermakers,* "there is no reason to create an incentive for an employer artfully to precipitate a strike." 858 F.2d at 768–69. We used this rationale in *Boilermakers* to conclude that it is permissible for an employer to use temporary replacements during a lockout. *Boilermakers* contains dictum to the effect that the same reasoning might not apply to the case of permanent replacements. We suggested that permanent replacement raises somewhat different considerations because, if permanent replacements are available, employees may accept the employer's terms no matter what—thus making it impossible for the employer to precipitate a strike. The point we made in *Boilermakers* suggests that an employer may have greater difficulty precipitating a strike if the labor market can provide permanent instead of temporary replacements. Nonetheless in both instances the identical concern exists that the employer will attempt to precipitate a strike while purporting to be engaged in good faith bargaining. Thus both cases raise the problem of employer brinkmanship that may "poison the atmosphere" of collective bargaining. Meltzer, *The Lockout Cases*, 1965 Sup. Ct. Rev. at 105.[5]

Having found that IP's conduct had a comparatively slight impact on employee rights, we now address whether IP met its burden in showing that its implementation of the permanent subcontract was based on legitimate and substantial business reasons.

The record shows that IP enjoyed several economic benefits by implementing the permanent subcontract during the lockout. It cut its overtime costs and eliminated the costs it had been incurring in maintaining an on-site facility where temporary replacements ate and lived. By implementing the permanent subcontract, IP was also able to obtain a reduction in BE&K's "multiplier," the number by which BE&K multiplied its costs to determine the price it charged IP. Finally, the record shows that after three years the permanent subcontract would save IP $7.2

---

[5]   In *Boilermakers* we also discussed whether a "lockout, followed by permanent replacements, might too easily become a device for union busting." 858 F.2d at 769 (quoting Meltzer, *The Lockout Cases*, 1965 Sup. Ct. Rev. at 104).

million per year compared to the cost of continuing maintenance in-house. Because of transition costs the savings in the first three years were projected to be $842,000, $5.42 million and $5.541 million respectively. By implementing the permanent subcontract during the lockout, as opposed to waiting until the lockout ended, IP would have been able to realize the maximum savings of the permanent subcontract sooner. We conclude that these economic reasons constituted legitimate and substantial business justifications for IP's conduct, which conduct, as discussed earlier, had a comparatively slight effect on employee rights.

NOTES

1. *Why allow permanent replacement of locked out workers?* Under the reasoning of *Mackay Radio*, should the right to hire permanent replacements during a strike be extended to a lockout? Should it matter why the employer locked out its employees? If you were reasoning from first principles, would you conclude that the employer may lock out its employees and then permanently replace them?

2. *Is subcontracting work different from replacing workers?* Should the use of subcontracting during a lockout be treated differently than the hiring of replacement workers? Should it matter whether the subcontracting or the hiring is temporary or permanent? Can you reconcile the Board's view that permanent replacement of locked out workers is unlawful with the D.C. Circuit's opinion in *International Paper*?

3. *Impasse before a lockout?* Recall the distinction between mandatory and permissive subjects of bargaining covered in Chapter 5. An employer is obligated to bargain to impasse over any mandatory subject of bargaining before unilaterally changing that term. As the court explained in *International Paper*, subcontracting of bargaining unit work is usually a mandatory subject of bargaining under *Fibreboard*. But elimination of bargaining unit work is not a mandatory subject when it is a core entrepreneurial decision, as shown in *First National Maintenance*. How should lockouts and the subsequent use of replacements be treated? Should it be necessary for an employer to bargain to impasse before locking out its employees? It is not necessary for a union to bargain to impasse before striking, but is there an argument for a different treatment of lockouts? If you conclude that it is NOT necessary for the employer to bargain to impasse before locking out its employees, should it be necessary to bargain to impasse before permanently replacing them? *See Land Air Delivery v. NLRB*, 862 F.2d 354 (D.C. Cir. 1988) (employer must bargain to impasse before replacing locked out workers).

4. *Incentives to negotiate vs. incentives to stall.* A determinedly anti-union employer has an incentive to prolong negotiations as long as possible—but certainly beyond the one-year certification bar period—and then encourage employees who are dissatisfied with the union's failure to negotiate a contract to file a petition to decertify the union. The Board and the Court have recognized this incentive and have, in some cases, recognized the need to

interpret the NLRA in ways that give employers incentives to negotiate rather than to stall and try to break the union. *See, e.g., Brooks v. NLRB*, 348 U.S. 96 (1954) (employer has duty to bargain with union for one year after certification even if employees repudiated the union); *NLRB v. Curtin Matheson Scientific, Inc.*, 494 U.S. 775 (1990) (NLRB reasonably refuses to presume that striker replacements oppose union, for purposes of determining whether employer may withdraw recognition based on good faith reasonable doubt about union's continuing majority status).

5.   *Is permanent replacement different from firing?* Could an employer whose employees have recently voted to unionize lock out its bargaining unit employees and permanently replace them during negotiations for a first collective bargaining agreement? What is the distinction between this and simply informing them that, because they have unionized, they will all be fired? Would it matter what the employer's motive was for locking out and replacing its workforce? In a footnote in *International Paper*, the court addressed this argument as follows:

> Ability to bust a union, presumably, turns primarily on whether the union presses demands vastly out of line with available alternatives. . . . Employer conduct [that has] comparatively slight [effect on employees' rights] may nonetheless violate the Act if the employer fails to prove that it had a legitimate and substantial business justification for its conduct. Additionally, even if an employer has a legitimate and substantial business justification, thereby putting the burden on the union to prove antiunion animus that arises from conduct with a comparatively slight effect, the court may nonetheless consider *direct* evidence of improper motivation for the employer's conduct. These constraints should still any apprehension that our holding today may give an employer a tool by which a union can simply be removed in its discretion.

How significant are these constraints? How would a union prove that the employer had an improper motive? What if the evidence were that the employer strenuously opposed the union but lost the election, and the employer insisted that it locked out its employees in order to extract the lowest possible wages and the greatest flexibility in managing its workforce? What if, conveniently, the replacement workers voted to decertify the union thus achieving the employer's goals of ensuring low wages and flexibility?

6.   *Puppets.* In 2015 the American Guild of Variety Artists won an NLRB election to represent puppeteers at Disneyland. Shortly thereafter, Disney cancelled the puppet show entirely and prevented the employees from working in other areas of the park. After the Guild filed two NLRB complaints against Disney alleging retaliatory action, the parties settled for a total of $167,000 in back pay. http://www.latimes.com/business/hollywood/la-fi-ct-disneyland-puppets-20170208-story.html. The settlement did not require Disney to continue the puppet show. Had the case not settled, what should have been the outcome?

7. *Effect of replacement workers on locked out employees' right to vote in a decertification election.* In *Harter Equipment, Inc.,* 280 N.L.R.B. 597 (1986), the Board held that hiring temporary replacements for locked out workers was permissible. The Third Circuit upheld the Board's new rule on a petition for review. In *Harter Equipment,* one of the "temporary" replacement workers filed a decertification petition. Should the replacement workers be eligible to vote in the decertification election, held five years after the employer first locked out its employees?

E. STATUTORY PROTECTIONS FOR EMPLOYERS: SECONDARY ACTIVITY

The Coalition of Immokalee Workers (CIW) wants a wage increase for the workers who harvest tomatoes in South Florida. The workers are employed by labor contractors, which provide seasonal labor to growers to harvest the crops. The growers sell the tomatoes to distributors and processors who in turn contract with Taco Bell and other restaurant chains and grocery stores to provide the tons of tomatoes served or sold each week in Taco Bell and other restaurant franchises across the country. Taco Bell is owned by Yum! Inc., a company that owns a number of fast-food chains. Efforts to persuade the labor contractors to increase wages are unsuccessful, as the contractors claim that if they increase wages, other contractors paying lower wages will bid for and get the contracts with the growers. The growers similarly resist pleas to raise wages, arguing that the price per pound of tomatoes is dictated by the distributors and that other tomato growers elsewhere will supply the tomatoes if they don't. The distributors and processors resist requests to increase the price per pound for tomatoes on the ground that the price is dictated by Taco Bell. Taco Bell resists a polite request to increase wages on the grounds that its business model is to sell food as cheaply as possible and it so dominates the market in many sectors that it has the market power to secure the lowest possible prices.

CIW decides that the only effective way to increase wages for tomato workers is to conduct a nationwide corporate social responsibility campaign and consumer boycott of Taco Bell. After four years of nationwide protests, including a successful campaign (known as Boot the Bell) to have Taco Bell banned from university campuses, pressure from shareholders at the Yum! corporation's annual meeting, and boycotts from the national organizations of several Christian denominations, CIW persuades Taco Bell to deal only with Immokalee tomato suppliers who pay workers an additional penny per pound of tomatoes harvested, which amounts to a 75 percent wage increase. CIW also persuades Taco Bell to add language to its Supplier Code of Conduct prohibiting indentured servitude and child labor and promising strict compliance with all labor laws.

The success of the CIW campaign against Taco Bell led to the creation of the Fair Food Program, a worker-driven social responsibility program that is a partnership between CIW, growers, and retail food companies. Participating businesses agree to abide by a Fair Food Code of Conduct, which goes beyond the requirements of law in demanding decent wages and working conditions for farm workers. Increased wages for farmworkers are funded by a slight increase in the price consumers pay for Fair Food Program certified products. This slightly higher price, which is advertised to consumers as a "fair food premium," is passed down through multiple layers in the supply chain through growers and farm labor contractors to pay a decent wage. The system is monitored by workers, who are trained to understand their rights under the Code of Conduct and the law, and by a system of audits. See www.fairfoodprogram.org.

Unions have long recognized the utility of economic pressure on businesses other than the ones whose employees they seek immediately to represent or on behalf of whom they bargain. For over a hundred years, garment workers unions have recognized that because of cut-throat competition in garment manufacturing, to improve working conditions in the small shops where clothes are cut and sewn, the unions must persuade (or force) the clothing "labels" or the retail stores to increase what they pay for the clothes. The desire of workers to pressure multiple businesses in a supply chain has only intensified as companies have contracted out significant parts of their operations and attempted to become more flexible, by building "value chains" to enable "just-in-time inventory." Unions recognize that the vulnerability of firms is not *within* firms but in the links *between* them. "A small, unexpected delay in one key location along the chain can cause more damage than a large, predictable strike." Charles Heckscher, *Organizations, Movements, and Networks*, 50 N.Y.L. Sch. L. Rev. 313, 322–23 (2005).

1. THE PRIMARY-SECONDARY DISTINCTION

Any successful strike will cause economic harm to businesses that depend on the employer that is the subject of the strike. Unions count not only on the economic pressure inflicted by lost sales but also on complaints from disgruntled suppliers and customers to induce the employer to settle the strike on terms favorable to the union. Similarly, a successful boycott of an employer will cause inconvenience to other businesses that wish to use the boycotted product or to provide goods or services to the boycotted producer.

Labor law distinguishes between economic pressure directed at "primary" employers (which is legal) and "secondary" or "neutral" employers (which is often illegal). The primary employer is the one who employs the workers whose working conditions are the subject of dispute. A primary strike is one by employees whose own working conditions are at issue. A primary boycott is a refusal to use or buy the products of the employer whose labor policies are at issue. Secondary activity is the application of economic pressure upon a person (the neutral or secondary) *Secondary* with whom the employees have no dispute regarding their own conditions of work in order to induce that person to cease doing business with another person (the primary) with whom the employees do have a dispute. For example, assume workers are on strike against Walmart over working conditions for the employees at Walmart. If workers picket Walmart stores and consumers honor the picket lines, the picket line is primary pressure. Moreover, although if the strike is successful, Walmart will sell less fruit and vegetables packed by Del Monte Foods Corp., the harm to Del Monte *— key language* is merely the lawful incidental effect of the union's primary strike against Walmart.

By contrast, a secondary strike is one by employees whose own working conditions are not at issue. A secondary boycott is a refusal to do business with an employer whose working conditions are not in issue, usually to get that employer to pressure the other. Assume that the strike at Walmart was not effective because Walmart continues its operations with supervisors and replacement workers and consumers are willing to cross the picket lines and shop at Walmart. Assume further that the UFCW, which is affiliated with OUR Walmart, also represents employees at Del Monte processing plants. If the UFCW threatens to strike the Del Monte plant unless Del Monte curtails sales to Walmart until Walmart agrees to recognize OUR Walmart or to a code of conduct governing conditions at Walmart, the UFCW would be engaging in secondary activity. Similarly, if the UFCW asks the Teamsters Union to ask its drivers not to deliver Del Monte products to get Del Monte to pressure Walmart to settle with the UFCW, that too is secondary pressure.

The Wagner Act did not prohibit secondary tactics. Pre-Wagner Act cases had treated secondary boycotts as violations of state tort law and federal antitrust law. With the enactment of the Norris-LaGuardia Act of 1932, however, it appeared that secondary boycotts and strikes against secondary employers could no longer be enjoined. And the protection of "concerted activity for mutual aid and protection" in section 7 of the Wagner Act appeared to protect secondary activity as well. Secondary activity was made illegal under the NLRA when Congress enacted the Taft-Hartley Act in 1947. But nowhere in the statute is the distinction between primary and secondary activity described; indeed, the statute does not even use the term "secondary." Section 8(b)(4)(A), as originally written, made it *8(b)(4)* an unfair labor practice "to engage in . . . a strike or a concerted refusal to use, manufacture, process, transport, or otherwise handle or work on any goods . . . where an object thereof is . . . forcing or requiring any employer or other person . . . to cease doing business with any other person."

A number of policies underlie the NLRA's proscription of secondary pressure. First, some thought it unfair to involve a "stranger" or a "neutral" *— why unfair* employer in a labor dispute. Second, Congress thought secondary activity proliferates labor unrest which disrupts the economy and inconveniences the public. Third, Congress believed that secondary boycotts gave some unions too much power. The Teamsters Union was of particular concern, as it was uniquely able to use secondary pressure, given the importance of trucking to the national economy. When a union that controls an artery of commerce happens to be corrupt, as was the case with some Teamsters locals in the 1950s, it seemed obvious to Congress that the power of unions needed to be curtailed.

The Railway Labor Act does not prohibit secondary boycotts. However, the NLRA treats employers covered under the RLA as neutrals who are protected under the NLRA. Section 8(b)(4) prohibits secondary activity by "any individual employed by any person." Secondary activity that enmeshes RLA employers can therefore be punished under § 8(b)(4). *See United Steelworkers v. NLRB* (Carrier Corp.), 376 U.S. 492 (1964).

Note that the § 8(b)(4) prohibition clearly does *not* apply to the UFCW's strike and picketing of Walmart or to the incidental harm to Del Monte caused by the picket at Walmart, even though the strike causes fewer people to buy Del Monte goods sold by Walmart. The prohibition clearly *does* apply to the UFCW's threat to strike Del Monte to get Del Monte to pressure Walmart. Assume that the International Brotherhood of Teamsters represents Del Monte's truck drivers. Teamster drivers refuse to cross the UFCW's picket lines at Walmart and thereby refuse to make deliveries to Walmart, which obviously affects both Walmart and Del Monte. Is this an illegal secondary boycott?

The Supreme Court addressed this issue in *NLRB v. International Rice Milling*, 341 U.S. 665 (1951). The driver of a delivery truck refused to cross a picket line at the primary employer's place of business. The Supreme Court held that the effect on the truck drivers, employees of the neutral employer, was simply the incidental effect of a primary strike. Although neutral employees' observance of a picket line does have the effect of causing the neutral employer not to do business with the primary employer, the Court held that this was a legal effect of a primary strike. *International Rice Milling* was decided the same day as *NLRB v. Denver Building & Construction Trades Council*, reproduced below, which drew a distinction between picket lines at a place of business occupied solely by the primary employer, where it would be acceptable to urge "neutral" employees not to cross, and picket lines at work sites shared by many employers, where it is not.

The law of secondary activity is extremely important for the modern labor lawyer to know. In the first place, with businesses increasingly using networks of contractors to obtain labor and materials and to distribute their products, what appears to the public and may be experienced by workers as a single business enterprise in fact involves multiple separate legal entities. The use of pressure to improve working conditions may therefore involve secondary activity. Second, the remedies for unlawful secondary activity are the harshest and most effective in all of federal labor law. Unlike most NLRB remedies, which are mild and slow to obtain, the remedies for violations of § 8(b)(4) are both strong and available quickly. In addition, secondary boycotts under § 8(b)(4)(B) are the only violations of the Act for which violations can be compensated by a private action for damages brought directly in court rather than through the NLRB.

— harsh remedies

The usual NLRB remedies apply to violations of § 8(b)(4): a cease and desist order. To make the penalties more vigorous, under § 10(*l*), in the case of secondary boycott charges under § 8(b)(4)(A) and (B) and under § 8(e), as well as recognitional picketing under § 8(B)(4)(C) and § 8(b)(7), "preliminary investigation of such charge shall be made forthwith and given priority over all other cases." If the Regional office finds "reasonable cause to believe such charge is true," the office is *required* to seek an injunction from the federal district court. The § 10(*l*) injunction process is more vigorous than the usual process for the Regions seeking injunctions under § 10(j) in two respects: the investigation must be given priority and the Region has no discretion about seeking an injunction; it must seek the injunction if it finds reasonable cause.

In addition to the usual Board remedies and the expedited § 10(*l*) injunction, the Act contains a final powerful remedy: under § 303, any person "injured in his business or property" by a union's violation of § 8(b)(4) may sue the union in federal court and recover damages and the costs of suit. The damages remedy is not limited to employers covered by the NLRA. And the damages are tort damages, not the contract damages available generally under the NLRA. As a consequence, violations of § 8(b)(4) can be punished by multimillion dollar awards that can be devastating for a union. *See, e.g., Fidelity Interior Constr. Inc. v. Southeastern Carpenters Regional Council*, 675 F.3d 1250 (11th Cir. 2012) (upholding a $1.7 million judgment against a union).

— 3rd party action

Students should read section 8(b)(4)(A) and (B) extremely closely at this point with particular attention to the structure of the statute's categories. (Subsections (C) and (D) are not covered in this chapter.) The following synopsis may be helpful:

It is an unfair labor practice for a labor organization or its agents—

(i) to engage in or to induce or encourage an employee to engage in a strike or refusal in the course of employment to use, manufacture, process, transport, or otherwise handle or work on any goods, etc., or to perform services;

or

(ii) to threaten, coerce, or restrain any person engaged in an industry affecting commerce where in either case an object thereof is

(A) requiring any employer or self-employed person to join any labor or employer organization or to enter into a "hot cargo" agreement prohibited by section 8(e)

or

(B) requiring any person to cease using, selling, etc., the products of any other producer, processor or manufacturer,

or to cease doing business with any other person,

or requiring any other employer to recognize or bargain with a union unless such union has been certified as the representative of those employees,

Provided, That nothing contained in this clause (B) shall be construed to make unlawful, where not otherwise unlawful, any primary strike or primary picketing

Proviso, Nothing in 8(b) shall be construed to prohibit a refusal to enter premises of any employer where such employer's employees are engaged in a strike authorized by the employees' union

Further proviso, Nothing in 8(b)(4) shall be construed to prohibit publicity, *other than picketing,*

for the purpose of truthfully advising the public,

that a product is produced by an employer with whom the union has a primary dispute and is distributed by another employer,

as long as such publicity does not have an effect of inducing any individual employed by any person other than the primary employer in the course of his employment to refuse to pick up, deliver, or transport any goods, or to refuse to perform services at the establishment of the employer engaged in such distribution.

Notice that section 8(b)(4) first describes two forms of prohibited *conduct* in subsections (i) and (ii). The prohibited conduct in (i) is engaging in or inducing work stoppages. The prohibited conduct in (ii) is broader: "to threaten, coerce or restrain." The *conduct* is prohibited only if it has one of the four prohibited *objects* described in subsections (A) through (D). Finally, there are two provisos at the end that carve out *exceptions* to the prohibitions. The first proviso is to protect the right of workers to refuse to cross picket lines. The second proviso applies *only* to subsection 4 (the secondary activity provision) and protects the right of workers to make appeals to consumers to boycott. The consumer appeal proviso is discussed below at pp. 842–859.

In analyzing any potential secondary boycott problem, the first step is to identify the primary employer. The primary employer is the entity with whom the union has a dispute. This is often the party whose employees the union represents, but it is not always so. For example, a union that pickets a non-union employer demanding recognition or protesting the employer's payment of substandard wages is engaged in a dispute with an employer whose employees it does not represent. Indeed, the "primary employer" need not be an employer: in *International Longshoremen's Association v. Allied International,* 456 U.S. 212 (1982) (which involved a refusal of American longshoremen to load or unload ships bound to or from the Soviet Union; the case is excerpted above in the section on First Amendment protection for labor protest), the "primary employer" was the Soviet Union because the dispute was over its invasion of Afghanistan. As shown by the *Denver Building Trades* case excerpted below, determining who is the primary employer often turns on how the court or the NLRB characterizes the nature of the dispute. Thus, the first step of the analysis involves two inquiries: (1) What is the dispute? (2) With whom does the union have a dispute? The first two parts of the analysis focus on distinguishing the "neutral" employer from the "primary" employer, which is the crucial distinction drawn in the prohibited objects outlined in subsections (B), and is conceptually the most difficult part of the law of secondary boycotts.

Once the primary and neutral employers are identified, the next step is to determine whether the union is coercing a neutral in order to force it to cease dealing with the primary. This requires analysis of two more factors: (1) Who is the target of or is affected by the union's activity? and (2) If the union's activity is directed at or affects a neutral employer, is the union coercing that person or entity? The last step in the analysis focuses on whether the conduct is prohibited. As reflected in *International Rice Milling,* this requires determining whether the neutral is being coerced or is simply feeling the incidental effects of lawful primary activity. This can be particularly problematic in situations where the primary and the neutral share a common work site.

Finally, remember that the § 8(b) prohibition on secondary boycotts applies only to labor organizations. Subject to the law of antitrust or state economic tort law, groups other than labor organizations are free to engage in secondary boycotts, and their involvement may sometimes be an effective tactic. For example, the problem that began this section was drawn from a real campaign that began in 2005, in which the Coalition of Immokalee Workers (CIW) organized a nationwide boycott against Taco Bell to protest the wages and working conditions of the immigrant workers who harvest tomatoes in Florida. The workers were employed by labor contractors who in turn contracted with an agricultural company which in turn contracted with Taco Bell, which itself is a subsidiary of Yum! Brands, Inc., a restaurant conglomerate that also owns Kentucky Fried Chicken, A & W, and Pizza Hut. The CIW, in partnership with a number of immigrant organizations, churches and student groups, boycotted Taco Bell, but also pressured Yum! The campaign ultimately succeeded. CIW reached an agreement with local tomato growers, several major purchasers of tomatoes, including McDonald's, Burger King, and grocery chains including Whole Foods, in which purchasers agreed to pay an additional penny per pound and the Florida Tomato Growers Exchange, the trade association that acted as a middleman, agreed to pass on the price difference to workers. As one CIW volunteer explained, CIW wisely resisted offers to merge with the United Farm Workers or other labor organizations because had it done so its secondary boycott would have been illegal. Elly Leary, *Immokalee Workers Take Down Taco Bell*, 57 Monthly Rev. 11 (October 2005). *See also* Kristofer Rios, *After Long Fight, Farmworkers in Florida Win an Increase in Pay*, N.Y. Times (Jan. 18, 2011); Gustavo Arellano, *Now We Have Faith*, OC Weekly (March 18, 2005).

2.   COMMON WORK SITES

a.   Identifying the Primary Employer

The first step in any secondary activity problem is to identify the primary employer. As noted, the primary is the entity with which the union has a dispute over working conditions. When an entity has effective control over the working conditions of a group of employees but does not directly employ them itself, and instead hires a subcontractor who is the technical employer, one might think that the union has a dispute with the entity that effectively controls the working conditions. After all, its decisions about which subcontractor to hire or what to pay the subcontractor are what the union finds problematic. In the following case, which arose during a period of business history in which only the construction industry and the garment industry commonly used subcontracting of labor and most large entities directly employed most of the workers, the Supreme Court held that only the entity that directly employs the workers is the primary.

NLRB v. DENVER BUILDING & CONSTRUCTION TRADES COUNCIL

341 U.S. 675 (1951)

JUSTICE BURTON delivered the opinion of the Court:

The principal question here is whether a labor organization committed an unfair labor practice, within the meaning of § 8(b)(4) by engaging in a strike, an object of which was to force the general contractor on a construction project to terminate its contract with a certain subcontractor on that project. For the reasons hereafter stated, we hold that such an unfair labor practice was committed.

In September, 1947, Doose & Lintner was the general contractor for the construction of a commercial building in Denver, Colorado. It awarded a subcontract for electrical work on the building to Gould & Preisner. The latter's employees proved to be the only nonunion workmen on the project. Those of the general contractor and of the other subcontractors were members of unions affiliated with the respondent Denver Building and Construction Trades Council. [A] representative of one of those unions told Gould that he did not see how the job could progress with Gould's nonunion men on it.

[T]he Council posted a picket at the project carrying a placard stating "This Job Unfair to Denver Building and Construction Trades Council." [While the picket was present] the only persons who reported for work were the nonunion electricians of Gould & Preisner. [The general contractor] notified it to get off the job so that Doose & Lintner could continue with the project. [T]he Council removed its picket and shortly thereafter the union employees resumed work on the project.

The language of [the statute] which is here essential is as follows: "(b) It shall be an unfair labor practice for a labor organization . . . (4) to engage in . . . a strike . . . where an object thereof is: (A) forcing or requiring . . . any employer or other person . . . to cease doing business with any other person. . . ." While § 8 (b)(4) does not expressly mention "primary" or "secondary" disputes, strikes or boycotts, that section often is referred to in the Act's legislative history as one of the Act's "secondary boycott sections."

At the same time that §§ 7 and 13 safeguard collective bargaining, concerted activities and strikes between the primary parties to a labor dispute, § 8(b)(4) restricts a labor organization and its agents in the use of economic pressure where an object of it is to force an employer or other person to boycott someone else.

We must first determine whether the strike in this case had a proscribed object. The conduct which the Board here condemned is readily distinguishable from that which it declined to condemn in the *Rice Milling* case. There the accused union sought merely to obtain its own recognition by the operator of a mill, and the union's pickets near the mill sought to influence two employees of a customer of the mill not to cross the picket line. In that case we supported the Board in its conclusion that such conduct was no more than was traditional and permissible in a primary strike. The union did not engage in a strike against the customer. It did not encourage concerted action by the customer's employees to force the customer to boycott the mill. It did not commit any unfair labor practice proscribed by § 8(b)(4).

In the background of the instant case there was a long-standing labor dispute between the Council and Gould & Preisner due to the latter's practice of employing non-union workmen on construction jobs in Denver. The respondent labor organizations contend that they engaged in a primary dispute with Doose & Lintner alone, and that they sought simply to force Doose & Lintner to make the project an all-union job. If there had been no contract between Doose & Lintner and Gould & Preisner there might be substance in their contention that the dispute involved no boycott. If, for example, Doose & Lintner had been doing all the electrical work on this project through its own nonunion employees, it could have replaced them with union men and thus disposed of the dispute. However, the existence of the Gould & Preisner subcontract presented a materially different situation. The nonunion employees were employees of Gould & Preisner. The only way that respondents could attain their purpose was to force Gould & Preisner itself off the job. This, in turn, could be done only through Doose & Lintner's termination of Gould & Preisner's subcontract. The result is that the Council's strike, in order to attain its ultimate purpose, must have included among its objects that of forcing Doose & Lintner to terminate that subcontract.

We hold also that a strike with such an object was an unfair labor practice within the meaning of § 8(b)(4)(A). It is not necessary to find that the *sole* object of the strike was that of forcing the contractor to terminate the subcontractor's contract. This is emphasized in the legislative history of the section.

We agree with the Board also in its conclusion that the fact that the contractor and subcontractor were engaged on the same construction project, and that the contractor had some supervision over the subcontractor's work, did not eliminate the status of each as an independent contractor or make the employees of one the employees of the other. The business relationship between independent contractors is too well established in the law to be overridden without clear language doing so. The Board found that the relationship between Doose & Lintner and Gould & Preisner was one of "doing business" and we find no adequate reason for upsetting that conclusion.

Finally, § 8(c) safeguarding freedom of speech has no significant application to the picket's placard in this case. Section 8(c) does not apply to a mere signal by a labor organization to its members, or to the members of its affiliates, to engage in an unfair labor practice such as a strike proscribed by § 8(b)(4)(A). That the placard was merely such a signal, tantamount to a direction to strike, was found by the Board.

Not only are the findings of the Board conclusive with respect to questions of fact in this field when supported by substantial evidence on the record as a whole, but the Board's interpretation of the Act and the Board's application of it in doubtful situations are entitled to weight. In the views of the Board as applied to this case we find conformity with the dual congressional objectives of preserving the right of labor organizations to bring pressure to bear on offending employers in primary labor disputes and of shielding unoffending employers and others from pressures in controversies not their own.

JUSTICE DOUGLAS, with whom JUSTICE REED joins, dissenting:

The employment of union and nonunion men on the same job is a basic protest in trade union history. That was the protest here. The union was not out to destroy the contractor because of his antiunion attitude. The union was not pursuing the contractor to other jobs. All the union asked was that union men not be compelled to work alongside nonunion men on the same job.

The picketing would undoubtedly have been legal if there had been no subcontractor involved—if the general contractor had put nonunion men on the job. The presence of a subcontractor does not alter one whit the realities of the situation; the protest of the union is precisely the same. In each the union was trying to protect the job on which union men were employed. If that is forbidden, the Taft-Hartley Act makes the right to strike, guaranteed by § 13, dependent on fortuitous business arrangements that have no significance so far as the evils of the secondary boycott are concerned. I would give scope to both § 8(b)(4) and § 13 by reading the restrictions of § 8(b)(4) to reach the case where an industrial dispute spreads from the job to another front.

NOTES

1. *Who is neutral?* From the union's perspective, what was the dispute? With whom did the union have that dispute? How did the Court characterize the parties to the dispute? In the Court's view, why was Doose & Lintner neutral? Do you agree?

2. *Controversy in the construction trades.* Construction unions considered the ruling in *Denver Building* to be an outrage because it forced union workers to work alongside workers whom they considered to be disloyal to the cause of improved working conditions. They sought legislative change. A bill to permit "common situs" picketing in the construction industry, and thus overrule *Denver Building*, passed both houses of Congress in 1975. *See* H.R. 5900 (1975) (the bill); 121 Cong. Rec. 40067 (House); 40553 (Senate). The votes could not be mustered to override President Ford's veto. 121 Cong. Rec. 42015–16 (presidential veto message). John Dunlop resigned as Secretary of Labor in protest of President Ford's veto.

3. *Networks of contracts in supply chains.* In holding that only the subcontractor was the primary in *Denver Building* the Court created a rule that has significant implications in today's economy as companies outsource production but workers cannot legally pressure entities above their own employer in the supply chain. The Coalition of Immokalee Workers found that tomato pickers' wages could be improved only by persuading grocery stores and restaurants to pay more and to pass the increase down through one or more levels of the supply chain. Similarly, Warehouse Workers United found that the wages and working conditions in warehouses are effectively dictated not by the labor contractors, nor even by logistics companies that hire labor contractors, but rather by the major retailers like Walmart which hire the

logistics companies. Yet, under the rationale of *Denver Building* pressure on growers in Florida or food suppliers or grocers or restaurant chains would be secondary, as would be pressure on logistics companies or Walmart.

* * *

The distinction drawn between permissible incidental effects of a picket line at a worksite occupied solely by one employer, as in *International Rice Milling*, and the illegal secondary effects of a picket line at a worksite occupied by multiple employers, as in *Denver Building*, has become enormously significant in contemporary labor law because of changes in the business structure of firms. In 1951, when *International Rice Milling* and *Denver Building* were decided, the most common worksite was owned by a single corporation which employed all the people who worked on the premises. Construction sites were one of the few circumstances in which multiple firms connected by a network of contracts employed workers who all worked on a common site. There were others, of course, including office buildings, but unions were uncommon in those industries. In the densely unionized manufacturing and mining industries, single employer worksites were the most common and so the Court might have imagined that its definition of illegal secondary boycotts in *Denver Building* would apply only in the construction business and would leave most employees free to picket at their place of work. Today, many employees work on sites occupied by the employees of multiple firms. Widespread subcontracting, shopping malls, industrial office parks, and other business models that were either unknown or uncommon in 1951 are ubiquitous. Even commercial office buildings are more commonly the site of unionization efforts as low-wage service workers (including janitors and security guards) are seeking to unionize. Establishing a picket line on the public property just outside an employer's place of business is far more likely to implicate neutral employers and their workers. If the *Denver Building* rule were applied to every worksite at which employees of two or more companies work, would picketing at the worksite commonly be secondary?

In sorting out when picketing at a site occupied by multiple employers is secondary, the NLRB and the courts have not relied primarily on either *International Rice Milling* or *Denver Building*. Instead, they have turned to the following decision, which involved a site where unionization was common in the early years of federal labor law and multiple employers shared premises—a shipyard.

b. The General Rule for Common Work Sites

SAILORS' UNION OF THE PACIFIC (MOORE DRY DOCK CO.)
92 N.L.R.B. 547 (1950)

[An American ship employing members of the Sailors' Union lost a contract to transport gypsum to a Panamanian ship employing non-union sailors who had agreed to work for less than half the wages of the unionized American sailors. The Panamanian ship, the *S.S. Phopho*, was owned by the Samsoc Corporation. The *Phopho* was tied up at the Moore Dry Dock where it was being converted to carry gypsum and where the crew was training, cleaning the ship, and preparing for the voyage. Samsoc refused the Sailors' Union request to recognize it to represent the crew, so the union sent pickets to the entrance of Moore Dry Dock carrying signs saying that the *Phopho* was unfair. The pickets requested permission to picket on Moore property close to the *Phopho*, but Moore refused. The *Phopho* crew did not cease work, as they were quartered on the ship and did not have to cross the picket line and their contracts required resolution of all labor disputes by Panamanian officials. The Moore Dry Dock employees, however, in response to a letter sent by the Sailors' Union to their union, refused to work on the *Phopho* but continued to work on all other ships at the dock. Moore Dry Dock filed charges under Section 8(b)(4).]

Section 8(b)(4)(A) is aimed at secondary boycotts and secondary strike activities. It was not intended to proscribe primary action by a union having a legitimate labor dispute with an employer. Picketing at the premises of a primary employer is traditionally recognized as primary action even though it is "necessarily designed to induce and encourage third persons to cease doing business with the picketed employer."

Section 8(b)(4)(A) was intended only to out-law certain *secondary* boycotts, whereby unions sought to enlarge the economic battleground beyond the premises of the primary Employer. When picketing is wholly at the premises of the employer with whom the union is engaged in a labor dispute, it cannot be called "secondary" even though, as is virtually always the case, an object of the picketing is to dissuade all persons from entering such premises for business reasons.

Hence, if Samsoc, the owner of the S.S. *Phopho*, had had a dock of its own in California to which the *Phopho* had been tied up while undergoing conversion by Moore Dry Dock employees, picketing by the Respondent at the dock site would unquestionably have constituted *primary* action, even though the Respondent might have expected that the picketing would be more effective in persuading Moore employees not to work on the ship than to persuade the seamen aboard the *Phopho* to quit that vessel. The difficulty in the present case arises therefore, not because of any difference in picketing objectives, but from the fact that the *Phopho* was not tied up at its own dock, but at that of Moore, while the picketing was going on in front of the Moore premises.

In the usual case, the *situs* of a labor dispute is the premises of the primary employer. Picketing of the premises is also picketing of the *situs*. But in some cases the *situs* of the dispute may not be limited to a fixed location; it may be ambulatory. Thus in the *Schultz* case, a majority of the Board held that the truck upon which a truck driver worked was the *situs* of a labor dispute between him and the owner of the truck. Similarly, we hold in the present case that, as the *Phopho* was the place of employment of the seamen, it was the *situs* of the dispute between Samsoc and the Respondent over working conditions aboard that vessel.

When the *situs* is ambulatory, it may come to rest temporarily at the premises of another employer. The perplexing question is: Does the right to picket follow the *situs* while it is stationed at the premises of a secondary employer, when the only way to picket that *situs* is in front of the secondary employer's premises? Admittedly, no easy answer is possible. Essentially the problem is one of balancing the right of a union to picket at the site of its dispute as against the right of a secondary employer to be free from picketing in a controversy in which it is not directly involved.

When a secondary employer is harboring the *situs* of a dispute between a union and a primary employer, the right of neither the union to picket nor of the secondary employer to be free from picketing can be absolute. The enmeshing of premises and *situs* qualifies both rights. In the kind of situation that exists in this case, we believe that picketing of the premises of a secondary employer is primary if it meets the following conditions: (a) The picketing is strictly limited to times when the *situs* of dispute is located on the secondary employer's premises; (b) at the time of the picketing the primary employer is engaged in its normal business at the *situs*; (c) the picketting is limited to places reasonably close to the location of the *situs*; and (d) the picketing discloses clearly that the dispute is with the primary employer. All these conditions were met in the present case.

(a) During the entire period of the picketing the *Phopho* was tied up at a dock in the Moore shipyard.

(b) Under its contract with Samsoc, Moore agreed to permit the former to put a crew on board the *Phopho* for training purposes during the last 2 weeks before the vessel's delivery to Samsoc. At the time the picketing started, 90 percent of the conversion job had been completed, practically the entire crew had been hired, the ship's oil bunkers had been filled, and other stores were shortly to be put aboard. The various members of the crew commenced work as soon as they reported aboard the *Phopho*. Those in the deck department did painting and cleaning up; those in the steward's department, cooking and cleaning up; and those in the engine department, oiling and cleaning up. The crew were thus getting the ship ready for sea. They were on board to serve the purposes of Samsoc, the

Phopho's owners, and not Moore. The normal business of a ship does not only begin with its departure on a scheduled voyage. The multitudinous steps of preparation, including hiring and training a crew and putting stores aboard, are as much a part of the normal business of a ship as the voyage itself. We find, therefore, that during the entire period of the picketing, the *Phopho* was engaged in its normal business.

(c) Before placing its pickets outside the entrance to the Moore shipyard, the Respondent Union asked, but was refused, permission to place its pickets at the dock where the *Phopho* was tied up. The Respondent therefore posted its pickets at the yard entrance which, as the parties stipulated, was as close to the *Phopho* as they could get under the circumstances.

(d) Finally, by its picketing and other conduct the Respondent was scrupulously careful to indicate that its dispute was solely with the primary employer, the owners of the *Phopho*. Thus the signs carried by the pickets said only that the *Phopho* was unfair to the Respondent. The *Phopho* and not Moore was declared "hot." Similarly, in asking cooperation of other unions, the Respondent clearly revealed that its dispute was with the *Phopho*. Finally, Moore's own witnesses admitted that no attempt was made to interfere with other work in progress in the Moore yard.

NOTES

1.   Although *Moore Dry Dock* referred to the worksite of the sailors as "ambulatory" and the case is sometimes referred to as establishing the ambulatory situs rule, it is the dominant rule for dealing with any common work site.

2.   How does the issue in *Moore Dry Dock* differ from the issue in *Denver Building*? Is there any dispute about who the primary employer is?

3.   HERE is on strike against a restaurant. HERE members picket the customer entrance and the loading dock. Because the Teamsters drivers won't cross the picket line at the loading dock, the restaurant owner drives to a supplier's warehouse to pick up the deliveries himself. HERE members follow the restaurant owner and picket while he is at the warehouse. The warehouse workers refuse to cross the picket line. Has HERE engaged in a secondary boycott?

4.   What if the union in a common situs picketing case complies with the four *Moore Dry Dock* requirements but writes a letter to the neutral employer saying that the picketing will stop when the union's demands are met? The Board has held that the letter indicates the union's intent to enmesh the neutral and thus establishes a violation of § 8(b)(4). Why?

5.   To continue operations during a strike, Verizon arranged for employees from its non-unionized operations across the United States to travel to New York to perform struck work. Striking Verizon workers noisily picketed the hotels where the striker replacements were staying, but picketed only

when the replacements were in the hotel (in the evenings and early mornings). Is the picketing at the hotels secondary? Is there another basis on which either Verizon or the hotels could have the picketing enjoined? (Hint: think about state law.) *See Paulson v. Communications Workers of America* (EDNY, 2016), https://www.bloomberglaw.com/document/X1Q6NLVB0382?fmt=pdf (granting § 10(*l*) injunction against picketing at hotels).

c. Separate Gates

Employers with employees on common work sites seized on the idea expressed in *Moore Dry Dock* that picketing must be confined to the place nearest the dispute. Employers established separate gates for entry to the common site and required employees of each employer to use a separate gate. By this device they hoped to be able to confine picketing of any particular employer to the single gate used by the employees of that employer and thus to allow the rest of the business to survive a strike without interruption of pick-ups, deliveries, or the other employees working on the premises. The following case established some ground rules for the use of separate gates to localize picketing.

LOCAL 761, INTERNATIONAL UNION OF ELECTRICAL WORKERS V. NLRB (GENERAL ELECTRIC CORP.)
366 U.S. 667 (1961)

JUSTICE FRANKFURTER delivered the opinion of the Court:

General Electric Corporation operates a plant outside of Louisville, Kentucky, where it manufactures washers, dryers, and other electrical household appliances. The square-shaped, thousand-acre, unfenced plant is known as Appliance Park. A large drainage ditch makes ingress and egress impossible except over five roadways across culverts, designated as gates.

Since 1954, General Electric sought to confine the employees of independent contractors who work on the premises of the Park, to the use of Gate 3-A and confine its use to them. The undisputed reason for doing so was to insulate General Electric employees from the frequent labor disputes in which the contractors were involved. Gate 3-A is 550 feet away from the nearest entrance available for General Electric employees, suppliers, and deliverymen. Since January 1958, a prominent sign has been posted at the gate which states: "GATE 3-A FOR EMPLOYEES OF CONTRACTORS ONLY—G.E. EMPLOYEES USE OTHER GATES." On rare occasions, it appears, a General Electric employee was allowed to pass the guardhouse, but such occurrence was in violation of company instructions. There was no proof of any unauthorized attempts to pass the gate during the strike in question.

The independent contractors are utilized for a great variety of tasks on the Appliance Park premises. Some do construction work on new buildings; some install and repair ventilating and heating equipment; some engage in retooling and rearranging operations necessary to the manufacture of new models; others do "general maintenance work." These services are contracted to outside employers either because the company's employees lack the necessary skill or manpower, or because the work can be done more economically by independent contractors. The latter reason determined the contracting of maintenance work for which the Central Maintenance department of the company bid competitively with the contractors. While some of the work done by these contractors had on occasion been previously performed by Central Maintenance, the findings do not disclose the number of employees of independent contractors who were performing these routine maintenance services, as compared with those who were doing specialized work of a capital-improvement nature.

The Union, petitioner here, is the certified bargaining representative for the production and maintenance workers who constitute approximately 7,600 of the 10,500 employees of General Electric at Appliance Park. On July 27, 1958, the Union called a strike because of 24 unsettled grievances with the company. Picketing occurred at all the gates, including Gate 3-A, and continued until August 9 when an injunction was issued by a Federal District Court. The signs carried by the pickets at all gates read: "LOCAL 761 ON STRIKE G.E. UNFAIR." Because of the picketing, almost all of the employees of independent contractors refused to enter the company premises.

Neither the legality of the strike or of the picketing at any of the gates except 3-A nor the peaceful nature of the picketing is in dispute. The sole claim is that the picketing before the gate exclusively used by employees of independent contractors was conduct proscribed by § 8(b)(4).

The Trial Examiner recommended that the Board dismiss the complaint. He concluded that the limitations on picketing which the Board had prescribed in so-called "common situs" cases were not applicable to the situation before him, in that the picketing at Gate 3-A represented traditional primary action which necessarily had a secondary effect of inconveniencing those who did business with the struck employer. He reasoned that if a primary employer could limit the area of picketing around his own premises by constructing a separate gate for employees of independent contractors, such a device could also be used to isolate employees of his suppliers and customers, and that such action could not relevantly be distinguished from oral appeals made to secondary employees not to cross a picket line where only a single gate existed.

The Board rejected the Trial Examiner's conclusion. It held that, since only the employees of the independent contractors were allowed to use Gate 3-A, the Union's object in picketing there was to enmesh these employees of the neutral employers in its dispute with the Company, thereby constituting a violation of § 8(b)(4)(A) because the independent employees were encouraged to engage in a concerted refusal to work "with an object of forcing the independent contractors to cease doing business with the Company."

Section 8(b)(4)(A) of the National Labor Relations Act provides that it shall be an unfair labor practice for a labor organization "to engage in . . . a strike . . . where an object thereof is . . . forcing any . . . person . . . to cease doing business with any other person." This provision could not be literally construed; otherwise it would ban most strikes historically considered to be lawful, so-called primary activity.

But not all so-called secondary boycotts were outlawed in § 8(b)(4)(A). The section does not speak generally of secondary boycotts. It describes and condemns specific union conduct directed to specific objectives. Employees must be induced; they must be induced to engage in a strike or concerted refusal; an object must be to force or require their employer or another person to cease doing business with a third person. Thus, much that might argumentatively be found to fall within the broad and somewhat vague concept of secondary boycott is not in terms prohibited.

Important as is the distinction between legitimate "primary activity" and banned "secondary activity," it does not present a glaringly bright line. The objectives of any picketing include a desire to influence others from withholding from the employer their services or trade. *See Sailors' Union of the Pacific* (Moore Dry Dock). Intended or not, sought for or not, aimed for or not, employees of neutral employers do take action sympathetic with strikers and do put pressure on their own employers. It is clear that, when a union pickets an employer with whom it has a dispute, it hopes, even if it does not intend, that all persons will honor the picket line, and that hope encompasses the employees of neutral employers who may in the course of their employment (deliverymen and the like) have to enter the premises. Almost all picketing, even at the situs of the primary employer and surely at that of the secondary, hopes to achieve the forbidden objective, whatever other motives there may be and however small the chances of success. But picketing which induces secondary employees to respect a picket line is not the equivalent of picketing which has an object of inducing those employees to engage in concerted conduct against their employer in order to force him to refuse to deal with the struck employer. *NLRB v. International Rice Milling.*

However difficult the drawing of lines more nice than obvious, the statute compels the task. Accordingly, the Board and the courts have attempted to devise reasonable criteria drawing heavily upon the means to which a union resorts in promoting its cause.

The nature of the problem, as revealed by unfolding variant situations, inevitably involves an evolutionary process for its rational response, not a quick, definitive formula as a comprehensive answer. And so, it is not surprising that the Board has more or less felt its way during the fourteen years in which it has had to apply § 8(b)(4)(A), and has modified and reformed its standards on the basis of accumulating experience. "One of the purposes which lead to the creation of such boards is to have decisions based upon evidential facts under the particular statute made by experienced officials with an adequate appreciation of the complexities of the subject which is entrusted to their administration." *Republic Aviation Corp. v. NLRB.*

The early decisions of the Board following the Taft-Hartley amendments involved activity which took place around the secondary employer's premises. For example, in *Wadsworth Building Co.* the union set up a picket line around the situs of a builder who had contracted to purchase prefabricated houses from the primary employer. The Board found this to be illegal secondary activity. In contrast, when picketing took place around the premises of the primary employer, the Board regarded this as valid primary activity. In *Oil Workers International Union* (Pure Oil Co.), Pure had used Standard's dock and employees for loading its oil onto ships. The companies had contracted that, in case of a strike against Standard, Pure employees would take over the loading of Pure oil. The union struck against Standard and picketed the dock, and Pure employees refused to cross the picket line. The Board held this to be a primary activity, although the union's action induced the Pure employees to engage in a concerted refusal to handle Pure products at the dock. The fact that the picketing was confined to the vicinity of the Standard premises influenced the Board not to find that an object of the activity was to force Pure to cease doing business with Standard, even if such was a secondary effect.

In *United Electrical Workers (Ryan Construction Corp.)*, 85 N.L.R.B. 417 (1949), Ryan had contracted to perform construction work on a building adjacent to the Bucyrus plant and inside its fence. A separate gate was cut through the fence for Ryan's employees which no employee of Bucyrus ever used. The Board concluded that the union—on strike against Bucyrus—could picket the Ryan gate, even though an object of the picketing was to enlist the aid of Ryan employees, since Congress did not intend to outlaw primary picketing.

However, the impact of the new situations made the Board conscious of the complexity of the problem by reason of the protean forms in which it appeared. This became clear in the "common situs" cases—situations where two employers were performing separate tasks on common premises. The *Moore Dry Dock* case laid out the Board's new standards in this area. These tests were widely accepted by reviewing federal courts. As is too often the way of law or, at least, of adjudications, soon the *Dry Dock* tests were mechanically applied so that a violation of one of the standards was taken to be presumptive of illegal activity. For example, failure of picket signs clearly to designate the employer against whom the strike was directed was held to be violative of § 8 (b)(4)(A).[4]

The Board's application of the *Dry Dock* standards to picketing at the premises of the struck employer was made explicit in *Retail Fruit & Vegetable Clerks (Crystal Palace Market),* 116 N.L.R.B. 856 (1956). The owner of a large common market operated some of the shops within, and leased out others to independent sellers. The union, although given permission to picket the owner's individual stands, chose to picket outside the entire market. The Board held that this action was violative of § 8(b)(4)(A) in that the union did not attempt to minimize the effect of its picketing, as required in a common-situs case, on the operations of the neutral employers utilizing the market. [The Board stated that the *Dry Dock*] principles should apply to all common situs picketing, including cases where, as here, the picketed premises are owned by the primary employer. The Board made clear that its decision did not affect situations where picketing which had effects on neutral third parties who dealt with the employer occurred at premises occupied solely by him.

In rejecting the ownership test in situations where two employers were performing work upon a common site, the Board was naturally guided by this Court's opinion in *Rice Milling,* in which we indicated that the location of the picketing at the primary employer's premises was "not necessarily conclusive" of its legality. Where the work done by the secondary employees is unrelated to the normal operations of the primary employer, it is difficult to perceive how the pressure of picketing the entire situs is any less on the neutral employer merely because the picketing takes place at property owned by the struck employer. The application of the *Dry Dock* tests to limit the picketing effects to the employees of the employer against whom the dispute is directed carries out the "dual congressional objectives of preserving the right of labor organizations to bring pressure to bear on offending employers in primary labor disputes and of shielding unoffending employers and others from pressures in controversies not their own." *NLRB v. Denver Bldg. Council.*

From this necessary survey of the course of the Board's treatment of our problem, the precise nature of the issue before us emerges. With due regard to the relation between the Board's function and the scope of judicial review of its rulings, the question is whether the Board may apply the *Dry Dock* criteria so as to make unlawful picketing at a gate utilized exclusively by employees of independent contractors who work on the struck employer's premises. The effect of such a holding would not bar the union from picketing at all gates used by the employees, suppliers, and customers of the struck employer. Of course an employer may not, by removing all his

---

[4]   The *Dry Dock* criteria had perhaps their widest application in the trucking industry. There, unions on strike against truckers often staged picketing demonstrations at the places of pickup and delivery. Compare *Int'l Bhd. of Teamsters (Schultz Refrigerated Service, Inc.),* 87 N.L.R.B. 502, with *Int'l Bhd. of Teamsters (Sterling Beverages, Inc.),* 90 N.L.R.B. 401.

employees from the situs of the strike, bar the union from publicizing its cause. The basis of the Board's decision in this case would not remotely have that effect, nor any such tendency for the future.

The Union claims that, if the Board's ruling is upheld, employers will be free to erect separate gates for deliveries, customers, and replacement workers which will be immunized from picketing. This fear is baseless. The key to the problem is found in the type of work that is being performed by those who use the separate gate. It is significant that the Board has since applied its rationale, first stated in the present case, only to situations where the independent workers were performing tasks unconnected to the normal operations of the struck employer—usually construction work on his buildings. In such situations, the indicated limitations on picketing activity respect the balance of competing interests that Congress has required the Board to enforce. On the other hand, if a separate gate were devised for regular plant deliveries, the barring of picketing at that location would make a clear invasion on traditional primary activity of appealing to neutral employees whose tasks aid the employer's everyday operations.

The foregoing course of reasoning would require that the judgment below sustaining the Board's order be affirmed but for one consideration, even though this consideration may turn out not to affect the result. The legal path by which the Board and the Court of Appeals reached their decisions did not take into account that if Gate 3-A was in fact used by employees of independent contractors who performed conventional maintenance work necessary to the normal operations of General Electric, the use of the gate would have been a mingled one outside the bar of § 8(b)(4)(A). In short, such mixed use of this portion of the struck employer's premises would not bar picketing rights of the striking employees. While the record shows some such mingled use, it sheds no light on its extent. It may well turn out to be that the instances of these maintenance tasks were so insubstantial as to be treated by the Board as *de minimis*. We cannot here guess at the quantitative aspect of this problem. It calls for Board determination. For determination of the questions thus raised, the case must be remanded by the Court of Appeals to the Board.

NOTES

1.   *General Electric* said that neutral employers who are part of the regular operations of a primary employer may be picketed at the work site they share with the primary employer. Is that consistent with *Denver Building*?

2.   On remand from the Supreme Court, the NLRB determined that the picketing at Gate 3-A was primary and therefore legal. The Board found that the repair and construction work was not *de minimis* as measured by the labor costs and that it was part of GE's normal operations because it was the same

type of work that had previously been performed by GE employees. *Local 761, Int'l Union of Elec. Workers,* 138 N.L.R.B. 342 (1962).

3.   In *United Steelworkers v. NLRB* (Carrier Corp.), 376 U.S. 492 (1964), employees of the Carrier Corporation picketed several entrances to their employer's plant, including a 35-foot railroad right-of-way used by the railroad for deliveries to Carrier and to three other companies in the area. The railroad spur was on property owned by the railroad but ran through a gate in a continuous chain-link fence which enclosed both the property of Carrier Corporation and the railroad right-of-way. The gate was locked when the spur was not in use and was accessible only to railroad employees. The pickets allowed the train through when it was destined for the neutral companies but prevented it passing when the cars were intended to pick up or deliver to Carrier. The Board found that the picketing was intended to interfere with the operations of the railroad, a neutral employer. The Supreme Court disagreed, ruling that the effort to stop the rail cars was an incident of the primary strike against Carrier:

> The primary strike is aimed at applying economic pressure by halting the day-to-day operations of the struck employer. But Congress not only preserved the right to strike; it also saved "primary picketing" from the secondary ban. Picketing has traditionally been a major weapon to implement the goals of a strike and has characteristically been aimed at all those approaching the situs whose mission is selling, delivering or otherwise contributing to the operations which the strike is endeavoring to halt. In light of this traditional goal of primary pressures we think Congress intended to preserve the right to picket during a strike a gate reserved for employees of neutral delivery men furnishing day-to-day service essential to the plant's regular operations.

The Court also rejected the contention that the rail spur was a common situs:

> Nor may the *General Electric* case be put aside for the reason that the picketed gate in the present case was located on property owned by New York Central Railroad and not upon property owned by the primary employer. The railroad gate adjoined company property and was in fact the railroad entrance gate to the Carrier plant. For the purposes of § 8(b)(4) picketing at a situs so proximate and related to the employer's day-to-day operations is no more illegal than if it had occurred at a gate owned by Carrier.

4.   Chemstor is a chemical storage company located on the Gulf of Mexico. Abutting Chemstor's property is Dock 5, a dock owned by Texas Terminal Company. Chemstor and two other businesses used Dock 5 to load and unload cargo for ocean-going vessels. Only one company may use the dock at any particular time. Dock 5 may be accessed by a private ramp owned by Chemstor leading from Chemstor's property and used solely by Chemstor employees when loading chemicals, and a second concrete ramp extending to the dock from a public access road. Those using the ramp from the public access

road include employees of the ship, federal and local officials, and various vendors of the vessel and pilots.

The union struck Chemstor alleging unfair labor practices and began picketing at the main entrance of Chemstor, as well as at the base of the concrete ramp leading to the dock from the public access road. The picketing at the ramp occurred only when there was a ship at the dock loading Chemstor material. The union also picketed the dock from the water in a small motor driven craft. The boat picketed both a ship already docked at Dock 5, but also to prevent other ships from entering Dock 5. Displayed from the boat was a sign reading "To the Public, OCAW Local 4–449 on Strike Against Chemstor. OCAW Local 4–449 does not have a dispute with any other employer."

By law as well as custom, a pilot licensed by the State is required to direct the ship from the Gulf to the dock and to take the ship from the dock out to sea. These pilots are members both of the Galveston-Texas City Pilots and the Master Mates and Pilots Union Local 100, affiliated with the International Association of Master Mates and Pilots. The pilots honored the picket line at the ramp of Dock 5. The pilots also refused to assist vessels scheduled for Chemstor's use from arriving at or departing from Dock 5. Is the picketing a violation of section 8(b)(4)? Which applies: the *Moore Dry Dock* or the *General Electric* rule? *See Anchortank, Inc. v. NLRB,* 601 F.2d 233 (5th Cir. 1979) (Dock 5 is not a common situs, therefore *Moore Dry Dock* does not apply, and under *General Electric* work on the ships at the dock is part of primary employer's normal operations).

BUILDING & CONSTRUCTION TRADES COUNCIL
(MARKWELL & HARTZ, INC.)
155 N.L.R.B. 319 (1965)

In the period covered by the complaint, Markwell & Hartz [M & H] was the general contractor on a project for expansion of a filtration plant in Jefferson Parish, Louisiana. M & H decided to perform about 80 percent of the project with its own employees while subcontracting the balance. Included in the work contracted out was the piledriving awarded to Binnings, and the electrical work awarded to Barnes. Both Binnings and Barnes employ members of craft unions affiliated with Respondent.

The East Jefferson Water Works is surrounded by a chain-link fence, with two vehicular gates on Jefferson Highway which bounds the property on the north, and two additional gates on Arnoult Road. [One gate is called the main gate, one gate is called the warehouse gate, and one gate is called the rear gate.]

At all times material, Respondent has been engaged in a primary labor dispute with M & H, and has had no dispute with either Binnings or Barnes.

On October 17, in connection with its dispute with M & H, Respondent commenced picketing the gates leading to the jobsite. The picketing took place during normal workhours, with the number of pickets varying from one to three individuals. The picket sign listed both the rates that should be paid on the job and carried the following message:

MARKWELL AND HARTZ

GENERAL CONTRACTOR DOES NOT HAVE A SIGNED
AGREEMENT WITH THE BUILDING AND CONSTRUCTION
TRADES COUNCIL OF NEW ORLEANS AFL-CIO

The picketing continued until enjoined in the § 10(*l*) proceeding. At no time during the picketing did employees of Binnings or Barnes cross the picket line to perform work in connection with their employers' subcontract.

The validity of Respondent's picketing prior to October 23 is not in issue. However, on that date M & H posted the two gates on Jefferson Highway and the warehouse gate on Arnoult Road, reserving them for use of subcontractors and persons making deliveries to the project, and prohibiting their use by M & H's employees. The rear gate on Arnoult Road was designated for exclusive use of the latter.

That morning, when Respondent's picket encountered the newly marked gates, he moved to the rear gate which was reserved for M & H's employees. As a result, piledriving crews employed by Binnings entered the main gate and began working. About an hour and a half later the picket returned to the main gate, and Binnings' employees walked off. M & H then decided to remove its employees, with the exception of the superintendent and project engineer, in the hope that Binnings would then be able to complete the piledriving work. By 10 o'clock that morning its employees were off the site. Though Respondent was notified of the absence of the primary employees, the picketing continued. When Binnings' crews again honored the picket line, M & H recalled its employees. They reported to work on October 24 at 10 a.m. to complete the piledriving work themselves.

On November 14, M & H changed the signs on the Jefferson Highway gates to indicate that these entrances were not to be used by employees of M & H or carriers and suppliers making deliveries to M & H, and that such persons were to use the rear gate on Arnoult Road. M & H informed Respondent of these changes and notified suppliers to use the rear gate only. Identical changes were made at the warehouse gate on November 16, and on December 6 the rear gate was marked as reserved for use of employees of M & H and suppliers and carriers making deliveries to M & H.

On these facts, we are asked to decide whether a union, in furtherance of a primary dispute with a general contractor in the construction industry, may lawfully engage in jobsite picketing at gates reserved and set apart for exclusive use of neutral subcontractors.

Without passing upon whether the subcontractor gates involved herein were established and maintained in accordance with the *General Electric* requirements, we are of the opinion that the principles expressed in that case are inapposite in determining whether a union may lawfully extend its dispute with a general contractor on a construction site by picketing gates reserved for exclusive use of subcontractors also engaged on that project. Rather, we believe that this issue must be resolved in the light of the *Moore Dry Dock* standards, traditionally applied by the Board in determining whether picketing at a common situs is protected primary activity.

Unlike *General Electric,* which involved picketing *at the premises of a struck manufacturer,* the picketing in the instant case occurred at a construction project on which M & H, the primary employer, was but one of several employers operating on premises owned and operated by a third party, the Jefferson Parish Water Works. Picketing of neutral and primary contractors under such conditions has been traditionally viewed as presenting a "common situs" problem.

[T]he Board, in determining whether a labor organization, when picketing a common situs, has taken all reasonable precaution to prevent enmeshment of neutrals, traditionally applies the limitations set forth in the *Moore Dry Dock* case. In our opinion application of these standards to all common situs situations, including those, which like the instant case, involve picketing of gates reserved exclusively for neutral contractors on a construction project, serves the . . . congressional objectives underlying the boycott provisions of the Act.

Nor do[es] the Supreme Court's decision in *General Electric* detract from our conclusions in this regard; for, the mere fact that picketing of a neutral gate *at premises of a struck employer,* may in proper circumstances be lawful primary action, does not require a like finding when a labor organization applies *direct* pressure upon secondary employers engaged on a common situs. That the Supreme Court had no intention of overriding this historic distinction is evidenced by its express approval of the *Moore Dry Dock* standards, and its observation that the *General Electric* case did not present a common situs situation to which the *Moore Dry Dock* standards should apply.

Applying the *Moore Dry Dock* standards to the instant case requires the timing and location of the picketing and the legends on the picket signs to be tailored to reach the employees of the primary employer, rather than those of the neutral employer, and deviations from these requirements establish the secondary object of the picketing and render it unlawful. Since Respondent's picketing at the neutral gates of Binnings and Barnes continued after November 16, we find that the picketing after that date failed to comply with the *Moore Dry Dock* requirement that such action take place reasonably close to the situs of Respondent's dispute with M &

H. We are completely satisfied that Respondent's picketing at the subcontractor gates was to induce strike action by employees of subcontractors with whom Respondent had no dispute. By such conduct, Respondent unlawfully sought to disrupt the operations of the neutral subcontractors and their employees and to enmesh them in the primary dispute in a manner which could not be condoned as an unavoidable by-product of legitimate primary picketing.

The dissent's analysis, although well-stated and on first reading not unreasonable as an application of *General Electric* standards in a construction industry setting, nevertheless runs counter to firmly established principles governing common situs picketing in that industry. Given the close relation—which is not only characteristic of but almost inevitable at many stages of a building construction project—of the work duties of the various other employees with those of the primary subcontractor, the principle of the dissent would also permit picket line appeals to the employees of the neutral general contractor and other subcontractors whatever the situation as to common or separate gates.

But it was precisely this claim, that the *close* working relations of various building construction contractors on a common situs involved them in a common undertaking which destroyed the neutrality and thus the immunity of secondary employers and employees to picket line appeals, that the Supreme Court rejected in *Denver Building Trades*. And there is not the slightest intimation by the Court in *General Electric* that it was reversing or revising the rule in *Denver*. [T]he theory of the dissent, if logically extended, is one that would in effect reverse *Denver* not only where the overarching general contractor on the building site is the primary employer, but also, where the intertwined work of a construction *sub*contractor is the primary target.

MEMBERS FANNING and JENKINS, dissenting:

In our view, the majority has inferred that Respondent's picketing was for an unlawful object simply from the fact that the reserved gates were used only by secondary employees, without inquiry into the question of whether the appeals to such employees, were, in the circumstances of this case, permissible primary activity.

[The Supreme] Court [in *General Electric*] reminded the Board that

> Almost all picketing, even at the situs of the primary employer and surely at that of the secondary, hopes to achieve the forbidden objective, whatever other motives there may be and however small the chances of success. *But picketing which induces secondary employees to respect a picket line is not the equivalent of picketing which has an object of inducing those employees to engage in concerted conduct against their employer in order to force him to refuse to deal with the struck employer.*

The italicized sentence from the above quotation succinctly states the issue which the Board must decide in this case: was Respondent's picketing for an object of inducing employees of the neutral subcontractors to take action to force their employers to cease dealing with M & H; or was its object merely to induce such employees to respect the picket line thrown up around M & H's operations, and, if so, does such activity constitute legitimate primary activity? This issue is no different from the issue posed by the facts in the *General Electric* case itself, for there the Board inferred an unlawful object simply from the fact that the picketing called into question by the complaint occurred at a gate not used by primary employees, and was directed solely to neutral employees. The whole thrust of the Court's *General Electric* decision is that the inference of unlawful object cannot be based simply on the fact that the picketing occurs at gates used solely by neutral employees. [T]he Court firmly established the proposition that direct appeals to employees of neutrals "whose mission is selling, delivering or otherwise contributing to the operations which the strike is endeavoring to halt" constitute protected primary activity.

But it is not only direct appeals to employees of suppliers and deliverymen which were found to constitute direct primary action. The *General Electric* case involved appeals to employees of neutral subcontractors and the Court, noting that "the key to the problem is found in the type of work that is being performed by those who use the separate gate," held that, before such appeals may be ruled unlawful under Section 8(b)(4)(B),

> There must be a separate gate, marked and set apart from other gates; the work done by the men who use the [separate] gate must be unrelated to the normal operations of the employer, and the work must be of a kind that would not, if done when the plant were engaged in its regular operations, necessitate curtailing those operations.

The crucial consideration regarding this holding is not, as the majority apparently views it, that it was made with respect to conduct occurring in connection with a strike at an industrial plant, but that it held that appeals to respect a picket line made to employees of secondary employers whose operations do not meet the tests stated above constitute legitimate primary activity just as do similar appeals to employees of neutral suppliers and deliverers.

The *Moore Dry Dock* standards were not designed to restrict primary activity at common situs disputes, but rather to assure that banned secondary activity would not be permitted.

Respondent had the right to appeal to employees delivering supplies and materials to M & H to respect the picket line. It undoubtedly is too late in the day to argue that appeals to employees making deliveries to a primary employer in the construction industry are not legitimate primary activity. Certainly, it cannot be so argued on the faulty premise that Congress intended "more lenient" treatment of picketing at industrial sites than it intended for picketing of sites in the building and construction industry.

Significantly, Congress has not seen fit to distinguish between industries, by adopting a more narrow definition of the lawful scope of picketing in the construction industry than is permitted in other industries. Certainly, the economic pressure sustained by neutral subcontractors as a consequence of reserved gate picketing on a construction job is no different from that imposed by like conduct upon neutral subcontractors performing work on premises occupied by a struck manufacturer. Nor is it any different from the pressures sustained by neutral suppliers making deliveries to the struck primary employer whether he be a manufacturer or a general contractor in the building and construction industry.

Nor do we regard the Court's decision in *Denver Building & Construction Trades Council* as precluding application of *General Electric* to the instant case. In *Denver*, the Court held that despite their close relationship, the several contractors on a construction job were not allies or a single employer for purposes of the boycott provisions of the Act.

In applying the *General Electric* standards to the instant case, we find that the work of Binnings and Barnes was related to the normal operations of M & H, the general contractor. In this connection it is relevant that employees of the named subcontractors were scheduled to work during the picketing period together with the employees of M & H in completing the filtration plant expansion job. In addition, during this period, M & H's project engineer and superintendent were to work with the subcontractors to insure that M & H's commitment to the owner was performed in compliance with project specifications. We find that M & H's portion of the work on this job was part of its normal operations, as was completion of the entire project, and that the work of the subcontractors was related to both M & H's work on the job and its responsibility to complete the project itself, and hence related to M & H's normal operations.

This being the case, the fact that such appeals were addressed to those employees at gates reserved for their exclusive use by M & H furnishes no basis for the majority's conclusion that the picketing after November 16 "failed to comply with the *Moore Dry Dock* requirement that such action take place reasonably close to the situs of Respondent's dispute with M & H." As the Supreme Court indicated in the *General Electric* decision, the barring of picketing through the device of a gate reserved for the exclusive use of secondary employees whose tasks aid the struck employer's every day operations constitutes a clear invasion of traditional primary activity. Furthermore, the *Moore Dry Dock* tests are utilized by the Board to aid it in determining whether certain kinds of picketing constitute proscribed secondary or protected primary activity whereas the *General Electric* tests are designed to aid in determining whether a union as the right to appeal directly to the secondary employees using a reserved gate. Accordingly, it seems obvious that the former tests must be applied in a manner which will give full effect to the latter tests. As we find that Respondent had the right to appeal to the employees of the neutral subcontractor, we find that the picketing at the reserved gates constituted compliance with the requirement that its picketing be limited to places reasonably close to the situs of Respondent's dispute with M & H. Accordingly, as the picketing also conformed to the other *Moore Dry Dock* tests, we perceive no basis on which to conclude that Respondent's object in picketing the reserved gates was to induce the employees of M & H's subcontractors to engage in a refusal to perform services with the object of forcing their employers to cease dealing with M & H.

NOTES

1. *Summing Up the Common Site and Separate Gates Rules.*

(a) When a primary employer works on a neutral's site, picketing the neutral's site in the course of a dispute with the primary is secondary unless the picketing union complies with *Moore Dry Dock*. To comply, (i) the picketing must take place as close as possible to the situs of the dispute and, if the neutral employer has reserved a gate for the primary's employees, picketing must be limited to that gate; (ii) the picketing may take place only when the primary's workers are on the site; (iii) the picketing may take place only when the primary is engaged in its normal operations; and (iv) the picket signs must disclose that the dispute is solely with the primary.

(b) When a neutral works on a primary's site, as in the case of subcontractors working in a manufacturing facility owned by another company, the use of separate gates is governed by *General Electric*. The employers can use reserved gates to immunize subcontractors from picketing, but not for work that is part of the normal operations of the primary (such as work that would have been done by the striking employees), and not for work that would require curtailing the normal operations of the primary.

(c) There is an exception to (b). In construction, when a neutral employer works on a site controlled by a primary employer and owned by a third party, and the primary reserves a gate for employees of the neutral, picketing the neutral reserved gate in the course of a dispute with the primary is secondary unless the picketing union complies with *Moore Dry Dock*. The employers can use a reserved gate and the picketing can occur only at the separate gate, only when the primary's workers are on site, only when the primary is engaged in its normal operations, and the signs must disclose that the dispute is with the primary. (See *Markwell & Hartz*.)

(d) In all reserved gate cases, the gates must be posted for the exclusive use of the primary or the neutral(s) and the reserved use must be enforced (no intermingling of employees).

2. *Struck Work and the Ally Doctrine.* The entire primary-secondary distinction rests on the notion that some employers are "neutral" and others are not. When a strike or lockout occurs, of course, employers whose workers continue to work often benefit from increased business, and sometimes employers anticipating a strike or a lockout will make arrangements in advance for their customers or suppliers to deal with other firms during the work stoppage. Two lines of cases have developed attempting to determine when an employer is so closely allied with a firm subject to a labor stoppage that it has lost its claim to neutrality; collectively the cases are known as the "ally doctrine." One line of cases concerns firms handling work that would ordinarily be done by employees of a firm on strike; this is the "struck work doctrine." When the struck employer arranges for another employer to perform work during a strike, the secondary employer loses its neutrality and may be picketed. *See Douds v. Metropolitan Fed'n of Architects*, 75 F.Supp. 672 (S.D.N.Y. 1948) (a design firm is not neutral when 75 percent of its work is subcontracted from another design firm whose employees are on strike and when supervisors of the struck firm inspected the subcontracted firm). A second line of cases concerns firms that are nominally separate (e.g., they are separate corporations with different names) but are in fact closely interrelated in their finances or management. This is known as the "alter ego" doctrine. The test for an "alter ego" is whether the two corporations share common ownership *and* common control of labor relations. *See South Prairie Constr. Co. v. Operating Eng'rs Local 627*, 425 U.S. 800 (1976) (defining the alter ego test).

If the neutral is an alter ego or becomes an ally by performing struck work, the strikers may picket the employer for all its work as if it were the primary—there is no requirement (as in *Moore Dry Dock*) that the picketers tailor their picketing to particular times or places.

3. PERMISSIBLE SECONDARY APPEALS

a. Consumer Appeals Under the Proviso

Not all activity that has the prohibited secondary "object" of "forcing or requiring any person to . . . cease doing business with any other person" is prohibited by section 8(b)(4): only strikes, threats, or coercion are prohibited. Until 1959, only coercion directed at getting workers to cease working was prohibited: picketing targeted at consumers was legal under federal law, although state courts sometimes enjoined it. In 1959, however, Congress added the language that now appears in § 8(b)(4) which prohibits coercive behavior with the object of "forcing . . . any person . . . to cease doing business with any other person." Read literally, of course, that would outlaw all product boycotts. Some in Congress were concerned with protecting the traditional product boycott, and so added a proviso to § 8(b)(4) which protects consumer appeals. It states that § 8(b)(4) shall not be construed to prohibit publicity, other than picketing, for the purpose of truthfully advising the public, including consumers and members of a labor organization, that a product or products are produced by an employer with whom the labor organization has a primary dispute and are distributed by another employer, as long as such publicity does not have an effect of inducing any individual employed by any person other than the primary employer in the course of his employment to refuse to pick up, deliver, or transport any goods, or not to perform any services, at the establishment of the employer engaged in such distribution.

The consumer appeal proviso was construed in the following case:

NLRB v. FRUIT AND VEGETABLE PACKERS, LOCAL 760 (TREE FRUITS)
377 U.S. 58 (1964)

JUSTICE BRENNAN delivered the opinion of the Court:

Under section 8(b)(4)(ii)(B) of the National Labor Relations Act, it is an unfair labor practice for a union "to threaten, coerce, or restrain any person," with the object of "forcing or requiring any person to cease using, selling, handling, transporting, or otherwise dealing in the products of any other producer" or "to cease doing business with any other person." A proviso excepts, however, "publicity, other than picketing, for the purpose of truthfully advising the public . . . that a product or products are produced by an employer with whom the labor organization has a primary dispute and are distributed by another employer, as long as such publicity does not have an effect of inducing any individual employed by any person other than the primary employer in the course of his employment to refuse to pick up, deliver, or transport any goods, or not to perform any services, at the establishment of the employer engaged in such distribution." The question in this case is whether the respondent unions violated this section when they limited their secondary picketing of retail stores to an appeal to the customers of the stores not to buy the products of certain firms against which one of the respondents was on strike.

Respondent Local 760 called a strike against fruit packers and warehousemen doing business in Yakima, Washington. The struck firms sold Washington State apples to the Safeway chain of retail stores in and about Seattle, Washington. Local 760, aided by respondent Joint Council, instituted a consumer boycott against the apples in support of the strike. They placed pickets who walked back and forth before the customers' entrances of 46 Safeway stores in Seattle. The pickets—two at each of 45 stores and three at the 46th store—wore placards and distributed handbills which appealed to Safeway customers, and to the public generally, to refrain from buying Washington State apples, which were only one of numerous food products sold in the stores.[3]

Throughout the history of federal regulation of labor relations, Congress has consistently refused to prohibit peaceful picketing except where it is used as a means to achieve specific ends which experience has shown are undesirable. We have recognized this congressional practice and have not ascribed to Congress a purpose to outlaw peaceful picketing unless there is the clearest indication in the legislative history that Congress intended to do so as regards the particular ends of the picketing under review. Both the congressional policy and our adherence to this principle of interpretation reflect concern that a broad ban against peaceful picketing might collide with the guarantees of the First Amendment.

We have examined the legislative history of the amendments to § 8(b)(4), and conclude that it does not reflect with the requisite clarity a congressional plan to proscribe all peaceful consumer picketing at secondary sites, and, particularly, any concern with peaceful picketing when it is limited, as here, to persuading Safeway customers not to buy Washington State apples when they traded in the Safeway stores. All that the legislative history shows in the way of an isolated evil believed to require proscription of peaceful consumer picketing at secondary sites was its use to persuade the customers of the secondary employer to cease trading with him in order to force him to cease dealing with, or to put pressure upon, the primary employer. This narrow focus reflects the difference between such conduct and peaceful picketing at the secondary site directed only at the struck product. In the latter case, the union's appeal to the public is confined to its dispute with the primary employer, since the public is not asked to withhold its patronage from the secondary employer, but only to boycott the primary employer's goods. On the other hand, a union appeal to the public at the secondary site not to trade at all

---

[3]   The placard worn by each picket stated: "To the Consumer: Non-Union Washington State apples are being sold at this store. Please do not purchase such apples. Thank you. Teamsters Local 760, Yakima, Washington."

A typical handbill read:

DON'T BUY WASHINGTON STATE APPLES

THE 1960 CROP OF WASHINGTON STATE APPLES IS BEING PACKED BY NON-UNION FIRMS

Included in this non-union operation are twenty-six firms in the Yakima Valley with which there is a labor dispute. These firms are charged with being

UNFAIR

by their employees who, with their union, are on strike and have been replaced by non-union strikebreaking workers employed under substandard wage scales and working conditions.

In justice to these striking union workers who are attempting to protect their living standards and their right to engage in good-faith collective bargaining, we request that you

DON'T BUY WASHINGTON STATE APPLES

TEAMSTERS UNION LOCAL 760 YAKIMA, WASHINGTON

This is not a strike against any store or market

with the secondary employer goes beyond the goods of the primary employer, and seeks the public's assistance in forcing the secondary employer to cooperate with the union in its primary dispute. This is not to say that this distinction was expressly alluded to in the debates. It is to say, however, that the consumer picketing carried on in this case is not attended by the abuses at which the statute was directed.

The story of the 1959 amendments begins with the original § 8(b)(4) of the National Labor Relations Act. Its prohibition, in pertinent part, was confined to the inducing or encouraging of "the employees of any employer to engage in, a strike or a concerted refusal . . . to . . . handle . . . any goods" of a primary employer. This proved to be inept language. Three major loopholes were revealed. Since only inducement of "employees" was proscribed, direct inducement of a supervisor or the secondary employer by threats of labor trouble was not prohibited. Since only a "strike or a concerted refusal" was prohibited, pressure upon a single employee was not forbidden. Finally, railroads, airlines and municipalities were not "employers" under the Act and therefore inducement or encouragement of their employees was not unlawful.

When major labor relations legislation was being considered in 1958 the closing of these loopholes was important to the House and to some members of the Senate. We think it is especially significant that neither Senator, nor the Secretary of Labor in testifying in support of the Administration's bill, referred to consumer picketing as making the amendments necessary. It was the opponents of the amendments who, in expressing fear of their sweep, suggested that they might proscribe consumer picketing. But we have often cautioned against the danger, when interpreting a statute, of reliance upon the views of its legislative opponents. In their zeal to defeat a bill, they understandably tend to overstate its reach.

Peaceful consumer picketing to shut off all trade with the secondary employer unless he aids the union in its dispute with the primary employer is poles apart from such picketing which only persuades his customers not to buy the struck product. The proviso indicates no more than that the Senate conferees' constitutional doubts led Congress to authorize publicity other than picketing which persuades the customers of a secondary employer to stop all trading with him, but not such publicity which has the effect of cutting off his deliveries or inducing his employees to cease work. On the other hand, picketing which persuades the customers of a secondary employer to stop all trading with him was also to be barred.

We come then to the question whether the picketing in this case, confined as it was to persuading customers to cease buying the product of the primary employer, falls within the area of secondary consumer picketing which Congress did clearly indicate its intention to prohibit under § 8(b)(4)(ii). We hold that it did not fall within that area, and therefore did not "threaten, coerce, or restrain" Safeway. While any diminution in Safeway's purchases of apples due to a drop in consumer demand might be said to be a result which causes respondents' picketing to fall literally within the statutory prohibition, "it is a familiar rule that a thing may be within the letter of the statute and yet not within the statute, because not within its spirit nor within the intention of its makers." *Holy Trinity Church v. U.S.*, 143 U.S. 457, 459. When consumer picketing is employed only to persuade customers not to buy the struck product, the union's appeal is closely confined to the primary dispute. The site of the appeal is expanded to include the premises of the secondary employer, but if the appeal succeeds, the secondary employer's purchases from the struck firms are decreased only because the public has diminished its purchases of the struck product. On the other hand, when consumer picketing is employed to persuade customers not to trade at all with the secondary employer, the latter stops buying the struck product, not because of a falling demand, but in response to pressure designed to inflict injury on his business generally. In such case, the union does more than merely follow the struck product; it creates a separate dispute with the secondary employer.

JUSTICE BLACK, concurring:

Because of the language of § 8(b)(4)(ii)(B) of the National Labor Relations Act and the legislative history, I feel impelled to hold that Congress, in passing this section of the Act, intended to forbid the striking employees of one business to picket the premises of a neutral business where the purpose of the picketing is to persuade customers of the neutral business not to buy goods supplied by the struck employer. Construed in this way, as I agree with Brother Harlan that it must be, I believe, contrary to his view, that the section abridges freedom of speech and press in violation of the First Amendment.

"Picketing," in common parlance and in § 8(b)(4)(ii)(B), includes at least two concepts: (1) patrolling, that is, standing or marching back and forth or round and round on the street, sidewalks, private property, or elsewhere, generally adjacent to someone else's premises; (2) speech, that is, arguments, usually on a placard, made to persuade other people to take the picketers' side of a controversy. While "the dissemination of information concerning the facts of a labor dispute must be regarded as within that area of free discussion that is guaranteed by the Constitution," *Thornhill v. Alabama*, patrolling is, of course, conduct, not speech, and therefore is not directly protected by the First Amendment. It is because picketing includes patrolling that neither *Thornhill* nor cases that followed it lend support to the contention that peaceful picketing is beyond legislative control. However, when conduct not constitutionally protected, like patrolling, is intertwined, as in picketing, with constitutionally protected free speech and press, regulation of the non-protected conduct may at the same time encroach on freedom of speech and press. In such cases it is established that it is the duty of courts, before upholding regulations of patrolling, to weigh the circumstances and to appraise the substantiality of the reasons advanced in support of the regulation of the free enjoyment of the rights of speech and press.

Even assuming that the Federal Government has power to bar or otherwise regulate patrolling by persons on local streets or adjacent to local business premises in the State of Washington, it is difficult to see that the section in question intends to do anything but prevent dissemination of information about the facts of a labor dispute—a right protected by the First Amendment. The statute in no way manifests any government interest against patrolling as such, since the only patrolling it seeks to make unlawful is that which is carried on to advise the public, including consumers, that certain products have been produced by an employer with whom the picketers have a dispute. All who do not patrol to publicize this kind of dispute are, so far as this section of the statute is concerned, left wholly free to patrol. Thus the section is aimed at outlawing free discussion of one side of a certain kind of labor dispute and cannot be sustained as a permissible regulation of patrolling.

I cannot accept my Brother Harlan's view that the abridgment of speech and press here does not violate the First Amendment because other methods of communication are left open. This reason for abridgment strikes me as being on a par with holding that governmental suppression of a newspaper in a city would not violate the First Amendment because there continue to be radio and television stations. First Amendment freedoms can no more validly be taken away by degrees than by one fell swoop.

JUSTICE HARLAN, whom JUSTICE STEWART joins, dissenting:

The difference to which the Court points between a secondary employer merely lowering his purchases of the struck product to the degree of decreased consumer demand and such an employer ceasing to purchase one product because of consumer refusal to buy any products, is surely too refined in the context of reality. It can hardly be supposed that in all, or even most, instances the result of the type of picketing involved here will be simply that suggested by the Court. Because of the very nature of picketing there may be numbers of persons who will refuse to buy at all from a picketed store, either out of economic or social conviction or because they prefer to shop where they need not brave a picket line. Moreover, the public can hardly be expected always to know or ascertain the precise scope of a particular picketing operation. Thus in cases like this, the effect on the secondary employer may not always be limited to a decrease in his sales of the struck product. And even when that is the effect, the employer may, rather than simply reducing purchases from the primary employer, deem it more expedient to turn to another producer whose product is approved by the union.

The distinction drawn by the majority becomes even more tenuous if a picketed retailer depends largely or entirely on sales of the struck product. If, for example, an independent gas station owner sells gasoline purchased from a struck gasoline company, one would not suppose he would feel less threatened, coerced, or restrained by picket signs which said "Do not buy X gasoline" than by signs which said "Do not patronize this gas station." To be sure Safeway is a multiple article seller, but it cannot well be gainsaid that the rule laid down by the Court would be unworkable if its applicability turned on a calculation of the relation between total income of the secondary employer and income from the struck product.

Contrary to my Brother Black, I think the fact that Congress in prohibiting secondary consumer picketing has acted with a discriminating eye is the very thing that renders this provision invulnerable to constitutional attack. That Congress has permitted other picketing which is likely to have effects beyond those resulting from the "communicative" aspect of picketing does not, of course, in any way lend itself to the conclusion that Congress here has aimed to prevent dissemination of information about the facts of a labor dispute. Even on the highly dubious assumption that the "non-speech" aspect of picketing is always the same whatever the particular context, the social consequences of the "non-communicative" aspect of picketing may certainly be thought desirable in the case of "primary" picketing and undesirable in the case of "secondary" picketing, a judgment Congress has indeed made in prohibiting secondary but not primary picketing.

* * *

NLRB v. Retail Store Employees Union, Local No. 1001 (Safeco Title Ins. Co.), 447 U.S. 607 (1980), picked up on Justice Harlan's gas station hypothetical for cases in which the consumer appeal is directed at a secondary employer that is heavily dependent on the product of the primary employer. During a strike of Safeco Insurance Company, employees picketed at Safeco's offices as well as at five local title insurance companies whose business consisted almost entirely of selling Safeco insurance. The Supreme Court splintered, but upheld the Board's order enjoining the picketing. In a plurality opinion, the Court distinguished *Tree Fruits,* in which picketing was directed at one item of many being sold by the secondary retailer, and reasoned that picketing at the title insurance companies would be far more coercive than picketing at grocery stores in *Tree Fruits.* The consumer appeal directed at Safeco insurance "leaves responsive consumers no realistic option other than to boycott the title companies altogether." The plurality therefore ruled: "Product picketing that reasonably can be expected to threaten neutral parties with ruin or substantial loss simply does not square with the language or the purpose of § 8(b)(4)(ii)(B). Since successful secondary picketing would put the title companies to a choice between their survival and the severance of their ties with Safeco, the picketing plainly violates the statutory ban on the coercion of neutrals." The plurality suggested that in a case in which the consumer appeal is directed at a product that represents "a major portion of a neutral's business but significantly less than that represented by a single dominant product, neither *Tree Fruits* nor today's decision necessarily would control. The critical question would be whether, by encouraging customers to reject the struck product, the secondary appeal is reasonably likely to threaten the neutral party with ruin or substantial loss."

Justice Blackmun concurred in the judgment but faulted the plurality's "cursory discussion of what for me are difficult First Amendment issues" given the NLRA's "content-based ban on peaceful picketing." Noting that in *Chicago v. Mosley,* 408 U.S. 92 (1972), the Court had found unconstitutional a Chicago ordinance that prohibited picketing because of the content discrimination, Justice Blackmun said he was "reluctant to hold unconstitutional Congress' striking of the delicate balance between union freedom of expression and the ability of neutral employers, employees, and consumers to remain free from coerced participation in industrial strife. My vote should not be read as foreclosing an opposite conclusion where another statutory ban on peaceful picketing, unsupported by equally substantial governmental interests, is at issue."

Justices Brennan, White, and Marshall dissented. Pointing out that a successful primary strike can be quite devastating to neutral employers that are heavily dependent on the struck product even when there is no activity at the site of neutral employers at all, the dissent argued that the permissibility of consumer appeals should be judged on whether the union attempts to inflict harm on interests of neutral employers that are unrelated to the neutral's relationship to the primary. Economic damage inflicted on a neutral "solely by virtue of its dependence upon the primary employer's goods" should be permissible regardless of whether the union protests only at the primary employer's site or at the secondary employer's as well.

NOTES

1.   *Does a worker's honoring a consumer appeal make it unlawful?* The consumer appeal proviso protects publicity only if it does not have the effect of inducing a worker to refuse to work. What if a single truck driver, who will scrupulously honor any request of workers to boycott, refuses to make a delivery, even if the handbills explicitly say that they do not call for workers not to work?

2.   *The limits of the* Safeco *exception.* Under what circumstances do product boycotts "threaten neutral parties with ruin or substantial loss"? What

if the grocery retailer in *Tree Fruits* were a small market selling primarily produce?

3.   *The ally doctrine?* Why doesn't the ally doctrine apply to the *Safeco Title Insurance* scenario? Were the local title insurance companies whose businesses consisted primarily of selling Safeco insurance performing work that had been directed to them because of the Safeco strike? If they make all their money by selling a struck product, in what respects are they neutral? In what respects are they not neutral?

* * *

The consumer appeal proviso was written with the traditional product boycott in mind to allow workers protesting conditions under which items are manufactured to advise consumers at the place where they are sold. Congress did not consider other kinds of economic relationships in which workers might want to advise the public about labor disputes near a business that is not a distributor of a product. For example, when the SEIU wishes to inform the public about the working conditions of janitors who clean commercial office buildings, can the consumer appeal proviso shelter the union's appeal where neither the building owner nor the other tenants in the building can be said to "distribute" any "product" of the cleaning services company that employs the janitors?

That question was answered in a case in which a construction union representing workers of subcontractor hired to build a department store at a mall distributed handbills at the mall protesting their substandard wages. When charged with an unfair labor practice under § 8(b)(4), the union insisted that the leafleting was protected under the consumer appeal proviso. The Supreme Court disagreed, holding that even if the construction workers could be said to produce a "product" that was distributed by construction employers other than their own, it was not possible to find a producer-distributor relationship between the construction subcontractor and stores in the mall. The Court held that the consumer appeal proviso shelters only publicity other than picketing directed at secondary employers who have some economic relationship with the primary employer. *Edward J. DeBartolo Corp. v. NLRB,* 463 U.S. 147 (1983).

On remand, the union argued that even if the consumer appeal proviso did not shelter its distribution of leaflets, the statute was unconstitutional. The Court took the case again and delivered the following opinion.

EDWARD J. DEBARTOLO CORP. V. FLORIDA GULF COAST BUILDING & CONSTRUCTION TRADES COUNCIL

485 U.S. 568 (1988)

JUSTICE WHITE delivered the opinion of the Court:

This case centers around the respondent union's peaceful handbilling of the businesses operating in a shopping mall in Tampa, Florida, owned by petitioner, the Edward J. DeBartolo Corporation (DeBartolo). The union's primary labor dispute was with H. J. High Construction Company (High) over alleged substandard wages and fringe benefits. High was retained by the H. J. Wilson Company (Wilson) to construct a department store in the mall, and neither DeBartolo nor any of the other 85 or so mall tenants had any contractual right to influence the selection of contractors.

The union, however, sought to obtain their influence upon Wilson and High by distributing handbills asking mall customers not to shop at any of the stores in the mall "until the Mall's owner publicly promises that all construction at the Mall will be done using contractors who pay their employees fair wages and fringe benefits." [The handbills read, in part:

> The Wilson's Department Store under construction on these premises is being built by contractors who pay substandard wages and fringe benefits. In the past, the Mall's owner, The Edward J. DeBartolo Corporation, has supported labor and our local economy by insuring that the Mall and its stores be built by contractors who pay fair wages and fringe benefits. Now, however, and for no apparent reason, the Mall owners have taken a giant step backwards by permitting our standards to be torn down. The payment of substandard wages not only diminishes the working person's ability to purchase with earned, rather than borrowed, dollars, but it also undercuts the wage standard of the entire community.]

The handbills made clear that the union was seeking only a consumer boycott against the other mall tenants, not a secondary strike by their employees. At all four entrances to the mall for about three weeks in December 1979, the union peacefully distributed the handbills without any accompanying picketing or patrolling.

[The NLRB held that the handbilling violated § 8(b)(4) of the NLRA because it "coerced" customers to cease doing business with businesses other than High, who the Board deemed to be the target of the labor dispute.]

[T]he Board's construction of the statute, as applied in this case, poses serious questions of the validity of § 8(b)(4) under the First Amendment. The handbills involved here truthfully revealed the existence of a labor dispute and urged potential customers of the mall to follow a wholly legal course of action, namely, not to patronize the retailers doing business in the mall. The handbilling was peaceful. No picketing or patrolling was involved. On its face, this was expressive activity arguing that substandard wages should be opposed by abstaining from shopping in a mall where such wages were paid. Had the union simply been leafletting the public generally, including those entering every shopping mall in town, pursuant to an annual educational effort against substandard pay, there is little doubt that legislative proscription of such leaflets would pose a substantial issue of validity under the First Amendment. The same may well be true in this case, although here the handbills called attention to a specific situation in the mall allegedly involving the payment of unacceptably low wages by a construction contractor.

That a labor union is the leafletter and that a labor dispute was involved does not foreclose this analysis. We do not suggest that communications by labor unions are never of the commercial speech variety and thereby entitled to a lesser degree of constitutional protection. The handbills involved here, however, do not appear to be typical commercial speech such as advertising the price of a product or arguing its merits, for they pressed the benefits of unionism to the community and the dangers of inadequate wages to the economy and the standard of living of the populace. Of course, commercial speech itself is protected by the First Amendment.

The case turns on whether handbilling such as involved here must be held to "threaten, coerce, or restrain any person" to cease doing business with another, within the meaning of § 8(b)(4)(ii)(B). [M]ore than mere persuasion is necessary to prove a violation of § 8(b)(4)(ii): that section requires a showing of threats, coercion, or restraints. Those words, we have said, are "nonspecific, indeed vague," and should be interpreted with "caution" and not given a "broad sweep. . . ." There is no suggestion that the leaflets had any coercive effect on customers of the mall. There was no violence, picketing, or patrolling and only an attempt to persuade customers not to shop in the mall.

The Board nevertheless found that the handbilling "coerced" mall tenants and explained in a footnote that "appealing to the public not to patronize secondary employers is an attempt to inflict economic harm on the secondary employers by causing them to lose business."

[There is no] reason to find in the language of § 8(b)(4)(ii), standing alone, any clear indication that handbilling, without picketing, "coerces" secondary employers. The loss of customers because they read a handbill urging them not to patronize a business, and not because they are intimidated by a line of picketers, is the result of mere persuasion, and the neutral who reacts is doing no more than what its customers honestly want it to do.

The Board's reading of § 8(b)(4) would make an unfair labor practice out of any kind of publicity or communication to the public urging a consumer boycott of employers other than those the proviso specifically deals with. On the facts of this case, newspaper, radio, and television appeals not to patronize the mall would be prohibited; and it would be an unfair labor practice for unions in their own meetings to urge their members not to shop in the mall. Nor could a union's handbills simply urge not shopping at a department store because it is using a nonunion contractor, although the union could safely ask the store's customers not to buy there because it is selling mattresses not carrying the union label.

In our view, interpreting § 8(b)(4) as not reaching the handbilling involved in this case is not foreclosed either by the language of the section or its legislative history. That construction makes unnecessary passing on the serious constitutional questions that would be raised by the Board's understanding of the statute.

NOTES

1. *Summing up the consumer appeal rules.* After *DeBartolo*, it was clear that a consumer appeal could be protected under the NLRA *either* because it was protected by the proviso to § 8(b)(4) as an appeal to a consumer not to purchase products produced by the primary employer and distributed by a neutral, *or* because the appeal was not coercive and therefore not covered by either of the conduct prohibitions of § 8(b)(4)(i) or (ii). Non-coercive consumer appeals are protected under *DeBartolo* regardless of whether there is a "producer-distributor" relationship between the primary employer and the neutral.

2. *The practical effects.* If you were a mall owner and one of the stores in the mall was in a labor dispute, if you could not prohibit handbilling entirely, where would you prefer the handbilling to occur? In front of the target store only? At the entrance(s) to the mall from the parking lot? At the entrance to the parking lot?

3. *Constitutional avoidance.* Why did the Supreme Court go to such lengths to construe the NLRA as not reaching the handbilling? Why didn't the Court simply invalidate portions of § 8(b)(4)?

b. Consumer Appeals Not Covered by the Proviso

After *DeBartolo* made clear that § 8(b)(4) does not prohibit non-coercive consumer appeals, the NLRB and a number of courts attempted to define which union appeals short of a call for a strike of secondary employees are coercive and therefore fall into the § 8(b)(4)(B) prohibition. In the following cases, the Board, the Ninth Circuit, and the D.C. Circuit reached different results on the question whether displaying a banner, sending a union member to a job site dressed up in a rat costume, and staging a mock funeral are coercive (like picketing) or merely persuasive (like distribution of a leaflet or paying for an advertisement on a billboard or in a newspaper). The Board's current rule is that banners and rats are not coercive and, therefore, not unlawful. As you read the cases, consider whether the distinctions drawn are persuasive, and if the cases are not meaningfully distinguishable, which is the better result and reasoning.

United Bhd. of Carpenters, Local 1506 (Eliason & Knuth), 355 N.L.R.B. No. 159 (2010). In a number of incidents, union members displayed banners on public sidewalks outside of the secondary employers' facilities, facing automobile traffic on busy public streets. The banners were 4 feet high and either 16 or 20 feet long and read: "Shame on [secondary employer]" in large letters, flanked on either side by "Labor Dispute" in smaller letters. The banners were placed anywhere from 40 feet to 1 mile away from the entrances to the secondaries' establishments or jobsites. At each demonstration, two or three union representatives held up the banner, but did not move the banner around the location of the demonstration. The Board held that the display of banners is not coercive.

The union representatives also distributed handbills to anyone who approached them and inquired about the demonstration. The handbill was entitled "Shame on [secondary employer] for Desecration of the American Way of Life" and included a drawing of a rat gnawing on an American flag. The handbills stated that the Union had a labor dispute with the primary employer based on its failure to respect area labor standards and criticized the secondary employer for hiring the primary as a sub-contractor on the project in question. The banner bearers did not chant, yell, or march, and did not block the ingress or egress of any person wishing to enter or leave the secondaries' facilities.

The General Counsel and the Charging Parties asserted that the Union's display of banners violated Section 8(b)(4)(ii)(B) because it constituted coercive conduct that had an object of forcing the secondary employers to cease doing business with the primary employers. They also argued that "fraudulent" wording on the banners misled the public into believing that the Union had a primary labor dispute with the secondaries regarding the treatment of their employees. The General Counsel argued that "picketing exists where a union posts individuals at or near the entrance to a place of business for the purpose of influencing customers, suppliers, and employees to support the union's position in a labor dispute." The General Counsel added, "the posting of individuals in this fashion is inherently confrontational within the meaning of the Act."

The Board held that neither the use of banners itself nor the content of the banners violated section 8(b)(4). The use of banners is not picketing, and nor is it coercive within the meaning of the language of 8(b)(4). In the Board's view, Congress did not intend to include the display of banners or the distribution of handbills in the proscriptions. The Board reasoned: "The core conduct that renders picketing coercive under Section 8(b)(4)(ii)(B) is not simply the holding of signs (in contrast to the distribution of handbills), but the combination of carrying of picket signs and persistent patrolling of the picketers back and forth in front of an entrance to a work site, creating a physical or, at least, a symbolic confrontation between the picketers and those entering the worksite."

The Board also explained: "Our conclusion that the holding of a stationary banner does not violate Section 8(b)(4)(ii)(B) is supported, if not mandated, by the constitutional concerns that animated the Supreme Court's decision in *DeBartolo* and its precursors. To prohibit the holding of a stationary banner would raise serious constitutional questions under the First Amendment. Under the framework established in the series of decisions culminating in *DeBartolo*, we cannot so hold unless it is unavoidable, which it clearly is not in this case."

The Ninth Circuit had earlier reached the same result on similar facts, also involving the use of banners reading "Shame on __" outside the premises of secondary employers. *Overstreet v. United Brotherhood of Carpenters*, 409 F.3d 1199 (9th Cir. 2005). The court rejected Overstreet's contention that the presence of union protesters at the entrance to a business necessarily coerces: "[T]he reliance on the physical presence of speakers in the vicinity of the individuals they seek to persuade . . . is no basis for lowering the shield of the First Amendment or turning communication into statutory "coercion." The court then explained: "Nor are the union members' activities "coercive" for any reason *other* than their physical presence. The union members simply stood by their banners, acting as human signposts. Just as members of the public can "avert [their] eyes" from billboards or movie screens visible from a public street, they could ignore the Carpenters and the union's banners. If anything, the Carpenters' behavior involved *less* potential for "coercing" the public than the handbilling in *DeBartolo*, as there was no one-on-one physical interaction or communication."

As to whether the use of the term "labor dispute" on a banner with *only* the name of a secondary employer is "fraudulent," because it suggests that the union has a primary labor dispute with the secondary employer, the court explained that the statement was truthful because the union did have a dispute—a secondary dispute—with the targets. "Disputes, labor and otherwise, commonly spill over to affect secondary institutions, as individuals with strong opinions concerning the dispute seek to convince those with some prospect of influencing the outcome of the dispute to do so. Clothing manufacturers allegedly operate sweatshops, and activists protest institutions that buy clothing from those manufacturers. A nation takes controversial political or military actions, and activists pressure universities and other institutions to divest endowment or other funds from businesses supporting those actions. . . . [W]hen the specific dispute is whether the secondary institution should sever ties with another company so that the secondary institution does not undermine regional labor standards, "labor dispute" is a perfectly apt description."

San Antonio Community Hospital v. Southern California District Council of Carpenters, **125 F.3d 1230 (9th Cir. 1997).** The union displayed a banner publicizing its labor dispute with Best Interiors, a subcontractor engaged in a construction project at San Antonio Community Hospital. The banner said "THIS MEDICAL FACILITY IS FULL OF RATS" and in smaller letters, "CARPENTERS L.U. 1506 HAS A DISPUTE WITH Best FOR FAILING TO PAY PREVAILING WAGES TO ITS WORKERS." The banner's holders also distributed a handbill explaining that a "rat is a contractor that does not pay all of its employees prevailing wages or provide health and pension benefits to all of its employees." The district court granted a preliminary injunction. The Ninth Circuit in a 2–1 decision affirmed. Concluding that the only claim that would support an injunction was the hospital's defamation claim, the court determined that the union acted with knowledge or reckless disregard of the truth of the assertions in the banner. Although

> federal law gives a union license to use intemperate, abusive, or insulting language without fear of restraint or penalty if it believes such rhetoric to be an effective means to make its point, the license to use inflammatory rhetoric during a labor dispute is not unbridled. Where, as here, a union's fraudulent language is directed at an entity with which no labor dispute exists, the Norris-LaGuardia Act does not prevent a district court from exercising jurisdiction to issue an injunction prohibiting the fraudulent activity.

> The most natural reading of the Union's statement "THIS MEDICAL FACILITY IS FULL OF RATS" is that the Hospital has a rodent problem. This, the Union concedes, is not true, nor has the Union ever believed it to be true. The Union argues, however, that the term "rat" has deep historical meaning in the context of labor disputes. Most dictionaries, the Union points out, define "rat" not only as a type of rodent, but also as an employer who fails to pay prevailing wages or a worker who works for substandard wages. Because Best Interiors was not paying its workers prevailing wages, the Union argues that its statement was both literally and factually true—the Hospital *was* "full of rats".

The court distinguished *Old Dominion Branch, National Association of Letter Carriers v. Austin*, 418 U.S. 264 (1974), which had held that the term "scab" in a labor dispute could not be the subject of an action for libel. "Nobody would have understood the union in *Letter Carriers* to be referring to the non-union workers as "crusts of hardened blood and serum over a wound," or "scabies of domestic animals." By contrast, the manner in which the Union used the term "rat" on its banner could cause most—if not all— readers to be misled into believing that the banner meant that the Hospital had a rodent problem." The court also distinguished other cases in which unions had referred to employers as "rats" on the ground that no one would believe that the employer was a rodent. "The problem with the use of the term 'rats' in this case was not the mere use of the term, but the manner in which it was used. At no place in that phrase or in the entire banner does the Union identify Best Interiors as the 'rat contractor.' The term 'rats' is directed at the Hospital, not the contractor with whom the Union has the labor dispute."

Sheet Metal Workers' International Association, Local 15 v. NLRB, 491 F.3d 429 (D.C. Cir. 2007). The union distributed leaflets outside a hospital protesting the presence of non-union workers employed either by a temporary agency or by a building contractor which was using workers supplied by the agency. The handbills stated, "There's a 'Rat' at Brandon Regional Hospital" and showed a cartoon of a rat near the bed of a sick patient. The Union also inflated a 16-foot tall balloon in the shape of a cartoon rat about 100 feet from the main entrance to the hospital. On another day, the Union staged a "mock funeral" outside the Hospital and distributed leaflets headed "Going to Brandon Hospital Should Not Be a Grave Decision"; the leaflets detailed several malpractice suits against the Hospital. The "mock funeral," comprising one person in a "Grim Reaper" costume and four other people carrying a prop coffin, paraded back and forth over a distance of about 400 feet on a sidewalk across the street from the Hospital and about 100 feet from the entrance.

While the unfair labor practice complaint arising out of the mock funeral was pending before the ALJ, the Regional Director of the NLRB asked the U.S. District Court for the Middle District of Florida to enjoin the Union, pursuant to § 10(l) of the Act, from restaging the mock theater or otherwise picketing or patrolling at the Hospital on the ground those activities would violate § 8(b)(4)(ii)(B). *See* 29 U.S.C. § 160(l). The district court, after reviewing a Union-made videotape of the event, found the mock funeral had been "orderly" and that "[n]o traffic was blocked, pedestrians were not obstructed or challenged and there appeared to be no eye contact or verbal contact [between] any participant" [and any Hospital patron]. Likewise, "[t]he leafleters [at the mock funeral] were orderly, non-confrontational and did not interfere [with] or impede . . . the egress or ingress of any individuals to or from the hospital." Nonetheless, the district court enjoined the Union from "threatening, coercing or restraining [the Hospital] by staging street theater . . . [or] processions" or by "picketing, patrolling and/or any manner of conduct calculated to induce individuals not to patronize the hospital."

The Board found it unnecessary to pass on whether the inflation of the rat or an instance in which one protester used a leaflet as a placard violated § 8(b)(4)(ii)(B) the Act because it found those unfair labor practices, if they were indeed unfair labor practices, were cumulative of the mock funeral, which the Board found to violate § 8(b)(4)(ii)(B).

The court of appeals overturned the Board's decision. The court said:

> [T]he mock funeral was a combination of street theater and handbilling. The Eleventh Circuit and the Board deemed this the "functional equivalent of picketing," but did not distinguish ends from means. Clearly, the Union's end in conducting the mock funeral was to dissuade consumers from patronizing the secondary employer, and in that sense the funeral was the functional equivalent of picketing. Just as clearly, however, the mock funeral was not the functional equivalent of picketing as a means of persuasion because it had none of the coercive character of picketing, as the Eleventh Circuit itself found: Union members did not physically or verbally interfere with or confront Hospital patrons coming and going; nor, contrary to Member Liebman's description, did the mock funeral participants "patrol" the area in the sense of creating a symbolic barrier to those who would enter the Hospital. Had they done so, or in any other way interfered with or confronted patrons entering or leaving the Hospital, we would agree with the Board that the Union's conduct was the "functional equivalent of picketing," and therefore coercive and unlawful. Nor was there, in this case, any "signal picketing," which entails an implicit instruction to other union members, including union employees of secondary businesses, to stop work.
>
> No court has yet determined how the Supreme Court cases dealing with protests at abortion clinics apply to the question whether a particular labor protest is coercive. Recall the Board described the mock funeral as "patrolling," and *DeBartolo* suggests patrolling is per se coercive and therefore a violation of the Act. The mock funeral occurred about 100 feet from the Hospital and the Board does not claim the participants approached patrons any closer to the Hospital. Indeed, the Union's protest operated well within those limitations, for the videotape shows the mock funeral was a quiet affair, not at all like the charged atmosphere surrounding the abortion protests; the Union protesters came nowhere near blocking anyone's ingress or egress and did not even make eye contact with Hospital patrons. Their behavior was orderly, disciplined, even somber, as befits a funeral; nothing they did can realistically be deemed coercive, threatening, restraining, or intimidating as those terms are ordinarily understood-quite apart, that is, from any special understanding necessary to avoid infringing upon the Union members' right of free speech.

Nor was their "message"—Invoking the iconography of the funeral rite and stating that "Going to Brandon Hospital Should Not Be a Grave Decision"—one by which a person of ordinary fortitude would be intimidated. The procession was not only orderly, the protesters went out of their way to convey a law-abiding, and therefore nonthreatening, attitude; the participants politely pressed a "walk" button and waited for a "walk" signal at the crosswalk before crossing. Their message may have been unsettling or even offensive to someone visiting a dying relative, but unsettling and even offensive speech is not without the protection of the First Amendment.

On remand, the Board adopted a new approach to rat displays and protests like the "mock funeral," finding them not to be coercive and therefore not prohibited by section 8(b)(4). Sheet Metal Workers Local 15 (Brandon Regional Med Ctr), 356 NLRB No. 162 (2011).

NOTE

As the law now stands, picketing is coercive unless it is directed to consumers, but the display of banners, leafleting, and the use of the rat are not. In light of that, consider which of the following are "coercive"? (Note the similarity between the analysis used to identify what is "coercive" within the meaning of § 8(b)(4) and the analysis, see note 4 on p. 748 above, used to determine what is "picketing" that receives lesser First Amendment protection.)

(a) Two people walk up and down at the entrance to a building distributing leaflets. What if it is two dozen or two hundred people distributing leaflets? If a single person or a few people use picket signs instead, but make clear that the signs do not call for a work stoppage and instead are to appeal only to consumers, can they be enjoined under the reasoning of the D.C. Circuit?

(b) During a labor protest in an extremely cold climate, unionists build a snowman and gave him a picket sign. Would that be "coercive"? Would it matter whether unionists had been picketing themselves before it got too cold?

(c) The Service Employees International Union's "Justice for Janitors" campaign has conducted its protests outside of commercial office buildings employing janitors in substandard conditions by having lots of union members gather outside the building wearing distinctive union T-shirts and carrying brooms and mops. Are they coercive?

(d) The Hotel and Restaurant Employees' Union sought to publicize the difficult work of hotel maids by wheeling beds onto the public street outside a target hotel and having the workers make the beds. Is that coercive?

(e) One SEIU Justice for Janitors protest involved gathering a large number of employees on the sidewalk outside an office building where they sang folksongs to the strumming of a guitar. Is a sing-along coercive?

(f) The Communication Workers Union encourages its members and friends nationwide to email company officials complaining about the company's intransigence in contract negotiations and alleged unfair labor practices. The CWA provides email addresses. This "click it and picket" campaign is a success and the huge volume of email causes problems for the company server and clogs the email boxes of the recipients. Is this coercive?

(g) A representative of the Carpenters Union meets with a real estate developer to discuss hiring union contractors to build a new development. The union representative says that the developer can avoid "problems, including protests, work stoppages, and delivery issues" if the contractors use union labor. Are these statements coercive? See *NLRB v. Metro. Reg'l Council of Carpenters*, 316 Fed. App'x. 150, 157 (3d Cir. 2009) (finding statements coercive).

4. HOT CARGO AGREEMENTS

a. History and Contemporary Significance of Agreements

Unions have sometimes tried to convince employers to promise not to make their employees handle the goods of an employer involved in a labor dispute. Such provisions have come to be called "hot cargo agreements," a term derived from Teamster collective bargaining agreements in which trucking companies promised not to handle goods of employers whose employees were on strike; the goods were referred to as "hot cargo." Hot cargo agreements are a precursor of today's corporate codes of conduct; those concerned about working conditions often want to pressure a firm to insist that its contracting partners observe decent working conditions and to refuse to do business with those that do not. In the contemporary labor market in which firms increasingly subcontract, those who wish to improve working conditions need to consider how lawfully to pressure contracting parties throughout a chain of manufacturing and distribution. That is what the law of hot cargo agreements is about.

Local 1976, United Brotherhood of Carpenters v. NLRB (**Sand Door & Plywood Co.), 357 U.S. 93 (1958).** The Supreme Court held that unions could not "induce" the employees of secondary employers not to handle hot goods, but that the employers could voluntarily refuse to handle the hot goods. In other words, a hot cargo agreement was held not to be a defense to charge under section 8(b)(4) when the union struck to enforce it, but the Court held that the Act did not prohibit the agreement *per se* or the right of an employer voluntarily to abide by it.

> A boycott voluntarily engaged in by a secondary employer for his own business reasons, perhaps because the unionization of other employers will protect his competitive position or because he identifies his own interests with those of his employees and their union, is not covered by the statute. Likewise, a union is free to approach an employer to persuade him to engage in a boycott, so long as it refrains from the specifically prohibited means of coercion through inducement of employees.

Congress responded to the *Sand Door* decision by adding section 8(e) to the Act. It makes it an unfair labor practice "for any labor organization and any employer to enter into any contract . . . whereby such employer ceases . . . dealing in any of the products of any other employer, or . . . doing business with any other person."

Read literally, section 8(e) would prohibit many provisions commonly found in collective bargaining agreements, such as provisions restricting the subcontracting of bargaining unit work. Section 8(e), however, was a congressional reaction to *Sand Door*'s holding that an agreement by an employer not to deal with another employer because of the other employer's labor dispute was not a secondary boycott. Consequently, the Supreme Court has read the primary/secondary distinction into § 8(e). Agreements that are primary are those that concern the wages, hours, or working conditions of employees subject to the agreement. These agreements are lawful even though they prevent the employer from transacting business with another employer. Agreements that are secondary and unlawful under § 8(e) are those aimed at the labor relations of other employers. The distinction between primary and secondary objects must be made both in deciding whether the agreement is *itself* lawful, and in deciding whether a job action to enforce the agreement is lawful, and the distinction is not an easy one to draw. One must first analyze whether an agreement is lawful under § 8(e). A contract is permissible if it allows a union to protect the working conditions of its own members by allowing them to refuse to handle goods manufactured under circumstances that would undercut the union members' own standards. A contract has an illegal secondary object if it allows union members to protest *others'* working conditions by refusing to handle goods made by others.

Furthermore, as in *Sand Door,* the agreement may be lawful but a job action to enforce the agreement may be a secondary boycott. In determining whether the job action is lawful, use the same analysis as in other secondary boycott problems. First identify the primary employer. Then determine whether the union is coercing a neutral to get it to refuse to do business with the primary. Remember, too, that a strike to obtain a lawful hot cargo agreement is lawful, but a strike to obtain an unlawful hot cargo agreement violates § 8(b)(4)(A). Second, although a strike to *obtain* a legal hot cargo agreement is protected, a strike to *enforce* any hot cargo agreement is not. A union confronted with an employer breaching a hot cargo agreement may file a suit or demand arbitration, but cannot use a work stoppage or any form of threat or coercion to enforce it. Those nuances in hot cargo agreements are discussed in the cases that follow.

***National Woodwork Manufacturers Association v. NLRB*, 386 U.S. 612 (1967).** A collective bargaining agreement allowed carpenters to refuse to hang pre-fabricated doors. The National Woodwork Manufacturers Association argued that the agreement was an illegal hot cargo agreement because it obligated construction contractors to cease "dealing in" the products of pre-fabricated door manufacturers. The Court upheld the Board's conclusion that the objective of the agreement was the "preservation of work traditionally performed by the job-site carpenters," not to change the working conditions of pre-fab door manufacturers. The Court articulated a test for drawing the distinction: "whether, under all the surrounding circumstances, the Union's objective was preservation of work for [the contracting employer's] employees, or whether the agreements and boycott were tactically calculated to satisfy union objectives elsewhere." "The touchstone is whether the agreement or its maintenance is addressed to the labor relations of the contracting employer *vis à vis* his own employees."

***NLRB v. Enterprise Ass'n of Pipefitters, Local No. 638 (Austin Co.)*, 429 U.S. 507 (1977).** The Pipefitters union had a collective bargaining agreement with Hudik, a heating and air-conditioning contractor, providing that the cutting and threading of internal piping in units installed by Hudik would be done at the jobsite by Hudik's employees. Hudik bid on and obtained a construction subcontract with Austin, a general contractor, requiring the installation of pre-fabricated climate control units with internal piping already cut and threaded at the factory of the manufacturer, Slant/Fin. Hudik employees refused to install the units. The contract provision was intended to preserve work for Hudik's employees and therefore was lawful. A divided Supreme Court, however, upheld the Board's determination that the job action of refusing to install the pre-fabricated units was an illegal secondary boycott. The majority determined that the union's dispute was over who would perform the work of cutting and threading the piping on the units and therefore held that Austin (the general contractor) was the primary employer because it controlled the assignment of the piping work.

> It is [i]ncontrovertable that the work at this site could not be secured by pressure on Hudik alone and that the union's work objectives could not be obtained without exerting pressure on Austin as well. That the union may also have been seeking to enforce its contract and to convince Hudik that it should bid on no

> more jobs where pre-piped units were specified does not alter the
> fact that the union refused to install the Slant/Fin units and
> asserted that the piping work on the [construction] job belonged
> to its members.

The dissent emphasized the Board's finding that the pipefitting work was
traditionally done at the job-site by Hudik employees. "The job assignment
provision in the Hudik CBA was for the primary purpose of preserving
pipefitters work. [P]ressure brought to compel Hudik to agree to it would
have been primary; and pressure brought to enforce it when Hudik
breached it, whether by ordering prefabricated units himself, as in
National Woodwork, or by entering a contract that required him to breach
it, was no less primary."

There are three provisos to section 8(e). The first one allows
agreements between "a labor organization and an employer in the
construction industry relating to the contracting or subcontracting of work
to be done at the site of the construction, alteration, painting, or repair of
a building, structure or other work." This proviso allows for construction
jobs to be done on an all union or all nonunion basis so as to avoid the
necessity of union and nonunion employees of different contractors having
to work together. *See NLRB v. Denver Building & Const. Trades Council,*
341 U.S. 675 (1951), excerpted above at p. 820. This proviso shelters only
agreements to prohibit the employer from employing nonunion contractors
at the jobsite. An agreement to prevent the employer from using at the
jobsite materials made elsewhere at a nonunion company is *not* sheltered
by the proviso.

The second and third provisos to section 8(e) provide that the ban on
hot cargo agreements does not apply to "persons in the relation of a jobber,
manufacturer, contractor, or subcontractor working on the goods or
premises of the jobber or manufacturer or performing parts of an
integrated process of production in the apparel and clothing industry." In
the garment industry, both historically and today, manufacturers
frequently subcontract the work of cutting, sewing, and pressing clothes to
contractors whose operations are small, highly mobile (because there is
little equipment involved except sewing machines and presses), poorly
capitalized, and extremely difficult to unionize. A union victory at one
contractor would prompt an instant dissolution of the business; the owner
of the business would usually move its sewing machines to a new
warehouse nearby and start a new business a few days later with a new
name, a new corporation, a new nonunion workforce, and the same poor
pay and working conditions. A large supply of recent immigrant workers
who were desperate for any sort of work, even under appallingly bad
conditions, made unionizing and regulating working conditions in the
garment trades extremely difficult. *See* Steven Fraser, Labor Will Rule:
Sidney Hillman and the Rise of American Labor (Free Press, 1991). The

sweatshop problem in garment manufacturing has changed little since the early twentieth century, except now some sweatshops remain in the urban areas (New York and Los Angeles), but increasingly the garments are manufactured overseas.

The structure of the garment manufacturing industry suggests why Congress decided to allow secondary appeals. A pre-Taft-Hartley case upholding the right of the International Ladies Garment Workers Union to picket secondary employers, *Abeles v. Friedman*, 171 Misc. 1042, 14 N.Y.S.2d 252 (N.Y. Sup. Ct. 1939), describes the situation:

> [S]ome twenty years ago the manufacture of dresses was largely concentrated in "inside" shops operated by employers who were directly responsible both for manufacturing and for marketing the product and who dealt with labor directly; thereafter certain employers discovered what they believed to be a method of avoiding unionization and evading all direct responsibility to their workers and the duty to maintain uniform labor standards. Pursuant to this method, they abandoned their "inside" shops and had their garments produced by a new type of middleman in the industry who came to be known as a 'contractor'. The change was only an apparent one. The manufacturer who had given up inside production continued in business; he originated the garment and marketed it, except that he turned over the process of manufacture to the "contractor" whom he supplied with the material and who made up the garment for him at a stipulated price.

> The result was that there arose a new kind of manufacturer who came to be known in the industry as a "jobber." He ceased to have direct dealings with the workers; he was under no agreement with them as to wages, hours and other standards of labor and was not responsible to them for wages. All these obligations were shifted from him to the contractor, often a person without financial responsibility. A majority of the employees ceased to work for direct and responsible employers and were forced to deal with more or less irresponsible middlemen. This involved for the worker not only a general lowering of labor standards but also increased unemployment and uncertainty of tenure of employment. The jobber had no obligation to the workers. He could withdraw his work from any contractor, with or without cause, and thus indirectly throw an entire shop of employees out of work.

> [C]ontractors were constantly engaged in fierce competition with each other for the work of jobbers. Such competition was based almost entirely on labor costs, each contractor trying to secure the

maximum amount of work by offering to do it at a lower price, with the result that labor standards were depressed.

The Union realized that the industry could not be stabilized unless the evils of the irresponsible system of "jobbing-contracting" were eliminated. The Union demanded, in 1924, that the jobber assume the same responsibility towards the workers that the inside manufacturer had. It was prepared to declare a general strike to achieve that purpose. Governor Alfred E. Smith intervened and averted a strike by appointing what became known as the Governor's Advisory Commission in the cloak and suit industry. He directed them to make a complete, exhaustive survey of the industry.

[The Commission made findings along the lines of the facts discussed above.]

The Commission found further: "In determining the relationship between jobber, submanufacturer, and workers we should be concerned not so much with the form as with the substance. By whatever name he may call himself, the jobber controls working conditions; he controls employment, and that element of control imposes upon him the responsibility that he shall so conduct his business that proper working standards may be upheld instead of undermined, and that employment may be stabilized instead of demoralized."

It was this history that prompted Congress not only to authorize hot cargo agreements in the garment industry, but more generally to exempt the garment industry from § 8(b)(4)(A) and (B). Later chapters in the ongoing struggle to improve working conditions in garment manufacturing in urban American cities are told in *Greenstein v. National Skirt & Sportswear Ass'n, Inc.*, 178 F.Supp. 681 (S.D.N.Y. 1959), and in Scott Cummings, *Hemmed In: Legal Mobilization in the Los Angeles Anti-Sweatshop Movement*, 30 Berkeley J. Emp. & Lab. L. 1 (2009).

NOTES

1. *Networks, supply chains, and the secondary boycott problem.* The subcontracting system that has long dominated the garment industry now applies to many other forms of manufacturing, as well as to the provision of as many kinds of low-skilled service work as can be contracted out, including agricultural work, janitorial, maintenance, and security work, and some forms of construction work. Should the spread of subcontracting and the ensuing downward pressure on wages be grounds for change in the law of secondary boycotts and hot cargo agreements? Could that change be made by the Board, or would it have to be made by Congress?

2. *Generalizing from the garment industry exception to the prohibition on hot cargo agreements.* What light does the history of the garment industry

shed on contemporary efforts to improve working conditions in third-world manufacturing facilities that supply goods for sale to U.S. companies like Walmart? Would the Coalition of Immokalee Workers' Fair Food Program be a hot cargo agreement if CIW were a union?

3. *Hot cargo agreements and codes of conduct.* Imagine that American labor unions, in common with many other groups, have decided to publicize to American consumers the use of child labor in the manufacture of goods overseas. Could they do any of the following:

   a.   The unionized employees of a large chain of sporting goods stores would like to pressure their employer to agree not to sell soccer balls manufactured using child labor. Can they? (No.) What if the employees are not unionized? (Yes.)

   b.   The employer enters into an agreement with the employees promising not to sell products manufactured by children. The employees discover that a new shipment of soccer balls were sewn by children. Can the employees enforce the agreement by refusing to unpack them or sell them? (No.)

   c.   Can the Teamsters union agree with trucking employers that any employee with a conscientious objection to child labor may refuse to handle goods produced by children? (Yes.)

4. *The primary-secondary distinction in hot cargo agreements.* Is the distinction between *National Woodwork* and *Austin* one of fact or one of policy? Which view is better? What options would the Pipefitters union have to achieve its goals *vis a vis* Hudik?

5. *Is the policy of secondary boycotts served?* Recall that one goal of secondary boycott law is to reduce rather than to proliferate labor unrest. Is that goal achieved by the Court's conclusion that Austin is the primary employer?

6. *Work preservation vs. work claiming.* In *National Woodwork, supra,* and in *NLRB v. International Longshoremen's Association,* 473 U.S. 61 (1985), the Court drew a distinction between lawful agreements that *preserve* work for union members in the face of changes in business practice and unlawful agreements that attempt to *claim new work* for bargaining unit members. The distinction between work preservation and work claiming, however, is not entirely clear. In the *Longshoremen's* case, the Court upheld an agreement between the ILA and marine shipping companies that provided ILA members would handle certain work with respect to loading and unloading containers as they are transferred from trucks to docks to ships because the agreement was intended to preserve traditional longshore work rather than to claim work previously done by truckers and warehousers. The Court reasoned:

> Technological innovation will often by design eliminate some aspect of an industry's work. For example, in *National Woodwork* the agreement at issue strove to preserve carpentry work done by hand at the jobsite, even though new off-site machining techniques had

eliminated the necessity for much of this work. Yet the jobs of carpenters were no less threatened, nor was their attempt to preserve them any less primary, than if the contractor had decided to subcontract the cutting and fitting of doors to nonunion workers. Similarly, containers have eliminated some of the work of loading and unloading cargo by hand for all participants in the industry-longshoremen, truckers, and warehousers alike. "Elimination" of work in the sense that it is made unnecessary by innovation is not of itself a reason to condemn work preservation agreements under §§ 8(b)(4)(B) and 8(e); to the contrary, such elimination provides the very premise for such agreements. The crucial findings are that the ILA's objective consistently has been to preserve longshore work, and that the ILA's employers have the power to control assignment of that work.

The Court rejected the contention that the fact that the Containerization Rules assigned to ILA members work that had sometimes been done, in the era of containers, by some truckers and warehousers: "such extra-unit effects, no matter how severe, are irrelevant to the analysis."

7. In *Meat & Highway Drivers, Local Union 710 v. NLRB,* 335 F.2d 709 (D.C. Cir. 1964), the court dealt with three types of provisions attempting to respond to the movement of meat packing out of unionized Chicago into other regions. The first, a work allocation clause requiring that truck shipments by out-of-state meat packers through Chicago-area distributors to Chicago customers be made by drivers covered by the agreement was held permissible as it was work "fairly claimable" by the union. The second, a "union standards" clause, required that signatory employers could contract with cartage companies for deliveries in Chicago only if they paid union standard wages. This too was held permissible. Finally, a union signatory clause, which required contracts for Chicago area deliveries to be made only with employers whose employees were represented by the union, was held to be invalid.

8. *Hot cargo agreements and struck work.* A union and an employer include the following provision in their collective bargaining agreement: "The employer agrees that it will not agree to perform work where the work is normally performed by another employer's employees who are on strike." Does the provision violate § 8(e)? (It is permissible if it is to prevent employees from being compelled to perform struck work. It is impermissible if it is to pressure the other employer to settle the strike.)

9. *The construction industry proviso.* In *Woelke & Romero Framing, Inc. v. NLRB,* 456 U.S. 645 (1982), the Court interpreted the scope of the construction industry proviso to § 8(e). One construction union had obtained an agreement that the employer would not subcontract work done at the construction jobsite to nonunion firms; another construction union sought such an agreement and picketed, causing work stoppages, when the employer refused. The Court upheld the agreement even though the union did not demonstrate that it represented workers at a particular jobsite who would be upset by working alongside possible nonunion workers whom the employer

might hire. The Court only insisted that such an agreement be limited to employers and unions that had a collective bargaining relationship. Review *Denver Building*. Could the union and the general contractor validly enter an agreement that the general contractor would refuse to hire nonunion subcontractors? (Yes.) Could the union strike to obtain such an agreement? (Yes.) To enforce such an agreement? (No.)

b. Hot Cargo Agreements and Double-Breasting in Construction

In the construction industry, many unionized contractors want to be able to bid on construction jobs that will use union labor and on jobs that will use nonunion labor. They do so by setting up two companies; a union company and a nonunion company. This is known as double-breasting. Construction unions have attempted to limit the ability of unionized companies to set up non-union operations through collective bargaining agreement provisions. In the following case, one such effort was held to violate sections 8(b)(4) and 8(e).

SHEET METAL WORKERS LOCAL 91 V. NLRB
905 F.2d 417 (D.C. Cir. 1990)

EDWARDS, CIRCUIT JUDGE:

This case arises from International's concern with contractors who operate both unionized and nonunionized shops—so-called "double breasted" employers. Describing this phenomenon as "one of the most serious threats to the union sheet metal industry," International announced to its locals a policy designed to force employers to "make a decision that they are either 100% union or 100% non-union." The centerpiece of this policy was a proposed collective bargaining provision known as the "Integrity Clause." In three separate sections, the Integrity Clause defines a unionized contractor who also operates a nonunionized shop, or who is affiliated with a company operating a non-unionized shop, as a "bad faith employer" ("section one"); mandates that the contractor notify the local should the contractor become a "bad faith employer" ("section two"); and provides that in such an event the local is entitled to rescind the collective bargaining agreement ("section three"). Under the policy devised by International, locals were to demand that employers include the Integrity Clause as a part of existing collective bargaining agreements. Employers who refused were to be informed that they were no longer eligible for so-called "Resolution 78" relief, *i.e.,* discretionary wage and benefit concessions awarded by the Union to help individual employers remain competitive with nonunionized employers.

[W]e have little difficulty upholding the Board's conclusion that the Union violated section 8(e) by securing inclusion of the Integrity Clause as a part of its collective bargaining agreement with Winger. The Board reasonably determined that the Integrity Clause constitutes an agreement to "cease doing business" for purposes of the statute. This language has been construed to include more than just circumstances where a primary employer effects a "complete termination of [its] business relationship" with a neutral employer; the case law makes it clear that "cease doing business" also extends to situations where a primary employer exerts any pressure calculated to cause a significant change or disruption of the neutral employer's mode of business. Under the Integrity Clause, primary employers, upon pain of losing their collective bargaining agreements, are obliged either to terminate their relationships with their nonunionized affiliates or to induce those affiliates to *become* unionized. Either outcome is within the ambit of section 8(e).

The Union's argument that the Integrity Clause does not *require* contractors to discontinue their relations with nonunionized affiliates misconceives the scope of section 8(e). By prohibiting certain secondary activity based on "express *or* implied" agreements, section 8(e) was intended to close a loophole in section 8(b)(4)(ii)(B) through which unions used "hot cargo" clauses "to exert subtle pressures upon employers to engage in 'voluntary' boycotts." *National Woodwork.* In the instant case, the Board reasonably concluded that the contract-rescission mechanism of section three exerted the requisite degree of pressure not to deal with nonunionized contractors.

Employers in the contracting industry have a vital interest in receiving the benefits of their contracts, including the unions' obligations to furnish skilled labor and to refrain from striking. The Union conceded at oral argument that a clause that automatically doubled the wages of employees should the contractor become affiliated with a nonunionized contractor would be tantamount to an "agreement" to cease doing business for purposes of section 8(e). The threatened loss of a collective bargaining agreement is no less penal and hence no less of an implicit agreement not to deal with nonunionized contractors.

The Board also reasonably concluded that the Integrity Clause has a secondary object. Far from seeking to protect only the jobs or benefits of Local No. 91's members, the Integrity Clause *expressly* ties the rescission remedy to the employer's failure to extend collective bargaining benefits to the employees of *nonunionized* neutral employers. Section one defines a "bad faith" employer as one who either operates or is affiliated with a sheet metal contractor "using employees whose wage package, hours, and working conditions are inferior to those prescribed" by the collective bargaining agreement of the relevant local affiliated with International. Integrity Clause § 1.

The circumstances under which the Union proposed the Integrity Clause buttress the Board's determination that the provision has an unlawful secondary object. In transmitting the Clause to its locals,

International baldly characterized the provision as designed to force employers to become "either 100% union"—that is, unionized throughout their affiliated operations—"or 100% non-union." Policy Memorandum at 1, *reprinted in* J.A. 291. Local No. 91 confirmed this understanding of the Integrity Clause when it informed Schebler that it would become eligible for Resolution 78 relief only when it "guarantees Sheet Metal Workers *everywhere* [that Schebler is] a 100 percent union contractor." J.A. 295 (emphasis added). These statements furnish ample support for the Board's factual finding that the Union *intended* the Integrity Clause to have a secondary purpose, a determination to which we owe deference.

NOTES

1.   *Is the nonunion side of a double-breasted contractor neutral?* Recall that § 8(e) is designed, as with the rest of the secondary activity prohibitions in section 8, to protect neutral employers from labor disputes that do not involve their own working conditions. In what ways are the nonunion parts of double-breasted sheet metal contracting companies neutral? If the nonunionized side of a double-breasted contracting company constituted an "alter ego" of a unionized firm (see note 2 on p. 842 above) would the union's insistence on the Integrity Clause violate § 8(e)? *See Becker Elec. Co. v. IBEW Local 212*, 927 F.2d 895 (6th Cir. 1991) (holding that whether the nonunion affiliate is an alter ego is irrelevant to the § 8(e) analysis because the union's work preservation clause, which prohibits signatory employers from operating nonunion affiliates, does not violate § 8(e) because its intent is to preserve union jobs).

2.   *Achieving the union's goals.* Could you revise the Sheet Metal Workers' Integrity Clause to comport with the requirements of §§ 8(b)(4) and 8(e) and still achieve the union's stated goal of preserving union jobs by making it harder for unionized sheet metal contractors to operate non-union affiliates? If the agreement simply required the "neutral" employer to pay union standard wages, would it violate § 8(e)? *See American Fed. of Musicians* (Seattle Symphony Orchestra), 19–CE–96 (April 17, 1996) (NLRB General Counsel memorandum determining agreement to pay union wage scale does not violate § 8(e)).

3.   *Deference?* Notice that the Judge Edwards' opinion for the D.C. Circuit in *Sheet Metal Workers Local 91* deferred to the Board's interpretation of a secondary object and the Board's finding of facts. If the Board had reached a contrary conclusion, should the D.C. Circuit have deferred to that conclusion as well?

5.   WORK ASSIGNMENT DISPUTES

Sometimes two unions will seek to represent the same group of employees. The Act restricts, although does not completely prohibit, unions from using economic force to resolve the dispute. Section 8(b)(4)(D) prohibits work stoppages or coercion with the object of "forcing or requiring any employer to assign particular work to employees in a particular trade, craft, or class" unless the Board has certified the union as the representative of the employees. Under § 10(k) of the Act, the Board is "empowered and directed" upon the filing of a § 8(b)(4)(D) charge "to hear and determine the dispute out of which such unfair labor practice charge shall have arisen" unless the parties resolve the jurisdictional dispute themselves. The NLRB is obligated to resolve the jurisdictional dispute and award the work to one union or the other. *NLRB v. Radio and Television Broad. Eng'rs Union, Local 1212* (CBS), 364 U.S. 573 (1961). The Board decides each case on its facts, considering, among other things, "the skills and work involved, certifications by the Board, company and industry practice, agreements between unions and between employers and unions, awards of arbitrators, joint boards, and the AFL-CIO in the same or related cases, the assignment made by the employer, and the efficient operation of the employer's business." *Machinists Local 1743 (J.A. Jones Constr. Co.)*, 135 N.L.R.B. 1402 (1962). The Board's § 10(k) decision is not binding on anyone; only if a union subsequently is charged under § 8(b)(4)(D) will the Board's determination of which employees are entitled to the work have force. If the union that is charged under § 8(b)(4)(D) has won a previous § 10(k) ruling, the charges should be dismissed and the union will be free to use economic force to assert its workers rights to the work. If the union lost the prior § 10(k) proceeding, it will be subject to the usual § 8(b)(4) penalties, including a cease and desist order, an injunction under § 10(k), and damages under § 303.

CHAPTER 7

LIFE UNDER THE COLLECTIVE BARGAINING AGREEMENT

■ ■ ■

A. INTRODUCTION

Smith, a maintenance employee of Enderby Industries, Inc., and a member of a bargaining unit represented by the Steelworkers, bid on and was awarded a position as drill operator trainee. During his period as a trainee, Smith's supervisor counseled him on several occasions that he was producing too many defective parts. After giving Smith a final warning that his performance had to improve or he would be discharged, the company fired Smith when his performance failed to improve. Smith, who is African-American and was a union steward, disputes the company's claim that he produced excessive defective parts. He claims that his supervisor, who is white, was biased against him because of his race and because he vigorously pursued grievances as a union steward. The union also claims that in the past the company has allowed five drill operator trainees, four of whom were white and none of whom were active union officers, whose performances were substandard to return to their prior positions rather than fire them. The company disputes the claims of discrimination and maintains that Smith's deficiencies were far more egregious and numerous than any other trainee and that unlike the situation with the other five trainees, there was no opening in Smith's former job.

Once the parties have concluded a collective bargaining agreement, they enter a new phase of their relationship, often referred to as contract administration. The above scenario, adapted from *Alexander v. Gardner-Denver Co.*, 415 U.S. 36 (1974), illustrates some of the complexities involved in the process of contract administration. There are many ways that Smith and his union may seek to reverse his discharge. Either or both of them might file a lawsuit for breach of contract. They might lead a strike, refusing to return to work until the company reverses the discharge. If the contract has a grievance procedure, they might file a grievance. They might file charges with the NLRB alleging that the company discriminated against Smith for his protected concerted activity as a union steward. Smith might file a claim for racial discrimination in violation of Title VII of the 1964 Civil Rights Act or 42 U.S.C. § 1981.

Assuming that the contract has a grievance procedure, may Smith be compelled to use it or may he file a breach of contact case in court? If Smith files a grievance and the union and company agree to resolve it by returning Smith to his former maintenance position but Smith wishes to pursue his claim that he should be reinstated to the trainee position, does he have any legal recourse? What if instead of filing a lawsuit or a grievance, the union goes out on strike? Does the company have any recourse? Does it matter if Smith leads a wildcat strike, i.e., a strike not authorized by the union? Does it matter if the strike protests alleged unfair labor practices or Title VII violations? How should the availability of the grievance procedure, or its actual use, affect any unfair labor practice charges or Title VII claims? This chapter explores these and related questions.

B. WORKPLACE SELF-GOVERNANCE UNDER THE COLLECTIVE BARGAINING AGREEMENT

Consider some typical claims that arise under collective bargaining agreements:

- The agreement prohibits discipline without just cause and an employee suspended for three days claims the employer lacked just cause.

- The agreement conditions holiday pay on the employee's working the last regularly scheduled day before the holiday and the first regularly scheduled day after the holiday. An employee is injured on the job two days before a holiday and the employer's doctor refuses to allow the employee to work the following day. The employer denies holiday pay because the employee failed to work the day prior to the holiday.

- For the past 15 years, a hospital has had a policy requiring all employees to clock out when going on meal breaks and clock back in upon returning. Over that period, the hospital has never enforced the policy against its registered nurses and the nurses generally do not clock out and in for meal breaks. The hospital notifies all nurses that it will begin enforcing the meal clocking policy in two weeks. The nurses' union claims that this violates the agreement's provision that requires notice to the union and an opportunity to bargain if the hospital "wishes to change existing policies related to terms and conditions of employment."

The monetary value of these and many similar claims typically will not justify a lawsuit. Moreover, unions and employees generally do not want to wait the years it may take to resolve a lawsuit. Instead of looking to the courts, unless the collective bargaining agreement prohibits strikes, an aggrieved union and employee are more likely to look to self-help—a strike or other job action to pressure the employer to grant the claim.

Employers generally do not wish to be vulnerable to job actions during the term of the contract and they too do not want to get bogged down in lawsuits over small amounts of money. Consequently, the parties commonly agree that there will be no strikes during the term of the contract and that they will abide by a grievance procedure to resolve claims of breach.

The typical grievance procedure provides for several steps, with the grievance discussed at successively higher levels within the union and employer hierarchies. If the grievance remains unresolved at the highest step, the typical contract provides that a party may demand that it be submitted to a mutually-selected neutral arbitrator whose resolution is final and binding.

Consequently grievance arbitration differs dramatically from arbitration under a commercial or individual employment contract. In the latter, arbitration substitutes a private tribunal for the public courts. In the former, arbitration is the final step in a process of negotiation over disputes that have arisen during the term of the contract. It provides a substitute for strikes or other job actions as the method for resolving those disputes.

The grievance and arbitration procedure also reduces strikes by enabling the parties to reach agreement on the contract's terms short of economic warfare. To illustrate, consider that many collective bargaining agreements require the employer to post vacancies and allow employees to bid on posted vacancies during a specified posting period, such as one week. Such contracts further provide that in filling the vacancy, as between employees whose qualifications are relatively equal, seniority will govern. Imagine the negotiations that led to such a provision. The union probably demanded that vacancies be filled strictly by seniority and the employer probably demanded that they be filled based on qualifications as judged by management. They probably agreed on the "relatively equal" language even though they sharply disagreed on the appropriate mix of qualifications and seniority. To the employer, "relatively equal" probably means "almost identical," while to the union it probably means "both are breathing." Yet, their different philosophies may not produce differences in actual application. Often, the employer will decide that the most senior bidder is also the most qualified. Consequently, the parties probably do not want to impede agreement on a contract based on what may turn out to be a purely abstract dispute over the relative weight given to seniority and qualifications. The grievance and arbitration procedure enables the parties to agree on contract language even though they do not agree on what that language means, and defer further refinement of the language to case-by-case negotiation through the grievance procedure with the understanding that if they cannot reach agreement, they will abide by an arbitrator's resolution of their dispute. In other words, they agree that if they cannot reach agreement on what the contract means in the particular dispute, then the contract means whatever the parties' mutually selected arbitrator says it means.

The grievance and arbitration procedures thus represent more than a process for adjudicating claims by one party that the other party breached the collective bargaining agreement. It is the mechanism by which the parties continue the process of collective bargaining during the term of the contract.

The first documented grievance arbitration in the United States occurred in 1871 when the Committee of the Anthracite Board of Trade and the Committee of the Workingmen's Benevolent Association selected Judge William Elwell of Bloomsburg, Pennsylvania to settle disputes between the parties concerning work stoppages and discharges. Toward the end of the nineteenth and beginning of the twentieth centuries, companies and unions in the apparel, coal, entertainment and railroad industries commonly settled their disputes by arbitration. In 1937, the UAW and General Motors agreed to refer unresolved grievances to arbitration.

The development of grievance and arbitration procedures flourished during World War II. Concern that labor disputes threatened war-time production led President Roosevelt to create the War Labor Board (WLB) to assist in settlement of such disputes. The WLB encouraged parties to include arbitration provisions in their collective bargaining agreements and when one party resisted, the WLB usually ordered it. By 1944, 73% of collective bargaining agreements contained arbitration provisions and today the practice is almost universal.

The Labor Management Relations (Taft-Hartley) Act of 1947 further encouraged the development of grievance arbitration. Section 203(d) declared "[f]inal adjustment of a method agreed upon by the parties . . . to be the desirable method for settlement of grievance disputes arising over the application or interpretation of an existing collective-bargaining agreement." Section 301(a) provided, "Suits for violation of contracts between an employer and a labor organization . . . may be brought in any district court of the United States having jurisdiction of the parties, without respect to the amount in controversy or without regard to the citizenship of the parties."

Section 301 made collective bargaining agreements enforceable by granting subject matter jurisdiction to the federal district courts but did not expressly address what substantive law would govern such actions. In *Textile Workers Union v. Lincoln Mills*, 353 U.S. 448 (1957), however, the Supreme Court interpreted section 301 to be more than just a grant of jurisdiction to federal district courts. Rather, the Court held, section 301 is a mandate to the federal courts to develop a substantive federal law of collective bargaining agreements. The Court observed that a primary congressional purpose in enacting section 301 was to promote industrial peace by holding both parties responsible for performance of the contract. The Court further reasoned:

> Plainly, the agreement to arbitrate grievances is the *quid pro quo* for an agreement not to strike. Viewed in this light, the legislation does more than confer jurisdiction in the federal courts over labor organizations. It expresses a federal policy that federal courts should enforce these agreements on behalf of or against labor organizations and that industrial peace can be best obtained only in that way.

1. ENFORCING THE AGREEMENT TO ARBITRATE

Assume, in the problem that began this chapter, that Smith files a grievance contesting his discharge. Enderby presents the union with documentation and pictures of what Enderby characterizes as Smith's egregious performance deficiencies and his prior counseling and warnings. Nevertheless, the union demands arbitration but Enderby, arguing that the grievance is patently frivolous, refuses to arbitrate. Will a court compel Enderby to arbitrate? The following two cases, together with *United Steelworkers of America v. Enterprise Wheel & Car Corp.*, reproduced *infra*, are collectively known as the *Steelworkers Trilogy*. Decided on the same day by the Supreme Court, these three cases are widely regarded as the Court's seminal pronouncements on federal labor policy concerning grievance arbitration.

UNITED STEELWORKERS OF AMERICA V. AMERICAN MANUFACTURING CO.

363 U.S. 564 (1960)

JUSTICE DOUGLAS delivered the opinion of the Court:

This suit was brought by petitioner union in the District Court to compel arbitration of a "grievance" that petitioner, acting for one Sparks, a union member, had filed with the respondent, Sparks' employer.

The agreement provided that during its term there would be "no strike," unless the employer refused to abide by a decision of the arbitrator. The agreement sets out a detailed grievance procedure with a provision for arbitration (regarded as the standard form) of all disputes between the parties "as to the meaning, interpretation and application of the provisions of this agreement."

The agreement reserves to the management power to suspend or discharge any employee "for cause." It also contains a provision that the employer will employ and promote employees on the principle of seniority "where ability and efficiency are equal." Sparks left his work due to an injury and while off work brought an action for compensation benefits. The case was settled, Sparks' physician expressing the opinion that the injury had made him 25% "permanently partially disabled." That was on September 9. Two weeks later the union filed a grievance which charged that Sparks was entitled to return to his job by virtue of the seniority provision of the collective bargaining agreement. Respondent refused to arbitrate and this action was brought. The District Court held that Sparks, having accepted the settlement on the basis of permanent partial disability, was estopped to claim any seniority or employment rights and granted the motion for summary judgment. The Court of Appeals affirmed for different reasons. After reviewing the evidence it held that the grievance is "a frivolous, patently baseless one, not subject to arbitration under the collective bargaining agreement."

Section 203(d) of the Labor Management Relations Act, states, "Final adjustment by a method agreed upon by the parties is hereby declared to be the desirable method for settlement of grievance disputes arising over the application or interpretation of an existing collective-bargaining agreement." That policy can be effectuated only if the means chosen by the parties for settlement of their differences under a collective bargaining agreement is given full play.

The lower courts in the instant case had a preoccupation with ordinary contract law. The collective agreement requires arbitration of claims that courts might be unwilling to entertain. In the context of the plant or industry the grievance may assume proportions of which judges are ignorant. Yet, the agreement is to submit all grievances to arbitration, not merely those that a court may deem to be meritorious. There is no exception in the "no strike" clause and none therefore should be read into the grievance clause, since one is the quid pro quo for the other. The question is not whether in the mind of the court there is equity in the claim. Arbitration is a stabilizing influence only as it serves as a vehicle for handling any and all disputes that arise under the agreement.

The collective agreement calls for the submission of grievances in the categories which it describes, irrespective of whether a court may deem them to be meritorious. In our role of developing a meaningful body of law to govern the interpretation and enforcement of collective bargaining agreements, we think special heed should be given to the context in which collective bargaining agreements are negotiated and the purpose which they are intended to serve. The function of the court is very limited when the parties have agreed to submit all questions of contract interpretation to the arbitrator. It is confined to ascertaining whether the party seeking arbitration is making a claim which on its face is governed by the contract. Whether the moving party is right or wrong is a question of contract interpretation for the arbitrator. In these circumstances the moving party should not be deprived of the arbitrator's judgment, when it was his judgment and all that connotes that was bargained for.

The courts, therefore, have no business weighing the merits of the grievance, considering whether there is equity in a particular claim, or determining whether there is particular language in the written instrument which will support the claim. The agreement is to submit all grievances to arbitration, not merely those which the court will deem meritorious. The processing of even frivolous claims may have therapeutic values of which those who are not a part of the plant environment may be quite unaware.

The union claimed in this case that the company had violated a specific provision of the contract. The company took the position that it had not violated that clause. There was, therefore, a dispute between the parties as to "the meaning, interpretation and application" of the collective bargaining agreement. Arbitration should have been ordered. When the judiciary undertakes to determine the merits of a grievance under the guise of interpreting the grievance procedure of collective bargaining agreements, it usurps a function which under that regime is entrusted to the arbitration tribunal.

Reversed.

UNITED STEELWORKERS OF AMERICA V. WARRIOR & GULF NAVIGATION CO.
363 U.S. 574 (1960)

JUSTICE DOUGLAS delivered the opinion of the Court:

Respondent transports steel and steel products by barge and maintains a terminal at Chickasaw, Alabama, where it performs maintenance and repair work on its barges. The employees at that terminal constitute a bargaining unit covered by a collective bargaining agreement negotiated by petitioner union. Respondent between 1956 and 1958 laid off some employees, reducing the bargaining unit from 42 to 23 men. This reduction was due in part to respondent contracting maintenance work, previously done by its employees, to other companies. The latter used respondent's supervisors to lay out the work and hired some of the laid-off employees of respondent (at reduced wages). Some were in fact assigned to work on respondent's barges. A number of employees signed a grievance which petitioner presented to respondent, the grievance reading:

> We are hereby protesting the Company's actions, of arbitrarily and unreasonably contracting out work to other concerns, that could and previously has been performed by Company employees.

> This practice becomes unreasonable, unjust and discriminatory in lieu (sic) of the fact that at present there are a number of employees that have been laid off for about 1 and 1/2 years or more for allegedly lack of work.

Confronted with these facts we charge that the Company is in violation of the contract by inducing a partial lock-out, of a number of the employees who would otherwise be working were it not for this unfair practice.

The collective agreement had both a "no strike" and a "no lockout" provision. It also had a grievance procedure which provided in relevant part as follows:

Issues which conflict with any Federal statute in its application as established by Court procedure or matters which are strictly a function of management shall not be subject to arbitration under this section.

Should differences arise between the Company and the Union or its members employed by the Company as to the meaning and application of the provisions of this Agreement, or should any local trouble of any kind arise, there shall be no suspension of work on account of such differences but an earnest effort shall be made to settle such differences immediately in the following manner:

A.   For Maintenance Employees:

First, between the aggrieved employees, and the Foreman involved;

Second, between a member or members of the Grievance Committee designated by the Union, and the Foreman and Master Mechanic.

Fifth, if agreement has not been reached the matter shall be referred to an impartial umpire for decision. The parties shall meet to decide on an umpire acceptable to both. If no agreement on selection of an umpire is reached, the parties shall jointly petition the United States Conciliation Service for suggestion of a list of umpires from which selection shall be made. The decision of the umpire will be final.

Settlement of this grievance was not had and respondent refused arbitration. This suit was then commenced by the union to compel it.

The District Court granted respondent's motion to dismiss the complaint. It held after hearing evidence, much of which went to the merits of the grievance, that the agreement did not "confide in an arbitrator the right to review the defendant's business judgment in contracting out work." It further held that "the contracting out of repair and maintenance work, as well as construction work, is strictly a function of management not limited in any respect by the labor agreement involved here." The Court of Appeals affirmed by a divided vote, the majority holding that the collective agreement had withdrawn from the grievance procedure "matters which are strictly a function of management" and that contracting out fell in that exception. The case is here on a writ of certiorari.

[T]he run of arbitration cases, illustrated by *Wilko v. Swan*, 346 U.S. 427 (1953) becomes irrelevant to our problem. There the choice is between the adjudication of cases or controversies in courts with established procedures or even special statutory safeguards on the one hand and the settlement of them in the more informal arbitration tribunal on the other. In the commercial case, arbitration is the substitute for litigation. Here arbitration is the substitute for industrial strife. Since arbitration of labor disputes has quite different functions from arbitration under an ordinary commercial agreement, the hostility evinced by courts toward arbitration of commercial agreements has no place here. For arbitration of labor disputes under collective bargaining agreements is part and parcel of the collective bargaining process itself.

The collective bargaining agreement states the rights and duties of the parties. It is more than a contract; it is a generalized code to govern a myriad of cases which the draftsmen cannot wholly anticipate. *See* Shulman, Reason, *Contract, and Law in Labor Relations*, 68 Harv. L. Rev. 999, 1004–1005 (1954–55). The collective agreement covers the whole employment relationship. It calls into being a new common law—the common law of a particular industry or of a particular plant. As one observer has put it:

> (I)t is not unqualifiedly true that a collective-bargaining agreement is simply a document by which the union and employees have imposed upon management limited, express restrictions of its otherwise absolute right to manage the enterprise, so that an employee's claim must fail unless he can point to a specific contract provision upon which the claim is founded. There are too many people, too many problems, too many unforeseeable contingencies to make the words of the contract the exclusive source of rights and duties. One cannot reduce all the rules governing a community like an industrial plant to fifteen or even fifty pages. Within the sphere of collective bargaining, the institutional characteristics and the governmental nature of the collective-bargaining process demand a common law of the shop which implements and furnishes the context of the agreement. We must assume that intelligent negotiators acknowledged so plain a need unless they stated a contrary rule in plain words.

Cox, *Reflections Upon Labor Arbitration*, 72 Harv. L. Rev. 1482, 1498–1499 (1959).

A collective bargaining agreement is an effort to erect a system of industrial self-government. When most parties enter into contractual relationship they do so voluntarily, in the sense that there is no real compulsion to deal with one another, as opposed to dealing with other parties. This is not true of the labor agreement. The choice is generally not between entering or refusing to enter into a relationship, for that in all probability pre-exists the negotiations. Rather it is between having that relationship governed by an agreed-upon rule of law or leaving each and every matter subject to a temporary resolution dependent solely upon the relative strength, at any given moment, of the contending forces. The mature labor agreement may attempt to regulate all aspects of the complicated relationship, from the most crucial to the most minute over an extended period of time. Because of the compulsion to reach agreement and the breadth of the matters covered, as well as the need for a fairly concise and readable instrument, the product of negotiations (the written document) is, in the words of the late Dean Shulman, "a compilation of diverse provisions: some provide objective criteria almost automatically applicable; some provide more or less specific standards which require reason and judgment in their application; and some do little more than leave problems to future consideration with an expression of hope and good faith." Shulman, *supra*, at 1005. Gaps may be left to be filled in by reference to the practices of the particular industry and of the various shops covered by the agreement. Many of the specific practices which underlie the agreement may be unknown, except in hazy form, even to the negotiators. Courts and arbitration in the context of most commercial contracts are resorted to because there has been a breakdown in the working relationship of the parties; such resort is the unwanted exception. But the grievance machinery under a collective bargaining agreement is at the very heart of the system of industrial self-government. Arbitration is the means of solving the unforeseeable by molding a system of private law for all the problems which may arise and to provide for their solution in a way which will generally accord with the variant needs and desires of the parties. The processing of disputes through the grievance machinery is actually a vehicle by which meaning and content are given to the collective bargaining agreement.

Apart from matters that the parties specifically exclude, all of the questions on which the parties disagree must therefore come within the scope of the grievance and arbitration provisions of the collective agreement. The grievance procedure is, in other words, a part of the continuous collective bargaining process. It, rather than a strike, is the terminal point of a disagreement.

The labor arbitrator performs functions which are not normal to the courts; the considerations which help him fashion judgments may indeed be foreign to the competence of courts.

A proper conception of the arbitrator's function is basic. He is not a public tribunal imposed upon the parties by superior authority which the parties are obliged to accept. He has no general charter to administer justice for a community which transcends the parties. He is rather part of a system of self-government created by and confined to the parties. *Shulman, supra,* at 1016.

The labor arbitrator's source of law is not confined to the express provisions of the contract, as the industrial common law—the practices of the industry and the shop—is equally a part of the collective bargaining agreement although not expressed in it. The labor arbitrator is usually chosen because of the parties' confidence in his knowledge of the common law of the shop and their trust in his personal judgment to bring to bear considerations which are not expressed in the contract as criteria for judgment. The parties expect that his judgment of a particular grievance will reflect not only what the contract says but, insofar as the collective bargaining agreement permits, such factors as the effect upon productivity of a particular result, its consequence to the morale of the shop, his judgment whether tensions will be heightened or diminished. For the parties' objective in using the arbitration process is primarily to further their common goal of uninterrupted production under the agreement, to make the agreement serve their specialized needs. The ablest judge cannot be expected to bring the same experience and competence to bear upon the determination of a grievance, because he cannot be similarly informed.

The Congress, however, has by § 301 of the Labor Management Relations Act, assigned the courts the duty of determining whether the reluctant party has breached his promise to arbitrate. For arbitration is a matter of contract and a party cannot be required to submit to arbitration any dispute which he has not agreed so to submit. Yet, to be consistent with congressional policy in favor of settlement of disputes by the parties through the machinery of arbitration, the judicial inquiry under § 301 must be strictly confined to the question whether the reluctant party did agree to arbitrate the grievance or did agree to give the arbitrator power to make the award he made. An order to arbitrate the particular grievance should not be denied unless it may be said with positive assurance that the arbitration clause is not susceptible of an interpretation that covers the asserted dispute. Doubts should be resolved in favor of coverage.

We do not agree with the lower courts that contracting-out grievances were necessarily excepted from the grievance procedure of this agreement. To be sure, the agreement provides that "matters which are strictly a function of management shall not be subject to arbitration." But it goes on to say that if "differences" arise or if "any local trouble of any kind" arises, the grievance procedure shall be applicable.

Collective bargaining agreements regulate or restrict the exercise of management functions; they do not oust management from the performance of them. Management hires and fires, pays and promotes, supervises and plans. All these are part of its function, and absent a collective bargaining agreement, it may be exercised freely except as limited by public law and by the willingness of employees to work under the particular, unilaterally imposed conditions. A collective bargaining agreement may treat only with certain specific practices, leaving the rest to management but subject to the possibility of work stoppages. When, however, an absolute no-strike clause is included in the agreement, then in a very real sense everything that management does is subject to the agreement, for either management is prohibited or limited in the action it takes, or if not, it is protected from interference by strikes. This comprehensive reach of the collective bargaining agreement does not mean, however, that the language, "strictly a function of management," has no meaning.

"Strictly a function of management" might be thought to refer to any practice of management in which, under particular circumstances prescribed by the agreement, it is permitted to indulge. But if courts, in order to determine arbitrability, were allowed to determine what is permitted and what is not, the arbitration clause would be swallowed up by the exception. Every grievance in a sense involves a claim that management has violated some provision of the agreement.

Accordingly, "strictly a function of management" must be interpreted as referring only to that over which the contract gives management complete control and unfettered discretion. Respondent claims that the contracting out of work falls within this category. Contracting out work is the basis of many grievances; and that type of claim is grist in the mills of the arbitrators. A specific collective bargaining agreement may exclude contracting out from the grievance procedure. Or a written collateral agreement may make clear that contracting out was not a matter for arbitration. In such a case a grievance based solely on contracting out would not be arbitrable. Here, however, there is no such provision. Nor is there any showing that the parties designed the phrase "strictly a function of management" to encompass any and all forms of contracting out. In the absence of any express provision excluding a particular grievance from arbitration, we think only the most forceful evidence of a purpose to exclude the claim from arbitration can prevail, particularly where, as here, the exclusion clause is vague and the arbitration clause quite broad. Since any attempt by a court to infer such a purpose necessarily comprehends the merits, the court should view with suspicion an attempt to persuade it to become entangled in the construction of the substantive provisions of a labor agreement, even through the back door of interpreting the arbitration clause, when the alternative is to utilize the services of an arbitrator.

The grievance alleged that the contracting out was a violation of the collective bargaining agreement. There was, therefore, a dispute "as to the meaning and application of the provisions of this Agreement" which the parties had agreed would be determined by arbitration.

The judiciary sits in these cases to bring into operation an arbitral process which substitutes a regime of peaceful settlement for the older regime of industrial conflict. Whether contracting out in the present case violated the agreement is the question. It is a question for the arbiter, not for the courts.

Reversed.

[The dissenting opinion of JUSTICE WHITTAKER has been omitted.]

NOTES

1.   The collective bargaining agreement in *Warrior & Gulf* expressly provided that "matters which are strictly a function of management shall not be subject to arbitration," and the court of appeals found that subcontracting was strictly a function of management and held that the grievance was not arbitrable. On what basis did the Supreme Court reverse? In Justice Douglas's view, who should decide whether subcontracting is strictly a function of management—a court or an arbitrator?

2.   How might the parties have drafted the collective bargaining agreement to preclude arbitration of the grievance?

3.   Justice Douglas speaks in glowing terms of the arbitrator as "chosen because of the parties' confidence in his knowledge of the common law of the shop and their trust in his personal judgment to bring to bear considerations which are not expressed in the contract as criteria for judgment." Sometimes parties may choose arbitrators for the reasons Justice Douglas suggested but other times they may have other criteria, such as whether they think the arbitrator is likely to side with them in the dispute. Is the case for a heavy presumption of arbitrability weaker if parties are less high-minded about their choice of arbitrators?

4.   *Should a Court or an Arbitrator Decide Substantive Arbitrability?* In *Warrior & Gulf*, even though the agreement excluded from arbitration matters that were strictly a function of management, the Court found that the lower courts improperly encroached on the arbitrator's authority by deciding that subcontracting was strictly a function of management. Given the interplay between the question of arbitrability and the merits of the grievance, might it have been better for the Court to have required the parties to arbitrate the question of arbitrability? In *AT&T Technologies, Inc. v. Communication Workers of America,* 475 U.S. 643 (1986), the collective bargaining agreement contained a broad arbitration clause but also purported to exclude from arbitration matters encompassed within its management functions clause. The lower courts ordered the parties to submit to the arbitrator the question of whether the grievance was arbitrable. The Supreme Court reversed. It held that issues of substantive arbitrability are to be decided by the court "unless the parties provide otherwise." The Court reaffirmed the principles of the *Steelworker Trilogy* and remanded to the lower courts to apply those principles to the issue of arbitrability presented in the case.

In *Granite Rock Co. v. International Brotherhood of Teamsters,* 561 U.S. 287 (2010), the Supreme Court held that the question whether a ratification vote was valid and thus whether a contract was validly formed was to be decided by a court rather than an arbitrator. Following the expiration of a collective bargaining agreement and an impasse in negotiations, the local union called a strike on June 9, 2004. On July 2, 2004, the parties reached a tentative agreement. The local submitted the agreement to a ratification vote. Meanwhile, the international objected that the local had not obtained a back-to-work agreement holding harmless the union and the employees for damages that may have occurred during the strike and ordered the local to continue the strike until it received such an agreement. The local went back on strike on July 5. The employer sued for an injunction and damages, alleging that the strike breached the no strike clause in the new contract which it claimed had been ratified on July 2. The local called off the strike, mooting the injunction claim and asked the court to order the claim for damages to arbitration where the arbitrator would consider whether the contract was properly ratified on July 2 or at the second ratification vote.

The Court held that whether the contract was ratified on July 2 determined whether any contract, and thus any obligation to arbitrate, had been formed as of the time that the local resumed the strike. The Court reasoned:

> The parties agree that the CBA's arbitration clause pertains only to disputes that "arise under" the agreement. Accordingly, to hold the parties' ratification-date dispute arbitrable, the Court of Appeals had to decide whether the dispute could be characterized as "arising under" the CBA. [T]he Court of Appeals relied upon the ratification dispute's relationship to Granite Rock's claim that Local breached the CBA's no-strike clause (a claim the Court of Appeals viewed as clearly "arising under" the CBA) to conclude that the arbitration clause is certainly susceptible of an interpretation that covers Local's formation-date defense.

> The Court of Appeals overlooked the fact that this theory of the ratification dispute's arbitrability fails if the CBA was not formed at the time the unions engaged in the acts that gave rise to Granite Rock's strike claims. If, as Local asserts, the CBA containing the parties' arbitration clause was not ratified, and thus not formed, until August 22, there was no CBA for the July no-strike dispute to "arise under," and thus no valid basis for the Court of Appeals' conclusion that Granite Rock's July 9 claims arose under the CBA and were thus arbitrable along with, by extension, Local's formation date defense to those claims.

Can you reconcile the Court's holding in *Granite Rock* with its holding in *AT&T Technologies'* direction that in resolving issues of arbitrability courts should appl[y *Steelworker Trilogy* principles, i.e. a strong presumption of arbitrability that can be rebutted only when it can be said with positive assurance that the parties did not intend to make the dispute arbitrable?

5. A collective bargaining agreement provides, "The Company recognizes the Union as the exclusive bargaining agent for [the] employees . . ." It also provides, "The right to invoke arbitration shall extend only to matters which involve [t]he interpretation or application of any of the terms or provisions of this Agreement . . ." The employer changed its method of evaluating the performance of certain employees by imposing sales quotas. The contract contains no provisions expressly dealing with performance standards. The union alleges that the new sales quotas breached the recognition clause. If the employer refuses to arbitrate the grievance should a court order arbitration? In *International Brotherhood of Electrical Workers Local 21 v. Illinois Bell Telephone. Co.*, 491 F.3d 685 (7th Cir. 2007), by a 2–1 vote, the court compelled arbitration. The majority reasoned that an arbitrator could interpret the recognition clause to require the union's consent before performance standards could be changed. The dissent argued that such an interpretation was impossible and "would require the arbitrator to completely rewrite the recognition clause, engrafting a duty that is not there."

6. May an employer be compelled to arbitrate claims that arise after the expiration of the collective bargaining agreement? The Supreme Court has distinguished between claims that the contract conferred vested rights on the employees that survived contract expiration, which may be arbitrable, from other claims which are not. *Compare Nolde Brothers v. Bakery & Confectionary Workers Local 358*, 430 U.S. 243 (1977) (holding arbitrable a grievance for severance pay where employer ceased operations a few days after collective bargaining agreement expired because whether the severance pay provision created a vested right that survived contract expiration was a question for the arbitrator) *with Litton Fin. Printing Div. of Litton Bus. Sys., Inc. v. NLRB*, 501 U.S. 190 (1991) (holding grievance for retaining junior employees and laying off senior employees after collective bargaining agreement expired is not arbitrable).

7. Assume that the collective bargaining agreement provides a four step grievance procedure with arbitration as the fourth step. The contract further provides that if the union is dissatisfied with the employer's response at the third step, it must demand arbitration within 14 days of receipt of that response. The union demands arbitration 16 days after receiving the step three response. If the employer refuses to arbitrate, should a court compel it to do so? In *John Wiley & Sons, Inc. v. Livingston*, 376 U.S. 543 (1964), the Court held that issues of procedural arbitrability are for the arbitrator, rather than the court, to decide.

A NOTE ON ARBITRATION IN NON-UNION SETTINGS

In 1953, in *Wilko v. Swan*, cited in *Warrior & Gulf*, a securities purchaser had entered into a margin agreement with a brokerage firm that obligated the purchaser to arbitrate any claims that might arise. The Supreme Court held that the agreement, as applied to the purchaser's claim under the Securities Act of 1933, was unenforceable. The Court held that the waiver of access to a judicial forum was a stipulation to waive compliance with the Act and was void under section 14 of the Act. The Court reasoned that an agreement to arbitrate sacrificed advantages, such as a broad choice of venue, that the statute gave to securities purchasers and that arbitrators were not subject to judicial control over their legal rulings.

More than three decades later, in *Mitsubishi Motors Corp. v. Soler Chrysler-Plymouth, Inc.*, 473 U.S. 614 (1985), the Court held that an American auto dealer was obligated under its franchise agreement with a Japanese manufacturer to arbitrate its claims that the manufacturer violated the antitrust laws. Although the Court grounded its ruling in part on the international nature of the contract, its rationale swept more broadly. The Court characterized the agreement to arbitrate as not waiving substantive legal rights but as merely substituting the arbitral forum for the judicial. The Court extended its enforcement of pre-dispute agreements to arbitrate to claims under the Securities Exchange Act of 1934 and under RICO in *Shearson/American Express, Inc. v McMahon*, 482 U.S. 220 (1987). Two years later, in *Rodrigues de Quejas v. Shearson/American Express, Inc.*, 490 U.S. 477 (1989), the Court overruled *Wilko*. These commercial arbitration decisions set the stage for the Court in 1991 to hold that a securities industry employee's agreement in his securities exchange registration to arbitrate all claims arising out of his employment required him to arbitrate his claim under the Age Discrimination in Employment Act. *Gilmer v. Interstate Johnson/Lane Corp.*, 500 U.S. 20 (1991). In *Circuit City Stores, Inc. v. Adams*, 532 U.S. 105 (2001), the Court interpreted narrowly the Federal Arbitration Act's exclusion of "contracts of employment of seamen, railroad employees or any other class of workers engaged in foreign or interstate commerce," and held that arbitration agreements of most employees would be enforceable.

Reacting to *Gilmer* and *Circuit City*, many employers have imposed on their non-union employees as a condition of employment requirements to arbitrate all claims related to their employment. This has spawned a lively debate over whether such agreements inherently advantage employers or also benefit employees. For views critical of employer-imposed arbitration agreements, see Reginald Alleyne, *Statutory Discrimination Claims: Rights "Waived" and Lost in the Arbitration Forum*, 13 Hofstra Lab. & Emp. L.J. 381 (1996); Joseph D. Garrison, *Mandatory Binding Arbitration Constitutes Little More Than a Waiver of a Worker's Rights*, 52 Disp. Resol. J., Fall, 1997, at 15; Robert A. Gorman, *The* Gilmer *Decision and the Private Arbitration of Public Disputes*, 1995 U. Ill. L. Rev. 635; Joseph R. Grodin, *Arbitration of Employment Discrimination Claims: Doctrine and Policy in the Wake of* Gilmer, 14 Hofstra Lab. & Emp. L.J. 1 (1996); David S. Schwartz, *Mandatory Arbitration and Fairness,* 84 Notre Dame L. Rev. 1247 (2009); David S. Schwartz, *Enforcing Small Print to Protect Big Business: Employee and Consumer Rights in an Age of Compelled Arbitration*, 1997 Wis. L. Rev. 33; Jean R. Sternlight, *Panacea or Corporate Tool: Debunking the Supreme Court's Preference for Binding Arbitration*, 74 Wash. U.L.Q. 637 (1996); Katherine Van Wezel Stone, *Mandatory Arbitration of Individual Employment Rights: The Yellow Dog Contract of the 1990s*, 73 Denv. U. L. Rev. 1017 (1996). For views that arbitration can be beneficial for employees, see Susan A. FitzGibbon,

Reflections on Gilmer *and* Cole, 1 Emp. Rts. & Emp. Pol'y J. 221 (1997); Martin H. Malin, *Privatizing Justice—But By How Much? Questions* Gilmer *Did Not Answer,* 16 Ohio St. J. Dispute Resol. 589 (2001); Theodore J. St. Antoine, *Mandatory Arbitration: Why It's Better Than It Looks*, 41 U. Mich. J.L. Reform 783 (2008).

Proponents of the view that arbitration could be beneficial for employees presumed that courts would police employer-imposed arbitration mandates rigorously. Many courts policed these mandates through state contract law of unconscionability. However, in *A T & T Mobility, LLC v. Concepcion*, 563 U.S. 333 (2011), the Court held that state unconscionability law was preempted by the Federal Arbitration Act (FAA), reasoning that the FAA embodies a federal policy that arbitration agreements be enforced in accordance with their terms. *Concepcion*, which involved a consumer contract for a cell phone, held that this FAA policy preempted California law, which had held that provisions mandating arbitration on an individual basis only and waiving the right to bring or participate in class actions were unconscionable.

Courts also policed employer-imposed arbitration mandates under the requirement that claimants be able to effectively vindicate their statutory rights in the arbitral forum for the arbitration mandate to not amount to a waiver of those statutory rights. *See, e.g., Cole v. Burns Int'l Sec. Servs.*, 105 F.3d 1465 (D.C. Cir. 1997). But in *American Express Co. v. Italian Colors Restaurant*, 570 U.S. 228 (2013), a commercial case, the Court characterized the effective vindication requirement as dicta and held that the policy that arbitration agreements be enforced according to their terms required enforcement of an agreement provision mandating individual-only arbitration of Italian Color's antitrust claim against American Express even though Italian Colors's expert estimated that the cost of expert analysis necessary to prove the antitrust claims would range in six or seven figures while the maximum recovery for an individual plaintiff after trebling the damages would be $38,549. The Court opined that "the fact that it is not worth the expense involved in *proving* a statutory remedy does not constitute the elimination of the *right to pursue* that remedy." For a critique of this jurisprudence by a scholar who previously envisioned employment arbitration rigorously policed by the courts as beneficial to employers and employees see Martin H. Malin, *The Three Phases of the Supreme Court's Arbitration Jurisprudence: Empowering the Already Empowered*, 17 Nev. L.J. 23 (2016).

As discussed in Chapter 2, the NLRB had held that employer-imposed mandates that employees arbitrate their claims on an individual basis violated NLRB section 8(a)(1) but in *Epic Systems Corp. v. Lewis*, 138 S. Ct. 1612 (2018), the Supreme Court rejected that view, narrowing significantly the scope of what constitutes concerted activity for mutual aid and protection under section 7 of the NLRA. The Court again emphasized the federal policy favoring enforcing arbitration agreements in accordance with their terms.

There is considerable evidence that since *Concepcion* and *Italian Colors*, an increasing number of employers have imposed mandates that their employees arbitrate their statutory claims on an individual basis only. *See, e.g.*, Alexander J.S. Colvin, Economic Policy Institute, The Growing Use of Mandatory Arbitration, https://www.epi.org/publication/the-growing-use-of-mandatory-arbitration/ (2017); Jeane R. Sternlight, *Disarming Employees: How American Employers Are Using Mandatory Arbitration to Deprive Workers of Legal Protection*, 80 Brooklyn L. Rev. 1309, 1310 n.9 (2015) (reporting on a recent survey of corporate general counsel which found that the use of arbitration mandates with class-action prohibitions increased from 16.1 percent in 2012 to 42.7 percent in 2014). Recent empirical studies suggest that employees win less often in arbitration than in litigation, recover less when they do win and are far less likely to file arbitration claims than to sue. *See, e.g.*, Alexander J.S. Colvin, *Mandatory Arbitration and Inequality of Justice in Employment*, 35 Berkeley J. Emp. & Lab. L. 71 (2014); Cynthia Estlund, *The Black Hole of Mandatory Arbitration*, 96 N. Car. L. Rev. 679 (2018).

2. ENFORCING THE ARBITRATION AWARD

Assume that Enderby and the union arbitrate Smith's discharge grievance. Despite Enderby's documentation and pictures, the arbitrator finds that Enderby failed to prove that Smith's performance was deficient. Enderby contends that the arbitrator's finding is irrational and refuses to reinstate Smith. The union may file suit under section 301 to enforce the award. Alternatively, Enderby may file suit under section 301 asking the court to vacate the award. In the third case in the *Steelworkers Trilogy*, the Supreme Court addressed how courts should handle such cases.

UNITED STEELWORKERS OF AMERICA V. ENTERPRISE WHEEL & CAR CORP.
363 U.S. 593 (1960)

JUSTICE DOUGLAS delivered the opinion of the Court:

Petitioner union and respondent during the period relevant here had a collective bargaining agreement which provided that any differences "as to the meaning and application" of the agreement should be submitted to arbitration and that the arbitrator's decision "shall be final and binding on the parties." Special provisions were included concerning the suspension and discharge of employees.

A group of employees left their jobs in protest against the discharge of one employee. A union official advised them at once to return to work. An official of respondent at their request gave them permission and then rescinded it. The next day they were told they did not have a job any more "until this thing was settled one way or the other."

A grievance was filed; and when respondent finally refused to arbitrate, this suit was brought for specific enforcement of the arbitration provisions of the agreement. The District Court ordered arbitration. The arbitrator found that the discharge of the men was not justified, though their conduct, he said, was improper. In his view the facts warranted at most a suspension of the men for 10 days each. After their discharge and before the arbitration award the collective bargaining agreement had expired. The union, however, continued to represent the workers at the plant. The arbitrator rejected the contention that expiration of the agreement barred reinstatement of the employees. He held that the provision of the agreement above quoted imposed an unconditional obligation on the employer. He awarded reinstatement with back pay, minus pay for a 10-day suspension and such sums as these employees received from other employment.

Respondent refused to comply with the award. The District Court directed respondent to comply. The Court of Appeals, while agreeing that the District Court had jurisdiction to enforce an arbitration award under a collective bargaining agreement, held that an award for back pay subsequent to the date of termination of the collective bargaining agreement could not be enforced. It also held that the requirement for reinstatement of the discharged employees was likewise unenforceable because the collective bargaining agreement had expired. We granted certiorari.

The refusal of courts to review the merits of an arbitration award is the proper approach to arbitration under collective bargaining agreements. The federal policy of settling labor disputes by arbitration would be undermined if courts had the final say on the merits of the awards. As we stated in *United Steelworkers of America v. Warrior & Gulf Navigation Co.*, the arbitrators under these collective agreements are indispensable agencies in a continuous collective bargaining process. They sit to settle disputes at the plant level—disputes that require for their solution knowledge of the custom and practices of a particular factory or of a particular industry as reflected in particular agreements.

When an arbitrator is commissioned to interpret and apply the collective bargaining agreement, he is to bring his informed judgment to bear in order to reach a fair solution of a problem. This is especially true when it comes to formulating remedies. There the need is for flexibility in meeting a wide variety of situations. The draftsmen may never have thought of what specific remedy should be awarded to meet a particular contingency. Nevertheless, an arbitrator is confined to interpretation and application of the collective bargaining agreement; he does not sit to dispense his own brand of industrial justice. He may of course look for guidance from many sources, yet his award is legitimate only so long as it draws its essence from the collective bargaining agreement. When the arbitrator's words manifest an infidelity to this obligation, courts have no choice but to refuse enforcement of the award.

The opinion of the arbitrator in this case, as it bears upon the award of back pay beyond the date of the agreement's expiration and reinstatement, is ambiguous. It may be read as based solely upon the arbitrator's view of the requirements of enacted legislation, which would mean that he exceeded the scope of the submission. Or it may be read as embodying a construction of the agreement itself, perhaps with the arbitrator looking to "the law" for help in determining the sense of the agreement. A mere ambiguity in the opinion accompanying an award, which permits the inference that the arbitrator may have exceeded his authority, is not a reason for refusing to enforce the award. Arbitrators have no obligation to the court to give their reasons for an award. To require opinions free of ambiguity may lead arbitrators to play it safe by writing no supporting opinions. This would be undesirable for a well-reasoned opinion tends to engender confidence in the integrity of the process and aids in clarifying the underlying agreement. Moreover, we see no reason to assume that this arbitrator has abused the trust the parties confided in him and has not stayed within the areas marked out for his consideration. It is not apparent that he went beyond the submission. The Court of Appeals' opinion refusing to enforce the reinstatement and partial back pay portions of the award was not based upon any finding that the arbitrator did not premise his award on his construction of the contract. It merely disagreed with the arbitrator's construction of it.

The collective bargaining agreement could have provided that if any of the employees were wrongfully discharged, the remedy would be reinstatement and back pay up to the date they were returned to work. Respondent's major argument seems to be that by applying correct principles of law to the interpretation of the collective bargaining agreement it can be determined that the agreement did not so provide, and that therefore the arbitrator's decision was not based upon the contract. The acceptance of this view would require courts, even under the standard arbitration clause, to review the merits of every construction of the contract. This plenary review by a court of the merits would make meaningless the provisions that the arbitrator's decision is final, for in reality it would almost never be final. This underlines the fundamental error which we have alluded to in *United Steelworkers of America v. American Manufacturing Co.* As we there emphasized, the question of interpretation of the collective bargaining agreement is a question for the arbitrator. It is the arbitrator's construction which was bargained for; and so far as the arbitrator's decision concerns construction of the contract, the courts have no business overruling him because their interpretation of the contract is different from his.

NOTES

1.   The Court says that a court should enforce an arbitration award as long as the award "draws its essence" from the collective bargaining agreement. What is the rationale for such a deferential standard of review?

2.   Michigan Family Resources (MFR) runs the Head Start programs in western Michigan. SEIU Local 517M represents some of MFR's employees. The collective bargaining agreement provides:

> Bargaining unit members will receive the same cost of living increase pursuant to the directive of MFR's funding source. The parties understand the timing and amount of any such increase is entirely dictated by the funding source.
>
> During the fall semester of each year, bargaining unit members will be reviewed and will be considered for a merit increase. MFR will guarantee at least that for each bargaining unit employee, the sum of any COLA paid during the year and the merit increase will be as follows: 2002—4%; 2003—2.5%; 2004—3.5%. For example, if the COLA increase for 2004 is 2.5%, effective September 1, 2004, bargaining unit members will receive at least an additional 1%.

In May 2003, MFR notified bargaining unit employees of a 2.5% increase, 1.5% from the funding source (the federal government) and 1% funded by MFR. MFR also granted its non-union employees a 4% increase. The union grieved, arguing that MFR was obligated to grant bargaining unit employees the same increase as it granted non-union employees. An arbitrator, relying on evidence that MFR always granted wage increases across the board, never evaluated employee performance as a method for distributing increases and never in the past granted different increases to unit and non-unit employees, agreed and ordered MFR to give bargaining unit employees an additional 1.5% increase. If MFR refuses to comply, should a court enforce the award? *See Mich. Family Res., Inc. v. Serv. Employees Int'l Union Local 517M*, 475 F.3d 746 (6th Cir. 2007), *overruling Cement Div., Nat'l Gypsum Co. v. United Steelworkers of Am. Local 135*, 793 F.2d 759 (6th Cir. 1986), *and enforcing the award*.

3.   In *Brentwood Medical Associates v. United Mine Workers of America*, 396 F.3d 237 (3d Cir. 2005), the court, by a 2–1 vote, enforced an award even though the arbitrator relied on language that was not in the collective bargaining agreement. The grievance alleged that the employer violated the contract when it refused to allow an employee whose position was abolished to bump less senior employees within the bargaining unit but outside her classification. The arbitrator sustained the grievance. In an opinion accompanying the award, the arbitrator wrote, "The Company urges that the contract does not confer bumping rights. Although the contract does not expressly provide for bumping, Article 10, seniority, states, in part, 'Employees who exercise seniority rights and bump must have the skill, qualifications, ability and physical fitness to perform all of the work remaining in that classification.'" In fact, the contract contained no such language, although it did define seniority as the total amount of time an employee had been employed in the bargaining unit and the arbitrator also relied on the bargaining unit-wide definition of seniority in finding bumping rights. The majority considered this latter discussion as "alone provid[ing] ample basis to uphold the award." The dissent criticized the majority, "To forgive the arbitrator's Humpty Dumpty approach to the specific provision in play by

referring to a general statement on seniority is akin to decreeing that the general call for mercy expiates the specific commandment not to kill." Which do you regard as the better view?

4.   The "draws its essence from the collective bargaining agreement" test is the most deferential standard of review known in the law. Occasionally, however, courts find arbitrators crossed the line and dispensed their own brand of industrial justice. For example, in *Amax Coal Co. v. United Mine Workers*, 92 F.3d 571 (7th Cir. 1996), the contract provided that draglines would be staffed by an operator, an oiler, a groundman and "at least one additional Employee who shall be an operator, oiler, groundman or a mechanic, electrician or welder." The employer for many years used an oiler as the extra employee but changed to a welder to reduce the time it took to make repairs requiring welding. The oiler who had been the extra employee was unable to qualify as a welder and transferred in accordance with his seniority to another position that paid less than an oiler. The arbitrator upheld the employer's right to replace the oiler with a welder but ordered the employer to continue to pay the displaced employee as an oiler. The court, finding no provision in the contract that arguably supported the order, concluded that the arbitrator dispensed his own brand of industrial justice and vacated the award.

MAJOR LEAGUE BASEBALL PLAYERS ASSOCIATION V. GARVEY
532 U.S. 504 (2001)

PER CURIAM:

In the late 1980's, petitioner Major League Baseball Players Association (Association) filed grievances against the Major League Baseball Clubs (Clubs), claiming the Clubs had colluded in the market for free-agent services after the 1985, 1986, and 1987 baseball seasons, in violation of the industry's collective-bargaining agreement. A free agent is a player who may contract with any Club, rather than one whose right to contract is restricted to a particular Club. In a series of decisions, arbitrators found collusion by the Clubs and damage to the players. The Association and Clubs subsequently entered into a Global Settlement Agreement (Agreement), pursuant to which the Clubs established a $280 million fund to be distributed to injured players. The Association also designed a "Framework" to evaluate the individual player's claims, and, applying that Framework, recommended distribution plans for claims relating to a particular season or seasons.

The Framework provided that players could seek an arbitrator's review of the distribution plan. The arbitrator would determine "only whether the approved Framework and the criteria set forth therein have been properly applied in the proposed Distribution Plan." The Framework set forth factors to be considered in evaluating players' claims, as well as specific requirements for lost contract-extension claims. Such claims were cognizable "only in those cases where evidence exists that a specific offer of an extension was made by a club prior to collusion only to thereafter be withdrawn when the collusion scheme was initiated."

Respondent Steve Garvey, a retired, highly regarded first baseman, submitted a claim for damages of approximately $3 million. He alleged that his contract with the San Diego Padres was not extended to the 1988 and 1989 seasons due to collusion. The Association rejected Garvey's claim in February 1996, because he presented no evidence that the Padres actually offered to extend his contract. Garvey objected, and an arbitration hearing was held. He testified that the Padres offered to extend his contract for the 1988 and 1989 seasons and then withdrew the offer after they began colluding with other teams. He presented a June 1996 letter from Ballard Smith, Padres' President and CEO from 1979 to 1987, stating that, before the end of the 1985 season, Smith offered to extend Garvey's contract through the 1989 season, but that the Padres refused to negotiate with Garvey thereafter due to collusion.

The arbitrator denied Garvey's claim, after seeking additional documentation from the parties. In his award, he explained that "[t]here exists . . . substantial doubt as to the credibility of the statements in the Smith letter." He noted the "stark contradictions" between the 1996 letter and Smith's testimony in the earlier arbitration proceedings regarding collusion, where Smith, like other owners, denied collusion and stated that the Padres simply were not interested in extending Garvey's contract. The arbitrator determined that, due to these contradictions, he "must reject [Smith's] more recent assertion that Garvey did not receive [a contract] extension" due to collusion, and found that Garvey had not shown a specific offer of extension.

Garvey moved in Federal District Court to vacate the arbitrator's award, alleging that the arbitrator violated the Framework by denying his claim. The District Court denied the motion. The Court of Appeals for the Ninth Circuit reversed by a divided vote. The court acknowledged that judicial review of an arbitrator's decision in a labor dispute is extremely limited. But it held that review of the merits of the arbitrator's award was warranted in this case, because the arbitrator "dispensed his own brand of industrial justice." The court recognized that Smith's prior testimony with respect to collusion conflicted with the statements in his 1996 letter. But in the court's view, the arbitrator's refusal to credit Smith's letter was "inexplicable" and "border[ed] on the irrational," because a panel of arbitrators, chaired by the arbitrator involved here, had previously concluded that the owners' prior testimony was false. The court rejected the arbitrator's reliance on the absence of other corroborating evidence, attributing that fact to Smith and Garvey's direct negotiations. The court also found that the record provided "strong support" for the truthfulness of

Smith's 1996 letter. The Court of Appeals reversed and remanded with directions to vacate the award.

The District Court then remanded the case to the arbitration panel for further hearings, and Garvey appealed. The Court of Appeals, again by a divided vote, explained that "the conclusion that Smith made Garvey an offer and subsequently withdrew it because of the collusion scheme was the only conclusion that the arbitrator could draw from the record in the proceedings." Noting that its prior instructions might have been unclear, the court clarified that "our holding contemplated an award in Garvey's favor." The Court of Appeals reversed the District Court and directed that it remand the case to the arbitration panel with instructions to enter an award for Garvey in the amount he claimed.

Judicial review of a labor-arbitration decision pursuant to such an agreement is very limited. Courts are not authorized to review the arbitrator's decision on the merits despite allegations that the decision rests on factual errors or misinterprets the parties' agreement. *Paperworkers v. Misco, Inc.*, 484 U.S. 29, 36 (1987). We recently reiterated that if an " 'arbitrator is even arguably construing or applying the contract and acting within the scope of his authority,' the fact that 'a court is convinced he committed serious error does not suffice to overturn his decision.' " *E. Associated Coal Corp. v. Mine Workers*, 531 U.S. 57, 62 (2000). It is only when the arbitrator strays from interpretation and application of the agreement and effectively "dispense[s] his own brand of industrial justice" that his decision may be unenforceable. *Steelworkers v. Enter. Wheel & Car Corp.* When an arbitrator resolves disputes regarding the application of a contract, and no dishonesty is alleged, the arbitrator's "improvident, even silly, factfinding" does not provide a basis for a reviewing court to refuse to enforce the award. *Misco,* 484 U.S., at 39.

In discussing the courts' limited role in reviewing the merits of arbitration awards, we have stated that "courts . . . have no business weighing the merits of the grievance [or] considering whether there is equity in a particular claim." When the judiciary does so, "it usurps a function which . . . is entrusted to the arbitration tribunal." It is the arbitrator's construction [of the agreement] which was bargained for." Consistent with this limited role, we said in *Misco* that "[e]ven in the very rare instances when an arbitrator's procedural aberrations rise to the level of affirmative misconduct, as a rule the court must not foreclose further proceedings by settling the merits according to its own judgment of the appropriate result." That step, we explained, "would improperly substitute a judicial determination for the arbitrator's decision that the parties bargained for" in their agreement. Instead, the court should "simply vacate the award, thus leaving open the possibility of further proceedings if they are permitted under the terms of the agreement."

To be sure, the Court of Appeals here recited these principles, but its application of them is nothing short of baffling. The substance of the court's discussion reveals that it overturned the arbitrator's decision because it disagreed with the arbitrator's factual findings, particularly those with respect to credibility. The Court of Appeals, it appears, would have credited Smith's 1996 letter, and found the arbitrator's refusal to do so at worst "irrational" and at best "bizarre." But even "serious error" on the arbitrator's part does not justify overturning his decision, where, as here, he is construing a contract and acting within the scope of his authority.

The Court of Appeals both rejected the arbitrator's findings and went further, resolving the merits of the parties' dispute based on the court's assessment of the record before the arbitrator. For that reason, the court found further arbitration proceedings inappropriate. But again, established law ordinarily precludes a court from resolving the merits of the parties' dispute on the basis of its own factual determinations, no matter how erroneous the arbitrator's decision. Even when the arbitrator's award may properly be vacated, the appropriate remedy is to remand the case for further arbitration proceedings. The Court of Appeals usurped the arbitrator's role by resolving the dispute and barring further proceedings, a result at odds with this governing law.

JUSTICE STEVENS, dissenting:

It is well settled that an arbitrator "does not sit to dispense his own brand of industrial justice." Our cases, however, do not provide significant guidance as to what standards a federal court should use in assessing whether an arbitrator's behavior is so untethered to either the agreement of the parties or the factual record so as to constitute an attempt to "dispense his own brand of industrial justice." Nor, more importantly, do they tell us how, having made such a finding, courts should deal with "the extraordinary circumstance in which the arbitrator's own rulings make clear that, more than being simply erroneous, his finding is completely inexplicable and borders on the irrational." Because our case law is not sufficiently clear to allow me to conclude that the case below was wrongly decided—let alone to conclude that the decision was so wrong as to require the extraordinary remedy of a summary reversal—I dissent from the Court's disposition of this petition.

NOTES

1. May a court refuse to enforce an arbitrator's award where, in the language of Justice Stevens' dissent, the arbitrator's "finding is completely inexplicable and borders on the irrational?" Is there a difference between "silly" factfinding which is not a basis for vacating an award and "irrational" factfinding?

2. Enderby Industries discharged Sally Jones for excessive absenteeism. The union grieved her discharge, claiming that the company

lacked just cause. Just prior to arbitration, the parties settled the grievance, with the employer agreeing to reinstate Ms. Jones, "effective October 29 on a 'last chance' basis whereunder she will be required to maintain an acceptable attendance level and will be terminated in the event she is absent, for any reason whatsoever including illness, more than one day per month for the first six months following her reinstatement." Ms. Jones had obtained other employment and asked if she could give her other employer two weeks' notice before returning to her job at Enderby. Enderby agreed and Ms. Jones returned on November 12. On April 26, she was absent because she overslept. On May 5, she was absent because her child was too sick to attend school and she was unable to find childcare. Enderby discharged her for having two absences within one month, the union grieved and ultimately an arbitrator sustained the grievance and ordered Enderby to reinstate Ms. Jones with back pay. If Enderby refuses to comply with the award on the ground that the award conflicts with the last chance agreement, will a court enforce it? Does the arbitrator's rationale determine the outcome of the lawsuit? What if the arbitrator held that the six months began to run on October 29 and the May 5 absence fell outside of the six-month period? What if the arbitrator determined that Ms. Jones did not have more than one absence per month, even though the two absences fell within nine days of each other? What if the arbitrator found that Enderby routinely excused employees for absences due to ill children and held that it should have excused the May 5 absence? *See Tootsie Roll Indus., Inc. v. Local 1, Bakery, Confectionary & Tobacco Workers Int'l Union*, 832 F.2d 81 (7th Cir. 1987).

In *Associated Electric Cooperative, Inc. v. IBEW Local 53*, 751 F.3d 898 (8th Cir. 2014), an employee was selected for a random drug test. After providing a urine sample, the employee told the plant manager that he would test positive because he had smoked marijuana recently with family members while attending a funeral. The plant manager offered him union representation but he declined. He then signed the employer's standard last chance agreement (LCA) under which he agreed to undergo rehabilitation and that any future positive drug test would result in termination. The employer suspended the employee without pay until he would be cleared for return to work by the rehabilitation program. Later, the drug test came back negative.

Subsequently, the rehabilitation program cleared the employee to return to work but in his return to work drug test, he tested positive for a benzodiazepine drug that was different from the benzodiazepine that he was taking pursuant to a prescription. The union grieved the discharge, the arbitrator sustained the grievance and awarded that the employee be reinstated with back pay to the date he was initially suspended. The district court held that the award conflicted with the LCA and vacated it but the Eighth Circuit reversed. The Eighth Circuit distinguished its prior ruling in *Coca Cola Bottling Co. v. Teamsters Local 688*, 959 F.2d 1438 (8th Cir. 1992), which had vacated an arbitration award that conflicted with an LCA which had been agreed to by an employee, his union and the employer. The court distinguished the instant LCA on two grounds: 1. It had not been negotiated with the union and 2. It could be rescinded for mutual mistake because the employer and employee both believed that the employee would test positive at the time they entered into it.

3.   In *Northern States Power Co. v. International Brotherhood of Electrical Workers Local 160*, 711 F.3d 900 (8th Cir. 2013), the collective bargaining agreement required just cause for discharge. Northern States Power discharged an employee when it learned that the employee had been convicted of possession of child pornography and sentenced to probation with a condition of probation that he have no contact with a minor. Northern States Power determined that it could not guarantee that the employee would not in the course of his duties have contact with a minor. The arbitrator ordered the employee reinstated without back pay, reasoning that management "demonstrated justification for their decision" but adding that "the Union has presented convincing evidence which set forth a number of factors that existed which ultimately favor the imposition of" a lesser penalty. The court, by 2–1 vote, vacated the award. The majority concluded that the arbitrator implicitly found just cause for the employee's discharge and lacked authority to order his reinstatement. The dissent argued that the arbitrator did not find just cause and that the award should be enforced. Might the arbitrator have better crafted the award and avoided vacatur? If so, what does this suggest?

4.   In *Hamilton Park Health Ctr., Ltd. v. 1199 SEIU Health Care Workers East*, 817 F.3d 857 (3d Cir. 2016), the collective bargaining agreement ran through February 28, 2013 but allowed the union to reopen it in November 2011 for the final year of the contract. It further provided that if the parties did not reach agreement by February 28, 2012, the union could submit any dispute over the new terms to binding interest arbitration, i.e. arbitration to determine the terms of the new contract. The parties submitted disputes over, *inter alia*, wages and health insurance contributions to arbitration. The arbitrator issued an award that covered the period February 28, 2012 through June 2016. It provided for a two percentage point increase in employer contributions to health insurance at the outset and another 3.5 percentage point increase in March 2014. It also provided that in the final year of the contract the union could reopen it and submit any matters on which agreement could not be reached to interest arbitration.

The employer sought to vacate the award, arguing that the arbitrator exceeded his authority by imposing an award that went beyond February 28, 2013, and by imposing interest arbitration if the parties were unable to reach agreement should the union reopen the contract in its final year. The court rejected the first argument but agreed with the second.

The court agreed that the collective bargaining agreement only authorized a reopening, and thus restricted arbitrator authority, with respect to the terms for its final year, February 28, 2012–February 28, 2013. But the court accepted the arbitrator's findings that both parties consented to his issuing a multi-year award.

With respect to the interest arbitration provision, however, the court found that the employer never consented to that. The court also opined that without employer consent, the interest arbitration portion of the award was contrary to the NLRA. Under the NLRA, resort to interest arbitration is a permissive subject of bargaining. Consequently, the court reasoned, the employer had no duty to bargain over the inclusion of interest arbitration for the final year of the multi-year award, and thus the arbitrator had no authority to award it. The court expressed concern that "[i]f an arbitrator, once empowered to decide a particular dispute, could then require all future disputes to be arbitrated, a party that has once agreed to a limited arbitration provision could forever be held hostage to it."

5.   Should a court, and if so under what circumstances, vacate an arbitration award because of arbitrator bias? This issue played a key role in judicial review of the four game suspension that NFL Commissioner Roger Goodell imposed on New England Patriots quarterback Tom Brady resulting from the use of under-inflated footballs in the 2015 AFC championship game. Following an investigation, Goodell determined that Brady was involved in "deflategate" and imposed the suspension for engaging in "conduct detrimental to the integrity and public confidence in the game of professional football."

Pursuant to Article 46, Section 1(a) of the NFL's collective bargaining agreement with the NFL Players Association, Brady and the NFLPA appealed the decision to the Commissioner. The NFL-NFLPA contract expressly provided for such appeals and for the Commissioner to name a hearing officer to hear the appeal. Commissioner Goodell appointed himself to hear the appeal, a move expressly authorized in Article 46. Following a hearing, Goodell affirmed the suspension.

Brady and the NFLPA sued to vacate Goodell's decision. The U.S. District Court for the Southern District of New York agreed with them and vacated the decision. U.S. District Judge Richard Berman ruled that under the common law of the workplace as it developed under the NFL-NFLPA agreement, a player's failure to cooperate in an investigation was not grounds for a suspension. Judge Berman further ruled that Brady did not have sufficient notice that complicity in deflating footballs in a conference championship game could result in a suspension, rather than a fine. He criticized Commissioner Goodell's analogy of Brady's conduct to a player's use of prohibited steroids which also commanded a four game suspension for a first offense. He faulted Goodell for not allowing Brady and the NFLPA to call NFL Executive Vice President and General Counsel Jeff Pash as a witness and for not affording Brady access to the NFL's investigator's notes of witness interviews. He vacated the Goodell decision.

The U.S. Court of Appeals for the Second Circuit, by 2–1 vote, reversed. *National Football League v. National Football League Players Ass'n*, 820 F.3d 528 (2d Cir. 2016). The appeals court majority viewed the matter as calling for a straight forward application of well-established law governing judicial review of labor arbitration awards. The court regarded its role as "simply ensur[ing] that the arbitrator [Goodell] was 'even arguably construing or applying the contact and acting within the scope of his authority.'" The court observed that Goodell's "authority was especially broad. The Commissioner was authorized to impose discipline for, among other things, 'conduct detrimental to the integrity of, or public confidence, in the game of professional football.' In their collective bargaining agreement, the players and the League mutually decided many years ago that the Commissioner should investigate possible rules violations, should impose appropriate sanctions, and may preside at arbitrations challenging his discipline. Although this tripartite regime may appear somewhat unorthodox, it is the regime bargained for and agreed upon by the parties, which we can only presume they determined was mutually satisfactory."

Viewed in this light, the decision was an easy one. District Judge Berman clearly overstepped his role. He determined that Brady should have been allowed to call a witness and should have been given access to certain files but such procedural determinations are for the arbitrator to make and not the court. Judge Berman also determined that the NFL-NFLPA agreement, as interpreted in prior discipline cases, did not support the four-day suspension but here too, he intruded on the authority of the arbitrator.

What is controversial about the Brady case is that the arbitrator (or "hearing officer" in the language of the NFL-NFLPA agreement) was Commissioner Goodell, the same person who imposed the discipline that was the subject of the arbitration appeal. We usually expect an arbitrator to be a neutral who had nothing to do with the decision under review. The Code of Professional Responsibility for Arbitrators of Labor-Management Disputes expressly provides, "If the arbitrator believes or perceives that there is a clear conflict of interest, the arbitrator should withdraw, irrespective of the expressed desires of the parties."

The Second Circuit majority did not see the Commissioner's role reviewing the discipline that he imposed as a basis for vacating his award. The court wrote, "[A]rbitration is a matter of contract, and consequently, the parties to an arbitration can ask for no more impartiality than inheres in the method they have chosen. . . . Here the parties contracted . . . to specifically allow the Commissioner to sit as the arbitrator in all disputes brought pursuant to Article 46, Section 1(a). They did so knowing full well that the Commissioner had the sole power of determining what constitutes 'conduct detrimental,' and thus knowing that the Commissioner would have a stake both in the underlying discipline and in every arbitration brought pursuant to Section 1(a). Had the parties wished to restrict the Commissioner's authority, they could have fashioned a different agreement."

The Eighth Circuit followed the Second Circuit's approach in *National Football League Players Ass'n v. National Football League*, 831 F.3d 985 (8th Cir. 2016). The court enforced the decision of commissioner-appointed hearing officer Harold Henderson who had previously served for 16 years as the league's vice-president for labor relations. Henderson had upheld the commissioner's imposition of a suspension and fine equal to six games' pay on Minnesota Vikings running back Adrian Peterson after Peterson pled nolo contendere to misdemeanor reckless assault on one of his children,

* * *

In *Garvey*, the Ninth Circuit appeared to be appalled by the inconsistency between the arbitrator's credibility findings in the Garvey arbitration and his credibility findings in a prior proceeding. Courts more often are outraged by the results arbitrators reach rather than their factual findings. Under what circumstances should such outrage justify a refusal to enforce the award? If the award orders a party to do something illegal, such as discriminate on the basis of race, there is general agreement that the award violates public policy and a court should vacate it. What if the award orders something that the court considers irrational and injurious to the public, although not literally illegal, such as an award ordering a bus company to reinstate a driver discharged for driving under the influence of alcohol and causing an accident?

EASTERN ASSOCIATED COAL CO. v. UNITED MINE WORKERS
531 U.S. 57 (2000)

JUSTICE BREYER delivered the opinion of the Court:

Petitioner, Eastern Associated Coal Corp., and respondent, United Mine Workers of America, are parties to a collective-bargaining agreement with arbitration provisions. The agreement specifies that, in arbitration, in order to discharge an employee, Eastern must prove it has "just cause." Otherwise the arbitrator will order the employee reinstated. The arbitrator's decision is final.

James Smith worked for Eastern as a member of a road crew, a job that required him to drive heavy truck-like vehicles on public highways. As a truck driver, Smith was subject to Department of Transportation (DOT) regulations requiring random drug testing of workers engaged in "safety-sensitive" tasks. In March 1996, Smith tested positive for marijuana. Eastern sought to discharge Smith. The union went to arbitration, and the arbitrator concluded that Smith's positive drug test did not amount to "just cause" for discharge. Instead the arbitrator ordered Smith's reinstatement, provided that Smith (1) accept a suspension of 30 days without pay, (2) participate in a substance-abuse program, and (3) undergo drug tests at the discretion of Eastern (or an approved substance-abuse professional) for the next five years.

Between April 1996 and January 1997, Smith passed four random drug tests. But in July 1997 he again tested positive for marijuana. Eastern again sought to discharge Smith. The union again went to arbitration, and the arbitrator again concluded that Smith's use of marijuana did not amount to "just cause" for discharge, in light of two mitigating circumstances. First, Smith had been a good employee for 17 years. And, second, Smith had made a credible and "very personal appeal under oath

. . . concerning a personal/family problem which caused this one time lapse in drug usage."

The arbitrator ordered Smith's reinstatement provided that Smith (1) accept a new suspension without pay, this time for slightly more than three months; (2) reimburse Eastern and the union for the costs of both arbitration proceedings; (3) continue to participate in a substance-abuse program; (4) continue to undergo random drug testing; and (5) provide Eastern with a signed, undated letter of resignation, to take effect if Smith again tested positive within the next five years.

Eastern claims that considerations of public policy make the arbitration award unenforceable. In considering this claim, we must assume that the collective-bargaining agreement itself calls for Smith's reinstatement. That is because both employer and union have granted to the arbitrator the authority to interpret the meaning of their contract's language, including such words as "just cause." They have "bargained for" the "arbitrator's construction" of their agreement." Of course, an arbitrator's award "must draw its essence from the contract and cannot simply reflect the arbitrator's own notions of industrial justice." "But as long as [an honest] arbitrator is even arguably construing or applying the contract and acting within the scope of his authority," the fact that "a court is convinced he committed serious error does not suffice to overturn his decision." Eastern does not claim here that the arbitrator acted outside the scope of his contractually delegated authority. Hence we must treat the arbitrator's award as if it represented an agreement between Eastern and the union as to the proper meaning of the contract's words "just cause."

We must then decide whether a contractual reinstatement requirement would fall within the legal exception that makes unenforceable "a collective-bargaining agreement that is contrary to public policy." Any such public policy must be "explicit," "well defined," and "dominant." It must be "ascertained 'by reference to the laws and legal precedents and not from general considerations of supposed public interests.'" And, of course, the question to be answered is not whether Smith's drug use itself violates public policy, but whether the agreement to reinstate him does so. To put the question more specifically, does a contractual agreement to reinstate Smith with specified conditions run contrary to an explicit, well-defined, and dominant public policy, as ascertained by reference to positive law and not from general considerations of supposed public interests?

Eastern initially argues that the District Court erred by asking, not whether the award is "contrary to" public policy "as ascertained by reference" to positive law, but whether the award "violates" positive law, a standard Eastern says is too narrow. We agree, in principle, that courts' authority to invoke the public policy exception is not limited solely to instances where the arbitration award itself violates positive law.

Nevertheless, the public policy exception is narrow. Moreover, in a case like the one before us, where two political branches have created a detailed regulatory regime in a specific field, courts should approach with particular caution pleas to divine further public policy in that area.

Eastern asserts that a public policy against reinstatement of workers who use drugs can be discerned from an examination of that regulatory regime, which consists of the Omnibus Transportation Employee Testing Act of 1991 and DOT's implementing regulations. The Testing Act embodies a congressional finding that "the greatest efforts must be expended to eliminate the . . . use of illegal drugs, whether on or off duty, by those individuals who are involved in [certain safety-sensitive positions, including] the operation of . . . trucks." The Act adds that "increased testing" is the "most effective deterrent" to "use of illegal drugs." It requires the Secretary of Transportation to promulgate regulations requiring "testing of operators of commercial motor vehicles for the use of a controlled substance." It mandates suspension of those operators who have driven a commercial motor vehicle while under the influence of drugs. And DOT's implementing regulations set forth sanctions applicable to those who test positive for illegal drugs.

In Eastern's view, these provisions embody a strong public policy against drug use by transportation workers in safety-sensitive positions and in favor of random drug testing in order to detect that use. Eastern argues that reinstatement of a driver who has twice failed random drug tests would undermine that policy—to the point where a judge must set aside an employer-union agreement requiring reinstatement.

Eastern's argument, however, loses much of its force when one considers further provisions of the Act that make clear that the Act's remedial aims are complex. The Act says that "rehabilitation is a critical component of any testing program," that rehabilitation "should be made available to individuals, as appropriate," and that DOT must promulgate regulations for "rehabilitation programs." The DOT regulations specifically state that a driver who has tested positive for drugs cannot return to a safety-sensitive position until (1) the driver has been evaluated by a "substance abuse professional" to determine if treatment is needed, (2) the substance-abuse professional has certified that the driver has followed any rehabilitation program prescribed, and (3) the driver has passed a return-to-duty drug test. In addition, (4) the driver must be subject to at least six random drug tests during the first year after returning to the job. Neither the Act nor the regulations forbid an employer to reinstate in a safety-sensitive position an employee who fails a random drug test once or twice. The congressional and regulatory directives require only that the above-stated prerequisites to reinstatement be met.

Moreover, when promulgating these regulations, DOT decided not to require employers either to provide rehabilitation or to "hold a job open for a driver" who has tested positive, on the basis that such decisions "should be left to management/driver negotiation." That determination reflects basic background labor law principles, which caution against interference with labor-management agreements about appropriate employee discipline.

We believe that these expressions of positive law embody several relevant policies. As Eastern points out, these policies include Testing Act policies against drug use by employees in safety-sensitive transportation positions and in favor of drug testing. They also include a Testing Act policy favoring rehabilitation of employees who use drugs. And the relevant statutory and regulatory provisions must be read in light of background labor law policy that favors determination of disciplinary questions through arbitration when chosen as a result of labor-management negotiation.

The award before us is not contrary to these several policies, taken together. The award does not condone Smith's conduct or ignore the risk to public safety that drug use by truck drivers may pose. Rather, the award punishes Smith by suspending him for three months, thereby depriving him of nearly $9,000 in lost wages, it requires him to pay the arbitration costs of both sides; it insists upon further substance-abuse treatment and testing; and it makes clear (by requiring Smith to provide a signed letter of resignation) that one more failed test means discharge.

The award violates no specific provision of any law or regulation. It is consistent with DOT rules requiring completion of substance-abuse treatment before returning to work, for it does not preclude Eastern from assigning Smith to a non-safety-sensitive position until Smith completes the prescribed treatment program. It is consistent with the Testing Act's 1-year and 10-year driving license suspension requirements, for those requirements apply only to drivers who, unlike Smith, actually operated vehicles under the influence of drugs. The award is also consistent with the Act's rehabilitative concerns, for it requires substance-abuse treatment and testing before Smith can return to work.

The fact that Smith is a recidivist—that he has failed drug tests twice—is not sufficient to tip the balance in Eastern's favor. The award punishes Smith more severely for his second lapse. And that more severe punishment, which included a 90-day suspension, would have satisfied even a "recidivist" rule that DOT once proposed but did not adopt—a rule that would have punished two failed drug tests, not with discharge, but with a driving suspension of 60 days.

We recognize that reasonable people can differ as to whether reinstatement or discharge is the more appropriate remedy here. But both employer and union have agreed to entrust this remedial decision to an arbitrator. We cannot find in the Act, the regulations, or any other law or legal precedent an "explicit," "well defined," "dominant" public policy to which the arbitrator's decision "runs contrary." We conclude that the lower courts correctly rejected Eastern's public policy claim.

JUSTICE SCALIA, with whom JUSTICE THOMAS joins, concurring in the judgment:

I concur in the Court's judgment, because I agree that no public policy prevents the reinstatement of James Smith to his position as a truck driver, so long as he complies with the arbitrator's decision, and with those requirements set out in the Department of Transportation's regulations. I do not endorse, however, the Court's statement that "[w]e agree, in principle, that courts' authority to invoke the public policy exception is not limited solely to instances where the arbitration award itself violates positive law." No case is cited to support that proposition, and none could be. There is not a single decision, since this Court washed its hands of general common-lawmaking authority in which we have refused to enforce on "public policy" grounds an agreement that did not violate, or provide for the violation of, some positive law.

After its dictum opening the door to flaccid public policy arguments of the sort presented by petitioner here, the Court immediately posts a giant "Do Not Enter" sign. "[T]he public policy exception," it says, must satisfy the principles which require that the applicable public policy be "explicit," "well defined," "dominant," and "ascertained 'by reference to the laws and legal precedents and not from general considerations of supposed public interests.'" It is hard to imagine how an arbitration award could violate a public policy, identified in this fashion, without actually conflicting with positive law. If such an award could ever exist, it would surely be so rare that the benefit of preserving the courts' ability to deal with it is far outweighed by the confusion and uncertainty, and hence the obstructive litigation, that the Court's Delphic "agree[ment] in principle" will engender.

The problem with judicial intuition of a public policy that goes beyond the actual prohibitions of the law is that there is no way of knowing whether the apparent gaps in the law are intentional or inadvertent. The final form of a statute or regulation, especially in the regulated fields where the public policy doctrine is likely to rear its head, is often the result of compromise among various interest groups, resulting in a decision to go so far and no farther. One can, of course, summon up a parade of horribles, such as an arbitration award ordering an airline to reinstate an alcoholic pilot who somehow escapes being grounded by force of law. But it seems to me we set our face against judicial correction of the omissions of the political branches when we declined the power to define common-law offenses. Surely the power to invalidate a contract providing for actions that are not contrary to law (but "ought" to be) is less important to the public welfare than the power to prohibit harmful acts that are not contrary to law (but "ought" to be). And it is also less efficacious, since it depends upon the willingness of one of the parties to the contract to *assert* the public policy interest. (If the airline is not terribly concerned about reinstating an alcoholic pilot, the courts will have no opportunity to prevent the reinstatement.) The horribles that can be imagined—if they are really so horrible and ever come to pass—can readily be corrected by Congress or the agency, with no problem of retroactivity. Supervening law is always grounds for the dissolution of a contractual obligation.

NOTES

1.   If the statute and regulations did not reflect a policy favoring rehabilitation of employees, should the Court have enforced the award? What if the arbitrator had not punished Smith more severely for his second offense than for the first?

2.   In his concurring opinion, Justice Scalia speaks sarcastically about summoning up a parade of horribles such as an award reinstating an alcoholic pilot. Arbitrators have reinstated pilots who violated airline and Federal Aviation Authority regulations on pre-flight alcohol consumption. In cases decided before *Eastern Associated Coal*, courts divided over whether to enforce those awards. *Compare Delta Airlines, Inc. v. Air Line Pilots Ass'n*, 861 F.2d 665 (11th Cir. 1988) (holding that award overturning discharge of airline pilot who flew plane while intoxicated and ordering airline to provide pilot with rehabilitation was contrary to public policy but enforcing order that airline pay for pilot's rehabilitation) *with Northwest Airlines, Inc. v. Air Line Pilots Ass'n*, 808 F.2d 76 (D.C. Cir. 1987) (finding award overturning discharge of pilot who operated airplane under the influence of alcohol not contrary to public policy). Has the Court's decision in *Eastern Associated Coal* resolved the split in the circuits over the enforcement of awards reinstating pilots who operated planes under the influence?

3.   In *National Railroad Passenger Corp. v. Fraternal Order of Police, Lodge 189*, 855 F.3d 335 (D.C. Cir. 2017), the D.C. Circuit by a 2 to 1 vote vacated an arbitration award in favor of an Amtrak employee as contrary to public policy.

Amtrak is a "designated federal entity" subject to the Inspector General Act. The collective bargaining agreement covering Amtrak police officers gave officers under investigation a right to delay questioning to have a union representative present, to be given *Miranda* warnings if the officer is suspected of criminal activity and to have the interrogation recorded mechanically or by a stenographer. Both the Amtrak Police Department's Internal Affairs Unit and the Amtrak Inspector General received anonymous tips that a police officer jointly owned a home with her supervisor and was receiving favored treatment in the assignment of higher paid assignments. The Internal Affairs Unit interviewed the officer, complied with the collective bargaining agreement provision governing interrogations and closed its investigation without taking action. A few months later, an Inspector General investigator interviewed the officer, did not give her the required statement of her right to have a union representative present and did not record the interrogation. The Inspector General concluded that the officer lied in her earlier interview with Internal Affairs, and had falsified an affidavit claiming a tax exemption for first-time home buyers. After receiving the Inspector General's report, Amtrak fired the police officer. She grieved and her union processed the grievance to arbitration.

The arbitrator sustained the grievance and awarded reinstatement with full back pay because the Inspector General had not complied with the contractual restrictions on interrogations. The majority vacated the award as being in conflict with the Inspector General Act. The court accepted the arbitrator's interpretation that the contractual restrictions on interrogations applied to Inspector General interviews but held that as so interpreted, the contract conflicted with the Inspector General Act and was unenforceable. The majority held that a contract may not add to or subtract from an inspector general's investigative authority under the Act.

The dissent would have enforced the arbitration award. The dissent agreed that the arbitrator's reasoning that the contract applied to the Inspector General conflicted with the Act but argued that the issue for the court was whether the award itself and not the reasoning was contrary to public policy. In the dissent's view, the award, which reinstated the officer because her discharge was based on an interrogation in which she was not afforded her procedural right, did not require the Inspector General to bargain with the union and did not impose on the Inspector General a duty to comply with the collective bargaining agreement. It only precluded Amtrak from relying on an interrogation that did not comply with the contract's procedural protections to terminate an employee. Which view is more consistent with the majority opinion in *Eastern Associated Coal*? With Justice Scalia's concurring opinion?

3. A GLIMPSE AT ARBITRAL COMMON LAW

Arbitrators are selected jointly by the union and employer. Some parties have agreed in advance on a list of arbitrators that they will use for all of their grievances. Others select their arbitrators on an ad hoc basis for each case. They may mutually agree on a specific individual to hear a particular case or they may request a list of arbitrators from an arbitrator-appointing agency. The most common arbitrator-appointing agencies are the American Arbitration Association and the Federal Mediation and Conciliation Service. State government labor relations agencies also often provide lists of arbitrators. Parties use different methods to narrow the list to a single arbitrator, such as alternately striking names from the list or simultaneously ranking the names on the list.

A good portion of many labor lawyers' practices involves representing unions or employers in grievance arbitration. A thorough review of what the Court has called the common law of the shop is beyond the scope of this book. However, it is useful to explore a brief sample of the types of decisions to which courts routinely defer. Reproduced below are three representative awards, one involving the subcontracting of bargaining unit work and two involving discharges.

UNIROYAL, INC.[1]

76 Lab. Arb. (BNA) 1049 (1981)
(Dennis R. Nolan, Arbitrator)

Janitorial work at Uniroyal's Winnsboro plants has been divided up for many years between bargaining unit and non-unit employees and outside contractors. Prior to March 1, 1981, three bargaining unit employees, out of 25 employees in the maintenance department and 600 in the bargaining unit as a whole, did janitorial work in the plant area.

In early February, the three bargaining unit employees who had been performing janitorial work were informed that their jobs would be terminated as of March 1 and they would be laid off because their work was being subcontracted. Shortly thereafter, a company official reported to J. L. Dorrier, Industrial Relations Manager, that subcontracting would result in savings of over $11,000 per year.

The Union protested the Employer's plans and filed the instant grievance on February 24. Union and Employer representatives discussed the question at least once before March 1, but the Union did not offer any cost-saving alternatives and the Employer went ahead with the subcontracting arrangement.

[T]he problem to be resolved is this: in the absence of any express contractual prohibition, may the Employer subcontract bargaining unit work to save a substantial amount of money, if doing so requires layoffs?

This issue is a recurring one in labor arbitrations and it has been the source of much commentary. Without belaboring those fine discussions, suffice it to say that they offer a few general rules, a great many overlapping and sometimes contradictory guidelines, and far too many arbitration awards on both sides of the question to be of much help in resolving it.

Let us begin with the few general rules. Apart from partisan briefs, virtually all authorities agree that absent some explicit contractual prohibition management retains broad authority to subcontract work. Common sense tells us as much, else why would so many unions strive so vigorously to impose explicit contractual limitations on subcontracting? Similarly, virtually all authorities agree that even a silent contract imposes some limitations on management's freedom to subcontract. To take an extreme example, no one would seriously contend that immediately after signing a collective bargaining agreement an employer could lay off all

---

[1]   Reproduced with permission from Labor Relations Reporter-Labor Arbitration Reports, 76 LA 1049–1054. Copyright 1981 by The Bureau of National Affairs, Inc. (800-372-1033) http://www.bna.com.

employees and hire a subcontractor to perform all bargaining unit work simply to escape the burdens of the collective agreement.

Those then are the general rules. Now as to the guidelines. There are almost as many of these as there are arbitrators. Two cases cited by the Union boil the relevant factors down to five, but they are not the same five.

At the risk of simply adding another list to those already given, it seems to me that all of the cases in this area attempt to strike a fair balance by looking at three things: (1) the type of work subcontracted; (2) the reasons for and conditions of the subcontracting; and (3) the impact of the subcontracting on the bargaining unit and its members.

[T]here is no certainty in this area, no absolute truth. The most an arbitrator can do is to make a careful examination of the contract and the facts and try to render a decision which protects the Union's side of the bargain without depriving the Employer of its side.

(1) The type of work subcontracted. Janitorial work, to judge by the reported cases, is more often subcontracted than any other, and with good reason. It is usually not the primary object of the business, it is not an essential part of that business and it can often be done better and cheaper by outside specialists.

(2) The reasons for and conditions of the subcontracting. Numerous cases permit subcontracting for substantial reasons, particularly [if] the conditions of the subcontracting impose no harm and pose no threat to the Union. Neither of these conditions is present here, however. The Employer's true reason was simply an economic one: the collective bargaining agreement was costly and that burden could be reduced by subcontracting. In short, this subcontracting aimed at obtaining a substitute labor supply at lower wages and inferior standards.

There can be no doubt that the conditions under which the subcontracted work was performed were inferior. H_____ now does the same cleaning as an employee of the subcontractor that she did for Uniroyal, but more of it for less pay and no fringe benefits. Clearly this factor argues eloquently against the Employer's position.

(3) The impact of the subcontracting on the bargaining unit and its members. Three employees lost their jobs and, so far as the record shows, none of them have found comparable work and benefits.

The bargaining unit, too, has suffered. It has lost three jobs, a small part of the total work force but a significant part of one department. More importantly, it has lost a crucial element of its bargain with the Employer. Matthew Seibies, President of Local 1800, testified that the Union had deliberately structured wage settlements in recent years to benefit the lower-paid workers in general and these three employees in particular. If the Employer could, after signing the agreement, abolish those jobs it would deprive the Union indirectly of the benefits it agreed to provide. This factor too argues eloquently against the Employer's position.

We cannot know with certainty what the parties had in mind with regard to subcontracting when they negotiated the last contract, for they did not preserve their thoughts in writing. After looking carefully at the type of work subcontracted, the reasons given for the subcontracting, the conditions under which it was performed, and the impact of the subcontracting on the bargaining unit, however, I am confident in concluding that whatever their thoughts, they did not intend to permit the body blow to the contract by the Employer in this case. Subcontracting three jobs simply to save money by purchasing a cheaper labor force amounts to a serious breach of the Employer's implied obligations of good faith and fair dealing because it undercuts the very bargain which was at the heart of the contract.

KROGER LIMITED PARTNERSHIP[2]

122 Lab. Arb. (BNA) 413 (2006)
(Samuel J. Nicholas, Arbitrator)

Company operates retail grocery stores in the state of Tennessee. The setting of the instant dispute is store number 550 in Bellevue, which is in the Nashville area.

The retail grocery industry is highly competitive, and Company earns pennies on the dollar. Therefore, Management must be able to trust its employees, who work in a largely unsupervised setting. A long-standing Company policy holds that any form of dishonesty subjects an employee to immediate discharge without warning. This policy is stated in Article 7 of the parties' Agreement and is echoed in the employee rules and regulations, according to which, "Theft . . . will result in discharge, regardless of value of the property involved and regardless of the employee's length of service." Likewise, Company rules and regulations make clear that employees may not consume merchandise on Company property unless it has been previously paid for. Consumption of any merchandise not previously paid for is grounds for discharge.

Grievant was employed at Kroger store number 550 for almost five years when she was suspended pending investigation of an allegation of dishonesty for consuming a frozen entree before purchasing it. She worked the third shift, from 10:00 p.m. to about 6:30 a.m., as a night clerk stocking groceries except for a short period of time she worked in the bakery. Grievant's discipline record shows that between January 2001 and May 2004, she received warnings for discourtesy and failure to show up for her

---

scheduled shift as well as half a dozen warnings for failure to follow instructions.

The incident leading to Grievant's suspension and discharge occurred on January 12, 2005. That night, about 15 or 20 minutes before the 2:00 a.m. lunch break, she went to the frozen food section, selected a frozen Stouffer rigatoni with pesto sauce, and proceeded to the break room. She heated the food, leaving the box in the break room on a table next to the microwave, where it was visible to others. She then walked down aisle five, dinner in hand, to inform new Head Night Clerk Robert Tapp (who succeeded Storey Olson) that she needed to take her lunch break early because of prescription medication that she had taken. Grievant proceeded to the front of the store, set the entree down at a register and clocked out. She returned to the register to retrieve the food then went out to the foyer to eat. When she finished, she clocked in and returned to work.

At about the time that Grievant was on her way to or in the foyer, Head Night Clerk Tapp walked to the front of the store to announce over the public address system that he had opened the register so employees could purchase any merchandise th[ey] wanted to consume during the lunch break. Two employees, including Tapp, made purchases but Grievant did not. According to Grievant, she was wearing headphones connected to a portable CD player, and could not hear Tapp's announcement.

The rest of the night crew went on their lunch break at the regular time, about 2:00 a.m. After the lunch break, Tapp asked the three employees trained as cashiers whether they had rung up any purchases for Grievant. He was told they had not. At about 4:00 a.m., Tapp called another break and, again, Grievant made no purchases. Tapp retrieved the frozen entree box from the break room

At 7:00 a.m., when Co-Manager Jeff Fields arrived, Tapp gave him the empty box and told him that Grievant had consumed a product that she had not purchased. Fields went upstairs, reviewed the store surveillance cameras and saw Grievant walk to the front of the store, clock out and go outside without paying. [A]ccompanied by Union Steward Sharon Richards, he confronted Grievant on aisle nine where she was working. Fields showed Grievant the empty box and asked her if it belonged to her. She said it did. Fields asked her to provide her receipt. She said she could not because she had intended to pay for it after her shift.

At the hearing, Grievant testified that employees trained as cashiers were not always on the night shift, and that Storey Olson, who was the head night clerk before Tapp, was aware of employees consuming merchandise and paying for it at the end of the shift. She also testified that she never attempted to conceal the fact that she ate lunch before paying for it, and that doing so was a common practice at night.

Courtesy Clerk Ben Bond, whose shift starts at 6:00 a.m., testified that, at Grievant's request, he always set aside her empty frozen entrée box when he cleaned the break room. According to Bond, "I would clean the break room when I come in in the morning at 6:00 o'clock and clean them. And [Grievant] would come back there and say, 'Ben, you know, don't throw—those little frozen dinners.' She would come back there and say, don't throw them away. I'm going to take them up and pay for them. And then it got to the point where I would just set it aside, and she would come up, you know, and get them and take them up there."

However, Bond never personally witnessed Grievant paying for the entrées she had consumed. Likewise, Night Clerks Tapp, Conner and Conner said they never saw any empty containers in the break room before January 12, 2005.

Union witnesses Robert Castro and John Hoskins, daytime cashiers, confirmed that when the store began to close between midnight and 6:00 a.m. they frequently checked out empty containers in the morning for Grievant and other members of the night crew, believing that no till was available during the night. This practice stopped, they both said, after Grievant was discharged.

Union witness Joe E. Russell, Grievant's fiancé, testified that in 2004 and 2005 he transported Grievant to work and picked her up after her shift ended. When she worked overtime, Russell shopped while he waited for her. His purchases sometimes included an empty container that he received from Grievant, which was scanned along with his other groceries. He testified that one of the employees who sometimes checked out his groceries was Store Manager Gray. While Gray verified that in rare occasions he operated a register in the morning, and that he would scan any empty packages presented by a customer, he stated that he was not acquainted with Russell prior to the hearing nor did he recall ringing up groceries for anyone who claimed to be Grievant's fiancé.

Based on Management's investigation, Human Resources Director Alan Quinkert concluded that in consuming merchandise before purchasing it, Grievant had committed an act of dishonesty, violating the Agreement and Company rules. Accordingly, from this conclusion and Grievant's previous disciplinary record, Quinkert made the decision to terminate Grievant.

Clearly, Grievant's conduct was in violation of the Agreement and Company rules and regulations. In this connection, the Agreement states, "no warning notice need be given to an employee before he is discharged if the cause for such discharge is dishonesty." As stated in to the rules, "Dishonesty in any form or criminal conduct will not be tolerated and shall be cause for discharge, regardless of amount or length of service." The rules go on to define as theft "removal or utilization of any company property regardless of value or type" unless it is "accompanied by a sales receipt or written authorization from management." The penalty for violation is discharge, "regardless of the value of the property involved and regardless of the employee's length of service."

Grievant does not maintain that she was unfamiliar with the rules, thereby acknowledging that she was aware of the policy that Company claims she violated. Nevertheless, for reasons best known by her, she knowingly violated Company's rule against consuming merchandise before paying for it.

Management witnesses, including three of Grievant's coworkers who testified under subpoena, denied that consuming merchandise and paying for it at the end of the shift was a "common practice" that was acceptable to Management. While Union witnesses Hoskins and Castro, day shift cashiers, confirmed that they sometimes checked Grievant's purchases out at the end of her shift, they could not substantiate Union's claim that Management condoned this practice.

Other Union evidence, unfortunately, I find to be equally weak. Courtesy Clerk Bond seems to have set Grievant's empty containers aside in the break room in the belief that she would use the bar code to pay, but he never actually saw her pay for an empty box. And the fact that Grievant's fiancé may have "purchased" empty containers on her behalf, lends no credence in support of Union's "past practice" argument. Actually, it serves to invalidate it, for it gives the appearance that Grievant was concealing the fact that she had consumed the contents.

As the record shows, Management ensured there were procedures in place to enable night crew employees to make purchases when the store began closing from midnight to 6:00 a.m. A till was made available and two to four night crew employees trained to operate the registers were always scheduled on the night crew. In this regard, Company records also show, as Grievant admitted, that she made purchases at night as well as after her shift. This was consistent with Company rules, which state, "During the times a store is not open for regular business, employees are permitted to purchase merchandise through the cash register authorized by management."

It may well be that Grievant would have paid at the end of her shift for the entrée she had consumed earlier. Indeed, Company did not attempt to show that Grievant tried to conceal the fact that she consumed the frozen entrée before paying for it. Nor did Company argue that Grievant did not intend to pay for it. However, her actions gave the appearance of theft and compromised Management's confidence in her honesty. To be sure, confidence in an employee's honesty is essential for a meaningful and successful employer-employee relationship. Management's confidence had been eroded by Grievant's disciplinary record. As Human Resources Manager Quinkert pointed out, Grievant's record could not mitigate the imposed penalty because it documented a pattern of failing to comply with instructions.

Accordingly, for the reasons stated, the action taken must be allowed to stand.

BUCKEYE FEED MILL, INC.[3]

122 Lab. Arb. (BNA) 719 (2006)
(John J, Murphy, Arbitrator)

The Employer operates a feed mill that produces and distributes food for animals. The Employer has a process by which the manufacturing and processing employees represented by the Union may purchase the product of the feed mill on a wholesale basis.

The elements of the process known to the employees, including the Grievant, began with the employee's placing an order for the purchase with the "order entry"—an office that receives purchase requests from employees. The product is then moved by an Employer-designated employee to a position immediately inside the rear garage door of the warehouse at the feed mill. At the end of his shift, the purchasing employee typically drives from the employee parking lot slightly less than one-half mile to the warehouse in order to pick up the purchased product.

The Grievant acknowledged that on Tuesday, July 26, 2005, he took a 50-pound bag of high performance dog food from the place in the warehouse where dog food is stored. He then placed the bag at a point 10 or 15 feet to the left of the rear door to the warehouse. At the end of his shift he then placed the bag of dog food in his vehicle temporarily parked outside of the garage door. He acknowledged that he did not pay for the dog food.

The Grievant was discharged effective August 1, 2005.

The only issue with respect to whether the evidence supports the finding of a theft by the Grievant is the matter of the Grievant's state of mind during the course of the conduct that he admitted in the warehouse on July 26. The Union's position is that he did not possess willful and knowledgeable intent to deprive the Employer of its property; the Grievant simply forgot to pay. Indeed that was the testimony of the Grievant with respect to his state of mind.

The Union did establish that the Grievant suffered from memory lapses. The Grievant did have surgeries on his brain in the late 1980's—a fact that was known throughout the plant by members of management and the bargaining unit. Furthermore, the Union did establish that the Grievant did suffer from stress through difficulties with coworkers. While the Union did not raise the Grievant's memory problems or stress as "a path to steal," the Union argued that the stress and memory problems support the Grievant's assertion that he simply forgot to pay.

The difficulty with this claim is the undisputed admissions by the Grievant during the course of the investigation that he not only took the Employer's product but did not intend or plan to pay for it. He also stated during the investigation without any contradiction by Union representatives present at the investigatory meetings, that he knew what he was doing was wrong, but that he did not plan to do this again. While the Grievant did state at the arbitration hearing on November 16, 2005 that he did not pay for the product because "I just forgot to," the Grievant also acknowledged that he never made this claim while the Employer was investigating his conduct.

The late assertion by the Grievant of lapse of memory on July 26 is rejected primarily based upon the admissions by the Grievant to the contrary during the course of investigation that ended in his discharge on August 1. Consequently, the record does support a finding of proven theft by the Grievant of the Employer's product on July 26, 2005.

After the two investigatory meetings were completed on July 28 and July 29, and after the two remaining interviews were conducted on July 29, the Employer considered the penalty to be applied for a proven theft. Two, the shift supervisor and the production manager recommended discharge; the contract administrator and director of operations finally decided that the Grievant would be discharged on Monday, August 1.

The contract administrator summarized the analysis of all the management personnel who considered the appropriate penalty. Discharge is the inexorable, fixed consequence of proven theft. "And everybody agreed that zero tolerance was the way we always handled it (proven theft) before."

An Employer may draw a "line in the sand." The Employer may describe conduct with varying levels of specificity and connect that conduct to a specific penalty. The Employer then, with full warning, can apply this announcement.

There is, however, an overarching interest that must be observed in this process. That interest, among others, is that the employees must be given fair and reasonable notice of the fixed penalty that would flow from their described conduct. The evidence in this record does not support such a finding.

This finding could not be supported either by the text of the Employer's policy dealing with theft or by a claim of practice. The Grievant acknowledged receipt of the Employer's policy that lists theft as well as other events. These events are denominated "Severe Offenses" for which "Severe and immediate disciplinary actions will be administered." The policy then calls for immediate suspension, notification to necessary parties, and investigation and finally a meeting. The meeting is described as follows: "Company and Union representatives will meet to discuss results of the investigation report to determine if employee termination proceeding shall continue." There is nothing in this policy that automatically connects discharge to a proven theft.

The Employer treated this case as one in which its written policy was zero toleration for proven theft. The record does not support this assessment of the policy. One of the consequences, however, is that the Employer did not consider any other factors in the discharge of the Grievant other than the proven theft. As the management representative testified, he did not consider discipline less than discharge or any mitigating items such as work record, length of service, disciplinary record. The question now becomes whether the penalty of discharge is appropriate as that question is considered in light of mitigatory factors as well as lesser discipline than discharge.

Proven theft of the Employer's property is so destructive of the employment relationship that [it] can often be found to be subject to discipline even without an Employer rule prohibiting theft. In this case the Employer not only had a rule prohibiting theft, the rule denominated theft as a "Serious Offense" for which immediate and severe disciplinary action was threatened. The record establishes and the Grievant admitted an act of theft on July 26, 2005. But there is more.

The Grievant admitted both in direct and cross examination that he had taken the Employer's product without paying for it "once or twice" prior to July 26. This admission must be weighed in assessing the penalty in this case. While the record does not state the exact value of the bag of dog food stolen by the Grievant, it appears to be approximately ten dollars in value.

Countervailing against discharge for the theft are mitigatory factors such as long service approaching three decades, extraordinary record of attendance, and no criticism of the Grievant's productivity. The Grievant is an employee of 26.5 years of employment with the Employer. It was also undisputed that the Grievant called off work for only one day during his long service to the Employer. His supervisor for the last four years of his employment prior to his discharge testified that he had no problem with the Grievant's attendance, tardiness, or productivity.

Given the long-term service of this Grievant, the absence of a clear warning of automatic discharge for proven theft, and the strength of the mitigatory factors, this Grievant should be reinstated but without back pay or restoration of his contract benefits from the time of his termination to the time of his reinstatement. This is a long suspension of approximately six months, but the Grievant did commit acts of theft which he himself admitted was wrong.

NOTES

1.   After reading Arbitrator Nolan's award in *Uniroyal*, can you articulate a common law of the shop with respect to subcontracting?

2.   After reading the awards in *Kroger* and *Buckeye Feed Mill*, can you articulate a common law of the shop with respect to discharge? Would Arbitrator Murphy have reached the same result in *Kroger* as Arbitrator Nicholas? Would Arbitrator Nicholas have reached the same result in *Buckeye Feed Mill* as Arbitrator Murphy?

3.   The Court in *Enterprise Wheel* indicated that it would not enforce the award if the arbitrator sought to impose "his own brand of industrial justice," instead of following the parties' contract. However, when a contract uses a term as broad or vague as "just cause," is it possible to differentiate between the contract and the arbitrator's own brand of justice? Professor Edgar Jones has asked, "If the arbitrator 'does not sit to dispense his own brand of industrial justice,' what other brand is available for him to dispense?" Edgar A. Jones, *"His Own Brand of Industrial Justice": The Stalking Horse of Judicial Review of Labor Arbitration*, 30 UCLA L. Rev. 881, 886 (1983). Professor John Dunsford has observed that once selected to hear a case, an arbitrator's options in handling the matter are practically unlimited. The only meaningful restraints are those tacitly conveyed by the parties as to their expectations. As an arbitrator's reputation and docket grow, a reciprocal conditioning comes into play. The parties are presumed to be familiar with the arbitrator's conduct, rulings and decisions and, by their selection, represent the arbitrator's past performance to be their expected standard for the current matter. John E. Dunsford, *The Role and Function of the Labor Arbitrator*, 30 St. Louis U. L.J. 109, 112–13 (1985). Similarly, Professor Jones has commented on the link between the parties' selection process and the role of the arbitrator's personal values in resolving a grievance: "[I]n this process of competitive selection, 'his own brand' was analyzed and adopted [by the parties] as their own brand [of justice], whatever may have been their respective expectations . . .." Edgar A. Jones, Jr., *A Meditation on Labor Arbitration and "His Own Brand of Industrial Justice"*, Proc. 35th Mtg Nat'l Acad. Arb. 1, 11 (1982). Do you agree with the views of Jones and Dunsford? What may parties do if they want to constrain arbitral discretion?

For a comprehensive empirical study of discipline and discharge arbitrations in Minnesota, see Laura J. Cooper, Mario F. Bognano & Stephen F. Befort, More Than We Have Ever Known About Discipline and Discharge in Labor Arbitration: An Empirical Study (2015).

A NOTE ON THE RAILWAY LABOR ACT

Disputes over the interpretation and application of a collective bargaining agreement are termed "minor disputes" in the railroad and airline industries, in contrast to "major disputes" which are disputes over the terms of a new collective bargaining agreement. The Railway Labor Act (RLA) established the National Railroad Adjustment Board (NRAB) with jurisdiction over minor disputes in the railroad industry. The NRAB is divided into four divisions. The First Division has jurisdiction over the operating crafts, such as engineers and conductors. The Second Division has jurisdiction over the shop crafts, such as machinists and electricians. The Third Division has jurisdiction over the other non-operating crafts, such as maintenance of way employees and clerks. The Fourth Division has jurisdiction over any crafts not covered by the other three. Each division has an equal number of members appointed by and paid by the railroads and the unions. The NRAB does not conduct evidentiary hearings. Rather, its decisions are based on a review of a record developed through handling in the earlier stages of the grievance procedure established in the collective bargaining agreement. In discipline and discharge cases, the railroad will usually conduct an evidentiary hearing with a railroad manager serving as hearing officer. The hearing transcript is part of the record submitted for NRAB review. An individual employee has a right to bring a case before the NRAB without the intervention of the union. A majority vote is needed to decide a case. If the members of the division deadlock, the NMB appoints a neutral arbitrator to sit with the division as referee and cast the tie-breaking vote.

The RLA requires that claims (grievances) be discussed in a conference prior to their submission to the NRAB. In *Union Pacific RR. Co. v. Bhd. of Locomotive Engineers and Trainmen*, 558 U.S. 67 (2010), the Supreme Court held that the conferencing requirement is not jurisdictional in nature and that the NRAB erred in dismissing claims *sua sponte* where the record did not contain evidence that the claims had been conferenced. The Court reasoned that the requirement of conferencing was a claims processing rule, akin to a statute of limitations, was not jurisdictional in nature and could be waived by the parties' failure to raise it or cured while holding the arbitration in abeyance.

The RLA also authorizes parties to establish by agreement Special Boards of Adjustment (SBAs). An SBA typically has three members: one appointed by the railroad, one appointed by the union and a neutral arbitrator who serves as chair of the Board. Like the NRAB, the SBA does not conduct evidentiary hearings, but reviews the record developed in the earlier stages of the grievance procedure. The RLA also authorizes establishment of Public Law Boards (PLBs). Unlike SBAs, PLBs do not require agreement of both parties. A union or railroad can compel the creation of a PLB for any case that has been pending before the NRAB for more than twelve months. PLBs, like SBAs, typically have a railroad-appointed member, a union-appointed member and a neutral chair. They tend to operate in the same manner as SBAs.

The RLA authorized the NMB to create a National Airline Adjustment Board but the NMB has never done so. Instead, airlines and unions have created their own System Boards of Adjustment (SBAs). The typical airline SBA will have an equal number of airline and union members and a neutral chair. Unlike railroad boards, airline SBAs typically conduct evidentiary hearings.

A NOTE ON THE PUBLIC SECTOR

Most public sector jurisdictions prohibit strikes. Even those that recognize a public employee right to strike usually prohibit strikes during the term of a contract. Thus, it cannot be said in the public sector that the grievance and arbitration procedure is the quid pro quo for the no-strike clause. No-strike clauses are superfluous in the public sector. Furthermore, many public sector statutes require all collective bargaining agreements to contain grievance and arbitration procedures. In these jurisdictions, the parties cannot be said to have voluntarily agreed to grievance arbitration—the statute imposes it on them.

Nevertheless, most public sector jurisdictions have given at least lip service to the *Steelworkers Trilogy.* However, some courts, while claiming to apply the essence test, have reviewed arbitration awards in the public sector more closely. Public sector courts have also refused to enforce arbitration awards if they determine that the award resulted from an unlawful delegation of a public body's non-delegable responsibilities. Jurisdictions have disagreed over the proper relationship between grievance arbitration and procedures under civil service and tenure statutes. *See generally* Ann C. Hodges, *The Interplay of Civil Service Law and Collective Bargaining in Public Sector Employee Discipline Cases*, 32 B.C. L. Rev. 95 (1990). Additionally, public sector jurisdictions have differed on the scope of public policy review of arbitration awards, with many employing a wider scope of review than under *Eastern Associated Coal*. For example, in *AFSCME v. Dept. of Cent. Mgmt. Servs.*, 671 N.E.2d 668 (Ill. 1996), a caseworker with the Illinois Department of Children and Family Services (DCFS) reported in her official report that the children on whom she had checked were doing fine. In fact, the children had died in an accidental fire a month earlier. The arbitrator overturned the discharge and reinstated the caseworker with full back pay because the employer had not begun disciplinary proceedings within the time frame required by the collective bargaining agreement. The Illinois Supreme Court vacated the award as contrary to a public policy of accurate reporting by DCFS. Would the case have been decided in the same way had it arisen in the private sector? Does the difference in employers justify a different result in the public sector? Should arbitration over discipline of such public employees as teachers, police officers and fire fighters be restricted, or even prohibited? Why or why not?

C. THE COLLECTIVE BARGAINING AGREEMENT AND THE NORRIS-LAGUARDIA ACT

A lawsuit to compel a party to arbitrate or to enforce an arbitration award seeks equitable relief. It might be argued that a federal court's jurisdiction to award such relief is barred by the Norris-LaGuardia Act's withdrawal of federal jurisdiction to issue injunctions in labor disputes. In *Lincoln Mills*, the Court had little trouble disposing of this argument:

The failure to arbitrate was not a part and parcel of the abuses against which the Act was aimed. Section 8 of the Norris-LaGuardia Act does, indeed, indicate a congressional policy toward settlement of labor disputes by arbitration, for it denies injunctive relief to any person who has failed to make 'every reasonable effort' to settle the dispute by negotiation, mediation, or 'voluntary arbitration.' Though a literal reading might bring the dispute within the terms of the Act, we see no justification in policy for restricting § 301(a) to damage suits, leaving specific performance of a contract to arbitrate grievance disputes to the inapposite procedural requirements of that Act.

1. ENJOINING BREACHES OF THE NO STRIKE CLAUSE

Thus far, we have seen that in the problem that opened this chapter, Smith may grieve his discharge against Enderby and, if the union demands arbitration and Enderby refuses, a court will order Enderby to arbitrate. But what if instead the union strikes Enderby in an effort to compel Smith's reinstatement? Will the Norris-LaGuardia Act preclude Enderby from obtaining an injunction against the strike?

BOYS MARKETS, INC. v. RETAIL CLERKS UNION LOCAL 770
398 U.S. 235 (1970)

JUSTICE BRENNAN delivered the opinion of the Court:

In this case we re-examine the holding of *Sinclair Refining Co. v. Atkinson*, 370 U.S. 195 (1962), that the anti-injunction provisions of the Norris-LaGuardia Act preclude a federal district court from enjoining a strike in breach of a no-strike obligation under a collective-bargaining agreement, even though that agreement contains provisions, enforceable under § 301(a) of the Labor Management Relations Act, for binding arbitration of the grievance dispute concerning which the strike was called. The Court of Appeals for the Ninth Circuit, considering itself bound by *Sinclair* reversed the grant by the District Court for the Central District of California of petitioner's prayer for injunctive relief.

In February 1969, at the time of the incidents that produced this litigation, petitioner and respondent were parties to a collective-bargaining agreement which provided, *inter alia*, that all controversies concerning its interpretation or application should be resolved by adjustment and arbitration procedures set forth therein and that, during the life of the contract, there should be "no cessation or stoppage of work, lock-out, picketing or boycotts." The dispute arose when petitioner's frozen foods supervisor and certain members of his crew who were not members of the bargaining unit began to rearrange merchandise in the frozen food cases of one of petitioner's supermarkets. A union representative insisted that the food cases be stripped of all merchandise and be restocked by union personnel. When petitioner did not accede to the union's demand, a strike was called and the union began to picket petitioner's establishment. Thereupon petitioner demanded that the union cease the work stoppage and picketing and sought to invoke the grievance and arbitration procedures specified in the contract.

The following day, since the strike had not been terminated, petitioner filed a complaint in California Superior Court seeking a temporary restraining order, a preliminary and permanent injunction, and specific performance of the contractual arbitration provision. The state court issued a temporary restraining order forbidding continuation of the strike and also an order to show cause why a preliminary injunction should not be granted. Shortly thereafter, the union removed the case to the Federal District Court and there made a motion to quash the state court's temporary restraining order. In opposition, petitioner moved for an order compelling arbitration and enjoining continuation of the strike. Concluding that the dispute was subject to arbitration under the collective-bargaining agreement and that the strike was in violation of the contract, the District Court ordered the parties to arbitrate the underlying dispute and simultaneously enjoined the strike, all picketing in the vicinity of petitioner's supermarket, and any attempts by the union to induce the employees to strike or to refuse to perform their services.

Textile Workers Union of America v. Lincoln Mills held generally that the substantive law to apply in suits under § 301(a) is federal law, which the courts must fashion from the policy of our national labor laws, and more specifically that a union can obtain specific performance of an employer's promise to arbitrate grievances. We rejected the contention that the anti-injunction proscriptions of the Norris-LaGuardia Act prohibited this type of relief, noting that a refusal to arbitrate was not "part and parcel of the abuses against which the Act was aimed," and that the Act itself manifests a policy determination that arbitration should be encouraged. Subsequently in the *Steelworkers Trilogy* we emphasized the importance of arbitration as an instrument of federal policy for resolving disputes between labor and management and cautioned the lower courts against usurping the functions of the arbitrator.

Serious questions remained, however, concerning the role that state courts were to play in suits involving collective-bargaining agreements. Confronted with some of these problems in *Charles Dowd Box Co. v. Courtney*, 368 U.S. 502 (1962), we held that Congress clearly intended not to disturb the pre-existing jurisdiction of the state courts over suits for violations of collective-bargaining agreements.

Shortly after the decision in *Dowd Box*, we sustained, in *Local 174, Teamsters v. Lucas Flour Co.*, 369 U.S. 95 (1962), an award of damages by a state court to an employer for a breach by the union of a no-strike provision in its contract. While emphasizing that "in enacting § 301 Congress intended doctrines of federal labor law uniformly to prevail over inconsistent local rules," we did not consider the applicability of the Norris-LaGuardia Act to state court proceedings because the employer's prayer for relief sought only damages and not specific performance of a no-strike obligation.

Subsequent to the decision in *Sinclair*, we held in *Avco Corp. v. Aero Lodge 735*, that § 301(a) suits initially brought in state courts may be removed to the designated federal forum under the federal question removal jurisdiction delineated in 28 U.S.C. § 1441. In so holding, however, the Court expressly left open the questions whether state courts are bound by the anti-injunction proscriptions of the Norris-LaGuardia Act and whether federal courts, after removal of a § 301(a) action, are required to dissolve any injunctive relief previously granted by the state courts. Three Justices who concurred expressed the view that *Sinclair* should be reconsidered "upon an appropriate future occasion."

The decision in *Avco*, viewed in the context of *Lincoln Mills* and its progeny, has produced an anomalous situation which, in our view, makes urgent the reconsideration of *Sinclair*. The principal practical effect of *Avco* and *Sinclair* taken together is nothing less than to oust state courts of jurisdiction in § 301(a) suits where injunctive relief is sought for breach of a no-strike obligation. Union defendants can, as a matter of course, obtain removal to a federal court, and there is obviously a compelling incentive for them to do so in order to gain the advantage of the strictures upon injunctive relief which *Sinclair* imposes on federal courts. The sanctioning of this practice, however, is wholly inconsistent with our conclusion in *Dowd Box* that the congressional purpose embodied in § 301(a) was to supplement, and not to encroach upon, the pre-existing jurisdiction of the state courts.

On the other hand, to the extent that widely disparate remedies theoretically remain available in state, as opposed to federal, courts, the federal policy of labor law uniformity elaborated in *Lucas Flour Co.*, is seriously offended. This policy, of course, could hardly require, as a practical matter, that labor law be administered identically in all courts, for undoubtedly a certain diversity exists among the state and federal systems in matters of procedural and remedial detail, a fact that Congress evidently took into account in deciding not to disturb the traditional jurisdiction of the States. The injunction, however, is so important a remedial device, particularly in the arbitration context, that its availability or non-availability in various courts will not only produce rampant forum shopping and maneuvering from one court to another but will also greatly frustrate any relative uniformity in the enforcement of arbitration agreements.

It is undoubtedly true that each of the foregoing objections to *Sinclair-Avco* could be remedied either by overruling *Sinclair* or by extending that decision to the States. While some commentators have suggested that the solution to the present unsatisfactory situation does lie in the extension of the *Sinclair* prohibition to state court proceedings, we agree with Chief Justice Traynor of the California Supreme Court that "whether or not Congress could deprive state courts of the power to give such (injunctive) remedies when enforcing collective bargaining agreements, it has not attempted to do so either in the Norris-LaGuardia Act or section 301." *McCarroll v. L.A. County Dist. Council of Carpenters*, 49 Cal.2d 45, 63, 315 P.2d 322, 332 (1957), *cert. denied*, 355 U.S. 932 (1958).

An additional reason for not resolving the existing dilemma by extending *Sinclair* to the States is the devastating implications for the enforceability of arbitration agreements and their accompanying no-strike obligations if equitable remedies were not available. As we have previously indicated, a no-strike obligation, express or implied, is the quid pro quo for an undertaking by the employer to submit grievance disputes to the process of arbitration. *See Textile Workers Union of America v. Lincoln Mills, supra.* Any incentive for employers to enter into such an arrangement is necessarily dissipated if the principal and most expeditious method by which the no-strike obligation can be enforced is eliminated. While it is of course true, as respondent contends, that other avenues of redress, such as an action for damages, would remain open to an aggrieved employer, an award of damages after a dispute has been settled is no substitute for an immediate halt to an illegal strike. Furthermore, an action for damages prosecuted during or after a labor dispute would only tend to aggravate industrial strife and delay an early resolution of the difficulties between employer and union.

Even if management is not encouraged by the unavailability of the injunction remedy to resist arbitration agreements, the fact remains that the effectiveness of such agreements would be greatly reduced if injunctive relief were withheld. Indeed, the very purpose of arbitration procedures is to provide a mechanism for the expeditious settlement of industrial disputes without resort to strikes, lockouts, or other self-help measures. This basic purpose is obviously largely undercut if there is no immediate, effective remedy for those very tactics that arbitration is designed to obviate. Thus, because *Sinclair*, in the aftermath of *Avco*, casts serious doubt upon the effective enforcement of a vital element of stable labor-management relations—arbitration agreements with their attendant no-strike obligations—we conclude that *Sinclair* does not make a viable contribution to federal labor policy.

The literal terms of § 4 of the Norris-LaGuardia Act must be accommodated to the subsequently enacted provisions of § 301(a) of the Labor Management Relations Act and the purposes of arbitration.

Statutory interpretation requires more than concentration upon isolated words; rather, consideration must be given to the total corpus of pertinent law and the policies that inspired ostensibly inconsistent provisions.

The Norris-LaGuardia Act was responsive to a situation totally different from that which exists today. In the early part of this century, the federal courts generally were regarded as allies of management in its attempt to prevent the organization and strengthening of labor unions; and in this industrial struggle the injunction became a potent weapon that was wielded against the activities of labor groups. The result was a large number of sweeping decrees, often issued ex parte, drawn on an ad hoc basis without regard to any systematic elaboration of national labor policy.

In 1932 Congress attempted to bring some order out of the industrial chaos that had developed and to correct the abuses that had resulted from the interjection of the federal judiciary into union-management disputes on the behalf of management. *See* Norris-LaGuardia Act, § 2. Congress, therefore, determined initially to limit severely the power of the federal courts to issue injunctions "in any case involving or growing out of any labor dispute." § 4. Even as initially enacted, however, the prohibition against federal injunctions was by no means absolute. *See* Norris-LaGuardia Act, §§ 7, 8, 9. Shortly thereafter Congress passed the Wagner Act, designed to curb various management activities that tended to discourage employee participation in collective action.

As labor organizations grew in strength and developed toward maturity, congressional emphasis shifted from protection of the nascent labor movement to the encouragement of collective bargaining and to administrative techniques for the peaceful resolution of industrial disputes. This shift in emphasis was accomplished, however, without extensive revision of many of the older enactments, including the anti-injunction section of the Norris-LaGuardia Act. Thus it became the task of the courts to accommodate, to reconcile the older statutes with the more recent ones.

[W]e have frequently noted, in such cases as *Lincoln Mills*, the *Steelworkers Trilogy*, and *Lucas Flour*, the importance that Congress has attached generally to the voluntary settlement of labor disputes without resort to self-help and more particularly to arbitration as a means to this end. Indeed, it has been stated that *Lincoln Mills*, in its exposition of § 301(a), "went a long way towards making arbitration the central institution in the administration of collective bargaining contracts."

The *Sinclair* decision, however, seriously undermined the effectiveness of the arbitration technique as a method peacefully to resolve industrial disputes without resort to strikes, lockouts, and similar devices. Clearly employers will be wary of assuming obligations to arbitrate specifically enforceable against them when no similarly efficacious remedy is available to enforce the concomitant undertaking of the union to refrain from striking. On the other hand, the central purpose of the Norris-LaGuardia Act to foster the growth and viability of labor organizations is hardly retarded—if anything, this goal is advanced—by a remedial device that merely enforces the obligation that the union freely undertook under a specifically enforceable agreement to submit disputes to arbitration. We conclude, therefore, that the unavailability of equitable relief in the arbitration context presents a serious impediment to the congressional policy favoring the voluntary establishment of a mechanism for the peaceful resolution of labor disputes, that the core purpose of the Norris-LaGuardia Act is not sacrificed by the limited use of equitable remedies to further this important policy, and consequently that the Norris-LaGuardia Act does not bar the granting of injunctive relief in the circumstances of the instant case.

The dissenting opinion in *Sinclair* suggested the following principles for the guidance of the district courts in determining whether to grant injunctive relief—principles that we now adopt:

> A District Court entertaining an action under § 301 may not grant injunctive relief against concerted activity unless and until it decides that the case is one in which an injunction would be appropriate despite the Norris-LaGuardia Act. When a strike is sought to be enjoined because it is over a grievance which both parties are contractually bound to arbitrate, the District Court may issue no injunctive order until it first holds that the contract does have that effect; and the employer should be ordered to arbitrate, as a condition of his obtaining an injunction against the strike. Beyond this, the District Court must, of course, consider whether issuance of an injunction would be warranted under ordinary principles of equity—whether breaches are occurring and will continue, or have been threatened and will be committed; whether they have caused or will cause irreparable injury to the employer; and whether the employer will suffer more from the denial of an injunction than will the union from its issuance.

In the present case there is no dispute that the grievance in question was subject to adjustment and arbitration under the collective-bargaining agreement and that the petitioner was ready to proceed with arbitration at the time an injunction against the strike was sought and obtained. The District Court also concluded that, by reason of respondent's violations of its no-strike obligation, petitioner "has suffered irreparable injury and will continue to suffer irreparable injury." Since we now overrule *Sinclair*, the holding of the Court of Appeals in reliance on *Sinclair* must be reversed. Accordingly, we reverse the judgment of the Court of Appeals and remand the case with directions to enter a judgment affirming the order of the District Court.

[The dissenting opinion of JUSTICE BLACK has been omitted.]

NOTES

1.   What is the Court's rationale for enjoining strikes in breach of a contractual no-strike clause? How did the Court reconcile its holding with the Norris-LaGuardia Act? Is this an appropriate role for a Court?

2.   Consider the following criticism of *Boys Market* by an attorney who, during the 1970s, was staff counsel for the United Mine Workers:

In 1969, in the *Boys Market* case, the Supreme Court held that it would now issue injunctions to enforce no-strike clauses in contracts.... The Court reasoned that we didn't need strikes anymore and everything could be decided by a neutral arbitrator. So if miners worried about a safety problem, they couldn't go on strike, at least during the contract. They had to arbitrate like civilized people.

The problem is, it's not so civilized down there. The *Boys Market* case changed the balance of power between the UMW and the companies. Previously, the companies could only bring damage suits (which for quickie "twenty-four hour strikes" were pointless), but now they could get TROs, with immediate fines. Now they could sit on grievances for years. They could change the safety rules, fire militants, and know that the union couldn't strike, or do anything except wait and wait and wait.

Thomas Geoghegan, Which Side Are You On? Trying to be for Labor When It's Flat on Its Back 31 (1991).

3.   The Court in *Boys Market* expressed concern that if injunctions were not available in federal court, state court concurrent jurisdiction would be defeated because unions would reflexively remove state court actions to federal court. Injunctions, however, are not necessarily available as a matter of course in state courts. Many states have "mini-Norris LaGuardia Acts," which severely restrict state court authority to issue injunctions in labor disputes.

BUFFALO FORGE CO. v. UNITED STEELWORKERS OF AMERICA
428 U.S. 397 (1976)

JUSTICE WHITE delivered the opinion of the Court:

The Buffalo Forge Co. (employer) operates three separate plant and office facilities in the Buffalo, N.Y., area. For some years production and maintenance (P&M) employees at the three locations have been represented by the United Steelworkers of America, AFL-CIO, and its Local Unions No. 1874 and No. 3732 (hereafter sometimes collectively Union). The United Steelworkers is a party to the two separate collective-bargaining agreements between the locals and the employer. The contracts contain identical no-strike clauses, as well as grievance and arbitration provisions for settling disputes over the interpretation and application of each contract.

Shortly before this dispute arose, the United Steelworkers and two other locals not parties to this litigation were certified to represent the employer's "office clerical-technical" (O&T) employees at the same three locations. On November 16, 1974, after several months of negotiations looking toward their first collective-bargaining agreement, the O&T employees struck and established picket lines at all three locations. On November 18, P&M employees at one plant refused to cross the O&T picket line for the day. Two days later, the employer learned that the P&M employees planned to stop work at all three plants the next morning. In telegrams to the Union, the employer stated its position that a strike by the P&M employees would violate the no-strike clause and offered to arbitrate any dispute which had led to the planned strike. The next day, at the Union's direction, the P&M employees honored the O&T picket line and stopped work at the three plants. They did not return to work until December 16, the first regular working day after the District Court denied the employer's prayer for a preliminary injunction.

The employer's complaint under § 301(a) of the Labor Management Relations Act claimed the work stoppage was in violation of the no-strike clause. The Union's position was that the work stoppage did not violate the no-strike clause. It offered to submit that question to arbitration "on one day's notice," but opposed the prayer for injunctive relief.

[T]he District Court concluded that the P&M employees were engaged in a sympathy action in support of the striking O&T employees. The District Court then held itself forbidden to issue an injunction by § 4 of the Norris-LaGuardia Act because the P&M employees' strike was not over an "arbitrable grievance" and hence was not within the "narrow" exception to the Norris-LaGuardia Act established in *Boys Markets v. Retail Clerks Union*.

The Court of Appeals affirmed. It held that enjoining this strike, which was not "over a grievance which the union has agreed to arbitrate," was not permitted by the *Boys Markets* exception to the Norris-LaGuardia Act.

As a preliminary matter, certain elements in this case are not in dispute. The Union has gone on strike not by reason of any dispute it or any of its members has with the employer, but in support of other local unions of the same international organization that were negotiating a contract with the employer and were out on strike. The parties involved here are bound by collective-bargaining contracts each containing a no-strike clause which the Union claims does not forbid sympathy strikes. The employer has the other view, its complaint in the District Court asserting that the work stoppage violated the no-strike clause. Each of the contracts between the parties also has an arbitration clause broad enough to reach not only disputes between the Union and the employer about other provisions in the contracts but also as to the meaning and application of the no-strike clause itself. Whether the sympathy strike the Union called violated the no-strike clause, and the appropriate remedies if it did, are subject to the agreed-upon dispute-settlement procedures of the contracts and are ultimately issues for the arbitrator. The employer thus was entitled to invoke the arbitral process to determine the legality of the sympathy strike and to obtain a court order requiring the Union to arbitrate if the Union refused to do so. Furthermore, were the issue arbitrated and the strike found illegal, the relevant federal statutes as construed in our cases would permit an injunction to enforce the arbitral decision.

The issue in this case arises because the employer not only asked for an order directing the Union to arbitrate but prayed that the strike itself be enjoined pending arbitration and the arbitrator's decision whether the strike was permissible under the no-strike clause. Contrary to the Court of Appeals, the employer claims that despite the Norris-LaGuardia Act's ban on federal-court injunctions in labor disputes the District Court was empowered to enjoin the strike by § 301 of the Labor Management Relations Act as construed by *Boys Markets v. Retail Clerks Union.*

The driving force behind *Boys Markets* was to implement the strong congressional preference for the private dispute settlement mechanisms agreed upon by the parties. Only to that extent was it held necessary to accommodate § 4 of the Norris-LaGuardia Act to § 301 of the Labor Management Relations Act and to lift the former's ban against the issuance of injunctions in labor disputes. Striking over an arbitrable dispute would interfere with and frustrate the arbitral processes by which the parties had chosen to settle a dispute. The quid pro quo for the employer's promise to arbitrate was the union's obligation not to strike over issues that were subject to the arbitration machinery. Even in the absence of an express no-strike clause, an undertaking not to strike would be implied where the strike was over an otherwise arbitrable dispute. Otherwise, the employer would be deprived of his bargain and the policy of the labor statutes to implement private resolution of disputes in a manner agreed upon would seriously suffer.

Boys Markets plainly does not control this case. The District Court found, and it is not now disputed, that the strike was not over any dispute between the Union and the employer that was even remotely subject to the arbitration provisions of the contract. The strike at issue was a sympathy strike in support of sister unions negotiating with the employer; neither its causes nor the issue underlying it was subject to the settlement procedures provided by the contracts between the employer and respondents. The strike had neither the purpose nor the effect of denying or evading an obligation to arbitrate or of depriving the employer of its bargain. Thus, had the contract not contained a no-strike clause or had the clause expressly excluded sympathy strikes, there would have been no possible basis for implying from the existence of an arbitration clause a promise not to strike that could have been violated by the sympathy strike in this case.

Nor was the injunction authorized solely because it was alleged that the sympathy strike called by the Union violated the express no-strike provision of the contracts. Section 301 of the Act assigns a major role to the courts in enforcing collective-bargaining agreements, but aside from the enforcement of the arbitration provisions of such contracts, within the limits permitted by *Boys Markets*, the Court has never indicated that the courts may enjoin actual or threatened contract violations despite the Norris-LaGuardia Act. In the course of enacting the Taft-Hartley Act, Congress rejected the proposal that the Norris-LaGuardia Act's prohibition against labor-dispute injunctions be lifted to the extent necessary to make injunctive remedies available in federal courts for the purpose of enforcing collective-bargaining agreements. The allegation of the complaint that the Union was breaching its obligation not to strike did not in itself warrant an injunction.

The contracts here at issue, however, also contained grievance and arbitration provisions for settling disputes over the interpretation and application of the provisions of the contracts, including the no-strike clause. That clause, like others, was subject to enforcement in accordance with the procedures set out in the contracts. Here the Union struck, and the parties were in dispute whether the sympathy strike violated the Union's no-strike undertaking. Concededly, that issue was arbitrable. It was for the arbitrator to determine whether there was a breach, as well as the remedy for any breach, and the employer was entitled to an order requiring the Union to arbitrate if it refused to do so. However, it does not follow that the District Court was empowered not only to order arbitration but to enjoin the strike pending the decision of the arbitrator, despite the express prohibition of § 4(a) of the Norris-LaGuardia Act against injunctions prohibiting any person from "[c]easing or refusing to perform any work or to remain in any relation of employment." If an injunction could issue against the strike in this case, so in proper circumstances could a court enjoin any other alleged breach of contract pending the exhaustion of the applicable grievance and arbitration provisions even though the injunction would otherwise violate one of the express prohibitions of § 4. The court in such cases would be permitted, if the dispute was arbitrable, to hold hearings, make findings of fact, interpret the applicable provisions of the contract and issue injunctions so as to restore the status quo, or to otherwise regulate the relationship of the parties pending exhaustion of the arbitration process. This would cut deeply into the policy of the Norris-LaGuardia Act and make the courts potential participants in a wide range of arbitrable disputes under the many existing and future collective-bargaining contracts, not just for the purpose of enforcing promises to arbitrate, which was the limit of *Boys Markets,* but for the purpose of preliminarily dealing with the merits of the factual and legal issues that are subjects for the arbitrator and of issuing injunctions that would otherwise be forbidden by the Norris-LaGuardia Act.

This is not what the parties have bargained for. Surely it cannot be concluded here, as it was in *Boys Markets*, that such injunctions pending arbitration are essential to carry out promises to arbitrate and to implement the private arrangements for the administration of the contract. As is typical, the agreements in this case outline the pre-arbitration settlement procedures and provide that if the grievance "has not been satisfactorily adjusted," arbitration may be had. Nowhere do they provide for coercive action of any kind, let alone judicial injunctions, short of the terminal decision of the arbitrator. The parties have agreed to submit to grievance procedures and arbitrate, not to litigate. They have not contracted for a judicial preview of the facts and the law. Had they anticipated additional regulation of their relationships pending arbitration, it seems very doubtful that they would have resorted to litigation rather than to private arrangements.

Injunctions against strikes, even temporary injunctions, very often permanently settle the issue; and in other contexts time and expense would be discouraging factors to the losing party in court in considering whether to relitigate the issue before the arbitrator.

With these considerations in mind, we are far from concluding that the arbitration process will be frustrated unless the courts have the power to issue interlocutory injunctions pending arbitration in cases such as this or in others in which an arbitrable dispute awaits decision. We agree with the Court of Appeals that there is no necessity here, such as was found to be the case in *Boys Markets*, to accommodate the policies of the Norris-LaGuardia Act to the requirements of § 301 by empowering the District Court to issue the injunction sought by the employer.

[The dissenting opinion of JUSTICE STEVENS, with whom JUSTICE BRENNAN, JUSTICE MARSHALL, and JUSTICE POWELL joined, has been omitted.]

NOTES

1.   If the employer is denied injunctive relief for strikes which are not over arbitral issues, hasn't it been denied part of the benefit of its bargain in agreeing to a grievance and arbitration provision? Won't this deter employers from agreeing to grievance and arbitration clauses?

2.   If an employer is unable to obtain an injunction, what remedies are available to it? A strike in breach of a no-strike clause generally is not protected by the NLRA. Consequently, the employer usually may discipline or discharge the striking employees. Of course, the union may grieve such actions under the contract's grievance procedure, particularly if the contract restricts discipline and discharge to instances of just cause.

Whether the employer may sue the union for damages for breach of the collective bargaining agreement depends on the wording of the grievance procedure. Some contracts provide only for unions or unions and employees to file grievances. Under such contracts, employers are not bound to grieve union breaches but may sue under section 301. Other contracts provide that employers may also file and arbitrate grievances. In such cases, the employer must bring its claim for damages for breach of the no-strike clause through the grievance and arbitration procedure. *See Atkinson v. Sinclair Refining Co.*, 370 U.S. 238 (1962); *Drake Bakeries, Inc. v. Am. Bakery & Confectionary Workers Local 50*, 370 U.S. 254 (1962). To recover, the employer must prove that the union authorized or ratified the strike. The local and the international unions are considered separate legal entities. Consequently, an employer who wishes to hold the international liable for a strike called by a local must prove that the international authorized or ratified the strike *See Carbon Fuel Co. v. United Mine Workers*, 444 U.S. 212 (1979). The employer may not recover damages against the individual strikers. *See Complete Auto Transit, Inc. v. Reis*, 451 U.S. 401 (1981).

In *Granite Rock Co. v. Int'l Bhd. of Teamsters*, 561 U.S. 287 (2010), the Supreme Court held that there is no cause of action under Section 301 for intentional interference with a contract's no strike obligation. After a local union reached tentative agreement with the employer and the union members ratified the agreement ending a strike, the international directed the local to resume the strike unless and until the employer agreed to hold harmless the union and the employees for any damages incurred during the strike. The employer sued the international for *inter alia* intentional interference with the local's obligation under the no strike clause under the new contract. The Court held that Section 301 encompasses contractual claims, not tort claims, and reasoned that the employer failed to show that its remedies available for breach of contract or otherwise were sufficiently defective to warrant implying a claim for intentional interference under Section 301.

3.   You represent an association of new car transport companies that service auto plants in and around Detroit, Michigan. Your client's collective bargaining agreement with Teamsters Local 299, which represents its drivers, was expiring, when your client and the union agreed to extend the contract, including its broad no-strike clause, and agreed that when a new contract was reached, all improvements in wages and benefits would be retroactive to the original expiration date of the old contract. The parties reached agreement on a new contract but the union membership rejected it in the ratification vote. The parties again agreed to extend the old contract and that all improvements eventually agreed to would be retroactive. When this agreement was announced, the drivers, led by the Teamsters for a Democratic Union, went on a wildcat strike. Their literature and picket signs complain of corrupt union leadership, inadequate representation over grievances and sweetheart contract deals. Your client's members are shut down by the strike and the auto companies have warned them that if they can't solve their labor problems, the auto companies will start shipping new cars by train. What rights and

remedies does your client have? *See Auto Transit, Inc. v. Ferdinance*, 420 F. Supp. 75 (E.D. Mich.1976).

* * *

Gateway Coal Co. v. United Mine Workers, 414 U.S. 368 (1974). The union struck during the term of the collective bargaining agreement to protest the return of two foremen who had been suspended and were being prosecuted criminally for falsifying company safety records. The union maintained that the return of the foremen constituted a safety hazard. The contract contained a grievance and arbitration procedure but did not have an express no-strike clause. The Supreme Court, in an opinion authored by Justice Powell, held the strike enjoinable under *Boys Markets*. The Court applied the *Steelworkers Trilogy's* presumption of arbitrability to find the dispute over the foremen arbitrable. It then held that the grievance and arbitration provisions contained an implied no-strike obligation.

> An arbitration agreement is usually linked with a concurrent no-strike obligation, but the two issues remain analytically distinct. Ultimately, each depends on the intent of the contracting parties. It would be unusual, but certainly permissible, for the parties to agree to a broad mandatory arbitration provision yet expressly negate any implied no-strike obligation. Such a contract would reinstate the situation commonly existing before our decision in *Boys Markets*. Absent an explicit expression of such an intention, however, the agreement to arbitrate and the duty not to strike should be construed as having coterminous application.

The Court also reversed the lower court's holding that section 502 of the LMRA precluded enjoining a strike over a safety dispute:

> The Court of Appeals majority also based its denial of injunctive relief on § 502 of the Labor Management Relations Act, which provides in part:
>
>> [N]or shall the quitting of labor by an employee or employees in good faith because of abnormally dangerous conditions for work at the place of employment of such employee or employees be deemed a strike under this chapter.
>
> This section provides a limited exception to an express or implied no-strike obligation. The Court of Appeals held that "a refusal to work because of good faith apprehension of physical danger is protected activity and not enjoinable, even where the employees have subscribed to a comprehensive no-strike clause in their labor contract." We agree with the main thrust of this statement—that a work stoppage called solely to protect employees from immediate danger is authorized by § 502 and cannot be the basis for either a damages award or a *Boys Markets* injunction.

The Court of Appeals majority erred, however, in concluding that an honest belief, no matter how unjustified, in the existence of "abnormally dangerous conditions for work" necessarily invokes the protection of § 502. If the courts require no objective evidence that such conditions actually obtain, they face a wholly speculative inquiry into the motives of the workers. [T]he difficulty occasioned by this view is especially apparent where, as here, the claim concerns not some identifiable, presently existing threat to the employees' safety, but rather a generalized doubt in the competence and integrity of company supervisors. Any employee who believes a supervisor or fellow worker incompetent and who honestly fears that at some future time he may commit some unspecified mistake creating a safety hazard could demand his colleague's discharge and walk off the job despite the contractual agreement not to do so. Absent the most explicit statutory command, we are unwilling to conclude that Congress intended the public policy favoring arbitration and peaceful resolution of labor disputes to be circumvented by so slender a thread as subjective judgment, however honest it may be. [A] union seeking to justify a contractually prohibited work stoppage under § 502 must present "ascertainable, objective evidence supporting its conclusion that an abnormally dangerous condition for work exists." We find this reading of the statute consistent both with common sense and with its previous application.

2. ENJOINING EMPLOYER CONDUCT PENDING ARBITRATION

A company has operated in a vertically integrated fashion, fabricating all of its parts. The company has now advised the union that it intends to purchase parts from outside vendors, either because it can no longer fabricate its own parts profitably or because it can increase its profit by purchasing from outside vendors. The company plans to streamline its operation to be primarily an assembly and distribution plant. Consequently, the jobs of most skilled machinists will be eliminated. Equipment will be sold, and buildings will be sold as operations are consolidated. The union files a grievance maintaining that the company's actions violate contractual restrictions on subcontracting. The company maintains that it is not subcontracting but that even if it is, its actions do not breach the collective bargaining agreement. As the union demands arbitration, the company enters into agreements with suppliers for parts and with a liquidator to sell most of its fabricating equipment.

If the union sues under section 301 to enjoin the company's actions, the court faces a dilemma. On the one hand, if it denies injunctive relief, by the time the grievance is heard by an arbitrator, the company may have sold the buildings and equipment and the arbitrator will be unable to put

Humpty Dumpty back together again and award effective relief. On the other hand, for the court to find injunctive relief appropriate, it will have to interpret the collective bargaining agreement, thereby invading the arbitrator's jurisdiction. May a court invade an arbitrator's jurisdiction to save the arbitrator's jurisdiction, or is such action so far afield from enjoining a breach of the no-strike clause that the Norris-LaGuardia Act precludes the exercise of jurisdiction?

LEVER BROTHERS CO. v. INTERNATIONAL CHEMICAL WORKERS UNION LOCAL 217

554 F.2d 115 (4th Cir. 1976)

HALL, CIRCUIT JUDGE:

This civil action was brought under Section 301 of the Labor Management Relations Act of 1947, by Local 217 of the International Chemical Workers Union against Lever Brothers Company seeking injunctive relief to prevent the Company from transferring its Baltimore, Maryland, soap production operation to Hammond, Indiana, until the Company complied with what the Union contended were certain specified contractual prerequisites to the move. The District Court granted a temporary restraining order and then a preliminary injunction enjoining the plant relocation pending the completion of arbitration to construe certain terms of the labor contract.

The Company unsuccessfully moved to dissolve the injunction, the Union initiated grievance was found to be arbitrable, and an award was rendered in favor of the Company. The preliminary injunction expired, as ordered, and the Company presumably has relocated its plant facility. The Company appeals seeking a determination that the preliminary injunction was wrongfully issued. We affirm.

The Company and the Union had entered into a collective bargaining agreement covering its plant located at Baltimore, Maryland. On October 28, 1975, the Company advised the Union that it was permanently closing its Baltimore plant and transferring that production to its Hammond, Indiana facility which was represented by the Oil, Chemical and Atomic Workers union. The Union argued that since the Hammond plant was represented by a union other than the International Chemical Workers, then the Company action constituted "outside contracting" under the collective bargaining agreement, and the Union was entitled to "due consideration" before the actual assignment of work to the outside contractors (i.e., the transfer to Indiana) occurred. The Company argued that the transfer was an "elimination" under the collective bargaining agreement, requiring only two weeks written notice to the Union in advance of the move, which notice it had given. Thus, the release of "full information," necessary when there was a "contracting out," was not required.

Before issuing the preliminary injunction, the court below analyzed the prerequisites to the issuance of injunctive relief and concluded that as to the first prerequisite, the Union had shown a "probable right," that is, a likelihood that the Union would prevail at a trial on the merits. The court equated this with the likelihood that the Union would prevail in its contention that the dispute in issue was one for the arbitrator. Thus, the preliminary injunction was issued halting the transfer of the plant and insuring the maintenance of the status quo until the arbitration could be completed.

The Union contends that the injunction properly issued to protect its contractual right to arbitrate grievances and had it prevailed in the arbitration, it would have been provided with "full information" regarding the reasons for the transfer and would have marshaled economic evidence to attempt to persuade the Company not to make the transfer. Thus, the injunction preserved the status quo in order to save the arbitration clause. The Company contends that although injunctive relief may have appropriately issued to require arbitration, it was inappropriate to also enjoin the transfer of the plant, since the arbitrator could not halt the transfer.

A plaintiff, without regard to whether he is the employer or the union, seeking to maintain the status quo pending arbitration pursuant to the principles of *Boys Markets* need only establish that the position he will espouse in arbitration is sufficiently sound to prevent the arbitration from being a futile endeavor. If there is a genuine dispute with respect to an arbitrable issue, the barrier (to the issuance of an injunction) we believe appropriately (sic) has been cleared. The District Judge did not abuse his discretion by issuing the preliminary injunction preserving the status quo until the completion of the pending arbitration.

The district court correctly issued the preliminary injunction to preserve the status quo pending the completion of arbitration. It did not order the plant moved to Indiana. It did not order the plant to remain in Baltimore. It simply preserved a status of neutrality so the parties could arbitrate the underlying differences between them as to the interpretation of the collective bargaining agreement. Had the district court not preserved the status quo, Lever Brothers would have permanently transferred their plant from Baltimore, Maryland, to Hammond, Indiana. If the union then prevailed in the arbitration, they would have had a double burden to satisfy first, to convince the company that it should not have moved the plant to Hammond, Indiana, a *fait accompli*, and then it would have had the burden to convince the company to move the plant back to Baltimore, Maryland. The arbitration in this sense would undoubtedly have been "but an empty victory" for the union.

In the instant case, had there not been an injunction pending arbitration to preserve the status quo, the employees at the Baltimore plant would have been totally and permanently deprived of their employment, and, as above noted, if the union prevailed at the arbitration, would have had a double burden of convincing the company not only not to move, which it had already done, but to return the plant. It was incumbent upon the union to prevail at arbitration, obtain the "full information" which they sought, and then seek to convince the company not to move its plant.

Further, the rule contained in this case is obviously a two-sided coin. An injunction to preserve the status quo pending arbitration may be issued either against a company or against a union in an appropriate *Boys Markets* case where it is necessary to prevent conduct by the party enjoined from rendering the arbitral process a hollow formality in those instances where, as here, the arbitral award when rendered could not return the parties substantially to the status quo ante.

NOTES

1.   Assume that the collective bargaining agreement exempted the limitations on subcontracting from the grievance and arbitration procedure. What advice would you give the union as to how it might fight the employer's decision? In *Aeronautical Industrial Dist. Lodge 91, Int'l Ass'n of Machinists v. United Technologies Corp.*, 230 F.3d 569 (2d Cir. 2000), the union sued the employer for breach of the provisions of the collective bargaining agreement restricting subcontracting. The district court found a breach and enjoined the subcontracting. The Second Circuit affirmed.

2.   Federal Rule of Civil Procedure Rule 65(c) provides for the district court to require the party seeking the injunction to post a bond to secure payment of damages suffered by the other party if it is found to have been wrongfully enjoined. The union ultimately lost the arbitration. Should the company have recourse against the bond the union posted? In a portion of the opinion not reproduced, the court in *Lever Brothers* held that the employer may only have recourse against the bond if the preliminary injunction is found to have been granted improperly. The outcome of the underlying arbitration is not relevant.

D.   THE INDIVIDUAL AND THE COLLECTIVE PROCESS

To this point, we have examined the law as it pertains to efforts by Smith's union to reverse Enderby's decision to discharge him. But what if Smith wants to go it alone, either because he does not trust the union, believes the union officials are not competent, or because the union has refused to press Smith's grievance to arbitration? May Smith sue Enderby on his own?

Section 301 of the LMRA provides, "Suits for violation of contracts between an employer and a labor organization . . . may be brought in any district court of the United States." In *Smith v. Evening News Ass'n*, 371

U.S. 195 (1962), the Supreme Court interpreted the word "between" as modifying "contracts" rather than "suits." Had the Court concluded that "between" modified "suits," section 301 would have been limited to lawsuits by unions to enforce collective bargaining agreements. Instead, the Court held that individual employees may sue under section 301. However, in *Republic Steel Corp. v. Maddox*, 379 U.S. 650 (1965), the Court held that implicit in its holding in *Smith* was a requirement that the employee exhaust the contractual grievance procedure before bringing suit under section 301. Most collective bargaining agreements vest exclusive control over the grievance procedure in the union rather than the individual employee. In *Vaca v. Sipes*, reproduced below, the Supreme Court held that an employee may proceed against the employer for breach of contract where the union's handling of the employee's grievance was tainted by a breach of the union's duty of fair representation. In *Hines v. Anchor Motor Freight, Inc.*, 424 U.S. 554 (1976), the Court held that an employer may still be sued for breach of contract even though it prevailed in arbitration, if the arbitration was tainted by a union's duty of fair representation breach.

1. THE UNION'S DUTY OF FAIR REPRESENTATION

a. Origins of the Duty of Fair Representation

It is now well-established that along with the statutory grant to a union of the status of exclusive bargaining representative comes a duty to represent all employees in the bargaining unit fairly. The law governing the union's duty of fair representation (DFR) traces its origins to the 1940s. At that time, many unions, particularly those in the railroad industry, admitted only whites to membership, even though the bargaining units they represented contained African-Americans as well. Union racial discrimination was not expressly outlawed by a statute until Congress enacted the Civil Rights Act of 1964. However, in the wake of World War II, the hypocrisy of the United States fighting in Europe against racist actions by Nazi Germany while maintaining its own racism at home was not lost on many people, particularly the justices of the Supreme Court.

**THE SUPREME COURT AND THE DUTY
OF FAIR REPRESENTATION**

Martin H. Malin
27 Harv. C.R.–C.L. L. Rev. 127 (1992)

The Supreme Court first recognized a cause of action for a DFR breach in *Steele v. Louisville and Nashville Railroad*, 323 U.S. 192 (1944). Black locomotive firemen sued the all-white union that represented their bargaining unit for negotiating a series of contract modifications intended to replace the black workers with whites. The plaintiffs attacked the constitutionality of the Railway Labor Act's requirement of exclusive representation, where the exclusive representative negotiated a racially discriminatory contract. The Court, however, avoided the constitutional issue by implying in the statutory grant of exclusive representative status a correlative duty to represent fairly all employees. It recognized that a union may agree to contracts which have unfavorable effects on some of the employees it represents, but opined that in making such agreements, the union must base its decisions on relevant considerations rather than factors such as race which are "obviously irrelevant and invidious."

During its first twenty years of DFR jurisprudence, all Supreme Court DFR cases except one involved racial discrimination. In this context, the Court established broad parameters governing a union's DFR liability. Specifically, it held that the DFR applies to unions acting under the National Labor Relations Act, as well as the Railway Labor Act; that the DFR applies to contract administration, as well as contract negotiation; that the claim arises under federal law and is actionable in federal court; and that remedies for DFR breaches include damages and injunctions.

Steele was litigated as a civil rights case. The Court's creation of the DFR enabled it to avoid the plaintiffs' attack on the constitutionality of the Railway Labor Act. The union's negotiation to eliminate the jobs of black workers and replace them with whites was illegal not because it denied black workers equal protection, but because it based an employment decision on a distinction, *i.e.*, race, that was not relevant to the workplace. This judicial creativity in statutory construction enabled the Court to respond to post World War II heightened concerns with racial discrimination in a non-racially based manner. It also enabled the Court to craft a tool for combating union-management discrimination without reaching unilateral union conduct.

The Court's efforts to develop a cause of action for union-management discrimination, couched in language of a general duty, led it to retreat from *Steele* in *Ford Motor Co. v Huffman*, 345 U.S. 330 (1953), where the Court held that the union did not breach its DFR by agreeing to grant seniority credit for pre-employment military service. The Court, however, never explained why pre-employment military service, regardless of the similarity between the military position and the job, was relevant for making seniority distinctions in the workplace. Strong arguments can be made that because of the importance of seniority rights to the job security of the individual employee, courts should closely scrutinize agreements which effectively reduce those rights, and that pre-employment military service is no more relevant for distinguishing seniority rights than race.

The parties argued that they needed the flexibility to grant seniority credit for pre-employment military service to prevent potential unrest in the bargaining unit resulting from the military veterans' belief that they were entitled to seniority credit for their military service regardless of whether they had worked for the company before joining the military. The

Court appeared to accept this argument, for it opined that unions must be given "[a] wide range of reasonableness . . . in serving the bargaining unit . . ."

NOTES

1.   In *Bhd. of Ry. Trainmen v. Howard*, 343 U.S. 768 (1952), the Court held that the union which represented brakemen employed by the Frisco Railroad breached its duty of fair representation when it negotiated a provision in its collective bargaining agreement prohibiting the employer from allowing porters to perform brakemen's work. The railroad segregated its employees by race, hiring only whites as brakemen and African-Americans as porters. Porters performed the same duties as brakemen but also helped passengers board and alight from the trains and worked only at the head end. Porters were represented by a different union. Nevertheless, the Court held the Trainmen's union breached its DFR because it negotiated a provision that caused the porters to lose their jobs only because they were not white. The Court reasoned, "Bargaining agents who enjoy the advantages of the Railway Labor Act's provisions must execute their trust without lawless invasions of the rights of other workers."

2.   Are there circumstances where an employer may wish to cooperate with plaintiffs bringing a duty of fair representation lawsuit? In *Steele*, although the plaintiffs included the railroad as a defendant, they did not seek damages against the railroad, but only against the union. The plaintiffs also received the tacit approval of the railroad before filing suit and an understanding that the railroad would not retaliate against them. At the time, locomotive engineer jobs were reserved for whites only. White firemen used that job as a stepping stone to engineer positions. African-American firemen, in contrast, stayed in firemen jobs for long periods of time. Consequently, many of the railroad's best firemen were African-Americans and the railroad did not want to see them bumped by inexperienced whites. The railroad used the pending lawsuit as a justification for ignoring the contract. *See* Deborah C. Malamud, *The Story of* Steele v. Louisville & Nashville Railroad*: White Unions, Black Unions and the Struggle for Racial Justice on the Rails*, *in* Labor Law Stories 55 (Laura J. Cooper & Catherine L. Fisk eds. 2005).

3.   Title VII of the 1964 Civil Rights Act expressly prohibits discrimination by labor organizations. Title VII is in many ways a more effective tool than the duty of fair representation for policing racial discrimination by labor unions. For example, unlike the duty of fair representation, Title VII prohibits union racial discrimination in admitting members. Moreover, today, African-American workers are more likely than whites to be union members. If the duty of fair representation is no longer a primary vehicle for policing racial discrimination, what should its purpose be? Should courts police union discrimination on grounds that are not recognized as invidious?

4.   Professor Matthew Finkin has suggested that the only distinction between *Steele* and *Huffman* is the Court's view of social policy, which at the

time condemned racial discrimination but supported returning veterans. Matthew Finkin, *The Limits of Majority Rule in Collective Bargaining*, 64 Minn. L. Rev. 183 (1980). Do you agree?

b.   The Duty of Fair Representation: Substantive Standards of Conduct

VACA V. SIPES
386 U.S. 171 (1967)

JUSTICE WHITE delivered the opinion of the Court:

On February 13, 1962, Benjamin Owens filed this class action against petitioners, as officers and representatives of the National Brotherhood of Packinghouse Workers and of its Kansas City Local No. 12, in the Circuit Court of Jackson County, Missouri. Owens, a Union member, alleged that he had been discharged from his employment at Swift & Company's Kansas City Meat Packing Plant in violation of the collective bargaining agreement then in force between Swift and the Union, and that the Union had "arbitrarily, capriciously and without just or reasonable reason or cause" refused to take his grievance with Swift to arbitration under the fifth step of the bargaining agreement's grievance procedures.

After a jury trial, a verdict was returned awarding Owens $7,000 compensatory and $3,300 punitive damages. The trial judge set aside the verdict and entered judgment for petitioners on the ground that the NLRB had exclusive jurisdiction over this controversy, and the Kansas City Court of Appeals affirmed. The Supreme Court of Missouri reversed and directed reinstatement of the jury's verdict. During the appeal, Owens died and respondent, the administrator of Owens' estate, was substituted.

In mid-1959, Owens, a long-time high blood pressure patient, became sick and entered a hospital on sick leave from his employment with Swift. After a long rest during which his weight and blood pressure were reduced, Owens was certified by his family physician as fit to resume his heavy work in the packing plant. However, Swift's company doctor examined Owens upon his return and concluded that his blood pressure was too high to permit reinstatement. After securing a second authorization from another outside doctor, Owens returned to the plant, and a nurse permitted him to resume work on January 6, 1960. However, on January 8, when the doctor discovered Owens' return, he was permanently discharged on the ground of poor health.

Armed with his medical evidence of fitness, Owens then sought the Union's help in securing reinstatement, and a grievance was filed with Swift on his behalf. By mid-November 1960, the grievance had been processed through the third and into the fourth step of the grievance procedure established by the collective bargaining agreement. Swift adhered to its position that Owens' poor health justified his discharge, rejecting numerous medical reports of reduced blood pressure proffered by Owens and by the Union. Swift claimed that these reports were not based upon sufficiently thorough medical tests.

On February 6, 1961, the Union sent Owens to a new doctor at Union expense "to see if we could get some better medical evidence so that we could go to arbitration with his case." This examination did not support Owens' position. When the Union received the report, its executive board voted not to take the Owens grievance to arbitration because of insufficient medical evidence. Union officers suggested to Owens that he accept Swift's offer of referral to a rehabilitation center, and the grievance was suspended for that purpose. Owens rejected this alternative and demanded that the Union take his grievance to arbitration, but the Union refused. With his contractual remedies thus stalled at the fourth step, Owens brought this suit.

[T]he question which the Missouri Supreme Court thought dispositive of the issue of liability was whether the evidence supported Owens' assertion that he had been wrongfully discharged by Swift, regardless of the Union's good faith in reaching a contrary conclusion. This was also the major concern of the plaintiff at trial: the bulk of Owens' evidence was directed at whether he was medically fit at the time of discharge and whether he had performed heavy work after that discharge.

A breach of the statutory duty of fair representation occurs only when a union's conduct toward a member of the collective bargaining unit is arbitrary, discriminatory, or in bad faith. There has been considerable debate over the extent of this duty in the context of a union's enforcement of the grievance and arbitration procedures in a collective bargaining agreement. Some have suggested that every individual employee should have the right to have his grievance taken to arbitration. Others have urged that the union be given substantial discretion (if the collective bargaining agreement so provides) to decide whether a grievance should be taken to arbitration, subject only to the duty to refrain from patently wrongful conduct such as racial discrimination or personal hostility.

Though we accept the proposition that a union may not arbitrarily ignore a meritorious grievance or process it in perfunctory fashion, we do not agree that the individual employee has an absolute right to have his grievance taken to arbitration regardless of the provisions of the applicable collective bargaining agreement. In providing for a grievance and arbitration procedure which gives the union discretion to supervise the grievance machinery and to invoke arbitration, the employer and the union contemplate that each will endeavor in good faith to settle grievances short of arbitration. Through this settlement process, frivolous grievances are ended prior to the most costly and time-consuming step in the grievance procedures. Moreover, both sides are assured that similar complaints will be treated consistently, and major problem areas in the interpretation of the collective bargaining contract can be isolated and perhaps resolved. And finally, the settlement process furthers the interest of the union as statutory agent and as coauthor of the bargaining agreement in representing the employees in the enforcement of that agreement.

If the individual employee could compel arbitration of his grievance regardless of its merit, the settlement machinery provided by the contract would be substantially undermined, thus destroying the employer's confidence in the union's authority and returning the individual grievant to the vagaries of independent and unsystematic negotiation. Moreover, under such a rule, a significantly greater number of grievances would proceed to arbitration. This would greatly increase the cost of the grievance machinery and could so overburden the arbitration process as to prevent it from functioning successfully. It can well be doubted whether the parties to collective bargaining agreements would long continue to provide for detailed grievance and arbitration procedures of the kind encouraged by L.M.R.A. § 203(d), if their power to settle the majority of grievances short of the costlier and more time-consuming steps was limited by a rule permitting the grievant unilaterally to invoke arbitration. Nor do we see substantial danger to the interests of the individual employee if his statutory agent is given the contractual power honestly and in good faith to settle grievances short of arbitration. For these reasons, we conclude that a union does not breach its duty of fair representation, and thereby open up a suit by the employee for breach of contract, merely because it settled the grievance short of arbitration.

For these same reasons, the standard applied here by the Missouri Supreme Court cannot be sustained. For if a union's decision that a particular grievance lacks sufficient merit to justify arbitration would constitute a breach of the duty of fair representation because a judge or jury later found the grievance meritorious, the union's incentive to settle such grievances short of arbitration would be seriously reduced. The dampening effect on the entire grievance procedure of this reduction of the union's freedom to settle claims in good faith would surely be substantial. Since the union's statutory duty of fair representation protects the individual employee from arbitrary abuses of the settlement device by providing him with recourse against both employer (in a § 301 suit) and union, this severe limitation on the power to settle grievances is neither necessary nor desirable. Therefore, we conclude that the Supreme Court of Missouri erred in upholding the verdict in this case solely on the ground that the evidence supported Owens' claim that he had been wrongfully discharged.

Applying the proper standard of union liability to the facts of this case, we cannot uphold the jury's award, for we conclude that as a matter of federal law the evidence does not support a verdict that the Union breached its duty of fair representation. As we have stated, Owens could not have established a breach of that duty merely by convincing the jury that he was in fact fit for work in 1960; he must also have proved arbitrary or bad-faith conduct on the part of the Union in processing his grievance. The evidence revealed that the Union diligently supervised the grievance into the fourth step of the bargaining agreement's procedure, with the Union's business representative serving as Owens' advocate throughout these steps. When Swift refused to reinstate Owens on the basis of his medical reports indicating reduced blood pressure, the Union sent him to another doctor of his own choice, at Union expense, in an attempt to amass persuasive medical evidence of Owens' fitness for work. When this examination proved unfavorable, the Union concluded that it could not establish a wrongful discharge. It then encouraged Swift to find light work for Owens at the plant. When this effort failed, the Union determined that arbitration would be fruitless and suggested to Owens that he accept Swift's offer to send him to a heart association for rehabilitation. At this point, Owens' grievance was suspended in the fourth step in the hope that he might be rehabilitated.

In administering the grievance and arbitration machinery as statutory agent of the employees, a union must, in good faith and in a nonarbitrary manner, make decisions as to the merits of particular grievances. In a case such as this, when Owens supplied the Union with medical evidence supporting his position, the Union might well have breached its duty had it ignored Owens' complaint or had it processed the grievance in a perfunctory manner. But here the Union processed the grievance into the fourth step, attempted to gather sufficient evidence to prove Owens' case, attempted to secure for Owens less vigorous work at the plant, and joined in the employer's efforts to have Owens rehabilitated. Only when these efforts all proved unsuccessful did the Union conclude both that arbitration would be fruitless and that the grievance should be dismissed. There was no evidence that any Union officer was personally hostile to Owens or that the Union acted at any time other than in good faith. Having concluded that the individual employee has no absolute right to have his grievance arbitrated under the collective bargaining agreement at issue, and that a breach of the duty of fair representation is not established merely by proof that the underlying grievance was meritorious, we must conclude that that duty was not breached here.

[The dissenting opinion by JUSTICE BLACK has been omitted.]

Air Line Pilots Ass'n v. O'Neill, **499 U.S. 65 (1991).** The Air Line Pilots Ass'n (ALPA) struck Continental Airlines but, using replacements and crossovers, Continental continued to operate. Continental announced a system-wide bid for a large number of positions (the 85–5 bid). ALPA authorized striking pilots to participate in the bid but Continental refused to allow them to do so. ALPA and Continental then settled the strike, giving striking pilots three options: participate in the bid with the first 100 captain positions going to working pilots, the next 70 going to the most senior strikers, and the remaining allocated 1-for-1 to strikers and working pilots; resignation and severance pay; and continuation of individual claims against Continental but going to the end of the list for positions. The Fifth Circuit held that ALPA breached its duty of fair representation because the striking pilots would have fared better than under the settlement agreement had ALPA simply called off the strike and the pilots returned and participated in the bid with their seniority. The Supreme Court, in an opinion by Justice Stevens, reversed.

Initially, The Court rejected an argument by ALPA that in negotiating a contract, the union's duty of fair representation is breached only by bad faith or discriminatory conduct. The Court held that contract negotiation, just like contract administration, is subject to a standard of arbitrary, discriminatory or bad faith conduct. Justice Stevens continued:

> Congress did not intend judicial review of a union's performance to permit the court to substitute its own view of the proper bargain for that reached by the union. Rather, Congress envisioned the relationship between the courts and labor unions as similar to that between the courts and the legislature. Any substantive examination of a union's performance, therefore, must be highly deferential, recognizing the wide latitude that negotiators need for the effective performance of their bargaining responsibilities. For that reason, the final product of the bargaining process may constitute evidence of a breach of duty only if it can be fairly characterized as so far outside a "wide range of reasonableness," it is wholly "irrational" or "arbitrary."

> The approach of the Court of Appeals is particularly flawed because it fails to take into account either the strong policy favoring the peaceful settlement of labor disputes or the importance of evaluating the rationality of a union's decision in light of both the facts and the legal climate that confronted the negotiators at the time the decision was made.

> For purposes of decision, we may assume that the Court of Appeals was correct in its conclusion that, if ALPA had simply surrendered and voluntarily terminated the strike, the striking pilots would have been entitled to reemployment in the order of seniority. Moreover, we may assume that Continental would have responded to such action by rescinding its assignment of all of the 85–5 bid positions to working pilots. After all, it did rescind about half of those assignments pursuant to the terms of the settlement. Thus, we assume that the union made a bad settlement—one that was even worse than a unilateral termination of the strike.

Nevertheless, the settlement was by no means irrational. A settlement is not irrational simply because it turns out *in retrospect* to have been a bad settlement. Viewed in light of the legal landscape at the time of the settlement, ALPA's decision to settle rather than give up was certainly not illogical. At the time of the settlement, Continental had notified the union that all of the 85–5 bid positions had been awarded to working pilots and was maintaining that none of the strikers had any claim on any of those jobs.

A comparable position had been asserted by United Air Lines in litigation in the Northern District of Illinois. Because the District Court in that case had decided that such vacancies were not filled until pilots were trained and actually working in their new assignments, the Court of Appeals here concluded that the issue had been resolved in ALPA's favor when it agreed to the settlement with Continental. But this reasoning overlooks the fact that the validity of the District Court's ruling in the other case was then being challenged on appeal.

Moreover, even if the law had been clear that the 85–5 bid positions were vacancies, the Court of Appeals erroneously assumed that the existing law was also clarion that the striking pilots had a right to those vacancies because they had more seniority than the crossover and replacement workers. The court relied for the latter proposition solely on our cases interpreting the National Labor Relations Act. We have made clear, however, that National Labor Relations Act cases are not necessarily controlling in situations, such as this one, which are governed by the Railway Labor Act.

Given the background of determined resistance by Continental at all stages of this strike, it would certainly have been rational for ALPA to recognize the possibility that an attempted voluntary return to work would merely precipitate litigation over the right to the 85–5 bid positions. Because such a return would not have disposed of any of the individual claims of the pilots who ultimately elected option one or option two of the settlement, there was certainly a realistic possibility that Continental would not abandon its bargaining position without a complete settlement. At the very least, the settlement produced certain and prompt access to a share of the new jobs and avoided the costs and risks associated with major litigation. Moreover, since almost a third of the striking pilots chose the lump-sum severance payment rather than reinstatement, the settlement was presumably more advantageous than a surrender to a significant number of striking pilots. In labor disputes, as in other kinds of litigation, even a bad settlement may be more advantageous in the long run than a good lawsuit. In all events, the resolution of the dispute over the 85–5 bid vacancies was well within the "wide range of reasonableness," that a union is allowed in its bargaining.

Humphrey v. Moore, **375 U.S. 335 (1964).** The union represented employees of Dealers and E & L, both new car transport companies servicing Ford Motor Co. out of Louisville, Kentucky. Dealers acquired E & L, which led to a dispute over whether to dovetail or endtail seniority lists. Both employers were party to a multi-employer, multi-local collective bargaining agreement. The union president interpreted the contract to require dovetailing and so recommended to a joint labor-management committee considering the issue. The committee ordered dovetailing. Employees of the acquiring company sued and the Kentucky Court of Appeals held, inter alia, that the union breached its duty of fair representation by simultaneously representing two groups of employees with antagonistic interests. The Supreme Court, in an opinion written by Justice White, reversed:

> The Kentucky court made much of the antagonistic interests of the E & L and Dealers drivers, both groups being represented by the same union, whose president supported one group and opposed the other at the hearing before the Joint Conference Committee. But we are not ready to find a breach of the collective bargaining agent's duty of fair representation in taking a good faith position contrary to that of some individuals whom it represents nor in supporting the position of one group of employees against that of another. In *Ford Motor Co. v. Huffman,* the Court found no breach of duty by the union in agreeing to an amendment of an existing collective bargaining contract, granting enhanced seniority to a particular group of employees and resulting in layoffs which otherwise would not have occurred. "Inevitably differences arise in the manner and degree to which the terms of any negotiated agreement affect individual employees and classes of employees. The mere existence of such differences does not make them invalid. The complete satisfaction of all who are represented is hardly to be expected. A wide range of reasonableness must be allowed a statutory bargaining representative in serving the unit it represents, subject always to complete good faith and honesty of purpose in the exercise of its discretion." Just as a union must be free to sift out wholly frivolous grievances which would only clog the grievance process, so it must be free to take a position on the not so frivolous disputes. Nor should it be neutralized when the issue is chiefly between two sets of employees. Conflict between employees represented by the same union is a recurring fact. To remove or gag the union in these

cases would surely weaken the collective bargaining and grievance processes.

As far as this record shows, the union took its position honestly, in good faith and without hostility or arbitrary discrimination. After Dealers absorbed the Louisville business of E & L, there were fewer jobs at Dealers than there were Dealers and E & L drivers. One group or the other was going to suffer. If any E & L drivers were to be hired at Dealers either they or the Dealers drivers would not have the seniority which they had previously enjoyed. Inevitably the absorption would hurt someone. By choosing to integrate seniority lists based upon length of service at either company, the union acted upon wholly relevant considerations, not upon capricious or arbitrary factors. The evidence shows no breach by the union of its duty of fair representation.

NOTES

1.   Consider the potential purposes of the duty of fair representation. One purpose, exemplified by *Steele* is to effect institutional change. If this is the primary purpose, what types of institutional change should the duty effect? A second potential purpose is to deter union conduct to the end of having unions act more carefully. If this is the primary purpose of the duty, what standard of care should be imposed on unions? A third way of viewing the duty of fair representation is that its purpose is to compensate employees harmed by union misfeasance or malfeasance. If this is the primary purpose, in what types of cases should compensation be paid?

2.   Should a union be liable when a steward fails to file a grievance in a timely manner or a union business representative fails to demand arbitration in a timely manner? Should the reasons for the missed deadline matter? The courts have reached conflicting results. *See Vencl v Int'l Union of Operating En'rs, Local 8*, 137 F.3d 420 (6th Cir. 1998); *Zuniga v. United Can Co.*, 812 F.2d 443 (9th Cir. 1987); *Ruzica v. Gen. Motors Corp.*, 707 F.2d 259 (6th Cir. 1983); *Graff v. Elgin, Joliet & Eastern Ry*, 697 F.2d 771 (7th Cir. 1983).

3.   Banks and Davis became involved in an altercation while on duty at Bethlehem Steel. Davis, a former boxer, struck Banks knocking him unconscious. Bethlehem discharged both employees. Both employees filed grievances. Banks maintained that Davis was the aggressor and that Banks was innocent of any wrong-doing. He also maintained that several employees who witnessed the incident would support his claim. The local union president, however, refused to interview the employees because he interpreted the union constitution as prohibiting any union member from testifying in a manner that would harm another union member. Any employee whose testimony would help Banks, the local president reasoned, would necessarily harm Davis. Eventually, the union settled both grievances for conversion of the employees' discharges to resignations and payment of $3,000 to each. Has the union

breached its duty of fair representation to Banks? *See Banks v. Bethlehem Steel Corp.*, 870 F.2d 1438 (9th Cir. 1989) (holding a blanket refusal to interview witnesses amounted to arbitrary and perfunctory processing of the grievance).

4.   The collective bargaining agreement provides for posting of all bargaining unit vacancies with employees given two weeks to bid on a vacancy. It further provides that the company will award the vacancy to the most qualified bidder but where qualifications are relatively equal, seniority will govern. Whenever the company awards a vacancy to a junior bidder, the union takes up the case of the senior bidder pursuant to a policy that favors seniority. The union does not examine the junior bidder's qualifications. As long as the senior bidder desires, the union will take the case through to arbitration. Does the union breach any duty to the junior bidder who is awarded the position? *See Smith v. Hussmann Refrigerator Co.*, 619 F.2d 1229 (8th Cir. 1980) (multiple conflicting opinions from a divided court).

c.   Duty of Fair Representation: Enforcement Procedures and Remedies

Duty of fair representation claimants have to navigate a procedural minefield. One study found that most duty of fair representation plaintiffs lose and about half lose on procedural grounds. Michael J. Goldberg, *The Duty of Fair Representation: What the Courts Do in Fact*, 34 Buffalo L. Rev. 89 (1985).

A breach of the duty of fair representation is an unfair labor practice under the NLRA. In *Vaca v. Sipes, supra*, the Supreme Court held that an employee may also bring a private cause of action in federal district court. Some public sector jurisdictions, however, hold that a DFR claim may only be brought as an unfair labor practice charge before the jurisdiction's labor board. *See, e.g., Karahalios v. Nat'l Fed'n of Fed. Employees*, 489 U.S. 527 (1989) (holding Federal Labor Relations Authority jurisdiction is exclusive under Federal Sector Labor Management Relations Statute)*; Brown v. Me. State Employees Ass'n*, 690 A.2d 956 (Me. 1997). Some find exclusive jurisdiction in the state courts to the exclusion of the labor board. *See Ziccardi v. Commonwealth*, 456 A.2d 979 (Pa. 1982). Still others provide that the labor board has exclusive jurisdiction over the DFR claim against the union, but the court has jurisdiction over the breach of collective bargaining agreement claim against the employer. *See O'Hara v. State*, 642 N.W.2d 303 (Iowa 2002).

In *Clayton v. United Auto Workers*, 451 U.S. 679 (1981), the Supreme Court held that a DFR claimant must first exhaust internal union remedies where the remedies could provide the claimant with complete relief or could reactivate the claimant's grievance against the employer. Because the duty of fair representation is a judicially created cause of action, it has no express statute of limitations. In *DelCostello v. Int'l Bhd. of Teamsters*, 462 U.S. 151 (1983), the Court held that DFR lawsuits are subject to the six month limitations period that the NLRA sets for filing an unfair labor practice charge. In *Terry v. Int'l Bhd. of Teamsters*, 494 U.S. 558 (1990), the Court held that there is a right to jury trial in DFR actions seeking damages.

The Supreme Court has also addressed issues of remedy. In *Int'l Bhd. of Electrical Workers v. Foust*, 442 U.S. 42 (1979), the Court held that punitive damages are unavailable in a DFR case. The most common DFR lawsuit is by a discharged employee against the union for failure to represent fairly and against the employer for breach of contract. If the employee is successful, the Court has held, damages for lost wages are to be apportioned between the union and employer. The employer is liable for lost compensation up to the point where it would have reinstated the employee had the union not breached its duty. The union is liable for lost compensation beyond that point. *Bowen v. U.S. Postal Serv.*, 459 U.S. 212 (1983).

Claims brought against the union for breach of the duty of fair representation and against the employer for breach of the collective bargaining agreement are often called "hybrid DFR/301" actions. This is because the action against the union arises under the NLRA while the action against the employer is brought under section 301 of the LMRA. But, to be able to press a claim against the employer, the plaintiff must establish that the union breached its duty of fair representation, even if the union is not named as a party. In *Yeftich v. Navistar, Inc.*, 772 F.3d 911 (7th Cir. 2013), the plaintiffs alleged that Navistar violated the collective bargaining agreement by laying them off while subcontracting their work to nonunion plants. They also claimed that they had filed numerous grievances and that union officials had told them the grievances were being processed when, in fact, they were diverted and stalled. The court affirmed the district court's dismissal of their complaint because they failed to allege a duty of fair representation breach with sufficient specificity as required generally by the Supreme Court's interpretation of Fed. R.Civ. Pro. 12(b)(6) in *Ashcroft v. Iqbal*, 556 U.S. 662 (2009) and *Bell Atl. Corp. v. Twonbley*, 550 U.S. 554 (2007). The court faulted the plaintiffs for failing to supply factual detail in support of their conclusory allegations that union officials acted invidiously or arbitrarily. The plaintiffs failed to allege who filed grievances, the dates and contents of the grievances, which union officials told them the grievances were being processed, how long they waited before concluding that their grievances had been abandoned or why the period of time they waited was an abnormal and arbitrary delay.

2. RIGHTS OF RETIREES

As seen in Chapter 5, in *Allied Chemical & Alkalai Workers Local 1 v. Pittsburgh Plate Glass Division*, 404 U.S. 157 (1971), the Supreme Court held that medical and other benefits provided by the employer to retirees are not mandatory subjects of bargaining. The Court reasoned that retirees were no longer part of the bargaining unit and, therefore, no longer represented exclusively by the union. Because retirees are no longer exclusively represented by the union, they are not bound to grieve and arbitrate claims against the employer when the employer reduces retiree benefits or imposes costs on retirees that exceed those provided for in the collective bargaining agreement that was in effect when they retired. Instead, the retirees may sue the employer under section 301.

The principal issue in such litigation is usually whether the collective bargaining agreement in effect when the retirees retired provided that the retiree benefits were vested for life or were subject to unilateral change or discontinuance by the employer. The courts took divergent approaches. The Courts of Appeals for the Sixth and Seventh Circuit represented opposite ends of the spectrum of opinion. In *United Auto Workers v. Yard-Man, Inc.*, 716 F.2d 1476 (6th Cir. 1983), the collective bargaining agreement provided, "The Company will provide insurance benefits equal to the active group benefits . . . for the former employee and his spouse." The court found this language ambiguous as to duration of the benefits. The Sixth Circuit ruled:

> [E]xamination of the context in which these benefits arose demonstrates the likelihood that continuing insurance benefits for retirees were intended. Benefits for retirees are only permissive not mandatory subjects of bargaining. As such, it is unlikely that such benefits, which are typically understood as a form of delayed compensation or reward for past services would be left to contingencies of future negotiations. The employees are presumably aware that the union owes no obligation to bargain for continued benefits for retirees. If they forgo wages now in expectation of retiree benefits, they would want assurance that once they retire they will continue to receive such benefits regardless of the bargain reached in subsequent agreements. . . .

> Further, retiree benefits are in a sense "status" benefits which, as such, carry with them an inference that they continue so long as the prerequisite is maintained. Thus when the parties contract for benefits which accrue upon achievement of retiree status, there is an inference that the parties likely intended those benefits to continue as long as the beneficiary remains a retiree.

In *Cherry v. Auburn Grear, Inc.*, 441 F.3d 476 (7th Cir. 2006), the Seventh Circuit held that there is a presumption that, absent express language in the contract that provides otherwise, retiree benefits do not vest but terminate upon expiration of the collective bargaining agreement. The court stated that the presumption "imposes a high burden of proof upon the retirees." It distinguished language that provides for benefit eligibility (language that the Sixth Circuit relied on in finding an intent to vest) from language of benefits duration, stating, "It is well established that 'lifetime' benefits can be limited to the duration of a contract." The Supreme Court resolved the conflict in the following decision.

M & G POLYMERS USA, LLC v. TACKETT

135 S. Ct. 926 (2015)

JUSTICE THOMAS delivered the opinion of the Court:

I

A

Respondents Hobert Freel Tackett, Woodrow K. Pyles, and Harlan B. Conley worked at (and retired from) the Point Pleasant Polyester Plant in Apple Grove, West Virginia (hereinafter referred to as the Plant). During their employment, respondent United Steel, Paper and Forestry, Rubber, Manufacturing, Energy, Allied Industrial and Service Workers International Union, AFL–CIO–CLC, or its predecessor unions (hereinafter referred to as the Union), represented them in collective bargaining. Tackett and Pyles retired in 1996, and Conley retired in 1998. They represent a class of retired employees from the Plant, along with their surviving spouses and other dependents. Petitioner M & G Polymers USA, LLC, is the current owner of the Plant.

When M & G purchased the Plant in 2000, it entered a master collective-bargaining agreement and a Pension, Insurance, and Service Award Agreement (P & I agreement) with the Union, generally similar to agreements the Union had negotiated with M & G's predecessor. The P & I agreement provided for retiree health care benefits as follows:

> "Employees who retire on or after January 1, 1996 and who are eligible for and receiving a monthly pension under the 1993 Pension Plan . . . whose full years of attained age and full years of attained continuous service . . . at the time of retirement equals 95 or more points will receive a full Company contribution towards the cost of [health care] benefits described in this Exhibit B-1. . . . Employees who have less than 95 points at the time of retirement will receive a reduced Company contribution. The Company contribution will be reduced by 2% for every point less than 95. Employees will be required to pay the balance of the health care contribution, as estimated by the Company annually in advance, for the [health care] benefits described in this Exhibit B-1. Failure to pay the required medical contribution will result in cancellation of coverage."

Exhibit B-1, which described the health care benefits at issue, opened with the following durational clause: "Effective January 1, 1998, and for the duration of this Agreement thereafter, the Employer will provide the following program of hospital benefits, hospital-medical benefits, surgical benefits and prescription drug benefits for eligible employees and their dependents. . . ." The P & I agreement provided for renegotiation of its terms in three years.

B

In December 2006, M & G announced that it would begin requiring retirees to contribute to the cost of their health care benefits. Respondent retirees, on behalf of themselves and others similarly situated, sued M & G and related entities, alleging that the decision to require these contributions breached both the collective-bargaining agreement and the P & I agreement, in violation of § 301 of the Labor Management Relations Act, 1947 (LMRA) and § 502(a)(1)(B) of the Employee Retirement Income Security Act of 1974 (ERISA), 88 Stat. 891. Specifically, the retirees alleged that M & G had promised to provide lifetime contribution-free health care benefits for them, their surviving spouses, and their dependents. They pointed to the language in the 2000 P & I agreement providing that employees with a certain level of seniority "will receive a full Company contribution towards the cost of [health care] benefits described in . . . Exhibit B-1." The retirees alleged that, with this promise, M & G had created a vested right to such benefits that continued beyond the expiration of the 2000 P & I agreement.

The District Court dismissed the complaint for failure to state a claim. It concluded that the cited language unambiguously did not create a vested right to retiree benefits.

The Court of Appeals reversed based on the reasoning of its earlier decision in *Yard-Man*. *Yard-Man* involved a similar claim that an employer had breached a collective-bargaining agreement when it terminated retiree benefits. Although the court found the text of the provision in that case ambiguous, it relied on the "context" of labor negotiations to resolve that ambiguity in favor of the retirees' interpretation. Specifically, the court inferred that parties to collective bargaining would intend retiree benefits to vest for life because such benefits are "not mandatory" or required to be included in collective-bargaining agreements, are "typically understood as a form of delayed compensation or reward for past services," and are keyed to the acquisition of retirement status. The court concluded that these inferences "outweigh[ed] any contrary implications [about the termination of retiree benefits] derived from" general termination clauses.

Applying the *Yard-Man* inferences on review of the District Court's dismissal of the action, the Court of Appeals concluded that the retirees had stated a plausible claim. *Tackett I,* 561 F.3d, at 490. "Keeping in mind the context of the labor-management negotiations identified in *Yard-Man*," the court found "it unlikely that [the Union] would agree to language that ensures its members a 'full Company contribution,' if the company could unilaterally change the level of contribution." The court construed the language about "employees" contributing to their health care premiums as limited to employees who had not attained the requisite seniority points to be entitled to a full company contribution. And it discerned an intent to vest lifetime contribution-free health care benefits from provisions tying eligibility for health care benefits to eligibility for pension benefits.

On remand, the District Court conducted a bench trial and ruled in favor of the retirees. It declined to revisit the question whether the P & I agreement created a vested right to retiree benefits, concluding that the Court of Appeals had definitively resolved that issue. It then issued a permanent injunction ordering M & G to reinstate contribution-free health care benefits for the individual respondents and similarly situated retirees.

The Court of Appeals affirmed, concluding that, although the District Court had erred in treating *Tackett I* as a conclusive resolution of the meaning of the P & I agreement, it had not erred in "presum[ing]" that, "in the absence of extrinsic evidence to the contrary, the agreements indicated an intent to vest lifetime contribution-free benefits." And because the District Court had concluded that the proffered extrinsic evidence was inapplicable, it had not clearly erred in finding that the agreement created those vested rights.

We granted certiorari, and now vacate and remand.

II

This case is about the interpretation of collective-bargaining agreements that define rights to welfare benefits plans. The LMRA grants federal courts jurisdiction to resolve disputes between employers and labor unions about collective-bargaining agreements. 29 U.S.C. § 185. When collective-bargaining agreements create pension or welfare benefits plans, those plans are subject to rules established in ERISA. ERISA defines pension plans as plans, funds, or programs that "provid[e] retirement income to employees" or that "resul[t] in a deferral of income." § 1002(2)(A). It defines welfare benefits plans as plans, funds, or programs established or maintained to provide participants with additional benefits, such as life insurance and disability coverage. § 1002(1).

ERISA treats these two types of plans differently. Although ERISA imposes elaborate minimum funding and vesting standards for pension plans, §§ 1053, 1082, 1083, 1084, it explicitly exempts welfare benefits plans from those rules, §§ 1051(1), 1081(a)(1). Welfare benefits plans must be "established and maintained pursuant to a written instrument," § 1102(a)(1), but "[e]mployers or other plan sponsors are generally free under ERISA, for any reason at any time, to adopt, modify, or terminate welfare plans,". As we have previously recognized, "[E]mployers have large leeway to design disability and other welfare plans as they see fit.". And, we have observed, the rule that contractual "provisions ordinarily should be enforced as written is especially appropriate when enforcing an ERISA [welfare benefits] plan.". That is because the "focus on the written terms of the plan is the linchpin of a system that is not so complex that administrative costs, or litigation expenses, unduly discourage employers from offering [welfare benefits] plans in the first place."

We interpret collective-bargaining agreements, including those establishing ERISA plans, according to ordinary principles of contract law, at least when those principles are not inconsistent with federal labor policy. "Where the words of a contract in writing are clear and unambiguous, its meaning is to be ascertained in accordance with its plainly expressed intent." In this case, the Court of Appeals applied the *Yard-Man* inferences to conclude that, in the absence of extrinsic evidence to the contrary, the provisions of the contract indicated an intent to vest retirees with lifetime benefits. As we now explain, those inferences conflict with ordinary principles of contract law.

III

A

1

The Court of Appeals has long insisted that its *Yard-Man* inferences are drawn from ordinary contract law. In *Yard-Man* itself, the court purported to apply "traditional rules for contractual interpretation." The court first concluded that the provision governing retiree insurance benefits—which stated only that the employer "will provide" such benefits—was ambiguous as to the duration of those benefits. To resolve that ambiguity, it looked to other provisions of the agreement. The agreement included provisions for terminating active employees' insurance benefits in the case of layoffs and for terminating benefits for a retiree's spouse and dependents in case of the retiree's death before the expiration of the collective-bargaining agreement, but no provision specifically addressed the duration of retiree health care benefits. From the existence of these termination provisions and the absence of a termination provision specifically addressing retiree benefits, the court inferred an intent to vest those retiree benefits for life.

The court then purported to apply the rule that contracts should be interpreted to avoid illusory promises. It noted that the retiree insurance provisions "contain[ed] a promise that the company will pay an early retiree's insurance upon such retiree reaching age 65 but that the retiree must bear the cost of company insurance until that time.". Employees could retire at age 55, but the agreement containing this promise applied only for a 3-year term. Thus, retirees between the ages of 55 and 62 would not turn 65 and become eligible for the company contribution before the 3-year agreement expired. In light of this fact, the court reasoned that the promise would be "completely illusory for many early retirees under age 62" if the retiree benefits terminated when the contract expired.

Finally, the court turned to "the context" of labor negotiations. It observed that "[b]enefits for retirees are . . . not mandatory subjects of collective bargaining" and that "employees are presumably aware that the union owes no obligation to bargain for continued benefits for retirees." Based on these observations, the court concluded that "it is unlikely that such benefits . . . would be left to the contingencies of future negotiations." It also asserted that "retiree benefits are in a sense 'status' benefits which, as such, carry with them an inference that they continue so long as the prerequisite status is maintained."

Although the contract included a general durational clause—meaning that the contract itself would expire at a set time—the court concluded that these contextual clues "outweigh[ed] any contrary implications derived from a routine duration clause."

B

We disagree with the Court of Appeals' assessment that the inferences applied in *Yard-Man* and its progeny represent ordinary principles of contract law.

As an initial matter, *Yard-Man* violates ordinary contract principles by placing a thumb on the scale in favor of vested retiree benefits in all collective-bargaining agreements. That rule has no basis in ordinary principles of contract law. And it distorts the attempt "to ascertain the intention of *the parties*." *Yard-Man*'s assessment of likely behavior in collective bargaining is too speculative and too far removed from the context of any particular contract to be useful in discerning the parties' intention.

And the Court of Appeals derived its assessment of likely behavior not from record evidence, but instead from its own suppositions about the intentions of employees, unions, and employers negotiating retiree benefits. For example, it asserted, without any foundation, that, "when . . . parties contract for benefits which accrue upon achievement of retiree status, there is an inference that the parties likely intended those benefits to continue as long as the beneficiary remains a retiree." Although a court may look to known customs or usages in a particular industry to determine the meaning of a contract, the parties must prove those customs or usages using affirmative evidentiary support in a given case. *Yard-Man* relied on no record evidence indicating that employers and unions in that industry customarily vest retiree benefits. Worse, the Court of Appeals has taken the inferences in *Yard-Man* and applied them indiscriminately across industries.

Because the Court of Appeals did not ground its *Yard-Man* inferences in any record evidence, it is unsurprising that the inferences rest on a shaky factual foundation. For example, *Yard-Man* relied in part on the premise that retiree health care benefits are not subjects of mandatory collective bargaining. Parties, however, can and do voluntarily agree to make retiree benefits a subject of mandatory collective bargaining. Indeed, the employer and union in this case entered such an agreement in 2001. *Yard-Man* also relied on the premise that retiree benefits are a form of deferred compensation, but that characterization is contrary to Congress' determination otherwise. In ERISA, Congress specifically defined plans that "resul[t] in a deferral of income by employees" as pension plans, § 1002(2)(A)(ii), and plans that offer medical benefits as welfare plans, § 1002(1)(A). Thus, retiree health care benefits are not a form of deferred compensation.

Further compounding this error, the Court of Appeals has refused to apply general durational clauses to provisions governing retiree benefits. Having inferred that parties would not leave retiree benefits to the contingencies of future negotiations, and that retiree benefits generally last as long as the recipient remains a retiree, the court in *Yard-Man* explicitly concluded that these inferences "outweigh[ed] any contrary implications derived from a routine duration clause terminating the agreement generally." The court's subsequent decisions went even further, requiring a contract to include a specific durational clause for retiree health care benefits to prevent vesting. These decisions distort the text of the agreement and conflict with the principle of contract law that the written agreement is presumed to encompass the whole agreement of the parties.

Perhaps tugged by these inferences, the Court of Appeals misapplied other traditional principles of contract law, including the illusory promises doctrine. That doctrine instructs courts to avoid constructions of contracts that would render promises illusory because such promises cannot serve as consideration for a contract. But the Court of Appeals construed provisions that admittedly benefited some class of retirees as "illusory" merely because they did not equally benefit *all* retirees. That interpretation is a contradiction in terms—a promise that is "partly" illusory is by definition not illusory. If it benefits some class of retirees, then it may serve as consideration for the union's promises. And the court's interpretation is particularly inappropriate in the context of collective-bargaining agreements, which are negotiated on behalf of a broad category of individuals and consequently will often include provisions inapplicable to some category of employees.

The Court of Appeals also failed even to consider the traditional principle that courts should not construe ambiguous writings to create lifetime promises. The court recognized that "traditional rules of contractual interpretation require a clear manifestation of intent before conferring a benefit or obligation," but asserted that "the duration of the benefit once clearly conferred is [not] subject to this stricture." In stark contrast to this assertion, however, the court later applied that very stricture to noncollectively bargained contracts offering retiree benefits.

The different treatment of these two types of employment contracts only underscores *Yard-Man*'s deviation from ordinary principles of contract law.

Similarly, the Court of Appeals failed to consider the traditional principle that "contractual obligations will cease, in the ordinary course, upon termination of the bargaining agreement." That principle does not preclude the conclusion that the parties intended to vest lifetime benefits for retirees. Indeed, we have already recognized that "a collective-bargaining agreement [may] provid[e] in explicit terms that certain benefits continue after the agreement's expiration." But when a contract is silent as to the duration of retiree benefits, a court may not infer that the parties intended those benefits to vest for life.

C

There is no doubt that *Yard-Man* and its progeny affected the outcome here. As in its previous decisions, the Court of Appeals here cited the "context of . . . labor-management negotiations" and reasoned that the Union likely would not have agreed to language ensuring its members a "full Company contribution" if the company could change the level of that contribution. It similarly concluded that the tying of eligibility for health care benefits to receipt of pension benefits suggested an intent to vest health care benefits. And it framed its analysis from beginning to end in light of the principles it announced in *Yard-Man* and its progeny.

We reject the *Yard-Man* inferences as inconsistent with ordinary principles of contract law. We vacate the judgment of the Court of Appeals and remand the case for that court to apply ordinary principles of contract law in the first instance.

(The concurring opinion of JUSTICE GINSBURG joined by JUSTICES BREYER, SOTOMAYOR and KAGAN has been omitted.)

NOTES

1.   In *CNH Industrial N.V. v. Reese*, 138 S. Ct. 761 (2018), the Sixth Circuit in a post-*Tackett* decision found that a collective bargaining agreement's provisions concerning whether retiree medical benefits vested for life were ambiguous. Although the contract contained a general duration clause, the court found the language ambiguous on the grounds that (1) the contract specified that life insurance benefits ceased at a different time, and (2) the contract tied eligibility for health care benefits to pension eligibility. In a per curium decision, the Supreme Court reversed, holding that the Sixth Circuit's decision was inconsistent with *Tackett*. The Court reasoned that for ambiguity to exist contact language must be reasonably susceptible to two different interpretations and the presumptions rejected by the Court in *Tackett* could not be used to find ambiguity. The contract could only be ambiguous if it could reasonably be read as vesting medical benefits for life but *Tackett* rejected the *Yardman* presumptions as inconsistent with ordinary principles

of contract interpretation. Consequently, using the *Yardman* presumptions to find the contract ambiguous was inconsistent with *Tackett*.

2.   Compare the Court's views in *Tackett* and *CNH* that collective bargaining agreements are to be interpreted applying ordinary principles of contract interpretation with its view of interpretation of collective bargaining agreements by arbitrators expressed in the *Steelworkers Trilogy*. If the issue of lifetime vesting of retiree medical benefits comes before an arbitrator, is the arbitrator bound by the Court's decisions in *Tackett and CNH*?

3.   Assume that after the collective bargaining agreement under which certain employees retired expired, the employer eliminated retiree medical benefits. The union filed a grievance under the expired collective bargaining agreement and demanded arbitration. The employer refused to arbitrate. Should a court order the employer to arbitrate? If a court orders the employer to arbitrate and the arbitrator holds for the employer, are the retirees who do not participate in the arbitration bound by the award?

Courts have taken different approaches. In *Cleveland Electric Illuminating Co. v. Utility Workers Union of America*, 440 F.3d 809 (6th Cir. 2006), the parties had submitted the arbitrability issue to the arbitrator. After the arbitrator found the union's grievance arbitrable, the employer sued to vacate the award. The court applied the *Steelworkers Trilogy*'s presumption of arbitrability and reviewed the arbitrator's determination under the draws its essence from the contract standard. But the court held that for the union to represent the retirees in arbitration, the union had to secure their consent. The court left it to the arbitrator to decide the nature and extent of the consent requirement, including whether the union had to secure consent of all retirees or of only a percentage and, if the latter, what percentage. In *International Brotherhood of Electrical Workers v. Citizens Telecommunications Co.*, 549 F.3d 781 (9th Cir. 2008), the employer eliminated retiree medical benefits and the union grieved and demanded arbitration. The employer opposed arbitration unless the retirees consented to representation by the union. The Ninth Circuit held that such consent was not necessary, reasoning that the elimination of retiree medical benefits also adversely affected active employees for whom the union was the exclusive representative. The court further opined that an arbitration award would rarely "if at all" bind individual retirees who were not parties to the arbitration. In *Exelon Generation Co. v. Local 15, International Brotherhood of Electrical Workers*, 540 F.3d 640 (7th Cir. 2008), the Seventh Circuit held that a union may only arbitrate on behalf of retirees who consent, thereby suggesting that if no retirees consent, the union may not arbitrate. In *Local Union No. 13417, United Steelworkers v. Kansas Gas Service Co.*, 193 LRRM 2324, 2012 WL 1435305 (D. Kan. 2012), the district court followed *Exelon* and opined that retirees who did not consent to the union arbitrating would retain their rights to sue their former employer under section 301 of the Labor Management Relations Act.

4.   Assume that in their latest round of negotiations, an employer and union tackled issues related to the rising cost of health insurance. Among other things, they agreed to a provision in the new collective bargaining agreement

that reads, "Beginning with the effective date of this collective bargaining agreement, retirees shall pay monthly premiums of $50.00 for individual coverage and $100.00 for family coverage. Retirees shall be subject to annual deductibles of $200.00 per person and $400.00 per family." Prior to this agreement, retirees paid no premiums for individual coverage and $50.00 per month for family coverage, and were not subject to deductibles. The parties never discussed whether "retirees" referred only to those employees who would retire after the contract took effect or included those who already were retired. The union's negotiators, in good faith, believed that they were only discussing future retirees while the employer's negotiators, in good faith, believed that they were discussing current as well as future retirees. When the employer applied the new premiums and deductibles to existing retirees, the retirees complained to the union. As counsel for the union, what would you advise your client to do? As counsel to the employer, if the union grieves and demands arbitration, how should you respond?

3. SUPER-SENIORITY AND HIRING HALLS

As seen in Chapter 4, Section 8(a)(3) prohibits employer discrimination to discourage membership in a labor organization. It also prohibits employer discrimination to encourage membership in a labor organization and section 8(b)(2) prohibits union efforts to have employers violate section 8(a)(3). Two areas which raise issues of unlawful encouragement of union membership are special benefits provided to union stewards and employer use of union-operated hiring halls.

Stewards are the union's front line in contract administration. They provide representation when employees are called in for investigatory interviews and frequently are present when discipline is administered. They typically are the union representatives who counsel employees on filing grievances and who handle grievances in the earliest steps in the grievance procedure. Because of their roles in contract administration, both parties have a legitimate interest in maintaining continuity among stewards and in having the stewards readily available in the workplace. For this reason, the NLRB has held that the parties may confer super-seniority on union stewards and other union officials who perform steward-like functions. The typical super-seniority clause provides that the stewards shall be placed at the top of the seniority list regardless of their actual length of service with the employer. Such grants of super-seniority must be limited to purposes of layoff and recall to be justified by the interests in labor relations stability. Grants of super-seniority for other purposes, such as for computing fringe benefits or for such matters as picking vacation schedules, and grants of super-seniority to union officials who do not perform steward-like functions discriminate on the basis of protected activity and violate sections 8(a)(3) and 8(b)(2). *See Gulton-Electro Voice, Inc.*, 266 N.L.R.B. 406 (1983), *enf'd sub nom Int'l Union of*

Elec., Radio & Machine Workers, Local 900 v. NLRB, 727 F.2d 1114 (D.C. Cir. 1984).

In many industries, particularly those such as construction and long shoring that are characterized by short-term employment assignments, unions operate hiring halls and employers agree in the collective bargaining agreement to use them. Hiring halls may be exclusive, where the employer agrees to hire its employees only through the hiring hall, or they may be non-exclusive, where the employer retains the right to hire employees directly or through other sources. Exclusive hiring halls encourage workers to become members of the union. Nevertheless, in *Local 357, International Brotherhood of Teamsters v. NLRB*, 365 U.S. 367 (1961), the Supreme Court held that exclusive hiring halls do not per se violate the NLRA. The Court, in an opinion written by Justice Douglas, reasoned:

> It may be that the very existence of the hiring hall encourages union membership. We may assume that it does. The very existence of the union has the same influence. When a union engages in collective bargaining and obtains increased wages and improved working conditions, its prestige doubtless rises and, one may assume, more workers are drawn to it. When a union negotiates collective bargaining agreements that include arbitration clauses and supervises the functioning of those provisions so as to get equitable adjustments of grievances, union membership may also be encouraged. The truth is that the union is a service agency that probably encourages membership whenever it does its job well. But, the only encouragement or discouragement of union membership banned by the Act is that which is "accomplished by discrimination." Nothing is inferable from the present hiring-hall provision except that employer and union alike sought to route "casual employees" through the union hiring hall and required a union member who circumvented it to adhere to it.

> The present agreement for a union hiring hall has a protective clause in it, and there is no evidence that it was in fact used unlawfully. We cannot assume that a union conducts its operations in violation of law or that the parties to this contract did not intend to adhere to its express language. Yet we would have to make those assumptions to agree with the Board that it is reasonable to infer the union will act discriminatorily.

In *Breininger v. Sheet Metal Workers International Ass'n Local 6*, 493 U.S. 67 (1989), the Supreme Court held that an employee may sue a union for breach of the duty of fair representation as a result of its operation of a non-exclusive hiring hall. Breininger alleged that the union refused to honor employer requests for his referral and passed him over for other referrals because he was not part of a faction of workers aligned with the local's business manager. The Court, in an opinion written by Justice Brennan, held that he stated a cause of action. The Court reasoned:

> Only because of its status as a Board-certified bargaining representative and by virtue of the power granted to it by the collective-bargaining agreement does a union gain the ability to refer workers for employment through a hiring hall. Together with this authority comes the responsibility to exercise it in a nonarbitrary and nondiscriminatory fashion, because the members of the bargaining unit have entrusted the union with the task of representing them. That the particular function of job referral resembles a task that an employer might perform is of no consequence. The key is that the union is administering a provision of the contract, something that we have always held is subject to the duty of fair representation. "The undoubted broad authority of the union as exclusive bargaining agent in the negotiation *and administration* of a collective bargaining contract is accompanied by a responsibility of equal scope, the responsibility and duty of fair representation."

> In *Vaca v. Sipes*, for example, we held that a union has a duty of fair representation in grievance arbitration, despite the fact that NLRA § 9(a) expressly reserves the right of "any individual employee or group of employees . . . to present grievances to their employer and to have such grievances adjusted, without the intervention of the bargaining representative, as long as the adjustment is not inconsistent with the terms of a collective-bargaining contract or agreement then in effect." The union in *Vaca* exercised power over grievances because the contract so provided, not because the NLRA required such an arrangement. Hence, the observation that a contract might provide for the operation of a hiring hall directly by a consortium of interested employers rather than a union is irrelevant; the same might have been said about the system for processing grievances in *Vaca*. In short, a union does not shed its duty of fair representation merely because it is allocating job openings among competing applicants, something that might be seen as similar to what an employer does.

> The union's assumption in the hiring hall of what respondent believes is an employer's role in no way renders the duty of fair representation inapplicable. When management administers job rights outside the hiring hall setting, arbitrary or discriminatory acts are apt to provoke a strong reaction through the grievance mechanism. In the union hiring hall, however, there is no balance of power. If respondent is correct that in a hiring hall the union has assumed the mantle of employer, then the individual

employee stands alone against a single entity: the joint union/ employer. An improperly functioning hiring hall thus resembles a closed shop, "'with all of the abuses possible under such an arrangement, including discrimination against employees, prospective employees, members of union minority groups, and operation of a closed union.'" In sum, if a union does wield additional power in a hiring hall by assuming the employer's role, its responsibility to exercise that power fairly *increases* rather than *decreases*.

JACOBY V. NLRB

233 F.3d 611 (D.C. Cir. 2000)

WILLIAMS, CIRCUIT JUDGE:

Under a labor agreement governing construction work at a refinery jobsite in California, Steamfitters Local Union No. 342 held an exclusive right to dispatch workers to subcontractor Contra Costa Electric. Petitioner Joe Jacoby, a member of the union for 27 years, registered for employment through the union's hiring hall; due to his skills and experience, his name was placed on the highest priority "A" list. For a period the union mistakenly dispatched several lower-priority individuals ahead of Jacoby. On discovery of the error, it dispatched Jacoby. All parties agree, for current purposes at least, that the priority mix-up was merely negligent, and reflected no intentional wrongdoing.

Jacoby filed an unfair labor practice charge with the National Labor Relations Board, and the Board's General Counsel issued a complaint. After a hearing an administrative law judge found that the union's negligent deviation from established hiring hall rules breached its duty of fair representation and thereby violated §§ 8(b)(1)(A) & (2) of the National Labor Relations Act. The Board reversed, ruling that the union's negligence violated neither the duty of fair representation nor the Act. Although the Board agreed that the ALJ had correctly applied the Board's previous decision in *Iron Workers Local 118 (California Erectors)*, 309 N.L.R.B. 808 (1992), it reasoned that that decision, as well as the ALJ's findings, were inconsistent with the Supreme Court's pronouncements about the duty of fair representation in *United Steelworkers of America v. Rawson*, 495 U.S. 362 (1990), and *Air Line Pilots Ass'n, Int'l v. O'Neill*, 499 U.S. 65 (1991).

[T]he Board's interpretation of the duty of fair representation is entitled to deference under *Chevron, U.S.A., Inc. v. NRDC*, 467 U.S. 837 (1984), when the Board enforces that duty as part of its jurisdiction to identify and remedy unfair labor practices. We shall explain why this is so despite the fact that the duty *also* exists as a judge-made, court-enforced duty. But *Chevron* does not help an agency that rests its decision on a misinterpretation of Supreme Court precedent, as the Board did here.

Accordingly, we reverse and remand the case to the Board for it to address the duty of fair representation anew.

The duty of fair representation originated in the context of the Railway Labor Act, judicially inferred from that statute and enforceable in the courts. A union breaches this duty when its actions are "arbitrary, discriminatory, or in bad faith."

Originally, the duty was the exclusive province of the courts, falling within the federal courts' general federal question jurisdiction. Beginning with its decision in *Miranda Fuel Co.,* 140 N.L.R.B. 181 (1962), however, the NLRB has enforced the duty of fair representation itself as part of its authority to identify and remedy unfair labor practices. We have upheld this branch of the Board's unfair labor practice jurisdiction.

At the same time, the Supreme Court refused to find that the Board's enforcement of the duty of fair representation preempted judicial jurisdiction over the duty of fair representation inferred from the NLRA. As a result the duty is subject to a kind of dyarchy. The Board is entitled to *Chevron* deference when it interprets the duty as part of its unfair labor practice jurisdiction, yet many cases involving the duty continue to originate in the courts.

And it is important to emphasize that for these court adjudicated cases the *Board's* definition of the duty of fair representation for purposes of adjudicating unfair labor practices appears only marginally relevant. The Supreme Court in *Breininger* explicitly "reject[ed] the proposition that the duty of fair representation should be defined in terms of what is an unfair labor practice." Thus, for cases arising in the courts, NLRB interpretations are relevant for what they may contribute on their intellectual merits, enjoying deference to the extent of their "power to persuade." Nonetheless, the Board's decision here is reviewable under the *Chevron* doctrine.

The duty of fair representation clearly extends to a union's operation of an exclusive hiring hall. Prior decisions of the Board described the duty, in the hiring hall context, in rather demanding terms. Ruling in favor of the Board in such a case, we said:

> [A]ny departure from established exclusive hiring hall procedures which results in a denial of employment to an applicant falls within that class of discrimination which inherently encourages union membership, breaches the duty of fair representation owed to all hiring hall users, and violates Section 8(b)(1)(A) and (2), unless the union demonstrates that its interference with employment was pursuant to a valid union-security clause or was necessary to the effective performance of its representative function.

Boilermakers Local No. 374 v. NLRB, 852 F.2d 1353, 1358 (D.C. Cir. 1988). And we also said that breach of the duty required no evidence of intent to discriminate:

> No specific intent to discriminate on the basis of union membership or activity is required; a union commits an unfair labor practice if it administers the exclusive hall arbitrarily or without reference to objective criteria and thereby affects the employment status of those it is expected to represent. "By wielding its power arbitrarily, the Union gives notice that its favor must be curried, thereby encouraging membership and unquestioned adherence to its policies."

The Board itself, applying the standard that we upheld in *Boilermakers,* found a breach of the duty (and an unfair labor practice) in circumstances virtually identical to the present ones. In *Iron Workers Local 118 (California Erectors),* 309 N.L.R.B. 808, it ruled that union officials breached their duty of representation when, "through mistake and inadvertence," they failed to dispatch a worker to a job to which he should have been referred under exclusive hiring hall procedures. Unsurprisingly, the ALJ applied *California Erectors* in its decision below.

In reversing the ALJ, the Board here acknowledged that her reading of that case was "correct," but found that continued application of *California Erectors* would be inconsistent with the Supreme Court decisions in *Rawson* and *O'Neill.*

There is undoubtedly language in these Supreme Court decisions supporting the Board's view. Both explicate the standard earlier laid down by the Court in *Vaca v. Sipes,* which said that a union breached the duty of fair representation when its actions were "arbitrary, discriminatory, or in bad faith." In *Rawson,* the Court rejected a claim that a union breached the duty when it negligently performed mine-safety related duties pursuant to a collective bargaining agreement. The Court observed that "[t]he courts have in general assumed that mere negligence, even in the enforcement of a collective-bargaining agreement, would not state a claim for breach of the duty of fair representation, and we endorse that view today."

O'Neill involved a claim that the Air Line Pilots Association breached its duty of fair representation in its negotiation and acceptance of a strike settlement. The Court held that the *Vaca* standard "applies to all union activity, including contract negotiation." Moreover, it explained that "a union's actions are arbitrary only if, in light of the factual and legal landscape at the time of the union's actions, the union's behavior is so far outside a 'wide range of reasonableness' as to be irrational."

But as Jacoby points out, the Board's reading of *Rawson* and *O'Neill* cannot be reconciled with our decision in *Plumbers & Pipe Fitters Local 32 v. NLRB,* 50 F.3d 29 (D.C. Cir. 1995). There we considered and rejected the argument that *O'Neill* undermined the standard governing a union's operation of an exclusive hiring hall—specifically the principle that a union operate a hiring hall by "reference to objective criteria."

In support of this conclusion we relied on the drastic difference in context. In *O'Neill* the Court's focus was on "protecting the content of negotiated agreements from judicial second-guessing." The operation of a hiring hall, by contrast, was one "where the union has assumed the role of employer, as well as representative, and where the risk of judicial second-guessing of a negotiated agreement that was of such concern to the Court in *O'Neill* is simply not present." We also relied on the Supreme Court's decision in *Breininger,* issued only one year before *Rawson* and two years before *O'Neill,* where the Court said that the imbalance of power and possibilities for abuse created by union operation of a hiring hall were such that "if a union does wield additional power in a hiring hall by assuming the employer's role, its responsibility to exercise that power fairly *increases* rather than *decreases.*"

The question before us today differs from that in *Plumbers & Pipe Fitters* primarily with regard to two details, both ultimately insignificant. First, this case turns on a different aspect of the legal standard defined in *Boilermakers.* Whereas *Plumbers & Pipe Fitters* involved the operation of a hiring hall "without reference to objective criteria," the facts here implicate the rule precluding departures "from established exclusive hiring hall procedures." But this distinction does nothing to help the Board's position. That position is premised on the conclusion that *O'Neill* generally precludes heightened scrutiny in the hiring hall context, but in *Plumbers & Pipe Fitters* we concluded that the "Court did not intend to weaken the standard of review applied to a union's operation of a hiring hall."

In addition, one might argue that in the present context the *Boilermakers* standard is more vulnerable to the claim of erasure by *O'Neill* and *Rawson,* as this case involves a claim of negligence, thus encountering *Rawson*'s conclusion that "mere negligence" did not violate the duty of fair representation in the contract administration context. But the Board's application of *Rawson* relies exclusively on the type of "one-size-fits-all" theory that *Plumbers & Pipe Fitters* rejected. And, once again, *Rawson* is not a hiring hall case. It concerned the specific question of whether a union violates the duty of fair representation through negligent enforcement of a collective bargaining agreement. Thus we see no reason why *Rawson*'s general statements on negligence should be regarded as any less subject to qualification than *O'Neill*'s statements about "behavior so far outside a range of reasonableness as to be irrational."

The Board's reliance on its mistaken analysis of *O'Neill* and *Rawson* compels a remand. "An agency action, however permissible as an exercise of discretion, cannot be sustained 'where it is based not on the agency's own judgment but on an erroneous view of the law.'" On remand, the Board must consider whether, given the union's heightened duty of fair dealing in the context of a hiring hall, the union's negligent failure to adhere to its referral standards was an unfair labor practice. In remanding, of course, we express no opinion on the validity of any alternate grounds that the Board might use to overrule *California Erectors*.

NOTES

1.   On remand, the NLRB reiterated its position that negligence in administering hiring hall referrals did not breach the duty of fair representation. *Steamfitters Local 342 (Contra Costa Electric, Inc.)*, 336 N.L.R.B. 549 (2001). A different panel of the D.C. Circuit, in an opinion written by Judge Edwards, affirmed, *Jacoby v. NLRB*, 325 F.3d 301 (D.C. Cir. 2003), reasoning:

> We are aware of no judicial decision—and petitioner cites us to none—in which a court has held that a union violates its duty of fair representation if it commits a single act of simple negligence or inadvertent error in the administration of an exclusive hiring hall. Indeed, we are unaware of *any case* in which a court has found a breach of the DFR based on a single act of simple negligence, where the record is devoid of evidence that the union acted pursuant to ill will, discrimination, unlawful favoritism, or other obviously unreasonable business practices. Therefore, there was no obvious legal impediment to the Board's holding in this case. The only intriguing question in this case is whether the Board's holding satisfies the "heightened duty of fair dealing" standard, which is unique to the hiring hall context.
>
> In *Boilermakers*, this court set forth the parameters of the heightened duty standard in hiring hall cases. The court made it clear that "a union commits an unfair labor practice if it administers the exclusive hall arbitrarily or without reference to objective criteria and thereby affects the employment status of those it is expected to represent." Under this precept, a union must operate a hiring hall with "objective, consistent standards," without discrimination, and without "caus[ing] or attempt[ing] to cause an employer to discriminate against an employee" in regard to employment so as to encourage union membership. The heightened duty standard does not mean, however, that a single, unintentional error by a union is a breach of the DFR. Nothing in *Boilermakers* suggests that, where a hiring hall is administered pursuant to objective and consistent standards, an act of simple negligence, unaccompanied by ill will, discrimination, unlawful favoritism, or other obviously unreasonable business practices, violates the "heightened duty" standard.

What remains of the "heightened duty" standard of fair representation in the operation of a hiring hall? Recall note 2 on p. 948 concerning union liability when a steward neglects to file a grievance within the contractually-established time limits. Are there reasons to judge some union conduct by a negligence standard or a standard that requires greater culpability than negligence but less than arbitrary or intentional misconduct?

2.   Should the status of the hiring hall as exclusive or non-exclusive make a difference in the level of scrutiny a court or the NLRB gives to its operation?

E. THE CONTRACTUAL GRIEVANCE PROCEDURE AND "EXTERNAL" PUBLIC LAW

In the problem that opened this chapter, Smith believes that Enderby fired him because of his activity as a shop steward which was protected by Section 7 of the NLRA. He also believes that Enderby fired him because of his race, in violation of Title VII of the Civil Rights Act of 1964. May Smith pursue these claims without first grieving his discharge under the collective bargaining agreement? If he grieves under the contract and loses, may he nonetheless pursue his claims under the NLRA and Title VII?

When the Supreme Court decided the *Steelworkers Trilogy*, very few statutes regulated the workplace. The Fair Labor Standards Act mandated minimum wage rates and premium pay for hours worked in excess of forty in a week and prohibited most forms of child labor. The NLRA protected concerted worker activity. These statutes notwithstanding, the primary regulations of the workplace was the collective bargaining agreement, as enforced through the grievance and arbitration procedure. Professor David Feller referred to this period as the golden age of labor arbitration. David Feller, *The Coming End of Arbitration's Golden Age*, in Arbitration 1976: Proceedings of the 29th Annual Meeting, National Academy of Arbitrators 97 (Barbara D. Dennis & Gerald G. Somers, eds. 1976).

Beginning in the mid 1960s, Congress enacted a plethora of statutes regulating the workplace. These statutes include the Equal Pay Act (which prohibits sex discrimination in pay), Title VII of the 1964 Civil Rights Act (which prohibits discrimination in hiring, firing, or any term of employment on the basis of race, religion, gender, and national origin), the Occupational Safety and Health Act (which regulates workplace safety), the Age Discrimination in Employment Act (which prohibits discrimination against employees over 40 years old), the Employment Retirement Income Security Act (which regulates employer provided benefit plans), the Americans with Disabilities Act (which prohibits discrimination based on disability in any term of employment), the Employee Polygraph Protection Act (which prohibits using lie detector tests to determine suitability for employment), the Worker Adjustment Retraining and Notification Act (which requires employers to give advance notice of plant closures and mass layoffs), and the Family and Medical Leave Act (which requires employers to give unpaid leave to employees for health care and family care). In addition, many states regulate many aspects of the work relationship that federal law does not regulate. In today's workplace, the parties' system of self-governance through the collective bargaining agreement and its grievance and arbitration procedure occurs in a setting of detailed and pervasive government regulation. This section first considers the interplay of the grievance and arbitration procedure with the NLRB and then examines its interplay with the broader panoply of public laws governing the workplace.

1. THE GRIEVANCE PROCEDURE AND THE NLRB

The same transaction may implicate the collective bargaining agreement and the NLRA. For example, an employer may change a working condition during the term of the contract. The union may allege that the employer breached its statutory duty to bargain by making a unilateral change in a mandatory subject of bargaining without first negotiating to impasse. The union may also allege that the change violated the contract. On the other hand, the employer may defend against the failure to bargain charge by pointing to the collective bargaining agreement, arguing that the contract gave it the right to act as it did. Similarly, discipline or discharge of an employee may give rise to a claim of breach of contract on the ground that the employer lacked just cause, and to interference with protected concerted activity and discrimination to discourage union activity. For instance, in *NLRB v. City Disposal Systems, Inc.*, 465 U.S. 822 (1984), *supra* Chapter 2, the employer fired a truck driver who refused to drive a truck that he believed to be unsafe. The Court held that the driver's refusal was protected by section 7 because the collective bargaining agreement gave all employees in the workplace the right to refuse to drive an unsafe truck.

During the debates over the Taft-Hartley Act, Congress rejected an amendment that would have given the NLRB jurisdiction over claims of breaches of collective bargaining agreements. Section 10(a) of the NLRA provides that the NLRB's power to prevent unfair labor practices "shall not be affected by any other means of adjustment or prevention that has been or may be established by agreement, law or otherwise."

In *NLRB v. C. & C. Plywood Corp.*, 385 U.S. 421 (1967), the Supreme Court held that the NLRB has authority to interpret collective bargaining agreements where necessary to resolve unfair labor practice complaints. Conversely, in *Carey v. Westinghouse Electric Corp.*, 375 U.S. 261 (1964), the Court held that an arbitrator may resolve a grievance even though the same transaction may give rise to proceedings before the Board.

The NLRB's interaction with the grievance process may arise in three situations. The NLRB may be called upon to adjudicate an unfair labor practice complaint after an arbitrator has ruled on the grievance. It may be called upon to adjudicate an unfair labor practice complaint while the grievance process is pending. Finally, a charging party may not have filed a grievance at all even though it could have done so.

In 1955, the NLRB addressed the situation where it is called upon to adjudicate the unfair labor practice after an arbitrator has ruled on a related grievance. In *Spielberg Manufacturing Co.*, 112 N.L.R.B. 1080 (1955), the Board held that it would defer to the arbitration award as long as the parties had agreed to be bound, the proceedings were fair and regular and the result was not clearly repugnant to the NLRA. When the Board defers to an arbitration award, it does not merely give collateral estoppel effect to arbitral findings. It completely dismisses the unfair labor practice complaint.

Controversy since *Spielberg* has centered on the degree to which the arbitrator must have considered the unfair labor practice. Initially, the Board refused to defer where the unfair labor practice had not been presented to the arbitrator. However, in *Electronic Reproduction Service Corp.*, 213 N.L.R.B. 757 (1974), the Board held that it would "give full effect to arbitration awards dealing with discipline or discharge cases, under *Spielberg,* except when unusual circumstances are shown which demonstrate that there were bona fide reasons, other than a mere desire on the part of one party to try the same set of facts before two forums, which caused the failure to introduce such evidence at the arbitration proceeding."

Six years later, in *Suburban Motor Freight, Inc.*, 247 N.L.R.B. 146 (1980), the Board overruled *Electronic Reproduction Services*, reasoning that the latter case as an "impermissible delegation of the Board's exclusive jurisdiction under Section 10(a) of the Act to decide unfair labor practice issues." The Board stated it could "no longer adhere to a doctrine which forces employees in arbitration proceeding to seek simultaneous vindication of private contractual rights and public statutory rights, or risk waiving the latter."

Four years later, in *Olin Corp.*, 268 N.L.R.B. 573 (1984), the Board reversed *Suburban Motor Freight*. It held that it would defer to an arbitration award as long as the grievance was factually parallel to the unfair labor practice and the arbitrator was presented with facts generally relevant to the unfair labor practice. The Board also interpreted *Speilberg's* concern that the award not be clearly repugnant to the Act to mean that the award may not be palpably wrong, i.e. not susceptible to an interpretation consistent with the Act.

In *Babcock & Wilcox Construction Co.*, 361 N.L.R.B. 1127 (2014), the Board overruled *Olin*. The Board held that it will only defer to an arbitration award where: the parties explicitly authorized the arbitrator to resolve the unfair labor practice issue either through authorization for that case or through a provision, such as a prohibition on discrimination for union activity, in the collective bargaining agreement; the arbitrator has been presented with and considered the unfair labor practice or was prevented from doing so by the party opposing deferral; and NLRB law reasonably permits the award. The new standards apply only to 8(a)(1) and 8(a)(3) charges, not to 8(a)(5) charges, *See also* General Counsel Memo 15–02 (Feb. 10, 2015) (guidelines for applying *Babcock & Wilcox*).

The Board confronted the question of how to handle an unfair labor practice while related grievance proceedings were pending in 1963. In *Dubo Manufacturing Corp.*, 142 N.L.R.B. 431 (1963), the Board held that it would stay unfair labor practice proceedings pending the outcome of the grievance. The Board's *Dubo* deferral policy has not been controversial. It conserves Board and party resources to await the outcome of a grievance proceeding that may resolve the unfair labor practice or otherwise render it moot.

The Board confronted a situation where the charging party could have but did not file a grievance in *Collyer Insulated Wire*, 192 N.L.R.B. 837 (1971). The union charged that Collyer had unilaterally changed wage rates without bargaining to impasse. Collyer asked the Board to refrain from deciding the case unless and until the union took its complaint through the contractual grievance procedure. The Board agreed. It reasoned:

> The courts have long recognized that an industrial relations dispute may involve conduct which, at least arguably, may contravene both the collective agreement and our statute. When the parties have contractually committed themselves to mutually agreeable procedures for resolving their disputes during the period of the contract, we are of the view that those procedures should be afforded full opportunity to function. The long and successful functioning of grievance and arbitration procedures suggests to us that in the overwhelming majority of cases, the utilization of such means will resolve the underlying dispute and make it unnecessary for either party to follow the more formal, and sometimes lengthy, combination of administrative and judicial litigation provided for under our statute. At the same time, by our reservation of jurisdiction, we guarantee that there will be no sacrifice of statutory rights if the parties' own processes fail to function in a manner consistent with the dictates of our law. This approach, we believe, effectuates the salutary policy announced in *Spielberg* of not requiring the "serious machinery of the Board where the record indicates that the parties are in the process of resolving their dispute in a manner sufficient to effectuate the policies of the Act."

Board Members Fanning and Jenkins vehemently dissented. They accused the majority of imposing "compulsory arbitration" and abdicating the

Board's statutory responsibility to adjudicate unfair labor practice complaints.

Despite the Fanning and Jenkins dissents, *"Collyerizing"* a case has become accepted Board practice. The Board will not *Collyerize*, however, where the party seeking deferral refuses to waive procedural obstacles to arbitration, such as the expiration of contractual time limits. The major controversy involving *Collyer* has focused on whether the Board should *Collyerize* 8(a)(1) and (3) claims as well as 8(a)(5) charges. In *National Radio Co.*, 198 N.L.R.B. 527 (1972), the Board extended *Collyer* to 8(a)(3) discrimination charges. Five years later, in *General American Transportation Corp.*, 228 N.L.R.B. 808 (1977), the Board overruled *National Radio* and again confined *Collyer* to 8(a)(5) cases. Seven years later, in *United Technologies Corp.*, 268 N.L.R.B. 557 (1984), the Board overruled *General American Transportation* and again *Collyerized* 8(a)(3) cases. In *Babcock & Wilcox Construction Co.*, 361 N.L.R.B. 1127 (2014), the Board indicated it will not defer 8(a)(1) and 8(a)(3) charges under *Dubo* and *Collyer* unless the parties have explicitly authorized the arbitrator to resolve the unfair labor practice issue either through authorization for that case or through a provision, such as a prohibition on discrimination for union activity, in the collective bargaining agreement.

The controversies over Board deferral to arbitration reflect deep divisions over matters of policy and statutory construction. The multiple opinions in the following case explore these issues.

HAMMONTREE V. NLRB
925 F.2d 1486 (D.C. Cir. 1991)

WALD, CIRCUIT JUDGE:

I.   Background

A.   *Factual Background*

Hammontree is employed as a truck driver by intervenor Consolidated Freightways ("CF"); he drives "peddle" runs—short roundtrips of less than 200 miles.

In late 1985, Hammontree filed a grievance ("Grievance 180") claiming that his seniority rights had been violated by peddle-run assignment practices. Pursuant to the CBA, Hammontree's grievance was heard by a "Multi-State Grievance Committee" composed of an equal number of union and management representatives. This committee failed to resolve the grievance, which Hammontree then pursued to the next level, the Southern Area Grievance Committee. That committee sustained Hammontree's claim and awarded him damages.

Thereafter, CF stopped posting run departure times. Hammontree then filed a second grievance ("Grievance 101") claiming, *inter alia,* that the removal of run times violated the maintenance of standards provision. The first-level grievance committee denied the claim. Hammontree then filed an unfair labor practice ("ULP") charge, and the NLRB's General Counsel issued a complaint, alleging that by removing departure times in response to Hammontree's exercise of his grievance rights (in Grievance 180) and by assigning Hammontree less desirable runs, CF had violated §§ 8(a)(1) and 8(a)(3) of the NLRA.

The Board held that under its policy set forth in *United Technologies Corp.*, Hammontree was required to exhaust the grievance procedures established by the CBA. Hammontree seeks review of the Board's order.

B.   *The NLRB's "Deferral" Policies*

This case concerns one of the Board's two "deferral" policies, its so-called "pre-arbitral deferral" policy. Under this policy, the Board refers complaints filed by the General Counsel to arbitration procedures established in the governing CBA; in doing so, the Board *defers* or delays its consideration of the complaint. Under a separate, so-called "post-arbitral deferral" policy, not directly implicated in this case, the Board shows limited *deference* to decisions made through grievance and arbitration processes pursuant to collective bargaining provisions.

Pre-arbitral deferral (what we will, for clarity's sake, call "*deferment*") resembles the exhaustion requirements often found in administrative regimes and the abstention doctrines employed by federal courts. Post-arbitral deferral (what we will call "*deference*") resembles appellate judicial deference.

1.   *The Board's Deferment Policy*

In *Collyer Insulated Wire,* the Board considered a § 8(a)(5) claim arising out of an alleged unilateral change of working conditions by an employer. The Board ruled that it would require exhaustion of CBA-provided arbitration remedies before it considered a § 8(a)(5) claim, if certain conditions are met. Such deferment is appropriate, the Board ruled, if

(i)   there is a long-standing bargaining relationship between the parties;

(ii)   there is no enmity by the employer toward the employee's exercise of rights;

(iii)   the employer manifests a willingness to arbitrate;

(iv)   the CBA's arbitration clause covers the dispute at issue; and

(v)   the contract and its meaning lie at the center of the dispute.

The Board extended this deferment policy to § 8(a)(1) and § 8(a)(3) complaints in *National Radio Co.* After a temporary contraction of the policy, the Board reaffirmed the *National Radio* policy in its 1984 decision in *United Technologies Corp.*

2.   *The Board's Deference Policy*

The critical NLRB decision involving the Board's policy of deference to arbitration awards is *Spielberg Manufacturing Co.* In *Spielberg,* the Board ruled that it would give deference to an arbitrator's resolution of an unfair labor practice claim if certain conditions are met. As refined in subsequent cases, the Board's policy is to defer if:

(i)   the ULP issue was presented to and considered by the arbitrator;

(ii)   the arbitration proceedings were fair and regular;

(iii)   the parties agreed to be bound by the arbitration award; and

(iv)   the arbitration award was not clearly repugnant to the purposes and policies of the NLRA.

II.   Analysis

The central issue in this case, whether the Board may require an individual employee to exhaust grievance procedures prior to filing a ULP charge, is governed by the now-familiar two-step analysis set forth in *Chevron U.S.A., Inc. v. Natural Resources Defense Council,* 467 U.S. 837 (1984). Under *Chevron,* we first determine "whether Congress has directly spoken to the precise question at issue"; if it has, then "that intention is the law and must be given effect." If the statute is "silent or ambiguous with respect to the specific issue," and if "the agency's answer is based on a permissible construction of the statute," we must defer.

A.   Chevron I *Analysis*

1.   *Section 10(a) of the NLRA*

Section 10(a) of the NLRA provides that the Board's power to "prevent . . . unfair labor practice[s]" "shall not be affected by any other means of adjustment or prevention that has been or may be established by agreement, law, or otherwise. . . ."

Hammontree first contends that the plain language of § 10(a) prohibits Board deferment of his claim; he reads that section as providing that no one (not even the Board itself) may diminish the Board's authority to resolve and prevent ULPs in the first instance. Although read literally and in isolation, § 10(a) might permit such an interpretation, a far more natural reading is that § 10(a) is an affirmative grant of authority to the Board, not an express limitation on the Board's authority. In other words, a more plausible reading of § 10(a) is that no one *other than* the Board shall diminish the Board's authority over ULP claims.

This latter interpretation is supported by a contemporary congressional analysis which explained that the contested sentence "is intended to make it clear that although *other* agencies may be established by code, agreement, or law to handle labor disputes, such *other* agencies can never divest the National Labor Relations Board of jurisdiction which it would otherwise have." Staff of Senate Comm. on Education and Labor, 74th Cong., 1st Sess., Comparison of S. 2926 (73d Congress) and S. 1958 (74th Congress) at 3 (Comm. Print 1935) (emphasis supplied) [hereinafter "Comparison"] reprinted in NLRB, 1 Legislative History of the National Labor Relations Act 1319, 1323 (1949) [hereinafter "Leg.Hist. of the NLRA"].

Hammontree also maintains that the legislative history of § 10 indicates Congress' express intention to preclude Board deferment. In particular, Hammontree relies on Congress' elimination of a provision (in earlier bills and earlier drafts of the Act) which expressly stated that the "Board may, in its discretion, defer its exercise of jurisdiction over any such unfair labor practice in any case where there is another means of prevention provided for by agreement. . . ." S. 1958, § 10(b) (1935); *reprinted in* 1 Leg.Hist. of the NLRA 1295, 1301.

An equally plausible reading of Congress' deletion of the proposed language, however, is that Congress deemed it superfluous in light of the sweeping language of § 10(a) itself. [T]here is strong evidence that Congress deleted the proposed section on grounds of redundancy. Certainly, we cannot say that the legislative history of § 10 reflects a specific congressional intention to foreclose Board deferment; at best, we can only say that Congress' intention in deleting the proposed section is ambiguous.

2. *Section 203(d) of the LMRA*

Hammontree also argues that the Board's deferment authority is limited by § 203(d) of the LMRA, which provides that "[f]inal adjustment by a method agreed upon by the parties is declared to be the desirable method for settlement of grievance disputes *arising over the application or interpretation* of an existing collective-bargaining agreement." (emphasis supplied). Hammontree contends that his claim does not "arise over" the interpretation of the CBA and thus that deferment of his claim is not authorized by § 203(d)'s mandate.

Initially, we observe that § 203(d) reads most naturally as a general policy statement in favor of private dispute resolution, not as any kind of limitation on Board authority. But even if we were to assume *arguendo* that § 203(d) does in some way limit the Board's deferment authority, Hammontree's argument fails on its own terms, for his § 8(a)(3) claim *does* "aris[e] over [contract] application or interpretation." Hammontree's discrimination claim, although raised under §§ 8(a)(1) and 8(a)(3), is also actionable under the contract. Article 21 of the CBA prohibits "discrimination against any employee because of Union membership or activities" and Article 37 of the CBA bars "discriminatory acts prohibited by law." These provisions led the Board to conclude that the alleged discrimination "is clearly prohibited by the contract."

3. *Section 10(m) of the NLRA*

Section 10(m) of the NLRA provides, in relevant part, that

> [w]henever it is charged that any person has engaged in an unfair labor practice within [§ 8(a)(3) or § 8(b)(2)] . . ., such charge shall be given priority over all other cases except cases of like character . . . and cases given priority under [§ 10](*l*). . . .

Although "to give priority" could conceivably be interpreted as an imperative to the Board that it must hear and decide all § 8(a)(3) and § 8(b)(2) claims before it hears any other claims, that phrase can just as easily be understood as a direction to the Board that it ensure the most expeditious processing of § 8(a)(3) and § 8(b)(2) claims consistent with its expertise and other statutory responsibilities.

The Board's deferment policy is animated by this latter interpretation of § 10(m). Deferment, the Board reasonably argues, facilitates the expeditious processing of § 8(a)(3) and § 8(b)(2) claims by generally resolving complaints more quickly than Board proceedings could. The Board's treatment of Hammontree's claim is part of a systematic policy designed to accommodate its various statutory obligations pursuant to §§ 10(a), 203(d), and 10(m) and although *individual* claims may be left unresolved by arbitration so that deferment effectively delays the ultimate resolution of those claims, on the whole the policy of deferment expedites the resolution of the *class* of claims identified in § 10(m). Thus the Board's deferment policy is fully consistent with the priority mandate of § 10(m).

Given the realities of the Board's workload, an "imperative" interpretation of § 10(m) unrealistically restricts the Board's prerogative to regulate its own work. The NLRB processes more than 10,000 § 8(a)(3) and § 8(b)(2) claims every year; requiring the Board to process and hear every one of these claims before it hears any other claim would postpone (perhaps indefinitely) the resolution of the thousands of claims not involving § 8(a)(3) and § 8(b)(2).

In sum, the language and legislative history of §§ 10(a), 203(d), and 10(m) do not persuade us that Congress "has directly spoken to the precise question" of whether the Board may require an employee to exhaust grievance remedies before filing a ULP charge of discrimination. On that basis, we reject the petitioner's several *Chevron I* arguments.

B. Chevron II *Analysis*

1. *Limitations on the Board's Deferment Authority*

Hammontree argues under the second prong of *Chevron* that the Board's action in his case is based on an impermissible construction of the Board's authority under those statutes. Hammontree contends that Board deferment in cases in which individual employee rights are at stake is inconsistent with a series of Supreme Court decisions beginning with *Alexander v. Gardner-Denver Co.,* 415 U.S. 36 (1974). We find the alleged conflict illusory.

In *Alexander,* the Supreme Court held that Title VII creates individual statutory rights that supplement, rather than supplant, contractual rights under a CBA. Accordingly, the Court held that an employee's use of arbitration procedures did not bar a subsequent action, based on the same facts, brought in federal court under Title VII. The Court reached a similar conclusion in *Barrentine v. Arkansas-Best Freight System, Inc.,* 450 U.S. 728 (1981) (considering an analogous claim brought under the Fair Labor Standards Act ("FLSA")) and in *McDonald v. West Branch,* 466 U.S. 284 (1984) (considering a first amendment claim brought under 42 U.S.C. § 1983). In each of these cases, the Court ruled that Congress provided a public forum for individual-rights claims and that participation in private arbitration must not diminish one's right to such a forum. Hammontree maintains that these cases limit the Board's discretion to defer claims in which an individual seeks to vindicate personal rights under the NLRA.

We disagree. In *Alexander, Barrentine,* and *McDonald,* the Supreme Court held that, when individual statutory rights are at stake, arbitration of a contractual claim does not preclude a subsequent statutory claim. In this case, however, we consider not the preclusive effect of arbitration awards but rather the Board's authority to require the exhaustion of arbitration remedies. These issues are analytically distinct. To give an arbitration award preclusive effect would destroy an individual's right to a public forum for the protection of her statutory rights; Board deferment does not similarly nullify an employee's rights under the Act.

Moreover, Title VII and the NLRA differ in several critical ways. First, under Title VII, Congress has expressly recognized that private dispute resolution and statutory relief are distinct and independent remedies; in contrast, under the NLRA, Congress has expressly legislated a preference for the use of private remedies, whenever feasible, before the resort to public remedies. § 203(d)'s express preference for private remedies reflects Congress' considered view that, with regard to NLRA rights, private and public dispute resolution were *not* independent, but interdependent. Thus, although under Title VII an exhaustion requirement may be impermissible, § 203(d) expressly authorizes such a requirement in the redress of NLRA rights.

This distinction reflects broader conceptual differences between the remedial regimes created by Title VII and the NLRA. Title VII established nonwaivable individual rights, redressable in federal court; the NLRA established waivable group and individual rights, redressable in a complex administrative scheme. In contrast to courts, which, under Title VII, are charged with adjudicating individual discrimination claims, the Board, under the NLRA, is charged with the overall administration of labor-management relations; accordingly, access to the Board in the first instance may be rationed differently, and exhaustion requirements in these two systems need not be identical.

The Board's deferment policy simultaneously recognizes the need for the prompt resolution of ULP claims, the importance of individual statutory rights, the limitations on Board resources, and the salutary effects of arbitration and minimal governmental intervention in labor disputes. Accordingly, the Board's deferment policy constitutes a reasonable accommodation of its multiple statutory obligations.

III. Conclusion

In summary, we find that the NLRA and the LMRA do not preclude the Board from requiring a claimant to exhaust contractual grievance remedies before the Board hears a § 8(a)(3) discrimination claim. We also find that the Board's deferment policy is reasonable and is informed by a permissible construction of the Board's various statutory obligations, and that the Board's order in this case was wholly consistent with that policy. Accordingly, we deny the petition for review.

EDWARDS, CIRCUIT JUDGE, concurring:

I agree with the majority that the Supreme Court's decisions in *Alexander, Barrentine* and *McDonald,* denying deference or preclusive effect to arbitral awards, do not control the disposition of this case.

Under Title VII, the FLSA and section 1983, Congress emphasized that private dispute resolution mechanisms and statutory claims are separate and independent remedies; under the collective bargaining statutes, however, as manifested in section 203(d) of the LMRA, Congress expressed a strong preference for the use of private remedies. And while rights protected by Title VII, the FLSA and section 1983 are individual in nature, the NLRA and the LMRA are designed to protect both individual and collective rights, and have as their paramount goal the promotion of labor peace through the collective efforts of labor and management. Thus, while courts have the undivided responsibility to adjudicate claims of individual discrimination under Title VII and section 1983, the Board is charged with fostering the overall well-being of labor-management relations, which may be best accomplished by requiring the parties to seek to resolve their disputes through contractual dispute resolution mechanisms.

Most tellingly, in the *Alexander* line of cases, the Supreme Court has flatly rejected arguments suggesting that statutory rights may be waived by an agreement to arbitrate disputes arising under a collective bargaining agreement.

In stark contrast, the Court has explicitly recognized that, because a union represents collective interests, it may waive certain NLRA rights of its members. In *Metropolitan Edison Co. v. NLRB,* 460 U.S. 693 (1983), the Court stated that it had long "recognized that a union may waive a member's statutorily protected rights. . . . Such waivers are valid because they rest on the premise of fair representation and presuppose that the selection of the bargaining representative remains free. . . ." Thus a union may bargain away its members' economic rights, but it may not surrender rights that impair the employees' choice of their bargaining representative. The Court rejected the argument that only collective, as opposed to individual, NLRA rights are subject to union waiver, expressly distinguishing its holding in *Alexander* that a union cannot waive its employees' individual Title VII rights. The Court indicated that the possibility of waiver of statutory rights depends upon the "purposes of the statute at issue," and stated that, unlike Title VII, the NLRA "contemplates that individual rights may be waived by the union so long as the union does not breach its duty of good-faith representation."

I believe that, in light of the parties' agreement prohibiting discrimination and requiring arbitration, Hammontree was properly required by the Board to arbitrate his grievance pursuant to the terms of the collective bargaining contract. The parties to the collective agreement chose to supplant statutory rights with analogous rights created under the contract, and they provided that disputes concerning those rights would be resolved pursuant to an agreed-upon grievance procedure. Giving legal effect to that agreement respects the private ordering of rights and responsibilities established through collective bargaining and fosters the strong labor policy of promoting industrial peace through arbitration. Consequently, Board deferment in the case is clearly permissible.

Furthermore, even if it might be argued that there was no "clear and unmistakable" waiver of statutory rights in this case, the Board could still require deferment. This is so because the Supreme Court has said in other contexts that, even when parties do not forgo substantive rights afforded by statute, they still may be required to adhere to an agreement to arbitrate a statutory claim. In such a situation, the parties simply submit the resolution of their dispute "in an arbitral, rather than a judicial, forum." And, as the Court noted, "[h]aving made the bargain to arbitrate, the party should be held to it unless Congress itself has evinced an intention to preclude a waiver of judicial remedies for the statutory rights at issue." Thus, absent a finding of the sort underlying *Alexander, i.e.,* that statutory and contractual rights are "distinctly separate" and that arbitration cannot adequately substitute for adjudication as a means of enforcing statutory rights, deferment is clearly appropriate.

The rationale behind our holding today, as well as the prior precedent of this court, indicate quite clearly that the Board may accord considerable deference to the decision reached by the grievance committee in the event that Hammontree pursues his contract remedies and then brings his claim once again before the Board.

Since the Board does not grant *de novo* review to claims which have been considered in arbitration, the Board's decision to defer a claim to arbitration inevitably diminishes the claimant's ability to have the Board determine his claim.

In this case the collective bargaining agreement prohibits precisely the type of discrimination Hammontree alleges in his statutory claim. Hammontree cannot be allowed to nullify his contractual claim simply by pursuing a statutory claim. His allegations of discrimination state a claim under the contract as well as under the NLRA, and Congress has indicated its preference for private resolution of labor disputes. Consequently, the Board may properly defer Hammontree's claim to arbitration, notwithstanding that the arbitral award "may be dispositive of the unfair labor practice claim."

CHIEF JUDGE MIKVA, dissenting:

Paul Hammontree works as a truck driver for Consolidated Freightways. The Teamsters Union is the bargaining representative for Consolidated's employees. Hammontree is a dissident member of the union, having disagreed with Teamster officials on numerous occasions. The Teamsters had an understanding with Consolidated whereby the union promised not to press any employee grievances based on certain seniority rights if Consolidated would post departure times for available trucking assignments called peddle runs. Hammontree nevertheless filed a grievance based on his seniority rights and won, but Consolidated then discontinued its practice of posting times and, after Hammontree unsuccessfully challenged that action at a second grievance proceeding, the company retaliated by assigning him several undesirable runs.

The court today tells Mr. Hammontree that he must take his complaints for alleged violations of his rights under the national labor laws to a grievance committee composed of members half from the union's hierarchy and half from the employer. (It is as if a new kid at school was told to try and work things out with the two bullies who beat him up rather than have the principal intervene and discipline the ruffians.) Inexplicably, the court repeatedly suggests that the "parties" consented to such arbitration in this case, when in fact the "party" most concerned with and affected by the unlawful discrimination against him never consented to such arbitration and instead expressly chose to pursue a complaint arising solely under the National Labor Relations Act.

Mr. Hammontree is consigned to a never-never land of partisan proceedings where his rights under the law may *never* be adjudicated before the Board. If he works long enough, and is persistent enough, the Board might someday review (without the benefit of any explanation or record) a decision of the grievance committee. I think my colleagues are wrong.

A.   *Congressional Enactments*

1.   The Wagner Act.

There can be no dispute that the Wagner Act gave the Board exclusive power to prevent unfair labor practices. The court contends that the section [10(a)] merely "empowers" the Board and in no way constrains its discretion to defer disputes to private arbitration. If this is correct, it is hard to understand why the proviso in the second sentence was even necessary. In fact, a review of the Act's legislative history demonstrates an alternative motivation, namely a clear directive *not* to let private parties interfere with the Board's congressionally mandated function. Furthermore, contrary to the majority's suggestion, the legislative history of the Act and its subsequent amendments confirms that there is no generalized preference for arbitration that would trump an individual employee's right under § 10(a) to have the Board consider his discrimination charges.

2.   The Taft-Hartley Act.

The preference for arbitration of disputes involving the application or interpretation of a collective bargaining agreement was added by § 203(d) of the Labor-Management Relations ("Taft-Hartley") Act in 1947. After initially charging the Board with preventing unfair labor practices through the Wagner Act, Congress subsequently carved out a limited preference for allowing parties to a collective bargaining agreement to resolve any disputes over that agreement in a manner agreed upon by them.

The majority contends that § 10(a) is ambiguous in light of this competing congressional directive to promote collective bargaining. Indeed, one of the concurring judges finds this an easy case because the "parties to the collective agreement chose to supplant statutory rights with analogous rights created under the contract. . . ."

But this case does not require any application or interpretation of the collective bargaining agreement, and Hammontree never agreed to give up his statutory protections against discrimination by the very parties to the collective bargaining agreement. There is nothing that would dilute the unambiguous command of § 10(a). In fact, § 203(d) is not the generalized preference for private dispute resolution that the court suggests. The version of the Taft-Hartley Act that passed the House would have deleted the sentence of § 10(a) that limits the Board's ability to defer, but the Conference Committee retained the sentence in order to prevent private rights of action from supplanting existing remedies.

The preference for arbitration is simply not involved in a case where the employee has not voluntarily submitted his discrimination claim to arbitration. Hammontree has not "nullified" his rights under the collective bargaining agreement; he has consciously decided not to invoke them.

3.   The Landrum-Griffin Act.

Perhaps nowhere is congressional concern for the well-being of the individual employee vis-a-vis the powerful union more manifest than in the Landrum-Griffin Act (the Labor-Management Reporting and Disclosure Act of 1959). The Act was passed at a time when union corruption was perceived to be widespread and individual employees were powerless to prevent abusive union tactics.

In addition to codifying the rights of union members and regulating the internal affairs of unions in order to stamp out racketeering and corruption, Landrum-Griffin also added § 10(m) to the National Labor Relations Act, providing that the Board should give discriminatory unfair labor practice claims arising under § 8(a)(3) priority over all other cases except secondary boycotts. According to Senator Mundt, who introduced this amendment, § 10(m) was intended to redress the problem of the individual employee who loses his job or wages as a result of discriminatory behavior; he explained that the Board often delays hearing such cases: "At present, a vast majority of these cases are left hanging on the vine for a period, sometimes amounting to years." 105 Cong. Rec. 6044 (1959) (remarks of Sen. Mundt), *reprinted in* History of Landrum-Griffin, at 1253. By introducing this measure, Senator Mundt sought to extend to the individual the same priority treatment that the Board accorded companies faced with secondary boycotts.

The court speculates that, by deferring as many § 8(a)(3) claims as possible, the Board is better able to expedite such claims in the aggregate. I do not doubt that sweeping deferral of unfair labor practice claims will clear the Board's docket more expeditiously, just as I am sure the courts could do some docket clearing by deferring anytime the defendant wanted to go to an arbitrator of his or her choosing. But administrative efficiency was certainly not the goal expressed by Congress in § 10(m). Hammontree has an individual right to priority treatment by the Board that cannot be sacrificed just so the discrimination claims brought by others can be processed more easily.

B.   *Statutory Interpretation and Agency Practice*

There are cases where the tension created by the twin policies expressed in the Act can best be resolved by deferring to a grievance proceeding. This court has allowed the Board to defer unfair labor practice claims that require contract interpretation. Likewise, other circuits have permitted the Board to defer where the *employee* has requested arbitration on the very issue before it, and the employee has not withdrawn that request. But until this case, no court has ever sanctioned deferral where the employee did *not* request arbitration and no portion of the claims rested upon a contractual matter. We have never before allowed the Board to defer *individual, non-contractual* unfair labor practice claims to arbitration.

C. *The Waiver Doctrine*

No one disputes the fact that Hammontree's unfair labor practice charges properly arise under the substantive prohibitions contained in sections 7 and 8(a) of the Act. A waiver of an employee's statutory rights may not be found unless it is "established clearly and unmistakably." Nor does the arbitration provision by itself waive the statutory rights that might be settled in a grievance proceeding.

The majority maintains that because Articles 21 and 37 in the collective bargaining agreement parallel the nondiscrimination guarantees in the Act, Hammontree's claims of retaliation can properly be submitted to arbitration. However, the fact that the union claims to have bolstered employees' protection against discrimination by negotiating the inclusion of these provisions in the contract would not deprive Hammontree of his preexisting statutory right to bring a claim under section 8(a)(1) and (3) before the Board. An individual's right to freely engage in union activities without fear of retaliation exists independently of any contract and cannot be diminished or diffused by its reiteration in a collective bargaining agreement

D. *Exhaustion of Remedies*

The court contends that this is solely an exhaustion of remedies question and does not foreclose subsequent judicial review in case the grievance committee rejects Hammontree's unfair labor practice claim and the Board summarily affirms that decision. While that characterization may ease the court's conscience, it ignores reality. The Board's precedents amply suggest what will happen if Hammontree's grievance proceeding is ever concluded: it will no doubt defer yet again, according significant deference to the arbitrator's decision. A challenger to an arbitration decision bears the burden of showing that it was repugnant to the Act or that the statutory issues were not fairly decided. In cases such as this, where the risk of structural bias against an aggrieved employee is obvious, even careful review on appeal will not assure that the employee's statutory rights, including the priority expressed in § 10(m), are fully protected. Under the method used by the Teamster Joint Arbitration Committee, a "bi-partite" panel consisting of an equal number of union and employer representatives hears the employee's grievance. If the initial panel is deadlocked, the grievance proceeds to the next level, and so on up the line.

There is no telling how much time will elapse before Hammontree has fully exhausted this private dispute resolution machinery and can once again appear before the Board if and when his discrimination charges are rejected. Such an arrangement fails to satisfy the requirements of diligence imposed on the Board by the Landrum-Griffin Act.

There are other deficiencies in the Teamsters' grievance mechanism that may well hamper effective review after exhaustion. This is not arbitration in the traditional sense where parties submit their dispute to a neutral third party. After hearing the individual's claim, the joint committee meets in private and either grants or denies the claim without a word of explanation for its decision. Since no record is kept, there is simply no way of knowing that the individual's claim has been fairly decided, let alone the grounds for the court decision. Such a scenario is particularly unacceptable if the individual employee is, as in this case, at odds with his union leadership. As there is no way to ensure that the employee will be adequately represented or that the arbitrator will properly interpret the governing statute, deferring an individual discrimination case to arbitration denies the employee the legal protection that he would receive if his case were heard *de novo* by the Board

Although the Board assures Mr. Hammontree that it retains ultimate jurisdiction to ensure that the result reached is not repugnant to the Act, the deferential standard of review makes it extremely unlikely that an arbitration decision will be overturned or thoroughly reviewed, to say nothing of the extensive delay that Congress specifically legislated against in the Landrum-Griffin Act. Indeed, under the Teamsters' grievance system, the goal of expediting employees' discrimination claims is turned on its head.

NOTES

1.   Consider the relevant issues of statutory interpretation and policy discussed in the three *Hammontree* opinions. Even Judge Mikva would allow the NLRB to *Collyerize* 8(a)(5) cases. Can his distinction be reconciled with his interpretation of section 10(a) of the NLRA? If not, does this support Judge Wald's view of section 10(a)?

2.   As a matter of policy, does *Collyerization* further or inhibit federal policies favoring resolution of disputes through the grievance procedure? Is *Collyerization* an appropriate tool for the Board to use in allocating its resources? Does it deprive the charging party of a choice of forum? Does a charging party have a right to choose the forum in which the dispute will be resolved?

3.   Should the Board consider backlogs or other delays in the parties' grievance process when deciding whether to *Collyerize* an unfair labor practice charge? In Memorandum GC 12–01 (Jan. 20, 2012), the NLRB's Acting General Counsel opined that the Board should no longer routinely *Collyerize*

charges where it appears that the grievance and arbitration will not be completed within one year. The Acting General Counsel instructed the regions that when *Collyerizing* a charge, they should monitor the grievance process and, if it appears that the grievance and arbitration process will exceed a year in length, they should refer the matter to the Advice Division of the General Counsel's office.

4.   Judge Edwards' view that the collective bargaining agreement substitutes contractual rights and remedies for statutory rights and remedies under the NLRA is contained in greater detail in his law review article. Harry T. Edwards, *Deferral to Arbitration and Waiver of the Duty to Bargain: A Possible Way Out of Everlasting Confusion at the NLRB*, 46 Ohio St. L.J. 23 (1985).

5.   Teamster contracts, and those of some other unions, often provide for grievances to be adjudicated by a joint committee, consisting of an equal number of union and employer representatives. The grievance goes to an independent arbitrator only if the committee deadlocks. Should the Board defer to decisions of such joint committees? Should the Board defer to grievance settlements arrived at by the employer and union short of arbitration?

2. GRIEVANCE ARBITRATION AND STATUTORY CLAIMS

In *Alexander v. Gardner-Denver Co.*, 415 U.S. 36 (1974), Alexander grieved his discharge and the union took the matter to arbitration where it lost. Alexander subsequently brought a Title VII lawsuit. The Court of Appeals for the Tenth Circuit held that the adverse arbitration award barred Alexander's lawsuit but the Supreme Court reversed. The Court held that the Title VII claim and the grievance were independent of each other. Consequently, Alexander could try his Title VII claim de novo even though his union had lost the grievance in arbitration. The Court applied *Gardner-Denver* to hold that an employee may bring an action under the Fair Labor Standards Act without first resorting to the collective bargaining agreement's grievance procedure in *Barrentine v. Arkansas-Best Freight System, Inc.*, 450 U.S. 728 (1981). In *McDonald v. City of West Branch*, 466 U.S. 284 (1984), the Court extended its holdings to actions under 42 U.S.C. § 1983.

The Court in *Gardner-Denver* offered several rationales for its holding. The Court observed that arbitration is intended to resolve claims under the collective bargaining agreement rather than claims under a statute that are independent of the contract. The Court also expressed concern that the union, rather than the individual employee, controlled the grievance process. The Court focused a good deal of its rationale, however, on the inappropriateness of arbitration for resolving statutory claims.

In *Gilmer v. Interstate/Johnson Lane Corp.*, 500 U.S. 20 (1991), a case arising in a non-union environment, the Supreme Court held that an agreement contained in a securities exchange's registration obligated an employee to arbitrate his Age Discrimination in Employment Act claim against his employer. The Court criticized *Gardner-Denver's* "mistrust of the arbitral process" as inconsistent with the Court's more recent commercial arbitration decisions and opined, "We are well past the time when judicial suspicion of the desirability of arbitration and of the competence of arbitral tribunals inhibited the development of arbitration as an alternative means of dispute resolution."

Gilmer led to a split in the lower courts over whether an employee covered by a collective bargaining agreement could be compelled to submit a statutory claim through the contractual grievance procedure. In *Wright v. Universal Maritime Service Corp.*, 525 U.S. 70 (1998), the Court declined to rule whether a collective bargaining agreement could waive the employee's right to litigate a statutory claim in court but held that any purported waiver must be clear and unmistakable. The Court considered the issue it left open in *Wright* in the following case.

14 PENN PLAZA, LLC v. PYETT
556 U.S. 247 (2009)

JUSTICE THOMAS delivered the opinion of the Court:

The question presented by this case is whether a provision in a collective-bargaining agreement that clearly and unmistakably requires union members to arbitrate claims arising under the Age Discrimination in Employment Act of 1967 (ADEA) is enforceable. The United States Court of Appeals for the Second Circuit held that this Court's decision in *Alexander v. Gardner-Denver Co.*, 415 U.S. 36 (1974), forbids enforcement of such arbitration provisions. We disagree and reverse the judgment of the Court of Appeals.

I

Respondents are members of the Service Employees International Union, Local 32BJ (Union). Since the 1930's, the Union has engaged in industry-wide collective bargaining with the Realty Advisory Board on Labor Relations, Inc. (RAB), a multiemployer bargaining association for the New York City real-estate industry. The agreement between the Union and the RAB is embodied in their Collective Bargaining Agreement for Contractors and Building Owners (CBA). The CBA requires union members to submit all claims of employment discrimination to binding arbitration under the CBA's grievance and dispute resolution procedures:

> "§ 30 NO DISCRIMINATION. There shall be no discrimination against any present or future employee by reason of race, creed, color, age, disability, national origin, sex, union membership, or any other characteristic protected by law, including, but not limited to, claims made pursuant to Title VII of the Civil Rights

Act, the Americans with Disabilities Act, the Age Discrimination in Employment Act, the New York State Human Rights Law, the New York City Human Rights Code, . . . or any other similar laws, rules, or regulations. All such claims shall be subject to the grievance and arbitration procedures (Articles V and VI) as the sole and exclusive remedy for violations. Arbitrators shall apply appropriate law in rendering decisions based upon claims of discrimination."

Petitioner 14 Penn Plaza LLC is a member of the RAB. It owns and operates the New York City office building where, prior to August 2003, respondents worked as night lobby watchmen and in other similar capacities. Respondents were directly employed by petitioner Temco Service Industries, Inc. (Temco), a maintenance service and cleaning contractor. In August 2003, with the Union's consent, 14 Penn Plaza engaged Spartan Security, a unionized security services contractor and affiliate of Temco, to provide licensed security guards to staff the lobby and entrances of its building. Because this rendered respondents' lobby services unnecessary, Temco reassigned them to jobs as night porters and light duty cleaners in other locations in the building. Respondents contend that these reassignments led to a loss in income, caused them emotional distress, and were otherwise less desirable than their former positions.

At respondents' request, the Union filed grievances challenging the reassignments. The grievances alleged that petitioners: (1) violated the CBA's ban on workplace discrimination by reassigning respondents on account of their age; (2) violated seniority rules by failing to promote one of the respondents to a handyman position; and (3) failed to equitably rotate overtime. After failing to obtain relief on any of these claims through the grievance process, the Union requested arbitration under the CBA.

After the initial arbitration hearing, the Union withdrew the first set of respondents' grievances—the age-discrimination claims—from arbitration. Because it had consented to the contract for new security personnel at 14 Penn Plaza, the Union believed that it could not legitimately object to respondents' reassignments as discriminatory. But the Union continued to arbitrate the seniority and overtime claims, and, after several hearings, the claims were denied.

In May 2004, while the arbitration was ongoing but after the Union withdrew the age-discrimination claims, respondents filed a complaint with the Equal Employment Opportunity Commission (EEOC) alleging that petitioners had violated their rights under the ADEA. Approximately one month later, the EEOC issued a Dismissal and Notice of Rights, which explained that the agency's " 'review of the evidence . . . fail[ed] to indicate that a violation ha[d] occurred,' " and notified each respondent of his right to sue.

Respondents thereafter filed suit against petitioners in the United States District Court for the Southern District of New York, alleging that their reassignment violated the ADEA and state and local laws prohibiting age discrimination. Petitioners filed a motion to compel arbitration of respondents' claims pursuant to § 3 and § 4 of the Federal Arbitration Act (FAA). The District Court denied the motion because under Second Circuit precedent, "even a clear and unmistakable union-negotiated waiver of a right to litigate certain federal and state statutory claims in a judicial forum is unenforceable."

The Court of Appeals affirmed According to the Court of Appeals, it could not compel arbitration of the dispute because *Gardner-Denver*, which "remains good law," held "that a collective bargaining agreement could not waive covered workers' rights to a judicial forum for causes of action created by Congress."

II

A

[T]he Union and the RAB, negotiating on behalf of 14 Penn Plaza, collectively bargained in good faith and agreed that employment-related discrimination claims, including claims brought under the ADEA, would be resolved in arbitration. This freely negotiated term between the Union and the RAB easily qualifies as a "conditio[n] of employment" that is subject to mandatory bargaining. The decision to fashion a CBA to require arbitration of employment-discrimination claims is no different from the many other decisions made by parties in designing grievance machinery

Respondents, however, contend that the arbitration clause here is outside the permissible scope of the collective-bargaining process because it affects the "employees' individual, non-economic statutory rights." We disagree. Parties generally favor arbitration precisely because of the economics of dispute resolution. As in any contractual negotiation, a union may agree to the inclusion of an arbitration provision in a collective-bargaining agreement in return for other concessions from the employer. Courts generally may not interfere in this bargained-for exchange. "Judicial nullification of contractual concessions . . . is contrary to what the Court has recognized as one of the fundamental policies of the National Labor Relations Act-freedom of contract."

As a result, the CBA's arbitration provision must be honored unless the ADEA itself removes this particular class of grievances from the NLRA's broad sweep. It does not. This Court has squarely held that the ADEA does not preclude arbitration of claims brought under the statute.

In *Gilmer*, the Court determined that "nothing in the text of the ADEA or its legislative history explicitly precludes arbitration." The Court also concluded that arbitrating ADEA disputes would not undermine the statute's "remedial and deterrent function."

The *Gilmer* Court's interpretation of the ADEA fully applies in the collective-bargaining context. Nothing in the law suggests a distinction between the status of arbitration agreements signed by an individual employee and those agreed to by a union representative. This Court has required only that an agreement to arbitrate statutory antidiscrimination claims be "explicitly stated" in the collective-bargaining agreement. The CBA under review here meets that obligation. Respondents incorrectly counter that an individual employee must personally "waive" a "[substantive] right" to proceed in court for a waiver to be "knowing and voluntary" under the ADEA. As explained below, however, the agreement to arbitrate ADEA claims is not the waiver of a "substantive right" as that term is employed in the ADEA,

B

The CBA's arbitration provision is also fully enforceable under the *Gardner-Denver* line of cases. Respondents interpret *Gardner-Denver* and its progeny to hold that "a union cannot waive an employee's right to a judicial forum under the federal antidiscrimination statutes" because "allowing the union to waive this right would substitute the union's interests for the employee's antidiscrimination rights." The "combination of union control over the process and inherent conflict of interest with respect to discrimination claims," they argue, "provided the foundation for the Court's holding [in *Gardner-Denver*] that arbitration under a collective-bargaining agreement could not preclude an individual employee's right to bring a lawsuit in court to vindicate a statutory discrimination claim." We disagree.

1

The holding of *Gardner-Denver* is not as broad as respondents suggest. The employee in that case was covered by a collective-bargaining agreement that prohibited "discrimination against any employee on account of race, color, religion, sex, national origin, or ancestry" and that guaranteed that "[n]o employee will be discharged . . . except for just cause." The agreement also included a "multistep grievance procedure" that culminated in compulsory arbitration for any "differences aris[ing] between the Company and the Union as to the meaning and application of the provisions of this Agreement" and "any trouble aris[ing] in the plant."

The employee was discharged for allegedly producing too many defective parts while working for the respondent as a drill operator. He filed a grievance with his union claiming that he was " 'unjustly discharged' " in violation of the " 'just cause' " provision within the CBA. Then at the final prearbitration step of the grievance process, the employee added a claim that he was discharged because of his race.

The arbitrator ultimately ruled that the employee had been " 'discharged for just cause,' " but "made no reference to [the] claim of racial discrimination." After obtaining a right-to-sue letter from the EEOC, the employee filed a claim in Federal District Court, alleging racial discrimination in violation of Title VII of the Civil Rights Act of 1964. The District Court issued a decision, affirmed by the Court of Appeals, which granted summary judgment to the employer because it concluded that "the claim of racial discrimination had been submitted to the arbitrator and resolved adversely to [the employee]."

This Court reversed the judgment on the narrow ground that the arbitration was not preclusive because the collective-bargaining agreement did not cover statutory claims. As a result, the lower courts erred in relying on the "doctrine of election of remedies" to bar the employee's Title VII claim. "That doctrine, which refers to situations where an individual pursues remedies that are legally or factually inconsistent" with each other, did not apply to the employee's dual pursuit of arbitration and a Title VII discrimination claim in district court. The employee's collective-bargaining agreement did not mandate arbitration of statutory antidiscrimination claims. "As the proctor of the bargain, the arbitrator's task is to effectuate the intent of the parties." Because the collective-bargaining agreement gave the arbitrator "authority to resolve only questions of contractual rights," his decision could not prevent the employee from bringing the Title VII claim in federal court "regardless of whether certain contractual rights are similar to, or duplicative of, the substantive rights secured by Title VII." *See id.,* at 46, n. 6 ("[W]e hold that the federal policy favoring arbitration does not establish that an arbitrator's resolution of a *contractual* claim is dispositive of a statutory claim under Title VII" (emphasis added)).

2

We recognize that apart from their narrow holdings, the *Gardner-Denver* line of cases included broad dicta that was highly critical of the use of arbitration for the vindication of statutory antidiscrimination rights. That skepticism, however, rested on a misconceived view of arbitration that this Court has since abandoned.

First, the Court in *Gardner-Denver* erroneously assumed that an agreement to submit statutory discrimination claims to arbitration was tantamount to a waiver of those rights. The Court was correct in concluding that federal antidiscrimination rights may not be prospectively waived, but it confused an agreement to arbitrate those statutory claims with a prospective waiver of the substantive right. The decision to resolve ADEA claims by way of arbitration instead of litigation does not waive the statutory right to be free from workplace age discrimination; it waives only the right to seek relief from a court in the first instance. The suggestion in *Gardner-Denver* that the decision to arbitrate statutory discrimination claims was tantamount to a substantive waiver of those rights, therefore, reveals a distorted understanding of the compromise made when an employee agrees to compulsory arbitration.

Second, *Gardner-Denver* mistakenly suggested that certain features of arbitration made it a forum "well suited to the resolution of contractual disputes," but "a comparatively inappropriate forum for the final resolution of rights created by Title VII." According to the Court, the "factfinding process in arbitration" is "not equivalent to judicial factfinding" and the "informality of arbitral procedure . . . makes arbitration a less appropriate forum for final resolution of Title VII issues than the federal courts." The Court also questioned the competence of arbitrators to decide federal statutory claims. In the Court's view, "the resolution of statutory or constitutional issues is a primary responsibility of courts, and judicial construction has proved especially necessary with respect to Title VII, whose broad language frequently can be given meaning only by reference to public law concepts."

These misconceptions have been corrected. For example, the Court has "recognized that arbitral tribunals are readily capable of handling the factual and legal complexities of antitrust claims, notwithstanding the absence of judicial instruction and supervision" and that "there is no reason to assume at the outset that arbitrators will not follow the law." An arbitrator's capacity to resolve complex questions of fact and law extends with equal force to discrimination claims brought under the ADEA. Moreover, the recognition that arbitration procedures are more streamlined than federal litigation is not a basis for finding the forum somehow inadequate; the relative informality of arbitration is one of the chief reasons that parties select arbitration. Parties "trad[e] the procedures and opportunity for review of the courtroom for the simplicity, informality, and expedition of arbitration."

Third, the Court in *Gardner-Denver* raised in a footnote a "further concern" regarding "the union's exclusive control over the manner and extent to which an individual grievance is presented." The Court suggested that in arbitration, as in the collective-bargaining process, a union may subordinate the interests of an individual employee to the collective interests of all employees in the bargaining unit.

We cannot rely on this judicial policy concern as a source of authority for introducing a qualification into the ADEA that is not found in its text. Absent a constitutional barrier, "it is not for us to substitute our view of . . . policy for the legislation which has been passed by Congress."

The conflict-of-interest argument also proves too much. Labor unions certainly balance the economic interests of some employees against the needs of the larger work force as they negotiate collective-bargaining agreements and implement them on a daily basis. But this attribute of organized labor does not justify singling out an arbitration provision for disfavored treatment. This "principle of majority rule" to which respondents object is in fact the central premise of the NLRA. *Emporium Capwell Co. v. Western Addition Community Organization*, 420 U.S. 50, 62 (1975). "In establishing a regime of majority rule, Congress sought to secure to all members of the unit the benefits of their collective strength and bargaining power, in full awareness that the superior strength of some individuals or groups might be subordinated to the interest of the majority." It was Congress' verdict that the benefits of organized labor outweigh the sacrifice of individual liberty that this system necessarily demands. Respondents' argument that they were deprived of the right to pursue their ADEA claims in federal court by a labor union with a conflict of interest is therefore unsustainable; it amounts to a collateral attack on the NLRA.

In any event, Congress has accounted for this conflict of interest in several ways. [T]he NLRA has been interpreted to impose a "duty of fair representation" on labor unions, which a union breaches "when its conduct toward a member of the bargaining unit is arbitrary, discriminatory, or in bad faith." Thus, a union is subject to liability under the NLRA if it illegally discriminates against older workers in either the formation or governance of the collective-bargaining agreement, such as by deciding not to pursue a grievance on behalf of one of its members for discriminatory reasons. Given this avenue that Congress has made available to redress a union's violation of its duty to its members, it is particularly inappropriate to ask this Court to impose an artificial limitation on the collective-bargaining process.

In addition, a union is subject to liability under the ADEA if the union itself discriminates against its members on the basis of age. Union members may also file age-discrimination claims with the EEOC and the National Labor Relations Board, which may then seek judicial intervention under this Court's precedent. In sum, Congress has provided remedies for the situation where a labor union is less than vigorous in defense of its members' claims of discrimination under the ADEA.

III

Respondents argue that the CBA operates as a substantive waiver of their ADEA rights because it not only precludes a federal lawsuit, but also allows the Union to block arbitration of these claims. Petitioners contest this characterization of the CBA, and offer record evidence suggesting that the Union has allowed respondents to continue with the arbitration even though the Union has declined to participate, But not only does this question require resolution of contested factual allegations, it was not fully briefed to this or any court and is not fairly encompassed within the question presented. Thus, although a substantive waiver of federally protected civil rights will not be upheld, we are not positioned to resolve in the first instance whether the CBA allows the Union to prevent respondents from "effectively vindicating" their "federal statutory rights in the arbitral forum,"

IV

We hold that a collective-bargaining agreement that clearly and unmistakably requires union members to arbitrate ADEA claims is enforceable as a matter of federal law. The judgment of the Court of Appeals is reversed, and the case is remanded for further proceedings consistent with this opinion.

JUSTICE SOUTER, with whom JUSTICE STEVENS, JUSTICE GINSBURG, and JUSTICE BREYER join, dissenting.

The issue here is whether employees subject to a collective-bargaining agreement (CBA) providing for conclusive arbitration of all grievances, including claimed breaches of the Age Discrimination in Employment Act of 1967 (ADEA) lose their statutory right to bring an ADEA claim in court. Under the 35-year-old holding in *Alexander v. Gardner-Denver Co.,* 415 U.S. 36 (1974), they do not, and I would adhere to *stare decisis* and so hold today.

Gardner-Denver considered the effect of a CBA's arbitration clause on an employee's right to sue under Title VII. One of the employer's arguments was that the CBA entered into by the union had waived individual employees' statutory cause of action subject to a judicial remedy for discrimination in violation of Title VII. [W]e unanimously held that "the rights conferred" by Title VII (with no exception for the right to a judicial forum) cannot be waived as "part of the collective bargaining process," *id.* at 51. We stressed the contrast between two categories of rights in labor and employment law. There were "statutory rights related to collective activity," which "are conferred on employees collectively to foster the processes of bargaining[, which] properly may be exercised or relinquished by the union as collective-bargaining agent to obtain economic benefits for union members." *Ibid.* But "Title VII . . . stands on plainly different [categorical] ground; it concerns not majoritarian processes, but an individual's right to equal employment opportunities." *Ibid.* Thus, as the Court previously realized, *Gardner-Denver* imposed a "seemingly absolute prohibition of union waiver of employees' federal forum rights." *Wright v. Universal Maritime Service Corp.,* 525 U.S. 70, 80 (1998).

We supported the judgment with several other lines of complementary reasoning. First, we explained that antidiscrimination statutes "have long evinced a general intent to accord parallel or overlapping remedies against discrimination," and Title VII's statutory scheme carried "no suggestion . . . that a prior arbitral decision either forecloses an individual's right to sue or divests federal courts of jurisdiction." *Gardner-Denver,* 415 U.S. at 47. We accordingly concluded that "an individual does not forfeit his private cause of action if he first pursues his grievance to final arbitration under the nondiscrimination clause of a collective-bargaining agreement." *Id.* at 49.

Second, we rejected the District Court's view that simply participating in the arbitration amounted to electing the arbitration remedy and waiving the plaintiff's right to sue. We said that the arbitration agreement at issue covered only a contractual right under the CBA to be free from discrimination, not the "independent statutory rights accorded by Congress" in Title VII. *Id.* at 49–50. Third, we rebuffed the employer's argument that federal courts should defer to arbitral rulings. We declined to make the "assumption that arbitral processes are commensurate with judicial processes," *id.* at 56, and described arbitration as "a less appropriate forum for final resolution of Title VII issues than the federal courts," *id, at 58.*

Finally, we took note that "[i]n arbitration, as in the collective bargaining process, the interests of the individual employee may be subordinated to the collective interests of all employees in the bargaining unit," *ibid.* n. 19, a result we deemed unacceptable when it came to Title VII claims. In sum, *Gardner-Denver* held that an individual's statutory right of freedom from discrimination and access to court for enforcement were beyond a union's power to waive.

Our analysis of Title VII in *Gardner-Denver* is just as pertinent to the ADEA in this case. Once we have construed a statute, stability is the rule, and "we will not depart from [it] without some compelling justification." There is no argument for abandoning precedent here, and *Gardner-Denver* controls.

II

The majority evades the precedent of *Gardner-Denver* as long as it can simply by ignoring it. The Court never mentions the case before concluding that the ADEA and the National Labor Relations Act "yiel[d] a straightforward answer to the question presented," that is, that unions can bargain away individual rights to a federal forum for antidiscrimination claims. If this were a case of first impression, it would at least be possible to consider that conclusion, but the issue is settled and the time is too late by 35 years to make the bald assertion that "[n]othing in the law suggests a distinction between the status of arbitration agreements signed by an individual employee and those agreed to by a union representative." In fact, we recently and unanimously said that the principle that "federal forum rights cannot be waived in union-negotiated CBAs even if they can be waived in individually executed contracts . . . assuredly finds support in" our case law, *Wright,* 525 U.S. at 77, and every Court of Appeals save one has read our decisions as holding to this position

Equally at odds with existing law is the majority's statement that "[t]he decision to fashion a CBA to require arbitration of employment-discrimination claims is no different from the many other decisions made by parties in designing grievance machinery." That is simply impossible to square with our conclusion in *Gardner-Denver* that "Title VII . . . stands on plainly different ground" from "statutory rights related to collective activity": "it concerns not majoritarian processes, but an individual's right to equal employment opportunities."

When the majority does speak to *Gardner-Denver,* it misreads the case in claiming that it turned solely "on the narrow ground that the arbitration was not preclusive because the collective-bargaining agreement did not cover statutory claims." That, however, was merely one of several reasons given in support of the decision, and we raised it to explain why the District Court made a mistake in thinking that the employee lost his Title VII rights by electing to pursue the contractual arbitration remedy. One need only read *Gardner-Denver* itself to know that it was not at all so narrowly reasoned, and later cases have made this abundantly clear.

Nor, finally, does the majority have any better chance of being rid of another of *Gardner-Denver's* statements supporting its rule of decision, set out and repeated in previous quotations: "in arbitration, as in the collective-bargaining process, a union may subordinate the interests of an individual employee to the collective interests of all employees in the bargaining unit," an unacceptable result when it comes to "an individual's right to equal employment opportunities." The majority tries to diminish this reasoning, and the previously stated holding it supported, by making the remarkable rejoinder that "[w]e cannot rely on this judicial policy concern as a source of authority for introducing a qualification into the ADEA that is not found in its text." It is enough to recall that respondents are not seeking to "introduc[e] a qualification into" the law; they are justifiably relying on statutory-interpretation precedent decades old, never overruled, and serially reaffirmed over the years. With that precedent on the books, it makes no sense for the majority to claim that "judicial policy concern[s]" about unions sacrificing individual antidiscrimination rights should be left to Congress.

Congress apparently does not share the Court's demotion of *Gardner-Denver's* holding to a suspect judicial policy concern: "Congress has had [over] 30 years in which it could have corrected our decision . . . if it disagreed with it, and has chosen not to do so. We should accord weight to this continued acceptance of our earlier holding."

(The separate dissenting opinion of JUSTICE STEVENS has been omitted.)

NOTES

1.   In the *Steelworkers Trilogy*, the Court regarded grievance arbitration as a substitute for workplace strife and a vehicle for workplace self-governance. The Court contrasted grievance arbitration with commercial arbitration which the Court regarded as a substitute for litigation. How does the Court view grievance arbitration in *Pyett*? What are the implications, if any, for the Court's change in perspective?

2.   What are the advantages and disadvantages to employers of having provisions in their collective bargaining agreements that clearly and unambiguously waive the employees' rights to litigate their statutory claims and require them to take their claims through the grievance and arbitration procedure? What are the advantages and disadvantages to unions?

3.   Is a union that has a collective bargaining agreement waiving the employees' right to sue obligated to grieve and arbitrate all statutory claims raised by members of the bargaining unit regardless of its assessment of the claims' merits? If the union decides not to pursue an employee's statutory claim, does this mean that the union has effectively waived the employee's substantive rights unless the employee is allowed to bring the claim in court? In *Kravar v. Triangle Services, Inc.*, 2009 WL 1392595 (S.D.N.Y. May 19, 2009), the court faced the same SEIU Local 32BJ-RAB collective bargaining agreement. The court refused to compel the plaintiff to arbitrate her claim of disability discrimination under the Americans with Disabilities Act. The court found that under the collective bargaining agreement, the union had the exclusive right to advance a grievance to arbitration and that the union refused to process the plaintiff's disability discrimination claim. The court concluded that the union's refusal to arbitrate the plaintiff's disability discrimination claim meant that if not allowed to proceed in court, she would not be able to bring her claim in any forum. Under the circumstances, the court opined, the collective bargaining agreement amounted to a waiver of plaintiff's substantive rights and was not enforceable. However, in *Duraku v. Tishman Speyer Properties, Inc.*, 714 F.Supp.2d 470 (S.D.N.Y. 2010), the court required plaintiffs to arbitrate their discrimination claims in light of a February 2010 supplemental agreement between RAB and Local 32BJ that expressly provides that an employee may proceed to arbitration if the union declines to do so.

The supplemental agreement relied on in *Duraku* has since been incorporated into the parties' collective bargaining agreement and is called the "No Discrimination Protocol." For many years, the parties have had an Office of the Contract Arbitrator (OCA), a separate legal entity that they jointly created to administer their contract. OCA has its own office and staff and an agreed-on panel of arbitrators.

Under the No Discrimination Protocol, any employee or the union may file a claim of discrimination. The parties established a separate panel of mediators for purposes of mediating discrimination claims. When a claim is filed, the OCA administrator appoints a mediator selected randomly from the panel. The mediator must schedule a pre-mediation conference within thirty days. At the conference, dates are established for exchange of information and position statements and for the mediation. At the mediation, the parties may present witnesses and exhibits and the mediator may meet separately with each party to discuss settlement. The mediator may, at the conclusion of the mediation, make a recommendation for settlement. Local 32BJ and RAB share the costs of the mediator and language interpreters, if needed, regardless of whether the union decided to pursue the claim.

If the matter is not resolved in mediation and the union decides not to pursue the claim, the individual employee, with or without counsel, may pursue the claim to arbitration before an arbitrator from a special panel selected jointly by Local 32BJ and RAB from a list of arbitrators qualified to hear discrimination claims provided by the American Arbitration Association (AAA). The manner by which the arbitrator is selected from the panel and the handling of the arbitrator's fee is left to agreement between the individual employee and the RAB member respondent, but in practice the employer has paid the entire fee of the arbitrator. The arbitration proceeds according to AAA's Employment Arbitration Rules except with respect to case administration, which is provided by OCA rather than AAA. The Protocol provides that the union is not a party to the arbitration and the arbitrator may not order relief that would require amendment of the collective bargaining agreement.

4.   How should the union's conduct in pursuing an employee's statutory claim be evaluated? Should it be subject to the duty of fair representation's standard of arbitrary, discriminatory or bad faith conduct, or should a higher standard of care be used?

5.   A collective bargaining agreement provides, "Employees are permitted leaves of absence to the extent required by, and in accordance with the terms of, the Family Medical Leave Act (FMLA). All requests for FMLA leave, and the terms of such leave are governed by the FMLA." Another section of the agreement provides, "Claims of discrimination arising within the employment relationship between the Company and the Employees, whether such claims are made under the collective bargaining agreement or in state or federal court and alleged to be violations of state or federal law are to be addressed, resolved and finalized solely under Section V—Grievance and/or [Section] VI—Arbitration of the Agreement; by the terms of the Collective Bargaining Agreement each Employee waives each and every cause of action and remedies provided under these statutes and common law frameworks." An employee sues alleging that he was fired in retaliation for exercising his right to leave under the Family Medical Leave Act. Should the court dismiss the suit? See Thompson v. Air Transport International, LLC, 664 F.3d 723 (11th Cir. 2011) (court dismissed the suit but plaintiff conceded that the contract required him to arbitrate his FMLA claim; court rejected plaintiff's argument that the contract was an unconscionable and unenforceable waiver of his FMLA rights).

6.   In Miami Dolphins, Ltd. v. Newson, 783 F.Supp.2d 769 (W.D.Pa. 2011), Newson, a player for the Miami Dolphins football team, filed a claim under the Pennsylvania workers compensation statute for an injury he sustained in Pennsylvania. The collective bargaining agreement between the National Football League and the NFL Players Association required that in any state where a club was excluded from workers compensation coverage, the team would either obtain voluntary coverage or guarantee equivalent benefits to its players which would be determined under the contract's non-injury grievance procedure. Because Florida excluded the club from coverage, the

NFL and NFLPA agreed that Dolphins' players would be entitled to the benefits equivalent to those set forth in the Florida Workers' Compensation Law with disputes to be resolved by a member of a three arbitrator local panel that the parties established for such claims. The Dolphins asked the court to enforce the arbitration agreement by enjoining Newson from proceeding on his Pennsylvania workers compensation claim. The court refused to do so, observing that an arbitration proceeding was pending concerning whether Newson breached the contract by filing the Pennsylvania claim and reasoning, *inter alia* that there could not be a clear and unmistakable waiver of the claim under the Pennsylvania statute as long as the arbitration proceeding was pending.

7.   Is waiver of the judicial forum for statutory claims and submission of those claims to the grievance procedure a mandatory subject of bargaining? If so, may an employer insist on such a waiver to the point of impasse? If the parties are at impasse, may the employer unilaterally impose such a waiver on the employees? Can a waiver unilaterally imposed by an employer be "clear and unmistakable?"

8.   In Canada, statutory discrimination claims are adjudicated by administrative tribunals rather than in court. They may also be pursued in arbitration under collective bargaining agreements. For a systematic comparison of the handling of such claims in arbitration in Ontario with their handling before the Human Rights Tribunal of Ontario see Martin H. Malin & Jon M. Werner, *14 Penn Plaza LLC v. Pyett: Oppression or Opportunity for U.S. Workers; Learning from Canada*, 2017 U. Chicago Legal Forum 347.

A NOTE ON THE PRECLUSIVE EFFECT OF ARBITRATION

Assume that the collective bargaining agreement prohibits discrimination on the basis of race, national origin, religion, sex, age and disability and also requires just cause for discipline and discharge. A terminated employee files a grievance and the union arbitrates the grievance contending that the employer lacked just cause. An arbitrator denies the grievance, finding that the employee engaged in misconduct and that the misconduct provided cause for discharge. Should the arbitration award preclude the employee from bringing any claims in subsequent statutory litigation that could have been brought before the arbitrator? Should it preclude the employee from litigating any issue that the arbitrator already resolved?

Gardner-Denver held that an employee may pursue a statutory claim in court *de novo*, although the arbitration award may be introduced as evidence in the litigation. In *Pyett*, Justice Thomas suggested in a footnote that *Gardner-Denver* may be a strong candidate for being overruled.

* * *

***Collins v. New York City Transit Authority*, 305 F.3d 113 (2d Cir. 2002).** Collins grieved his discharge and his union pursued his grievance to arbitration where an arbitrator upheld the discharge. Collins then sued under Title VII, alleging that he was discharged because of his race. The court affirmed a trial court decision that granted summary judgment to the Transit Authority.

> Generally speaking, a plaintiff's burden of establishing a prima facie case in the context of employment discrimination law is "minimal." However, appellant has not met even this low threshold, because the circumstances of his termination do not give rise to or support an inference of discrimination or retaliation. Appellant challenged the Transit Authority's decision to fire him and was finally discharged only after the arbitration board made an independent inquiry, including the taking of evidence, and authorized termination because it found that appellant had assaulted [his supervisor]. Appellant does not suggest that the arbitration board was not a fully independent and unbiased decision-maker in affirming his termination or that his claims of bias and of [his supervisor]'s faking an assault was not fully aired before the board.

> Appellant's termination occurred, therefore, only after a decision, based on substantial evidence, of an undisputedly independent, neutral, and unbiased adjudicator that had the power to prevent the termination. This fact is highly probative of the absence of discriminatory intent in that termination. Collins has offered insufficient evidence of causation linking his termination to motives of retaliation or discrimination to overcome the cumulative probative weight of the evidence of a legitimate reason for his discharge and of the final termination decision by the arbitration board.

> In sum, a negative arbitration decision rendered under a CBA does not preclude a Title VII action by a discharged employee. However, a decision by an independent tribunal that is not itself subject to a claim of bias will attenuate a plaintiff's proof of the requisite causal link. Where, as here, that decision follows an evidentiary hearing and is based on substantial evidence, the Title VII plaintiff, to survive a motion for summary judgment, must present strong evidence that the decision was wrong as a matter of fact—e.g. new evidence not before the tribunal—or that the impartiality of the proceeding was somehow compromised.

***Mathews v. Denver Newspaper Agency*, 649 F.3d 1199 (10th Cir. 2011).** Plaintiff grieved his demotion on grounds that included allegations of national origin discrimination and retaliation for filing a prior discrimination complaint. The collective bargaining agreement contained a non-discrimination clause but did not obligate employees to bring their statutory claims through the grievance procedure. Plaintiff arbitrated represented by his own attorney rather than a union advocate and the arbitrator denied his grievance. The district court interpreted *Pyett* as modifying *Gardner-Denver* and concluded, in light of the arbitration, that plaintiff's Title VII and § 1981 actions were barred by the doctrine of *res judicata*, i.e. claim preclusion. The Court of Appeals for the Tenth Circuit reversed.

Applying Supreme Court precedent to the facts of Mathews's case, it is evident no waiver of judicial forum has occurred. Again, such a waiver may only occur where the arbitration agreement expressly grants the arbitrator authority to decide statutory claims. The arbitration clause of the CBA, from which the arbitrator derived all authority, states that "[t]he arbitrator shall have no power to add to, subtract from, change or modify any provision of this Agreement, *but shall be authorized only to resolve the dispute submitted to him or her.*" CBA, Article XIII (emphasis added). The dispute submitted to arbitration by Mathews asserted a violation of Article II, Section 11 of the CBA and a vague complaint of retaliation, but no statutory claims under Title VII. Because the arbitration agreement empowered the arbitrator to resolve only the dispute submitted, and because the dispute submitted made no mention of statutory claims, the arbitral decision could in no way determine the question of Mathews's statutory rights.

[N]o preclusive effect should be accorded to the arbitral decision. Again, nothing in the arbitration agreement permitted or required Mathews to submit statutory claims to the arbitrator, nothing in the amended grievance purports to do so, and the arbitration agreement nowhere empowered the arbitrator to decide questions of statutory rights. The facts of Mathews's case thus mirror those of *Gardner-Denver* in all relevant aspects.

Mathews has presented some evidence that other employees were not demoted for their objectionable conduct. Such evidence can, in some circumstances, provide a sufficient showing that an employer's proffered explanation is pretextual to avoid summary judgment. The Agency, however, urges this court to hold Mathews to a more stringent standard in light of the arbitrator's prior adverse ruling. Specifically, the Agency cites to Second Circuit case law holding that, where a plaintiff's statutory discrimination or retaliation claims have previously been rejected in an arbitral proceeding following an evidentiary hearing and based upon substantial evidence, the plaintiff, "to survive a motion for summary judgment, must present strong evidence that the decision was wrong as a matter of fact—e.g. new evidence not before the tribunal—or that the impartiality of the proceeding was somehow compromised."

This court has not adopted the Second Circuit's per se "strong evidence" standard, and there is no need to do so now. In *Gardner-Denver* the Supreme Court counseled that, when evaluating a plaintiff's statutory discrimination claims arising out of the same facts as a previously arbitrated contract dispute, the arbitrator's prior decision "may be admitted as evidence and accorded such weight as the court deems appropriate." 415 U.S. at 60. The Court clarified that it could prescribe no fixed standard as to the probative weight accorded to such an arbitral decision, "since this must be determined in the [trial] court's discretion with regard to the facts and circumstances of each case." *Id.* at 60 n.21. Certainly, " '[w]here an arbitral determination gives full consideration to an employee's [Title VII] rights, a court may properly accord it great weight,' " but the court must also consider the " 'degree of procedural fairness in the arbitral forum, adequacy of the record with respect to the issue of discrimination, and the special competence of particular arbitrators.' " In light of the Supreme Court's clear directive to accord weight to prior arbitral decisions on a case-by-case basis, a per se standard is inappropriate and we will not affirm the grant of summary judgment on that basis.

NOTES

1. Can the two decisions be reconciled? If not, which presents the better view? Have the Supreme Court's decisions in *Gilmer* and *Pyett* undermined *Gardner-Denver's* holding that a Title VII claim may be litigated in court despite an adverse arbitration award?

2. Assume that at the arbitration hearing, Collins had been represented by a non-lawyer union business representative. Should that affect the weight that the court should accord the arbitration award?

3. In footnote 21 of *Gardner Denver*, cited in *Mathews*, the Court addressed the role of the arbitration award in subsequent Title VII litigation:

We adopt no standards as to the weight to be accorded an arbitral decision, since this must be determined in the court's discretion with regard to the facts and circumstances of each case. Relevant factors include the existence of provisions in the collective-bargaining agreement that conform substantially with Title VII, the degree of procedural fairness in the arbitral forum, adequacy of the record with respect to the issue of discrimination, and the special competence of particular arbitrators. Where an arbitral determination gives full consideration to an employee's Title VII rights, a court may properly accord it great weight. This is especially true where the issue is solely one of fact, specifically addressed by the parties and decided by the arbitrator on the basis of an adequate record. But courts should be ever the mindful that Congress, in enacting Title VII, thought it necessary to provide a judicial forum for the ultimate resolution of discriminatory employment claims. It is the duty of courts to assure the full availability of this forum.

Are the courts' decisions in line with this footnote?

3. ARBITRAL CONSIDERATION OF PUBLIC LAW CLAIMS

THE EVOLVING ROLE OF THE LABOR ARBITRATOR
Martin H. Malin & Jeanne M. Vonhof
21 Ohio State Journal on Dispute Resolution 199 (2005)

Their increasing contact with external law led to a recurring debate among labor arbitrators about how to handle these problems. The debate is often referred to as the "Meltzer-Howlett debate," after a famous exchange between Professor Bernard Meltzer and arbitrator Robert Howlett at the twentieth annual meeting of the National Academy of Arbitrators. Meltzer acknowledged that where an arbitrator faces two interpretations of a collective bargaining agreement, one of which is repugnant to a statute, "the statute is a relevant factor for interpretation." However, he continued, "Where . . . there is an irrepressible conflict, the arbitrator, in my opinion, should respect the agreement and ignore the law."

Meltzer reasoned that arbitrators could not be credited "with any competence, let alone any special expertise, with respect to the law, as distinguished from the agreement." Arbitrators deciding cases on the law instead of the contract, in Meltzer's view, "would be deciding issues that go beyond not only the submission agreement but also arbitral competence. Arbitrators would, moreover, be doing so within a procedural framework different from that applicable to official tribunals. Finally, they would be impinging on an area in which courts or other official tribunals are granted plenary authority."

In a subsequent article, Meltzer explained that his contention that arbitrators lack competence to resolve statutory claims referred to arbitrators' institutional competence rather than individual arbitrators' personal abilities. The problem of institutional competence arose from the underlying purpose of arbitration. It is a vehicle for resolving disputes under the CBA and the arbitrator's presumed expertise and the parties' consent to be bound by the arbitrator's judgment were limited to the CBA. In addition, many arbitrators lacked legal training.

Howlett, on the other hand, argued that "arbitrators *should* render decisions on the issues before them *based on both contract language and law.*" He maintained that the law is incorporated into every agreement, and that "[t]he law is part of the 'essence [of the] collective bargaining agreement' to which Mr. Justice Douglas has referred."

Howlett also considered arbitrators obligated to probe for statutory issues even those that the parties have not raised. In Howlett's view, where an arbitrator's probing uncovers issues that are better resolved by external legal authority, the arbitrator should so advise the parties and withdraw from the case.

In attendance discipline and discharge cases the simple fact [is] that an employer cannot operate its attendance plan anymore without significantly taking into account the [Family Medical Leave Act] FMLA,[4] and, therefore, it does not make sense to operate the disciplinary system as if this elephant were not standing in the middle of the room. Regardless of whether one agrees with Howlett's general contention that the law is incorporated into every contract, the FMLA is clearly implicated—and with increasing frequency expressly incorporated—into every contract's just cause provision. Consequently, the most recent edition of the leading treatise on labor arbitration observes, "In the majority of cases involving the FMLA, arbitrators rely on the provisions of the FMLA and the Department of Labor regulations without regard to whether the collective bargaining agreement says anything about the FMLA."

NOTES

1. Has the increasing level of legal regulation of the workplace effectively resolved the Meltzer-Howlett debate? Has Meltzer lost the debate? Professor Malin argues that he has. Martin H. Malin, *Revisiting the Meltzer-Howlett Debate over External Law in Labor Arbitration: Time for Courts to Declare Howlett the Winner?*, 24 Lab. Law. 1 (2008).

2. An employer has an attendance control plan that assesses points for every absence, tardiness and early departure. At designated point accumulations, an employee receives a verbal warning, written warning, suspension and discharge. An employee with poor attendance worked her way through the system, receiving the warnings and then the suspension. She did not grieve any of that discipline. When she was fired, she grieved. None of the absences leading to the discharge were FMLA-protected but the union seeks to introduce evidence in the arbitration over the discharge that two of the absences that led to the suspension were FMLA-protected. The employer objects to the evidence on the ground that the time for grieving the suspension has long expired. However, the statute of limitations under the FMLA has not yet expired. How should the arbitrator rule?

3. An employee was terminated for excessive absenteeism. At the arbitration hearing, evidence established that the employee's most recent absences which led to the termination resulted from illness that would have qualified as a serious health condition entitling the employee to leave under

---

[4]   **Editors' note.** The FMLA gives covered employees a right to up to 12 weeks of unpaid leave within 12 months of the birth or adoption of a child, or when needed to care for a parent, spouse or minor child who has a serious health condition, or for the employee's own serious health condition.

the FMLA. The employee's personnel record, introduced into evidence, reflects no FMLA leave ever taken by the employee. The evidence at the hearing further reflects that the employee made the employer aware of the medical condition that was responsible for the absences but there is no evidence that the employer ever raised the subject of FMLA leave. The union argues that the discharge lacked just cause but does not argue that the discharge violated the FMLA. Should the arbitrator raise the issue?

* * *

Recall the suggestion in *Enterprise Wheel*, that an arbitrator who bases an award "solely upon the arbitrator's view of the requirements of enacted legislation, would [have] exceeded the scope of the submission." Does this dicta continue to apply in today's environment? Consider the following case.

COASTAL OIL OF NEW ENGLAND, INC. V. TEAMSTERS LOCAL NO. 25
134 F.3d 466 (1st Cir. 1998)

CHIEF JUDGE TORRUELLA:

Appellant operates three separate facilities in Massachusetts, including one in Revere and one in Chelsea. Although they are all represented for collective bargaining purposes by appellee, the employees in each of the three facilities belong to separate bargaining units and are covered by discrete collective bargaining agreements.

Joseph Abruzzese, a yardman within the Revere bargaining unit, was injured in a work-related accident in 1991, forcing him to take a leave of absence, during which he received benefits under the Massachusetts Worker's Compensation Act. In August 1995, when Abruzzese sought to return to work, no job openings were available in the Revere unit. Nevertheless, appellant and appellee reached an agreement that Abruzzese would be reinstated to the next available position. Subsequently, Abruzzese learned that a yardman position was available in the Chelsea unit, the same job that he had previously had in the Revere unit. He applied for that slot through his union, appellee. Appellant refused the request, contending that Abruzzese only had a right to reinstatement in the Revere unit. After appellant hired someone else to the Chelsea position, appellee filed a grievance pursuant to the Revere contract.

Eventually, the dispute was heard before an arbitrator. After hearing the evidence, the arbitrator concluded that the issue to be decided was "whether the Company violated the [Revere] Agreement when it refused to place Joseph Abruzzese . . . in a position of yardman at the Company's Chelsea terminal. . . ." Thereafter, the arbitrator concluded that Article XIV, Section 10(a) of the Revere Agreement, which incorporated the Massachusetts Worker's Compensation Law, mandated the employment of

Abruzzese at the open position in Chelsea. Appellant was thus ordered to reinstate him to the Chelsea position and to make him whole as to back pay and lost benefits.

Appellant's challenge to the district court's rulings stems from its contention that the arbitrator exceeded his authority under the Revere collective bargaining agreement by ordering the employment of a member of that unit into the Chelsea unit. As a corollary to that issue, appellant claims that the arbitrator lacked authority to interpret the Worker's Compensation Act.

We commence our quest for the answers to the issues raised by this appeal with a reading of Article XVIII of the Revere Agreement entitled "Grievance Procedure," which provides in Section 2, in effect, that in exchange for labor peace "during the life of this Agreement[,] . . . any question of interpretation, enforcement, adjustment or grievance . . . between the employer and the Union and his employees which cannot be adjusted[,] . . . shall be referred . . . to . . . arbitration[,] . . . [which] . . . decision . . . shall be final and binding upon both parties."

We next proceed to the specific provision upon which the arbitrator relied for his ruling, Article XIV, Section 10(a) of the Revere contract. It states that:

> The Company shall either carry worker's compensation or, in the event of an injury to an employee, shall provide said employee with the same benefits and payments and in the same manner as provided by the provisions of the Worker's Compensation Law (Massachusetts G.L., Chapter 152) and Amendments thereto, up to and including the date of the signing of this Agreement.

We thus come to Section 75A of the Massachusetts Worker's Compensation statute, which the arbitrator found applicable to the submitted grievance under the previously cited contractual provision, and which he interpreted to require that Abruzzese be reinstated to the Chelsea position notwithstanding his previous employment outside that unit. Section 75A reads as follows:

> Any person who has lost a job as a result of an injury compensable under this chapter shall be given preference in hiring by the employer for whom he worked at the time of compensable injury over any persons not at the time of application for re-employment employed by such employer; provided, however, that a suitable job is available. Actions may be filed under this section with the superior court department of the trial court for the county in which the alleged violation occurred. An employer found to have violated this section shall be exclusively liable to pay to the employee lost wages, shall grant the employee a suitable job, and shall reimburse such reasonable attorney fees incurred in the

protection of rights granted by this section as shall be determined by the court. In the event that any right set forth in this section is inconsistent with an applicable collective bargaining agreement or chapter thirty-one, the collective bargaining agreement or said chapter thirty-one shall prevail.

Although we have often stated the following principle, due to the number of groundless appeals that have come before us challenging arbitration awards, it bears repeating that: "[j]udicial review of an arbitration award is among the narrowest known to the law." For courts "do not sit to hear claims of factual or legal error by an arbitrator[,] as an appellate court does in reviewing decisions of lower courts." In fact, "[f]ederal court review of arbitral decisions is extremely narrow and extraordinarily deferential."

"[A] court should uphold an award that depends on the arbitrator's interpretation of a collective bargaining agreement if it can find, within the four corners of the agreement, any plausible basis for that interpretation." That a court would have decided an issue differently is not a basis for overruling an arbitrator if the arbitrator "even arguably acted within the scope of his authority."

Although the scope of the reinstatement remedy provided through an arbitral award is usually limited to the contractual bargaining unit from which the grievance arises, a contrary result is not unheard of where the parties have bargained to grant the arbitrator such power. The parties to the collective bargaining agreement, the same entities presently before us, voluntarily contracted to submit to final and binding arbitration any question of interpretation of that agreement, or any grievance involving employees. It cannot be seriously contended that the underlying controversy submitted to, and litigated before, the arbitrator does not concern both the interpretation of the collective bargaining agreement as well as a grievance involving an employee. How can the arbitrator, in determining whether appellant lived up to the contractual obligations mandated by Section 10(a) of Article XIV of the Revere Agreement, fail to address whether the provisions of the Massachusetts Worker's Compensation Law, incorporated into that agreement by Section 10(a), have been met?

The response to this question as well as to appellant's challenge to the arbitrator's authority to interpret the aforementioned Massachusetts statute is self-evident. Obviously, the arbitrator acted properly and within the scope of his delegated authority. We can perceive of no valid reason why the parties could not also agree to have statutory rights enforced before an arbitral forum.

A cursory reading of that statute leads to the inevitable conclusion that the arbitrator's ruling in this case was not only clearly within the powers granted to him in the collective bargaining agreement, it is substantially the remedy that the Massachusetts Superior Court would likely have felt required to grant Joseph Abruzzese given that the appellant is a single, unitary employer, for workman's compensation purpose. As a result, its trinary profile, for labor relations purposes, is presently irrelevant. We note that our views as to the legal soundness of the arbitrator's conclusions are largely gratuitous, for as previously stated, even an erroneous interpretation of the law by an arbitrator is not subject to judicial review if that authority has been delegated to the arbitrator, as it was in this case.

NOTES

1.   Would the result have been the same if the collective bargaining agreement made no express reference to the Massachusetts Worker's Compensation Act? In *Sheriff of Suffolk County v. AFSCME Council 93*, 856 N.E.2d 194 (Mass. App. 2006), a corrections officer had retired on full disability pension as a result of an on-duty injury. A Massachusetts statute allowed employees who retired due to disability to return to their former positions or similar positions if they recovered sufficiently to perform the essential functions of their job. The grievant returned to work under this statutory provision but was placed in a position that he believed was lower than the position to which his seniority entitled him. The union pursued his grievance to arbitration. The arbitrator determined that the parties had not contemplated this type of situation and, hence, the contract did not control. Relying on the statute, the arbitrator concluded that the grievant was entitled to a higher position by virtue of his seniority and required the employer to upgrade him. The Massachusetts Appeals Court concluded that, by relying on the statute, the arbitrator exceeded his authority.

2.   How should a court review an arbitrator's award that is clearly inconsistent with a statute or with judicial decisions interpreting the statute? In *American Postal Workers Union v. U.S. Postal Service*, 789 F.2d 1 (D.C. Cir. 1986), Judge Edwards opined:

> When construction of the contract implicitly or directly requires an application of "external law," i.e., statutory or decisional law, the parties have necessarily bargained for the arbitrator's interpretation of the law and are bound by it. Since the arbitrator is the "contract reader," his interpretation of the law becomes part of the contract and thereby part of the private law governing the relationship to the contract. Thus, the parties may not seek relief from the courts for an alleged mistake of law by the arbitrator. . . . The parties' remedy in such cases is the same remedy they possess whenever they are not satisfied with the arbitrator's performance of his or her job: negotiate a modification of the contract or hire a new arbitrator.

Do you agree with this approach? Should it apply to cases where the collective bargaining agreement clearly and unmistakably waived the employee's rights to sue in court and the employee has no choice but to submit the statutory claim to the grievance procedure? For example, should a court vacate an arbitrator's award denying an employee's claim under the Age Discrimination in Employment Act because the employee was "only 45 years old"?

3.   Assume that the NLRB *Collyerizes* an unfair labor practice charge. The arbitrator hearing the grievance finds no breach of the collective bargaining agreement but finds a violation of the NLRA and orders relief. Should a court enforce the award? *See Roadmaster Corp. v. Prod. & Maint. Employees Local 504*, 851 F.2d 886 (7th Cir. 1988) (vacating award, holding that arbitrator was plainly wrong in relying on NLRA).

CHAPTER 8

COLLECTIVE ACTIVISM: THE EXPANDING BOUNDARIES OF THE MODERN LABOR LAW PRACTICE

■ ■ ■

Unions, worker organizations, and community groups in cities across the United States have identified low wages, the absence of sick leave and other benefits, and erratic schedules in the retail and food industries as a major source of economic and social distress. They seek to improve conditions locally, through enacting local ordinances regulating wages, schedules, and sick leave. They also seek a viable way to improve conditions throughout the national and global supply chains. One way to do that is to mobilize consumers to focus on the high cost of low prices and to use their buying power to leverage improvements in working conditions for workers in sweatshops the world over and workers on farms. The activists are also concerned about the proliferation of app-based services that are driving down wages for workers in the transportation industry, delivery services, and even restaurants where employers can use an app to find servers, cooks, and other restaurant staff on an as-needed independent contractor basis.

You have been consulted by unions and other worker organizations, along with groups focused on labor abuses in global and national supply chains, for both legal and political advice. Can or should the unions, in coalition with other organizations, do any of the following:

- *Lobby local governments to enact ordinances requiring restaurants and retail establishments to pay a minimum wage higher than the federal minimum wage, to provide paid sick leave to all employees, and to require businesses to give all workers regular schedules that are announced at least two weeks in advance?*

- *Lobby the local government to enact a law providing for some form of process by which workers in app-based gig economy jobs like driving, delivery, or other services can negotiate collectively with the platforms through which they provide services?*

- *Support the Fair Food Program, a partnership among farmers, farm workers, retail food companies, and the Coalition of Immokalee Workers—a worker center of South Florida farmworkers—that attempts to ensure decent wages for farmworkers by requiring participating retail food companies to ensure that a small premium paid by consumers for fair food certified products is passed down through the supply chain to farm workers, and to boycott growers that do not pay the premium to the farmworkers?*

- *Offer legal, financial, and/or staff support to groups (who are not labor unions) to assist them in conducting protest marches and staging a series of one-day strikes?*

- *Spend members' dues on political activities, including lobbying and organizing nonunion workers? Recent cases from the U.S. Supreme Court have imposed increasingly severe restrictions on unions' ability to collect money from workers whom they represent. How should unions respond to these cases and to the workers they represent who don't share the goals and political sensibilities of the union's leadership and members?*

What legal arguments would you anticipate counsel for nationwide retail and food service companies to make in response to these forms of activism? In this chapter, we provide the tools to analyze these and myriad other problems that confront the modern labor law practitioner.

A. INTRODUCTION

Among the most important contemporary functions of labor unions is to represent the voice of workers in local, state, and national politics. Although unions today represent less than seven percent of the private sector workforce, they nevertheless remain a disproportionally large and influential political voice on behalf of workers. For one thing, union membership is substantially higher in key states. The US Bureau of Labor Statistics reports that in 2017 in California, 17 percent of workers were unionized, in Hawaii, 23 percent of workers belong to unions, and in Washington state, 20 percent do. Union political influence is substantial because union members tend to be active and informed on the issues that concern them, and they vote. In areas or in elections where the electorate is closely divided and voter turn-out is low, union support for candidates or ballot measures is often the margin of victory. Although union financial support of candidates and issues matters, labor's strength in politics rests primarily on its ability to mobilize voters; in contributing money, business contributions dwarf labor contributions by fifteen to one. *See* Jake Rosenfeld, What Unions No Longer Do (2014); Marick F. Masters & John T. Delaney, Organized Labor's Political Scorecard, in What Do Unions Do? A Twenty-Year Perspective (J. Bennett & B. Kaufman eds. 2007). Studies of union political activity and spending since 1947 have shown that unions tend to succeed in political activity only when they support broad social issues rather than issues that are perceived to affect unions' own power. At the national level since 1970, unions have enjoyed no success in gaining new *pro-union* legislation, but only in blocking anti-union legislation and in promoting general social welfare legislation, such as raising the minimum wage.

With no realistic prospect for a dramatic near-term increase in union density, private sector unions' most significant role in the near future may not be as bargaining agents, but rather as members-only groups whose principal impact will be in the form of sophisticated and relatively well-financed advocacy for worker protection through legislation, litigation, and community organizing. Unions coordinate and support minimum wage, family and paid sick leave, and other minimum labor standards campaigns in local areas. They organize immigrants in support of liberalizing immigration laws. They research and publicize workplace dangers to health and safety. They work in coalition with local grassroots worker groups and church groups in gaining national attention for low wages and lack of affordable health care. The activism is not always on issues supported by the Democratic Party: unions in the construction trades often support building projects that they expect to generate jobs, sometimes over the objection of environmental organizations. Unions representing police and prison guards are politically engaged on issues of criminal law and punishment. Increasingly, unions are not tied to specific industries, occupations, or workplaces, but instead—like Fight for 15, Caring Across Generations, Working America, and coalitions representing low-wage immigrant workers—are developing themselves into groups of "citizen workers." Institutionally, however, one difficulty unions face in moving beyond contract negotiation and administration to a larger agenda of political work is that unions are membership organizations that depend on dues and, as we will see later in this chapter, federal law strictly limits how unions can raise and spend money for purposes other than contract negotiation and enforcement.

In the public sector, the political role of unions is even harder to separate from their role as bargaining and contract enforcement agents. A union concerned about the working conditions or pay of public school teachers, firefighters, police officers, or government clerical employees must think about not only how to protect and serve their members in negotiating and administering a contract, but also whether political strategies to obtain the same goals through legislative or administrative action might be more effective. If teachers are concerned about the harm to themselves and their students by having too many students in a classroom, should they support legislation capping class size, or should they negotiate to hire more teachers at an individual school? If a union representing public safety officers is concerned about whether the retirement age is too high and leaves too many workers with difficult or dangerous jobs that they are no longer able to perform, should they negotiate for early retirement at the bargaining table or lobby for it at the legislature? But the recent upsurge of concern about the power of public sector unions suggests that some skeptics have concluded that unions wield too much power both in negotiations and in political activism and that they are protecting their members at the expense of the public fisc or public welfare. A vexing question we will consider is whether law can regulate unions to prevent abuses of political or other power while still allowing them to perform those functions that the majority may consider legitimate.

This chapter will acquaint the student with the role of contemporary unions and other worker organizations in federal, state and local politics and in community organizing. The first part of the chapter surveys some of the major recent initiatives of labor organizations on local, national, and international issues of workplace justice. Although the statutory and common law protections for individual workers are often taught in an Employment Law course distinct from the Labor Law course, the reality is that the two subjects are deeply connected. The goal of this chapter is to show how much of contemporary labor organizing involves both political activity and enforcement of employment law rights of workers. As we will see, a modern labor law practice also calls upon lawyers to become familiar with a wide array of federal, state, and local laws. Lawyers involved in the campaigns described at the beginning of this chapter developed expertise in laws regulating food safety, franchising, campaign finance, business organizations, local government, international human rights, and a host of other subjects.

Innovative legal and political campaigns related to labor are not initiated only by worker activists. Lawyers and strategists representing businesses have waged a number of high-profile legal and political campaigns targeting the political and other activities of unions, have eliminated the right of some employees to bargain collectively in some states (such as in Indiana and Wisconsin), have changed the landscape of bargaining and of union-member relations in other states (such as in Tennessee and Michigan), and have sometimes tried to limit the political activities of unions and their members (for example in Alabama). As a consequence, the law governing campaign finance generally, the political activities of unions specifically, and the relations between unions and their members has become increasingly important for labor law practitioners. The last two sections of the chapter examine the pertinent law of campaign finance, as well as the federal regulation of the internal affairs of unions under the NLRA and under the Labor Management Reporting and Disclosure Act.

B. NEW LABOR ORGANIZATIONS AND NEW FORMS OF WORKER ACTIVISM

Worker organizing has almost always involved community activism that mobilizes workers and consumers while also publicizing to consumers and regulators the labor conditions that animate the organizing. What is new today is the power that national brands have to influence consumer behavior and the ability of a worker campaign to tarnish the value of a brand. Just as corporations seek to create value in the brand by touting their corporate social responsibility, workers seek to use the brand to gain publicity about labor practices, often by calling for consumer boycotts, picketing the employer's premises, persuading major suppliers, commercial customers, and financiers to sever ties with the target or to force it to change its practices, and seeking increased regulatory oversight over the employer's operations. Workers also apply political pressure (such as lobbying, tweeting or letter-writing, and legislative testimony) at whatever level of government appears to have influence over the employer's operations.

Unions have always used publicity to persuade employers to unionize, to rally support for their cause, to encourage their supporters to refrain from patronizing companies that are unfair to labor, and to negotiate contracts. In the 1930s, San Francisco culinary unions trying to organize department and variety stores sought to embarrass the employers and enlist public support by attending the Stanford-UCLA football game and passing out "score cards" asking the public to help the workers "hold that line." Activists also had boats cruise the San Francisco Bay during the annual Columbus Day celebration with a large sign urging people not to patronize certain employers. Although corporate campaigns are not new, they have grown in size, scope, sophistication, and visibility with the advent of TV, the Internet, and the globalization of business.

As will be seen below, in light of the vogue for corporations to advertise their corporate culture and to market their corporate social responsibility campaigns, only substantial worker involvement (what is known as worker-driven corporate social responsibility) provides transparency and accountability in corporate claims about social responsibility. This raises additional questions about how, if at all, the expansion of corporations' own conceptions of their social responsibility and their marketing of themselves as being socially responsible should affect the legality of what unions or worker centers and their members and allies can do in publicizing corporate practices.

Thus Part B first provides an overview of new forms of labor organization and then briefly profiles how two such organizations engaged in organizing and mobilization over workplace issues. It then considers three sets of legal issues under the NLRA about these approaches to worker organization.

1. NEW FORMS OF LABOR ORGANIZATION

In the 1970s and 1980s, as industries de-unionized even while they grew (hospitality, building service, taxis, delivery driving) and other industries that unions had never organized grew (especially domestic and health care work), a new form of worker organization emerged. These worker centers were based in communities rather than in workplaces or industries. The earliest were organized by black worker activists in North and South Carolina, immigrant activists based in food service and garment manufacturing in New York's and San Francisco's Chinatowns, and among Central American refugees in Los Angeles and Mexican workers in south Texas. Janice Fine, *Worker Centers: Organizing Communities at the Edge of the Dream* (2006). Restaurant Opportunities Center (ROC) began as a union-sponsored effort to help the families of restaurant workers killed in the World Trade Center towers on September 11. The National Day Laborers Organizing Network (NDLON) began when day laborers congregated together and discussed issues of wage theft, safety, and respect in day labor markets near home improvement centers and lumber yards.

Worker centers focused on providing education and services for immigrant workers particularly. *See* Ruth Milkman, Joshua Bloom & Victor Narro, *Working for Justice: The L.A. Model of Organizing and Advocacy* (2010) (case studies of eleven worker centers and their organizing campaigns in Los Angeles); Ruth Milkman & Ed Ott, *New Labor in New York: Precarious Workers and the Future of the Labor Movement* (2014) (case studies of thirteen organizing campaigns in New York). Worker centers, especially in the early years but still today, tend to be grass-roots organizations with loose membership structures, few paid staff and small budgets dependent on foundation grants and philanthropy rather than member dues. As Janice Fine explained, worker centers provide support to low-wage workers through three major approaches:

- *Service delivery.* Worker centers provide legal representation to recover unpaid wages. They offer English classes and worker rights education. They offer access to health clinics, bank accounts, and loans.

- *Advocacy:* Worker centers research and publish studies exposing conditions in low-wage industries. Based on this, they lobby for new laws regulating work and partner with government agencies to improve monitoring and grievance processes. They also sue employers that are the most serious violators of minimum labor standards.

- *Organizing:* Worker centers engage in leadership development among workers to take action on their own for economic and political change.

Until the second decade of the twenty-first century, worker centers were relatively small and local. Most focused their work in a single immigrant community and in a particular city or neighborhood. Workers would come to a worker center because they lived or worked in the neighborhood, not because they worked in a particular occupation or industry. Worker centers emphasized that membership was a privilege that was earned by taking classes and becoming involved. Staff and leaders sought to use the privilege of membership, and the legal representation and other free services that came with membership, as an incentive to encourage workers to learn their rights, to tell co-workers about their rights, and thereby to encourage others to insist on better working conditions. As Fine explained:

> Among the services currently offered at worker centers, legal help stands out. It is the one in greatest demand and also the most developed aspect of most centers' service work. . . .
>
> Most workers are unaware of their rights and will not learn about them at their workplaces. They don't know the locations of the government agencies where they can go to seek help. Undocumented workers often don't go to them for fear of "outing themselves" and being arrested and deported. Despite the fact that undocumented immigrants are covered by the same labor and employment laws as other American workers, federally funded legal service organizations are required by law to turn them away if they do come in seeking help. . . .
>
> Unlike government agencies or conventional legal clinics, most centers see their mission as empowering workers and aggressively look for ways to involve them in resolving their employment problems. If more than one worker has been affected by the problem, center staff encourage workers to go back and recruit their colleagues. If they do so, groups of workers are supported in filing class-action-type suits and in devising collective strategies for dealing with their employers.

Id. at 74, 81.

Worker center staff recognized that worker centers could improve conditions for low-wage immigrant workers by working with federal, state, and local agencies and public interest lawyers to improve enforcement of minimum labor standards laws and to persuade agencies and advocates to target the industries with the most egregious and widespread non-compliance: restaurants, ethnic markets, day labor, domestic work. In several cities, worker center leaders from different communities formed coalitions to speak with one voice to local governments and labor agency staff in order to develop specific recommendations for changes in law and changes in enforcement in order to combat systemic problems like wage theft and health and safety issues. As Fine explains about an early worker center coalition effort in California:

> The coalition's first significant accomplishment was the state secretary of labor's establishment of a low-wage worker advisory

board, which was made up of [the coalition's] member organizations. The advisory board met quarterly with the labor secretary advising him on enforcement issues. In addition, [the coalition] began to work quite closely with Henry Huerta, a senior deputy labor commissioner and a twenty-four-year veteran of labor standards enforcement in California. He became a key ally in [the coalition's] efforts to improve enforcement. "I tried to work with them to develop a better working relationship between advocacy groups and the agency because traditionally it had been very hostile. Some things were attitudinal. Investigators were putting the burden on low-wage immigrant workers to complete their claims without considering the level of education and the workers' fear of dealing with a government agency."

Id. at 164–65. After publication of a study documenting widespread violations of labor laws in low-wage industries and a dramatic decline in enforcement of state labor laws, *see* Annette Bernhardt, *et al.,* Broken Laws, Unprotected Workers (UCLA Labor Center 2009), and after the state agency was reorganized to create a new enforcement arm and the appointment of a crusading new state labor commissioner (a former workers' rights lawyer), worker centers continued to work with the newly empowered agency to develop very specific recommendations for operational changes in the approach to low-wage industry enforcement. The new enforcement strategy aimed to correct the longstanding problem that agencies conducted sweeps of workplaces or resolved individual wage claims but did little investigation or follow-up and failed to collect penalties. *Id.*

Worker centers have also played a crucial role in organizing efforts to pass new laws that would benefit low-wage workers. In the first two decades of the twenty-first century, dozens of state and local governments enacted higher minimum wage laws. Unions strongly supported these efforts, and devoted resources to lobbying for them, but worker centers' ties to low-wage industries enabled them to provide spokespersons who could explain the financial and family hardships endured by low-wage workers and who would directly benefit from increases in the minimum wage, paid sick leave, and other ordinances.

A first step for successful labor organizing among low-wage and immigrant workers is often developing a worker center. Chesa Boudin & Rebecca Scholtz, *Strategic Options for Development of a Worker Center*, 13 Harv. Latino L. Rev. 91, 104 (2010). Worker centers offer unique advantages over traditional unions. As worker centers may not be subject to the NLRA, they have the freedom to engage in creative organizing strategies that are prohibited by the NLRA's restrictions on secondary boycotts and recognitional picketing. Additionally, worker centers allow their members to tailor the organization to meet their goals and foster a sense of community. Finally, they promote democratic governance and provide leadership training. *Id.* at 104–105. As traditional unions and worker centers are not mutually exclusive, a group of workers can enlist the assistance of both to reach its goals. Modest-sized, community-based organizations of low-wage workers that focus on work/wage issues through service, advocacy, and organizing have mostly succeeded in raising wages and improving conditions via public policy, not direct intervention in labor markets. Janice Fine, Community Unions and the Revival of the American Labor Movement, 33.1 Politics & Society 153, 153 (2005).

One challenge faced by worker centers and unions alike is building a sustainable organization with the funding and social and political power to deal effectively with large, politically sophisticated, and well-financed employers and employer groups that oppose increases in labor costs. Matthew Ginsburg, *Nothing New Under the Sun: The "New Labor Law" Must Still Grapple With the Traditional Challenges of Firm-Based Organizing and Building Self-Sustainable Worker Organizations*, 126 Yale L.J. Forum 488 (2017). As will be seen, unions and worker centers approach that challenge differently: unions rely on dues paid by members; worker centers rely on foundation and government grants

As the number of worker centers grew (by 2015, there were an estimated 250 individual worker centers spread across the United States and five national networks of worker centers), the range of issues they took on and strategies they used grew dramatically. Some continued to focus on local legislation and improving enforcement of local and state law. They increasingly have done so through formal partnerships with state and local labor agencies. *See* Seema N. Patel & Catherine L. Fisk, *California Co-Enforcement Initiatives That Facilitate Worker Organizing*, Harv. L. & Pol'y Rev. (2017).

Others launched national campaigns, often with substantial financial, logistical and staff assistance from national unions. For example, Caring Across Generations is a project of the National Domestic Workers Alliance in partnership with many organizations, including unions, to provide more support for families to provide in-home care for young, old, and ailing people, to provide good jobs for caregivers, and to provide good choices for seniors or people who need or want in-home care. *See* https://caring across.org. The Fight for $15 movement, which began in 2012 with a wave of high-profile protests and strikes by fast food workers, managed to make $15 an hour the normal standard for a decent hourly wage. *See* Michael M. Oswalt, *Improvisational Unionism*, 104 California L. Rev. 597 (2016); Kate Andrias, *The New Labor Law*, 126 Yale L.J. 2 (2016); Kimberly M. Sanchez Ocasio & Leo Gertner, *Fighting for the Common Good: How Low Wage Workers' Identities are Shaping Labor Law*, 126 Yale L.J. Forum 503 (2017). The Restaurant Opportunities Center, which began as a project of the Hotel and Restaurant Employees Union to help the families of restaurant workers who died in the World Trade Center on September 11,

2001, launched a major national campaign to partner with responsible restaurants that pay decent wages, to target the major national chain restaurants such as Olive Garden that pay low wages, and to eliminate the subminimum wage for tipped employees. *See* Saru Jayaraman, Forked: A New Standard for American Dining (2016). Various groups, including the Coalition of Immokalee Workers, Migrant Justice, and many others focus on getting major food companies, including grocery stores, food manufacturers, and restaurants to ensure decent wages and working conditions at all companies in their supply chains. Many of these organizations work in partnership with labor unions. All focus on educating and organizing workers and consumers to demand corporate policies and legislation to establish minimum standards for wages, safety, and scheduling. A description of some of these organizations and their members, and the gains they have secured, is provided in Kimberly M. Sanchez Ocasio & Leo Gertner, Fighting for the Common Good: How Low Wage Workers' Identities Are Shaping Labor Law, *supra.*

In addition, a number of groups, including the Freelancers Union, focus on improving conditions in the so-called "gig economy" or "on demand economy" (including Uber and other ride services) whose business model deems all workers independent contractors. On some of the legal issues that arise when (in)dependent contractors organize, see Sanjukta Paul, *Uber as For Profit Hiring Hall: A Price-Fixing Paradox and Its Implications*, 38 Berkeley J. Emp. & Lab. L. 233 (2017); Seth Harris & Alan Kreuger, *A Proposal for Modernizing Labor Laws for Twenty-First-Century Work: The "Independent Worker"* (Hamilton Project Dec. 2015, http://www. hamiltonproject.org/assets/files/modernizing_labor_laws_for_twenty_ first_century_work_krueger_harris.pdf; Scott L. Cummings, *Preemptive Strike: Law in the Campaign for Clean Trucks*, 4 UC Irvine L. Rev. 939 (2014); Elizabeth Kennedy, *Freedom from Independence: Collective Bargaining Rights for "Dependent Contractors,"* 26 Berkeley J. Emp. & Lab. L. 143 (2005). *See also* Benjamin Sachs, *A New Category of Worker for the On-Demand Economy?*, Onlabor.org (June 22, 2015), available at http://onlabor.org/2015/06/22/a-new-category-of-worker-for-the-on- demand-economy/; Benjamin Sachs, *Do We Need a New Independent Worker Category?* Onlabor.org (Dec. 5, 2015) (questioning Harris-Kreuger thesis).

NOTES

1.   *What can unions learn from worker centers? Are smaller unions necessarily weaker?* The fact that the percentage of American workforce that are union members has been declining since the 1950s is often taken as proof that unions are weak and that collective action among workers is declining. In what respects is the size of the membership of an organization a reflection of its strength, and in what respects does strength come from other things, like commitment, effective communication, and activism?

2.   *The power of a network.* It has been argued that because of the power of loose networks to mobilize support through rapid communication and to exploit news media, and the ability of networks to wage effective publicity campaigns, "[t]he key question is not how many members you have, but who you can mobilize. A small number at the right time can have more effect than a large mass, and they need not be "members" in the sense of "signing up" for a permanent organization." Charles Heckscher, *Organizations, Movements, and Networks*, 50 N.Y.L. Sch. L. Rev. 313 (2005). What light is shed on this argument by the description of worker centers and the examples given by Professor Fine?

3.   *Mobilizing lawyers.* How should workers centers mobilize lawyers in addition to mobilizing members? If you were a lawyer for a worker center, how would you think about using law to empower the workers as opposed to disempower them? On legal strategies of worker centers, see Julie Yates Rivchin, *Colloquium: Building Power Among Low-Wage Immigrant Workers: Some Legal Considerations for Organizing Structures and Strategies*, 28 N.Y.U. Rev. L. & Soc. Change 397 (2004). Some worker centers do not use legal strategies, but instead emphasize direct action such as picketing and boycotts. The various approaches used by different worker centers are surveyed in Eli Naduris-Weissman, *The Worker Center Movement and Traditional Labor Law: A Contextual Analysis*, 30 Berkeley J. Emp. & Lab. L. 232 (2009).

2.   NEW FORMS OF WORKER ACTIVISM

The first excerpt below describes the process by which workers can leverage their organizing efforts to become involved in monitoring and enforcing contractual agreements to improve labor standards in the United States and in the global supply chain. The second describes a more locally focused campaign. Both describe different phases and forms of organizing among low-wage workers in the U.S. and abroad.

THE PROBLEM WITH CORPORATE SOCIAL RESPONSIBILITY

Jennifer Gordon
https://wsr-network.org/wp-content/uploads/2017/07/Gordon-
CSR-vs-WSR-FINAL-July-2017.pdf (2017)

In the 1980s, as the flight of manufacturing jobs from high-wage countries accelerated, activists in those nations began to pressure brands to answer for their global contractors' treatment of workers abroad. As consumers began to pay attention, corporations responded by creating codes of conduct that required their suppliers to meet certain workplace standards. Within a decade, the field of Corporate Social Responsibility grew from a sideline into a multi-billion dollar industry.

Unilateral corporate codes quickly came under fire for being promotional efforts that sought to protect brand reputations and pacify consumers without truly addressing the underlying problems that workers faced. For example, when Nike was targeted for boycott in the 1990s for paying pennies an hour to workers in Vietnam, it responded by creating its own code of conduct and hiring its own accountants to verify its compliance. Few people were persuaded that Nike—and the many companies that followed a similar path—had changed much of anything other than its publicity materials.

What's Wrong with Corporate Social Responsibility?

First, **corporate participation is always voluntary**. Centuries of labor history affirm that corporations rarely make truly voluntary efforts to improve the conditions of the lowest-wage workers, particularly those whose work is subcontracted rather than employed directly. Instead, working conditions improve when there is sustained pressure that threatens a company's bottom line.

Furthermore, **[m]onitoring is intermittent and ineffectual, and standards are not legally binding**. Compliance is almost always determined by private auditors. It is most often the brands being audited for compliance that pay the monitors. Importantly, codes do not include provisions that give workers or others the right to sue for compliance.

Finally, **brands simultaneously demand compliance with labor standards and pressure subcontractors to ignore them**. Codes impose expensive requirements on suppliers, but brands have not traditionally paid more per contract to cover those costs.

A New Approach: Worker-Driven Corporate Social Responsibility

While Corporate Social Responsibility is motivated by a brand's desire to protect its reputation among consumers, Worker-Driven Social Responsibility is generated by workers and their allies.

The Fair Food Program designed by the Coalition of Immokalee Workers in Florida has led this new approach. The Coalition describes itself as a farmworker-based human rights organization. It is located in Immokalee, Florida, where 90% of the winter tomatoes in the United States are grown. In 2010, after 17 years of organizing with farmworkers and tens of thousands of students, people of faith, and consumers across the United States, the Coalition won and began implementing the Program.

The Fair Food Program requires that participating brands like McDonalds and Walmart pay a small premium of one to four cents per pound of produce to their growers, who must pass the money through to workers, keeping a small percentage to offset the additional payroll taxes created by the bonus payments. More than $20 million has gone into farmworkers' pockets through this program over its first six years. Participating brands can only buy from growers who have signed the Fair Food Code, which mandates a range of improvements in working conditions. The design of the code, and the provisions in it, grew out of the experiences of Coalition members—mostly immigrant tomato pickers—

with sexual harassment, systemic underpayment, and dangerous conditions in the fields. The Fair Food Buyer Agreements are legally enforceable contracts. Experienced workers have taught 45,000 others about their rights under the Code on paid work time, and all actively monitor their employers for code violations. The Fair Food Standards Council carries out intensive audits of participating growers, now in three crops in seven states.

Another example of Worker-driven Social Responsibility is the 2013 Accord on Fire and Building Safety in Bangladesh, adopted in the wake of the building collapse at Rana Plaza, and recently renewed and extended to 2021. The groundwork for the Accord was laid over decades by advocates who pressured brands to sign binding agreements, and the agreement itself was drafted with the participation of Bangladeshi as well as global unions two years before the collapse. Until the tragedy, however, only two brands had been willing to sign. That number rose to 218 following Rana Plaza and the ensuing public outcry.

The Accord makes brands co-responsible for safety conditions in the factories, and requires them to commit to fully fund the cost of the safety improvements at their Bangladeshi contractors. The repairs and upgrades that the Accord mandates target the life-threatening dangers that Bangladeshi garment workers have long faced on the job, and are coupled with protection against retaliation in a context where workers who speak up risk physical violence. The Accord also requires that suppliers pay workers for up to six months during closure for safety renovations, and seek to place them elsewhere if orders drop at a renovated factory. At the factory level, the Accord calls for the establishment of labor-management health and safety committees. The commitments of the signatory corporations are legally enforceable, a fact that led several American brands, most notably Walmart and Gap, to refuse to participate, choosing a less binding alternative instead. Despite challenges in implementation, the Accord has carried out initial inspections at all of the more than 1600 factories covered by the Agreement, and identified over 122,000 violations. Although progress toward full compliance has been slow, 75% of the factories report taking steps toward remedying the dangers identified, offering increased protections to over 2 million workers.

The participation of workers and their representatives ensures that codes of conduct reflect on-the-ground knowledge about repeat problems. Worker-driven Social Responsibility places primary responsibility for these violations at the door of multinational corporations, whose consolidated power at the top of supply chains allows them to demand ever-lower prices from their suppliers. [W]orkers themselves do peer education, monitor for violations, and file complaints that trigger enforcement.

NOTES

1.   *Why does worker involvement matter?* Professor Gordon describes the difference between corporate social responsibility and worker-driven corporate social responsibility. What failures of corporate social responsibility does worker involvement address?

2.   *Compare and contrast the Fair Food Program with the Accord.* How do the FFP and the Bangladesh Accord resemble and differ from each other? What accounts for the differences?

* * *

In 2006, approximately 120,000 workers in the United States were seeking or performing work in which they were hired by the day. They were predominantly male, Latino, and immigrants, although about 7% of those surveyed were born in the U.S. and 40% had lived in the U.S. for more than six years. Most day laborers are hired to work on residential construction and remodeling jobs, often to replace crew members who call in sick, to finish detail work or to clean a construction site, or sometimes just to reduce labor costs. Abel Valenzuela, *et al.,* On the Corner: Day Labor in the United States, UCLA Center for the Study of Urban Poverty (2006). One major national network of worker centers is the National Day Laborer Organizing Network (NDLON), which coordinated the efforts of many local groups to help a low-wage workforce whom the construction unions had long ignored or tried to suppress, believing them to pose a threat to union wage and safety protections. The following account of NDLON's organizing illustrates an approach still used by many worker centers.

IMPACTING NEXT WAVE ORGANIZING: CREATIVE CAMPAIGN STRATEGIES OF THE LOS ANGELES WORKER CENTERS

Victor Narro
50 N.Y.L. Sch. L. Rev. 465 (2005)

The National Day Laborer Organizing Network (NDLON) was founded in 2001 as a national collaborative of day laborers and day laborer advocacy organizations. The mission of NDLON is to strengthen and expand the work of local day-laborer organizing groups in order to become more effective and strategic in building leadership, advancing low-wage worker and immigrant rights, and developing successful models for organizing immigrant contingent and temporary workers.

Since its formation, NDLON has promoted its mission through the following two basic and immediate goals: 1) form worker centers as humane and dignified spaces where day laborers can work collectively to improve their working conditions and increase wages, and assimilate productively into their host communities; and 2) eliminate local laws that restrict day laborers' rights to seek work in public in the absence of city-sanctioned, day-laborer worker centers.

For at least twenty years, day laborers had congregated on two main intersections in Redondo Beach, California, to seek and receive work to feed their families; on any given day, between 20 to 150 men wait for work. Day laborers are not the only people to utilize these locations: hundreds of subcontractors, entrepreneurs, and small businesses make a regular practice of meeting and hiring workers to do a variety of different kinds of work, including construction, demolition, lawn care, masonry, carpentry, tiling, painting, roofing, drywall construction, and landscaping, among others.

NDLON staff first met with the day laborers in Redondo Beach in September 2004. NDLON organizers visited the corners in Redondo Beach as part of a survey of the Los Angeles area to determine whether local police were enforcing, or threatening to enforce, ordinances [that prohibit solicitation on the street]. During the visits, workers assured NDLON staff that there was no police harassment. Relations on the corner were relatively harmonious, and workers reported extremely high rates of employment.

On October 6, 2004, one month after NDLON completed its survey, the City of Redondo Beach initiated a massive crackdown on day laborers. During the course of a month-long effort, over sixty workers were arrested, detained, and charged with violations of a municipal law forbidding the "solicitation of employment from streets." Through a series of sting operations, local undercover police officers dressed as contractors and posed as potential employers of day laborers. They offered to hire the day laborers, and when the workers got in the unmarked police trucks, they were driven straight to the police station and placed in custody. The organizing and litigation response that followed marked a historic turning point not only in the advocacy work for the rights of day laborers, but in the exercise of power by an organization that had only been in existence for three years. In an initial two-day sting operation, undercover police officers arrested thirty-seven men for seeking work on a public sidewalk in violation of a local municipal ordinance.

Many of the arrested workers were very recently arrived immigrants who were unaware of efforts to organize and work collectively to defend their rights. After prolonged discussions about whether it was worth the effort to assert their rights, workers on the corner voted unanimously to join together and form the "Comité de Jornaleros de Redondo Beach" (Comité). The Comité decided to serve as plaintiff in the federal lawsuit and act as the vehicle for collective action and responses.

NDLON staff quickly gathered testimonies and evidence from local day laborers to prepare a lawsuit against Redondo Beach. Through this process and during a series of "corner meetings," workers were consulted about the preparations for litigation challenging the "anti-day laborer solicitation" ordinance on First Amendment grounds. In a few weeks, the federal complaint was ready, and the workers prepared for a march to announce the filing of the lawsuit. Meetings were held in a nearby Catholic church where workers prepared protest signs and informed each other about developments in the campaign.

On November 17, 2004, Redondo Beach day laborers publicly launched their response against Redondo Beach city officials. Approximately 250 day laborers, union supporters, community organization representatives, and others staged an enormous march down the Pacific Coast Highway. NDLON member organizations from around Los Angeles brought carloads of day laborers from their centers to march in solidarity with the arrested workers. For two miles, workers walked and chanted "trabajo sí, policía no" ("work yes, police no").

The march ended with a press conference and rally in front of Redondo Beach City Hall, where a group of day laborers symbolically served the lawsuit complaint to the City, initiating the legal battle. Arrested workers gave speeches and testimonials to denounce their treatment by local police. Attorneys explained the basis for the lawsuit, that solicitation of work in public areas is protected free speech under the First and Fourteenth Amendments. NDLON members from around the country sent emails and letters demanding that Redondo Beach cease enforcement of its anti-solicitation law. During the press conference, a clear message for the campaign emerged: Looking for work is not a crime. Media coverage of the story was extensive. In a city where day laborers are a familiar sight, the protest garnered major media and public attention. Almost all of the local television, radio, and print media outlets and affiliates picked up the story. Workers from Redondo Beach, briefed on the specific details of the complaint and the campaign, provided interviews on television and on radio talk shows. The City defended its actions to the press by asserting that the day laborers littered, urinated in public, and threatened passersby. Workers responded by noting that if those accusations were true, the City need not arrest them for merely seeking work. In a very short period of time, the workers had shifted the terms of the debate from one about the concerns of local businesses to one highlighting the human right and First Amendment right to seek jobs in public areas to earn a living.

On December 6, 2004, the Redondo Beach day laborers won a major victory in federal court. Federal District Court Judge Consuelo Marshall issued a temporary restraining order to halt future citations and arrests by the City. The judge found "serious questions" about the constitutionality of the ordinance and noted that the balance of hardships in the lawsuit favored temporarily siding with the day laborers. Shortly thereafter, NDLON and the Comité scored a second court victory when Judge Marshall issued a preliminary injunction to allow the day laborers to continue seeking employment while the litigation continued. In her decision, she expressed her concerns over the constitutionality of the ordinance.

NDLON organizers and the workers continue[d] to meet and work together to seek a long-term resolution to the conflict. The court victory provided them with the opportunity to establish the strategic analysis and framework for a political and community organizing campaign in Redondo Beach. The legal victory also created tremendous leverage for day laborers to negotiate possible solutions with city officials, police, businesses, and community residents.

NOTES

1. *First Amendment victory in court.* The victory secured by Comité de Jornaleros in the trial court was eventually upheld by the Ninth Circuit *en banc*, which held that the Redondo Beach ordinance prohibiting solicitation was not narrowly tailored to serve the city's articulated interest in facilitating traffic flow. *Comité de Jornaleros v. City of Redondo Beach*, 657 F.3d 936 (9th Cir. 2011) (*en banc*). In *Valle del Sol, Inc. v. Whiting*, 709 F.3d 808 (9th Cir. 2013), the Ninth Circuit struck down under the First Amendment an Arizona law prohibiting a motor vehicle occupant from hiring a person for work and prohibiting any person from seeking to be hired in such a manner. The court held that Arizona had failed to show that targeting and penalizing day labor solicitation was necessary to protect public safety, rather than enforcing existing traffic laws.

2. *Is NDLON a labor organization?* Recall the discussion above in the section on worker centers about the distinction between a worker center and a labor organization and the legal consequences that flow from it. Is NDLON a "labor organization" within the meaning of section 2(5) of the NLRA? Would the interests of day laborers be better served if NDLON were subject to secondary boycott and other restrictions imposed on labor organizations?

3. *Learning from successes and failures.* Can you generalize about what makes local labor campaigns more or less likely to succeed? There have been a number of studies of what makes labor-community coalitions work, and also what factors contribute to union success in mobilizing community support to obtain recognition or a collective bargaining agreement after winning a certification election. *See* Chris Rhomberg & Louise Simmons, *Beyond Strike Support: Labor-Community Alliances and Democratic Power in New Haven*, 30 Labor Studies J. 21 (2005); Bruce Nissen, *The Effectiveness and Limits of Labor-Community Coalitions: Evidence from South Florida*, 29 Labor Studies J. 67 (2004).

A study described the success of a campaign by the Paper, Allied-Chemical, and Energy Workers union against Crown Central Petroleum. The campaign involved filing charges with relevant government agencies reporting pollution and discrimination, collaborating with oil workers in Norway, and traveling the country to speak at churches to start a consumer boycott. The campaign eventually ended a lockout of 252 union members at a Texas refinery by causing share prices to fall and preventing the sale of the company. Robert Hickey, *Preserving the Pattern: Membership Mobilization and Union Revitalization at PACE Local 4–227*, 29 Labor Studies J. 1 (2004). A book-length study of a successful union campaign that included a corporate social responsibility element is Tom Juravich and Kate Bronfenbrenner, Ravenswood: The Steelworkers' Victory and the Revival of American Labor (Cornell University Press 1999). Some studies have been highly critical of the utility and legality of such campaigns. *See* Herbert R. Northrup & Charles H. Steen, *Union "Corporate Campaigns" as Blackmail: The RICO Battle at Bayou Steel*, 22 Harv. J.L. & Pub. Pol'y 771 (1999); Jarol B. Manheim, The Death of a Thousand Cuts: Corporate Campaigns and the Attack on the Corporation (Lawrence Earlbaum Assocs., Inc. 2001).

3. NLRA PROTECTIONS FOR AND RESTRICTIONS ON WORKER CENTERS AND WORKER-DRIVEN CORPORATE SOCIAL RESPONSIBILITY CAMPAIGNS

The new forms of labor organization and worker-driven corporate social responsibility campaigns raise three set of questions for the NLRA: (a) Does section 7 protect this activism, given that much of it is not aimed at forming a union with exclusive representation and bargaining rights and much of it is focused on changing or enforcing state and local law? (b) Does section 8 preempt all or part of state and local laws enacted in support of worker centers or other new worker formations? (c) Does section 8(b) restrict the protest and the worker-consumer boycotts that are often at the heart of the economic and political leverage the campaigns exert? Each of those issues is addressed below.

a. Section 7 Protection for Worker Campaign Activism

Recall that the Court held in *Eastex, Inc. v. NLRB*, 437 U.S. 556 (1978), that certain political activity is protected under section 7. (The case is excerpted in Chapter 2). In that case, employees sought to distribute a union newsletter urging employees to support the union, to register to vote, and to urge legislators to oppose a proposal to add the state "right-to-work" statute into the state constitution, and to oppose a Presidential veto of an increase in the federal minimum wage. The Court rejected the employer's argument that the newsletter was not protected because it did not relate to a "specific dispute" between employees and their own employer "over an issue which the employer has the right or power to affect":

> We find no warrant for petitioner's view that employees lose their protection under the "mutual aid or protection" clause when they seek to improve terms and conditions of employment or otherwise improve their lot as employees through channels outside the immediate employee-employer relationship. The 74th Congress knew well enough that labor's cause often is advanced on fronts

other than collective bargaining and grievance settlement within the immediate employment context. [I]t has been held that the "mutual aid or protection" clause protects employees from retaliation by their employers when they seek to improve working conditions through resort to administrative and judicial forums, and that employees' appeals to legislators to protect their interests as employees are within the scope of this clause. To hold that activity of this nature is entirely unprotected—irrespective of location or the means employed—would leave employees open to retaliation for much legitimate activity that could improve their lot as employees.

Both workers and companies resort to law other than labor law in the effort to exert leverage. Workers, for example, will report every safety violation they find to the state or federal Occupational Safety and Health Administration or to state safety agencies. Workers will file complaints of unlawful discrimination on the basis of race, religion, sex, national origin, disability, etc. Workers will file reports of alleged environmental problems with state and federal environmental protection agencies.

Workers sometimes face retaliation for filing such charges. The scope of anti-retaliation provisions under environmental, discrimination, or health and safety laws varies widely, as does protection available under whistleblower statutes. One question is whether the filing of complaints is protected under section 7. Although there is no mention of whether the nurses in the case below were involved in a union or any form of worker organization, the issue in the case—whether NLRA section 7 protects employees against retaliation for filing charges with agencies other than the NLRB—is important for any form of worker organizing.

ORCHARD PARK HEALTH CARE CENTER

341 N.L.R.B. 642 (2004)

CHAIRMAN BATTISTA and MEMBERS LIEBMAN, SCHAUMBER, WALSH, and MEISBURG:

[Two nurses in New York called the New York State Department of Health Patient Care Hotline to report excessive heat in the nursing home where they worked. The nursing home did not have air conditioning and during a July heat wave, four patients were sent to the hospital with dehydration. One nurse "observed that the patients were refusing to eat and drink, were unresponsive, and were taking off their clothes." There was no bottled water available for the staff. After discussion among nurses about the miserable heat, two nurses got together and called the hotline to report these conditions; the one who spoke falsely identified herself as a relative of a resident.]

Reed and Gunnersen explicitly disclaimed an interest in their own working conditions when they called the hotline. Reed called the hotline to express their concern about patients, as distinguished from an effort to improve their lot as employees. Indeed, Reed went out of her way, to the point of lying, to tell the authorities that she was a relative of a resident. If Reed wanted to complain about employee conditions, she need only have truthfully identified herself as an employee. In addition, it is significant that the hotline that she called was the "Patient Care Hotline."

[The majority then turned to a discussion of Board precedent. It deduced from these cases that] employee concerns for the quality of care and the welfare of their patients are not interests encompassed by the mutual aid or protection clause. The fact that Reed and Gunnersen were reporting to State authorities does not make the activity protected. In *Autumn Manor*, 268 N.L.R.B. 239 (1983), nursing home employees testified at the nursing home's relicensing hearing before the Kansas Department of Health and Environment about alleged patient abuse. The Board found that the employees' testimony about management's treatment of patients "had no direct relationship to the working conditions of employees." *Id.* As with the employees' testimony in *Autumn Manor*, the hotline call to the New York State Department of Health has no direct relationship to the working conditions of employees.

Reed and Gunnersen were concerned about the quality of the care and welfare of the residents, not their own working conditions. Indeed, as noted above, they conceded at the hearing in this matter that they did not call the hotline to address their own working conditions. Gunnersen testified, "[W]hen we used the line that day, it wasn't for working conditions. It wasn't meant for the staff members. It was about what was going on with the residents." When Reed was asked what was the focus of the state requirements, she responded: "[a]ny and all concerns with regards to the patients." Our dissenting colleagues would have us ignore Reed and Gunnersen's testimony about their motive for calling the hotline because employees' subjective characterizations of their conduct are not determinative of the conduct's protected status. We agree that if, on the objective facts, the phone call had been to protect employee working conditions, Reed and Gunnersen's testimony to the contrary would not necessarily remove the conduct from the protection of the Act. However, as discussed, the objective facts are the other way, and the Reed and Gunnersen testimony supports the objective facts.

[The Board then distinguished cases on which the dissent relied in which nurses' complaints about staffing levels having an impact on patients were directly related to their own working conditions:] By analogy if, in the instant case, the employees were complaining that their own thirst was making them unable to care for patients, that could be protected activity. Here, Reed and Gunnersen did not call the hotline because of a perception that their ability to deliver patient care was impaired or imperiled. Further, there is no showing that using or failing to use the hotline to complain about the heat would have any real or potential impact on Reed and Gunnersen's employment.

[Two members dissented. The dissent emphasized that one of the nurses who made the call complained that she was feeling ill on account of the heat. A notice posted in the nursing home] required employees and licensed health professionals, pursuant to the New York State Public Health Law, "to report any instance of patient physical abuse, mistreatment or neglect' to the New York State Department of Health. [T]he severity of the heat directly affected the manner in which the nursing home employees carried out their resident-care duties. Resident care, after all, is the responsibility of the nurses and nursing assistants, and the conditions that affect the residents surely have a profound effect on how the nurses and nursing assistants carry out that duty.

[The dissent then addressed the question whether the nurses' testimony that they called the hotline out of concern for the residents rather than for themselves vitiated the protection of section 7.] The motive of the actor in a labor dispute must be distinguished from the purpose for his activity. The motives of the participants are irrelevant in terms of determining the scope of Section 7 protections; what is crucial is that the purpose of the conduct relate to collective bargaining, working conditions and hours, or other matters of "mutual aid or protection" of employees. [The Seventh Circuit has held in *NLRB v. Parr Lance Ambulance Serv.*, 723 F.2d 575, 578 (7th Cir. 1983), that] concern over the adequacy of medical equipment qualified as a working condition. The court stated: "Even if a health care employee phrases a complaint about a situation solely in terms of its effect on patient welfare, the employee is protected if the situation relates to a working condition."

NOTES

1. *The difference between "I" and "we."* If the nurses had complained to the Hotline that they were suffering health effects from excessive heat and lack of water, would they be protected under section 7? What if the nurse who made the call had truthfully identified herself as a nurse rather than a relative of a patient and had said that they were concerned both for themselves and for the patients? *See Summit Healthcare Assoc.*, 357 NLRB 1614 (2011) (distinguishing *Orchard Park* and finding that when nurse complained about patient conditions that related to working conditions, the complaint was for mutual aid and protection). What if the nurse testified at the hearing that she had identified herself as a relative because she feared retaliation and had said that she and the other nurses were concerned about their working conditions but had focused on patients because patients are of foremost importance? Because changing a word or two would change the legal outcome, lawyers preparing employees to testify in these proceedings should be careful. While of

course it is unethical to encourage a witness to testify falsely about what she said, it is also important to be precise about exactly what the employee said if the outcome of a case turns on whether the employee said "I" or "we" when raising concerns about workplace safety. *See Holling Press*, 343 N.L.R.B. 301 (2004) (whether action is protected under section 7 turns on whether employee said "I" or "we").

2. *Section 7 and other anti-retaliation protections.* Apart from the reasons given in the majority opinion, why might the majority have been concerned about reading section 7 to protect employees against retaliation for invoking state laws protecting nursing home patients? Should that same concern extend to reading section 7 to protect employees against retaliation for invoking state laws protecting employees? Federal, state and local anti-retaliation statutes are often an extremely important source of legal rights in a comprehensive campaign.

3. *Immigration raids as a form of retaliation.* Among the various forms of alleged employer retaliation against employees for engaging in union activity, none has generated more high-profile recent legal controversy than the use of employer-instigated workplace immigration raids to arrest undocumented workers. Under the Immigration Reform and Control Act of 1986 it is illegal for employers to *knowingly* hire undocumented immigrant workers. An unscrupulous employer can, however, turn a blind eye to the immigration status of workers until the workers assert their labor rights, at which point the employer can trigger a raid of its own worksite and the arrest of its employees, but assert that it did not know its workers were unauthorized. Employer sanctions for violation of IRCA are relatively rare, but worksite raids, which typically entail mass arrest of workers followed by criminal prosecution and/or rapid removal from the United States, are not. *See* Stephen Lee, *Monitoring Immigration Enforcement*, 53 Ariz. L. Rev. 1089 (2011); Stephen Lee, *Private Immigration Screening in the Workplace*, 61 Stan. L. Rev. 1103 (2009). How should the immigration law prohibitions on unauthorized work be reconciled with the labor law rights of all workers? How, if at all, should immigration authorities prevent the strategic use of immigration enforcement to quell worker organizing and facilitate exploitative working conditions?

Since the Trump Administration has made immigration a central policy focus, states and cities have responded by adopting "sanctuary" laws and policies limiting local law enforcement cooperation with ICE. Even in sanctuary jurisdictions, however, ICE exercises the power to raid workplaces.

4. *Applying the law to a campaign.* The UFCW is trying to organize the Smithfield slaughterhouse and pork processing plant in Tar Heel, North Carolina. Workplace injuries concern the workers most because wages at the plant are a few dollars an hour above the minimum, which is better than most of the jobs in the local area. But injuries are very common because the slaughtering and dismembering work involves dangerously large and sharp knives and the dis-assembly line runs extremely fast, which leads to repetitive motion injuries.

a. A UFCW organizer helps injured workers file workers' compensation claims and has encouraged them to contact the Occupational Safety and Health Administration to inspect the plant. The employee who calls OSHA is subsequently fired, ostensibly for tardiness. He files a charge under § 8(a)(1) and 8(a)(3). What arguments would you expect the company to make in the ULP proceeding?

b. A few days after the OSHA inspection, federal immigration enforcement agents come to the plant and round up several undocumented workers. The following week, a supervisor calls a meeting of all the day-shift workers, including the new hires who replaced the undocumented workers who were arrested in the immigration raid. The supervisor says: "If there is any trouble here, the company will insist on strict enforcement of immigration laws." Can a union supporter file a § 8(a)(1) charge?

* * *

Grassroots protest and litigation aimed at large and well-financed entities sometimes prompts the targets of the protest to file litigation in retaliation. If one assumes that the litigation has merit, or that the protest organization and the target both have roughly equal litigation resources, the use of litigation to respond to harassing workplace protests may seem uncontroversial. But workplace protesters often do not have the litigation resources of the large corporations they target, and the possibility of even frivolous litigation being filed against them may prompt them to refrain from legally protected protest for fear of incurring legal bills they cannot pay. To protect the grassroots David from the chilling effect of the threat of expensive litigation brought by the corporate or government Goliath, some states, including California, have enacted legislation designed to make it difficult to file litigation aiming to silence protest. These are known as anti-SLAPP statutes (SLAPP is an acronym for Strategic Litigation Against Public Protest). The contours of anti-SLAPP legislation vary among jurisdictions and are complex. It is sufficient at this point simply to know that they might be helpful in the context of a comprehensive campaign. There is no federal anti-SLAPP statute, which means that the availability of protection against retaliatory lawsuits is judged under the usual federal procedural rules for judging meritless litigation. The following excerpt summarizes the development and prospects of the federal labor law on this issue.

PROTECTIONS AGAINST RETALIATORY EMPLOYER LAWSUITS AFTER *BE & K CONSTRUCTION V. NLRB*

Paul More
25 Berkeley J. Emp. & Lab. L. 205 (2004)

Employers have responded to a resurgent labor movement by taking unions, their employees, and individual workers to court. In *BE&K Construction v. NLRB*, 536 U.S. 516 (2002), the Supreme Court addressed the authority of the National Labor Relations Board (NLRB) to adjudicate and sanction such retaliatory lawsuits. The suit underlying BE&K Construction involved a non-union contractor's claim that a regional building trades council and other local unions had violated federal labor and antitrust law by opposing the contractor's permits, lobbying for a toxic waste ordinance, and suing the contractors for environmental violations. Although the contractor's claims were dismissed on summary judgment, the litigation lasted for several years, imposing a significant burden on the unions involved. After the suit was completed, the unions brought a claim before the NLRB, alleging that the contractor's suit had been brought to interfere with workers' rights protected under the National Labor Relations Act (NLRA). The Board agreed and the case eventually proceeded to the Supreme Court.

The Court altered the standard applied by the Board and courts alike for twenty years in adjudicating employers' retaliatory lawsuits. Previously, under the standard set forth in *Bill Johnson's Restaurants v. NLRB*, 461 U.S. 731 (1983), the Board found employer lawsuits to be unfair labor practices where they were unsuccessful and were brought with an intent to interfere with rights protected under § 7 of the Act. *BE&K Construction* holds that the Board must find that the employer's lawsuit was brought for "subjectively non-genuine" reasons, rather than with an intent to interfere with rights protected under the NLRA, in order to sanction the suit. Although the Court did not define the precise scope of "subjectively non-genuine litigation," it held that the Board must now find that the employer intended to use the court process itself, as opposed to the outcome of the litigation, to interfere with § 7 rights.

The issue of the Board's ability to address employer lawsuits that attack workers and their unions for engaging in protected activity arises at an important time. Due to a confluence of factors, unions have broadened their organizing tactics beyond the traditional strike and picket line to incorporate a wider range of strategies, such as legislative lobbying and lawsuits, shareholder actions, and creative media work. The broadening of unions' organizing tactics, sometimes termed the shift to "comprehensive campaigns," has been a crucial component of some of organized labor's most successful and most visible campaigns during the last two decades. Employers have developed legal theories to respond to the effectiveness of comprehensive campaigns and the broadening of union organizing tactics generally. Employers have used state law torts, such as defamation and tortious interference with business relations, to attack unions' use of the media, leafleting and public demonstrations. More recently, employers have sued unions under federal antitrust law to attack unions' ability to form coalitions with community and environmental groups, and under the RICO Act against unions' appeals to regulatory agencies. While such lawsuits have not met with much success to date, they can delay and distract union campaigns and impose substantial costs on unions that are forced to defend against them. For employers whose main advantage over a union is financial leverage, imposing such costs can be a victory in itself, regardless of the fate of the legal claim. Although the *Bill Johnson's* unfair labor practice charge has deterred much meritless employer litigation, future employer challenges to comprehensive campaigns can be expected to take place in the courtroom.

NOTES

1.   *The Board's rule.* When *BE&K* was remanded, a 3–2 majority of the Board held that a reasonably based lawsuit—whether pending or completed—could not be found to be an unfair labor practice regardless of its motive. *BE&K Construction Co.*, 351 N.L.R.B. No. 29 (2007). The *BE&K* rule is a two-way street for unions, as it also protects their ability to file allegedly retaliatory litigation against employers. *See Village Construction*, 351 N.L.R.B. 606 (2007); *Petrochem Insulation v. NLRB*, 340 F.3d 26 (D.C. Cir. 2001).

2.   *RICO Suits.* One common form of retaliatory litigation are suits filed under the civil provisions of the Racketeer Influenced and Corrupt Organizations (RICO) Act, 18 U.S.C. § 1962, which prohibit extortion. Most conduct in comprehensive campaigns is legal—including lobbying local governments, issuing press releases, picketing and other forms of peaceful expressive protest, and filing charges with state and federal workplace safety and environmental protection agencies. The theory is that the comprehensive campaigns are extortion because their purpose is to coerce the employer into recognizing a union. *See, e.g., Smithfield Foods, Inc. v. United Food & Commercial Workers*, 593 F. Supp. 2d 840 (E.D. Va. 2008); Adam Liptak, A Corporate View of Mafia Tactics: Protesting, Lobbying, and Citing Upton Sinclair, N.Y. Times (Feb. 5, 2008). Unions have argued in response that the lobbying, protest and publicity is not conduct that RICO prohibits and is not "extortionate," which is what RICO requires. Unions also argue that, even if the conduct were covered by RICO, it is protected under the First Amendment. Much of the conduct in a comprehensive campaign is also protected by § 7 under *Eastex*. Should RICO be read as a limit on the scope of § 7 protections?

Although the district court denied the union's motion to dismiss the RICO suit in the *Smithfield* case and the case ultimately settled, other courts have held that RICO may not be used to challenge corporate campaigns because the labor activists' conduct is not a predicate act (such as extortion). *See, e.g., Cintas Corp. v. UNITE HERE*, 601 F. Supp. 2d 571 (S.D.N.Y.), *aff'd*, 355 F. App'x 508 (2d Cir. 2009); *Wackenhut Corp. v. SEIU*, 593 F. Supp. 2d 1289 (S.D.

Fla. 2009); *Cook-Illinois Corp. v. Teamsters Local No. 777*, 2012 WL 1655976 (N.D. Ill. 2012).

On the history and contemporary uses of RICO against labor unions, see James J. Brudney, *Collateral Conflict: Employer Claims of RICO Extortion Against Union Comprehensive Campaigns*, 83 S. Cal. L. Rev. 731 (2010).

3. *Defamation suits.* As mentioned in the excerpt above, employers sometimes bring defamation suits against the employees or their union, charging that the criticism of the company is defamation. Assuming the employer can prove the falsity of union statements, in some states the litigation turns on whether the false statements are directed at a "public figure," in which case the employer must prove actual malice—*i.e.*, that the statements were either knowingly false or were made with reckless disregard of the truth. (In some states, such as California, the target must prove actual malice regardless of whether he, she or it is a public figure.) How would you go about deciding whether a company or its top management is a public figure? The contours of defamation law and the First Amendment protection for labor speech are often quite important to the permissibility of some aspects of a comprehensive campaign.

4. *The strategic costs and benefits of litigation.* Apart from the merits of the legal theory, why might both unions and employers favor the use of litigation as a tactic in an ongoing struggle over organization or contract negotiation? Consider the benefits of publicity, the costs of litigation, and the burdens of pretrial discovery of facts.

b. NLRA Preemption and New Collective Activism

As noted above, much worker center and recent union activism has been focused on state and local law. This is, in a way, a return to an earlier period of labor history. Labor organizing and activism had generally been local in the nineteenth and early twentieth centuries. It focused on the workplace, the region, or an industry. From 1932 through the 1980s, labor efforts to gain legal reforms were often focused on Congress, and labor had many successes. The failure of Congress to enact any significant workplace reform since the early 1990s, and the Republican control of either the White House or the Congress for most of the four decades after 1980, prompted worker groups to shift focus for legal reform from Congress to state and local governments.

Preemption of state and local law has emerged as a huge issue in efforts to address labor standards at the local level. Efforts to avoid preemption by choosing legal strategies that are least likely to affect any federal regulatory scheme have become a crucial aspect of nearly every campaign, both those initiated by groups seeking improved labor standards and by those seeking to prevent the hiring of immigrants lacking proper work authorizations. *See* Benjamin I. Sachs, *Despite Preemption: Making Labor Law in Cities and States*, 124 Harv. L. Rev. 1153 (2011); Catherine L. Fisk, *The Anti-Subordination Principle of Labor and Employment Law*

Preemption, 5 Harv. L. & Policy Rev. 17 (2011). Many federal laws regulating working conditions, including federal wage and hour laws and anti-discrimination laws, do not broadly preempt state law. The NLRA, however, preempts state and local law that regulate union organizing and bargaining. Other federal law, notably the Employee Retirement Income Security Act, preempts state law even more broadly than does the NLRA. But preemption doctrine, as we will see in Chapter 10, is complex and results are hard to predict. A Los Angeles ordinance aimed at preventing erosion of labor standards in the grocery industry by requiring any employer over a certain size that acquires a grocery store to retain the labor force for three months was upheld against a preemption challenge. *California Grocers Ass'n v. City of Los Angeles*, 52 Cal. 4th 177 (2011). So, too, was an ordinance regulating big-box retail stores based on environmental issues. *Wal-Mart Stores, Inc. v. City of Turlock*, 138 Cal. App. 4th 273 (2006). In contrast, another Los Angeles law, which attempted to address pollution and poor labor standards at the huge and busy Port of Los Angeles by requiring trucking companies using the port (a City property) to employ truck drivers rather than use independent contractors and which regulated traffic to reduce emissions and noise, was held to be preempted by a federal statute regulating long-distance trucking. *American Trucking Ass'ns, Inc. v. City of Los Angeles*, 569 U.S. 641 (2013).

Results in cases involving local efforts to regulate or restrict immigrant labor have also varied. Arizona, Alabama and some other states and localities enacted harsh measures restricting the employment of unauthorized immigrant workers, as well as prohibiting them from entering into contracts and engaging in other aspects of daily life, including sending their children to school. Arizona S.B. 1070, Ariz. Laws 2010 Ch. 113, Ariz. Rev. Stat. § 11–1051; Acts of Alabama 2011–535, Ala. Code § 31–13–1. The U.S. Supreme Court held that federal immigration law preempts most provisions of the Arizona law, S.B. 1070. *Arizona v. United States*, 567 U.S. 387 (2012). Most provisions of the Alabama law were also held to be preempted. *United States v. Alabama*, 691 F.3d 1269 (11th Cir. 2012), *cert. denied*, 569 U.S. 968 (2013). However, the Court also has upheld against preemption challenges some state and local laws restricting the hiring of unauthorized immigrants. *Chamber of Commerce v. Whiting*, 563 U.S. 582 (2011).

In the long political struggle over working conditions, the balance of power between federal, state, and local governments has always been an issue. Whenever one side in the conflict succeeds in enacting legislation to protect its interests, the adversary may seek to invalidate the law as being beyond the power of the legislature to enact. Early in the twentieth century, employers tended to argue that state and local laws protecting workers were unconstitutional. After 1937, when the federal courts became reluctant to declare that state and local labor laws violated due process, other arguments came to the fore. The law of preemption became a dominant one. After the NLRA was enacted, unions began to worry that conservative state and local legislatures would undermine its protections by prohibiting picketing and other conduct that the NLRA protected, so they filed suits challenging state and local laws as being preempted by the NLRA. As is explained more fully in Chapter 10, early labor preemption cases broadly preempted state law based on the assumption that federal labor law reflected the most carefully considered policy, and labor unions were generally content with the results.

By the late twentieth century, the tables began to turn. Many labor supporters felt that Congress, the NLRB, and the federal courts were out of step with the needs of workers, had not kept labor law up to date, and were significantly less friendly to the cause of labor than some state and local legislatures and judges. As a result, whereas in the 1950s and 1960s preemption was usually an argument favored by unions, preemption is now an argument much more likely to be made by employers seeking to invalidate legislation favorable to worker interests.

As you will see when you read Chapter 10, most significant recent NLRA preemption cases involve employer efforts to invalidate state and local laws enacted during organizing or negotiating battles. One example is *Golden State Transit Corp. v. City of Los Angeles*, 475 U.S. 608 (1986), which arose from the refusal of the City of Los Angeles to renew a taxicab franchise until a labor dispute was settled. The Teamsters, which represented the drivers, opposed any extension of the Yellow Cab franchise, stating that such action would simply lengthen the strike and keep the drivers out of work. The Court held, under *Machinists v. Wisconsin Employment Relations Comm'n*, 427 U.S. 132 (1976), that the City was prohibited from using the license renewal to "impos[e] additional restrictions on economic weapons of self-help, such as strikes or lockouts. . . ." Of course, political leverage can be used in the public sector free of any federal preemption concerns, because the NLRA does not apply to public sector employment.

Another example of the significance of preemption arose from a prolonged organizing campaign among taxi and app-based for-hire car drivers in Seattle. The city enacted an ordinance providing for collective bargaining on behalf of drivers who are independent contractors. Taxi companies, along with Uber, Lyft, and other app-based services, have strenuously argued that their drivers are independent contractors, not employees, and therefore ineligible for a host of legal protections, including the right to organize under the NLRA. Taking the companies at their word, Seattle created a legal framework for collective bargaining. When it appeared that a majority of drivers would vote to bargain collectively, the Chamber of Commerce and the National Right to Work committee filed suit to enjoin enforcement of the Seattle independent contractor collective bargaining ordinance. Among their legal arguments is that the NLRA preempts state laws allowing bargaining by any worker who might arguably be an employee under the NLRA. As of this writing, that argument was rejected by the Ninth Circuit. *See Chamber of Commerce v. City of Seattle*, 890 F.3d 769 (9th Cir. 2018). Other arguments included that collective bargaining by independent contractors violates both the antitrust laws and the NLRA. Those arguments have not been resolved as of this writing. The Seattle ordinance litigation is discussed in Chapters 9 and 10 below.

NOTE

1. *Is preemption always bad for alternative forms of organizing?* UNITE-HERE sent a postcard to 11,000 patients and prospective patients of a Northern California hospital chain's maternity ward. The postcard warned: "You might be bringing home more than your baby" from the hospital because the hospital's laundry contractor's poor health and safety record and bad working conditions fail to ensure that " 'clean' linens are free of blood, feces and harmful pathogens." The hospital sued for defamation. UNITE-HERE defended on the grounds that mailing the postcards was protected concerted activity and, in addition, that the statements were true, citing reports of OSHA violations and health department inspections of the laundry contractor. The judge rejected the preemption argument and sent the case to the jury, which awarded $17 million, about $1500 per postcard. On appeal, the court held that a communication that is made as part of a labor dispute is not defamatory unless the target proves actual malice, regardless of whether the target is a public figure. *Sutter Health v. UNITE-HERE*, 186 Cal. App. 4th 1193 (2010). (The litigation later settled and the union apologized for the postcard.) As a matter of policy, should the NLRA preempt this application of the state law of defamation? Why or why not?

c. NLRA (and Other) Restrictions on Worker Centers and New Forms of Activism

Recall from Chapter 4 the definition of a labor organization under section 2(5). A "labor organization" is defined broadly to include any organization "in which employees participate and which exists for the purpose, in whole or in part, of dealing with employers concerning grievances, labor disputes, wages, rates of pay, hours of employment, or conditions of work." Recall from Chapter 6 that only labor organizations are subject to the prohibitions of section 8(b), including limits on secondary activity imposed by section 8(b)(4). And, as we will see later in this chapter, only labor organizations are required to file elaborate disclosure documents and adhere to the other requirements of the Taft-Hartley Act and the Labor-Management Reporting and Disclosure Act. There are good reasons, therefore, for worker centers to resist being deemed "labor organizations" under the NLRA.

The NLRB's General Counsel has issued two advice memoranda on worker centers. (An advice memo is a device by which the agency makes policy.) The advice memos reach opposite conclusions as to whether two different worker groups were unions subject to the NLRA (and, presumably, the LMRDA). In one, the General Counsel determined that Restaurant Opportunities Center New York was not a labor organization because it did not "deal with" restaurants on behalf of workers, but instead confined itself to employment law advocacy. *See* Restaurant Opportunities Center of New York, Advice Memorandum No. 2-CP-1067 (Nov. 30, 2006). In another, the General Counsel determined that OUR Wal-Mart, which was affiliated with a union but was not itself a union, was part of a labor organization, even though it did not deal with an employer on behalf of workers. *See* Advice Memorandum (April 10, 2013), available at www.nlrb.gov. A sustained analysis of whether worker centers should be deemed to be labor organizations under the NLRA and LMRDA is Thomas I.M. Gottheil, *Note, Part of the Bargain: Worker Centers and Labor Law in Sociohistorical Context*, 89 N.Y.U. L. Rev. 2228 (2014); *see also* Kim Bobo & Marien Casillas Pabellon, The Worker Center Handbook: A Practical Guide for Starting and Building the New Labor Movement (2016); Eli Naduris-Weissman, *The Worker Center Movement and Traditional Labor Law: A Contextual Analysis*, 30 Berkeley J. Emp. & Lab. L. 232 (2009); David Rosenfeld, *Worker Centers: Emerging Labor Organizations—Until They Confront the National Labor Relations Act*, 27 Berkeley J. Emp. & Lab. L. 469 (2006).

However, labor organizations do enjoy one significant advantage over other groups under federal labor law. Labor organizations are exempt from antitrust scrutiny so long as their concerted activity is within traditional bounds. Occasionally, employers may counter creative coalitions between labor and other community groups under federal antitrust law. Paul Salvatore & Brian Rauch, Taking A Page From The Unions' Playbook: Employers Litigating Against Union Corporate Campaigns, 15.4 Metropolitan Corporate Counsel 49 (2007). Although labor groups are generally exempt from antitrust regulations, they may lose their exemptions by exceeding the scope of unions' traditional roles and activities, most notably by colluding with non-labor organizations or engaging in secondary boycotts not subject to NLRA protection during corporate campaigns. Under federal antitrust law, courts may subject a union that conspires with religious or community organizations to the same scrutiny as a union that conspires with other non-labor groups.

The contours of the labor exemption from federal antitrust scrutiny is covered in Chapter 9.

C. UNIONS AND INTERNATIONAL LAW

Globalization has transformed American labor markets, consumer behavior, and immigration patterns and has also shaped the agenda and the practices of labor unions throughout the world. Unions have forged international ties at least since the late nineteenth century as wars, colonialism, and migrations of people fleeing repressive governments and economic collapse brought workers from many parts of the world together. United States labor unions had significant international ties early in the last century; they focused heavily on the domestic agenda for much of the century, but returned to a more international focus at the end of the twentieth century as it became painfully obvious that improved communications and transportation enabled significant mobility of capital to low-wage labor markets in China and the global South, threatening the standard of living that U.S., Canadian, and European unions had fought so hard to secure. As corporations became global, unions and worker groups too were forced to become global in their organizing and in their efforts to protect workers. *See* Harry Arthurs, *Global Corporations and Global Unions, Reinventing Labor Law for the Global Economy: The Benjamin Aaron Lecture*, 22 Berkeley J. Emp. & Lab. L. 271 (2001); Peter Fairbrother & Nikolaus Hammer, Global Unions: Past Efforts and Future Prospects, 60 Relations Industrielles (July 2005), available at 2005 WLNR 19080665.

The forms of international cooperation and activism concerning labor standards are many and varied. Companies with international operations or that produce goods through international supply chains work with a variety of business groups and NGOs to manage and monitor working conditions in their operations or in those of their contracting partners in the supply chain. When factories in Bangladesh producing garments for sale in U.S. and European stores collapsed and burned, killing thousands of workers, American and European NGOs joined efforts to hold the American and European brands and retailers accountable for the dangerous working conditions. *See* Worker Rights Consortium, www. workersrights.org. When American workers at a Japanese-owned hotel in Los Angeles were locked in struggle over their efforts to unionize, the union called for an international boycott of the hotel by its international clientele, picketed the Los Angeles location, and also picketed the offices of the company in Tokyo. John Sweeney, the head of the AFL-CIO at the time, even joined the picket line in Tokyo. (This is the story of the *New Otani Hotel* case in Chapter 4.) *See also* Fran Ansley, *Inclusive Boundaries and Other (Im)Possible Paths Toward Community Development in a Global World*, 150 U. Pa. L. Rev. 353 (2001) (Tennessee garment workers went to visit a Mexican maquiladora and meet the workers who performed the work they once had done).

Consider a single example of the many possible sources of regulation and fora relevant to a claim of forced labor and unsafe conditions and suppression of union organizing in a Korean-owned sportswear garment factory in Mexico producing goods for sale under U.S. labels in U.S. and European retail stores:

- The U.S. Office of Trade Agreement Implementation or the Canadian Office of Inter-American Labour Cooperation under the North American Free Trade Agreement (NAFTA). NAFTA is a trade treaty between Canada, the U.S., and Mexico. As part of NAFTA, the three countries pledged to adhere to certain dispute resolution measures for claims that poor labor standards give one country an unfair advantage in trade.

- The International Labor Organization's (ILO) Committee on Freedom of Association under ILO Conventions 87 and 88. The ILO was created at the end of World War I to address global labor practices.

- The Organization for Economic Cooperation and Development (OECD) under its Guidelines on Multinational Enterprises. The OECD, whose predecessor organization was created in 1948 as part of the Marshall Plan, is an organization of 37 member countries (mainly wealthy countries) to promote trade and economic development.

- The World Bank under a labor standards clause in its International Finance Corporation's private sector loans program. The World Bank is an international financial institution that provides loans to developing countries to promote economic development and fight poverty.

- The social compliance office of each multinational corporation under whose brand the garments are labeled or sold.

- The annual meetings of each of those corporations under shareholder resolutions submitted by socially responsible investors.

- The Fair Labor Association, the Worker Rights Consortium, or other NGOs who maintain "stakeholder" coalition codes of conduct.

- The Inter-American Court of Human Rights or the Inter-American Commission on Human Rights. These institutions were formed (in 1979 and 1959, respectively) under the 1948 American Declaration of the Rights and Duties of Man and a 1959 American Convention on Human Rights, which are international charters to protect human rights in the Americas.

- United States federal or state courts under claims that the American corporations violated human rights (especially if the victims are U.S. nationals) under the Alien Tort Statute or under common law tort claims.

- Media campaigns publicizing the working conditions and seeking boycotts, including by efforts to ban sales of the goods at retail establishments that may be especially sensitive to human rights issues, such as college and university bookstores.[1]

This section examines three of the principal legal regimes addressing labor standards on a global basis. The first are the formal international treaties articulating labor rights and human rights and the agencies that are tasked to implement them. The second are treaties regulating international trade; some couple trade preferences with respect for basic labor rights. The third subsection examines other legal strategies used recently, including litigation in U.S. courts under the federal Alien Tort Statute and anti-trafficking statutes, and the use of codes of conduct and other private law and voluntary measures.

1. INTERNATIONAL AGENCIES AND LABOR STANDARDS

The international law that was established in the aftermath of the world wars of the twentieth century declared workers' rights are human rights. The principal international entity that regulates labor rights is the International Labor Organization (ILO), created by the Treaty of Versailles at the end of World War I. The ILO survived the disintegration of the League of Nations (the entity established by the Treaty of Versailles to articulate and enforce international law, which itself did not survive the unwillingness of the United States to join the League). The ILO became a specialized agency of the United Nations after World War II. The ILO is the only major international body in which civil society groups (union and employer representatives) are part of the governing apparatus. It has promulgated a number of conventions for implementation by its 187 member states. ILO conventions and recommendations do not have the force of law; these conventions bind a member country only when the country has ratified them, creating an obligation to enact domestic legislation to implement them.

A number of international treaties protect labor rights as human rights, including the Universal Declaration of Human Rights (1948), the International Covenant on Civil and Political Rights (1966), and the International Covenant on Economic, Social and Cultural Rights (1966). Labor provisions in treaties, like the ILO conventions and

---

[1] This case study is drawn from James Atleson, *et al.,* International Labor Law: Cases and Materials on Workers' Rights in the Global Economy 12–13 (2008).

recommendations, operate largely at the level of rhetoric and moral suasion rather than as coercive law. Countries, including the United States, that are signatories to the various human rights treaties and members of the ILO are frequently accused of violating the provisions stated therein.

The norms articulated in the various human rights treaties and by the ILO range from the very general (freedom of association), to the very abstract (declarations of a right to decent work and freedom from poverty), to the technical and—in some places—controversial (such as the ILO Hours of Work Convention, adopted in the early years of the ILO's existence, which mandated eight-hour workdays and restricted night work for women and young people).

"Core" labor standards are defined in the ILO Declaration of Fundamental Principles and Rights of Work as: (1) freedom of association and effective recognition of the right to bargain collectively; (2) elimination of all forms of forced labor; (3) effective abolition of child labor; and (4) elimination of discrimination in employment and occupation.[2] These "core" labor rights have been designated by the ILO as the four fundamental rights that all members of the ILO are obligated "to respect, promote and realize in good faith," regardless of whether the member has ratified relevant ILO conventions.

Core labor rights focus on freedom, not on low wages. The ILO and other treaties do not challenge the differential in wages due to the availability of cheap labor which gives low wage countries a comparative advantage in international trade. Although some assert that observance of core labor rights does not significantly increase labor costs, except of course to prohibit extreme abuses such as slavery or child labor, others disagree. Some believe that if countries actually respected freedom of association, labor costs might go up because workers could effectively demand adherence to minimum legal standards and could bargain collectively for better wages. Many important and widely recognized labor rights are not "core" labor rights, including the right to a safe and healthful workplace, limits on the hours of work, and protection against abuse.

The ILO has no enforcement powers. It can investigate and make findings and recommendations, but it cannot impose sanctions. However, in at least one instance, when a government (Burma) defied the ILO's repeated efforts to end the practice of forced labor in 2006, the ILO Governing Body took the hitherto unprecedented step of referring the matter to the International Court of Justice, which does have enforcement

---

[2]   The 1998 ILO Declaration of Fundamental Principles and Rights at Work commits ILO member states to respect and promote principles and rights in these four categories, regardless of whether they have ratified the relevant Conventions. It reflects a new approach to the challenge of articulating fundamental labor rights in a world in which different levels of economic development and different political cultures makes it difficult to get binding commitments to respect labor rights. *See* http://www.ilo.org/declaration/lang--en/index.htm.

powers. *See* James Atleson, *et al.*, International Labor Law: Cases and Materials on Workers' Rights in the Global Economy 101 (2008).

Although the ILO has no enforcement powers of its own, its norms appear to be influencing domestic labor law. One study found that ILO norms on child labor law and freedom of association appears to have prompted changes in executive, legislative, and court-made law, along with soft-law mechanisms in response to trade agreements, in twenty countries in the Americas between 1990 and 2017. James J. Brudney, *The Internationalization of Sources of Labor Law*, 39 U. Pa. J. Int'l L. 1 (2017).

2. PROTECTING WORKERS' RIGHTS THROUGH INTERNATIONAL TRADE AGREEMENTS

The absence of meaningful enforcement of ILO and treaty provisions has prompted human rights and labor activists to search for mechanisms under international law that have real leverage in forcing countries to enact and enforce domestic laws regulating working conditions. In the late 1980s and early 1990s, activists identified international trade laws as a promising strategy. There are a number of multi-lateral trade treaties and agreements, and they are periodically discussed by representatives of many countries in what are known as "rounds of negotiations." The purpose of the negotiations is to find agreement about whether countries will impose tariffs on imports in order to protect their domestic industries or instead will reduce tariffs and other restrictions on imported goods, services, and industry (what is known as "free trade"). In the 1994 Uruguay Round, the United States proposed a study committee on the relation of free trade to basic labor rights, but the developing countries opposed it, arguing that the ILO, rather than trade, is the place to deal with labor rights. A global organization that emerged to manage trade negotiations is the World Trade Organization (WTO), and it was widely perceived as favoring reduced barriers to trade. In the 1990s, people concerned about what they considered the deleterious effects of global trade on environmental and working conditions both in the industrial and post-industrial global North and in the industrializing global South began to focus their concern on the WTO and its support for reduced restrictions on trade.

A highly-publicized and acrimonious debate followed. On the one hand, developing countries asserted that protection of workers' rights would provide a guise for developed countries to deprive developing countries of their competitive advantage of low labor costs. This, they contended, would stifle developing countries' ability to develop industries and raise living standards. In particular, they feared that the economically powerful countries, particularly the United States and the European Union, would, under political pressure from industry and unions, find ways to use labor rights to engage in protectionism. They also feared that investors would move capital from countries that adhered to minimum labor standards to those that did not, which made developing countries reluctant to enter bilateral agreements on labor rights. Developing countries also protested that enforcing core labor rights would invade their sovereignty. Conditioning free trade on recognition of labor rights means, in effect, that an importing country may inquire into and indirectly regulate labor conditions in an exporting country. Exporting employers would be required to observe standards set by a foreign country. And investors from developed countries encouraged developing countries in their opposition to agreements enforcing minimum labor standards, seeing it a threat to their profits.

On the other side, developed countries insisted on tying free trade to core labor rights for economic and non-economic reasons of their own. Labor unions raised general and legitimate concerns for the welfare of workers worldwide, seeing it as a moral issue, requiring a response beyond the bounds of economic self-interest.

The debate over free trade and labor has surface repeatedly in the United States, most recently early in the Trump Administration as leaders debated whether President Trump should abandon the trade treaty President Obama had negotiated with Asia, the Trans Pacific Partnership. The issue surfaced again in spring 2018 when President Trump imposed tariffs on certain imports in the name of protecting U.S. jobs in steel and manufacturing, and then other trading partners promptly announced tariffs on U.S. products they import, including bourbon and motorcycles.

The debate over trade and labor was explained succinctly by the late Professor Clyde Summers:

> The first core labor right—and the one considered the most fundamental—is the right to associate freely, to organize and bargain collectively. U.S. unions may hope that the organization of unions in developing countries will give workers more bargaining power and enable them to push up wages, thereby reducing their comparative advantage. They may also hope that unions in other countries will support them in disputes with U.S. employers.

> For the same reason, the developing countries may resist enforcement of the rights of freedom of association and collective bargaining. They may see unionization and collective bargaining as potentially reducing their competitive advantage in international trade. The calculations of both would seem questionable, for the unions in most developing countries are now, and will be for the foreseeable future, too economically weak to compel large wage increases. Moreover, they are not likely to bargain away all of their competitive advantage, making exports

unprofitable and destroying their jobs, even if they become strong enough to do so.

Some developing countries may have a greater and more realistic fear of enforcing this core labor right for political reasons. Unions provide a major base for popular organization, and they regularly focus on political concerns as well as economic concerns. In developing countries, their political function may be more important than their economic function. They will, therefore, constitute a challenge to entrenched power of political leaders and insist on increased recognition of democratic rights.

[However, one] of the most energizing motives in [the U.S.] for such vocal opposition to free trade [is] U.S. workers' fear that competing goods imported from low wage countries will rob the U.S. workforce of countless jobs. The free movement of capital, made more free and protected by the WTO, has aggravated those fears as U.S. employers have closed plants, moved production to countries with low labor costs, and shipped the products back to this country to compete with products made here.

This perspective requires us to examine more carefully the underlying premise of comparative advantage, which is accepted almost universally by economists, and is not directly challenged by those who would impose restrictions on free trade. I am not prepared to question here the general theory that if each country can produce the goods in which it has a comparative advantage and freely exchange them for goods in which another country has a comparative advantage, the overall economic welfare of both counties will benefit. The theory of comparative advantage, however, gives us limited guidance on the question of whether free trade should be tied to certain labor rights, because it focuses only on economic efficiency and excludes consideration of societal values.

First, the theory omits consideration of the distribution of economic gains. Each country may have a net economic gain, but there are inevitably winners and losers in each country. Goods imported into the United States, particularly those from developing countries, are predominantly labor intensive goods that can be produced by lower skilled and unskilled workers: shoes, textiles, clothing, toys, and assembly of cars, household appliances and electronics. As a result, the losers in the United States at the present time are primarily workers in manufacturing industries, particularly those with fewer skills. The winners are those hired in the new jobs created by increased exports, which are predominantly in capital-intensive industries.

They are predominantly the highly trained workers who are higher paid and in short supply in the present job market.

There are also winners and losers in the developing countries. Those who obtain jobs in the export industries are the winners; although their wages are low, they often earn more than they would elsewhere. Those who do not obtain jobs are not so much losers as left behind. The losers in many developing countries are those who go to the cities with the expectation of jobs, only to find unemployment, hunger, and squalid living conditions and are often worse off than they were before. As in the United States, the effect is to increase the inequality in society. Studies have shown that in most developing countries, inequality between the bottom forty percent and the top sixty percent has significantly increased with free trade. That inequality must be counted as a social cost of free trade.

Does the availability of slave labor entitle a country to claim that its comparative advantage gained by such labor should not be denied by restrictions on free trade in the products of slave labor? The same problem is posed by other labor conditions that may affect the costs of production—dangerous and unhealthy work, long hours of work, lack of rest periods. [E]conomists do not tell us what should or should not count as a comparative advantage when dealing with the labor factor of production.

Clyde Summers, *The Battle in Seattle: Free Trade, Labor Rights, and Societal Values*, 22 U. Pa. J. Int'l Econ. L. 61 (2001).

Regional trade agreements. Although efforts to incorporate workers' rights into the global WTO trade agreements failed, the United States has negotiated labor rights provisions into bilateral and regional trade agreements, including NAFTA, CAFTA-DR (the Central American Free Trade Agreement), and agreements with many other countries (including, at various points, Colombia, Singapore, Jordan, Chile, Bahrain, Australia, Oman, Panama, Peru, and South Korea). The enforcement is weak, however. Nevertheless, Jeffrey Vogt has found that trade and labor linkages in U.S. and E.U. trade treaties have had a positive effect on commitments to labor rights but "fall well short of ensuring compliance with ILO fundamental labor rights in law or in practice. At best, and particularly in the U.S., the leverage created by the negotiation of trade agreements has been used to compel partners to introduce important reforms to labor laws and regulations before the ratification of these agreements." He also reports that "complaints filed under the labor chapters of trade agreements post-ratification, almost entirely under U.S. agreements, have achieved limited results to date." Jeffrey S. Vogt, *The Evolution of Labor Rights and Trade—A Transatlantic Comparison and*

Lessons for the Transatlantic Trade and Investment Partnership, 18 J. Int'l Econ. L. 827 (2016).

Another scholar argued that those seeking to improve compliance with labor standards internationally should focus on systems that are bilateral and regional, that pursue development objectives, and "that experiment with using non-state, private regulatory regimes that harness the power of non-state actors to effectively regulate labor along global supply chains." Kevin Kolben, *The WTO Distraction*, 21 Stan. L. & Pol'y Rev. 461 (2010). On the analysis of Vogt and Kolben, thus, it appears that trade agreements can be useful leverage for labor activists to push for improved labor standards but that the labor provisions in such agreements by themselves seem not to have dramatically improved labor standards.

Opponents of linking trade agreements to labor rights argue that trade sanctions are inefficient, reduce total wealth, and do not help their intended beneficiaries. Indian trade unions opposed efforts to include labor rights provisions in the WTO on these grounds, and also argued that labor rights in trade treaties recapitulate India's colonial history by depriving India of the ability to govern itself.

3. CROSS-BORDER COALITIONS AND OTHER HUMAN RIGHTS STRATEGIES

Protecting workers in a global economy is challenging because of the workers' precarious immigration status (as in the case of undocumented workers in the U.S. or migrant workers anywhere). It is also challenging because companies either ignore labor legislation or threaten to eliminate jobs and move production if workers insist on compliance. Two of the most prominent strategies to address these difficulties are litigation in United States courts and development of fair trade agreements.

a. Alien Tort Statute

The Alien Tort Statute ("ATS" or "ATCA," the Alien Tort Claims Act), 28 U.S.C. § 1350, provides, in full: "The district courts shall have original jurisdiction of any civil action by an alien for a tort only, committed in violation of the law of nations or a treaty of the United States." The ATS was enacted by the first Congress in 1789, but twentieth century globalization revived interest in it. The ATS held out great promise as a way to force multinational corporations to respect human rights, including labor rights, in their global operations. Human rights lawyers brought a number of such suits in U.S. courts. One especially significant and potentially pathbreaking suit challenged forced and exploitative labor by UNOCAL in the construction of an oil pipeline in Burma. Although the suit settled before a court issued a major substantive ruling, *see Doe v. UNOCAL*, 963 F. Supp. 880 (C.D. Cal. 1997), *aff'd in part and reversed in part*, 395 F.3d 932 (9th Cir. 2002), *dismissed following hearing en banc*,

403 F.3d 708 (9th Cir. 2005), the settlement created important institutions to protect workers' rights in Burma. Another suit challenged forced labor and other exploitative conditions at a rubber plantation operated by Bridgestone-Firestone in Liberia. *See Roe v. Bridgestone Corp.*, 492 F. Supp. 2d 988 (S.D. Ind. 2007). Courts dismissed some claims and other cases settled.

But as the human rights promise of the ATS became apparent, multinational corporations fought (and, to a substantial extent, won) a litigation campaign to limit its scope and power. Two of the major issues about ATS were what standards should be used to determine what kind of conduct is a "violation of the law of nations" and where and whom can be sued. As to the first, the ATS says nothing. Today it may seem odd to enact a statute providing for suit without clearly stating what standards of conduct the law requires. In 1789, it was not regarded as problematic for Congress to enact a jurisdictional statute without simultaneously enacting a body of substantive law for courts to apply under it, for Congress imagined courts looking to the common law, or in this case, to the law of nations, for legal principles to decide cases. Indeed, as we saw in Chapter 7, this was the approach followed by Congress in 1947 when it enacted section 301 of the Taft-Hartley Act, which does nothing other than provide jurisdiction to sue for enforcement of collective bargaining agreements without providing a substantive law to apply. Whatever may have been the consensus about the content of the law of nations in 1789, today there is substantial controversy about the content of the law of nations generally, and, most pertinent to labor cases, which kinds of labor exploitation or human rights abuses of workers, and by whom, constitute violations of the law of nations.

For a time, the Supreme Court decided the ATS authorized suits in U.S. courts for violations of the law of nations when the claim rested on "a norm of international character accepted by the civilized world and defined with a specificity comparable to the features of the eighteenth-century paradigm" as articulated in Blackstone's famous *Commentaries,* a British treatise on the common law that was first published in the United States in 1803. *Sosa v. Alvarez-Machain*, 542 U.S. 692, 725 (2004). The Court in *Sosa* noted that Blackstone mentioned actions for injuries to ambassadors, for piracy, and for violation of the right of safe passage. Some scholars argued that the ATS should be limited to those sorts of claims, *see* Thomas H. Lee, *The Safe Conduct Theory of the Alien Tort Statute*, 106 Colum. L. Rev. 830 (2006), but others argued that both the language and the original meaning of the ATS, along with sound policy and the Supreme Court's decision in *Sosa*, suggest that any violation of the law of nations is actionable under the ATS so long as it is specific and a "norm of international character accepted by the civilized world." An account of the history of the Alien Tort Statute in the twentieth century can be found in Jeffrey Davis, Justice Across Borders (2008).

As the composition of the Supreme Court changed, the meaning of the ATS changed too. In particular, the Court decided two cases dramatically reducing the power of the ATS to protect international human rights. *Jesner v. Arab Bank*, 138 S. Ct. 1386 (2018); *Kiobel v. Royal Dutch Petroleum*, 569 U.S. 108 (2013).

In *Jesner*, the Supreme Court held that non-U.S. corporations cannot be sued under the ATS. In *Kiobel*, the Supreme Court sharply limited the use of the ATS in any case in which the foreign defendants committed conduct outside the territory of the United States that did not affect United States nationals.

Although the Supreme Court limited the reach of the ATS by limiting who could be sued and over what conduct, substantive questions remain about the scope of the ATS in labor cases in which United States companies commit harms against U.S. nationals or within U.S. territory. One such question is which abuses of workers constitute violations of the law of nations. For example, while slavery is universally condemned, is the systematic failure to pay wages and the use of force to keep workers from leaving their jobs tantamount to slavery? One court found a violation. *See Iwanowa v. Ford Motor Co.*, 67 F. Supp. 2d 424, 433–34 (D.N.J. 1999) (plaintiff was abducted by Nazi troops in Russia and sent to work in a plant in Germany). Another court rejected a claim alleging systematic failure to pay wages and other forms of exploitation because "[s]uch a rule would support a federal claim for relief whenever any employee was denied pay or otherwise subject to economic coercion while living under difficult economic circumstances." *Doe v. Wal-Mart Stores, Inc.*, 2007 WL 5975664 (C.D. Cal. 2007), *dismissed*, 572 F.3d 677 (9th Cir. 2009).

b. Worker Driven Social Responsibility Campaigns in the International Context

Worker-driven social responsibility campaigns use public pressure to force companies to agree to a code of conduct and monitoring of the labor conditions in their and their contractors' overseas operations. These so-called "soft-law" mechanisms harness worker organizing and consumer outrage over human rights abuses in the foreign manufacture of products sold in the U.S. *See, e.g.*, First Tier Garment Exporters in Delhi: Industry and Company Perspectives, A Collaboration Between United Students Against Sweatshops, Jobs with Justice, Society for Labour and Development (March 2007). Experience has shown that such codes of conduct protect workers only when workers are involved in their design, monitoring, and enforcement.

Another system, one that has not been implemented because statutory changes to U.S. immigration law have not passed Congress, would harness immigration law to protect workers in the global labor supply chain. Professor Jennifer Gordon has proposed a system of "transnational labor citizenship" that would require migrant workers coming to the United States to join a cross-border worker organization in lieu of the current requirement of having a job offer from an employer. Jennifer Gordon, *Transnational Labor Citizenship*, 80 S. Cal. L. Rev. 503 (2007). Her proposal would facilitate the enforcement of labor rights and allow migrants to carry benefits and services with them as they move. She says:

> In practical terms, transnational labor citizenship would permit its holder to work for any employer in the United States with full labor rights and eventual conversion to permanent residence if the migrant so desired.

> [E]ach migrant would be asked to take a "solidarity oath" as a condition of membership, promising to take no job that violated basic workplace laws or that paid less than the minimum set by the transnational labor organizations, to report employer violators to their transnational labor organizations once discovered, and to uphold union solidarity with other workers (for example, refusing to cross picket lines). Failure to adhere to these requirements would be grounds for removal from membership in the transnational labor organizations and withdrawal of the visa.

> When the migrants arrived in the United States, the U.S. transnational labor organizations in their area would hold welcome meetings, orienting them to the region, laying out the options for membership, and inviting the migrants to know-your-rights classes, English classes, and social, cultural, and organizing activities. In the best-organized sectors, the transnational labor organizations would be administering collective bargaining agreements that covered transnational labor citizens together with other workers. In those areas, transnational labor organization staff would also provide copies of the contract and explain its benefits and grievance process to the new arrivals.

> As migrants returned home, the Mexican transnational labor organizations would staff ongoing organizing and leadership development efforts and provide critical links between and support for ongoing organizing campaigns and lawsuits related to the migrants' work in the United States. Transnational labor citizens would be able to draw on the transnational labor organizations' legal resources (either from within the United States or from the sending country) to pursue claims against employers in the United States for violations of workplace law, from being paid less than minimum wage, to denials of workers compensation for on-the-job injury, to sexual harassment. They would also have access to a variety of other services, from

notarization, to English classes, to health care accessible in both countries.

U.S. and Mexican transnational labor organizations would be linked through a network that enabled them to collaborate to defend the rights of their members through a combination of government enforcement, lawsuits, and collective pressure.

NOTES

1.   *Mixing immigration law and labor law.* What are the advantages and disadvantages of Professor Gordon's proposals? On the whole, would they benefit American and migrant workers in the U.S.? What about firms? Would providing information about labor standards and worker organizations help, even if the system has no mechanism to force employers to adhere to minimum labor standards or workers to adhere to the promises made at the time of immigration?

2.   *Global production and the migration of American workers to foreign destinations.* In some cases, when jobs left the United States, American workers have followed the jobs. Some unions fear that the migration of American workers following runaway jobs contributes to the undermining of labor standards in the U.S. Film production is an example. As major motion picture companies moved film production to Canada where labor costs are lower because the collective bargaining agreements do not apply, Hollywood unions found their members working in Canada for less than they would have been paid if the film had been made in the U.S. Hollywood unions are stymied in their efforts to prevent production companies from shifting the jobs overseas because the NLRA does not apply outside the U.S. and the production is done by the non-U.S. subsidiaries of the multinational companies that own Hollywood production companies. The union representing actors applied to its members working in Canada the longstanding union rule prohibiting work for employers who have not signed a collective bargaining agreement with the union. Violation of the rule prohibiting nonunion work can be punished by reprimand, fine, suspension or even expulsion from the union. As a matter of tactics, should Hollywood unions discipline their members for working on nonunion jobs outside the U.S.? As a matter of law, does the enforcement of the rule violate § 8(b)(1)(A), which makes it an unfair labor practice for a union "to restrain or coerce employees in the exercise of rights guaranteed" by § 7? (You may wish to return to this issue after reading Section D.4 below, which covers the law restricting the power of unions to implement rules disciplining members for doing work that is contrary to interests of union members.) *See* Gail Frommer, *Hooray for . . . Toronto? Hollywood, Collective Bargaining, and Extraterritorial Union Rules in an Era of Globalization,* 6 U. Pa. J. Lab. & Emp. L. 55 (2003).

D. REGULATION OF UNION POLITICAL ACTIVITY, UNION SECURITY, AND UNION FINANCES

1. A CAMPAIGN FINANCE PRIMER: POLITICAL ACTIVITY, EXPENDITURES, AND FUNDRAISING BY UNIONS AND OTHER GROUPS

One of the most vibrant and significant contemporary forms of labor activism is in the realm of political activity. Whether organizing protests, lobbying state and local legislatures, urging agencies to enforce laws, or preparing reports on working conditions, unions use political activity to achieve workplace gains.

Unions play many important roles in politics, as do organizations on a variety of other issues, including the Chamber of Commerce, the National Association of Manufacturers, bar associations, environmental associations, and special interest associations on every topic ranging from guns to religion. They act as lobbyists. They provide financial support to candidates and on legislation or ballot initiatives. They do extensive advertising on political candidates and issues. They are conduits of information to voters. And they get out the vote.

Union political activity is regulated as is the political activity of corporations, associations, and individuals. But unions face restrictions that other political actors do not. A lawyer who represents labor unions or who works in the legislative field in which labor unions are active needs to know not only the labor law regulation of unions' political activity discussed below, but also the basics of election law. While a full treatment of election law is beyond the scope of this book, a brief examination of the subject illustrates the range of issues that labor lawyers should consider.

Those concerned about the influence of money on politics tend to be particularly concerned about the power of large organizations—corporations, special interest groups, and unions—to concentrate their impact by collecting and expending large sums on politics. Since 1947, federal law has prohibited unions from making contributions directly to parties or candidates in elections, but has permitted them to contribute to Political Action Committees (PACs). (Corporations never had such a restriction.) A series of federal and state laws attempted to restrict donations and expenditures of money in politics, particularly focusing on large donations that are thought to dwarf the efforts of individuals and on large expenditures that are thought to give disproportionate power in politics to the wealthy. The Federal Election Campaign Act of 1971, as amended in 1974, 2 U.S.C. § 441 *et seq.*, for example, limited contributions by individuals or groups to candidates for federal office, imposed a ceiling on expenditures by candidates, imposed disclosure requirements for individuals and committees contributing to political campaigns, and created public funding for presidential elections. In the seminal decision in *Buckley v. Valeo*, 424 U.S. 1 (1976), the Supreme Court held that the First Amendment protection of freedom of speech applies to the expenditure of money in politics because spending money is a form of political speech. The Court upheld contribution limits but held that limits on expenditures are unconstitutional.

Other legislative efforts to restrict campaign contributions or expenditures by large organizations and corporations have been declared unconstitutional too. In *First National Bank of Boston v. Bellotti*, 435 U.S. 765 (1978), the Supreme Court held unconstitutional a Massachusetts law that prohibited banks or businesses from making contributions or expenditures in connection with ballot initiatives and referenda. The Court said:

> If the speakers here were not corporations, no one would suggest that the State could silence their proposed speech. It is the type of speech indispensable to decision-making in a democracy, and this is no less true because the speech comes from a corporation rather than an individual. The inherent worth of the speech in terms of its capacity for informing the public does not depend upon the identity of its source, whether corporation, association, union, or individual.

In subsequent cases, the Supreme Court continued to strike down statutory limits on expenditures by individuals, parties, and political action committees, but to uphold limits on contributions. In 2002, Congress enacted the Bipartisan Campaign Finance Reform Act of 2002 (the so-called McCain-Feingold Act) restricting issue advertisements by corporations and unions that mention a federal candidate and are targeted to the relevant electorate in the period just before an election. The McCain-Feingold Act was the result of years of hearings and debate and sought to close loopholes that had emerged under the *Buckley* framework. First, the law sought to restrict "soft money," which is money raised and spent by political parties that was not covered by limits on contributions to candidates or Political Action Committees. Soft money had increased from $21.6 million in 1984 to $498 million in 2000. Moreover, the top five corporate soft-money donors gave a total of more than $9 million in nonfederal funds to the two national political party candidates, and in the 2002 election cycle, "the political parties raised almost $600 million—60% of their total soft-money fundraising—from just 800 donors, each of which contributed a minimum of $120,000." *McConnell v. Federal Election Commission,* 540 U.S. 93, 124 (2003). In addition, the McCain-Feingold Act restricted issue advertisements that mention a federal candidate and are targeted to the relevant electorate within 30 days of a primary election or 60 days of a general election.

In *Citizens United v. Federal Election Commission*, 558 U.S. 310 (2010), the Supreme Court overruled its prior decisions upholding parts of the McCain-Feingold law and held that most of its provisions violated the First Amendment. The Court struck down the restrictions on independent expenditures by corporations and unions, but upheld the disclosure requirements. As a result, corporations are now free to make unlimited political expenditures from their general treasuries for candidates and issues. Unions are too, although federal labor law restricts unions' expenditures of money for purposes not germane to collective bargaining (see *infra*, Part D.2) and no similar legal restrictions exist for corporations. Some scholars have argued that corporate shareholders ought to have the same rights to opt out of financially supporting corporate political spending that employees represented by a union have to opt out of union political spending. *See* Benjamin I. Sachs, *Unions, Corporations, and Political Opt-Out Rights After Citizens United*, 112 Colum. L. Rev. 800 (2012); Victor Brudney, *Business Corporations and Stockholders' Rights Under the First Amendment*, 91 Yale L. J. 235 (1981) (arguing that for publicly held business corporations not engaged in the communications business, the First Amendment does not preclude laws requiring stockholder consent for some or all noncommercial speech). In every Congress since *Citizens United* was decided, members of Congress have introduced a Shareholder Protection Act to require shareholder authorization for political expenditures by public companies. H.R. 376, 115th Cong. (2017). Some scholars have suggested that neither unionized employees nor shareholders should have a constitutional right to opt out of political expenditures, arguing that statutory regulation of organizational political activity raises no First Amendment problems. Catherine L. Fisk & Erwin Chemerinsky, *Political Speech and Association Rights After Knox v. SEIU, Local 1000*, 98 Cornell L. Rev. 1023 (2013).

In *Federal Election Commission v. National Right to Work Committee*, 459 U.S. 197 (1982), the Court upheld a federal law that prohibited corporations and unions from making political contributions from general funds. The law allowed them to create separate funds to solicit and spend money in connection with federal elections. Unions raise money from members separately from union dues and agency fees to fund contributions and advertisements in federal elections.

In *Davenport v. Washington Education Ass'n*, 551 U.S. 177 (2007), the Supreme Court upheld a Washington state law that required labor unions to obtain advance permission from members and non-member fee payers before spending any union general treasury funds (that is, money paid in member dues and fees) on politics. The law did not apply any such restriction to corporations' use of general funds. Because the NLRA preempts state regulation of member dues expenditures, the law applied only to public sector unions not covered by the NLRA. The Washington Supreme Court held that the state law unconstitutionally infringed the right of a teachers' union to engage in political activity. The Washington court reasoned that the law restricted "speech" (expenditure of money on political activity and expression) and targeted only a single type of speaker (labor unions) and therefore violated the First Amendment.

The Supreme Court reversed, holding that the law was valid as applied to union expenditure of money raised from represented employees who were not union members but who paid only a fee for representation services. In explaining why the Court's campaign finance cases were not on point, the Court said:

> For purposes of the First Amendment, it is entirely immaterial that [the Washington law] restricts a union's use of funds only after those funds are already within the union's lawful possession under Washington law. What matters is that public-sector agency fees are in the union's possession only because Washington and its union-contracting government agencies have compelled their employees to pay those fees. The cases upon which [the union] relies deal with governmental restrictions on how a regulated entity may spend money that has come into its possession without the assistance of governmental coercion of its employees. As applied to public sector unions, [the Washington law] is not fairly described as a restriction on how the union can spend 'its' money; it is a condition placed upon the union's extraordinary *state* entitlement to acquire and spend *other people's* money.

In addition to general federal and state campaign finance laws, a number of federal and state laws restrict union fundraising for political purposes. The efforts to enact these laws are framed in terms of protecting individual workers' rights, but they are supported by employer associations. Not surprisingly, business interests, like lobbyists everywhere, often prefer that their adversaries not be heard in the legislative process. Some business interests embraced the idea that unions should be prohibited from using the dues of members to seek state and local legislation, or to support or oppose candidates for elected office. They have therefore advocated for protecting the right of unionized employees to be free from subsidizing political activities with which they disagree.

These laws are generally known by their supporters as "paycheck protection" measures and by their detractors as "paycheck deception" laws. They aim to make it more difficult for unions to collect dues and fees from both members and nonmembers by requiring unions to get specific authorization from each employee before collecting dues, rather than (as is currently the practice under most collective bargaining agreements) requiring employees to opt out of automatic dues collection through payroll deduction. Although most such measures have been defeated at the polls or in the legislature, they have arguably served a political purpose: forcing unions to spend considerable money and staff resources in defeating the measure. Even when such ballot measures fail, the mere threat of them succeeds in drawing away the adversary's resources, thereby demonstrating how ballot measures can be used strategically to undercut one's opponents. *See* Brian D. Olney, *Paycheck Protection or Paycheck Deception? When Government "Subsidies" Silence Political Speech*, 4 U.C. Irvine L. Rev. 881 (2013); Hank Dempsey, *The "Overlooked Hermaphrodite" of Campaign Finance: Candidate Controlled Ballot Measure Committees in California Politics*, 95 Cal. L. Rev. 123 (2007).

NOTES

1.   *Is political giving or spending speech?* In striking down limits on political expenditures, the Supreme Court has adhered to the view that spending money is a form of speech protected by the First Amendment. Do you agree?

2.   *Are unions, corporations, and other political groups all the same?* As a matter of First Amendment law, or as a matter of statutory election law, should corporate political expenditures and union political expenditures be treated the same as each other? Why or why not? What about expenditures of other organizations, like the ACLU, the National Rifle Association, the NAACP, the Chamber of Commerce, or worker advocacy groups?

3.   *Does requiring employee or shareholder consent for organizational political spending infringe the First Amendment rights of the organization?* The claim that shareholders and employees should have a right to prevent a corporation or union from spending money on politics without consent rests on the idea that the individual constituent's free speech rights are infringed when the organization spends money. Do you agree? Might a requirement that constituents opt into political spending (or be permitted to opt out) infringe the speech rights of the organization?

2. THE REGULATION OF UNION SECURITY AND UNION DUES: HISTORY AND OVERVIEW

As explained in Chapter 7, under federal labor law, the union is the exclusive representative of the employees in the bargaining unit, which means that the union alone has the power to negotiate with the employer over terms of employment and to enforce the collective bargaining agreement. Both in negotiating the collective bargaining agreement and in enforcing it, the union owes a duty of fair representation to every employee in the bargaining unit. Not every employee will be a supporter of every choice the union makes. If a union negotiates health benefits at the expense of a wage increase, or if a union agrees to concessions in favor of a struggling firm in exchange for a promise to keep the plant open, or if a union negotiates for promotions based on seniority rather than "merit," some employees will be disappointed. Unions must make trade-offs, and some employees will therefore become disaffected. Even employees who oppose the union entirely are still owed a duty of fair representation.

Unions have often considered employees who do not support the union to be a threat to their power to secure the best possible working conditions. Since the power of the union comes from its ability to speak with one voice on behalf of all workers, many unions considered it desirable to allow only union members to work in the bargaining unit. Unions, like the professions of today, also have thought that a monopoly on who can practice a certain trade or profession would protect the consumers of the product or service from poor quality work. For all these reasons, in some occupations labor organizations (sometimes with and sometimes without the support of employers) insisted on employment rules making it necessary to be a member of the union, craft, or guild in order to work in a particular job. These "closed shop" agreements gave unions power that they sometimes abused. Some blackballed employees by refusing them membership and thereby preventing them from being hired by unionized employers. Some got employees fired by expelling them from union membership.

Nothing in the original Wagner Act changed the legality of these "closed shop" rules. Section 8(3) as originally written prohibited "discrimination in regard to hire or tenure of employment . . . to encourage or discourage membership in any labor organization," but contained a proviso "[t]hat nothing in this Act, or in any other statute of the United States, shall preclude an employer from making an agreement with a labor organization . . . to require as a condition of employment membership therein. . . ." In the railroad industry, where closed shops were uncommon, the Railway Labor Act of 1926 did not address the permissibility of closed shops where they existed.

When the Taft-Hartley Act amended the Wagner Act with a series of provisions creating legal rights for employers to resist unionization, it added to section 7 the right of employees "to refrain from [concerted activities] except to the extent that such right may be affected by an agreement requiring membership in a labor organization as a condition of employment" as authorized in section 8(a)(3). It also amended section 8(a)(3) to prohibit the "closed shop" by prohibiting rules requiring union membership at the time of initial employment. The Taft-Hartley Act amendments were a product of congressional concern about the power of unions to interrupt the operation of basic industry in the post-War period and also to coerce union members and other employees. But Congress also understood the union concern that without some rule requiring employees to pay dues to the union that owes a duty of representation, employees who did not join the union by becoming members will get a "free ride" by sharing the benefits of what unions are able to accomplish though collective bargaining without paying for them. The revised section 8(a)(3) prohibited a "closed shop" but enabled unions and firms to agree to require employees to join the union 30 days after becoming employed (a "union shop"). In a union shop, an employee can be fired for a loss of union membership only when it results from a failure to pay union dues or fees to cover the employee's pro rata share of the cost of negotiating and administering the collective bargaining agreement. Thus, there are two key differences between the union shop allowed under the Taft-Hartley Act and the closed shop: (1) the obligation to become a union member does not begin until 30 days after hiring, which precludes the union from blackballing anyone; and (2) an employee may not be fired for lack of union membership except where it results from a failure to pay dues or fees, which prevents a firing simply because the employee has not abided by the union's by-laws or other rules.

A variation on the union shop clause is a "maintenance of membership" clause, whereby employees who have chosen to join a union are required to maintain their membership during the term of the contract but have the option to withdraw during a period after the contract expires. Another variation is an "agency fee" arrangement, which obligates nonmembers to pay the equivalent of union dues and fees for the union's services. As we will see, when the Supreme Court in the 1960s expanded individual freedoms of speech and association through new interpretations of the First Amendment, the Court further restricted the ability of unions and employers to require employees to join unions. Under current law, the most that a union and employer can enforce against an objecting employee is an "agency fee" arrangement.

When Congress amended section 8(a)(3) to ban the closed shop, it went further and added section 14(b), which allows states the power to restrict or prohibit union security agreements altogether, an exception to the general rule of NLRA preemption. Section 14(b) provides:

> Nothing in this Act shall be construed as authorizing the execution or application of agreements requiring membership in a labor organization as a condition of employment in any State or Territory in which such execution or application is prohibited by State or Territorial law.

When section 14(b) was enacted, twelve states already outlawed or restricted union security devices. In 2018, twenty-eight states, mainly in the southeast, southwest, and west, have exercised this power, and their resulting statutes make up what is colloquially known as "right-to-work" laws.[3] Although states differ in the extent to which they utilize section 14(b) to restrict security agreements, every state with a right-to-work law prohibits unions and employers from conditioning employment on any type of union "membership." In so doing, state right-to-work laws—either

---

[3]   The following states have enacted "right-to-work" provisions: Alabama, Arizona, Arkansas, Florida, Georgia, Idaho, Indiana, Iowa, Kansas, Kentucky, Louisiana, Michigan, Mississippi, Missouri, Nebraska, Nevada, North Carolina, North Dakota, Oklahoma, South Carolina, South Dakota, Tennessee, Texas, Utah, Virginia, West Virginia, Wisconsin, and Wyoming.

explicitly or as interpreted judicially—bar most union security agreements, including agency fee arrangements.

There have been numerous efforts to extend the right-to-work regime nationally by introducing legislation in Congress to ban all union security arrangements. A nonprofit organization, the National Right-to-Work Committee, has pushed for over fifty years to enact right-to-work legislation both at the state level and nationally. Those allied with the labor movement vigorously oppose the right-to-work regime, arguing that workers in right-to-work states tend to earn less than workers in other states. *See* Michael M. Oswalt, *Note, The Grand Bargain: Revitalizing Labor Through NLRA Reform and Radical Workplace Relations*, 57 Duke L.J. 691 (2007) (reporting data showing lower union density in states with right-to-work laws and also reporting a study showing an increase in shareholder wealth after the passage of right-to-work laws, an effect that was attributed to labor's weakened bargaining position).

There is a narrow but significant exception to the section 8(a)(3) rules for union security agreements in the construction industry. Because employment in construction is generally short term, with construction employees working for one contractor and then another at different job sites, construction employers and unions are allowed to enter into "pre-hire agreements" which require employees to join the union or become agency fee payers within seven days, rather than the usual 30 under section 8(a)(3), after commencing employment. Section 8(f) reads, in pertinent part:

> It shall not be an unfair labor practice . . . for an employer engaged primarily in the building and construction industry to make an agreement covering employees engaged (or who, upon their employment, will be engaged) in the building and construction industry with a labor organization of which building and construction employees are members (not established, maintained, or assisted by any action defined in section 8(a) of this Act as an unfair labor practice) because (1) the majority status of such labor organization has not been established under the provisions of section 9 of this Act prior to the making of such agreement, or (2) such agreement requires as a condition of employment, membership in such labor organization after the seventh day following the beginning of such employment or the effective date of the agreement, whichever is later. . . .

The law governing union security was originally different under the Railway Labor Act. Unlike the NLRA, which evolved from closed shop to union shop, the RLA evolved from open shop to union shop. Union density was quite high on the railroads, and union security agreements were rare because employees had no reason to fear the threat of low-wage non-union competition. During World War II, when some railroad unions made an unsuccessful attempt to obtain union security, the unions pledged not to strike for the duration of the war and argued that they were therefore justified in seeking to maintain their positions by union security arrangements. A Presidential Emergency Board rejected the claim that union security was necessary to protect the bargaining position of the unions: "The unions are not suffering from a falling off in members. On the contrary, membership has been growing and at the present time appears to be the largest in railroad history, with less than 10 percent nonmembership among the employees here represented."

The "agency fee" system, which essentially limits what an employer and union can require employees to pay in fees to the union in support of only the negotiation and administration of the collective bargaining agreement, was developed largely in response to two related strands of Supreme Court cases in the 1960s and 1970s. The cases arose because the RLA, unlike the NLRA, preempts state right-to-work laws. The first strand began with *Railway Employees Dept. v. Hanson,* 351 U.S. 225 (1956). In *Hanson*, an employer association known as the National Right to Work Committee argued that the RLA was unconstitutional because it preempted a Nebraska right-to-work law and therefore compelled employees to support unions with which they did not wish to associate. The Supreme Court made two significant holdings. First, the Court agreed with the plaintiffs that the RLA's preemption of state right-to-work laws was sufficient state action to subject the union security agreement between the private union and the private railroad to constitutional scrutiny. Second, the Court held that the compelled subsidization of the employee's exclusive bargaining representative did not violate the employees' First Amendment rights. But the Court reserved the issue of whether the expenditure of those employees' dues/fees over their objection on political candidates violated their First Amendment rights.

The Court reached the issue it reserved in *Hanson* in *International Association of Machinists v. Street,* 367 U.S. 740 (1961). To avoid the question whether compulsory dues violated the First Amendment, the Court interpreted the RLA not to require dissenting employees to provide financial support for union political speech. In an opinion by Justice Brennan, the Court noted the statutorily prescribed involvement of unions in the Presidential Emergency Boards that adjudicate bargaining disputes and grievances in the railway industry. The Court also emphasized the importance of unions' role

> in effectuating the basic congressional policy of stabilizing labor relations in the industry. It is fair to say that every stage in the evolution of this railroad labor code was progressively infused with the purpose of securing self-adjustment between the effectively organized railroads and the equally effective railroad unions and, to that end, of establishing facilities for such self-

adjustment by the railroad community of its own industrial controversies.

The Court quoted a House of Representatives committee report stating that about 75% or 80% of all railroad employees were believed to belong to a union, and that nonunion members "share in the benefits derived from collective agreements negotiated by the railway labor unions but bear no share of the cost of obtaining such benefits." The Court continued:

> Section 2, Eleventh contemplated compulsory unionism to force employees to share the costs of negotiating and administering collective agreements, and the costs of the adjustment and settlement of disputes. One looks in vain for any suggestion that Congress also meant in § 2, Eleventh to provide the unions with a means for forcing employees, over their objection, to support political causes which they oppose.

The Court also noted:

> many of the expenditures involved in the present case are made for the purpose of disseminating information as to candidates and programs and publicizing the positions of the unions on them. As to such expenditures an injunction would work a restraint on the expression of political ideas which might be offensive to the First Amendment. For the majority also has an interest in stating its views without being silenced by the dissenters. To attain the appropriate reconciliation between majority and dissenting interests in the area of political expression, we think the courts in administering the Act should select remedies which protect both interests to the maximum extent possible without undue impingement of one on the other.

Therefore, the Court refused to construe the RLA to allow compulsory payment of dues to support political activity.

The second strand of cases began with *Abood v. Detroit Board of Education*, 431 U.S. 209 (1977). The Michigan courts had held the state public sector labor statute to allow an agency shop and to allow unions to spend agency shop fees on political activities. The Court therefore could not avoid the constitutional question through statutory interpretation and held that government employees have First Amendment rights to refuse to join the unions that represent them and to refuse to provide financial support to their unions' political activities unrelated to the union's duties in negotiating and enforcing the collective bargaining agreement.

The notion embraced in both *Street* and *Abood* that contractually required union membership involved compelled speech in violation of the First Amendment produced sharp dissent from some Justices. As Justice Frankfurter (joined by Justice Harlan) stated in dissent in *Street*, the provision of the Railway Labor Act allowing union security arrangements cannot be meaningfully construed except against the background and presupposition of what is loosely called political activity of American trade unions in general and railroad unions in particular—activity indissolubly relating to the immediate economic and social concerns that are the raison d'etre of unions. It would be pedantic heavily to document this familiar truth of industrial history and commonplace of trade-union life. To write the history of the Brotherhoods, the United Mine Workers, the Steel Workers, the Amalgamated Clothing Workers, the International Ladies Garment Workers, the United Auto Workers, and leave out their so-called political activities and expenditures for them, would be sheer mutilation. Suffice it to recall a few illustrative manifestations. The AFL, surely the conservative labor group, sponsored as early as 1893 an extensive program of political demands calling for compulsory education, an eight-hour day, employer tort liability, and other social reforms. More specifically, the weekly publication "Labor"—an expenditure under attack in this case—has since 1919 been the organ of the railroad brotherhoods which finance it. Its files through the years show its preoccupation with legislative measures that touch the vitals of labor's interests and with the men and parties who effectuate them. This aspect—call it the political side—is as organic, as inured a part of the philosophy and practice of railway unions as their immediate bread-and-butter concerns.

Justices Frankfurter and Harlan insisted that the use of union dues to support political activity did not constitute compelled speech:

The use of union dues to promote relevant and effective means of realizing the purposes for which unions exist does not constitute a utilization of dues "as a cover for forcing ideological conformity" in any fair reading of those words. Plaintiffs here are in no way subjected to such suppression of their true beliefs or sponsorship of views they do not hold. Nor are they forced to join a sham organization which does not participate in collective bargaining functions, but only serves as a conduit of funds for ideological propaganda. No one's desire or power to speak his mind is checked or curbed. The individual member may express his views in any public or private forum as freely as he could before the union collected his dues. Federal taxes also may diminish the vigor with which a citizen can give partisan support to a political belief, but as yet no one would place such an impediment to making one's views effective within the reach of constitutionally protected free speech.

It is a commonplace of all organizations that a minority of a legally recognized group may at times see an organization's funds used for promotion of ideas opposed by the minority. The analogies are numerous. On the largest scale, the Federal Government expends revenue collected from individual taxpayers to propagandize ideas which many taxpayers oppose. To come closer to the heart of the immediate matter, is the union's choice of when to picket or to go out on strike unconstitutional? Picketing is still deemed also a form of speech, but surely the union's decision to strike under its statutory aegis as a bargaining unit is not an unconstitutional compulsion forced upon members who strongly oppose a strike, as minorities not infrequently do. Indeed, legislative reform intended to insure the fair representation of the minority workers in internal union politics would be redundant if, despite all precautions, the union were constitutionally forbidden because of minority opposition to spend money in accordance with the majority's desires.

Outside the context of public sector unions, where it is state law that mandates the payment of fees and thus there is obvious state action in compelling a government employee to support a union, the argument for the unconstitutionality of union security provisions is complex because a union security clause is a private agreement between a private employer and a private association of employees. The Supreme Court nevertheless applied the concepts of compelled speech and compelled association to agreements negotiated by unions and employers in the private sector. This has been one of the most hotly contested areas of labor law for at least a generation and has produced a number of recent Supreme Court decisions on the First Amendment issues in union representation under a regime of exclusive representation.

3. PUBLIC SECTOR UNION SECURITY AND DUES

After the Supreme Court in *Abood* upheld the constitutionality of a Michigan law authorizing public sector unions and employers to agree to require workers to pay a fee for representation services, the question whether such contracts would exist was left to state law. Fierce battles were fought in state legislatures and in state ballot measures over whether to enact a so-called right-to-work law prohibiting contracts requiring payment of agency or fair share fees. By 2018, 28 states had enacted laws prohibiting fair share fees. Litigation battles were fought in states that allowed fair share fees over the size of the permissible fees and how to calculate which services could be charged to non-member fee payers. *See, e.g., Lehnert v. Ferris Faculty Assn.*, 500 U.S. 507 (1991). As the composition of the Supreme Court changed, union opponents—who once focused on lobbying to abolish fair share fees or litigating to restrict the amount of fees—saw a litigation opportunity to make fair share fees unconstitutional nationwide.

The constitutional attack on fair share fees gained steam in *Knox v. Service Employees International Union Local 1000*, 567 U.S. 298 (2012), in which the issue was whether the default rule should be that unions can charge the employees they represent for the cost of all union activities, thus forcing dissenting employees to opt out of supporting the union's expenditures that are not germane to collective bargaining (as was then the law), or whether the default rule should be that unions can gather money from employees to support the full range of union activity, including organizing, political expenditures, and contract bargaining and administration, only if employees opt in. For a while, the National Right to Work legal challenges—both in litigation and through legislation like that at issue in *Knox*—focused on moving the law to require that employees opt in rather than allowing unions and employers to negotiate a contract that requires employees to opt out. In *Knox,* the Supreme Court required opt in (for public sector employees and for special assessments) as a matter of federal constitutional requirement rather than, as in *Davenport v. Washington Education Association*, 551 U.S. 177 (2007), as a matter of legislative enactment.

Although the holding in *Knox* was narrow—unions must gain consent from fee payers before spending money on special assessments—language in Justice Alito's opinion in the sharply divided 5–4 decision was very broad. The opinion called into question the constitutionality of any public sector law or contract that required payment of representation fees by union-represented workers who choose not to become union members. Not surprisingly, union opponents represented by the National Right to Work Legal Foundation filed a host of cases in federal courts across the country seeking to have any form of representation fee declared unconstitutional. In *Harris v. Quinn*, 573 U.S. ___, 134 S.Ct. 2618 (2014), the Court, again 5–4 with Justice Alito writing for the majority, invalidated an Illinois statute allowing fair share fee provisions for home health aides paid with Medicaid funds. *Harris* emphasized that home health aides work for private households and, therefore, the government's interest in bargaining with a union over their working conditions was less than in the situation of other government employees.

For a time observers believed that *Harris* indicated that the Court might not overrule *Abood* because it could have done so in *Harris* and chose not to. That changed very shortly after, when the Court granted review in *Friedrichs v. California Teachers Ass'n*, 576 U.S. ___, 135 S.Ct. 2933 (2015), to consider a constitutional challenge to fair share fees in California teachers' union contracts. Justice Scalia died a month after oral argument in *Friedrichs*, and the lower court decision was affirmed by an equally divided Court. 578 U.S. ___, 136 S.Ct. 1083 (2016). But the Court quickly granted review in another case challenging all fair share fee provisions governing Illinois public employees and overruled *Abood*.

JANUS V. AMERICAN FEDERATION OF STATE, COUNTY & MUNICIPAL EMPLOYEES, COUNCIL 31

138 S. Ct. 2448 (2018)

JUSTICE ALITO delivered the opinion of the Court:

In *Abood,* the main defense of the agency-fee arrangement was that it served the State's interest in "labor peace." By "labor peace," the *Abood* Court meant avoidance of the conflict and disruption that it envisioned would occur if the employees in a unit were represented by more than one union. In such a situation, the Court predicted, "inter-union rivalries" would foster "dissension within the work force," and the employer could face "conflicting demands from different unions." Confusion would ensue if the employer entered into and attempted to "enforce two or more agreements specifying different terms and conditions of employment."

We assume that "labor peace," in this sense of the term, is a compelling state interest, but *Abood* cited no evidence that the pandemonium it imagined would result if agency fees were not allowed, and it is now clear that *Abood*'s fears were unfounded. The *Abood* Court assumed that designation of a union as the exclusive representative of all the employees in a unit and the exaction of agency fees are inextricably linked, but that is simply not true.

The federal employment experience is illustrative. Under federal law, a union chosen by majority vote is designated as the exclusive representative of all the employees, but federal law does not permit agency fees. See 5 U.S.C. §§ 7102, 7111(a), 7114(a). Nevertheless, nearly a million federal employees—about 27% of the federal work force—are union members. The situation in the Postal Service is similar. Although permitted to choose an exclusive representative, Postal Service employees are not required to pay an agency fee, 39 U.S.C. §§ 1203(a), 1209(c), and about 400,000 are union members. Likewise, millions of public employees in the 28 States that have laws generally prohibiting agency fees are represented by unions that serve as the exclusive representatives of all the employees.

In addition to the promotion of "labor peace," *Abood* cited "the risk of 'free riders' " as justification for agency fees. Petitioner strenuously objects to this free-rider label. He argues that he is not a free rider on a bus headed for a destination that he wishes to reach but is more like a person shanghaied for an unwanted voyage.

Whichever description fits the majority of public employees who would not subsidize a union if given the option, avoiding free riders is not a compelling interest. Many private groups speak out with the objective of obtaining government action that will have the effect of benefiting nonmembers. Suppose that a particular group lobbies or speaks out on behalf of what it thinks are the needs of senior citizens or veterans or physicians, to take just a few examples. Could the government require that all seniors, veterans, or doctors pay for that service even if they object? It has never been thought that this is permissible.

[I]t is simply not true that unions will refuse to serve as the exclusive representative of all employees in the unit if they are not given agency fees. Even without agency fees, designation as the exclusive representative confers many benefits. [T]hat status gives the union a privileged place in negotiations over wages, benefits, and working conditions. Not only is the union given the exclusive right to speak for all the employees in collective bargaining, but the employer is required by state law to listen to and to bargain in good faith with only that union. Designation as exclusive representative thus results in a tremendous increase in the power of the union.

These benefits greatly outweigh any extra burden imposed by the duty of providing fair representation for nonmembers. [T]he union's bargaining latitude would be little different if state law simply prohibited public employers from entering into agreements that discriminate in that way. [I]t is questionable whether the Constitution would permit a public-sector employer to adopt a collective-bargaining agreement that discriminates against nonmembers.

What about the representation of nonmembers in grievance proceedings? Unions do not undertake this activity solely for the benefit of nonmembers—which is why Illinois law gives a public-sector union the right to send a representative to such proceedings even if the employee declines union representation. Representation of nonmembers furthers the union's interest in keeping control of the administration of the collective-bargaining agreement, since the resolution of one employee's grievance can affect others.

In any event, whatever unwanted burden is imposed by the representation of nonmembers in disciplinary matters can be eliminated through means significantly less restrictive of associational freedoms than the imposition of agency fees. Individual nonmembers could be required to pay for that service or could be denied union representation altogether.

Nor can such fees be justified on the ground that it would otherwise be unfair to require a union to bear the duty of fair representation. That duty is a necessary concomitant of the authority that a union seeks when it chooses to serve as the exclusive representative of all the employees in a unit.

The principal defense of *Abood* advanced by respondents and the dissent is based on our decision in *Pickering v. Bd. of Ed.,* 391 U.S. 563 (1968), which held that a school district violated the First Amendment by firing a teacher for writing a letter critical of the school administration. Under *Pickering* and later cases in the same line, employee speech is largely unprotected if it is part of what the employee is paid to do, see *Garcetti v. Ceballos,* 547 U.S. 410 (2006), or if it involved a matter of only private concern.

[T]he *Pickering* framework was developed for use in a very different context—in cases that involve "one employee's speech and its impact on that employee's public responsibilities." *United States v. Treasury Employees,* 513 U.S. 454 (1995). This case, by contrast, involves a blanket requirement that all employees subsidize speech with which they may not agree. A speech-restrictive law with "widespread impact," we have said, "gives rise to far more serious concerns than could any single supervisory decision."

The core collective-bargaining issue of wages and benefits illustrates this point. Suppose that a single employee complains that he or she should have received a 5% raise. This individual complaint would likely constitute a matter of only private concern and would therefore be unprotected under *Pickering.* But a public-sector union's demand for a 5% raise for the many thousands of employees it represents would be another matter entirely. Granting such a raise could have a serious impact on the budget of the government unit in question, and by the same token, denying a raise might have a significant effect on the performance of government services. When a large number of employees speak through their union, the category of speech that is of public concern is greatly enlarged.

Pickering is based on the insight that the speech of a public-sector employee may interfere with the effective operation of a government office. When a public employer does not simply restrict potentially disruptive speech but commands that its employees mouth a message on its own behalf, the calculus is very different. Of course, if the speech in question is part of an employee's official duties, the employer may insist that the employee deliver any lawful message. Otherwise, however, it is not easy to imagine a situation in which a public employer has a legitimate need to demand that its employees recite words with which they disagree. And we have never applied *Pickering* in such a case.

[T]he union speech paid for by agency fees is not [speech as part of the employees' official duties] controlled by *Garcetti.* [We therefore] move on to the next step of the *Pickering* framework and ask whether the speech is on a matter of public or only private concern. It is impossible to argue that the level of state spending for employee benefits is not a matter of great public concern.

Illinois, like some other States and a number of counties and cities around the country, suffers from severe budget problems. As of 2013, Illinois had nearly $160 billion in unfunded pension and retiree healthcare liabilities. By 2017, that number had only grown, and the State was grappling with $15 billion in unpaid bills. We are told that a "quarter of the budget is now devoted to paying down" those liabilities.

The State claims that its employment-related debt is squeezing core programs in education, public safety, and human services, in addition to limiting the State's ability to pay its bills. And the State's desire for savings in fact drove its bargaining positions on matters such as health-insurance benefits and holiday, overtime, and promotion policies. But when the State offered cost-saving proposals on these issues, the Union countered with very different suggestions. Among other things, it advocated wage and tax increases, cutting spending "to Wall Street financial institutions," and reforms to Illinois' pension and tax systems (such as closing "corporate tax loopholes," "[e]xpanding the base of the state sales tax," and "allowing an income tax that is adjusted in accordance with ability to pay". To suggest that speech on such matters is not of great public concern—or that it is not directed at the "public square," *post* (KAGAN, J., dissenting)—is to deny reality.

In addition to affecting how public money is spent, union speech in collective bargaining addresses many other important matters. [U]nions express views on a wide range of subjects—education, child welfare, healthcare, and minority rights, to name a few. Take the example of education. The public importance of subsidized union speech is especially apparent in this field, since educators make up by far the largest category of state and local government employees, and education is typically the largest component of state and local government expenditures.

Speech in this area also touches on fundamental questions of education policy. Should teacher pay be based on seniority, the better to retain experienced teachers? Or should schools adopt merit-pay systems to encourage teachers to get the best results out of their students? Should districts transfer more experienced teachers to the lower performing schools that may have the greatest need for their skills, or should those teachers be allowed to stay where they have put down roots? Should teachers be given tenure protection and, if so, under what conditions? On what grounds and pursuant to what procedures should teachers be subject to discipline or dismissal? How should teacher performance and student progress be measured—by standardized tests or other means?

Even union speech in the handling of grievances may be of substantial public importance and may be directed at the public square. For instance, the Union respondent in this case recently filed a grievance seeking to compel Illinois to appropriate $75 million to fund a 2% wage increase.

[D]efenders of *Abood* have asserted a different state interest—the State's "interest in bargaining with an adequately funded exclusive bargaining agent." Although the dissent would accept without any serious independent evaluation the State's assertion that the absence of agency fees would cripple public-sector unions and thus impair the efficiency of government operations, ample experience shows that this is questionable.

An important factor in determining whether a precedent should be overruled is the quality of its reasoning, and *Abood* was poorly reasoned. *Abood* went wrong at the start when it concluded that two prior decisions, *Railway Employes' Dep't v. Hanson,* 351 U.S. 225 (1956), and *Machinists v. Street,* 367 U.S. 740 (1961), appeared to require validation of the agency-shop agreement before the Court. *Abood* failed to appreciate that a very different First Amendment question arises when a State *requires* its employees to pay agency fees. [N]either *Hanson* nor *Street* gave careful consideration to the First Amendment. *Abood* also did not sufficiently take into account the difference between the effects of agency fees in public- and private-sector collective bargaining. In the public sector, core issues such as wages, pensions, and benefits are important political issues, but that is generally not so in the private sector.

Abood's line between chargeable and nonchargeable union expenditures has proved to be impossible to draw with precision. The Court's experience with union lobbying expenses illustrates the point. In *Knox,* for example, we confronted a union's claim that the costs of lobbying the legislature and the electorate about a ballot measure were chargeable expenses under *Lehnert v. Ferris Faculty Assn.,* 500 U.S. 507 (1991). The Court rejected this claim out of hand. And in the present case, nonmembers are required to pay for unspecified "lobbying" expenses and for "services" that "may ultimately inure to the benefit of the members of the local bargaining unit." That formulation is broad enough to encompass just about anything that the union might choose to do.

Objecting employees also face a daunting and expensive task if they wish to challenge union chargeability determinations. While *Hudson* requires a union to provide nonmembers with sufficient information to gauge the propriety of the union's fee, the *Hudson* notice in the present case and in others that have come before us do not begin to permit a nonmember to make such a determination. How could any nonmember determine whether [the] numbers [provided in the *Hudson* notice] are even close to the mark without launching a legal challenge and retaining the services of attorneys and accountants? The Union argues that challenging its chargeability determinations is not burdensome because the Union pays for the costs of arbitration, but objectors must still pay for the attorneys and experts needed to mount a serious challenge.

It is also significant that the Court decided *Abood* against a very different legal and economic backdrop. Public-sector unionism was a relatively new phenomenon in 1977. Since then, public-sector union membership has come to surpass private-sector union membership, even though there are nearly four times as many total private-sector employees as public-sector employees. This ascendance of public-sector unions has been marked by a parallel increase in public spending. In 1970, total state and local government expenditures amounted to $646 per capita in nominal terms, or about $4,000 per capita in 2014 dollars. By 2014, that figure had ballooned to approximately $10,238 per capita. ProQuest, Statistical Abstract of the United States: 2018, pp. 17, Table 14, 300, Table 469. Not all that increase can be attributed to public-sector unions, of course, but the mounting costs of public-employee wages, benefits, and pensions undoubtedly played a substantial role. Unsustainable collective-bargaining agreements have also been blamed for multiple municipal bankruptcies. These developments, and the political debate over public spending and debt they have spurred, have given collective-bargaining issues a political valence that *Abood* did not fully appreciate.

Abood particularly sticks out when viewed against our cases holding that public employees generally may not be required to support a political party. See *Elrod v. Burns,* 427 U.S. 347 (1976). The Court reached that conclusion despite a long tradition of political patronage in government. It is an odd feature of our First Amendment cases that political patronage has been deemed largely unconstitutional, while forced subsidization of union speech (which has no such pedigree) has been largely permitted.

In some cases, reliance provides a strong reason for adhering to established law, and this is the factor that is stressed most strongly by respondents, their *amici,* and the dissent. [P]ublic-sector unions have been on notice for years regarding this Court's misgivings about *Abood.* In *Knox,* decided in 2012, we described *Abood* as a First Amendment "anomaly." Two years later in *Harris,* we were asked to overrule *Abood,* and while we found it unnecessary to take that step, we cataloged *Abood*'s many weaknesses. In 2015, we granted a petition for certiorari asking us to review a decision that sustained an agency-fee arrangement under *Abood. Friedrichs v. California Teachers Assn.,* 576 U.S. ___. After exhaustive briefing and argument on the question whether *Abood* should be overruled, we affirmed the decision below by an equally divided vote. 578 U.S. ___ (2016). During this period of time, any public-sector union seeking an agency-fee provision in a collective-bargaining agreement must have understood that the constitutionality of such a provision was uncertain. But even if an agreement antedates those decisions, the union was able to protect itself if an agency-fee provision was essential to the overall bargain.

We recognize that the loss of payments from nonmembers may cause unions to experience unpleasant transition costs in the short term, and may require unions to make adjustments in order to attract and retain members. But we must weigh these disadvantages against the considerable windfall that unions have received under *Abood* for the past 41 years. It is hard to estimate how many billions of dollars have been taken from nonmembers and transferred to public-sector unions in violation of the First Amendment. Those unconstitutional exactions cannot be allowed to continue indefinitely.

JUSTICE KAGAN, with whom JUSTICE GINSBURG, JUSTICE BREYER, and JUSTICE SOTOMAYOR join, dissenting.

Abood's reasoning about governmental interests has three connected parts. First, exclusive representation arrangements benefit some government entities because they can facilitate stable labor relations. In particular, such arrangements eliminate the potential for inter-union conflict and streamline the process of negotiating terms of employment. Second, the government may be unable to avail itself of those benefits unless the single union has a secure source of funding. The various tasks involved in representing employees cost money; if the union doesn't have enough, it can't be an effective employee representative and bargaining partner. And third, agency fees are often needed to ensure such stable funding. That is because without those fees, employees have every incentive to free ride on the union dues paid by others.

The majority stakes everything on the third point—the conclusion that maintaining an effective system of exclusive representation often entails agency fees. *Ante* (It "is simply not true" that exclusive representation and agency fees are "inextricably linked").

But basic economic theory shows why a government would think that agency fees are necessary for exclusive representation to work. What ties the two together, as *Abood* recognized, is the likelihood of free-riding when fees are absent. Remember that once a union achieves exclusive-representation status, the law compels it to fairly represent all workers in the bargaining unit, whether or not they join or contribute to the union. Because of that legal duty, the union cannot give special advantages to its own members. And that in turn creates a collective action problem of nightmarish proportions. Everyone—not just those who oppose the union, but also those who back it—has an economic incentive to withhold dues; only altruism or loyalty—as *against* financial self-interest—can explain why an employee would pay the union for its services. And so emerged *Abood*'s rule allowing fair-share agreements: That rule ensured that a union would receive sufficient funds, despite its legally imposed disability, to effectively carry out its duties as exclusive representative of the government's employees.

The majority's initial response to this reasoning is simply to dismiss it. "[F]ree rider arguments," the majority pronounces, "are generally insufficient to overcome First Amendment objections." But that disregards the defining characteristic of *this* free-rider argument—that unions, unlike other private groups, must serve members and non-members alike. Groups advocating for "senior citizens or veterans" (to use the majority's examples) have no legal duty to provide benefits to all those individuals: They can spur people to pay dues by conferring all kinds of special advantages on their dues-paying members. Unions are—by law—in a different position, as this Court has long recognized. Justice Scalia, responding to the same argument as the majority's, may have put the point best. In a way that is true of no other private group, the "law *requires* the union to carry" non-members—"indeed, requires the union to *go out of its way* to benefit [them], even at the expense of its other interests." *Lehnert v. Ferris Faculty Assn.,* 500 U.S. 507 (1991) (opinion concurring in part and dissenting in part). That special feature was what justified *Abood*: "Where the state imposes upon the union a duty to deliver services, it may permit the union to demand reimbursement for them."

The majority's fallback argument purports to respond to the distinctive position of unions, but still misses *Abood*'s economic insight. The gist of the account is that "designation as the exclusive representative confers many benefits," which outweigh the costs of providing services to non-members. But that response avoids the key question, which is whether unions without agency fees will be *able to* (not whether they will *want to*) carry on as an effective exclusive representative. And as to that question, the majority again fails to reckon with how economically rational actors behave—in public as well as private workplaces. Without a fair-share agreement, the class of union non-members spirals upward. Employees (including those who love the union) realize that they can get the same benefits even if they let their memberships expire. And as more and more stop paying dues, those left must take up the financial slack (and anyway, begin to feel like suckers)—so they too quit the union. And when the vicious cycle finally ends, chances are that the union will lack the resources to effectively perform the responsibilities of an exclusive representative—or, in the worst case, to perform them at all. The result is to frustrate the interests of every government entity that thinks a strong exclusive-representation scheme will promote stable labor relations.

In many cases over many decades, this Court has addressed how the First Amendment applies when the government, acting not as sovereign but as employer, limits its workers' speech. Those decisions have granted substantial latitude to the government, in recognition of its significant interests in managing its workforce so as to best serve the public. *Abood* fit neatly with that caselaw, in both reasoning and result. Indeed, its reversal today creates a significant anomaly—an exception, applying to union fees alone, from the usual rules governing public employees' speech.

In striking the proper balance between employee speech rights and managerial interests, the Court has long applied a test originating in *Pickering v. Board of Ed.,* 391 U.S. 563 (1968). [In] the *Pickering* inquiry, the Court first asks whether the employee spoke as a citizen on a matter of public concern. If she did not—but rather spoke as an employee on a workplace matter—she has no "possibility of a First Amendment claim": A public employer can curtail her speech just as a private one could. But if she did speak as a citizen on a public matter, the public employer must demonstrate an adequate justification for treating the employee differently from any other member of the general public.

Like *Pickering, Abood* drew the constitutional line by analyzing the connection between the government's managerial interests and different kinds of expression. The Court [understood] collective bargaining, contract administration, and grievance adjustment (really, who would not?) as intimately tied to the workplace and employment relationship. The speech was about working conditions, pay, discipline, promotions, leave, vacations, and terminations; the speech occurred (almost always) in the workplace; and the speech was directed (at least mainly) to the employer. And so *Abood* allowed the government to mandate fees for collective bargaining—just as *Pickering* permits the government to regulate employees' speech on similar workplace matters.

Abood thus dovetailed with the Court's usual attitude in First Amendment cases toward the regulation of public employees' speech. That attitude is one of respect—even solicitude—for the government's prerogatives as an employer. And when the regulated expression concerns the terms and conditions of employment—the very stuff of the employment relationship—the government really cannot lose. Except that today the government does lose, in a first for the law. Now, the government can constitutionally adopt all policies regulating core workplace speech in pursuit of managerial goals—save this single one.

The majority claims it is not making a special and unjustified exception. First, the majority says, this case involves a "blanket" policy rather than an individualized employment decision. Second, the majority asserts, the regulation here involves compelling rather than restricting speech. And finally, the majority claims that even under the solicitous *Pickering* standard, the government should lose, because the speech here involves a matter of public concern and the government's managerial interests do not justify its regulation. The majority goes wrong at every turn.

First, this Court has applied the same basic approach whether a public employee challenges a general policy or an individualized decision. In fact, the majority cannot come up with any case in which we have *not* done so. All it can muster is one case in which *while* applying the *Pickering* test to a broad rule—barring any federal employee from accepting any payment for any speech or article on any topic—the Court noted that the policy's breadth would count against the government at the test's second step. See *United States v. Treasury Employees,* 513 U.S. 454 (1995). Nothing in *Treasury Employees* suggests that the Court defers only to ad hoc actions, and not to general rules, about public employee speech. That would be a perverse regime. So I would wager a small fortune that the next time a general rule governing public employee speech comes before us, we will dust off *Pickering*.

Second, the majority's distinction between compelling and restricting speech also lacks force. The majority posits that compelling speech always works a greater injury, and so always requires a greater justification. But the only case the majority cites for that reading of our precedent is possibly (thankfully) the most exceptional in our First Amendment annals: It involved the state forcing children to swear an oath contrary to their religious beliefs. [I]f anything, the First Amendment scales tip the opposite way when (as here) the government is not compelling actual speech, but instead compelling a subsidy that others will use for expression. So when a government mandates a speech subsidy from a public employee—here, we might think of it as levying a tax to support collective bargaining—it should get at least as much deference as when it restricts the employee's speech.

The majority mainly argues that union speech in collective bargaining is a matter of great public concern because it affects how public money is spent and addresses "other important matters" like teacher merit pay or tenure. The question is not, as the majority seems to think, whether the public is, or should be, interested in a government employee's speech. Instead, the question is whether that speech is about and directed to the workplace—as contrasted with the broader public square.

Consistent with that focus, speech about the terms and conditions of employment—the essential stuff of collective bargaining—has never survived *Pickering*'s first step. This Court has rejected all attempts by employees to make a "federal constitutional issue" out of basic "employment matters, including working conditions, pay, discipline, promotions, leave, vacations, and terminations." Of course, most of those issues have budgetary consequences: They affect how public money is spent. And some raise important non-budgetary disputes; teacher merit pay is a good example. But arguing about the terms of employment is still arguing about the terms of employment: The workplace remains both the context and the subject matter of the expression.

[T]he majority subverts all known principles of *stare decisis*. *Abood* is not just any precedent: It is embedded in the law (not to mention in the world) in a way not many decisions are. Over four decades, this Court has cited *Abood* favorably many times, and has affirmed and applied its central distinction between the costs of collective bargaining (which the government can charge to all employees) and those of political activities (which it cannot). [Here Justice Kagan cites seven Supreme Court cases upholding the chargeability of public sector fair share fees, compelled state bar dues, public university student activity fees, and commercial advertising for agricultural coops.]

[T]he majority suggests that *Abood* conflicts with "our political patronage decisions." *Ante*. But in fact those decisions strike a balance much like *Abood*'s. On the one hand, the Court has enabled governments to compel policymakers to support a political party, because that requirement (like fees for collective bargaining) can reasonably be thought to advance the interest in workplace effectiveness. On the other hand, the Court has barred governments from extending that rule to non-policymaking employees because that application (like fees for political campaigns) can't be thought to promote that interest; the government is instead trying to "leverage the employment relationship" to achieve other goals. So all that the majority has left is *Knox* and *Harris*. Dicta in those recent decisions indeed began the assault on *Abood* that has culminated today. But neither actually addressed the extent to which a public employer may regulate its own employees' speech. Relying on them is bootstrapping—and mocking *stare decisis*. Don't like a decision? Just throw some gratuitous criticisms into a couple of opinions and a few years later point to them as "special justifications."

The majority is likewise wrong to invoke "workability" as a reason for overruling *Abood*. Does *Abood* require drawing a line? Yes, between a union's collective-bargaining activities and its political activities. Is that line perfectly and pristinely precise, as the majority demands? Well, not quite that—but as exercises of constitutional line drawing go, *Abood* stands well above average. In the 40 years since *Abood,* this Court has had to resolve only a handful of cases raising questions about the distinction. To my knowledge, the circuit courts are not divided on any classification issue; neither are they issuing distress signals of the kind that sometimes prompt the Court to reverse a decision. There may be some gray areas (there always are), but in the mine run of cases, everyone knows the difference between politicking and collective bargaining. The majority cites some disagreement in two of the classification cases this Court decided—as if non-unanimity among Justices were something startling. And it notes that a dissenter in one of those cases called the Court's approach "malleable" and "not principled"—as though those weren't stock terms in dissenting vocabulary. If the kind of hand-wringing about blurry lines that the majority offers were enough to justify breaking with precedent, we might have to discard whole volumes of the U.S. Reports.

Twenty-two States, the District of Columbia, and Puerto Rico, plus another two States for police and firefighter unions, [some with] multiple statutory provisions [and] with variations for different categories of public employees will now need to come up with new ways—elaborated in new statutes—to structure relations between government employers and their workers. Still more, thousands of current contracts covering millions of workers provide for agency fees. The majority undoes bargains reached all over the country. It prevents the parties from fulfilling other commitments they have made based on those agreements. It does so knowing that many of the parties will have to revise (or redo) multiple contracts simultaneously. (New York City, for example, has agreed to agency fees in 144 contracts with 97 public-sector unions.) It does so knowing that those renegotiations will occur in an environment of legal uncertainty, as state governments scramble to enact new labor legislation. It does so with no real clue of what will happen next—of how its action will alter public-sector labor relations. It does so even though the government services affected— policing, firefighting, teaching, transportation, sanitation (and more)— affect the quality of life of tens of millions of Americans. [T]he majority's ruling does more than advance by a few years a future renegotiation (though even that would be significant). In most cases, it commands new bargaining over how to replace a term that the parties never expected to change.

There is no sugarcoating today's opinion. The majority overthrows a decision entrenched in this Nation's law—and in its economic life—for over 40 years. As a result, it prevents the American people, acting through their state and local officials, from making important choices about workplace governance. And it does so by weaponizing the First Amendment, in a way that unleashes judges, now and in the future, to intervene in economic and regulatory policy. The majority has overruled *Abood* for no exceptional or special reason, but because it never liked the decision. It has overruled *Abood* because it wanted to.

Because, that is, it wanted to pick the winning side in what should be—and until now, has been—an energetic policy debate. Today, that healthy—that democratic—debate ends. The majority has adjudged who should prevail.

And maybe most alarming, the majority has chosen the winners by turning the First Amendment into a sword, and using it against workaday economic and regulatory policy. Today is not the first time the Court has wielded the First Amendment in such an aggressive way. See, *e.g.,* *National Institute of Family and Life Advocates v. Becerra* (invalidating a law requiring medical and counseling facilities to provide relevant information to users); *Sorrell v. IMS Health Inc.,* 564 U.S. 552 (2011) (striking down a law that restricted pharmacies from selling various data). And it threatens not to be the last. Speech is everywhere—a part of every human activity (employment, health care, securities trading, you name it). For that reason, almost all economic and regulatory policy affects or touches speech. So the majority's road runs long. And at every stop are black-robed rulers overriding citizens' choices.

NOTES

1.   *Is this a matter of compelled speech?* In what respect is the dissenting employee's right to free speech curtailed by the union's use of money to advocate positions with which he disagrees?

2.   *What is the future of exclusive representation?* The majority suggests that a public employee union facing a large number of free riders could elect not to represent them in grievances or not to represent them at all. Assuming

state law would allow that choice (which will need to be determined in the new constitutional framework *Janus* created), what would you advise a union or a government agency to consider before negotiating such a contract?

3. *Should unions have the choice whether to bargain for members only?* If fair share fees subsidize constitutionally protected speech in the public sector because all government employee wages and working conditions raise issues of public policy, should exclusive representation be unconstitutional? Federal courts of appeals have thus far rejected calls to find exclusive representation unconstitutional in the public sector. *Hill v. Serv. Employees Int'l Union*, 850 F.3d 861 (7th Cir. 2016); *D'Agostino v. Baker*, 812 F.3d 240 (1st Cir.), *cert. denied*, 136 S. Ct. 2473 (2016); *Jarvis v. Cuomo*, 660 Fed. Appx. 72 (2d Cir. 2016), *cert. denied*, 137 S. Ct. 1204 (2017). On the constitutional issues in the new wave of challenges to exclusive representation, see Cynthia Estlund, *Are Unions a Constitutional Anomaly?* 114 Mich. L. Rev. 169 (2015).

4. *Payment directly to the union?* Could a state re-write its public sector labor law to provide that the union's cost of representing workers will be paid directly by the government to the union? If the money never goes into the employees' paycheck (and then back out again in the form of union dues or fees), can the entire First Amendment compelled speech issue be avoided? *See* Benjamin I. Sachs, *Agency Fees and the First Amendment*, 131 Harv. L. Rev. 1046 (2018). Scholars disagree about the wisdom and viability of post-*Janus* solutions to the unions' collective action problems. *See* Catherine L. Fisk & Martin H. Malin, *After Janus*, 107 Cal. L. Rev. ___ (forthcoming 2019); Aaron Tang, *Life After Janus*, 119 Colum. L. Rev. ___ (forthcoming 2019).

5. *What about the First Amendment rights of unions and union supporters?* The majority in *Janus* says that unions cannot discriminate in contract negotiation and grievance arbitration against free-riding nonmembers. If the duty of fair representation compels them to continue to represent the nonpayers and, therefore, provide them free legal services, are the First Amendment rights of unions or union members infringed? Why does it violate the First Amendment rights of nonmembers to pay for services of members (as well as themselves) but not violate the rights of members to pay for services for nonmembers? *See* Catherine L. Fisk & Margaux Poueymirou, *Harris v. Quinn and the Contradictions of Compelled Speech*, 48 Loyola L.A. L. Rev. 439 (2015).

6. *Should dissenting shareholders have the same rights as dissenting employees?* The debate about union expenditure of dues for political purposes sometimes turns on whether one regards union political expenditures as being akin to corporate political expenditures. In what respects is the method by which unions raise and spend money on politics similar to the method by which corporations raise and spend money on politics. In what respects is it different? Many public employees have pension plans in which, as a condition of employment, the state takes a portion of their wages and either directly invests it, or requires it to be invested, in shares of stock in publicly traded corporations. Under *Citizens United*, this money is now available for corporate political activity including the direct support of particular candidates some

public employees might not support. Currently there are no reporting requirements so that the employees can know to what political ends their retirement savings might be used and there are no opt out procedure so they can avoid such use. Isn't this forced association in violation of the First Amendment? Benjamin I. Sachs, *Unions, Corporations, and Political Opt-Out Rights After Citizens United*, 112 Colum. L. Rev. 800 (2012). Should we require corporations to account for political spending in much the same way we require unions to account for such spending? Could we give dissenting shareholders the right to opt out of political expenditures, and receive an annual dividend equal to the percent the firm corporations spend on politics, in much the same way we allow dissenting employees to opt out of union political spending? Would mutual funds comprised of shares that opt-out of political spending be an attractive retirement investment?

4. UNION SECURITY UNDER THE NLRA

Outside public sector labor relations, in which a union contract requiring a worker to pay dues to a union is state action, there is no obvious reason why compelling worker membership or financial support for a union should raise any constitutional issues because a collective bargaining agreement is a private agreement between a private employer and a union. As we saw above, however, the Supreme Court suggested in *Hanson* and held in *Street* that the Railway Labor Act's preemption of state right-to-work laws imbued the union security provisions in railroad industry collective bargaining agreements with the aura of state action. (That is an expansive approach to the state action doctrine that the Court shortly thereafter repudiated. But it never overruled *Hanson* or *Street*.) Nevertheless, the Supreme Court construed the NLRA to require unions to allow dissenting employees to refuse to join the union and to refuse to pay dues to support unions' political activities. The case in which it created a statutory restriction on compulsory union membership follows.

NLRB v. GENERAL MOTORS CORP.
373 U.S. 734 (1963)

JUSTICE WHITE delivered the opinion of the Court:

[The United Automobile Workers proposed an agency fee arrangement for the Indiana plants in its multi-plant bargaining unit (union shop clauses are illegal under Indiana law). The UAW contract with GM in other states required maintenance of membership and provided for a union shop. Under the UAW proposal for Indiana, the Court explained,

> Employees choosing not to join would make the required payments and, in accordance with union custom, would share in union expenditures for strike benefits, educational and retired member benefits, and union publications and promotional activities, but they would not be entitled to attend union meetings,

vote upon ratification of agreements negotiated by the union, or have a voice in the internal affairs of the union. The respondent made no counterproposal, but replied to the union's letter that the proposed agreement would violate the National Labor Relations Act and that respondent must therefore "respectfully decline to comply with your request for a meeting" to bargain over the proposal.

In essence, GM's position was that the proviso to section 8(a)(3) of the NLRA allowed a union shop, but nothing less than that, and if a union shop provision was unconstitutional (or illegal in any state), then nothing short of a union shop provision was permissible.]

We find nothing in the legislative history of the Act indicating that Congress intended the amended proviso to § 8(a)(3) to validate only the union shop and simultaneously to abolish, in addition to the closed shop, all other union-security arrangements permissible under state law. There is much to be said for the Board's view that, if Congress desired in the Wagner Act to permit a closed or union shop and in the Taft-Hartley Act the union shop, then it also intended to preserve the status of less vigorous, less compulsory contracts which demanded less adherence to the union.

[T]he 1947 [Taft-Hartley Act] amendments not only abolished the closed shop but also made significant alterations in the meaning of "membership" for the purposes of union-security contracts. Under the second proviso to § 8(a)(3), the burdens of membership upon which employment may be conditioned are expressly limited to the payment of initiation fees and monthly dues. It is permissible to condition employment upon membership, but membership, insofar as it has significance to employment rights, may in turn be conditioned only upon payment of fees and dues. "Membership" as a condition of employment is whittled down to its financial core.

The proposal for requiring the payment of dues and fees imposes no burdens not imposed by a permissible union shop contract and compels the performance of only those duties of membership which are enforceable by discharge under a union shop arrangement. If an employee in a union shop unit refuses to respect any union-imposed obligations other than the duty to pay dues and fees, and membership in the union is therefore denied or terminated, the condition of "membership" for § 8(a)(3) purposes is nevertheless satisfied and the employee may not be discharged for nonmembership even though he is not a formal member. Of course, if the union chooses to extend membership even though the employee will meet only the minimum financial burden, and refuses to support or "join" the union in any other affirmative way, the employee may have to become a "member" under a union shop contract, in the sense that the union may be able to place him on its rolls. The agency shop arrangement proposed here removes that choice from the union and places the option of membership in the employee while still requiring the same monetary support as does the union shop. Such a difference between the union and agency shop may be of great importance in some contexts, but for present purposes it is more formal than real. To the extent that it has any significance at all it serves, rather than violates, the desire of Congress to reduce the evils of compulsory unionism while allowing financial support for the bargaining agent.

* * *

Having held in *General Motors* that private sector employees cannot be required to join a union, for twenty-five years the law was settled that private sector employees could not be required to join a union but could be required to pay full dues, even if the union spent some portion of the revenue from dues on political activity, unless the employee worked in a state that had enacted a so-called right-to-work law prohibiting any payment of fees. In the following case, the Court extended to all employees covered by the NLRA the right it had previously created in *Street* and *Abood* to pay less than full dues.

COMMUNICATION WORKERS OF AMERICA V. BECK
487 U.S. 735 (1988)

[The CWA had negotiated a union-security clause in the collective bargaining agreement with AT&T under which all represented employees, including those who did not wish to become union members, must pay the union "agency fees" in amounts equal to the periodic dues paid by union members. Twenty employees sued, alleging that the union's expenditure of their fees on activities such as organizing the employees of other employers, lobbying for labor legislation, and participating in social, charitable, and political events violated petitioners' duty of fair representation, § 8(a)(3) of the NLRA, the First Amendment, and various common-law fiduciary duties. The Court avoided the First Amendment issue by interpreting the Taft-Hartley Act amendments to the NLRA to prohibit the expenditure of dues on activities not germane to collective bargaining.]

JUSTICE BRENNAN delivered the opinion of the Court:

Petitioners claim that the union-security provisions of the RLA and NLRA can and should be read differently in light of the vastly different history of unionism in the industries the two statutes regulate. Thus they note the long-standing tradition of voluntary unionism in the railway industry prior to 1951 and the fact that in 1934 Congress had expressly endorsed an "open shop" policy in the RLA. The history of union security in industries governed by the NLRA was precisely the opposite: under the Wagner Act of 1935, all forms of compulsory unionism, including the closed shop, were permitted. Petitioners accordingly argue that the inroads

Congress made in 1947 on the policy of compulsory unionism were likewise limited, and were designed to remedy only those carefully defined abuses of the union shop system that Congress had expressly identified. Because agreements requiring the payment of uniform dues were not among these specified abuses, petitioners contend that § 8(a)(3) cannot plausibly be read to prohibit the collection of fees in excess of those necessary to cover the costs of collective bargaining.

We find this argument unpersuasive. Congress did not set out in 1947 simply to tinker in some limited fashion with the NLRA's authorization of union-security agreements. Rather, to the extent Congress preserved the status quo, it did so because of the considerable evidence adduced at congressional hearings indicating that such agreements promoted stability by eliminating free riders, and Congress accordingly gave unions the power to contract to meet that problem while withholding from unions the power to cause the discharge of employees for any other reason.

[H]owever much union-security practices may have differed between the railway and NLRA-governed industries prior to 1951, it is abundantly clear that Congress itself understood its actions in 1947 and 1951 to have placed these respective industries on an equal footing insofar as compulsory unionism was concerned.

Petitioners also deem it highly significant that prior to 1947 unions rather typically used their members' dues for a variety of purposes in addition to meeting the costs of collective bargaining, and yet Congress, which was presumably well aware of the practice, in no way limited the uses to which unions could put fees collected from nonmembers. The short answer to this argument is that Congress was equally well aware of the same practices by railway unions. We see no reason to give greater weight to Congress' silence in the NLRA than we did in the RLA, particularly where such silence is again perfectly consistent with the rationale underlying § 8(a)(3): prohibiting the collection of fees that are not germane to representational activities would have been redundant if Congress understood § 8(a)(3) simply to enable unions to charge nonmembers only for those activities that actually benefit them.

We conclude that § 8(a)(3), like its statutory equivalent, § 2, Eleventh of the RLA, authorizes the exaction of only those fees and dues necessary to performing the duties of an exclusive representative of the employees in dealing with the employer on labor-management issues.

JUSTICE KENNEDY took no part in the consideration or decision of this case.

JUSTICE BLACKMUN, with whom JUSTICE O'CONNOR and JUSTICE SCALIA join, concurring in part and dissenting in part:

The Court's conclusion that § 8(a)(3) prohibits petitioners from requiring respondents to pay fees for purposes other than those "germane" to collective bargaining, contract administration, and grievance adjustment simply cannot be derived from the plain language of the statute. In effect, the Court accepts respondents' contention that the words "dues" and "fees," as used in § 8(a)(3), refer not to the periodic amount a union charges its members but to the portion of that amount that the union expends on statutory collective bargaining. Not only is this reading implausible as a matter of simple English usage, but it is also contradicted by the decisions of this Court and of the NLRB interpreting the section. Section 8(a)(3) does not speak of "dues" and "fees" that employees covered by a union-security agreement may be required to tender to their union representative; rather, the section speaks only of "the periodic dues and the initiation fees *uniformly required as a condition of acquiring or retaining membership*" (emphasis added). Thus, the section, by its terms, defines "periodic dues" and "initiation fees" as those dues and fees "uniformly required" of all members, not as a portion of full dues. By virtue of § 8(a)(3), such dues may be required from *any* employee under a union-security agreement. Nothing in § 8(a)(3) limits, or even addresses, the purposes to which a union may devote the moneys collected pursuant to such an agreement.

The NLRA does not share the RLA's underlying policy, which propelled the Court's interpretation of § 2, Eleventh in *Street*. Indeed, the history of the NLRA points in the opposite direction: the original policy of the Wagner Act was to permit all forms of union-security agreements, and such agreements were commonplace in 1947. [T]he 1947 amendments to § 8(a)(3) were designed to make an inroad into a preexisting policy of the absolute freedom of private parties under federal law to negotiate union-security agreements.

NOTES

1.   *Why do union security and union dues matter?* In *General Motors* and *Beck*, the Supreme Court decided the NLRA limited the ability of unions and employers to agree to union security and to establish contractual mechanisms obligating employees in the bargaining unit to provide financial support to the union in the form of dues. Can you understand why private sector union security and union dues have been such an extraordinarily important and contentious issue to firms, employees, and unions, and even to the Republican and Democratic Parties?

2.   *Private sector union security after* Janus. Does the Supreme Court's opinion in *Janus* offer any guidance about the continuing legality of agency fee agreements in the private sector?

3.   *Is union security bad for unions?* It has been suggested that elimination of any form of union security agreement from a collective bargaining relationship is not all bad for unions because an open shop rule forces unions to be more attentive to the interests of their members and to communicate more effectively with them; in essence, the argument goes, the absence of union security forces the union to be more like a social movement

and less like an institution. *See* Michael M. Oswalt, *Note, The Grand Bargain: Revitalizing Labor Through NLRA Reform and Radical Workplace Relations*, 57 Duke L.J. 691 (2007). Do you agree?

A NOTE ON THE EFFECT OF RIGHT-TO-WORK LAWS ON UNION MEMBERS

In the 28 states that prohibit unions and employers from agreeing to require employees to pay any fees or dues to the union for the services the union is compelled by the duty of fair representation to provide, the union is obligated to provide contract negotiation and administration services to nonmembers for free. The union is required to represent all workers in the bargaining unit equally, and may not discriminate between those who become union members and those who do not. The duty extends not just to collective bargaining—where the union cannot bargain terms that favor members over nonmembers—but to disciplinary matters as well. The union must grieve and arbitrate on behalf of nonmembers just as zealously (and, more to the point, as expensively) as they do on behalf of members. In *non*-right-to-work states, federal law enables unions to require that nonmembers pay for the services they receive. In right-to-work states, on the other hand, the union still bears the same federal duty to represent nonmembers, but state law precludes a requirement that the nonmembers pay for that representation.

Two scholars have argued that the confluence of state law allowing workers to refuse to pay for union representation and federal law requiring the union nonetheless to provide equal representation to the non-paying nonmember creates a serious inequity because it forces union members to subsidize free legal services for their nonunion coworkers. *See* Catherine Fisk & Benjamin Sachs, *Restoring Equity in Right to Work Law*, 4 U.C. Irvine L. Rev. 859 (2014). They propose three legal approaches to eliminate the inequity.

First, they argue that section 14(b) of the NLRA—the provision in the federal statute that allows states to pass right-to-work laws—should not be read to allow states to prohibit agreements under which nonmembers are compelled to pay dues and fees *lower* than those required of members.

Second, in any state where employees are permitted to avoid paying anything to the union, Fisk and Sachs argue that federal law ought to relax the requirement of exclusive representation and allow unions to organize, bargain on behalf of, and represent only those workers who affirmatively choose to become members. In brief, if workers exercise their right not to be represented by a union and not to pay for the union's services, federal law ought to allow the union to construct a bargaining unit that does not include those workers. This proposal would implement a members-only bargaining regime in right-to-work states.

Third, they suggest the Board could maintain the principle of exclusive representation in right-to-work states but change slightly the union's duties with respect to nonmembers in those states. In particular, the NLRB should abandon its rule forbidding unions from charging nonmembers a fee for representation services that the union provides directly and individually to the nonmember. Under the Board's current rule—which is dictated neither by statute nor judicial interpretation—a union violates § 8(b)(1)(A) of the federal law if it insists that nonmembers pay for representation in disciplinary matters, even in right-to-work states where the nonmember has a right not to pay for the representation. *See Furniture Workers Div.*, 291 N.L.R.B. 182 (1988); *Columbus Area Local, Am. Postal Workers Union*, 277 N.L.R.B. 541 (1985); *Int'l Ass'n of Machinists, Local 697*, 223 N.L.R.B. 832 (1976). In their view, in right-to-work states, it ought to be within a union's discretion to charge non-paying nonmembers if those nonmembers wish to have the union represent them in disciplinary matters. Unlike the NLRB's current position, they believe that charging someone the fair price of a union service does *not* coerce that person, within the meaning of § 8(b)(1)(A), to become a union member or restrain his or her ability to refuse to support the union.

Do you agree with Professors Fisk and Sachs? If so, which of their proposed changes in the law seems most sensible? If not, why do you disagree? Nebraska, a right-to-work state, has adopted in its public sector labor law the third approach that Professors Fisk and Sachs propose. Under Nebraska law, "[a]ny employee may choose his or her own representative in any grievance or legal action regardless of whether or not an exclusive collective-bargaining agent has been certified. If an employee who is not a member of the labor organization chooses to have legal representation from the labor organization in any grievance or legal action, such employee shall reimburse the labor organization for his or her pro rata share of the actual legal fees and court costs incurred by the labor organization in representing the employee in such grievance or legal action." Neb. Rev. Stat. 48–838. Anecdotal reports of the experience of public school teachers in Nebraska suggests that many are union members and some speculate it is because they find it impossible to find private lawyers to handle their grievance arbitrations at a price they can afford and find that paying union dues or agency fees is more affordable than paying a fee to either the union or to a private lawyer for contract administration services.

In April 2015, the NLRB invited briefing on whether to abandon its rule forbidding unions from charging nonmembers in right-to-work states (*i.e.*, those who receive representation services without paying anything) a fee for representation services provided individually to the nonmember, such as in grievance handling and arbitration. *United Steel Local 1192 (Buckeye Florida Corp.)*, No. 12-CB-109654. The matter settled without the issue being resolved. If the number of right-to-work jurisdictions grows and union finances fall, the issue may surface again.

* * *

Issues involving union security and agency fee provisions under the NLRA fall into two categories. The first category involves the administration of the fee provision. This issue is addressed in the following case. The second category concerns which expenditures are chargeable to dissenting fee payers. That issue will be covered afterward.

CHICAGO TEACHERS UNION V. HUDSON
475 U.S. 292 (1986)

JUSTICE STEVENS delivered the opinion of the Court:

The Chicago Teachers Union has acted as the exclusive collective-bargaining representative of the Board's educational employees continuously since 1967. Approximately 95% of the 27,500 employees in the bargaining unit are members of the Union. Until December 1982, the Union members' dues financed the entire cost of the Union's collective bargaining and contract administration. Nonmembers received the benefits of the Union's representation without making any financial contribution to its cost.

In an attempt to solve this "free rider" problem, the Union made several proposals for a "fair share fee" clause in the labor contract. Because the Illinois School Code did not expressly authorize such a provision, the Board rejected these proposals until the Illinois General Assembly amended the School Code in 1981. In the following year, the Chicago Teachers Union and the Chicago Board of Education entered into an agreement requiring the Board to deduct "proportionate share payments" from the paychecks of nonmembers.

For the 1982–1983 school year, the Union determined that the "proportionate share" assessed on nonmembers was 95% of union dues. At that time, the union dues were $17.35 per month for teachers and $12.15 per month for other covered employees; the corresponding deduction from the nonmembers' checks thus amounted to $16.48 and $11.54 for each of the 10 months that dues were payable.

Union officials computed the 95% fee on the basis of the Union's financial records for the fiscal year ending on June 30, 1982. They identified expenditures unrelated to collective bargaining and contract administration (which they estimated as $188,549.82). They divided this amount by the Union's income for the year ($4,103,701.58) to produce a percentage of 4.6%; the figure was then rounded off to 5% to provide a "cushion" to cover any inadvertent errors.

The Union also established a procedure for considering objections by nonmembers. Before the deduction was made, the nonmember could not raise any objection. After the deduction was made, a nonmember could object to the "proportionate share" figure by writing to the Union President within 30 days after the first payroll deduction. The objection then would meet a three-stage procedure. First, the Union's Executive Committee would consider the objection and notify the objector within 30 days of its decision. Second, if the objector disagreed with that decision and appealed within another 30 days, the Union's Executive Board would consider the objection. Third, if the objector continued to protest after the Executive Board decision, the Union President would select an arbitrator from a list maintained by the Illinois Board of Education. The Union would pay for the arbitration, and, if there were multiple objections, they could be consolidated. If an objection was sustained at any stage of the procedure, the remedy would be an immediate reduction in the amount of future deductions for all nonmembers and a rebate for the objector.

In October 1982, the Union formally requested the Board to begin making deductions and advised it that a hearing procedure had been established for nonmembers' objections. The Board accepted the Union's 95% determination without questioning its method of calculation and without asking to review any of the records supporting it. The Board began to deduct the fee from the paychecks of nonmembers in December 1982. The Board did not provide the nonmembers with any explanation of the calculation, or of the Union's procedures. The Union did undertake certain informational efforts. It asked its member delegates at all schools to distribute flyers, display posters, inform nonmembers of the deductions, and invite nonmembers to join the Union with an amnesty for past fines. It also described the deduction and the protest procedures in the December issue of the Union newspaper, which was distributed to nonmembers.

Three nonmembers—Annie Lee Hudson, K. Celeste Campbell, and Walter Sherrill—sent identical letters of protest to the Union stating that they believed the Union was using part of their salary for purposes unrelated to collective bargaining and demanding that the deduction be reduced. A fourth nonmember—Beverly Underwood—objected to any deduction from her paycheck. The Union's response to each of the four briefly explained how the proportionate-share fee had been calculated, described the objection procedure, enclosed a copy of the Union Implementation Plan, and concluded with the advice that "any objection you may file" would be processed in compliance with that procedure. None of the letters was referred to the Executive Committee. Only Hudson wrote a second letter; her request for detailed financial information was answered with an invitation to make an appointment for an "informational conference" at the Union's office, at which she could review the Union's financial records. The four nonmembers made no further effort to invoke the Union procedures; instead, they challenged the new procedure in court.

The question presented in this case is whether the procedure used by the Chicago Teachers Union and approved by the Chicago Board of Education adequately protects the basic distinction drawn in *Abood*. "[T]he objective must be to devise a way of preventing compulsory subsidization of ideological activity by employees who object thereto without restricting the Union's ability to require every employee to contribute to the cost of collective-bargaining activities."

Procedural safeguards are necessary to achieve this objective for two reasons. First, although the government interest in labor peace is strong enough to support an "agency shop" notwithstanding its limited infringement on nonunion employees' constitutional rights, the fact that those rights are protected by the First Amendment requires that the procedure be carefully tailored to minimize the infringement. Second, the nonunion employee—the individual whose First Amendment rights are being affected—must have a fair opportunity to identify the impact of the governmental action on his interests and to assert a meritorious First Amendment claim.

The procedure that was initially adopted by the Union and considered by the District Court contained three fundamental flaws. First, a remedy which merely offers dissenters the possibility of a rebate does not avoid the risk that dissenters' funds may be used temporarily for an improper purpose. "[T]he Union should not be permitted to exact a service fee from nonmembers without first establishing a procedure which will avoid the risk that their funds will be used, even temporarily, to finance ideological activities unrelated to collective bargaining." *Abood*, 431 U.S. at 244 (concurring opinion). The amount at stake for each individual dissenter does not diminish this concern. For, whatever the amount, the quality of respondents' interest in not being compelled to subsidize the propagation of political or ideological views that they oppose is clear.

Second, the "advance reduction of dues" was inadequate because it provided nonmembers with inadequate information about the basis for the proportionate share. In *Abood*, we reiterated that the nonunion employee has the burden of raising an objection, but that the union retains the burden of proof: " 'Since the unions possess the facts and records from which the proportion of political to total union expenditures can reasonably be calculated, basic considerations of fairness compel that they, not the individual employees, bear the burden of proving such proportion.' " Basic considerations of fairness, as well as concern for the First Amendment rights at stake, also dictate that the potential objectors be given sufficient information to gauge the propriety of the union's fee. Leaving the nonunion employees in the dark about the source of the figure for the agency fee— and requiring them to object in order to receive information—does not adequately protect the careful distinctions drawn in *Abood*.

In this case, the original information given to the nonunion employees was inadequate. Instead of identifying the expenditures for collective bargaining and contract administration that had been provided for the benefit of nonmembers as well as members—and for which nonmembers as well as members can fairly be charged a fee—the Union identified the amount that it admittedly had expended for purposes that did not benefit dissenting nonmembers. An acknowledgment that nonmembers would not be required to pay any part of 5% of the Union's total annual expenditures was not an adequate disclosure of the reasons why they were required to pay their share of 95%.

Finally, the original Union procedure was also defective because it did not provide for a reasonably prompt decision by an impartial decision-maker. The nonunion employee, whose First Amendment rights are affected by the agency shop itself and who bears the burden of objecting, is entitled to have his objections addressed in an expeditious, fair, and objective manner.[20]

The Union's procedure does not meet this requirement. As the Seventh Circuit observed, the "most conspicuous feature of the procedure is that from start to finish it is entirely controlled by the union, which is an interested party, since it is the recipient of the agency fees paid by the dissenting employees." 743 F.2d at 1194–1195. The initial consideration of the agency fee is made by Union officials, and the first two steps of the review procedure (the Union Executive Committee and Executive Board) consist of Union officials. The third step—review by a Union-selected arbitrator—is also inadequate because the selection represents the Union's unrestricted choice from the state list.[21]

The Union has not only created an escrow of 100% of the contributions exacted from the respondents, but has also advised us that it would not object to the entry of a judgment compelling it to maintain an escrow system in the future. The Union takes the position that because a 100% escrow completely avoids the risk that dissenters' contributions could be used improperly, it eliminates any valid constitutional objection to the procedure and thereby provides an adequate remedy in this case. We reject this argument.

Although the Union's self-imposed remedy eliminates the risk that nonunion employees' contributions may be temporarily used for impermissible purposes, the procedure remains flawed in two respects. It does not provide an adequate explanation for the advance reduction of dues, and it does not provide a reasonably prompt decision by an impartial decision-maker. We reiterate that these characteristics are required

---

[20] We reject the Union's suggestion that the availability of ordinary judicial remedies is sufficient. This contention misses the point. Since the agency shop itself is a significant impingement on First Amendment rights, the government and union have a responsibility to provide procedures that minimize that impingement and that facilitate a nonunion employee's ability to protect his rights. We are considering here the procedural adequacy of the agency shop arrangement itself; we presume that the courts remain available as the ultimate protectors of constitutional rights. Clearly, however, if a State chooses to provide extraordinarily swift judicial review for these challenges, that review would satisfy the requirement of a reasonably prompt decision by an impartial decision-maker.

[21] We do not agree, however, with the Seventh Circuit that a full-dress administrative hearing, with evidentiary safeguards, is part of the "constitutional minimum." Indeed, we think that an expeditious arbitration might satisfy the requirement of a reasonably prompt decision by an impartial decision-maker, so long as the arbitrator's selection did not represent the Union's unrestricted choice. In contrast to the Union's procedure here, selection of an arbitrator frequently does not represent one party's unrestricted choice from a list of state-approved arbitrators.

because the agency shop itself impinges on the nonunion employees' First Amendment interests, and because the nonunion employee has the burden of objection. The appropriately justified advance reduction and the prompt, impartial decision-maker are necessary to minimize both the impingement and the burden.

We need not hold, however, that a 100% escrow is constitutionally required. Such a remedy has the serious defect of depriving the Union of access to some escrowed funds that it is unquestionably entitled to retain. If, for example, the original disclosure by the Union had included a certified public accountant's verified breakdown of expenditures, including some categories that no dissenter could reasonably challenge, there would be no reason to escrow the portion of the nonmember's fees that would be represented by those categories. On the record before us, there is no reason to believe that anything approaching a 100% "cushion" to cover the possibility of mathematical errors would be constitutionally required. Nor can we decide how the proper contribution that might be made by an independent audit, in advance, coupled with adequate notice, might reduce the size of any appropriate escrow.

NOTES

1.   *Arbitration is not required.* In *Air Line Pilots Ass'n v. Miller*, 523 U.S. 866 (1998), the Court held that a dissenting fee payer need not institute a proceeding before the neutral decision-maker required by *Hudson* before filing suit in court challenging the union's administration of the agency fee provision.

2.   *Union notice obligations.* In *Philadelphia Sheraton Corp.*, 136 N.L.R.B. 888 (1962), the Board held that the union must notify an employee how much dues or fees are, how dues or fees are computed, the date by which the employee must pay them, and that the employee will be terminated pursuant to the union security provision of the collective bargaining agreement if he fails to pay. The Board has taken the position that the burden is on the union to prove it gave proper notice.

3.   *Public Sector v. Private Sector* Hudson *notices.* After *Janus*, it would appear that public sector *Hudson* notices should advise union-represented employees of their rights to resign their union membership and to pay nothing to the union, but issues over chargeability of particular expenses may no longer arise because nonmembers can no longer be required to pay fees. *Hudson* notices in the private sector in states that still allow fair share fees must continue to provide notice as described in *Hudson*.

* * *

The second category of issues arising under agency fee provisions concerns the allocation of union expenses as either political (and thus not chargeable to dissenting workers) or germane to contract negotiation and administration (and thus chargeable). In the following case, the Court attempted to explain why certain expenditures are on each side of the line.

ELLIS V. BROTHERHOOD OF RAILWAY CLERKS
466 U.S. 435 (1984)

JUSTICE WHITE delivered the opinion of the Court:

Petitioners are present or former clerical employees of Western [Airlines] who objected to the use of their compelled dues for specified union activities. They [also] contend . . . that they can be compelled to contribute no more than their pro rata share of the expenses of negotiating agreements and settling grievances with Western Airlines [and that the union's practice of collecting agency fees equivalent to full union dues and then rebating a portion to objecting employees is illegal.]

By exacting and using full dues, then refunding months later the portion that it was not allowed to exact in the first place, the union effectively charges the employees for activities that are outside the scope of the statutory authorization. The cost to the employee is, of course, much less than if the money was never returned, but this is a difference of degree only. The harm would be reduced were the union to pay interest on the amount refunded, but respondents did not do so. Even then the union obtains an involuntary loan for purposes to which the employee objects.

The only justification for this union borrowing would be administrative convenience. But there are readily available alternatives, such as advance reduction of dues and/or interest-bearing escrow accounts, that place only the slightest additional burden, if any, on the union. Given the existence of acceptable alternatives, the union cannot be allowed to commit dissenters' funds to improper uses even temporarily. A rebate scheme reduces but does not eliminate the statutory violation.

We remain convinced that Congress' essential justification for authorizing the union shop was the desire to eliminate free riders— employees in the bargaining unit on whose behalf the union was obliged to perform its statutory functions, but who refused to contribute to the cost thereof. Only a union that is certified as the exclusive bargaining agent is authorized to negotiate a contract requiring all employees to become members of or to make contributions to the union. Until such a contract is executed, no dues or fees may be collected from objecting employees who are not members of the union; and by the same token, any obligatory payments required by a contract authorized by § 2, Eleventh terminate if the union ceases to be the exclusive bargaining agent. Hence, when employees such as petitioners object to being burdened with particular union expenditures, the test must be whether the challenged expenditures are necessarily or reasonably incurred for the purpose of performing the duties of an exclusive representative of the employees in dealing with the employer on labor-management issues. Under this standard, objecting employees may be compelled to pay their fair share of not only the direct costs of negotiating and administering a collective-bargaining contract and of settling grievances and disputes, but also the expenses of activities or undertakings normally or reasonably employed to implement or effectuate the duties of the union as exclusive representative of the employees in the bargaining unit.

With these considerations in mind, we turn to the particular expenditures for which petitioners insist they may not be charged.

1. **Conventions.** Every four years, BRAC holds a national convention at which the members elect officers, establish bargaining goals and priorities, and formulate overall union policy. We have very little trouble in holding that petitioners must help defray the costs of these conventions. Surely if a union is to perform its statutory functions, it must maintain its corporate or associational existence, must elect officers to manage and carry on its affairs, and may consult its members about overall bargaining goals and policy. Conventions such as those at issue here are normal events about which Congress was thoroughly informed and seem to us to be essential to the union's discharge of its duties as bargaining agent. We cannot fault it for choosing to elect its officers at a convention rather than by referendum.

2. **Social Activities.** Approximately 0.7% of Grand Lodge expenditures go toward purchasing refreshments for union business meetings and occasional social activities. These activities are formally open to nonmember employees. Petitioners insist that these expenditures are entirely unrelated to the union's function as collective-bargaining representative and therefore could not be charged to them. While these affairs are not central to collective bargaining, they are sufficiently related to it to be charged to all employees. As the Court of Appeals noted, "[t]hese small expenditures are important to the union's members because they bring about harmonious working relationships, promote closer ties among employees, and create a more pleasant environment for union meetings."

3. **Publications.** The Grand Lodge puts out a monthly magazine, the Railway Clerk/interchange, paid for out of the union treasury. The magazine's contents are varied and include articles about negotiations, contract demands, strikes, unemployment and health benefits, proposed or recently enacted legislation, general news, products the union is boycotting, and recreational and social activities. The Court of Appeals found that the magazine "is the union's primary means of communicating information concerning collective bargaining, contract administration, and employees' rights to employees represented by BRAC." Under the union's rebate policy, objecting employees are not charged for that portion of the magazine devoted to "political causes." The rebate is figured by calculating the number of lines that are devoted to political issues as a proportion of the total number of lines.

The union must have a channel for communicating with the employees, including the objecting ones, about its activities. Congress can be assumed to have known that union funds go toward union publications; it is an accepted and basic union activity. The magazine is important to the union in carrying out its representational obligations and a reasonable way of reporting to its constituents.

Respondents' limitation on the publication costs charged [to] objecting employees is an important one, however. If the union cannot spend dissenters' funds for a particular activity, it has no justification for spending their funds for writing about that activity. By the same token, the Act surely allows it to charge objecting employees for reporting to them about those activities it can charge them for doing.

4. **Organizing.** The Court of Appeals found that organizing expenses could be charged to objecting employees because organizing efforts are aimed toward a stronger union, which in turn would be more successful at the bargaining table. Despite this attenuated connection with collective bargaining, we think such expenditures are outside Congress' authorization. Several considerations support this conclusion.

First, the notion that § 2, Eleventh would be a tool for the expansion of overall union power appears nowhere in the legislative history. Nor was any claim seriously advanced that the union shop was necessary to hold or increase union membership. Thus, organizational efforts were not what Congress aimed to enhance by authorizing the union shop.

Second, where a union shop provision is in place and enforced, all employees in the relevant unit are already organized. By definition, therefore, organizing expenses are spent on employees outside the collective-bargaining unit already represented. Using dues exacted from an objecting employee to recruit members among workers outside the bargaining unit can afford only the most attenuated benefits to collective bargaining on behalf of the dues payer.

Third, the free-rider rationale does not extend this far. The image of the smug, self-satisfied nonmember, stirring up resentment by enjoying benefits earned through other employees' time and money, is completely out of place when it comes to the union's overall organizing efforts. If one accepts that what is good for the union is good for the employees, a proposition petitioners would strenuously deny, then it may be that employees will ultimately ride for free on the union's organizing efforts outside the bargaining unit. But the free rider Congress had in mind was the employee the union was required to represent and from whom it could not withhold benefits obtained for its members. Nonbargaining unit organizing is not directed at that employee. Organizing money is spent on people who are not union members, and only in the most distant way works to the benefit of those already paying dues. Any free-rider problem here is roughly comparable to that resulting from union contributions to pro-labor political candidates.

5.   **Litigation.** The expenses of litigation incident to negotiating and administering the contract or to settling grievances and disputes arising in the bargaining unit are clearly chargeable to petitioners as a normal incident of the duties of the exclusive representative. The same is true of fair representation litigation arising within the unit, of jurisdictional disputes with other unions, and of any other litigation before agencies or in the courts that concerns bargaining unit employees and is normally conducted by the exclusive representative. The expenses of litigation not having such a connection with the bargaining unit are not to be charged to objecting employees. Contrary to the view of the Court of Appeals, therefore, unless the Western Airlines bargaining unit is directly concerned, objecting employees need not share the costs of the union's challenge to the legality of the airline industry mutual aid pact; of litigation seeking to protect the rights of airline employees generally during bankruptcy proceedings; or of defending suits alleging violation of the nondiscrimination requirements of Title VII of the Civil Rights Act of 1964.

Petitioners' primary argument is that for the union to compel their financial support of these [five] activities violates the First Amendment. We need only address this contention with regard to the three activities for which, we have held, the RLA allows the union to use their contributions. We perceive no constitutional barrier.

The First Amendment does limit the uses to which the union can put funds obtained from dissenting employees. But by allowing the union shop at all, we have already countenanced a significant impingement on First Amendment rights. The dissenting employee is forced to support financially an organization with whose principles and demands he may disagree. It has long been settled that such interference with First Amendment rights is justified by the governmental interest in industrial peace. At a minimum, the union may constitutionally expend uniform exactions under the union-shop agreement in support of activities germane to collective bargaining.

Petitioners do not explicitly contend that union social activities implicate serious First Amendment interests. We need not determine whether contributing money to such affairs is an act triggering First Amendment protection. To the extent it is, the communicative content is not inherent in the act, but stems from the union's involvement in it. The objection is that these are union social hours. Therefore, the fact that the employee is forced to contribute does not increase the infringement of his First Amendment rights already resulting from the compelled contribution to the union. Petitioners may feel that their money is not being well-spent, but that does not mean they have a First Amendment complaint.

The First Amendment concerns with regard to publications and conventions are more serious; both have direct communicative content and involve the expression of ideas. Nonetheless, we perceive little additional infringement of First Amendment rights beyond that already accepted, and none that is not justified by the governmental interests behind the union shop itself. The very nature of the free-rider problem and the governmental interest in overcoming it require that the union have a certain flexibility in its use of compelled funds. These expenses are well within the acceptable range.

NOTES

1.   *The chargeability of litigation expenses.* In *Lehnert v. Ferris Faculty Association*, 500 U.S. 507 (1991), the Supreme Court addressed an important question about how costs should be allocated between national unions and various local affiliates. For some unions, the largest chunk of fees goes to the state affiliate rather than the national union. The National Right to Work Committee had argued that chargeability determinations must be made by bargaining unit; under that approach, employees in a bargaining unit whose contract was not up for renewal would not have to pay anything to support negotiations for other bargaining units. Such a system would drastically reduce the money available to a union during negotiations, and would also impose a significantly greater accounting burden on the union. The Court rejected the argument and approved the cost pool method of allocating charges. Thus, a state affiliate, or a national or international union, can make a single chargeability determination and apply it across the board. *Locke v. Karass*, 555 U.S. 207 (2009), held that local unions can charge non-members for litigation by the national union with which they are affiliated as long as the litigation would have been chargeable if it were undertaken by the local. Although these cases involved public sector employment, where fair share fees are no longer permissible after *Janus*, the principles still apply to private sector unions.

2.   *Accounting requirements.* In order to comply with their obligations to fair share fee payers, unions keep careful records of their finances so that they can determine the source and amount of funds used to support candidates for public office (which funds, for some unions, are collected separately from members and maintained in separate political action committees), the source and amount of funds used for other political activities (such as for research on issues of public policy, lobbying for legislation, providing information to members and to the public, and getting out the vote), the source and amount of funds used for negotiating and administering collective bargaining agreements, and even the source and amount of funds used to prepare for strikes and other concerted activities. Based on the determination of the accountants as to the proportion of the unions' funds that are spent on purposes not "germane to collective bargaining," as that term has been defined by the courts and the Board, unions are permitted to require nonmember dissenters to pay a fair share fee that is only that same proportion of the amount of dues charged to members. Fair share fees are usually about 85% to 95% of full dues.

3.   *Organizing as chargeable expenses.* May unionized grocery store employees who are concerned about the effect on their standard of living of the

arrival of non-union low-wage big box stores charge dissenting members for the cost of engaging in area standards picketing outside such low-wage stores? May the union charge dissenting members for the costs associated with trying to organize non-union stores in the same area? *See Food & Commercial Workers Locals 951, 1036 & 7 (Meijer Inc.)*, 329 N.L.R.B. 730 (1999), *enf'd, Food & Commercial Workers Local 1036 v. NLRB*, 284 F.3d 1099 (9th Cir. 2002) (en banc) (yes). (The en banc court adopted the analysis proposed in Christopher David Ruiz Cameron, *The Labyrinth of Solidarity: Why the Future of the American Labor Movement Depends on Latino Workers*, 53 U. Miami L. Rev. 1089 (1999).) What if the stores that the union were trying to organize were 80 miles from the nearest unionized store?

4. *When is political activity chargeable?* If the cost of organizing and area standards picketing are chargeable, why may the union not charge dissenting members the costs associated with trying to achieve the same result by picketing outside the city hall when the city hall is considering living wage legislation that would have the same effect as successful picketing outside the big box store?

A NOTE ON THE UNION'S DUTY TO DISCLOSE BECK RIGHTS

One source of controversy after *Beck* was whether unions must notify all employees in the bargaining unit of their right to refuse to be a union member and their right to decline to pay dues. A related issue is how much information unions are obligated to provide to agency fee payers about the unions' accounting and expenditures of funds so as to enable dissenters to determine whether the calculation of the amount of the agency fee is acceptable. In two cases after *Beck*, the Court and the Board considered whether a union breaches its duty of fair representation in failing to provide employees with sufficiently clear or detailed descriptions of their rights to become agency fee payers.

In *Marquez v. Screen Actors Guild, Inc.*, 525 U.S. 33 (1998), the Screen Actors Guild agreement with motion picture and television producers contained a standard union security clause, providing that any performer who worked under the agreement must be "a member of the Union in good standing." The clause quoted verbatim the language from the provisos to § 8(a)(3) about employees having 30 days to join the union and the prohibition on denying membership for reasons other than failure to pay dues. The clause did not explain that cases interpreting § 8(a)(3) had determined that union *membership* is not in fact required under law, and that all that is necessary is that the agency fee be paid. The Court rejected the employee's argument that it was "irrational to negotiate a clause that cannot be enforced as written," by saying that "this clause *can* be enforced as written, because by tracking the statutory language, the clause incorporates all of the refinements that have become associated with that language." "After we stated that the statutory language incorporates an employee's right not to 'join' the union (except by paying fees and dues) and an employee's right to pay for only representational activities, we cannot fault SAG for using this very language to convey these very concepts." The Court also rejected the employee's contention that the union acted in bad faith by using the language of the statute without explaining how its meaning had been modified by subsequent cases "even if the union always informs workers of their rights and even if it enforces the union security clause in conformity with federal law." The Court thought a union might choose to use the statutory language as "shorthand" to refer by implication to all the nuances that had been read into the language in cases "precisely *because* it incorporates all of the refinements."

California Saw & Knife Works, 320 N.L.R.B. 224 (1995), the Board's first decision after *Beck*, addressed a number of issues about union dues that the Supreme Court had not resolved. The Board reviewed a voluntary *Beck* program set up by the International Association of Machinists and Aerospace Workers. The Board held that challenges to the expenditure of union dues could be brought under the duty of fair representation, but rejected the dissenting employees' argument that challenges to the collection and expenditure of union dues for unions governed by the NLRA could be made under the First Amendment. The Board then made the following specific rulings:

(1)   The union must provide notice to nonunion members of the right to object to payment of full fees, and to fee payment objectors regarding the use of such fees. The IAM published the *Beck* notice annually in the December issue of its monthly magazine, which it mailed to the last known address of all union member and nonmember bargaining unit employees. The Board held that a union does not have an obligation under the duty of fair representation to issue an additional notice of *Beck* rights to new nonmember employees at the time they resign their union membership. The Board held that a union must give *Beck* rights notice to both newly hired nonmember employees at the time the union seeks to obligate these newly hired employees to pay dues and to currently employed employees at the time they become nonmembers if these currently employed employees have not been sent a copy of the magazine containing the *Beck* notice. The notice must inform employees that they have the right to be or remain a nonmember and that nonmembers have the right to object to paying for union activities not germane to the union's duties as bargaining agent and to obtain a reduction in fees for such activities.

(2)   The Board invalidated in part the IAM's policy that all dues objections be filed during a "window period" consisting of the month of January. The Board accepted that objections could be confined to a limited window period and that 30 days is a reasonable period. The Board held that the window period was invalid solely as applied to employees who resign their membership following the expiration of the January window period because it compels the employee to continue to pay full dues even though no longer a union member, and operates as an arbitrary restriction on the right to resign from union membership. The Board also invalidated the requirements that objections be sent by certified mail and in an individual envelope.

(3)   The Board held that a union need not calculate and disclose its Beck dues reductions on a unit-by-unit basis. The Board suggested that some litigation expenses incurred outside the bargaining unit would be properly

chargeable as benefiting the unit and others would not: "union litigation of issues arising in connection with collective-bargaining agreements may confer benefits on employees beyond those units immediately affected."

(4) The Board held that the IAM provided objectors with sufficient information to determine whether to challenge the dues-reduction calculations. The IAM sent objectors information detailing the percentage reduction in dues based on the previous year's expenses, as well as a summary of the major categories of expenditures, showing how the reduction was calculated. All challenges were consolidated in a single arbitral proceeding. The IAM bore the burden of justifying its dues-reduction calculations before an arbitrator chosen through the American Arbitration Association's Rules for Impartial Determination of Union Fees.

(5) The Board found it acceptable to have the audits of District and Local Lodges performed by in-house auditors employed by the IAM rather than by outside certified auditors.

(6) The Board declined to adopt a rule requiring a union to bear the travel costs of challengers to attend the arbitration hearing on challenges to dues-reduction calculations. Challengers were permitted to present their case before the arbitrator personally or in writing or via conference call.

NOTES

1. *Winners and losers.* Who gains (other than lawyers and accountants) and who loses under the Board's approach to *Beck* rights in *California Saw*?

2. *Who cares?* Why is the issue of notice to nonmembers of their rights to refuse to pay dues, and to challenge the union's expenditures, of such intense interest to unions, to firms, and to the National Right to Work Committee?

3. *Renewal of dues objection.* A union requires dissenting employees to renew their objection to dues payment annually. Under what circumstances would the requirement of annual renewal of *Beck* objections be permissible? Under what circumstances would it be impermissible? What standard should the Board use to determine whether a union violates section 8(b)(1)(A) by requiring annual renewal—should it be under the deferential arbitrary, discriminatory, or bad faith standard ordinarily used in duty of fair representation cases, or should it be a more rigorous standard? *See Int'l Ass'n of Machinists (L-3 Communications)*, 355 N.L.R.B. 1062 (2010) (where employee asked in writing that his *Beck* objection be continuing, union violated section 8(b)(1)(A) by requiring annual renewal, but Board declined to adopt a per se rule prohibiting unions from requiring annual renewal and determined that the arbitrary, discriminatory, and bad faith standard of DFR cases applies).

4. *Is there a better way?* Can you think of a better way to accommodate the rights of union dissenters and the rights of union supporters than the complex body of rules governing expenditures and accounting that the Board and the courts have created?

5.   *Are notice requirements compelled speech?* The battle over requiring unions to notify employees of their *Beck* rights has generally overlooked the question whether the NLRA authorizes the Board to require unions to notify employees of their rights. However, when the Board issued a rule requiring employers to notify employees of their section 7 rights to join or to refrain from joining unions, the Chamber of Commerce and the National Association of Manufacturers challenged the rule on the grounds that it exceeded the Board's statutory rulemaking authority and that the notice was compelled speech in violation of section 8(c) of the NLRA and the First Amendment. Two courts of appeals found the Board's rule requiring employers to notify employees of their rights invalid on the ground that it exceeds the Board's rulemaking authority and also that the Board does not have the power to require employers to notify employees of their rights. *Chamber of Commerce v. NLRB,* 721 F.3d 152 (4th Cir. 2013); *National Ass'n of Mfrs. v. NLRB,* 717 F.3d 947 (D.C. Cir. 2013), *overruled on other grounds by American Meat Inst. v. U.S. Dept. of Ag.,* 760 F.3d 18 (2014). Although neither court explicitly ruled on the employers' First Amendment objections, the D.C. Circuit found that the notice-posting requirement violated section 8(c) because it compelled employers to disseminate a message and thus violated the statutory free speech protection of section 8(c).

If the Board lacks the authority to require employers to notify employees of their rights under section 7 (both to join unions and to refrain from doing so), on what basis does federal labor law authorize the Board (or the Supreme Court) to require unions to notify employees of their rights? Are unions and employers differently situated with respect to compulsory notice requirements? If the statute authorizes the different treatment of employers and unions with respect to compulsory notice of statutory rights, is there any argument that the different rules are viewpoint-based discrimination between different types of compelled speech?

5.   OTHER RIGHTS OF UNION MEMBERS VIS À VIS THE UNION UNDER THE NLRA

Unions, like other membership organizations, create rules for getting and keeping a membership. The validity of those rules is tested under § 8(b)(1), usually when a union wishes to punish a dissident for crossing picket lines or challenging other important decisions the union leadership has made. Section 8(b)(1) prohibits unions from coercing or restraining workers who refuse to exercise § 7 rights, but protects the right of unions to maintain reasonable rules governing union membership. Additionally, when the Landrum-Griffin Act created rights of members against their unions, it recognized that unions may fine, suspend, expel, or otherwise discipline members, so long as prescribed procedures were observed. In *NLRB v. Allis-Chalmers,* 388 U.S. 175 (1967), the Court upheld the power of a union to fine members for crossing a picket line. A lower court had held that the discipline coerced employees in violation of § 8(b)(1)(A), but the Supreme Court disagreed:

The requirements of adherence to democratic principles, fair procedures and freedom of speech apply to the election of union officials and extend into all aspects of union affairs. In the present case the procedures followed for calling the strikes and disciplining the recalcitrant members fully comported with these requirements, and were in every way fair and democratic. Whether § 8(b)(1)(A) proscribes arbitrary imposition of fines, or punishment for disobedience of a fiat of a union leader, are matters not presented by this case.

After *Allis-Chalmers*, a union member who wished to cross a picket line without facing discipline under union rules could do so only if he or she unconditionally resigned membership in the union before crossing the picket line. To prevent that from happening, some unions adopted rules restricting the ability of members to resign during strikes. In *Pattern Makers' League v. NLRB,* 473 U.S. 95 (1985), the Court addressed union restrictions on resignation during strikes. During a long strike, 10 of 40 striking union members resigned from the striking local unions and returned to work. The unions refused to accept the resignations and fined the workers approximately the equivalent of their earnings during the strike. The employers challenged the union rule allowing the fine as an unfair labor practice under § 8(b)(1)(A). The Court held that imposing fines on employees for returning to work "restrains" the exercise of their § 7 rights. The Court noted that, "if the terms "refrain" and "restrain or coerce" are interpreted literally, fining employees to enforce compliance with any union rule or policy would violate the Act," and declined to go so far. The Court reasoned that because employees are entitled not to join a union, "§ 8(a)(3) protects the employment rights of the dissatisfied member, as well as those of the worker who never assumed full union membership. By allowing employees to resign from a union at any time, § 8(a)(3) protects the employee whose views come to diverge from those of his union."

The union argued that its rule did not interfere with workers' employment rights because offending members were not discharged, but only fined. They further argued that the proviso to § 8(b)(1)(A) expressly allows unions to place restrictions on the right to resign. The proviso states that nothing in § 8(b)(1)(A) shall "impair the right of a labor organization to prescribe its own rules with respect to the acquisition or retention of membership therein." The Court rejected the arguments. The proviso allows unions to maintain rules that provide for the expulsion of employees from the union, but not for the discharge or fining of employees who are expelled. The Court also emphasized that it was deferring to the Board's interpretation of the Act as prohibiting the union's rule:

The Board has the primary responsibility for applying the general provisions of the Act to the complexities of industrial life. In this case, two factors suggest that we should be particularly reluctant to hold that the Board's interpretation of the Act is impermissible. First, in related cases this Court invariably has yielded to Board decisions on whether fines imposed by a union "restrain or coerce" employees. Second, the Board consistently has construed § 8(b)(1)(A) as prohibiting the imposition of fines on employees who have tendered resignations invalid under a union constitution. Therefore, we conclude that the Board's decision here is entitled to our deference.

As Justice White explained in his concurring opinion, the proviso to § 8(b)(1)(A), which preserves the union's right to prescribe its own rules with respect to the acquisition or retention of membership, "might be read as permitting restrictions on resignation during a strike, since they would seem to relate to the "retention" of membership. But it can also be sensibly read to refer only to the union's right to determine who shall be allowed to join and to remain in the union. The latter is the Board's interpretation. . . . Where the statutory language is rationally susceptible to contrary readings, and the search for congressional intent is unenlightening, deference to the Board is not only appropriate, but necessary."

The four dissenting justices argued that "[u]nless internal rules can be enforced, the union's status as bargaining representative will be eroded, and the rights of the members to act collectively will be jeopardized. Union activity, by its very nature, is group activity, and is grounded on the notion that strength can be garnered from unity, solidarity, and mutual commitment. This concept is of particular force during a strike, where the individual members of the union draw strength from the commitments of fellow members, and where the activities carried on by the union rest fundamentally on the mutual reliance that inheres in the pact." In their view, the rule allowing for fines for employees who refuse to honor a strike "stands for the proposition that to become a union member one must be willing to incur a certain obligation upon which others may rely; as such, it is a rule literally involving the acquisition and retention of membership. . . . To be effective, the decision to strike, like the decision to bargain collectively, must be respected by the minority until democratically revoked. The employees' collective decision to strike is not taken lightly, and entails considerable costs. Before workers undertake such a course, it is reasonable that they have some assurance that collectively they will have the means to withstand the pressures the employer is able lawfully to impose on them. A voluntarily and democratically adopted rule prohibiting resignations during a strike is one such means."

NOTES

1. *Deference to a divided Board.* Justice White emphasized the importance of deference to the Board; the dissenting opinion noted that the Board was divided on its interpretation. Should split Board decisions draw less deference than unanimous decisions?

2. *Deference to an old rule.* Justice White said he would defer to whatever rule the Board reached. What if the Board were to reach a contrary rule today, after more than two decades under the old rule? Should old rules receive more deference than new rules? Should it matter that an old rule was controversial at its inception? *See Nat'l Cable & Telecomm. Ass'n v. Brand X Internet Servs.*, 545 U.S. 967, 981 (2005) (courts should defer to reasonable agency interpretations even where agency changes its policy in response to changed factual circumstances or a change in administrations).

3. *Struck work.* During the Hollywood writers' strike of 2007–08, it was suspected that some striking writers were covertly performing some struck work. Under the *Pattern Makers* reasoning, what could the Writers' Guild of America, Inc., do to those members? Union membership is an extremely valuable commodity in Hollywood, as it facilitates getting work and is required for participation in health and retirement benefit funds. Could the WGA expel those members who performed struck work? Should the WGA attempt to do so? Does it benefit a union to expel members when doing so still allows them to work without paying dues?

4. *Doing nonunion work.* Issues about union discipline of members arise not only in the context of strikes, as in *Allis-Chalmers*, *Pattern Makers,* and the Hollywood guilds, but also in the construction industry and other short-term employment when union members may be tempted to work non-union. Construction unions authorize fines of members who work for non-union contractors in areas in which union contractors compete, which sometimes results in litigation over whether the union's procedure for imposing fines are fair. The LMRDA requires unions to create internal grievance procedures to challenge discipline. A member who is disciplined must exhaust his union's internal procedures before bringing suit. Failure to exhaust internal remedies precludes a suit under the LMRDA unless the dissatisfied member proves that the union's procedures fail to comply with LMRDA § 411(a)(5), which requires notice of charges, time to prepare a defense, and opportunity to receive a hearing. *See McPhetridge v. IBEW, Local Union No. 53*, 578 F.3d 886, 889 (8th Cir. 2009) (declining to grant an injunction against disciplining union members for working for non-union contractors).

5. *What kinds of membership rules coerce?* How should the Board decide which union rules coerce? The dissent in *Pattern Makers* offered a distinction between rules that affect only relations between the member and the union and rules that affect the relation between the member and the employer. Is that a useful distinction? Under the majority's reasoning, would a union rule requiring every striking employee to take a turn on picket line duty and fining those who refuse violate the member's right to "refrain from" concerted activity?

E. UNION GOVERNANCE AND ELECTIONS UNDER THE LMRDA

Unions began as voluntary associations of workers who joined together for a common purpose in the way that people everywhere form associations ranging from bowling leagues to reading groups to churches. At some point in the development of any association of people, the group becomes an institution and the question of the institution's legal status and its rights and obligations vis à vis both its members and third parties arises. The legal status of labor unions has been profoundly shaped by their history, and in particular the history of judicial hostility to unions. Union leaders early decided that they were far better off with no legal recognition.

But as unions gained strength and numbers in the 1930s and 1940s, and in particular gained the right to be the exclusive representative of all employees in the bargaining unit and the legal obligation to do so fairly, legislators gained interest in regulating the internal affairs of unions so as to protect employees from unfairness and corruption. Early common law doctrines that treated the union's legal status as a contract with its members, along with the smattering of state laws regulating non-profit associations generally, seemed to critics inadequate to the task of regulating entities that had the economic and political power and social importance that unions had in the 1950s. Moreover, corruption in the large and powerful Teamsters Union invited congressional action. Of course, those who believed that union power was bad for business were happy to support any effort to curtail the autonomy of unions. All of these goals are reflected in the Labor Management Reporting and Disclosure Act, popularly known as the Landrum-Griffin Act, which Congress enacted in 1959. A major goal was to regulate internal union affairs by protecting the rights of union members to participate in the governance of the union and to enable the United States Department of Labor to inspect the finances of unions.

Martin H. Malin, Individual Rights Within the Union 33 (BNA 1988) summarizes the LMRDA:

> Titles I through VI of the LMRDA are the first and only comprehensive federal regulation of the internal affairs of labor unions. Title I contains a bill of rights for union members. Title II contains reporting requirements for unions, their officers, certain employers, and employer persuaders. Title III regulates trusteeships imposed by internationals or intermediate bodies over subordinate bodies. Title IV regulates elections of union officers. Title V imposes fiduciary duties on union officials. Title VI contains miscellaneous "housekeeping" provisions, including a grant of general investigative power to the Secretary of Labor and a prohibition of retaliation against those who exercise their rights under the act.

The LMRDA represents an attempt to draw a fine line between the need to protect internal union democracy and the desire to avoid undue government interference in internal union affairs.

The LMRDA confers rights only on the union "member," who is defined as "any person who has fulfilled the requirements for membership in such organization, and who neither has voluntarily withdrawn from membership nor been expelled or suspended from membership." 29 U.S.C. § 402(*o*). The LMRDA is enforced by litigation brought by private individuals, as well as by investigations and litigation brought by the United States Department of Labor. In addition, the Department of Labor has promulgated regulations interpreting and enforcing the statute. *See* 29 C.F.R. Part 401, *et seq.*

1. UNION GOVERNANCE

Bill of Rights. Title I of the LMRDA, dubbed in the statute as the "Union Members Bill of Rights," confers several rights on union members and reads like the U.S. Constitution's bill of rights that inspired it. It grants members rights to equal treatment, to free speech and assembly, to run for union office, to approve dues increases through direct votes or delegate conventions, to sue their union, to due process in disciplinary proceedings, to obtain a copy of the collective bargaining agreement, to be informed by the union about rights under the LMRDA, and to freedom from retaliation by the union for attempting to exercise rights under the LMRDA. 29 U.S.C. §§ 411–415, 431, 529, 530. In *Sheet Metal Workers v. Lynn*, 488 U.S. 347 (1989), one of the leading cases interpreting Title I protections, the Supreme Court held that an elected union official could not be removed in retaliation for expression of views critical of a proposed dues increase. Title I may be enforced by an individual's bringing a private right of action.

In addition to the LMRDA protections, section 8(b)(1)(A), which was added by the Taft-Hartley Act, protects the section 7 right of workers to refrain from participating in unions. As we saw above in Chapter 7, the duty of fair representation as enforced under section 8(b)(1)(A) regulates union discipline of members.

Union Elections. Title IV of the LMRDA contains detailed requirements governing the election of union officers. It requires that labor organizations (including local unions, intermediate organizations such as regional labor federations, and national or international unions) conduct elections every certain number of years (three, four or five years, depending on the type of labor organization). 29 U.S.C. § 481. It requires that elections be by secret ballot, it prohibits the use of union or employer funds to support candidates for union office, and it requires that unions mail candidates' literature to union members at the candidates' expense.

Title IV also allows unions to enforce only "reasonable requirements uniformly imposed" on eligibility to run for office. 29 U.S.C. § 481(e). In *Local 3489, United Steelworkers v. Usery*, 429 U.S. 305 (1977), the Supreme Court invalidated a provision of the Steelworkers' union constitution that limited eligibility for local union office to members who had attended at least one-half of the regular monthly meetings of the local for three years previous to the election unless prevented by union activities or working hours. The Court concluded that the rule was not a "reasonable requirement" because it rendered 96 percent of union members ineligible and required potential candidates to plan their candidacies as early as 18 months in advance of an election. The Court reasoned:

> the rule has a restrictive effect on union democracy. In the absence of a permanent "opposition party" within the union, opposition to the incumbent leadership is likely to emerge in response to particular issues at different times, and member interest in changing union leadership is therefore likely to be at its highest only shortly before elections.

The Court rejected the union's contention that there was no evidence that the rule entrenched incumbents and that it was justified by the desire to encourage attendance at union meetings and to ensure that those elected to union office were dedicated and knowledgeable about union governance.

Criticism of the *Local 3489* approach to judging the reasonableness of union rules for eligibility to stand for election has focused on its indeterminacy about how many must be ineligible before the rule becomes unreasonable and on its alleged underestimation of the importance of having potential candidates be regular attendees at union meetings. *See Herman v. Local 1011, United Steelworkers*, 207 F.3d 924 (7th Cir. 2000) (finding unreasonable an eligibility rule requiring attendance at 8 monthly meetings in 2 years when it disqualified 92% of local's 3000 members); *Herman v. Springfield Mass., Local 497 Postal Workers*, 201 F.3d 1 (1st Cir. 2000) (finding reasonable a rule requiring attendance at 3 monthly meetings in 12 months even though it disqualified 96% of membership).

Title IV, like much of the LMRDA, is enforced by the United States Department of Labor, not the NLRB. Except for the requirement that unions mail union election literature to the members, individuals may not bring private rights of action to enforce Title IV. When the Department of Labor brings a proceeding to challenge the validity of a union election, the election is presumed valid and the winners remain in office while the action is pending. A finding of a violation produces a rerun election conducted under Labor Department supervision.

Union Mergers and Reorganizations. In recent years, a number of large and small unions have proposed or effected mergers or reorganizations in order to gain the strength of numbers, the ability to negotiate large national or regional contracts with large national and regional employers, and to minimize jurisdictional disputes among unions representing employees in the same economic sector, craft, or industry in the same geographic area. For example, the SEIU was created through the gradual merger of smaller separate unions in the service, clerical, health care, and building maintenance industries. It has periodically reorganized its local affiliates in ways that created large local unions representing employees in the same industry across a region or state in place of smaller, geographically specific local unions. *See* UHW-W Urges Members to Boycott SEIU Advisory Vote on Reorganization, Daily Lab. Report at p. A-11 (Nov. 26, 2008); SEIU Plans to Hold Advisory Vote Among California Health Care Workers at p. A-8 (Sept. 15, 2008). UNITE (the union representing workers in the garment industry and needle trades) merged with HERE (the hotel and restaurant employees' union) because both represent low-wage, immigrant workers in urban areas. In some cases, the mergers are controversial and litigation ensues. The LMRDA stipulates the processes unions must use to approve a merger and to restructure their operations.

In reviewing a matter of governance under LMRDA § 411, including a merger, the election of union leadership, reorganizations, and changes to the union constitution and by-laws, courts often defer to unions. This is because, "[w]hile the rights guaranteed under Section 411 are designed to ensure that unions adhere to certain basic democratic principles, courts are instructed not to read the broad language of Section 411(a) as a mandate for courts to impose on labor unions whatever procedures or practices they regard as democratic. . . . Federal courts have applied a long-standing policy of avoiding judicial interference in a union's self-governance and internal affairs." *Shelley v. Am. Postal Workers Union*, 775 F. Supp. 2d 197, 207 (D.D.C. 2011) (declining to grant a preliminary injunction delaying a CBA ratification vote in order to allow the objectors to communicate their concerns to fellow union members).

A court may agree to enjoin a union from removing *elected* officials. In *Babler v. Futhey*, 618 F.3d 514, 525 (6th Cir. 2010), the court enjoined the retaliatory removal of officers who opposed union policies and exercised LMRDA rights. Because the removal might chill free speech and discourage LMRDA enforcement, the public interest weighed in favor of protecting officers' rights over noninterference with internal union management. However, a court is unlikely to enjoin a union from removing *appointed* officials. In *Vasquez v. Central States Joint Bd.*, 692 F. Supp. 2d 968, 976 (N.D. Ill. 2010), the court declined to enjoin the alleged removal of officers for opposing union corruption: "To the extent the [LMRDA] limits action taken as part of a purposeful and deliberate attempt . . . to suppress dissent within the union, it doesn't do that at the expense of the freedom of an elected union leader to choose a staff whose views are compatible with his own."

NOTES

1.   *Conflicts.* Unions, like other organizations, have long dealt with internal struggles over leadership and direction. As we saw in Chapter 1, the AFL-CIO was formed in 1955 to resolve a longstanding struggle over philosophies of organizing between unions affiliated with the AFL and those affiliated with the CIO and to end jurisdictional fights. When some unions left the AFL-CIO to form Change to Win in the early 2000s, the split was over leadership and direction, particularly with respect to organizing. The LMRDA was enacted, in part, to enable rank-and-file union members to have more control over leadership, but of course its provisions can become weapons in the internal struggles. Outside counsel for unions have often played informal roles in mediating disputes. They are able to do so in part because a single law firm typically represents multiple different unions. Union clients are reluctant to fire outside counsel because of the expertise and institutional knowledge their lawyers acquire over many years of representation. As a result, union lawyers are uniquely positioned to try to resolve conflicts among their clients, even when the lawyer is faced with what might be considered a conflict of interest under legal ethics rules.

2.   *What internal union requirements for office holders are reasonable?* A union represents a multi-racial and multi-lingual workforce, including bargaining units that may be predominantly Spanish-speaking recent immigrants, predominantly African-American, predominantly female of many races and ethnicities, or predominantly white. Responding to criticism that the white male leaders of some local unions were unable effectively to mobilize or organize nonwhite and female workforces, the international union adopted a rule requiring every local to insure that the local's officers were "representative of the diversity of its members." In compliance with that requirement, a local that represents a substantial number of Spanish-speaking Latinas has adopted a rule stating that any person who runs for local union office must be fluent in Spanish and that half of all officers must be female and half must be Latino/a. Is the rule valid under the LMRDA?

3.   *RICO and the LMRDA.* The LMRDA is not the only federal statute that has been used to target corruption in unions. The Racketeer Influenced and Corrupt Organizations Act (RICO), which contains civil and criminal prohibitions of conspiracies involving bribery, extortion, and other conduct, has also been used to police internal union affairs. Indeed, one of its original purposes was to provide federal law enforcement greater power to root out corruption in both unions and businesses that had close ties to the Mafia. For a thorough discussion of the use of RICO against the Teamsters union and the administration of the resulting consent decree, see James B. Jacobs & Kerry T. Cooperman, Breaking the Devil's Pact: the Battle to Free the Teamsters from the Mob (2011); Michael J. Goldberg, *Cleaning Labor's House: Institutional Reform Litigation in the Labor Movement*, 1989 Duke L.J. 903.

4.   *LMRDA Rights for Nonmembers?* Only union members have the right to vote in union elections under the LMRDA. Fee-payers do not because the statute does not confer such a right on them and most union constitutions and

bylaws give nonmember fee payers no right to vote on union governance or contract ratification. Union-represented employees thus face a choice: join the union and pay full dues or pay a fair share fee (or nothing at all in right-to-work states) and have no say in the union's operation or on the contract. Could you argue that, in the public sector, requiring employees to make this choice violates the employees' First Amendment rights because they only way they can vote on union governance and contract ratification is to pay dues that subsidize political speech with which they disagree?

2. TRUSTEESHIPS

As with any organization, internecine struggles for control of unions—whether control over the money or control over the ability to set policy and direct the activities of the group—are a serious issue. A trusteeship is the legal device that unions have used to enable the national or international union to control a local union or an intermediate body, such as regional labor union. The parent union appoints a trustee who is authorized to remove the lower body's officers and direct its affairs, and thus the "labor organization suspends the autonomy otherwise available to a subordinate body under its constitution or bylaws." 29 U.S.C. § 402(h). Trusteeships have been used to prevent or root out corruption, to address mismanagement, or to settle a disastrous strike. Trusteeships have also enabled national union leadership to loot the treasury of local unions and to suppress dissent. Title III of the LMRDA attempts to prevent the latter and enable the former by permitting a labor organization to impose a trusteeship only in accordance with the parent union's constitution and bylaws and only for one of four purposes: to correct local corruption or financial malpractice; to assure the performance of the collective bargaining agreement or other duties of the bargaining representative; to restore democratic procedures; or to "otherwise carry[ ] out the legitimate objects of such labor organization." 29 U.S.C. § 462. Once a trusteeship is imposed in accordance with the organization's constitution and after a fair hearing, it is presumptively valid for 18 months and may not be attacked "except upon clear and convincing proof that the trusteeship was not established or maintained in good faith for a purpose allowable under [the LMRDA]." 29 U.S.C. § 464(c). After 18 months, the presumption is reversed and the trusteeship must be discontinued absent proof by the labor organization that it is necessary. The requirements and procedures for the imposition of trusteeships have been the subject of extensive litigation. *See* William W. Osborne, Jr., ed., Labor Union Law and Regulation 557–582 (BNA 2003).

NOTES

1. *A trusteeship to settle a controversial strike.* Citing nonunion competition, Geo. A. Hormel & Company, the well-known meat packing firm, sought drastic wage cuts in negotiations for a new collective bargaining

agreement. A local affiliated with the United Food & Commercial Workers International Union, Local P-9, resisted and voted to strike. During the course of the strike, the company hired permanent replacements. As the strike dragged on, UFCW International pressured Local P-9 to settle the strike by accepting the company's offer. The leaders of Local P-9 refused. UFCW International leaders believed that P-9 was being unrealistic in continuing a disastrous strike, that Hormel workers would never get their jobs back, and that the efforts of P-9 employees to gain support for their cause by sending roving pickets to other Hormel plants were unlawful and would cause UFCW employees at other Hormel plants to lose their jobs. The International put the local into trusteeship and accepted the company's offer to settle the strike. Was this a proper purpose for a trusteeship? *See Hansen v. Guyette*, 636 F. Supp. 907 (D. Minn. 1986), *aff'd*, 814 F.2d 547 (8th Cir. 1987). A documentary film by noted film maker Barbara Kopple, *American Dream* (1990), tells the story of the strike and the relationship between Local P-9 and UFCW International.

2. *A trusteeship to replace local leadership.* Consider note 2 above (on the local union rule restricting eligibility to run for office based on gender, language ability, and ethnic origin). Imagine the international union was concerned that the predominantly white and male leadership of a local that represents Latina women janitors had lost touch with the changing demographics of the industry, as evidenced by the union leadership's refusal to conduct meetings in Spanish or with live Spanish translation and refusal to prioritize immigration-related issues in its negotiations with employers. The international wishes to replace the local leadership with new leaders whom it thinks will more effectively organize and represent the Latina workforce. Can it use a trusteeship to achieve its goal?

3. UNION FINANCES

Among the things that generated the most interest in the 1957–1958 hearings of the Permanent Subcommittee on Labor Legislation of the Senate Committee on Labor and Public Welfare, commonly known as the McClellan Committee, were abuses and corruption in the handling of union money. The McClellan Committee investigated the Teamsters Union's finances at length, and dwelt extensively on evidence of corruption in the handling of money and the involvement of the Mafia in the Teamsters. For example, the McClellan Committee reported that when a Teamsters local in Pontiac, Michigan revolted against four union officials whom they accused of extortion, the international union put the local under the trusteeship of Jimmy Hoffa who then put two of the four allegedly corrupt local officials in charge of the local.

One of the principal goals of the LMRDA, which was the result of the McClellan Committee hearings, was to enact Title V, which imposes fiduciary duties on union officials handling union finances. Section 501 of the LMRDA, which imposes the fiduciary duty, provides for both civil and criminal enforcement. The criminal provisions are significantly different from the civil prohibitions. It is a crime for a union officer or a person employed by a union to take funds belonging to a labor organization with intent to defraud, 29 U.S.C. § 501, or to accept a loan of union funds of more than $2000, 29 U.S.C. § 503. In addition, a violation of section 501 is a predicate act under the federal Racketeer Influenced and Corrupt Organizations (RICO) Act, 18 U.S.C. §§ 1961–1968.

Another LMRDA requirement to promote honesty in union finances is that every union official or employee who handles union funds must be bonded "to provide protection against loss by reason of acts of fraud or dishonesty on his party directly or through connivance with others." 29 U.S.C. § 502.

4. UNION DISCLOSURE

Title II of LMRDA was intended to root out corruption and enhance union democracy by requiring unions to report information to members and to disclose it to the Department of Labor. Section 431(a) requires that "every labor organization shall adopt a constitution and bylaws and shall file a copy thereof with the Secretary [of Labor], together with a report" stating the union's name and address, the name and title of union officers, the initiation fees and dues required of members, and detailed information about the union's rules with respect to qualification for membership, meetings, selection and removal of officers, discipline of members, ratification of contracts, and strike authorizations. Section 431(b) requires labor organizations to file annual financial reports with the Department of Labor. 29 U.S.C. § 431. These reports, known as LM-2 Reports, are available for every union going back many years on the DoL website. There is no equivalent corporate disclosure required, even in the 10(k) filings that the Securities Exchange Commission requires of corporations.

The LMRDA also requires disclosure of payments received and money spent by persons or entities retained by employers in connection with anti-union campaigns. Section 203 requires disclosure by those hired "to persuade employees to exercise or not to exercise, or persuade employees as to the manner of exercising, the right to organize and bargain collectively through representatives of their own choosing" or those hired "to supply an employer with information concerning the activities of employees or a labor organization in connection with a labor dispute involving such employer." In *Marshall v. Stevens People & Friends for Freedom,* 669 F.2d 171 (4th Cir. 1981), the court held that disclosure may be required not only by law firms or other consultants hired to conduct anti-union campaigns or to monitor employees supporting the union, but also by organizations of employees who oppose the union; the object of the disclosure in that case was to determine the source of funds for the group in the hard-fought campaign to unionize textile mills operated by J.P. Stevens in North Carolina. (This campaign was the subject of the 1979 film

Norma Rae.) In *Donovan v. The Rose Law Firm,* 768 F.2d 964 (8th Cir. 1985), the court held that a law firm that was hired to conduct an anti-union campaign need only disclose payments and disbursements in connection with the engagement with that employer, not those in connection with all of the firm's labor relations work. Other circuits have reached contrary decisions, and the Department of Labor's enforcement policy is to require more disclosure than the Eight Circuit required in the *Rose Law Firm* case.

In 2016, the U.S. Department of Labor issued a rule defining the required disclosure obligation under section 203. The rule never went into effect because it was enjoined by a federal court and then the Trump Administration rescinded it. The so-called "persuader" rule would have required disclosure of any agreement to retain a consultant to engage in any actions, conduct or communications on behalf of an employer that would directly or indirectly persuade workers concerning their rights to organize and bargain collectively, regardless of whether or not the consultant has direct contact with workers. The rule would also have required disclosure of any agreement under which a consultant plans or orchestrates a campaign or program to avoid or counter a union organizing or collective bargaining effort. In essence, the rule would have narrowed an exception to the disclosure requirement under which lawyers and labor relations consultants hired to "advise" an employer in conducting a union avoidance campaign are exempt from the disclosure requirement unless the lawyer or consultant itself communicates directly with the employees orally or in writing. According to the Obama DoL, the rule was necessary because the current interpretation of section 203 "has resulted in significant underreporting of employer and consultant persuader agreements. Better disclosure is critical to helping workers make informed decisions about their right to organize and bargain collectively." News Release: US Labor Department Announces Proposed Rule Concerning Reporting on Use of Labor Relations Consultants (2011). The rule addressed concerns about attorney-client privilege by not requiring disclosure of the substantive information provided by the consultant, only the fact that the consultant was hired, the purpose of the hiring agreement, and the fees paid pursuant to the agreement, none of which is protected from disclosure by the attorney-client privilege.

According to the AFL-CIO, the underreporting of the use of union avoidance consultants in organizing campaigns is possible under current law because the employers claim that the consultants—who often are management-side labor lawyers—are providing legal or labor relations advice to the company rather than being hired to persuade the employees. In organized labor's view, the so-called "advice" exception has effectively swallowed the disclosure rule. Employees should have a right to know (through DoL disclosure requirements) whether the employer has hired any entity to advise it in a union avoidance campaign, regardless of whether the consultant communicates directly to the employees or simply creates a campaign that is executed by the employer's supervisory employees. According to the AFL-CIO, the union avoidance consultants are hired to persuade employees: they often script supervisors' conversations with employees and train supervisors how to elicit (and shape) employees' attitudes toward unions by asking carefully framed questions and reading employees' verbal and non-verbal reactions. At least one law firm representing management has published a comprehensive book on how to beat unions in NLRB elections. *See* J.D. Robert Lewis & Jackson Lewis, Winning NLRB Elections: Avoiding Unionization Through Preventive Employee Programs (1997).

Management, not surprisingly, strenuously opposed the new rule, insisting that it would dissuade companies from obtaining legitimate labor relations advice. In addition, the ABA asserted in its comment on the proposed rule that the rule would require lawyers and their clients to disclose confidential information in violation of Rule 1.6 of the Model Rules of Professional Conduct, including "the identity of the client as well as other information related to the legal representation, including, for example, the nature of the representation and the amount of legal fees paid by the client to the lawyer."

NOTES

1. *The purpose of union disclosure.* What is the purpose of the Section 431 required disclosure, which compels unions to file with DoL copies of the union constitution, bylaws and annual financial reports?

2. *The purpose of employer disclosure.* What is the purpose of the Section 203 required disclosure of "persuader" agreements? Does the current rule, which exempts any agreement in which the lawyer or consultant is hired only to advise and requires disclosure only when the consultant is itself directly communicating with the employees, adequately serve the statutory purpose?

3. *Confidentiality when "persuaders" are lawyers.* When the "persuader" is a lawyer or law firm, should the facts that the law firm has been retained and the amount of fees paid be deemed confidential? What about the subject matter of the representation? Generally, the fact that a lawyer has been hired and the identity of the client are not privileged under the attorney-client privilege, although the scope of confidentiality under Model Rule 1.6 is broader. But Model Rule 1.6(b)(6) provides that lawyers may reveal confidential information "to comply with other law or court order." The ABA's comment did not explain why lawyers should not be required to disclose the fact of representation, the identity of the client, and the fees paid in connection with the persuader rule. What might such arguments be? What are the counter-arguments?

5. PROHIBITIONS ON EMPLOYER CONTRIBUTIONS TO UNIONS

One reform aimed at union and employer corruption was the Taft-Hartley Act's prohibition in section 302 of the payment of or request for bribes. In an effort to stamp out all forms of shady financial dealings between employers and unions, section 302 defines the prohibited employer financial contributions to unions fairly broadly. In addition to prohibiting financial contributions or loans to unions and employee representatives, section 302 also prohibits paying "any employee or group or committee of employees of such employer" anything "in excess of their normal compensation for the purpose of causing such employee or group or committee . . . to influence any other employees in the exercise of the right to organize and bargain collectively." Section 302(c) contains a number of important exceptions. For example, § 302(c)(1) allows employers to pay their employees "whose established duties include acting openly for such employers in matters of labor relations" (thus enabling employers to pay their human relations staff). Among the most financially significant of the section 302(c) exceptions is subsection (c)(5), which allows employers to make contributions to benefit funds (such as health, disability and retirement funds). This is the origin of federal statutory regulation of the employer-provided benefit fund, which today is covered mainly by the Employee Retirement Income Security Act (ERISA) and is an enormously complex field of law. Section 302(c)(5) imposes requirements on any union employee benefit fund: in particular, it must be operated as a trust, and employees and employers must be "equally represented in the administration of such fund." Hence, employee benefit plans in the unionized sectors of the economy are often known as "Taft-Hartley funds" or "jointly trusteed funds."

The Secretary of Labor may institute civil or criminal proceedings for making payments prohibited under section 302.

NOTES

1. *Are worker centers labor organizations under the LMRDA?* The LMRDA does not define what is a labor organization subject to the extensive reporting and disclosure requirements and other provisions of the statute. This is likely because, at the time it was enacted, there was no form of worker organization other than traditional labor unions. It was simply assumed that any labor union representing private sector employees was covered. As worker centers and other formations with different financial and membership models have grown, the question has arisen whether worker centers should be covered by its regulatory provisions. What are the arguments for and against subjecting all worker centers to the LMRDA? *See* Catherine L. Fisk, Workplace Democracy and Democratic Worker Organizations: Notes on Worker Centers, 17 Theoretical Inquiries in Law 101 (2016).

2.   *Should worker centers be subject to section 302?* Some worker centers have developed innovative programs with employers who adhere to high labor standards under which the employer and the worker center jointly sponsor programs to educate workers and their rights and train them in job-relevant skills. The programs are typically funded by the employer or jointly by the employer and the worker center or a foundation. Some such programs do not appear to fall into any of the section 302(c) exceptions. If worker centers are labor organizations under the NLRA or the LMRDA or both, it would appear that such payments, and the programs they fund, are unlawful. How can (or should) the anti-corruption goals of section 302 and the LMRDA be achieved without sacrificing such programs?

CHAPTER 9

ENDING THE COLLECTIVE BARGAINING RELATIONSHIP

■ ■ ■

A. INTRODUCTION

"It is bankruptcy by design."[1]

—A union representative at Eastern

Enderby Industries is a multinational conglomerate that owns a variety of concerns including transportation and shipping companies. Recently it has expanded its holdings in the trucking industry by buying up smaller trucking firms. To further these takeovers, Enderby set up two holding companies: Enderby Trucking, which owns the trucking operations and Enderby Ground Capital, which owns physical assets such as trucks, terminals and computer systems. The management lynchpin of the company's trucking operations is the president of Enderby Ground Capital, Frank Lozano.

Among Enderby's recent acquisitions were Eastern Van Lines and New York Truck Lines. Eastern Van Lines is a major unionized carrier that handles a substantial amount of freight on the east coast. Eastern Van Lines is on the verge of bankruptcy, primarily because it overextended its credit on new truck and terminal acquisitions and committed to an across-the-board pay hike just as other carriers began to adopt the market strategy of aggressive price discounting. New York Truck Lines (NYTL) is a small, nonunion regional cartage carrier that operates in the northeast United States. NYTL uses many owner-operators between terminals, but employees for local pick-up and delivery. New York Truck Lines' maintenance work is mostly handled through subcontracting arrangements in each of the terminals. NYTL also uses only temporary drivers to handle seasonal fluctuations. Although NYTL also has problems with profitability, its business along the New York and Boston corridor is very lucrative.

The employees of Eastern Van Lines are represented by two different unions: the International Brotherhood of Teamsters (IBT), which represents the company's 8,000 drivers and warehouse workers, and the International Association of Machinists (IAM), which represents the company's 800

---

[1]   This hypothetical problem involving Eastern Van Lines is based on the real-life facts and litigation involving Eastern Airlines. *See* John Summa, Bleeding the Assets, Blaming the Unions, 10 Multinat'l Monitor No. 3 (Mar. 1989) (remarks of IAM official Jim Conley), http://www.multi nationalmonitor.org/hyper/issues/1989/03/summa.html.

mechanics and office employees. Soon after Enderby purchased Eastern, a group of mechanics approached Frank Lozano to tell him that many mechanics no longer supported the IAM as their representative. They claimed that the union had ignored the realities of the marketplace for too long, and had won only very modest wage increases, and even those were at the cost of employment and job security. They felt they would be better on their own, dealing with Lozano directly. After the visit, Lozano consulted with his attorneys about what he should do. They advised him about the law related to employer withdrawal of recognition, and counseled him about the decertification process.

Later, representatives of the Teamsters met with Lozano. They wanted to know whether Lozano intended to honor the collective bargaining agreement that had been negotiated with the previous owners of Eastern. They also asked some general questions about the health of the company and Lozano's management philosophy, because their contract is up for renegotiation in a year. Lozano ignored questions about the collective bargaining agreement, but instead prepared the union representatives for some potentially drastic cost-cutting measures. Claiming that Eastern has been losing $20 million a year, Lozano said that the workers will need to make major pay concessions in the range of 20% to 40% to match the wages of New York Truck Lines, his nonunion company. After the meeting with the Teamsters was over, Lozano consulted his legal counsel about whether he was bound to recognize the union at all, much less follow the collective bargaining agreement negotiated by the previous owner.

In the year leading up to negotiations for the next contract, Lozano did several things that the unions viewed as undermining their representational and bargaining positions. He authorized the sale of Eastern's automated customer ordering and invoicing system to Enderby Ground Capital at the bargain price of $20 million. (The IAM estimated that the system was worth five times what Enderby Ground Capital had paid for it, and noted that the transfer required Eastern to pay Enderby $5 million dollars a year to use a system that it used to own.) The presidents of both unions also maintained that Lozano transferred truck terminals and many other assets to Enderby Ground Capital as part of a plan to pay off its debts—and to de-unionize Eastern. Later, when Eastern sold or transferred trucks to Enderby Ground Capital or New York Truck Lines, union labor was replaced by lower-paid nonunion labor. These changes had a negative impact on the balance sheet of Eastern and the red ink began to flow.

The union presidents say that Lozano has turned Eastern into a "cash cow" which he milks of all its profits. They say Lozano and Enderby "bought Eastern to dismantle it" and thereby eliminate the competition that Eastern presented to New York Truck Lines. Lozano has transferred assets and "literally stolen [from Eastern]" say Machinists' representatives.

NOTES

1.   Suppose that Enderby's strategy in purchasing both Eastern Van Lines and New York Trucking was to reduce labor costs by merging their separate operations to increase efficiencies. Does the NLRA interfere with Enderby's freedom to manage operations as it likes? First, are there any constraints with respect to the nonunion operation? Next, what are the possible constraints on the unionized side of the house? Can Enderby avoid preexisting labor agreements and union bargaining obligations if it decides to restructure all of the operations of both entities by merging them into one large company, Enderby Trucking? Was there something Enderby might have done initially to structure the deal so that its labor obligations would be cut off? What result if it had been a straight stock purchase? An asset purchase? Recall the division between Enderby Ground Capital and Enderby Trucking. What if Enderby had spun off all of the capital assets of Eastern and New York Truck Lines to Enderby Capital, but kept the routes and drivers in Enderby Trucking? Could it tell the union that Enderby Trucking has little value, and therefore, must reduce drivers' and warehouse workers' wages?

2.   What strategy should the workers adopt in responding to this situation? Should the nonunion workers be concerned? Should they be happy? If they know that Lozano has an anti-labor strategy, then how will they benefit? Are their wages likely to increase as Enderby tries to make unionization less attractive? Or will there be a balancing of wages toward the lower end of the scale once Eastern and New York are merged? What steps should the unions take first? Was it wise for mechanics represented by the IAM to suggest that they wanted to decertify? Should the Teamsters have played their hand differently? Instead of asking Lozano whether Enderby would honor the existing agreement, should they have pressed for immediate negotiations for a new contract? Should they be prepared now to seek arbitration under the predecessor agreement if Enderby imposes new terms that are not to their liking?

* * *

In the past quarter century, perhaps no issue has proved more vexing for American labor than how unions maintain their status as exclusive bargaining representative in the face of management hostility backed by the ability to change capital structure and organization. Questions about the continuity of collective bargaining relationships and agreements in the new economy invariably arise whenever there is a change in ownership or a transfer of work. Many of these changes have an impact on the existing labor force, and can result in labor changes significant enough to raise questions about an existing union's continued majority support. Labor instability caused by change can also by itself cause a shift in workers' attitudes toward their union. When have circumstances changed so much that the employees might be asked for a new expression of union support under the relevant labor statute? What weight should be given to the views of new employees, who may have different preferences? Or should union support be presumed unless and until the employees themselves raise the question? Is a change in the nature of the operation enough of a change to raise these questions? What about how the work is done—for example, what if a new employer has the capital to automate a substantial amount of existing labor? What about a massive layoff? What about a fairly minor reduction in force? A change of location? New offices? May the employer simply refuse to bargain with a union thought to have lost majority support among the employees, or should the employer or dissident employees have to file for a decertification election? If the employer may raise representation issues merely by rearranging its business and shuffling assets or customers from one pocket to another, how can our labor laws be used to promote stability in bargaining relationships and industrial peace? In this Chapter we explore the various ways in which the collective bargaining relationship can be continued or terminated in the face of changed circumstances and firm structures, including the traditional avenue of a decertification election and the newer channels of corporate restructuring and transfer of capital.

Starting as early as the mid-1960s, but catching a full head of steam in the 1980s, the increasing ease with which capital could be transferred to other countries resulted in creative uses of the corporate form, sometimes to evade labor obligations, that the authors of the NLRA hardly could have anticipated. Many in the labor movement have pinned their woes squarely on the way that business is now conducted, in both the United States and around the world. They have decried that a statutory scheme crafted in the 1930s and 1940s is ill-suited to deal with the new world corporate order, as illustrated by the following excerpt.

Hiding Behind the Corporate Veil: Employer Abuse of the Corporate Form to Avoid or Deny Workers' Collectively Bargained and Statutory Rights

Grant Crandall, Sarah J. Starrett & Douglas L. Parker
100 W. Va. L. Rev. 537 (1998)

In a 1996 speech on "corporate citizenship," Secretary of Labor Robert B. Reich lamented the passing of a bygone era when chief executives of large corporations gave greater consideration to the consequences of corporate actions on workers and their communities. Reich quoted from a 1951 address by Frank Abrams, then Chief Executive Officer of Standard Oil of New Jersey: "The job of management is to maintain an equitable and working balance among the claims of the various directly interested groups . . . stockholders, employees, customers and the public at large." Reich asserted that this balancing of interests was the product of an implicit social compact between companies, workers, and the communities that so long as a company made a respectable profit, it could be relied upon to remain in the community and employees could depend on keeping their jobs; anything less was "un-American."

Today this social compact has unraveled. The principal causes, according to Reich, include deregulation of a number of key industries, information technology that speeds commercial transactions to levels unimaginable in previous eras, the growing demands of shareholders to maximize profits, and of course the globalization of markets for capital, goods, and services. . . .

Companies are increasingly using aggressive tactics to shed their collective bargaining obligations. [One way employers do this is by selling their business, raising] the vexing problem of ***successorship***, and workers' ability to maintain their jobs and their collective bargaining agreement during the transfer of their work site to another employer. [Another way employers shed their collective bargaining obligations is by adding or changing corporate forms and changing the way they do business to the disadvantage of their union workers.] "[D]ouble-breasting"—the practice by employers of operating two companies, one union and one nonunion— [is used] to drain away the work of unionized employees into the nonunion firm to reduce labor costs and enhance management control. [Finally,] subcontracting [work to nonunion companies is also used] to avoid liabilities [under union contracts].

"[S]uccessorship" in labor law parlance [is] the problem of what happens to determine the legal status of employees, their bargaining unit, and their collective bargaining agreement when their work site changes hands. In some respects [unions can] "bargain around" this problem, [by securing a] contract clause that requires employers to secure any purchasers' promise to honor the [union's] contract as a "successor" if it decides to sell its operations. However, few labor union[s] have enough leverage to negotiate such terms.

Under "successorship," a series of Supreme Court cases have outlined the basic analysis for determining the degree to which a successor employer must honor a predecessor's collective bargaining agreement or recognize the bargaining unit of a newly acquired venture. As a general matter, the National Labor Relations Board considers four basic issues in determining whether a new employer must recognize the collective bargaining unit of the predecessor employer: (1) whether there is "continuity in the workforce," (2) whether there is continuity in the employing industry, (3) whether there is "continuity in the bargaining unit," and (4) whether and how long the work site has been idled prior to the takeover of the new employer.

What matters most is that the determining factors are all within the exclusive control of the new management. They are all subject to the decision of the new employer because under current law the employer is in control of the makeup of the new workforce. It is essentially within the new employer's discretion whether to structure the workforce and the workplace in a way that avoids successor liability.

One of the most egregious examples of contract avoidance occurs when companies engage in **intra-corporate transfers** to avoid the application of collective bargaining agreements. In such an instance, a[n] operation is transferred from a company that is a signatory to the contract to a related nonsignatory company that attempts to operate the site nonunion. [The only remedies unions have for such strategies is to negotiate work preservation provisions in their collective bargaining agreements to prevent or limit the reassignment of their work or to organize the employees to whom the work has been transferred.]

In the latter half of the 1980s, the [American economy] saw an increasing number of companies opening nonunion [operations] themselves rather than through subcontracting or leasing, in effect engaging in **double-breasting**. Where a company had historically depended on production from its [union facilities] to fill its contracts, it now could draw from both its [union]-represented operations and nonunion operations to meet its sales commitments. The company could shift production from its union [facilities] to its nonunion [facilities], resulting in the shutdown of the union [operation] or [its] slower but inevitable demise.

Another increasingly common strategy used by companies to insulate themselves from employee-related liabilities is **subcontracting**. In this strategy, companies limit their own exposure and maximize profits by [under-taking the most profitable portions of production] themselves, and contracting out smaller, [less profitable, projects] to independent operators. As one commentator has explained [in relation to the coal industry], "Contracting is a one-sided relationship. Big companies own the coal. They sell the coal. And they decide how much they will pay contractors, who actually mine the coal."

[As you might imagine, one critical issue in all of these situations is the definition of "employer" under the NLRA—based on whether the definition is viewed expansively or narrowly, the entity receiving union work may be held liable or avoid liability under the NLRA. However,] the NLRB has traditionally taken a narrow view in interpreting the . . . term under the NLRA. Section 2(2) of that law defines the term "employer" as including "any person acting as an agent of an employer, directly or indirectly," but does not further define the term. As a result, the NLRB has developed (and federal courts have approved) a number of indicia to determine "employer" identity, focusing on whether the entity has the right of control over essential terms and conditions of employment, such as hiring, firing, supervision, wages, and hours. However, instead of simply applying a single definition, as [at least one state court has] done, the Board has developed at least six distinct tests or analytical frameworks for use in varying factual scenarios. Among these are "joint employers," "single employer," "alter ego," "piercing the corporate veil," and the "ally" doctrine, in addition to the "successorship" doctrine. Although each is applied somewhat differently, all of these tests essentially seek to evaluate whether and to what extent two nominally separate entities actually function as a single entity, or whether they should properly both be considered the employer of a certain employee and should be bound by each others' agreements.

[H]aving identified some examples of the problems workers face in winning economic security, it is appropriate to also identify some broad principles which should guide any attempt at systematic legal reform. First, under current law, collective bargaining alone does not offer sufficient economic security to workers. Given the legal restraints on the economic weapons a union may use to pressure an employer, most employees do not have the leverage to negotiate contracts that sufficiently ensure job security. Second, laws protecting workers' rights have not kept pace with changes in the nature and speed of economic activity. Reform must effectively deal with the consequences of recent deregulation, globalization of markets, and the view that fiduciary duties run only to shareholders. Finally, any reform should address the failure of current formal rules to reflect the realities of the workplace or the corporate world. Courts are often restrained from ruling in favor of workers because companies have the ability to avoid liabilities by re-structuring their corporate form and their transactions. Even though worker protection laws are numerous, they are all too easy to thwart with expensive and creative legal advice. Instead of such formal rules, labor laws should take a functional look at the employer-employee relationship.

NOTE

The forgoing excerpt was written by the former general counsel and two staff attorneys of the United Mine Workers Union. The United Mine Workers has been particularly hard hit by corporate restructuring and also the decline of the coal industry. To what extent do you agree with their descriptions, outlook, and reasoning? What about their proposed suggestions for reform? Are their suggestions helpful, or too general? What concrete actions would you recommend to accomplish their objectives? At what cost?

* * *

This Chapter, which deals with the impact of the corporate strategies noted above on the collective bargaining relationship covers five distinct but related topics: withdrawal of recognition of an existing collective bargaining representative; decertification of such a representative; corporate successorship doctrine; the rejection of collective bargaining agreements in bankruptcy proceedings; and the complex interrelationship between antitrust and labor law, with its implications for ending the collective bargaining relationship. (Double-breasting, including the alter ego and single employer doctrines, is treated in Chapter 3, *supra* p. 341.)

B. WITHDRAWAL OF RECOGNITION

Recall from Chapter 4 that a newly-certified exclusive bargaining representative is conclusively presumed to have the support of a majority of the employees for one year and a newly-recognized exclusive representative is presumed to have majority support for a reasonable period of time. After the conclusive presumption period expires, the presumption becomes rebuttable. There is also a rebuttable presumption of majority support after a contract expires. The primary question for this section is: what sort of evidence does the employer need to rebut this presumption and withdraw recognition?

In the problem that opened this chapter, a group of mechanics approached Lozano and told him that many of them no longer supported the IAM as their bargaining representative. The mechanics could have gathered signatures and filed a decertification petition with the NLRB, but often employees are not aware of this option. Employees are generally more aware today because of the internet, but it is more likely that they will turn to their employer. How may the employer respond? May it simply withdraw recognition of the union? May it conduct a poll to determine whether the union continues to enjoy majority support? May it encourage the employees to file a decertification petition? May it file its own petition asking the Board to conduct an election? Consider the following case.

ALLENTOWN MACK SALES & SERVICE, INC. V. NLRB
522 U.S. 359 (1998)

JUSTICE SCALIA delivered the opinion of the Court.

Under longstanding precedent of the National Labor Relations Board, an employer who believes that an incumbent union no longer enjoys the support of a majority of its employees has three options: to request a formal, Board-supervised election, to withdraw recognition from the union and refuse to bargain, or to conduct an internal poll of employee support for the union. The Board has held that the latter two are unfair labor practices unless the employer can show that it had a "good-faith reasonable doubt" about the union's majority support. We must decide whether the Board's standard for employer polling is rational and consistent with the National Labor Relations Act, and whether the Board's factual determinations in this case are supported by substantial evidence in the record.

I

Mack Trucks, Inc., had a factory branch in Allentown, Pennsylvania, whose service and parts employees were represented by Local Lodge 724 of the International Association of Machinists, AFL-CIO (Local 724). Mack notified its Allentown managers in May 1990 that it intended to sell the branch, and several of those managers formed Allentown Mack Sales &

Service, Inc., the petitioner here, which purchased the assets of the business on December 20, 1990, and began to operate it as an independent dealership. From December 21, 1990, to January 1, 1991, Allentown hired 32 of the original 45 Mack employees.

During the period before and immediately after the sale, a number of Mack employees made statements to the prospective owners of Allentown Mack Sales suggesting that the incumbent union had lost support among employees in the bargaining unit. In job interviews, eight employees made statements indicating, or at least arguably indicating, that they personally no longer supported the union. In addition, Ron Mohr, a member of the union's bargaining committee and shop steward for the Mack Trucks service department, told an Allentown manager that it was his feeling that the employees did not want a union, and that "with a new company, if a vote was taken, the Union would lose." And Kermit Bloch, who worked for Mack Trucks as a mechanic on the night shift, told a manager that the entire night shift (then five or six employees) did not want the union.

On January 2, 1991, Local 724 asked Allentown Mack Sales to recognize it as the employees' collective-bargaining representative, and to begin negotiations for a contract. The new employer rejected that request by letter dated January 25, claiming a "good faith doubt as to support of the Union among the employees." The letter also announced that Allentown had "arranged for an independent poll by secret ballot of its hourly employees to be conducted under guidelines prescribed by the National Labor Relations Board." The poll, supervised by a Roman Catholic priest, was conducted on February 8, 1991; the union lost 19 to 13. Shortly thereafter, the union filed an unfair-labor-practice charge with the Board.

The Administrative Law Judge (ALJ) concluded that Allentown was a "successor" employer to Mack Trucks, Inc., and therefore inherited Mack's bargaining obligation and a presumption of continuing majority support for the union. The ALJ held that Allentown's poll was conducted in compliance with the procedural standards enunciated by the Board in *Struksnes Constr. Co.*, 165 N.L.R.B. 1062 (1967), but that it violated §§ 8(a)(1) and 8(a)(5) of the National Labor Relations Act (Act) because Allentown did not have an "objective reasonable doubt" about the majority status of the union. The Board adopted the ALJ's findings and agreed with his conclusion that Allentown "had not demonstrated that it harbored a reasonable doubt, based on objective considerations, as to the incumbent Union's continued majority status after the transition." The Board ordered Allentown to recognize and bargain with Local 724. [T]he Court of Appeals for the District of Columbia Circuit enforced the Board's bargaining order, over a vigorous dissent.

II

Allentown challenges the Board's decision in this case on several grounds. First, it contends that because the Board's "reasonable doubt" standard for employer polls is the same as its standard for unilateral withdrawal of recognition and for employer initiation of a Board-supervised election (a so-called "Representation Management," or "RM" election), the Board irrationally permits employers to poll only when it would be unnecessary and legally pointless to do so. Second, Allentown argues that the record evidence clearly demonstrates that it had a good-faith reasonable doubt about the union's claim to majority support. Finally, it asserts that the Board has, *sub silentio* (and presumably in violation of law), abandoned the "reasonable doubt" prong of its polling standard, and recognizes an employer's "reasonable doubt" only if a majority of the unit employees renounce the union.

While the Board's adoption of a unitary standard for polling, RM elections, and withdrawals of recognition is in some respects a puzzling policy, we do not find it so irrational as to be "arbitrary [or] capricious" within the meaning of the Administrative Procedure Act. The Board believes that employer polling is potentially "disruptive" to established bargaining relationships and "unsettling" to employees, and so has chosen to limit severely the circumstances under which it may be conducted. The unitary standard reflects the Board's apparent conclusion that polling should be tolerated only when the employer might otherwise simply withdraw recognition and refuse to bargain.

It is true enough that this makes polling useless as a means of insulating a contemplated withdrawal of recognition against an unfair-labor-practice charge-but there is more to life (and even to business) than escaping unfair-labor-practice findings. An employer concerned with good employee relations might recognize that abrupt withdrawal of recognition—even from a union that no longer has majority support—will antagonize union supporters, and perhaps even alienate employees who are on the fence. Preceding that action with a careful, unbiased poll can prevent these consequences. The "polls are useless" argument falsely assumes, moreover, that every employer will want to withdraw recognition as soon as he has enough evidence of lack of union support to defend against an unfair-labor-practice charge. It seems to us that an employer whose evidence met the "good-faith reasonable doubt" standard might nonetheless want to withdraw recognition only if he had conclusive evidence that the union in fact lacked majority support, lest he go through the time and expense of an (ultimately victorious) unfair-labor-practice suit for a benefit that will only last until the next election. And finally, it is probably the case that, though the standard for conviction of an unfair labor practice with regard to polling is identical to the standard with regard to withdrawal of recognition, the chance that a charge will be filed is significantly less with regard to the polling, particularly if the union wins.

It must be acknowledged that the Board's avowed preference for RM elections over polls fits uncomfortably with its unitary standard; that preference should logically produce a more rigorous standard for polling. But there are other reasons why the standard for polling ought to be less rigorous than the standard for Board elections. For one thing, the consequences of an election are more severe: If the union loses an employer poll it can still request a Board election, but if the union loses a formal election it is barred from seeking another for a year. If it would be rational for the Board to set the polling standard either higher or lower than the threshold for an RM election, then surely it is not irrational for the Board to split the difference.

III

The Board held Allentown guilty of an unfair labor practice in its conduct of the polling because it "ha[d] not demonstrated that it held a reasonable doubt, based on objective considerations, that the Union continued to enjoy the support of a majority of the bargaining unit employees." We must decide whether that conclusion is supported by substantial evidence on the record as a whole.

Before turning to that issue, we must clear up some semantic confusion. The Board asserted at argument that the word "doubt" may mean either "uncertainty" or "disbelief," and that its polling standard uses the word only in the latter sense. We cannot accept that linguistic revisionism. "Doubt" is precisely that sort of "disbelief" (failure to believe) which consists of an uncertainty rather than a belief in the opposite. If the subject at issue were the existence of God, for example, "doubt" would be the disbelief of the agnostic, not of the atheist. A doubt is an uncertain, tentative, or provisional disbelief.

The question presented for review, therefore, is whether, on the evidence presented to the Board, a reasonable jury could have found that Allentown lacked a genuine, reasonable uncertainty about whether Local 724 enjoyed the continuing support of a majority of unit employees. In our view, the answer is no. The Board's finding to the contrary rests on a refusal to credit probative circumstantial evidence, and on evidentiary demands that go beyond the substantive standard the Board purports to apply.

The Board adopted the ALJ's finding that 6 of Allentown's 32 employees had made "statements which could be used as objective considerations supporting a good-faith reasonable doubt as to continued majority status by the Union." And it presumably accepted the ALJ's assessment that "7 of 32, or roughly 20 percent of the involved employees" was not alone sufficient to create "an objective reasonable doubt of union majority support." The Board did not specify how many express disavowals would have been enough to establish reasonable doubt, but the number must presumably be less than 16 (half of the bargaining unit), since that would establish reasonable certainty. Still, we would not say that 20% first-hand-confirmed opposition (even with no countering evidence of union support) is alone enough to require a conclusion of reasonable doubt. But there was much more.

For one thing, the ALJ and the Board totally disregarded the effect upon Allentown of the statement of an eighth employee, Dennis Marsh, who said that "he was not being represented for the $35 he was paying." The ALJ, whose findings were adopted by the Board, said that this statement "seems more an expression of a desire for better representation than one for no representation at all." It seems to us that it is, more accurately, simply an expression of dissatisfaction with the union's performance—which could reflect the speaker's desire that the union represent him more effectively, but could also reflect the speaker's desire to save his $35 and get rid of the union. The statement would assuredly engender an uncertainty whether the speaker supported the union, and so could not be entirely ignored.

But the most significant evidence excluded from consideration by the Board consisted of statements of two employees regarding not merely their own support of the union, but support among the work force in general. Kermit Bloch, who worked on the night shift, told an Allentown manager "the entire night shift did not want the Union." The ALJ refused to credit this, because "Bloch did not testify and thus could not explain how he formed his opinion about the views of his fellow employees." Unsubstantiated assertions that other employees do not support the union certainly do not establish the fact of that disfavor with the degree of reliability ordinarily demanded in legal proceedings. But under the Board's enunciated test for polling, it is not the fact of disfavor that is at issue (the poll itself is meant to establish that), but rather the existence of a reasonable uncertainty on the part of the employer regarding that fact. On that issue, absent some reason for the employer to know that Bloch had no basis for his information, or that Bloch was lying, reason demands that the statement be given considerable weight.

Another employee who gave information concerning overall support for the union was Ron Mohr, who told Allentown managers that "if a vote was taken, the Union would lose" and that "it was his feeling that the employees did not want a union." The ALJ again objected irrelevantly that "there is no evidence with respect to how he gained this knowledge." In addition, the Board held that Allentown "could not legitimately rely on [the statement] as a basis for doubting the Union's majority status," because Mohr was "referring to Mack's existing employee complement, not to the individuals who were later hired by [Allentown]." This basis for disregarding Mohr's statements is wholly irrational. Local 724 had never won an election, or even an informal poll, within the actual unit of 32 Allentown employees. Its claim to represent them rested entirely on the Board's presumption that the work force of a successor company has the same disposition regarding the union as did the work force of the predecessor company, if the majority of the new work force came from the old one. The Board cannot rationally adopt that presumption for purposes of imposing the duty to bargain, and adopt precisely the opposite presumption (i.e., contend that there is no relationship between the sentiments of the two work forces) for purposes of determining what evidence tends to establish a reasonable doubt regarding union support. Such irrationality is impermissible even if it would further the Board's political objectives. It must be borne in mind that the issue here is not whether Mohr's statement clearly establishes a majority in opposition to the union, but whether it contributes to a reasonable uncertainty whether a majority in favor of the union existed. We think it surely does.

Giving fair weight to Allentown's circumstantial evidence, we think it quite impossible for a rational factfinder to avoid the conclusion that Allentown had reasonable, good-faith grounds to doubt—to be uncertain about—the union's retention of majority support.

That conclusion would make this a fairly straightforward administrative-law case, except for the contention that the Board's factfinding here was not an aberration. Allentown asserts that, although "the Board continues to cite the words of the good faith doubt branch of its withdrawal of recognition standard," a systematic review of the Board's decisions will reveal that "it has in practice eliminated the good faith doubt branch in favor of a strict head count." That the current decision may conform to a long pattern is also suggested by academic commentary. One scholar, after conducting "[a] thorough review of the withdrawal of recognition case law," concluded:

> "[C]ircumstantial evidence, no matter how abundant, is rarely, if ever, enough to satisfy the good-faith doubt test. In practice, the Board deems the test satisfied only if the employer has proven that a majority of the bargaining unit has expressly repudiated the union. Such direct evidence, however, is nearly impossible to gather lawfully. Thus, the Board's good-faith doubt standard, although ostensibly a highly fact-dependent totality-of-the-circumstances test, approaches a per se rule in application. . . ." Flynn, *The Costs and Benefits of "Hiding the Ball": NLRB Policymaking and the Failure of Judicial Review*, 75 B.U.L. Rev. 387, 394–395 (1995).

The Administrative Procedure Act, which governs the proceedings of administrative agencies and related judicial review, establishes a scheme of "reasoned decisionmaking." Not only must an agency's decreed result be within the scope of its lawful authority, but the process by which it reaches that result must be logical and rational. Courts enforce this principle with regularity when they set aside agency regulations which, though well within the agencies' scope of authority, are not supported by the reasons that the agencies adduce. The National Labor Relations Board has chosen to promulgate virtually all the legal rules in its field through adjudication rather than rulemaking. But adjudication is subject to the requirement of reasoned decisionmaking as well. It is hard to imagine a more violent breach of that requirement than applying a rule of primary conduct or a standard of proof which is in fact different from the rule or standard formally announced.

Reasoned decisionmaking, in which the rule announced is the rule applied, promotes sound results, and unreasoned decisionmaking the opposite. The evil of a decision that applies a standard other than the one it enunciates spreads in both directions, preventing both consistent application of the law by subordinate agency personnel (notably ALJ's), and effective review of the law by the courts. Because reasoned decisionmaking demands it, and because the systemic consequences of any other approach are unacceptable, the Board must be required to apply in fact the clearly understood legal standards that it enunciates in principle, such as good-faith reasonable doubt and preponderance of the evidence. Reviewing courts are entitled to take those standards to mean what they say, and to conduct substantial-evidence review on that basis. Even the most consistent and hence predictable Board departure from proper application of those standards will not alter the legal rule by which the agency's factfinding is to be judged.

For the foregoing reasons, we need not determine whether the Board has consistently rejected or discounted probative evidence so as to cause "good-faith reasonable doubt" or "preponderance of the evidence" to mean something more than what the terms connote. The line of precedents relied on by the ALJ and the Court of Appeals could not render irrelevant to the Board's decision, and hence to our review, any evidence that tends to establish the existence of a good-faith reasonable doubt. It was therefore error for the ALJ to discount Ron Mohr's opinion about lack of union support because of "the Board's historical treatment of unverified assertions by an employee about another employee's sentiments." Of course, the Board is entitled to be skeptical about the employer's claimed reliance on second-hand reports when the reporter has little basis for knowledge, or has some incentive to mislead. But that is a matter of logic and sound inference from all the circumstances, not an arbitrary rule of disregard to be extracted from prior Board decisions. The same is true of the Board precedents holding that "an employee's statements of dissatisfaction with the quality of union representation may not be treated as opposition to union representation," and that "an employer may not rely on an employee's anti-union sentiments, expressed during a job interview in which the employer has indicated that there will be no union."

We conclude that the Board's "reasonable doubt" test for employer polls is facially rational and consistent with the Act. But the Board's factual finding that Allentown Mack Sales lacked such a doubt is not supported by substantial evidence on the record as a whole. The judgment of the Court of Appeals for the District of Columbia Circuit is therefore reversed, and the case is remanded with instructions to deny enforcement.

[In a separate opinion Chief Justice Rehnquist, joined by Justices O'Connor, Kennedy and Thomas, concurred with Parts I, III and IV of the opinion of the Court but dissented from Part II's holding that the Board could rationally apply the same standard to an employer's polling of employees as to an employer's withdrawal of recognition. They urged, among other things:

["[T]he Board's rationale gives short shrift to the Act's goal of protecting employee choice. By ascertaining employee support for the union, a poll indirectly promotes this goal. Employees are not properly represented by a union lacking majority support. Employers also have a legitimate, recognized interest in not bargaining with a union lacking majority support. The ability to poll employees thus provides the employer (and the employees) with a neutral and effective manner of obtaining information relevant to determining the employees' proper representative and the employer's bargaining obligations. Stability, while an important goal of the Act, is not its be-all and end-all. That goal would not justify, for example, allowing a nonmajority union to remain in place (after a certification or contract bar has expired) simply by denying employers any effective means of ascertaining employee views. I conclude that the Board's standard restricts polling in the absence of coercion or restraint of employee rights and therefore is contrary to the Act.

[Quite apart from the lack of statutory authority for the Board's treatment of polling, this treatment irrationally equates employer polls, RM elections, and unilateral withdrawals of recognition. The Board argues that having the same standard for polls and unilateral withdrawals is reasonable because the employer can still use polls to confirm a loss of majority support. As a practical matter, this leaves little room for polling. But even conceding some remaining value to polling, the Board's rationale fails to address the basic inconsistency of imposing the same standard on two actions having dramatically different effects. Surely a unilateral withdrawal of recognition creates a greater disruption of the bargaining relationship and greater "doubts" in the minds of employees than does a poll. Consistent with the Board's reliance on such disruption to justify its polling standard, the standard for unilateral withdrawals should surely be higher.

[Justice Breyer, in an opinion joined by Justices Stevens, Souter and Ginsberg, concurred in Parts I and II, but dissented from Parts III and IV. They argued that the Court had improperly changed the Board's standard of objectively based good faith reasonable doubt to reasonable uncertainly and that the decision by the Board that Allentown Mack lacked an objectively reasonable good faith doubt was supported by substantial evidence in the record as a whole.]

NOTES

1.   *Balancing fundamental principles.* The employer's decision to end the bargaining relationship based on lack of union support touches on two fundamental principles of the NLRA that are in tension and must be balanced: the desire to promote stability in labor relations and the principle of employee free choice. It would frustrate the purposes of the Act to allow an employer to refuse to bargain with a union at any sign of employee discontent with the union. Indeed to uphold the value of stability in bargaining relationships, the Board and Court have developed the doctrine of the presumption of continuing majority status by the union. *See* Julius G. Getman, Bertrand B. Pogrebin & David L. Gregory, Labor Management Relations and the Law 29–34 (2d ed. 1999). On the other hand, if the employer bargaining with a union which the employer knew did not have majority support, this would frustrate the principle of employee free choice under the NLRA. In balancing these two principles sometimes one clearly dominates. For example, the presumption of continuing majority status is irrebutable at certain times, such as within the period of an election or contract bar, discussed in Chapter 4, *supra* p. 540. The primary question in *Allentown Mack* is not only what proof is required but also who bears the burden of proof. The Court addressed the question of, in the absence of a total bar, what sort of evidence the employer must offer to rebut the continuing presumption of majority status. Did the Court get the balance right?

2.   *The Board's unitary standard.* In *Allentown Mack*, the employer had to decide what to do when confronted with evidence that the union no longer represented a majority of employees in the unit. Why should an employer get involved in the matter at all if it is purely a question of employee free choice? Why should an employer have any interest in this? In seeking to end the bargaining relationship the employer might have undertaken three different options: (1) poll its employees to determine majority status, (2) initiate a "representation management," or "RM" election, or (3) unilaterally withdraw recognition without a poll or election. As the Court discusses, prior to *Allentown Mack*, the Board applied the same "unitary standard" of looking to see whether the employer had a "good faith reasonable doubt" based on "objective evidence" as to the union's majority status in determining whether employer actions were justified in all three of these cases. Although all three options might ultimately lead to the withdrawal of recognition from the union, they would seem to involve different levels of certainty and fairness in their procedures. Does it make sense to apply a unified standard to all three cases? Both the majority opinion and Chief Justice Rehnquist's opinion suggest that it would be rational for the Board to require a higher evidentiary standard for unilateral withdrawal of recognition; do you agree? A unitary standard makes

the choice between the three options less important doesn't it? What does the Court tell us is the Board's reason for a unified standard? Does this make sense under the NLRA?

3. *Reasonable doubt vs. reasonable uncertainty.* In *Allentown*, Justice Scalia criticized the Board's use of the term "disbelief" to explain the reasonable doubt standard, equating: (1) "disbelief" with "belief in the opposite" and (2) "doubt" with "uncertainty." Justice Scalia then argued that if one disbelieves, he or she must believe the opposite and so cannot be uncertain. As a result, Justice Scalia concluded that the term doubt cannot be usefully used to describe the reasonable doubt standard which must be equated with reasonable uncertainty. Are these semantic exercises useful in understanding the concept of good faith reasonable doubt? *See* Richard E. Levy & Robert L. Glicksman, *Agency-Specific Precedents,* 89 Tex. L. Rev. 499, 533–34 (2011). The examples of uncertainty and disbelief that Justice Scalia gave are an agnostic, who is uncertain about the existence of God, and an atheist, who disbelieves in God as a matter of faith. Is this a useful example for understanding the concept of "doubt" in the context of labor relations? Don't you think most employers would prefer a decertification election to simply withdrawing recognition given the certainty of the former?

4. *Evidence to support good faith reasonable doubt.* What sort of "objective evidence" can an employer use to support a good faith reasonable doubt? Signed statements from a majority of employees? Complaints from the employees about the union? Reports from employees on the desires of other employees? If the report is from a long-time union opponent, is that "objective evidence"? Do these statements and reports have to be unequivocal statements that the employee does not support the union? What if the union produces conflicting reports on employee support? In *Allentown Mack,* Justice Scalia criticized the Board for applying general rules to certain categories of evidence in applying a "totality of the circumstances" approach in weighing evidence. Are these approaches really inconsistent? Aren't general rules on the value of certain kinds of evidence exactly the sort of rules a specialized agency charged with enforcing a law should adopt? Won't such general rules give better notice to employers than Scalia's "holistic" approach? Did the Court give proper deference to the Board in this case?

5. *Determining majority status through unfair labor practice proceeding or election.* The Board's unitary standard gives no preference for determining the representation question through election as opposed to an unfair labor practice charge adjudication. Is this a sound policy? In formulating your answer, consider the subsequent facts in the *Allentown Mack* case. After Allentown withdrew recognition, the union collected cards, petitioned for a representation election and won the election. Should an employer be required to petition for a decertification election before withdrawing recognition?

In response to *Allentown Mack*, the Board issued the following decision.

LEVITZ FURNITURE CO.
333 N.L.R.B. 717 (2001)

By CHAIRMAN TRUESDALE and MEMBERS LIEBMAN, HURTGEN and WALSH:

In this case we reconsider whether, and under what circumstances, an employer may lawfully withdraw recognition unilaterally from an incumbent union. The Board has long held that an employer may withdraw recognition by showing either that the union has actually lost the support of a majority of the bargaining unit employees or that it has a good-faith doubt, based on objective considerations, of the union's continued majority status. *Celanese Corp.*, 95 N.L.R.B. 664 (1951). On the same showing of good-faith doubt, an employer may test an incumbent union's majority status by petitioning for a Board-conducted (RM) election, or by polling its employees to ascertain their union sentiments.

While this case was pending, the Supreme Court issued *Allentown Mack Sales & Service v. NLRB*, 522 U.S. 359 (1998), which addressed the Board's good-faith doubt standard. The Court held that maintaining a unitary standard for an employer's withdrawal of recognition, filing an RM petition, and polling its employees was rational, but indicated that the Board also could rationally adopt a nonunitary standard, including, in theory, imposing more stringent requirements for withdrawal of recognition. The Court also held that the Board's "good-faith doubt" standard must be interpreted to permit the employer to act where it has a "reasonable uncertainty" of the union's majority status, rejecting the Board's argument that the standard required a good-faith disbelief of the union's majority support.

In addressing the arguments concerning the *Celanese* rule and the standards for holding RM elections, then, we must take into account the Court's teachings in *Allentown Mack*. In particular, we must avoid the confusion over terminology which the Court identified in our application of the good-faith doubt standard.

After careful consideration, we have concluded that there are compelling legal and policy reasons why employers should not be allowed to withdraw recognition merely because they harbor uncertainty or even disbelief concerning unions' majority status. We therefore hold that an employer may unilaterally withdraw recognition from an incumbent union only where the union has actually lost the support of the majority of the bargaining unit employees, and we overrule *Celanese* and its progeny insofar as they permit withdrawal on the basis of good-faith doubt. Under our new standard, an employer can defeat a postwithdrawal refusal to bargain allegation if it shows, as a defense, the union's actual loss of majority status.

We have also decided to allow employers to obtain RM elections by demonstrating good-faith reasonable uncertainty (rather than disbelief) as to unions' continuing majority status. We adopt this standard to enable employers who seek to test a union's majority status to use the Board's election procedures—in our view the most reliable measure of union support—rather than the more disruptive process of unilateral withdrawal of recognition.

II. FACTS

The Respondent and the Union were parties to a collective-bargaining agreement that was effective from February 1, 1992, to and including January 31, 1995. On about December 1, 1994, the Respondent received a petition bearing what it concluded to be the signatures of a majority of the unit employees, stating that they no longer desired to be represented by the Union for purposes of collective bargaining. By letter dated December 2, 1994, the Respondent informed the Union that it had obtained objective evidence that the Union no longer represented a majority of the employees in the unit. The Respondent advised the Union that it would be withdrawing recognition from the Union effective February 1, 1995, but that it would continue to honor the agreement until it expired on January 31, 1995.

By letter dated December 14, 1994, the Union informed the Respondent that it was disputing the Respondent's claim that it had objective evidence that the Union no longer represented a majority of the unit employees. The letter also stated, "To the contrary, we are in possession of objective evidence that Local 101 does represent a majority of the bargaining unit employees at the South San Francisco facility. The Union is ready at any time to demonstrate this fact to you." By letter dated December 21, 1994, the Respondent acknowledged to the Union that it had received the Union's December 14 letter, but reiterated that the Respondent had received objective evidence from which it had concluded that the Union no longer represented a majority of the unit. The letter further stated that, except as required by the contract, the Respondent would no longer recognize the Union. At no time did the Respondent examine or request to examine the Union's alleged evidence of majority status. The record does not indicate the nature of the Union's evidence.

The Respondent continued to honor the terms of the contract until it expired on January 31, 1995; the contract was not renewed. When the agreement expired, the Respondent withdrew recognition from the Union as the collective-bargaining representative of the unit employees. Since February 1, 1995, the Respondent has failed and refused to bargain with the Union as the representative of the unit employees.

IV. HISTORICAL DEVELOPMENT OF THE GOOD-FAITH DOUBT STANDARD

Employers have always been able to rebut the presumption of continued majority status, and withdraw recognition by showing that a union has actually lost majority support. A harder question is raised when an employer cannot prove that the union no longer commands majority support but has a good-faith reason to be unsure of the union's majority status.

Under the Wagner Act, an employer who questioned a union's majority support was left to his own devices. At that time, an employer could not petition for a Board election unless two or more unions were vying to represent the same employees. Unless the union or the employees filed an election petition, the only way for such an employer to have the issue decided was to refuse to bargain and raise the union's lack of majority support as a defense in an unfair labor practice proceeding.

In that context, the Board held that an employer could lawfully refuse to recognize and bargain with either an incumbent union or a union seeking initial recognition, regardless of the union's actual degree of support, if the employer had a good-faith doubt as to the union's majority support and had not engaged in illegal conduct tending to erode the union's support. As we discuss below, that standard lacked a specific statutory basis, and it also allowed employers to refuse to recognize unions that actually had majority support. However, there was then at least some arguable basis for affording employers this means of resolving their uncertainties concerning unions' support, in the absence of any way to secure a Board election.

In 1947, as part of the Taft-Hartley amendments, Congress added Section 9(c)(1)(B), which provides for employer-filed RM petitions. Ever since, employers have had access to the Board's election procedures both when one union demands initial recognition and when employers doubt the majority support of incumbent unions. In early cases under Taft-Hartley, the Board rejected employers' claims that they had withdrawn recognition lawfully, in part because they had not availed themselves of the Board's election procedures. The Board held that the failure to invoke those procedures indicated that the employers' refusals to bargain were not based on doubts raised in good faith, but instead were motivated by a desire to evade their statutory duty to bargain.

In 1951, however, despite the Taft-Hartley Act's expansion of Section 9(c) to include RM petitions, the Board in *Celanese* abandoned this approach. Instead, the Board majority adhered to the Wagner Act policy of allowing withdrawals of recognition pursuant to the employer's good-faith doubt of the union's majority support. The majority held that there were two prerequisites to a finding of good faith: that the employer have some reasonable grounds for believing that the union had lost majority status, and that the employer not raise the issue in a context of illegal activities aimed at causing disaffection from the union. The majority indicated that the employer's failure to petition for a Board election might be "some evidence of bad faith," but held that the employer was not required to file an RM petition in order to demonstrate its good faith. The majority specifically held that withdrawal of recognition was lawful if done in good faith, regardless of whether the union actually did have majority support.

In applying the good-faith doubt standard, the Board generally required a showing of disbelief, not merely uncertainty, regarding a union's majority status. In fact, the Board (and some reviewing courts) used the terms "doubt" and "[dis]belief" interchangeably, sometimes in the same opinions.

Although the Board abandoned the good-faith doubt standard in the initial recognition setting some 30 years ago, it continued to adhere to that standard (as set forth in *Celanese*) in the withdrawal of recognition context. The standard came under criticism because it was the same standard that the Board required employers to meet in order to petition for an RM election and to poll their employees concerning their support for unions. Some commentators argued that applying the same standard to all three kinds of conduct would tend to discourage employers from petitioning for elections, and that this was inconsistent with the Board's preference for elections as the optimal means of testing employees' support for unions. Employers also criticized the Board's application of the standard. They contended that the Board erroneously refused to consider certain kinds of evidence tending to establish good-faith doubt, and even suggested that the Board had, *sub silentio*, abandoned the good-faith doubt standard and in practice required employers to prove actual loss of majority status in order to withdraw recognition.

In *Allentown Mack*, a case involving polling, the Supreme Court addressed those concerns. The Court held that the Board had not acted irrationally in adopting a "unitary standard" for polling, withdrawal of recognition, and petitioning for RM elections, although it indicated that the Board could have adopted a more stringent standard for either withdrawing recognition or polling. However, the Court agreed with several of the criticisms of the Board's application of the good-faith doubt standard. Initially, the Court held that, having enunciated the standard in terms of good-faith doubt, the Board must interpret the standard to mean uncertainty, not disbelief. Second, the Court found that under that standard, the employer, which had refused to bargain and conducted a private poll of its employees (which the union lost), had harbored a genuine, reasonable uncertainty about the union's continued majority support.

The Court's decision in *Allentown Mack* had a significant impact on the Board's long established scheme. As a result of that decision, employers may now withdraw recognition from unions based on reasonable uncertainty, a less stringent standard than the Board's disbelief standard. At the same time, the Court indicated that the Board has substantial flexibility in this area to devise a scheme that promotes the Act's policies of promoting stable collective bargaining and employee free choice. Thus, we read the Court as permitting us to depart from our historic unitary standard and to impose a more stringent requirement in withdrawal of recognition cases.

V. ANALYSIS

A. New Standards for Withdrawing Recognition and Filing RM Petitions

Withdrawals of recognition. The fundamental policies of the Act are to protect employees' right to choose or reject collective-bargaining representatives, to encourage collective bargaining, and to promote stability in bargaining relationships. If employees' exercise of the right to choose union representation is to be meaningful, their choices must be respected by employers. That means that employers must not be allowed to refuse to recognize unions that are, in fact, the choice of a majority of their employees. It also means that collective-bargaining relationships must be given an opportunity to succeed, without continual baseless challenges. These considerations underlie the presumption of continuing majority status:

> The presumption of continuing majority status essentially serves two important functions of Federal labor policy. First, it promotes continuity in bargaining relationships. The resulting industrial stability remains a primary objective of the Wagner Act, and to an even greater extent, the Taft-Hartley Act. Second, the presumption of continuing majority status protects the express statutory right of employees to designate a collective-bargaining representative of their own choosing, and to prevent an employer from impairing that right without some objective evidence that the representative the employees have designated no longer enjoys majority support. *Pennex Aluminum Corp.*, 288 N.L.R.B. 439, 441 (1988), *enf'd*, 869 F.2d 590 (3d Cir. 1989)

In view of these considerations, we are persuaded that *Celanese* and its progeny do not further important statutory goals insofar as they hold that an employer may lawfully withdraw recognition on the basis of good-faith doubt (either uncertainty or disbelief) concerning the union's continued majority support.

To begin, the *Celanese* rule is not compelled by the text of the Act. There is no suggestion in the text that an employer may ever, even in good faith, withdraw recognition of an incumbent union that actually enjoys majority support. Allowing employers to withdraw recognition from majority unions undermines central policies of the Act. It wrongfully destroys the parties' bargaining relationship and, as a result, frustrates the exercise of employee free choice. Nor is unilateral withdrawal of recognition based on the employer's good-faith disbelief or uncertainty as to the union's majority status necessary to give effect to other policies under the Act. Such withdrawals are not necessary to ensure that employees can freely reject an incumbent union. If a majority of the unit employees present evidence that they no longer support their union, their employer may lawfully withdraw recognition. Even absent such a showing, if 30 percent of unit employees are unhappy with their union, they can file a decertification (RD) petition and the Board will determine in a secret ballot election whether the union will continue as their representative-all without any assistance from the employer.

For all of these reasons, we hold that an employer may rebut the continuing presumption of an incumbent union's majority status, and unilaterally withdraw recognition, only on a showing that the union has, in fact, lost the support of a majority of the employees in the bargaining unit. We overrule *Celanese* and its progeny insofar as they hold that an employer may lawfully withdraw recognition on the basis of a good-faith doubt (uncertainty or disbelief) as to the union's continued majority status.

We emphasize that an employer with objective evidence that the union has lost majority support—for example, a petition signed by a majority of the employees in the bargaining unit—withdraws recognition at its peril. If the union contests the withdrawal of recognition in an unfair labor practice proceeding, the employer will have to prove by a preponderance of the evidence that the union had, in fact, lost majority support at the time the employer withdrew recognition. If it fails to do so, it will not have rebutted the presumption of majority status, and the withdrawal of recognition will violate Section 8(a)(5).

RM elections. Given our ruling above regarding withdrawals of recognition, we think it appropriate to reconsider the showing that we shall require for holding employer-requested elections. After careful consideration of all the options, we have decided to adopt the lower—uncertainty—standard. The Board and the courts have consistently said that Board elections are the preferred method of testing employees' support for unions. And we think that processing RM petitions on a lower showing of good-faith uncertainty will provide a more attractive alternative to unilateral action. By contrast, were we to require employers to demonstrate a higher showing of good-faith belief of lost majority support in order to obtain an RM election, we might encourage some employers instead to withdraw recognition rather than seeking an election. Thus, by liberalizing the standard for holding RM elections, we are promoting both employee free choice (by making it easier to ascertain employees' support for unions via Board elections) and stability in collective-bargaining relationships (which remain intact during representation proceedings).

B.   Evidence Required to Establish Good-Faith Reasonable Uncertainty

We turn now to the kinds of evidence that employers may present to establish good-faith reasonable uncertainty. Clearly, antiunion petitions signed by unit employees and firsthand statements by employees concerning personal opposition to an incumbent union could contribute to employer uncertainty.

Prior to *Allentown Mack*, the Board consistently declined to rely on certain kinds of evidence to establish a good-faith doubt. For example, the Board did not consider employees' unverified statements regarding other employees' antiunion sentiments to be reliable evidence of opposition to the union. Similarly, the Board viewed employees' statements expressing dissatisfaction with the union's performance as the bargaining representative as not showing opposition to union representation itself. The Board's treatment of such evidence was consistent with the good-faith disbelief standard that the Board applied. But, as the Court held in *Allentown Mack*, the Board's good-faith doubt standard could only mean good-faith uncertainty, and either of those kinds of statements could contribute to such uncertainty.

We therefore hold that statements of the type described above should be considered by the regional offices when processing RM petitions. The regional offices should take into account all of the evidence which, viewed in its entirety, might establish uncertainty as to unions' continued majority status. In RM cases, the regional offices should determine whether good-faith uncertainty exists on the basis of evidence that is objective and that reliably indicates employee opposition to incumbent unions—i.e., evidence that is not merely speculative. The specific types of evidence that are probative of such uncertainty, and the weight to be afforded each type under the circumstances, will be decided on a case-by-case basis.

MEMBER HURTGEN, concurring:

Under previously established principles of law, an employer can withdraw recognition from an incumbent union if the employer has a good-faith uncertainty as to the union's majority status.

In the decision issued today, my colleagues overrule this principle. Hereafter, an employer can withdraw recognition only if the employer correctly determines that the union has lost majority status.

I disagree. As my colleagues recognize, they are reversing legal principles which go back half-a-century. Indeed, in recognition of that sharp reversal, my colleagues apply previously extant law to this case and dismiss the complaint.

[M]y colleagues mandate continued recognition of the union, even where the employer has a good-faith belief that the union has lost majority status. My colleagues do this in the interest of fostering the collective bargaining process. In this regard, they rely upon the preamble to the Act which states that the policy of the United States is to "encourage the practice and procedure of collective bargaining." However, the Act itself, in its substantive provisions, gives employees the fundamental right to choose whether to engage in collective bargaining or not. The preamble and the substantive provisions of the Act are not inconsistent. Read together, they pronounce a policy under which our nation protects and encourages the practice and procedure of collective bargaining *for those employees who have freely chosen to engage in it.* My colleagues, by relying on the preamble, have diminished the importance of the latter part of this principle. The result, I fear, is to impose a union on nonconsenting employees. I would retain the extant rule which balances the interests of collective bargaining and the Section 7 rights of employees.

[M]y colleagues have subjected employers to a guessing game. If the employer guesses wrongly, the employer violates the Act, notwithstanding his good faith. I prefer that these matters not be the subject of a guessing game. They should be a matter of good faith. If the employer has a good-faith uncertainty as to majority status, the employer can withdraw recognition. If the employer has a good-faith belief of majority status, he can continue recognition.

My colleagues say that there is a way out of the dilemma, viz, the employer can file an RM petition and obtain a Board election. And, in this regard, they say that they would permit the processing of an RM petition if there is uncertainty as to the Union's majority status. I agree with this RM standard. However, I do not agree that the RM petition offers a solution to the problem discussed above. That is, it does not obviate the necessity for the extant rule which grants employers the option of withdrawal of recognition on a showing of uncertainty as to the union's majority status. My reasons are set forth below.

RM petitions are subject to the "blocking charge" principle. Faced with an RM petition, unions can file charges to forestall or delay the election. Concededly, in some situations, the Regional Director can dismiss the charges or can decide that the charges, even if meritorious, would not preclude a valid election. However, that determination requires investigatory time. *During that time, the employer must continue recognition of the incumbent Union.*

Further, the Regional Director also has the power to issue complaint, and the authority to conclude that the charges *do* preclude a valid election. The Board has no power to review the former determination, and the Board reviews the latter only under an "abuse of discretion" standard. If the Regional Director so concludes, the charge will block the election for the prolonged period during which the charge/complaint is litigated. Although the employer could settle the case, he may not wish to do so if he believes that he has a valid defense. Further, even if the employer litigates and wins after prolonged litigation, the block will be removed only after that litigation. *In the meantime, the employer must continue recognition of the incumbent.*

In addition, even if there is no blocking charge, or if the block is removed, the election will not necessarily resolve the question concerning representation. In those cases where the union loses the election, the union can file objections and/or challenges. There is often a prolonged period for the litigation of these matters. *The employer must recognize the incumbent during the period of this litigation.*

In sum, the RM road can be a long and difficult one. During this prolonged period, the employer must continue recognition, even though there is good-faith uncertainty as to the union's majority status. In my view, it is far better to resolve the matter by having an RC election. That is, after the employer has withdrawn recognition based on a good-faith uncertainty (a lawful withdrawal in my view), the union can immediately file an RC petition. Although the union could file blocking charges, its interest presumably would be to have a quick election and resume its representation status. Further, the Board correctly gives a high priority to processing such petitions as expeditiously as possible. Thus, I would continue this approach. It comports with current law and procedures, and it is not shown to be deficient.

NOTES

1.   In *Allentown Mack*, a majority of the Court held that the Board may apply the same standard in judging the validity of an employer's withdrawal of recognition, an employer's polling of its employees concerning whether they wish to continue to be represented, and an employer's filing of an RM petition. In *Levitz*, the Board majority decided to abandon that approach. Who does this favor? The union, employees, or employer? Which approach is preferable? What should the standards be?

2.   What arguments might you raise for the proposition that an employer should only be allowed to file an RM petition and should never be allowed to unilaterally withdraw recognition?

3.   As Member Hurtgen observed in his concurring opinion, the Board announced its new rule that an employer may only withdraw recognition when the union has in fact lost majority support among the employees, but did not apply the rule to the case before it. Recall from Chapter 4 that the Board did the same thing in *Excelsior Underwear*. Later, a Supreme Court majority opined that the *Excelsior* Board had engaged in rulemaking in violation of the Administrative Procedures Act (APA) by not following the statutory requirements. However, a different majority of the Court held that in the case before it the Board did engage in appropriate adjudication. Thus, the Board could effectively engage in rulemaking, bypass the APA's rulemaking procedures and still apply the rule in subsequent cases. Is this appropriate? Note that rulemaking under state administrative procedure acts may allow less leeway. *See, e.g., Snohomish Cty. Pub. Transp. Ben. Area v. PERB,* 173 Wash. App. 504, 518–21, 294 P.3d 803, 811–12 (2013) (Washington state law takes narrower approach to rulemaking by adjudication).

4. If an employer unilaterally withdraws recognition, a union may respond by filing a Section 8(a)(5) charge contesting the validity of the withdrawal or by filing a new representation petition seeking to reestablish its majority support. Which is the better strategy for the union? In light of the *Levitz* decision, what is the best strategy for an employer who believes that the union no longer has the support of a majority of its employees? In *Scomas of Sausalito v. NLRB,* 849 F.3d 1147 (D.C. Cir. 2017), the court overruled an NLRB decision and order imposing a bargaining order as a remedy for employer withdrawal of recognition of a union enjoying majority support. The union filed a ULP when the employer withdrew recognition. The court agreed that the employer had violated the law under *Levitz* by withdrawing recognition without knowing that the union had "in fact" lost majority support. *Id.* at 1151. However, the court stated that a bargaining order is an extraordinary remedy and should not be imposed in a case like *Scomas* where six employees revoked signatures on a decertification petition and "the Union withheld information about its restored majority status." *Id.* at 1156.

5. Is employer polling to test the continuing support of an incumbent union qualitatively different from employer polling to test the support of a union seeking to organize unrepresented employees? An employer might eliminate some risk by polling employees *after* a decertification attempt in order to assure itself that in fact the union no longer is supported by a majority. *See, e.g., Unifirst Corp.,* 346 N.L.R.B. 591 (2006). What arguments support allowing employers liberally to poll when they believe an incumbent union has lost the support of a majority of employees? What arguments support prohibiting employers from ever polling where there is an incumbent union? After *Levitz,* the standard for employer conduct during a decertification effort is high. In fact, polling is seldom used by employers because of the risks and difficulties. See the discussion of polling in Chapter 4E. In *Bradford Printing & Finishing, LLC,* 356 N.L.R.B. 899 (2011), the Board found that continuous statements by the employer that a union is "unnecessary" along with an ongoing refusal to recognize and bargain with the union is "conduct [that] tainted the employee petition." Therefore, the employer was precluded from using an employee petition as a reason for its refusal to recognize and bargain with the union. Assume that the union has gone on strike, a sizable minority of employees have crossed the picket line, and the employer has permanently replaced most of the remaining strikers. Should there be any presumption concerning the replacements' or the crossovers' support for continued representation by the union? Is it likely that incumbent employees cross the picket line because they no longer desire representation? Because they cannot afford financially to remain on strike? Because they disagree with their union's bargaining position but still desire union representation? What about the sentiments of permanent replacements, considering that most unions demand as a condition of a strike settlement that replacements be bumped by returning strikers? Do any policy considerations about the collective bargaining process affect your answers to these questions? How might a presumption that replacements or crossovers are opposed to continued union representation affect the behavior of the union and the employer in negotiations? How might

such a presumption affect the likelihood that a union will strike or that an employer will provoke a strike? *See NLRB v. Curtin Matheson Scientific, Inc.*, 494 U.S. 775 (1990) (Board's refusal to presume that striker replacements oppose union, for purpose of determining whether employer had good-faith doubt as to union's majority status, was rational and consistent with the NLRA).

C. DECERTIFICATION

Section 9(c)(1)(A)(ii) of the NLRA allows an employee or a group of employees to file a petition asserting that an existing exclusive bargaining representative no longer enjoys majority support. The NLRB will typically order a decertification election so long as (1) the petition is supported by a "substantial" number of employees, and (2) there is no existing bar to an election. When an incumbent union is able successfully to negotiate successive labor contracts, for example, the "contract bar" rule will prevent a valid decertification petition except during the 30 day period that falls 90 to 60 days before the expiration date of a given labor contract. But, what happens if the decertification process is tainted by employer unfair labor practices that might lead one to question whether a substantial number of employees actually support the petition?

SFO GOOD-NITE INN, LLC
357 N.L.R.B. 79 (2011)

By Chairman Liebman and Members Pearce and Hayes:

The National Labor Relations Board has delegated its authority in this proceeding to a three-member panel.

The Board has considered the judge's decision and the record in light of the exceptions and briefs and has decided to affirm the judge's rulings, findings, and conclusions[, but as] to the Respondent's withdrawal of recognition, discussed in section III of the prior decision, we adopt the judge's recommended Order only for the reasons explained below.

The judge concluded that the Respondent violated Section 8(a)(5) and (1) of the Act by withdrawing recognition from the Union on September 14, 2005, after committing a number of unfair labor practices directly related to encouraging its employees' decertification efforts. Applying the causation analysis in *Master Slack Corporation (Master Slack)*, 271 NLRB 78 (1984), he found that the Respondent's unlawful conduct tainted employee petitions disavowing support for the Union. In limited cross-exceptions, the General Counsel argues that, besides the judge's *Master Slack* causation analysis, the Respondent's misconduct *per se* precluded its reliance on the petitions as a valid basis for withdrawing recognition. We agree. As we explain below, the disposition of this case is properly controlled by *Hearst Corp.*, 281 NLRB 764 (1986), enfd. Mem. 837 F.3d

1088 (5th Cir. 1988), holding that an employer may not withdraw recognition based on a petition that it unlawfully assisted, supported, or otherwise unlawfully encouraged, even absent specific proof of the misconduct's effect on employee choice.

I

An incumbent union enjoys a continuing presumption of majority status, which is irrebuttable during a union's first year following certification or the first 3 years of a collective-bargaining agreement. When the presumption is rebuttable, an employer may withdraw recognition from an incumbent union upon receiving proof that an actual majority of its unionized employees no longer desire union representation. That privilege, however, is not absolute. Rather, it is well settled that an employer may only withdraw recognition if the expression of employee desire to decertify represents "the free and uncoerced act of the employees concerned."

Both *Master Slack* and *Hearst* apply that limitation, but in two different contexts. As the Fourth Circuit recently observed, *Master Slack* prescribes a four-part causation analysis to determine whether there is "a causal link between decertification efforts and *other* unfair labor practices distinct from any unlawful assistance by the employer in the actual decertification petition." *Narricot Industries v. NLRB*, 587 F.3d 654, 664–665 (4th Cir. 2009). In *Master Slack* itself, the Board considered whether the employer's threats of plant closure and discriminatory discharges of 28 employees, among other things, that occurred almost 10 years before the withdrawal of recognition affected the employees' rejection of the union, and concluded that they did not. In such cases, there is no straight line between the employer's unfair labor practices and the decertification campaign, and the *Master Slack* test must be used to draw one, if it exists.

By contrast, *Hearst* applies when an employer has engaged in unfair labor practices directly related to an employee decertification effort, such as "actively soliciting, encouraging, promoting, or providing assistance in the initiation, signing, or filing of an employee petition seeking to decertify the bargaining representative." Wire Products Mfg. Co., 326 NLRB 625, 640 (1998). In those situations, the employer's unfair labor practices are not merely coincident with the decertification effort; rather, they directly instigate or propel it. The Board therefore presumes that the employer's unlawful meddling tainted any resulting expression of employee disaffection, without specific proof of causation, and precludes the employer from relying on that expressed disaffection to overcome the union's continuing presumption of majority support.

II.

Here, the Respondent unlawfully attempted to coerce three of its housekeepers to sign employee decertification petitions and threatened another employee with discipline for speaking against decertification. Specifically, the judge made the following findings:

- In late August 2005, Respondent's general manager and banquet manager called housekeepers Christina Valencia and Maria Maldonado—whom the Respondent later unlawfully terminated for their union support—to a meeting, told them that the Union was "no good," and unlawfully attempted to coerce them to sign a petition to "deunionize."

- Immediately thereafter, another manager approached housekeeper Margarita Taloma, asked her to sign a decertification petition, threatened that the Union might attempt to reduce her hours, and promised that the Respondent would protect her from the Union's efforts, if Taloma signed the petition. When Taloma demurred, the same manager later unlawfully pressured Taloma at her home.

- As the decertification campaign picked up in early September 2005, Respondent's general manager and one of its owners unlawfully threatened room inspectress and union negotiating committee member Consuelo Contreras with discharge for urging her coworkers not to sign the decertification petition, despite the absence of any rule against such solicitation during work hours.

The judge found that all of those acts violated Section 8(a)(1), and we agree.

After committing these violations, the Respondent withdrew recognition on September 14, 2005, based on petitions signed by 14 of the 24 unit employees. The Respondent's unfair labor practices were obviously directly related to furthering the employees' decertification campaign. Consequently, we agree with the General Counsel that the judge should have applied *Hearst*, rather than a *Master Slack* analysis. Doing so, we find that the Respondent's violations tainted the resulting employee petitions and rendered them an unreliable indicator of employee choice. The Respondent's withdrawal of recognition based on those petitions therefore violated Section 8(a)(5) and (1) of the Act.

III.

Despite its unlawful attempts to coerce employees to sign decertification petitions and its threat to discipline an employee for opposing decertification, the Respondent argues that its withdrawal of recognition from the Union was lawful because neither Valencia, Maldonado, nor Taloma actually succumbed to its coercion, and there was no evidence that any of the 14 employees who did add his name to the decertification petitions knew about the Respondent's coercive acts. The Board's decision in *Hearst* forecloses that argument, however. In *Hearst*, the Board rejected an employer's attempt to resuscitate the reliability of a decertification petition by proving that a majority of petition signers were unaware of its unfair labor practices. There, the employer's violations were similar to the Respondent's here—promising better benefits if employees rejected the union, interrogating employees about their union sympathies, explicitly soliciting union repudiation, and threatening employees to keep away from union representatives, among other things. The employer pointed to testimony from 19 employees (out of a unit of 56) that they were unaware of the unfair labor practices, suggesting that the decertification petition signers expressed an untainted desire to repudiate the union.

The Board rejected counting the number of petition signers the unfair labor practices affected. The Board made clear that, where "an employer engages in unlawful activity aimed specifically at causing employee disaffection with their union, its misconduct . . . will bar any reliance on an expression of disaffection by its employees, notwithstanding that some employees may profess ignorance of their employer's misconduct." 281 NLRB at 765. Justifying the rule, the Board explained that, when an employer unlawfully foists itself into an employee decertification campaign, it "cannot expect to take advantage of the chance occurrence that some of its employees may be unaware of its actions," but rather "must be held responsible for the foreseeable consequence of its conduct." *Id.*

Hearst thus creates a conclusive presumption that an employer's commission of unfair labor practices assisting, supporting, encouraging, or otherwise directly advancing an employee decertification effort taints a resulting petition. As described, this presumption is based on the predictable result of an employer's unlawful, direct participation in an employee decertification effort—a petition plagued with uncertainty because of the very nature of the employer's unfair labor practices, which is *per se* insufficient to rebut the presumption of continuing majority status. We reaffirm the *Hearst* presumption today. . . .

[W]e emphasize the narrow role the *Hearst* presumption plays in the mechanics of how and when a bargaining relationship may be ended. . . .We are . . . dealing only with the narrow circumstance where an employer unlawfully instigates or propels a decertification campaign, and then invokes the results of that campaign to justify its unilateral withdrawal of recognition from its employees' representative. In that circumstance, it is particularly appropriate, as the Court stated in *Auciello Iron Works v. NLRB,* to give a "short leash to the employer as vindicator of its employees' organizational freedom." 581 U.S. 781, 790 (1986). Thus, as the Court further observed in *Auciello*, "[t]he Board is accordingly entitled to suspicion when faced with an employer's benevolence as its workers' champion against their certified union, which is subject to a decertification petition from the workers if they want to file one." *Id.*

Nevertheless, the *Hearst* presumption is not the product of mere suspicion. Rather, it is grounded in the Board's approach, in all cases, of objectively assessing whether an employer's unlawful interference with employee rights likely undermined the reliability of an expression of employee choice. Unlike a *Master Slack* situation, however, when an employer unlawfully thrusts itself into its employees' decertification debate there is little need for extended analysis of the likely impact of the employer's misconduct. As recognized in *Hearst* and in other cases, the objective "foreseeable consequence" of such misconduct—and frequently its purpose—is "an inherent tendency to contribute to the union's loss of majority status." 281 NLRB at 765. Thus, no direct proof of the unfair labor practices' effect on petition signers is necessary to conclude that the violations likely interfered with their choice.

Further, as a matter of policy, to the extent *Hearst* broadly prohibits employers from withdrawing recognition based on decertification petitions that they themselves unlawfully assisted, it provides a strong incentive to employers to steer clear of potentially unlawful conduct. Any other rule would condone the employer's unlawful acts, allowing it to take advantage of its coercion so long as its victims remained silent. . . . The likelihood that employees would remain silent about their employer's unlawful conduct and/or its impact on their choice is quite real, moreover. To the extent that an employer seeks to elicit employee testimony about their reasons for signing documents supporting or rejecting a union, the Board and the courts have long recognized the inherent unreliability of such testimony. As the Supreme Court observed in upholding the Board's rule prohibiting employers from demanding employee testimony explaining why they signed authorization cards, "employees are more likely than not, many months after a card drive and in response to questions by company counsel, to give testimony damaging to the union, particularly where company officials have previously threatened reprisals for union activity in violation of § 8(a)(1)." *NLRB v. Gissel Packing Co.*, 395 U.S. 575, 608 (1969). Consequently, in logic that applies equally here, the Court explained that questioning employees about the subjective motives for their representation preferences would result in "endless and unreliable inquiry." *Id.* For those reasons, as well, we are unwilling to subject petition signers to *ex post facto* examination about their reasons for supporting decertification.

MEMBER HAYES, concurring in part and dissenting in part.

I agree with my colleagues that the Respondent's unlawful involvement with the employees' petition tainted its reliability as an indicator of disaffection with the Union. However, I believe that the *Hearst* presumption of taint should be rebuttable rather than irrebuttable, thereby raising the possibility in future cases that the representational desires of a majority of employees unaffected by, or possibly even unaware of, unlawful employer involvement can be honored.

In my view, the evidentiary issue of whether an employer's unlawful involvement in decertification taints a petition stands at midpoint between

Master Slack, 271 NLRB 78 (1984), where the General Counsel bears the burden of proving that unfair labor practices caused employee disaffection, and *Lee Lumber & Building Material Corp.*, 322 NLRB 175, 177 (1996) (*Lee Lumber II*), enfd. in relevant part and remanded in part 117 F.3d 1454 (D.C. Cir. 1997), where the presumption of taint in a showing of disaffection after an unlawful withdrawal of recognition is irrebuttable. In the former instance, there is no warrant for presuming that *any* unfair labor practice, no matter how remote in time from the employee petition or limited in degree or scope, has an impact on employee free choice. In the latter instance, there are sound policy reasons for denying an employer from even attempting to prove that its unlawful withdrawal of recognition, which necessarily impacts the entire bargaining unit, had no impact on a subsequent showing of disaffection.

There are, as well, valid policy reasons for discouraging material employer involvement in employee decertification efforts. Those reasons support a presumption of taint arising from unlawful involvement, shifting the evidentiary burden to the wrongdoing employer to present objective proof that its misconduct did not cause or further disaffection with an incumbent bargaining representative. However, unlike in refusal to recognize and bargain situations, the employer's unlawful conduct does not necessarily impact all bargaining unit employees. It remains possible, even if not likely, that subsequent evidence of disaffection by an employee majority is an accurate and reliable expression of free choice on the issue of continued collective-bargaining representation. I therefore disagree with my colleagues that in such circumstances employee free choice must be denied or deferred as the result of an irrebuttable presumption of taint.

The difference between a rebuttable presumption and an irrebuttable presumption is of no significance in the present case, where the Respondent has failed to show that its misconduct could not have tainted the employees' petition. I therefore agree that its withdrawal of recognition based on this petition violated Section 8(a)(5) and (1) of the Act.

NOTES

1. The *Hearst* presumption was viewed by the majority in *SFO Good-Nite* to be rebuttable, prompting disagreement by Member Hayes in his concurring opinion. The Hayes view that the *Hearst* presumption should be rebuttable is likely to carry the day with more conservative Boards. Indeed, in *Linwood Care Center,* 2016 WL 627282 (Feb. 17, 2016), a more conservative Board panel (Pearce, Miscimarra, Hirozawa) dismissed an employer petition seeking reversal of a Regional Director decision in a decertification case while expressly finding it "unnecessary to rely on *SFO Good-Nite Inn*" in so doing. *Id.* at 627282 n.1.

2. In the problem that opened this chapter, a group of mechanics approached Lozano and told him that many mechanics no longer wished to be

represented by the IAM. Assume that Lozano does not want to withdraw recognition, poll or even file an RM petition. He prefers that the employees take action themselves. Lozano likely does nothing objectionable by referring the employees to the regional office of the NLRB. May Lozano do more? May he explain the decertification process to the employees? May he have his lawyer draft the decertification petition? If Lozano involves his lawyer, does that raise an ethical issue for the lawyer? May Lozano take the completed petition to the regional office to file it as a convenience to the employees? May he actively encourage employees to support the decertification effort?

3. *"Decertification" under the Railway Labor Act.* The language of the RLA does not seem to envision a nonunion environment. The rights and duties under that statute run only to a "representative." Unlike the NLRA, the RLA has no statutory provision providing for decertification of a bargaining representative. As a result, a technique adopted by those seeking to "decertify" under the RLA involves running a single worker against the union in an election, commonly referred to as a "straw man," who, immediately upon prevailing, would renounce any interest in representing the workers and ask to terminate the collective bargaining relationship. Thus, in *Russell v. NMB*, 714 F.2d 1332 (5th Cir. 1983), the court faced a situation in which the National Mediation Board (NMB), the federal agency having exclusive jurisdiction to decide representational matters under the Act, had refused to process the representation application of a "straw man" who had agreed to stand for election. According to the court,

> that Russell did not "intend to represent" his fellow employees in the accustomed fashion, however, does not mean that he did not "intend to represent" them within the meaning of the Act. Section 1, Sixth, defines "representative" as "any person or persons, labor union, organization, or corporation designated either by a carrier . . . or by its . . . employees, to act for it or them." There are no qualifiers attached to the Act's simple definition of "representative." The "representative" of a craft of employees is, simply, a person or union designated to act on their behalf, to accomplish what they seek to accomplish, and is not necessarily a man for all seasons. [T]he Act nowhere requires collective representation. To accept the Board's definition of "intent to represent" would be to impose such a requirement. A claimed majority of the craft here wanted Russell, apparently, to terminate collective bargaining. Torturous interpretations of "representation" aside, Russell fits the bill.

Id. at 1341–42.

DECERTIFICATION ELECTIONS AND INDUSTRIAL STABILITY: NEED FOR REFORM

Douglas E. Ray
1984 Ariz. St. L.J. 257 (1984)

Decertification is important because it intersects with two major labor policies. Although decertification directly fosters employees' section 7 rights to refrain from union activities, decertification can be a threat to industrial stability, one of the prime goals of the labor laws. [E]mployees' statutory right to decertify their collective bargaining representative has been interpreted and administered in a manner that neither fosters employees' rights to refrain from union activity nor preserves industrial stability.

To enable the decertification process to become the primary means by which an incumbent union may be removed, employees need to be furnished with adequate information as to their rights. First, the appropriate party to provide information needs to be determined. Possible providers of information include the employer, the union and the NLRB. Of the three alternatives, the employer is the least appropriate. An employer providing employees with information on how to decertify their union violates its duty to bargain with that union in good faith and may interfere with employee rights. Instead either the union or the NLRB should advise employees of their rights.

The union could have an incentive to provide the information. The employer might be denied the opportunity to withdraw recognition if the union posted notices advising employees of their rights and the employees took no steps to decertify. The present rules for determining the legality of an employer's withdrawal of recognition could apply, however, were the union not to post such notice. To require the union to advise employees of their decertification rights, however, is to ask it to act contrary to its best interests. This may not be practical.

The preferred alternative is for the NLRB to require the posting of official notices advising employees of their rights. Such notice is not entirely unprecedented. The notices, of course, should neither encourage nor discourage the filing of petitions. Again, if with full knowledge of their rights, employees fail to take steps to decertify, an employer ought to be barred from determining, on its own, that such employees do not want representation.

The first and primary impact of using the decertification system to indicate employees' wishes should be limiting or eliminating the employer's right to independently withdraw recognition. An employer that withdraws recognition from an incumbent union can forestall bargaining for years by arguing its case before the NLRB and one of the courts of appeals. Whatever the outcome, the passing years deprive employees of the services of their designated collective bargaining representative.

Irrespective of the outcome of the case, when an employer withdraws recognition, costs are imposed on employees, the union, and even the employer. Employees lose because they are deprived of a representative during the years that litigation may consume. Even if employees oppose the current representative, operation of the Board's blocking charge doctrine deprives them of the right to select another representative or to decertify their representative where the employer has been charged with unlawfully withdrawing recognition.

The union's ability to represent its members is clearly destroyed by an employer's unwillingness to deal with it during the long period when the legality of the withdrawal of recognition is being tested. Even a union that enjoys majority support at the time recognition is withdrawn may find its support eroded by the time bargaining is once again ordered. Employees who are denied the services of a representative over time or who are hired while withdrawal of recognition is being litigated may well have less strong feelings for the union than employees who are continually served and represented.

Finally, the uncertainty of the current system may actually impose costs on the employer withdrawing recognition. During the pendency of unfair labor practice charges, it may be dangerous and costly for an employer to change or adjust employee benefits. If it is ultimately determined that recognition was unlawfully withdrawn, the employer can be ordered to restore any benefits changed without bargaining. If an employer wrongfully withdraws recognition in a strike situation, the unlawful withdrawal may convert an economic strike into an unfair labor practice strike with possibly expensive repercussions to the employer.

Compared to this uncertainty and delay, the election process is far better suited to measure the level of employee support. The Supreme Court has acknowledged the superiority of elections over unfair labor practice proceedings in a similar context.

There must be substantial safeguards to ensure that any decertification petition filed is not the result of employer interference. The employer may not solicit, encourage or induce employees to file a petition, nor may it provide any more than "ministerial aid" with regard to the filing of the petition.

At the first stage, it is necessary to examine the entire chain of events that leads to the petition's filing. Although an employer does not violate the Act by referring an employee to the National Labor Relations Board in response to a request for advice regarding removal of the union as bargaining representative, it may not solicit, support or assist in the initiation, signing or filing of a petition. The employer must bear in mind that the incumbent union is the exclusive representative of the employees. Thus, the employer may not deal directly with employees over wages and benefits, nor may it promise improvements if they take steps to decertify their representative.

Once the petition has been filed, another set of considerations must be applied with regard to any employer involvement in "campaigning" prior to the election. One might well argue that, for practical reasons, an employer should desist from any involvement in the pre-election campaign. One could persuasively argue that the employer's duty to deal in good faith with the exclusive representative of its employees carries with it a concomitant duty not to participate in any campaign seeking to undermine the union. This, however, does not seem to be the current state of the law.

Should the proposal that employees be provided more information be adopted, the above safeguards will be of critical importance. The employer should not be allowed to encourage decertification activity nor should it be permitted to impair the freedom of the election process.

NOTES

1.   What do you think of Professor Ray's proposal? Should the NLRA be amended to require that decertification elections are the primary, or only, means of withdrawing recognition from a union? How do we ensure that employees have adequate knowledge of their right to decertify a union, and adequate opportunity to file decertification petitions, without unnecessarily destabilizing the collective bargaining relationship?

2.   Professor Ray's article was written well before *SFO Good-Nite Inn* and more current caselaw on decertification and withdrawal of recognition. Is his idea of an election as the preferred way to terminate recognition closer or further from gaining traction as a result of that decision? Apparently, there are lots of reasons why unions might prefer decertification elections to employer estimations of support for the purpose of withdrawing recognition. One might say the circumstances would be the exact opposite of the initial union election. In the decertification context the union, not the employer, may be the party that most needs and wants the time to plead its case and mount a union campaign in its favor. Why would an employer ever prefer a decertification election? Are you convinced by Professor Ray's argument about the potential pitfalls of withdrawing recognition without an election? Would you change your mind if the employer were subject to more substantial penalties under the Act for guessing wrong?

D. SUCCESSORSHIP

Corporate changes, including purchases, mergers, sales, spin-offs and so on are now commonplace due, at least in part, to increasing control of business by finance capital. When entities engage in such transactions, they have to consider the impact of various laws, including tax laws, environmental responsibilities, obligations to third parties among others. These arrangements can often contemplate complicated deals, including lengthy legal documents. One of the aspects to consider, of course, is the labor and employment law impacts of such transactions. Under labor law, this is known as "successorship," and the rules under the Act may defer to those under other legal regimes that apply in any such transactions. Sometimes they conflict.

At times employers will structure their deals to avoid the union to the extent legally possible, and in other cases employers will recognize that the union will have to come along with the workers. Where the employer intentionally structures a deal to avoid successorship, there is a certain cost to the employer in the disruption. And furthermore, it is often difficult for the union to prove such intent since it is kept secret and there are not enough outward indications of the unlawful purpose.

One of the more complicated issues in labor law arises when Company A merges with Company B, particularly if Company A is unionized and Company B is not. Recall the Enderby problem, in which Eastern Van Lines, a larger unionized company, and New York Trucking, a smaller nonunion company, were both purchased by Enderby. Frank Lozano, Enderby's president, is interested in knowing whether, and to what extent, he has an obligation either to abide by Eastern's contract with the Teamsters or even to recognize the Teamsters as the exclusive representative of the company's drivers and warehouse workers. Many questions arise. Is Enderby Eastern's successor, or does Eastern merely continue to exist as a separate company held by Enderby with no other changes? What are the labor law implications of one versus the other? Does Enderby plan to merge Eastern and New York? If so, which company is the survivor, or is the merged entity a completely new company—called, say, Enderby Van Lines? There can be a substantial difference in how the entities are structured for labor law obligations, and these will be explored in this section.

The first, and perhaps most critical, question for labor law is this: is the purchasing entity a labor law successor? If the answer is yes, then other questions must follow. First, must the successor follow the preexisting collective bargaining agreement between the predecessor company and the incumbent union? Second, if not, must the successor nonetheless arbitrate grievances that arose under the predecessor's collective bargaining agreement. What about a grievance involving the successor's acquisition of the company? Third, if the successor has no obligation under the prior union contract, then is the successor required to recognize and bargain with the predecessor union or unions? Finally, what are the successor's obligations regarding the predecessor's unfair labor practices? As you read the cases below, think about the answers to these questions in relation to Enderby.

NLRB v. BURNS INT'L SECURITY SERVICES
406 U.S. 272 (1972)

JUSTICE WHITE delivered the opinion of the Court:

Burns International Security Services, Inc. (Burns), replaced another employer, the Wackenhut Corp. (Wackenhut), which had previously provided plant protection services for the Lockheed Aircraft Service Co. (Lockheed) located at the Ontario International Airport in California. When Burns began providing security service, it employed 42 guards; 27 of them had been employed by Wackenhut. Burns refused, however, to bargain with the United Plant Guard Workers of America (UPG) which had been certified after a National Labor Relations Board (Board) election as the exclusive bargaining representative of Wackenhut's employees less than four months earlier. The issues presented in this case are whether Burns refused to bargain with a union representing a majority of employees in an appropriate unit and whether the National Labor Relations Board could order Burns to observe the terms of a collective-bargaining contract signed by the union and Wackenhut that Burns had not voluntarily assumed.

I

The Wackenhut Corp. provided protection services at the Lockheed plant for five years before Burns took over this task. On February 28, 1967, a few months before the changeover of guard employers, a majority of the Wackenhut guards selected the union as their exclusive bargaining representative in a Board election after Wackenhut and the union had agreed that the Lockheed plant was the appropriate bargaining unit. On March 8, the Regional Director certified the union as the exclusive bargaining representative for these employees, and, on April 29, Wackenhut and the union entered into a three-year collective-bargaining contract.

Meanwhile, since Wackenhut's one-year service agreement to provide security protection was due to expire on June 30, Lockheed had called for bids from various companies supplying these services, and both Burns and Wackenhut submitted estimates. At a pre-bid conference attended by Burns on May 15, a representative of Lockheed informed the bidders that Wackenhut's guards were represented by the union, that the union had recently won a Board election and been certified, and that there was in existence a collective-bargaining contract between Wackenhut and the union. Lockheed then accepted Burns' bid, and on May 31 Wackenhut was notified that Burns would assume responsibility for protection services on July 1. Burns chose to retain 27 of the Wackenhut guards, and it brought in 15 of its own guards from other Burns locations.

During June, when Burns hired the 27 Wackenhut guards, it supplied them with membership cards of the American Federation of Guards (AFG), another union with which Burns had collective-bargaining contracts at other locations, and informed them that they had to become AFG members to work for Burns, that they would not receive uniforms otherwise, and that Burns "could not live with" the existing contract between Wackenhut and the union. On June 29, Burns recognized the AFG on the theory that it had obtained a card majority. On July 12, however, the UPG demanded that Burns recognize it as the bargaining representative of Burns' employees at Lockheed and that Burns honor the collective-bargaining agreement between it and Wackenhut. When Burns refused, the UPG filed unfair labor practice charges, and Burns responded by challenging the appropriateness of the unit and by denying its obligation to bargain. The Board, adopting the trial examiner's findings and conclusions, found the Lockheed plant an appropriate unit and held that Burns had violated §§ 8 (a)(2) and 8 (a)(1) of the National Labor Relations Act by unlawfully recognizing and assisting the AFG, a rival of the UPG; and that it had violated §§ 8 (a)(5) and 8 (a)(1) by failing to recognize and bargain with the UPG and by refusing to honor the collective-bargaining agreement that had been negotiated between Wackenhut and UPG.

II

The Board, without revision, accepted the trial examiner's findings and conclusions with respect to the duty to bargain, and we see no basis for setting them aside. In an election held but a few months before, the union had been designated bargaining agent for the employees in the unit and a majority of these employees had been hired by Burns for work in the identical unit. It is undisputed that Burns knew all the relevant facts in this regard and was aware of the certification and of the existence of a collective-bargaining contract. In these circumstances, it was not unreasonable for the Board to conclude that the union certified to represent all employees in the unit still represented a majority of the employees and that Burns could not reasonably have entertained a good-faith doubt about that fact. Burns' obligation to bargain with the union over terms and conditions of employment stemmed from its hiring of Wackenhut's employees and from the recent election and Board certification.

It goes without saying, of course, that Burns was not entitled to upset what it should have accepted as an established union majority by soliciting representation cards for another union and thereby committing the unfair labor practice of which it was found guilty by the Board. That holding was not challenged here and makes it imperative that the situation be viewed as it was when Burns hired its employees for the guard unit, a majority of whom were represented by a Board-certified union.

It would be a wholly different case if the Board had determined that because Burns' operational structure and practices differed from those of Wackenhut, the Lockheed bargaining unit was no longer an appropriate one. Likewise, it would be different if Burns had not hired employees already represented by a union certified as a bargaining agent. But where the bargaining unit remains unchanged and a majority of the employees hired by the new employer are represented by a recently certified bargaining agent there is little basis for faulting the Board's implementation of the express mandates of § 8 (a)(5) and § 9 (a) by ordering the employer to bargain with the incumbent union.

III

It does not follow, however, from Burns' duty to bargain that it was bound to observe the substantive terms of the collective-bargaining contract the union had negotiated with Wackenhut and to which Burns had in no way agreed. Section 8(d) of the Act expressly provides that the existence of such bargaining obligation "does not compel either party to agree to a proposal or require the making of a concession." Congress has consistently declined to interfere with free collective bargaining and has preferred that device, or voluntary arbitration, to the imposition of compulsory terms as a means of avoiding or terminating labor disputes.

[T]he Board's prior decisions, which until now have consistently held that, although successor employers may be bound to recognize and bargain with the union, they are not bound by the substantive provisions of a collective-bargaining contract negotiated by their predecessors but not agreed to or assumed by them. As the Court of Appeals said in this case, "The successor has always been held merely to have the duty of bargaining with his predecessor's union."

The Board, however, has now departed from this view and argues that the same policies that mandate a continuity of bargaining obligation also require that successor employers be bound to the terms of a predecessor's collective-bargaining contract. It asserts that the stability of labor relations will be jeopardized and that employees will face uncertainty and a gap in the bargained—for terms and conditions of employment, as well as the possible loss of advantages gained by prior negotiations, unless the new employer is held to have assumed, as a matter of federal labor law, the obligations under the contract entered into by the former employer.

Here, Burns had notice of the existence of the Wackenhut collective-bargaining contract, but it did not consent to be bound by it. The source of its duty to bargain with the union is not the collective-bargaining contract but the fact that it voluntarily took over a bargaining unit that was largely intact and that had been certified within the past year. Nothing in its actions, however, indicated that Burns was assuming the obligations of the contract, and "allowing the Board to compel agreement when the parties themselves are unable to agree would violate the fundamental premise on which the Act is based—private bargaining under governmental supervision of the procedure alone, without any official compulsion over the actual terms of the contract." *H. K. Porter Co. v. NLRB*, 397 U.S. at 108.

We also agree with the Court of Appeals that holding either the union or the new employer bound to the substantive terms of an old collective-bargaining contract may result in serious inequities. A potential employer may be willing to take over a moribund business only if he can make changes in corporate structure, composition of the labor force, work location, task assignment, and nature of supervision. Saddling such an employer with the terms and conditions of employment contained in the old collective-bargaining contract may make these changes impossible and may discourage and inhibit the transfer of capital. On the other hand, a union may have made concessions to a small or failing employer that it would be unwilling to make to a large or economically successful firm.

The Board's position would also raise new problems, for the successor employer would be circumscribed in exactly the same way as the predecessor under the collective-bargaining contract. It would seemingly follow that employees of the predecessor would be deemed employees of the successor, dischargeable only in accordance with provisions of the contract and subject to the grievance and arbitration provisions thereof. Burns would not have been free to replace Wackenhut's guards with its own except as the contract permitted. Given the continuity of employment relationship, the pre-existing contract's provisions with respect to wages, seniority rights, vacation privileges, pension and retirement fund benefits, job security provisions, work assignments and the like would devolve on the successor. Nor would the union commit a § 8(b)(3) unfair labor practice if it refused to bargain for a modification of the agreement effective prior to the expiration date of the agreement. A successor employer might also be deemed to have inherited its predecessor's pre-existing contractual obligations to the union that had accrued under past contracts and that had not been discharged when the business was transferred. "[A] successor may well acquire more liabilities as a result of Burns than appear on the face of a contract." Finally, a successor will be bound to observe the contract despite good-faith doubts about the union's majority during the time that the contract is a bar to another representation election. For the above reasons, the Board itself has expressed doubts as to the general applicability of its Burns rule.

In many cases, of course, successor employers will find it advantageous not only to recognize and bargain with the union but also to observe the pre-existing contract rather than to face uncertainty and turmoil. Also, in a variety of circumstances involving a merger, stock acquisition, reorganization, or assets purchase, the Board might properly find as a matter of fact that the successor had assumed the obligations under the old contract. Such a duty does not, however, ensue as a matter of law from the mere fact than an employer is doing the same work in the same place with the same employees as his predecessor, as the Board had recognized until its decision in the instant case. We accordingly set aside the Board's finding of a § 8 (a)(5) unfair labor practice insofar as it rested on a conclusion that

Burns was required to but did not honor the collective-bargaining contract executed by Wackenhut.

IV

Although a successor employer is ordinarily free to set initial terms on which it will hire the employees of a predecessor, there will be instances in which it is perfectly clear that the new employer plans to retain all of the employees in the unit and in which it will be appropriate to have him initially consult with the employees' bargaining representative before he fixes terms. In other situations, however, it may not be clear until the successor employer has hired his full complement of employees that he has a duty to bargain with a union, since it will not be evident until then that the bargaining representative represents a majority of the employees in the unit as required by § 9 (a) of the Act. Here, for example, Burns' obligation to bargain with the union did not mature until it had selected its force of guards late in June. The Board quite properly found that Burns refused to bargain on July 12 when it rejected the overtures of the union. It is true that the wages it paid when it began protecting the Lockheed plant on July 1 differed from those specified in the Wackenhut collective-bargaining agreement, but there is no evidence that Burns ever unilaterally changed the terms and conditions of employment it had offered to potential employees in June after its obligation to bargain with the union became apparent. If the union had made a request to bargain after Burns had completed its hiring and if Burns had negotiated in good faith and had made offers to the union which the union rejected, Burns could have unilaterally initiated such proposals as the opening terms and conditions of employment on July 1 without committing an unfair labor practice. The Board's order requiring Burns to make whole its employees for any losses suffered by reason of Burns' refusal to honor and enforce the contract, cannot therefore be sustained on the ground that Burns unilaterally changed existing terms and conditions of employment, thereby committing an unfair labor practice which required monetary restitution in these circumstances.

NOTES

1.   Although a new employer is free to hire its own workforce, it cannot in so doing discriminate against workers because of their union membership or because it generally wishes to avoid dealing with a union. Thus, the Board will impose a bargaining order on a successor who violates Section 8(a)(3) in hiring workers where the new employer's unfair labor practices result in less than a majority of predecessor workers being hired. *See Grane Health Care Co.*, 357 NLRB 1412 (2011), *enfd*, 712 F.3d 145 (3d Cir. 2013) (change from public to private status, successorship applies); *A. J. Myers & Sons, Inc.*, 362 NLRB No. 51 (2015) (successor for part of bargaining unit); *AG Communication Systems Corp.*, 350 NLRB 168 (2007), *review denied, IBEW, Local 21 v. NLRB*, 563 F.3d 418 (D. C. Cir 2009); *Daufuskie Island Club & Resort*, 328 N.L.R.B.

415 (1999); *Inland Container Corp.*, 275 N.L.R.B. 378 (1985). If Enderby decided to merge Eastern and New York after acquisition, and announced to all current employees of both firms that they would have to apply anew for jobs with the new entity, what advice would you give about the hiring process? What about the practical impact of such a decision? Would it hurt morale? If Lozano told you directly that he would like the new entity to be a nonunion operation, what advice would you give? Note that the presence of a "successor clause" in the collective bargaining agreement may affect the analysis. When an employer integrated operations and employees of one of its wholly owned subsidiaries into two other wholly-owned subsidiaries, the court enforced an arbitrator's award against the employer on the basis that the restructuring triggered the collective bargaining agreement's successorship clause. The court even allowed the employer to be "created" as a party by the arbitrator. *See Equitable Resources Inc. v. United Steel, Local 8-512*, 621 F.3d 538 (6th Cir. 2010). How can a successor clause be binding on a successor who is not obligated to accept the collective bargaining agreement? Successor clauses appear in many collective bargaining agreements, but not often enforceable.

2.   If a purchasing entity is a "successor," then the incumbent union will enjoy a presumption of continued majority support. In 1999, the Board adopted a "successor bar" rule providing unions a reasonable time to negotiate a new contract with a successor before facing any challenge to majority status. *See St. Elizabeth Manor*, 329 N.L.R.B. 341 (1999) (Clinton Board). In 2002, however, the Board reversed itself and found that an incumbent union enjoys no extra protection in the successorship context, only a rebuttable presumption of majority status, and therefore can face an otherwise valid challenge to majority status at any time. *See MV Transportation*, 337 N.L.R.B. 770 (2002) (Bush Board). In 2010, the Board agreed to reconsider its decision in *MV Transportation* and to consider returning to the rule set out in *St. Elizabeth Manor*. It issued a notice and invitation to file briefs on whether or not it should modify or overrule *MV Transportation*. *See UGL-UNICCO Serv. Co.*, 355 N.L.R.B. No. 155 (2010). The Board subsequently overruled *MV Transportation* in *Lamons Gasket Co.*, 357 N.L.R.B. No. 72 (2011) (Liebman Board), which restored the law as set forth in *St. Elizabeth Manor*, 329 N.L.R.B. 341 (1999). As the Board explained:

> Finally, prior to *MV Transportation*, which we also overrule today, when a new employer assumed an operation and the conditions for successorship were satisfied so that the new employer also assumed a legally enforceable duty to recognize and bargain with a union that represented its predecessor's employees, the Board barred any challenge to the union's representative status for a similar reasonable period of time. *St. Elizabeth Manor, Inc.*, 329 N.L.R.B. 341 (1999).

Lamons Gasket, 357 NLRB 739, 744 (2011).

The complete decision in *Lamons Gasket Co.* is reprinted in Chapter 4, *supra*.

3.   Recall the Enderby problem, in which Enderby "acquired" Eastern Van Lines. If the acquisition was of the entire company by stock purchase, then it seems clear that Enderby must not only recognize and bargain with the union, but also abide by any existing collective bargaining agreement. In such a case, Enderby is not technically a successor. *See TKB International Corp.*, 240 N.L.R.B. 1082 (1979) (stock purchase involves continued "existence of legal entity, albeit under new ownership."). But if, after a stock purchase, Enderby immediately were to change or merge operations, then successorship rules might apply. *See EPE, Inc. v. NLRB*, 845 F.2d 483, 490 (4th Cir. 1988). If Enderby merely acquired Eastern's assets, however, then *Burns* would seem squarely to apply, meaning that Enderby would not inherit the existing union contract, and its obligation, if any, to recognize and bargain with the union would rest on the continuity of the workforce.

Note that there is an important distinction between stock purchases and asset purchases. An employer can engage in an asset purchase to avoid the consequences of being stuck with the union contract. In a stock purchase, the employer is stuck with all the contracts, including the labor agreement. You can't carve out the labor agreement from the stock purchase. Stock purchases go on all the time with respect to public or privately traded companies. That's why a stock purchase doesn't affect any contracts between the entity and third parties, including the collective bargaining agreements. How should unions deal with these potential transactions. Should they try to bargain over the decision and the effects of such a sale? Should they try to get copies of the underlying agreements to determine what their rights are with respect to the predecessors and the successor?

* * *

Burns answered a lot of questions about successorship, and has become the leading Supreme Court case on the subject. Nonetheless, after *Burns*, many questions remained regarding technical issues affecting the union's majority status and the continuity of the workforce. When is majority status determined? Can a bargaining obligation attach before a majority of former union members is hired by the successor? If so, under what circumstances? What would be the effect of a hiatus in operations on the union's presumed majority? The following case provides some insights into these questions. As you read the case, notice the prominence of *Burns* in the Court's discussion.

 ### FALL RIVER DYEING V. NLRB
482 U.S. 27 (1987)

JUSTICE BLACKMUN delivered the opinion of the Court:

In this case we are confronted with the issue whether the National Labor Relations Board's decision is consistent with *NLRB v. Burns International Security Services, Inc.*, 406 U.S. 272 (1972). In *Burns*, this Court ruled that the new employer, succeeding to the business of another, had an obligation to bargain with the union representing the predecessor's employees. We first must decide whether *Burns* is limited to a situation where the union only recently was certified before the transition in employers, or whether that decision also applies where the union is entitled to a presumption of majority support. Our inquiry then proceeds to three questions that concern rules the Labor Board has developed in the successorship context. First, we must determine whether there is substantial record evidence to support the Board's conclusion that petitioner was a "successor" to Sterlingwale Corp., its business predecessor. Second, we must decide whether the Board's "substantial and representative complement" rule, designed to identify the date when a successor's obligation to bargain with the predecessor's employees' union arises, is consistent with *Burns*, is reasonable, and was applied properly in this case. Finally, we must examine the Board's "continuing demand" principle to the effect that, if a union has presented to a successor a premature demand for bargaining, this demand continues in effect until the successor acquires the "substantial and representative complement" of employees that triggers its obligation to bargain.

I

For over 30 years before 1982, Sterlingwale operated a textile dyeing and finishing plant in Fall River, Mass. Its business consisted basically of two types of dyeing, called, respectively, "converting" and "commission." Under the converting process, which in 1981 accounted for 60% to 70% of its business, Sterlingwale bought unfinished fabrics for its own account, dyed and finished them, and then sold them to apparel manufacturers. In commission dyeing, which accounted for the remainder of its business, Sterlingwale dyed and finished fabrics owned by customers according to their specifications. The financing and marketing aspects of converting and commission dyeing are different. Converting requires capital to purchase fabrics and a sales force to promote the finished products. The production process, however, is the same for both converting and commission dyeing.

In the late 1970's the textile-dyeing business, including Sterlingwale's, began to suffer from adverse economic conditions and foreign competition. After 1979, business at Sterlingwale took a serious turn for the worse because of the loss of its export market, and the company reduced the number of its employees. Finally, in February 1982, Sterlingwale laid off all its production employees, primarily because it no longer had the capital to continue the converting business. It retained a skeleton crew of workers and supervisors to ship out the goods remaining on order and to maintain the corporation's building and machinery. In the months following the layoff, Leonard Ansin, Sterlingwale's president, liquidated the inventory of the corporation and, at the same time, looked for a business partner with whom he could "resurrect the business." Ansin felt that he owed it to the community and to the employees to keep Sterlingwale in operation.

For almost as long as Sterlingwale had been in existence, its production and maintenance employees had been represented by the United Textile Workers of America, AFL-CIO, Local 292 (Union). The most recent collective-bargaining agreement before Sterlingwale's demise had been negotiated in 1978 and was due to expire in 1981. By an agreement dated October 1980, however, in response to the financial difficulties suffered by Sterlingwale, the Union agreed to amend the 1978 agreement to extend its expiration date by one year, until April 1, 1982, without any wage increase and with an agreement to improve labor productivity. In the months following the final February 1982 layoff, the Union met with company officials over problems involving this job action, and, in particular, Sterlingwale's failure to pay premiums on group-health insurance. In addition, during meetings with Ansin, Union officials told him of their concern with Sterlingwale's future and their interest in helping to keep the company operating or in meeting with prospective buyers.

In late summer 1982, however, Sterlingwale finally went out of business. It made an assignment for the benefit of its creditors, primarily Ansin's mother, who was an officer of the corporation and holder of a first mortgage on most of Sterlingwale's real property and the Massachusetts Capital Resource Corporation (MCRC), which held a security interest on Sterlingwale's machinery and equipment. Ansin also hired a professional liquidator to dispose of the company's remaining assets, mostly its inventory, at auction.

During this same period, a former Sterlingwale employee and officer, Herbert Chace, and Arthur Friedman, president of one of Sterlingwale's major customers, Marcamy Sales Corporation (Marcamy), formed petitioner Fall River Dyeing & Finishing Corp. Chace and Friedman formed petitioner with the intention of engaging strictly in the commission-dyeing business and of taking advantage of the availability of Sterlingwale's assets and work force. Chace became petitioner's vice president in charge of operations and Friedman became its president.

In September 1982, petitioner began operating out of Sterlingwale's former facilities and began hiring employees. It advertised for workers and supervisors in a local newspaper, and Chace personally got in touch with several prospective supervisors. Petitioner hired 12 supervisors, of whom 8 had been supervisors with Sterlingwale and 3 had been production employees there. In its hiring decisions for production employees, petitioner took into consideration recommendations from these supervisors and a prospective employee's former employment with Sterlingwale. Petitioner's initial hiring goal was to attain one full shift of workers, which meant from 55 to 60 employees. Petitioner planned to "see how business would be" after this initial goal had been met and, if business permitted, to expand to two shifts. The employees who were hired first spent approximately four to six weeks in start-up operations and an additional month in experimental production.

By letter dated October 19, 1982, the Union requested petitioner to recognize it as the bargaining agent for petitioner's employees and to begin collective bargaining. Petitioner refused the request, stating that, in its view, the request had "no legal basis." At that time, 18 of petitioner's 21 employees were former employees of Sterlingwale. By November of that year, petitioner had employees in a complete range of jobs, had its production process in operation, and was handling customer orders by mid-January 1983, it had attained its initial goal of one shift of workers. Of the 55 workers in this initial shift, a number that represented over half the workers petitioner would eventually hire, 36 were former Sterlingwale employees. Petitioner continued to expand its work force, and by mid-April 1983, it had reached two full shifts. For the first time, ex-Sterlingwale employees were in the minority but just barely so (52 or 53 out of 107 employees). Although petitioner engaged exclusively in commission dyeing, the employees experienced the same conditions they had when they were working for Sterlingwale. The production process was unchanged and the employees worked on the same machines, in the same building, with the same job classifications, under virtually the same supervisors. Over half the volume of petitioner's business came from former Sterlingwale customers, and, in particular, Marcamy.

On November 1, 1982, the Union filed an unfair labor practice charge with the Board, alleging that in its refusal to bargain petitioner had violated §§ 8(a)(1) and (5) of the National Labor Relations Act (NLRA). After a hearing, the Administrative Law Judge (ALJ) decided that, on the facts of the case, petitioner was a successor to Sterlingwale. Petitioner thus committed an unfair labor practice in refusing to bargain. In a brief decision and order, the Board, with one member dissenting, affirmed this decision. The Court of Appeals for the First Circuit, also by a divided vote, enforced the order.

II

Fifteen years ago in *NLRB v. Burns International Security Services, Inc.*, this Court first dealt with the issue of a successor employer's obligation to bargain with a union that had represented the employees of its predecessor. When the union that had represented the Wackenhut employees brought unfair labor practice charges against Burns, this Court agreed with the Board's determination that Burns had an obligation to bargain with this union.

Although our reasoning in *Burns* was tied to the facts presented there, we suggested that our analysis would be equally applicable even if a union with which a successor had to bargain had not been certified just before the transition in employers. We cited with approval, Board and Court of Appeals decisions where it "ha[d] been consistently held that a mere change of employers or of ownership in the employing industry is not such an 'unusual circumstance' as to affect the force of the Board's certification within the normal operative period if a majority of employees after the change of ownership or management were employed by the preceding employer. Several of these cases involved successorship situations where the union in question had not been certified only a short time before the transition date.

Moreover, in defining "the force of the Board's certification within the normal operative period," we referred in *Burns* to two presumptions regarding a union's majority status following certification. First, after a union has been certified by the Board as a bargaining-unit representative, it usually is entitled to a conclusive presumption of majority status for one year following the certification. Second, after this period, the union is entitled to a rebuttable presumption of majority support.

During a transition between employers, a union is in a peculiarly vulnerable position. It has no formal and established bargaining relationship with the new employer, is uncertain about the new employer's plans, and cannot be sure if or when the new employer must bargain with it. While being concerned with the future of its members with the new employer, the union also must protect whatever rights still exist for its members under the collective-bargaining agreement with the predecessor employer. Accordingly, during this unsettling transition period, the union needs the presumptions of majority status to which it is entitled to safeguard its members' rights and to develop a relationship with the successor.

The position of the employees also supports the application of the presumptions in the successorship situation. If the employees find themselves in a new enterprise that substantially resembles the old, but without their chosen bargaining representative, they may well feel that their choice of a union is subject to the vagaries of an enterprise's transformation. This feeling is not conducive to industrial peace. In addition, after being hired by a new company following a layoff from the old, employees initially will be concerned primarily with maintaining their new jobs. In fact, they might be inclined to shun support for their former union, especially if they believe that such support will jeopardize their jobs with the successor or if they are inclined to blame the union for their layoff and problems associated with it. Without the presumptions of majority support and with the wide variety of corporate transformations possible, an employer could use a successor enterprise as a way of getting rid of a labor contract and of exploiting the employees' hesitant attitude towards the union to eliminate its continuing presence.

In addition to recognizing the traditional presumptions of union majority status, however, the Court in *Burns* was careful to safeguard "the rightful prerogative of owners independently to rearrange their businesses." We observed in *Burns* that, although the successor has an obligation to bargain with the union, it "is ordinarily free to set initial terms on which it will hire the employees of a predecessor," and it is not bound by the substantive provisions of the predecessor's collective-bargaining agreement. We further explained that the successor is under no obligation to hire the employees of its predecessor, subject, of course, to the restriction that it not discriminate against union employees in its hiring. Thus, to a substantial extent the applicability of *Burns* rests in the hands of the successor. If the new employer makes a conscious decision to maintain generally the same business and to hire a majority of its employees from the predecessor, then the bargaining obligation of § 8 (a)(5) is activated. This makes sense when one considers that the employer intends to take advantage of the trained work force of its predecessor.

We now hold that a successor's obligation to bargain is not limited to a situation where the union in question has been recently certified. Where, as here, the union has a rebuttable presumption of majority status, this status continues despite the change in employers. And the new employer has an obligation to bargain with that union so long as the new employer is in fact a successor of the old employer and the majority of its employees were employed by its predecessor.

III

We turn now to the three rules, as well as to their application to the facts of this case, that the Board has adopted for the successorship situation.

A

In *Burns* we approved the approach taken by the Board and accepted by courts with respect to determining whether a new company was indeed the successor to the old. This approach, which is primarily factual in nature and is based upon the totality of the circumstances of a given situation, requires that the Board focus on whether the new company has "acquired substantial assets of its predecessor and continued, without interruption or substantial change, the predecessor's business operations." Hence, the focus is on whether there is "substantial continuity" between the enterprises. Under this approach, the Board examines a number of factors: whether the business of both employers is essentially the same; whether the employees of the new company are doing the same jobs in the same working conditions under the same supervisors; and whether the new entity has the same production process, produces the same products, and basically has the same body of customers.

In conducting the analysis, the Board keeps in mind the question whether "those employees who have been retained will understandably view their job situations as essentially unaltered." This emphasis on the employees' perspective furthers the Act's policy of industrial peace. If the employees find themselves in essentially the same jobs after the employer transition and if their legitimate expectations in continued representation by their union are thwarted, their dissatisfaction may lead to labor unrest. Although petitioner does not challenge the Board's "substantial continuity" approach, it does contest the application of the rule to the facts of this case. [W]e find that the Board's determination that there was "substantial continuity" between Sterlingwale and petitioner and that petitioner was Sterlingwale's successor is supported by substantial evidence in the record. Petitioner acquired most of Sterlingwale's real property, its machinery and equipment, and much of its inventory and materials. It introduced no new product line. Of particular significance is the fact that, from the perspective of the employees, their jobs did not change. Although petitioner abandoned converting dyeing in exclusive favor of commission dyeing, this change did not alter the essential nature of the employees' jobs, because both types of dyeing involved the same production process. The job classifications of petitioner were the same as those of Sterlingwale; petitioner's employees worked on the same machines under the direction of supervisors most of whom were former supervisors of Sterlingwale. The record, in fact, is clear that petitioner acquired Sterlingwale's assets with the express purpose of taking advantage of its predecessor's work force.

We do not find determinative of the successorship question the fact that there was a 7-month hiatus between Sterlingwale's demise and petitioner's start-up. Petitioner argues that this hiatus, coupled with the fact that its employees were hired through newspaper advertisements— not through Sterlingwale employment records, which were not transferred to it—resolves in its favor the "substantial continuity" question. Yet such a hiatus is only one factor in the "substantial continuity" calculus and thus is relevant only when there are other indicia of discontinuity. Conversely, if other factors indicate a continuity between the enterprises, and the hiatus is a normal start-up period, the "totality of the circumstances" will suggest that these circumstances present a successorship situation.

Accordingly, we hold that, under settled law, petitioner was a successor to Sterlingwale. We thus must consider if and when petitioner's duty to bargain arose.

B

In *Burns*, the Court determined that the successor had an obligation to bargain with the union because a majority of its employees had been employed by Wackenhut. The Court, however, did not have to consider the question when the successor's obligation to bargain arose: Wackenhut's contract expired on June 30 and *Burns* began its services with a majority of former Wackenhut guards on July 1. In other situations, as in the present case, there is a start-up period by the new employer while it gradually builds its operations and hires employees. In these situations, the Board, with the approval of the Courts of Appeals, has adopted the "substantial and representative complement" rule for fixing the moment when the determination as to the composition of the successor's work force is to be made. If, at this particular moment, a majority of the successor's employees had been employed by its predecessor, then the successor has an obligation to bargain with the union that represented these employees.

This rule represents an effort to balance "the objective of insuring maximum employee participation in the selection of a bargaining agent against the goal of permitting employees to be represented as quickly as possible." In deciding when a "substantial and representative complement" exists in a particular employer transition, the Board examines a number of factors. It studies "whether the job classifications designated for the operation were filled or substantially filled and whether the operation was in normal or substantially normal production." In addition, it takes into consideration "the size of the complement on that date and the time expected to elapse before a substantially larger complement would be at work . . . as well as the relative certainty of the employer's expected expansion."

We hold that the Board's "substantial and representative complement" rule is reasonable in the successorship context. Moreover, its application to the facts of this case is supported by substantial record evidence. The Court of Appeals observed that by mid-January petitioner "had hired employees in virtually all job classifications, had hired at least fifty percent of those it would ultimately employ in the majority of those classifications, and it employed a majority of the employees it would eventually employ when it reached full complement." At that time petitioner had begun normal production. Although petitioner intended to expand to two shifts, and, in fact, reached this goal by mid-April, that expansion was contingent expressly upon the growth of the business. Accordingly, as found by the Board and approved by the Court of Appeals, mid-January was the period when petitioner reached its "substantial and representative complement." Because at that time the majority of petitioner's employees were former Sterlingwale employees, petitioner had an obligation to bargain with the Union then.

C

We also hold that the Board's "continuing demand" rule is reasonable in the successorship situation. The successor's duty to bargain at the "substantial and representative complement" date is triggered only when the union has made a bargaining demand. Under the "continuing demand" rule, when a union has made a premature demand that has been rejected by the employer, this demand remains in force until the moment when the employer attains the "substantial and representative complement."

The judgment of the Court of Appeals is *affirmed*.

[A dissenting opinion by JUSTICE POWELL, joined by CHIEF JUSTICE REHNQUIST and JUSTICE O'CONNOR is omitted.]

NOTES

1.   From Fall River's perspective, this was an entirely new enterprise. The new management had purchased the plant and equipment after Sterlingwale had been liquidated and hired its employees "off the street." It engaged only in commission-dyeing. From the employees' perspective, they were doing the same work in the same structure under the same working conditions as when they worked for Sterlingwale. Why decide the successorship issue from the employees' perspective? Are there any policy arguments for approaching the issue from the new employer's perspective?

2.   Although a successor employer may be required to bargain with the existing union, it does not necessarily have an obligation to adhere to the existing contract terms, at least initially. *See Burns.* Whether it does depends on whether it is "perfectly clear" that the new employer plans to hire predecessor employees. Where the employer actively or by tacit inference leads predecessor employees to believe they will be hired without change to their terms or conditions of employment, it is "perfectly clear" that they are a *Burns* successor. However, where such hiring is contingent on predecessor employees accepting changed terms and conditions of employment it will not be "perfectly clear" that a majority of such employees will be hired. Accordingly, there is no obligation to bargain with the union over the initial or "start up" terms and conditions of employment. *See Spruce-Up Corp.,* 209 N.L.R.B. 194 (1974); *see also* Drew Willis & Richard Bales, *Interpreting* NLRB v. Burns: *The Not So "Perfectly Clear" Successor Exception,* 7 Seton Hall Circuit Rev. 1, 2–25 (2010) (discussing three-way circuit split interpreting meaning of "perfectly clear").

On December 1, 2017, the Board's General Counsel Peter Robb issued a Memorandum, *Mandatory Submissions to Advice, Memorandum GC 18–02,* setting out examples of cases in which the General Counsel's Office may want to provide alternative analyses to the Board along with a complaint. In the *Memorandum,* the General Counsel targets three successorship cases involving the "perfectly clear" exception to *Burns.* Those three cases were: 1) *GVS Properties, LLC,* 362 N.L.R.B. No. 194 (2015), in which the Board found that it was "perfectly clear" that an employer intended to hire the predecessor's employees despite the fact that intent could not really be evaluated since state law required the employer to retain the predecessor's employees for a period of 90 days after assuming control of predecessor's business. However, the Board's order was later vacated as moot. *GVS Properties,* 2017 WL 1462124 (April 20, 2017); 2) *Creative Vision Resources,* 364 N.L.R.B. No. 91 (2016), in which the Board found that the timing and clarity of the successor's express intent concerning existing terms and conditions of employment established that the purchaser was a "perfectly clear" successor despite the fact that the Union failed to make a bargaining demand until several days after the successor began operation. 3) *Nexeo Solutions, LLC,* 364 NLRB No. 44 (2016), in which the Board found the Purchase Agreement and several communications authorized, approved, and ratified by the purchaser made it "perfectly clear" that the purchaser was a successor intent on retaining predecessor employees. Dissenting Member Miscimarra maintained successorship was not perfectly clear because the Purchase Agreement allowed purchaser to set initial terms and was not received by employees until after they received offers of employment, and because all communications about hiring and terms were made by the predecessor, not the successor. It seems perfectly clear these decisions of the prior Board do not sit well with the Trump Board's General Counsel.

3.   *Duty to arbitrate grievances filed against predecessor.* In the first successorship case to go the U.S. Supreme Court, a union pressed a claim to arbitrate against a successor employer based on the predecessor's labor contract. Although the acquiring larger employer was nonunionized at the time of acquisition and then merger, the Court found that the employer was obligated to arbitrate under the predecessor's collective bargaining agreement because it had hired half of the predecessor's workforce, a substantial number. *See John Wiley & Sons v. Livingston*, 376 U.S. 543 (1964).

In 1974, another Supreme Court successor arbitration case, *Howard Johnson Co. v. Hotel & Restaurant Employees,* 417 U.S. 249 (1974), reached a different result when change resulted from a purchase of assets. There the Court made plain that the logic of *Burns* would prevail. In *Howard Johnson,* a franchisee sold to Howard Johnson Co. all the personal property assets of a Howard Johnson restaurant and motel, leasing the real property back to Howard Johnson, which resumed operations with 45 employees. However, only 9 of the 45 had been employed by the predecessor. The union filed an action compelling arbitration on the issue of the successor's failure to hire a large number of former employees, claiming that it violated the contract's no lockout provision. The Supreme Court, applying *Burns*, found that the successor was not obligated to arbitrate. The Court distinguished *Wiley* indicating that in *Wiley* the former company had been swallowed up by the purchasing company which had then hired all of the employees of the former company. By contrast, *Howard Johnson* involved a purchase of assets, and the continuity of operation of the former business. According to the Court,

> We do not believe that *Wiley* requires a successor employer to arbitrate in the circumstances of this case. The Court there held that arbitration could not be compelled unless there was "substantial continuity of identity in the business enterprise" before and after a change of ownership, for otherwise the duty to arbitrate would be "something imposed from without, not reasonably to be found in the particular bargaining agreement and the acts of the parties involved." This continuity of identity in the business enterprise necessarily includes, we think, a substantial continuity in the identity of the work force across the change in ownership.

Id. at 263–264.

4. *Liability for predecessor's unfair labor practices.* To ensure the fullest protection of workers under the NLRA, the Supreme Court has resisted allowing unfair labor practices committed by a predecessor employer to be detached from the successor, which could occur if corporate law concepts were strictly adhered to. In *Golden State Bottling Co. v. NLRB,* 414 U.S. 168 (1973), the Court held that a successor is required to remedy the unfair labor practices of a predecessor so long as it had adequate notice of them at the time of acquisition. Presumably, with adequate notice, the successor could make contractual arrangements with the predecessor—in the form of increased purchase price and the like—to deal with potential liability. But *Golden State* sends a strong signal that unfair labor practices are not easily evaded. Corporate transactions implicating successorship typically require notice to all involved. A purchaser has an obligation to due diligence and in that process can often discover any pending unfair labor practices.

E. REJECTION OF COLLECTIVE BARGAINING AGREEMENTS IN BANKRUPTCY

1. LABOR'S FEARS ABOUT BANKRUPTCY

During the recessions of the late 1970s and early 1980s, labor leaders watched anxiously as federal bankruptcy judges threw out collective bargaining agreements with major employers that had filed for reorganization under Chapter 11 of the U.S. Bankruptcy Code. Among the many industries so affected were air passenger service, food processing, interstate ground transportation, and steel manufacturing. During the recession that afflicted the American economy during the late 2000s, employers in many of these same industries again contemplated Chapter 11—and the possibility of rejecting their CBAs.

In each uncertain era, employers defended their attacks on the fruits of collective bargaining by arguing they could not compete with nonunion competitors, either at home or abroad, unless high costs imposed by labor contracts were drastically reduced. The only alternative to reorganization under Chapter 11, they argued, was liquidation under Chapter 7, which would shut down the affected businesses and cause the loss of every job.

In 1983, in what became the most notorious bankruptcy of the earlier era, Texas Air Corporation chief Frank Lorezno filed a petition plunging his subsidiary, Continental Airlines, into Chapter 11 so he could lay off nearly two-thirds of the carrier's unionized workforce and cut their wages in half. *See* Iver Peterson, *Leaner Continental Resumes Flights*, N.Y. Times, Sept. 28, 1983. Over objections by unions representing flight attendants, mechanics, and pilots, the bankruptcy court permitted Lorenzo to act unilaterally, which helped transform Continental into a low-cost, low-fare carrier that could compete with start-ups. *See In re Continental Airlines,* 38 Bankr. 67 (Bankr. S.D. Tex. 1984). Lorenzo and his actions at Continental—which included purchasing and then stripping away many of the assets of now-defunct Eastern Airlines to benefit Continental—inspired the Enderby problem and its protagonist Frank Lozano, whose exploits are outlined at the beginning of this Chapter, see *supra* p. 1115.

Organized labor's fears about bankruptcy were attributable largely to the rejection power granted by the Bankruptcy Code. Under Section 365(a), 11 U.S.C. § 365(a), the debtor-employer—whether operated by incumbent management or a court-appointed trustee—is given the power to reject any "executory" contract that is deemed to burden the debtor's estate. (An "executory" contract is an agreement that remains at least partially unperformed by both parties. The collective bargaining agreement has been long assumed to be a type of executory contract.) Under an equitable principle known as the "business judgment rule," once the debtor has filed a petition for reorganization under Chapter 11, it enjoys broad discretion to determine which executory contracts are burdensome and therefore should be rejected, and which are beneficial and therefore should be assumed, and their breaches cured. In most reorganization proceedings, it is rare for an independent trustee to be appointed; in practice, the business is operated by the debtor "in possession," which means that incumbent management continues to call the shots. This has caused some prominent bankruptcy scholars to question whether the managers who steered the company into bankruptcy in the first place are capable of steering it out. *See, e.g.*, Lynn M. LoPucki & William C. Whitford, *Corporate Governance in the Bankruptcy Reorganizations of Large Publicly-Held Companies*, 141 U. Pa. L. Rev. 669 (1993).

From labor's perspective, rejection was problematic for at least two reasons. First, it was too easy to qualify for, because the business judgment rule erected such a low barrier. Second, rejection transformed generous contract rights into unattractive "pre-petition" claims for unsecured damages, which are typically paid last and at a fraction of their actual value. By contrast, higher priority claims, such as secured interests and post-petition administrative costs of the estate, are typically paid first and at full value. As a result, labor leaders accused employers of filing for Chapter 11 solely for the purpose of shredding their union contracts.

In 1984, the Supreme Court decided *NLRB v. Bildisco & Bildisco*, 465 U.S. 513 (1984), a case that seemed to confirm organized labor's worst fears about the pro-employer tilt of the bankruptcy laws. Although the Court unanimously agreed that the business judgment rule set too low a standard, the justices stopped short of raising the bar to the high level demanded by union advocates, who argued that rejection should be approved only when essential to ensure the success of the debtor-employer's plan of reorganization. Moreover, by a closer 5 to 4 vote, the Court held that the unilateral act of rejection prior to bankruptcy court approval did not itself constitute a violation of the duty to bargain—

effectively preempting NLRA remedies as to any debtor-employer that had filed a petition to reorganize its financial affairs under Chapter 11.

To organized labor, *Bildisco* had unfairly changed the rules of the collective bargaining game by encouraging unilateral self-help at the expense of arms-length negotiations. By claiming economic hardship, an employer-debtor could change the terms and conditions of employment first and seek court approval later, all while ignoring its union bargaining partner. By contrast, federal labor policy, as explained in Chapter 5, *supra* p. 636, requires the opposite: the employer must bargain with the union first, and absent an agreement, must continue bargaining until impasse before it may implement changes. In fact, unilateral modifications during the term of a collective bargaining agreement may constitute both a breach of contract and an unfair labor practice under Section 8(a)(5). In the context of a bankruptcy proceeding, however, *Bildisco* impaired each of these remedies without giving labor much in return. *See, e.g.*, David L. Gregory, *Labor Contract Rejection in Bankruptcy: The Supreme Court's Attack on Labor in NLRB v. Bildisco*, 25 B.C.L. Rev. 539, 554–55 & n.75 (1984); James J. White, *The Bildisco Case and the Congressional Response*, 30 Wayne L. Rev. 1169, 1202–03 (1984).

2. THE LAW RESPONDS

a. In the Private Sector: Section 1113

Labor's criticism of *Bildisco* was so swift and effective that a bill to deal with the decision was introduced the same day it was announced. Less than five months later, in practically record time for Congress, the bill became law. Section 1113 of the Bankruptcy Code was part of comprehensive reform legislation known as the Bankruptcy Amendments and Federal Judgeship Act, Pub. L. No. 98–353, 98 Stat. 333, *codified as amended* at 11 U.S.C. §§ 1101–1114.

Section 1113 was designed to meet labor's twin goals of reversing the right of debtor-employers to engage in economic self-help during Chapter 11, and making it tougher for bankruptcy courts to approve the rejection of collective bargaining agreements. As to the former, Section 1113(d)(1), 11 U.S.C. § 1113(d)(1), requires notice and a hearing, and Section 1113(f), 11 U.S.C. § 1113(f), requires bankruptcy court approval, *before* the employer may reject a labor contract. As to the latter, the statute conditions such approval on the completion of nine steps. As explained by *In re American Provision Co.*, 44 B.R. 907 (Bankr. D. Minn.1984), the case most frequently cited to explain Section 1113, the debtor must: (1) offer the union a proposal that (2) is based on the most complete information available, (3) provides for such modifications in the existing contract as are necessary to permit the debtor's reorganization, and (4) assures that all creditors, the debtor, and all affected parties are treated fairly and equitably. The debtor must also: (5) provide the union with such relevant information as is necessary to evaluate the proposal and (6) meet and confer with the union (7) in good faith. If the union (8) has refused to accept such proposal without good cause, and if (9) the balance of equities clearly favors rejection, then and only then may the bankruptcy judge issue an order granting rejection. *See* 11 U.S.C. §§ 1113(b)(1)(A)–(B), 1113(b)(2), 1113(c)(3). (A parallel provision, Section 1114, 11 U.S.C. § 1114, makes it similarly more difficult to reject pension and benefit fund obligations.)

The statute's nine steps make Section 1113 a unique piece of labor legislation in three respects.

First, Section 1113 is the only federal labor law governing the private sector that allows the government, in the guise of the courts, to decide whether the employer's bargaining proposals are meritorious, and therefore, adoptable by the union. For example, in step 3, rejection is conditioned on the debtor's establishing that his proposed changes are "necessary" to permit the debtor's reorganization. Similarly, steps 4, 8, and 9 focus on the merits of the parties' bargaining positions. By contrast, under the NLRA, the government, in the guise of the NLRB, is never allowed to pass upon the merits of the employer's bargaining proposals, or to state whether the union is justified in refusing them. The NLRB may supervise the process, but not the product, of collective bargaining.

Second, the statute reallocates responsibility for regulating collective bargaining, at least between Chapter 11 employers and their unions, from a forum of experts in labor relations (the NLRB) to a forum of nonexperts (the federal bankruptcy courts). Under Section 1113, an employer seeking to reject, or a union seeking to defend, a labor contract has to persuade a bankruptcy judge who may have no training in or sympathy for the principles of freedom of association and self-organization enshrined in the NLRA. Indeed, the two forums have different missions. Whereas the Board's job is to ensure employee free choice in exercising the rights guaranteed by the NLRA, the bankruptcy judge's job in a reorganization proceeding is to give the debtor wide latitude—the term of art is called "breathing space"—to get back on its financial feet. Here the statute codifies rather than overturns *Bildisco*, which effectively ousted the NLRB of its heretofore exclusive jurisdiction to decide unfair labor practice charges under Section 8(a)(5).

Finally, Section 1113 redefines the once-settled meaning of the employer's duty to bargain. Although steps 1, 2, 5, 6, and 7 certainly impose a type of duty to bargain with language borrowed from the traditional law of collective bargaining procedure, similar terms found in the NLRA do not mean the same thing in Section 1113. Whereas the duty to bargain under the NLRA is open-ended, the duty to bargain under Section 1113 is truncated by time and procedure. For example, once the debtor-employer's application to reject has been filed, bargaining must take place within a brief, statutorily defined period of time, whose length and duration is controlled primarily by the employer. If time runs out before the union is satisfied with the product of negotiations, the debtor may be permitted to implement its proposal anyway—even if impasse, the traditional point at which the duty to bargain is suspended under the NLRA, has not yet been reached. For a discussion of the statute's unique attributes, see Christopher D. Cameron, *How "Necessary" Became the Mother of Rejection: An Empirical Look at the Fate of Collective Bargaining Agreements on the Tenth Anniversary of Section 1113*, 34 Santa Clara L. Rev. 841, 873–74 (1994).

In an early and influential application of Section 1113 to the post-*Bildisco* world, a bankruptcy court held that the operator of a bus transportation service between New York City's major airports had taken the nine steps and qualified for the right to reject a pair of collective bargaining agreements with the Teamsters Union.

IN RE CAREY TRANSPORTATION, INC.

50 Bankr. 203 (Bankr. S.D.N.Y. 1985), *aff'd*, 816 F.2d 82 (2d Cir. 1986)

BURTON R. LIFLAND, BANKRUPTCY JUDGE:

This contested matter was brought on by the application of Carey Transportation, Inc., the debtor-in-possession ("Carey" or "the Debtor"), to reject two collective bargaining agreements with Bus Drivers and Truck Drivers Local Union No. 807, International Brotherhood of Teamsters, Chauffeurs, Warehouse workers and Helpers of America ("Local 807" or "the Union"). One of the agreements covers about 105 drivers; the other covers 10 station personnel.

Carey filed a voluntary petition for reorganization under [Chapter 11]. The Debtor is a privately held company whose primary business operations are providing bus service from and between New York City and John F. Kennedy International Airport and LaGuardia Airport. A major portion of Carey's business is in connection with permit and franchise arrangements it has negotiated with the Port Authority of New York and New Jersey ("Port Authority") and the City of New York. Carey attributes its "present financial difficulties to excessive operating costs. In significant part, these high costs of operation are attributable to the terms of [the] collective bargaining agreements covering the debtor's drivers and station personnel." Carey further traces its present fiscal problems to a 64-day strike in 1982 by a majority of the employees covered by the Local 807 agreements. Carey indicates that the loss of ridership during the strike has had long-term adverse effects which were only partially mitigated by the Debtor's successful efforts at recapturing passengers. Carey also points to its higher than average labor costs. Testimony was adduced to the effect that, given its present cash flow situation, Carey anticipates its vendors refusing to provide services within the next thirty days.

The Debtor has produced evidence to substantiate its averment that it has negotiated with the Union pre-and post-petition and has instituted across the board economies.

Pre-petition, Carey and the Union engaged in negotiations that resulted in a Supplement modifying the terms of the collective bargaining agreements. The Supplement terms pertained to all full-time drivers above the contract minimum hired after July 1, 1984. They included: establishment of a two-tier wage schedule permitting new drivers to start at a lower rate; reduction of overtime pay and vacations; elimination of sick days and reduction in fringe benefit contributions. In addition, Carey reduced its number of management, supervisory and nonunion employees, and streamlined its operation.

Carey's financial and operations officers testified that although savings were achieved by instituting the terms of the Supplement, further modifications in the collective bargaining agreements were needed. Negotiations with the Union during the first quarter of 1985, however, were fruitless.

Post-petition, Carey's proposal of necessary modifications included:

- Freezing all wages for second tier drivers and reducing hourly wages for first tier drivers for a period of three years.

- Reducing overtime, vacation and fringe benefit contributions.

- Eliminating sick days.

- Guaranteeing a minimum number of full-time drivers.

The Union's rejection of this proposal prompted the present application. In addition, a majority of the drivers covered by the Local 807 collective bargaining agreement, believing themselves disaffected, organized into a Drivers Ad Hoc Committee ("the Drivers"). The Drivers, acting independently of their designated collective bargaining agent, for the most part boycotted the negotiating sessions between Carey and the Union. Ultimately they submitted counter-proposals, which are discussed below. After the third day of this hearing, the Union submitted its counter-proposal, similar to the one Carey had made (and the Union had rejected 82 to 7), pre-petition.

This Court must decide whether Carey has complied with the requirements of Code § 1113 which permits the bankruptcy court to approve an application to reject a collective bargaining agreement.

The Supreme Court's decision in *NLRB v. Bildisco & Bildisco*, 465 U.S. 513, 104 S. Ct. 1188, 79 L. Ed. 2d 482 (1984), ruled that a bankruptcy court should permit rejection if the debtor can show that the contract burdens the estate and that, after careful scrutiny, the equities balance in favor of rejection. That decision further held that a debtor which unilaterally terminated or modified provisions of the agreement prior to obtaining court approval to reject the collective bargaining agreement did not commit an unfair labor practice under the National Labor Relations Act.

Congress' response to *Bildisco* is contained in Code § 1113, which in part overturns the Supreme Court's decision by forbidding unilateral rejection prior to a hearing [by a bankruptcy judge] and ruling upon an application to reject a collective bargaining agreement. Furthermore, Code § 1113 requires the debtor to propose modifications to the union post-petition before seeking approval to reject its collective bargaining agreements. 11 U.S.C. § 1113(b)(1)(A). The proposal may contain only "those necessary modifications . . . that are necessary to permit the reorganization of the debtor and assures that all creditors, the debtor and all of the affected parties are treated fairly and equitably." *Id.* The debtor also must confer with the union representative in good faith in attempting to reach mutually satisfactory modifications of the collective bargaining agreement. 11 U.S.C. § 1113(b)(2). The standard for rejection is provided by § 1113(c), which allows the court to approve an application to reject a collective bargaining agreement only if it finds that the applicant has complied with § 1113(b)(1); the union representative has refused without good cause to accept the proposal; and the balance of equities clearly favors rejection. 11 U.S.C. § 1113(c).

Section 1113 was enacted reactively with little or no accompanying legislative history. Congress did not agree upon a committee report to accompany this section; there are only statements read into the Congressional Record by various members of Congress on the date the statute was enacted, June 29, 1984.

This Court declines to give substantial weight to the aforementioned legislative statements and instead will be guided by the plain meaning of the statutory language and what little case law exists.

An early case construing § 1113, *In re American Provision Co.*, 44 B.R. 907 (Bankr. D. Minn.1984), extracts nine elements from the language of § 1113(b) and (c) that must be satisfied before a court may approve rejection of collective bargaining agreements. Because the case provides a convenient framework in which to examine the Debtor's evidence, it will be utilized to that extent. It will be noted that, where appropriate, certain of *American Provision*'s elements are dealt with in tandem.

The nine elements in Code § 1113(b) and (c) are:

1. The debtor in possession must make a proposal to the Union to modify the collective bargaining agreement.

2. The proposal must be based on the most complete and reliable information available at the time of the proposal.

3. The proposed modifications must be necessary to permit the reorganization of the debtor.

4. The proposed modifications must assure that all creditors, the debtor and all of the affected parties are treated fairly and equitably.

5. The debtor must provide to the Union such relevant information as is necessary to evaluate the proposal.

6. Between the time of the making of the proposal and the time of the hearing on approval of the rejection of the existing collective bargaining agreement, the debtor must meet at reasonable times with the Union.

7. At the meetings the debtor must confer in good faith in attempting to reach mutually satisfactory modifications of the collective bargaining agreement.

8. The Union must have refused to accept the proposal without good cause.

9. The balance of the equities must clearly favor rejection of the collective bargaining agreement.

THE DEBTOR'S (1) PROPOSAL TO MODIFY THE COLLECTIVE BARGAINING AGREEMENT (2) MUST BE BASED ON THE MOST COMPLETE AND RELIABLE INFORMATION AVAILABLE AT THE TIME OF THE PROPOSAL

Carey's controller testified, and evidence was advanced, that the Debtor has operated at a loss since December 31, 1981. For the fiscal year ending February 28, 1985, the Debtor's loss amounted to approximately $2.5 million, and the Debtor projected a loss for the fiscal year ending February 28, 1986 of $746,000.

Carey's controller testified that the proposal given to the Union was based upon the following cost savings, which were instituted pre-petition:

- Elimination of through-service to Port Authority Bus Terminal and replacement of that service with a shuttle, resulting in a projected savings of $264,000 annually.

- Elimination of Carey's Pier 60 maintenance and storage facility as well as removal of its administrative, marketing and financial office to a less costly location, resulting in a net annual savings of $225,000.

- Settlement of a dispute with the Metropolitan Transportation Authority over the amount of tolls Carey paid at the Queens-Midtown Tunnel, resulting in an estimated annual savings of $264,000.

Carey's chief operating officer testified that pre-petition negotiations with the Port Authority, concerning equipment leases, license fees and other charges will result in a combined annual savings of about $886,000. Carey's proposal to the Union was based, in addition, upon these savings.

In response to Carey's proposals, which would result in projected economies of $1.8 million for each of the next three fiscal years, the Union, after the third day of this hearing, submitted counter-proposals. These would result in estimated annual savings of $750,000. The Drivers, in fragmented fashion and [despite] the negotiations being conducted by their certified representative, also submitted various counter-proposals in response to Carey.

The Drivers assert that Carey's failure to provide financial information about potential revenues to be gained from instituting a children's half-fare policy (children currently ride free of charge) as well as Carey's failure to provide information regarding inter-company transactions prevents this Court from finding that Carey's proposal complies with Code § 1113. The child half-fare policy was not contained in Carey's proposal.

While claiming an initial lack of supplied relevant financial information, the Union chose not to avail itself of Carey's offer to permit the Union's auditors to examine the Debtor's books and records on location. The Union never contended that Carey failed to supply financial information necessary to evaluate Carey's proposal. Indeed, most of the Union's rebuttal evidence was based upon management-supplied information. That the Union is not satisfied with the Debtor's proposals and that the Debtor did not adopt one of the Driver's counter-proposals are insufficient bases to support a finding that Carey failed to provide relevant financial information. This Court finds that the relevant information developed at the evidentiary hearing was available pre-hearing.

(3) PROPOSED MODIFICATIONS MUST BE NECESSARY TO PERMIT THE DEBTOR'S REORGANIZATION

The Debtor's financial and operating officers testified generally but credibly that the proposed modifications are necessary to rehabilitate the debtor into a competitive business enterprise in its particular market and to provide for a successful reorganization. The Union argued to the contrary without developing any factual contradiction. The Union's conclusory statements are insufficient to disprove that Carey's proposals are necessary.

Nevertheless, neither side discussed what Code § 1113(b)(1)(A) means by "necessary modifications." For example, in *Allied Delivery System Co.*, 49 Bankr. 700 (Bankr. N.D. Ohio 1985), the bankruptcy court concluded that " 'necessary' must be read as a term of lesser degree than 'essential' [used in § 1113(e)]." The court reasoned that "the subsequent requirement of good faith negotiation" would otherwise be "meaningless, since the debtor would thereby be subject to a finding that any substantial lessening of the demands made in the original proposal [would prove] that the original proposal's modifications were not 'necessary.' " That court found the proposed modifications "necessary" based upon the fact that 87% of the debtor's gross revenues went toward union labor costs.

The *American Provision* court, on the other hand, found that a proposed savings amounting to 2% of the debtor's monthly operating expenses (it is unclear whether the figures used were gross or net) was not "necessary to permit the reorganization of the debtor." It is unclear what proportion of the debtor's total revenues went toward union labor expenses in *American Provision*. While this Court agrees that where the proportion of labor costs to total revenues is as high as it was in the *Allied Delivery* case, modifications are clearly necessary, it is hesitant to quantify what proportion of costs to revenues would be de minimis and thus not necessary to permit a reorganization. There can be no pat formula. Any analysis must be undertaken on a case by case basis with due consideration given to the nature of the business and industry patterns. In other words, the § 1113 process is designed to encourage selective, necessary contract modification rather than a total elimination of all provisions in the collective bargaining agreement. Complete de novo negotiation would be wasteful and counterproductive.

The evidence presented by Carey indicates that "the proposed modifications [impact] upon the debtor's operations." The Union's failure to specifically contradict this evidence requires this Court to find that the proposed modifications are necessary for Carey's reorganization.

(4) THE PROPOSAL MUST ASSURE THAT ALL CREDITORS, THE DEBTOR AND ALL OF THE AFFECTED PARTIES ARE TREATED FAIRLY AND EQUITABLY

A significant number of management personnel have dual employment with the Debtor's affiliated companies. Carey's chief financial officers testified that the percentage of managerial and supervisory salaries allocated to Carey is smaller than the percentage of time spent by those personnel on Carey business. Testimony was also adduced indicating that Carey's pay scale for its managers and supervisors was lower than comparable rates in similar enterprises. Pre-petition, Carey reduced the number of these personnel from twenty-three to fifteen. Two of these personnel received raises of $4,000 and $1,600 in fiscal 1985, reflecting increased responsibilities. Carey maintains five company automobiles for these personnel. In addition, Carey made the following pre-petition reductions and modifications: decreased the number of its other nonunion personnel from fifteen to twelve; reduced the number of people in its financial group from eight to six as a result of consolidating its accounting operations with those of one of its affiliates; reduced the number of airport customer service agents; and made fare increases.

The Union's main objection to Carey's proposal is that its employees bear the brunt, if not all, of the cost-cutting measures in Carey's proposal. In addition to the salary raises and company cars, the Union notes that in 1984, Carey made a 6% contribution to the profit sharing plan enjoyed by eight management personnel, while the only increase enjoyed by Union members for the remainder of the term of the collective bargaining agreement (8 months) is a 10per hour increase in pension fund contributions. The Union asserts that the "fair and equitable" language in § 1113(b)(1)(A) requires this Court to deny Carey's motion because its proposal does not include concomitant wage cuts and other economies for management, supervisory and other nonunion personnel.

Equity requires management to tighten its belt along with labor, and the record herein supports a finding that Carey has complied with this requirement. These pruning efforts may occur prior to or concurrent with the Chapter 11 filing.

It is rare that management approaches labor seeking economic concessions without being able to demonstrate that it has already taken steps to cut excess costs and overhead. Section 1113(b)(1)(A) requires the debtor who seeks to reject a collective bargaining agreement to "make a proposal to the authorized representative of the employees covered by [the collective bargaining agreement] which provides for those necessary modifications in the employees benefits and protections and assures that all creditors, the debtor and all of the affected parties are treated fairly and equitably." 11 U.S.C. § 1113(b)(1)(A). The courts have considered whether all of the " 'affected parties' [are] shouldering a [proportionate] burden of the debtor's cost-cutting efforts." Although Carey has not reduced the wages and salaries of its remaining managerial and supervisory employees, it has gradually reduced the number of these personnel by approximately 65%, which has certainly resulted in economies of scale. Nowhere does the Union demonstrate that Carey's administrative expenses are disproportionate to an operation of this kind, or that management was enjoying an extravagant corporate lifestyle. It merely calls management costs "excessive," by selectively highlighting purported examples. To the contrary, counsel for the Union conceded in his post-trial summation that the 2% management raises in 1985 "were not the biggest," and did not contradict testimony that the value of services received in some instances exceeded Carey's allocable share of salary. As one court stated, "[f]air and equitable treatment does not of necessity mean identical or equal treatment."

Carey's evidence of efforts at streamlining its management and supervisory staff, its agreements negotiated with its creditors the Port Authority and the MTA, and the concessions negotiated with the union covering its mechanics, District 15, all lead ineluctably to the conclusion that Carey's proposal treats all affected parties fairly and equitably, without placing a disproportionate burden on the members of the Union.

(6) THE DEBTOR MUST MEET WITH THE UNION AT REASONABLE TIMES BETWEEN THE MAKING OF ITS PROPOSAL AND THE TIME OF THE HEARING ON THE APPLICATION TO REJECT THE COLLECTIVE BARGAINING AGREEMENT

There is no question that Carey complied with this requirement. Although Carey and the Union met at least 9 times between the date the Debtor made its proposal and the date this hearing concluded, the Drivers, apparently acting on the advice of nonunion affiliated counsel, "stonewalled" these meetings. That the negotiating sessions were not fruitful is irrelevant and perhaps inevitable.

(7) THE DEBTOR MUST CONFER IN GOOD FAITH IN ATTEMPTING TO REACH MUTUALLY SATISFACTORY MODIFICATIONS OF THE COLLECTIVE BARGAINING AGREEMENT

The Union bases its contention that Carey failed to confer in good faith on the fact that Carey rejected the Union's last minute counter-proposal. Furthermore, Carey's testimony stands uncontradicted that the Union's counter-proposal does not contain sufficient savings to permit reorganization. The parties' failure to reach an agreement in this case appears to be partially the result of the internecine conflict involving the Union and its membership.

Regarding the good faith negotiating requirement of § 1113, the court noted in *Salt Creek*, "the failure to reach agreement appears to be the result of the difficultness of the task, rather than the lack of 'good faith' of either party." The *American Provision* court stated that "once the debtor has shown that it has met with the Union representatives, it is incumbent upon the Union to produce evidence that the debtor did not confer in good faith."

Carey has discharged its burdens of production and persuasion; the Union has produced no credible evidence demonstrating Carey's bad faith.

(8) THE UNION MUST HAVE REFUSED TO ACCEPT THE PROPOSAL WITHOUT GOOD CAUSE

Carey asserts that it has discharged its burden of proof on this issue merely by pointing to the Union's counter-proposal. Because there is no committee report accompanying Code § 1113, the meaning of "good cause" must be found from the statutory language and the sparse case law.

For example, the bankruptcy court in *In re K & B Mounting Co.*, 50 Bankr. 460 (Bankr. N.D. Ind. 1985), found that the Union had good cause to refuse to accept the debtor's proposal where the debtor failed to provide sufficient financial information and failed to make a proposal which treated all parties fairly and equitably. The *Allied Delivery* court enunciated a definition of "good cause" that flows from the requirements of § 1113(b), stating: "If the proposal is necessary and is fair and equitable then the Union's refusal to accept it on the basis that the proposal is unjust is not for good cause." The *Salt Creek* court stated:

> [I]n order to approve an application for rejection, it is not necessary to find that a Union has rejected a debtor's proposal in "bad faith" or for some contrary motive. In fact, the Union may often have a principled reason for deciding to reject the debtor's proposal and which may, when viewed subjectively and from the viewpoint of its self-interest, be a perfectly good reason. However, the court must review the Union's rejection utilizing an objective standard which narrowly construes the phrase "without good cause" in light of the main purpose of Chapter 11, namely reorganization of financially distressed businesses.

In re Salt Creek Freightways, 47 Bankr. 835, 840 (Bankr. D. Wy. 1985).

As in the *Salt Creek* case, there is no testimony concerning the Union's specific reasons for refusing to accept Carey's proposal. Having found that Carey's proposal contained necessary modifications and was fair and equitable when all the economies made by Carey pre-petition are combined with those proposed post-petition, it must be found that the Union's refusal to accept Carey's proposal was without good cause within the meaning of the statute.

(9) THE BALANCE OF THE EQUITIES MUST CLEARLY FAVOR REJECTION OF THE COLLECTIVE BARGAINING AGREEMENT

Carey has produced testimony tending to show that its previous pattern of annual losses, its projected although decreased loss for the coming fiscal year, its excessive labor costs and its tight cash flow situation formed the basis for filing its petition. The Debtor's financial officers have testified that the liquidation value of Carey is about $250,000, which would be consumed by administration and liquidation costs, leaving little if anything for unsecured creditors and equity shareholders. Further, Carey indicated that $70,000 of pre-petition claims owed to the Union's pension and welfare funds would exhaust the priority treatment afforded these claims under Code § 507(a)(3) and (4). Carey has also indicated its recognition of the fact that if its Application is granted, it will still have a duty to bargain in good faith with the Union toward achieving a new contract. Finally, if Carey were forced to liquidate, the Union members would be unemployed. The Union has not produced any credible rebuttal evidence.

The balancing of the equities test is largely a codification of the standard for rejecting a collective bargaining agreement adopted by the

Supreme Court in *Bildisco*. The Supreme Court indicated that this test is "higher than that of the 'business judgment' rule. This test is a broad equitable one, lacking rigidity." By inserting language in § 1113(c)(3) permitting rejection only where the balance of the equities "clearly" favors it, "Congress intended to clarify that rejection was only appropriate where the equities balance decidedly in favor of rejection." In *Salt Creek*, the equities to be balanced involved the interests of the affected parties—the debtor, creditors, and employees. The Bankruptcy Court must consider the likelihood and consequences of liquidation for the debtor absent rejection, the reduced value of the creditors' claims that would follow from affirmance and the hardship that would impose on them, and the impact of rejection on the employees. In striking the balance, the Bankruptcy Court must consider not only the degree of hardship faced by each party, but also any qualitative difference between the types of hardship each may face.

In balancing the equities, "a Bankruptcy Court must focus on the goal of Chapter 11 when considering those equities, and must consider only how the equities relate to the success [and policy] of reorganization."

Factors found relevant to this balancing test by the *Salt Creek* court included: whether the policy of reorganization will be furthered by the rejection of the collective bargaining agreement; whether the Union asserted that the debtor filed solely to disencumber itself from the collective bargaining agreement; and how damage claims resulting from the rejection would be treated under Code § 502(c).

While this Court concurs that the first and third factors above described are relevant for purposes of § 1113, it is loathe to attach any significance to whether or not the Union asserts a claim that the case was filed solely to jettison its union contract. That issue is more appropriate fodder for dismissal considerations under § 1112(b) of the Code, or for a motion by a party in interest such as the Union here, or to appoint a trustee or examiner under Code § 1104. The *Salt Creek* court's willingness to emphasize an unadvanced assertion is unjustified and dubious at best. Unlike the *Salt Creek* union, the Union in the case at bar did assert that Carey filed for Chapter 11 solely to reject its collective bargaining agreement; in fact, nothing in the record supports this assertion.

Code § 502(c) requires claims for damages resulting from the rejection of an executory contract to be estimated for purposes of determining allowed claims. As to the treatment of claims under § 502(c), Carey has indicated that because of the priority scheme of the Code and the small projected liquidation value of the company, such claims would not be likely to receive a dividend.

A final factor to be considered is that "[t]he impact of the cost savings which can be realized from further cutting the nonunion employees would be minute." Similar to the conclusion reached by that court is the one reached herein: "The evidence clearly demonstrate[s] that the financial drain on this debtor is enormous. The cutting of labor costs is essential. There has been no showing of any other area in which substantial savings could be realized by the debtor."

Carey attests that its labor costs were approximately 60% higher than the industry average. Because 66% of Carey's employees are unionized there is no way to avoid the conclusion that a substantial proportion of the Debtor's cost-saving measures will have to be borne by Local 807 members. In balancing the equities, then, and having considered all the factors of Code § 1113 as reiterated by the court in *American Provision*, this Court concludes that the balance of the equities clearly favors rejection of Carey's collective bargaining agreements with Local 807.

Based upon the testimony and evidence adduced at the hearing on this Application and the record in this case, the Court finds that the special requirements for rejection of a collective bargaining agreement have been met. The Debtor's application for rejection pursuant to § 1113 of the Bankruptcy Code is granted.

NOTES

1.   Section 1113 "created an expedited form of collective bargaining with several safeguards designed to insure that employers did not use Chapter 11 as medicine to rid themselves of corporate indigestion." *Century Brass Products, Inc. v. United Auto Workers*, 795 F.2d 265, 272 (2d Cir. 1986). Of the 9 steps to rejection contemplated by *American Provision Co.*, 44 Bankr. 907 (Bankr. D. Minn. 1984), step 3, the requirement that changes in the collective bargaining agreements be "necessary" for reorganization, is thought by commentators to be the most important. *See, e.g.*, Carlos J. Cuevas, *Necessary Modifications and Section 1113 of the Bankruptcy Code: A Search for the Substantive Standard for Modification of a Collective Bargaining Agreement in a Corporate Reorganization*, 64 Am. Bankr. L. J. 133, 135 & n.5 (1990). At least one empirical study of cases decided under Section 1113 seems to confirm this. *See* Christopher D. Cameron, *How "Necessary" Became the Mother of Rejection: An Empirical Look at the Fate of Collective Bargaining Agreements on the Tenth Anniversary of Section 1113*, 34 Santa Clara L. Rev. 841, 906–07 (1994).

Does the step 3 "necessary" requirement—or for that matter, any of Section 1113's other steps—make it harder for a debtor-employer to reject a collective bargaining agreement? The answer is a qualified yes. Before Section 1113, about 67% of all applications to reject union contracts were granted; in the first decade after the statute became law, 58% of all applications were granted. *See* Cameron, *supra*, at 892–93. Moreover, according to at least one other empirical study, in considering applications to reject union contracts that turn on step 3, bankruptcy courts nearly always interpret "necessary" in a manner that results in rejection. *See* Andrew B. Dawson, *Collective Bargaining Agreements in Corporate Reorganization*, 84 Am. Bankr. L.J. 103, 104 (2010); *see also* Babette A. Ceccotti, *Lost in Transformation: The Disappearance of*

Labor Policies in Applying Section 1113 of the Bankruptcy Code, 15 Am. Bankr. Inst. L. Rev. 415, 427–35 (2007) (documenting tendency of bankruptcy courts to subordinate labor policies to bankruptcy policies in considering applications to reject); *cf.* William T. Bodoh & Beth A. Buchanan, *Ignored Consequences— The Conflicting Policies of Labor Law and Business Reorganization and Its Impact on Organized Labor*, 15 Am. Bankr. Inst. L. Rev. 395, 411 (2007) (concluding that, contrary to the intentions of its sponsors, Section 1113 has weakened the position of labor in reorganization proceedings).

Of course, 58% still represents a lot of rejections. Many reasons could explain this. Could one of them be the different—and perhaps conflicting— purposes that underlie the NLRA and the Bankruptcy Code? For example, whereas Section 201(a) of the NLRA "encourage[s] employers and the representatives of their employees to reach and maintain agreements," 29 U.S.C. § 175(a), the automatic stay provision of Section 362(a) of the Bankruptcy Code, 11 U.S.C. § 362(a), is designed to give debtors "breathing space" from creditors seeking to enforce agreements of all types, *Bildisco*, 465 U.S. at 532, so they can get back on their financial feet. And whereas the NLRA is interpreted by a (hopefully) neutral agency having expertise in labor relations, the Bankruptcy Code is interpreted by a bench having a stake in successful employer reorganizations, irrespective of the contractual rights of nondebtor parties. *See* Cameron, *supra*, at 926–27.

2.   *Masterpiece theater?* By tradition, the bankruptcy court is a court of equity, so it is not surprising that the language of equity appears throughout Section 1113. Sometimes, this language seems redundant, which is why at least one bankruptcy judge has said the statute "is not a masterpiece of draftsmanship." *American Provision Co.*, 44 Bankr. at 909. For example, step 4 requires the debtor's proposal to treat all parties "fairly and equitably"; step 9 requires that the "balance of equities" clearly favor rejection. Are these two separate steps, or just the same thing expressed two different ways?

3.   *Of equities and iniquities.* One of the grounds on which the Union and Drivers Ad Hoc Committee opposed Carey's proposal to implement substantial wage and benefit cuts was their inequity as applied to different segments of the workforce; nonunion workers were not asked to make proportionately similar sacrifices. Indeed, the compensation of some managers was raised, ostensibly to compensate them for picking up the slack attributable to laid off managers, whose ranks were reduced by 65%. In addressing step 9, that the balance of equities must clearly favor rejection, Judge Lifland noted: "Carey attests that its labor costs were approximately 60% higher than the industry average. Because 66% of Carey's employees are unionized there is no way to avoid the conclusion that a substantial proportion of the Debtor's cost-saving measures will have to be borne by Local 807 members." Something similar could be said of the labor cost structure borne by employers in many unionized industries. If so, what stops employers in those industries from declaring bankruptcy for the purpose of rejecting their collective bargaining agreements too?

4. *Concession bargaining.* In addressing step 4—that the that the debtor's proposal must treat all parties fairly and equitably—Judge Lifland observed: "It is rare that management approaches labor seeking economic concessions without being able to demonstrate that it has already taken steps to cut excess costs and overhead." Is this statement true of midterm collective bargaining outside the context of a Chapter 11 proceeding?

Recall your study of the duty to bargain in good faith in Chapter 5, *supra* p. 636. Under the NLRA, it is clear that an employer runs afoul of Section 8(a)(5) if it abrogates an existing collective bargaining agreement, no matter how dire the financial circumstances; a union is free to accede to the employer's request to engage in "midterm" bargaining, but has no duty to do so. Even after the term of a contract is ended, the employer must first bargain to impasse before implementing unilateral changes.

But must the employer "demonstrate that it has already taken steps to cut excess costs and overhead," as Judge Lifland put it, before demanding concessions at the bargaining table? Must the employer demonstrate economic distress at all? Is the duty to bargain in "good faith" under Section 8(a)(5) the same as step 7's duty to confer in "good faith"? Absent bankruptcy, would a union be entitled to obtain financial information backing up the employer's demand for concessions? Would such information have to be "the most complete and reliable information available at the time of the proposal," as contemplated by step 2? If the standards are different depending on whether the employer is in or out of Chapter 11, does that make sense to you?

b. In the Public Sector: Chapter 9

Due to the relatively higher proportion of labor costs paid by employers in the public as opposed to the private sector, municipal governments facing serious financial setbacks have little choice but to try to persuade public employee unions that their wage and benefit packages should be reduced. Even so, bankruptcy filings by cities, counties, and other local government entities are extremely rare; since the last major reform of the Bankruptcy Code in 1978, only a handful have filed for reorganization under the special provisions codified by Congress in Chapter 9. *See* 11 U.S.C. §§ 901–944. One important reason for the relative rarity of Chapter 9 filings has to do with principles of federalism and state sovereignty. As a creation of state government, a failing municipality operating under Chapter 9 cannot readily be liquidated and its assets sold to pay creditors, as would be the case for a failed private company whose reorganization under Chapter 11 did not pan out. (The remedy for a failed Chapter 11 is to convert the proceeding and liquidate the debtor under Chapter 7.) Certainly, grave constitutional implications would arise if any federal bankruptcy court attempted to undertake so drastic a step. *Compare, e.g., Ashton v. Cameron County Water District No. 1*, 298 U.S. 513 (1936) (striking down pre-reform predecessor to Chapter 9 for unconstitutionally encroaching on state power), *with United States v. Bekins*, 304 U.S. 27

(1938) (upholding post-reform predecessor to Chapter 9 against similar attack).

For most of Chapter 9's existence, the lone reported decision addressing a municipal employer's attempt to abrogate a public sector collective bargaining agreement—often called a memorandum of understanding (MOU)—arose out of the bankruptcy declared by Orange County, Calif. In 1994, Orange County, facing general fund losses of $527 million and investment pool losses of $1.7 billion, filed under Chapter 9. In hopes of saving millions of dollars immediately, County officials sought to abrogate scheduled pay raises and to lay off 186 employees out of seniority order, both in breach of MOUs between the County and 10 separate unions representing deputy sheriffs, deputy fire marshals, clerical staff, and other employees. Union creditors said they were willing to discuss concessions as to the scheduled pay hikes, but refused to give up the rights of employees to be laid off in seniority order, and sought to preserve employment of senior workers by invoking provisions permitting them to "bump" junior employees from lower classified positions.

Granting a motion filed by a coalition formed by the 10 public employee unions, the bankruptcy court enjoined the County from imposing unilateral changes to the MOUs. *See In re County of Orange*, 179 Bankr. 177 (Bankr. C.D. Cal. 1995). Although Bankruptcy Judge Ryan rejected the coalition's argument that Section 1113 governed the rejection of collective bargaining agreements in Chapter 9 as well as Chapter 11 proceedings, he did forbid the County from making unilateral mid-term modifications unless and until it had both established the existence of a fiscal "emergency" under a multi-factor test established by the applicable California public sector labor relations statute, and bargained with the coalition over possible compromises. Explained Judge Ryan:

> In my view, any unilateral action by a municipality to impair a contract with its employees must satisfy these factors if not as a legal matter, certainly from an equitable standpoint. In applying these factors, the County declared its fiscal emergency and the evidence adequately supports the declaration. The action is designed for the social good of the County and not for the benefit of an individual. However, in my view, the emergency did not necessitate the complete abrogation of seniority and grievance procedures without first attempting to negotiate acceptable changes. Also, the action did not indicate that it was for a temporary time, but given the County's fiscal situation, the exigency is likely to continue until the bankruptcy is resolved.

In re County of Orange, 179 Bankr. at 184. Accordingly, a temporary restraining order issued against the County, and the parties were required to negotiate, especially with regard to seniority issues. Eventually, the coalition gave up the scheduled pay raises in exchange for adherence to seniority principles and modified application of the "bumping" procedures called for by the MOUs.

In 2008, Vallejo, Calif., filed for Chapter 9 protection and sought rejection of MOUs with unions representing police, firefighters, managerial and other workers. The bankruptcy court granted rejection, and the district court affirmed. *See In re City of Vallejo*, 432 Bankr. 262 (E.D. Cal. 2010). While agreeing with *In re County of Orange* that Section 1113 was inapplicable, the two *In re City of Vallejo* judges ruled that the pre-Section 1113 principles announced in *NLRB v. Bildisco & Bildisco*, 465 U.S. 513 (1984), rather than state collective bargaining law, set forth the appropriate standards for determining rejection.

News reports suggested that Vallejo might be the first of numerous municipalities to deal with times of want by seeking to reject pension and benefit obligations agreed to by public officials during times of plenty. *See, e.g.*, Jesse McKinley, *City Council in Bay Area Declares Bankruptcy*, N.Y. Times, May 8, 2008; *see also* Edward Iwata, Economy Hobbles Calif. Town, USA Today, July 27, 2008. But municipal bankruptcies have remained rare; Vallejo was only the second city ever to file under Chapter 9. To date, only a handful of public entities of any type—whether city, county, township, school board, special assessment district, etc.—has ever filed for such protection.

In 2012, Stockton, Calif., and in 2013, San Bernardino, Calif., and Detroit, Mich., each filed under Chapter 9. The key issue in each proceeding was whether vested pension and benefit obligations could be reduced through voluntary negotiations, or whether they would have to be rejected through the Chapter 9 process.

In the California municipal bankruptcies, the trend seemed to favor rejection. Stockton successfully sought reduction of retirees' health benefit payments. *See In re City of Stockton*, 478 Bankr. 8 (E.D. Cal. 2012). San Bernardino successfully sought rejection of both wage and benefit provisions in its firefighters' MOU. *See In re City of San Bernardino*, 530 Bankr. 474 (C.D. Cal. 2015). Both outcomes generated bad feelings. In *In re San Bernardino*, the district court affirmed the bankruptcy court's rejection of the firefighters' MOU on the ground that the city had shouldered its burdens under *Bildisco*, which requires the debtor seeking rejection under Section 365(a) to show three things: (1) "reasonable efforts to negotiate a voluntary modification have been made, and are not likely to produce a prompt and satisfactory solution," (2) the agreement is a burden on the debtor, and (3) the balance of the equities weighs in favor of the rejection. *Bildisco*, 465 U.S. at 526. The city met this burden by showing that it had spent almost two years trying to negotiate voluntary wage and benefit reductions with the union. These efforts included mediating before two separate judges on at least four occasions; meeting outside the mediation process on at least three occasions; and exchanging numerous emails and telephone calls. But the union largely rebuffed these efforts, and insisted on rolling back unilaterally-adopted reductions before it would enter into serious negotiations for relief from the MOU. In what may be regarded as a classic example of how **_not_** to avoid rejection of collectively-bargaining obligations in the context of a municipal bankruptcy, the union made several arguments that the district court characterized as "legally unsupported and lazy" and "vapid." *In re City of Bernardino*, 530 Bankr. at 482. The least impressive of these arguments was that the firefighters' MOU could not be evaluated as burdensome until reductions to all other MOUs had been factored in. As the district court put it:

> The Court is appalled that the Union would suggest that the cuts to other labor unions must be considered before its own MOU is deemed a burden. There is no law anywhere that allows a creditor to sandbag the bankruptcy process and then claim its debt is not a burden because other creditors already took cuts. The Union is not entitled to preferential treatment because it held out the longest and refused to negotiate. This sly attempt to discredit the worth of the other public sector labor unions is astounding.

In re City of San Bernardino, 530 Bankr. at 484.

In the Detroit municipal bankruptcy, however, the city's unions avoided having to fight and risk losing similar rejection battles by agreeing to a "grand bargain" that incorporated negotiated cuts in wages and benefits, including reduced pensions for retirees, into a plan of adjustment. *See In re City of Detroit, Mich.*, 524 Bankr. 147, 169–70 (Bankr. E.D. Mich. 2014). For a general discussion of the problems posed by bankruptcies in the public sector, see Martin M. Malin, Ann C. Hodges, Joseph Slater & Jeffrey M. Hirsch, Public Sector Employment: Cases and Materials 325–45 (3d ed. 2016). For a thoughtful discussion of a failed attempt by a bankrupt school district in San Jose, Calif., to abrogate its MOUs, see Barry Winograd, *San Jose Revisited: A Proposal for Negotiated Modification of Public Sector Bargaining Agreements Rejected Under Chapter 9 of the Bankruptcy Code*, 37 Hast. L.J. 231 (1985).

3. THE AFTERMATH: WHAT REJECTION MEANS

Of the many changes worked by the rejection of a collective bargaining agreement in bankruptcy, three are particularly important.

First, as noted above, *supra* p. 1170, the union creditor loses the full benefit of its bargain. Rejection transforms the rights created by an executory contract into less attractive "pre-petition" claims for unsecured damages. In the typical bankruptcy, an unsecured, pre-petition claim is worth just a fraction of its actual value; this type of claim is low priority, and can be honored only if assets remain in the debtor's estate after creditors having higher priority claims have been paid. The priority scheme, which is somewhat complicated, is set forth in the Bankruptcy

Code. *See* 11 U.S.C. § 507. Examples of higher priority claims include the liens of secured creditors and the expenses associated with the post-petition administration of the estate. The latter include fees charged by professionals, such as accountants, attorneys, and consultants hired to sort out the debtor's affairs and help prepare a plan of reorganization. An example of a lower priority claim is unpaid wages, which are limited to wages earned up to 180 days before the Chapter 11 filing, and are capped at $12,850 per individual claimant. If a debtor-employer decided to get back on its financial feet by slashing the negotiated hourly wage in half, its employees, or their union, would have unsecured claims for the difference, but it is unlikely such claimants would recover much if anything. *See generally* Daniel Keating, *The Fruits of Labor: Worker Priorities in Bankruptcy*, 35 Ariz. L. Rev. 905 (1993).

Second, even if funds are available to pay unsecured creditors, many of the rights created by collective bargaining agreements are unique, and therefore difficult to treat as compensable claims. Typical of the nonmonetary rights that unions extract from employers at the bargaining table are the following: prohibition on the subcontracting out of bargaining unit work; respect for seniority rights, as illustrated by the Orange County case; the requirement of "just cause" to support management's discipline or discharge of employees; grievance arbitration and other mechanisms for adjusting disputes over the application of "just cause" and other contractual rights; and the no-strike clause. The monetary value of claims arising out of the elimination of such rights can be so hard to liquidate that some bankruptcy judges may estimate their value at $0, or simply disallow them altogether. *See, e.g., In re Northwest Airlines Corp.*, 366 Bankr. 270 (Bankr. S.D.N.Y. 2007); *In re Continental Air Lines*, 60 Bankr. 466 (Bankr. S.D. Tex. 1986).

Third, rejection of the entire collective bargaining agreement may result in the industrial equivalent of a nuclear holocaust: a strike that delivers the final, fatal blow to the troubled debtor-employer. Unable to operate even temporarily, the struck company may have to shut down, thereby eliminating all the jobs the union was fighting to save in the first place. This is possible because complete rejection means the elimination of the contractual obligations of both parties—including union's obligations under the no-strike clause. The abrogation of the no-strike clause would free the union and the employees it represents to exercise their Section 7 rights to withhold their labor. With some exceptions for strike-related violence discussed in Chapter 1, *supra* p. 20, and Chapter 10, *infra* p. 1206, federal courts are all but powerless to enjoin strike activity governed by the NLRA save when the union has entered into a bargain in exchange for giving up the right to strike, as in the case of a *Boys Market* injunction, discussed in Chapter 7, *supra* p. 921. *See Buffalo Forge Co. v. United Steelworkers*, 428 U.S. 397 (1976); *accord Jacksonville Bulk Terminals, Inc. v. International Longshoremen's Ass'n*, 457 U.S. 702 (1982). So when that bargain is off, all bets on the debtor's ability to enjoin a strike are off too. *See generally* Norris-LaGuardia Act, 29 U.S.C. § 101–116. It is well-established that the financial exigencies attending bankruptcy proceedings do not alter the right of the debtor's workers to strike. *See, e.g., In re Royal Composing Room, Inc.,* 62 Bankr. 403, 405 (Bankr. S.D.N.Y.1986), *aff'd,* 78 Bankr. 671 (S.D.N.Y. 1987), *aff'd,* 848 F.2d 345 (2d Cir.1988); *Briggs Transp. Co. v. Int'l Brotherhood of Teamsters,* 739 F.2d 341, 344 (8th Cir. 1984).

An important exception to the rule that a bankruptcy court lacks the power to enjoin a strike during reorganization proceedings is found in the railway and airline industries. Following the disruptions in commercial aviation that came after the events of September 11, 2001, and during the economic downturn that plagued the industry during the late 2000s, several air carriers filed for reorganization under Chapter 11. Unions representing employees of at least two of these carriers called a strike, or threatened to call a strike, which the carriers sought to enjoin. *See In re Northwest Airlines Corp.,* 346 Bankr. 333 (S.D.N.Y.), *rev'd,* 483 F.3d 160 (2d Cir. 2007); *In re Mesaba Aviation Inc.,* 350 Bankr. 112 (Bankr. D. Minn. 2006).

In *Northwest Airlines,* the more prominent case, the Second Circuit reversed the district court's denial of an injunction against a strike called by the union representing the carrier's flight attendants. After filing for Chapter 11, Northwest had persuaded the bankruptcy court to grant a Section 1113 application for rejection of a collective bargaining agreement with the Association of Flight Attendants (AFA), but only after flight attendants represented by the AFA had voted not to ratify an interim agreement for concessions that had been negotiated between the union and the carrier. Responding to the rejection of the labor contract, the AFA called a strike. As explained in Chapter 5, *supra* p. 644, the Railway Labor Act (RLA), which governs labor relations in the railway and airline industries, requires a party who wants to modify a collective bargaining agreement to serve a notice of intent on the other party. Thereafter, the parties are obligated to maintain the status quo until they exhaust the extensive negotiation and mediation procedures mandated by the RLA. Upon exhaustion, they may be "released" to use their economic weapons, including the strike weapon, by the National Mediation Board (NMB). This status quo, the Second Circuit explained, ceases to exist upon abrogation of a collective bargaining agreement under Section 1113. But the RLA's duty that the parties "exert every reasonable effort to make and maintain agreements" continues to apply. The court held that the AFA's threatened strike breached this duty, in part because no release had been issued by the NMB. As a result, the Norris-LaGuardia Act did not prevent the issuance of a strike injunction. *See In re Northwest Airlines Corp.,* 483 F.3d 160 (2d Cir. 2007). According to the Second Circuit: "There is no need at this point to decide when and if the AFA will have fulfilled its duty; it has not done so yet." *Id.* at 175. The problem was that the AFA had sought neither "to persuade its members to 'face up to economic reality,' " nor to mediate the dispute before the NMB, as required by the RLA. *Id.* at 176.

NOTES

1.   With the jobs of rank-and-file members hanging in the balance, why on earth would a union ever call a strike against an employer whose finances were so dire that it was compelled to file for bankruptcy protection? Can you think of any circumstances that would cause a union to call a strike anyway, and risk the company's liquidation? *See In re Horsehead Industries, Inc.*, 300 Bankr. 573, 587 (Bankr. S.D.N.Y. 2003) (observing that a strike "is an inherent risk in every § 1113 motion").

2.   *Choose your (economic) weapons.* Outside the railway and airline industries, it is settled that the debtor-employer's bankruptcy does not affect the union's right to deploy its economic weapons, including the strike. Should the converse be true as to the employer's economic weapons? Suppose that, after a Chapter 11 petition is filed by a health care facility, a strike is called by a union representing nurses. In an effort to continue providing patient care, the health care facility seeks to hire replacement nurses. Can it be prevented from doing so? *Cf. New England Health Care Employees Union, District 1199 v. Rowland*, 221 F. Supp. 2d 297 (D. Conn. 2002) (holding preempted governor's intervention in nursing home employees' strike by using state vehicles to transport nonstriking and replacement workers to job sites).

3.   *Flying the not-so-friendly skies.* As we have just seen, inside the railway and airline industries, whose labor relations are governed by the RLA, a bankrupt carrier may be able to enjoin a strike, and thereby undermine the union's attempt to apply economic pressure. Should the converse be true as to the debtor's attempt to apply economic pressure by unilaterally reducing employees' wages, benefits, and working conditions? Suppose that, during bargaining for a first contract, but before the mediation procedures required by the RLA have been exhausted, an airline operating in Chapter 11 attempts to save money by drastically altering the pay rates, flying schedules, and other working conditions of pilots. The union seeks an injunction preserving the status quo until RLA procedures are exhausted. Should the injunction issue? *See International Brotherhood of Teamsters v. North American Airlines*, 518 F.3d 1052 (9th Cir. 2008) (denying injunction to pilots who sued carrier for unilaterally altering rates of pay and work rules after commencement of negotiations but before agreement reached).

F. ANTITRUST AND THE END OF THE COLLECTIVE BARGAINING RELATIONSHIP

1. STATUTORY AND NONSTATUTORY LABOR ANTITRUST EXEMPTIONS

Without antitrust immunity, practically every collective bargaining agreement, and practically every action undertaken to secure the terms of one, would constitute a "contract, combination . . . or conspiracy" in restraint of trade in violation of Section 1 of the Sherman Antitrust Act, 15 U.S.C. § 1.[2]

At common law in most states, concerted activities by workers—including strikes, picketing, boycotts, and other weapons deployed to demand that employers recognize unions and enter into collective bargaining agreements with them—were considered unlawful, enjoinable conspiracies to restrain trade. *See, e.g., Vegelahn v. Guntner*, 167 Mass. 92, 44 N.E. 1077 (1896), discussed in Chapter 1, *supra* p. 20. For many years after the enactment the Sherman Act, which imposed criminal as well as civil penalties (the latter in the form of treble damages), the federal courts continued to adhere to the common law view, despite the objections of organized labor that the Act was intended to outlaw combinations, contracts and conspiracies to restrain trade by business enterprises only. *See, e.g., Loewe v. Lawlor (The Danbury Hatters Case)*, 208 U.S. 274 (1908). Even the statute's amendment by Sections 6 and 20 of the Clayton Act of 1914, 15 U.S.C. §§ 6, 20, which were expressly designed to give labor immunity from antitrust liability, failed to dampen the enthusiasm of federal judges for declaring most concerted activities to be illegal restraints on competition, and for enjoining workers and their unions from engaging in them. *See, e.g., Duplex Printing Press Co. v. Deering*, 254 U.S. 443 (1921). This state of affairs did not begin to change until the enactment of the Norris-LaGuardia Act of 1932, 29 U.S.C. §§ 101–115, which ousted the federal courts of jurisdiction over most labor disputes. It took nearly a decade after that for the Supreme Court finally to hold that taken together the Sherman, Clayton, Norris-LaGuardia Acts create for workers and unions a "statutory" immunity, or exemption, from federal antitrust liability. *See United States v. Hutcheson*, 213 U.S. 219 (1941). With limited exceptions not relevant here, this exemption has shielded labor from most antitrust liability for over 80 years.

---

[2] Which helps explain why, since practically the enactment of the Sherman Act in 1890, Major League Baseball employers have enjoyed broad antitrust immunity from liability for the anticompetitive harms caused by "the business of baseball," ranging from the reserve clause restricting the employment of individual players, *see, e.g., Federal Base Ball Club of Baltimore, Inc. v. National League of Professional Base Ball Clubs*, 259 U.S. 200 (1922), to league rules restricting the rights of franchises to relocate, *see City of San Jose v. Office of Commissioner of Baseball*, 776 F.3d 686 (9th Cir. 2015).

The statutory labor antitrust exemption may be asserted by a union when two conditions are met: first, the restraint of trade at issue is of legitimate interest to labor; second, it is not sought at the behest of nonlabor groups. *See, e.g., H.A. Artists & Associates, Inc. v. Actors' Equity Ass'n*, 451 U.S. 704, 714–15 (1981); *United States v. Hutcheson*, 312 U.S. 219, 229–30 (1941). Contract terms setting minimum wages, maximum hours, and other mandatory subjects of bargaining typically satisfy both conditions.

With the spread of multiemployer bargaining practices, or "pattern bargaining," in major U.S. industries, especially after World War II, came the need to create a corresponding antitrust immunity to shield the parties sitting on the other side of the bargaining table—namely, employers. Pattern bargaining is still common in industries affecting aerospace, automobile manufacturing, film and television entertainment, retail food, and major league team sports, among others. The need for a "nonstatutory" exemption arose from the tension between the free market principles embodied in the antitrust laws and national labor policy favoring collective bargaining codified in the NLRA. In 1965, the Supreme Court obliged by recognizing a nonstatutory antitrust exemption. *See Local Union No. 189, Amalgamated Meat Cutters & Butcher Workmen v. Jewel Tea Co.*, 381 U.S. 676 (1965); *United Mine Workers v. Pennington*, 381 U.S. 657 (1965) *see also Connell Constr. Co. v. Plumbers & Steamfitters Local Union No. 100*, 421 U.S. 616 (1975). As the Court later explained:

> As a matter of logic, it would be difficult, if not impossible, to require groups of employers and employees to bargain together, but at the same time to forbid them to make among themselves or with each other any of the competition-restricting agreements potentially necessary to make the process work or its results mutually acceptable.

Brown v. Pro Football Inc., 518 U.S. 231, 237 (1996).

The nonstatutory labor antitrust exemption may be asserted by an employer or group of employers when at least two conditions are met: first, the restraint at issue primarily affects the parties to the collective bargaining relationship; and second, such restraint constitutes a mandatory subject of bargaining under the NLRA. *See Mackey v. NFL*, 543 F.2d 606, 614 (8th Cir. 1976). Although there is a split of authority, a third condition may have to be met too: the restraint must be the product of bona fide, arms-length negotiations. *Compare, e.g., Mackey* (adopting third condition), *with, e.g., Clarett v. NFL*, 306 F. Supp. 2d 379 (S.D.N.Y. 2004) (rejecting third condition), *rev'd in part, vacated on other grounds*, 369 F.3d 124 (2d Cir. 2004), *cert. denied*, 544 U.S. 961 (2005); *see also California ex rel. Lockyer v. Safeway Inc.*, 371 F. Supp. 2d 1179, 1185 n.5 (C.D. Cal. 2005) (reasoning *that Brown v. Pro Football* overruled requirement that *Mackey's* third condition be met), *aff'd sub nom. California ex rel. Harris v. Safeway*

Inc., 651 F.3d 1118 (9th Cir. 2011) (en banc). As in the case of the statutory exemption, agreements by employers to set minimum wages, maximum hours, and other mandatory subjects of bargaining generally satisfy the conditions for the nonstatutory labor antitrust exemption.

2. APPLICATION TO MULTIEMPLOYER BARGAINING IN GENERAL

The parties to litigation raising claims under Section 1 of the Sherman Antitrust Act must deal with up to three crucial issues affecting the employer's potential liability.

First, as noted above, the defendant employer may argue that it is exempt under the nonstatutory labor antitrust exemption. A successful defense under this exemption turns on whether the two (or three) conditions relating to this exemption have been satisfied.

Second, if the exemption arguably applies, then the plaintiff union may rebut by arguing that the defendant's conduct exceeded the proper scope of the exemption. It is now recognized that the scope of the nonstatutory labor antitrust exemption is limited by subject matter; it shields concerted activity affecting labor relations as undertaken by a multiemployer group. It does not shield all tangentially-related commercial activities, such as an exclusive licensing agreement to manufacture clothing bearing the group's logo or other intellectual property for the consumer market. *See American Needle Inc. v. NFL*, 130 S. Ct. 2201 (2010). Nor does it shield a mutual assistance pact among four grocery store employers calling for each employer to subsidize the others for losses caused by a particular labor dispute, if one of the employers is not involved in such labor dispute. *See California ex rel. Harris v. Safeway Inc.* 651 F.3d 1118 (9th Cir. 2011) (en banc). It is also recognized that the scope of this exemption is limited by duration; it expires when the collective bargaining relationship ends, as indicated by decertification or some other event confirming the union's loss of majority support among employees. It does not expire when either the union contract terminates or the parties reach impasse in negotiations for a new contract. *See Brown v. Pro Football Inc.*, 518 U.S. 231 (1996).

Third, if the exemption and scope of exemption arguments are unavailing, the parties may argue the merits. Either of two means may be used to establish a Section 1 claim under the Sherman Antitrust Act: the per se approach or the rule-of-reason analysis. Historically, the per se approach was preferred. A Section 1 claim was considered meritorious if it fell into one of the categories of anticompetitive practices that are considered illegal per se, such price-fixing, engaging in a group boycott, entering into any contract "tying" the buyer to a promise not to deal with the seller's competitors, or agreeing to a horizontal division of markets. In the world of multiemployer bargaining, the most common activity by employers that could give rise to potential antitrust liability is setting limits on wages—the salary cap found in professional team sports is such a limit—because wage-fixing is equivalent to price-fixing. *See Brown v. Pro Football Inc.*, 141 L.R.R.M. (BNA) 2942 (D.D.C. 1992). Modernly, however, the rule of reason analysis has become predominant. This is a case-by-case test that balances the anticompetitive harm caused by the restraint against its procompetitive benefits, tempered by the availability of less restrictive means of accomplishing those benefits. *See National College Athletic Ass'n v. Board of Regents*, 468 U.S. 85 (1984).

For a summary of applicable labor antitrust law, see Douglas E. Ray, William R. Corbett & Christopher David Ruiz Cameron, Labor-Management Relations: Strikes, Lockouts and Boycotts § 9:14 (2017–18).

3. APPLICATION TO WORKERS CHARACTERIZED AS INDEPENDENT CONTRACTORS

The nonstatutory labor antitrust exemption is generally not available to protect workers who are legally classified as independent contractors, on the theory that any collective action by them is anti-competitive and therefore repugnant to the principle that markets, not conspirators, should set prices in the marketplace. The Sherman Act "reflects a legislative judgment that ultimately competition will produce not only lower prices, but also better goods and services." *National Society of Professional Engineers v. United States,* 435 U.S. 679, 695 (1978).

Independent contractors ranging from business consultants, gardeners, and musicians to solo law practitioners, street vendors, and Uber drivers may be self-employed business actors, but they are in business nonetheless. Businesses are not allowed to fix or attempt to fix the price of their products and services, at least not outside the context of arms-length bargaining with unions representing their employees. For example, lawyers in private practice who act as court-appointed counsel for indigent defendants in criminal cases were found to have violated the federal antitrust laws by organizing and participating in a boycott designed to pressure the system to increase their fees. *See Federal Trade Commission v. Superior Court Trial Lawyers' Ass'n*, 493 U.S. 411 (1990).

As Professor Sanjukta Paul has noted, the contemporary service economy seems to create an antitrust paradox. If the members of a hiring hall, whether operated by a union or directly by workers, were considered independent contractor service providers, then they would be engaged in impermissible price-fixing under the conventional interpretation of antitrust law. But so far Uber has been permitted to engage in precisely this sort of price coordination between independent contractors—for its own economic benefit, rather than that of the drivers who do the work. To address the paradox, she advances the argument that Uber and other "app"-based service providers are essentially modern-day hiring halls whose workers should be permitted to engage in collective bargaining. *See* Sanjukta Paul, *Uber as For-Profit Hiring Hall: A Price-Fixing Paradox and Its Implications*, 38 Berkeley J. of Emp. & Lab. L. 233 (2017).

Responding to the antitrust paradox in their own way, a handful of local governments have enacted legislation to confer collective bargaining rights on the drivers of ride-hailing companies.

In 2016, Seattle Ordinance No. 124968 went into effect. The ordinance provides a mechanism through which for-hire drivers in Seattle can collectively bargain with the companies that hire, contract with, and/or partner with them. The ordinance applies only to for-hire drivers who are independent contractors, not employees. Pursuant to the procedures codified in the ordinance, Teamsters Local 117 notified three members of the local Chamber of Commerce that it wished to represent their drivers in collective bargaining. The Chamber, acting on behalf of its members, filed an action challenging the ordinance on several grounds, including that it violated the Sherman Act and was preempted by the NLRA. A federal district judge rejected these challenges. *See Chamber of Commerce of U.S. v. City of Seattle*, 274 F. Supp. 3d 1155 (W.D. Wash. 2017). However, on appeal, the court remanded the antitrust claims for further proceedings reversing the district court, but upheld the lower court in dismissing the NLRA preemption claim. *See Chamber of Commerce v. City of Seattle,* 890 F.3d 769 (9th Cir. 2018).

Among the remedies available to persons or businesses who claim to have been damaged by price-fixing among independent contractors include suing for antitrust damages under the Sherman and Clayton Acts, 15 U.S.C. §§ 1–2, 15; suing for secondary boycott damages under Section 303 of the Taft-Hartley Act, 29 U.S.C. § 187; and seeking injunctive relief from the courts or through the NLRB under Section 10(*l*) of the NLRA, 29 U.S.C. § 160(*l*). As to the latter, however, it should be noted that the federal courts are generally prohibited from issuing inunctions to enjoin activities relating to labor disputes. *See* Norris-LaGuardia Act of 1932, 29 U.S.C. §§ 401–531. Apparently, the prohibition of injunctive relief applies equally to such relief whether sought against workers, *see, e.g., Milk Wagon Drivers' Union Local No. 753 v. Lake Valley Farm Products, Inc.*, 311 U.S. 91 (1940), as universally understood, or business owners, *see Brady v. NFL*, 644 F.3d 661 (8th Cir. 2011), as more recently articulated by the Eighth Circuit.

4. APPLICATION TO MULTIEMPLOYER BARGAINING IN PROFESSIONAL TEAM SPORTS

The nonstatutory labor antitrust exemption is especially important to the business model found in major league team sports. In the U.S. and Canada, these sports are generally considered to be the ones operated by Major League Baseball (MLB), the National Basketball Association (NBA), the National Football League (NFL), and the National Hockey League (NHL). (This list does not yet include the sport operated by Major League Soccer (MLS) due to its smaller size and unique ownership practices, including the league's ownership of a percentage of each franchise.) Unlike most business enterprises, multiemployer coordination is essential to the operation of the MLB, NBA, NFL, and NHL. This is because each league, by definition, is a joint venture. The joint venturers are the clubs or franchises. Although clubs certainly engage in economic competition, they also undertake substantial economic coordination. They must agree to be paired with each other in order to compete on the field; they play under a common set of rules; they share television and other revenues generated by the games they play. Indeed, the product sold to live spectators and television audiences alike is not the performance of individual clubs playing by themselves, but rather the exhibition of games or matches between clubs played under the foregoing conditions. Without the nonstatutory antitrust exemption, collectively-bargained agreements by league owners as to the perennial, hot-button labor issues—such as the rookie draft, the reserve clause, minimum salary, free agency, salary arbitration, and the salary cap—would likely fall under the weight of treble damages imposed by the Sherman Act.

Thus the continued existence of the nonstatutory labor antitrust exemption has become a staple of labor relations in professional team sports. In recent years, the players, taking their cue from *Brown v. Pro Football*, have called the same basic play: if the union fails to achieve its goals at the bargaining table, or on the picket line, then it turns instead to the courts. Initially, negotiations are held. If they prove fruitless, then mediation may follow. If that doesn't work, then the parties they may draw their economic weapons and prepare to fight. For players, this usually means calling a strike during the playoffs; for owners, it usually means locking the players out of training camp and all the games at the start of the regular reason. If economic weapons don't work, then the players hold a pro forma decertification vote. Once it passes, the union, acting now as a voluntary membership organization rather than as the exclusive bargaining representative, proceeds to help individual players prepare and file lawsuits under the Sherman Act against the affected league and all club owners. Perhaps one side will file with the NLRB unfair labor practice charges against the other. Rarely does either set of litigation proceed to conclusion. But without the shield afforded by the nonstatutory antitrust exemption, the owners are exposed to treble damage liability in the Sherman Act litigation. This exposure is used by the players to leverage owners into settling on terms more favorable than would have been agreed to absent the gambit of antitrust litigation. These terms—which will include withdrawal of the pending antitrust claims and ULP charges—are incorporated into a new collective bargaining agreement, which is subject to approval by the players. The players then vote both to recertify the union as their collective bargaining agent and to approve the new collective bargaining agreement. Afterward, play can resume and life in the league can go on. With some variations, every major league team sport in North America has contemplated this scenario.

As a result, strikes and lockouts, together with the resulting litigation, often draw more attention from the public when they occur in major league team sports than they when they occur in other industries. A labor dispute in professional sports has the potential to shut down an entire sports industry. The shutdown can last from a single game to a full season or longer.

In the summer of 2011, season-threatening lockouts by owners of clubs in both the NFL and the NBA commanded the public's attention. *See* Howard Beck, *Two Lockouts, Each with a Different Playbook*, N.Y. Times, Jul. 10, 2011, at p. SP8.

Take the NFL labor dispute, which arose first. When negotiations for a new contract between club owners and the National Football League Players Association (NFLPA) went nowhere, the owners filed unfair labor practice charges alleging that the NFLPA did not bargain in good faith. In particular, they argued that the NFLPA's aim from the get-go was to fail to reach an agreement so that the union could call the play outlined above. While ULP charges were pending, the union rejected the owners' last, best, and final offer, and the players voted to decertify the union. The decertification vote set the stage for the players to argue that, bereft of a collective bargaining relationship and the nonstatutory labor exemption that comes with it, the owners were violating the antitrust laws, and therefore, exposed to substantial damages. The owners responded by locking the players out of training camp. Then a group of players, led by star quarterback Tom Brady of the New England Patriots, filed a class action lawsuit alleging claims under the Sherman Act and seeking injunctive relief and damages. A federal district judge granted the players' motion for a preliminary injunction ending the lockout, but refused to stay her order pending the owners' appeal. A panel of the U.S. Court of Appeals for the Eighth Circuit, however, granted temporary and permanent stays, and by a 2 to 1 vote, dissolved the preliminary injunction on the ground that it had been issued in violation of the Norris-LaGuardia Act. The Eighth Circuit did not reach the merits of the parties' arguments about the status of the nonstatutory labor antitrust exemption. *See Brady v. NFL*, 779 F. Supp. 2d 992 (D. Minn.), *stay denied*, 779 F. Supp. 2d 1043 (D. Minn.), *stay granted*, 638 F.3d 1004 (8th Cir.) *stay granted*, 640 F.3d 785 (8th Cir.), *preliminary injunction vacated*, 644 F.3d 661 (8th Cir. 2011).

Ultimately, both of the major league labor disputes in 2011 were settled in time for regular season play.

After a four-month dispute, the NFL and NFLPA entered into a 10-year collective bargaining agreement and went on to play a full regular season plus the playoffs; the deal included complete withdrawal of all antitrust litigation with no settlement payments, together with a supplemental revenue-sharing plan for owners. *See* Judy Battista, *N.F.L. Owners Vote for Tentative Labor Deal*, N.Y. Times, July 21, 2011, http://www.nytimes.com/2011/07/22/sports/football/NFL-Union-Labor-Deal.html?pagewanted=all.

After a five-month dispute, the NBA and NBAPA entered into a 10-year collective bargaining agreement that salvaged 66 of 82 regular season games plus the playoffs; the price of the deal included reducing the players' share of league revenues from 57% to 50%. *See* Howard Beck, *N.B.A. Reaches a Tentative Deal to Save the Season*, N.Y. Times, Nov. 26, 2011, http://www.nytimes.com/2011/11/27/sports/basketball/nba-and-basketball-players-reach-deal-to-end-lockout.html?_r=1&scp=10&sq=nba%20labor%20settlement&st=Search.

CHAPTER 10

PREEMPTION

∎ ∎ ∎

A. INTRODUCTION

Ron's Food Warehouse is the brand name of a chain of retail food stores owned and operated by Rons Grocery Company in the western and central United States. Rons advertises that it is able to offer low prices on food items because it is a no-frills operation that strictly controls labor costs. Some of Rons' stores are unionized, but most are not.

A year ago, a group of employees working in the company's Torrance, California store approached Frank Reese, president of Local 17 of the Retail Clerks Union, about the possibility of organizing the Torrance store. One of those employees was Teresa Salazar, a cashier. Salazar told Reese that on average Rons pays a dollar an hour less to its food clerks than other area grocery stores, does not offer health benefits, and has a history of ignoring female employees' complaints about sexual harassment by supervisors. (Like most Rons stores, the Torrance store's hourly nonexempt workforce is predominantly female, but the store manager and his assistants are mostly male.) Reese advised Salazar that, due to the higher wages and benefits historically negotiated by Local 17 on behalf of employees working in the industry, her group should expect a difficult fight. If the employees were serious about getting organized, then Local 17 would be happy to help— provided that Salazar and her group first do some of the "leg work" by encouraging their co-workers to demand union representation.

Salazar and her group began holding meetings in employees' homes to discuss their complaints about Rons and what a union might be able to do about them. Reese and other Local 17 staff attended these meetings. One day, Salazar and Odessa Marshall, a "box" person (or grocery bagger), brought union authorization cards to work. They asked co-workers to sign the cards. On the same day, Ken Johnson, the store manager, found out about this and confiscated the cards. Within earshot of other employees, Johnson told Salazar and Marshall, "Rons doesn't want any union in here. You'd better think twice before pulling a stunt like this again." A few days later, Salazar was discharged.

Local 17 filed unfair labor practice charges challenging both the confiscation of cards from Salazar and Marshall and Salazar's discharge. Local 17 immediately undertook a corporate campaign in which it used social media, handbilling outside the store, and community leaders to urge consumers to boycott all stores operated by Rons. After the Regional Director determined the charges to be meritorious and directed the issuance of a complaint, Rons agreed to settle the charges by reinstating Salazar and remaining neutral during a "card count." The count showed strong support for Local 17, and Rons responded by agreeing to bargain with Local 17. Shortly thereafter, Rons signed a "me too" agreement, in which the company consented at its Torrance store to be bound by the terms of conditions of the multiemployer collective bargaining agreement (CBA) to which Local 17 and other retail food chains were already parties in the Torrance area. The CBA contained two relevant provisions. The first provision stated: "Any grievance not satisfactorily settled or resolved through informal discussions shall be submitted to arbitration for final determination upon the written demand of either party." The second provision stated: "To the extent required by Federal or State laws, the Union and the Employer agree not to discriminate against any employee or applicant for employment because of race, creed, religion, color, national origin, handicap, age or sex."

Within a week of her reinstatement, Salazar hired her own lawyer and filed in state court against Rons a lawsuit alleging that for years she was subjected to a hostile work environment created by Albert Tsukahara, the assistant store manager who was her immediate supervisor. The complaint alleged that Salazar was the victim of harassment based on both her union organizing activities and her sex, each of which sounded in tort in violation of California public policy. (Fearing that she would not beat the statute of limitations, Salazar did not sue directly under either state or federal antidiscrimination law.) In particular, the complaint alleged that Tsukahara had continuously leered at Salazar, "sexted" her by sending a text message with a photograph of his genitalia, and asked her out on a date. (She declined.)

Can Salazar's lawsuit proceed?

NOTES

1.   Teresa Salazar's state court lawsuit raises two claims that potentially conflict with federal labor policy: her claim that she was harassed based on her union organizing activities, and her claim that she was harassed on the basis of sex. The first claim is clearly preempted by the NLRA. This is indicated not only by the filing and settlement in her favor of unfair labor practice charges challenging Johnson's confiscation of the union authorization cards and her subsequent discharge, but also by the long-settled principle that the Act precludes state law claims regulating conduct that is "arguably" protected by Section 7 or prohibited as an unfair labor practice under Section 8. *See San Diego Building Trades Council v. Garmon*, 359 U.S. 236 (1959), discussed *infra* p. 1206. Why might somebody standing in Salazar's shoes attempt to pursue a state law remedy—assuming one is available—when federal law purports to

address the same harm? Could it be because the NLRA provides no private right of action, judicial forum, or consequential or punitive damages? Are there any other reasons?

The second claim, however, presents a closer question. On the one hand, the claim is arguably barred by Section 301 of the Taft-Hartley Act, which precludes state law claims that depend upon the meaning of a collective bargaining agreement. *See, e.g., Lingle v. Norge Division of Magic Chef, Inc.*, 486 U.S. 399 (1988), discussed *infra* p. 1235. By incorporating the anti-discrimination provisions of "Federal or State laws" into their CBA—including California's employee-friendly laws prohibiting sexual harassment—the parties clearly and unmistakably intended that Salazar pursue such a claim exclusively through the grievance and arbitration machinery of the CBA. *See, e.g., 14 Penn Plaza, LLC v. Pyett*, 556 U.S. 247 (2009), discussed in Chapter 7, *supra* p. 986. On the other hand, the claim is arguably independent of the CBA. California's law governing sexual harassment—including its providing a judicial forum in which to adjudicate such claims—exists separate and apart from any contract between Rons and Local 17. Thus the application of California law hardly "depends" on the interpretation of the CBA. Moreover, it cannot be assumed that the union waived Salazar's right to have a judge and jury determine her claim. *See, e.g., Wright v. Universal Maritime Service Corp.*, 525 U.S. 70 (1998), discussed in Chapter 7, *supra* p. 986.

Note that Salazar herself is not a party to the CBA. What impact, if any, does this fact have on the preemption issue? If she is a party, then clearly she could waive her right to have her claim adjudicated a judicial forum. *See, e.g., Gilmer v. Interstate Johnson/Lane Corp.*, 500 U.S. 20 (1991), discussed in Chapter 7, *supra* pp. 888, 985. But if she isn't, then we have to ask whether Local 17 could grant such a waiver, even if she objected.

2. *Stain removal?* Assume that Rons prefers to defend Salazar's lawsuit in federal rather than state court. Assume also that there is no diversity of citizenship, because both plaintiff and defendant are citizens of California. Could Rons remove the case on the theory that its federal preemption defense creates federal question jurisdiction? Ordinarily, the answer would be no; under the well-pleaded complaint rule, *see Louisville & Nashville Railroad Co. v. Mottley*, 211 U.S. 149 (1908), a federal question must be an element of the plaintiff's claim rather than the defendant's defense. Might the removal question be resolved differently under Section 301, which completely precludes claims for breach of a labor contract? *See Caterpillar, Inc. v. Williams*, 482 U.S. 386 (1987) (holding state law wrongful termination claims of downgraded managers to be neither completely preempted by, nor removable under, Section 301).

3. *State contract law: breach of contract, or into the breach?* Suppose California had enacted a separate statute prohibiting any private employer holding a state government contract from spending state treasury funds received under that contract to encourage or discourage workers from forming or joining unions. Assume Rons held such a contract. Would the statute run

afoul of labor preemption principles? If so, then which type of preemption—
Garmon, Section 301, or something else? In exercising the power of its purse,
should a state be free to attach whatever strings it wishes? *See Chamber of
Commerce v. Brown*, 128 S. Ct. 2408 (2008) (holding similar California law to
be preempted), discussed *infra* p. 1225.

* * *

The importance of federal labor preemption is undeniable. No issue in
the field of collective bargaining has been presented to the Supreme Court
more often. From 1943 to 1993 alone, the Court devoted substantial
discussion to labor preemption in over 90 cases, *see* Henry H. Drummonds,
*The Sister Sovereign States: Preemption and the Second Twentieth Century
Revolution in the Law of the American Workplace*, 62 Fordham L. Rev. 469,
560 n.509 (1993), and the Court has addressed the issue many times since
then. Moreover, the doctrine is complex; Justice Frankfurter once
described the contours of labor preemption as being "of a Delphic nature,
to be translated into concreteness by the process of litigating elucidation."
International Ass'n of Machinists v. Gonzales, 356 U.S. 617, 619 (1958).
Even experienced counsel for employees and employers alike can
unwittingly run afoul of preemption rules. *See, e.g.*, Stephen F. Befort,
Demystifying Federal Labor and Employment Law Preemption, 13 Lab.
Law. 429 (1998).

As the Salazar problem illustrates, applying competing federal and
state laws can give rise to conflicting or potentially conflicting regulation
of labor relations. Although our complex system of government may
actually encourage such conflicts—it is famously said that "a single,
courageous state may serve as a laboratory . . . to try novel social and
economic experiments," *New State Ice Co. v. Liebmann*, 285 U.S. 262, 311
(1932) (Brandeis, J., dissenting)—Congress may identify some areas in
which no federal-state conflict will be tolerated. In such areas, any attempt
by a state to regulate is preempted by supervening federal policy. The
preemption power derives from the Supremacy Clause in Article VI of the
U.S. Constitution, which declares federal law to be the supreme law of the
land. Where preemption prevails, the relevant state rule will not be
permitted to have any force or effect upon the matter in question.

Many federal workplace protections, such as the minimum wage and
overtime requirements of the Fair Labor Standards Act, 29 U.S.C. § 201 *et
seq.*, and the prohibitions on race, religious, gender, and national origin
discrimination under Title VII of the Civil Rights Act of 1964, 42 U.S.C.
§ 2000e *et seq.*, operate as floors rather than ceilings of worker protection;
these statutes preempt only those state laws that would permit what
federal law prohibits. They do not preempt state laws that offer greater
protection to employees, such as state minimum wage laws that set higher
wages than the federal minimum, or state laws that prohibit employment

discrimination on the basis of sexual orientation, which for years was considered to be beyond the protection of federal law.

Federal preemption of state laws attempting to regulate the workplace can be much broader than the minimum-standards form of conflict preemption that applies under the FLSA and Title VII. Some of these broader forms of federal preemption include:

- Preemption by various provisions of the National Labor Relations Act of all laws regulating union organizing and collective bargaining, even where state law and federal law do not conflict. NLRA preemption is the focus of this Chapter. For the most part, these preemption principles are consistent with those applicable to the railway and airline industries under the Railway Labor Act (RLA), 45 U.S.C. §§ 151–188. *See, e.g., Sullivan v. American Airlines, Inc.*, 424 F.3d 267 (2d Cir. 2005).

- Preemption of all claims that relate to benefit plans under Section 502(a)(1)(B) of the Employee Retirement Income Security Act (ERISA), 29 U.S.C. § 1132(a)(1)(B). ERISA is the exclusive source of regulation of all employee benefit plans covered by ERISA. *See, e.g., Aetna Health Inc. v. Davila*, 542 U.S. 200 (2004) (preempting claim under Texas law by plan participant against administrator who denied health care coverage). *But see, e.g., Calop Business Systems Inc. v. City of Los Angeles,* 614 Fed. Appx. 867 (9th Cir. 2015), *aff'g in relevant part* 984 F. Supp. 2d 981 (C.D. Cal. 2013) (not preempting Los Angeles' "living wage" ordinance for certain city contractors, on ground it had no "reference to" any ERISA-covered plan).

- Preemption by federal immigration law of state legislation that criminalizes efforts by undocumented immigrants to seek work, *see Arizona v. United States*, 132 S. Ct. 2492 (2012) (preempting Arizona statute making it misdemeanor for alien to look for work, or otherwise be present in state, without carrying required federal documents).

- Preemption by federal statutes having apparently little to do with the law of the workplace of state or local efforts to regulate working conditions in particular industries. For example, in *American Trucking Ass'n, Inc. v. City of Los Angeles*, 133 S. Ct. 2096 (2013), and *American Trucking Ass'n, Inc. v. City of Los Angeles*, 559 F.3d 1046 (9th Cir. 2009), the courts held that a federal statute regulating interstate transportation preempted ordinances enacted by

Los Angeles, California, in an effort to improve labor and environmental conditions at the Port of Los Angeles.

As applied by the Supreme Court, NLRA preemption consists of three basic types: *Garmon* preemption, which precludes state regulation of conduct that is "arguably" protected by Section 7 or prohibited as an unfair labor practice under Section 8, as illustrated by the Teresa Salazar case; *Machinists* preemption, which precludes state regulation of areas that Congress intended to leave unregulated; and Section 301 preemption, also illustrated by the Salazar problem, which precludes state law claims whose resolution is "inextricably intertwined" with the interpretation of a collective bargaining agreement covering the same employee rights. (The first and second forms of preemption are named for the seminal Supreme Court cases, both reproduced below, in which those forms of preemption were most forcefully articulated; the third is named for the statute that gave rise to it.) All three types of NLRA preemption are discussed below.

B. GARMON PREEMPTION

Under *Garmon* preemption, conduct that is "arguably" protected by Section 7 or prohibited by Section 8 of the NLRA may not be regulated by state law. An aggrieved party's only remedy is to file an unfair labor practice charge with the NLRB's General Counsel, who in his or her sole discretion may (or may not) pursue an unfair labor practice complaint. But *Garmon* preemption has two major exceptions: matters "deeply rooted" in local interests, and matters that are merely "peripheral" to the NLRA, may be regulated by the states. For example, strike-related picket line violence—which is usually subject to state civil remedies for tort damages, and often, state criminal penalties—is thought to come within the former, if not the latter, exception.

Among the tools historically used by states to regulate conduct that is arguably protected or prohibited by the NLRA are the picketing injunction and the tort damages action, as illustrated by the *Garmon* case itself.

SAN DIEGO BUILDING TRADES COUNCIL V. GARMON
359 U.S. 236 (1959)

JUSTICE FRANKFURTER delivered the opinion of the Court:

The present litigation began with a dispute between the petitioning unions and respondents, co-partners in the business of selling lumber and other materials in California. Respondents began an action in the Superior Court for the County of San Diego, asking for an injunction and damages. Upon hearing, the trial court found the following facts. The unions sought from respondents an agreement to retain in their employ only those workers who were already members of the unions, or who applied for membership within thirty days. Respondents refused, claiming that none of their employees had shown a desire to join a union, and that, in any event, they could not accept such an arrangement until one of the unions had been designated by the employees as a collective bargaining agent. The unions began at once peacefully to picket the respondents' place of business, and to exert pressure on customers and suppliers in order to persuade them to stop dealing with respondents. The sole purpose of these pressures was to compel execution of the proposed contract. The unions contested this finding, claiming that the only purpose of their activities was to educate the workers and persuade them to become members. On the basis of its findings, the court enjoined the unions from picketing and from the use of other pressures to force an agreement, until one of them had been properly designated as a collective bargaining agent. The court also awarded $1,000 damages for losses found to have been sustained.

At the time the suit in the state court was started, respondents had begun a representation proceeding before the National Labor Relations Board. The Regional Director declined jurisdiction, presumably because the amount of interstate commerce involved did not meet the Board's monetary standards in taking jurisdiction.

We granted certiorari to determine whether the California court had jurisdiction to award damages arising out of peaceful union activity which it could not enjoin.

The case before us concerns one of the most teasing and frequently litigated areas of industrial relations, the multitude of activities regulated by §§ 7 and 8 of the National Labor Relations Act. These broad provisions govern both protected "concerted activities" and unfair labor practices. They regulate the vital, economic instruments of the strike and the picket line, and impinge on the clash of the still unsettled claims between employers and labor unions. The extent to which the variegated laws of the several States are displaced by a single, uniform, national rule has been a matter of frequent and recurring concern.

When the exercise of state power over a particular area of activity threatened interference with the clearly indicated policy of industrial relations, it has been judicially necessary to preclude the States from acting. However, due regard for the presuppositions of our embracing federal system, including the principle of diffusion of power not as a matter of doctrinaire localism but as a promoter of democracy, has required us not to find withdrawal from the States of power to regulate where the activity regulated was a merely peripheral concern of the Labor Management Relations Act. Or where the regulated conduct touched interests so deeply rooted in local feeling and responsibility that, in the absence of compelling congressional direction, we could not infer that Congress had deprived the States of the power to act.

When it is clear or may fairly be assumed that the activities which a State purports to regulate are protected by § 7 of the National Labor Relations Act, or constitute an unfair labor practice under § 8, due regard for the federal enactment requires that state jurisdiction must yield. To leave the States free to regulate conduct so plainly within the central aim of federal regulation involves too great a danger of conflict between power asserted by Congress and requirements imposed by state law. Nor has it mattered whether the States have acted through laws of broad general application rather than laws specifically directed towards the governance of industrial relations.

At times it has not been clear whether the particular activity regulated by the States was governed by § 7 or § 8 or was, perhaps, outside both these sections. But courts are not primary tribunals to adjudicate such issues. It is essential to the administration of the Act that these determinations be left in the first instance to the National Labor Relations Board. What is outside the scope of this Court's authority cannot remain within a State's power and state jurisdiction too must yield to the exclusive primary competence of the Board.

The case before us is such a case. The adjudication in California has throughout been based on the assumption that the behavior of the petitioning unions constituted an unfair labor practice. This conclusion was derived by the California courts from the facts as well as from their view of the Act. It is not for us to decide whether the National Labor Relations Board would have, or should have, decided these questions in the same manner. When an activity is arguably subject to § 7 or § 8 of the Act, the States as well as the federal courts must defer to the exclusive competence of the National Labor Relations Board if the danger of state interference with national policy is to be averted.

To require the States to yield to the primary jurisdiction of the National Board does not ensure Board adjudication of the status of a disputed activity. If the Board decides, subject to appropriate federal judicial review, that conduct is protected by § 7, or prohibited by § 8, then the matter is at an end, and the States are ousted of all jurisdiction. Or, the Board may decide that an activity is neither protected nor prohibited, and thereby raise the question whether such activity may be regulated by the States. However, the Board may also fail to determine the status of the disputed conduct by declining to assert jurisdiction, or by refusal of the General Counsel to file a charge, or by adopting some other disposition which does not define the nature of the activity with unclouded legal significance.

In the light of these principles the case before us is clear. Since the National Labor Relations Board has not adjudicated the status of the conduct for which the State of California seeks to give a remedy in damages, and since such activity is arguably within the compass of § 7 or § 8 of the Act, the State's jurisdiction is displaced.

Nor is it significant that California asserted its power to give damages rather than to enjoin what the Board may restrain though it could not compensate. Our concern is with delimiting areas of conduct which must be free from state regulation if national policy is to be left unhampered. Such regulation can be as effectively exerted through an award of damages as through some form of preventive relief.

It is true that we have allowed the States to grant compensation for the consequences, as defined by the traditional law of torts, of conduct marked by violence and imminent threats to the public order. We have also allowed the States to enjoin such conduct. State jurisdiction has prevailed in these situations because the compelling state interest, in the scheme of our federalism, in the maintenance of domestic peace is not overridden in the absence of clearly expressed congressional direction.

JUSTICE HARLAN, with whom JUSTICES CLARK, WHITTAKER, and STEWART join, concurring:

I concur in the result upon the narrow ground that the Unions' activities for which the State has awarded damages may fairly be considered protected under the Taft-Hartley Act, and that therefore state action is precluded until the National Labor Relations Board has made a contrary determination respecting such activities.

The threshold question in every labor preemption case is whether the conduct with respect to which a State has sought to act is, or may fairly be regarded as, federally protected activity. Because conflict is the touchstone of preemption, such activity is obviously beyond the reach of all state power.

The Court's opinion in this case cuts deeply into the ability of States to furnish an effective remedy under their own laws for the redress of past nonviolent tortious conduct which is not federally protected, but which may be deemed to be, or is, federally prohibited. Henceforth the States must withhold access to their courts until the National Labor Relations Board has determined that such unprotected conduct is not an unfair labor practice, a course which, because of unavoidable Board delays, may render state redress ineffective. And in instances in which the Board declines to exercise its jurisdiction, the States are entirely deprived of power to afford any relief. Moreover, since the reparation powers of the Board, as we observed in *Russell*, are narrowly circumscribed, those injured by nonviolent conduct will often go remediless even when the Board does accept jurisdiction.

NOTES

1.   The essence of Justice Frankfurter's opinion is this:

When it is clear or may fairly be assumed that the activities which a State purports to regulate are protected by § 7 of the National Labor Relations Act, or constitute an unfair labor practice under § 8, due regard for the federal enactment requires that state jurisdiction must yield. To leave the States free to regulate conduct so plainly within the central aim of federal regulation involves too great a danger of conflict between power asserted by Congress and requirements imposed by state law.

This language has been used as the basis for the shorthand test of "arguably" protected by Section 7 or prohibited by Section 8, which has been applied by courts since *Garmon.*

Recall the basic Section 7 rights, as discussed in Chapter 2, the violation of which are prohibited by Section 8. Any state legislation attempting to expand, contract, modify, or enforce these rights is likely to be preempted. Among these are the rights of employees to:

- Self-organization

- Form, join, or assist labor organizations

- Bargain collectively through representatives of their own choosing

- Engage in concerted activities for mutual aid or protection

- Not do any of these

But *Garmon's* reach is limited by its exceptions, which no doubt contribute to its complexity. State regulation is permitted where the activity regulated is of "merely peripheral concern" to the NLRA, such as an action for breach of contract due to the expulsion of a member from his union, *see, e.g., International Ass'n of Machinists v. Gonzales*, 356 U.S. 617 (1958), or touches interests "deeply rooted in local feeling and responsibility," such as tort damages caused by violence and imminent threats to the public order that sometimes accompany strikes, lockouts, boycotts, and related concerted activities, *see, e.g., UAW v. Russell*, 356 U.S. 634 (1958); *United Constr. Workers v. Laburnum Constr. Corp.*, 347 U.S. 656 (1954); *see also Youngdahl v. Rainfair Inc.*, 355 U.S. 131 (1957) (allowing state to enjoin such activity); *UAW v. Wis. Employment Relations Bd.*, 351 U.S. 266 (1956) (same).

More recently, Walmart Stores Inc. successfully pursued in the California state courts a civil trespass action seeking damages from and declaratory and injunctive relief against a union that had organized in-store demonstrations as part of a nationwide campaign to induce the company to offer better pay and working conditions. The trial court found that the union and its supporters committed and threatened to commit "unlawful acts," such as "blocking ingress and egress and aisle ways and customers' mobility inside the store, littering balloons and flyers throughout stores, and blowing air horns, screaming, and conducting "flash mobs." A state appellate court rejected the union's defense that the action was precluded by *Garmon* and its progeny. *See Walmart Stores, Inc. v. United Food & Commercial Workers Int'l Union*, 4 Cal.App.5th 194 (Cal. Ct. App. 2016). The company has pursued similar litigation in other venues, but not always successfully. *See, e.g., Walmart Stores, Inc. v. United Food & Commercial Workers Int'l Union*, 190 Wash. App. 14, 354 P.3d 31 (2015) (holding trespass claim to be preempted by *Garmon*), *review denied*, 185 Wash. 2d 1013, 367 P.3d 1084 (2016).

2. Suppose that State X, eager to supplement the limited make-whole remedies available under the National Labor Relations Act, enacts a statute directing its Department of Labor to maintain a list of every person or firm found by judicially-enforced orders of the NLRB to have violated federal labor law at least three times within a five-year period. Suppose further that the statute forbids state procurement agents to purchase any product known to be manufactured or sold by anyone included on the violators' list, and requires that a violator's name must remain on the list for three years. Is the State X statute preempted by *Garmon*? Is there a difference between state regulation seeking to add or subtract liability for unfair labor practices, and state regulation seeking to enhance or reduce the penalties for committing ULPs? *See Wisconsin Dep't of Indus., Labor & Human Relations v. Gould, Inc.*, 475 U.S. 282 (1986) (holding preempted similar statute enacted by Wisconsin).

3. Suppose that a State Y statute authorizes the state's courts to intervene in labor disputes by issuing injunctions against mass picketing and intimidation of passersby. Shortly after a union started an organizing campaign among a supermarket's meat cutters, the supermarket began interrogating them about their union preferences, engaging in surveillance of union meetings, and threatening active union adherents with discharge. The union responded by filing unfair labor practice charges under Section 8(a)(1) that were upheld by the administrative law judge, and set up a picket line advising customers about its legal action. The supermarket responded by petitioning a State Y court to limit the number of picketers and to enjoin them from both passing out handbills containing certain messages and speaking with customers. Although it found neither violence nor a breach of the peace, the State Y court issued the injunction. Meanwhile, the NLRB adopted the administrative law judge's findings and recommendations, and issued a cease and desist order. The Board now files suit in federal district court to restrain enforcement of the State Y court's injunction on the ground that the NLRB has exclusive jurisdiction to adjudicate and remedy unfair labor practices. Should the Board prevail? *See NLRB v. Nash-Finch Co.*, 404 U.S. 138 (1971) (finding implied authority for agency to bring such suit). Could State Y enjoin the picketing instead on the ground that it was in aid of an illegal secondary boycott? Or that it constituted trespassing on private property? *See Sears, Roebuck & Co. v. San Diego County Dist. Council of Carpenters*, 436 U.S. 180 (1978) (permitting California courts to enjoin picketing based on its trespassory location, but not due to its alleged secondary objective).

4.   Suppose a state enacts a law prohibiting any "job targeting" or
"market recovery" program. In such programs, funds from union members'
wages are spent to subsidize the winning construction bids of unionized
contractors—a tactic that construction unions have used successfully to
organize various building projects. *See generally* Herbert R. Northrup &
Augustus T. White, *Subsidizing Contractors to Gain Employment:
Construction Union "Job Targeting,"* 17 Berkeley J. Emp. & Lab. L. 62 (1996).
Is the law preempted? *See Idaho Bldg. & Constr. Trades Council v. Wasden*,
801 F.3d 950 (9th Cir. 2015) (holding such program not preempted).

5.   Typically, *Garmon* addresses federal labor preemption of conflicting
state regulation. But is there such a thing as federal labor preemption of
conflicting "other" federal regulation? Recall the case of Teresa Salazar, *supra*
p. 1201. Local 17 is attempting to help Salazar and her group organize the Rons
Grocery Company's Torrance store. To get around the company's restrictions
on physical access to the store and its employees by non-employer organizers,
as discussed in Chapter 4, see *supra* p. 461, the union compiles a list of the
names and addresses of Rons workers by "tagging" the license numbers of cars
parked in the facility's parking lot, then obtaining matching personal
information from a database maintained by the state's department of motor
vehicles (DMV). Although the union is entitled to obtain the names and home
addresses of workers under *Excelsior Underwear*, 156 N.L.R.B. 1236 (1966),
the DMV tactic is arguably illegal under the Driver's Privacy Protection Act
(DPPA) of 1994, 18 U.S.C. §§ 2721 2725. If so, is the DPPA, a sister federal
statute, "preempted" by *Garmon*? Professor Michael Duff thinks it might be.
See Michael C. Duff, *What Brady v. NFL Teaches About the Devolution of Labor
Law*, 52 Washburn L.J. 429, 460–63 (2013); *compare, e.g., Pichler v. UNITE*,
585 F.3d 741 (3d Cir. 2009) (upholding denial of protective order that would
have prevented disclosure of such information), *with e.g., Trollinger v. Tyson
Foods, Inc.*, 370 F.3d 602 (6th Cir. 2004) (holding not preempted action by
former employees who alleged employer hired undocumented immigrants as
part of conspiracy to depress wages in violation of Racketeer Influenced
Corrupt Organizations (RICO) Act).

6.   An exception to NLRA preemption is found in Section 14(b) of the
Taft-Hartley Act, which allows states to enact laws prohibiting unions and
employers from agreeing to any contract term requiring employees to join or
pay any fees to the union that represents them. Absent Section 14(b), state
prohibitions on union security provisions would be preempted by the NLRA.
Retail Clerks Int'l Ass'n, Local 1625, AFL-CIO v. Schermerhorn, 373 U.S. 746
(1963). About half the states have adopted laws outlawing union security or
agency fee provisions in collective bargaining agreements; these states are
known as "right to work" (RTW) states. In states with RTW laws, unions are
obligated by the federal duty of fair representation to negotiate and administer
collective bargaining agreements on behalf of everyone in the designated
bargaining unit, even employees who refuse to pay anything for the services
the union is required to provide. This effectively means that union members
must subsidize free legal services for their co-workers. Two scholars have

argued that the preemptive scope of Section 14(b) should be limited: it should allow states to enact laws requiring employees to join unions or pay an amount equivalent to union dues, but it should preclude the enforcement of any state laws banning agreements requiring employees to pay only their pro rata share of the costs of negotiating and administering collective bargaining agreements. Catherine L. Fisk & Benjamin I. Sachs, *Restoring Equity in the Right to Work*, 4 U.C. Irvine L. Rev. 857 (2014). Can or should Section 14(b) be read this way?

Can a union deal with the "free rider" problem by requiring non-member employees to pay a "service" or "representation" fee set at, say, 50% or less of the regular fair share fee? *See Sweeney v. Pence*, 767 F.3d 654 (7th Cir. 2014) (rejecting union's argument that Indiana's RTW statute violated Takings Clause of Fifth Amendment); *International Union of Operating Engineers Local 370 v. Wasden*, 217 F. Supp. 3d 1209 (D. Idaho 2016) (same as to Idaho's RTW statute). Could a union argue that requiring it to represent a free-rider in a grievance proceeding constitutes compelled speech under the First Amendment? Could a municipal government in a non-RTW state enact an ordinance establishing a RTW regime limited to its own backyard? *See* Ariana R. Levinson, Alyssa Hare & Travis Fiechter, *Federal Preemption of Local Right-to-Work Ordinances*, 54 Harv. J. Leg. 402 (2017) (arguing such ordinance would be preempted by *Garmon* and *Machinists* doctrines).

7.   Even nations that, like the U.S., adhere to a federalized system of government have not necessarily adopted the complicated form of preemption doctrine that is associated with the NLRA. For example, in the labor law regimes of Canada and Mexico, preemption problems of the type contemplated by *Garmon* are largely absent, but for different reasons.

In Canada, a common law jurisdiction, the federal government and the provincial governments each exercise sovereign power over the labor relations of industries falling within their respective spheres, as codified by Sections 91 and 92 of the Canadian Constitution. *See Toronto Elec. Comm'rs v. Snider*, [1925] A.C. 396 (Privy Council). In practice, this has meant that most labor law is provincial law; only 10 percent of the private sector workforce is governed by federal labor statutes. *See* Donald Carter, Geoffrey England, Brian Etherington & Gilles Trudeau, Labour Law in Canada 62 (5th ed. 2002). Industries subject to federal regulation include inter-provincial and international trade; broadcasting and communications; uranium mining; some areas of defense; and federal employment. *See* Ron McCallum, *Plunder Down Under: Transplanting the Anglo-American Labor Law Model to Australia*, 26 Comp. Lab. L. & Policy J. 381, 391–92 (2005) (discussing Canadian scheme). Thus drawing the boundary between federal and provincial regimes is more a matter of understanding the constitutional division of legislative powers than interpreting U.S.-style preemption doctrine. Even so, in "borderline cases," it can be difficult to determine "what is federal and what is provincial." Labour and Employment Law: Cases, Materials and Commentary ch. 1, § 800 (Labour Law Casebook Group eds., 7th ed. 2004).

In Mexico, a civil law jurisdiction, all labor law is federal. The basic labor law is codified in Article 123 of the Mexican Constitution of 1917, which was amended in 1929 to make federal law exclusive of state law. *See* Stephen Zamora, José Ramón Cossío, Leonel Pereznieto, José Roldán-Xopa & David Lopez, Mexican Law 110 (2004). But the enforcement of federal labor law is divided between federal and state authorities. Federal authorities apply the law to workers in industries whose scope is national; state authorities apply the law to workers in industries who scope is more local. The national-versus-local boundary, however, is not always applied in a way that makes sense to outsiders. For example, despite their links to the global economy, most of the thousands of *maquiladora* plants in the U.S.-Mexico border region come within the purview of state labor law authorities. These authorities are called Conciliation and Arbitration Boards (CABs). Whether federal or state, a CAB is a tripartite, quasi-judicial entity including representatives from government, management, and labor. The CAB decides labor disputes of all types: from collective issues (involving organizing, bargaining, and strikes) to individual grievances (including overtime pay, seniority violations, maternity leave, unjust discharge, and failure to pay severance). *See* Lance Compa, Justice for All: The Struggle for Worker Rights in Mexico 10 (2003).

8. Various international conventions attempt to establish universal principles that must be adhered to throughout society, including the workplace. One of these conventions is the International Covenant on Civil and Political Rights of 1992 (ICCPR), discussed in Chapter 3, *supra* p. 296. Among other things, the ICCPR guarantees workers freedom of association, which includes the right to form or join labor unions. Suppose that State Z, citing the ICCPR, passes the Workers' Safe Haven Act, a law that not only declares State Z to be a sanctuary for undocumented laborers, but also provides the remedies of reinstatement and back pay to such persons when they are fired for attempting to organize a union, both in contravention of *Hoffman Plastic Compounds, Inc. v. NLRB*, 535 U.S. 137 (2002), discussed *supra* p. 286. Is the Safe Haven Act preempted by *Garmon*? If so, would the application of preemption principles place the U.S. in violation of the ICCPR? Should an undocumented worker whose State Z rights under the Safe Haven Act are preempted nevertheless be able to bring a private right of action under the ICCPR? If so, in what forum? *See* Justin D. Cummins, *Invigorating Labor: A Human Rights Approach in the United States*, 19 Emory Int'l L. Rev. 1, 48–49 (2005) (discussing possibility of bringing private rights of action under Alien Tort Claims Act, 28 U.S.C. § 1350; Section 1983 of Civil Rights Act of 1871, 42 U.S.C. § 1983; and doctrine of *jus cogens*).

C. MACHINISTS PREEMPTION

Under *Machinists* preemption, conduct that is neither protected nor prohibited by either Section 7 or Section 8 of the NLRA is precluded from state regulation. Instead, Congress is considered to have "occupied the field" to the exclusion of treatment by the states. In earlier cases applying this form of preemption, the object of state regulation tended to be the parties' peaceful use of economic weapons, including the strike by labor and the lockout by management. Here the effect of preemption is to permit, as the Court put it in the *Machinists* case itself, "the uncontrolled power of management and labor to further their respective interests." In later cases, however, the goal of state regulation has been to prevent the use of state treasury funds to take sides in either potential or ongoing labor disputes. Examples of each follow.

LODGE 76, INTERNATIONAL ASSOCIATION OF MACHINISTS & AEROSPACE WORKERS v. WISCONSIN EMPLOYMENT RELATIONS COMMISSION
427 U.S. 132 (1976)

JUSTICE BRENNAN delivered the opinion of the Court:

The question to be decided in this case is whether federal labor policy preempts the authority of a state labor relations board to grant an employer covered by the National Labor Relations Act an order enjoining a union and its members from continuing to refuse to work overtime pursuant to a union policy to put economic pressure on the employer in negotiations for renewal of an expired collective-bargaining agreement.

A collective-bargaining agreement between petitioner Lodge 76 (Union) and respondent Kearney & Trecker (Employer) was terminated by the Employer pursuant to the terms of the agreement on June 19, 1971. Good-faith bargaining over the terms of a renewal agreement continued for over a year thereafter, finally resulting in the signing of a new agreement effective July 23, 1972. A particularly controverted issue during negotiations was the Employer's demand that the provision of the expired agreement under which, as for the prior 17 years, the basic workday was 7½ hours, Monday through Friday, and the basic workweek was 37½ hours, be replaced with a new provision providing a basic workday of 8 hours and a basic workweek of 40 hours, and that the terms on which overtime rates of pay were payable be changed accordingly.

A few days after the old agreement was terminated the Employer unilaterally began to make changes in some conditions of employment provided in the expired contract, e.g., eliminating the checkoff of Union dues, eliminating the Union's office in the plant, and eliminating Union lost time. No immediate change was made in the basic workweek or workday, but in March 1972, the Employer announced that it would unilaterally implement, as of March 13, 1972, its proposal for a 40-hour week and 8-hour day. The Union response was a membership meeting on March 7 at which strike action was authorized and a resolution was adopted binding Union members to refuse to work any overtime, defined as work in excess of 7½ hours in any day or 37½ hours in any week. Following the strike vote, the Employer offered to "defer the implementation" of its workweek proposal if the Union would agree to call off the concerted refusal to work overtime. The Union, however, refused the offer and indicated its intent to continue the concerted ban on overtime. Thereafter, the Employer did not make effective the proposed changes in the workday and workweek before the new agreement became effective on July 23, 1972. Although all but a very few employees complied with the Union's resolution against acceptance of overtime work during the negotiations, the Employer did not discipline, or attempt to discipline, any employee for refusing to work overtime.

Instead, while negotiations continued, the Employer filed a charge with the National Labor Relations Board that the Union's resolution violated § 8(b)(3) of the National Labor Relations Act, 29 U.S.C. § 158(b)(3). The Regional Director dismissed the charge. The Employer also filed a complaint before the Wisconsin Employment Relations Commission charging that the refusal to work overtime constituted an unfair labor practice under state law. The Union filed a motion before the Commission to dismiss the complaint [because] "the activity complained of [is] preempted" by the National Labor Relations Act. The motion was denied and the Commission adopted the Conclusion of Law of its Examiner finding that the Union's concerted refusal to work overtime was a concerted effort to interfere with production and constituted an unfair labor practice within the meaning of Section 111.06(2)(h) of the Wisconsin Statutes.[1] The Wisconsin Supreme Court affirmed. We granted certiorari. We reverse.

I.

The national Act leaves much to the states, though Congress has refrained from telling us how much. We must spell out from conflicting indications of congressional will the area in which state action is still permissible. Federal labor policy as reflected in the NLRA has been construed not to preclude the States from regulating aspects of labor relations that involve "conduct touch[ing] interests so deeply rooted in local feeling and responsibility that . . . we could not infer that Congress had deprived the States of the power to act." *San Diego Building Trades Council v. Garmon*, 359 U.S. 236, 244 (1959). Policing of actual or threatened violence to persons or destruction of property has been held most clearly a matter for the States. Similarly, the federal law governing labor relations does not withdraw "from the States power to regulate where the activity regulated is a merely peripheral concern of the Labor Management Relations Act." *Id.* at 243.

Cases that have held state authority to be preempted by federal law tend to fall into one of two categories: (1) those that reflect the concern that

---

[1]   Wisconsin Stat. § 111.06(2) (1974) provides: "It shall be an unfair labor practice for an employee individually or in concert with others . . . (h) To take unauthorized possession of property of the employer or to engage in any concerted effort to interfere with production except by leaving the premises in an orderly manner for the purpose of going on strike."

one forum would enjoin, as illegal, conduct which the other forum would find legal and (2) those that reflect the concern that the application of state law by state courts would restrict the exercise of rights guaranteed by the Federal Acts. In referring to decisions holding state laws preempted by the NLRA, care must be taken to distinguish preemption based on federal protection of the conduct in question from that based predominantly on the primary jurisdiction of the National Labor Relations Board although the two are often not easily separable. Each of these distinct aspects of labor law preemption has had its own history in our decisions, to which we now turn.

The first preemption approach is based predominantly on the primary jurisdiction of the Board. This line of preemption analysis was developed in *Garmon*.

A second line of preemption analysis has been developed in cases focusing upon the crucial inquiry whether Congress intended that the conduct involved be unregulated because left "to be controlled by the free play of economic forces." *NLRB v. Nash-Finch Co.*, 404 U.S. 138, 144 (1971).[4]

II.

NLRB v. Insurance Agents International Union, 361 U.S. 477 (1960), involved a charge of a refusal by the union to bargain in good faith in violation of § 8(b)(3) of the Act. The charge was based on union activities that occurred during good faith bargaining over the terms of a collective bargaining agreement. During the negotiations, the union directed concerted on-the-job activities by its members of a harassing nature designed to interfere with the conduct of the Employer's business, for the avowed purpose of putting economic pressure on the Employer to accede to the union's bargaining demands. The harassing activities, all peaceful, by the member insurance agents included refusal for a time to solicit new business, and refusal (after the writing of new business was resumed) to comply with the Employer insurance company's reporting procedures; refusal to participate in a company campaign to solicit new business; reporting late at district offices the days the agents were scheduled to attend them; refusing to perform customary duties at the office, instead engaging there in "sit-in-mornings," "doing what comes naturally," and leaving at noon as a group; absenting themselves from special business conferences arranged by the company; picketing and distributing leaflets outside the various offices of the company on specified days and hours as

---

[4]   *See* Archibald Cox, *Labor Law Preemption Revisited*, 85 Harv. L. Rev. 1337, 1352 (1972): "An appreciation of the true character of the national labor policy expressed in the NLRA and the LMRA indicates that in providing a legal framework for union organization, collective bargaining, and the conduct of labor disputes, Congress struck a balance of protection, prohibition, and laissez-faire in respect to union organization, collective bargaining, and labor disputes that would be upset if a state could also enforce statutes or rules of decision resting upon its views concerning accommodation of the same interests."

directed by the union; distributing leaflets each day to policyholders and others and soliciting policyholders' signatures on petitions directed to the company; and presenting the signed policyholders' petitions to the company at its home office while simultaneously engaging in mass demonstrations there. We held that such tactics would not support a finding by the NLRB that the union had failed to bargain in good faith as required by § 8(b)(3) and rejected the per se rule applied by the Board that use of "economically harassing activities" alone sufficed to prove a violation of that section. The Court assumed "that the activities in question here were not 'protected' under § 7 of the Act," but held that the per se rule was beyond the authority of the NLRB to apply.

> The scope of § 8(b)(3) and the limitations on Board power which were the design of § 8(d) are exceeded, we hold, by inferring a lack of good faith not from any deficiencies of the union's performance at the bargaining table by reason of its attempted use of economic pressure, but solely and simply because tactics designed to exert economic pressure were employed during the course of the good-faith negotiations. Our labor policy is not presently erected on a foundation of government control of the results of negotiations. Nor does it contain a charter for the National Labor Relations Board to act at large in equalizing disparities of bargaining power between employer and union.

361 U.S. at 490.

We noted further that "Congress has been rather specific when it has come to outlaw particular economic weapons on the part of unions" and "the activities here involved have never been specifically outlawed by Congress." Accordingly, the Board's claim "to power . . . to distinguish among various economic pressure tactics and brand the ones at bar inconsistent with good-faith collective bargaining," was simply inconsistent with the design of the federal scheme in which "the use of economic pressure by the parties to a labor dispute is . . . part and parcel of the process of collective bargaining." *Id.* at 495.

The Court had earlier recognized in preemption cases that Congress meant to leave some activities unregulated and to be controlled by the free play of economic forces. "It is implicit in the Act that the public interest is served by freedom of labor to use the weapon of picketing. For a state to impinge on the area of labor combat designed to be free is quite as much an obstruction of federal policy as if the state were to declare picketing free for purposes or by methods which the federal Act prohibits."

But the analysis of *Insurance Agents* came full bloom in the preemption area in *Teamsters v. Morton*, 377 U.S. 252 (1964), which held preempted the application of state law to award damages for peaceful union secondary picketing. Although *Morton* involved conduct neither "protected nor prohibited" by § 7 or § 8 of the NLRA, we recognized the necessity of an inquiry whether " 'Congress occupied this field and closed it to state regulation.' " 377 U.S. at 258. Central to *Morton*'s analysis was the observation that "[i]n selecting which forms of economic pressure should be prohibited Congress struck the 'balance between the uncontrolled power of management and labor to further their respective interests.' "

Although many of our past decisions concerning conduct left by Congress to the free play of economic forces address the question in the context of union and employee activities, self-help is of course also the prerogative of the employer because he, too, may properly employ economic weapons Congress meant to be unregulable.

"[R]esort to economic weapons should more peaceful measures not avail" is the right of the employer as well as the employee, and the State may not prohibit the use of such weapons or "add to an employer's federal legal obligations in collective bargaining" any more than in the case of employees. Cox, *supra*, at 1365 n.4. Whether self-help economic activities are employed by employer or union, the crucial inquiry regarding preemption is the same: whether the exercise of plenary state authority to curtail or entirely prohibit self-help would frustrate effective implementation of the Act's processes.

III.

There is simply no question that the Act's processes would be frustrated in the instant case were the State's ruling permitted to stand. The Employer in this case invoked the Wisconsin law because it was unable to overcome the Union tactic with its own economic self-help means. Although it did employ economic weapons putting pressure on the Union when it terminated the previous agreement, it apparently lacked sufficient economic strength to secure its bargaining demands under "the balance of power between labor and management expressed in our national labor policy." But the economic weakness of the affected party cannot justify state aid contrary to federal law for, as we have developed, "the use of economic pressure by the parties to a labor dispute is not a grudging exception [under] the Act; it is part and parcel of the process of collective bargaining." It is clear beyond question that Wisconsin "[entered] into the substantive aspects of the bargaining process to an extent Congress has not countenanced." *NLRB v. Insurance Agents*, 361 U.S. at 498.

Our decisions hold that Congress meant that these activities, whether of employer or employees, were not to be regulable by States any more than by the NLRB, for neither States nor the Board is "afforded flexibility in picking and choosing which economic devices of labor and management shall be branded as unlawful." Rather, both are without authority to attempt to "introduce some standard of properly 'balanced' bargaining power" or to define "what economic sanctions might be permitted negotiating parties in an 'ideal' or 'balanced' state of collective bargaining."[11]

Reversed.

JUSTICE POWELL, with whom CHIEF JUSTICE BURGER joins, concurring:

The Court correctly identifies the critical inquiry with respect to preemption as whether "the exercise of plenary state authority to curtail or entirely prohibit self-help would frustrate effective implementation of the Act's processes."

This is equally true whether the self-help activities are those of the employer or the Union. I agree with the Court that the Wisconsin law, as applied in this case, is preempted since it directly curtails the self-help capability of the Union and its members, resulting in a significant shift in the balance of free economic bargaining power struck by Congress. I write to make clear my understanding that the Court's opinion does not, however, preclude the States from enforcing, in the context of a labor dispute, "neutral" state statutes or rules of decision: state laws that are not directed toward altering the bargaining positions of employers or unions but which may have an incidental effect on relative bargaining strength.[36] Except where Congress has specifically provided otherwise, the States generally should remain free to enforce, for example, their law of torts or of contracts, and other laws reflecting neutral public policy.

With this understanding, I join the opinion of the Court.

JUSTICE STEVENS, with whom JUSTICES STEWART and JUSTICE REHNQUIST join, dissenting:

If Congress had focused on the problems presented by partial strike activity, and had enacted special legislation dealing with this subject matter, but left the form of the activity disclosed by this record unregulated, the Court's conclusion would be supported by *Teamsters Union v. Morton.* But this is not such a case. Despite the numerous statements in the Court's opinion about Congress' intent to leave partial strike activity wholly unregulated, I have found no legislative expression of any such intent nor any evidence that Congress has scrutinized such activity.

---

[11]   It must be realized that collective bargaining, under a system where the Government does not attempt to control the results of negotiations, cannot be equated with an academic collective search for truth or even with what might be thought to be the ideal of one. . . . The system has not reached the ideal of the philosophic notion that perfect understanding among people would lead to perfect agreement among them on values. The presence of economic weapons in reserve, and their actual exercise on occasion by the parties, is part and parcel of the system that the Wagner and Taft-Hartley Acts have recognized. *Insurance Agents,* 361 U.S. at 488–89.

[36]   State laws should not be regarded as neutral if they reflect an accommodation of the special interests of employers, unions, or the public in areas such as employee self-organization, labor disputes, or collective bargaining.

If this Court had previously held that the no-man's land in which conduct is neither arguably protected nor arguably prohibited by federal law is nevertheless preempted by an unexpressed legislative intent, I would follow such a holding. But none of the cases reviewed in the Court's opinion so holds.

I am not persuaded that partial strike activity is so essential to the bargaining process that the States should not be free to make it illegal.

NOTES

1.   The object of much concerted activity, including the partial strike in *Machinists*, is to pressure employers to increase the wages and benefits of represented employees. Does this mean that the social safety net traditionally erected by the states in the form of fair labor standards—such as the minimum wage, overtime compensation, and mandatory rest periods—is preempted? *Cf. Metropolitan Life Insurance Co. v. Massachusetts*, 471 U.S. 724 (1985) (holding not preempted Massachusetts statute requiring mandatory minimum health benefits in general insurance policies). For example, suppose Maine enacted a statute requiring every employer to provide a one-time severance benefit to its employees in the event of a plant closing. Would such a statute run afoul of *Machinists*, or is Maine's establishment of labor standards, which falls within the traditional police power of the state, entitled to deference? *See Fort Halifax Packing Co. v. Coyne*, 482 U.S. 1 (1987) (holding preempted such statute).

2.   One of the reasons traditionally offered for *Machinists* preemption is that states should not take sides in labor disputes in which strikes, lockouts, boycotts, and other economic weapons are deployed. For example, New York, unlike many states, authorizes the payment of unemployment compensation to strikers. (Ordinarily, unemployment compensation is paid to employees who are involuntarily separated from employment, not to those who choose to stop working.) New York's scheme, like that of most states, is a form of insurance financed primarily by taxes assessed against employers. Is paying unemployment compensation under such circumstances a form of impermissible side-taking, and therefore, preempted? *See New York Tel. Co. v. New York State Dep't of Labor*, 440 U.S. 519 (1979) (plurality opinion) (holding preempted such statute). What if instead of authorizing unemployment compensation for strikers, the state barred it? Would that be preempted? *See Baker v. General Motors Corp.*, 478 U.S. 621 (1986) (finding not preempted Michigan statute denying unemployment insurance benefits to strikers who had "financed" strike by payment of "emergency" strike fund dues).

3.   Suppose Michigan enacts a statute denying welfare assistance to strikers because the state cannot afford to subsidize activity that is harmful to the state's economy, even though the NLRA clearly guarantees strikers the right to inflict such harm. Would such a statute be preempted? *Cf. Lyng v. Automobile Workers,* 485 U.S. 360 (1988) (upholding against First Amendment challenge federal statute precluding household from receiving food stamps if household member goes on strike).

4.   From time to time, state or local governments may consider proposals attempting to limit the settled NLRA rights of employers to hire permanent or temporary replacements during labor disputes. Suppose that, after the commencement of a strike, a paper mill hired over 500 replacement workers and housed them in dozens of mobile homes set up near the mill. The town in which the mill is located responds by enacting three ordinances: (1) the Professional Strikebreaker Ordinance, which prohibits any firm from hiring or offering to hire employees who have twice before been hired for jobs ordinarily performed by striking workers; (2) the Environmental Protection Ordinance, which requires town officials to take extra care to enforce existing federal, state and local environmental laws, and creates a special fund to pay for enforcement efforts; and (3) the Temporary Housing Ordinance, which prohibits town property owners from constructing temporary or mobile living quarters housing 10 or more tenants. The mill responds by bringing in federal district court a declaratory judgment action seeking to void the legislation as preempted. How should the district court rule as to each ordinance? *See International Paper Co. v. Town of Jay,* 672 F. Supp. 29 (D. Me. 1987) (without ruling on the preemption issues, the court found the challenge to the Professional Strikebreaker Ordinance not ripe for adjudication, refused to enjoin the Environmental Protection Ordinance because it did nothing other than commit the city to enforce existing environmental laws, and temporarily enjoined the Temporary Housing Ordinance). Would your answer be different if the ordinances were passed by popular referendum, after being placed on the ballot by a board that included some of the striking mill workers? *See International Paper Co. v. Town of Jay,* 736 F. Supp. 359 (D. Me. 1990) (holding not preempted Environmental Protection Ordinance, even though it may have been motivated by desire to pressure company with respect to strike, because it had no effect on either negotiations or company's use of striker replacements), *aff'd,* 928 F.2d 480 (1st Cir. 1991).

* * *

As the paper mill problem suggests, organized labor can exercise considerable influence on politics, especially at the state and local levels. In big cities, small townships, and other places where labor typically flexes its political muscles, worker-and union-friendly referendums, statutes, and ordinances sometimes are proposed and passed into law. (The living wage movement, discussed in Chapter 8, *supra* p. 1025, illustrates how this political power may be exercised.) To many commentators, these state law initiatives can be understood as organized labor's creative response to the twin diagnoses offered to explain why the NLRA is a "failed" regime: it is both too weak to fulfill its own goals of preserving workers' rights to freedom of association and self-organization, and too rigid to adapt to the needs of workers and firms in the modern workplace. *See, e.g.,* Benjamin I. Sachs, *Employment Law as Labor Law,* 29 Cardozo L. Rev. 2685, 2686 (2008); *see also, e.g.,* Katherine V.W. Stone, From Widgets to Digits: Employment Regulation for the Changing Workplace 87–119 (2004).

An important consequence of these state law developments has been to turn the politics of labor law preemption upside-down. In the early years of the NLRA, preemption was raised mainly as a shield by unions. During the 1950s, 1960s, and 1970s, organized labor perceived state authorities as hostile because management often tried to use state laws and state courts to reduce the effectiveness of strikes, picketing, and other concerted activities. *Garmon* and *Machinists* are examples of this approach. In more recent years, however, preemption has been wielded mainly as a sword by employers. During the 1980s, 1990s, and 2000s, the following beliefs became articles of faith among labor leaders: the NLRB could not be counted on to embrace pro-labor interpretations of the Act; even if the Board followed labor's lead, conservative judges appointed by Republican Presidents would refuse to enforce its orders; and Congress would fail to act on most of labor's proposals to beef up the statute. So union officials turned their attention to state capitols and city halls where their reform agenda might be more warmly received. As a result, today organized labor often pursues state and local initiatives to overcome the "ossification" of federal labor law. *See* Cynthia Estlund, *The Ossification of American Labor Law*, 102 Colum. L. Rev. 1527, 1609 (2002); *see also, e.g.*, Michael Gottesman, *Rethinking Labor Law Preemption: State Laws Facilitating Unionization*, 7 Yale J. on Reg. 355 (1990). In this environment, management has responded by arguing preemption as a means to avoid or undermine the application of labor-friendly state and local legislation.

In recent years, California has been one of the states serving as a sort of laboratory for testing whether and to what extent pro-labor legislation enacted at the subfederal level can survive federal preemption scrutiny. One recent experiment from this laboratory is the neutrality statute tested in *Chamber of Commerce v. Brown*, discussed *infra* p. 1225.

Several state or local initiatives supported by labor have been tied to the power of the purse: as a condition of receiving public funds under a government contract, the firm must agree to do (or not to do) certain things in the workplace. For example, participation by private firms in a large government construction project might be conditioned on compliance with the terms of a project labor agreement (PLA), which seeks to ensure that all work is performed by union labor in exchange for the unions' long-term promise to refrain from strikes, boycotts, and other concerted activities that could increase costs by disrupting progress and delaying completion. The PLA operates as a sort of super collective bargaining agreement governing the entire project; every contractor providing goods or services must sign it or lose out on participating in the project.

The U.S. Supreme Court rejected a *Machinists*-style challenge to a PLA in *Building & Construction Trades Council v. Associated Builders & Contractors of Massachusetts/Rhode Island, Inc. (Boston Harbor)*, 507 U.S. 218 (1993). In *Boston Harbor*, the Massachusetts Water Resources

Authority required participation in a PLA as part of the bid specifications for work undertaken during the 1980s and 1990s on the region's "Big Dig," a massive, $6.1 billion water pollution cleanup and transportation improvement project in the Boston Harbor area. The ostensible purpose of requiring contractors to enter into the PLA was to avoid delays in complying with court orders to clean up the polluted waterway. In rejecting a preemption challenge brought by nonunion contractors who refused to become union signatories, the Supreme Court explored an important wrinkle in the application of *Machinists* doctrine: the market participation exception. Under this exception, a bid specification requiring adherence to a PLA will not be preempted so long as the state, in setting conditions, is acting in a proprietary rather than a regulatory capacity. The Court reasoned that whereas public sector proprietors are permitted to attach strings to the conditions of their participation in the labor market affecting public works projects, public sector regulators are not. A state actor loses the benefit of the market participation exception when it attempts to regulate within "a zone protected and reserved for market freedom," as held by *Machinists*. Because the Commonwealth of Massachusetts was acting in its capacity as proprietor rather than regulator, it was entitled to claim the market participation exception, and thereby avoid *Machinists* preemption. Relying on *Boston Harbor*, federal courts have upheld most PLAs that could be characterized as falling within the market participation exception. *See, e.g., Building Industry Electrical Contractors Ass'n v. New York*, 678 F.3d 184 (2d Cir. 2012) (holding not preempted 6 PLAs covering some 32,000 workers employed on an estimated $6 billion worth of electrical construction projects to be undertaken in New York City over 5-year period).

Following *Boston Harbor*, organized labor and supportive scholars searched for state, local, and other non-NLRA means to preserve workers' rights, including their access to collective bargaining.

For example, in 2017, a labor law reform symposium devoted to this search—presented by the Harvard Labor and Worklife Program, the Economic Policy Institute, and the Harvard Law and Policy Review—was held in Cambridge, Mass. It produced the following papers: Charlotte Garden, *The Seattle Solution: Collective Bargaining by For-Hire Drivers & Prospects for Pro-Labor Federalism*, available at http://harvardlpr.com/wp-content/uploads/2018/01/Garden-SeattleSolution.pdf; Jose Garza, *Outrunning the Devil: Considering the Implications of Relaxing the NLRA's Preemption Scheme for Working Texas Families*, available at http://harvard lpr.com/wp-content/uploads/2018/01/Garza-Outrunning.pdf; Kate Andrias, *Social Bargaining in States and Cities: Toward a More Egalitarian and Democratic Workplace Law*, available at http://harvardlpr.com/wp-content/uploads/2018/01/Andrias-Social.pdf; Seema N. Patel & Catherine L. Fisk, *California Co-Enforcement Initiatives That Facilitate Worker Organizing*, available at http://harvardlpr.com/wp-content/uploads/2017/11/Patel-Fisk-CoEnforcement.pdf.

An earlier result of this search for alternative means to preserve workers' rights was the neutrality provision. Under a neutrality provision, the employer must agree to remain neutral while the union attempts to collect union authorization cards. (Recall Teresa Salazar's organizing efforts at Rons Grocery Company, which eventually produced this outcome.) Often, the employer stands to gain something from agreeing to neutrality: for example, labor peace, or in the case of a government contractor, coveted public sector business—in the form of state or local expenditures on the government contract. In the latter case, the employer must agree not to spend those funds to oppose or support unionization.

Although the stated purpose of neutrality agreements in the public sector is to ensure the cost-efficient and on-time completion of public works projects, the effect is often to encourage unionization among the employees of private contractors; workers are more likely to choose unions when organizers face no formal opposition. The following case illustrates a successful preemption attack on this device.

CHAMBER OF COMMERCE V. BROWN
554 U.S. 60 (2008)

JUSTICE STEVENS delivered the opinion of the Court:

A California statute known as Assembly Bill 1889 (AB 1889) prohibits several classes of employers that receive state funds from using the funds "to assist, promote, or deter union organizing." *See* Cal. Gov't Code Ann. §§ 16645–16649 (West Supp. 2008). The question presented to us is whether two of its provisions—§ 16645.2, applicable to grant recipients, and § 16645.7, applicable to private employers receiving more than $10,000 in program funds in any year—are preempted by federal law mandating that certain zones of labor activity be unregulated.

I.

As set forth in the preamble, the State of California enacted AB 1889 for the following purpose:

> It is the policy of the state not to interfere with an employee's choice about whether to join or to be represented by a labor union. For this reason, the state should not subsidize efforts by an employer to assist, promote, or deter union organizing. It is the intent of the Legislature in enacting this act to prohibit an employer from using state funds and facilities for the purpose of influencing employees to support or oppose unionization and to prohibit an employer from seeking to influence employees to

support or oppose unionization while those employees are performing work on a state contract.

2000 Cal. Stats. ch. 872, § 1.

AB 1889 forbids certain employers that receive state funds—whether by reimbursement, grant, contract, use of state property, or pursuant to a state program—from using such funds to "assist, promote, or deter union organizing." Cal. Gov't Code Ann. §§ 16645.1 to 16645.7. This prohibition encompasses "any attempt by an employer to influence the decision of its employees" regarding "[w]hether to support or oppose a labor organization" and "[w]hether to become a member of any labor organization." § 16645(a). The statute specifies that the spending restriction applies to "any expense, including legal and consulting fees and salaries of supervisors and employees, incurred for . . . an activity to assist, promote, or deter union organizing." § 16646(a).

Despite the neutral statement of policy quoted above, AB 1889 expressly exempts "activit[ies] performed" or "expense[s] incurred" in connection with certain undertakings that promote unionization, including "[a]llowing a labor organization or its representatives access to the employer's facilities or property," and "[n]egotiating, entering into, or carrying out a voluntary recognition agreement with a labor organization." §§ 16647(b), (d).

To ensure compliance with the grant and program restrictions at issue in this case, AB 1889 establishes a formidable enforcement scheme. Covered employers must certify that no state funds will be used for prohibited expenditures; the employer must also maintain and provide upon request "records sufficient to show that no state funds were used for those expenditures." §§ 16645.2(c), 16645.7(b)–(c). If an employer commingles state and other funds, the statute presumes that any expenditures to assist, promote, or deter union organizing derive in part from state funds on a pro rata basis. § 16646(b). Violators are liable to the State for the amount of funds used for prohibited purposes plus a civil penalty equal to twice the amount of those funds. §§ 16645.2(d), 16645.7(d). Suspected violators may be sued by the state attorney general or any private taxpayer, and prevailing plaintiffs are "entitled to recover reasonable attorney's fees and costs." § 16645.8(d).

II.

Today we hold that §§ 16645.2 and 16645.7 are preempted under *Machinists v. Wisconsin Employment Relations Comm'n*, 427 U.S. 132, 140 (1976), because they regulate within "a zone protected and reserved for market freedom." *Bldg. & Constr. Trades Council v. Associated Builders & Contractors of Mass./R I., Inc.*, 507 U.S. 218, 227 (1993) (*Boston Harbor*). We do not reach the question whether the provisions would also be preempted under *Garmon*.

III.

Among the frequently litigated issues under the Wagner Act were charges that an employer's attempts to persuade employees not to join a union—or to join one favored by the employer rather than a rival—amounted to a form of coercion prohibited by § 8. The NLRB took the position that § 8 demanded complete employer neutrality during organizing campaigns, reasoning that any partisan employer speech about unions would interfere with the § 7 rights of employees.

Concerned that the Wagner Act had pushed the labor relations balance too far in favor of unions, Congress passed the Labor Management Relations (Taft-Hartley) of 1947. The Taft-Hartley Act amended §§ 7 and 8 in several key respects. [Among other things] it added § 8(c), 29 U.S.C. § 158(c), which protects speech by both unions and employers from regulation by the NLRB. Specifically, § 8(c) provides:

> The expressing of any views, argument, or opinion, or the dissemination thereof, whether in written, printed, graphic, or visual form, shall not constitute or be evidence of an unfair labor practice under any of the provisions of this subchapter, if such expression contains no threat of reprisal or force or promise of benefit.

Enactment [of section 8(c)] manifested a "congressional intent to encourage free debate on issues dividing labor and management." It is indicative of how important Congress deemed such "free debate" that Congress amended the NLRA rather than leaving to the courts the task of correcting the NLRB's decisions on a case-by-case basis. We have characterized this policy judgment as "favoring uninhibited, robust, and wide-open debate in labor disputes," stressing that "freewheeling use of the written and spoken word . . . has been expressly fostered by Congress and approved by the NLRB."

Congress' express protection of free debate forcefully buttresses the preemption analysis in this case. Under *Machinists,* congressional intent to shield a zone of activity from regulation is usually found only "implicit[ly] in the structure of the Act." In the case of noncoercive speech, however, the protection is both implicit and explicit. Sections 8(a) and 8(b) demonstrate that when Congress has sought to put limits on advocacy for or against union organization, it has expressly set forth the mechanisms for doing so. Moreover, the amendment to § 7 calls attention to the right of employees to refuse to join unions, which implies an underlying right to receive information opposing unionization. Finally, the addition of § 8(c) expressly precludes regulation of speech about unionization "so long as the communications do not contain a "threat of reprisal or force or promise of benefit." *Gissel Packing,* 395 U.S. at 618.

The explicit direction from Congress to leave noncoercive speech unregulated makes this case easier, in at least one respect, than previous NLRA cases because it does not require us "to decipher the presumed intent of Congress in the face of that body's steadfast silence." California's policy judgment that partisan employer speech necessarily "interfere[s] with an employee's choice about whether to join or to be represented by a labor union," 2000 Cal. Stats. ch. 872, § 1, is the same policy judgment that the NLRB advanced under the Wagner Act, and that Congress renounced in the Taft-Hartley Act. To the extent §§ 16645.2 and 16645.7 actually further the express goal of AB 1889, the provisions are unequivocally preempted.

IV.

The Court of Appeals concluded that *Machinists* did not preempt §§ 16645.2 and 16645.7 for three reasons: (1) the spending restrictions apply only to the *use* of state funds, (2) Congress did not leave the zone of activity free from *all* regulation, and (3) California modeled AB 1889 on federal statutes. We find none of these arguments persuasive.

Use of State Funds

California plainly could not directly regulate noncoercive speech about unionization by means of an express prohibition. It is equally clear that California may not indirectly regulate such conduct by imposing spending restrictions on the use of state funds.

In *Wisconsin Dep't of Industry v. Gould, Inc.*, 475 U.S. 282, 287–89 (1986), we held that Wisconsin's policy of refusing to purchase goods and services from three-time NLRA violators was preempted under *Garmon* because it imposed a "supplemental sanction" that conflicted with the NLRA's "integrated scheme of regulation." Wisconsin protested that its debarment statute was "an exercise of the State's spending power rather than its regulatory power," but we dismissed this as "a distinction without a difference." "[T]he point of the statute [was] to deter labor law violations," and "for all practical purposes" the spending restriction was "tantamount to regulation." Wisconsin's choice "to use its spending power rather than its police power d[id] not significantly lessen the inherent potential for conflict" between the state and federal schemes; hence the statute was preempted.

We distinguished *Gould* in *Boston Harbor*, holding that the NLRA did not preclude a state agency supervising a construction project from requiring that contractors abide by a labor agreement. We explained that when a State acts as a "market participant with no interest in setting policy," as opposed to a "regulator," it does not offend the preemption principles of the NLRA. 507 U.S. at 229.

It is beyond dispute that California enacted AB 1889 in its capacity as a regulator rather than a market participant. AB 1889 is neither "specifically tailored to one particular job" nor a "legitimate response to state procurement constraints or to local economic needs." As the statute's preamble candidly acknowledges, the legislative purpose is not the efficient procurement of goods and services, but the furtherance of a labor policy. *See* 2000 Cal. Stats. ch. 872, § 1. Although a State has a legitimate proprietary interest in ensuring that state funds are spent in accordance with the purposes for which they are appropriated, this is not the objective of AB 1889.

California's reliance on a "use" restriction rather than a "receipt" restriction is, at least in this case, no more consequential than Wisconsin's reliance on its spending power rather than its police power in *Gould*. As explained below, AB 1889 couples its "use" restriction with compliance costs and litigation risks that are calculated to make union-related advocacy prohibitively expensive for employers that receive state funds. By making it exceedingly difficult for employers to demonstrate that they have not used state funds and by imposing punitive sanctions for noncompliance, AB 1889 effectively reaches beyond the use of funds over which California maintains a sovereign interest.

NLRB Regulation

The NLRB has policed a narrow zone of speech to ensure free and fair elections under the aegis of § 9 of the NLRA, 29 U.S.C. § 159. Whatever the NLRB's regulatory authority within special settings such as imminent elections, however, Congress has clearly denied it the authority to regulate the broader category of noncoercive speech encompassed by AB 1889. It is equally obvious that the NLRA deprives California of this authority, since "[t]he States have no more authority than the Board to upset the balance that Congress has struck between labor and management."

Federal Statutes

Finally, the Court of Appeals reasoned that Congress could not have intended to preempt AB 1889 because Congress itself has imposed similar restrictions. Specifically, three federal statutes include provisions that forbid the use of particular grant and program funds "to assist, promote, or deter union organizing."[2] We are not persuaded that these few isolated restrictions, plucked from the multitude of federal spending programs, were either intended to alter or did in fact alter the "wider contours of federal labor policy."

---

[2]   *See* 29 U.S.C. § 2931(b)(7) ("Each recipient of funds under [the Workforce Investment Act] shall provide to the Secretary assurances that none of such funds will be used to assist, promote, or deter union organizing"); 42 U.S.C. § 9839(e) ("Funds appropriated to carry out [the Head Start Programs Act] shall not be used to assist, promote, or deter union organizing"); 42 U.S.C. § 12634(b)(1) ("Assistance provided under [the National Community Service Act] shall not be used by program participants and program staff to . . . assist, promote, or deter union organizing").

A federal statute will contract the preemptive scope of the NLRA if it demonstrates that "Congress has decided to tolerate a substantial measure of diversity" in the particular regulatory sphere. In *New York Telephone Co. v. New York State Dep't of Labor*, 440 U.S. 519, 546 (1979) (plurality opinion), an employer challenged a state unemployment system that provided benefits to employees absent from work during lengthy strikes. The employer argued that the state system conflicted with the federal labor policy "of allowing the free play of economic forces to operate during the bargaining process." We upheld the statute on the basis that the legislative histories of the NLRA and Social Security Act, which were enacted within six weeks of each other, confirmed that "Congress intended that the States be free to authorize, or to prohibit, such payments."

The three federal statutes relied on by the Court of Appeals neither conflict with the NLRA nor otherwise establish that Congress "decided to tolerate a substantial measure of diversity" in the regulation of employer speech. Unlike the States, Congress has the authority to create tailored exceptions to otherwise applicable federal policies, and (also unlike the States) it can do so in a manner that preserves national uniformity without opening the door to a 50-state patchwork of inconsistent labor policies. Consequently, the mere fact that Congress has imposed targeted federal restrictions on union-related advocacy in certain limited contexts does not invite the States to override federal labor policy in other settings.

Had Congress enacted a federal version of AB 1889 that applied analogous spending restrictions to *all* federal grants or expenditures, the preemption question would be closer. But none of the cited statutes is Government-wide in scope, none contains comparable remedial provisions, and none contains express pro-union exemptions.

The Court of Appeals' judgment reversing the summary judgment entered for the Chamber of Commerce is reversed, and the case is remanded for further proceedings consistent with this opinion.

JUSTICE BREYER, with whom JUSTICE GINSBURG joins, dissenting:

The question before us is whether California's spending limitations amount to *regulation* that the NLRA preempts. In my view, they do not.

First, the only relevant Supreme Court case that found a State's labor-related spending limitations to be preempted differs radically from the case before us. In that case, *Wisconsin Dept. of Industry v. Gould Inc.*, 475 U.S. 282 (1986), the Court considered a Wisconsin statute that prohibited the State from doing business with firms that repeatedly violated the NLRA. The Court said that the statute's "manifest purpose and inevitable effect" was "to enforce" the NLRA's requirements, which "role Congress reserved exclusively for the [National Labor Relations Board]." In a word, the Wisconsin statute sought "to *compel* conformity with the NLRA."

California's statute differs from the Wisconsin statute because it does not seek to compel labor-related activity. Nor does it seek to forbid labor-related activity. It permits all employers who receive state funds to "assist, promote, or deter union organizing." It simply says to those employers, do not do so on our dime. I concede that a federal law that forces States to pay for labor-related speech from public funds would encourage *more* of that speech. But no one can claim that the NLRA is such a law. And without such a law, a State's refusal to pay for labor-related speech does not *impermissibly* discourage that activity. To refuse to pay for an activity (as here) is not the same as to compel others to engage in that activity (as in *Gould*).

Second, California's operative language does not weaken or undercut Congress' policy of "encourag[ing] free debate on issues dividing labor and management." For one thing, employers remain free to spend *their own* money to "assist, promote, or deter" unionization. More importantly, I cannot conclude that California's statute would weaken or undercut any such congressional policy because Congress itself has enacted three statutes that, *using identical language,* do precisely the same thing. Congress has forbidden recipients of Head Start funds from using the funds to "assist, promote, or deter union organizing." 42 U.S.C. § 9839(e). It has forbidden recipients of Workforce Investment Act of 1998 funds from using the funds to "assist, promote, or deter union organizing." 29 U.S.C. § 2931(b)(7). And it has forbidden recipients of National Community Service Act of 1990 funds from using the funds to "assist, promote, or deter union organizing." 42 U.S.C. § 12634(b)(1). Could Congress have thought that the NLRA would prevent the States from enacting the very same kinds of laws that Congress itself has enacted? Far more likely, Congress thought that directing government funds away from labor-related activity was *consistent,* not *inconsistent,* with, the policy of "encourag[ing] free debate" embedded in its labor statutes.

Finally, the law normally gives legislatures broad authority to decide how to spend the People's money. A legislature, after all, generally has the right *not* to fund activities that it would prefer not to fund—even where the activities are otherwise protected. *See, e.g., Regan v. Taxation With Representation of Wash.,* 461 U.S. 540, 549 (1983) ("We have held in several contexts that a legislature's decision not to subsidize the exercise of a fundamental right does not infringe the right").

As far as I can tell, States that *do* wish to pay for employer speech are generally free to do so. They might make clear, for example, through grant-related rules and regulations that a grant recipient can use the funds to pay salaries and overhead, which salaries and overhead might include expenditures related to management's role in labor organizing contests. If so, why should States that do *not* wish to pay be deprived of a similar freedom? Why should they be conscripted into paying?

NOTES

1.   In holding the California statute preempted, the Court reasoned that, although the state had a legitimate interest in ensuring that state funds are spent consistent with the purposes for which they are appropriated, the objective of AB 1889 was to impose "a targeted negative restriction on employer speech about unionization," which is not a permissible state objective. Would the result have been different if AB 1889 had been better drafted? How might the statute be rewritten to satisfy the Court's concerns? To what extent did the statute's penalties influence the outcome? Should any attention be paid to modifying them? If so, how?

2.   Like California, scores of authorities at the state and local levels have attempted to condition acceptance of taxpayers' money—including payments made pursuant to government contracts—on agreement by private employers to remain neutral in the event of union organizing activities, often in exchange for promises by unions to refrain from strikes, picketing, and other activity that might disrupt the construction or operation of major public works. Such agreements have been required by municipalities as diverse as Pittsburgh, Pennsylvania; Seward, Alaska; and Milwaukee, Wisconsin. Although the Third and Ninth Circuits rejected *Machinists* preemption attacks in the first two cases, the Seventh Circuit upheld such an attack in the third case. *Compare Hotel Employees & Rest. Employees Union Local 57 v. Sage Hospitality Res. LLC*, 390 F.3d 206 (3d Cir. 2004), *and Associated Bldrs. & Contractors, Inc. v. City of Seward*, 966 F.2d 492 (9th Cir. 1992), *with Metro. Milwaukee Ass'n of Commerce v. Milwaukee County*, 431 F.3d 277 (7th Cir. 2005).

Does *Chamber of Commerce v. Brown* signal that such neutrality agreements are now more likely to be preempted by *Machinists*, or may municipalities continue to insist on neutrality agreements as a condition of accepting disbursements from state treasuries? In other words, was the Seventh Circuit right, and were the Third and Ninth Circuits wrong? Is there a difference between requiring contractors to hire union labor and requiring them to remain neutral in labor disputes? Is *Boston Harbor* consistent with, or distinguishable from, *Chamber of Commerce v. Brown*?

3.   Suppose a city passes an ordinance refusing to renew the Yellow Cab Company's taxi franchise at the airport unless and until it settles an ongoing labor dispute with drivers represented by the Teamsters Union. The Teamsters supports the ordinance on the ground that franchise renewal would simply stiffen Yellow Cab's resolve at the bargaining table and lengthen the strike. Is the city acting in its capacity as market participant (in which case *Machinists* preemption is inapplicable) or market regulator (in which case *Machinists* preemption applies)? Does the city have the right to assure its residents that taxi service will not be interrupted by the strike? *See Golden State Transit Corp. v. City of L.A.* (*Golden State I*), 475 U.S. 608 (1986) (holding preempted such ordinance); *see also Division 1287 of Amalgamated Ass'n of St., Elec. Ry. and Motor Coach Emp. of America v. Missouri*, 374 U.S. 74 (1963) (holding preempted Missouri statute both empowering state's governor to seize and

operate utility threatened by strike, and authorizing injunction against such strike).

4.   As noted in Chapter 8, *supra* p. 1025, during the 1990s and 2000s hundreds of cities and counties across the country enacted "living wage" ordinances. Often these laws were passed as the result of campaigns led by workers' centers, church groups, and other community advocates, including some labor unions. Typically, a living wage ordinance requires government contractors, and occasionally large private firms operating within city limits, to pay minimum wages that more accurately reflect the true costs of living in that community. As a result, the living wage is often substantially higher than the minimum wage required by federal law. *See* Fair Labor Standards Act, 29 U.S.C. §§ 201–219. (In most industries, the federal minimum wage was set at $7.25 effective July 24, 2009. Although there have been calls to raise for raising the minimum wage, Congress has refused to do so. As of 2018, however, at least 29 states have set their minimum wage above the federal rate.)

Suppose a city passes an ordinance requiring workers in the hospitality industry to be paid a living wage. Suppose further that the union representing such employees had tried and failed in negotiations to secure contract terms setting the minimum wage at the level that the ordinance now mandates. Ordinarily, state wage regulation is not preempted under a *Machinists* theory because it simply imposes minimum labor standards that form the baseline beyond which parties bargain. *Livadas v. Bradshaw,* 512 U.S. 107 (1994); *Fort Halifax Packing Co. v. Coyne,* 482 U.S. 1 (1987); *Metropolitan Life Ins. v. Mass.,* 471 U.S. 724 (1985). Is the fact that the union secured through legislation that which it could not obtain through bargaining enough to justify preemption? *Compare 520 S. Michigan Avenue Assocs., Ltd. v. Shannon,* 549 F.3d 1119 (7th Cir. 2008) (holding preempted Illinois One Day Rest in Seven Act because it applied only to Chicago hotel employees), *with Dillingham v. Sonoma County,* 190 F.3d 1034, 1041 (9th Cir.1999) (holding not preempted minimum standards that applied only to apprentices in skilled construction trades); *Nat. Broadcasting Co. v. Bradshaw,* 70 F.3d 69, 71–72 (9th Cir.1995) (holding not preempted California regulation applying only to broadcast employees); *and Wash. Serv. Contractors Coalition v. District of Columbia,* 54 F.3d 811, 819 (D.C.Cir.1995) (holding not preempted regulation applying only to food and janitorial workers).

5.   Suppose a city enacted an ordinance providing a mechanism through which for-hire drivers can collectively bargain with Lyft, Uber, and the other companies that hire, contract with, and/or partner with them. The ordinance applies only to for-hire drivers who are independent contractors, not employees. Suppose further that, pursuant to the procedures codified in the ordinance, a union notified three members of the local Chamber of Commerce that it wished to represent their drivers in collective bargaining. The Chamber, acting on behalf of its members, responds by filing an action challenging the ordinance on several grounds, including that it was preempted by *Garmon,* *Machinists,* or both. How would you rule on these challenges, and why? *See*

Chamber of Commerce of U.S. v. City of Seattle, 274 F. Supp. 3d 1155 (W.D. Wash. 2017) (rejecting both preemption challenges).

6.   Successorship obligations arising out of the sale or transfer of a business, which are discussed in Chapter 9, *supra* p. 1151, can raise preemption issues. For example, a successor employer may seek to lower its labor costs, and thereby reduce its exposure to liability for employment-related claims, by attempting to rid itself of collective bargaining obligations that the predecessor employer had incurred. Suppose that, to combat this tactic, a city enacts an ordinance requiring the purchasers of large grocery stores to employ the predecessor owner's employees for at least 90 days following the transfer. Is this preempted? *See California Grocers Ass'n v. City of Los Angeles*, 52 Cal. 4th 177 (2011) (ordinance not preempted by NLRA), *cert. denied*, 132 S. Ct. 1144 (2012).

D. SECTION 301 PREEMPTION

Under Section 301 preemption, any state claim or cause of action that depends upon the meaning of a collective bargaining agreement is precluded, and uniform federal labor law principles must be applied instead. In the typical Section 301 preemption case, the aggrieved party's exclusive remedy—say, for discharge from employment without good cause—is to pursue a grievance under the alternative dispute resolution procedures set forth in the collective bargaining agreement, rather than to file a lawsuit in state (or federal) court. This form of preemption indicates a preference for remedies negotiated through private ordering over those made available by the government in public forums, including courts of law.

Questions of Section 301 preemption are often inseparable from the parties' tactical choice of forum. Whereas plaintiff-employees usually prefer to bring state law claims in state court, defendant-employers prefer, if possible, to remove and defend those claims under federal labor law principles in federal court. But federal courts are courts of limited jurisdiction; they may not entertain claims lacking proper jurisdiction over the subject matter. In most labor cases, subject matter jurisdiction is based on the existence of a federal question. (Owing to the arcana of applicable doctrine and the unincorporated status of many unions, subject matter jurisdiction based on complete diversity of citizenship, the other major pathway to federal court, rarely exists.) Moreover, under the "well pleaded complaint" rule, federal defenses such as preemption cannot be anticipated to create federal question jurisdiction; ordinarily, a question of federal law must be part of the plaintiff's claim to qualify for federal court. But there is an important exception to the well-pleaded complaint rule: under the "complete preemption" doctrine, "the preemptive force of § 301 is so powerful as to displace entirely any state cause of action for violation of contracts between an employer and a labor organization." *Franchise Tax*

Bd. v. Construction Laborers Vacation Trust for S. Cal., 463 U.S. 1, 23 (1983).

Thus Section 301 preemption can transform a claim bearing a state law label into a claim that turns out to raise a federal question, which is now properly removable to federal court. Accordingly, to create removal jurisdiction, a defendant usually attempts to reframe the plaintiff's claims as raising federal rather than state law questions—even if federal questions appear nowhere on the face of the plaintiff's complaint, as demonstrated by the following case.

LINGLE V. NORGE DIVISION OF MAGIC CHEF, INC.
486 U.S. 399 (1988)

JUSTICE STEVENS delivered the opinion for a unanimous Court:

In Illinois an employee who is discharged for filing a worker's compensation claim may recover compensatory and punitive damages from her employer. The question presented in this case is whether an employee covered by a collective bargaining agreement that provides her with a contractual remedy for discharge without just cause may enforce her state-law remedy for retaliatory discharge. The Court of Appeals held that the application of the state tort remedy was preempted by § 301 of the Labor Management Relations Act. We disagree.

I.

Petitioner was employed in respondent's manufacturing plant in Herrin, Ill. On December 5, she notified respondent that she had been injured in the course of her employment and requested compensation for her medical expenses pursuant to the Illinois Workers' Compensation Act. On December 11, respondent discharged her for filing a "false worker's compensation claim."

The union representing petitioner promptly filed a grievance pursuant to the collective bargaining agreement that covered all production and maintenance employees in the Herrin plant. The agreement protected those employees, including petitioner, from discharge except for "proper" or "just" cause and established a procedure for the arbitration of grievances. The term "grievance" was broadly defined to encompass "any dispute between the Employer and any employee, concerning the effect, interpretation, application, claim of breach or violation of this Agreement." Ultimately, an arbitrator ruled in petitioner's favor and ordered respondent to reinstate her with full back pay.

Meanwhile petitioner commenced this action against respondent by filing a complaint in the Illinois Circuit Court for Williamson County, alleging that she had been discharged for exercising her rights under the Illinois workers' compensation laws. Respondent removed the case to federal district court on the basis of diversity of citizenship, and then filed a motion praying that the court either dismiss the case on preemption grounds or stay further proceedings pending the completion of the arbitration. Relying on our decision in *Allis-Chalmers Corp. v. Lueck*, 471 U.S. 202 (1985), the district court dismissed the complaint. It concluded that the "claim for retaliatory discharge is 'inextricably intertwined' with the collective bargaining provision prohibiting wrongful discharge or discharge without just cause" and that allowing the state-law action to proceed would undermine the arbitration procedures set forth in the parties' contract.

II.

Section 301(a) of the Labor Management Relations Act of 1947, 29 U.S.C. § 185(a), provides:

> Suits for violation of contracts between an employer and a labor organization representing employees in an industry affecting commerce as defined in this Act, or between any such labor organizations, may be brought in any district court of the United States having jurisdiction of the parties, without respect to the amount in controversy or without regard to the citizenship of the parties.

In *Textile Workers v. Lincoln Mills*, 353 U.S. 448 (1957), we held that § 301 not only provides federal court jurisdiction over controversies involving collective bargaining agreements, but also "authorizes federal courts to fashion a body of federal law for the enforcement of these collective bargaining agreements."

In *Teamsters v. Lucas Flour Co.*, 369 U.S. 95 (1962), we were confronted with a straightforward question of contract interpretation: whether a collective-bargaining agreement implicitly prohibited a strike that had been called by the union. The Washington Supreme Court had answered that question by applying state-law rules of contract interpretation. We rejected that approach, and held that § 301 mandated resort to federal rules of law in order to ensure uniform interpretation of collective-bargaining agreements, and thus to promote the peaceable, consistent resolution of labor-management disputes.[3]

---

[3]   [There we said]: "It was apparently the theory of the Washington court that, although *Lincoln Mills* requires the federal courts to fashion, from the policy of our national labor laws, a body of federal law for the enforcement of collective-bargaining agreements, nonetheless, the courts of the States remain free to apply individualized local rules when called upon to enforce such agreements. This view cannot be accepted. The dimensions of § 301 require the conclusion that substantive principles of federal labor law must be paramount in the area covered by the statute. Comprehensiveness is inherent in the process by which the law is to be formulated under the mandate of *Lincoln Mills*, requiring issues raised in suits of a kind covered by § 301 to be decided according to the precepts of federal labor policy."

In *Allis-Chalmers Corp. v. Lueck*, 471 U.S. 202 (1985), we considered whether the Wisconsin tort remedy for bad-faith handling of an insurance claim could be applied to the handling of a claim for disability benefits that were authorized by a collective-bargaining agreement. We began by examining the collective-bargaining agreement, and determined that it provided the basis not only for the benefits, but also for the right to have payments made in a timely manner. We then analyzed the Wisconsin tort remedy, explaining that it "exists for breach of a 'duty devolv[ed] upon the insurer by reasonable implication from the express terms of the contract,' the scope of which, crucially, is 'ascertained from a consideration of the contract itself.'" Since the "parties' agreement as to the manner in which a benefit claim would be handled [would] necessarily [have been] relevant to any allegation that the claim was handled in a dilatory manner," we concluded that § 301 preempted the application of the Wisconsin tort remedy in this setting.

Thus, *Lueck* faithfully applied the principle of § 301 preemption developed in *Lucas Flour*. If the resolution of a state-law claim depends upon the meaning of a collective-bargaining agreement, the application of state law (which might lead to inconsistent results since there could be as many state-law principles as there are States) is preempted and federal labor-law principles—necessarily uniform throughout the Nation—must be employed to resolve the dispute.

III.

Illinois courts have recognized the tort of retaliatory discharge for filing a worker's compensation claim and have held that it is applicable to employees covered by union contracts. "[T]o show retaliatory discharge, the plaintiff must set forth sufficient facts from which it can be inferred that (1) he was discharged or threatened with discharge and (2) the employer's motive in discharging or threatening to discharge him was to deter him from exercising his rights under the [Illinois Workers' Compensation] Act or to interfere with his exercise of those rights." Each of these purely factual questions pertains to the conduct of the employee and the conduct and motivation of the employer. Neither of the elements requires a court to interpret any term of a collective-bargaining agreement. To defend against a retaliatory discharge claim, an employer must show that it had a nonretaliatory reason for the discharge; this purely factual inquiry likewise does not turn on the meaning of any provision of a collective-bargaining agreement. Thus, the state-law remedy in this case is "independent" of the collective-bargaining agreement in the sense of "independent" that matters for § 301 preemption purposes: resolution of the state-law claim does not require construing the collective-bargaining agreement.

Petitioner points to the fact that the Illinois right to be free from retaliatory discharge is nonnegotiable and applies to unionized and nonunionized workers alike. While it may be true that most state laws that are not preempted by § 301 will grant nonnegotiable rights that are shared by all state workers, we note that neither condition ensures nonpreemption. It is conceivable that a State could create a remedy that, although nonnegotiable, nonetheless turned on the interpretation of a collective-bargaining agreement for its application. Such a remedy would be preempted by § 301. Similarly, if a law applied to all state workers but required, at least in certain instances, collective-bargaining agreement interpretation, the application of the law in those instances would be preempted. Conversely, a law could cover only unionized workers but remain unpreempted if no collective-bargaining agreement interpretation was needed to resolve claims brought thereunder.

IV.

The result we reach today is consistent both with the policy of fostering uniform, certain adjudication of disputes over the meaning of collective-bargaining agreements and with cases that have permitted separate fonts of substantive rights to remain unpreempted by other federal labor-law statutes.

There is nothing novel about recognizing that substantive rights in the labor relations context can exist without interpreting collective-bargaining agreements. "This Court has, on numerous occasions, declined to hold that individual employees are, because of the availability of arbitration, barred from bringing claims under federal statutes." *See, e.g., Alexander v. Gardner-Denver Co.*, 415 U.S. 36 (1974).

V.

In sum, we hold that an application of state law is preempted by § 301 of the Labor Management Relations Act of 1947 only if such application requires the interpretation of a collective-bargaining agreement.[12]

NOTES

1.   The result in *Lingle* avoided finding preemption of an employee's state law claim for retaliation due to his exercise of rights guaranteed by the Illinois worker's compensation scheme. But the result in *Lueck*, cited in *Lingle*, found preemption as to a worker's state law tort claim under Wisconsin law for bad faith handling of a claim relating to insurance benefits created by a

---

[12]   A collective-bargaining agreement may, of course, contain information such as rate of pay and other economic benefits that might be helpful in determining the damages to which a worker prevailing in a state-law suit is entitled. Although federal law would govern the interpretation of the agreement to determine the proper damages, the underlying state-law claim, not otherwise preempted, would stand. Thus, as a general proposition, a state-law claim may depend for its resolution upon both the interpretation of a collective-bargaining agreement and a separate state-law analysis that does not turn on the agreement. In such a case, federal law would govern the interpretation of the agreement, but the separate state-law analysis would not be thereby preempted. As we said in *Allis-Chalmers Corp. v. Lueck*, "not every dispute . . . tangentially involving a provision of a collective-bargaining agreement, is preempted by § 301."

collective bargaining agreement. Can the two cases be harmonized? Can they be distinguished? How?

2.   The holding of *Lingle* elaborates on the "inextricably intertwined" test of *Lueck*: if "the resolution of a state-law claim depends upon the meaning of a collective-bargaining agreement," then the state law claim is preempted. This standard has generated a substantial body of case law. Applying *Lingle*, the courts have found preempted numerous state statutory and common law claims against employers (and unions). Among these are: contract claims alleging that the employer breached a promise of job security made to an employee covered by a collective bargaining agreement, *see, e.g., Dougherty v. AT & T*, 902 F.2d 201 (2d Cir. 1990); tort claims alleging a union's failure to fulfill its duty under a collective bargaining agreement to maintain a safe working environment, *see, e.g., United Steelworkers v. Rawson*, 495 U.S. 362 (1990); *IBEW v. Hechler*, 481 U.S. 851 (1987); and claims alleging breach of the implied covenant of good faith and fair dealing implied in every individual employment contract, *see, e.g., Fox v. Parker Hannifin Corp.*, 914 F.2d 795 (6th Cir. 1990); *Newberry v. Pac. Racing Ass'n*, 854 F.2d 1142 (9th Cir. 1988).

Suppose you were general counsel to an employer faced with a variety of claims brought by disgruntled employees. After *Lingle*, which of the following are preempted:

- Religious or disability discrimination claims based on state antidiscrimination statutes? *See, e.g., Cook v. Lindsay Olive Growers*, 911 F.2d 233 (9th Cir. 1990) (holding not preempted statutory religious discrimination claim, but holding preempted tort claim alleging breach of covenant of good faith and fair dealing); *Ackerman v. Western Elec. Co.*, 860 F.2d 1514 (9th Cir. 1988) (holding not preempted disability discrimination claim).

- Whistleblower claims, in which an employee alleges retaliatory discharge for reporting an employer's violation of state or federal law? *See, e.g., Brevik v. Kite Painting, Inc.*, 416 N.W.2d 714 (Minn. 1987) (holding not preempted private right of action under state occupational safety and health act).

- State law tort claims alleging that the employer's handling of discipline caused the employee to suffer intentional infliction of emotional distress? *Compare, e.g., Hanks v. General Motors Corp.*, 906 F.2d 341 (8th Cir. 1990) (holding not preempted IIED claim requiring no interpretation of collective agreement), *with Douglas v. Am. Info. Techs. Corp.*, 877 F.2d 565 (7th Cir. 1989) (holding preempted IIED claim, because court cannot decide whether employer's conduct was "extreme and outrageous"—the applicable legal standard for the tort of IIED—without interpreting the collective bargaining agreement, claim). What about a state law tort claim by an employee alleging that his union caused him to suffer IIED? *See Farmer v. United Bhd. of*

Carpenters & Joiners, Local 25, 430 U.S. 290 (1977) (holding not preempted IIED claim under California law).

• State law wage claims by nurses for premium pay due to extra hours worked, after a grievance filed and pursued by their union under the CBA did not obtain full relief? *See Kobold v. Good Samaritan Regional Medical Center*, 832 F.3d 1024 (9th Cir. 2016) (holding preempted such claim).

3. Recall the case of Teresa Salazar that opened this chapter. The second of Salazar's two state law claims alleged that Rons Grocery Company had created a hostile work environment in violation of California law condemning discrimination based on sex. In particular, Salazar accused Albert Tsukahara, the assistant store manager, of continuously leering at her, "sexting" her by sending a text message with a photograph of his genitalia, and asking her out on a date, which she declined. Is this claim "inextricably intertwined" with the CBA between Rons and Local 17? Why or why not? Before answering, review the two key provisions of the CBA identified in the case, see *supra* p. 1202.

* * *

A related doctrine that can affect the tactics and strategy of labor-related litigation is known as complete preemption. It arises in the context of the removal to federal court of an action that was initiated in state court. It is possible that Salazar's claim is completely preempted under Section 301.

The general removal statute, 28 U.S.C. § 1441, permits a defendant to remove only if the plaintiff originally could have filed her action in federal court at the start of the litigation. One of the bases supporting such a move is called federal question jurisdiction. Under federal question jurisdiction, the doors of the federal courthouse always are open to hear a federal question claim. A federal question claim is a claim involving federal business: any claim arising under the Constitution, laws, or treaties of the United States. So defendants who feel they would be better off dealing with federal question claims in the federal courts routinely remove actions including one or more such claims once plaintiffs have attempted to pursue them in the state courts. But there's a catch: generally, a defendant is not permitted to invoke federal question jurisdiction—and thereby remove an action initiated in state court—when the federal question is an element of his federal *defense* rather than an element of the plaintiff's state law *claim*. This catch is known as the well-pleaded complaint rule. *See Louisville & Nashville R.R. v. Mottley*, 211 U.S. 149 (1908). Ordinarily, preemption is a federal defense that cannot be used to establish federal question jurisdiction, and hence, a basis for removal.

The complete preemption doctrine is an exception to the well-pleaded complaint rule. It applies in those rare circumstances in which the preemptive force of federal law is "so powerful as to displace entirely any state cause of action." *Franchise Tax Board v. Construction Laborers Vacation Trust*, 463 U.S. 1, 23 (1983). Section 301 preemption has been held to satisfy this test and thereby open the door to removal. *See Avco Corp. v. Aero Lodge No. 735*, 390 U.S. 557 (1968). ERISA preemption, *see Metropolitan Life Insurance Co. v. Taylor*, 481 U.S. 58 (1987), and National Banking Act preemption, *see Beneficial National Bank v. Anderson*, 539 U.S. 1 (2003), are two other rare circumstances that satisfy this test and achieve the same end.

For a thoughtful discussion of the doctrine of complete preemption and its flaws, see Gil Seinfeld, *The Puzzle of Complete Preemption*, 155 Mich. L. Rev. 537 (2007).

INDEX

References are to Pages

DISCLOSURES

DISCRIMINATION

Productivity benchmarks, 24
Progressive era, 25
Public sector labor relations acts, 79
Pullman workers' strike, 26
Race and the labor movement, 100
Racketeering, labor, 77
Radical and reform political programs, 13
Radicalism, 23
Railway strike of 1877, 15, 31
RICO trusteeships, 77
RLA, 36
Scientific management and personnel
      management theories, 23
Secondary boycotts, 21
Sedition and Espionage Act, 27
Service economy, development of, 91
Sherman Act litigation, 33
Sit ins, 16
Skilled workers era, 12, 22
Socialism, 23
Spies, 22
State and federal power conflicts, 1034
Steel seizure case, 74
Strikebreaker era, 22
Subcontracting, 92
Syndicalism, 26
Taft-Walsh War Labor Conference Board,
      27
Taylorism, 24, 61
Temporary restraining orders, 35
Time and motion studies, 24
Trade societies, 12
Transborder labor, 92
United Mine Workers, 13
Vertical integration of production, 72
Walkouts, 118
War Labor Board, 62
World War II
      Reconstruction era, 72
      War production measures, 62
Yellow-dog contracts, 26, 29, 32

HOME HEALTH CARE PROVIDERS
Employee status, 224

HOSPITALS
Bargaining unit determinations, 516

HOT CARGO AGREEMENTS
Generally, 860
Double-breasting, 867
Jurisdictional disputes, 862

HOURS OF WORK
Eight-hour day movement, 16
History of labor law, 15

IMMIGRANT WORKERS
See Transborder Workers, this index

IMPASSE
See Collective Bargaining, this index

INDEPENDENT CONTRACTORS
See also Subcontractors, this index

Employee status, 225, 228 et seq.
Taft-Hartley Act amendments, 246

INDIVIDUAL BARGAINING
Collective bargaining compared, regulatory
      policies, 10

INDIVIDUAL CONTRACTS
Collective bargaining agreements
      inconsistent with, 418

INDUSTRIAL ERA OF LABOR LAW
Generally, 22 et seq., 61

**INDUSTRIAL WORKERS OF THE
      WORLD (IWW)**
Generally, 23, 26

INFORMATION TECHNOLOGY
Collective action tools, 107
Organizational uses, 107

INJUNCTIONS
      See also Judicial Review, this index
Arbitration injunctions
      Generally, 920
      Employer conduct restraints pending,
            934
      Norris-LaGuardia Act, 920 et seq.
Bonds, 937
CBA enforcement, 921 et seq.
Clayton Act limitations, 34
Conspiracy injunctions, 31
Employer conduct restraints pending
      arbitration, 934
Governance by injunction era, 31
History of labor law, 31, 925
Interference claims, 20
National emergency, 67
Norris-LaGuardia Act restrictions
      Generally, 41, 43
      CBA enforcement, 921 et seq.
No-strike clauses, enforcement, 43, 921 et seq.
Picket lines, 215
Picketing, 18, 742
Strikes
            Generally, 772
      National security, 769
      No-strike clause enforcement, 921 et
            seq.
Taft-Hartley Amendments, 67

INTERFERENCE TORTS
Injunctions against picketing, 20

INTERNAL AFFAIRS
See Governance, Union, this index

INTERNAL LABOR MARKETS
Generally, 72

**INTERNATIONAL ASSOCIATION OF
      MACHINISTS**
History of labor law, 13